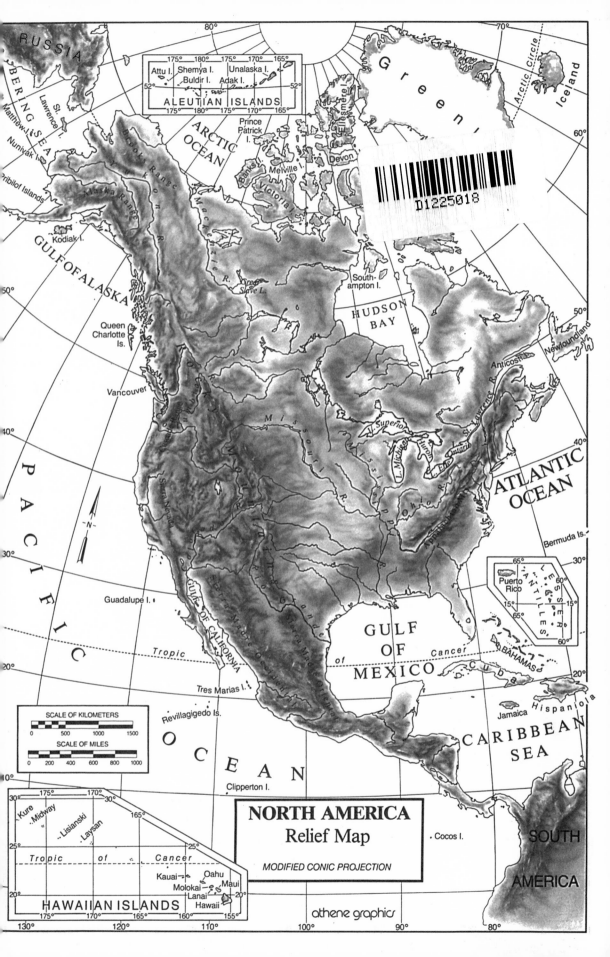

NORTH AMERICA
Relief Map

MODIFIED CONIC PROJECTION

athene graphics

Ex Libris

Wm. M. Shepherd

CHECK-LIST

OF

NORTH AMERICAN BIRDS

**

The Species of Birds of North America
from the Arctic through Panama,
Including the West Indies and Hawaiian Islands

**

PREPARED BY

THE COMMITTEE ON CLASSIFICATION AND NOMENCLATURE

OF THE

AMERICAN ORNITHOLOGISTS' UNION

**

SEVENTH EDITION

1998

Zoölogical nomenclature is a means, not an end, to Zoölogical Science

---

PUBLISHED BY THE

AMERICAN ORNITHOLOGISTS' UNION

1998

ISBN Number: 1-891276-00-X

1998. Preferred citation:

American Ornithologists' Union. 1983. *Check-list of North American Birds.* 7th edition. American Ornithologists' Union, Washington, D.C.

Printed by Allen Press, Inc.
Lawrence, Kansas, U.S.A.

CONTENTS

DEDICATION

BURT L. MONROE, JR.
1930–1994

To Dr. Burt L. Monroe, Jr., Past Chairman of the Committee on Classification and Nomenclature, whose encyclopedic knowledge of avian taxonomy, nomenclature, and distribution were indispensable in the preparation of the initial draft of the present volume. As Chair, he led the Committee with patience and efficient diplomacy, gaining our friendship and deep respect. A skilled communicator, he corresponded globally with both scientists and amateurs in a highly productive effort to standardize English names, a task in which he enthusiastically welcomed the views of everyone. During the waning months of his tenure, while enduring the constant pain and fatigue of terminal illness, Burt labored selflessly toward the completion of this Check-list, a significant portion of which represents one of his many lasting contributions to ornithology.

PREFACE TO THE SEVENTH EDITION

Background

Soon after publication of the sixth edition of the Check-list in 1983, members of the reconstituted Committee on Classification and Nomenclature began preparing this seventh edition. A primary goal of the Committee was to produce a volume that would emphasize information on the nature and extent of geographic variation in each included species and relate that variation to subspecific nomenclature. Each Committee member accepted responsibility for particular groups of birds. Draft species accounts were sent to Chairman Burt L. Monroe, Jr., for compilation and distribution to other committee members for review. Although subspecies-level accounts were written for almost half of the species in the Check-list area, it eventually became clear that a volume at that level would not be completed within acceptable time limits. In 1991, the Committee reluctantly decided to postpone that edition and instead to work toward a new edition at the species level.

Concurrently with work on the subspecies edition, the Committee pursued two other goals: (1) to maintain the currency of the sixth edition by evaluating newly published studies in taxonomy and nomenclature, accepting those recommendations or findings based on sound data analysis, and (2) to maintain the accuracy of distributional data for species known to occur in North America as defined in the Check-list or in particular political subdivisions (countries, states, or provinces) thereof. Beginning in 1984, the Committee met twice annually, in mid-winter (a few meetings skipped) and at the annual A.O.U. meeting. In preparation for a meeting, a member of the Committee would distribute a detailed analysis of published evidence for proposed changes in existing classification or for range extensions that added species to the A.O.U. area or to North America north of Mexico. In December 1995, the Committee began a series of ballots by mail, after distribution of such analyses. When a vote from either a meeting or a mail ballot resulted in a change in species limits or nomenclature, or the addition of a species to the known avifauna of the Check-list area or to the geographic area of the fifth and earlier editions of the Check-list (thus requiring the assignment of an A.O.U. or World number), the decision was included in a Supplement to the Check-list. Supplements were published in the July issue of *The Auk* in each odd-numbered year after the publication of the sixth edition until the publication of the seventh. A list of all Supplements to the Check-list since the first edition in 1886 appears at the end of this volume. Proposals not adopted by the Committee at any given meeting remained available for future consideration and reanalysis. Unresolved matters generally are reflected by alternative treatments mentioned with citations in "Notes" at the end of species accounts in this edition. On a few occasions, the Committee generated proposals on its own, concerning reevaluations of previously published analyses. These generally were reviews of decisions made for the sixth edition, and they usually resulted in the reversal of earlier decisions that had been made without adequate documentation.

In 1992, Monroe sent copies of a revised species-level manuscript to regional distributional authorities in states and provinces, Mexico, Central America, and the Caribbean. When most of those authorities had reviewed the manuscript for species in their areas, Monroe sent the updated manuscript to the Committee members for taxonomic review and refinement. Committee members, each concentrating on particular taxonomic groups of birds, sent their comments or revisions to Monroe, who maintained the master manuscript in a computer file. Monroe's health was failing in this period, and production of the revised edition went very slowly. When Burt Monroe died in May 1994 (Able 1996), Committee members became acutely aware of their dependence on him to carry the burden of the new edition.

In 1994, the A.O.U. Council authorized funds for the Committee to employ Andrew J. Kratter to assume the responsibility of maintaining the manuscript as members submitted new information and the Committee made taxonomic decisions. Kratter remained under contract, on a part time basis, from January 1995 until May 1996, after which the manuscript file and the responsibility of maintaining it were transferred to J. V. Remsen.

This edition includes taxonomic decisions made by the Committee up to March 1997. In general, taxonomic and systematic literature published after 1996 has not been reviewed. An important exception to that cutoff date is Ornithological Monographs no. 48, the contents of which were well known to the Committee because of editorial overlap. No new distributional information was included after about 31 December 1996. Because of the considerable gap between return of the reviews of distributional information by regional authorities and the publication of this volume, it is likely that some important distributional records have been overlooked.

This edition of the Check-list contains 2,008 species, a significant increase from the 1,913 in the sixth edition. Of the total, 991 are nonpasserines; of the 1,017 passerines, 254 are suboscines and 763 are oscines. Of the latter, 315 are nine-primaries oscines. There are 83 additional species in part 1 of the Appendix, and 34 in part 2.

Taxonomic Philosophy

Since publication of the sixth edition of this Check-list, the Committee has studied a flood of new publications on the systematic status and taxonomic relationships of birds. Much of this literature has involved the examination of traditional morphologic data through the application of phylogenetic systematic or cladistic approaches. Increasingly, molecular systematic techniques, such as DNA-DNA hybridization, allozyme electrophoresis, restriction fragment length polymorphisms (RFLP), and direct sequencing of DNA bases, have been brought to bear on long-standing problems in classification and relationships, from subspecific to ordinal levels. The addition of molecular data to traditional information not only has provided a healthy multidisciplinary perspective heretofore lacking but also has given results that are based on independent data sets. In many instances the new techniques have provided conclusions entirely supportive of traditional taxonomies. In other examples, conflicting findings point to the need for further investigation. Throughout the species accounts of this check-list, we cite literature pertinent to our decisions on change in classification. Consequently, the Literature Cited is a reasonably comprehensive bibliography of recent literature on the systematics and taxonomy of North American birds and thus a major resource not found in previous editions of the Check-list.

As an official source on the taxonomy of North American birds, the Check-list of the American Ornithologists' Union is relied on by a variety of professional biologists, including museum curators, journal editors, state, provincial, and federal government wildlife managers and scientists, law enforcement personnel, and ornithologists in general. In addition, the Check-list is a basic resource for most of the technical and semi-popular references used by bird watchers. Because of wide acceptance of the Check-list as an authoritative standard, the Committee responsible for its preparation feels it necessary to avoid hasty decisions that risk quick reversal, thereby fostering instability. Following the time-honored tradition of previous Committees, our general stance has been conservative and cautious when judging recently published proposals for novel classifications, schemes of relationship, and species limits. We routinely have tabled recommendations for which supporting data were inconclusive and that lacked a consensus among the Committee. Such proposals can be reconsidered later in the light of additional relevant information.

Changes from the Sixth Edition

Higher-level classification.—The Committee established a policy for this edition whereby changes in classification of major groups require concordant evidence from two or more independent data sets. Among the more important changes in nonpasserines are the transfer of the family Cathartidae from the Falconiformes to the Ciconiiformes, the elevation of the New World Quail to the level of family (Odontophoridae), the removal of the family Pteroclididae from the Columbiformes to a position *incertae sedis* between the Charadriiformes and the Columbiformes, removing the family Upupidae from the Coraciiformes and raising it to the level of order (Upupiformes), and the separation of Old World and New World barbets (Capitonidae), with the latter placed as a subfamily (Capitoninae) in the family Ramphastidae.

In the suboscine passerines, the subfamily Thamnophilinae is elevated to the level of family (Thamnophilidae). In the Tyrannidae, we recognize a subfamily Platyrinchinae but not the subfamily Tityrinae. Several genera formerly scattered among the families Tyrannidae, Cotingidae, and Pipridae are removed from their former respective families and placed together *incertae sedis* before the Cotingidae.

In the oscine passerines, major changes include recognition of a corvine assemblage (the parvorder Corvida of Sibley and Ahlquist [1990]) of primarily Australasian families separate from other oscines. The Family Pycnonotidae is moved to follow the families Troglodytidae and Cinclidae, rather than precede them. The family Sturnidae is moved to a position following the Mimidae. The subfamilies of the sixth edition's Muscicapidae and Emberizidae are returned to their former rank as families; the kinglets, genus *Regulus,* are removed from the Muscicapidae and elevated to the rank of family (Regulidae). The genus *Peucedramus* is removed from the Parulidae and placed in a monotypic family (Peucedramidae), ahead of the Parulidae.

The many changes at lower taxonomic levels are summarized in Supplements published since the sixth edition.

A.O.U. numbers.—A system of numbering the species in the Check-list was established in the first edition and carried through, with necessary modifications, into the sixth. That system was applied only to those species that occurred in the geographic area covered by the first five editions, Canada and the continental United States plus Baja California, Mexico, and Greenland. Species in the sixth edition that occurred only in Hawaii, the Caribbean, Mexico, or Central America remained numberless. When an "extralimital" species was documented as occurring in the old Check-list area, the Committee assigned it a number. Any original significance of the sequence of numbers was lost as the classification changed over the years and as new species were interspersed. The original A.O.U. numbers retained usefulness in marking and organizing egg collections and other data sets or in administrative record keeping, but to an extent much limited by the geographic coverage. In 1990, Sibley and Monroe used a World List numbering system originally devised by P. William Smith, based on the old A.O.U. numbers but expanded to provide a number for each species of bird in the world. In the 38th Supplement to the Check-list (A.O.U. 1991), the Committee announced that it would adopt the World List numbering system in this seventh edition. Difficulties in applying that system as species were split or lumped over the next several years led the Committee to reevaluate what by default had become a commitment to maintain the system for a significant portion of the avian world. In 1995, the Committee decided to abandon any numbering system in the seventh edition, a decision noted in the 41st Supplement (A.O.U. 1997). The A.O.U. numbers for North American species in the sixth edition are still available and useful for those who see a need for a numbering system, as are those for the world list of birds in Sibley and Monroe (1990, 1993).

Statements of habitat.—Descriptions of habitat in the sixth edition were inconsistent and generalized, particularly for Neotropical species with which the Committee was less familiar. For the present edition we have adopted the standardized nomenclature for tropical American habitats used by Stotz et al. (1996) to compile ecological databases for all Neotropical bird species. Habitat terms that are initially capitalized here are from Stotz et al. (1996), and we refer readers to that publication for detailed botanical descriptions of those habitats.

Citations to literature.—As mentioned several times herein, the "Notes" sections at the ends of many species accounts have been expanded. We have attempted to provide references to document statements on alternative systematic treatments or nomenclature. We assume that most users of the Check-list are familiar with the historical literature on avian systematics, and will automatically refer to the classic compendia by Ridgway, Hellmayr, and Peters (as these series are generally known, although other authors also were involved). Those works, and the major scientific books on birds of the various Central American countries, may not always be cited in this Check-list, but they should always be consulted by researchers initiating taxonomic or distributional studies. Sibley and Ahlquist (1990) provided thorough historical reviews of the history of higher-level classification, which should be consulted by anyone interested in the classification of birds. That resource permits our "Notes" sections for higher-level categories to be brief.

French names.—A new feature of this edition is a list of French names for all included species. The French names used are derived from "Noms Français des Oiseaux du Monde," 1993, Commission internationale des noms français des oiseaux, Sainte-Foy, Canada, Éditions MultiMondes. Additional or modified French names necessitated by taxonomic changes adopted in the Check-list since 1993 were provided by the North American representatives of the International Committee on French names.

Appendix.—The three major appendices (A, B and C) of the sixth edition have been combined into a single Appendix for this volume. The Appendix includes species of birds whose names have been mentioned in the literature in a way suggesting that they are a part of the avifauna of the area covered but that the Committee finds inadmissible to the main list for reasons indicated. The Appendix consists of two parts—species reported with insufficient evidence, and named forms of doubtful status or hybrid origin. Appendix D of the sixth edition, unestablished introductions, has been omitted.

Taxonomic Categories

In general, our classification scheme uses only the familiar formal categories of Order, Suborder, Superfamily, Family, Subfamily, Tribe, Genus, and Species. We do not use the Superspecies as a taxonomic category as advocated by Amadon (1966) and as used by Sibley and Monroe (1990). In Notes at the end of many accounts, however, we indicate that species have been considered or treated as allospecies of superspecies by some authorities. The Committee believes that many such treatments are more conjectural than factual. An informal category that we invoke is that of Group, also used extensively by Sibley and Monroe (1990). A Group typically is a geographic portion (one or more subspecies) of a polytypic species that was previously treated as a separate species but that has been merged with another Group under the biological species concept (BSC). The use of the Group concept is helpful in tracing the nomenclatural history of a species and in many instances provides names for use if and when the species is redivided. Many mergers in the early days of the biological species concept were not based on strong biological evidence. We have retained the merged species because in most instances strong evidence for re-division has not been presented. In a few instances, recent studies have suggested, without thorough analysis, that populations long considered to be conspecific should perhaps be split into two or more species. We have in some such instances used the term Group prospectively rather than retrospectively. In a sense, each mention of a Group is an invitation for research into the relationships of the populations involved.

Recognition of subspecies.—As in the sixth edition, for reasons of expediency, the Committee reluctantly excluded treatment of subspecies in the current volume. Their omission should not be interpreted as a devaluation of the importance of that taxonomic rank. To the contrary, the Committee strongly and unanimously continues to endorse the biological reality and practical utility of subspecies. Subspecies names denote geographic segments of species' populations that differ abruptly and discretely in morphology or coloration; these differences often correspond with differences in behavior and habitat. Such populations are thus flagged for the attention of evolutionists, ecologists, and conservationists. Some subspecies also are "species-in-the-making" and therefore constitute a significant element of newly evolving biodiversity. The Committee's endorsement of subspecies as entities worthy of scientific inquiry carries with it our realization that an uncertain number of currently recognized subspecies, especially those formally named early in this century, probably cannot be validated by rigorous modern techniques. The opposite is also true; after careful study an unknown number of present subspecies probably will be unmasked as cryptic biological species. This point further emphasizes the important role of this taxonomic rank in calling attention to examples of avian diversity deserving additional investigation.

Geographic Coverage

The geographic area covered by this edition is the same as that in the sixth edition— North and Middle America including the adjacent islands under the jurisdiction of the included nations; the Hawaiian Islands; Clipperton Island; Bermuda; the West Indies, including the Bahama Islands, the Greater Antilles, Leeward and Windward islands of the Lesser Antilles; and Swan, Providencia, and San Andrés islands in the Gulf of Mexico. In the Bering Sea the boundary is that delimiting the United States from Russia, which is also the International Date Line. To the east the boundary is the boundary between Canada and Greenland. The southern boundary in Middle America is the border between Panama and Colombia; in the Lesser Antilles, Grenada is the southernmost island included. Records of occurrence within 160 kilometers (100 miles) offshore from any coast in the Check-list area are included unless the locality of the records lies outside the specified limits in that region (e.g., an international boundary).

Criteria for Inclusion

All species for which there is a published record or report of occurrence within the Check-list area are included, either in the main list or in the Appendix. For inclusion in the main text, records of occurrence must be documented by a specimen or an unequivocally identifiable photograph. A recording of vocalizations diagnostic for a species could constitute equally valid documentation, but no species are included on that basis. Properly labeled specimens deposited in a public museum provide the best evidence of occurrence because they can be reexamined and verified in many ways (see beyond). Identifiable photographs, preferably published, that are deposited in a museum or photographic archive are the next best kind of evidence, and several species are included on the basis of such evidence. Once a species is admitted to the Check-list area, additional distributional data may be based on sight reports, but if the occurrence would constitute an addition to a national list, especially for the United States or Canada, documentation must be as firm as for addition to the entire list. For states and provinces in the United States and Canada, and for other political units where it might apply, this Committee has cooperated extensively with the Check-list Committee of the American Birding Association, which also is stringent in its assessment of the documentation of records. We note that a properly verified record of a species does not validate either earlier or later poorly documented or undocumented sight reports.

Species that have been introduced by humans, either deliberately or accidentally, are considered to be established if there are persistent records for at least ten years and satisfactory evidence that they are maintaining a reasonably stable or increasing population through successful reproduction. Ornithologists and birders are urged to pay close attention to species introduced in their areas and to document constancy of occurrence and changes in population size. Introduced species often are neglected, although they provide opportunity for fascinating research.

Format

Scientific names.—The Check-list follows the third edition of the International Code of Zoological Nomenclature, published in 1985, and decisions of the International Commission on Zoological Nomenclature as published in the Bulletin of Zoological Nomenclature.

Citation.—Each generic and specific scientific name is followed by the name of the author (original describer) of the name. If the author's name is in parentheses, the species was originally described in a genus different from that to which it is currently assigned. Each generic or specific name is further followed by the date (year, occasionally month and year) in which it was first published and the name of the publication in which the name appeared. This is followed by a statement of the type species (of a genus) or type locality (of a species). Where more than one year is given, the one in parentheses is the ostensible date of publication, usually as on the cover or title page, and the one without parentheses is the actual date of publication as determined by other evidence. Some publication dates have been changed from the sixth edition because of the studies of Browning and Monroe (1991) or others. In a few instances, the change of a date has necessitated the change (from previous editions) of a citation or even of the name itself because of the Law of Priority as set forth in the Code. We are especially grateful to Alan P. Peterson for assistance in obtaining correct dates of publication.

English names.—We have followed the guidelines on English names set forth in the Preface to the sixth edition, with some exceptions. For species of primarily Eurasian distribution that are on the American list as a result of vagrancy, we have accepted the English name used by the B.O.U. (1992). An extensive suite of changes was published in the 40th Supplement (A.O.U. 1995). When a species was divided into two or more distinct species, we have used former English names, if available, for the resultant taxa. In general, we have followed the policy that no English name should be used for both a combined species and one of the components (Groups). However, we often have retained a well-known English name for a widespread North American form when a taxon that is either extralimital or restricted in distribution is separated from it. An example is the retention of the name Red-winged Blackbird for *Agelaius phoeniceus* when the Cuban population was separated as *A. assimilis* and named the Red-shouldered Blackbird.

Species Concepts

The Committee strongly and unanimously continues to endorse the biological species concept (BSC), in which species are considered to be genetically cohesive groups of populations that are reproductively isolated from other such groups. According to the BSC, geographic isolation leads to genetic change and potentially to the reproductive isolation of sister taxa. If and when these closely related forms later coexist, reproductive isolating mechanisms such as distinctive displays and vocalizations serve to maintain the essential genetic integrity of the newly formed biological species. In recent decades the BSC has been criticized because of several purported weaknesses (Cracraft 1983, McKitrick and Zink 1988). These problems fall into three categories (Zink 1996): interpretation of hybridization, the supposed recognition of nonhistorical groups, and the treatment of allopatric populations. Although space does not permit a thorough analysis of the relevant issues here, the Committee believes that the supposed weaknesses of the BSC have been overstated, as the following brief comments explain.

Regarding the interpretation of hybridization, we emphasize that a significant number of undisputed biological species of birds long retain the capacity for at least limited interbreeding with other species, even non-sister taxa (Prager and Wilson 1975, Grant and Grant 1992). Therefore, the occasional occurrence of hybridization, even between taxa that the Committee has long recognized as species, by no means diminishes the biological reality of their *essential* reproductive isolation. In practice, interbreeding has not been the ironclad determinate of conspecificity that some would believe. Thus, essential (lack of free interbreeding) rather than complete reproductive isolation has been and continues to be the fundamental operating criterion for species status by workers adhering to the BSC. In particular, hybridization of two forms across narrow and stable contact zones–once viewed as a sufficient criterion for treatment as one species–is now viewed as evidence for *lack* of free interbreeding. As a consequence, many pairs of sister taxa that were merged in the sixth edition have been resplit in this edition of the Check-list.

The BSC also has been criticized because it supposedly cannot correctly reflect the historical relationships of taxa. Admittedly, occasional examples of massive hybridization have led this Committee and previous ones (prior to the availability of molecular phylogenetic information) improperly to combine into single species probable non-sister taxa. Nonetheless, the BSC can readily accommodate new data on historical relationships of taxa as better estimates become available. Such estimates are now commonplace for many taxa, reflecting the widespread application of molecular systematic techniques appropriate to phylogenetic recovery.

Finally, the subjective treatment of allopatric populations, which by definition cannot pass the test of sympatry by proving their reproductive isolation, has been claimed to be a weakness of the BSC. In fact, modern technology has removed much of the taxonomic treatment of such populations from the realm of subjectivity and opinion. Quantified study of vocalizations and detailed investigation of genetic distances of allopatric populations, for example, provide data for quantitative comparison with levels of difference seen in the same features among sympatric biological species. When allopatric taxa demonstrate either similarities or differences in features related to reproductive isolation, such as song and genetic distance, taxonomic rank can be assigned by appropriate, objective criteria rather than through guesses as to their capacity for interbreeding with allopatric relatives.

Cracraft (1983) proposed a "phylogenetic species concept" (PSC) for ornithology, which narrowly defines species as "the smallest diagnosable cluster of individual organisms within which there is a parental pattern of ancestry and descent." Using this definition, many groups of populations recognized as subspecies under the BSC would become species under the PSC. For strongly characterized subspecies or "near species" under the BSC, diagnosis as phylogenetic species presents no serious problem. But to elevate to species status the plethora of subspecies of birds exhibiting distinct but trivial, or geographically chaotic, variation would represent extreme retrogression to the typological species concepts of more than a century ago. The PSC would be reduced to absurdity when species status is granted to tiny clusters of individuals now diagnosable through sophisticated molecular approaches. Furthermore, use of diagnostic characters does not necessarily guarantee accurate phylogenetic construction. Moreover, we regard as indefensible the identification of species by what are essentially phenetic criteria. A final major problem with the PSC is its lack of a distinctly biological foundation. This is revealed clearly by the fact that the PSC can apply equally well to either animate or inanimate objects, both categories of which include members that are diagnosable at some level and also have a history.

The Committee recognizes that essential genetic isolation is the indispensable feature of biological species and that this independence from all other living genetic systems is a consequence of reproductive isolation. The latter is, therefore, the main engine that propels the evolution of biodiversity, including that of birds. That one can observe directly and measure the reproductive isolating mechanisms that protect the essential genetic integrity of biological species of birds in natural environments is further reason to apply the BSC to members of this Class. Application of the BSC has the undeniable biological appeal of allowing the behavior of the populations themselves to determine taxonomic rank.

Collection of Specimens

The Committee strongly and unanimously supports the judicious and ethical collection of birds for scientific purposes. Specimens are indispensable for the investigation of a multitude of unsolved problems of relationship, evolutionary history, structure, and geographic occurrence. Existing collections are an irreplaceable foundation for present taxonomy and distribution. Nonetheless, most specimens in such collections were obtained decades ago when standards for systematic analysis were different from those at present. Because of discoloration resulting from age, inadequate reproductive data, and poor initial preparation– as well as ongoing evolutionary change–present collections, even when considered together, nearly always must be supplemented by new material for comprehensive systematic studies (Winker 1996). Furthermore, most current collections either lack or have an inadequate representation of preserved tissue necessary for the application of molecular systematic approaches.

We emphasize that the recognition, description, and conservation of all biodiversity, including that of birds, depends ultimately on proper taxonomic analyses. The latter, in turn, cannot be conducted without adequate scientific collections of specimens (Remsen 1995).

The Committee unanimously recognizes the contributions of an increasing number of serious amateurs and other workers with excellent skills in field identification who continue to add significant distributional information for the large number of easily identifiable kinds of birds. Despite such contributions, however, scientific collecting continues to play a crucial role in the proper documentation of avian distribution. Many species of birds in some plumages, and some species in all plumages, cannot be identified safely in the field, the increased sophistication of field skills notwithstanding. The Committee deplores the invasion of the primary distributional literature by an increasing volume of poorly documented reports of the latter two categories of species, resulting in a significant general decline in quality of the scientific database for avian distribution. For many taxa of birds, judicious scientific collecting is necessary to provide full and proper documentation for dependable distributional records.

Acknowledgments

It is difficult to think of an ornithologist or birder who is interested in avian systematics or distribution who has not helped us in some way, directly or indirectly, in the preparation of this volume.

Jon L. Dunn provided detailed reviews of the distribution sections for many families. M. Ralph Browning, Steven W. Cardiff, Roger B. Clapp, Donna L. Dittmann, and Curtis A. Marantz reviewed early drafts of many family accounts. The Committee wishes to acknowledge its great debt to the following additional individuals for providing diverse kinds of important assistance: John Arvin, G. C. Banks, Jon C. Barlow, John M. Bates, Louis Bevier, Paul A. Buckley, R. Wayne Campbell, Carla Cicero, José A. Colon, Paul A. DeBenedictis, Richard A. Erickson, Ted Eubanks, Robert C. Fleischer, Kimball Garrett, John A. Gerwin, Daniel D. Gibson, Helen F. James, Greg W. Lasley, Paul Lehman, Joe T. Marshall, Jr., Joseph Morlan, Storrs L. Olson, Michael A. Patten, Alan P. Peterson, H. Douglas Pratt, Robert L. Pyle, Mark B. Robbins, Kenneth V. Rosenberg, Thomas S. Schulenberg, P. William Smith, Ted Snetsinger, Douglas F. Stotz, John Tomer, Philip Unitt, and Robert M. Zink.

Because of the untimely death of Burt Monroe, we were unable to construct a complete list of those who contributed or corrected distributional information in early reviews of the manuscript. We apologize to any who were omitted from the following list: Gordon Berkey (North Dakota), Laurence C. Binford (California, Illinois, Michigan, Oaxaca), Eriik A. T. Blom (Delaware, Maryland), Steven W. Cardiff (Louisiana), Charles M. Carlson (Montana), Paul A. DeBenedictis (New York), James J. Dinsmore (Iowa), Donna L. Dittmann (Louisiana), David O. Easterla (Missouri), Charles Ely (Kansas), Richard A. Erickson (California), Kimball L. Garrett (California), Orlando Garrido (Cuba), Sidney A. Gauthreaux (South Carolina), Daniel D. Gibson (Alaska), Bernie Gollop (Saskatchewan), Joseph A. Grzybowski (Oklahoma), George A. Hall (West Virginia), C. Stuart Houston (Prairie provinces), S. N. G. Howell (Guatemala, Mexico), John P. Hubbard (New Mexico), Thomas A. Imhof (Alabama), Ross D. James (Ontario), Robert B. Janssen (Minnesota), Charles E. Keller (Indiana), Allan A. Keith (Lesser Antilles), Rudolf F. Koes (Manitoba), Ed Kurac (Texas), Greg W. Lasley (Texas), Catherine Levy (Jamaica), Curtis A. Marantz (Louisiana), Bruce McGillivray (Alberta), J. Michael Meyers (Puerto Rico), Russell E. Mumford (Indiana), Robert Nero (Manitoba), Blair Nikula (New England), Robert L. Norton (West Indies), Michael A. Patten (California), Dennis Paulson (British Columbia, Idaho, Oregon, Washington), Robert B. Payne (Michigan), Raul Perez-Rivera (Puerto Rico), Bruce Peterjohn (Ohio), H. Douglas Pratt (Hawaii), Jack Redall (Colorado), Robert R. Reid (Alabama), Robert S. Ridgely (Panama), Chandler S. Robbins (Delaware, D.C., Maryland), W. B. Robertson (Florida), Gary H. Rosenberg (Arizona, Costa Rica), Ella Sorenson (Utah), Max C. Thompson (Kansas), Walter Thurber (El Salvador), Nathaniel R. Whitney (South Dakota), Morris D. Williams (Tennessee), Sartor O. Williams, III (New Mexico), Glen E. Woolfenden (Florida), and Phillip L. Wright (Montana).

> *Committee:* Richard C. Banks, *Chairman, 1995–1998*
> John W. Fitzpatrick
> Thomas R. Howell
> Ned K. Johnson
> † Burt L. Monroe, Jr., *Chairman, 1983–1994*
> Henri Ouellet
> J. V. Remsen, Jr.
> Robert W. Storer

---

† Deceased

LIST OF THE 2,008 BIRD SPECIES (WITH SCIENTIFIC AND ENGLISH NAMES) KNOWN FROM THE A.O.U. CHECK-LIST AREA.

Notes: "(A)" = accidental/casual in A.O.U. area; "(H)" = recorded in A.O.U. area only from Hawaii; "(I)" = introduced into A.O.U. area; "(N)" = has not bred in A.O.U. area but occurs regularly as nonbreeding visitor; "†" preceding name = extinct.

TINAMIFORMES
TINAMIDAE
Tinamus major Great Tinamou.
Nothocercus bonapartei Highland Tinamou.
Crypturellus soui Little Tinamou.
Crypturellus cinnamomeus Thicket Tinamou.
Crypturellus boucardi Slaty-breasted Tinamou.
Crypturellus kerriae Choco Tinamou.
GAVIIFORMES
GAVIIDAE
Gavia stellata Red-throated Loon.
Gavia arctica Arctic Loon.
Gavia pacifica Pacific Loon.
Gavia immer Common Loon.
Gavia adamsii Yellow-billed Loon.
PODICIPEDIFORMES
PODICIPEDIDAE
Tachybaptus dominicus Least Grebe.
Podilymbus podiceps Pied-billed Grebe.
†*Podilymbus gigas* Atitlan Grebe.
Podiceps auritus Horned Grebe.
Podiceps grisegena Red-necked Grebe.
Podiceps nigricollis Eared Grebe.
Aechmophorus occidentalis Western Grebe.
Aechmophorus clarkii Clark's Grebe.
PROCELLARIIFORMES
DIOMEDEIDAE
Thalassarche chlororhynchos Yellow-nosed Albatross. (A)
Thalassarche cauta Shy Albatross. (A)
Thalassarche melanophris Black-browed Albatross. (A)
Phoebetria palpebrata Light-mantled Albatross. (A)
Diomedea exulans Wandering Albatross. (A)
Phoebastria immutabilis Laysan Albatross.
Phoebastria nigripes Black-footed Albatross.
Phoebastria albatrus Short-tailed Albatross. (N)
PROCELLARIIDAE
Fulmarus glacialis Northern Fulmar.
Pterodroma neglecta Kermadec Petrel. (A)
Pterodroma arminjoniana Herald Petrel. (A)
Pterodroma ultima Murphy's Petrel. (N)
Pterodroma inexpectata Mottled Petrel. (A)
Pterodroma cahow Bermuda Petrel.
Pterodroma hasitata Black-capped Petrel.
Pterodroma externa Juan Fernandez Petrel. (N)
Pterodroma phaeopygia Dark-rumped Petrel.
Pterodroma cervicalis White-necked Petrel. (H)
Pterodroma hypoleuca Bonin Petrel. (H)
Pterodroma nigripennis Black-winged Petrel. (H, A)
Pterodroma cookii Cook's Petrel. (N)
Pterodroma longirostris Stejneger's Petrel. (A)

Bulweria bulwerii Bulwer's Petrel. (H)
Bulweria fallax Jouanin's Petrel. (H, A)
Procellaria parkinsoni Parkinson's Petrel. (N)
Calonectris leucomelas Streaked Shearwater. (A)
Calonectris diomedea Cory's Shearwater. (N)
Puffinus creatopus Pink-footed Shearwater. (N)
Puffinus carneipes Flesh-footed Shearwater. (N)
Puffinus gravis Greater Shearwater. (N)
Puffinus pacificus Wedge-tailed Shearwater.
Puffinus bulleri Buller's Shearwater. (N)
Puffinus griseus Sooty Shearwater. (N)
Puffinus tenuirostris Short-tailed Shearwater. (N)
Puffinus nativitatis Christmas Shearwater. (H)
Puffinus puffinus Manx Shearwater.
Puffinus auricularis Townsend's Shearwater.
Puffinus opisthomelas Black-vented Shearwater.
Puffinus lherminieri Audubon's Shearwater.
Puffinus assimilis Little Shearwater. (A)

HYDROBATIDAE
Oceanites oceanicus Wilson's Storm-Petrel. (N)
Pelagodroma marina White-faced Storm-Petrel. (A)
Hydrobates pelagicus European Storm-Petrel. (A)
Oceanodroma furcata Fork-tailed Storm-Petrel.
Oceanodroma leucorhoa Leach's Storm-Petrel.
Oceanodroma homochroa Ashy Storm-Petrel.
Oceanodroma castro Band-rumped Storm-Petrel. (N)
Oceanodroma tethys Wedge-rumped Storm-Petrel. (N)
Oceanodroma melania Black Storm-Petrel.
†*Oceanodroma macrodactyla* Guadalupe Storm-Petrel.
Oceanodroma markhami Markham's Storm-Petrel. (A)
Oceanodroma tristrami Tristram's Storm-Petrel. (H)
Oceanodroma microsoma Least Storm-Petrel.

PELECANIFORMES
PHAETHONTIDAE
Phaethon lepturus White-tailed Tropicbird.
Phaethon aethereus Red-billed Tropicbird.
Phaethon rubricauda Red-tailed Tropicbird.

SULIDAE
Sula dactylatra Masked Booby.
Sula nebouxii Blue-footed Booby.
Sula variegata Peruvian Booby. (A)
Sula leucogaster Brown Booby.
Sula sula Red-footed Booby.
Morus bassanus Northern Gannet.

PELECANIDAE
Pelecanus erythrorhynchos American White Pelican.
Pelecanus occidentalis Brown Pelican.

PHALACROCORACIDAE
Phalacrocorax penicillatus Brandt's Cormorant.
Phalacrocorax brasilianus Neotropic Cormorant.
Phalacrocorax auritus Double-crested Cormorant.
Phalacrocorax carbo Great Cormorant.
Phalacrocorax urile Red-faced Cormorant.
Phalacrocorax pelagicus Pelagic Cormorant.

ANHINGIDAE
Anhinga anhinga Anhinga.

FREGATIDAE
Fregata magnificens Magnificent Frigatebird.

Fregata minor Great Frigatebird.
Fregata ariel Lesser Frigatebird. (A)

CICONIIFORMES
  ARDEIDAE
    Botaurus pinnatus Pinnated Bittern.
    Botaurus lentiginosus American Bittern.
    Ixobrychus sinensis Yellow Bittern. (A)
    Ixobrychus exilis Least Bittern.
    Tigrisoma lineatum Rufescent Tiger-Heron.
    Tigrisoma fasciatum Fasciated Tiger-Heron.
    Tigrisoma mexicanum Bare-throated Tiger-Heron.
    Ardea herodias Great Blue Heron.
    Ardea cinerea Gray Heron. (A)
    Ardea cocoi Cocoi Heron.
    Ardea alba Great Egret.
    Egretta eulophotes Chinese Egret. (A)
    Egretta garzetta Little Egret. (A)
    Egretta gularis Western Reef-Heron. (A)
    Egretta thula Snowy Egret.
    Egretta caerulea Little Blue Heron.
    Egretta tricolor Tricolored Heron.
    Egretta rufescens Reddish Egret.
    Bubulcus ibis Cattle Egret.
    Butorides virescens Green Heron.
    Butorides striatus Striated Heron.
    Agamia agami Agami Heron.
    Pilherodius pileatus Capped Heron.
    Nycticorax nycticorax Black-crowned Night-Heron.
    Nyctanassa violacea Yellow-crowned Night-Heron.
    Cochlearius cochlearius Boat-billed Heron.
  THRESKIORNITHIDAE
    Threskiornithinae
      Eudocimus albus White Ibis.
      Eudocimus ruber Scarlet Ibis. (A)
      Plegadis falcinellus Glossy Ibis.
      Plegadis chihi White-faced Ibis.
      Mesembrinibis cayennensis Green Ibis.
      Theristicus caudatus Buff-necked Ibis. (A)
    Plataleinae
      Ajaia ajaja Roseate Spoonbill.
  CICONIIDAE
    Jabiru mycteria Jabiru.
    Mycteria americana Wood Stork.
  CATHARTIDAE
    Coragyps atratus Black Vulture.
    Cathartes aura Turkey Vulture.
    Cathartes burrovianus Lesser Yellow-headed Vulture.
    Gymnogyps californianus California Condor.
    Sarcoramphus papa King Vulture.

PHOENICOPTERIFORMES
  PHOENICOPTERIDAE
    Phoenicopterus ruber Greater Flamingo.

ANSERIFORMES
  ANATIDAE
    Dendrocygninae
      Dendrocygna viduata White-faced Whistling-Duck.
      Dendrocygna autumnalis Black-bellied Whistling-Duck.
      Dendrocygna arborea West Indian Whistling-Duck.

Dendrocygna bicolor Fulvous Whistling-Duck.
Anserinae
    Anser fabalis Bean Goose. (A)
    Anser brachyrhynchus Pink-footed Goose. (A)
    Anser albifrons Greater White-fronted Goose.
    Anser erythropus Lesser White-fronted Goose. (A)
    Chen canagica Emperor Goose.
    Chen caerulescens Snow Goose.
    Chen rossii Ross's Goose.
    Branta canadensis Canada Goose.
    Branta sandvicensis Hawaiian Goose. (H)
    Branta bernicla Brant.
    Branta leucopsis Barnacle Goose. (A)
    Cygnus olor Mute Swan. (I)
    Cygnus buccinator Trumpeter Swan.
    Cygnus columbianus Tundra Swan.
    Cygnus cygnus Whooper Swan.
Tadorninae
    Sarkidiornis melanotos Comb Duck.
    Neochen jubata Orinoco Goose. (A)
Anatinae
    Cairina moschata Muscovy Duck.
    Aix sponsa Wood Duck.
    Anas strepera Gadwall.
    Anas falcata Falcated Duck. (A)
    Anas penelope Eurasian Wigeon. (N)
    Anas americana American Wigeon.
    Anas rubripes American Black Duck.
    Anas platyrhynchos Mallard.
    Anas fulvigula Mottled Duck.
    Anas wyvilliana Hawaiian Duck. (H)
    Anas laysanensis Laysan Duck. (H)
    Anas poecilorhyncha Spot-billed Duck. (A)
    Anas discors Blue-winged Teal.
    Anas cyanoptera Cinnamon Teal.
    Anas clypeata Northern Shoveler.
    Anas bahamensis White-cheeked Pintail.
    Anas acuta Northern Pintail.
    Anas querquedula Garganey. (N)
    Anas formosa Baikal Teal. (A)
    Anas crecca Green-winged Teal.
    Aythya valisineria Canvasback.
    Aythya americana Redhead.
    Aythya ferina Common Pochard. (A)
    Aythya collaris Ring-necked Duck.
    Aythya fuligula Tufted Duck.
    Aythya marila Greater Scaup.
    Aythya affinis Lesser Scaup.
    Polysticta stelleri Steller's Eider.
    Somateria fischeri Spectacled Eider.
    Somateria spectabilis King Eider.
    Somateria mollissima Common Eider.
    Histrionicus histrionicus Harlequin Duck.
  †*Camptorhynchus labradorius* Labrador Duck.
    Melanitta perspicillata Surf Scoter.
    Melanitta fusca White-winged Scoter.
    Melanitta nigra Black Scoter.
    Clangula hyemalis Oldsquaw.

Bucephala albeola Bufflehead.
Bucephala clangula Common Goldeneye.
Bucephala islandica Barrow's Goldeneye.
Mergellus albellus Smew. (N)
Lophodytes cucullatus Hooded Merganser.
Mergus merganser Common Merganser.
Mergus serrator Red-breasted Merganser.
Nomonyx dominicus Masked Duck.
Oxyura jamaicensis Ruddy Duck.

FALCONIFORMES
ACCIPITRIDAE
Pandioninae
Pandion haliaetus Osprey.
Accipitrinae
Leptodon cayanensis Gray-headed Kite.
Chondrohierax uncinatus Hook-billed Kite.
Elanoides forficatus Swallow-tailed Kite.
Gampsonyx swainsonii Pearl Kite.
Elanus leucurus White-tailed Kite.
Rostrhamus sociabilis Snail Kite.
Rostrhamus hamatus Slender-billed Kite.
Harpagus bidentatus Double-toothed Kite.
Ictinia mississippiensis Mississippi Kite.
Ictinia plumbea Plumbeous Kite.
Haliaeetus leucocephalus Bald Eagle.
Haliaeetus albicilla White-tailed Eagle.
Haliaeetus pelagicus Steller's Sea-Eagle. (A)
Busarellus nigricollis Black-collared Hawk.
Circus cyaneus Northern Harrier.
Accipiter soloensis Gray Frog-Hawk. (H, A)
Accipiter superciliosus Tiny Hawk.
Accipiter striatus Sharp-shinned Hawk.
Accipiter cooperii Cooper's Hawk.
Accipiter gundlachi Gundlach's Hawk.
Accipiter bicolor Bicolored Hawk.
Accipiter gentilis Northern Goshawk.
Geranospiza caerulescens Crane Hawk.
Leucopternis plumbea Plumbeous Hawk.
Leucopternis princeps Barred Hawk.
Leucopternis semiplumbea Semiplumbeous Hawk.
Leucopternis albicollis White Hawk.
Asturina nitida Gray Hawk.
Buteogallus anthracinus Common Black-Hawk.
Buteogallus subtilis Mangrove Black-Hawk.
Buteogallus urubitinga Great Black-Hawk.
Buteogallus meridionalis Savanna Hawk.
Parabuteo unicinctus Harris's Hawk.
Harpyhaliaetus solitarius Solitary Eagle.
Buteo magnirostris Roadside Hawk.
Buteo lineatus Red-shouldered Hawk.
Buteo ridgwayi Ridgway's Hawk.
Buteo platypterus Broad-winged Hawk.
Buteo brachyurus Short-tailed Hawk.
Buteo swainsoni Swainson's Hawk.
Buteo albicaudatus White-tailed Hawk.
Buteo albonotatus Zone-tailed Hawk.
Buteo solitarius Hawaiian Hawk. (H)
Buteo jamaicensis Red-tailed Hawk.

Buteo regalis Ferruginous Hawk.
Buteo lagopus Rough-legged Hawk.
Morphnus guianensis Crested Eagle.
Harpia harpyja Harpy Eagle.
Aquila chrysaetos Golden Eagle.
Spizastur melanoleucus Black-and-white Hawk-Eagle.
Spizaetus tyrannus Black Hawk-Eagle.
Spizaetus ornatus Ornate Hawk-Eagle.

FALCONIDAE
Micrasturinae
Micrastur ruficollis Barred Forest-Falcon.
Micrastur mirandollei Slaty-backed Forest-Falcon.
Micrastur semitorquatus Collared Forest-Falcon.
Caracarinae
Daptrius americanus Red-throated Caracara.
Caracara plancus Crested Caracara.
Milvago chimachima Yellow-headed Caracara.
Falconinae
Herpetotheres cachinnans Laughing Falcon.
Falco tinnunculus Eurasian Kestrel. (A)
Falco sparverius American Kestrel.
Falco columbarius Merlin.
Falco subbuteo Eurasian Hobby. (A)
Falco femoralis Aplomado Falcon.
Falco rufigularis Bat Falcon.
Falco deiroleucus Orange-breasted Falcon.
Falco rusticolus Gyrfalcon.
Falco peregrinus Peregrine Falcon.
Falco mexicanus Prairie Falcon.

GALLIFORMES
CRACIDAE
Ortalis vetula Plain Chachalaca.
Ortalis cinereiceps Gray-headed Chachalaca.
Ortalis ruficauda Rufous-vented Chachalaca.
Ortalis wagleri Rufous-bellied Chachalaca.
Ortalis poliocephala West Mexican Chachalaca.
Ortalis leucogastra White-bellied Chachalaca.
Penelope purpurascens Crested Guan.
Chamaepetes unicolor Black Guan.
Penelopina nigra Highland Guan.
Oreophasis derbianus Horned Guan.
Crax rubra Great Curassow.
PHASIANIDAE
Phasianinae
Alectoris chukar Chukar. (I)
Francolinus pondicerianus Gray Francolin. (H, I)
Francolinus francolinus Black Francolin. (H, I)
Francolinus erckelii Erckel's Francolin. (H, I)
Tetraogallus himalayensis Himalayan Snowcock. (I)
Perdix perdix Gray Partridge. (I)
Coturnix japonica Japanese Quail. (H, I)
Gallus gallus Red Junglefowl. (H, I)
Lophura leucomelanos Kalij Pheasant. (H, I)
Phasianus colchicus Ring-necked Pheasant. (I)
Pavo cristatus Common Peafowl. (I)
Tetraoninae
Bonasa umbellus Ruffed Grouse.
Centrocercus urophasianus Sage Grouse.

Falcipennis canadensis Spruce Grouse.
Lagopus lagopus Willow Ptarmigan.
Lagopus mutus Rock Ptarmigan.
Lagopus leucurus White-tailed Ptarmigan.
Dendragapus obscurus Blue Grouse.
Tympanuchus phasianellus Sharp-tailed Grouse.
Tympanuchus cupido Greater Prairie-Chicken.
Tympanuchus pallidicinctus Lesser Prairie-Chicken.
Meleagridinae
Meleagris gallopavo Wild Turkey.
Meleagris ocellata Ocellated Turkey.
Numidinae
Numida meleagris Helmeted Guineafowl. (I)
ODONTOPHORIDAE
Dendrortyx barbatus Bearded Wood-Partridge.
Dendrortyx macroura Long-tailed Wood-Partridge.
Dendrortyx leucophrys Buffy-crowned Wood-Partridge.
Oreortyx pictus Mountain Quail.
Callipepla squamata Scaled Quail.
Callipepla douglasii Elegant Quail.
Callipepla californica California Quail.
Callipepla gambelii Gambel's Quail.
Philortyx fasciatus Banded Quail.
Colinus virginianus Northern Bobwhite.
Colinus nigrogularis Black-throated Bobwhite.
Colinus cristatus Crested Bobwhite.
Odontophorus gujanensis Marbled Wood-Quail.
Odontophorus melanotis Black-eared Wood-Quail.
Odontophorus dialeucos Tacarcuna Wood-Quail.
Odontophorus leucolaemus Black-breasted Wood-Quail.
Odontophorus guttatus Spotted Wood-Quail.
Dactylortyx thoracicus Singing Quail.
Cyrtonyx montezumae Montezuma Quail.
Cyrtonyx ocellatus Ocellated Quail.
Rhynchortyx cinctus Tawny-faced Quail.
GRUIFORMES
RALLIDAE
Coturnicops noveboracensis Yellow Rail.
Micropygia schomburgkii Ocellated Crake. (A)
Laterallus ruber Ruddy Crake.
Laterallus albigularis White-throated Crake.
Laterallus exilis Gray-breasted Crake.
Laterallus jamaicensis Black Rail.
Crex crex Corn Crake. (A)
Rallus longirostris Clapper Rail.
Rallus elegans King Rail.
Rallus limicola Virginia Rail.
Aramides axillaris Rufous-necked Wood-Rail.
Aramides cajanea Gray-necked Wood-Rail.
Amaurolimnas concolor Uniform Crake.
†*Porzana palmeri* Laysan Rail. (H)
Porzana porzana Spotted Crake. (A)
Porzana carolina Sora.
†*Porzana sandwichensis* Hawaiian Rail. (H)
Porzana flaviventer Yellow-breasted Crake.
Neocrex colombianus Colombian Crake.
Neocrex erythrops Paint-billed Crake.
Cyanolimnas cerverai Zapata Rail.

Pardirallus maculatus Spotted Rail.
Porphyrula martinica Purple Gallinule.
Porphyrula flavirostris Azure Gallinule. (A)
Gallinula chloropus Common Moorhen.
Fulica atra Eurasian Coot. (A)
Fulica alai Hawaiian Coot. (H)
Fulica americana American Coot.
Fulica caribaea Caribbean Coot.

HELIORNITHIDAE
Heliornis fulica Sungrebe.

EURYPYGIDAE
Eurypyga helias Sunbittern.

ARAMIDAE
Aramus guarauna Limpkin.

GRUIDAE
Gruinae
Grus canadensis Sandhill Crane.
Grus grus Common Crane. (A)
Grus americana Whooping Crane.

CHARADRIIFORMES
BURHINIDAE
Burhinus bistriatus Double-striped Thick-knee.

CHARADRIIDAE
Vanellus vanellus Northern Lapwing. (A)
Vanellus chilensis Southern Lapwing. (N)
Pluvialis squatarola Black-bellied Plover.
Pluvialis apricaria European Golden-Plover. (A)
Pluvialis dominica American Golden-Plover.
Pluvialis fulva Pacific Golden-Plover.
Charadrius mongolus Mongolian Plover. (N)
Charadrius collaris Collared Plover.
Charadrius alexandrinus Snowy Plover.
Charadrius wilsonia Wilson's Plover.
Charadrius hiaticula Common Ringed Plover.
Charadrius semipalmatus Semipalmated Plover.
Charadrius melodus Piping Plover.
Charadrius dubius Little Ringed Plover. (A)
Charadrius vociferus Killdeer.
Charadrius montanus Mountain Plover.
Charadrius morinellus Eurasian Dotterel.

HAEMATOPODIDAE
Haematopus ostralegus Eurasian Oystercatcher. (A)
Haematopus palliatus American Oystercatcher.
Haematopus bachmani Black Oystercatcher.

RECURVIROSTRIDAE
Himantopus himantopus Black-winged Stilt. (A)
Himantopus mexicanus Black-necked Stilt.
Recurvirostra americana American Avocet.

JACANIDAE
Jacana spinosa Northern Jacana.
Jacana jacana Wattled Jacana.

SCOLOPACIDAE
Tringa nebularia Common Greenshank. (N)
Tringa melanoleuca Greater Yellowlegs.
Tringa flavipes Lesser Yellowlegs.
Tringa stagnatilis Marsh Sandpiper. (A)
Tringa totanus Common Redshank. (A)
Tringa erythropus Spotted Redshank. (N)

Tringa glareola Wood Sandpiper.
Tringa ochropus Green Sandpiper. (A)
Tringa solitaria Solitary Sandpiper.
Catoptrophorus semipalmatus Willet.
Heteroscelus incanus Wandering Tattler.
Heteroscelus brevipes Gray-tailed Tattler. (N)
Actitis hypoleucos Common Sandpiper. (N)
Actitis macularia Spotted Sandpiper.
Xenus cinereus Terek Sandpiper. (N)
Bartramia longicauda Upland Sandpiper.
Numenius minutus Little Curlew. (A)
Numenius borealis Eskimo Curlew.
Numenius phaeopus Whimbrel.
Numenius tahitiensis Bristle-thighed Curlew.
Numenius madagascariensis Far Eastern Curlew. (N)
Numenius tenuirostris Slender-billed Curlew. (A)
Numenius arquata Eurasian Curlew. (A)
Numenius americanus Long-billed Curlew.
Limosa limosa Black-tailed Godwit. (N)
Limosa haemastica Hudsonian Godwit.
Limosa lapponica Bar-tailed Godwit.
Limosa fedoa Marbled Godwit.
Arenaria interpres Ruddy Turnstone.
Arenaria melanocephala Black Turnstone.
Aphriza virgata Surfbird.
Calidris tenuirostris Great Knot. (A)
Calidris canutus Red Knot.
Calidris alba Sanderling.
Calidris pusilla Semipalmated Sandpiper.
Calidris mauri Western Sandpiper.
Calidris ruficollis Red-necked Stint.
Calidris minuta Little Stint. (N)
Calidris temminckii Temminck's Stint. (A)
Calidris subminuta Long-toed Stint. (N)
Calidris minutilla Least Sandpiper.
Calidris fuscicollis White-rumped Sandpiper.
Calidris bairdii Baird's Sandpiper.
Calidris melanotos Pectoral Sandpiper.
Calidris acuminata Sharp-tailed Sandpiper. (N)
Calidris maritima Purple Sandpiper.
Calidris ptilocnemis Rock Sandpiper.
Calidris alpina Dunlin.
Calidris ferruginea Curlew Sandpiper.
Calidris himantopus Stilt Sandpiper.
Eurynorhynchus pygmeus Spoonbill Sandpiper. (A)
Limicola falcinellus Broad-billed Sandpiper. (A)
Tryngites subruficollis Buff-breasted Sandpiper.
Philomachus pugnax Ruff.
Limnodromus griseus Short-billed Dowitcher.
Limnodromus scolopaceus Long-billed Dowitcher.
Lymnocryptes minimus Jack Snipe. (A)
Gallinago gallinago Common Snipe.
Gallinago stenura Pin-tailed Snipe. (A)
Scolopax rusticola Eurasian Woodcock. (A)
Scolopax minor American Woodcock.
Phalaropus tricolor Wilson's Phalarope.
Phalaropus lobatus Red-necked Phalarope.
Phalaropus fulicaria Red Phalarope.

GLAREOLIDAE
  Glareolinae
    Glareola maldivarum Oriental Pratincole. (A)
LARIDAE
  Stercorariinae
    Catharacta skua Great Skua. (N)
    Catharacta maccormicki South Polar Skua. (N)
    Stercorarius pomarinus Pomarine Jaeger.
    Stercorarius parasiticus Parasitic Jaeger.
    Stercorarius longicaudus Long-tailed Jaeger.
  Larinae
    Larus atricilla Laughing Gull.
    Larus pipixcan Franklin's Gull.
    Larus minutus Little Gull.
    Larus ridibundus Black-headed Gull.
    Larus philadelphia Bonaparte's Gull.
    Larus heermanni Heermann's Gull.
    Larus modestus Gray Gull. (A)
    Larus belcheri Band-tailed Gull. (A)
    Larus crassirostris Black-tailed Gull. (A)
    Larus canus Mew Gull.
    Larus delawarensis Ring-billed Gull.
    Larus californicus California Gull.
    Larus argentatus Herring Gull.
    Larus cachinnans Yellow-legged Gull. (A)
    Larus thayeri Thayer's Gull.
    Larus glaucoides Iceland Gull.
    Larus fuscus Lesser Black-backed Gull. (N)
    Larus schistisagus Slaty-backed Gull.
    Larus livens Yellow-footed Gull.
    Larus occidentalis Western Gull.
    Larus glaucescens Glaucous-winged Gull.
    Larus hyperboreus Glaucous Gull.
    Larus marinus Great Black-backed Gull.
    Xema sabini Sabine's Gull.
    Rissa tridactyla Black-legged Kittiwake.
    Rissa brevirostris Red-legged Kittiwake.
    Rhodostethia rosea Ross's Gull.
    Pagophila eburnea Ivory Gull.
  Sterninae
    Sterna nilotica Gull-billed Tern.
    Sterna caspia Caspian Tern.
    Sterna maxima Royal Tern.
    Sterna elegans Elegant Tern.
    Sterna bergii Great Crested Tern. (H, A)
    Sterna sandvicensis Sandwich Tern.
    Sterna dougallii Roseate Tern.
    Sterna hirundo Common Tern.
    Sterna paradisaea Arctic Tern.
    Sterna forsteri Forster's Tern.
    Sterna albifrons Little Tern. (H, A)
    Sterna antillarum Least Tern.
    Sterna superciliaris Yellow-billed Tern. (A)
    Sterna aleutica Aleutian Tern.
    Sterna lunata Gray-backed Tern. (H)
    Sterna anaethetus Bridled Tern.
    Sterna fuscata Sooty Tern.
    Phaetusa simplex Large-billed Tern. (A)

Chlidonias leucopterus White-winged Tern. (A)
Chlidonias hybridus Whiskered Tern. (A)
Chlidonias niger Black Tern.
Larosterna inca Inca Tern. (A)
Anous stolidus Brown Noddy.
Anous minutus Black Noddy.
Procelsterna cerulea Blue-gray Noddy. (H)
Gygis alba Common White-Tern. (H)
Rynchopinae
Rynchops niger Black Skimmer.
ALCIDAE
Alle alle Dovekie.
Uria aalge Common Murre.
Uria lomvia Thick-billed Murre.
Alca torda Razorbill.
†*Pinguinus impennis* Great Auk.
Cepphus grylle Black Guillemot.
Cepphus columba Pigeon Guillemot.
Brachyramphus perdix Long-billed Murrelet. (A)
Brachyramphus marmoratus Marbled Murrelet.
Brachyramphus brevirostris Kittlitz's Murrelet.
Synthliboramphus hypoleucus Xantus's Murrelet.
Synthliboramphus craveri Craveri's Murrelet.
Synthliboramphus antiquus Ancient Murrelet.
Ptychoramphus aleuticus Cassin's Auklet.
Aethia psittacula Parakeet Auklet.
Aethia pusilla Least Auklet.
Aethia pygmaea Whiskered Auklet.
Aethia cristatella Crested Auklet.
Cerorhinca monocerata Rhinoceros Auklet.
Fratercula arctica Atlantic Puffin.
Fratercula corniculata Horned Puffin.
Fratercula cirrhata Tufted Puffin.
Family *INCERTAE SEDIS*
PTEROCLIDIDAE
Pterocles exustus Chestnut-bellied Sandgrouse. (H, I)
COLUMBIFORMES
COLUMBIDAE
Columba livia Rock Dove. (I)
Columba cayennensis Pale-vented Pigeon.
Columba speciosa Scaled Pigeon.
Columba squamosa Scaly-naped Pigeon.
Columba leucocephala White-crowned Pigeon.
Columba flavirostris Red-billed Pigeon.
Columba inornata Plain Pigeon.
Columba fasciata Band-tailed Pigeon.
Columba caribaea Ring-tailed Pigeon.
Columba subvinacea Ruddy Pigeon.
Columba nigrirostris Short-billed Pigeon.
Streptopelia orientalis Oriental Turtle-Dove. (A)
Streptopelia risoria Ringed Turtle-Dove. (I)
Streptopelia turtur European Turtle-Dove. (A)
Streptopelia decaocto Eurasian Collared-Dove. (I)
Streptopelia chinensis Spotted Dove. (I)
Geopelia striata Zebra Dove. (H, I)
Zenaida asiatica White-winged Dove.
Zenaida aurita Zenaida Dove.
Zenaida auriculata Eared Dove.

Zenaida macroura Mourning Dove.
Zenaida graysoni Socorro Dove.
†*Ectopistes migratorius* Passenger Pigeon.
Columbina inca Inca Dove.
Columbina passerina Common Ground-Dove.
Columbina minuta Plain-breasted Ground-Dove.
Columbina talpacoti Ruddy Ground-Dove.
Claravis pretiosa Blue Ground-Dove.
Claravis mondetoura Maroon-chested Ground-Dove.
Leptotila verreauxi White-tipped Dove.
Leptotila rufaxilla Gray-fronted Dove.
Leptotila wellsi Grenada Dove.
Leptotila jamaicensis Caribbean Dove.
Leptotila cassini Gray-chested Dove.
Geotrygon veraguensis Olive-backed Quail-Dove.
Geotrygon chrysia Key West Quail-Dove.
Geotrygon mystacea Bridled Quail-Dove.
Geotrygon albifacies White-faced Quail-Dove.
Geotrygon chiriquensis Chiriqui Quail-Dove.
Geotrygon carrikeri Tuxtla Quail-Dove.
Geotrygon lawrencii Purplish-backed Quail-Dove.
Geotrygon costaricensis Buff-fronted Quail-Dove.
Geotrygon goldmani Russet-crowned Quail-Dove.
Geotrygon caniceps Gray-headed Quail-Dove.
Geotrygon versicolor Crested Quail-Dove.
Geotrygon violacea Violaceous Quail-Dove.
Geotrygon montana Ruddy Quail-Dove.
Starnoenas cyanocephala Blue-headed Quail-Dove.

PSITTACIFORMES
PSITTACIDAE
Platycercinae
Melopsittacus undulatus Budgerigar. (I)
Psittacinae
Psittacula krameri Rose-ringed Parakeet. (I)
Arinae
Pyrrhura picta Painted Parakeet.
Pyrrhura hoffmanni Sulphur-winged Parakeet.
Myiopsitta monachus Monk Parakeet. (I)
†*Conuropsis carolinensis* Carolina Parakeet.
Aratinga holochlora Green Parakeet.
Aratinga strenua Pacific Parakeet.
Aratinga finschi Crimson-fronted Parakeet.
Aratinga chloroptera Hispaniolan Parakeet.
Aratinga euops Cuban Parakeet.
Aratinga nana Olive-throated Parakeet.
Aratinga canicularis Orange-fronted Parakeet.
Aratinga pertinax Brown-throated Parakeet.
Ara severa Chestnut-fronted Macaw.
Ara militaris Military Macaw.
Ara ambigua Great Green Macaw.
Ara chloropterus Red-and-green Macaw.
Ara macao Scarlet Macaw.
†*Ara tricolor* Cuban Macaw.
Ara ararauna Blue-and-yellow Macaw.
Rhynchopsitta pachyrhyncha Thick-billed Parrot.
Rhynchopsitta terrisi Maroon-fronted Parrot.
Bolborhynchus lineola Barred Parakeet.
Forpus passerinus Green-rumped Parrotlet.

Forpus cyanopygius Mexican Parrotlet.
Forpus conspicillatus Spectacled Parrotlet.
Brotogeris jugularis Orange-chinned Parakeet.
Brotogeris versicolurus White-winged Parakeet. (I)
Touit costaricensis Red-fronted Parrotlet.
Touit dilectissima Blue-fronted Parrotlet.
Pionopsitta pyrilia Saffron-headed Parrot.
Pionopsitta haematotis Brown-hooded Parrot.
Pionus menstruus Blue-headed Parrot.
Pionus senilis White-crowned Parrot.
Amazona albifrons White-fronted Parrot.
Amazona xantholora Yellow-lored Parrot.
Amazona leucocephala Cuban Parrot.
Amazona collaria Yellow-billed Parrot.
Amazona ventralis Hispaniolan Parrot.
Amazona vittata Puerto Rican Parrot.
Amazona agilis Black-billed Parrot.
Amazona viridigenalis Red-crowned Parrot.
Amazona finschi Lilac-crowned Parrot.
Amazona autumnalis Red-lored Parrot.
Amazona farinosa Mealy Parrot.
Amazona oratrix Yellow-headed Parrot.
Amazona auropalliata Yellow-naped Parrot.
Amazona ochrocephala Yellow-crowned Parrot.
Amazona arausiaca Red-necked Parrot.
Amazona versicolor St. Lucia Parrot.
Amazona guildingii St. Vincent Parrot.
Amazona imperialis Imperial Parrot.

CUCULIFORMES
CUCULIDAE
Cuculinae
Cuculus canorus Common Cuckoo. (A)
Cuculus saturatus Oriental Cuckoo. (A)
Coccyzinae
Coccyzus erythropthalmus Black-billed Cuckoo.
Coccyzus americanus Yellow-billed Cuckoo.
Coccyzus euleri Pearly-breasted Cuckoo. (A)
Coccyzus minor Mangrove Cuckoo.
Coccyzus ferrugineus Cocos Cuckoo.
Coccyzus melacoryphus Dark-billed Cuckoo. (A)
Saurothera merlini Great Lizard-Cuckoo.
Saurothera vetula Jamaican Lizard-Cuckoo.
Saurothera longirostris Hispaniolan Lizard-Cuckoo.
Saurothera vieilloti Puerto Rican Lizard-Cuckoo.
Hyetornis rufigularis Bay-breasted Cuckoo.
Hyetornis pluvialis Chestnut-bellied Cuckoo.
Piaya cayana Squirrel Cuckoo.
Piaya minuta Little Cuckoo.
Neomorphinae
Tapera naevia Striped Cuckoo.
Dromococcyx phasianellus Pheasant Cuckoo.
Morococcyx erythropygus Lesser Ground-Cuckoo.
Geococcyx velox Lesser Roadrunner.
Geococcyx californianus Greater Roadrunner.
Neomorphus geoffroyi Rufous-vented Ground-Cuckoo.
Crotophaginae
Crotophaga major Greater Ani.
Crotophaga ani Smooth-billed Ani.
Crotophaga sulcirostris Groove-billed Ani.

STRIGIFORMES
TYTONIDAE
Tyto alba Barn Owl.
Tyto glaucops Ashy-faced Owl.
STRIGIDAE
Otus flammeolus Flammulated Owl.
Otus sunia Oriental Scops-Owl. (A)
Otus kennicottii Western Screech-Owl.
Otus asio Eastern Screech-Owl.
Otus seductus Balsas Screech-Owl.
Otus cooperi Pacific Screech-Owl.
Otus trichopsis Whiskered Screech-Owl.
Otus choliba Tropical Screech-Owl.
Otus barbarus Bearded Screech-Owl.
Otus guatemalae Vermiculated Screech-Owl.
Otus clarkii Bare-shanked Screech-Owl.
Otus nudipes Puerto Rican Screech-Owl.
Otus lawrencii Cuban Screech-Owl.
Lophostrix cristata Crested Owl.
Pulsatrix perspicillata Spectacled Owl.
Bubo virginianus Great Horned Owl.
Nyctea scandiaca Snowy Owl.
Surnia ulula Northern Hawk Owl.
Glaucidium gnoma Northern Pygmy-Owl.
Glaucidium jardinii Andean Pygmy-Owl.
Glaucidium griseiceps Central American Pygmy-Owl.
Glaucidium sanchezi Tamaulipas Pygmy-Owl.
Glaucidium palmarum Colima Pygmy-Owl.
Glaucidium brasilianum Ferruginous Pygmy-Owl.
Glaucidium siju Cuban Pygmy-Owl.
Micrathene whitneyi Elf Owl.
Athene cunicularia Burrowing Owl.
Ciccaba virgata Mottled Owl.
Ciccaba nigrolineata Black-and-white Owl.
Strix occidentalis Spotted Owl.
Strix varia Barred Owl.
Strix fulvescens Fulvous Owl.
Strix nebulosa Great Gray Owl.
Asio otus Long-eared Owl.
Asio stygius Stygian Owl.
Asio flammeus Short-eared Owl.
Pseudoscops clamator Striped Owl.
Pseudoscops grammicus Jamaican Owl.
Aegolius funereus Boreal Owl.
Aegolius acadicus Northern Saw-whet Owl.
Aegolius ridgwayi Unspotted Saw-whet Owl.
CAPRIMULGIFORMES
CAPRIMULGIDAE
Chordeilinae
Lurocalis semitorquatus Short-tailed Nighthawk.
Chordeiles acutipennis Lesser Nighthawk.
Chordeiles minor Common Nighthawk.
Chordeiles gundlachii Antillean Nighthawk.
Caprimulginae
Nyctidromus albicollis Common Pauraque.
Phalaenoptilus nuttallii Common Poorwill.
†*Siphonorhis americanus* Jamaican Pauraque.
Siphonorhis brewsteri Least Pauraque.

Nyctiphrynus mcleodii Eared Poorwill.
Nyctiphrynus yucatanicus Yucatan Poorwill.
Nyctiphrynus ocellatus Ocellated Poorwill.
Caprimulgus carolinensis Chuck-will's-widow.
Caprimulgus rufus Rufous Nightjar.
Caprimulgus cubanensis Greater Antillean Nightjar.
Caprimulgus salvini Tawny-collared Nightjar.
Caprimulgus badius Yucatan Nightjar.
Caprimulgus ridgwayi Buff-collared Nightjar.
Caprimulgus vociferus Whip-poor-will.
Caprimulgus noctitherus Puerto Rican Nightjar.
Caprimulgus saturatus Dusky Nightjar.
Caprimulgus cayennensis White-tailed Nightjar.
Caprimulgus maculicaudus Spot-tailed Nightjar.
Caprimulgus indicus Jungle Nightjar. (A)

NYCTIBIIDAE
Nyctibius grandis Great Potoo.
Nyctibius griseus Common Potoo.
Nyctibius jamaicensis Northern Potoo.

STEATORNITHIDAE
Steatornis caripensis Oilbird. (A)

APODIFORMES
APODIDAE
Cypseloidinae
Cypseloides niger Black Swift.
Cypseloides storeri White-fronted Swift.
Cypseloides cryptus White-chinned Swift.
Cypseloides cherriei Spot-fronted Swift.
Streptoprocne rutila Chestnut-collared Swift.
Streptoprocne zonaris White-collared Swift.
Streptoprocne semicollaris White-naped Swift.
Chaeturinae
Chaetura pelagica Chimney Swift.
Chaetura vauxi Vaux's Swift.
Chaetura chapmani Chapman's Swift. (A)
Chaetura brachyura Short-tailed Swift.
Chaetura andrei Ashy-tailed Swift. (A)
Chaetura spinicauda Band-rumped Swift.
Chaetura cinereiventris Gray-rumped Swift.
Chaetura martinica Lesser Antillean Swift.
Hirundapus caudacutus White-throated Needletail. (A)
Aerodramus bartschi Guam Swiftlet. (H, I)
Apodinae
Apus apus Common Swift. (A)
Apus pacificus Fork-tailed Swift. (A)
Apus melba Alpine Swift. (A)
Aeronautes saxatalis White-throated Swift.
Panyptila cayennensis Lesser Swallow-tailed Swift.
Panyptila sanctihieronymi Great Swallow-tailed Swift.
Tachornis phoenicobia Antillean Palm-Swift.

TROCHILIDAE
Phaethornithinae
Glaucis aenea Bronzy Hermit.
Glaucis hirsuta Rufous-breasted Hermit.
Threnetes ruckeri Band-tailed Barbthroat.
Phaethornis guy Green Hermit.
Phaethornis superciliosus Long-tailed Hermit.
Phaethornis anthophilus Pale-bellied Hermit.

Phaethornis longuemareus Little Hermit.
Eutoxeres aquila White-tipped Sicklebill.
Trochilinae
Androdon aequatorialis Tooth-billed Hummingbird.
Doryfera ludovicae Green-fronted Lancebill.
Phaeochroa ~~cuvieri~~ cuvierii Scaly-breasted Hummingbird.   *cuvieirii* cuvierii
Campylopterus curvipennis Wedge-tailed Sabrewing.
Campylopterus excellens Long-tailed Sabrewing.
Campylopterus rufus Rufous Sabrewing.
Campylopterus hemileucurus Violet Sabrewing.
Florisuga mellivora White-necked Jacobin.
Colibri delphinae Brown Violet-ear.
Colibri thalassinus Green Violet-ear.
Anthracothorax prevostii Green-breasted Mango.
Anthracothorax nigricollis Black-throated Mango.
Anthracothorax veraguensis Veraguan Mango.
Anthracothorax dominicus Antillean Mango.
Anthracothorax viridis Green Mango.
Anthracothorax mango Jamaican Mango.
Eulampis jugularis Purple-throated Carib.
Eulampis holosericeus Green-throated Carib.
Chrysolampis mosquitus Ruby-topaz Hummingbird.
Orthorhyncus cristatus Antillean Crested Hummingbird.
Klais guimeti Violet-headed Hummingbird.
Abeillia abeillei Emerald-chinned Hummingbird.
Lophornis brachylopha Short-crested Coquette.
Lophornis delattrei Rufous-crested Coquette.
Lophornis helenae Black-crested Coquette.
Lophornis adorabilis White-crested Coquette.
Discosura conversii Green Thorntail.
Chlorostilbon auriceps Golden-crowned Emerald.
Chlorostilbon forficatus Cozumel Emerald.
Chlorostilbon canivetii Canivet's Emerald.
Chlorostilbon assimilis Garden Emerald.
Chlorostilbon ricordii Cuban Emerald.
†*Chlorostilbon bracei* Brace's Emerald.
Chlorostilbon swainsonii Hispaniolan Emerald.
Chlorostilbon maugaeus Puerto Rican Emerald.
Cynanthus sordidus Dusky Hummingbird.
Cynanthus latirostris Broad-billed Hummingbird.
Cyanophaia bicolor Blue-headed Hummingbird.
Thalurania ridgwayi Mexican Woodnymph.
Thalurania colombica Violet-crowned Woodnymph.
Thalurania fannyi Green-crowned Woodnymph.
Panterpe insignis Fiery-throated Hummingbird.
Damophila julie Violet-bellied Hummingbird.
Lepidopyga coeruleogularis Sapphire-throated Hummingbird.
Hylocharis grayi Blue-headed Sapphire.
Hylocharis eliciae Blue-throated Goldentail.
Hylocharis leucotis White-eared Hummingbird.
Hylocharis xantusii Xantus's Hummingbird.
Goldmania violiceps Violet-capped Hummingbird.
Goethalsia bella Rufous-cheeked Hummingbird.
Trochilus polytmus Streamertail.
Amazilia candida White-bellied Emerald.
Amazilia luciae Honduran Emerald.
Amazilia amabilis Blue-chested Hummingbird.
Amazilia decora Charming Hummingbird.

Amazilia boucardi Mangrove Hummingbird.
Amazilia cyanocephala Azure-crowned Hummingbird.
Amazilia cyanifrons Indigo-capped Hummingbird.
Amazilia beryllina Berylline Hummingbird.
Amazilia cyanura Blue-tailed Hummingbird.
Amazilia saucerrottei Steely-vented Hummingbird.
Amazilia edward Snowy-bellied Hummingbird.
Amazilia tzacatl Rufous-tailed Hummingbird.
Amazilia yucatanensis Buff-bellied Hummingbird.
Amazilia rutila Cinnamon Hummingbird.
Amazilia violiceps Violet-crowned Hummingbird.
Amazilia viridifrons Green-fronted Hummingbird.
Eupherusa eximia Stripe-tailed Hummingbird.
Eupherusa cyanophrys Blue-capped Hummingbird.
Eupherusa poliocerca White-tailed Hummingbird.
Eupherusa nigriventris Black-bellied Hummingbird.
Elvira chionura White-tailed Emerald.
Elvira cupreiceps Coppery-headed Emerald.
Microchera albocoronata Snowcap.
Chalybura buffonii White-vented Plumeleteer.
Chalybura urochrysia Bronze-tailed Plumeleteer.
Lampornis viridipallens Green-throated Mountain-gem.
Lampornis sybillae Green-breasted Mountain-gem.
Lampornis amethystinus Amethyst-throated Hummingbird.
Lampornis clemenciae Blue-throated Hummingbird.
Lampornis hemileucus White-bellied Mountain-gem.
Lampornis calolaema Purple-throated Mountain-gem.
Lampornis castaneoventris White-throated Mountain-gem.
Lamprolaima rhami Garnet-throated Hummingbird.
Heliodoxa jacula Green-crowned Brilliant.
Eugenes fulgens Magnificent Hummingbird.
Haplophaedia aureliae Greenish Puffleg.
Heliothryx barroti Purple-crowned Fairy.
Heliomaster longirostris Long-billed Starthroat.
Heliomaster constantii Plain-capped Starthroat.
Calliphlox evelynae Bahama Woodstar.
Calliphlox bryantae Magenta-throated Woodstar.
Calliphlox mitchellii Purple-throated Woodstar.
Doricha enicura Slender Sheartail.
Doricha eliza Mexican Sheartail.
Tilmatura dupontii Sparkling-tailed Hummingbird.
Calothorax lucifer Lucifer Hummingbird.
Calothorax pulcher Beautiful Hummingbird.
Archilochus colubris Ruby-throated Hummingbird.
Archilochus alexandri Black-chinned Hummingbird.
Mellisuga minima Vervain Hummingbird.
Mellisuga helenae Bee Hummingbird.
Calypte anna Anna's Hummingbird.
Calypte costae Costa's Hummingbird.
Stellula calliope Calliope Hummingbird.
Atthis heloisa Bumblebee Hummingbird.
Atthis ellioti Wine-throated Hummingbird.
Selasphorus platycercus Broad-tailed Hummingbird.
Selasphorus rufus Rufous Hummingbird.
Selasphorus sasin Allen's Hummingbird.
Selasphorus flammula Volcano Hummingbird.
Selasphorus ardens Glow-throated Hummingbird.
Selasphorus scintilla Scintillant Hummingbird.

TROGONIFORMES
  TROGONIDAE
    Trogoninae
      Priotelus temnurus Cuban Trogon.
      Priotelus roseigaster Hispaniolan Trogon.
      Trogon melanocephalus Black-headed Trogon.
      Trogon citreolus Citreoline Trogon.
      Trogon viridis White-tailed Trogon.
      Trogon bairdii Baird's Trogon.
      Trogon violaceus Violaceous Trogon.
      Trogon mexicanus Mountain Trogon.
      Trogon elegans Elegant Trogon.
      Trogon collaris Collared Trogon.
      Trogon aurantiiventris Orange-bellied Trogon.
      Trogon rufus Black-throated Trogon.
      Trogon melanurus Black-tailed Trogon.
      Trogon massena Slaty-tailed Trogon.
      Trogon clathratus Lattice-tailed Trogon.
      Euptilotis neoxenus Eared Trogon.
      Pharomachrus auriceps Golden-headed Quetzal.
      Pharomachrus mocinno Resplendent Quetzal.
UPUPIFORMES
  UPUPIDAE
      Upupa epops Eurasian Hoopoe. (A)
CORACIIFORMES
  TODIDAE
      Todus multicolor Cuban Tody.
      Todus subulatus Broad-billed Tody.
      Todus angustirostris Narrow-billed Tody.
      Todus todus Jamaican Tody.
      Todus mexicanus Puerto Rican Tody.
  MOMOTIDAE
      Hylomanes momotula Tody Motmot.
      Aspatha gularis Blue-throated Motmot.
      Momotus mexicanus Russet-crowned Motmot.
      Momotus momota Blue-crowned Motmot.
      Baryphthengus martii Rufous Motmot.
      Electron carinatum Keel-billed Motmot.
      Electron platyrhynchum Broad-billed Motmot.
      Eumomota superciliosa Turquoise-browed Motmot.
  ALCEDINIDAE
    Cerylinae
      Ceryle torquata Ringed Kingfisher.
      Ceryle alcyon Belted Kingfisher.
      Chloroceryle amazona Amazon Kingfisher.
      Chloroceryle americana Green Kingfisher.
      Chloroceryle inda Green-and-rufous Kingfisher.
      Chloroceryle aenea American Pygmy Kingfisher.
PICIFORMES
  BUCCONIDAE
      Nystalus radiatus Barred Puffbird.
      Notharchus macrorhynchos White-necked Puffbird.
      Notharchus pectoralis Black-breasted Puffbird.
      Notharchus tectus Pied Puffbird.
      Malacoptila panamensis White-whiskered Puffbird.
      Micromonacha lanceolata Lanceolated Monklet.
      Nonnula ruficapilla Gray-cheeked Nunlet.
      Monasa morphoeus White-fronted Nunbird.

GALBULIDAE
    Brachygalba salmoni Dusky-backed Jacamar.
    Galbula ruficauda Rufous-tailed Jacamar.
    Jacamerops aurea Great Jacamar.
RAMPHASTIDAE
  Capitoninae
    Capito maculicoronatus Spot-crowned Barbet.
    Eubucco bourcierii Red-headed Barbet.
  Semnornithinae
    Semnornis frantzii Prong-billed Barbet.
  Ramphastinae
    Aulacorhynchus prasinus Emerald Toucanet.
    Pteroglossus torquatus Collared Aracari.
    Pteroglossus frantzii Fiery-billed Aracari.
    Selenidera spectabilis Yellow-eared Toucanet.
    Ramphastos sulfuratus Keel-billed Toucan.
    Ramphastos swainsonii Chestnut-mandibled Toucan.
PICIDAE
  Jynginae
    Jynx torquilla Eurasian Wryneck. (A)
  Picumninae
    Picumnus olivaceus Olivaceous Piculet.
    Nesoctites micromegas Antillean Piculet.
  Picinae
    Melanerpes lewis Lewis's Woodpecker.
    Melanerpes herminieri Guadeloupe Woodpecker.
    Melanerpes portoricensis Puerto Rican Woodpecker.
    Melanerpes erythrocephalus Red-headed Woodpecker.
    Melanerpes formicivorus Acorn Woodpecker.
    Melanerpes chrysauchen Golden-naped Woodpecker.
    Melanerpes pucherani Black-cheeked Woodpecker.
    Melanerpes striatus Hispaniolan Woodpecker.
    Melanerpes radiolatus Jamaican Woodpecker.
    Melanerpes chrysogenys Golden-cheeked Woodpecker.
    Melanerpes hypopolius Gray-breasted Woodpecker.
    Melanerpes pygmaeus Red-vented Woodpecker.
    Melanerpes rubricapillus Red-crowned Woodpecker.
    Melanerpes uropygialis Gila Woodpecker.
    Melanerpes hoffmannii Hoffmann's Woodpecker.
    Melanerpes aurifrons Golden-fronted Woodpecker.
    Melanerpes carolinus Red-bellied Woodpecker.
    Melanerpes superciliaris West Indian Woodpecker.
    Sphyrapicus thyroideus Williamson's Sapsucker.
    Sphyrapicus varius Yellow-bellied Sapsucker.
    Sphyrapicus nuchalis Red-naped Sapsucker.
    Sphyrapicus ruber Red-breasted Sapsucker.
    Xiphidiopicus percussus Cuban Green Woodpecker.
    Dendrocopos major Great Spotted Woodpecker. (A)
    Picoides scalaris Ladder-backed Woodpecker.
    Picoides nuttallii Nuttall's Woodpecker.
    Picoides pubescens Downy Woodpecker.
    Picoides villosus Hairy Woodpecker.
    Picoides stricklandi Strickland's Woodpecker.
    Picoides borealis Red-cockaded Woodpecker.
    Picoides albolarvatus White-headed Woodpecker.
    Picoides tridactylus Three-toed Woodpecker.
    Picoides arcticus Black-backed Woodpecker.
    Veniliornis fumigatus Smoky-brown Woodpecker.

Veniliornis kirkii Red-rumped Woodpecker.
Piculus simplex Rufous-winged Woodpecker.
Piculus callopterus Stripe-cheeked Woodpecker.
Piculus chrysochloros Golden-green Woodpecker.
Piculus rubiginosus Golden-olive Woodpecker.
Piculus auricularis Gray-crowned Woodpecker.
Colaptes punctigula Spot-breasted Woodpecker.
Colaptes auratus Northern Flicker.
Colaptes chrysoides Gilded Flicker.
Colaptes fernandinae Fernandina's Flicker.
Celeus loricatus Cinnamon Woodpecker.
Celeus castaneus Chestnut-colored Woodpecker.
Dryocopus lineatus Lineated Woodpecker.
Dryocopus pileatus Pileated Woodpecker.
Campephilus haematogaster Crimson-bellied Woodpecker.
Campephilus melanoleucos Crimson-crested Woodpecker.
Campephilus guatemalensis Pale-billed Woodpecker.
Campephilus principalis Ivory-billed Woodpecker.
Campephilus imperialis Imperial Woodpecker.
PASSERIFORMES
FURNARIIDAE
Synallaxis albescens Pale-breasted Spinetail.
Synallaxis brachyura Slaty Spinetail.
Synallaxis erythrothorax Rufous-breasted Spinetail.
Cranioleuca erythrops Red-faced Spinetail.
Cranioleuca vulpina Rusty-backed Spinetail.
Xenerpestes minlosi Double-banded Graytail.
Premnoplex brunnescens Spotted Barbtail.
Margarornis bellulus Beautiful Treerunner.
Margarornis rubiginosus Ruddy Treerunner.
Pseudocolaptes lawrencii Buffy Tuftedcheek.
Hyloctistes subulatus Striped Woodhaunter.
Syndactyla subalaris Lineated Foliage-gleaner.
Anabacerthia variegaticeps Scaly-throated Foliage-gleaner.
Philydor fuscipennis Slaty-winged Foliage-gleaner.
Philydor rufus Buff-fronted Foliage-gleaner.
Automolus ochrolaemus Buff-throated Foliage-gleaner.
Automolus rubiginosus Ruddy Foliage-gleaner.
Thripadectes rufobrunneus Streak-breasted Treehunter.
Xenops minutus Plain Xenops.
Xenops rutilans Streaked Xenops.
Sclerurus mexicanus Tawny-throated Leaftosser.
Sclerurus albigularis Gray-throated Leaftosser.
Sclerurus guatemalensis Scaly-throated Leaftosser.
Lochmias nematura Sharp-tailed Streamcreeper.
DENDROCOLAPTIDAE
Dendrocincla fuliginosa Plain-brown Woodcreeper.
Dendrocincla anabatina Tawny-winged Woodcreeper.
Dendrocincla homochroa Ruddy Woodcreeper.
Sittasomus griseicapillus Olivaceous Woodcreeper.
Deconychura longicauda Long-tailed Woodcreeper.
Glyphorynchus spirurus Wedge-billed Woodcreeper.
Xiphocolaptes promeropirhynchus Strong-billed Woodcreeper.
Dendrocolaptes sanctithomae Northern Barred-Woodcreeper.
Dendrocolaptes picumnus Black-banded Woodcreeper.
Xiphorhynchus picus Straight-billed Woodcreeper.
Xiphorhynchus susurrans Cocoa Woodcreeper.
Xiphorhynchus flavigaster Ivory-billed Woodcreeper.

Xiphorhynchus lachrymosus Black-striped Woodcreeper.
Xiphorhynchus erythropygius Spotted Woodcreeper.
Lepidocolaptes leucogaster White-striped Woodcreeper.
Lepidocolaptes souleyetii Streak-headed Woodcreeper.
Lepidocolaptes affinis Spot-crowned Woodcreeper.
Campylorhamphus trochilirostris Red-billed Scythebill.
Campylorhamphus pusillus Brown-billed Scythebill.

THAMNOPHILIDAE

Cymbilaimus lineatus Fasciated Antshrike.
Taraba major Great Antshrike.
Thamnophilus doliatus Barred Antshrike.
Thamnophilus nigriceps Black Antshrike.
Thamnophilus bridgesi Black-hooded Antshrike.
Thamnophilus atrinucha Western Slaty-Antshrike.
Xenornis setifrons Spiny-faced Antshrike.
Thamnistes anabatinus Russet Antshrike.
Dysithamnus mentalis Plain Antvireo.
Dysithamnus striaticeps Streak-crowned Antvireo.
Dysithamnus puncticeps Spot-crowned Antvireo.
Myrmotherula brachyura Pygmy Antwren.
Myrmotherula surinamensis Streaked Antwren.
Myrmotherula fulviventris Checker-throated Antwren.
Myrmotherula axillaris White-flanked Antwren.
Myrmotherula schisticolor Slaty Antwren.
Herpsilochmus rufimarginatus Rufous-winged Antwren.
Microrhopias quixensis Dot-winged Antwren.
Formicivora grisea White-fringed Antwren.
Terenura callinota Rufous-rumped Antwren.
Cercomacra tyrannina Dusky Antbird.
Cercomacra nigricans Jet Antbird.
Gymnocichla nudiceps Bare-crowned Antbird.
Myrmeciza longipes White-bellied Antbird.
Myrmeciza exsul Chestnut-backed Antbird.
Myrmeciza laemosticta Dull-mantled Antbird.
Myrmeciza immaculata Immaculate Antbird.
Hylophylax naevioides Spotted Antbird.
Myrmornis torquata Wing-banded Antbird.
Gymnopithys leucaspis Bicolored Antbird.
Phaenostictus mcleannani Ocellated Antbird.

FORMICARIIDAE

Formicarius analis Black-faced Antthrush.
Formicarius nigricapillus Black-headed Antthrush.
Formicarius rufipectus Rufous-breasted Antthrush.
Pittasoma michleri Black-crowned Antpitta.
Grallaria guatimalensis Scaled Antpitta.
Hylopezus perspicillatus Streak-chested Antpitta.
Hylopezus dives Thicket Antpitta.
Grallaricula flavirostris Ochre-breasted Antpitta.

RHINOCRYPTIDAE

Scytalopus panamensis Tacarcuna Tapaculo.
Scytalopus chocoensis Choco Tapaculo.
Scytalopus argentifrons Silvery-fronted Tapaculo.

TYRANNIDAE

Elaeniinae

Ornithion semiflavum Yellow-bellied Tyrannulet.
Ornithion brunneicapillum Brown-capped Tyrannulet.
Camptostoma imberbe Northern Beardless-Tyrannulet.
Camptostoma obsoletum Southern Beardless-Tyrannulet.

Phaeomyias murina Mouse-colored Tyrannulet.
Nesotriccus ridgwayi Cocos Flycatcher.
Capsiempis flaveola Yellow Tyrannulet.
Tyrannulus elatus Yellow-crowned Tyrannulet.
Myiopagis gaimardii Forest Elaenia.
Myiopagis caniceps Gray Elaenia.
Myiopagis cotta Jamaican Elaenia.
Myiopagis viridicata Greenish Elaenia.
Elaenia martinica Caribbean Elaenia.
Elaenia flavogaster Yellow-bellied Elaenia.
Elaenia chiriquensis Lesser Elaenia.
Elaenia frantzii Mountain Elaenia.
Elaenia fallax Greater Antillean Elaenia.
Serpophaga cinerea Torrent Tyrannulet.
Mionectes olivaceus Olive-striped Flycatcher.
Mionectes oleagineus Ochre-bellied Flycatcher.
Leptopogon amaurocephalus Sepia-capped Flycatcher.
Leptopogon superciliaris Slaty-capped Flycatcher.
Phylloscartes flavovirens Yellow-green Tyrannulet.
Phylloscartes superciliaris Rufous-browed Tyrannulet.
Phyllomyias burmeisteri Rough-legged Tyrannulet.
Phyllomyias griseiceps Sooty-headed Tyrannulet.
Zimmerius vilissimus Paltry Tyrannulet.
Sublegatus arenarum Northern Scrub-Flycatcher.
Pseudotriccus pelzelni Bronze-olive Pygmy-Tyrant.

Platyrinchinae

Myiornis atricapillus Black-capped Pygmy-Tyrant.
Lophotriccus pileatus Scale-crested Pygmy-Tyrant.
Lophotriccus pilaris Pale-eyed Pygmy-Tyrant.
Oncostoma cinereigulare Northern Bentbill.
Oncostoma olivaceum Southern Bentbill.
Poecilotriccus sylvia Slate-headed Tody-Flycatcher.
Todirostrum cinereum Common Tody-Flycatcher.
Todirostrum nigriceps Black-headed Tody-Flycatcher.
Cnipodectes subbrunneus Brownish Flycatcher.
Rhynchocyclus brevirostris Eye-ringed Flatbill.
Rhynchocyclus olivaceus Olivaceous Flatbill.
Tolmomyias sulphurescens Yellow-olive Flycatcher.
Tolmomyias assimilis Yellow-margined Flycatcher.
Platyrinchus cancrominus Stub-tailed Spadebill.
Platyrinchus mystaceus White-throated Spadebill.
Platyrinchus coronatus Golden-crowned Spadebill.

Fluvicolinae

Onychorhynchus coronatus Royal Flycatcher.
Terenotriccus erythrurus Ruddy-tailed Flycatcher.
Myiobius villosus Tawny-breasted Flycatcher.
Myiobius sulphureipygius Sulphur-rumped Flycatcher.
Myiobius atricaudus Black-tailed Flycatcher.
Myiophobus fasciatus Bran-colored Flycatcher.
Lathrotriccus euleri Euler's Flycatcher.
Aphanotriccus capitalis Tawny-chested Flycatcher.
Aphanotriccus audax Black-billed Flycatcher.
Xenotriccus callizonus Belted Flycatcher.
Xenotriccus mexicanus Pileated Flycatcher.
Mitrephanes phaeocercus Tufted Flycatcher.
Contopus cooperi Olive-sided Flycatcher.
Contopus pertinax Greater Pewee.
Contopus lugubris Dark Pewee.

Contopus ochraceus Ochraceous Pewee.
Contopus sordidulus Western Wood-Pewee.
Contopus virens Eastern Wood-Pewee.
Contopus cinereus Tropical Pewee.
Contopus caribaeus Cuban Pewee.
Contopus pallidus Jamaican Pewee.
Contopus hispaniolensis Hispaniolan Pewee.
Contopus latirostris Lesser Antillean Pewee.
Empidonax flaviventris Yellow-bellied Flycatcher.
Empidonax virescens Acadian Flycatcher.
Empidonax alnorum Alder Flycatcher.
Empidonax traillii Willow Flycatcher.
Empidonax albigularis White-throated Flycatcher.
Empidonax minimus Least Flycatcher.
Empidonax hammondii Hammond's Flycatcher.
Empidonax wrightii Gray Flycatcher.
Empidonax oberholseri Dusky Flycatcher.
Empidonax affinis Pine Flycatcher.
Empidonax difficilis Pacific-slope Flycatcher.
Empidonax occidentalis Cordilleran Flycatcher.
Empidonax flavescens Yellowish Flycatcher.
Empidonax fulvifrons Buff-breasted Flycatcher.
Empidonax atriceps Black-capped Flycatcher.
Sayornis nigricans Black Phoebe.
Sayornis phoebe Eastern Phoebe.
Sayornis saya Say's Phoebe.
Pyrocephalus rubinus Vermilion Flycatcher.
Fluvicola pica Pied Water-Tyrant.
Colonia colonus Long-tailed Tyrant.
Machetornis rixosus Cattle Tyrant. (A)
Tyranninae
Attila spadiceus Bright-rumped Attila.
Sirystes sibilator Sirystes.
Rhytipterna holerythra Rufous Mourner.
Myiarchus yucatanensis Yucatan Flycatcher.
Myiarchus barbirostris Sad Flycatcher.
Myiarchus tuberculifer Dusky-capped Flycatcher.
Myiarchus panamensis Panama Flycatcher.
Myiarchus cinerascens Ash-throated Flycatcher.
Myiarchus nuttingi Nutting's Flycatcher.
Myiarchus crinitus Great Crested Flycatcher.
Myiarchus tyrannulus Brown-crested Flycatcher.
Myiarchus nugator Grenada Flycatcher.
Myiarchus validus Rufous-tailed Flycatcher.
Myiarchus sagrae La Sagra's Flycatcher.
Myiarchus stolidus Stolid Flycatcher.
Myiarchus antillarum Puerto Rican Flycatcher.
Myiarchus oberi Lesser Antillean Flycatcher.
Deltarhynchus flammulatus Flammulated Flycatcher.
Pitangus lictor Lesser Kiskadee.
Pitangus sulphuratus Great Kiskadee.
Megarynchus pitangua Boat-billed Flycatcher.
Myiozetetes cayanensis Rusty-margined Flycatcher.
Myiozetetes similis Social Flycatcher.
Myiozetetes granadensis Gray-capped Flycatcher.
Conopias albovittata White-ringed Flycatcher.
Myiodynastes hemichrysus Golden-bellied Flycatcher.
Myiodynastes chrysocephalus Golden-crowned Flycatcher.

Myiodynastes maculatus Streaked Flycatcher.
Myiodynastes luteiventris Sulphur-bellied Flycatcher.
Legatus leucophaius Piratic Flycatcher.
Empidonomus varius Variegated Flycatcher. (A)
Tyrannus melancholicus Tropical Kingbird.
Tyrannus couchii Couch's Kingbird.
Tyrannus vociferans Cassin's Kingbird.
Tyrannus crassirostris Thick-billed Kingbird.
Tyrannus verticalis Western Kingbird.
Tyrannus tyrannus Eastern Kingbird.
Tyrannus dominicensis Gray Kingbird.
Tyrannus caudifasciatus Loggerhead Kingbird.
Tyrannus cubensis Giant Kingbird.
Tyrannus forficatus Scissor-tailed Flycatcher.
Tyrannus savana Fork-tailed Flycatcher.
Genera *INCERTAE SEDIS*
Sapayoa aenigma Sapayoa.
Schiffornis turdinus Thrush-like Schiffornis.
Piprites griseiceps Gray-headed Piprites.
Lipaugus unirufus Rufous Piha.
Laniocera rufescens Speckled Mourner.
Pachyramphus versicolor Barred Becard.
Pachyramphus rufus Cinereous Becard.
Pachyramphus cinnamomeus Cinnamon Becard.
Pachyramphus polychopterus White-winged Becard.
Pachyramphus albogriseus Black-and-white Becard.
Pachyramphus major Gray-collared Becard.
Pachyramphus aglaiae Rose-throated Becard.
Pachyramphus homochrous One-colored Becard.
Pachyramphus niger Jamaican Becard.
Tityra semifasciata Masked Tityra.
Tityra inquisitor Black-crowned Tityra.
COTINGIDAE
Cotinga amabilis Lovely Cotinga.
Cotinga ridgwayi Turquoise Cotinga.
Cotinga nattererii Blue Cotinga.
Carpodectes hopkei Black-tipped Cotinga.
Carpodectes antoniae Yellow-billed Cotinga.
Carpodectes nitidus Snowy Cotinga.
Querula purpurata Purple-throated Fruitcrow.
Cephalopterus glabricollis Bare-necked Umbrellabird.
Procnias tricarunculata Three-wattled Bellbird.
PIPRIDAE
Chloropipo holochlora Green Manakin.
Manacus candei White-collared Manakin.
Manacus aurantiacus Orange-collared Manakin.
Manacus vitellinus Golden-collared Manakin.
Corapipo altera White-ruffed Manakin.
Chiroxiphia lanceolata Lance-tailed Manakin.
Chiroxiphia linearis Long-tailed Manakin.
Pipra pipra White-crowned Manakin.
Pipra coronata Blue-crowned Manakin.
Pipra erythrocephala Golden-headed Manakin.
Pipra mentalis Red-capped Manakin.
OXYRUNCIDAE
Oxyruncus cristatus Sharpbill.
MELIPHAGIDAE
†*Moho braccatus* Kauai Oo. (H)

†*Moho apicalis* Oahu Oo. (H)
† *Moho bishopi* Bishop's Oo. (H)
†*Moho nobilis* Hawaii Oo. (H)
†*Chaetoptila angustipluma* Kioea. (H)
LANIIDAE
Lanius cristatus Brown Shrike. (A)
Lanius ludovicianus Loggerhead Shrike.
Lanius excubitor Northern Shrike.
VIREONIDAE
Vireo brevipennis Slaty Vireo.
Vireo griseus White-eyed Vireo.
Vireo crassirostris Thick-billed Vireo.
Vireo pallens Mangrove Vireo.
Vireo bairdi Cozumel Vireo.
Vireo caribaeus St. Andrew Vireo.
Vireo modestus Jamaican Vireo.
Vireo gundlachii Cuban Vireo.
Vireo latimeri Puerto Rican Vireo.
Vireo nanus Flat-billed Vireo.
Vireo bellii Bell's Vireo.
Vireo atricapillus Black-capped Vireo.
Vireo nelsoni Dwarf Vireo.
Vireo vicinior Gray Vireo.
Vireo osburni Blue Mountain Vireo.
Vireo flavifrons Yellow-throated Vireo.
Vireo plumbeus Plumbeous Vireo.
Vireo cassinii Cassin's Vireo.
Vireo solitarius Blue-headed Vireo.
Vireo carmioli Yellow-winged Vireo.
Vireo huttoni Hutton's Vireo.
Vireo hypochryseus Golden Vireo.
Vireo gilvus Warbling Vireo.
Vireo leucophrys Brown-capped Vireo.
Vireo philadelphicus Philadelphia Vireo.
Vireo olivaceus Red-eyed Vireo.
Vireo flavoviridis Yellow-green Vireo.
Vireo altiloquus Black-whiskered Vireo.
Vireo magister Yucatan Vireo.
Hylophilus flavipes Scrub Greenlet.
Hylophilus ochraceiceps Tawny-crowned Greenlet.
Hylophilus aurantiifrons Golden-fronted Greenlet.
Hylophilus decurtatus Lesser Greenlet.
Vireolanius melitophrys Chestnut-sided Shrike-Vireo.
Vireolanius pulchellus Green Shrike-Vireo.
Vireolanius eximius Yellow-browed Shrike-Vireo.
Cyclarhis gujanensis Rufous-browed Peppershrike.
CORVIDAE
Perisoreus canadensis Gray Jay.
Cyanocitta stelleri Steller's Jay.
Cyanocitta cristata Blue Jay.
Calocitta colliei Black-throated Magpie-Jay.
Calocitta formosa White-throated Magpie-Jay.
Cyanocorax dickeyi Tufted Jay.
Cyanocorax affinis Black-chested Jay.
Cyanocorax yncas Green Jay.
Cyanocorax morio Brown Jay.
Cyanocorax melanocyaneus Bushy-crested Jay.
Cyanocorax sanblasianus San Blas Jay.

Cyanocorax yucatanicus Yucatan Jay.
Cyanocorax beecheii Purplish-backed Jay.
Cyanolyca cucullata Azure-hooded Jay.
Cyanolyca pumilo Black-throated Jay.
Cyanolyca nana Dwarf Jay.
Cyanolyca argentigula Silvery-throated Jay.
Cyanolyca mirabilis White-throated Jay.
Aphelocoma coerulescens Florida Scrub-Jay.
Aphelocoma insularis Island Scrub-Jay.
Aphelocoma californica Western Scrub-Jay.
Aphelocoma ultramarina Mexican Jay.
Aphelocoma unicolor Unicolored Jay.
Gymnorhinus cyanocephalus Pinyon Jay.
Nucifraga columbiana Clark's Nutcracker.
Pica pica Black-billed Magpie.
Pica nuttalli Yellow-billed Magpie.
Corvus monedula Eurasian Jackdaw. (A)
Corvus brachyrhynchos American Crow.
Corvus caurinus Northwestern Crow.
Corvus palmarum Palm Crow.
Corvus nasicus Cuban Crow.
Corvus leucognaphalus White-necked Crow.
Corvus jamaicensis Jamaican Crow.
Corvus imparatus Tamaulipas Crow.
Corvus sinaloae Sinaloa Crow.
Corvus ossifragus Fish Crow.
Corvus hawaiiensis Hawaiian Crow. (H)
Corvus cryptoleucus Chihuahuan Raven.
Corvus corax Common Raven.

MONARCHIDAE
Chasiempis sandwichensis Elepaio. (H)

ALAUDIDAE
Alauda arvensis Sky Lark.
Eremophila alpestris Horned Lark.

HIRUNDINIDAE
Hirundininae
Progne subis Purple Martin.
Progne cryptoleuca Cuban Martin.
Progne dominicensis Caribbean Martin.
Progne sinaloae Sinaloa Martin.
Progne chalybea Gray-breasted Martin.
Progne elegans Southern Martin.
Progne tapera Brown-chested Martin.
Tachycineta bicolor Tree Swallow.
Tachycineta albilinea Mangrove Swallow.
Tachycineta euchrysea Golden Swallow.
Tachycineta thalassina Violet-green Swallow.
Tachycineta cyaneoviridis Bahama Swallow.
Pygochelidon cyanoleuca Blue-and-white Swallow.
Notiochelidon pileata Black-capped Swallow.
Neochelidon tibialis White-thighed Swallow.
Stelgidopteryx serripennis Northern Rough-winged Swallow.
Stelgidopteryx ruficollis Southern Rough-winged Swallow.
Riparia riparia Bank Swallow.
Petrochelidon pyrrhonota Cliff Swallow.
Petrochelidon fulva Cave Swallow.
Hirundo rustica Barn Swallow.
Delichon urbica Common House-Martin. (A)

PARIDAE
Poecile carolinensis Carolina Chickadee.
Poecile atricapillus Black-capped Chickadee.
Poecile gambeli Mountain Chickadee.
Poecile sclateri Mexican Chickadee.
Poecile rufescens Chestnut-backed Chickadee.
Poecile hudsonicus Boreal Chickadee.
Poecile cinctus Gray-headed Chickadee.
Baeolophus wollweberi Bridled Titmouse.
Baeolophus inornatus Oak Titmouse.
Baeolophus griseus Juniper Titmouse.
Baeolophus bicolor Tufted Titmouse.
REMIZIDAE
Auriparus flaviceps Verdin.
AEGITHALIDAE
Psaltriparus minimus Bushtit.
SITTIDAE
Sittinae
Sitta canadensis Red-breasted Nuthatch.
Sitta carolinensis White-breasted Nuthatch.
Sitta pygmaea Pygmy Nuthatch.
Sitta pusilla Brown-headed Nuthatch.
CERTHIIDAE
Certhiinae
Certhia americana Brown Creeper.
TROGLODYTIDAE
Donacobius atricapillus Black-capped Donacobius.
Campylorhynchus albobrunneus White-headed Wren.
Campylorhynchus zonatus Band-backed Wren.
Campylorhynchus megalopterus Gray-barred Wren.
Campylorhynchus chiapensis Giant Wren.
Campylorhynchus rufinucha Rufous-naped Wren.
Campylorhynchus gularis Spotted Wren.
Campylorhynchus jocosus Boucard's Wren.
Campylorhynchus yucatanicus Yucatan Wren.
Campylorhynchus brunneicapillus Cactus Wren.
Salpinctes obsoletus Rock Wren.
Catherpes mexicanus Canyon Wren.
Hylorchilus sumichrasti Sumichrast's Wren.
Hylorchilus navai Nava's Wren.
Thryothorus spadix Sooty-headed Wren.
Thryothorus atrogularis Black-throated Wren.
Thryothorus fasciatoventris Black-bellied Wren.
Thryothorus nigricapillus Bay Wren.
Thryothorus semibadius Riverside Wren.
Thryothorus leucopogon Stripe-throated Wren.
Thryothorus thoracicus Stripe-breasted Wren.
Thryothorus rutilus Rufous-breasted Wren.
Thryothorus maculipectus Spot-breasted Wren.
Thryothorus rufalbus Rufous-and-white Wren.
Thryothorus sinaloa Sinaloa Wren.
Thryothorus pleurostictus Banded Wren.
Thryothorus ludovicianus Carolina Wren.
Thryothorus felix Happy Wren.
Thryothorus leucotis Buff-breasted Wren.
Thryothorus modestus Plain Wren.
Thryomanes bewickii Bewick's Wren.
Thryomanes sissonii Socorro Wren.

Ferminia cerverai Zapata Wren.
Troglodytes aedon House Wren.
Troglodytes tanneri Clarion Wren.
Troglodytes rufociliatus Rufous-browed Wren.
Troglodytes ochraceus Ochraceous Wren.
Troglodytes troglodytes Winter Wren.
Cistothorus platensis Sedge Wren.
Cistothorus palustris Marsh Wren.
Uropsila leucogastra White-bellied Wren.
Thryorchilus browni Timberline Wren.
Henicorhina leucosticta White-breasted Wood-Wren.
Henicorhina leucophrys Gray-breasted Wood-Wren.
Microcerculus philomela Nightingale Wren.
Microcerculus marginatus Scaly-breasted Wren.
Cyphorhinus phaeocephalus Song Wren.

CINCLIDAE
Cinclus mexicanus American Dipper.

PYCNONOTIDAE
Pycnonotus cafer Red-vented Bulbul. (H, I)
Pycnonotus jocosus Red-whiskered Bulbul. (I)

REGULIDAE
Regulus satrapa Golden-crowned Kinglet.
Regulus calendula Ruby-crowned Kinglet.

SYLVIIDAE
Sylviinae
Cettia diphone Japanese Bush-Warbler. (H, I)
Locustella ochotensis Middendorff's Grasshopper-Warbler. (A)
Locustella lanceolata Lanceolated Warbler. (A)
Acrocephalus familiaris Millerbird. (H)
Phylloscopus sibilatrix Wood Warbler. (A)
Phylloscopus fuscatus Dusky Warbler. (A)
Phylloscopus borealis Arctic Warbler.

Polioptilinae
Microbates cinereiventris Tawny-faced Gnatwren.
Ramphocaenus melanurus Long-billed Gnatwren.
Polioptila caerulea Blue-gray Gnatcatcher.
Polioptila lembeyei Cuban Gnatcatcher.
Polioptila californica California Gnatcatcher.
Polioptila melanura Black-tailed Gnatcatcher.
Polioptila nigriceps Black-capped Gnatcatcher.
Polioptila albiloris White-lored Gnatcatcher.
Polioptila plumbea Tropical Gnatcatcher.
Polioptila schistaceigula Slate-throated Gnatcatcher.

MUSCICAPIDAE
Ficedula narcissina Narcissus Flycatcher. (A)
Ficedula mugimaki Mugimaki Flycatcher. (A)
Ficedula parva Red-breasted Flycatcher. (A)
Muscicapa sibirica Siberian Flycatcher. (A)
Muscicapa griseisticta Gray-spotted Flycatcher. (A)
Muscicapa dauurica Asian Brown Flycatcher. (A)

TURDIDAE
Luscinia calliope Siberian Rubythroat. (A)
Luscinia svecica Bluethroat.
Luscinia cyane Siberian Blue Robin. (A)
Tarsiger cyanurus Red-flanked Bluetail. (A)
Copsychus malabaricus White-rumped Shama. (H, I)
Oenanthe oenanthe Northern Wheatear.
Saxicola torquata Stonechat. (A)

Sialia sialis Eastern Bluebird.
Sialia mexicana Western Bluebird.
Sialia currucoides Mountain Bluebird.
Myadestes townsendi Townsend's Solitaire.
Myadestes occidentalis Brown-backed Solitaire.
Myadestes elisabeth Cuban Solitaire.
Myadestes genibarbis Rufous-throated Solitaire.
Myadestes melanops Black-faced Solitaire.
Myadestes coloratus Varied Solitaire.
Myadestes unicolor Slate-colored Solitaire.
Myadestes myadestinus Kamao. (H)
†*Myadestes woahensis* Amaui. (H)
Myadestes lanaiensis Olomao. (H)
Myadestes obscurus Omao. (H)
Myadestes palmeri Puaiohi. (H)
Catharus gracilirostris Black-billed Nightingale-Thrush.
Catharus aurantiirostris Orange-billed Nightingale-Thrush.
Catharus fuscater Slaty-backed Nightingale-Thrush.
Catharus occidentalis Russet Nightingale-Thrush.
Catharus frantzii Ruddy-capped Nightingale-Thrush.
Catharus mexicanus Black-headed Nightingale-Thrush.
Catharus dryas Spotted Nightingale-Thrush.
Catharus fuscescens Veery.
Catharus minimus Gray-cheeked Thrush.
Catharus bicknelli Bicknell's Thrush.
Catharus ustulatus Swainson's Thrush.
Catharus guttatus Hermit Thrush.
Hylocichla mustelina Wood Thrush.
Turdus merula Eurasian Blackbird. (A)
Turdus obscurus Eyebrowed Thrush. (N)
Turdus naumanni Dusky Thrush. (A)
Turdus pilaris Fieldfare. (A)
Turdus iliacus Redwing. (A)
Turdus nigrescens Sooty Robin.
Turdus infuscatus Black Robin.
Turdus plebejus Mountain Robin.
Turdus fumigatus Cocoa Thrush.
Turdus obsoletus Pale-vented Thrush.
Turdus grayi Clay-colored Robin.
Turdus nudigenis Bare-eyed Robin.
Turdus jamaicensis White-eyed Thrush.
Turdus assimilis White-throated Robin.
Turdus rufopalliatus Rufous-backed Robin.
Turdus rufitorques Rufous-collared Robin.
Turdus migratorius American Robin.
Turdus swalesi La Selle Thrush.
Turdus aurantius White-chinned Thrush.
†*Turdus ravidus* Grand Cayman Thrush.
Turdus plumbeus Red-legged Thrush.
Cichlherminia lherminieri Forest Thrush.
Ixoreus naevius Varied Thrush.
Ridgwayia pinicola Aztec Thrush.

TIMALIIDAE

Garrulax pectoralis Greater Necklaced Laughingthrush. (H, I)
Garrulax canorus Hwamei. (H, I)
Leiothrix lutea Red-billed Leiothrix. (H, I)
Chamaea fasciata Wrentit.

ZOSTEROPIDAE
    Zosterops japonicus Japanese White-eye. (H, I)
MIMIDAE
    Dumetella carolinensis Gray Catbird.
    Melanoptila glabrirostris Black Catbird.
    Mimus polyglottos Northern Mockingbird.
    Mimus gilvus Tropical Mockingbird.
    Mimus gundlachii Bahama Mockingbird.
    Oreoscoptes montanus Sage Thrasher.
    Mimodes graysoni Socorro Mockingbird.
    Toxostoma rufum Brown Thrasher.
    Toxostoma longirostre Long-billed Thrasher.
    Toxostoma guttatum Cozumel Thrasher.
    Toxostoma cinereum Gray Thrasher.
    Toxostoma bendirei Bendire's Thrasher.
    Toxostoma ocellatum Ocellated Thrasher.
    Toxostoma curvirostre Curve-billed Thrasher.
    Toxostoma redivivum California Thrasher.
    Toxostoma crissale Crissal Thrasher.
    Toxostoma lecontei Le Conte's Thrasher.
    Ramphocinclus brachyurus White-breasted Thrasher.
    Melanotis caerulescens Blue Mockingbird.
    Melanotis hypoleucus Blue-and-white Mockingbird.
    Margarops fuscus Scaly-breasted Thrasher.
    Margarops fuscatus Pearly-eyed Thrasher.
    Cinclocerthia ruficauda Brown Trembler.
    Cinclocerthia gutturalis Gray Trembler.
STURNIDAE
    Sturnus vulgaris European Starling. (I)
    Acridotheres tristis Common Myna. (I)
    Acridotheres cristatellus Crested Myna. (I)
    Gracula religiosa Hill Myna. (H, I)
PRUNELLIDAE
    Prunella montanella Siberian Accentor. (A)
MOTACILLIDAE
    Motacilla flava Yellow Wagtail.
    Motacilla citreola Citrine Wagtail. (A)
    Motacilla cinerea Gray Wagtail. (A)
    Motacilla alba White Wagtail.
    Motacilla lugens Black-backed Wagtail.
    Anthus trivialis Tree Pipit. (A)
    Anthus hodgsoni Olive-backed Pipit. (A)
    Anthus gustavi Pechora Pipit. (A)
    Anthus cervinus Red-throated Pipit.
    Anthus rubescens American Pipit.
    Anthus spragueii Sprague's Pipit.
    Anthus lutescens Yellowish Pipit.
BOMBYCILLIDAE
    Bombycilla garrulus Bohemian Waxwing.
    Bombycilla cedrorum Cedar Waxwing.
PTILOGONATIDAE
    Phainoptila melanoxantha Black-and-yellow Silky-flycatcher.
    Ptilogonys cinereus Gray Silky-flycatcher.
    Ptilogonys caudatus Long-tailed Silky-flycatcher.
    Phainopepla nitens Phainopepla.
DULIDAE
    Dulus dominicus Palmchat.

PEUCEDRAMIDAE
    Peucedramus taeniatus Olive Warbler.
PARULIDAE
    †*Vermivora bachmanii* Bachman's Warbler.
    Vermivora pinus Blue-winged Warbler.
    Vermivora chrysoptera Golden-winged Warbler.
    Vermivora peregrina Tennessee Warbler.
    Vermivora celata Orange-crowned Warbler.
    Vermivora ruficapilla Nashville Warbler.
    Vermivora virginiae Virginia's Warbler.
    Vermivora crissalis Colima Warbler.
    Vermivora luciae Lucy's Warbler.
    Parula gutturalis Flame-throated Warbler.
    Parula superciliosa Crescent-chested Warbler.
    Parula americana Northern Parula.
    Parula pitiayumi Tropical Parula.
    Dendroica petechia Yellow Warbler.
    Dendroica pensylvanica Chestnut-sided Warbler.
    Dendroica magnolia Magnolia Warbler.
    Dendroica tigrina Cape May Warbler.
    Dendroica caerulescens Black-throated Blue Warbler.
    Dendroica coronata Yellow-rumped Warbler.
    Dendroica nigrescens Black-throated Gray Warbler.
    Dendroica chrysoparia Golden-cheeked Warbler.
    Dendroica virens Black-throated Green Warbler.
    Dendroica townsendi Townsend's Warbler.
    Dendroica occidentalis Hermit Warbler.
    Dendroica fusca Blackburnian Warbler.
    Dendroica dominica Yellow-throated Warbler.
    Dendroica graciae Grace's Warbler.
    Dendroica adelaidae Adelaide's Warbler.
    Dendroica pityophila Olive-capped Warbler.
    Dendroica pinus Pine Warbler.
    Dendroica kirtlandii Kirtland's Warbler.
    Dendroica discolor Prairie Warbler.
    Dendroica vitellina Vitelline Warbler.
    Dendroica palmarum Palm Warbler.
    Dendroica castanea Bay-breasted Warbler.
    Dendroica striata Blackpoll Warbler.
    Dendroica cerulea Cerulean Warbler.
    Dendroica plumbea Plumbeous Warbler.
    Dendroica pharetra Arrowhead Warbler.
    Dendroica angelae Elfin-woods Warbler.
    Catharopeza bishopi Whistling Warbler.
    Mniotilta varia Black-and-white Warbler.
    Setophaga ruticilla American Redstart.
    Protonotaria citrea Prothonotary Warbler.
    Helmitheros vermivorus Worm-eating Warbler.
    Limnothlypis swainsonii Swainson's Warbler.
    Seiurus aurocapillus Ovenbird.
    Seiurus noveboracensis Northern Waterthrush.
    Seiurus motacilla Louisiana Waterthrush.
    Oporornis formosus Kentucky Warbler.
    Oporornis agilis Connecticut Warbler.
    Oporornis philadelphia Mourning Warbler.
    Oporornis tolmiei MacGillivray's Warbler.
    Geothlypis trichas Common Yellowthroat.
    Geothlypis beldingi Belding's Yellowthroat.

Geothlypis flavovelata Altamira Yellowthroat.
Geothlypis rostrata Bahama Yellowthroat.
Geothlypis semiflava Olive-crowned Yellowthroat.
Geothlypis speciosa Black-polled Yellowthroat.
Geothlypis nelsoni Hooded Yellowthroat.
Geothlypis aequinoctialis Masked Yellowthroat.
Geothlypis poliocephala Gray-crowned Yellowthroat.
Microligea palustris Green-tailed Warbler.
Teretistris fernandinae Yellow-headed Warbler.
Teretistris fornsi Oriente Warbler.
Leucopeza semperi Semper's Warbler.
Wilsonia citrina Hooded Warbler.
Wilsonia pusilla Wilson's Warbler.
Wilsonia canadensis Canada Warbler.
Cardellina rubrifrons Red-faced Warbler.
Ergaticus ruber Red Warbler.
Ergaticus versicolor Pink-headed Warbler.
Myioborus pictus Painted Redstart.
Myioborus miniatus Slate-throated Redstart.
Myioborus torquatus Collared Redstart.
Euthlypis lachrymosa Fan-tailed Warbler.
Basileuterus culicivorus Golden-crowned Warbler.
Basileuterus rufifrons Rufous-capped Warbler.
Basileuterus belli Golden-browed Warbler.
Basileuterus melanogenys Black-cheeked Warbler.
Basileuterus ignotus Pirre Warbler.
Basileuterus tristriatus Three-striped Warbler.
Phaeothlypis fulvicauda Buff-rumped Warbler.
Zeledonia coronata Wrenthrush.
Icteria virens Yellow-breasted Chat.
Granatellus venustus Red-breasted Chat.
Granatellus sallaei Gray-throated Chat.
Xenoligea montana White-winged Warbler.

COEREBIDAE
Coereba flaveola Bananaquit.

THRAUPIDAE
Conirostrum leucogenys White-eared Conebill.
Nesospingus speculiferus Puerto Rican Tanager.
Chlorospingus ophthalmicus Common Bush-Tanager.
Chlorospingus tacarcunae Tacarcuna Bush-Tanager.
Chlorospingus inornatus Pirre Bush-Tanager.
Chlorospingus pileatus Sooty-capped Bush-Tanager.
Chlorospingus flavigularis Yellow-throated Bush-Tanager.
Chlorospingus canigularis Ashy-throated Bush-Tanager.
Hemithraupis flavicollis Yellow-backed Tanager.
Chrysothlypis ~~chrysomelas~~ Black-and-yellow Tanager.   chrysomelaena
Phaenicophilus palmarum Black-crowned Palm-Tanager.
Phaenicophilus poliocephalus Gray-crowned Palm-Tanager.
Calyptophilus tertius Western Chat-Tanager.
Calyptophilus frugivorus Eastern Chat-Tanager.
Rhodinocichla rosea Rosy Thrush-Tanager.
Mitrospingus cassinii Dusky-faced Tanager.
Chlorothraupis carmioli Olive Tanager.
Chlorothraupis olivacea Lemon-spectacled Tanager.
Eucometis penicillata Gray-headed Tanager.
Lanio aurantius Black-throated Shrike-Tanager.
Lanio leucothorax White-throated Shrike-Tanager.
Heterospingus rubrifrons Sulphur-rumped Tanager.

Heterospingus xanthopygius Scarlet-browed Tanager.
Tachyphonus luctuosus White-shouldered Tanager.
Tachyphonus delatrii Tawny-crested Tanager.
Tachyphonus rufus White-lined Tanager.
Habia rubica Red-crowned Ant-Tanager.
Habia fuscicauda Red-throated Ant-Tanager.
Habia atrimaxillaris Black-cheeked Ant-Tanager.
Piranga roseogularis Rose-throated Tanager.
Piranga flava Hepatic Tanager.
Piranga rubra Summer Tanager.
Piranga olivacea Scarlet Tanager.
Piranga ludoviciana Western Tanager.
Piranga bidentata Flame-colored Tanager.
Piranga leucoptera White-winged Tanager.
Piranga erythrocephala Red-headed Tanager.
Ramphocelus sanguinolentus Crimson-collared Tanager.
Ramphocelus dimidiatus Crimson-backed Tanager.
Ramphocelus passerinii Passerini's Tanager.
Ramphocelus costaricensis Cherrie's Tanager.
Ramphocelus flammigerus Flame-rumped Tanager.
Spindalis zena Stripe-headed Tanager.
Thraupis episcopus Blue-gray Tanager.
Thraupis abbas Yellow-winged Tanager.
Thraupis palmarum Palm Tanager.
Bangsia arcaei Blue-and-gold Tanager.
Euphonia jamaica Jamaican Euphonia.
Euphonia affinis Scrub Euphonia.
Euphonia luteicapilla Yellow-crowned Euphonia.
Euphonia laniirostris Thick-billed Euphonia.
Euphonia hirundinacea Yellow-throated Euphonia.
Euphonia musica Antillean Euphonia.
Euphonia elegantissima Elegant Euphonia.
Euphonia fulvicrissa Fulvous-vented Euphonia.
Euphonia imitans Spot-crowned Euphonia.
Euphonia gouldi Olive-backed Euphonia.
Euphonia minuta White-vented Euphonia.
Euphonia anneae Tawny-capped Euphonia.
Euphonia xanthogaster Orange-bellied Euphonia.
Chlorophonia flavirostris Yellow-collared Chlorophonia. (A)
Chlorophonia occipitalis Blue-crowned Chlorophonia.
Chlorophonia callophrys Golden-browed Chlorophonia.
Tangara inornata Plain-colored Tanager.
Tangara cabanisi Azure-rumped Tanager.
Tangara palmeri Gray-and-gold Tanager.
Tangara florida Emerald Tanager.
Tangara icterocephala Silver-throated Tanager.
Tangara guttata Speckled Tanager.
Tangara gyrola Bay-headed Tanager.
Tangara lavinia Rufous-winged Tanager.
Tangara cucullata Lesser Antillean Tanager.
Tangara larvata Golden-hooded Tanager.
Tangara dowii Spangle-cheeked Tanager.
Tangara fucosa Green-naped Tanager.
Dacnis venusta Scarlet-thighed Dacnis.
Dacnis cayana Blue Dacnis.
Dacnis viguieri Viridian Dacnis.
Chlorophanes spiza Green Honeycreeper.
Cyanerpes lucidus Shining Honeycreeper.

Cyanerpes caeruleus Purple Honeycreeper.
Cyanerpes cyaneus Red-legged Honeycreeper.
Tersina viridis Swallow Tanager.
EMBERIZIDAE
Volatinia jacarina Blue-black Grassquit.
Sporophila schistacea Slate-colored Seedeater.
Sporophila americana Variable Seedeater.
Sporophila torqueola White-collared Seedeater.
Sporophila nigricollis Yellow-bellied Seedeater.
Sporophila minuta Ruddy-breasted Seedeater.
Oryzoborus nuttingi Nicaraguan Seed-Finch.
Oryzoborus funereus Thick-billed Seed-Finch.
Amaurospiza concolor Blue Seedeater.
Melopyrrha nigra Cuban Bullfinch.
Tiaris canora Cuban Grassquit.
Tiaris olivacea Yellow-faced Grassquit.
Tiaris bicolor Black-faced Grassquit.
Loxipasser anoxanthus Yellow-shouldered Grassquit.
Loxigilla portoricensis Puerto Rican Bullfinch.
Loxigilla violacea Greater Antillean Bullfinch.
Loxigilla noctis Lesser Antillean Bullfinch.
Euneornis campestris Orangequit.
Melanospiza richardsoni St. Lucia Black Finch.
Pinaroloxias inornata Cocos Finch.
Haplospiza rustica Slaty Finch.
Acanthidops bairdii Peg-billed Finch.
Diglossa baritula Cinnamon-bellied Flowerpiercer.
Diglossa plumbea Slaty Flowerpiercer.
Sicalis flaveola Saffron Finch.
Sicalis luteola Grassland Yellow-Finch.
Emberizoides herbicola Wedge-tailed Grass-Finch.
Paroaria coronata Red-crested Cardinal. (H, I)
Paroaria capitata Yellow-billed Cardinal. (H, I)
Lysurus crassirostris Sooty-faced Finch.
Pselliophorus tibialis Yellow-thighed Finch.
Pselliophorus luteoviridis Yellow-green Finch.
Pezopetes capitalis Large-footed Finch.
Atlapetes albinucha White-naped Brush-Finch.
Atlapetes pileatus Rufous-capped Brush-Finch.
Buarremon brunneinuchus Chestnut-capped Brush-Finch.
Buarremon virenticeps Green-striped Brush-Finch.
Buarremon torquatus Stripe-headed Brush-Finch.
Arremon aurantiirostris Orange-billed Sparrow.
Arremonops rufivirgatus Olive Sparrow.
Arremonops chloronotus Green-backed Sparrow.
Arremonops conirostris Black-striped Sparrow.
Melozone kieneri Rusty-crowned Ground-Sparrow.
Melozone biarcuatum Prevost's Ground-Sparrow.
Melozone leucotis White-eared Ground-Sparrow.
Pipilo chlorurus Green-tailed Towhee.
Pipilo ocai Collared Towhee.
Pipilo maculatus Spotted Towhee.
Pipilo erythrophthalmus Eastern Towhee.
Pipilo albicollis White-throated Towhee.
Pipilo fuscus Canyon Towhee.
Pipilo crissalis California Towhee.
Pipilo aberti Abert's Towhee.
Aimophila ruficauda Stripe-headed Sparrow.

Aimophila humeralis Black-chested Sparrow.
Aimophila mystacalis Bridled Sparrow.
Aimophila sumichrasti Cinnamon-tailed Sparrow.
Aimophila carpalis Rufous-winged Sparrow.
Aimophila cassinii Cassin's Sparrow.
Aimophila aestivalis Bachman's Sparrow.
Aimophila botterii Botteri's Sparrow.
Aimophila ruficeps Rufous-crowned Sparrow.
Aimophila rufescens Rusty Sparrow.
Aimophila notosticta Oaxaca Sparrow.
Aimophila quinquestriata Five-striped Sparrow.
Oriturus superciliosus Striped Sparrow.
Torreornis inexpectata Zapata Sparrow.
Spizella arborea American Tree Sparrow.
Spizella passerina Chipping Sparrow.
Spizella pallida Clay-colored Sparrow.
Spizella breweri Brewer's Sparrow.
Spizella pusilla Field Sparrow.
Spizella wortheni Worthen's Sparrow.
Spizella atrogularis Black-chinned Sparrow.
Pooecetes gramineus Vesper Sparrow.
Chondestes grammacus Lark Sparrow.
Amphispiza bilineata Black-throated Sparrow.
Amphispiza belli Sage Sparrow.
Calamospiza melanocorys Lark Bunting.
Passerculus sandwichensis Savannah Sparrow.
Ammodramus savannarum Grasshopper Sparrow.
Ammodramus bairdii Baird's Sparrow.
Ammodramus henslowii Henslow's Sparrow.
Ammodramus leconteii Le Conte's Sparrow.
Ammodramus nelsoni Nelson's Sharp-tailed Sparrow.
Ammodramus caudacutus Saltmarsh Sharp-tailed Sparrow.
Ammodramus maritimus Seaside Sparrow.
Xenospiza baileyi Sierra Madre Sparrow.
Passerella iliaca Fox Sparrow.
Melospiza melodia Song Sparrow.
Melospiza lincolnii Lincoln's Sparrow.
Melospiza georgiana Swamp Sparrow.
Zonotrichia capensis Rufous-collared Sparrow.
Zonotrichia albicollis White-throated Sparrow.
Zonotrichia querula Harris's Sparrow.
Zonotrichia leucophrys White-crowned Sparrow.
Zonotrichia atricapilla Golden-crowned Sparrow.
Junco vulcani Volcano Junco.
Junco hyemalis Dark-eyed Junco.
Junco phaeonotus Yellow-eyed Junco.
Calcarius mccownii McCown's Longspur.
Calcarius lapponicus Lapland Longspur.
Calcarius pictus Smith's Longspur.
Calcarius ornatus Chestnut-collared Longspur.
Emberiza leucocephalos Pine Bunting. (A)
Emberiza pusilla Little Bunting. (A)
Emberiza rustica Rustic Bunting. (A)
Emberiza aureola Yellow-breasted Bunting. (A)
Emberiza variabilis Gray Bunting. (A)
Emberiza pallasi Pallas's Bunting. (A)
Emberiza schoeniclus Reed Bunting. (A)
Plectrophenax nivalis Snow Bunting.
Plectrophenax hyperboreus McKay's Bunting.

CARDINALIDAE
Saltator albicollis Lesser Antillean Saltator.
Saltator striatipectus Streaked Saltator.
Saltator coerulescens Grayish Saltator.
Saltator maximus Buff-throated Saltator.
Saltator atriceps Black-headed Saltator.
Saltator grossus Slate-colored Grosbeak.
Caryothraustes poliogaster Black-faced Grosbeak.
Caryothraustes canadensis Yellow-green Grosbeak.
Rhodothraupis celaeno Crimson-collared Grosbeak.
Cardinalis cardinalis Northern Cardinal.
Cardinalis sinuatus Pyrrhuloxia.
Pheucticus chrysopeplus Yellow Grosbeak.
Pheucticus tibialis Black-thighed Grosbeak.
Pheucticus ludovicianus Rose-breasted Grosbeak.
Pheucticus melanocephalus Black-headed Grosbeak.
Cyanocompsa cyanoides Blue-black Grosbeak.
Cyanocompsa parellina Blue Bunting.
Guiraca caerulea Blue Grosbeak.
Passerina rositae Rose-bellied Bunting.
Passerina amoena Lazuli Bunting.
Passerina cyanea Indigo Bunting.
Passerina versicolor Varied Bunting.
Passerina leclancherii Orange-breasted Bunting.
Passerina ciris Painted Bunting.
Spiza americana Dickcissel.

ICTERIDAE
Dolichonyx oryzivorus Bobolink.
Agelaius phoeniceus Red-winged Blackbird.
Agelaius assimilis Red-shouldered Blackbird.
Agelaius tricolor Tricolored Blackbird.
Agelaius humeralis Tawny-shouldered Blackbird.
Agelaius xanthomus Yellow-shouldered Blackbird.
Nesopsar nigerrimus Jamaican Blackbird.
Sturnella militaris Red-breasted Blackbird.
Sturnella magna Eastern Meadowlark.
Sturnella neglecta Western Meadowlark.
Xanthocephalus xanthocephalus Yellow-headed Blackbird.
Dives dives Melodious Blackbird.
Dives atroviolacea Cuban Blackbird.
Euphagus carolinus Rusty Blackbird.
Euphagus cyanocephalus Brewer's Blackbird.
Quiscalus quiscula Common Grackle.
Quiscalus major Boat-tailed Grackle.
Quiscalus mexicanus Great-tailed Grackle.
†*Quiscalus palustris* Slender-billed Grackle.
Quiscalus nicaraguensis Nicaraguan Grackle.
Quiscalus niger Greater Antillean Grackle.
Quiscalus lugubris Carib Grackle.
Molothrus bonariensis Shiny Cowbird.
Molothrus aeneus Bronzed Cowbird.
Molothrus ater Brown-headed Cowbird.
Scaphidura oryzivora Giant Cowbird.
Icterus dominicensis Black-cowled Oriole.
Icterus laudabilis St. Lucia Oriole.
Icterus oberi Montserrat Oriole.
Icterus bonana Martinique Oriole.
Icterus wagleri Black-vented Oriole.

Icterus maculialatus Bar-winged Oriole.
Icterus spurius Orchard Oriole.
Icterus cucullatus Hooded Oriole.
Icterus chrysater Yellow-backed Oriole.
Icterus auricapillus Orange-crowned Oriole.
Icterus mesomelas Yellow-tailed Oriole.
Icterus icterus Troupial. (I)
Icterus pustulatus Streak-backed Oriole.
Icterus auratus Orange Oriole.
Icterus leucopteryx Jamaican Oriole.
Icterus pectoralis Spot-breasted Oriole.
Icterus gularis Altamira Oriole.
Icterus graduacauda Audubon's Oriole.
Icterus galbula Baltimore Oriole.
Icterus bullockii Bullock's Oriole.
Icterus abeillei Black-backed Oriole.
Icterus parisorum Scott's Oriole.
Amblycercus holosericeus Yellow-billed Cacique.
Cacicus uropygialis Scarlet-rumped Cacique.
Cacicus cela Yellow-rumped Cacique.
Cacicus melanicterus Yellow-winged Cacique.
Psarocolius decumanus Crested Oropendola.
Psarocolius wagleri Chestnut-headed Oropendola.
Psarocolius montezuma Montezuma Oropendola.
Psarocolius guatimozinus Black Oropendola.
FRINGILLIDAE
Fringillinae
Fringilla coelebs Common Chaffinch. (A)
Fringilla montifringilla Brambling.
Carduelinae
Leucosticte tephrocotis Gray-crowned Rosy-Finch.
Leucosticte atrata Black Rosy-Finch.
Leucosticte australis Brown-capped Rosy-Finch.
Pinicola enucleator Pine Grosbeak.
Carpodacus erythrinus Common Rosefinch. (N)
Carpodacus purpureus Purple Finch.
Carpodacus cassinii Cassin's Finch.
Carpodacus mexicanus House Finch.
Loxia curvirostra Red Crossbill.
Loxia leucoptera White-winged Crossbill.
Carduelis flammea Common Redpoll.
Carduelis hornemanni Hoary Redpoll.
Carduelis spinus Eurasian Siskin. (A)
Carduelis pinus Pine Siskin.
Carduelis atriceps Black-capped Siskin.
Carduelis notata Black-headed Siskin.
Carduelis xanthogastra Yellow-bellied Siskin.
Carduelis cucullata Red Siskin. (I)
Carduelis dominicensis Antillean Siskin.
Carduelis psaltria Lesser Goldfinch.
Carduelis lawrencei Lawrence's Goldfinch.
Carduelis tristis American Goldfinch.
Carduelis carduelis European Goldfinch. (I)
Carduelis sinica Oriental Greenfinch. (A)
Serinus mozambicus Yellow-fronted Canary. (I)
Serinus canaria Common Canary. (I)
Pyrrhula pyrrhula Eurasian Bullfinch. (A)
Coccothraustes abeillei Hooded Grosbeak.

Coccothraustes vespertinus Evening Grosbeak.
Coccothraustes coccothraustes Hawfinch. (A)
Drepanidinae
Telespiza cantans Laysan Finch.
Telespiza ultima Nihoa Finch.
Psittirostra psittacea Ou.
†*Dysmorodrepanis munroi* Lanai Hookbill.
Loxioides bailleui Palila.
†*Rhodacanthis flaviceps* Lesser Koa-Finch.
†*Rhodacanthis palmeri* Greater Koa-Finch.
†*Chloridops kona* Kona Grosbeak.
Pseudonestor xanthophrys Maui Parrotbill.
Hemignathus virens Hawaii Amakihi.
Hemignathus flavus Oahu Amakihi.
Hemignathus kauaiensis Kauai Amakihi.
Hemignathus parvus Anianiau.
†*Hemignathus sagittirostris* Greater Amakihi.
†*Hemignathus obscurus* Lesser Akialoa.
Hemignathus ellisianus Greater Akialoa.
Hemignathus lucidus Nukupuu.
Hemignathus munroi Akiapolaau.
Oreomystis bairdi Akikiki.
Oreomystis mana Hawaii Creeper.
Paroreomyza maculata Oahu Alauahio.
Paroreomyza flammea Kakawahie.
Paroreomyza montana Maui Alauahio.
Loxops caeruleirostris Akekee.
Loxops coccineus Akepa.
†*Ciridops anna* Ula-ai-hawane.
Vestiaria coccinea Iiwi.
†*Drepanis pacifica* Hawaii Mamo.
†*Drepanis funerea* Black Mamo.
Palmeria dolei Akohekohe.
Himatione sanguinea Apapane.
Melamprosops phaeosoma Poo-uli.
PASSERIDAE
Passer domesticus House Sparrow. (I)
Passer montanus Eurasian Tree Sparrow. (I)
PLOCEIDAE
Ploceinae
Ploceus cucullatus Village Weaver. (I)
Euplectes franciscanus Orange Bishop. (I)
Euplectes afer Yellow-crowned Bishop. (I)
ESTRILDIDAE
Estrildinae
Uraeginthus bengalus Red-cheeked Cordonbleu. (H, I)
Estrilda caerulescens Lavender Waxbill. (H, I)
Estrilda melpoda Orange-cheeked Waxbill. (I)
Estrilda troglodytes Black-rumped Waxbill. (I)
Estrilda astrild Common Waxbill. (I)
Amandava amandava Red Avadavat. (I)
Lonchura malabarica Warbling Silverbill. (I)
Lonchura cucullata Bronze Mannikin. (I)
Lonchura punctulata Nutmeg Mannikin. (I)
Lonchura malacca Chestnut Mannikin. (I)
Padda oryzivora Java Sparrow. (I)
Viduinae
Vidua macroura Pin-tailed Whydah. (I)

THE CHECK-LIST: SPECIES

Class **AVES**: Birds

Subclass **NEORNITHES**: True Birds

Superorder **PALEOGNATHAE**: Ratites and Tinamous

Order **TINAMIFORMES**: Tinamous

Family **TINAMIDAE**: Tinamous

Genus *TINAMUS* Hermann

Tinamus Hermann, 1783, Tabula Affinit. Anim., pp. 164, 235. Type, by subsequent designation (Apstein, 1915), "Le Magoua" Buffon = *Tetrao major* Gmelin.

Tinamus major (Gmelin). Great Tinamou.

Tetrao major Gmelin, 1789, Syst. Nat. l(2): 767. Based largely on "Le Magoua" Buffon, Hist. Nat. Ois. 4: 507, pl. 24. (in Americæ australis, praesertim Cayennæ et Gujanæ = Cayenne.)

Habitat.—Tropical Lowland Evergreen Forest, River-edge Forest, Secondary Forest (0–1000 m; Tropical and lower Subtropical zones).

Distribution.—*Resident* from southern Veracruz and northern Oaxaca (possibly southeastern Puebla, at least formerly) south along the Gulf-Caribbean slope of Tabasco, Chiapas, southern Campeche, southern Quintana Roo, Guatemala, Belize, Honduras, and Nicaragua, on both slopes of Costa Rica (absent from dry northwest) and Panama (except the drier central regions), and in South America from Colombia, Venezuela, and the Guianas south, west of the Andes to western Ecuador, and east of the Andes to central Bolivia and central Brazil.

Genus *NOTHOCERCUS* Bonaparte

Nothocercus Bonaparte, 1856, C. R. Acad. Sci. Paris 42: 881. Type, by subsequent designation (Salvadori, 1895), *Tinamus julius* Bonaparte.

Nothocercus bonapartei (Gray). Highland Tinamou.

Tinamus Bonapartei G. R. Gray, 1867, List Birds Brit. Mus., pt. 5, p. 97. (valley of Aragua, Venezuela.)

Habitat.—Montane Evergreen Forest, especially in ravines (1300–2500 m; upper Tropical, Subtropical, and Temperate zones).

Distribution.—*Resident* in the highlands of Costa Rica (north to Cordillera de Guanacaste) and extreme western Panama (Volcán de Chiriquí massif); and mountains from Colombia and western and northern Venezuela south through Ecuador to northwestern Peru.

Genus *CRYPTURELLUS* Brabourne and Chubb

Crypturellus Brabourne and Chubb, 1914, Ann. Mag. Nat. Hist. (8)14: 322. Type, by original designation, *C. tataupa* (Temminck) = *Tinamus tataupa* Temminck.

1

Crypturellus soui (Hermann). Little Tinamou.

> *Tinamus soui* Hermann, 1783, Tabula Affinit. Anim., p. 165. Based on "Le Soui" Buffon, Hist. Nat. Ois. 4: 512, and "Le Soui ou Petit Tinamou, de Cayenne" Daubenton, Planches Enlum., pl. 829. (Cayenne.)

Habitat.—Tropical Lowland Evergreen Forest Edge, Secondary Forest, River-edge Forest, (0–1500 m; Tropical and lower Subtropical zones).

Distribution.—*Resident* on the Gulf-Caribbean slope from southern Veracruz and northern Oaxaca south through Tabasco, northern Chiapas, southern Campeche, southern Quintana Roo, Guatemala, Belize, Honduras, and Nicaragua, on both slopes of Costa Rica (absent from dry northwest) and Panama (including Isla del Rey in the Pearl Islands, where probably introduced), and in South America from Colombia, Venezuela, Trinidad, and the Guianas south, west of the Andes to western Ecuador, and east of the Andes to central Bolivia and central and southeastern Brazil.

Crypturellus cinnamomeus (Lesson). Thicket Tinamou.

> *Tinamus (nothura) cinnamomea* Lesson, 1842, Rev. Zool. [Paris] 5: 210. (La Union, Centre Amérique = La Unión, El Salvador.)

Habitat.—Gallery Forest, Tropical Deciduous Forest, Secondary Forest (0–1850 m; Tropical and lower Subtropical zones).

Distribution.—*Resident* on the Pacific slope of Middle America from central Sinaloa (absent from Pacific Oaxaca) south to northwestern Costa Rica (Guanacaste), and on the Gulf-Caribbean slope from northern Tamaulipas and southeastern San Luis Potosí south to the Yucatan Peninsula, northern Guatemala (Petén), Belize, and the interior valleys of eastern Chiapas, central Guatemala, and northern Honduras.

Notes.—Also known as Rufescent Tinamou. Vocal differences between northern and southern populations in eastern Mexico suggest that two species may be involved. May hybridize with *Crypturellus boucardi* in Honduras (Monroe 1968), but this possibility has been questioned (Howell and Webb 1995). *Crypturellus idoneus* (Todd, 1919), a Colombian endemic once treated as a subspecies of *C. cinnamomeus,* appears to be a subspecies of *C. erythropus* (Pelzeln, 1863) based on ectoparasite data (fide Carriker *in* Blake 1977) and voice (P. Schwartz, unpubl.).

Crypturellus boucardi (Sclater). Slaty-breasted Tinamou.

> *Tinamus boucardi* (Sallé MS) Sclater, 1859, Proc. Zool. Soc. London, p. 391. (In statu Oaxaca reipublicae Mexicanae . . . Playa Vicente . . . and . . . Teotalcingo = Teotalcingo, Oaxaca; Binford, 1989, Ornithol. Monogr. 43, p. 336.)

Habitat.—Tropical Lowland Evergreen Forest, Secondary Forest (0–800 m; Tropical and lower Subtropical zones).

Distribution.—*Resident* from southern Veracruz and northern Oaxaca south along the Gulf-Caribbean slope (also Pacific slope of Sierra Madre de Chiapas) of Tabasco, Chiapas, southern Quintana Roo, Guatemala, Belize, Honduras, and Nicaragua to Costa Rica (to the latitude of Puerto Limón, occurring also on the Pacific slope of the Cordillera de Guanacaste).

Notes.—Also known as Boucard's Tinamou. *Crypturellus boucardi* and *C. kerriae* are closely allied and constitute a superspecies (Sibley and Monroe 1990). The relationships of the northern Colombian *C. columbianus* (Salvadori, 1895), variously treated as a separate species, a race of *C. boucardi,* or a race of the South American *C. erythropus* (Pelzeln, 1863), remain uncertain (see Blake 1977). See comments under *C. cinnamomeus.*

Crypturellus kerriae (Chapman). Choco Tinamou.

> *Crypturus kerriae* Chapman, 1915, Bull. Amer. Mus. Nat. Hist. 34: 636. (Baudó, Chocó, Colombia.)

Habitat.—Tropical Lowland Evergreen Forest (300–800 m; upper Tropical and lower Subtropical zones).

Distribution.—*Resident* in extreme eastern Panama (Río Mono to Cerro Quía in south-eastern Darién) and northwestern Colombia (foothills of the Serranía de Baudó in Chocó). **Notes.**—See comments under *C. boucardi.*

Superorder NEOGNATHAE: Typical Birds

Order GAVIIFORMES: Loons

Notes.—The phylogenetic relationships of the Gaviiformes are highly controversial (see Sibley and Ahlquist 1990 and references therein); although they are probably close to the Procellariiformes or Charadriiformes, we retain them in their current position until their relationships are resolved.

Family GAVIIDAE: Loons

Genus *GAVIA* Forster

Gavia J. R. Forster, 1788, Enchirid. Hist. Nat., p. 38. Type, by subsequent designation (Allen, 1908), *Colymbus imber* Gunnerus = *Colymbus immer* Brünnich.

Notes.—Authors in the Old World use the group name Diver for species in this genus. *Colymbus* Linnaeus, 1758, has been used in Old World literature for *Gavia* but has been suppressed (I.C.Z.N. 1956a).

Gavia stellata (Pontoppidan). Red-throated Loon.

Colymbus Stellatus Pontoppidan, 1763, Dan. Atlas 1: 621. Based on *Colymbus maximus stellatus* Willughby, Ornithology, p. 256, pl. 62. (Tame River, Warwickshire, England.)

Habitat.—Ponds and shallow lakes in coastal and alpine tundra, and in coastal flats south of tundra, sometimes in wooded areas (breeding); primarily bays, inlets, estuaries, and seacoasts, occasionally on lakes and rivers (nonbreeding).

Distribution.—*Breeds* in North America on Arctic coasts and islands from Alaska to Ellesmere Island, south along the Pacific coast through the Aleutian Islands to the Queen Charlotte and Vancouver islands, in the interior of the continent to central Yukon, southern Mackenzie, northeastern Alberta (probably), northern Saskatchewan, around Hudson Bay, and along the Atlantic coast to southeastern Quebec (including Anticosti Island), Miquelon Island, and northern Newfoundland (Grey Island); and in Eurasia from Greenland, Iceland, and Arctic islands and coasts south to the British Isles, southern Scandinavia, northern Russia, Lake Baikal, Sakhalin, the Kuril Islands, Kamchatka, and the Commander Islands. Non-breeding birds may remain on the wintering grounds through the summer as far south as California on the Pacific coast and Chesapeake Bay on the Atlantic coast.

Winters in North America primarily along the Pacific coast from Alaska south to Baja California and northwestern Sonora, and on the Atlantic coast from Newfoundland south to northeastern Florida, ranging casually or rarely to the Gulf coast of Alabama, Mississippi, and Florida; and in Eurasia south to the Mediterranean, Black, and Caspian seas, and along the western Pacific coast to China and Taiwan.

Migrates through south-central Canada and the Great Lakes region (commonly Lake Ontario, uncommonly or rarely elsewhere), rarely through the upper Ohio and Mississippi valleys and Appalachian region, and casually or rarely elsewhere in the interior of North America south to southern California, Arizona, New Mexico, Texas, and the Gulf coast.

Casual in Hidalgo.

Gavia arctica (Linnaeus). Arctic Loon.

Colymbus arcticus Linnaeus, 1758, Syst. Nat. (ed. 10) 1: 135. (in Europa & America boreali = Sweden.)

Habitat.—Lakes in tundra and taiga (breeding); primarily bays, estuaries, and seacoasts, rarely on lakes and rivers (nonbreeding).

Distribution.—*Breeds* [*arctica* group] in Eurasia from the British Isles east across Arctic coasts to the Lena River, and south to southern Scandinavia, central Russia, and Lake Baikal; and [*viridigularis* group] in eastern Siberia (east of *arctica,* but not in the Arctic east of the Indigirka River) south to Transbaicalia, Amurland, Sakhalin, and Kamchatka, and in western Alaska from the Cape Prince of Wales region to Cape Krusenstern and (possibly) Safety Sound.

Winters [*arctica* group] in Eurasia south to the Mediterranean, Black, Caspian, and Aral seas; and [*viridigularis* group] in Eurasia from the breeding range south to coastal eastern China, Ussuriland, Japan, and the Kuril Islands, probably also to Korea, and casually in North America in western and southern Alaska and California (Sonoma, Marin, and San Luis Obispo counties).

Notes.—Known also as Black-throated Loon or Black-throated Diver. The two groups were once regarded as distinct species, *G. viridigularis* Dwight, 1918 [Green-throated Loon] and *G. arctica* [Black-throated Loon], but the two appear to intergrade in eastern Siberia (east of the Lena River and Lake Baikal); however, the level of hybridization is insufficiently known and obscured by individual variation (Vaurie 1965, Cramp and Simmons 1977). See also *G. pacifica.*

Gavia pacifica (Lawrence). Pacific Loon.

Colymbus pacificus Lawrence, 1858, in Baird, Cassin, and Lawrence, Rep. Explor. Surv. R. R. Pac. 9: 889. (Coast of California; Puget's Sound. Restricted to San Diego, San Diego County, California, by Grinnell, 1932, Univ. Calif. Publ. Zool 38: 260.)

Habitat.—Lakes in tundra and taiga (breeding); primarily seacoasts (often at considerable distance from shore), bays, upwellings, and estuaries, rarely on lakes and rivers (non-breeding).

Distribution.—*Breeds* in eastern Siberia from the Arctic coast (west to the Indigirka River) south to Anadyrland, and in North America from the Arctic coast of Alaska and Canada, and Banks, Prince of Wales, Victoria, and northern Baffin islands south to St. Lawrence Island, southern Alaska (Alaska and Kenai peninsulas), southwestern Yukon, northwestern British Columbia, southern Mackenzie, northeastern Alberta, northern Manitoba, northern Ontario, Belcher Islands, and northwestern Quebec. Nonbreeding birds may summer along the Pacific coast (south to Baja California), in Colorado, northern Alberta, and northwestern Saskatchewan, and north to Melville Island.

Winters from Siberia south to Japan, along the Pacific coast of North America from Alaska south to southern Baja California and southern Sonora, and (more frequently as migrants) in the interior of western North America south to southern California, Arizona, New Mexico, and Texas.

Casual in central and eastern North America east to the Great Lakes region, southern Ontario, southern Quebec, and Maine, and south irregularly to the Gulf coast and southern Florida; as a vagrant, most frequently recorded along the Atlantic coast from Maine to Virginia, rarely (species uncertain, possibly *G. arctica*) to the Hawaiian Islands (Oahu) and Bermuda. Accidental in western Greenland.

Notes.—In the Old World known as Pacific Diver. *Gavia pacifica* has been frequently treated as a subspecies of *G. arctica,* but sympatric breeding occurs widely in eastern Siberia and probably also western Alaska (Vaurie 1965, Stepanyan 1975, Kistchinski 1980); probable hybrids have been reported (Storer 1978).

Gavia immer (Brünnich). Common Loon.

Colymbus Immer Brünnich, 1764, Ornithol. Bor., p. 38. (Faeroes = Faeroe Islands.)

Habitat.—Large and small lakes and ponds, occasionally rivers, from tundra south in primarily forested situations (breeding); primarily seacoasts, bays, inlets, and estuaries, less frequently along lakes and rivers, rarely or uncommonly to the shelf break ca. 100 km off North Carolina (nonbreeding).

Distribution.—*Breeds* from western and central Alaska (Seward Peninsula, western Aleutian Islands, and the Brooks Range), northern Yukon, northwestern and southern Mackenzie, central Keewatin, northern Manitoba, northern Ontario, southern Baffin Island, Labrador, and Newfoundland south to northeastern California (at least formerly), Nevada, northwestern Montana, western Wyoming, northern North Dakota, northern Iowa (formerly), northern Wisconsin, northern Illinois (formerly), northern Indiana (formerly), southern Ontario, northern New York, southern New England, and Nova Scotia; also both coasts of Greenland, Iceland, Scotland (in 1970), and (probably) Bear Island (south of Spitsbergen). Nonbreeding birds summer regularly outside the breeding range south, at least casually, to southern California, Sonora, Texas, the Gulf coast, and Florida, in northern Europe, and on Jan Mayen.

Winters in North America primarily along the Pacific coast from the Aleutian Islands south to Baja California and Colima, and along the Atlantic and Gulf coasts from Newfoundland south to southern Florida and west to Tamaulipas, less frequently (especially in the north) on inland waters through most of the continental United States; and in the western Palearctic along the Atlantic coast south to northwestern Africa, casually to the eastern Atlantic islands and through Europe to the Mediterranean and Black seas.

Casual in Coahuila, Bermuda, and Cuba (Havana); sight reports for Hidalgo and México.

Notes.—In the Old World known as Great Northern Diver. *Gavia immer* and *G. adamsii* constitute a superspecies (Mayr and Short 1970; Storer *in* Mayr and Cottrell 1979).

Gavia adamsii (Gray). Yellow-billed Loon.

> *Colymbus adamsii* G. R. Gray, 1859, Proc. Zool. Soc. London, p. 167. (Russian America = Alaska.)

Habitat.—Tundra lakes (breeding); seacoasts, bays, and estuaries, less frequently on lakes (nonbreeding).

Distribution.—*Breeds* in North America from northern and western Alaska (south to St. Lawrence Island and the southern Seward Peninsula) east to Banks, Victoria, and Prince of Wales islands and northern Keewatin, and south to east-central Mackenzie and east-central Keewatin; and in Eurasia from extreme northwestern Russia east to Siberia (including Novaya Zemlya). Nonbreeding individuals summer outside the breeding range east to northeastern Keewatin (Melville Peninsula) and northern Baffin Island, and south to southwestern British Columbia, southern Mackenzie (Great Slave Lake), and southern Keewatin, casually to coastal California.

Winters in North America along the Pacific coast of Alaska and British Columbia, casually south in coastal areas to California, and inland to Alberta; and in Eurasia in the breeding range, casually west to Greenland and south to southern Europe, China, Korea, and Japan.

Casual or accidental in inland California, Saskatchewan, northern Manitoba, northern Baja California, Arizona, Nevada, Utah, Montana, Colorado, New Mexico, Kansas, Oklahoma, Texas, Minnesota, Illinois, Missouri, Quebec, and New York (Long Island); sight reports for Idaho, Wyoming, Arkansas, and Ontario.

Notes.—Known in the Old World as White-billed Diver. See comments under *G. immer.*

Order PODICIPEDIFORMES: Grebes

Family PODICIPEDIDAE: Grebes

Notes.—The classification here follows Storer *in* Mayr and Cottrell (1979). For a summary of the relationships among the genera and species of grebes, see Vlug and Fjeldså (1990).

Genus *TACHYBAPTUS* Reichenbach

> *Tachybaptus* Reichenbach, 1853, Handb, Spec. Ornithol., Die Vögel, pt. 3 (1852), p. iii. Type, by monotypy, *Colymbus minor* Gmelin = *Colymbus ruficollis* Pallas.
> *Limnodytes* Oberholser, 1974, Bird Life Texas 1: 63; 2: 970. Type, by original designation, *Colymbus dominicus* Linnaeus.

Notes.—For recognition of *Tachybaptus,* see Storer (1976).

Tachybaptus dominicus (Linnaeus). Least Grebe.

Colymbus dominicus Linnaeus, 1766, Syst. Nat. (ed. 12) 1: 223. Based on "La Grèbe de rivière de S. Domingue" Brisson, Ornithologie 6: 64, pl. 5, fig. 2. (in Dominica = Haiti, *fide* D. Wetherbee.)

Habitat.—Freshwater Marshes, Freshwater Lakes and Ponds, temporary bodies of water, generally in slow-flowing or still waters with emergent vegetation, occasionally mangrove swamps (0–2600 m; Tropical to lower Temperate zones).

Distribution.—*Resident* locally from southern Baja California, southern Sonora (Pacific lowlands), southern Texas (Gulf lowlands), and the Bahamas (except Grand Bahama) south along both slopes of Middle America (including Cozumel Island), the Greater Antilles (east to Virgin Gorda and St. Croix in the Virgin Islands), and South America (also Trinidad and Tobago) to central Argentina.

Casual north to southeastern California (including one breeding record), southern Arizona, and central and eastern Texas. Accidental in Louisiana (Baton Rouge) and southern Florida (Big Pine Key).

Genus *PODILYMBUS* Lesson

Podilymbus Lesson, 1831, Traité Ornithol. 8: 595. Type, by monotypy, *Podiceps carolinensis* Latham = *Colymbus podiceps* Linnaeus.

Podilymbus podiceps (Linnaeus). Pied-billed Grebe.

Colymbus Podiceps Linnaeus, 1758, Syst. Nat. (ed. 10) 1: 136. Based on "The Pied-Bill Dopchick" Catesby, Nat. Hist. Carolina, p. 91, pl. 91. (in America septentrionali = South Carolina.)

Habitat.—Lakes, ponds, sluggish streams, and marshes, usually with tall emergent vegetation; in migration and winter also in brackish bays, lagoons, and estuaries.

Distribution.—*Breeds* in the Hawaiian Islands (Hawaii, since 1985; 1985; Amer. Birds 40: 161) and south-coastal Alaska (Copper River region, once), and from central and northeastern British Columbia, south-central Mackenzie, northern Alberta, northern Saskatchewan, northern Manitoba, central Ontario, southern Quebec, Maine, New Brunswick, Prince Edward Island, and Nova Scotia south locally through North America, Middle America, Bermuda (casually, where common as a migrant), the West Indies, and South America to central Chile and southern Argentina.

Winters in southeastern Alaska (rarely), through most of the breeding range from the Queen Charlotte Islands and southern British Columbia, the central United States, lakes Erie and Ontario, and New York southward (casually farther north), and on Bermuda (uncommonly). Northern populations are migratory, at least in part, and winter south to Panama; tropical populations are essentially sedentary.

Casual on the Hawaiian Islands of Kauai and Oahu, and on the continent north to southern Alaska, southern Yukon, southern Baffin Island, northern Labrador, Newfoundland, in the Revillagigedo Islands (Socorro Island), and western Europe; accidental on the Azores and Canary Islands. *Podilymbus podiceps*

Notes.—*Podiceps podiceps* and *P. gigas* are closely allied and may constitute a superspecies (Mayr and Short 1970; Storer *in* Mayr and Cottrell 1979) although both were reported to have bred on Lake Atitlán, Guatemala.

†*Podilymbus gigas* Griscom. Atitlan Grebe.

Podilymbus gigas Griscom, 1929, Amer. Mus. Novit., no. 379, p. 5. (Panajachel, 5300 ft., north shore of Lake Atitlan, Guatemala.)

Habitat.—Reed and cattail beds, less frequently open water, on a single lake (1555 m; Subtropical Zone).

Distribution.—Apparently EXTINCT (Hunter 1988); formerly *resident* on Lake Atitlán, Guatemala (elevation, 1555 meters).

Notes.—Also known as Giant Pied-billed Grebe. See comments under *P. podiceps*.

Genus *PODICEPS* Latham

Podiceps Latham, 1787, Gen. Synop. Birds, suppl. 1: 294. Type, by subsequent des-
ignation (G. R. Gray, 1840), *Colymbus cristatus* Linnaeus.
Dytes Kaup, 1829, Skizz. Entw.-Ges. Eur. Thierw., p. 41. Type, by subsequent desig-
nation (G. R. Gray, 1841), *Dytes cornutus* Kaup = *Colymbus auritus* Linnaeus.
Pedetaithya Kaup, 1829, Skizz. Entw.-Ges. Eur. Thierw., p. 44. Type, by monotypy,
Colymbus subcristatus Jacquin = *Colymbus grisegena* Boddaert.
Proctopus Kaup, 1829, Skizz. Entw.-Ges. Eur. Thierw., p. 49. Type, by monotypy,
Colymbus auritus Linnaeus.

Notes.—*Podiceps* has been considered by many authors to be a junior synonym of *Colymbus* Linnaeus, 1758, but the latter name has been officially suppressed (see comments
under *Gavia*).

Podiceps auritus (Linnaeus). Horned Grebe.

Colymbus auritus Linnaeus, 1758, Syst. Nat. (ed. 10) 1: 135. (in summis Europæ &
Americæ lacubus = Vaasa, Finland.)

Habitat.—Marshes, ponds, and lakes, occasionally along sluggish streams (breeding);
bays, inlets, estuaries, and in migration commonly in inland fresh-water
habitats, especially lakes and rivers (nonbreeding).
Distribution.—*Breeds* from central Alaska, northern Yukon, northwestern and southern
Mackenzie, southern Keewatin, and northern Manitoba south to eastern Washington, south-
central Oregon, northeastern Idaho, northern Montana, northwestern Wyoming, northern
South Dakota, northwestern Minnesota (rarely), central Wisconsin, northwestern Ontario
(Fort Severn), and southeastern Quebec (Anticosti and Magdalen islands), and formerly (at
least locally) from central Ontario, southern Quebec, and New Brunswick south to north-
central Nebraska, and northern Indiana (once); reports of breeding in New England not
substantiated; also breeds in northern Eurasia from Iceland, northern Scotland, and Scandinavia east across northern Russia and northern Siberia, south to central Russia, Lake Baikal,
Amurland, Sakhalin, and Kamchatka.
Winters in North America on the Pacific coast from the Aleutians and south-coastal Alaska
south to northern Baja California, and on the Atlantic and Gulf coasts from Nova Scotia
south to southern Florida and west to southern Texas, more uncommonly on inland waters
from southern Canada and the Great Lakes southward, uncommonly to Bermuda, casually
to the Hawaiian Islands (Kauai) and the Gulf of California; and in Eurasia from the seas
off Iceland, the Faeroe Islands, British Isles, and Norway south to the northern Mediterranean,
Black, and Caspian seas, casually to Madeira, the Azores, and northern Africa, and on the
Pacific coast from Japan south to Korea.
Migrates regularly through interior North America, and in western Europe.
Casual north to Labrador, Newfoundland, Greenland, Jan Mayen, and Spitsbergen, and
to the Commander Islands; a sight report for the northern Gulf of California.
Notes.—Known in the Old World as Slavonian Grebe.

Podiceps grisegena (Boddaert). Red-necked Grebe.

Colymbus grisegena Boddaert, 1783, Table Planches Enlum., p. 55. Based on "Le
Jougris" Daubenton, Planches Enlum., pl. 931. (No locality given = France.)

Habitat.—Lakes and large ponds, occasionally along quiet rivers (breeding); primarily
seacoasts, bays, inlets, and estuaries, less frequently large inland bodies of water, in migration
regularly on lakes, ponds, and rivers (nonbreeding).
Distribution.—*Breeds* in North America from western and central Alaska, central Yukon,
northwestern and southern Mackenzie, northwestern Saskatchewan, central Manitoba, and
western and central Ontario south to St. Lawrence Island (at least formerly), the Alaska
Peninsula, central Washington, northern Idaho, northern Montana, northwestern Wyoming,
central and eastern North Dakota, northeastern South Dakota, central Minnesota, and northwestern and southeastern Wisconsin, locally to southwestern Oregon, and rarely to northern
Michigan, southern Ontario, southern Quebec, southwestern New Brunswick (formerly), and

New Hampshire; and in western Eurasia from Scandinavia and western Russia south to eastern Europe and Asia Minor, and in eastern Asia west to long. 115° E. and south to northern Japan.

Winters in North America from the Aleutian Islands south on the Pacific coast to southern California (rarely), and from the Bay of Fundy south on the Atlantic coast to South Carolina and Florida (where casual at best; no verifiable records), casually north in interior North America to northwestern Montana and north-central Colorado, and rarely to casually west along the Gulf coast to Texas; and in Eurasia primarily along the coasts of Norway and the North, Baltic, Caspian, Aegean, Adriatic, and Black seas, rarely to the Mediterranean, and in eastern Asia from Kamchatka south to eastern China (Fukien), Korea, and southern Japan.

Migrates regularly through the Great Lakes region, rarely through the Ohio and upper Mississippi valleys, and casually elsewhere in interior North America.

Casual in the Hawaiian Islands (Kauai) and Bermuda, and north to Hudson Bay, Labrador, Greenland, Iceland, the Faeroe Islands, and Spitsbergen.

Notes.—Reasons for not accepting Bochenski's (1994) proposal to split *P. g. grisegena* from *P. g. holboellii* are explained in Storer (1996).

Podiceps nigricollis Brehm. Eared Grebe.

> *Podiceps nigricollis* C. L. Brehm, 1831, Handb. Naturgesch. Vögel Dtsch., p. 963. (Germany.)

Habitat.—Marshes, large ponds, and lakes, generally with emergent vegetation (breeding); in migration and winter also in salt lakes, bays, estuaries, seacoasts, and inland reservoirs.

Distribution.—*Breeds* in North America from central interior and northeastern British Columbia, southern Yukon, northwestern and central Alberta, central Saskatchewan, southern Manitoba, and western Minnesota south locally to northern Baja California, central and southeastern Arizona, Chihuahua, Nayarit, Jalisco, Puebla, Distrito Federal, and south-central Texas, east to northeastern Illinois (Cook County, casually), northern Iowa, eastern Nebraska, central Kansas, and western Oklahoma (Panhandle); in Eurasia locally from the British Isles, southern Scandinavia, central Russia, and eastern Siberia south to the Mediterranean region, northern Africa (formerly), Asia Minor, and Ussuriland; and locally in eastern and southern Africa.

Winters from southern British Columbia, northern Nevada, northern Utah, Montana, Colorado (casually), and Kansas (irregularly) south through the western United States and most of Mexico to Guatemala and El Salvador, in the southern and eastern United States from Kansas and Maryland south to the Gulf coast (rarely east of southwestern Louisiana); in Eurasia from the British Isles south to the Mediterranean Sea, Iran, and northern India, and on the Pacific coast from Japan south to southern China; and in eastern and southern Africa.

Casual in the Hawaiian Islands (Oahu), southern Mackenzie, eastern North America (from the Great Lakes, southern Quebec, New York, and New England southward), Costa Rica, Greenland, Madeira, and the Canary Islands.

Notes.—Also known as Black-necked Grebe. The distinct, isolated, rufous-necked form in Colombia, *P. andinus* (Meyer de Schauensee, 1959, now apparently extinct), has sometimes been treated as a race of *P. nigricollis* (e.g., Blake 1977), but see Fjeldså (1982a) and Hilty and Brown (1986). *Podiceps nigricollis, P. andinus,* the South American *P. occipitalis* Garnot, 1826, and possibly *P. taczanowskii* Berlepsch and Stolzmann, 1894, appear to constitute a superspecies (Storer *in* Mayr and Cottrell 1979; Sibley and Monroe 1990). *Podiceps caspicus* (Hablitzl, 1783), used by some past authors for *P. nigricollis,* has been officially suppressed (I.C.Z.N. 1956b: 121).

Genus *AECHMOPHORUS* Coues

> *Aechmophorus* Coues, 1862, Proc. Acad. Nat. Sci. Philadelphia 14: 229. Type, by original designation, *Podiceps occidentalis* Lawrence.

Aechmophorus occidentalis (Lawrence). Western Grebe.

> *Podiceps occidentalis* Lawrence, 1858, in Baird, Cassin, and Lawrence, Rep. Explor. Surv. R. R. Pac. 9: liv, 892, 894. (Pacific coast from Washington Territory to California = Fort Steilacoom, Washington.)

Habitat.—Marshes, lakes, and bays, generally with emergent vegetation (breeding); in migration and winter also in sheltered marine and brackish seacoasts, bays, inlets, channels, and lagoons, less frequently on inland reservoirs and lakes, and along rivers (Subtropical and Temperate zones).

Distribution.—*Breeds* from extreme southwestern mainland and south-central British Columbia, central Alberta, central Saskatchewan, and southern Manitoba south locally to southern California, Arizona (except southwestern), southern Colorado, western Minnesota, and east-central Wisconsin (Rush Lake).

Resident in Mexico south to Guerrero and western Puebla, and north of Mexico on some lakes that do not freeze over in the winter (e.g., Clear Lake, California).

Winters from southeastern Alaska, coastal southern British Columbia, Montana (casually), southern Utah, Colorado, New Mexico and western and (rarely) southern Texas south to the west coast of Mexico (southern Baja California, Sonora, Sinaloa), casually east to Nuevo León and Coahuila (sight).

Casual or accidental north to southern Yukon, and to Colorado, the Great Lakes, southwestern Quebec, upper Mississippi Valley, and southeastern Texas, also casually to the Atlantic and Gulf coasts from Nova Scotia and New England to Florida, and west to Texas. Most records, especially those from the north and east, refer to *A. occidentalis* (see note).

Notes.—This species and the next were formerly considered color morphs of a single species *(A. occidentalis),* and thus most authors did not distinguish between them. Records of occurrence in the literature may refer to either or both species. The most consistent differences between the two species appear to be bill color, facial pattern, number of notes in the advertising call, and foraging behavior (Ratti 1979, Nuechterlein 1981, Nuechterlein and Storer 1982, Storer and Nuechterlein 1985); DNA-DNA hybridization studies also indicate a species-level distinction (Ahlquist et al. 1987). Limited hybridization between the species (ca. 1%) occurs in some populations, and intermediates are known; the extent of hybridization in Mexico is unknown, although both species are resident on the Mexican Plateau. The only breeding record of the genus in Texas was reported to be a mixed pair *A. occidentalis* x *A. clarkii* at Lake Balmorhea in October 1991 (1992, Amer. Birds 46: 118).

Aechmophorus clarkii (Lawrence). Clark's Grebe.

> *Podiceps clarkii* Lawrence, 1858, in Baird, Cassin and Lawrence, Rep. Explor. Surv. R. R. Pac. 9: 895. (California and New [sic] Mexico = Laguna Santa María, Chihuahua, Mexico; restricted by Dickerman, 1963, Condor 65: 66–67.)

Habitat.—Marshes, lakes, and bays, generally with emergent vegetation; in migration and winter also sheltered seacoasts, less frequently on inland reservoirs and along rivers (Subtropical and Temperate zones).

Distribution.—*Breeds* from south-central British Columbia, southern Alberta, southern Saskatchewan, southwestern Manitoba, south-central North Dakota, and South Dakota south to southern California (casually), Arizona (except southwestern), southwestern and northeastern New Mexico, southern Colorado; essentially sympatric with *A. occidentalis,* although rare in the northern and eastern parts of its range.

Resident in Mexico south to Guerrero and western Puebla, and north of Mexico on some lakes that do not freeze over in the winter (e.g., Clear Lake, California).

Winters from central California (casually north to southern British Columbia) and Colorado (rarely) south to southern Baja California.

Casual east to Minnesota, Missouri, and Texas; there are sight reports east to Illinois and Tennessee.

Notes.—See comments under *A. occidentalis.*

Order **PROCELLARIIFORMES**: Tube-nosed Swimmers

Family **DIOMEDEIDAE**: Albatrosses

Notes.—We follow Nunn et al. (1996) for genus-level taxonomy and the linear sequence of taxa in the Diomedeidae.

Genus *THALASSARCHE* Reichenbach

Thalassarche Reichenbach, 1853, Handb. spec. Ornithol., lfr. 3, Die Vogel, p. 5. Type, by original designation, *Diomedea melanophrys* Temminck.

Thalassarche chlororhynchos (Gmelin). Yellow-nosed Albatross.

Diomedea chlororhynchos Gmelin, 1789, Syst. Nat. 1(2): 568. Based on the "Yellow-nosed Albatross" Latham, Gen. Synop. Birds 3(1): 309, pl. 94. (ad caput bonae spei, et in mari australi extra tropicos = off Cape of Good Hope.)

Habitat.—Pelagic Waters; breeds on islands.

Distribution.—*Breeds* on islands in the South Atlantic and southern Indian oceans, and *ranges* widely at sea in these southern oceans east to Australian and New Zealand waters.

Casual or accidental in Quebec (Gulf of St. Lawrence), New Brunswick (near head of Bay of Fundy, Moncton), Maine (East Fryeburg), New York (off Freeport, Long Island, and up the Hudson River), Maryland (Ocean City), Florida (St. Marks, Key Largo), Louisiana (Holly Beach), Texas (South Padre Island), and Greenland; sight reports offshore from Newfoundland and Maine south to Florida.

Thalassarche cauta (Gould). Shy Albatross.

Diomedea cauta Gould, 1841, Proc. Zool. Soc. London (1840), p. 177. (Bass's Straits [off southeastern Australia].)

Habitat.—Pelagic Waters; breeds on islands.

Distribution.—*Breeds* on islands off southern Australia and New Zealand, and *ranges* widely in the southern Pacific and Indian oceans, less commonly in the South Atlantic.

Accidental off the coast of Washington (lat. 47°55' N., long. 125°37' W., ca. 39 miles west of the mouth of Quillayute River, 1 September 1951; Slipp 1952) and in the Gulf of Aqaba, Elat, Israel.

Notes.—Also known as White-capped Albatross.

Thalassarche melanophris (Temminck). Black-browed Albatross.

Diomedea melanophris Temminck, 1828, Planches Color., livr. 77, p. 456 and text. (Cap. Nouvelle Hollande, et mers antarctiques = Cape of Good Hope.)

Habitat.—Pelagic Waters; breeds on islands.

Distribution.—*Breeds* on islands off southern South America, Kerguelen in the southern Indian Ocean, and islands off southern New Zealand, and *ranges* at sea in southern oceans generally north to the Tropic of Capricorn.

Casual in the British Isles; accidental on Martinique (Vauclin, 12 November 1956; Bond 1959), near Greenland, and in Iceland, the Faeroe Islands, Spitsbergen, Norway, Germany, and Spain; sight reports, none satisfactory, for waters off the Atlantic coast of North America from Newfoundland to Florida.

Notes.—Although emended to *D. melanophrys* by Temminck in 1839, the consistent use of the acceptable spelling *melanophris* by him in 1828 renders the former an unjustified emendation.

Genus *PHOEBETRIA* Reichenbach

Phoebetria Reichenbach, 1853, Handb. spec. Ornithol., lfr. 3, Die Vogel, p. 5. Type, by original designation, *Diomedea fuliginosa* Gmelin = *Diomedea palpebrata* Forster.

Phoebetria palpebrata (Forster). Light-mantled Albatross.

Diomedea palpebrata J. R. Forster, 1785, Mém. Math. Phys. Acad. Sci. Paris 10: 571, pl. 15. (depuis le degré quarante-septième de latitude austral jusqu'au soixante-onzième & dix minutes = south of Prince Edward and Marion islands.)

Habitat.—Pelagic Waters; breeds on islands.

Distribution.—*Breeds* on subantarctic islands (Tristan da Cunha group, Prince Edward, Marion, Crozet, Kerguelen, Amsterdam, and St. Paul islands). *Ranges* at sea in southern oceans between latitude 30° S. and the edge of the pack ice.

Accidental off central California (Cordell Banks), 17 July 1994 (Stallcup and Terrill 1996; photograph). A specimen taken by Townsend near the "mouth of the Columbia River, Oregon" is the only specimen from northern waters; the locality, however, is regarded as erroneous (A.O.U. 1957).

Notes.—Also known as Light-mantled Sooty-Albatross.

Genus *DIOMEDEA* Linnaeus

Diomedea Linnaeus, 1758, Syst. Nat. (ed. 10) 1: 132. Type, by subsequent designation (G. R. Gray, 1840), *Diomedea exulans* Linnaeus.

Diomedea exulans Linnaeus. Wandering Albatross.

Diomedea exulans Linnaeus, 1758, Syst. Nat. (ed. 10) 1: 132. Based primarily on "The Albatross" Edwards, Nat. Hist. Birds 2: 88, pl. 88. (intra tropicos Pelagi & ad Cap. b. Spei = Cape of Good Hope.)

Habitat.—Pelagic Waters; breeds on islands.

Distribution.—*Breeds* on subantarctic islands from the South Atlantic east to the Auckland, Campbell, and Antipodes islands in the South Pacific, and *ranges* at sea generally throughout the southern oceans north to lat. 30° S.

Accidental in California (The Sea Ranch, Sonoma County, 11–12 July 1967; Paxton 1968), Panama (Bay of Panama, August 1937; Murphy 1938), and Japan; two old reports from Florida are unsatisfactory (Robertson and Woolfenden 1992). Although the possibility that Northern Hemisphere records may have been human-assisted cannot always be excluded, vagrancy to the N. Hemisphere by other southern albatrosses (e.g., *Thalassarche chlororhynchos, T. cauta,* and *T. melanophris*) lend support to the belief that the California and Panama reports are based on natural wanderings.

Genus *PHOEBASTRIA* Reichenbach

Phoebastria Reichenbach, 1853, Handb. spec. Ornithol., lfr. 3, Die Vogel, p. 5. Type, by original designation, *Diomedea brachyura* Temminck = *Diomedea albatrus* Pallas.

Phoebastria immutabilis (Rothschild). Laysan Albatross.

Diomedea immutabilis Rothschild, 1893, Bull. Brit. Ornithol. Club 1: 48. (Laysan Island.)

Habitat.—Pelagic Waters, mainly beyond continental shelf; breeds on the ground in open areas on oceanic islands.

Distribution.—*Breeds* on most of the northwestern Hawaiian Islands (Kure east to Kauai and Oahu), in the Ogasawara Islands (on Torishima), and, at least formerly, in the Seven Islands of Izu (on Torishima), and on Marcus, Johnston and Wake islands; also off Baja California (Guadalupe Island, since 1986; Alijos Rocks off Baja California) and in the Revillagigedo Islands (Clarión, since 1988; San Benedicto, 1992).

Ranges at sea in the Bering Sea, and in the North Pacific from the Gulf of Alaska south to the coast of California and Baja California, and Gulf of California, and from Kamchatka and the Kuril Islands south to the coast of Japan.

Casual in interior California (Palm Springs area, Salton Sea); accidental in Arizona (Yuma).

Notes.—Occasional hybrids between *P. immutabilis* and *P. nigripes* have been reported from the northwestern Hawaiian Islands (Midway).

Phoebastria nigripes (Audubon). Black-footed Albatross.

Diomedea nigripes Audubon, 1839, Ornithol. Biogr. 5: 327. (Pacific Ocean, lat. 30°44' N., long. 146° [W].)

Habitat.—Pelagic Waters, mainly over continental shelf; nests on open sand on oceanic islands.

Distribution.—*Breeds* in the northwestern Hawaiian Islands (Kure east to Kaula), and on Torishima in the Seven Islands of Izu; bred formerly in the northern Bonin Islands (Muko-shima), Volcano Islands (Iwo Jima), Marianas (Agrihan), Marshall Islands (Taongi), and on Marcus, Wake, and Johnston islands.

Ranges at sea in the Bering Sea, and in the North Pacific from the Gulf of Alaska south to Baja California, and from Kamchatka south to the coast of China and the Caroline Islands.

Notes.—See comments under *P. immutabilis*.

Phoebastria albatrus (Pallas). Short-tailed Albatross.

> *Diomedea albatrus* Pallas, 1769, Spic. Zool., 1 (5): 28. (ad oram Kamtschatcae orientalum . . . ad Insulam Beringii = in the Bering Sea off Kamchatka.)

Habitat.—Pelagic Waters; breeds on small oceanic islands.

Distribution.—*Breeds* in small but increasing numbers on Torishima, in the Seven Islands of Izu; formerly bred on Kita-no-shima (in the Parry group), Kobishi (in the Senkaku Archipelago, southern Ryukyu Islands) and Nishi-no-shima, Tome-shima, and Muko-shima (in the Bonin Islands). Occurs during the breeding season in the northwestern Hawaiian Islands (Midway, more than two individuals annually); reported breeding from Wake Island is erroneous, being based on *D. immutabilis*.

Ranges at sea (commonly prior to 1900, casually in the 20th Century) from Siberia, the Bering Sea and Gulf of Alaska south to the China coast and through the North Pacific to the northwestern Hawaiian Islands and southern Baja California; a sight report for the Revillagigedo Islands.

Family **PROCELLARIIDAE**: Shearwaters and Petrels

Genus *FULMARUS* Stephens

> *Fulmarus* Stephens, 1826, in Shaw, Gen. Zool. 13(1): 233. Type, by subsequent designation (G. R. Gray, 1855), *Procellaria glacialis* Linnaeus.
> *Priocella* Hombron and Jacquinot, 1844, C. R. Acad. Sci. Paris 18: 357. Type, by monotypy, *Priocella garnotii* Hombron and Jacquinot = *Procellaria glacialoides* Smith.

Fulmarus glacialis (Linnaeus). Northern Fulmar.

> *Procellaria glacialis* Linnaeus, 1761, Fauna Svecica (ed. 2): 51. Based primarily on "Mallemucke" Martens, Spitsbergen Groenland Reise, p. 68, pl. N, fig. c. (in mari septentrionali intra circulum arcticum = Spitsbergen.)

Habitat.—Pelagic Waters; nests primarily on sea cliffs, less frequently on low and flat rocky islands.

Distribution.—*Breeds* in western North America on islands in the Bering Sea (Hall, St. Matthew, and the Pribilofs), in the Aleutians (Buldir, Davidof, Gareloi, Bobrof, and Chagulak islands), in the northern Gulf of Alaska (on Seal, Semidi, Barren, and Chiswell islands); in the Canadian Arctic on Devon Island, eastern Baffin Island (south to Cumberland Sound and Admiralty Bay), and Labrador (Gannet Islands), and in Newfoundland (since 1973); in the Palearctic on northeastern Greenland, Spitsbergen, Franz Josef Land, Bear Island, Novaya Zemlya, and along the coast of Koryakland and the Chukotski Peninsula (Plover Bay) south to Jan Mayen, Iceland, the Faeroes, the British Isles, and northern France (Brittany and Normandy). Summers regularly outside the breeding range in the Bering and Chukchi seas, off the Pacific coast of Washington, Oregon, and California, in Arctic Canada west to Banks and Melville islands, in the Gulf of St. Lawrence, south to the English Channel, northwestern France, northwestern Germany, and the North Sea, and along the coast of Kamchatka.

Winters in the North Pacific south to Japan and Baja California, and in the North Atlantic from Greenland, Labrador, Spitsbergen, and northern Norway south to the Newfoundland

Banks, Georges Bank off Massachusetts, and northern France, less commonly but regularly off the east coast of the United States to South Carolina.

Casual in the Hawaiian Islands, Ontario, Quebec, northern New York, and continental Europe; sight reports for Yukon, the Gulf of California, Alabama, and the Bahama Islands.

Notes.—Known in Old World literature as the Fulmar. *Fulmarus glacialis* and *F. glacialoides* appear to constitute a superspecies (Mayr and Short 1970).

Genus *PTERODROMA* Bonaparte

Pterodroma Bonaparte, 1856, C. R. Acad. Sci. Paris 42: 768. Type, by subsequent designation (Coues, 1866), *Procellaria macroptera* Smith.

Pterodroma neglecta (Schlegel). Kermadec Petrel.

Procellaria neglecta Schlegel, 1863, Mus. Hist. Nat. Pays-Bas, livr. 4, Procell., p. 10. (Kermadec and Sunday Islands.)

Habitat.—Pelagic Waters; nests in burrows on islands.

Distribution.—*Breeds* on islands in the South Pacific (Kermadecs and Lord Howe east to the Juan Fernández group), and *ranges* at sea generally through the South Pacific.

Accidental in the Hawaiian Islands (Kure, 30 April 1923, specimen in U.S.N.M.; Gould and King 1967) and Pennsylvania (Heintzelman 1961, now considered definite as to species identification), with additional sight reports from Hawaiian waters and Mexican waters north to the Revillagigedo Islands. Reports from California and England cannot be verified.

Notes.—Also known as Variable Petrel and formerly treated under the name of *P. philippi* (G. R. Gray, 1862). Jouanin and Mougin *in* Mayr and Cottrell (1979) considered *P. neglecta, P. arminjoniana,* and *P. alba* (Gmelin, 1789) to constitute a superspecies.

Pterodroma arminjoniana (Giglioli and Salvadori). Herald Petrel.

Æstrelata arminjoniana Giglioli and Salvadori, 1869, Ibis, p. 62. (near Trinidad [= Trindade] Island, in the South Atlantic.)

Habitat.—Pelagic Waters; nests on bare rock under overhanging ledges or plants on islands.

Distribution.—*Breeds* [*arminjoniana* group] on islands in the South Atlantic (Trindade, Martin Vas Rocks) and Indian Ocean (Round Island off Mauritius) and [*heraldica* group] on islands in the tropical South Pacific; *ranges* at sea generally in the oceans near the respective breeding grounds.

Casual or accidental [*arminjoniana* group] in New York (near Ithaca [Allen 1934], the North Atlantic off North Carolina [Lee 1979], in Puerto Rico (Cayo Lobito, Culebra National Wildlife Refuge), northeast of the Lesser Antilles (lat. 21°51′ N., long. 43°35′ W.), and in England. Accidental [*heraldica* group] in the Hawaiian Islands (French Frigate Shoals, 14 March 1968; Amerson 1971: 125), with additional sight reports near Clipperton Island and north to the Revillagigedo Islands.

Notes.—Groups: *P. heraldica* (Salvin, 1888) [Herald Petrel] and *P. arminjoniana* [Trindade or South Trinidad Petrel]. Brooke and Rowe (1996) used genetic evidence to treat these groups as species, and to divide *heraldica* into two species. See comments under *P. neglecta.*

Pterodroma ultima Murphy. Murphy's Petrel.

Pterodroma ultima Murphy, 1949, in Mayr and Schuz (eds.), Ornithol. Biol. Wiss., p. 89. (Oeno Island, south Pacific.)

Habitat.—Pelagic Waters; nests in burrows on small islands.

Distribution.—*Breeds* in the south-central Pacific Ocean in the Austral, Tuamotu, and Pitcairn islands.

Ranges at sea in the northern and central Pacific Ocean north to the Hawaiian Islands (Kure, French Frigate Shoals, Kauai, off Oahu), and to the Pacific coast off California and Mexico (Revillagigedo Islands), where it is probably regular in spring, casually off Washington and Oregon.

Notes.—Jouanin and Mougin *in* Mayr and Cottrell (1979) considered *P. ultima, P. brevirostris* (Lesson, 1831), and *P. mollis* (including *P. feae* and *P. madeira*) to constitute a superspecies. Bretagnolle (1995) presented evidence indicating that *P. feae* (including *madeira*) is closer to *P. cahow* than to *P. mollis*.

Pterodroma inexpectata (Forster). Mottled Petrel.

Procellaria inexpectata J. R. Forster, 1844, Descr. Anim., p. 204. (in Oceano antarctico = Antarctic Ocean.)

Habitat.—Pelagic Waters; nests primarily along mountain bluffs and in burrows on small islands.

Distribution.—*Breeds* in the New Zealand region in the Snares Islands and on islets off Stewart Island, and formerly in the highlands of New Zealand (North and South islands).

Ranges at sea in Antarctic waters between New Zealand and South America, and throughout much of the Pacific from the southern Bering Sea and Gulf of Alaska south to the Hawaiian Islands and California (mostly far-offshore waters).

Casual along the Pacific coast from British Columbia to California, and in the vicinity of the Galapagos Islands. Accidental in New York (Mount Morris, Livingston County, 1880).

Notes.—Also known as Scaled Petrel.

Pterodroma cahow (Nichols and Mowbray). Bermuda Petrel.

Æstrelata cahow Nichols and Mowbray, 1916, Auk 33: 194. (Gurnet Head Rock, Bermuda.)

Habitat.—Pelagic Waters; nests in burrows in sandy areas on islets.

Distribution.—*Breeds* in Bermuda, persisting in small numbers on islets in Castle Roads, formerly also the Bahamas (Crooked Island, bone deposits in caves).

Ranges at sea but no confirmed records away from the breeding grounds; sightings have been reported off North Carolina.

Notes.—Also known as Cahow. See comments under *P. hasitata* and *P. ultima*.

Pterodroma hasitata (Kuhl). Black-capped Petrel.

Proc[ellaria] hasitata Kuhl, 1820, Beitr. Zool. 1: 142. (No locality given = Dominica.)

Habitat.—Pelagic Waters; nests in burrows at high elevations on island mountain summits.

Distribution.—*Breeds* on Hispaniola (Massif de La Selle east to western end of Sierra de Baorucó), Jamaica (Blue Mountains, formerly), Guadeloupe, Dominica (where probably extirpated), and (possibly) Martinique. Reports of breeding in Cuba are unsubstantiated.

Ranges at sea in the Caribbean and western Atlantic Ocean from about the Tropic of Cancer south to eastern Brazil, regularly in the Gulf Stream north to North Carolina, irregularly north to Maine.

Accidental in Ontario, Pennsylvania, New York, Massachusetts, western Virginia, Kentucky, Ohio, western Florida (Leon County), and England.

Notes.—The possibly extinct, dark form that bred on Jamaica may represent a distinct species, *Pterodroma caribbaea* Carte, 1866 [Jamaican Petrel]. Sibley and Monroe (1990) considered *P. hasitata* and *P. cahow* to constitute a superspecies; Jouanin and Mougin *in* Mayr and Cottrell (1979) also included *P. externa, P. baraui* (Jouanin, 1964), and *P. phaeopygia* in this superspecies. Bretagnolle (1995) presented evidence from vocalizations that suggests that *P. hasitata* is not closely related to *P. cahow* and *P. feae*.

Pterodroma externa (Salvin). Juan Fernandez Petrel.

Æstrelata externa Salvin, 1875, Ibis, p. 373. ("Islands of Masafuera and Juan Fernandez" = Más Afuera.)

Habitat.—Pelagic Waters; nests in burrows on islands.

Distribution.—*Breeds* on Más Afuera, in the Juan Fernández Islands, off Chile.

Ranges at sea in the eastern Pacific Ocean north to the Hawaiian Islands (off Kaula, on Oahu, with sight reports off Maui and Hawaii) and Middle America (north to Clipperton Island, apparently regular); a sight report off Washington.

Notes.—It is clear from Salvin's type description that the specimens on which the description was based came from Más Afuera. English names for this and *P. defilippiana* were confused in the 37th Supplement (A.O.U. 1989: 532, 537) but were subsequently corrected (A.O.U. 1990, 1991). See comments under *P. cervicalis* and *P. hasitata.*

Pterodroma phaeopygia (Salvin). Dark-rumped Petrel.

Æstrelata phaeopygia Salvin, 1876, Trans. Zool. Soc. London 9: 507, pl. 88, figs. 1 and 2. (Chatham Island, Galapagos.)

Habitat.—Pelagic Waters; nests in burrows at higher elevations on islands.

Distribution.—*Breeds* [*sandwichensis* group] in the interior highlands of the Hawaiian Islands (Kauai, Maui, and Hawaii, probably also on Lanai, possibly on Molokai); and [*phaeopygia* group] in the Galapagos Islands (Isabela, San Salvador, Santa Cruz, Floreana, and San Cristóbal).

Ranges at sea [*sandwichensis* group] in the central Pacific Ocean from 5° to 42° N. lat.; and [*phaeopygia* group] in the eastern Pacific Ocean from Clipperton Island and Costa Rica south to northern Peru; one record (photograph) [group uncertain] and two sight reports for California; one sight report for Oregon.

Notes.—Groups: *P. sandwichensis* (Ridgway, 1884) [Hawaiian Petrel] and *P. phaeopygia* [Galapagos Petrel]. See comments under *P. hasitata.*

Pterodroma cervicalis (Salvin). White-necked Petrel.

Æstrelata cervicalis Salvin, 1891, Ibis, p. 192. (Kermadec Islands.)

Habitat.—Pelagic Waters; nests in burrows on islands.

Distribution.—*Breeds* in the Kermadec Islands north of New Zealand, and *ranges* at sea in the central Pacific Ocean, principally between the Equator and the Hawaiian Islands.

Casual in the Hawaiian Islands (between Midway and Laysan, 3 November 1984, and ca. 16 km west-northwest of Tern Island, French Frigate Shoals, 16 November 1984, photographs; Pyle and Eilerts 1986: 182); there are also several sight reports off Hawaii.

Notes.—Often considered conspecific with *P. externa,* but these two species are apparently not closely related (Imber 1985).

Pterodroma hypoleuca (Salvin). Bonin Petrel.

Æstrelata hypoleuca Salvin, 1888, Ibis, p. 359. (Krusenstern Is., in North Pacific Ocean = Hawaiian Leeward Islands, probably Laysan; Murphy, 1951, Amer. Mus. Novit. 1512, p. 17–18.)

Habitat.—Pelagic Waters; nests in burrows on oceanic islands.

Distribution.—*Breeds* in the northwestern Hawaiian Islands (Kure east to Nihoa), and in the Bonin and Volcano islands.

Ranges at sea in the western North Pacific in the vicinity of the breeding grounds and from Sakhalin south to Taiwan and the Seven Islands of Izu.

Notes.—The relationships of this species and several closely allied forms that breed in southern waters from Australia and New Zealand east to South America remain uncertain.

Pterodroma nigripennis (Rothschild). Black-winged Petrel.

Æstrelata nigripennis Rothschild, 1893, Bull. Brit. Ornithol. Club 1: 57. (Kermadec Islands.)

Habitat.—Pelagic Waters; nests in burrows on islands.

Distribution.—*Breeds* on islands in the New Zealand region in the Kermadec, Austral, Three Kings, and Chatham islands, and on Lord Howe, Norfolk, and Portland islands, and *ranges* at sea, primarily in the South Pacific near the breeding grounds.

Casual in Hawaiian waters (ca. 60 miles west of Hawaii, 12 November 1965; Berger

1972) and in Maui (Kahului harbor, 11 October 1990, captured; 1991, Amer. Birds 45: 155); several other sight reports for Hawaiian waters.

Notes.—See comments under *P. hypoleuca.*

Pterodroma cookii (Gray). Cook's Petrel.

> *Procellaria Cookii* G. R. Gray, 1843, in Dieffenbach, Travels N. Z., 2, p. 199. (New Zealand.)

Habitat.—Pelagic Waters; nests in burrows on islands.

Distribution.—*Breeds* on islands off the coast of New Zealand (Little and Great Barrier, off North Island; and Codfish, off Stewart Island).

Ranges at sea from the northern and eastern Pacific Ocean south to New Zealand and Peru, and uncommonly to the Aleutians (near Adak), off California, and off Baja California; many of these reports are sight reports.

Accidental at sea in the northwestern Hawaiian Islands, and in Washington (Gray's Harbor), and interior southern California (Salton Sea).

Notes.—Also known as Blue-footed Petrel. Jouanin and Mougin *in* Mayr and Cottrell (1979) considered *P. cookii* to form a superspecies with *P. defilippiana* (Giglioli and Salvadori, 1869), *P. longirostris,* and *P. leucoptera* (Gould, 1844).

Pterodroma longirostris (Stejneger). Stejneger's Petrel.

> *Æstrelata longirostris* Stejneger, 1893, Proc. U. S. Natl. Mus. 16: 618. (Province of Mutzu, Hondo, Japan.)

Habitat.—Pelagic Waters; breeds on islands.

Distribution.—*Breeds* on Más Afuera, in the Juan Fernández group in the South Pacific off Chile, and *ranges* at sea in the North Pacific to waters off Japan and between the Hawaiian Islands and North America.

Accidental in the Hawaiian Islands (Lanai, 1914, a specimen previously misidentified as *P. hypoleuca*; [Clapp 1984]) and off California (35 miles southwest of Point Reyes, 17 November 1990, photograph; 1991, Amer. Birds 45: 146, 174; DeBenedictis 1994a); additional photographs and sight reports from off southern California (where species may prove to be regular) and south of Clipperton Island.

Notes.—Specimens taken in international waters more than 600 miles west of California (Moffitt 1938) were reported as *P. leucoptera masafuerae* Lönnberg, 1921, presently regarded as a synonym of *P. longirostris;* other reports of *P. leucoptera* between the Hawaiian Islands and California also pertain to *P. longirostris.* See comments under *P. cookii.*

Genus *BULWERIA* Bonaparte

> *Bulweria* Bonaparte, 1843, Nuovi Ann. Sci. Nat. Bologna (1842) 8: 426. Type, by monotypy, *Procellaria bulwerii* Jardine and Selby.

Bulweria bulwerii (Jardine and Selby). Bulwer's Petrel.

> *Procellaria bulwerii* Jardine and Selby, 1828, Illus. Ornithol. 2: pl. 65. (Madeira or the small islands adjacent.)

Habitat.—Pelagic Waters; nests in small holes in rocky areas and under plants on oceanic islands.

Distribution.—*Breeds* in the Pacific Ocean in the Hawaiian Islands (Pearl and Hermes Reef east to Kaula, and on small islets around the main islands), on small islands off the coast of China, in the Bonin, Volcano, Marquesas, and Phoenix islands, and on Johnston Island; and in the Atlantic Ocean in the Azores, Madeira, Canary, and Cape Verde islands.

Ranges at sea in the western Pacific Ocean in the breeding areas and from Japan to Taiwan and the Moluccas; casually in the eastern Atlantic Ocean north to England, the Mediterranean Sea and the western Atlantic (off Trinidad); and to the equatorial, western, and central Indian Ocean; sight reports from Florida.

Notes.—*Bulweria bulwerii* and *B. fallax* constitute a superspecies (Sibley and Monroe 1990); they have been considered conspecific, but see Zonfrillo (1988).

Bulweria fallax Jouanin. Jouanin's Petrel.

> *Bulweria fallax* Jouanin, 1955, Oiseau 25: 158, 159, 160. (en mer au point approximatif [lat.] 12°30′ N., [long.] 55° E. [northwestern Indian Ocean].)

Habitat.—Pelagic Waters.

Distribution.—*Breeds* presumably on small islands in the Indian Ocean off Arabia, and *ranges* at sea primarily in the northwestern Indian Ocean.

Accidental in the Hawaiian Islands (Lisianski Island, 4 September 1967).

Notes.—See comments under *B. bulwerii.*

Genus *PROCELLARIA* Linnaeus

> *Procellaria* Linnaeus, 1758, Syst. Nat. (ed. 10) 1: 131. Type, by subsequent designation (G. R. Gray, 1840), *Procellaria aequinoctialis* Linnaeus.
> *Adamastor* Bonaparte, 1856, C. R. Acad. Sci. Paris 43: 594. Type, by original designation, *Procellaria haesitata* Forster = *Procellaria cinerea* Gmelin.

Procellaria parkinsoni Gray. Parkinson's Petrel.

> *Procellaria parkinsoni* G. R. Gray, 1862, Ibis, p. 245. (New Zealand.)

Habitat.—Pelagic Waters; nests in burrows on islands and at high elevations in mountains.

Distribution.—*Breeds* on islands off New Zealand (Great Barrier and Little Barrier) and, at least formerly, in the mountainous interior ranges of both North and South islands, New Zealand.

Ranges at sea west to Australia and east, apparently regularly, to the vicinity of the Galapagos Islands and waters off Ecuador and the west coast of Middle America (ca. 50 miles off Guatemala, 14 April 1973, and 17 miles off the Nicoya Peninsula, Costa Rica, 21 April 1973, plus many sight reports between Mexico and Panama probably referable to this species; Jehl 1974), and South America south to Peru.

Notes.—Also known as Black Petrel. *Procellaria aequinoctialis* Linnaeus, 1758, *P. parkinsoni, and P. westlandica* Falla, 1946, of New Zealand, constitute a superspecies (Sibley and Monroe 1990).

Genus *CALONECTRIS* Mathews and Iredale

> *Calonectris* Mathews and Iredale, 1915, Ibis, pp. 590, 592. Type, by original designation, *Procellaria leucomelas* Temminck.

Notes.—For reasons for separation of *Calonectris* from *Puffinus,* see Kuroda 1954: 102–104, 117.

Calonectris leucomelas (Temminck). Streaked Shearwater.

> *Procellaria leucomelas* Temminck, 1835, Planches Color., livr. 99, pl. 587. (seas of Japan and Nagasaki Bay.)

Habitat.—Pelagic Waters; nests in burrows or occasionally under shrubs on small wooded islands.

Distribution.—*Breeds* on islands from the Bonin and Pescadores groups to the coast of Japan, and *ranges* at sea in the western Pacific Ocean from Korea and Japan to Borneo, Australia, New Guinea, and off Thailand.

Casual in California (Monterey Bay and Red Bluff), and the Hawaiian Islands (Laysan), and also to Sri Lanka.

Calonectris diomedea (Scopoli). Cory's Shearwater.

> *Procellaria diomedea* Scopoli, 1769, Annus I, Hist.-Nat., p. 74. (No locality given = Tremiti Islands, Adriatic Sea.)

Habitat.—Pelagic Waters, primarily warm water over continental shelf; nests in burrows or crevices on islands.

Distribution.—*Breeds* on islands in the eastern North Atlantic Ocean in the Azores, on Berlenga Island off Portugal, in the Madeira, Salvage, and Canary islands, and in the Mediterranean Sea from Gibraltar, Corsica, and Sardinia locally east to the Adriatic Sea, the Balkans, Turkey, and the Near East.

Ranges widely at sea in the Atlantic Ocean, including west to the North American coast from Newfoundland, Nova Scotia, and southern Quebec south to Florida, and west in the Gulf of Mexico to Texas.

Casual in the Bahamas (Grand Bahama), Cuba (off Gibara), Barbados, Trinidad, Brazil, Argentina, western Europe, Syria, South Africa, and New Zealand; sight reports off Cozumel Island and Panama.

Genus *PUFFINUS* Brisson

Puffinus Brisson, 1760, Ornithologie 1: 56; 6: 130. Type, by tautonymy, *Puffinus* Brisson
  = *Procellaria puffinus* Brünnich.
Ardenna Reichenbach, 1853, Hand. Spec. Ornithol., Die Vögel, pt. 3 (1852), p. iv.
  Type, by original designation, *Procellaria minor* Faber = *Procellaria gravis* O'Reilly.
Thyellodroma Stejneger, 1889, Proc. U. S. Natl. Mus. 11 (1888): 93. Type, by original
  designation, *Puffinus sphenurus* Gould = *Puffinus chlororhynchus* Lesson.
Neonectris Mathews, 1913, Austral Avian Rec. 2: 12. Type, by original designation,
  Puffinus brevicaudus Gould = *Procellaria tenuirostris* Temminck.
Hemipuffinus Iredale, 1913, Austral Avian Rec. 2: 20. Type, by original designation,
  Puffinus carneipes Gould.

Notes.—For assignment of species to subgenera, see Jouanin and Mougin *in* Mayr and Cottrell (1979).

Puffinus creatopus Coues. Pink-footed Shearwater.

Puffinus creatopus (Cooper MS) Coues, 1864, Proc. Acad. Nat. Sci. Philadelphia 16:
  131. (ex insula "San Nicholas" prope California = San Nicolas Island, California.)

Habitat.—Pelagic Waters, primarily over continental shelf; nests in burrows on islands.

Distribution.—*Breeds* on islands off Chile (Más á Tierra and Santa Clara in the Juan Fernández group, and Isla Mocha in Arauco Bay).

Ranges at sea off the Pacific coast of the Americas, north at least as far as south-coastal Alaska.

Notes.—*Puffinus creatopus* and *P. carneipes* constitute a superspecies (Sibley and Monroe 1990).

Puffinus carneipes Gould. Flesh-footed Shearwater.

Puffinus carneipes Gould, 1844, Ann. Mag. Nat. Hist. (1) 13: 365. (small islands off
  Cape Leeuwin, western Australia.)

Habitat.—Pelagic Waters; nests in burrows on islands.

Distribution.—*Breeds* on islands off the south coast of western Australia (from Cape Leeuwin to Archipelago of the Recherche), on Lord Howe Island, on islands off New Zealand (eastern coast of North Island), and on St. Paul Island in the Indian Ocean.

Ranges at sea from the breeding areas throughout most of the Pacific Ocean to the Hawaiian Islands, the west coast of North America (from the southern Bering Sea and Gulf of Alaska south, uncommonly, to California), waters off Japan and the Juan Fernández Islands off Chile, and to the Indian Ocean (north to the Arabian Sea and Sri Lanka); a sight report off northern Baja California.

Notes.—Also known as Pale-footed Shearwater. See comments under *P. creatopus*.

Puffinus gravis (O'Reilly). Greater Shearwater.

Procellaria Gravis O'Reilly, 1818, Voy. Greenland Adj. Seas, p. 140, pl. 12, fig. 1.
  (Latitude of Cape Farewell and Staten Hook, frequently Newfoundland in summer.)

Habitat.—Pelagic Waters, primarily cold water over continental shelf; nests in burrows on oceanic islands.

Distribution.—*Breeds* in the South Atlantic Ocean on Tristan da Cunha (Nightingale and Inaccessible islands), on Gough Island, and in the Falkland Islands.

Ranges at sea throughout the Atlantic Ocean from Greenland and Iceland south to Tierra del Fuego and South Africa, most numerous between May and October off the Atlantic coast of North America (rarely also the Gulf of St. Lawrence) from Newfoundland to Florida and the West Indies, and rarely in the Gulf of Mexico from southeastern Texas to Florida; in June in the Davis Strait off Labrador and Greenland; and between August and October off Iceland, the Faeroe Islands, and the west coast of Europe (including the western Mediterranean east to Algeria and Sardinia).

Casual in Trinidad and continental Europe; sight reports for interior New York (Albany) and the New Zealand region; accidental off California (photograph; Monterey Bay) and (doubtfully) Costa Rica (Tortuguero).

Notes.—Known in Old World literature as Great Shearwater.

Puffinus pacificus (Gmelin). Wedge-tailed Shearwater.

Procellaria pacifica Gmelin, 1789, Syst. Nat. 1(2): 560. Based on the "Pacific Petrel" Latham, Gen. Synop. Birds 3(2): 416. (circa insulam Europa aliasque maris pacifici = Kermadec Islands.)

Habitat.—Pelagic Waters; nests in burrows on islands.

Distribution.—*Breeds* on islands off the western coast of Mexico (on San Benedicto, in the Revillagigedo group), in the Hawaiian Islands (Kure east to Kauai and Oahu, and on small islets around the main islands), in the central and western Pacific Ocean (from the Pescadores and Bonin Islands south to the Tonga, Austral, and Pitcairn groups), in waters off southern Australia and around New Zealand, and in the Indian Ocean (from the Seychelles and Cocos-Keeling south to the Mascarenes and Western Australia).

Ranges at sea in the Pacific Ocean off the west coast of Middle America and South America (from southern Baja California and Colima south to Panama and Colombia) and throughout most of the central and western Pacific Ocean north to Japan and Taiwan; and in the Indian Ocean north to the Arabian and southern Red seas.

Casual in California (Monterey Bay [Stallcup et al. 1988] and inland at Salton Sea [McCaskie and Webster 1990]).

Puffinus bulleri Salvin. Buller's Shearwater.

Puffinus bulleri Salvin, 1888, Ibis, p. 354. (New Zealand.)

Habitat.—Pelagic Waters, especially near upwellings; nests in burrows or rocky crevices on islands.

Distribution.—*Breeds* on Poor Knights Islands, off North Island, New Zealand.

Ranges at sea in the Pacific Ocean off the west coast of North America (from the Gulf of Alaska south to Baja California), near the Hawaiian and Galapagos islands, off the Kuril Islands, and off the west coast of South America (from Ecuador to Chile).

Accidental inland in southern California (Salton Sea) and off New Jersey (off Barnegat); sight reports off Baja California.

Notes.—Also known as Gray-backed Shearwater or New Zealand Shearwater.

Puffinus griseus (Gmelin). Sooty Shearwater.

Procellaria grisea Gmelin, 1789, Syst. Nat. 1(2): 564. Based mainly on the "Grey Petrel" Latham, Gen. Synop. Birds 3(2): 399. (in hemisphaerio australi, inter 35° et 50° = New Zealand.)

Habitat.—Pelagic Waters, primarily cold water over continental shelf, often close to shore; nests in burrows or rock crevices on small islands.

Distribution.—*Breeds* on islands off southeastern Australia (off New South Wales and Tasmania) and widely in New Zealand waters (including Stewart, Snares, Auckland, and

Chatham islands); and off southern South America (Wollaston, Deceit, and Chiloé, probably also Huafo and Mocha, off Chile; off Tierra del Fuego); and in the Falkland Islands.

Ranges at sea throughout the Pacific Ocean north to the southern Bering Sea, Aleutian Islands, Kamchatka, Taiwan, and the Hawaiian Islands, and along the entire Pacific coast of the Americas; and in the Atlantic Ocean off the coast of North America (rarely also the Gulf of St. Lawrence) from Newfoundland south to Florida, the Bahamas, and Cuba (also in the Gulf of Mexico, casually west to Texas, and in the Lesser Antilles), off eastern South America north to Brazil, off the west coast of Europe from Greenland, Iceland, Norway, Sweden, and Denmark south to Portugal and the Mediterranean Sea (east to Algeria and Italy), and off the west coast of Africa north to Fernando Po and Angola.

Casual inland in the United States, mostly after storms, where recorded from southeastern California, southern Arizona, Alabama (Attalla), and North Carolina (Twin Oaks); accidental in Arabia.

Puffinus tenuirostris (Temminck). Short-tailed Shearwater.

Procellaria tenuirostris Temminck, 1835, Planches Color., livr. 99, text facing pl. 587. (dans les mers au nord du Japon et sur les côtes de la Corée = Japan.)

Habitat.—Pelagic Waters, primarily cold water over continental shelf; nests in burrows on small islands.

Distribution.—*Breeds* on islands off the coast (and locally along the mainland coast) of southern Australia from Archipelago of the Recherche east to Victoria and Tasmania, and north to New South Wales (Bateman's Bay).

Ranges at sea in southern Australian and New Zealand waters, and north through the Pacific Ocean to the Bering and Chukchi seas, and south along the west coast of North America to Baja California (Los Coronados Islands).

Casual in Hawaiian waters, in northern Canada (Northwest Territories), in the Gulf of California, off Nayarit and Guerrero, and in the Indian Ocean (Pakistan east to Sri Lanka and the Malay Peninsula); a questionable sight report from Costa Rican waters.

Notes.—Also known as Slender-billed Shearwater.

Puffinus nativitatis Streets. Christmas Shearwater.

Puffinus (Nectris) nativitatis Streets, 1877, Bull. U. S. Natl. Mus., no. 7, p. 29. (Christmas Island [Pacific Ocean].)

Habitat.—Pelagic Waters; nests under vegetation or in small burrows on oceanic islands.

Distribution.—*Breeds* in the Hawaiian Islands (from Kure east to Kauai, on Lehua off Niihau, and on Moku Manu off Oahu), in the Phoenix, Marquesas, Tuamotu, and Austral islands, and on Wake, Christmas, and Easter islands.

Ranges at sea in the tropical Pacific Ocean east to waters off southern Mexico between Nayarit and Oaxaca.

Puffinus puffinus (Brünnich). Manx Shearwater.

Procellaria Puffinus Brünnich, 1764, Ornithol. Bor., p. 29. (E Feroa & Norvegia = Faeroe Islands.)

Habitat.—Pelagic Waters; nests in burrows on grassy coastal islands, on cliffs of rocky islands, and occasionally inland in mountainous regions.

Distribution.—*Breeds* in the North Atlantic on islands off Newfoundland (since 1977) and Massachusetts (Penikese Island, 1973), and from Iceland and the Faeroe and Shetland islands south around most of the British Isles to western France (Brittany), and in Madeira and the Azores.

Ranges at sea to the western Atlantic along the coast of North America (recorded regularly at sea from Newfoundland south to Florida and Bermuda), rarely the Gulf of St. Lawrence, to the eastern Atlantic from Iceland and Norway south to the Canary Islands, and to the east coast of South America from Trinidad to Argentina.

Casual or accidental in Washington (off Westport), California (Monterey Bay region), on the Gulf coast of Texas, Alabama, and Florida, and in Belize, Puerto Rico, Grenada, Greenland, continental Europe, South Africa, and South Australia.

Notes.—Species limits in the superspecies complex that includes *P. puffinus,* the two following species, and two species from the Australian-New Zealand region, *P. gavia* (Forster, 1844) and *P. huttoni* Mathews, 1912, are uncertain. Varying treatments include the entire complex as a single species or the recognition of three species *(P. puffinus, P. gavia, and P. huttoni),* the other forms united with one of the three. Murphy (1952) united *auricularis* and *newelli* with the *puffinus* group, and *opisthomelas* with the *gavia* group. Bourne et al. (1988) treated the Mediterranean populations as a separate species, *P. yelkouan* (Acerbi, 1827), and genetic differences between these forms consistent with treatment as species have been shown by Wink et al. (1993).

Puffinus auricularis Townsend. Townsend's Shearwater.

> *Puffinus auricularis* C. H. Townsend, 1890, Proc. U. S. Natl. Mus. 13; 133. (Clarión Island, Revillagigedo Group.)

Habitat.—Pelagic Waters; nests in burrows on oceanic islands.

Distribution.—*Breeds* [*newelli* group] in the Hawaiian Islands on Kauai (possibly also on other main islands); and [*auricularis* group] in the Revillagigedo Islands (Socorro, and, at least formerly, Clarión and San Benedicto), off western Mexico.

Ranges at sea [*newelli* group] primarily near the Hawaiian Islands; and [*auricularis* group] from southern Baja California south to Clipperton Island, west to approximately 121° W. long., and along the coast of Mexico south to Oaxaca; sight reports from California, and from Oaxaca southward, require confirmation.

Accidental [*newelli* group] in the Marianas and American Samoa.

Notes.—Groups: *P. auricularis* [Townsend's Shearwater] and *P. newelli* Henshaw, 1900 [Newell's Shearwater]. See comments under *P. puffinus.*

Puffinus opisthomelas Coues. Black-vented Shearwater.

> *Puffinus opisthomelas* Coues, 1864, Proc. Acad. Nat. Sci. Philadelphia 16: 139. (Cape San Lucas, Baja California.)

Habitat.—Pelagic Waters, primarily warm water over continental shelf near shore; nests in burrows or rock crevices on islands.

Distribution.—*Breeds* off the Pacific coast of Baja California (on Guadalupe, San Martín, Natividad, and the San Benito islands).

Ranges at sea along the Pacific coast of North America from central California (casually north to Calvert and Vancouver islands, British Columbia) south to Baja California, Sonora, and (at least casually) Guerrero.

Notes.—See comments under *P. puffinus.*

Puffinus lherminieri Lesson. Audubon's Shearwater.

> *Puffinus* [sic] *Lherminieri* Lesson, 1839, Rev. Zool. [Paris] 2: 102. (ad ripas Antillarum = Straits of Florida.)

Habitat.—Pelagic Waters; nests in rock crevices or under dense vegetation on islands.

Distribution.—*Breeds* in the Caribbean and western Atlantic region on Crab Cay (off Isla Providencia east of Nicaragua), on Tiger Rock and other nearby islets (off the Caribbean coast of Bocas del Toro, Panama), on Los Hermanos and Islas Los Roques (off Venezuela), on Bermuda (formerly), in the Bahamas, near Puerto Rico (Mona Island, and Cayo del Agua, off Culebra), in the Virgin Islands, and widely in the Lesser Antilles (from St. Martin south to islets off Tobago); in the eastern Atlantic on the Cape Verde Islands; in the Indian Ocean (islands in the southern Persian Gulf south to the Mascarene, Seychelles, and Maldive groups); and in the Pacific Ocean from the Bonin and Volcano islands south to the Palau, Vanuatu, Samoa, Society, Tuamotu, and Galapagos islands.

Ranges at sea in the western Atlantic from Massachusetts (at least casually, sight reports north to Nova Scotia) south to Florida and throughout the West Indies to the Caribbean coast of Costa Rica and Panama, and in the Gulf of Mexico west (casually) to Louisiana and Texas; in the tropical Indian Ocean north to the Persian Gulf, Arabian Sea, and India; in the eastern Pacific along the Pacific coast of Mexico from Jalisco (sight report) south to northern South America in Colombia; and in the tropical Pacific from the general breeding range south to Indonesia, New Guinea, and northern Australia.

Accidental in Ontario (Almonte) and England.

Notes.—*Puffinus lherminieri* and *P. assimilis* constitute a superspecies (Sibley and Monroe 1990); they are often treated as conspecific.

Puffinus assimilis Gould. Little Shearwater.

> *Puffinus assimilis* Gould, 1838, Synop. Birds Aust., pt. 4, app., p. 7. (New South Wales = Norfolk Island.)

Habitat.—Pelagic Waters; nests in burrows or crevices on islands .

Distribution.—*Breeds* on islands in the eastern Atlantic (the Azores, Desertas, Salvage, and Canary islands), southern Indian Ocean (St. Paul, formerly Amsterdam), and off Australia and New Zealand (east to Lord Howe and Norfolk islands), and *ranges* at sea primarily in southern oceans.

Casual or accidental in the Hawaiian Islands, Nova Scotia, South Carolina, and continental Europe; sight reports for Puerto Rico and off North Carolina.

Notes.—Also known as Allied Shearwater. See comments under *P. lherminieri*.

Family **HYDROBATIDAE**: Storm-Petrels

Genus *OCEANITES* Keyserling and Blasius

> *Oceanites* Keyserling and Blasius, 1840, Wirbelth. Eur., pp. xciii, 131, 238. Type, by monotypy, *"Thalassidroma"* (= *Procellaria*) *wilsonii* Bonaparte = *Procellaria oceanica* Kuhl.

Oceanites oceanicus (Kuhl). Wilson's Storm-Petrel.

> *Procellaria oceanica* Kuhl, 1820, Beitr. Zool. 1: 136. (No locality given = South Georgia.)

Habitat.—Pelagic Waters, primarily over continental shelf, especially near upwellings; nests in burrows and cliff crevices on islands and in coastal areas.

Distribution.—*Breeds* on islands off southern South America (Wollaston, Deceit, Herschel, and the Falklands), South Georgia, South Sandwich, South Orkney, and South Shetland islands, on the Antarctic Peninsula, around Antarctica, and on the Crozets, Kerguelen, Heard, and probably other subantarctic islands.

Ranges widely at sea throughout the Atlantic Ocean, eastern Caribbean Sea, and Gulf of Mexico north to Texas, the Gulf coast, Labrador, and the British Isles, and east in the Mediterranean to Sardinia, throughout the Indian Ocean north to the Red Sea and Persian Gulf, in Australian and New Zealand waters north to Indonesia and New Guinea, and in the Pacific to Japan (rarely), and to central California, and along the west coast of South America from Peru and occasionally Ecuador southward.

Casual north in the Pacific Ocean off North and Middle America (Panama, sight reports from Washington, Oregon, northern Baja California, Guatemala, and Costa Rica). Accidental in the Hawaiian Islands (between Midway and Laysan), southern Ontario (Long Beach, Lake Muskoka), southwestern Quebec (Lake Deschênes), northern and western New York, and Pennsylvania (Greensburg, Reading). Reports from inland Florida and Mexico are regarded as unsatisfactory.

Genus *PELAGODROMA* Reichenbach

> *Pelagodroma* Reichenbach, 1853, Handb. Spec. Ornithol., Die Vögel, pt. 3 (1852), p. iv. Type, by original designation, *Procellaria marina* Latham.

Pelagodroma marina (Latham). White-faced Storm-Petrel.

> *Procellaria marina* Latham, 1790, Index Ornithol. 2: 826. Based on the "Frigate Petrel"
> Latham, Gen. Synop. Birds 3(2): 410. (in Mari australi; latitudine 37 = off the mouth
> of the Río de la Plata, lat. 35°-37° S.)

Habitat.—Pelagic Waters; nests in burrows under dense vegetation on islands.

Distribution.—*Breeds* on islands off Australia (from Abrolhos east to Bass Strait and Broughton Islands) and in New Zealand waters (Kermadec, Chatham, Auckland, and others near the mainland); in the eastern Atlantic Ocean on the Salvage, Canary (possibly), and Cape Verde islands, and on Tristan da Cunha and Gough Island in the South Atlantic; and in the southern Indian Ocean, at least formerly, on Amsterdam and St. Paul islands.

Ranges at sea in the Indian and Pacific oceans from the Arabian Sea south and east throughout the Australian and New Zealand breeding range across the Pacific to the Galapagos Islands and the west coast of South America (off Ecuador, at least casually); in the Atlantic from the Azores (casually north to the British Isles) south along the west coast of Africa to the South Atlantic and southern Indian Ocean, occurring west to the coasts of Uruguay and Argentina.

Casual in the western Atlantic off North America from Massachusetts south to North Carolina.

Genus *HYDROBATES* Boie

> *Hydrobates* Boie, 1822, Isis von Oken, col. 562. Type, by subsequent designation (Baird, Brewer and Ridgway, 1884), *Procellaria pelagica* Linnaeus.

Hydrobates pelagicus (Linnaeus). European Storm-Petrel.

> *Procellaria pelagica* Linnaeus, 1758, Syst. Nat. (ed. 10) 1: 131. (in albo Oceano = Sweden.)

Habitat—Pelagic Waters; nests in natural cavities, under stones, and burrows on small rocky islands.

Distribution.—*Breeds* on islands in the northern and eastern Atlantic Ocean and western Mediterranean Sea, and *ranges* at sea throughout the Mediterranean and Black seas and the eastern Atlantic and western Indian oceans.

Accidental in Nova Scotia (Sable Island, 10 August 1970; McNeil and Burton 1971); there is also an old specimen (USNM) from the "Bay of Fundy" lacking further data. A specimen taken at McClellanville, South Carolina, in 1972, and reported as *H. pelagicus,* was subsequently identified as *Oceanodroma castro* (1973, Amer. Birds 27: 44).

Notes.—Also known as British Storm-Petrel. Known in Old World literature as the Storm Petrel.

Genus *OCEANODROMA* Reichenbach

> *Oceanodroma* Reichenbach, 1853, Handb. Spec. Ornithol., Die Vögel, pt. 3 (1852), p. iv. Type, by original designation, *Procellaria furcata* Gmelin.
> *Cymochorea* Coues, 1864, Proc. Acad. Nat. Sci. Philadelphia 16: 75. Type, by original designation, *Procellaria leucorhoa* Vieillot.
> *Halocyptena* Coues, 1864, Proc. Acad. Nat. Sci. Philadelphia 16: 78. Type, by original designation, *Halocyptena microsoma* Coues.
> *Loomelania* Mathews, 1934, Bull. Brit. Ornithol. Club 54: 119. Type, by original designation, *Procellaria melania* Bonaparte.
> *Thalobata* Mathews, 1943, in Mathews and Hallstrom, Notes on Order Procellariiformes, p. 27. Type, by original designation, *Thalassidroma castro* Harcourt.

Oceanodroma furcata (Gmelin). Fork-tailed Storm-Petrel.

> *Procellaria furcata* Gmelin, 1789, Syst. Nat. 1(2): 561. Based on the "Fork-tail Petrel" Pennant, Arct. Zool. 2: 535. (in glacie maris, Americam & Asiam interfluentis = Bering Sea.)

Habitat.—Pelagic Waters; nests in burrows or under rocks or among drift logs on hilly, vegetated islands.

Distribution.—*Breeds* in the North Pacific from southern Alaska (the Aleutian Islands, islands in the Gulf of Alaska, and the Alexander Archipelago) south along the west coast of North America to islets off northern California (Del Norte and Humboldt counties), and in eastern Asia from the Commander Islands south to the Kuril Islands.

Ranges at sea from the Bering Sea (casually the southern Chukchi Sea) south through the North Pacific along the west coast of North America from southern Alaska south to central (casually southern) California, to Marcus Island, and west to Japan and the Volcano Islands; two sight reports from the Hawaiian Islands are poorly documented.

Oceanodroma leucorhoa (Vieillot). Leach's Storm-Petrel.

Procellaria leucorhoa Vieillot, 1818, Nouv. Dict. Hist. Nat. (nouv. éd.) 25 (1817): 422. (sur les bords maritimes de la Picardie, se tient sur l'Ocean, jusqu'au Brésil = Picardy, France.)

Habitat.—Pelagic Waters, especially upwellings; nests in burrows on islands.

Distribution.—*Breeds* in the North Pacific from the Aleutian and Shumagin islands and south-coastal Alaska south along the North American coast to Baja California (Los Coronados, San Benito, and Guadalupe islands, and Alijos Rocks), and from the Commander Islands south to the Kuril Islands and northern Hokkaido, Japan; and in the North Atlantic from southern Labrador (Gannet Islands) south to Gulf of St. Lawrence, Newfoundland, Maine (Casco Bay), and Massachusetts (Penikese Islands), and from southern Iceland, the Faeroe Islands, and Norway to northern Scotland.

Ranges at sea in the Pacific Ocean from the breeding areas south to the Hawaiian, Revillagigedo, and Galapagos islands, and in the western Pacific to Indonesia and New Guinea; and in the Atlantic Ocean south along both coasts to Florida, the West Indies, Caribbean Sea, South America (Venezuela east to eastern Brazil), and South Africa, also to the west coast of Greenland (rarely but regularly); casual to the eastern Atlantic islands, Mediterranean Sea and western Europe.

Casual or accidental in interior Oregon, interior California, Ohio, Baffin Island, southern Ontario, northern Quebec, northern New York, Vermont, the District of Columbia, along the Gulf coast (from Texas east to Florida), inland in Alabama (Eufaula), along the Pacific coast of Costa Rica (Cabo Velas), and in New Zealand.

Notes.—*Oceanodroma leucorhoa* and the closely allied *O. monorhis* (Swinhoe, 1867) of Japan and Korea, probably constitute a superspecies (Sibley and Monroe 1990). There are three breeding populations off western Mexico: one dark-rumped population on Socorro Island in the Isla Revillgigedo group (here regarded as a race of *O. leucorhoa* but which has been treated variously as a subspecies of *O. monorhis* or as a distinct species, *O. socorroensis* C. H. Townsend, 1890 [Dusky-rumped Storm-Petrel]); one variably, mostly white-rumped summer breeding population on Guadalupe Island; and a distinct, white-rumped, winter breeding population, also on Guadalupe Island. See Ainley (1980, 1983) and Bourne and Jehl (1982). Mayr and Short (1970) considered *O. leucorhoa* and *O. castro* to constitute a superspecies.

Oceanodroma homochroa (Coues). Ashy Storm-Petrel.

Cymochorea homochroa Coues, 1864, Proc. Acad. Nat. Sci. Philadelphia 16: 77. (Farallone Islands, Pacific coast of North America = Farallon Islands, California.)

Habitat.—Pelagic Waters; nests in natural crevices or burrows on rocky islands.

Distribution.—*Breeds* on islands off the coast of California (on Bird Island in Marin County, the Farallon Islands, and on San Miguel, Santa Barbara, and Santa Cruz islands in the Channel Islands) and, rarely, northern Baja California (Los Coronados Islands).

Ranges at sea off the coast of California and northern Baja California from Humboldt County south to the San Benito Islands.

Oceanodroma castro (Harcourt). Band-rumped Storm-Petrel.

> *Thalassidroma castro* Harcourt, 1851, Sketch Madeira, p. 123. (Deserta Islets, near Madeira.)

Habitat.—Pelagic Waters; nests in burrows or rock crevices on islands.

Distribution.—*Breeds* on islands in the Pacific Ocean in the Hawaiian Islands (no nest located, indirect evidence for nesting on Kauai and Hawaii, possibly also Maui), off Japan, in the Galapagos Islands, and possibly on Cocos Island, off Costa Rica; and in the Atlantic Ocean in the Azores (probably), Salvage, Madeira, Cape Verde, Ascension, and St. Helena islands.

Ranges at sea primarily in the vicinity of the breeding grounds, occurring uncommonly but regularly off the Atlantic coast of North America (Massachusetts to Florida).

Casual off the Pacific coast of Costa Rica, in the Gulf of Mexico (Texas, Florida; sight reports from Louisiana), and off Cuba, also off the coast of Brazil and the British Isles. Accidental inland in Missouri, Indiana, Ontario, Pennsylvania, the District of Columbia, South Carolina and Tennessee; a sight report for California.

Notes.—Also known as Madeira Storm-Petrel or Harcourt's Storm-Petrel. See comments under *O. leucorhoa.*

Oceanodroma tethys (Bonaparte). Wedge-rumped Storm-Petrel.

> *Thalassidroma Tethys* Bonaparte, 1852, Tagebl. Dtsch. Naturforsch. Aertze, Weisbaden, Beilage, no. 7, p. 89. (Galapagos Islands.)

Habitat.—Pelagic Waters; nests in burrows on islands.

Distribution.—*Breeds* in the Galapagos Islands (Tower and Pitt) and on islands off the coast of Peru (San Gallán and Pescadores).

Ranges at sea along the west coast of the Americas north to southern Baja California and south to the coast of Chile (lat. 20° S.), casually north to central California (Monterey Bay).

Notes.—Also known as Galapagos Storm-Petrel.

Oceanodroma melania (Bonaparte). Black Storm-Petrel.

> *Procellaria melania* Bonaparte, 1854, C. R. Acad. Sci. Paris 38: 662. (coast of California = vicinity of San Francisco.)

Habitat.—Pelagic Waters; nests in burrows or crevices on rocky islands.

Distribution.—*Breeds* on Sutil Island, adjacent to Santa Barbara Island in the Channel Islands, off southern California; on the Los Coronados and San Benito islands, off the Pacific coast of Baja California; and on islands in the northern third of the Gulf of California (Consag Rock, San Luis Islands, and Partida Island).

Ranges at sea along the Pacific coast of the Americas from northwestern Oregon south to Panama, Colombia, Ecuador, and Peru (to lat. 8° S.).

A sight report for interior southern California (Salton Sea).

Notes.—*Oceanodroma melania* and *O. matsudairae* Kuroda, 1922, of the Volcano Islands and Japanese waters, constitute a superspecies (Sibley and Monroe 1990).

†*Oceanodroma macrodactyla* Bryant. Guadalupe Storm-Petrel.

> *Oceanodroma leucorhoa macrodactyla* W. E. Bryant, 1887, Bull. Calif. Acad. Sci. 2: 450. (Guadalupe Island, Baja California.)

Habitat.—Pelagic Waters; nested in burrows among coniferous trees at high elevations.

Distribution.—EXTINCT. *Bred* formerly on Guadalupe Island, Baja California; not certainly recorded since 1912. Known only from the vicinity of the breeding grounds.

Oceanodroma markhami (Salvin). Markham's Storm-Petrel.

> *Cymochorea markhami* Salvin, 1883, Proc. Zool. Soc. London, p. 430. (coast of Peru, lat. 19°40' S., long. 75° W.)

Habitat—Pelagic Waters.

Distribution.—*Breeding* grounds unknown; *ranges* at sea along the Pacific coast of South America from northern Peru to central Chile, occasionally to the Galapagos Islands.

Casual north to Clipperton Island, western Costa Rica (Cocos Island), and western Panama.

Notes.—*Oceanodroma markhami* and *O. tristrami* constitute a superspecies (Sibley and Monroe 1990); if these two are considered conspecific, Sooty Storm-Petrel may be used for the broader specific unit.

Oceanodroma tristrami Salvin. Tristram's Storm-Petrel.

> *Oceanodroma tristrami* (Stejneger MS) Salvin, 1896, Cat. Birds Brit. Mus. 25: xiv, 347, 354. (Sendai Bay, [Honshu,] Japan.)

Habitat.—Pelagic Waters; nests in burrows and crevices among rocks on islands.

Distribution.—*Breeds* in the northwestern Hawaiian Islands (from Pearl and Hermes Atoll east to Nihoa, and possibly Kure and Lisianski), in the Seven Islands of Izu (Torishima), and in the Volcano Islands (Kita Iwo).

Ranges at sea from the Hawaiian Islands (east to Kauai) to Japanese waters and the Bonin Islands.

Notes.—See comments under *O. markhami.*

Oceanodroma microsoma (Coues). Least Storm-Petrel.

> *Halocyptena microsoma* Coues, 1864, Proc. Acad. Nat. Sci. Philadelphia 16: 79. (San Jose del Caba [sic], Lower California = San José del Cabo, Baja California.)

Habitat.—Pelagic Waters, primarily warm water over continental shelf; nests in crevices or among stones on rocky islets.

Distribution.—*Breeds* on the Pacific side of Baja California in the San Benito Islands and in the northern third of the Gulf of California (Consag Rock, and San Luis and Partida islands, probably other islands).

Ranges at sea along the west coast of North America from central California (Monterey Bay), south to Oaxaca, less frequently south as far as Panama and northern South America (Colombia and Ecuador, to lat. 2° S.).

Casual in northern and central southern California (Humboldt County, Salton Sea), and the lower Colorado river (in California and Arizona). Accidental in New Mexico (Silver City).

Notes.—This species was formerly treated in the monotypic genus *Halocyptena.*

Order **PELECANIFORMES**: Totipalmate Birds

Notes.—Because considerable controversy surrounds what is included in this order and the relationships among the groups included (Cracraft 1985, Sibley and Monroe 1990 and references therein), we retain the arrangement used in the Sixth Edition (AOU 1983).

Suborder PHAETHONTES: Tropicbirds

Family **PHAETHONTIDAE**: Tropicbirds

Genus *PHAETHON* Linnaeus

> *Phaëthon* Linnaeus, 1758, Syst. Nat. (ed. 10) 1: 134. Type, by subsequent designation (G. R. Gray, 1840), *Phaethon aethereus* Linnaeus.

Phaethon lepturus Daudin. White-tailed Tropicbird.

> *Phaëton* [sic] *lepturus* Daudin, 1802, in Buffon, Hist. Nat., ed. Didot, Quadr., 14: 319. (Mauritius.)

Habitat.—Pelagic Waters; nests on tropical islands in rocky crevices, holes, or caves, especially on cliffs, occasionally in trees.

Distribution.—*Breeds* on islands in the Atlantic Ocean and Caribbean Sea from Bermuda, the Bahamas, and throughout the Greater and Lesser Antilles south to islets off Tobago, Fernando de Noronha (off Brazil), Ascension Island, and islands in the Gulf of Guinea; in the Pacific Ocean from the Hawaiian Islands (main islands west to Kauai, occasionally on Midway) and the Bonin and Volcano islands south to New Caledonia and the Fiji, Marquesas, and Tuamotu islands; and in the Indian Ocean from the Seychelles and Andaman Islands south to the Mascarenes and Christmas Island.

Ranges at sea throughout the breeding areas and tropical waters in the western Atlantic, rarely north along the east coast of North America to North Carolina (casually to Nova Scotia), casually in the Gulf of Mexico (mostly off Florida, regularly at Dry Tortugas), and the Caribbean Sea (recorded off Cozumel Island and off northern Colombia); also in the western Pacific Ocean from Japan to Australia and (casually) New Zealand; and in the Indian Ocean south to South Africa.

Accidental in southern California (Orange County), Arizona (Scottsdale), Pennsylvania (Gettysburg), western New York, and Chiapas; a sight report for Panama.

Notes.—Also known as Yellow-billed Tropicbird.

Phaethon aethereus Linnaeus. Red-billed Tropicbird.

Phaëthon æthereus Linnaeus, 1758, Syst. Nat. (ed. 10) 1: 134. (in Pelago inter tropicos = Ascension Island.)

Habitat.—Pelagic Waters; nests in crevices and holes, usually on cliffs, on tropical islands.

Distribution.—*Breeds* on islands in the Caribbean region (on Culebra and Vieques off Puerto Rico, on small islets in the Virgin Islands and Lesser Antilles south to Tobago and Grenada, and on Swan Key in Almirante Bay, Panama, also on Los Hermanos and Los Roques off Venezuela), and on islands in the eastern Atlantic from the Cape Verde Islands south to islets off Senegal; in the eastern Pacific off Mexico (off Colima and probably Guerrero, and Revillagigedo, Tres Marías, and Isabela islands), in the Gulf of California (Consag and Alijos rocks, and San Pedro Mártir and San Jorge islands) and northern South America (the Galapagos and islands off the coast from Colombia to Ecuador and Peru); and in the northern Indian Ocean, Red Sea, and Persian Gulf.

Ranges at sea in the breeding areas in the western Atlantic region throughout the Lesser Antilles and off northern South America, less frequently through the Greater Antilles, casually north off the Atlantic coast of North America from Maine to Florida; in the Pacific regularly from Baja California south to Peru, irregularly north to California, west to the Hawaiian Islands (recorded French Frigate Shoals, Nihoa, and Kauai) and south to Chile; and in the tropical Indian Ocean.

Casual or accidental in Washington, interior southern California (Morongo Valley), southern Arizona, Texas (Houston, Zapata), Louisiana, Bermuda, Madeira, and southern Africa.

Phaethon rubricauda Boddaert. Red-tailed Tropicbird.

Phaeton [sic] *rubricauda* Boddaert, 1783, Table Planches Enlum., p. 57. Based on "Paille-en queue de l'Isle de France" Daubenton, Planches Enlum., pl. 979. (Mauritius.)

Habitat.—Pelagic Waters; nests on the ground on tropical islands.

Distribution.—*Breeds* on islands in the Pacific Ocean from the Hawaiian Islands (from Kure east to Kauai, Lanai, and Kahoolawe, on Manana Island off Oahu, and probably on islets off Molokai), and Bonin and Volcano islands south to northeastern Australia (Raine Island) and Lord Howe, Norfolk, Kermadec, Tuamotu, and Pitcairn islands; and in the Indian Ocean near Mauritius, in the Cocos-Keeling Islands, and off the northwestern coast of Australia.

Ranges at sea from Japan, Taiwan, and the Hawaiian Islands (throughout) south throughout the breeding range and east (at least casually) to waters well off California (including San Nicolas Island) and islands off Mexico (Guadalupe, Revillagigedo, Clipperton). Accidental on Vancouver Island and off the coast of Chile.

Suborder PELECANI: Boobies, Pelicans, Cormorants, and Darters

Family **SULIDAE**: Boobies and Gannets

Genus *SULA* Brisson

Sula Brisson, 1760, Ornithologie 1: 60; 6: 494. Type, by tautonymy, *Sula* Brisson = *Sula leucogaster* Boddaert.

Sula dactylatra Lesson. Masked Booby.

Sula dactylatra Lesson, 1831, Traité Ornithol. 8: 601. (L'île de l'Ascension = Ascension Island.)

Habitat.—Pelagic Waters; nests on the ground on low, flat oceanic islands.

Distribution.—*Breeds* in the Atlantic-Caribbean region off the Yucatan Peninsula (Cayo Arcas, Cayo Arenas, and Alacrán reef), in the Florida Keys (Dry Tortugas, occasionally), in the southern Bahamas (Santo Domingo Cay, formerly), on Cayman Brac in the Cayman Islands, southwest of Jamaica (the Pedro and Serranilla cays), off Puerto Rico (Monito Island, and off Culebra), in the Virgin Islands (Cockroach and Sula cays), in the Lesser Antilles (Dog Island off Anguilla, Sombrero Island, and in the Grenadines), off Venezuela (Islas de Aves east to Los Hermanos), and on islands off Brazil east to Ascension Island; in the Pacific off Mexico (on Alijos Rocks off southwestern Baja California, on Clarión and San Benedicto islands in the Revillagigedo group, and on Clipperton Island), from the Hawaiian (Kure east to Kaula Rock, Lehua off Niihau, and on Moku Manu off Oahu) and Ryukyu islands south to eastern Australia (Queensland) and the Kermadec, Tuamotu, and Easter islands, and in the Galapagos and on islands off Ecuador, Peru, and Chile (San Ambrosia and San Félix); and in the Indian Ocean from the Gulf of Aden and Cocos-Keeling and Christmas islands south to the Mascarenes and northwestern Australia.

Ranges at sea in the Atlantic-Caribbean region from the Bahamas, Antilles, and the Yucatan Peninsula south through the breeding range, rarely north through the Gulf of Mexico from Tamaulipas and Texas east to Florida, Bermuda (casually), along the Atlantic coast to North Carolina, and casually along the coast of Middle America; and in the Pacific and Indian oceans generally throughout the breeding range south to western Mexico (Oaxaca), eastern Australia, and South Africa.

Casual off central and southeastern California (north to Monterey County), northwestern Baja California (Los Coronados Islands); a sight report for Guatemala.

Notes.—Also known as Blue-faced Booby or White Booby.

Sula nebouxii Milne-Edwards. Blue-footed Booby.

Sula Nebouxii Milne-Edwards, 1882, Ann. Sci. Nat. (Zool.), (6)13: 37, pl. 14. (la côte pacifique de l'Amérique = Pacific coast of America, presumably Chile.)

Habitat.—Coastal Waters; nests on the ground on islands.

Distribution.—*Breeds* on islands in the Gulf of California (from Consag Rock and George Island southward), off western Mexico (Isabela, the Tres Marietas, and the Tres Marías islands), off Honduras (Los Farallones), in the Gulf of Panama (Isla Villa, Farallón del Chirú, and Isla Pachequilla in the Pearl Islands, and Isla Boná), in the Galapagos Islands, and along the coast of South America from Colombia to northern Peru.

Ranges at sea in the eastern Pacific from Baja California and the Gulf of California south along the coast of Middle America and South America to the Galapagos Islands and central Peru, casually north to central coastal California (San Francisco), southeastern California (mostly Salton Sea and lower Colorado River), southern Nevada (Lake Mead) and southwestern Arizona (lower Colorado River, Phoenix).

Accidental in Washington (Everett), interior central California, and Texas (Burnet and Cameron counties); a sight report for northwestern California (Del Norte County).

Sula variegata (Tschudi). Peruvian Booby.

Dasyporus variegatus Tschudi, 1843. Arch. Naturgesch. 9: 390. (coasts and islands of Pacific Ocean = islands off coast of Peru.)

Habitat.—Pelagic Waters; nests on islands.

Distribution.—*Breeds* on islands off coasts of Ecuador, Peru, and Chile, and *ranges* at sea off western South America.

Casual off the Pacific coast of Panama (Bay of Panama), where present in summer 1983 (maximum about 3500 individuals on 17 June) in apparent association with a major "El Niño Southern Oscillation" (Aid et al. 1985, Reed 1988).

Sula leucogaster (Boddaert). Brown Booby.

Pelecanus Leucogaster Boddaert, 1783, Table Planches Enlum, p. 57. Based on "Le Fou, de Cayenne" Daubenton, Planches Enlum., pl. 973. (No locality given = Cayenne.)

Habitat.—Coastal Waters, Pelagic Waters; nests on the ground on islands.

Distribution.—*Breeds* on islands in the Atlantic-Caribbean region from islets off the Yucatan Peninsula and Bahamas south through the Antilles (including Cayman Brac in the Cayman Islands) and along the coasts of Middle America and northern South America (east to Los Hermanos), and from the Cape Verde Islands and the Gulf of Guinea south to the coast of central Brazil and Ascension Islands; in the Pacific from Consag Rock and George Island in the Gulf of California south to Guerrero and the Revillagigedo and Clipperton islands, off Honduras (Los Farallones and Bird Island in Gulf of Fonseca), on islets off Costa Rica, in the Bay of Panama (Isla Boná, Farallon Rock, and the Pearl Islands), and off Colombia (Gorgona Island), and from the Hawaiian Islands (Kure east to Niihau and Moku Manu off Oahu), the Bonin and Volcano islands and the Seven Islands of Izu south to the South China Sea, northern Australia, New Caledonia, and the Tonga and Tuamotu islands; and in the Indian Ocean from the Red Sea and the Malay Peninsula south to the Seychelles, Cocos-Keeling, and Christmas islands.

Ranges at sea generally in the breeding range, and in the Atlantic-Caribbean region north (at least rarely) to the Gulf coast (Texas east to Florida), along the Atlantic coast north (at least casually) as far as New York, Massachusetts, and Nova Scotia, and to Bermuda; in the Pacific from Baja California south to northwestern South America, casually north along coast to central California, and inland in southeastern California (Salton Sea, Colorado River), southern Nevada (Lake Mead), and western and southern Arizona, and from Hawaiian waters and Japan south to Australia and (rarely) New Zealand; and in the Indian Ocean south to South Africa.

Notes.—Also known as White-bellied Booby.

Sula sula (Linnaeus). Red-footed Booby.

Pelecanus Sula Linnaeus, 1766, Syst. Nat. (ed. 12) 1: 218. Based in part on "The Booby" Catesby, Nat. Hist. Carolina 1: 87, pl. 87. (in Pelago indico = Barbados, Lesser Antilles.)

Habitat.—Pelagic Waters; nests in tress and shrubs on islands.

Distribution.—*Breeds* on islands in the Atlantic-Caribbean region off Yucatán (Alacrán reef), Belize (Half Moon Cay), in the Cayman Islands (Little Cayman), Bahama Islands (White Cay off San Salvador) Swan Islands (Little Swan), off Puerto Rico (Mona, Monito, Desecheo, and Culebra islands), in the Virgin Islands (Dutchcap, Frenchcap and, formerly, Cockroach and Sula cays), in the Grenadines (Battowia and Kick-'em-Jenny), off Venezuela (Los Roques east to Los Hermanos), and off Brazil (Fernando de Noronha and Trindade islands); in the Pacific off Mexico (the Tres Marías islands, Isla Isabela, and Clarión and San Benedicto in the Revillagigedo group), off Costa Rica (Cocos Island), in the Galapagos Islands, off Ecuador (Isla de la Plata), and from the Hawaiian (west to Kure, uncommon east of Oahu) and Bonin islands south to northern Australia, New Caledonia, and the Fiji, Samoa, and Tuamotu islands; and in the Indian Ocean from Aldabra east to Cocos-Keeling Island.

Ranges at sea in the breeding areas in the Atlantic-Caribbean region from Quintana Roo and Belize south along the coasts (rarely inshore) of Middle America and South America to eastern Brazil, casually north to the Gulf coast (from Texas east to western Florida) and through the Greater Antilles to southern Florida; in the Pacific throughout the Hawaiian Islands (rare east to Oahu) and (rarely inshore) along Pacific coast from Sinaloa south to Panama; and in the Indian Ocean north to the Bay of Bengal.

Casual in California (from Farallon Islands and Marin County south to the Channel Islands and Los Angeles) and Gulf of California; accidental in South Carolina (Edisto Island).

Genus *MORUS* Vieillot

Morus Vieillot, 1816, Analyse, p. 63. Type, by monotypy, "Fou de Bassan" Brisson = *Pelecanus bassanus* Linnaeus.

Notes.—*Morus* is recognized as a genus on the basis of Olson and Warheit (1988) and van Tets et al. (1988).

Morus bassanus (Linnaeus). Northern Gannet.

Pelecanus Bassanus Linnaeus, 1758, Syst. Nat. (ed. 10) 1: 133. (in Scotia, America = Bass Rock, Scotland.)

Habitat.—Pelagic, primarily over continental shelf; nests primarily on open ground on flat-topped islands, less frequently on rocky slopes and cliffs along coasts.

Distribution.—*Breeds* on islands in eastern North America in the Gulf of St. Lawrence (on Bonaventure, Anticosti, and Bird Rocks in the Magdalen Islands), off Quebec (Perroquet Island, formerly), and in Labrador (Ramah Bay) and Newfoundland (Cape St. Mary, and on Baccalieu and Funk islands), formerly in Nova Scotia (near Yarmouth) and off New Brunswick (Gannet Rock); and in Europe around Iceland, the Faeroe Islands, British Isles, northern France, and Norway.

Ranges at sea off eastern North America from southern Labrador, Greenland, and areas near the breeding range south along the Atlantic coast (regular inside Chesapeake Bay) to Florida, and west along the Gulf coast to Texas; and in Europe east and south to northern Russia, Scandinavia, the Baltic Sea, throughout the Mediterranean Sea, and along the Atlantic coast to northwestern Africa and (casually) the Cape Verde Islands.

Casual inland in the St. Lawrence Valley, New England, and the Great Lakes west to Michigan, Indiana, and Ohio; and in Eurasia to Spitsbergen, Bear Island, and continental Europe. Accidental on Victoria Island (Holman) and in Kentucky; sight reports for Manitoba, Illinois, Tennessee, Tamaulipas, Veracruz, and the Bahama Islands (Berry and Exuma islands).

Notes.—Known in most literature as the Gannet. The gannets of the world, *M. bassanus, M. capensis* (Lichtenstein, 1823) of South Africa, and *M. serrator* (G. R. Gray, 1843) of Australia and New Zealand, constitute a superspecies (Dorst and Mougin *in* Mayr and Cottrell 1979).

Family **PELECANIDAE**: Pelicans

Genus *PELECANUS* Linnaeus

Pelecanus Linnaeus, 1758, Syst. Nat. (ed. 10) 1: 132. Type, by subsequent designation (G. R. Gray, 1840), *Pelecanus onocrotalus* Linnaeus.

Cyrtopelicanus Reichenbach, 1853, Avium Syst. Nat. (1852), p. vii. Type, by original designation, *Pelecanus trachyrhynchus* Latham = *Pelecanus erythrorhynchos* Gmelin.

Leptopelicanus Reichenbach, 1853, Avium Syst. Nat. (1852), p. vii. Type, by original designation, *Pelecanus fuscus* Gmelin = *Pelecanus occidentalis* Linnaeus.

Pelecanus erythrorhynchos Gmelin. American White Pelican.

> *Pelecanus erythrorhynchos* Gmelin, 1789, Syst. Nat. 1(2): 571. Based on the "Rough-billed Pelican" Latham, Gen. Synop. Birds 3(2): 586. (in America septentrionali = Hudson Bay.)

Habitat.—Shallow lakes, rivers, and freshwater marshes, rarely around coastal islands; nests on the ground, usually on islands in inland lakes; in winter, primarily estuaries, bays, brackish marshes, and large lakes.

Distribution.—*Breeds* from south-central British Columbia (Stum Lake), northeastern Alberta, northwestern Saskatchewan, central Manitoba, and west-central Ontario south locally to northern California, western Nevada, northern Utah, central Colorado, Wyoming, northeastern South Dakota, and western Minnesota, with sporadic breeding on the central coast of Texas and from central to southern California (formerly on Salton Sea), also in Durango and Tamaulipas. Recorded in summer in southern Mackenzie (possibly breeding at Great Slave Lake), southern California (to Salton Sea), and coastal Mississippi and Alabama, also in many localities within the winter range.

Winters along the Pacific coast from central California and southern Arizona south along the Pacific lowlands (less frequently in the interior) of Mexico to Guatemala, El Salvador, and Nicaragua (sight reports for Costa Rica), and from Florida and the Gulf states south along the Gulf coast of Mexico to the Yucatan Peninsula, casually in the breeding range in western North America.

Wanders irregularly after the breeding season through most of eastern North America from Hudson Bay, Quebec, New Brunswick, Nova Scotia, and Newfoundland south to the Gulf coast and (rarely) the West Indies (Bimini and Great Inagua in the Bahamas, Grand Cayman, Cuba, Jamaica, and Puerto Rico). Accidental in Alaska (Petersburg), northern Mackenzie (Liverpool Bay), Victoria Island (Holman), Panama (Herrera), and the Lesser Antilles (Antigua).

Notes.—In American literature usually known as the White Pelican.

Pelecanus occidentalis Linnaeus. Brown Pelican.

> *Pelecanus occidentalis* Linnaeus, 1766, Syst. Nat. (ed. 12) 1: 215. Based mainly on "The Pelican of America" Edwards, Nat. Hist. Birds 2: 93, pl. 93. (in Africa, Asia, & in America = Jamaica.)

Habitat.—Coastal Waters; nests on islands on the ground or in small bushes and trees.

Distribution.—*Breeds* [*occidentalis* group] on islands along the Pacific coast of North America from central California (the Channel Islands, formerly north to Monterey County) south to Isabela and the Tres Marias Islands (and including islands in the Gulf of California), in the Bay of Fonseca (Honduras), off Costa Rica (Guayabo and Bolaños) and Panama (mostly in the Pearl Islands, and islets off Isla Coiba and in the Bay of Panama), in the Galapagos Islands, along the Atlantic, Gulf and Caribbean coasts from Maryland south around Florida (including inland at Lake Okeechobee) and west to southern Texas, in the northwestern Bahamas (Great Inagua, Caicos, and formerly Bimini), Greater Antilles (from Cuba east to the Virgin Islands and St. Martin), Lesser Antilles (St. Kitts), in southern Veracruz (Roca Partida), off the Yucatan Peninsula and Belize (Man-of-war Cay), and off the northern coast of Venezuela from Los Roques east to Tobago and Trinidad; and [*thagus* group] along the South American coast from northern Peru to southern Chile (Isla de Chiloé).

Ranges [*occidentalis* group] along on the Pacific coast of the Americas from southern British Columbia south to northern Peru, and inland to the great lakes of Nicaragua, southeastern California (Salton Sea), and southern Arizona, casually elsewhere in the interior of the southwestern United States, and throughout the Atlantic, Gulf, and Caribbean coastal and insular areas from southern New York (casually north to New England) south to eastern Venezuela (rarely to northern Brazil); and [*thagus* group] to coastal Ecuador.

Casual in North America north to Idaho, southeastern Wyoming, South Dakota, Iowa, Wisconsin, Michigan, Ontario, southern Quebec, and Nova Scotia; a sight report for North Dakota.

Notes.—Groups: *P. occidentalis* [Brown Pelican] and *P. thagus* Molina, 1782 [Peruvian Pelican].

Family **PHALACROCORACIDAE**: Cormorants

Genus *PHALACROCORAX* Brisson

Phalacrocorax Brisson, 1760, Ornithologie 1: 60; 6: 511. Type, by tautonymy, *Phalacrocorax* Brisson = *Pelecanus carbo* Linnaeus.

Notes.—Siegel-Causey (1988) split the family Phalacrocoracidae into two subfamilies and the genus *Phalacrocorax* into nine genera. The subfamily Phalacrocoracinae ("cormorants") contained the species listed herein through *P. carbo,* whereas the Leucocarboninae ("shags") contained the remaining species. The genera used were *Phalacrocorax (carbo), Hypoleucus (auritus, brasilianus), Compsohalieus (penicillatus, perspicillatus), Stictocarbo (pelagicus, urile, gaimardi), and Leucocarbo (bougainvillii).* We retain a more traditional classification because other data (e.g., DNA-DNA hybridization data, see Sibley and Ahlquist 1990: 851) suggest that the relationships among them differ from the Siegel-Causey arrangement.

Phalacrocorax penicillatus (Brandt). Brandt's Cormorant.

Carbo penicillatus M. Brandt, 1837, Bull. Sci. Acad. Imp. Sci. St.-Petersbourg 3: col. 55. (No locality given = Vancouver Island, British Columbia.)

Habitat.—Coastal Waters, ranging at sea as well as inshore on brackish bays; nests on open ground on rocky slopes.

Distribution.—*Breeds* along the Pacific coast in south-coastal Alaska (Seal Rocks, Hinchinbrook Entrance, Prince William Sound), and southeastern Alaska (Hazy Islands, St. Lazaria Island), south-coastal British Columbia (Vancouver Island), and Washington (Matia Island) south to Baja California (Isla Natividad, in San Cristobal Bay, and on Guadalupe Island, Pacific coast; and San Pedro Mártir, Salsipuedes, and Roca Blanca islands, Gulf of California).

Ranges generally near the breeding areas but occurs from southern Alaska south to southern Baja California (Cape San Lucas) and widely in the Gulf of California (rarely to the coast of Sonora), casually in interior California and to Nayarit (Isla Isabela).

Phalacrocorax brasilianus (Gmelin). Neotropic Cormorant.

Pelecanus brasilianus Gmelin, 1789, Syst. Nat. 1 (2): 564. Based on "Maiagué" Piso, Ind. utriusque Re Nat. Med., p. 83 = (northeastern Brazil.)

Habitat.— Freshwater Lakes and Ponds, Coastal Waters, Rivers; nests in trees and on rocks (0–3500 m; Tropical to Temperate zones).

Distribution.—*Resident* from Sonora, southwestern New Mexico, north-central and eastern Texas, Oklahoma (possibly), and southwestern Louisiana south through Middle America and South America (also islands north of Venezuela from Aruba to Trinidad) to Tierra del Fuego; also in the Bahama Islands (Great Inagua) and Cuba.

Ranges north to southeastern Arizona.

Casual north to southern Baja California, southeastern California, Colorado, Nebraska, South Dakota, southern Minnesota, and northern Illinois, and in Jamaica, Puerto Rico, and the Virgin Islands; a sight report for southern Nevada.

Notes.—Also known as Olivaceous Cormorant. For acceptance of the name *P. brasilianus* (Gmelin, 1789) over *P. olivaceus* (Humboldt, 1805) see Browning (1989a). See comments under *P. auritus.*

Phalacrocorax auritus (Lesson). Double-crested Cormorant.

Carbo auritus Lesson, 1831, Traité Ornithol. 8: 605. Based on "Le Cormoran dilophe" Vieillot, in Vieillot and Oudart, Gal. Ois. 2: pl. 275. (in Nouvelle-Zélande, error = upper Saskatchewan River, North America; restricted by Todd, 1963, Birds Labrador Peninsula, p. 105.)

Habitat.—Lakes, rivers, swamps, and seacoasts; nests on the ground or in trees in fresh-water situations, on coastal cliffs, and even on artificial structures.

Distribution.—*Breeds* in the southeastern Bering Sea (Cape Peirce), southern Alaska (from Carlisle Island in the eastern Aleutians east to Yakutat Bay, and inland to Lake Louise), and from southern British Columbia, northern Alberta, northwestern and central Saskatchewan, central Manitoba, southern James Bay, the north shore of the Gulf of St. Lawrence, and Newfoundland south, in isolated colonies, to Baja California, coastal Sonora, central Chihuahua, central Durango, southwestern and south-central Arizona, southern New Mexico, west-central and southern Texas, the Gulf coast, Florida, the northern Bahamas (south to Great Inagua and San Salvador), Cuba, the Isle of Pines, Yucatan Peninsula, and northern Belize.

Winters along the Pacific coast from the Aleutians and southern Alaska south to Baja California, Nayarit, and inland from east-central Washington and Montana (rarely) south locally to southeastern California (Salton Sea and southern Arizona); in the interior United States (casually farther north) from northeastern Colorado (rarely), southern Minnesota, and the southern Great Lakes south to New Mexico, Oklahoma, Texas, and the Gulf states, and in the Atlantic region from Lake Ontario and New England south to Florida, Bermuda (irregularly), the Bahamas, Greater Antilles (east, at least casually, to the Virgin Islands), the Yucatan Peninsula, and northern Belize.

Migrates regularly through the Great Plains and Mississippi and Ohio valleys, irregularly north to southern Mackenzie and Pribilof Islands.

Casual north to Yukon, Hudson Bay, Baffin Island, and Labrador, and in Bermuda and the Cayman Islands. Accidental in the Lesser Antilles (St. Martin) and England.

Notes.—In view of the description of a small race of this species on San Salvador Island in the Bahamas (Watson et al. 1991), breeding records of this species and of *P. brasilianus* in the Bahama Islands need to be reviewed and more data obtained.

Phalacrocorax carbo (Linnaeus). Great Cormorant.

Pelecanus Carbo Linnaeus, 1758, Syst. Nat. (ed. 10) 1: 133. (in Europa = Sweden.)

Habitat.—Coastal Waters; nests mostly on cliffs; in winter, occasionally on large rivers slightly inland. In Old World, also breeds on rivers and lakes, and nests in trees.

Distribution.—*Breeds* [*carbo* group] in northeastern North America from the north shore of the Gulf of St. Lawrence in Quebec (Lake, Outer Wapitagun, Anticosti, Magdalen, and St. Mary islands) and southwestern Newfoundland (Guernsey Island, Coal River, and Port au Prince Peninsula) south to Prince Edward Island (Cape Tryon and East Point), Nova Scotia (south to Shelburne County, formerly south to the Bay of Fundy), and Maine (Isle au Haut), casually to Massachusetts; and in the Palearctic from southern Greenland, Iceland, the Faeroe Islands, northern Scandinavia, and the Kola Peninsula south to the Mediterranean and southern Europe, and across central Asia to Sakhalin, Japan, Taiwan, and China; and in New Guinea, Australia, and New Zealand.

Winters [*carbo* group] in North America in the breeding range and south regularly to South Carolina, casually to southern Florida, the Gulf coast (west to Mississippi), and Bermuda, and inland to Lake Ontario; and in the Old World from the breeding range south to the Canary Islands, Mediterranean and Black seas, Persian Gulf, India, the Malay Peninsula, Sumatra, the Philippines, and Bonin Islands; and generally in the breeding range in the Australian region.

Resident [*lucidus* group] in the Cape Verde Islands and Africa.

Accidental [*carbo* group] in West Virginia.

Notes.—Also known as Black Cormorant or Common Cormorant and, in Old World literature, as the Cormorant. Groups: *P. carbo* [Great Cormorant] and *P. lucidus* (Lichtenstein, 1823) [White-breasted Cormorant]. *Phalacrocorax carbo* and *P. capillatus* (Temminck and Schlegel, 1850), of Japan and Korea, constitute a superspecies (Dorst and Mougin *in* Mayr and Cottrell 1979).

Phalacrocorax urile (Gmelin). Red-faced Cormorant.

Pelecanus Urile Gmelin, 1789, Syst. Nat. 1(2): 575. Based on the "Red-faced Cor-vorant" Pennant, Arct. Zool. 2: 584, and the "Red-faced Shag" Latham, Gen. Synop. Birds 3(2): 601. (in Camtschatcae rupestribus maritimis = Kamchatka.)

Habitat.—Coastal Waters; nests on cliffs or steep slopes.

Distribution.—*Breeds* in the southern Bering Sea (in the Pribilofs, on Cape Peirce, and in the Walrus Islands), throughout the Aleutian Islands, and east along the Alaska coast to Prince William Sound; also in the Commander Islands and off Japan (Hokkaido).

Winters generally throughout the breeding range, occurring casually north to St. Michael in Norton Sound, Alaska, and south to southeastern Alaska (Sitka) and Japan (Honshu).

Accidental in British Columbia (Queen Charlotte Islands).

Notes.—Dorst and Mougin *in* Mayr and Cottrell (1979) considered *P. urile* and *P. pelagicus* to constitute a superspecies, but overlap in breeding distribution appears extensive.

Phalacrocorax pelagicus Pallas. Pelagic Cormorant.

Phalacrocorax pelagicus Pallas, 1811, Zoogr. Rosso-Asiat. 2: 303. (maris Camtschatici orientalis et Americanarum insularum incola = Aleutian Islands.)

Habitat.—Coastal Waters; nests on cliffs on islands and along rocky coasts.

Distribution.—*Breeds* from the southern Chukchi Sea (Cape Lisburne and Cape Thompson, Alaska) south through the Bering Sea to the Aleutian Islands, and along the Pacific coast of North America to northern Baja California (Los Coronados Islands), and from Wrangel Island east along the Arctic coast of Siberia to the Bering Strait, and south to northern Japan (Honshu).

Winters from the Aleutian Islands and southern Alaska south to central Baja California (casually to Cape San Lucas), and from Kamchatka south to China.

Casual north to northern Alaska (Point Barrow). Accidental in the northwestern Hawaiian Islands (Midway, Laysan) and inland California (Mono County).

Notes.—See comments under *P. urile.*

Family **ANHINGIDAE**: Darters

Genus *ANHINGA* Brisson

Anhinga Brisson, 1760, Ornithologie 1: 60; 6: 476. Type, by tautonymy, *Anhinga* Brisson = *Plotus anhinga* Linnaeus.

Anhinga anhinga (Linnaeus). Anhinga

Plotus anhinga Linnaeus, 1766, Syst. Nat. (ed. 12) 1: 218. Based on the "Anhinga" Marcgrave, Hist. Nat. Bras., p. 218, and Brisson, Ornithologie 6: 476. (in America australi = Rio Tapajós, Pará, Brazil.)

Habitat.—Fresh-water swamps, lakes, and sluggish streams at low elevations and, in tropical regions, around brackish lagoons and in mangroves; nests in trees (0–900 m; Tropical and Subtropical zones).

Distribution.—*Breeds* from central and eastern Texas, southeastern Oklahoma, southern and eastern Arkansas, southeastern Missouri (formerly), western Tennessee, southern Illinois (formerly), north-central Mississippi, southern Alabama, southern Georgia, and coastal North Carolina south to southern Florida, Cuba, and the Isle of Pines, and from Sinaloa and the Gulf coast south along both lowlands of Mexico and through Central America and South America (including Trinidad and Tobago) west of the Andes to Ecuador and east of the Andes to northern Argentina and Uruguay.

Winters from central South Carolina, southern Georgia, Florida, and the Gulf coast southward, being essentially resident in Cuba, the Isle of Pines, and Middle America and South America.

Casual north to northern California, Arizona, Colorado, Nebraska, Illinois, Wisconsin, southern Ontario, Ohio, New Jersey, and Maryland, and to the Florida Keys, Bahamas (Andros), Cayman Islands, Haiti, and Grenada; sight reports for Massachusetts.

Notes.—Also known as American Darter. The relationship of *A. anhinga* to the Old World forms *A. rufa* (Daudin, 1802) of Africa, *A. melanogaster* Pennant, 1769, of Southeast Asia, and *A. novaehollandiae* (Gould, 1847) of the Australian region, remains in doubt; all forms constitute a superspecies (Mayr and Short 1970; Dorst and Mougin *in* Mayr and Cottrell 1979).

Suborder FREGATAE: Frigatebirds

Family **FREGATIDAE**: Frigatebirds

Genus *FREGATA* Lacépède

Fregata Lacépède, 1799, Tabl. Mamm. Ois., p. 15. Type, by subsequent designation (Daudin, 1802), *Pelecanus aquilus* Linnaeus.

Fregata magnificens Mathews. Magnificent Frigatebird.

Fregata minor magnificens Mathews, 1914, Austral Avian Rec. 2: 20. (Barrington, Indefatigable, Albemarle Islands = Barrington Island, Galapagos.)

Habitat.—Coastal Waters, Pelagic Waters, Mangrove Forest; nests on islands in low trees and shrubs.

Distribution.—*Breeds* in the Revillagigedo Islands (San Benedicto), off Baja California (Santa Margarita Island), Nayarit (Isabela and the Tres Marietas islands), Oaxaca (Natartiac Island in Laguna Superior; near Punta Paloma in Mar Muerte), Honduras (Isla Pájaro in the Gulf of Fonseca), Costa Rica (Isla Bolaños), Panama (many islets in the Gulf of Chiriquí and Bay of Panama), and South America (Colombia, Ecuador, and the Galapagos Islands); in the Atlantic-Caribbean region in Florida (Dry Tortugas and, formerly, Marquesas Key), on the central coast of Texas (Aransas County, formerly) and the coast of Veracruz (Laguna de Tamiahua, Roca Partida), off the Yucatan Peninsula and Belize (Man-of-war Cay), widely in the Bahamas and Antilles (south to St. Kitts and east to Barbuda in the northern Lesser Antilles), in the Cayman (Little Cayman) and Swan (Little Swan) islands, on islands north of Venezuela (Los Hermanos and Margarita east to Tobago), in the Grenadines of the southern Lesser Antilles, and locally along the South American coast to southern Brazil; and in the Cape Verde Islands, off western Africa.

Ranges at sea along the Pacific coast from Baja California (rarely from northern California and casually from the Alaska Peninsula) south to northern Peru, north through the Gulf of California, and inland to the great lakes of Nicaragua, southeastern California (Salton Sea), and southern Arizona; throughout the Gulf of Mexico, Caribbean Sea, Bermuda (rarely), and western Atlantic from North Carolina (casually from New England and Nova Scotia) south to northern Argentina; and in the eastern Atlantic in the vicinity of the Cape Verde Islands.

Casual or accidental in the remainder of interior North America, mostly after storms, north to central California, Colorado, Minnesota, Wisconsin, Ontario, Quebec, and Newfoundland, and in the British Isles, continental Europe, and the Azores; a sight report for Michigan.

Fregata minor (Gmelin). Great Frigatebird.

Pelecanus minor Gmelin, 1789, Syst. Nat. 1(2): 572. Based mainly on the "Lesser Frigate" Latham, Gen. Synop. Birds 3(2): 590. (No locality given = Christmas Island, eastern Indian Ocean.)

Habitat.—Pelagic Waters; nests on islands in trees or on low vegetation.

Distribution.—*Breeds* on islands in the Pacific Ocean from the Revillagigedo Islands (San Benedicto), off Costa Rica (Cocos Island), in the Galapagos Islands, and from the Hawaiian Islands (Kure east to Niihau) and South China Sea south to northeastern Australia (Raine Island), the Fiji and Tuamotu islands, and Sala-y-Gomez Island (off Chile); in the South Atlantic on Trindade Island and Martín Vas Rocks (off Brazil); and in the Indian Ocean from Aldabra and the Seychelles east to Christmas Island.

Ranges at sea generally in the vicinity of the breeding areas, and occurring throughout the Hawaiian Islands, north to Japan and south to southeastern Australia and New Zealand; not certainly recorded (sight reports only) from the Pacific coast of North or South America.

Accidental in Oklahoma (Perry, 3 November 1975; Bull. Okla. Ornith. Soc. 1977: 9–10; DeBenedictis 1992, Tomer et al. 1996) and California (Farallon Islands, 14 March 1992; Heindel and Patten 1996).

Fregata ariel (Gray). Lesser Frigatebird.

> *Atagen Ariel* (Gould MS) G. R. Gray, 1845, Genera Birds 3: [669], col. pl. [185]. (No locality given = Raine Island, Queensland.)

Habitat.—Pelagic Waters; nests on islands primarily in low bushes or trees.

Distribution.—*Breeds* in the South Pacific off northern Australia (northwestern West Australia east to Raine Island, Queensland), in New Caledonia, and from the Howland, Line and Marquesas islands south to the Fiji, Tonga, and Tuamotu islands; in the South Atlantic at Trindade Island and Martín Vas Rocks, off Brazil; and in the western Indian Ocean in the Aldabra Islands.

Ranges widely at sea, especially in the Pacific Ocean, north regularly through Indonesia, the South China Sea and western Pacific to Korea, Japan, and Kamchatka, and casually to the northwestern Hawaiian Islands (Kure, French Frigate Shoals); also recorded in the South Atlantic not far from the breeding grounds, and in the Indian Ocean in the Mascarene Islands.

Accidental in Maine (Deer Island, Hancock County, 3 July 1960; Snyder 1961) and Siberia.

Notes.—Also known as Least Frigatebird.

Order **CICONIIFORMES**: Herons, Ibises, Storks, American Vultures, and Allies

Notes.—The monophyly of the Ciconiiformes, the relationships among the subgroups within it, and the relationships between this order and others are by no means clear. For a summary of these problems, see Sibley and Ahlquist (1972).

Suborder ARDEAE: Herons, Bitterns, and Allies

Family **ARDEIDAE**: Herons, Bitterns, and Allies

Notes.—Recent studies of genetic and vocal characters (Sheldon 1987, Sheldon et al. 1995, McCracken and Sheldon 1997) support the traditional arrangement used here in most ways; the relationships of *Butorides* might be with the Nycticoracini rather than the Ardeini.

Tribe BOTAURINI: Bitterns

Genus **BOTAURUS** Stephens

> *Botaurus* Stephens, 1819, *in* Shaw, Gen. Zool. 11(2): 592. Type, by subsequent designation (G. R. Gray, 1840), *Ardea stellaris* Linnaeus.

Botaurus pinnatus (Wagler). Pinnated Bittern.

> *Ardea pinnata* (Lichtenstein MS) Wagler, 1829, Isis von Oken, col. 662. (Bahia, Brazil.)

Habitat.—Freshwater Marshes (0–2600 m; Tropical to Temperate zones).

Distribution.—*Resident* locally in the lowlands of Middle America in southeastern Mexico (Veracruz, Tabasco, Yucatan Peninsula, Chiapas), Belize, El Salvador (Laguna Jocotal), Nicaragua (Managua, Río San Juan), and Costa Rica (Río Frío district, Guanacaste, Turrialba); and locally in South America in central Colombia and western Ecuador, and east of the Andes from southern Venezuela and the Guianas south to northern Argentina, Uruguay, and southern Brazil (generally absent from Amazonia).

Notes.—Sibley and Monroe (1990) considered *B. pinnatus* and *B. lentiginosus* to represent a superspecies. Mayr and Short (1970) considered all species in *Botaurus* to represent a superspecies.

Botaurus lentiginosus (Rackett). American Bittern.

> *Ardea lentiginosa* Rackett, 1813, in Pulteney, Cat. Birds Shells Plants Dorsetshire, ed. 2, p. 14. (Piddletown, Dorset, England.)

Habitat.—Fresh-water and brackish marshes, usually with tall vegetation.

Distribution.—*Breeds* from extreme southeastern Alaska, central interior British Columbia, southern Mackenzie, northern Manitoba, northern Ontario, central Quebec, and Newfoundland south locally to southern California, central Arizona (formerly), southern New Mexico, Texas, central Arkansas, central and western Tennessee, western Kentucky, central Ohio, southern Pennsylvania, northeastern West Virginia, eastern Maryland, and eastern Virginia; at least formerly also bred in Louisiana, Florida, Puebla, and México.

Winters from east-central British Columbia, western Washington, western Oregon, northern Nevada, northern and central Utah, northern Arizona, central New Mexico, northern Texas, the Gulf states and southern New England (casually farther north) south to southern Mexico and Cuba, rarely (or formerly) to Costa Rica and Panama, and to the Swan and Cayman islands, Greater Antilles (east to the Virgin Islands), Bahamas, and Bermuda.

Casual or accidental north to Keewatin and Labrador, south to the Lesser Antilles (Martinique), on Clipperton Island, and in Greenland, Iceland, the Faeroe Islands, British Isles, continental Europe, the Azores, and Canary Islands.

Notes.—See comments under *B. pinnatus*.

Genus *IXOBRYCHUS* Billberg

Ixobrychus Billberg, 1828, Synop. Faunae Scand. (ed. 2) 1(2): 166. Type, by subsequent designation (Stone, 1907), *Ardea minuta* Linnaeus.

Ixobrychus sinensis (Gmelin). Yellow Bittern.

Ardea Sinensis Gmelin, 1789, Syst. Nat. 1(2): 642. Based on the "Chinese Heron" Latham, Gen. Synop. Birds, 3(1): 99. (China.)

Habitat.—Tall emergent vegetation in marshes (0–3100 m).

Distribution.—*Breeds* in Asia and the Australasian region from India, China, and southeastern Siberia south to Indonesia, New Guinea, and the Solomon Islands, and *winters* in the southern portion of the breeding range.

Accidental in Alaska (Attu, in the Aleutian Islands, 17–22 May 1989, specimen; Gibson and Kessel 1992).

Notes.—Also known as Chinese Little Bittern or Chinese Bittern. See comments under *I. exilis*.

Ixobrychus exilis (Gmelin). Least Bittern.

Ardea exilis Gmelin, 1789, Syst. Nat. 1(2): 645. Based on the "Minute Bittern" Latham, Gen. Synop. Birds 3(1): 66. (in Jamaica.)

Habitat.—Tall emergent vegetation in marshes, primarily fresh-water, reedbeds, sedges, less commonly in coastal brackish marshes and mangrove swamps (Tropical to Temperate zones).

Distribution.—*Breeds* locally in western North America in southern Oregon, interior and southern coastal California, southern Arizona, and Baja California; in central and eastern North America from southern Manitoba, northeastern and south-central North Dakota, northwestern Minnesota, northern Wisconsin, northern Michigan, southern Ontario, extreme southern Quebec, eastern Maine, and southern New Brunswick south to western and southern Texas, the Gulf coast, Florida, the Greater Antilles, and probably on Grand Cayman in the Cayman Islands, and west to southern Montana (probably), Utah (rare), northeastern Colorado (local), and south-central New Mexico; in western Mexico from Sonora (Kino Bay) south to Guerrero; in eastern Mexico south to southern Veracruz; in Central America in Guatemala, Belize, El Salvador (Lake Olomega, Laguna El Ocotal), Honduras (Lake Yojoa, Copén), Nicaragua, Costa Rica (Guanacaste), Panama (Canal area), and probably elsewhere in Middle America; in the Lesser Antilles on Guadeloupe and Marie Galante, probably also Dominica; and in South America in northern Colombia, northern Venezuela, Trinidad, the Guianas, coastal Peru, northern Bolivia, Paraguay, eastern Brazil, and northern Argentina.

Winters from southern and (rarely) central California, southwestern Arizona, southern Texas, northern Florida (rarely the Gulf coast), and Bermuda (rarely, uncommon in migration) south throughout the Greater Antilles and Middle America through the breeding range in

South America. Breeding populations south of the United States are mostly sedentary; North American breeding birds winter as far south as Panama and Colombia.

Casual north to southern British Columbia, southern Saskatchewan, southern Quebec, and Newfoundland, and throughout most western states where breeding has not been verified. Accidental on Clipperton Island, Bermuda, Iceland, and the Azores.

Notes.—*Ixobrychus exilis, I. sinensis,* and *I. minutus* (Linnaeus, 1766), including the Australasian *I. novaezelandiae* (Potts, 1871) constitute a superspecies (Mayr and Short 1970; Payne *in* Mayr and Cottrell 1979). Vocal differences among Neotropical populations (Behrstock 1996) suggest that more than one species may be involved. The rare, dark color-morph of *I. exilis* was once considered a separate species, *I. neoxena* [Cory's Least Bittern] (see summary in Pittaway and Burke 1996).

Tribe TIGRISOMATINI: Tiger-Herons

Genus *TIGRISOMA* Swainson

Tigrisoma Swainson, 1827, Zool. J. 3: 362. Type, by original designation, *Ardea tigrina* "Latham" [= Gmelin] = *Ardea lineata* Boddaert.
Heterocnus Sharpe, 1895, Bull. Brit. Ornithol. Club 5: xiv. Type, by original designation, *Tigrisoma cabanisi* Heine = *Tigrisoma mexicana* Swainson.

Notes.—Members of this genus are sometimes known under the group name Tiger-Bittern.

Tigrisoma lineatum (Boddaert). Rufescent Tiger-Heron.

Ardea lineata Boddaert, 1783, Table Planches Enlum., p. 52. Based on "L'Onoré rayé, de Cayenne" Daubenton, Planches Enlum., p. 860. (Cayenne.)

Habitat.—Interior of shaded forests and along forest streams, wooded swamps, open marshes (South America only), less commonly in mangroves (0–1000 m; Tropical Zone).

Distribution.—*Resident* [*lineatum* group] in Middle America on the Caribbean slope of extreme eastern Honduras (Gracias a Dios), Nicaragua, Costa Rica, and Panama (east to San Blas, also on the Pacific slope in Darién), and in South America from Colombia, Venezuela, and Trinidad south, west of the Andes to western Ecuador, and east of the Andes to northeastern Bolivia and Amazonian Brazil; and [*marmoratum* group] in Bolivia (except northeastern), eastern and southern Brazil, Paraguay, Uruguay, and northern Argentina.

Reports from Chiapas and Guatemala are unsatisfactory.

Notes.—Groups: *T. lineatum* [Lineated Tiger-Heron] and *T. marmoratum* (Vieillot, 1817) [Banded Tiger-Heron].

Tigrisoma fasciatum (Such). Fasciated Tiger-Heron.

Ardea fasciata Such, 1825, Zool. J. 2: 117. (Brazil.)

Habitat.—Rivers, Streams, in hilly regions (0–2400 m; Tropical and lower Subtropical zones).

Distribution.—*Resident* in Costa Rica (Caribbean slope foothills of the Cordillera Central and Cordillera Talamanca) and Panama (primarily Caribbean slope from Bocas del Toro to San Blas, and in Darién); and in South America from Colombia and Venezuela south, west of the Andes to western Ecuador and east of the Andes to northern Argentina and southeastern Brazil.

Notes.—For use of *T. fasciatum* instead of *T. salmoni* Sclater and Salvin, 1875, see Eisenmann (1965).

Tigrisoma mexicanum Swainson. Bare-throated Tiger-Heron.

Tigrisoma mexicana Swainson, 1834, in Murray, Encycl. Geogr., p. 1383. (Real del Monte, [Hidalgo,] Mexico.)

Habitat.—Freshwater Marshes, Rivers, Streams (0–800 m; Tropical Zone).

Distribution.—*Resident* from southern Sonora, southern San Luis Potosí, and southern Tamaulipas south along both slopes of Middle America to eastern Panama (Pacific slope throughout, including the Pearl Islands, Isla Coiba, and several smaller islets; Caribbean slope in San Blas) and northwestern Colombia (lower Atrato Valley).

Notes.—Formerly placed in the monotypic genus *Heterocnus*.

Tribe ARDEINI: Typical Herons

Genus *ARDEA* Linnaeus

Ardea Linnaeus, 1758, Syst. Nat. (ed. 10) 1: 141. Type, by subsequent designation (G. R. Gray, 1840), *Ardea cinerea* Linnaeus.

Casmerodius Gloger, 1841, Gemein. Handb. und Hilfsb. Naturgesch., p. 412. Type, by subsequent designation (Salvadori, 1882), *Ardea egretta* Gmelin (= *Ardea alba* Linnaeus).

Notes.—Studies by Payne and Risley (1976) of skeletal characters, and by Sheldon (1987) and Sibley and Ahlquist (1990) of DNA-DNA hybridization indicate that *Casmerodius* should not be separated from *Ardea*.

Ardea herodias Linnaeus. Great Blue Heron.

Ardea Herodias Linnaeus, 1758, Syst. Nat. (ed. 10) 1: 143. Based mainly on "The Ash-colour'd Heron of North-America" Edwards, Nat. Hist. Birds 3: 135, pl. 135. (in America = Hudson Bay.)

Habitat.—Fresh-water, brackish, and (rarely) salt marshes, along lakes, rivers, and lagoons, and mangroves; in winter also on seacoasts, shorelines of bays, and mudflats (0–2500 m; Tropical to Temperate zones).

Distribution.—*Breeds* [*herodias* group] from south-coastal and southeastern Alaska (west to Prince William Sound), coastal and southern interior British Columbia, northern Alberta, central Saskatchewan, northern Manitoba, northern Ontario, southern Quebec (Gaspé Peninsula), New Brunswick, Prince Edward Island, and Nova Scotia south, at least locally, throughout the United States and much of lowland Mexico to Nayarit, Tabasco, the Gulf coast, and interior southern Florida, also in the Galapagos Islands; and [*occidentalis* group] in southern coastal Florida (from Florida Keys north to the Tampa area and Key Biscayne), Cuba, the Isle of Pines, St. Thomas, Anegada (possibly), the coast of the Yucatan Peninsula, and Los Roques off the northern coast of Venezuela, with probable breeding elsewhere in the Greater Antilles and on other islands off Venezuela.

Winters [*herodias* group] from south-coastal and southeastern Alaska, the coast of British Columbia and Washington, Idaho, western and central Montana, northern Wyoming, central Nebraska, central Missouri, central Wisconsin (rarely), southern Michigan, the Ohio Valley, southern Ontario, and the southern New England coast (casually farther north) south throughout the southern United States, Middle America, Bermuda, and the West Indies to northern Colombia, northern Venezuela, and (rarely) to western Ecuador and the Galapagos Islands; and [*occidentalis* group] primarily in the vicinity of the breeding range and along the coasts of Venezuela and on islands offshore (east to Tobago and Trinidad).

Wanders widely [*herodias* group] west to Cook Inlet, Alaska, and north to the Arctic coast of Alaska (casually), southern Yukon, northern British Columbia, the Revillagigedo Islands, southern Keewatin, Hudson Bay (rarely), northern Quebec, Anticosti Island, and Newfoundland; and [*occidentalis* group] north in peninsular Florida and casually along the Gulf coast west to Texas and the Atlantic coast to North Carolina, and in the Bahamas. Casual or accidental [*herodias* group] in the Hawaiian Islands (from Kauai to Hawaii), northwestern Alaska (Wainwright), Clipperton Island, Greenland, the Azores, and Spain; and [*occidentalis* group] in Pennsylvania.

Notes.—The white and mixed white and blue forms have often been considered as a separate species, *A. occidentalis* Audubon, 1835 [Great White Heron], but are now generally regarded as being conspecific with *A. herodias* (Mayr 1956, Meyerriecks 1957); a juvenal white morph in an all-blue colony was discovered in Texas (McHenry and Dyes 1983).

Ardea cinerea, A. cocoi, and *A. herodias* constitute a superspecies (Payne *in* Mayr and Cottrell 1979).

Ardea cinerea Linnaeus. Gray Heron.

> *Ardea cinerea* Linnaeus, 1758, Syst. Nat. (ed. 10) 1: 143. (in Europa = Sweden.)

Habitat.—*Breeds* in habitats similar to those of *A. herodias* .

Distribution.—*Breeds* from the British Isles and Scandinavia east to Sakhalin and through-out much of Eurasia south locally to South Africa and the East Indies, wandering within this range after the breeding season.

Casual in Greenland, the Lesser Antilles (Montserrat, Martinique, Barbados), Trinidad, French Guiana, and Amazonian Brazil.

Notes.—Known in Old World literature as the Heron. See comments under *A. herodias.*

Ardea cocoi Linnaeus. Cocoi Heron.

> *Ardea Cocoi* Linnaeus, 1766, Syst. Nat. (ed. 12) 1: 237. Based in part on "Le Herón hupé de Cayenne" Brisson, Ornithologie 5: 400. (in Cayana = Cayenne.)

Habitat.—Freshwater Marshes, Freshwater Lakes and Ponds, Rivers (0–900 m; Tropical to Temperate zones).

Distribution.—*Resident* in eastern Panama (eastern Panamá province and eastern Darién) and throughout lowland South America (including Trinidad) south to southern Chile and southern Argentina.

Casual in central Panama (west to the Canal area). Accidental in the Falkland Islands.

Notes.—Also known as White-necked Heron. See comments under *A. herodias.*

Ardea alba (Linnaeus). Great Egret.

> *Ardea alba* Linnaeus, 1758, Syst. Nat. (ed. 10) 1: 144. (in Europa = Sweden.)

Habitat.—Marshes, swampy woods, tidal estuaries, lagoons, mangroves, and along streams; in winter, also in roadside ditches, canals, and wet fields (0–1500 m; Tropical to Temperate zones).

Distribution.—*Breeds* in North America locally from central Washington, southern Oregon, and southern Idaho south through California, Nevada, and southwestern Arizona, and from southeastern Saskatchewan (rarely), southwestern Manitoba, South Dakota, central Minnesota, western and southern Wisconsin, northwestern and southern Michigan, northern Ohio, southern Ontario, southwestern Quebec (Dickerson Island), and New England south through the Gulf states, west locally to eastern Colorado, southern New Mexico, and south-central Texas, along both slopes of Mexico (also locally in the interior), and through the Bahamas, Antilles, Middle America and South America to southern Chile and southern Argentina, also the Galapagos Islands; in the Old World from central Europe east to Us-suriland and Japan, and south to Turkey, Iran, India, China, most of Southeast Asia, the East Indies, the Philippines, New Guinea, Australia, and New Zealand; and locally in Africa south of the Sahara and in Madagascar.

Winters in North America from coastal Oregon, northern California, central Nevada, central Utah, central New Mexico, central Texas, the Gulf coast region, coastal Maryland, and Bermuda (rarely) south throughout Mexico and the remainder of the breeding range in the Americas to the Straits of Magellan (casually the Falkland Islands); in the Old World from the Mediterranean coast of Africa, the Red Sea, Persian Gulf, central India, China, Korea, and Japan south through the breeding range in Southeast Asia to Australia and New Zealand; and in the breeding range in Africa and Madagascar.

Wanders north irregularly in North America to northwestern and central British Columbia, southern Alberta, southern Saskatchewan, southeastern Manitoba, south-coastal and eastern Quebec, Maine, and Newfoundland, casually to southern Alaska (west to Kodiak Island) and South Georgia; and in Europe to the British Isles, Scandinavia, and the Baltic states, casually to the Revillagigedo Islands (Socorro Island), Clipperton Island, the Canary Islands, and southern Africa.

Accidental in the Hawaiian Islands (Oahu, Maui).

Notes.—Formerly placed in the monotypic genus *Casmerodius*; placed by some authors (e.g., Blake 1977) in *Egretta*. Also known as Common Egret or American Egret and, in Old World literature, as Great White Heron.

Genus *EGRETTA* Forster

Egretta T. Forster, 1817, Synop. Cat. Brit. Birds, p. 59. Type, by monotypy, *Ardea garzetta* Linnaeus.

Demigretta Blyth, 1846, J. Asiat. Soc. Bengal. 15: 372. Type, by monotypy, *Demigretta concolor* Blyth = *Ardea sacra* Gmelin.

Florida Baird, 1858, in Baird, Cassin, and Lawrence, Rep. Explor. Surv. R. R. Pac. 9: xxi, xlv, 659, 671. Type, by monotypy, *Ardea caerulea* Linnaeus.

Hydranassa Baird, 1858, in Baird, Cassin, and Lawrence, Rep. Explor. Surv. R. R. Pac. 9: 660. Type, by original designation, *Ardea ludoviciana* Wilson = *Egretta ruficollis* Gosse = *Ardea tricolor* Müller.

Dichromanassa Ridgway, 1878, Bull. U. S. Geol. Geogr. Surv. Terr. 4: 224, 246. Type, by original designation, *Ardea rufa* Boddaert = *Ardea rufescens* Gmelin.

Leucophoyx Sharpe, 1894, Bull. Brit. Ornithol. Club 3: xxxix. Type, by original designation, *Ardea candidissima* Gmelin = *Ardea thula* Molina.

Egretta eulophotes (Swinhoe). Chinese Egret.

Herodias eulophotes Swinhoe, 1860, Ibis, p. 64. (Amoy, China.)

Habitat.—Shallow tidal estuaries, mudflats, bays.

Distribution.—Formerly bred from the mouth of the Amur River south along the coast of Asia to at least Hong Kong. Now drastically reduced in numbers, with breeding colonies in North Korea, South Korea, Shandong, and Hebei provinces in China, and possibly between the Amur River delta and Vladivostock and other parts of its former range.

Winters from the Malay Peninsula east to the Philippines and Sulawesi. Wanders widely from northern Japan southward, accidentally to Christmas Island (Indian Ocean).

Accidental in Alaska (Agattu Island in the Aleutians, 16 June 1974; Byrd et al. 1978).

Egretta garzetta (Linnaeus). Little Egret.

Ardea Garzetta Linnaeus, 1766, Syst. Nat. (ed. 12) 1: 237. (in Oriente = northeastern Italy.)

Habitat.—Marshy areas.

Distribution.—*Breeds* locally in southern Europe, Africa, Madagascar, and from Southeast Asia and Japan south to Australia and New Guinea.

Winters principally in Southeast Asia and the African and Australian regions.

Accidental in Quebec (Cacouna area), Newfoundland, Nova Scotia (Bon Portage Island), New Hampshire (Rye), Massachusetts (Plum Island, Nantucket), Virginia (Chincoteague), Bermuda, Puerto Rico (Culebra Island), St. Lucia, Martinique, Trinidad, and Surinam.

Notes.—*Egretta garzetta, E. gularis, E. dimorpha* Hartert, 1914, and *E. thula* appear to constitute a superspecies (Payne *in* Mayr and Cottrell 1979, Sibley and Monroe 1990).

Egretta gularis (Bosc). Western Reef-Heron.

Ardea gularis Bosc, 1792, Actes Soc. Hist. Nat. Paris 1: 4., pl. 2. (Senegal River.)

Habitat—Seacoasts, estuaries, and mudflats.

Distribution.—[*gularis* group] western Africa from Mauritania to Nigeria, ranging (at least casually) north to the Azores, Cape Verde Islands, and Spain, and south to Gabon; and [*schistacea* group] from the Red Sea and Persian Gulf to western India, ranging to southern India and Sri Lanka.

Accidental in Massachusetts (Nantucket, 12 April-September 1983, numerous observers and photos, dark-morph bird identifiable to *gularis;* Cardillo et al. 1983); in addition, several birds have been reported from Barbados, presumably also representing the *gularis* group

(1984, Amer. Birds 38: 361, 969; Smith and Hutt 1984), and Tobago. Sight reports for St. Lucia and Trinidad.

Notes.—Groups: *E. gularis* [Western Reef-Heron] and *E. schistacea* (Ehrenberg, 1828) [Indian Reef-Heron]. Individuals that escaped from captivity in Europe and had been considered as a possible source of the Massachusetts vagrant (1983, Amer. Birds 37: 1032) were *schistacea,* not *gularis.* This species was formerly placed in the genus *Demigretta.*(e.g., Peters 1931). See comments under *E. garzetta.*

Egretta thula (Molina). Snowy Egret.

Ardea Thula Molina, 1782, Saggio Stor. Nat. Chili, p. 235. (Chili = Chile.)

Habitat.—Marshes, lakes, ponds, lagoons, mangroves, and shallow coastal habitats (0–1500 m; Tropical to Temperate zones).

Distribution.—*Breeds* from eastern Oregon, northern California, northern Nevada, southeastern Idaho, Montana, North Dakota, South Dakota, central Kansas, central Oklahoma, Arkansas, southeastern Missouri, northeastern Wisconsin, southern Illinois, southern Ontario, northwestern Ohio, and the Gulf and Atlantic coasts (north to Maine) south, primarily in coastal lowlands (locally in the interior) through the United States, Greater Antilles, Cayman Islands, Middle America, and South America to southern Chile and central Argentina.

Winters from western Oregon (rarely), northern California, southwestern Arizona, Mexico, the Gulf coast, and coastal South Carolina south throughout the breeding range in the West Indies, Middle America, and South America.

Wanders irregularly north to southwestern British Columbia, southern Alberta, southern Saskatchewan, southern Manitoba, northern Ontario, southern Quebec, Nova Scotia, and Newfoundland; also to the Hawaiian Islands (Oahu, Maui, Hawaii), Bahamas, and throughout the Lesser Antilles, regularly to Bermuda, uncommonly to the Galapagos Islands. Accidental in Iceland and in the Revillagigedo Islands (Socorro Island; sight report), on Clipperton Island, Tristan da Cunha, and South Georgia; a sight report for southeastern Alaska.

Notes.—This species was formerly placed in the monotypic genus *Leucophoyx.* See comments under *E. garzetta.*

Egretta caerulea (Linnaeus). Little Blue Heron.

Ardea cærulea Linnaeus, 1758, Syst. Nat. (ed. 10) 1: 143. Based mainly on "The Blew Heron" Catesby, Nat. Hist. Carolina 1: 76, pl. 76. (in America septentrionali = South Carolina.)

Habitat.—Swamps, marshes, ponds, lakes, meadows, streams, and mangroves; primarily in fresh-water habitats (0–1500 m; Tropical to Temperate zones).

Distribution.—*Breeds* locally from southern California (rarely; since 1979), Baja California, southern Sonora, southern New Mexico (rarely), south-central Colorado (once), north-central Texas, central Oklahoma, central Kansas, southeastern Missouri, southern Illinois, west-central Indiana, northwestern Ohio, northern Alabama, southern Georgia, and the Atlantic coast (north to Maine), and south along both slopes of Mexico (also in the interior in Jalisco and Guanajuato) and Middle America, through the Gulf coast region and West Indies, and in South America (including Tobago and Trinidad) from Colombia, Venezuela, and the Guianas west of the Andes to central Peru and east of the Andes (mostly coastal lowlands) to eastern Bolivia, central Brazil, and Uruguay; also sporadically in North Dakota, South Dakota, and central Minnesota.

Winters from southwestern California, southern Sonora, the Gulf coast, and coastal Virginia south throughout most of the breeding range and South America (to northern Chile).

Wanders irregularly north to northern California, Oregon, southeastern Saskatchewan, southern Manitoba, northern Ontario, southern Quebec, southern Labrador, Newfoundland, and Nova Scotia. Casual or accidental in the Hawaiian Islands (Oahu), southwestern British Columbia, Washington, Idaho, Montana, Utah, Chile, western Greenland, and the Azores.

Notes.—This species was formerly placed in the monotypic genus *Florida.*

Egretta tricolor (Müller). Tricolored Heron.

Ardea tricolor P. L. S. Müller, 1776, Natursyst., Suppl., p. 111. Based on "La Demi-Aigrette" Buffon, Hist. Nat. Ois. 7: 378, and "Herón bleuâtre a ventre blanc, de Cayenne" Daubenton, Planches Enlum., pl. 350. (America = Cayenne.)

Habitat.—Primarily coastal marshes, but also locally inland in swamps, lakes, and rivers, especially near coast (0–700 m; Tropical and Subtropical zones).

Distribution.—*Breeds* from southern Sonora, southeastern New Mexico, north-central and northeastern Texas, southern Arkansas, the Gulf states, and the Atlantic coast (north to southern Maine) south along both slopes of Middle America (including Baja California) and South America (including interior) to central Peru and northeastern Brazil; and in the Bahamas, Greater Antilles (east to St. Thomas and St. Croix), and on Providencia and San Andrés islands in the western Caribbean Sea. Casual or rare breeding inland in North Dakota, South Dakota, and central Kansas.

Winters from Baja California, southern Sonora, southeastern Texas, the Gulf coast, and the Atlantic coast (north to New Jersey, casually farther) south through the remainder of the breeding range.

Wanders irregularly (or casually) north to California, Oregon, Utah, southern New Mexico, Colorado and, east of the Rockies, to southern Manitoba, northern Minnesota, northern Wisconsin, northern Michigan, Ontario, southern Quebec, southern New Brunswick, Nova Scotia, and Newfoundland, also to the Lesser Antilles (south to Barbados); a sight report for Socorro Island; accidental in the Azores.

Notes.—Also known as Louisiana Heron. This species was formerly placed in the monotypic genus *Hydranassa.*

Egretta rufescens (Gmelin). Reddish Egret.

Ardea rufescens Gmelin, 1789, Syst. Nat. 1(2): 628. Based on "Aigrette rousse" Buffon, Hist. Nat. Ois. 7: 378, and "L'Aigrette rousse, de la Louisiane" Daubenton, Planches Enlum., pl. 902. (in Louisiana.)

Habitat.—Brackish marshes, sandy beaches, and other shallow coastal habitats; suitable nesting habitat requires low trees, primarily red mangrove, for nest sites (Tropical Zone).

Distribution.—*Breeds* in Baja California (north to San Quintín on the Pacific coast and Isla San Luis in the Gulf of California), and along the coast of Sonora (Tobari Bay), Sinaloa (Isla Las Tunas), and Oaxaca (Mar Muerto); along the Gulf coast of Texas (Cameron to Chambers counties), Louisiana (vicinity of Chandeleur Sound), and Alabama (Cat Island); in southern Florida (north to Merritt Island and the Tampa area), the northwestern Bahamas (Grand Bahama, Abaco, Andros, and Great Inagua), Cuba, the Isle of Pines, and Hispaniola (formerly Jamaica); and on the coast of the Yucatan Peninsula (including offshore islands) and in northern Belize.

Winters primarily in the breeding range, north regularly (but rarely) to southwestern (casually central coastal) California; along the Gulf coast (from Texas to Florida) and Georgia (casually north to Delaware); and south along the Pacific coast to Costa Rica, and in the Caribbean to Belize, the Cayman Islands, Puerto Rico, the Virgin Islands, and the northern coast of Venezuela (also the Netherlands Antilles east to Margarita Island).

Casual inland, generally as postbreeding wanderers, north to Nevada, central Arizona, southern Colorado, western and central Texas, northwestern South Carolina, and Kentucky, and to Massachusetts, San Luis Potosí, Costa Rica (Caribbean coast), and Isla Coiba (off Panama); a sight report for New York. Accidental to Iowa, southeastern Illinois, northwestern Indiana, and southeastern Michigan (all fall 1993; 1994, Amer. Birds 48(1): 111, 114, 159).

Notes.—This species was formerly placed in the monotypic genus *Dichromanassa.*

Genus *BUBULCUS* Bonaparte

Bubulcus (Pucheran MS) Bonaparte, 1855, C. R. Acad. Sci. Paris 40: 722. Type, by subsequent designation (G. R. Gray, 1871), *Ardea ibis* "Hasselquist" [= Linnaeus].

Notes.—By some merged in the Old World genus *Ardeola* Boie, 1822, or in *Egretta* (e.g., Payne *in* Mayr and Cottrell 1979); affinities remain uncertain (Sheldon 1987).

Bubulcus ibis (Linnaeus). Cattle Egret.

> *Ardea Ibis* Linnaeus, 1758, Syst. Nat.(ed. 10) 1: 144. Based on *Ardea Ibis* Hasselquist,
> Iter Palaestinum, p. 248. (in Ægypto = Egypt.)

Habitat.—Primarily pastures, especially where cattle or horses are actively grazing, lawns, and roadsides; occasionally in flooded fields and marshes; requires low trees and bushes for nest sites (Tropical to Temperate zones).

Distribution.—*Breeds* [*ibis* group] in the Western Hemisphere locally from central (casually northwestern) California, eastern Oregon, southern Idaho, northern Utah, Colorado, North Dakota, southern Saskatchewan (rarely), Minnesota, Wisconsin, southern Michigan, southern Ontario, northern Ohio, eastern Pennsylvania, and Maine south, primarily in coastal lowlands (very scattered inland localities) through Middle America, the Gulf and Atlantic states, West Indies, and South America (including Tobago, Trinidad, and the Galapagos Islands) to northern Chile and northern Argentina, and in southern Europe from the Mediterranean region east to the Caspian Sea, and south throughout most of Africa (except the Sahara), including Madagascar and islands in the Indian Ocean; and [*coromanda* group] in Southeast Asia from India east to eastern China, Japan, and the Ryukyu Islands, and south throughout the Philippines and East Indies to New Guinea and Australia.

Winters [*ibis* group] in the Americas through much of the breeding range from western Oregon, northern California, coastal Texas, the Gulf states, and Florida south through the West Indies, Middle America, and South America; frequent vagrant to Bermuda; and in the Old World from southern Spain and northern Africa south and east through the remainder of the breeding range in Africa and southwestern Asia; and [*coromanda* group] from southern Asia and the Philippines south throughout Indonesia and the Australian region.

Wanders [*ibis* group] to Clipperton Island and South Georgia, and north, at least casually, to southeastern Alaska, northern Mackenzie, southern Canada (from British Columbia east to Nova Scotia and Newfoundland); also to Eurasia north to Iceland, the British Isles, continental Europe, and the eastern Atlantic islands; and [*coromanda* group] to Johnston Island, Micronesia (east to Pohnpei), and New Caledonia; accidental [*coromanda* group] in Alaska (Agattu, in the Aleutians, 19 June 1988; Gibson and Kessel 1992).

Introduced [*ibis* group] (in 1959) and established on most of the larger Hawaiian Islands, wandering to French Frigate Shoals and Midway.

Notes.—Also known as Buff-backed Heron. Groups: *B. ibis* [Common Cattle-Egret] and *B. coromanda* (Boddaert, 1783) [Eastern Cattle-Egret]. This species apparently spread to the New World (Guianas in South America) in the late 1870's, reaching Florida by the early 1940's; the range is still expanding.

Genus *BUTORIDES* Blyth

> *Butorides* Blyth, 1852, Cat. Birds Mus. Asiat. Soc. (1849), p. 281. Type, by monotypy,
> *Ardea javanica* Horsfield = *Ardea striata* Linnaeus.

Notes.—Sometimes merged with the Old World *Ardeola* Boie, 1822 (e.g., Payne *in* Mayr and Cottrell 1979).

Butorides virescens (Linnaeus). Green Heron.

> *Ardea virescens* Linnaeus, 1758, Syst. Nat. (ed. 10) 1: 144. Based on "The small
> Bittern," *Ardea stellata minima* Catesby, Nat. Hist. Carolina, 4: 80, pl. 80. (America
> = coast of South Carolina.)

Habitat.—Primarily wooded wetlands, especially swamps, ponds, rivers, lakes, lagoons, marshes, and mangroves (Tropical to Temperate zones).

Distribution.—*Breeds* from extreme southwestern British Columbia (including southeastern Vancouver Island), western Washington, western Oregon, northern California, west-central and southern Nevada, southern Idaho (probably), southern Utah, western and central Arizona, north-central New Mexico, the western edge of the Great Plains states (north to eastern Colorado, eastern North Dakota, eastern South Dakota), southern Manitoba, northern Wisconsin, northern Michigan, southern Ontario, southern Quebec, and southern New Brunswick south through Middle America, the eastern United States and West Indies to eastern

Panama (including the Pearl Islands), islands off the north coast of Venezuela (Aruba east to La Tortuga and Blanquilla), and Tobago.

Winters from southwestern British Columbia, coastal and southeastern California, southern Arizona, southern Texas, the Gulf states (casually Tennessee), northern Florida, South Carolina, and Bermuda (rarely, regular on migration) south throughout the breeding range (also in the Bahama Islands) to northern Colombia and northern Venezuela.

Wanders north to southeastern Alaska, southern and eastern British Columbia, eastern Washington, Idaho, southern Alberta, southern Saskatchewan, central Ontario, Nova Scotia, and southwestern Newfoundland, on Clipperton Island, and south to Surinam. Accidental in the Hawaiian Islands, Greenland, England, and the Azores.

Notes.—See comments under *B. striatus*.

Butorides striatus (Linnaeus). Striated Heron.

Ardea striata Linnaeus, 1758, Syst. Nat. (ed. 10) 1: 144. (in Surinami = Surinam.)

Habitat.—Freshwater Marshes, Saltwater/Brackish Marshes, Mangrove Forest, Rivers, Streams (0–1900 m; Tropical to Temperate zones).

Distribution.—*Resident* in the Americas from eastern Panama (eastern Panamá province and Darién), Colombia, Venezuela (including Margarita Island), and Trinidad south to southern Peru, Chile (rarely), central Argentina and Uruguay, also in the Galapagos Islands; and in the Old World from the Red Sea to the Gulf of Aden, in Africa south of the Sahara, on islands in the Indian Ocean, and from northern China, the Amur Valley and Japan (northern populations in eastern Asia are migratory) south throughout Southeast Asia, the East Indies and Philippines to Australia and southern Polynesia.

Wanders north to Costa Rica (Guanacaste, Cocos Island) and St. Vincent (Lesser Antilles).

Notes.—*Butorides virescens* was considered conspecific with *B. striatus* (A.O.U. 1983) because intermediate specimens have been reported (Payne 1974); however, hybridization in zones of contact is limited without demonstrated introgression, and no mixed pairings are known (Monroe and Browning 1992). When the two species are considered conspecific, Green-backed Heron, Striated Heron, or Little Heron have been used as the English name. *Butorides sundevalli* (Reichenow, 1877) of the Galapagos Islands is sometimes considered conspecific with *striatus* (e.g., Payne *in* Mayr and Cottrell 1979).

Genus *AGAMIA* Reichenbach

Agamia Reichenbach, 1853, Avium Syst. Nat. (1852), p. xvi. Type, by original designation, *Agamia picta* Reichenbach = *Ardea agami* Gmelin.

Agamia agami (Gmelin). Agami Heron.

Ardea Agami Gmelin, 1789, Syst. Nat. 1(2): 629. Based on "Agami" Buffon, Hist. Nat. Ois., 7, p. 382, and "Le Heron Agami de Cayenne" Daubenton, Planches Enlum., pl. 859. (in Cayanna = Cayenne.)

Habitat.—River-edge Forest, Gallery Forest, Freshwater Lakes and Ponds (0–600 m; Tropical, occasionally to Subtropical and lower Temperate zones).

Distribution.—*Resident* locally from southern Veracruz, Tabasco, Chiapas (including Pacific coast), southern Campeche, and Quintana Roo south through eastern Guatemala (Petén), Belize, northern Honduras (La Ceiba), Costa Rica, and Panama (not recorded Nicaragua), and in South America from Colombia, Venezuela, Trinidad, and the Guianas south, west of the Andes to northwestern Ecuador and east of the Andes to central Bolivia and Amazonian Brazil.

Casual in Nuevo León (Contreras B. 1988, a specimen record, contra Howell and Webb 1995).

Notes.—Also known as Chestnut-bellied Heron.

Genus *PILHERODIUS* Bonaparte

Pilherodius Bonaparte, 1855, Consp. Gen. Avium 2(1857): 139. Type, by monotypy, *Ardea alba* var. ß Gmelin = *Ardea pileata* Boddaert.

Pilherodius pileatus (Boddaert). Capped Heron.

Ardea pileata Boddaert, 1783, Table Planches Enlum., p. 54. Based on "Heron blanc, hupé de Cayenne" Daubenton, Planches Enlum., pl. 907. (Cayenne.)

Habitat.—Freshwater Marshes, Freshwater Lakes and Ponds, Rivers (0–900 m; Tropical Zone).

Distribution.—*Resident* from eastern Panama (primarily in Darién but recorded west to Canal area), Colombia, Venezuela, and the Guianas south, east of the Andes, to central Bolivia, northern Paraguay, and eastern Brazil (to Santa Catarina).

Tribe NYCTICORACINI: Night-Herons

Genus *NYCTICORAX* Forster

Nycticorax T. Forster, 1817, Synop. Cat. Brit. Birds, p. 59. Type, by tautonymy, *Nycticorax infaustus* Forster = *Ardea nycticorax* Linnaeus.

Nycticorax nycticorax (Linnaeus). Black-crowned Night-Heron.

Ardea Nycticorax Linnaeus, 1758, Syst. Nat. (ed. 10) 1: 142. (in Europa australi = southern Europe.)

Habitat.—Marshes, swamps, ponds, lakes, rivers, streams, lagoons, and mangroves (0–440 m; Tropical to Temperate zones).

Distribution.—*Breeds* in the Western Hemisphere from extreme southwestern British Columbia (Reifel Island), central Washington, southern Idaho, Montana, east-central Alberta, central Saskatchewan, southern Manitoba, northwestern and central Minnesota, central Wisconsin, northern Michigan, southern Ontario, southern Quebec, northeastern New Brunswick, and Nova Scotia south locally through the United States, Middle America, the Bahamas, Greater Antilles, and South America to Tierra del Fuego and the Falkland Islands; and in the Old World from the Netherlands, central and southern Europe and northwestern Africa east to south-central Russia, and south locally through East and South Africa, on Madagascar, and from Asia Minor east across Southeast Asia to eastern China and Japan, and south to the Philippines and East Indies.

Winters in the Western Hemisphere from western Washington, southern Oregon, southern Nevada, northern Utah, Colorado, southern Texas, the southern Great Lakes and southern New England (casually farther north) south throughout the breeding range, becoming more widespread in winter (including Bermuda, Cayman Islands, and through the Lesser Antilles); and in the Old World in Africa south of the Sahara (most European populations), and from Asia Minor across Southeast Asia to Japan, and southward.

Resident in the Pacific from the Hawaiian Islands (west to Niihau) south locally through the islands of Polynesia.

Wanders north in North America to southern British Columbia, northern Wisconsin, central Ontario, central Quebec, and Newfoundland; and in Europe to Iceland, the Faeroe Islands, British Isles, Scandinavia, and the eastern Atlantic islands. Casual in the western Hawaiian Islands (Kure, Midway), southern Alaska (St. Paul Island in the Pribilofs; Attu, Shemya, and Atka in the Aleutians; and at Juneau), Clipperton Island, and Greenland.

Notes.—Also known as Night Heron in European literature. *Nycticorax nycticorax* and *N. caledonicus* (Gmelin, 1789), of Polynesia and the Australian region, constitute a superspecies (Mayr and Short 1970; Payne *in* Mayr and Cottrell 1979).

Genus *NYCTANASSA* Stejneger

Nyctanassa Stejneger, 1887, Proc. U. S. Natl. Mus. 10: 295, note. Type, by original designation, *Ardea violacea* Linnaeus.

Nyctanassa violacea (Linnaeus). Yellow-crowned Night-Heron.

Ardea violacea Linnaeus, 1758, Syst. Nat. (ed. 10) 1: 143. Based on "The Crested Bittern" Catesby, Nat. Hist. Carolina 1: 79, pl. 79. (in America septentrionali = South Carolina.)

Habitat.—Primarily wooded wetlands, especially swamps, lakes, lagoons, and mangroves; sometimes nests in wooded suburbs (Tropical to lower Temperate zones).

Distribution.—*Breeds* from central Baja California (both slopes), central Sonora, central and northeastern Texas, central Oklahoma, east-central Colorado (rarely), Kansas, southeastern Nebraska, southern and eastern Iowa, southeastern Minnesota, southern Wisconsin, southern Michigan, the lower Ohio Valley, eastern Tennessee, southeastern Pennsylvania, Massachusetts, and southern Maine (rarely) south along both slopes of Mexico, the Gulf coast, Bahamas, Antilles, Middle America (including Socorro Island in the Revillagigedo Islands and Isla María Madre in the Tres Marías Islands), and South America (including the Galapagos Islands) on the Pacific coast to extreme northern Peru and on the Caribbean-Atlantic coast to eastern Brazil.

Winters from central Baja California, central Sonora, the Gulf coast (locally), and coastal South Carolina south throughout the remainder of the breeding range.

Introduced and breeding in Bermuda (since 1979), where formerly considered casual.

Wanders, at least casually, north as far as central California, southern Arizona, southern New Mexico, Montana, North Dakota, southern Saskatchewan, southern Manitoba, southern Ontario, southern Quebec, southern New Brunswick, Newfoundland, and Nova Scotia, and to Clipperton Island.

Notes.—This species was placed in the genus *Nycticorax* in the 6th edition but was subsequently (A.O.U. 1989: 533) treated in *Nyctanassa,* based on Sheldon (1987).

Tribe COCHLEARIINI: Boat-billed Herons

Genus *COCHLEARIUS* Brisson

Cochlearius Brisson, 1760, Ornithologie 1: 48; 5: 506. Type, by tautonymy, *Cochlearius* Brisson = *Cancroma cochlearia* Linnaeus.

Cochlearius cochlearius (Linnaeus). Boat-billed Heron.

Cancroma Cochlearia Linnaeus, 1766, Syst. Nat. (ed. 12) 1: 233. Based on "La Cuillière" Brisson, Ornithologie 5: 506. (in Guiana = Cayenne.)

Habitat.—Freshwater Lakes and Ponds, Rivers, Mangrove Forest (0–800 m; Tropical Zone).

Distribution.—*Resident* [*zeledoni* group] from Sinaloa in the Pacific lowlands and Tamaulipas in the Gulf-Caribbean lowlands south through Middle America (including islands off the Yucatan Peninsula) to El Salvador (at least formerly) and northern Honduras; and [*cochlearius* group] in Costa Rica, Panama, and South America from Colombia, Venezuela, Trinidad, and the Guianas south, west of the Andes to western Ecuador and east of the Andes to central Bolivia, northeastern Argentina and eastern Brazil.

Notes.—Groups: *C. zeledoni* (Ridgway, 1885) [Northern Boat-billed Heron] and *C. cochlearius* [Southern Boat-billed Heron].

Suborder THRESKIORNITHES: Ibises and Spoonbills

Family **THRESKIORNITHIDAE**: Ibises and Spoonbills

Subfamily THRESKIORNITHINAE: Ibises

Genus *EUDOCIMUS* Wagler

Eudocimus Wagler, 1832, Isis von Oken, col. 1232. Type, by subsequent designation (Reichenow, 1877), *Scolopax rubra* Linnaeus.

Eudocimus albus (Linnaeus). White Ibis.

Scolopax alba Linnaeus, 1758, Syst. Nat. (ed. 10) 1: 145. Based on "The White Curlew" Catesby, Nat. Hist. Carolina 1: 82, pl. 82. (in America· = South Carolina.)

Habitat.—Marshes, mangroves, lagoons, and shallow lake margins; nests primarily in wooded swamps; often also in flooded and wet fields (Tropical and lower Subtropical zones).

Distribution.—*Resident* from central Baja California (lat. 27° N.), central Sinaloa, southern and eastern Texas, Louisiana, central Alabama, Florida, southeastern Georgia, and coastal North Carolina (rarely Virginia) south along both slopes of Middle America, through the Greater Antilles (Cuba, the Isle of Pines, Jamaica, and Hispaniola), and along the coasts of South America to northwestern Peru and French Guiana.

Wanders to the Cayman Islands and north, at least casually, to southern California, southern Arizona, and central New Mexico, and east of the Rockies to southeastern South Dakota, southern Michigan, southern Ontario, southern Quebec, and Nova Scotia; reports from northern (and possibly some from southern) California may be based on escapes. Casual on Clipperton Island, and in southern Idaho, Bermuda, and Puerto Rico; sight reports from Wyoming, Manitoba, North Dakota, Wisconsin, the Bahamas, and Barbados.

Notes.—Despite slight overlap in mixed colonies in Venezuela, *E. albus* and *E. ruber* appear to constitute a superspecies (Steinbacher *in* Mayr and Cottrell 1979). Hybridization between the two occurs in captivity and among the mixed Florida colony, also occasionally (but at a low level) under natural conditions in South America. Ramo and Busto (1985, 1987) proposed conspecificity for *E. albus* and *E. ruber* on the basis of interbreeding of the two forms in mixed colonies in Venezuela. The White Ibis population in these colonies is only about 10% of the total of thousands of birds, and the maximum number of mixed pairs *(albus* x *ruber)* recorded per year is less than 0.3% of the number of pairs breeding. As yet there is not conclusive evidence of random or nonassortative mating nor any data on the relative viability and fertility of the offspring of mixed pairs. Pending the acquisition of such information, we retain the two forms as separate species.

Eudocimus ruber (Linnaeus). Scarlet Ibis.

> *Scolopax rubra* Linnaeus, 1758, Syst. Nat. (ed. 10) 1: 145. Based mainly on "The Red Curlew" Catesby, Nat. Hist. Carolina 1: 84, pl. 84. (in America.)

Habitat.—Primarily in coastal swamps and lagoons, mangroves, and occasionally along rivers and marshes in drier interior areas (Tropical Zone).

Distribution.—*Resident* coastally from northern Colombia east through Venezuela (including Margarita Island), Trinidad, and the Guianas to northeastern and southern Brazil.

Accidental in Florida (1874), Grenada, and eastern Ecuador; reports from Nova Scotia, Texas, Louisiana, the Bahamas, Cuba, Jamaica, Honduras, and Costa Rica are all open to question. Attempted introductions by placing eggs in nests of *E. albus* in southern Florida have been generally unsuccessful.

Notes.—See comments under *E. albus*.

Genus *PLEGADIS* Kaup

> *Plegadis* Kaup, 1829, Skizz. Entw.-Ges. Eur. Thierw., p. 82. Type, by monotypy, *Tantalus falcinellus* Linnaeus.

Plegadis falcinellus (Linnaeus). Glossy Ibis.

> *Tantalus Falcinellus* Linnaeus, 1766, Syst. Nat. (ed. 12) 1: 241. Based mostly on *Numenius rostro arcuato* Kramer, Elench. Veget. Anim. Austriam Inf. Obsv., p. 350, and "Le Courly verd" Brisson, Ornithologie 5: 326, pl. 27, fig. 2. (in Austria, Italia = Neusiedler See, Lower Austria.)

Habitat.—Marshes, swamps, lagoons, and margins of shallow lakes, and flooded and wet fields, with reed beds, low trees, or bushes for nest sites (Tropical to Temperate zones).

Distribution.—*Breeds* in North America locally from Maine (Stratton Island) and Rhode Island south to Florida, and west on the Gulf coast to south-central Louisiana (Avery Island), although largely absent between St. Mark's, Florida, and southeastern Louisiana, also inland (formerly) in Arkansas; in southwest Campeche; in Yucatan Peninsula (including Cozumel Island); in northwestern Costa Rica (Guanacaste, since 1978); in the Greater Antilles (Cuba, Hispaniola, and Puerto Rico); in South America in northern Venezuela (Aragua); and locally in the Old World from southeastern Europe east to eastern China, India, and the Malay Peninsula, and south through East Africa to South Africa and Madagascar, and through the East Indies to Australia. Reported breeding in eastern Texas has not been verified; a breeding attempt in New Brunswick was unsuccessful.

Winters in the Americas from northern Florida and the Gulf coast of Louisiana south through the Greater Antilles (casually the Bahamas, the Cayman Islands, and northern Lesser Antilles), and in northwestern Costa Rica, Panama, and northern Venezuela; and in the Old World from the Mediterranean region east to Southeast Asia and south widely through Africa, the East Indies, and Australia.

In North America wanders, at least casually, west to Kansas and central Oklahoma, north to Saskatchewan, southern Manitoba, Minnesota, Wisconsin, central Michigan, southern Ontario, southern Quebec, Prince Edward Island, New Brunswick, Nova Scotia, and Newfoundland, east to Bermuda, and south to southeastern Mexico (Chiapas, Quintana Roo), and San Andrés; and in Eurasia to Iceland, the Faeroe Islands, British Isles, and Scandinavia. Frequent vagrant to Bermuda. Casual in Colombia and the eastern Atlantic islands; sight reports from Wyoming, Colorado, Belize, Honduras, and Costa Rica (away from Guanacaste) are not certainly identifiable to species.

Notes.—*Plegadis falcinellus* and *P. chihi* were formerly considered conspecific, but sympatric breeding occurs in Louisiana (Avery Island). Despite limited sympatry, the two constitute a superspecies (Mayr and Short 1970; Steinbacher *in* Mayr and Cottrell 1979).

Plegadis chihi (Vieillot). White-faced Ibis.

Numenius chihi Vieillot, 1817, Nouv. Dict. Hist. Nat. (nouv. éd.) 8: 303. Based on "Cuello jaspeado" Azara, Apunt. Hist. Nat. Páx. Parag. 3: 197 (no. 364). (Paraguay et dans les plaines de Buenos-Ayres = Paraguay and the campos of Buenos Aires, Argentina.)

Habitat.—Marshes, swamps, margins of shallow lakes and rivers, mostly in fresh-water areas, and flooded and wet fields (Tropical to Temperate zones).

Distribution.—*Breeds* in North America locally from northern California, eastern Oregon, southern Idaho, Montana, southern Alberta (rarely), north-central North Dakota, and (formerly) southwestern Minnesota south to Durango, Jalisco (perhaps elsewhere on Mexican Plateau), southern and eastern Texas, southern Louisiana (east to Avery Island), coastal Alabama (rarely), and occasionally (or formerly) in northwestern Iowa (Spirit Lake) and possibly Florida (Brevard County and Lake Okeechobee); and in South America west of the Andes in northern and central Chile, and east of the Andes from central Bolivia, Paraguay, and extreme southern Brazil south to central Chile and central Argentina.

Winters from central California, southwestern Arizona, and the Gulf coast of Texas and southern Louisiana south through Mexico (including Baja California) to the Pacific lowlands of Guatemala; and in the general breeding range in South America.

Wanders, at least casually, to the Hawaiian Islands, north to southern British Columbia, southern Saskatchewan, southern Manitoba, Minnesota, Wisconsin, Michigan, Ohio, Ontario (sight report), New York (Long Island), and Massachusetts, and along the Gulf coast to Florida, and south to southwestern Campeche and, at least formerly, El Salvador and Costa Rica (Térraba Valley), also to Clipperton Island.

Notes.—See comments under *P. falcinellus*.

Genus *MESEMBRINIBIS* Peters

Mesembrinibis Peters, 1930, Occas. Pap. Boston Soc. Nat. Hist. 5: 256. Type, by original designation, *Tantalus cayennensis* Gmelin.

Mesembrinibis cayennensis (Gmelin). Green Ibis.

Tantalus cayennensis Gmelin, 1789, Syst. Nat. 1(2): 652. Based mainly on "Courly verd de Cayenne" Daubenton, Planches Enlum., pl. 820. (in Cayanna = Cayenne.)

Habitat.—River-edge Forest, Gallery Forest, Freshwater Marshes, Freshwater Lakes and Ponds, Rivers (0–1200 m; Tropical Zone).

Distribution.—*Resident* from Costa Rica (Caribbean lowlands), Panama, Colombia, southern Venezuela, and the Guianas south, east of the Andes, to central Bolivia, Paraguay, northeastern Argentina and extreme southeastern Brazil; sight reports for Nicaragua (Río San Juan) and northeastern Honduras (Río Platano).

Genus *THERISTICUS* Wagler

Theristicus Wagler, 1832, Isis von Oken, col. 1231. Type, by monotypy, *Tantalus melanopis* Gmelin.

Theristicus caudatus (Boddaert). Buff-necked Ibis.

Scolopax caudatus Boddaert, 1783, Table Planches Enlum., p. 57. Based on "Courly à col blanc de Cayenne" Daubenton, Planches Enlum., pl. 976. (Cayenne.)

Habitat.—Low Seasonally Wet Grassland, Pastures/Agricultural Lands (0–1200 m)

Distribution.—*Resident* in the open areas that ring Amazonia from northern and eastern Colombia, northern Venezuela, and the Guianas south through interior and eastern Brazil to eastern Bolivia, Paraguay, and northern Argentina.

Accidental in Panama (near Pacora, eastern Panamá province; Wetmore 1965).

Notes.—*Theristicus caudatus,* the southern South American *T. melanopis* (Gmelin, 1789), including the high Andean *T. branickii* Berlepsch and Stolzmann, 1894, constitute a superspecies (Steinbacher *in* Mayr and Cottrell 1979).

Subfamily PLATALEINAE: Spoonbills

Genus *AJAIA* Reichenbach

Ajaia Reichenbach, 1853, Avium Syst, Nat., pt. 3 (1852), p. xvi. Type, by original designation, *Ajaia rosea* Reichenbach = *Platalea ajaja* Linnaeus.

Ajaia ajaja (Linnaeus). Roseate Spoonbill.

Platalea Ajaja Linnaeus, 1758, Syst. Nat. (ed. 10) 1: 140. Based mainly on *Aiaia Brasiliensibus* Marcgrave, Hist. Nat. Bras., p. 204. (in America australi = Rio São Francisco, eastern Brazil.)

Habitat.—Marshes, swamps, ponds, margins of rivers, and lagoons; breeding habitat requires low trees and bushes for nest sites (0–800 m; Tropical and Subtropical zones).

Distribution.—*Resident* locally from northern Sinaloa, the Gulf coast of Texas, and southwestern Louisiana (Cameron Parish), and central and southern Florida south along both slopes of Middle America and through the Greater Antilles (Cuba, the Isle of Pines, and Hispaniola), Bahamas (Great Inagua), and South America to central Chile and central Argentina.

Wanders north to interior Louisiana east in the Gulf states to northern Florida, and north along the Atlantic coast to North Carolina; in interior Mexico north to central Durango; also widely through much of the West Indies (rare in Cayman Islands and Lesser Antilles). Casual or accidental north to central and southern California, southern Nevada, southwestern Arizona, central New Mexico, northwestern Utah, Colorado, Nebraska, Kansas, Wisconsin, Iowa, Indiana, Ohio, Pennsylvania, New York, and the Pacific coast of Baja California south to southern Chile and the Falkland Islands.

Notes.—This species is sometimes placed in the genus *Platalea* (e.g., Payne *in* Mayr and Cottrell 1979).

Suborder CICONIAE: Storks and American Vultures

Family **CICONIIDAE**: Storks

Tribe LEPTOPTILINI: Jabirus and Allies

Genus *JABIRU* Hellmayr

Jabiru Hellmayr, 1906, Abh. Math. Phys. Kl. Bayr. Akad. Wiss. 22: 711. Type, by original designation, *Ciconia mycteria* Lichtenstein.

Jabiru mycteria (Lichtenstein). Jabiru.

> *Ciconia mycteria* Lichtenstein, 1819, Abh. Phys. Kl. Akad. Wiss. Berlin (1816–17), p. 163. Based on "Jabirú" Marcgrave, Hist. Nat. Bras., p. 200. (northeastern Brazil.)

Habitat.—Low Seasonally Wet Grassland, Freshwater Marshes, Freshwater Lakes, and Ponds (0–700 m; Tropical Zone).

Distribution.—*Resident* locally in Middle America from Tabasco, Chiapas, Campeche, and Quintana Roo south through Central America (not recorded Guatemala) to Panama, and in South America from Colombia, Venezuela, and the Guianas south, mostly east of the Andes, to southern Bolivia, northeastern Argentina, and Uruguay.

Wanders casually north to Veracruz (Cosamaloapan) and Texas (Kleberg, Brooks, and Hidalgo counties, Houston and Corpus Christi as well as an 1867 record from Austin). Accidental in Oklahoma (near Tulsa).

Tribe MYCTERIINI: Wood Storks

Genus *MYCTERIA* Linnaeus

> *Mycteria* Linnaeus, 1758, Syst. Nat. (ed. 10) 1: 140. Type, by monotypy, *Mycteria americana* Linnaeus.

Mycteria americana Linnaeus. Wood Stork.

> *Mycteria americana* Linnaeus, 1758, Syst. Nat. (ed. 10) 1: 140. Based mainly on "Jabiru-guaçu" Marcgrave, Hist. Nat. Bras., p. 201. (in America calidiore = Brazil.)

Habitat.—Freshwater Marshes, Saltwater/Brackish Marshes, Freshwater Lakes, and Ponds, occasionally flooded fields (0–800 m; Tropical and lower Subtropical zones).

Distribution.—*Resident* (but breeding very locally in colonies only) from southern Sonora, the Gulf coast (from eastern Texas to Florida), and the Atlantic coast (from South Carolina to southern Florida) south locally along both lowlands of Middle America (including many offshore islands), in Cuba and Hispaniola (Dominican Republic, including Saona Island), and through South America west of the Andes to western Ecuador and east of the Andes to northern Argentina.

Wanders north to southeastern California (rarely, breeding attempted), southwestern Arizona, in the Gulf states to southern Oklahoma, Arkansas, and western Tennessee, and in the Atlantic states to North Carolina, casually north to northern California, southern Idaho, Montana, northwestern Wyoming, northeastern Colorado, South Dakota, Iowa, Wisconsin, Indiana, central Michigan, southern Ontario, New York, Maine, Magdalen Island, and southern New Brunswick. Casual in Jamaica and Grand Bahama; accidental in northwestern British Columbia (Telegraph Creek) and Chile.

Notes.—Also known as Wood Ibis.

Family **CATHARTIDAE**: New World Vultures

Notes.—A relationship between the New World vultures and storks was suggested by Ligon (1967) and supported by additional analyses of anatomy, morphology, and behavior (König 1982, Rea 1983), chemical composition of the uropygial gland (Jacob 1983), DNA-DNA hybridization studies (Sibley and Ahlquist 1990, Harshman 1994), and mitochondrial DNA sequences (Wink 1995). For a critique of many of these analyses and a contrary opinion (to retain the Cathartidae in the Falconiformes), see Griffiths (1994).

Genus *CORAGYPS* Geoffroy

> *Coragyps* Geoffroy, 1853, in Le Maout, Hist. Nat. Ois., p. 66. Type, by monotypy, *Vultur urubu* Vieillot = *Vultur atratus* Bechstein.

Coragyps atratus (Bechstein). Black Vulture.

Vultur atratus Bechstein, 1793, in Latham, Allg. Uebers. Vögel 1 (Anh.): 655. Based on "The black vulture or carrion crow" Bartram, Travels Carolina, pp. 152, 289. (St. John's River, Florida.)

Habitat.—Nearly everywhere except in heavily forested regions and open plains, primarily in lowlands; especially common in cattle country and, in tropics, around garbage dumps and towns (0–2800 m; Tropical to Temperate zones).

Distribution.—*Resident* from southern Arizona, Chihuahua, western Texas, eastern Oklahoma, eastern Kansas (formerly), southern Missouri, southern Illinois, southern Indiana, central Ohio, south-central Pennsylvania, and New Jersey south to the Gulf coast and southern Florida, and throughout Middle America and South America (including Trinidad and Margarita Island, off Venezuela) to central Chile and central Argentina. Recorded in summer (and possibly breeding) north to southeastern New York and southern Maine.

Wanders casually north to southwestern Yukon, Saskatchewan (sight report), North Dakota, Wisconsin, southern Ontario, southern Quebec, New Brunswick, Prince Edward Island, and Nova Scotia, and south to the Bahamas (Bimini); also questionably recorded (sight reports only) from California, New Mexico, and the Antilles (Cuba, Jamaica, Barbados, Grenada). Some populations appear to be partly migratory, especially the northernmost ones in the eastern United States.

Genus *CATHARTES* Illiger

Cathartes Illiger, 1811, Prodromus, p. 236. Type, by subsequent designation (Vigors, 1825), *Vultur aura* Linnaeus.

Cathartes aura (Linnaeus). Turkey Vulture.

Vultur Aura Linnaeus, 1758, Syst. Nat. (ed. 10) 1: 86. Based mainly on the "Tzopilotle s. Aura" Hernandez, Nova Plant Anim. Min. Mex. Hist., p. 331. (in America calidiore = state of Veracruz.)

Habitat.—Primarily areas of open woodland and open country, generally near wooded areas or cliffs for roosting and nesting, from lowlands to mountains; avoids dense forest; regularly over small coastal islands (0–2500 m; Tropical to Temperate zones).

Distribution.—*Breeds* from south-coastal and southern British Columbia (including Vancouver Island), central Alberta, central Saskatchewan, southern Manitoba, western Ontario, northern Minnesota, northern Wisconsin, northern Michigan, southern Ontario, southwestern Quebec, New York, southern Vermont, southwestern and eastern New Hampshire and southern Maine south throughout the remaining continental United States, Middle America and South America (including Trinidad and Margarita Island, off Venezuela) to the Straits of Magellan; also in the Greater Antilles (Cuba, the Isle of Pines, and Jamaica). Recorded in summer (and possibly breeding) in the Cayman Islands (Cayman Brac) and north to northern Manitoba, northern Vermont, and southwestern Nova Scotia.

Winters mainly from northern California, Arizona, Chihuahua, Texas, the Ohio Valley, and Maryland (casually north to southern Canada) south to the Gulf coast, Florida, and the northern Bahamas (casually to Bimini, New Providence, and Andros), and through the breeding range in Middle America, the Greater Antilles, and South America.

Introduced and established in Puerto Rico.

Casual north to east-central Alaska, northern Ontario, central Quebec, Labrador, and Newfoundland, and on Bermuda, Hispaniola, St. Croix (in the Virgin Islands), and the Cayman Islands. Accidental on South Georgia.

Cathartes burrovianus Cassin. Lesser Yellow-headed Vulture.

Cathartes Burrovianus Cassin, 1845, Proc. Acad. Nat. Sci. Philadelphia 2: 212. (in the vicinity of Vera Cruz = near Veracruz Llave, Veracruz.)

Habitat.—Low Seasonally Wet Grassland, Second-growth Scrub, Saltwater/Brackish Marshes (0–1000 m; Tropical Zone).

Distribution.—*Resident* locally in eastern and southern Mexico (southern Tamaulipas, Veracruz, Tabasco, Chiapas, the Yucatan Peninsula, and on both slopes of Oaxaca), Belize, Guatemala (Petén), eastern Honduras (Mosquitia), northeastern Nicaragua, and Costa Rica (Río Frío region, recorded rarely elsewhere), and from Panama (both slopes) south through most of nonforested South America east of the Andes to northern Argentina and Uruguay.

Genus *GYMNOGYPS* Lesson

Gymnogyps Lesson, 1842, Echo Monde Savant (2)6: col. 1037. Type, by monotypy, *Vultur californianus* Shaw.

Gymnogyps californianus (Shaw). California Condor.

Vultur californianus Shaw, 1798, in Shaw and Nodder, Naturalists' Misc. 9: pl. 301 and text. (coast of California = Monterey.)

Habitat.—Mountainous country at low and moderate elevations, especially rocky and brushy areas with cliffs for nest sites; forages in grasslands, oak savanna, mountain plateaus, ridges, and canyons.

Distribution.—*Resident* formerly (last living birds removed from the wild in 1987) in the coastal ranges of California from Monterey and San Benito counties south to Ventura County, ranging, at least casually, north to Santa Clara and San Mateo counties, and east to the western slope of the Sierra Nevada (north as far as Fresno County) and the Tehachapi Mountains, with breeding sites apparently confined to Los Padres National Forest in Santa Barbara, Ventura, and extreme northern Los Angeles counties. Formerly resident (before 1900) along the Pacific coast and in part inland west of the Cascade-Sierra Nevada ranges, apparently from southwestern British Columbia south to northern Baja California (although there are no confirmed breeding records outside of California). Recent reports of condors east to southeastern Arizona, as well as within or around the former range in Baja California, seem to be without foundation. Reintroduced into the wild in southern California (Los Padres National Forest) in 1992 and in northern Arizona (Grand Canyon area) in 1996.

Genus *SARCORAMPHUS* Duméril

Sarcoramphus Duméril, 1806, Zool. Anal., p. 32. Type, by subsequent designation (Vigors, 1825), *Vultur papa* Linnaeus.

Sarcoramphus papa (Linnaeus). King Vulture.

Vultur Papa Linnaeus, 1758, Syst. Nat. (ed. 10) 1: 86. Based on "The Warwovwen, or Indian Vulture" Albin, Nat. Hist. Birds 2: 4, pl. 4, and "The King of the Vultures" Edwards, Nat. Hist. Birds 1: 2, pl. 2. (in India occidentali, error = Surinam.)

Habitat.—Tropical Lowland Evergreen Forest, Tropical Deciduous Forest, Gallery Forest, Low Seasonally Wet Grassland (0–1500 m; Tropical and lower Subtropical zones).

Distribution.—*Resident* from Sinaloa (at least formerly), Guerrero, and Veracruz south through Middle America and South America west of the Andes to northwestern Peru and east of the Andes to northern Argentina and Uruguay; former occurrence in Florida is not convincing (Robertson and Woolfenden 1992: 184, *contra* Harper 1936).

Casual in Trinidad; a sight report for San Luis Potosí.

Order **PHOENICOPTERIFORMES**: Flamingos

Notes.—The taxonomic position of the flamingos is uncertain; some evidence suggests a relationship with the Charadrii of the Charadriiformes (see Olson and Feduccia 1980), whereas other data support a relationship with the Ciconiiformes (see Sibley and Ahlquist 1990: 516–527) or Anseriformes (Hagey et al. 1990).

Family **PHOENICOPTERIDAE**: Flamingos

Genus *PHOENICOPTERUS* Linnaeus

Phoenicopterus Linnaeus, 1758, Syst. Nat. (ed. 10) 1: 139. Type, by monotypy, *Phoenicopterus ruber* Linnaeus.

Phoenicopterus ruber Linnaeus. Greater Flamingo.

Phoenicopterus ruber Linnaeus, 1758, Syst. Nat. (ed. 10) 1: 139. Based largely on "The Flamingo" Catesby, Nat. Hist. Carolina 1: 73, pl. 73. (in Africa, America, rarius in Europa = Bahamas.)

Habitat.—Coastal Waters, mud flats, lagoons. and lakes, generally of high salinity; nests on mud mounds in shallow water.

Distribution.—*Resident* [*ruber* group] locally in the Americas along the northern coast of the Yucatan Peninsula (Celestún, Río Lagartos), in the Greater Antilles (Cuba, Hispaniola, and probably Gonâve and Beata islands), in the southern Bahamas (Acklins Island and Great Inagua), in the Netherlands Antilles (Bonaire) and in the Galapagos Islands; and [*roseus* group] in the Old World locally along the coasts of the Mediterranean and northwest Africa, in the rift lakes of East Africa, in South Africa, and from southern Russia and the Caspian Sea south to the Persian Gulf and northwestern India. Formerly bred [*ruber* group] in the Florida Keys (once, possibly), widely in the Bahamas, locally from Culebra and Anegada to the Virgin Islands, along the north coast of South America from Colombia to the Guianas; and [*roseus* group] in the Cape Verde Islands.

Wanders [*ruber* group] to southern Florida (where captive flocks are also established), widely through the Bahamas and Antilles, along the east coast of the Yucatan Peninsula (including Cozumel Island) and northeastern South America from Colombia to northern Brazil; and [*roseus* group] widely through Europe and to the Canary Islands. Casual or accidental (but many if not all probably pertaining to escaped individuals) [*ruber* group] along the Gulf coast from Texas to Florida, inland north to Kansas, Michigan, Ontario, and southern Quebec, along the Atlantic coast north to New Brunswick and Nova Scotia, and to Bermuda and the Cayman Islands; reports from Washington, California, and Nevada almost certainly pertain to escaped individuals.

Notes.—Known in Old World literature as the Flamingo. Groups: *P. ruber* [American Flamingo] and *P. roseus* Pallas, 1811 [Greater Flamingo]. *Phoenicopterus ruber* (including *roseus*) and the South American *P. chilensis* Molina, 1782, appear to constitute a superspecies (Sibley and Monroe 1970). See also *P. chilensis* (Appendix).

Order **ANSERIFORMES**: Screamers, Swans, Geese, and Ducks

Notes.—The following classification and sequence are based on a series of studies by Livezey (especially 1991, 1995a, b, c, 1996a, b), although they differ in some details. Subtribes and subgeneric categories are omitted.

Suborder ANSERES: Waterfowl

Superfamily ANATOIDEA: Typical Waterfowl

Family **ANATIDAE**: Ducks, Geese, and Swans

Subfamily DENDROCYGNINAE: Whistling-Ducks and Allies

Tribe DENDROCYGNINI: Whistling-Ducks

Genus *DENDROCYGNA* Swainson

Dendrocygna Swainson, 1837, Class. Birds 2: 365. Type, by subsequent designation (Eyton, 1838), *Anas arcuata* Horsfield.
Lamprocygna Boetticher, 1949, Beitr. Gattungssystematik Vögel, p. 25. Type, by original designation, *Anas autumnalis* Linnaeus.
Nesocygna Boetticher, 1949, Beitr. Gattungssystematik Vögel, p. 24. Type, by original designation, *Anas arborea* Linnaeus.
Prosopocygna Boetticher, 1949, Beitr. Gattungssystematik Vögel, p. 23. Type, by original designation, *Anas viduata* Linnaeus.

Notes.—The group name Tree-Duck was formerly used for members of this genus.

Dendrocygna viduata (Linnaeus). White-faced Whistling-Duck.

Anas viduata Linnaeus, 1766, Syst. Nat. (ed. 12) 1: 205. (in Carthagenæ lacubus = Cartagena, Colombia.)

Habitat.—Freshwater Marshes, Freshwater Lakes and Ponds, Streams (0–1000 m; Tropical Zone).
Distribution.—*Resident* locally in Costa Rica (Guanacaste and the Gulf of Nicoya area, at least formerly) and irregularly in eastern Panama (eastern Panamá province, wandering casually to the Canal area); locally through savanna regions of South America from Colombia, Venezuela (including Curaçao), Trinidad, and Guyana south to central Bolivia, northern Argentina, Uruguay, and southern Brazil; in Africa south of the Sahara to Angola in the west and Natal in the east; and in Madagascar and the Comoro Islands.
Casual in the Antilles (Cuba, the Dominican Republic on Hispaniola, and Barbados).

Dendrocygna autumnalis (Linnaeus). Black-bellied Whistling-Duck.

Anas autumnalis Linnaeus, 1758, Syst. Nat. (ed. 10) 1: 127. (in America = West Indies.)

Habitat.—Freshwater Marshes, shallow freshwater lakes (0–1500 m; Tropical and Subtropical zones).
Distribution.—*Resident* from central Sonora, southern Arizona, central and southeastern Texas, and southwestern Louisiana (Lacassine Refuge) south through most of Middle America and South America (including Trinidad) west of the Andes to northwestern Peru and east of the Andes (except locally in Amazonia) to northern Argentina, Paraguay, and southern Brazil. Some withdrawal in winter at northern periphery of breeding range, e.g., Arizona and southwestern Louisiana.
Established in central and southern Florida, perhaps from a mixture of escaped captives and natural colonizers (Robertson and Woolfenden 1992), and in Cuba.
Casual in southeastern California, southern Baja California, southern New Mexico, western Texas, Oklahoma, Kansas, Ontario, Minnesota, Arkansas, Mississippi, Alabama, Virginia, South Carolina, Baja California (Cape district), Valley of México, Puerto Rico, the Virgin Islands, and Lesser Antilles; sight reports for Missouri, Georgia, the Bahama Islands, and the Cayman Islands.

Dendrocygna arborea (Linnaeus). West Indian Whistling-Duck.

Anas arborea Linnaeus, 1758, Syst. Nat. (ed. 10) 1: 128. Based mainly on "The Black-billed Whistling Duck" Edwards, Nat. Hist. Birds 4: 193, pl. 193. (in America = Jamaica.)

Habitat.—Primarily mangroves and forested swamps.

Distribution.—*Resident* in the Bahamas (Andros, Exuma, Great Inagua, and Middle Caicos islands, and probably Eleuthera; vagrant elsewhere), throughout the Greater Antilles (including the Isle of Pines, Grand Cayman, and île-à-Vache off Hispaniola), in the Virgin Islands (formerly), and in the northern Lesser Antilles (at least on Barbuda and Antigua, formerly on Martinique and probably St. Kitts).

Accidental in Bermuda; sight reports from Florida may be of natural vagrants.

Dendrocygna bicolor (Vieillot). Fulvous Whistling-Duck.

Anas bicolor Vieillot, 1816, Nouv. Dict. Hist. Nat. (nouv. éd.) 5: 136. Based on "Pato roxo y negro" Azara, Apunt. Hist. Nat. Páx. Parag. 3: 443 (no. 436). (Paraguay.)

Habitat.—Shallow waters (both fresh and brackish), preferring marshes, lagoons, and wet and flooded cultivated fields (primarily Tropical Zone.)

Distribution.—*Breeds* in the Hawaiian Islands (Oahu); in North America from southeastern California (formerly north to Merced County), central and eastern Texas, and southwestern Louisiana south at least to Nayarit, Jalisco (Lake Chapala, at least formerly) and Veracruz; locally in central and southern Florida, the West Indies (from Cuba, Hispaniola, Puerto Rico, and Grand Bahama south to Barbados, Grenada, Tobago, and Trinidad), El Salvador, central Honduras (Lake Yojoa) and, probably, northwestern Costa Rica; in South America from Colombia, northern Venezuela, and the Guianas south, west of the Andes to northwestern Peru, and east of the Andes to southern Bolivia, Paraguay, and northeastern Argentina; and in the Old World in East Africa, Madagascar, India, Sri Lanka, and southwestern Burma.

Winters in the Hawaiian Islands (Oahu, occasionally reaching other main islands), from southeastern California (casually), southern Arizona (at least formerly), the Gulf coast, and central and southern Florida south to Oaxaca, Tabasco, and Quintana Roo, and in the breeding range elsewhere in the American tropics, South America, and the Old World.

Casual north to southern British Columbia, western Washington, coastal Oregon, Nevada, Utah, Colorado (sight report), North Dakota, Minnesota, Wisconsin, Michigan, southern Ontario, southern Quebec, Maine, southern New Brunswick, Prince Edward Island, and Nova Scotia; also from the Valley of México to Guatemala (Lago de Retana), and to Nicaragua (sight report), Bermuda, Grand Cayman, central Chile, central Argentina, and Morocco. Accidental in Panama (La Jagua, eastern Panamá province), presumably from South American populations.

Notes.—*Dendrocygna bicolor* and *D. arcuata* (Horsfield, 1824), of the Australian region, may constitute a superspecies (Mayr and Short 1970; Johnsgard *in* Mayr and Cottrell 1979).

Subfamily ANSERINAE: Geese and Swans

Tribe ANSERINI: True Geese

Genus *ANSER* Brisson

Anser Brisson, 1760, Ornithologie 1: 58; 6: 261. Type, by tautonymy, *Anser domesticus* Brisson = *Anas anser* Linnaeus.

Notes.—See comments under *Chen.*

Anser fabalis (Latham). Bean Goose.

Anas Fabalis Latham, 1787, Gen. Synop. Birds (suppl.) 1: 297. (Great Britain.)

Habitat.—Tundra tand taiga watercourses, open heath, and grassy plains; in winter, brackish and marine situations as well as fresh-water lakes and ponds.

Distribution.—*Breeds* from Scandinavia, northern Russia (including Novaya Zemlya) and northern Siberia south to northern Mongolia, Lake Baikal, Amurland, and Anadyrland. *Winters* south to the Mediterranean Sea, Iran, China, and Japan.

Migrates regularly in spring east to the western Aleutian Islands (east casually as far as Adak), and casually to the Pribilofs, St. Lawrence Island, and the mainland coast of southern Alaska (Safety Sound, Hooper Bay).

Casual to Iceland, the eastern Atlantic islands and northern Africa. Accidental in Quebec (Cap-Tourmente) and on the Iowa-Nebraska border.

Notes.—*Anser fabalis* and *A. brachyrhynchus* constitute a superspecies; they are regarded as conspecific by some authors (e.g., Vaurie 1965).

Anser brachyrhynchus Baillon. Pink-footed Goose.

Anser Brachyrhynchus Baillon, 1834, Mém. Soc. R. Emulation Abbeville, sér. 2, no. 1 (1833), p. 74. (Abbeville, lower Somme River, France.)

Habitat.—River gorges, low heathy mounds and ridges, and boggy grasslands; in winter, estuarine flats and sandbanks, and freshwater lakes.

Distribution.—*Breeds* in eastern Greenland, Iceland, Spitsbergen, and possibly also Franz Josef Land and the Kola Peninsula, and *winters* in northwestern Europe.

Accidental in Newfoundland (St. Anthony, 10 May-3 June 1980, photograph; 1980, Amer. Birds 34: 755; also spring 1995, Nat. Aud. Soc. Field Notes 49: 221) and Quebec (Cap-Tourmente, 6–21 October 1988, photograph; 1989, Amer. Birds 43: 68); sight reports from Quebec; reports from New York and Massachusetts are doubtful.

Anser albifrons (Scopoli). Greater White-fronted Goose.

Branta albifrons Scopoli, 1769, Annus I, Hist.-Nat., p. 69. (No locality given = northern Italy.)

Habitat.—Arctic tundra and open areas in subarctic forest zone, often along small lakes and ponds, in deltas and estuaries; winters in inland and coastal marshes, pastureland, and open terrain with small bodies of water; in migration often in flooded fields.

Distribution.—*Breeds* in North America from northern Alaska south to Bristol Bay in the Cook Inlet region, and east across northern Yukon, northern Mackenzie, and southern Victoria Island to northern Keewatin; in western Greenland; and in northern Eurasia from the Kanin Peninsula east to Anadyrland. Recorded in summer on Melville Island.

Winters in North America from southern British Columbia south (mostly through the Pacific states) to Baja California, Sinaloa, on the Mexican Plateau to Jalisco and México, in the Gulf region from Texas, Oklahoma, Kansas, Arkansas, and Louisiana south to Veracruz and (casually) Campeche, and rarely (or locally) in the eastern United States from the Great Lakes south to Mississippi and Florida; and in Eurasia from the British Isles and southern Scandinavia south to the eastern Atlantic islands (rarely), Mediterranean Sea, Asia Minor, India, and from Manchuria and Japan south to eastern China.

Migrates through most of North America primarily west of the Mississippi River, and rarely to casually in eastern North America from Ontario, Quebec, and Labrador south to Florida and North Carolina, casually to Cuba.

Casual in the Hawaiian Islands, Aleutians (Attu, Amchitka, Adak), Pribilofs (St. Paul), southern Arizona, Bermuda, and Belize.

Notes.—Usually known as White-fronted Goose. The form *elgasi* Delacour and Ripley, 1975 (= *gambelli* auct., not Hartlaub, 1852) [Tule Goose] differs in behavior and ecology, and may represent a distinct species that breeds in the Cook Inlet area of southern Alaska and winters in the Sacramento Valley of California (Krogman 1978, 1979, Bauer 1979). Johnsgard *in* Mayr and Cottrell (1979) considered *A. albifrons* and *A. erythropus* to consitute a superspecies.

Anser erythropus (Linnaeus). Lesser White-fronted Goose.

Anas erythropus Linnaeus, 1758, Syst. Nat., (ed. 10) 1: 123. (in Europa septentrionali = northern Sweden.)

Habitat.—Breeds in taiga; winters on marshes, lakes, and ponds.

Distribution.—*Breeds* from Scandinavia to eastern Siberia, and *winters* from eastern Europe and the eastern Mediterranean region east to India and eastern China.

Accidental in Alaska (Attu Island, 5 June 1994; spec., Univ. Alaska Mus. #6518; 1994, Amer. Birds 48: 330). Earlier North American records from British Columbia, North Dakota, Ohio, western Pennsylvania, and Delaware likely involve escapes from captivity rather than natural vagrancy.

Notes.—See comments under *A. albifrons*.

Genus *CHEN* Boie

Chen Boie, 1822, Isis von Oken, col. 563. Type, by monotypy, *Anser hyperboreus* Pallas = *Anas caerulescens* Linnaeus.

Exanthemops Elliot, 1868, Birds N. Amer. 2 (9): pl. 44. Type, by monotypy, *Anser rossii* Cassin.

Philacte Bannister, 1870, Proc. Acad. Nat. Sci. Philadelphia 22: 131. Type, by monotypy, *Anas canagica* Sevastianov.

Notes.—Most authors, including Livezey (1996a), merge *Chen* into *Anser,* where it may be treated as a subgenus.

Chen canagica (Sevastianov). Emperor Goose.

Anas Canagica Sevastianov, 1802, Nova Acta Acad. Sci. Imp. Petropolitanae 13: 349, pl. 10. (Kanaga Island, Aleutian Islands.)

Habitat.—Arctic tundra in lowland marsh areas, generally not far from the coast, commuting to upland areas to forage; winters in salt-water areas along reefs and rocky beaches.

Distribution.—*Breeds* along the coast of western Alaska from Kotzebue Sound south to Kuskokwim Bay, on St. Lawrence and Nunivak islands, and in northeastern Siberia from Koliutschin Bay east to East Cape and south to the Gulf of Anadyr.

Winters throughout the Aleutians, along the Alaska Peninsula (east to Sanak Island and Bristol Bay), on Kodiak Island, irregularly south along the Pacific coast from southeastern Alaska and British Columbia to northern California (casually south to Orange County), and in Kamchatka and the Commander Islands.

Casual in the Hawaiian Islands (Midway, Laysan, and the main islands from Kauai east to Hawaii) and northern Alaska (east to Barrow). Accidental in Greenland.

Notes.—This species is frequently placed in the monotypic genus *Philacte*.

Chen caerulescens (Linnaeus). Snow Goose.

Anas cærulescens Linnaeus, 1758, Syst. Nat. (ed. 10) 1: 124. (in Canada = Hudson Bay, northeastern Manitoba.)

Habitat.—Open tundra, nesting on raised hummocks and ridges, generally near water and usually near coast; winters in both fresh-water and salt marshes, wet prairies, and extensive sandbars, foraging also in pastures, cultivated lands, and flooded fields.

Distribution.—*Breeds* from northern Alaska (Sagavanirktok River delta) east along the Arctic coast and islands of Canada to northwestern Greenland and Ellesmere and Baffin islands, south to Southampton Island, and along both coasts of Hudson Bay to mid James Bay (Akimiski Island), also in northeastern Siberia (Wrangel Island, possibly also on the Chukotski Peninsula); isolated breeding reports from Oregon (Malheur Lake), northern California (Tule Lake), North Dakota (Arrowwood), and southern Quebec (near Quebec City).

Winters in western North America from protected coastal waters of British Columbia and Washington south to the interior valleys and the southern coast of California, northern Baja California, northwestern Sonora, southwestern Arizona, and (rarely) eastern Colorado; from Chihuahua and southern (rarely northeastern) New Mexico south to Jalisco (where locally common) and to (locally and rarely) Durango and Guanajuato; from Nebraska, Iowa, and the Great Lakes south to the Gulf coast (from Florida to northern Veracruz), most commonly from Louisiana and Texas south to northern Tamaulipas; on the Atlantic coast from New

York (casually north to the St. Lawrence River and New England) to Florida (primarily from Chesapeake Bay to North Carolina); and in eastern Asia in Japan and eastern China.

Migrates chiefly along the Pacific coast and through Alberta and western Saskatchewan, occurring widely in the United States west of the Rocky Mountains; and through the Great Plains and Mississippi Valley, with large staging areas in Montana, the Dakotas, Minnesota, Nebraska, and Iowa; and through Quebec, Ontario, New Brunswick, Nova Scotia, and Vermont to the Atlantic wintering ground.

Casual south to southern Mexico (Tabasco), Belize, the Greater Antilles (east to the Virgin Islands), and the Bahamas; also in the Hawaiian Islands (Midway, Oahu, Maui), Aleutians (Attu, Alaid), Pribilofs (St. Paul), New England (coastal area), Greenland, Iceland, the British Isles, continental Europe, the Azores, and Korea. Accidental in Honduras (Campín, near La Lima) and the Marshall Islands.

Notes.—The "blue" morph and "white" morph were formerly considered distinct species, *C. caerulescens* [Blue Goose] and *C. hyperborea* [Snow Goose]; see Cooke and Cooch (1968) and Cooke et al. (1988, 1995).

Chen rossii (Cassin). Ross's Goose.

Anser Rossii Cassin, 1861, Proc. Acad. Nat. Sci. Philadelphia 13: 73. (Great Slave Lake.)

Habitat.—Arctic tundra, usually flat and with mix of grass and stunted shrubs, often near lakes and ponds, frequently associated with *C. caerulescens;* in migration and winter in both fresh-water and brackish marshes and wet prairies, foraging in grassy areas, pastures, and cultivated fields.

Distribution.—*Breeds* primarily in the Queen Maud Gulf area of northern Mackenzie (probably also Banks Island in Franklin District), northwestern Keewatin, southern Southampton Island, and along the west coast of Hudson Bay south to James Bay (Akimiski Island), also once in northern Alaska (Sagavanirktok River delta).

Winters mainly in the interior valleys of California (rarely to coastal California and southern Arizona), and to Chihuahua, Durango, southern (casually northern) New Mexico, Colorado, Oklahoma, Missouri, Arkansas, and southwestern Louisiana, casual east to inland Mississippi and Alabama.

Migrates primarily from Alberta, western Montana, and western Saskatchewan south through the interior western states (rarely west to British Columbia and Washington, and east to Wyoming, Colorado, and Utah), and through the Great Plains (uncommonly east to southern Manitoba, Minnesota, Missouri, and Arkansas, rarely to Michigan, Illinois, Indiana, Kentucky, and Tennessee).

Casual in northern Alaska (Barrow, Teshekpuk Lake, Canning River Delta), southeastern Alaska (Stikine River Delta), northern Baja California (sight report), Jalisco, Ohio, Quebec, Vermont, and along the Atlantic and Gulf coasts from New York (sight reports) and Pennsylvania (rare and regular in recent years in New Jersey and Delaware) to Florida.

Genus *BRANTA* Scopoli

Branta Scopoli, 1769, Annus I, Hist.-Nat., p. 67. Type, by subsequent designation (Bannister, 1870), *Anas bernicla* Linnaeus.

Leucopareia Reichenbach, 1853, Handb. Spec., Ornithol., Die Vögel, pt. 3 (1852), p. ix. Type, by monotypy, *Anas leucopsis* Bechstein.

Leucoblepharon Baird, 1858, in Baird, Cassin, and Lawrence, Rep. Explor. Surv. R. R. Pac. 9: xlix, 763. Type, by subsequent designation, *Anas canadensis* Linnaeus.

Nesochen Salvadori, 1895, Cat. Birds Brit. Mus. 27: xii, 81, 126. Type, by original designation, *N. sandvicensis* = *Bernicla sandvicensis* Vigors.

Eubranta Verheyen, 1955, Bull. Inst. R. Sci. Nat. Belg. 31(36): 9. Type, by subsequent designation (Parkes, 1958), *Anas leucopsis* Bechstein.

Branta canadensis (Linnaeus). Canada Goose.

Anas canadensis Linnaeus, 1758, Syst. Nat. (ed. 10) 1: 123. Based mainly on "The Canada Goose" Catesby, Nat. Hist. Carolina 1: 92, pl. 92. (in Canada = City of Quebec.)

Habitat.—A variety of habitats near water, from temperate regions to tundra; winters from tidewater areas and marshes to wooded inland lakes and flooded and cultivated fields, increasingly in areas with large lawns in urban areas, such as parks and golf courses.

Distribution.—*Breeds* from the Arctic coast of Alaska and northern Canada east to southern Baffin Island, western Greenland, and Labrador, and south to the Commander Islands (formerly), Aleutians (Buldir), central and northeastern California, central Utah, southern New Mexico, northern Texas, Arkansas, western Tennessee, western Kentucky, Ohio, New York, and Virginia.

Winters from south-coastal and southeastern Alaska (west to Prince William Sound), British Columbia, southern Alberta, southern Saskatchewan, southern Manitoba, the Great Lakes region and Atlantic coast of Newfoundland south to central Baja California, the northern Mexican states (casually south to Jalisco and Veracruz), Texas, and southwestern Louisiana, and to (rare) Mississippi, Alabama, and northern Florida (casually to the Florida Keys), formerly also to Kamchatka and Japan.

Introduced and established in Iceland, the British Isles, Sardinia, and New Zealand; in addition, there are many feral, usually nonmigratory (although free-flying) populations in the United States, both within and outside the normal breeding range, and often of a subspecies other than that expected in the wild.

Casual north to Melville Island, and in the Hawaiian Islands, central Siberia, and Japan. Accidental in Bermuda, the Bahamas (Andros, New Providence, Eleuthera), Cuba, and the Dominican Republic; there are records in Jamaica and Puerto Rico of birds of questionable origin.

Notes.—The northern populations of small Canada Geese have been variously treated taxonomically as three separate species, *B. hutchinsii* (Richardson, 1832) [Hutchins's or Richardson's Goose], *B. minima* Ridgway, 1885 [Cackling Goose], and *B. leucopareia* (Brandt, 1836) [Aleutian Goose]; as a single species under the name *B. hutchinsii*; or as one or more subspecies of *B. canadensis*. Relationships between breeding populations and groups are still uncertain, but this complex probably consists of at least two species, a large one, *B. canadensis* [Canada Goose], and a small one, *B. hutchinsii* [Tundra Goose], that includes the other two groups (Aldrich 1946, supported by mtDNA data in Quinn et al. 1991).

Branta sandvicensis (Vigors). Hawaiian Goose.

> *Bernicla sandvicensis* Vigors, 1834, Proc. Zool. Soc. London, p. 43 (Olson, 1989, Bull. Brit. Ornithol. Club 109: 201–205). (in insulis Sandvicensibus et in Owyhee = island of Hawaii.)

Habitat.—Uplands, primarily sparsely vegetated lava flows with no standing water.

Distribution.—*Resident* in the Hawaiian Islands on Hawaii (population small and locally distributed, the surviving native populations having been increased by introductions from captive stock); recently introduced in the Haleakala area of Maui, where it may formerly have bred, and on Kauai.

Notes.—Formerly placed in the monotypic genus *Nesochen*. Quinn et al. (1991) indicated that this species is closely related to *B. canadensis*. Also known as Nene.

Branta bernicla (Linnaeus). Brant.

> *Anas Bernicla* Linnaeus, 1758, Syst. Nat. (ed. 10) 1: 124. (in Europa boreali = Sweden.)

Habitat.—Arctic tundra, near coast and often in river deltas; winters primarily in coastal marshes, lagoons, estuaries, and shallow bays.

Distribution.—*Breeds* [*bernicla* group] in North America from Prince Patrick, Melville, and Ellesmere islands south to northern Keewatin (Adelaide Peninsula), Prince of Wales Island (probably), and Southampton, Coats, and western Baffin islands, and in the Palearctic in northern Greenland, Spitsbergen, and Franz Josef Land east to the Taimyr Peninsula; and [*nigricans* group] in North America from western (Kuskokwim Bay) and northern Alaska east to northern Mackenzie and Banks, Melville, and Prince Patrick islands (probably also Victoria Island), and in the Palearctic along the coast of Siberia east of the Taimyr Peninsula to the Bering Strait, Wrangell Island, and the Chukotski Peninsula.

Winters [*bernicla* group] in eastern North America along the Atlantic coast from New York, New Brunswick, and Nova Scotia south to Florida, and in western Eurasia south to the coasts of northwestern Europe, rarely on the Pacific coast from southern British Columbia to California, and to the Azores; and [*nigricans* group] in western North America along the Pacific coast from British Columbia (including Queen Charlotte Islands) south to southern Baja California, Sonora, and Sinaloa, casually north to southeastern Alaska and to southern Arizona, and in eastern Eurasia south, at least rarely, to the coast of northern China and Korea.

Migrates [*bernicla* group] regularly through eastern Ontario, Quebec, the Gulf of St. Lawrence, New England, and lakes Ontario and Erie, especially in fall; and [*nigricans* group] through southern California (Salton Sea), otherwise casual in interior California.

Casual [*bernicla* group] on the coast of northwestern Alaska, elsewhere in interior North America from northern California, eastern Colorado, South Dakota, Manitoba, Wisconsin, Michigan, and southwestern Ontario south to Texas, Arkansas, Kentucky, northern Alabama, and West Virginia (a report from Barbados is unsatisfactory), and in Bermuda; and [*nigricans* group] in the Hawaiian Islands, western North America east to Saskatchewan, Minnesota, Iowa, and Kansas, and south to New Mexico, Texas, and Louisiana, along the Atlantic coast from Massachusetts to Virginia, Bermuda, and in Iceland, the British Isles, and northern continental Europe; sight reports for Nayarit, Guerrero, and the Yucatan Peninsula.

Notes.—Known in Old World literature as Brent Goose. Groups: *B. bernicla* [White-bellied Brant] and *B. nigricans* (Lawrence, 1846) = *B. orientalis* Tougarinov, 1941 [Black Brant]. Delacour and Zimmer (1952) suggested that the name *nigricans* applies to an eastern, perhaps extinct, dark-bellied form and that the Black Brant of the Pacific should be known as *orientalis* Tougarinov, 1941. Handley (1950) reported that pale-bellied and dark-bellied birds coexist without interbreeding on Prince Patrick Island, although others (e.g., Manning et al. 1956) reported many intermediates in the western Canadian archipelago. Shields (1990) has shown that birds from Melville Island differ in mitochondrial DNA from Alaskan birds referred to *nigricans*, and that both differ markedly from light-bellied birds from eastern Canada.

Branta leucopsis (Bechstein). Barnacle Goose.

Anas leucopsis Bechstein, 1803, Ornithol. Taschenb. Dtsch. 2: 424. (auf dem Zuge, Deutschland = Germany.)

Habitat.—Rivers and marshes in Arctic regions, nesting primarily on rocky outcrops, ledges and crevices, less frequently on low islands; in winter, marshes and grasslands, generally near the coast.

Distribution.—*Breeds* in eastern Greenland, Spitsbergen, and southern Novaya Zemlya. *Winters* in the British Isles and Netherlands.

Casual in North America, from Labrador west to Baffin Island and James Bay, and south to Quebec, New Brunswick, and Nova Scotia, along the Atlantic coast south to South Carolina, and on rare occasions inland as far as eastern Washington, California, Oklahoma, Illinois, Missouri, Kentucky, Manitoba (sight report), Michigan, and Pennsylvania, and south to the Gulf coast (recorded Texas and Alabama); and in the Old World to Bear Island, the Mediterranean region, the Azores, and northern Africa. Many North American vagrant records almost certainly represent escapees from captivity, especially away from the Atlantic coast of northeastern North America; nevertheless, the seasonal pattern of distribution suggests that many are natural vagrants (Szantyr 1985).

Tribe CYGNINI: Swans

Genus *CYGNUS* Bechstein

Cygnus Bechstein, 1803, Ornithol. Taschenb. Dtsch. 2: 404, footnote. Type, by monotypy, *Anas olor* Gmelin.

Olor Wagler, 1832, Isis von Oken, col. 1234. Type, by subsequent designation (G. R. Gray, 1840), *Cygnus musicus* Bechstein = *Anas cygnus* Linnaeus.

Clangocycnus Oberholser, 1908, Emu 8: 3. Type, by monotypy, *Cygnus buccinator* Richardson.

Cygnus olor (Gmelin). Mute Swan.

Anas Olor Gmelin, 1789, Syst. Nat. 1(2): 501. Based in part on the "Mute Swan" Latham, Gen. Synop. Birds 3(2): 436, and Pennant, Arct. Zool. 2: 543. (in Russia, Sibiria, Persico etiam littore maris caspii = Russia.)

Habitat.—Open and quiet waters of lakes, ponds, marshes, and sluggish rivers, especially where reed beds and similar emergent vegetation provide nesting habitat; winters also in brackish and protected marine situations.

Distribution.—*Breeds* from the British Isles, southern Scandinavia and Russia southeast through central Europe to Asia Minor, and east to eastern Siberia and Ussuriland.

Winters from the breeding range south to the Mediterranean, Black, and Caspian seas and northwestern India, and from Korea south to eastern China, wintering casually to the Azores, northern Africa, Japan, and the Seven Islands of Izu.

Introduced and established in North America, with breeding recorded locally from southwestern British Columbia, southwestern Montana, southern Saskatchewan (formerly), northern Minnesota, northern Wisconsin, northern Michigan, southern Ontario, central and southeastern New York, and southern New England (east to Cape Cod) south to central Missouri, central Illinois, northern Indiana, northwestern Ohio and Virginia, also in southern Alabama; and in the Old World in the Faeroe Islands, South Africa, Australia, and New Zealand. Recorded after the breeding season from the breeding range and Maine south to the Ohio Valley; also Bermuda. Some of these records, as well as numerous reports elsewhere in North America, pertain to local escapes from captivity.

Notes.—This species and the next three have been treated as 1–4 species (Johnsgard 1974, Johnsgard *in* Mayr and Cottrell 1979).

Cygnus buccinator Richardson. Trumpeter Swan.

Cygnus buccinator Richardson, 1831, *in* Wilson and Bonaparte, Amer. Ornithol. (Jameson ed.) 4: 345. (Hudson's Bay.)

Habitat.—Ponds, lakes, marshes, and slow-moving rivers, especially where reeds, sedges, or similar emergent vegetation that provide nesting habitat, occasionally in brackish situations; winters on open lakes and bays, occasionally ponds, and often feeds in agricultural fields.

Distribution.—*Breeds* in northern Alaska (casually, from the Canning River east to Demarcation Point), in western Alaska (Noatak River Valley, Seward Peninsula, and Yukon-Kuskokwim Delta), widely in central and southern Alaska (from the middle Yukon River south to the Kenai Peninsula and Yakutat Bay, casually southeastern), northern British Columbia, southwestern Mackenzie, northwestern Alberta, western and central Montana, and southern Saskatchewan. Formerly bred from northern Yukon, northern Mackenzie, northern Manitoba, and James Bay south to Nebraska, Iowa, Missouri, central Illinois, Indiana, and (probably) New Brunswick.

Winters from southern Alaska, western and central British Columbia, southern Alberta (rarely), and Montana south to southern California, Arizona, New Mexico, and southern Texas (casually), and east to eastern Colorado and Minnesota; formerly wintered south to the Mexican border (one record from Tamaulipas), the Gulf coast of Texas and Louisiana, Mississippi Valley, and Atlantic coast to North Carolina.

Introduced and established locally from southern British Columbia, southeastern Alberta, and southwestern Saskatchewan south to southeastern Oregon, eastern Idaho, western Montana, and northwestern Wyoming, also in Nevada (Ruby Lake), southwestern South Dakota, northwestern Nebraska, and the Great Lakes region, with wintering to Texas, Kansas, Missouri, Arkansas, Indiana, Ohio, and New York; sight reports from Mississippi.

Cygnus columbianus (Ord). Tundra Swan.

Anas Columbianus Ord, 1815, in Guthrie, Geogr (ed. 2, Amer.) 2: 319. (below the great narrows of the Columbia River = The Dalles, Oregon.)

Habitat.—Open tundra ponds, lakes, and sluggish streams, occasionally swampy bogs, often near coast; winters primarily in shallow lakes, slow-moving rivers, less frequently on bays and estuaries, and in flooded and agricultural fields.

Distribution.—*Breeds* [*columbianus* group] from northwestern Alaska (Point Barrow and Cape Prince of Wales) south to St. Lawrence Island and the Alaska Peninsula, and east near the Arctic coast (including Banks Island) to Baffin Island, thence south to Churchill, the Belcher Islands, Cape Henrietta Maria, and Quebec (Hudson Bay, coast of the Ungava Peninsula), also on the Chukotski Peninsula in eastern Siberia; and [*bewickii* group] from northern Russia east along the Arctic coast (including Novaya Zemlya and other islands) to northern Siberia.

Winters [*columbianus* group] on the Pacific coast of North America from coastal and southern interior British Columbia south to southern California, in the interior through the valleys of California to northern Baja California (casually), in western Nevada, northern Utah, Montana, and Wyoming, and rarely to southern Arizona, southern New Mexico, and Chihuahua; the Great Lakes region; and also commonly along the Atlantic coast and Piedmont from southeastern Pennsylvania and Maryland to North Carolina, casually north to Maine and south to Florida, and in the interior of North America south of the Great Lakes region; casual on the Gulf coast and inland in the Gulf states from southern Texas to Florida; and [*bewickii* group] in Eurasia south to the British Isles, northern Europe, the Caspian Sea, Japan, Korea, and the coast of China.

Migrates [*columbianus* group] widely through the interior of North America on large bodies of water, primarily in the Great Basin, upper Mississippi Valley and Great Lakes, also across the Appalachians in southern Pennsylvania and northern West Virginia.

Casual or *accidental* [*columbianus* group] in the Hawaiian Islands (Midway, Maui), Bermuda, Cuba, Puerto Rico, the Virgin Islands (St. Thomas), Newfoundland, England, Japan, and the Commander Islands; and [*bewickii* group] in the Aleutians (Adak), British Columbia, Washington, Oregon, California, Saskatchewan, Pennsylvania, Maryland, and Labrador (some of these reports are probably based on escaped individuals, although the bird from Adak and one from California were recoveries of birds banded in Siberia), and in the Old World in Iceland, the British Isles, Netherlands, and Sweden.

Notes.—The two groups have been considered (e.g., Johnsgard 1978) as distinct species, *C. columbianus* [Whistling Swan] and *C. bewickii* Yarrell, 1830 [Bewick's Swan], but are generally treated as conspecific (e.g., Palmer 1976, Cramp and Simmons 1977, Sibley and Monroe 1990, del Hoyo et al. 1992) despite lack of a thorough, published analysis, and despite Johnsgard's (1974) suggestion that each might be more closely related to other species of *Cygnus* than to each other.

Cygnus cygnus (Linnaeus). Whooper Swan.

> *Anas Cygnus* Linnaeus, 1758, Syst. Nat. (ed. 10) 1: 122. (in Europa, America septentrionali = Sweden.)

Habitat.—Lakes, ponds, marshes, and quiet-flowing rivers; winters also in bays and estuaries.

Distribution.—*Breeds* from Greenland (formerly; currently a visitor only), Iceland, the Faeroe Islands (formerly), Scotland, Scandinavia, and northern Russia east to Anadyrland and Kamchatka, and south to Poland, the Caspian Sea, Turkestan, and Ussuriland. One breeding record on Attu, Aleutian Islands, May 1996 (1996, N.A.S. Field Notes 50: 319).

Winters south to central Europe, the eastern Mediterranean, Black and Caspian seas; and from Korea and Japan south to eastern China (casually to India and the Bonin Islands), and east to the central Aleutian Islands (at least as far as Atka).

Casual in the Pribilof Islands, western and south-coastal Alaska, Jan Mayen, Spitsbergen, Bear Island, and south to northern Africa. Accidental in Maine (Washington County, 1903); the origin of this bird and of individuals recorded in Oregon and California is controversial.

Subfamily TADORNINAE: Shelducks and Allies

Tribe PLECTROPTERINI: Pied Shelducks

Genus *SARKIDIORNIS* Eyton

Sarkidiornis Eyton, 1838, Monogr. Anatidae, p. 20. Type, by original designation, *Anser melanotos* Pennant.

Sarkidiornis melanotos (Pennant). Comb Duck.

Anser melanotos Pennant, 1769, Indian Zool., p. 12, pl. 11. (Ceylon.)

Habitat.—Freshwater Lakes and Ponds, Freshwater Marshes (0–1200 m; Tropical to Temperate zones).

Distribution.—*Resident* [*sylvicola* group] locally in tropical America from eastern Panama (Río Chucunaque in eastern Darién, casually west to La Jagua, eastern Panamá province) south through northern South America to northwestern Peru, central Bolivia (rarely), northern Argentina, and Uruguay (generally absent from Amazonia); and [*melanotos* group] in the Old World in Africa (south of the Sahara), Madagascar, and from India east to southeastern China and Sri Lanka.

Notes.—Groups: *S. sylvicola* Ihering and Ihering, 1907 [American Comb-Duck] and *S. melanotos* [African Comb-Duck].

Tribe TADORNINI: True Shelducks and Sheldgeese

Genus *NEOCHEN* Oberholser

Neochen Oberholser, 1918, J. Wash. Acad. Sci., 8, p. 571. Type, by original designation, *Anser jubatus* Spix.

Neochen jubata (Spix). Orinoco Goose.

Anser jubatus Spix, 1825, Avium Nov. Spec. Bras., 2, p. 84, pl. 108. (Ad ripam fl. Solimoëns in insula Praya das Onças.)

Habitat.—Riverine Sand Beaches, Freshwater Marshes (Tropical Zone).

Distribution.—*Resident* in South America east of the Andes from eastern Colombia, central Venezuela, and the Guianas south to southern Bolivia, Paraguay, and northwestern Argentina.

Accidental in Barbados (19–29 March 1995, photograph) and Jamaica (1865).

Subfamily ANATINAE: True Ducks

Tribe ANATINI: Surface-feeding Ducks

Genus *CAIRINA* Fleming

Cairina Fleming, 1822, Philos. Zool. 2: 260. Type, by monotypy, *Anas moschata* Linnaeus.

Cairina moschata (Linnaeus). Muscovy Duck.

Anas moschata Linnaeus, 1758, Syst. Nat. (ed. 10) 1: 124. (in India, error = Brazil.)

Habitat.—Freshwater Lakes and Ponds, Rivers, Freshwater Marshes (0–1000 m; Tropical Zone).

Distribution.—*Resident* in the lowlands from Sinaloa and Tamaulipas south through most of Middle America (including Cozumel Island) and South America south, west of the Andes to western Ecuador and east of the Andes to northern Argentina and Uruguay.

Rare visitor or resident on the Rio Grande in Texas (Hidalgo, Starr, and Zapata counties), where breeding was reported in 1994 (T.O.S. 1995); established in Florida from feral stock, some hybridized with domestic *Anas platyrhynchos* (Robertson and Woolfenden 1992). Also established from feral stock in Cuba. Feral birds found widely in North America, including lower Rio Grande Valley.

Casual in Trinidad and western Peru.

Notes.—Also known as Muscovy.

Genus *AIX* Boie

Aix Boie, 1828, Isis von Oken, col. 329. Type, by subsequent designation (Eyton, 1838), *Anas sponsa* Linnaeus.

Aix sponsa (Linnaeus). Wood Duck.

Anas Sponsa Linnaeus, 1758, Syst. Nat. (ed. 10) 1: 128. Based mainly on "The Summer Duck" Catesby, Nat. Hist. Carolina 1: 97, pl. 97. (in America septentrionali = South Carolina.)

Habitat.—Inland waters near woodland, such as swamps, flooded forest, ponds, marshes, and along slow-moving streams and rivers, where nesting in holes in trees and bird boxes; winters mainly on fresh-water marshes, ponds, streams, and occasionally brackish marshes and estuaries.

Distribution.—*Breeds* from southern British Columbia, southern Alberta, east-central Saskatchewan, central and southeastern Manitoba, central Ontario, southern Quebec, New Brunswick, Prince Edward Island, Nova Scotia, and (possibly) Newfoundland south to central (rarely southern) coastal and interior California, west-central Nevada, central Arizona, central (rarely southern) New Mexico, central and southeastern Texas, the Gulf coast, southern Florida, and Cuba.

Winters at least irregularly throughout the breeding range in western North America (most commonly near coastal areas and in the interior valleys of California, casually south to Jalisco, Guerrero, and Distrito Federal); in eastern North America primarily in the southern parts of the breeding range north to eastern Colorado, southern Kansas, southern Minnesota, the Ohio River Valley, and New England (casually farther north); and in Cuba and the Bahamas.

Casual in southeastern Alaska (Juneau, Stikine River, Ketchikan), northeastern British Columbia, northern Baja California (sight report), Veracruz, the Yucatan Peninsula, Bermuda, Jamaica (at least formerly), and the Cayman Islands (Little Cayman). Accidental in Hispaniola, Puerto Rico, the Lesser Antilles (Saba), and Azores; European reports almost certainly based mostly on escapes.

Genus *ANAS* Linnaeus

Anas Linnaeus, 1758, Syst. Nat. (ed. 10) 1: 122. Type, by subsequent designation (Lesson, 1828), *Anas boschas* Linnaeus = *Anas platyrhynchos* Linnaeus.

Spatula Boie, 1822, Isis von Oken, col. 564. Type, by monotypy, *Anas clypeata* Linnaeus.

Dafila Stephens, 1824, in Shaw, Gen. Zool. 12(2): 126. Type, by monotypy, *Dafila caudacuta* Stephens = *Anas acuta* Linnaeus.

Mareca Stephens, 1824, in Shaw, Gen. Zool. 12(2): 130. Type, by subsequent designation (Eyton, 1838), *Mareca fistularis* Stephens = *Anas penelope* Linnaeus.

Querquedula Stephens, 1824, in Shaw, Gen. Zool. 12(2): 142. Type, by tautonymy, *Anas circia* Linnaeus = *Anas querquedula* Linnaeus.

Nettion Kaup, 1829, Skizz. Entw.-Ges. Eur. Thierw., p. 95. Type, by monotypy, *Anas crecca* Linnaeus.

Chaulelasmus "G. R. Gray" Bonaparte, 1838, Geogr. Comp. List, p. 56. Type, by monotypy, *Anas strepera* Linnaeus.

Eunetta Bonaparte, 1856, C. R. Acad. Sci. Paris 43: 650. Type, by monotypy, *Anas falcata* Georgi.

Notes.—*Mareca* is treated as a genus by Livezey (1991), with *Chaulelasmus* and *Eunetta* as subgenera. The remaining synonyms have been used for genera or subgenera.

Anas strepera Linnaeus. Gadwall.

> *Anas strepera* Linnaeus, 1758, Syst. Nat. (ed. 10) 1: 125. (in Europæ aquis dulcibus = Sweden.)

Habitat.—Shallow lakes and marshes with grassy margins; in winter, fresh-water and brackish marshes, shallow lakes, and wet and flooded fields.

Distribution.—*Breeds* [*strepera* group] in North America from southern Alaska (the Alaska Peninsula, and east to Prince William Sound and, rarely, southeastern Alaska), southern Yukon, northeastern British Columbia, central Saskatchewan, central Manitoba, central Ontario, southwestern Quebec, Prince Edward Island, Anticosti Island (rarely), and New Brunswick south locally to southern California, southern Nevada, northern Arizona, southern New Mexico, south-central Texas, southern Kansas, northern Iowa, central Minnesota, southern Wisconsin, northern Ohio, northern Pennsylvania (formerly) and, on the Atlantic coast, to North Carolina, with one isolated breeding in northern Alabama (Wheeler Refuge); and in Eurasia from Iceland, the British Isles, and southern Scandinavia east to eastern Siberia, and south to the Mediterranean region, Algeria, Turkey, Iran, Afghanistan, northern China, and Sakhalin.

Winters [*strepera* group] in the Hawaiian Islands (rarely); in North America from southern Alaska (west to the Aleutian and Kodiak islands), southern British Columbia, Idaho, Montana, southern South Dakota, southeastern Minnesota, the southern Great Lakes, and southern New England (rarely from New Brunswick and Nova Scotia) south to northern Baja California, Oaxaca, México, Puebla, Veracruz, Tabasco, Yucatán, the Gulf coast throughout, Florida, the Bahamas (New Providence, Andros), western Cuba, Jamaica (formerly), and Puerto Rico; and in Eurasia from the British Isles, central Europe, and the Black and Caspian seas south to northern and eastern Africa, and east to India, Burma, eastern China, and Japan.

Resident [*couesi* group] formerly in the southern Indian Ocean on the Crozets and Kerguelen Island (now extinct).

Casual or accidental [*strepera* group] in the Hawaiian Islands, Pribilofs, western and northern Alaska, northern Manitoba, Bermuda, Greenland, the Faeroe Islands, Nigeria, Sri Lanka, and the Marshall Islands; a sight report from the Cayman Islands.

Notes.—Groups: *A. strepera* [Common Gadwall] and *A. couesi* (Streets, 1876) [Coues's Gadwall]. This species was long placed in the genus *Chaulelasmus*; Livezey (1991) placed it in *Mareca*.

Anas falcata Georgi. Falcated Duck.

> *Anas falcata* Georgi, 1775, Bemerk. Reise Russ. Reich. 1: 167. (Baikal region, Siberia.)

Habitat.—Primarily in fresh-water on and around ponds, small lakes and quiet rivers; forages and winters also in rice fields.

Distribution.—*Breeds* in eastern Siberia from the Yenisei River east to the Sea of Okhotsk and Kamchatka, and south to Lake Baikal, Mongolia, Amurland, Sakhalin, and Japan.

Winters from Japan south to Korea and eastern China, less frequently to Iran, India, Burma, Vietnam, and southeastern China, rarely to Thailand.

Casual in Alaska in the Pribilof (St. George, St. Paul) and Aleutian islands (Attu, Shemya, Amchitka, Adak), and in the Commander Islands. Reports from British Columbia, Washington (Willapa Bay), and California (San Francisco, Newport Bay) are considered to be of uncertain origin; records from Virginia, North Carolina, and Europe almost certainly are of escapes.

Notes.—Also known as Falcated Teal. Placed in the genus *Mareca* by Livezey (1991).

Anas penelope Linnaeus. Eurasian Wigeon.

> *Anas Penelope* Linnaeus, 1758, Syst. Nat. (ed. 10) 1: 126. Based on "The Wigeon or Whewer" Albin, Nat. Hist. Birds 2: 88, pl. 99. (in Europæ maritimis & paludibis = Sweden.)

Habitat.—Marshes and lakes with substantial vegetation along shores, mainly in taiga and forested areas, less commonly in open moors and cultivated country; in winter, lakes, ponds, marshes, and estuaries (in North America, usually in association with American Wigeon).

Distribution.—*Breeds* in Eurasia from Iceland, the British Isles, and Scandinavia east to eastern Siberia and Kamchatka, south to northern Europe, central Russia, and Transcaucasia.

Winters in the Old World from Iceland, the British Isles, northern Europe, southern Russia, and Japan south to the eastern Atlantic islands, northern and eastern Africa, Arabia, India, the Malay Peninsula, southern China, Taiwan, and the Philippines, casually to Sri Lanka, Borneo, Sulawesi, and Greenland; and regularly in small numbers in North America, mostly on the Pacific coast from southeastern Alaska south to northern Baja California, and (less frequently) on the Atlantic-Gulf coast from Labrador and Newfoundland south to Florida, and in the Hawaiian Islands.

Migrates regularly (primarily in the spring) through southwestern Alaska (rare elsewhere in Alaska) and coastal British Columbia, and irregularly in the interior of North America from the southern parts of the Canadian provinces southward.

Casual or accidental throughout most of interior North America from southern Yukon to the Mexican border and the Gulf coast, Bermuda, the Antilles (Hispaniola, Puerto Rico, Barbuda, and Barbados), Jan Mayen, Spitsbergen, Bear Island, and the Caroline and Marshall Islands; sight reports from southern Baja California, Sonora, and Clipperton Island.

Notes.—Also known as European Wigeon and, in Old World literature, as the Wigeon. *Anas penelope* and *A. americana* constitute a superspecies (Mayr and Short 1970; Johnsgard *in* Mayr and Cottrell 1979); occasional hybrids between the two species have been reported. Both species were placed in the genus *Mareca* in the past, and are so treated by Livezey (1991).

Anas americana Gmelin. American Wigeon.

Anas americana Gmelin, 1789, Syst. Nat. 1(2): 526. Based on "Le Canard jensen, de la Louisiane" Daubenton, Planches Enlum., pl. 955, and the "American Wigeon" Pennant, Arct. Zool. 2: 567. (in America a Cayenna insulisque vicini Oceani ad sinum Hudsonis usque = New York.)

Habitat.—Large marshes and shallow lakes; in winter, lakes, ponds, marshes, sloughs, and estuaries, also golf courses and parks with extensive lawns.

Distribution.—*Breeds* from central (rarely western) Alaska, central Yukon, northwestern and central Mackenzie, southern Keewatin, northeastern Manitoba, northern Ontario, southern Quebec, New Brunswick, Prince Edward Island, Newfoundland, and Nova Scotia south to south-coastal Alaska (Cook Inlet east to Yakutat Bay) and coastal British Columbia, in the interior through much of British Columbia, northwestern and eastern Washington, and eastern Oregon to northeastern (rarely central) California, northern Nevada, northern Utah, eastern Arizona (formerly) northern New Mexico, central Colorado, northwestern Nebraska, South Dakota, northern Minnesota, southern Wisconsin, southern Michigan, southern Ontario, northwestern Ohio, and northern New York, sporadically to the Atlantic coast (recorded breeding in Maine, Massachusetts, and Delaware); the breeding range east of Manitoba and Minnesota is highly local.

Winters in the Hawaiian Islands; and from southern Alaska, southern British Columbia, Washington, Idaho, southern Utah, and Colorado sporadically across the central United States to the southern Great Lakes region, Ohio River Valley, and Atlantic coast (north to Nova Scotia), south throughout the southern United States, Bermuda (rare), Middle America, and the West Indies to Panama, northern Colombia, northern Venezuela (rarely), Tobago, and Trinidad.

Regular migrant in the Pribilof Islands. Casual or accidental in the Aleutians, Banks Island, Greenland, Iceland, Europe, the Azores, Japan, and the Commander, Caroline, and Marshall islands; a sight report for Clipperton Island.

Notes.—See comments under *A. penelope*.

Anas rubripes Brewster. American Black Duck.

Anas obscura (not Linnaeus, 1761) Gmelin, 1789, Syst. Nat. 1(2): 541. Based on the "Dusky Duck" Latham, Gen. Synop. Birds 3(2): 545, and Pennant, Arct. Zool. 2: 564. (in Noveboraco = New York.)

Anas obscura rubripes Brewster, 1902, Auk 19: 184. (Lake Umbagog, New Hampshire shore.)

Habitat.—A variety of wetland habitats in both fresh-water and marine situations, in and around marshes, swamps, ponds, lakes, bays, estuaries, and tidal flats, favoring wooded swamps for breeding; in winter, primarily estuaries, tidal marshes, lakes, and ponds.

Distribution.—*Breeds* from northern Saskatchewan (rarely), northern Manitoba, northern Ontario, northern Quebec, Labrador, and Newfoundland south to northern South Dakota, northern Minnesota, southern Wisconsin, northern Illinois, central Indiana, northern Ohio, central West Virginia, and on the Atlantic coast to North Carolina; also sporadic breeding west to southern Alberta and south to the northern Gulf states, Georgia, northern Florida, and Bermuda.

Winters from southeastern Minnesota, central Wisconsin, central Michigan, southern Ontario, southern Quebec, New Brunswick, Nova Scotia, and southern Newfoundland south to Texas (perhaps only casual now), the northern portions of the Gulf coastal states, and Bermuda.

Introduced and established in British Columbia (Vancouver area) and Washington (Everett).

Casual visitant (in summer in the northern areas, in migration and winter in western and southern localities) from central Alaska, northern Mackenzie, Keewatin, and Baffin Island south to northern California, Wyoming, Colorado (at least formerly), and western Texas, and along Gulf Coast and southern Florida. Accidental in Puerto Rico, Iceland, the British Isles, northern continental Europe, the Azores, and Korea; some extralimital records and peripheral reports in the southwest may pertain to escaped or released individuals.

Notes.—Formerly known in American literature as the Black Duck. See comments under *A. platyrhynchos*.

Anas platyrhynchos Linnaeus. Mallard.

Anas platyrhynchos Linnaeus, 1758, Syst. Nat. (ed. 10) 1: 125. (in Europæ maritimis = Sweden.)

Habitat.—Shallow waters such as ponds, lakes, marshes, and flooded fields; in winter, mostly in fresh-water and cultivated fields, less commonly in brackish situations; [*diazi* group] Freshwater Marshes (800–1800 m)

Distribution.—*Breeds* [*platyrhynchos* group] in North America from northern Alaska, northern Yukon, northwestern and southern Mackenzie, southern Keewatin, northeastern Manitoba, northern Ontario, southern Quebec, and southern Maine south to the Aleutian and Pribilof islands, northern Baja California, Arizona, southern New Mexico, and from Oklahoma east through the Ohio River Valley to Virginia, with local breeding (probably through introduction or semi-domestic stock) to the Gulf coast and Florida, and in the Palearctic in southwestern Greenland, Iceland, and from Scandinavia east to eastern Siberia and south to the Mediterranean region, central Asia, and Japan; and [*diazi* group] from southeastern Arizona, southern New Mexico, and west-central Texas south in the highlands of Mexico to Jalisco, Michoacán, México, Distrito Federal, Tlaxcala, and Puebla.

Winters [*platyrhynchos* group] in North America generally from southern Alaska (west coastally to the Aleutian Islands, rare in central Alaska) and southern Canada south to central Mexico (at least formerly to Michoacán, México, and Veracruz), the Gulf coast, southern Florida, and Bermuda (rare), and in Eurasia from Iceland, the British Isles, southern Scandinavia, and the southern part of the breeding range south to the eastern Atlantic islands, northern Africa, India, Burma, and Borneo; and [*diazi* group] east to southern Coahuila, San Luis Potosí, and western Tamaulipas.

Introduced and established [*platyrhynchos* group] in the Virgin Islands, Hawaiian Islands, Australia, and New Zealand; in addition, wild populations throughout most of the normal range are supplemented frequently by escapes from captivity.

Casual or accidental [*platyrhynchos* group] in Guatemala, Honduras, Nicaragua, Costa Rica (near Turrialba), Panama (Canal area), the Bahamas (Andros, New Providence), Cuba, the Cayman Islands, Puerto Rico, the Virgin Islands (St. Croix), Trinidad, Spitsbergen, Bear Island, and the Marshall and Gilbert [= Kiribati] islands.

Notes.—The two groups were formerly recognized as distinct species, *A. platyrhynchos* and *A. diazi* Ridgway, 1886 [Mexican Duck] (e.g., Aldrich and Baer 1970), but extensive hybridization in southeastern Arizona, southern New Mexico, and west-central Texas compels merger into a single species (Hubbard 1977). *Anas platyrhynchos* (including *diazi*), *A. fulvigula*, *A. rubripes*, *A. wyvilliana*, *A. laysanensis,* and possibly several Old World forms are all closely related; at least the first three appear to constitute a superspecies (Johnsgard *in* Mayr and Cottrell 1979). In various treatments, some or even all the taxa mentioned are treated as conspecific under the name *A. platyrhynchos* (e.g., Johnsgard 1961, 1967). *Anas rubripes* hybridizes frequently with *A. platyrhynchos* in an area of broad overlap, largely the result of introductions of the latter in the range of the former. These two forms differ somewhat behaviorally and tend to segregate as species (Brodsky and Weatherhead 1984, Hepp et al. 1988), although genetically they are virtually identical (Ankney et al. 1986, Ankney and Dennis 1988, Avise et al. 1990).

Anas fulvigula Ridgway. Mottled Duck.

> *Anas obscura,* var. *fulvigula* Ridgway, 1874, Amer. Nat. 8: 111. (St. John's river, Florida = Dummits, Brevard County.)

Habitat.—Fresh-water and brackish marshes and ponds, usually treeless, foraging also in wet and flooded fields, especially rice.

Distribution.—*Breeds* along the Gulf coast from northwestern Florida, southern Alabama, southern Louisiana, and Texas south to Tamaulipas; in peninsular Florida from Alachua County south to Cape Sable; and locally inland in central Kansas and northeastern Texas.

Winters in the breeding range and along the entire Gulf coast from western Florida to central Texas and south to Veracruz.

Introduced and established in South Carolina.

Casual in the Great Plains region from Nebraska south to northern Texas, and southern Florida (Key Largo); a sight report for Nuevo León.

Notes.—Some individuals taken in the Great Plains region from Kansas to Oklahoma show indications of hybridization with *A. platyrhynchos* (Hubbard 1977).

Anas wyvilliana Sclater. Hawaiian Duck.

> *Anas wyvilliana* Sclater, 1878, Proc. Zool. Soc. London, p. 350. (Hawaiian Islands.)

Habitat.—Coastal lagoons, marshes, and mountain streams.

Distribution.—*Resident* in the Hawaiian Islands (Kauai and possibly Niihau, formerly on all main islands except Lanai and Kahoolawe); recent introductions from captive stocks to Oahu and Hawaii have bred successfully.

A record from Sinaloa (Mazatlán, prior to 1859 = type of *A. aberti* Ridgway, 1878) is almost certainly based on a mislabeled specimen.

Notes.—Also known as Koloa. See comments under *A. platyrhynchos.*

Anas laysanensis Rothschild. Laysan Duck.

> *Anas laysanensis* Rothschild, 1892, Bull. Brit. Ornithol. Club 1: 17. (Island of Laysan.)

Habitat.—Brackish lagoons, and adjacent dense brush and sedges.

Distribution.—*Resident* in small numbers on Laysan Island, in the Hawaiian Islands.

Notes.—Also known as Laysan Teal. See comments under *A. platyrhynchos.*

Anas poecilorhyncha Forster. Spot-billed Duck.

> *Anas poecilorhyncha* J. R. Forster, 1781, Zool. Indica, p. 23, pl. 13, fig. 1. (Ceylon.)

Habitat.—Small streams and ponds.

Distribution.—*Breeds* in eastern Asia from Siberia and Sakhalin south to India, Sri Lanka, and Southeast Asia, and *winters* south to the Philippines.

Casual in Alaska in the Aleutians (Attu, Adak) and on Kodiak Island.

Anas discors Linnaeus. Blue-winged Teal.

Anas discors Linnaeus, 1766, Syst. Nat. (ed. 12) 1: 205. Based mainly on "The White-face Teal" Catesby, Nat. Hist. Carolina 1: 100, pl. 100. (in America septentrionali = South Carolina.)

Habitat.—Fresh-water and brackish marshes, ponds, sloughs, lakes, and sluggish streams, with emergent vegetation; in winter, primarily fresh-water and brackish marshes, also in wet and flooded fields.

Distribution.—*Breeds* from east-central Alaska, southern Yukon, southern Mackenzie, northern Saskatchewan, central Manitoba, northern Ontario, southern Quebec, New Brunswick, Prince Edward Island, Nova Scotia, and southwestern Newfoundland south to northeastern California, central Nevada, north-central Arizona, southern New Mexico, western and southern Texas, Louisiana (locally), eastern Arkansas, central Tennessee, and eastern North Carolina, locally to north-central Arizona, the Gulf coast, and central Florida, casually to southern California and in central Mexico (Distrito Federal).

Winters from northern California, southern Arizona, central New Mexico, western and southern Texas, the Gulf coast, and North Carolina on the Atlantic coast (casually north to Montana, the southern Great Lakes, and Chesapeake Bay) south throughout Middle America and the West Indies to central Peru, central Argentina, and southern Brazil.

Casual in the Hawaiian Islands (bred twice on Hawaii), north to the Aleutians (Adak), northern Alaska, northern Mackenzie, Anticosti Island, and southern Labrador; and to Clipperton Island, Bermuda, southern Argentina, Uruguay, Greenland, the British Isles, and South Georgia. Accidental in Iceland, Europe, and the Azores; a sight report for the Galapagos Islands.

Notes.—*Anas discors* and *A. cyanoptera* are closely related and natural hybrids are known (e.g., Anderson and Miller 1953).

Anas cyanoptera Vieillot. Cinnamon Teal.

Anas cyanoptera Vieillot, 1816, Nouv. Dict. Hist. Nat. (nouv. éd.) 5: 104. Based on "Pato Alas azules" Azara, Apunt. Hist. Nat. Páx. Parag. 3: 437 (no. 434). (dans l'Amérique meridionale sur la rivière de la Plata et à Buenos Ayres = Río de la Plata and Buenos Aires, Argentina.)

Habitat.—Shallow lakes, ponds, sluggish streams, and marshes (Tropical to Temperate zones).

Distribution.—*Breeds* in North America from coastal and southern interior British Columbia, central Alberta, southwestern Saskatchewan, central North Dakota, southwestern South Dakota (probably), western Nebraska, and central Kansas south to northern Baja California, central Mexico (to Jalisco, Valley of México, and Hidalgo) and central Texas (formerly); also one breeding record for Ontario (Amherstburg).

Winters from northern California, southern Nevada, Utah (rarely), southeastern Arizona, southern New Mexico, and central Texas south through Middle America to Colombia, northern Venezuela, and northern Ecuador (at least formerly).

Resident in South America in Colombia (Eastern Andes, and the Cauca and Magdalena valleys), and from central Peru, Bolivia, Paraguay, and southern Brazil south to the Straits of Magellan.

Casual in the Hawaiian Islands (Kauai, Molokai, Maui, Hawaii), and from northern Alaska, southern Yukon, central British Columbia, central Alberta, central Saskatchewan, southern Manitoba, western and southern Ontario, southern Quebec, New Brunswick, New York, and New Jersey south to the Gulf coast, Florida, the Bahamas (Grand Bahama), Cuba, Jamaica, and the Virgin Islands (St. Croix); a sight report for Clipperton Island.

Notes.—See comments under *A. discors*.

Anas clypeata Linnaeus. Northern Shoveler.

> *Anas clypeata* Linnaeus, 1758, Syst. Nat. (ed. 10) 1: 124. (in Europæ maritimis = southern Sweden.)

Habitat.—Shallow lakes and ponds with emergent vegetation, especially in muddy, sluggish water situations; in winter, both fresh-water and brackish marshes, shallow lakes, and flooded fields.

Distribution.—*Breeds* in North America from northern Alaska, northern Yukon, northwestern and southern Mackenzie, northern Manitoba, and northern Ontario (casually east to southern Quebec, Prince Edward Island, New Brunswick, and Nova Scotia) south to southern California (rarely west of the coast ranges from central British Columbia southward), Utah, central Arizona (possibly), northern Colorado, northwestern Oklahoma, central Kansas, northern Missouri, central Illinois, northern Indiana, central Ohio, western Pennsylvania, New York, northeastern Maryland, and Delaware, also in southern New Mexico and southeastern Texas, and casually to northern Alabama; and in Eurasia from Iceland, the British Isles, and Scandinavia east across northern Russia and Siberia to Kamchatka and the Commander Islands, and south to the Mediterranean, Black, and Caspian seas, southern Russia, Mongolia, Transbaicalia, and Sakhalin.

Winters in the Hawaiian Islands, and from coastal and southern British Columbia, western Washington, Idaho, western Montana, Colorado, central Texas, the Gulf coast, and Maryland on the Atlantic coast south through Middle America, Bermuda, and the West Indies to Colombia, the Netherlands Antilles, and Trinidad, rarely in southern Alaska (in the Aleutians, on Kodiak Island, and in southeastern Alaska), and north to Iowa, the Great Lakes, and New England; and in the Old World from the British Isles, central Europe, southern Russia, eastern China, and Japan south to northern and eastern Africa, the Indian Ocean, Malay Peninsula, Borneo, the Philippines, and Micronesia.

Migrates regularly through the Aleutian Islands.

Casual or accidental in Clipperton Island, Labrador, Newfoundland, Greenland, Spitsbergen, Bear Island, the eastern Atlantic islands, South Africa, and the Gilbert Islands.

Notes.—Known in Old World literature as the Shoveler.

Anas bahamensis Linnaeus. White-cheeked Pintail.

> *Anas bahamensis* Linnaeus, 1758, Syst. Nat. (ed. 10) 1: 124. (in Bahama = Bahama Islands.)

Habitat.—Freshwater Marshes, Coastal Saltwater Marshes, Freshwater Lakes and Ponds, Alkaline Lakes, Coastal Waters, sometimes foraging in cultivated fields.

Distribution.—*Resident* [*bahamensis* group] in the Bahamas (from Abaco south to the Caicos), Greater Antilles, northern Lesser Antilles (south to Guadeloupe), islands off the north coast of Venezuela (Netherlands Antilles east to Tobago and Trinidad), and along the coasts (mostly) of South America south to northern Chile and northeastern Argentina; and [*galapagensis* group] in the Galapagos Islands.

Casual [*bahamensis* group] in peninsular Florida, the Florida Keys, and the Cayman Islands (Grand Cayman). Accidental [*bahamensis* group] in Wisconsin (Lake Winneconne), Illinois (Steward Lake), Texas (Laguna Atascosa), Alabama (Magnolia Springs), Virginia (Pungo, Chincoteague), and Delaware (Assawoman); most or all of these reports, as well as those from California and one from New Jersey representing a South American race, probably pertain to escapes from captivity.

Notes.—Also known as Bahama Pintail or Bahama Duck. Groups: *A. bahamensis* [White-cheeked Pintail] and *A. galapagensis* (Ridgway, 1889) [Galapagos Pintail].

Anas acuta Linnaeus. Northern Pintail.

> *Anas acuta* Linnaeus, 1758, Syst. Nat. (ed. 10) 1: 126. (in Europæ maritimis = Sweden.)

Habitat.—Lakes, rivers, marshes, and ponds in grasslands, barrens, dry tundra, open boreal forest, and cultivated fields; in winter, shallow lakes, ponds, marshes, and estuaries.

Distribution.—*Breeds* in North America from northern Alaska, northern Yukon, northern

Mackenzie, southwestern Banks Island, southern Victoria Island, northern Keewatin, Southampton Island, northern and eastern Quebec, central Labrador, New Brunswick, and Nova Scotia south, at least locally, to southwestern and south-coastal Alaska, along the Pacific coast to southern California, and to northern Arizona, southern New Mexico, western Oklahoma (Panhandle), Kansas, northwestern Missouri, northern Iowa, northern Illinois, northern Indiana, northern Ohio, northern New York, and Massachusetts, casually or sporadically to western Kentucky and Virginia, also once on Ellesmere Island and recorded in summer casually to Banks and Baffin islands, and in Newfoundland; and in the Palearctic from western Greenland, Iceland, the Faeroe Islands, Spitsbergen, and Scandinavia east across Arctic areas to the Chukotski Peninsula, Kamchatka, and the Commander Islands, and south to the British Isles, central Europe, Caspian Sea, Transcaucasia, and the Kuril Islands.

Winters in the Hawaiian Islands; in the Americas from southern Alaska (coastal areas west to the Aleutian and Kodiak islands), coastal and southern interior British Columbia, central Washington, southern Idaho, Montana, eastern Colorado, Nebraska, central Missouri, the southern Great Lakes, and along the Atlantic coast from Massachusetts, south throughout the southern United States, Middle America, Bermuda, and the West Indies (south at least to Guadeloupe) to northern Colombia, northern Venezuela, and the Guianas; and in the Old World from the British Isles, southern Scandinavia, southern Russia, Turkestan, and Japan south to northern and eastern Africa, the Indian Ocean, Borneo, the Philippines, and islands of Micronesia.

Migrates regularly in the Aleutians, Labrador, and Newfoundland.

Casual to Clipperton Island, Bear Island, Madeira, and the Azores.

Notes.—*Anas eatoni* (Sharpe, 1875) of Kerguelen Island (including *A. drygalskii* Reichenow, 1904 of the Crozet Islands) is often (e.g., A.O.U. 1983) considered conspecific with *A. acuta,* but has been separated by Stahl et al. (1984) [Eaton's Pintail]. Also known as Common Pintail and, in Old World literature, as the Pintail. Johnsgard *in* Mayr and Cottrell (1979) considered *A. acuta* and South American *A. georgica* Gmelin, 1789 to constitute a superspecies.

Anas querquedula Linnaeus. Garganey.

> *Anas Querquedula* Linnaeus, 1758, Syst. Nat. (ed. 10) 1: 126. (in Europæ aquis dulcibus = Sweden.)

Habitat.—Shallow inland lakes, ponds, and streams bordered with dense emergent vegetation, reed beds or marshes; winters primarily on fresh-water but also in marine or brackish situations.

Distribution.—*Breeds* from the British Isles, southern Scandinavia, central Russia, and eastern Siberia (east to Amurland and Kamchatka) south to southern Europe, the Black and Caspian seas, Turkey, Transcaucasia, Mongolia, and Ussuriland.

Winters in the Hawaiian Islands (rarely), and from the Mediterranean Sea (rarely), Iraq, Arabia, India, eastern China, Taiwan, and Japan south to southern Africa, the Maldive Islands, Sri Lanka, Greater Sunda Islands, New Guinea, and Australia.

Migrates regularly through the western Aleutians (casually as far east as Adak, in the Pribilofs, and at Middleton Island).

Casual (mainly as spring migrant) in Iceland, the Faeroe Islands, Azores, and widely in continental North America from southern British Columbia, Alberta, Saskatchewan, Manitoba, Ontario, Minnesota, Quebec, New Brunswick, Prince Edward Island, and Nova Scotia south to California, Arizona, New Mexico, Texas, Oklahoma, Kansas, Iowa, Illinois, and North Carolina. Accidental in Bermuda, Puerto Rico, and Barbados; sight reports for Sinaloa and Missouri.

Anas formosa Georgi. Baikal Teal.

> *Anas formosa* Georgi, 1775, Bemerk. Reise Russ. Reich. 1: 168. (um Irkutsk . . . und dem ganzen südlichen Baikal = Lake Baikal, Siberia.)

Habitat.—Small ponds, pools or edges of streams, generally in forested areas.

Distribution.—*Breeds* in eastern Siberia from the Yenisei River east to western Anadyrland and Kamchatka, and south to Lake Baikal, Transbaicalia, and the Sea of Okhotsk.

Winters from eastern China, Korea, and Japan south (currently rare) to India, Burma, and Thailand.

Casual in western and northern Alaska from Wainwright south to the Pribilofs, Nanvak Bay, and the Aleutians (Attu), and in fall and winter on the Pacific coast from British Columbia south to southern California. Birds reported from Colorado, Oklahoma, Ohio, Pennsylvania, New Jersey, North Carolina, and Europe may be escaped individuals.

Anas crecca Linnaeus. Green-winged Teal.

> *Anas Crecca* Linnaeus, 1758, Syst. Nat. (ed. 10) 1: 126. (in Europæ aquis dulcibus = Sweden.)

Habitat.—Shallow lakes, marshes, ponds, pools, and shallow streams with emergent vegetation; in winter, both fresh-water and brackish situations around marshes, shallow lakes, estuaries, and wet and flooded fields.

Distribution.—*Breeds* [*crecca* group] in North America in the Pribilof Islands and Aleutian Islands (east to Akutan), Greenland (casually), and in Eurasia from the British Isles east to eastern Siberia and the Commander, Kuril, and Bering islands, and south to the Mediterranean, Black, and Caspian seas, Mongolia, Manchuria, Ussuriland, and Japan; and [*carolinensis* group] in North America from western and northern Alaska (including the eastern Aleutians), northern Yukon, northwestern and southern Mackenzie, southern Keewatin, northeastern Manitoba, northern Ontario, northern Quebec, north-central Labrador, and Newfoundland south to western Washington, central Oregon, northern Nevada, northern Utah (rarely), Colorado, South Dakota, southern Minnesota, southern Ontario, southern Quebec, Massachusetts, and Nova Scotia, with sporadic local breeding south to southern California, northeastern Arizona, southern New Mexico, Kansas, northern Iowa, northern Illinois, northern Indiana, northern Ohio, Pennsylvania, northeastern West Virginia, and on the Atlantic coast to Maryland and Delaware.

Winters [*crecca* group] in North America in the Aleutians, and in Eurasia from Iceland, the British Isles, northern Europe, the Black and Caspian seas, Korea, and Japan south to tropical Africa, India, Sri Lanka, the Malay Peninsula, southeastern China, and the Philippines; and [*carolinensis* group] in the Hawaiian Islands, and in North America from southern Alaska (Kodiak Island), southern British Columbia, central Montana, South Dakota, southern Minnesota, southern Wisconsin, the Great Lakes, New York, New England, New Brunswick, and Nova Scotia south to Baja California, Oaxaca, the Gulf coast, southern Florida, Bermuda, and the Bahamas, rarely to northern Central America (El Salvador, northern Honduras, and Belize), the Antilles (recorded south to Tobago), the Cayman Islands, and Bermuda.

Migrates [*crecca* group] in small numbers through Greenland.

Casual [*crecca* group] in the Hawaiian Islands (Midway, Oahu), in continental North America from Alaska and Labrador south on the Pacific coast to southern California, in the interior to Nevada, Ohio, and Pennsylvania, and on the Atlantic coast to Florida, and in Micronesia, Jan Mayen, Spitsbergen, and the eastern Atlantic islands; and [*carolinensis* group] in Nicaragua, Costa Rica, Colombia, Greenland, the British Isles, continental Europe, Morocco, and Japan.

Notes.—Known in Old World literature as the Teal. The two groups within the species were formerly considered as separate species, *A. crecca* [Common Teal] and *A. carolinensis* Gmelin, 1789 [Green-winged Teal], but are now generally treated as conspecific (e.g., Palmer 1976, Cramp and Simmons 1977, Sibley and Monroe 1990, del Hoyo et al. 1992). No analysis, however, has been published concerning the nature of variation in the region where the groups are parapatric, and only a few intergrades have been documented (Palmer 1976). Johnsgard *in* Mayr and Cottrell (1979), considered *A. crecca* and South American *A. flavirostris* Vieillot, 1816, to constitute a superspecies.

Tribe AYTHYINI: Pochards and Allies

Genus *AYTHYA* Boie

> *Aythya* Boie, (before May) 1822, Tageb. Reise Norwegen, p. 351. Type, by monotypy, *Anas marila* Linnaeus.

Nyroca Fleming, (June) 1822, Philos. Zool. 2: 260. Type, by tautonymy, *Anas nyroca* Güldenstädt.

Aristonetta Baird, 1858, in Baird, Cassin, and Lawrence, Rep. Explor. Surv. R. R. Pac. 9: 793. Type, by original designation, *Anas valisineria* Wilson.

Perissonetta Oberholser, 1921, Proc. Ind. Acad. Sci. (1920), p. 110. Type, by original designation, *Anas collaris* Donovan.

Notes.—Livezey (1996b) recognized *Aristonetta* as a genus for the species *valisineria, americana,* and *ferina.*

Aythya valisineria (Wilson). Canvasback.

Anas valisineria Wilson, 1814, Amer. Ornithol. 8: 103, pl. 70, fig. 5. (United States.)

Habitat.—Fresh-water marshes and lakes with emergent vegetation; winters on deep, fresh-water lakes, rivers, and marshes as well as on bays and estuaries.

Distribution.—*Breeds* from central Alaska, northern Yukon, western and southern Mackenzie, central Saskatchewan, central and northeastern Manitoba, and western Ontario south to south-coastal Alaska (Anchorage area east to Bering River delta), and locally in inland areas to northeastern (casually central) California, northern Nevada, northern Utah (rarely), central New Mexico, central Kansas, northwestern Iowa, southwestern Ontario, Wisconsin, Michigan, and central New York. Occurs in summer in Alaska west to Seward Peninsula.

Winters along the Pacific coast from the central Aleutians (in small numbers west to Adak) and south-coastal Alaska south to Baja California, and from interior Washington, Idaho, western Montana, Colorado, Nebraska, Iowa, the Great Lakes and, on the Atlantic coast, from New England (sporadically north in the western states to southern Canada) south to southern Mexico (Veracruz and the Yucatan Peninsula), the Gulf coast, and Florida.

Migrates through southern Ontario and southwestern Quebec.

Casual or accidental in the Hawaiian Islands, western Aleutians, Pribilofs (St. Paul), Clipperton Island, Guatemala, Honduras, eastern Canada (north to New Brunswick and Nova Scotia), Bermuda, Cuba, Puerto Rico, the Marshall Islands, Iceland, and Germany; sight reports from Nicaragua, and the Bahama and Swan islands.

Notes.—See comments under *A. ferina.*

Aythya americana (Eyton). Redhead.

Fuligula americana Eyton, 1838, Monogr. Anatidae, p. 155. (North America.)

Habitat.—Extensive fresh-water marshes; in winter, mostly brackish and marine lagoons, estuaries, and bays, less frequently in fresh-water lakes and marshes.

Distribution.—*Breeds* locally in interior south-central and southeastern Alaska, and from central and northeastern British Columbia, southwestern Mackenzie, northern Saskatchewan, west-central and southern Manitoba, and northwestern and central Minnesota south to southern California, central (rarely southern) Arizona, central (rarely southern) New Mexico, northern Texas (Panhandle), central Kansas, and northern Iowa, sporadically in eastern North America from Wisconsin, Michigan, southern Ontario, southern Quebec, New Brunswick, and Nova Scotia south to northern Illinois, northwestern Indiana, northern Ohio, western Pennsylvania (formerly), and central and southeastern New York, also in interior Mexico in Jalisco and Distrito Federal.

Winters from coastal and southern interior British Columbia, Washington, Idaho, western Montana, Colorado, Kansas, the middle Mississippi and Ohio river valleys, and the Great Lakes (occasionally north to North Dakota and the upper Great Lakes), and from New England on the Atlantic coast south throughout the southern United States and most of Mexico to Guatemala, Jamaica, Bermuda (rare), and the Bahamas.

Casual in the Hawaiian Islands, northern and western Alaska, southern Yukon, Nicaragua, Cuba, Greenland, and Sweden; a sight report for Guam.

Notes.—See comments under *A. ferina.*

Aythya ferina (Linnaeus). Common Pochard.

> *Anas ferina* Linnaeus, 1758, Syst. Nat. (ed. 10) 1: 126. (in Europæ maritimis = Sweden.)

Habitat.—Fresh-water marshes and lakes with emergent vegetation; winters in fresh-water and brackish areas, rarely in bays and estuaries.

Distribution.—*Breeds* from Iceland, the British Isles, southern Scandinavia, central Russia, and southern Siberia south to Spain, central Europe, Tunisia (formerly), the Black and Caspian seas, Turkey, and Lake Baikal.

Winters from the British Isles, central Europe, southern Sweden, and southern Russia south to the Mediterranean region, northern Africa, Arabia, India, Burma, eastern China, and Japan, rarely to the eastern Atlantic islands, Taiwan, and the Philippines.

Migrates regularly through the western Aleutian Islands (east to Adak), casually in the Pribilof Islands (St. Paul, St. George) and on St. Lawrence Island.

Casual or accidental in the northwestern Hawaiian Islands (Midway), western (near Nome) and south-coastal Alaska (Homer), California (Silver Lakes), the Faeroe Islands, and Guam.

Notes.—Known in Old World literature as the Pochard. Relationships among *A. ferina*, *A. valisineria* and *A. americana* are close (Livezey 1996a); Johnsgard *in* Mayr and Cottrell (1979) considered *A. ferina* and *A. valisineria* to constitute a superspecies.

Aythya collaris (Donovan). Ring-necked Duck.

> *Anas collaris* Donovan, 1809, Nat. Hist. Brit. Birds 6: 147 and text. (Lincolnshire, England, specimen found in Leadenhall market, London.)

Habitat.—Fresh-water marshes, sloughs, bogs, and swamps, usually in forested areas; in winter, primarily on lakes, ponds, slow-moving rivers, and (less frequently) marshes and estuaries.

Distribution.—*Breeds* in east-central and southeastern Alaska, and from northeastern British Columbia, southern Yukon, northwestern and southern Mackenzie, northern Saskatchewan, central Manitoba, northern Ontario, southern Quebec, Newfoundland, and Nova Scotia south to south-coastal British Columbia, northwestern Washington, eastern Oregon, northern California, central Nevada, eastern Arizona (rarely), western Colorado, northern Nebraska (formerly), northeastern South Dakota, northern Iowa, Wisconsin, northern Indiana, southern Ontario, western Pennsylvania (formerly), northern New York, Massachusetts (formerly), and Maine; also in Georgia (Augusta) and north-central Florida (Alachua County).

Winters in the Hawaiian Islands (rarely); and on the Pacific coast from southeastern Alaska, in the interior from Washington, Idaho, western Montana, Colorado, Oklahoma, the lower Mississippi and Ohio river valleys, the southern Great Lakes region, and New England south through the southern United States, Middle America, and the West Indies to Panama (east to eastern Panamá province) and Grenada.

Casual in northern, western, and southwestern Alaska, and in the Hawaiian Islands, Bermuda, Venezuela (including Margarita Island), Trinidad, Iceland, Europe, the Azores, and Japan; a sight report for Clipperton Island.

Aythya fuligula (Linnaeus). Tufted Duck.

> *Anas Fuligula* Linnaeus, 1758, Syst. Nat. (ed. 10) 1: 128. (in Europæ maritimis = Sweden.)

Habitat.—Primarily marshy ponds and small lakes; in winter, mostly in marine and brackish areas (European range), less commonly in fresh-water (most American records).

Distribution.—*Breeds* from Iceland, the Faeroe Islands, Bear Island (probably), and Scandinavia east to Ussuriland, Sakhalin, and the Commander Islands, and south to central Europe, the Mediterranean Sea (rarely), Syria, Transcaucasia, northern Mongolia, and Japan.

Winters from Iceland, the British Isles, southern Scandinavia, and Japan south to northern Africa, Arabia, India, the Malay Peninsula, eastern China, and the Philippines.

Migrates regularly through the western and central Aleutians, casually north to the Pribilofs, St. Lawrence Island, and Barrow, and east in southern Alaska to Unalaska, and Kodiak islands, and to Cordova.

Rare and irregular in the Hawaiian Islands; elsewhere along the Pacific coast of North America from southern British Columbia south to southern California, and inland to Montana (sight report), Saskatchewan (sight report), Wyoming, and Arizona; on the Atlantic coast from Newfoundland, Nova Scotia, Prince Edward Island, and Massachusetts to New Jersey and inland to the Great Lakes region, southern Ontario, southern Quebec, and central New York; and in Bermuda, Greenland, Spitsbergen, the eastern Atlantic islands, southern Africa, Seychelles, the Greater Sunda Islands, and Micronesia. Some records from eastern North America may pertain to escapees from captivity.

Aythya marila (Linnaeus). Greater Scaup.

Anas Marila Linnaeus, 1761, Fauna Svecica, ed. 2, p. 39. (in Lapponica = Lapland.)

Habitat.—Ponds and lakes primarily in taiga and tundra; in winter, mostly bays, estuaries, and lagoons, less commonly on fresh-water lakes.

Distribution.—*Breeds* from western Alaska (Kotzebue Sound south locally to the Aleutians, Alaska Peninsula, and Kodiak Island) east across northern Yukon, northwestern, north-central, and southern Mackenzie, southern Keewatin, around Hudson Bay, eastern James Bay, and northern Quebec (possibly also Labrador), casually or irregularly south to southeastern Alaska (Copper-Bering River deltas), central Manitoba, New Brunswick, Anticosti, and Magdalen islands, and Newfoundland (other southern reports open to question); and in Eurasia from Iceland, the Faeroe Islands (formerly), and Scandinavia east across Arctic Russia to eastern Siberia, Kamchatka, and the Commander Islands.

Winters in western North America from the Aleutians, southeastern Alaska, coastal and southern British Columbia, interior Washington, and western Montana south to northern Baja California, southeastern California, southwestern Arizona, and southern New Mexico, in central North America from the Great Lakes region and Ohio and lower Mississippi river valleys south to the Gulf coast (from southern Texas east to Florida), and on the Atlantic coast from Newfoundland south to central Florida and Bermuda (rare); and in Eurasia from the British Isles, southern Scandinavia, and the Baltic and North seas south to the Mediterranean, Black, and Caspian seas, the Persian Gulf, and northwestern India, and on the Pacific coast from Sakhalin and Japan south to Korea and eastern China, rarely to Taiwan and the Philippines.

Migrates regularly through throughout most of interior North America.

Casual in the Hawaiian Islands, the Bahamas (New Providence), Greenland, Jan Mayen and Bear islands, and south to the Azores and northern Africa; sight reports from Costa Rica and the Virgin Islands (St. Croix).

Notes.—Known in Old World literature as the Scaup.

Aythya affinis (Eyton). Lesser Scaup.

Fuligula affinis Eyton, 1838, Monogr. Anatidae, p. 157. (North America.)

Habitat.—Marshes, ponds, and small lakes; in winter, bays, estuaries, shallow water along coast, lakes, rivers, and ponds.

Distribution.—*Breeds* from central Alaska, central Yukon, northwestern and southern Mackenzie, northern Manitoba, and northern Ontario south through interior British Columbia, northern Idaho, northern Wyoming, North Dakota, northeastern South Dakota, and northwestern and (formerly) central Minnesota, casually or irregularly east to southern Ontario and central Quebec, and south to Washington, central California, northern Utah, western and central Colorado, central Nebraska, Kansas, northwestern Iowa, central Illinois, and western New York, formerly to northern Kentucky and northern Ohio. Occurs in summer in Alaska west to Seward Peninsula.

Winters in the Hawaiian Islands and southern Alaska (rare at Kodiak and Cordova), and from coastal and southern British Columbia, Washington, Idaho, Montana, northeastern Colorado, Kansas, Iowa, the southern Great Lakes region, and New England south throughout the southern United States, Middle America, Bermuda (rare), and the West Indies to northern Colombia, northern Venezuela, Tobago, and Trinidad (uncommon to rare from Costa Rica and the Lesser Antilles southward).

Migrates regularly east to New Brunswick, Nova Scotia, and Newfoundland.

Casual in Pribilof Islands, Clipperton Island, western Ecuador, Greenland, England, and Ireland; a sight report for Surinam.

Tribe MERGINI: Seaducks and Mergansers

Genus *POLYSTICTA* Eyton

Polysticta Eyton, 1836, Cat. Brit. Birds, p. 58. Type, by monotypy, *Anas stelleri* Pallas.

Polysticta stelleri (Pallas). Steller's Eider.

Anas Stelleri Pallas, 1769, Spic. Zool. 1(6): 35, pl. v. (E. Kamtschatka = Kamchatka.)

Habitat.—Arctic ponds and lakes; in winter, shallow marine habitats around bays, reefs, lagoons, and inlets.

Distribution.—*Breeds* in North America along the Arctic coast of Alaska from Point Barrow south to St. Lawrence Island and Hooper Bay; and in Eurasia along the Arctic coast of Siberia from the New Siberian Islands and Lena Delta (casually Scandinavia and Novaya Zemlya) east to the Chukotski Peninsula. Recorded in summer (and possibly breeding) in northern Yukon and northwestern Mackenzie.

Winters in North America in the Pribilof and Aleutian islands, and east along the southern coast of Alaska to Cook Inlet (rarely to Prince William Sound), casually south along the Pacific coast to northern California; and in Eurasia from Scandinavia and northern Siberia south to the Baltic Sea, southern Kamchatka, and the Commander and Kuril islands.

Casual or accidental in Quebec (Godbout), Maine (Scarborough), Massachusetts (off Scituate), Baffin Island, Greenland, Iceland, the British Isles, Spitsbergen, and northern continental Europe.

Genus *SOMATERIA* Leach

Somateria Leach, 1819, in Ross, Voy. Discovery, app., p. xlviii. Type, by monotypy, *Anas spectabilis* Linnaeus.

Eider Jarocki, 1819, Spis. Ptakow Gab. Zool. Krol. Warsz. Uniw., p. 62. Type, by monotypy, *Anas mollissima* "Gmelin" [= Linnaeus].

Lampronetta J. F. Brandt, 1847, Fuligulam (Lampronettam) Fischeri Nov. Avium Rossicarum Spec., pp. 18, 19 and plate. Type, by monotypy, *Fuligula (Lampronetta) fischeri* Brandt.

Somateria fischeri (Brandt). Spectacled Eider.

Fuligula Fischeri J. F. Brandt, 1847, Fuligulam (Lampronettam) Fischeri Nov. Avium Rossicarum Spec., p. 18, pl. 1. (St. Michael, Alaska.)

Habitat.—Arctic ponds, lakes, deltas, and tidal inlets with grass or sedge margins; in winter, primarily openings in pack ice.

Distribution.—*Breeds* on the Arctic coast of Alaska from Point Barrow south to St. Lawrence Island and the mouth of the Kuskokwim River, and along the Arctic coast of Siberia from the Yana Delta east to the Chukotski Peninsula. Populations declining dramatically in recent decades.

Winters in openings in the Bering Sea icepack; recorded irregularly in coastal Alaska.

Accidental in Norway; the origin of an individual supposedly taken in 1893 at Bitterwater Lake, San Benito County, California, is questionable.

Somateria spectabilis (Linnaeus). King Eider.

Anas spectabilis Linnaeus, 1758, Syst. Nat. (ed. 10) 1: 123. Based mainly on "The Gray-headed Duck" Edwards, Nat. Hist. Birds 3: 154, pl. 154. (in Canada, Svecia = Sweden.)

Habitat.—Arctic ponds and pools; in winter, primarily offshore along rocky coasts and in large bays.

Distribution.—*Breeds* in North America along the Arctic coast and islands from northern Alaska east to Greenland, the west coast of Hudson Bay, islands in Hudson and James bays, and (probably) northern Quebec, and south to islands in the Bering Sea (St. Lawrence, St. Matthews); and in Eurasia along the Arctic coast from northern Russia (including Spitsbergen and Novaya Zemlya) east to the Chukotski Peninsula.

Winters in the Pacific region from Kamchatka and the Bering Sea south to the Kuril, Aleutian and Shumagin islands, rarely to the southern mainland coast of Alaska, casually as far south on the Pacific coast as southern California; in the Atlantic from Labrador and Greenland south to New England, New York (Long Island), New Jersey, and Maryland, and casually as far south as Florida; in the interior of North America on open waters in Hudson and James bays, rarely to the Great Lakes, and casually to Kansas, Nebraska, Iowa, Illinois, Indiana, Kentucky, West Virginia, and central South Carolina; and in western Eurasia to Iceland and the Scandinavian and northern Russian coasts.

Casual in Alberta, Saskatchewan, Louisiana, the Faeroe Islands, British Isles, Jan Mayen, Bear Island, continental Europe, and Japan.

Somateria mollissima (Linnaeus). Common Eider.

> *Anas mollissima* Linnaeus, 1758, Syst. Nat. (ed. 10) 1: 124. Based on "The Great Black and White Duck" Edwards, Nat. Hist. Birds 2: 98, pl. 98. (in Europa boreali, pelagica = Island of Gotland, Sweden.)

Habitat.—Ponds and lagoons with outlets to the sea; in winter, primarily seacoasts, bays, and estuaries.

Distribution.—*Breeds* [*mollissima* group] on southern Ellesmere, Cornwallis, Devon, Somerset, and Baffin islands, along coasts of Hudson Bay, islands and east coast of James Bay, and along coasts from northern Quebec, Labrador, and Newfoundland south to eastern Quebec (mouth of St. Lawrence River), New Hampshire, Maine, and Nova Scotia, and in the western Palearctic from Greenland (both coasts), Iceland, the Faeroe Islands, Spitsbergen, and Franz Josef Land south to the northern British Isles, northern Europe, and southern Scandinavia, and in the northern Netherlands; and [*v-nigrum* group] in western North America from the Arctic coast of Alaska and Canada east to northeastern Mackenzie, on southern Banks and southern Victoria islands, and south (locally) in Alaska to the Aleutians, Alaska Peninsula, and south-coastal Alaska (east probably to Glacier Bay), and in the eastern Palearctic from Wrangel Island, the New Siberian Islands, and northeastern coast of Siberia south to Kamchatka and the Commander Islands.

Winters [*mollissima* group] in eastern North America in open water of Hudson and James bays, from Labrador south along the Atlantic coast to New York (Long Island), rarely to North Carolina (Outer Banks), and casually south as far as southern Florida and inland to the Great Lakes, and in the western Palearctic from the breeding range south to central Europe; and [*v-nigrum* group] in western North America from the Bering Sea ice pack south to the Aleutians and Cook Inlet, on the Pacific coast south (rarely) to southeastern Alaska, and in eastern Eurasia south to Kamchatka.

Introduced [*mollissima* group] in southeastern Massachusetts.

Casual [*mollissima* group] inland North America west to Nebraska, Wisconsin, and Illinois, and in the western Palearctic south to the Azores and southern Europe; and [*v-nigrum* group] in British Columbia and east to North Dakota, Minnesota, Iowa, and Kansas. Accidental [*v-nigrum* group] in Saskatchewan, Newfoundland, and western Greenland.

Notes.—Known in Old World literature as the Eider. Groups: *S. mollissima* [Common Eider] and *S. v-nigrum* Gray 1856 [Pacific Eider].

Genus *HISTRIONICUS* Lesson

> *Histrionicus* Lesson, 1828, Man. Ornithol. 2: 415. Type, by original designation, *Anas histrionica* Linnaeus.

Histrionicus histrionicus (Linnaeus). Harlequin Duck.

> *Anas histrionica* Linnaeus, 1758, Syst. Nat. (ed. 10) 1: 127. Based on "The Dusky and Spotted Duck" Edwards, Nat. Hist. Birds 2: 99, pl. 99. (in America = Newfoundland.)

Habitat.—Mountain streams and rivers, usually in forested regions; in winter, primarily turbulent coastal waters, especially in rocky regions.

Distribution.—*Breeds* in western North America from western Alaska, northern Yukon, northern British Columbia, and southern Alberta south to the Alaska Peninsula, southeastern Alaska, coastal British Columbia (including the Queen Charlotte and Vancouver islands), interior Washington, eastern Oregon, California (Sierra Nevada, at least formerly), central Idaho, western Wyoming, and (formerly) southwestern Colorado; in eastern North America from southern Baffin Island south to central western and eastern Quebec and eastern Labrador, possibly also Newfoundland; and in the Palearctic in Greenland and Iceland, and from the Lena River in Siberia east to Kamchatka, and south to northern Mongolia and the Kuril Islands.

Winters along the Pacific coast of North America from the Pribilof and Aleutian islands south to central (rarely southern) California; on the Atlantic coast from southern Labrador, Newfoundland, and Nova Scotia south to New York (Long Island), less commonly to the Great Lakes, casually farther inland to Nevada, Montana, northern New Mexico, Nebraska, Missouri, Tennessee, and West Virginia, on the Atlantic coast to Florida, and on the Gulf coast from western Florida to southeastern Texas; and in eastern Eurasia from Manchuria and Kamchatka south to Korea and southern Japan.

Casual or accidental in the Hawaiian Islands (Midway, Laysan), western Mackenzie, southern Canada (eastern Alberta east to Manitoba), Sonora (Puerto Peñasco), and widely through Europe.

Notes.—Known in Old World literature as the Harlequin.

Genus *CAMPTORHYNCHUS* Bonaparte

> *Camptorhynchus* "Eyton" Bonaparte, 1838, Geogr. Comp. List, p. 58. Type, by monotypy, *Anas labradoria* Gmelin.

†*Camptorhynchus labradorius* (Gmelin). Labrador Duck.

> *Anas labradoria* Gmelin, 1789, Syst. Nat. 1(2): 537. Based on "The Pied Duck" Pennant, Arct. Zool. 2: 559, and Edwards, Nat. Hist. Birds 2: 99, pl. 99. (in America boreali = Labrador.)

Habitat.—Breeding habitat unknown; winter habitat included sandy bays and estuaries.

Distribution.—EXTINCT. Alleged to have bred in Labrador. Recorded along the Atlantic coast from Nova Scotia and New Brunswick south to New York (Long Island) and New Jersey (also one report from Chesapeake Bay); and inland in Quebec (Laprairie near Montreal) and New York (Elmira), where the last known individual was taken on 12 December 1878.

Genus *MELANITTA* Boie

> *Melanitta* Boie, 1822 (before May), Tageb. Reise Norwegen, p. 351. Type, by subsequent designation (Eyton, 1838), *Anas fusca* Linnaeus.
> *Oidemia* Fleming, 1822 (May), Philos. Zool. 2: 260. Type, by subsequent designation (G. R. Gray, 1840), *Anas nigra* Linnaeus.
> *Pelionetta* Kaup, 1829, Skizz. Entw.-Ges. Eur. Thierw., p. 107. Type, by monotypy, *Anas perspicillata* Linnaeus.

Melanitta perspicillata (Linnaeus). Surf Scoter.

> *Anas perspicillata* Linnaeus, 1758, Syst. Nat. (ed. 10) 1: 125. Based on "The Great Black Duck from Hudson's-Bay" Edwards, Nat. Hist. Birds 2: 155, pl. 155. (in Canada = Hudson Bay.)

Habitat.—Lakes, ponds, or sluggish streams; in winter, primarily in shallow marine littoral areas, bays, and estuaries or occasionally on large lakes.

Distribution.—*Breeds* from the Mackenzie River delta east across central Mackenzie and northern Manitoba to Hudson Bay in northern Ontario and west-central Quebec, and south to western (from Kotzebue Sound to the Alaska Peninsula) and central Alaska, southern Yukon, northeastern British Columbia, central Alberta, and northern Saskatchewan; also in eastern Quebec and southern Labrador. Summers widely in northern Alaska, and across northern Canada from southern Keewatin east to Newfoundland, and along the Pacific coast south to California.

Winters primarily along the Pacific coast from the eastern Aleutian Islands and southeastern Alaska south to central Baja California and Sonora (also inland on the Salton Sea), in Utah (casually), on the Great Lakes (rarely), on the Atlantic coast from the Bay of Fundy to North Carolina, less commonly south to Florida, and rarely (but regularly) to the Gulf coast (Texas east to Florida).

Migrates regularly through Utah, the Dakotas, Great Lakes region, and rarely through the Mississippi and Ohio valleys.

Casual in eastern Siberia, St. Lawrence Island, the Pribilof Islands, central and western Aleutian Islands, and elsewhere throughout the interior of North America south to Arizona, New Mexico, Coahuila, and Texas, and in Bermuda, Greenland, Iceland, the Faeroe Islands, the British Isles, continental Europe, and the Azores; a sight report for Nayarit. Accidental in the Hawaiian Islands (Oahu) and Japan.

Melanitta fusca (Linnaeus). White-winged Scoter.

> *Anas fusca* Linnaeus, 1758, Syst. Nat. (ed. 10) 1: 123. (in oceano Europæo = Swedish coast.)

Habitat.—Lakes, ponds, and sluggish streams in tundra and prairie; in winter, mostly shallow marine littoral areas, bays, and estuaries, less commonly on large lakes.

Distribution.—*Breeds* [*deglandi* group] in North America from northern Alaska, northern Yukon, northwestern and southern Mackenzie, southern Keewatin, and northern Manitoba south to central Alaska, southern Yukon, interior British Columbia, southeastern Alberta, southern Saskatchewan, northern North Dakota (formerly), southern Manitoba, northern Ontario, and western Quebec, occurring in summer to northeastern Mackenzie and from Hudson Bay east to Labrador and Newfoundland, and in Asia from central and eastern Siberia south to Lake Baikal, Amurland, Sakhalin, and Kamchatka; and [*fusca* group] in Eurasia from Spitsbergen (formerly) and Scandinavia east across northern Russia to central Siberia, and south to west-central Russia.

Winters [*deglandi* group] in North America primarily on the Pacific coast from the Aleutians and Alaska Peninsula south to central California, less commonly south to northern Baja California, on the Great Lakes, and on the Atlantic coast from the Gulf of St. Lawrence and Newfoundland south to New Jersey, less commonly south to South Carolina (rarely to Florida), and in Asia from Kamchatka south to Korea, eastern China, and Japan; and [*fusca* group] in Eurasia from the breeding grounds south to the Mediterranean, Black, and Caspian seas.

Migrates [*deglandi* group] regularly through Utah, North Dakota, the Great Lakes region, and Mississippi and Ohio valleys.

Casual [*deglandi* group] on Melville Island, through the interior of North America south to southeastern California, Arizona, Sonora, New Mexico, southern Texas, and the Gulf coast (east to Florida), and in Greenland; accidental in Bermuda; and [*fusca* group] in Greenland, Iceland, the Faeroe Islands, Bear Island, Azores, northern Africa, and Afghanistan.

Notes.—Groups: *M. fusca* [Velvet Scoter] and *M. deglandi* (Bonaparte, 1850) [White-winged Scoter], the latter also including the eastern Asiatic form *M. stejnegeri* (Ridgway, 1887) [Asiatic Scoter] whose relationships appear to be with *deglandi* but whose status is uncertain.

Melanitta nigra (Linnaeus). Black Scoter.

> *Anas nigra* Linnaeus, 1758, Syst. Nat. (ed. 10) 1: 123. (in Lapponia, Anglia = Lapland and England.)

Habitat.—Lakes and pools on tundra and taiga; in winter, mostly shallow marine littoral areas and bays, less commonly on large lakes.

Distribution.—*Breeds* [*americana* group] in North America in Alaska (from Cape Lisburne and the Alaska Range south to the Alaska Peninsula and Kodiak Island) and scattered localities in central and eastern Canada (southern Keewatin, northern Quebec, and Newfoundland), with isolated breeding occurrences in Wisconsin (Door County) and North Carolina (Pamlico Sound), and from Siberia to Anadyrland, Sakhalin, Kamchatka, and the northern Kuril Islands; and [*nigra* group] in Eurasia from Iceland, the British Isles, Spitsbergen, and Scandinavia east across northern Russia. Summers widely from southern Yukon and southern Mackenzie east to Labrador and Newfoundland.

Migrates [*americana* group] regularly through the Dakotas, Great Lakes region, rarely through the Mississippi and Ohio valleys.

Winters [*americana* group] in North America primarily on the Pacific coast from the Pribilof and Aleutian islands south to southern California and (rarely) northern Baja California, on the Great Lakes (rarely), on the Atlantic coast from Newfoundland south to southern Florida, and rarely on the Gulf coast of Florida (rarely west to southern Texas), and in Korea, eastern China, and Japan; and [*nigra* group] in Eurasia from the breeding regions south to the Mediterranean, Black, and Caspian seas (casually to Greenland, northern Africa, and the eastern Atlantic islands).

Casual [*americana* group] elsewhere in the interior of North America south to Arizona, New Mexico, and Texas, and in Bermuda. Accidental [*americana* group] in the northwestern Hawaiian Islands (Midway).

Notes.—Also known as Common Scoter. Groups: *M. americana* (Swainson, 1832) [American Scoter] and *M. nigra* [Black Scoter].

Genus *CLANGULA* Leach

> *Clangula* Leach, 1819, in Ross, Voy. Discovery, app., p. xlviii. Type, by monotypy, *Anas glacialis* Linnaeus = *Anas hyemalis* Linnaeus.

Clangula hyemalis (Linnaeus). Oldsquaw.

> *Anas hyemalis* Linnaeus, 1758, Syst. Nat. (ed. 10) 1: 126. Based mainly on "The Longtailed Duck from Hudson's-Bay" Edwards, Nat Hist. Birds 3: 156, pl. 156. (in Europa & America arctica = northern Sweden.)

Habitat.—Shallow lakes in taiga and tundra; in winter, primarily on ocean near coast, also bays, pack ice, and less commonly on large inland lakes.

Distribution.—*Breeds* in North America from the Arctic coast of Alaska east across northern Canada and throughout the Arctic islands to Ellesmere and Baffin islands and Labrador, south to southern and central Alaska and northwestern British Columbia, and from eastern and south-central Mackenzie and most of Keewatin south around Hudson Bay, and the islands and northeastern coast of James Bay; and in the Palearctic from Greenland, Iceland, Spitsbergen, and Scandinavia east across Arctic Russia to the Chukotski Peninsula, Anadyrland, and the Commander Islands.

Winters from the Bering Sea south along the Pacific coast to Oregon, rarely to California and inland to Utah; along the Atlantic coast from Greenland and Labrador south to South Carolina; in the interior of North America on the Great Lakes, and rarely west to North Dakota and south through the Mississippi and Ohio river valleys to the Gulf region (from Arkansas and Texas east to Florida); in Europe from Iceland, the Faeroe Islands, Scandinavia, and western Russia south to central Europe and the Black Sea, casually to southern Europe, Madeira, and the Azores; and in Asia from Caucasia to Iran, Lake Baikal, Korea, eastern China, and Japan.

Casual elsewhere in the interior of North America from southern Canada south to southeastern California, southern Arizona, New Mexico, southern Texas, and southern Florida, and in Bermuda. Accidental in the Hawaiian Islands (Midway) and northwestern Sinaloa (near Guamuchil); sight reports for Baja California, Sonora, and Jalisco.

Notes.—Known in Old World literature as Long-tailed Duck.

Genus *BUCEPHALA* Baird

Bucephala Baird, 1858, in Baird, Cassin, and Lawrence, Rep. Explor. Surv. R. R. Pac. 9: xxiii, L, 787, 788, 795. Type, by original designation, *Anas albeola* Linnaeus.

Glaucionetta Stejneger, 1885, Proc. U. S. Natl. Mus. 8: 409. Type, by original designation, *Anas clangula* Linnaeus.

Clanganas Oberholser, 1974, Bird Life Texas, p. 974. Type, by original designation, *Anas islandica* Gmelin.

Bucephala albeola (Linnaeus). Bufflehead.

Anas Albeola Linnaeus, 1758, Syst. Nat. (ed. 10) 1: 124. Based on the "Little Black and White Duck" Edwards, Nat. Hist. Birds, p. 100, pl. 100. (in America = Newfoundland.)

Habitat.—Lakes and ponds, nesting in tree cavities in mixed coniferous-deciduous and deciduous woodland; in winter, bays, estuaries, lakes, and slow-moving rivers.

Distribution.—*Breeds* from central Alaska, southern Yukon, western and southern Mackenzie, southern Keewatin, northeastern Manitoba, and northern Ontario south locally to southern British Columbia (excluding Vancouver Island), northern Washington, western Montana, southern Alberta, southern Saskatchewan, southern Manitoba, northwestern Minnesota, central Ontario, and west-central Quebec; also locally (or formerly) south to the mountains of Oregon and northern California, and to northwestern Wyoming, central Colorado, north-central North Dakota, northwestern Iowa, and southeastern Wisconsin. Occurs in small numbers in summer on Bering Sea Islands and Seward Peninsula, Alaska.

Winters from the Aleutian Islands and the Alaska Peninsula on the Pacific coast, from Washington, Idaho, Montana, and the Great Lakes in the interior, and from New Brunswick, Nova Scotia, and Newfoundland on the Atlantic, south in coastal states and the Ohio and Mississippi river valleys (locally elsewhere in the interior) to the southern United States, northern Baja California, the interior of Mexico (to Jalisco, México, Distrito Federal, and Tamaulipas), the Gulf coast, Florida, and Bermuda.

Casual in the Hawaiian Islands, Yucatan Peninsula, Greater Antilles (Cuba, Jamaica, and Puerto Rico), Greenland, Iceland, the British Isles, continental Europe, Japan, and the Kuril and Commander islands; a sight report for the Bahama Islands (Eleuthera).

Bucephala clangula (Linnaeus). Common Goldeneye.

Anas Clangula Linnaeus, 1758, Syst. Nat. (ed. 10) 1: 125. (in Europa; sæpius maritima = Sweden.)

Habitat.—Forested ponds, lakes, rivers, and coastal bays, nesting in hollow trees and stubs near water, and in bird boxes; in winter, primarily bays, estuaries, and large lakes, less commonly on rivers.

Distribution.—*Breeds* in North America from western Alaska (Kotzebue Sound), northern Yukon, northwestern and southern Mackenzie, southwestern Keewatin, northern Manitoba, northern Ontario, northern Quebec, central Labrador, and Newfoundland south to central Alaska, southern British Columbia, northern Washington, central Montana, northwestern Wyoming, southern Saskatchewan (absent from grassland region of Alberta and Saskatchewan), northern North Dakota, northern Minnesota, northern Wisconsin, northern Michigan, southern Ontario, northern New York, northern Vermont, Maine, New Brunswick, and Nova Scotia; and in Eurasia from Scandinavia east across Russia and Siberia to Kamchatka, and south to northern Europe, Lake Baikal, Manchuria, and Sakhalin.

Winters in North America from the Aleutians and southeastern Alaska south to Baja California and Sonora, in the western interior from Washington and Idaho south to Utah, on the Great Lakes, and on the Atlantic-Gulf coasts from Newfoundland and Nova Scotia south to central Florida and west to Texas, less frequently but regularly elsewhere in the interior of the United States south to Arizona, New Mexico, Texas, the Gulf states, and Florida; and in Eurasia south to the Mediterranean Sea, Turkey, Iran, southeastern China, and Japan

Casual south to Sinaloa and Durango, and in the Hawaiian Islands (Maui, Molokai), Bermuda, Greenland, the Faeroe Islands, Azores, and northern Africa.

Notes.—Known in Old World literature as the Goldeneye.

Bucephala islandica (Gmelin). Barrow's Goldeneye.

> *Anas islandica* Gmelin, 1789, Syst. Nat. 1(2): 541. Based on "Hravn Oend" O. F. Müller, Zool. Dan. Prodromus, p. 16. (in Islandia = Iceland.)

Habitat.—Primarily forested lake, ponds, and rivers, nesting in tree cavities (occasionally in tundra on the ground); in winter, lakes, rivers, estuaries, and bays, especially where rocky.

Distribution.—*Breeds* from central and southwestern Alaska (base of the Alaska Peninsula), southern Yukon, western Mackenzie (probably), northern British Columbia, and west-central Alberta south to south-coastal and southeastern Alaska, southern interior British Columbia, and northern Washington, locally at higher elevations to eastern California (Sierra Nevada, at least formerly), eastern Oregon, western Montana, northwestern Wyoming, and northern (formerly southern) Colorado; in northern Labrador (probably); and in southwestern Greenland (formerly) and Iceland.

Winters primarily along the Pacific coast from south-coastal and southeastern Alaska (west to Kodiak Island) south to central (casually southern) California; in the interior of western North America locally from coastal and interior British Columbia, Idaho, and northern Montana south to southeastern California (Colorado River Valley), western Arizona, and northern New Mexico; and in the Atlantic region (primarily coastal) from the upper St. Lawrence drainage, Gulf of St. Lawrence, and Nova Scotia south to Rhode Island, rarely to New York (Long Island), and casually to South Carolina.

Casual in the Aleutian and Pribilof islands, to the eastern shore of Hudson Bay and Newfoundland, in the interior of North America from southern Canada south to Texas, Oklahoma, Missouri, Tennessee, and western North Carolina; also in the Faeroe Islands, British Isles, Spitsbergen, and continental Europe.

Genus *MERGELLUS* Selby

> *Mergellus* Selby, 1840, Cat. Generic Sub-Generic Types Aves, p. 47. Type, by monotypy, *Mergus albellus* Linnaeus.

Notes.—*Mergellus* and *Lophodytes* are sometimes merged into *Mergus* (e.g., Vaurie 1965).

Mergellus albellus (Linnaeus). Smew.

> *Mergus Albellus* Linnaeus, 1758, Syst. Nat. (ed. 10) 1: 129. (in Europa = Mediterranean, near Izmir, Turkey.)

Habitat.—Lakes, ponds, and rivers, nesting in the taiga in cavities in trees (rarely on the ground); in winter, lakes, bays, and rivers.

Distribution.—*Breeds* from Scandinavia east through northern Russia and Siberia to Kamchatka, south to southern Russia, Amurland, the Sea of Okhotsk, and northern Sakhalin.

Winters from Iceland, the British Isles, Scandinavia, Russia, and Kamchatka south to northwestern Africa, the Mediterranean Sea, Persian Gulf, eastern China, Korea, and Japan.

Migrates regularly through the Aleutian Islands (east to Adak, where casual at other seasons), casually to the Pribilof Islands (St. Paul, St. George) and east to Kodiak Island and the coast of British Columbia.

Casual or accidental in Washington (near Stevenson, McKenna), California (San Mateo County), southern Ontario, western New York, Rhode Island, Iceland, northern Africa, and Burma.

Genus *LOPHODYTES* Reichenbach

> *Lophodytes* Reichenbach, 1853, Handb. Spec. Ornithol., Die Vögel, pt. 3 (1852), p. ix. Type, by original designation, *Mergus cucullatus* Linnaeus.

Notes.—See comments under *Mergellus*.

Lophodytes cucullatus (Linnaeus). Hooded Merganser.

Mergus cucullatus Linnaeus, 1758, Syst. Nat. (ed. 10) 1: 129. Based on "The round-crested Duck" Catesby, Nat. Hist. Carolina 1: 94, pl. 94. (in America = South Carolina.)

Habitat.—Forested streams, lakes, swamps, and ponds, nesting in tree cavities; in winter, primarily wooded lakes and ponds, less commonly in marshes, estuaries, and bays.

Distribution.—*Breeds* from southeastern Alaska (north to the Taku and Chilkat rivers, casually to the Copper River delta), coastal and central interior British Columbia and northern Alberta (locally) south to southwestern Oregon, central Idaho, and western Montana (casually to northern California, north-central Colorado, and central New Mexico); and from central Saskatchewan, central Manitoba, central Ontario, southern Quebec, New Brunswick, and southern Nova Scotia south (primarily from the mountains of New England, New York, and the Appalachians westward) through central and eastern North Dakota, eastern South Dakota, Iowa, central Kansas, eastern Oklahoma, and Arkansas to northeastern Texas, northern Louisiana (locally), central Mississippi, southern Alabama, northern Georgia, and (rarely) central Florida. Occurs in summer north to southern Mackenzie, northern Ontario, central Quebec, and central Labrador.

Winters along the Pacific coast in south-coastal Alaska (rarely, Prince William Sound), and from southern British Columbia south to southern Baja California, on the Atlantic and Gulf coasts from New England south to Florida and west to Texas and Tamaulipas, locally in the interior from southern Canada south to northern Mexico (rare), casually farther (recorded Coahuila, Distrito Federal, and Veracruz), Bermuda (rare), and in the northern Bahamas.

Casual in southwestern Alaska (Alaska Peninsula at Katmai, and Izembek), the Pribilof islands (St. Paul), Aleutian Islands (Attu, Alaid, Adak), Hawaiian Islands (Oahu, Hawaii), Newfoundland, Cuba, Puerto Rico, the Virgin Islands, Martinique, Iceland, the British Isles, and continental Europe; a sight report for Quintana Roo.

Genus *MERGUS* Linnaeus

Mergus Linnaeus, 1758, Syst. Nat. (ed. 10) 1: 129. Type, by subsequent designation (Eyton, 1838), *Mergus castor* Linnaeus = *Mergus serrator* Linnaeus.

Notes.—See comments under *Mergellus*.

Mergus merganser Linnaeus. Common Merganser.

Mergus Merganser Linnaeus, 1758, Syst. Nat. (ed. 10) 1: 129. (in Europa = Sweden.)

Habitat.—Mostly lakes and rivers, nesting in tree cavities, nest boxes or cliff crevices, generally near clear waters in forested regions and mountainous terrain; in winter, primarily lakes and rivers.

Distribution.—*Breeds* in North America from central and south-coastal Alaska (west to the lower Kuskokwim River and Kodiak Island), southern Yukon, southern Mackenzie, northern Saskatchewan, northern Manitoba, northern Ontario, central Quebec, central Labrador, and Newfoundland south to the mountains of central California and in coastal region south to central California (Monterey County, casually to Santa Barbara County), central Nevada, central Arizona, southwestern Chihuahua, and southwestern and northern New Mexico, and east of the Rocky Mountains south to Montana, central Nebraska, southwestern South Dakota, northeastern Minnesota, northern Wisconsin, central Michigan, southern Ontario, New York, eastern Pennsylvania (probably), northwestern New Jersey, central Massachusetts, southern Maine, and west-central Nova Scotia, locally and casually farther south (recorded breeding in Tennessee, Virginia, North Carolina, and South Carolina; and in Eurasia from Iceland, the British Isles, and Scandinavia east across Russia and Siberia to Anadyrland and Kamchatka, and south to northern Europe, central Russia, the northern Himalayas, northern Mongolia, Ussuriland, and Sakhalin. Recorded in summer (and probably breeding) north to central Mackenzie, southern Keewatin, and northern Quebec.

Winters in North America from the Aleutian Islands, central (rarely) and south-coastal Alaska, and British Columbia east across southern Canada to Newfoundland, and south to southern California, northern Baja California (rarely), northern Mexico (Sonora east, rarely, to Tamaulipas; casually, at least formerly, to Jalisco, Guanajuato, and Distrito Federal) and (rarely) to the northern Gulf coast states (and casually farther south from southern Texas east to northern Florida); and in Eurasia from Iceland, the British Isles, Scandinavia, Japan, and the Kuril Islands south to the northern Mediterranean region, Black Sea, Iran, northern India, and eastern China.

Casual or accidental in the Hawaiian Islands (Kauai, Oahu, Maui), Pribilof Islands, Bermuda, the Cayman Islands, Greenland, the Faeroe Islands, Spitsbergen, Bear Island, northwestern Africa, Taiwan, and the Ryukyu Islands; a report from Puerto Rico is erroneous.

Notes.—Known in Old World literature as the Goosander.

Mergus serrator Linnaeus. Red-breasted Merganser.

Mergus Serrator Linnaeus, 1758, Syst. Nat. (ed. 10) 1: 129. (in Europa = Sweden.)

Habitat.—Rivers and lakes; in winter, mainly estuaries, bays, and shallow coastal waters, less frequently on deep lakes.

Distribution.—*Breeds* in North America from northern Alaska, northern Yukon, Northwest Territories (Axel Heiberg Island), northern Mackenzie, central Keewatin, northern Baffin Island, Labrador, and Newfoundland south to the Aleutian Islands, southern and southeastern Alaska, northwestern British Columbia (including the Queen Charlotte Islands), northern Alberta, southwestern and central Saskatchewan, southern Manitoba, northeastern Minnesota, northern Wisconsin, central Michigan, southern Ontario, northern New York, southern Quebec, northern Vermont, Maine, New Brunswick, and Nova Scotia, casually in northwestern Wyoming and northern Illinois, and south along the Atlantic coast to New York (Long Island) and New Jersey (Barnegat Bay); and in the Palearctic from Greenland, Iceland, the Faeroe Islands, British Isles, Scandinavia, and northern Europe east across northern Russia and Siberia to Kamchatka and the Commander Islands. Nonbreeding birds summer regularly south to the Gulf coast (from Texas east to Florida).

Winters in North America primarily along coasts and locally on large inland bodies of water from southern Alaska (west to the Aleutian Islands), coastal British Columbia, southern Canada, and the Great Lakes south to southern Baja California, northern Sonora, northern Chihuahua, and southern New Mexico, southern Texas, northern Tamaulipas, the Gulf coast (east to southern Florida), and Cuba (locally); and in the Old World from Iceland, the Faeroe Islands, British Isles, Scandinavia, Kamchatka, and the Kuril Islands south to the Mediterranean, Black, and Caspian seas, southern Russia, eastern China, and Japan.

Casual or accidental in the Hawaiian Islands (Oahu, Molokai, Hawaii), Pribilofs, Bermuda, the Bahamas, Puerto Rico (including Vieques and Mona islands), the Cayman Islands, Jan Mayen, Spitsbergen, the eastern Atlantic islands, and northern Africa; sight reports for southern Veracruz, Yucatán, and the Lesser Antilles (Antigua); a report from the Virgin Islands (St. Croix) is erroneous.

Tribe OXYURINI: Stiff-tailed Ducks

Genus *NOMONYX* Ridgway

Nomonyx Ridgway, 1880, Proc. U. S. Natl. Mus. 3: 15. Type, by original designation, *Anas dominica* Linnaeus.

Notes.—Recognition of the genus *Nomonyx* follows Livezey (1995b).

Nomonyx dominicus (Linnaeus). Masked Duck.

Anas dominica Linnaeus, 1766, Syst. Nat. (ed. 12) 1: 201. Based mainly on "La Sarcelle de S. Domingue" Brisson, Ornithologie 6: 472, pl. 41, fig. 2. (in America meridionali = Haiti ?, probably from elsewhere in West Indies, *fide* D. Wetherbee.)

Habitat.—Freshwater Marshes, usually with dense emergent vegetation, occasionally mangrove swamps and rice fields (0–800 m; primarily Tropical Zone, ranging locally to Temperate Zone).

Distribution.—*Resident* locally from Nayarit, the Gulf coast of Texas (at least formerly), the Greater Antilles south along both slopes of Middle America and through the Lesser Antilles, and in South America from Colombia, Venezuela, Trinidad, and the Guianas south, west of the Andes to western Ecuador, and east of the Andes to northern Argentina and Uruguay.

A nomadic and irregular wanderer casually to central Texas, southern Louisiana, Florida, the Bahamas, the Cayman Islands (Grand Cayman), and Tobago. Accidental in Wisconsin, Pennsylvania, Vermont, Massachusetts, Maryland, North Carolina, Georgia, and Tennessee.

Genus *OXYURA* Bonaparte

Oxyura Bonaparte, 1828, Ann. Lyc. Nat. Hist. N. Y. 2: 390. Type, by monotypy, A*nas rubidus* Wilson = *Anas jamaicensis* Gmelin.

Oxyura jamaicensis (Gmelin). Ruddy Duck.

Anas jamaicensis Gmelin, 1789, Syst. Nat. 1(2): 519. Based on the "Jamaica Shoveler" Latham, Gen. Synop. Birds 3(2): 513. (in Jamaica.)

Habitat.—Fresh-water marshes and lakes with dense emergent vegetation and open water; in winter, primarily lakes, ponds, estuaries, and bays (Temperate Zone).

Distribution.—*Breeds* in North America in east-central Alaska (casually), and from central and northeastern British Columbia, southwestern Mackenzie, northern Alberta, central Saskatchewan, and central and southeastern Manitoba south to southern California, southern Arizona, southern New Mexico, western and southern Texas, with scattered, sporadic or former breeding from central Ontario, southern Quebec, and Nova Scotia south to northern Iowa, southern Illinois, northern Indiana, northern Ohio, western Pennsylvania, Maryland, Delaware, South Carolina, also in southeastern Arkansas, southwestern Louisiana (formerly?), and central and northern Florida, Baja California, Jalisco, the Valley of México, Guatemala, El Salvador, and the Bahamas (New Providence, Eleuthera, possibly the Caicos Islands).

Winters from southern British Columbia, Idaho, western Montana (rarely), Colorado, Kansas, the Great Lakes, and on the Atlantic coast from Massachusetts south throughout the southern United States and most of Mexico to Honduras (also sight reports from Nicaragua and a doubtful record from Costa Rica), Bermuda (rare), and throughout the Bahamas.

Resident in the Greater Antilles and Lesser Antilles south to Grenada.

Migrates rarely east to the Maritime Provinces.

Introduced and established in England (where increasing).

Casual in the Hawaiian Islands (Oahu, Hawaii), southeastern Alaska, southern Yukon, Newfoundland, Georgia, and the Cayman Islands.

Notes.—The Andean species, *O. ferruginea* (Eyton, 1838), is sometimes regarded as conspecific with *O. jamaicensis* (e.g., Blake 1977), but see Siegfried (1976) and Livezey (1995b).

Order **FALCONIFORMES**: Diurnal Birds of Prey

Suborder ACCIPITRES: Kites, Eagles, Hawks, Secretarybirds, and Allies

Family **ACCIPITRIDAE**: Hawks, Kites, Eagles, and Allies

Subfamily PANDIONINAE: Ospreys

Genus *PANDION* Savigny

Pandion Savigny, 1809, Descr. Egypte 1: 69, 95. Type, by monotypy, *Pandion fluvialis* Savigny = *Falco haliaetus* Linnaeus.

Pandion haliaetus (Linnaeus). Osprey.

> *Falco Haliætus* Linnaeus, 1758, Syst. Nat. (ed. 10) 1: 91. (in Europa = Sweden.)

Habitat.—Estuaries, rivers, lakes, and extensive marshes (Tropical and Temperate zones).

Distribution.—*Breeds* in North America from northwestern Alaska, northern Yukon, western and southern Mackenzie, northern Saskatchewan, northern Manitoba, northern Ontario, central Quebec, central Labrador, and Newfoundland south locally (mostly in western North America, the upper Great Lakes, and coastally) to Baja California (both coasts), the Tres Marias Islands (off Nayarit), Sinaloa, central Arizona, southwestern and central New Mexico (at least formerly), southern Texas, the Gulf coast, and southern Florida, and in the Bahamas, on small cays off Cuba, along the coasts and on islands off the eastern coast of the Yucatan Peninsula and Belize, and in eastern Guatemala (Petén); and in the Old World from the British Isles, Scandinavia, northern Russia, and northern Siberia south, at least locally, through much of Eurasia and most of Africa and Australia to South Africa, the Himalayas, Tasmania, New Caledonia, and the Solomon Islands. Reintroductions in North America in areas where former breeding populations were reduced or eliminated through environmental contamination have been generally successful.

Winters in the Americas from central California (rarely Washington and Idaho), southern Arizona, southern Texas, the Gulf coast, Florida, and Bermuda (rarely north to southern New England) south through Middle America (including Cocos Island off Costa Rica, and in the Revillagigedos), the West Indies, and South America (also the Galapagos Islands) to southern Chile, northern Argentina, and Uruguay; and in the Old World from the Mediterranean, Black, and Caspian seas, India, and eastern China south throughout the remainder of the breeding range.

Migrates regularly through islands in the western Pacific from the Ryukyu and Bonin chains southward.

Casual in the Hawaiian Islands (Midway, and main islands from Kauai eastward), Aleutians and Pribilofs, St. Lawrence Island, and the Seward Peninsula, and north to northern Yukon and northern Quebec, on Guadalupe Island (off Baja California), Clipperton Island, and in Greenland, Iceland, the Faeroe Islands, and the eastern Atlantic islands.

Subfamily ACCIPITRINAE: Kites, Eagles, and Hawks

Genus *LEPTODON* Sundevall

> *Leptodon* Sundevall, 1836, Vetensk.-Akad. Handl. (1835), p. 114. Type, by monotypy, "*Falco cayanensis* et *palliatus* auct." = *Falco cayanensis* Latham.

Leptodon cayanensis (Latham). Gray-headed Kite.

> *Falco cayanensis* Latham, 1790, Index Ornithol. 1: 28. Based on the "Cayenne Falcon" Latham, Gen. Synop. Birds 1(1): 59. (in Cayana = Bahia, Brazil.)

Habitat.—Tropical Lowland Evergreen Forest, River-edge Forest, Tropical Deciduous Forest (0–1000 m; Tropical and Subtropical zones).

Distribution.—*Resident* locally from northern and southeastern Oaxaca, southern Tamaulipas (formerly), and southern Veracruz south through Middle America and South America (including Trinidad) west of the Andes to western Ecuador and east of the Andes to Paraguay, northern Argentina, and southern Brazil.

Genus *CHONDROHIERAX* Lesson

> *Chondrohierax* Lesson, 1843, Echo Monde Savant (2)7: col. 61. Type, by monotypy, *Chondrohierax erythrofrons* Lesson = *Falco uncinatus* Temminck.

Chondrohierax uncinatus (Temminck). Hook-billed Kite.

> *Falco uncinatus* (Illiger MS) Temminck, 1822, Planches Color., livr. 18, pls. 103–104. (Rio de Janeiro and Bahia, Brazil = Bahia.)

Habitat.—[*uncinatus* group] Tropical Lowland Evergreen Forest, Tropical Deciduous Forest, Gallery Forest, Montane Evergreen Forest (0–2800 m); [*wilsonii* group] Tropical Lowland Evergreen Forest (0–500 m); (Tropical to lower Subtropical zones).

Distribution.—*Resident* [*uncinatus* group] from southern Sinaloa, southern Texas (Falcon Dam to Santa Ana), and Tamaulipas south through Middle America and South America (including Grenada in the Lesser Antilles, and Trinidad), west of the Andes to western Ecuador, and east of the Andes to central Bolivia, northern Argentina, and southern Brazil; and [*wilsonii* group] in eastern Cuba.

Notes.—Groups: *C. uncinatus* [Hook-billed Kite] and *C. wilsonii* (Cassin, 1847) [Cuban Kite].

Genus *ELANOIDES* Vieillot

> *Elanoïdes* Vieillot, 1818, Nouv. Dict. Hist. Nat. (nouv. éd.) 24 (1817): 101. Type, by monotypy, "Milan de la Caroline" = *Falco forficatus* Linnaeus.

Elanoides forficatus (Linnaeus). Swallow-tailed Kite.

> *Falco forficatus* Linnaeus, 1758, Syst. Nat. (ed. 10) 1: 89. Based on "The Swallow tail'd Hawk" Catesby, Nat. Hist. Carolina 1: 4, pl. 4. (in America = South Carolina.)

Habitat.—Forested regions, often bottomland or riverine forest, also open pine woodland, Montane Evergreen Forest (Tropical and Subtropical zones).

Distribution.—*Breeds* locally from South Carolina south to the upper Florida Keys, and west to Louisiana and (formerly) central Texas (recent possible breeding records from eastern Texas); and from Chiapas south through most of Middle America (except El Salvador) and South America (including Trinidad), west of the Andes to northwestern Peru and east of the Andes to northern Argentina, Uruguay, and southern Brazil. Formerly bred north to Oklahoma, eastern Kansas, eastern Nebraska, northwestern Minnesota, southern Wisconsin, and Ohio.

Winters primarily in South America from Colombia and Venezuela southward; recorded occasionally in winter in Middle America. Several sight reports from Florida in December and January.

Migrates regularly through coastal Texas, Mexico (from Nuevo León and Tamaulipas south to the Distrito Federal and Veracruz, and eastward through the Yucatan Peninsula), the western Greater Antilles (Cuba, Jamaica), and the Cayman Islands.

Casual in New Mexico, eastern Colorado, southern Saskatchewan, southern Manitoba, northern Wisconsin, southern Michigan, southern Ontario, New York, Vermont, New Hampshire, Massachusetts, Nova Scotia, Oaxaca, and Bermuda. Accidental on Tobago and in England. Sight reports from the Bahama Islands (west of Grand Bahama and on Eleuthera).and southeastern Arizona.

Genus *GAMPSONYX* Vigors

> *Gampsonyx* Vigors, 1825, Zool. J. 2: 69. Type, by monotypy, *Gampsonyx swainsonii* Vigors.

Notes.—For inclusion of this genus in the Accipitridae, see Brodkorb (1960).

Gampsonyx swainsonii Vigors. Pearl Kite.

> *Gampsonyx swainsonii* Vigors, 1825, Zool. J. 2: 69. (tableland of Bahia, about ten leagues west-southwest from the Bay of San Salvador, Brazil.)

Habitat.—Tropical Lowland Evergreen Forest Edge, Tropical Deciduous Forest Edge, Secondary Forest, Low Seasonally Wet Grassland, Arid Lowland Scrub (0–1200 m; Tropical Zone).

Distribution.—*Resident* in western Nicaragua (Pacific slope from near Chinandega to Granada) and Panama (locally west to Bocas del Toro and Herrera); and in South America west of the Andes from western Colombia south to northwestern Peru, and east of the Andes from northern Colombia, Venezuela, Trinidad, and the Guianas south, locally, to southern Bolivia, Paraguay, northern Argentina, and southern Brazil.

Genus *ELANUS* Savigny

Elanus Savigny, 1809, Descr. Egypte 1: 69, 97. Type, by monotypy, *Elanus caesius* Savigny = *Falco caeruleus* Desfontaines.

Elanus leucurus (Vieillot). White-tailed Kite.

Milvus leucurus Vieillot, 1818, Nouv. Dict. Hist. Nat. (nouv. éd.) 24: 101. (Paraguay.)

Habitat.—Savanna, open woodland, marshes, desert grassland, partially cleared lands, and cultivated fields, mostly in lowlands (Tropical to Temperate zones).

Distribution.—*Resident* locally from southwestern Washington south (mostly west of the deserts) to Baja California, in southern Arizona, Sinaloa, Nayarit, and Chihuahua, in peninsular Florida, from northeastern Kansas, southern Oklahoma, southern Louisiana (sporadically), southwestern Mississippi, east-central and southern Texas, Tamaulipas, and southeastern Oaxaca south through Middle America (both slopes) to eastern Panama, thence eastward in northern South America to Surinam, from southern Bolivia and central and eastern Brazil south to central Argentina, and in central Chile. The range, especially in Middle America, has greatly expanded since 1960.

Casual or accidental north to Nevada, Idaho, Utah, New Mexico (regular?), western and northern Texas, Missouri, North Dakota, Wisconsin, central Illinois, Indiana, Tennessee, Massachusetts, Maryland, and Virginia (also sight reports north to British Columbia, Wyoming, Iowa, and New York), and to Yucatán, Isla Utila (in the Bay Islands, off Honduras), and Trinidad.

Notes.—*Elanus leucurus, E. caeruleus* (Desfontaines, 1789), and *E. axillaris* (Latham, 1801) constitute a superspecies (Amadon *in* Mayr and Cottrell 1979); they were formerly considered one species (e.g., A.O.U. 1983), but see Clark and Banks (1992).

Genus *ROSTRHAMUS* Lesson

Rostrhamus Lesson, 1830, Traité Ornithol., livr. 1, p. 55. Type, by monotypy, *Rostrhamus niger* Lesson = *Herpetotheres sociabilis* Vieillot.

Helicolestes Bangs and Penard, 1918, Bull. Mus. Comp. Zool. Harv. 62: 38. Type, by original designation, *Falco hamatus* Illiger = Temminck.

Rostrhamus sociabilis (Vieillot). Snail Kite.

Herpetotheres sociabilis Vieillot, 1817, Nouv. Dict. Hist. Nat. (nouv. éd.) 18: 318. Based on "Gavilan de Estero Sociable" Azara, Apunt. Hist. Nat. Páx. Parag. 1: 84 (no. 16). (Corrientes, near Río de la Plata, Argentina.)

Habitat.—Freshwater Marshes, Freshwater Lakes and Ponds (0–1000 m; Tropical, rarely Subtropical and lower Temperate zones).

Distribution.—*Resident* in Florida (Lake Okeechobee region, and locally throughout the Everglades basin, the upper St. John's River, and central Florida lakes), Cuba, and the Isle of Pines; locally from Guerrero, Oaxaca, Veracruz, and the Yucatan peninsula south to Nicaragua; in northwestern Costa Rica (Pacific lowlands around Gulf of Nicoya and Guanacaste); locally in Panama (recorded Chiriquí, eastern Panamá province and San Blas); and in South America from Colombia, Venezuela, and the Guianas south, west of the Andes to western Ecuador and east of the Andes throughout to northern Argentina, Uruguay, and southern Brazil.

Casual or accidental in southern Texas (Jim Wells County) and Trinidad; and north casually in Florida (primarily dispersal due to drought) to Wakulla, Alachua, Jefferson, Putnam, and Duval counties.

Notes.—Also known as Everglade Kite.

Rostrhamus hamatus (Temminck). Slender-billed Kite.

Falco hamatus (Illiger MS) Temminck, 1821, Planches Color., livr. 11, pl. 61 and text. (Brazil.)

Habitat.—River-edge Forest, Gallery Forest, Freshwater Marshes (0–800 m; Tropical Zone).

Distribution.—*Resident* in eastern Panama (Tuira Valley, along the Río Paya, Darién); and locally in South America east of the Andes from northern Colombia, northern Venezuela, and Surinam south to northern Bolivia and Amazonian Brazil.

Genus *HARPAGUS* Vigors

Harpagus Vigors, 1824, Zool. J. 1: 338. Type, by subsequent designation (G. R. Gray, 1840), *Falco bidentatus* Latham.

Harpagus bidentatus (Latham). Double-toothed Kite.

Falco bidentatus Latham, 1790, Index Ornithol. 1: 38. Based on the "Notched Falcon" Latham, Gen. Synop. Birds (suppl.) 1: 34. (in Cayana = Cayenne.)

Habitat.—Tropical Lowland Evergreen Forest, Montane Evergreen Forest (0–1500 m; Tropical and lower Subtropical zones).

Distribution.—*Resident* on the Pacific slope of Middle America in Guerrero and southeastern Oaxaca, and in the Gulf-Caribbean lowlands from northern Oaxaca, southern Veracruz, and Quintana Roo south to Honduras, on both slopes of Nicaragua, Costa Rica (rare in dry northwest), and Panama, and in South America from Colombia, Venezuela, Trinidad, and the Guianas south, west of the Andes to western Ecuador and east of the Andes to central Bolivia and east-central Brazil.

Genus *ICTINIA* Vieillot

Ictinia Vieillot, 1816, Analyse, p. 24. Type, by monotypy, "Milan cresserelle" Vieillot = *Falco plumbeus* Gmelin.

Ictinia mississippiensis (Wilson). Mississippi Kite.

Falco misisippiensis [sic] Wilson, 1811, Amer. Ornithol. 3: 80, pl. 25, fig. 1. (a few miles below Natchez [Mississippi].)

Habitat.—Riverine forest, open woodland, and prairies near riparian woodland; regularly in wooded suburbs in some portions of range.

Distribution.—*Breeds* from southern Arizona, central New Mexico, southeastern Colorado, north-central Kansas, southern Missouri, southern Illinois, southern Indiana, western Kentucky, western Tennessee, northwestern Mississippi, the coastal plain of the Gulf states, South Carolina, and (probably) North Carolina south to southern New Mexico, Texas, the Gulf coast, and north-central Florida, the range expanding along its borders in recent years; formerly bred north to central Colorado and Iowa.

Winters apparently for the most part in central South America, where recorded from Paraguay and northern Argentina; scattered sight reports suggest casual or occasional wintering north as far as southern Texas and Florida, but the vast majority lack documentation.

Migrates regularly from Nuevo León, Tamaulipas, and Chiapas (casually west to Baja California) south through Middle America, Colombia, and Bolivia.

Casual straggler north to northern California, southern Nevada, northern Colorado, northern Wyoming, southern Saskatchewan, Minnesota, Wisconsin, Michigan, southern Ontario, Ohio, Pennsylvania, New Jersey, New York, Massachusetts, and Nova Scotia; sight report for Maine.

Notes.—*Ictinia mississippiensis* and *I. plumbea* constitute a superspecies (Stresemann and Amadon *in* Mayr and Cottrell 1979; Amadon and Bull 1988).

Ictinia plumbea (Gmelin). Plumbeous Kite.

Falco plumbeus Gmelin, 1788, Syst. Nat. 1(1): 283. Based on the "Spotted-tailed Hawk" Latham, Gen. Synop. Birds 1(1): 106. (in Cayenna = Cayenne.)

Habitat.—Tropical Lowland Evergreen Forest, Tropical Deciduous Forest, Gallery Forest (0–1700 m; Tropical and Subtropical zones).

Distribution.—*Breeds* from southern Tamaulipas, southeastern San Luis Potosí, Veracruz, and northern and south-central Oaxaca south along both slopes of Middle America (including the Pearl Islands, where perhaps only a migrant), and in South America from Colombia, Venezuela, Trinidad, and the Guianas south, east of the Andes, to northern Argentina and southeastern Brazil.

Winters primarily in the South American portion of the breeding range, casually south to Buenos Aires. Winter reports from Middle America have not been substantiated.

An old specimen labeled "Indian Territory" was probably not taken in Oklahoma (Parker 1981).

Notes.—See comments under *I. mississippiensis*.

Genus *HALIAEETUS* Savigny

Haliaeetus Savigny, 1809, Descr. Egypte 1: 68, 85. Type, by monotypy, *Haliaeetus nisus* Savigny = *Falco albicilla* Linnaeus.

Haliaeetus leucocephalus (Linnaeus). Bald Eagle.

Falco leucocephalus Linnaeus, 1766, Syst. Nat. (ed. 12) 1: 124. Based on "The Bald Eagle" Catesby, Nat. Hist. Carolina 1: 1, pl. 1. (in America, Europa = South Carolina.)

Habitat.—Primarily near seacoasts, rivers, swamps, and large lakes.

Distribution.—*Breeds* from central Alaska (southern Brooks Range), northern Yukon, northwestern and southern Mackenzie, northern Saskatchewan, northern Manitoba, northern Ontario, central Quebec, Labrador, and Newfoundland south locally to the Commander Islands (formerly), southern Alaska (west to Buldir in the Aleutian Islands [once on Attu], and east along the southern coast), Baja California (Magdalena Bay, formerly elsewhere), Sonora (Rio Yaqui), central Arizona, southwestern and central New Mexico, central Texas, and the Gulf coast from southeastern Texas east to southern Florida (including the Florida Keys); absent as a breeding bird through much of the Great Basin (bred formerly) and most of the prairie and plains regions; very local in interior North America.

Winters generally throughout the breeding range but most frequently from southern Alaska and southern Canada southward.

Migrates widely but sporadically over most of the North American continent.

Casual along the Arctic coast of northeastern Siberia; a sight reports for Puerto Rico and Bermuda. Accidental in Ireland.

Notes.—*Haliaeetus leucocephalus* and *H. albicilla* appear to constitute a superspecies (Stresemann and Amadon *in* Mayr and Cottrell 1979; Amadon and Bull 1988).

Haliaeetus albicilla (Linnaeus). White-tailed Eagle.

Falco Albicilla Linnaeus, 1758, Syst. Nat. (ed. 10) 1: 89. (in Europa, America = Sweden.)

Habitat.—Rocky coasts, rivers, and large lakes, in regions of tundra, forests, deserts or mountains.

Distribution.—*Breeds* from western Greenland, Iceland, Scandinavia, northern Russia, and northern Siberia south to northern Europe (formerly to northeastern Africa), Syria, Iran, Turkestan, Kamchatka, and the Aleutian Islands (Attu); a report of breeding on Baffin Island (Cumberland Sound) has not been confirmed.

Winters in the breeding range and south, at least casually, to the Mediterranean and Red seas, India, Taiwan, Japan, and the Seven Islands of Izu.

Casual elsewhere in the Aleutian Islands (Shemya), off Massachusetts (near Nantucket

Lightship), and in eastern Greenland; an earlier report from the eastern Aleutian Islands (Unalaksa) is erroneous.

Notes.—Also known as White-tailed Sea-Eagle or Gray Sea-Eagle. See comments under *H. leucocephalus.*

Haliaeetus pelagicus (Pallas). Steller's Sea-Eagle.

Aquila pelagica Pallas, 1811, Zoogr. Rosso-Asiat. 1: 343 and plate. (in Insulis inter Camtshatcam et Continentem Americes, praesertim in infami naufragio et monte Beringii insula = Tauisk, on Sea of Okhotsk.)

Habitat.—Sea coasts and the lower portions of coastal rivers.

Distribution.—*Breeds* from northeastern Siberia (west to Yakutsk) and Kamchatka south to Sakhalin, possibly also in Korea.

Winters from the breeding range south to Korea, Japan, and the Seven Islands of Izu.

Casual or accidental in the Hawaiian Islands (Kure, Midway, French Frigate Shoals), Alaska (Attu, Unimak, Simeonof, and Kodiak islands, and Taku River near Juneau), the Commander Islands, and eastern China. A record for the Pribilofs is erroneous.

Genus *BUSARELLUS* Lesson

Busarellus "Lafresnaye" Lesson, 1843, Echo Monde Savant (2)7: col. 468. Type, by original designation, *Circus busarellus* Vieillot = *Falco nigricollis* Latham.

Notes.—For placement of this genus, see Olson (1982).

Busarellus nigricollis (Latham). Black-collared Hawk.

Falco nigricollis Latham, 1790, Index Ornithol. 1: 35. Based on the "Black-necked Falcon" Latham, Gen. Synop. Birds (suppl.) 1: 30. (in Cayana = Cayenne.)

Habitat.—River-edge Forest, Gallery Forest, Freshwater Marshes (0–800 m; Tropical Zone).

Distribution.—*Resident* from Sinaloa (but now rare in western Mexico), northern Oaxaca, and Veracruz south along both slopes of Middle America, and in South America from Colombia, Venezuela, Trinidad, and the Guianas south, east of the Andes, to northern Argentina and southern Brazil.

Genus *CIRCUS* Lacépède

Circus Lacépède, 1799, Tabl. Mamm. Ois., p. 4. Type, by subsequent designation (Lesson, 1828), *Falco aeruginosus* Linnaeus.

Circus cyaneus (Linnaeus). Northern Harrier.

Falco cyaneus Linnaeus, 1766, Syst. Nat. (ed. 12) 1: 126. Based on "The Blue Hawk" Edwards, Glean. Nat. Hist. 1: 33, pl. 225. (in Europa, Africa = vicinity of London, England.)

Habitat.—Primarily grassy marshes and wet prairie with tall grass (breeding); marshes, meadows, grasslands, and cultivated fields (nonbreeding).

Distribution.—*Breeds* [*hudsonius* group] in North America from northern Alaska, northern Yukon, northwestern and southern Mackenzie, northern Saskatchewan, northern Manitoba, northern Ontario, west-central Quebec, and Newfoundland south to northern Baja California, southern Arizona, southern New Mexico, central and eastern Texas, northwestern Arkansas, southern Illinois, central Kentucky, West Virginia, southeastern Virginia, and (formerly) Florida; and [*cyaneus* group] in Eurasia from the British Isles, Scandinavia, northern Russia, and northern Siberia south to the northern Mediterranean region, southern Russia, Turkestan, Amurland, Ussuriland, Sakhalin, and the Kuril Islands.

Winters [*hudsonius* group] in the Americas from Alaska (casually), southern British Columbia, southern Alberta, southern Saskatchewan (rarely), Montana, South Dakota, southern

Minnesota, southern Wisconsin, southern Michigan, southern Ontario, New York, and Massachusetts (casually farther north) south through the United States, Middle America and the Antilles (rare in the Cayman Islands and Lesser Antilles) to Panama and Barbados, casually to northern Colombia and northern Venezuela; and [*cyaneus* group] in Eurasia from the British Isles, southern Scandinavia and southern Japan south to northwestern Africa, Asia Minor, India, Burma, eastern China, Formosa, and the Ryukyu Islands.

Migrates casually [group unknown] through the Aleutian and Commander islands.

Casual or accidental [*hudsonius* group] in the Hawaiian Islands, Labrador, northern Quebec, the Revillagigedo Islands (Socorro Island; sight reports), Bermuda, and the Bahamas; and [*cyaneus* group] in Iceland and the Faeroe Islands.

Notes.—Groups: *C. cyaneus* [Hen Harrier] and *C. hudsonius* (Linnaeus, 1766) [American Harrier or Marsh Hawk]. *Circus cyaneus* and the South American *C. cinereus* Vieillot, 1816, constitute a superspecies (Mayr and Short 1970).

Genus *ACCIPITER* Brisson

Accipiter Brisson, 1760, Ornithologie 1: 28; 6: 310. Type, by tautonymy, *Accipiter* Brisson = *Falco nisus* Linnaeus.

Accipiter soloensis (Horsfield). Gray Frog-Hawk.

Falco Soloënsis Horsfield, 1821, Trans. Linn. Soc. London, 13: 137. (Solo, Java.)

Habitat.—Wooded country with adjacent swamps or rice fields.

Distribution.—*Breeds* in eastern and southern China, Taiwan, and Korea.

Winters principally in northern Sulawesi and the Philippines, also widely from the Andaman Islands, the Malay Peninsula, Sunda Islands, Moluccas, and Waigu off New Guinea to the Marianas (where rare). Accidental on Kure Atoll, Hawaii; one found alive 27 Sept. 1991 (specimen, Bishop Museum #178451).

Notes.—Also known as Chinese Goshawk or Blue Frog-Hawk.

Accipiter superciliosus (Linnaeus). Tiny Hawk.

Falco superciliosus Linnaeus, 1766, Syst. Nat. (ed. 12) 1: 128. (in Surinamo = Surinam.)

Habitat.—Tropical Lowland Evergreen Forest, Montane Evergreen Forest (0–1200 m; Tropical and lower Subtropical zones).

Distribution.—*Resident* from eastern Nicaragua (vicinity of Waspam and San Juan del Sur [Greytown]) south through Costa Rica, Panama, and South America west of the Andes to western Ecuador and east of the Andes to central Bolivia, northern and eastern Brazil, eastern Paraguay, and extreme northeastern Argentina.

Notes.—Stresemann and Amadon *in* Mayr and Cottrell (1979) considered *A. superciliosus* and *A. collaris* Sclater, 1860 of South America to constitute a superspecies.

Accipiter striatus Vieillot. Sharp-shinned Hawk.

Accipiter striatus Vieillot, 1808, Hist. Nat. Ois. Amer. Sept. 1 (1807): 42, pl. 14. (Santo Domingo = Haiti.)

Habitat.—Forest and open woodland, usually mixed coniferous-deciduous; in winter, often also suburbs [*striatus* group]; Pine Forest, Pine-Oak Forest, Montane Evergreen Forest, Tropical Deciduous Forest [*chionogaster* group] (500–3000 m); (Tropical to Temperate zones).

Distribution.—*Breeds* [*striatus* group] from western and central Alaska, northern Yukon, western and southern Mackenzie, northern Saskatchewan, central Manitoba, northern Ontario, central Quebec, southern Labrador, and Newfoundland south (locally) to central (casually south-central) California, central Arizona, southern New Mexico, north-central (formerly southern) Texas, the northern parts of the Gulf states, and South Carolina, and south through the highlands of Mexico to central Oaxaca; also in the Greater Antilles (Cuba, Hispaniola, and Puerto Rico).

Winters [*striatus* group] from southern Alaska, the southernmost portions of the Canadian provinces (casually), and Nova Scotia south through the United States and Middle America to central Panama, Bermuda, casually to the Bahamas, Jamaica, the Virgin Islands (St. John), and (probably) Mona Island off Puerto Rico; also in the breeding range in the Greater Antilles.

Resident [*chionogaster* group] in the highlands of eastern Oaxaca (Sierra Madre de Chiapas), Chiapas, Guatemala, El Salvador, Honduras, and north-central Nicaragua; and [*erythronemius* group] in South America in the mountains of Venezuela, the Andes from Colombia to southern Bolivia, and from central Brazil and Paraguay south to northern Argentina and Uruguay.

Casual or accidental [*striatus* group] in northern Alaska and on the Revillagigedo Islands (Socorro Island; sight report).

Notes.—Groups: *A. striatus* [Sharp-shinned Hawk], *A. chionogaster* (Kaup, 1852) [White-breasted Hawk], and *A. erythronemius* (Kaup, 1850) [Rufous-thighed Hawk].

Accipiter cooperii (Bonaparte). Cooper's Hawk.

> *Falco Cooperii* Bonaparte, 1828, Amer. Ornithol. 2: 1, pl. 10, fig. 1. (near Bordentown, New Jersey.)

Habitat.—Primarily mature forest, either broadleaf or coniferous, mostly the former, and riparian forest, usually with open country or edge nearby, occasionally also in suburbs; in winter, also in more open country (0–3000 m).

Distribution.—*Breeds* from central British Columbia, central Alberta, central Saskatchewan, central Manitoba, central Ontario, southern Quebec, and Maine (rarely New Brunswick and Nova Scotia) south to Baja California, Sinaloa, Chihuahua, Nuevo León, southern Texas, Louisiana, central Mississippi, central Alabama, and central Florida.

Winters from southern British Columbia, Washington, Idaho, western Montana, Colorado, Nebraska, southeastern Minnesota, southern Wisconsin, southern Michigan, southern Ontario, New York, and New England south through the southern United States and Mexico to Guatemala and Honduras, casually to Costa Rica and Colombia (Cundinamarca).

Sight reports for southeastern Alaska and on the Revillagigedo Islands (Socorro Island).

Notes.—*Accipiter cooperii*, *A. gundlachi*, and *A. bicolor* appear to constitute a superspecies (Stresemann and Amadon *in* Mayr and Cottrell 1979).

Accipiter gundlachi Lawrence. Gundlach's Hawk.

> *Accipiter Gundlachi* Lawrence, 1860, Ann. Lyc. Nat. Hist. N. Y. 7: 252. (Hanabana, Cuba.)

Habitat.—Tropical Lowland Evergreen Forest, Tropical Deciduous Forest, Pine Forest (0–900 m).

Distribution.—*Resident* on Cuba.

Notes.—See comments under *A. cooperii*.

Accipiter bicolor (Vieillot). Bicolored Hawk.

> *Sparvius bicolor* Vieillot, 1817, Nouv. Dict. Hist. Nat. (nouv. éd.) 10: 325. (Cayenne.)

Habitat.—Tropical Deciduous Forest, Gallery Forest, Tropical Lowland Evergreen Forest (0–2000 m; Tropical and lower Subtropical zones, in southern South America to Temperate Zone).

Distribution.—*Resident* [*bicolor* group] from northern Oaxaca, southern Tamaulipas, Veracruz, the Yucatan Peninsula, and Guatemala south through Middle America and South America to northeastern Bolivia, Amazonian and southeastern Brazil, and eastern Paraguay; [*guttifer* group] in Bolivia (except northeastern), western Brazil, western Paraguay, and northern Argentina; and [*chilensis* group] in Chile and extreme western Argentina north to about lat. 34°S.

Notes.—Groups: *A. bicolor* [Bicolored Hawk], *A. guttifer* Hellmayr, 1917 [Spotted Hawk] and *A. chilensis* R. A. Philippi and Landbeck, 1864 [Chilean Hawk]. See comments under *A. cooperii*.

Accipiter gentilis (Linnaeus). Northern Goshawk.

Falco gentilis Linnaeus, 1758, Syst. Nat. (ed. 10) 1: 89. (in Alpibus = Dalecarlian Alps, Sweden.)

Habitat.—Deciduous, coniferous, and mixed forest, forest edge and open woodland, foraging also in cultivated regions, primarily in mountains in the southern portions of range.

Distribution.—*Breeds* [*atricapillus* group] in North America from western and central Alaska, northern Yukon, western and southern Mackenzie, southern Keewatin (probably), northeastern Manitoba, northern Ontario, central and northeastern Quebec, Labrador, and Newfoundland south to southern Alaska (west to the base of the Alaska Peninsula), southern California (to San Jacinto Mountains and [formerly?] Cuyumaca Mountains), southern Nevada, southern Arizona, southern New Mexico, the eastern foothills of the Rockies (including the Black Hills of western South Dakota), central Alberta, southern Saskatchewan, southern Manitoba, northern Minnesota, northern Wisconsin, central Michigan, Pennsylvania, northern New Jersey, and northwestern Connecticut, in the Appalachian mountains south to West Virginia and western Maryland, and south in the Mexican highlands to Jalisco and (probably) Guerrero; and [*gentilis* group] in Eurasia from the British Isles (rarely), Scandinavia, northern Russia, and northern Siberia south to the Mediterranean region, Asia Minor, Iran, the Himalayas, eastern China, and Japan.

Winters throughout the breeding range, and [*atricapillus* group] in North America south irregularly south of breeding range, casually to southern California, northern Mexico, western and east-central Texas, the northern portions of the Gulf states, west-central Florida, and Bermuda and [*gentilis* group] in Eurasia casually to northern Africa, India, and Burma. A specimen (Univ. Mich. Mus. Zool. #62390) from Red Bay, Labrador, has been tentatively identified by E. Mayr as *A. g. gentilis* (Van Tyne 1943).

Notes.—Known in Old World literature as the Goshawk. Groups: *A. atricapillus* (Wilson, 1812) [American Goshawk] and *A. gentilis* [Eurasian Goshawk]. Stresemann and Amadon *in* Mayr and Cottrell (1979) considered *A. gentilis* and Old World *A. meyerianus* (Sharpe, 1878) to constitute a superspecies.

Genus *GERANOSPIZA* Kaup

Ischnosceles (not *Ischnoscelis* Burmeister, 1842) Strickland, 1844, Ann. Mag. Nat. Hist. (1)13: 409. Type, by original designation, *Falco gracilis* Temminck = *Sparvius caerulescens* Vieillot.

Geranospiza Kaup, 1847, Isis von Oken, col. 143. New name for *Ischnosceles* Strickland.

Notes.—*Ischnosceles* Strickland is not invalidated by *Ischnoscelis* Burmeister (Hellmayr and Conover 1949) and was used by Wetmore (1965). However, it is considered and treated as a *nomen oblitum* as provided for by Article 23 (b) of I.C.Z.N. (1964) by most authors (Monroe 1968, Blake 1977, Stresemann and Amadon *in* Mayr and Cottrell 1979, Amadon 1982).

Geranospiza caerulescens (Vieillot). Crane Hawk.

Sparvius cærulescens Vieillot, 1817, Nouv. Dict. Hist. Nat. (nouv. éd.) 10: 318. (l'Amérique méridionale = Cayenne.)

Habitat.—Tropical Deciduous Forest, Gallery Forest, River-edge Forest, Mangrove Forest (0–1500 m; Tropical and lower Subtropical zones).

Distribution.—Resident [*nigra* group] from Mexico (Sonora on the Pacific slope and Tamaulipas on the Gulf-Caribbean) south through Middle America and South America west of the Andes to northwestern Peru; [*caerulescens* group] in South America east of the Andes south to eastern Peru and Amazonian Brazil; and [*gracilis* group] in south-central South America from eastern Bolivia and south-central and eastern Brazil south to northern Argentina.

Accidental [*nigra* group] in southern Texas (Santa Ana; photo, 1987–88, Amer. Birds 42: 194, 288; DeBenedictis 1991).

Notes.—The three groups have been regarded as distinct species, *G. nigra* (Du Bus de

Gisignies, 1847) [Blackish Crane-Hawk], *G. caerulescens* [Gray Crane-Hawk], and *G. gracilis* (Temminck, 1821) [Banded Crane-Hawk], but color varies clinally from north to south (Amadon 1982).

Genus *LEUCOPTERNIS* Kaup

Leucopternis Kaup, 1847, Isis von Oken, col. 210. Type, by subsequent designation (G. R. Gray, 1844), *Falco melanops* Latham.

Leucopternis plumbea Salvin. Plumbeous Hawk.

Leucopternis plumbea Salvin, 1872, Ibis, p. 240, pl. 8. (Ecuador.)

Habitat.—Tropical Lowland Evergreen Forest (0–800 m; Tropical Zone).

Distribution.—Resident from Panama (from Veraguas eastward on the Caribbean slope, and on both slopes in Darién) south in the Pacific lowlands of South America to extreme northwestern Peru.

Notes.—*Leucopternis plumbea* and the South American *L. schistacea* (Sundevall, 1851) constitute a superspecies (Stresemann and Amadon *in* Mayr and Cottrell 1979; Amadon and Bull 1988).

Leucopternis princeps Sclater. Barred Hawk.

Leucopternis princeps Sclater, 1866, Proc. Zool. Soc. London (1865), p. 429, pl. 24. (Costa Rica, in montibus = Tucurrique, Costa Rica.)

Habitat.—Montane Evergreen Forest, Tropical Lowland Evergreen Forest (300–2500 m; upper Tropical and Subtropical zones).

Distribution.—*Resident* from Costa Rica (Caribbean slope of cordilleras Central and Talamanca) and Panama south through western Colombia to northern Ecuador.

Leucopternis semiplumbea Lawrence. Semiplumbeous Hawk.

Leucopternis semiplumbeus Lawrence, 1861, Ann. Lyc. Nat. Hist. N. Y. 7: 288. (Atlantic side of the Isthmus of Panama, along the line of the Panama Railroad.)

Habitat.—Tropical Lowland Evergreen Forest (0–1000 m; Tropical and lower Subtropical zones).

Distribution.—*Resident* locally in northeastern Honduras (Gracias a Dios), Nicaragua, Costa Rica (Caribbean slope), Panama, northern Colombia, and northwestern Ecuador.

Leucopternis albicollis (Latham). White Hawk.

Falco albicollis Latham, 1790, Index Ornithol. 1: 36. Based on the "White-necked Falcon" Latham, Gen. Synop. Birds (suppl.) 1: 30. (Cayenne.)

Habitat.—Tropical Lowland Evergreen Forest, Montane Evergreen Forest, Tropical Deciduous Forest (0–1500 m; Tropical and Subtropical zones).

Distribution.—*Resident* from northern Oaxaca, southern Veracruz, Tabasco, and Chiapas south (mostly on the Caribbean drainage) through Guatemala, Belize, and western El Salvador to Honduras, and both slopes of Nicaragua, Costa Rica, and Panama to South America, from Colombia, Venezuela, Trinidad, and the Guianas south locally, east of the Andes, to northern Bolivia and Amazonian Brazil.

Notes.—Stresemann and Amadon *in* Mayr and Cottrell (1979) considered *L. albicollis* and the South American *L. polionota* (Kaup, 1847) to constitute a superspecies.

Genus *ASTURINA* Vieillot

Asturina Vieillot, 1816, Analyse, pp. 24, 68. Type, by original designation, *Asturia* [sic] *cinerea* Vieillot = *Falco nitidus* Latham.

Notes.—Often treated in the genus *Buteo* (e.g., Johnson and Peeters 1963, A.O.U. 1983), but see Amadon (1982).

Asturina nitida (Latham). Gray Hawk.

> *Falco nitidus* Latham, 1790, Index Ornithol. 1: 41. Based on the "Plumbeous Falcon"
> Latham, Gen. Synop. Birds (suppl.) 1: 37. (in Cayana = Cayenne.)

Habitat.—Gallery Forest, Tropical Deciduous Forest, Tropical Lowland Evergreen Forest Edge, River-edge Forest (0–1300 m; Tropical and Subtropical zones).

Distribution.—*Resident* [*plagiata* group] from southern Arizona, Sonora, Tamaulipas, and western and southern Texas south through Middle America (including the Bay Islands, off Honduras) to northwestern Costa Rica (Gulf of Nicoya region); and [*nitida* group] in Costa Rica (except northwest), Panama, and South America from Colombia, Venezuela, Tobago, Trinidad, and the Guianas south, west of the Andes to western Ecuador and east of the Andes to northern Argentina, Paraguay, and southern Brazil. Northernmost breeding populations in Arizona and western Texas [*plagiata* group] are migratory southward in nonbreeding season.

Casual [*plagiata* group] in southern New Mexico; a sight report for northeastern Kansas.

Notes.—Groups: *A. plagiata* (Schlegel, 1862) [Gray Hawk] and *A. nitida* [Gray-lined Hawk].

Genus *BUTEOGALLUS* Lesson

> *Buteogallus* Lesson, 1830, Traité Ornithol., livr. 2, p. 83. Type, by monotypy, *Buteogallus cathartoides* Lesson = *Falco aequinoctialis* Gmelin.
> *Urubitinga* Lafresnaye, 1842, Dict. Univ. Hist. Nat. 2: 786. Type, by tautonymy, *Falco urubitinga* Gmelin.
> *Hypomorphnus* Cabanis, 1844, Arch. Naturgesch. 10: 263. Type, by original designation, *Falco urubitinga* Gmelin.
> *Heterospizias* Sharpe, 1874, Cat. Birds Brit. Mus. 1: x, 158, 160. Type, by monotypy, *Falco meridionalis* Latham.

Buteogallus anthracinus (Deppe). Common Black-Hawk.

> *Falco anthracinus* "Lichtenst[ein]." W. Deppe, 1830, Preis.-Verz. Säugeth. Vögel, etc., Mex., p. 3. (Veracruz = Tecolutla, Veracruz; Mauersberger and Neumann, 1986, Mitt. Zool. Mus. Berlin 62 Suppl. Ann. Orn. 10: 137–142.)

Habitat.—Tropical Deciduous Forest, Gallery Forest, Tropical Lowland Evergreen Forest, usually near water (0–1800 m; Tropical and lower Subtropical zones).

Distribution.—*Resident* [*anthracinus* group] from central (rarely northwestern) Arizona, southwestern Utah (rarely), southern (rarely central) New Mexico, and western and (formerly) southern Texas south through Middle America (including Cozumel and Cancun islands off Quintana Roo, and Utila and Guanaja islands off Caribbean Honduras) to northern Colombia, and east through coastal Venezuela and Trinidad to Guyana and French Guiana, and in the Lesser Antilles on St. Vincent; and [*gundlachii* group] in Cuba (including small coastal cays) and the Isle of Pines. Northernmost breeding populations in the southwestern United States and northwestern Mexico usually migrate southward in nonbreeding season.

Casual or accidental [*anthracinus* group] in southern Nevada (breeding attempted), north-central Texas (Lubbock), southern and western Texas away from breeding areas, and the Lesser Antilles (St. Lucia, the Grenadines, and Grenada); sight reports for southern California and northern Baja California; reports from Minnesota and southern Florida (Miami area) are probably based on escaped individuals, and may pertain in part to *B. urubitinga.*

Notes.—Also known as Black Hawk. Groups: *B. anthracinus* [Common Black-Hawk] and *B. gundlachii* (Cabanis, 1855) [Cuban Black-Hawk]; some authors (e.g., Blake 1977) have considered *B. subtilis* to be conspecific with *B. anthracinus,* although *B. subtilis* and the South American *B. aequinoctialis* (Gmelin, 1788) have been considered by others (e.g., Stresemann and Amadon *in* Mayr and Cottrell 1979) to constitute a superspecies.

Buteogallus subtilis (Thayer and Bangs). Mangrove Black-Hawk.

> *Urubitinga subtilis* Thayer and Bangs, 1905, Bull. Mus. Comp. Zool. Harv. 46: 94. (Gorgona Island, Colombia.)

Habitat.—Mangrove Forest (Tropical Zone).

Distribution.—*Resident* along the Pacific coast from Chiapas to Panama (including the Pearl Islands), Colombia (including coastal islands), Ecuador, and extreme northwestern Peru (Tumbes).

Notes.—See comments under *B. anthracinus.*

Buteogallus urubitinga (Gmelin). Great Black-Hawk.

Falco Urubitinga Gmelin, 1788, Syst. Nat. 1(1): 265. Based in part on the "Brasilian Eagle" Latham, Gen. Synop. Birds 1(1): 41. (in Brasilia = northeastern Brazil.)

Habitat.—Tropical Deciduous Forest, Tropical Lowland Evergreen Forest, Gallery Forest, River-edge Forest (0–1600 m; Tropical and occasionally lower Subtropical zones).

Distribution.—*Resident* from northern Mexico (southern Sonora on the Pacific slope and southern Tamaulipas on the Gulf-Caribbean) south through Middle America and South America (including Tobago and Trinidad) west of the Andes to northwestern Peru and east of the Andes to northern Argentina and Uruguay.

Buteogallus meridionalis (Latham). Savanna Hawk.

Falco meridionalis Latham, 1790, Index Ornithol. 1: 36. Based on the "Rufous-headed Falcon" Latham, Gen. Synop. Birds (suppl.) 1: 33. (in Cayana = Cayenne.)

Habitat.—Low Seasonally Wet Grassland, Second-growth Scrub (0–1200 m; Tropical Zone).

Distribution.—*Resident* from western Panama (from Chiriquí eastward, rare or absent from Darién) south in South America (including Trinidad) west of the Andes to northwestern Peru and east of the Andes to central Argentina .

Notes.—Often placed in the monotypic genus *Heterospizias,* but see Amadon (1982).

Genus *PARABUTEO* Ridgway

Parabuteo Ridgway, 1874, in Baird, Brewer, and Ridgway, Hist. N. Amer. Birds 3: 248, 250. Type, by monotypy, *Buteo harrisi* Audubon = *Falco unicinctus* Temminck.

Parabuteo unicinctus (Temminck). Harris's Hawk.

Falco unicinctus Temminck, 1824, Planches Color., livr. 53, p. 313. (Brésil . . . dans les environs du Rio-Grande, près Boa-Vista = Boa Vista, western Minas Gerais, Brazil.)

Habitat.—Arid Lowland Scrub, Arid Montane Scrub, Tropical Deciduous Forest, Low Seasonally Wet Grassland, recently in some suburbs of desert cities (0–1900 m; Tropical and Subtropical zones).

Distribution.—*Resident* in southern Kansas (Meade County and vicinity, casually or formerly), and from northern Baja California, southeastern California (formerly; recent re-introduction attempts along Colorado River), southern Arizona, southern New Mexico, and south-central Texas south through Middle America (rare and local from Chiapas to Nicaragua and in Panama, unrecorded in Belize and Honduras) and South America (including Margarita Island off Venezuela) to central Chile and central Argentina.

Casual in south-central California (increasingly regular, but origin controversial), northern and eastern Texas, southwestern Louisiana, Oklahoma, Kansas, Missouri, and Colorado; a sight report for southern Nevada. Stragglers reported from Iowa (Hillsboro), Ohio (Harrisburg), and several localities in Florida are probably escapes from captivity.

Notes.—Also known as Bay-winged Hawk.

Genus *HARPYHALIAETUS* Lafresnaye

Harpyhaliœtus Lafresnaye, 1842, Rev. Zool. [Paris] 5: 173. Type, by original designation, *Harpyia coronata* Vieillot.

Urubitornis J. Verreaux, 1856, Proc. Zool. Soc. London, p. 145. Type, by original designation, *Circaetus solitarius* Tschudi.

Harpyhaliaetus solitarius (Tschudi). Solitary Eagle.

Circaëtus solitarius Tschudi, 1844, Arch. Naturgesch. 10: 264. (Republica Peruana = Río Chanchamayo, Junín, Peru.)

Habitat.—Montane Evergreen Forest, Tropical Evergreen Forest (600–2200 m; upper Tropical and Subtropical zones).

Distribution.—*Resident* locally in Mexico (recorded southeastern Sonora, Coahuila, Jalisco, and Oaxaca), Guatemala (San Gerónimo), Honduras (Valle de Talanga), Costa Rica (Cordillera Central, Cordillera Talamanca, and Golfo Dulce), Panama (Veraguas, eastern Panamá province, and Darién) and South America, mainly in foothills of Andes, from Colombia and northern Venezuela south to northwestern Argentina. Although often listed for Nicaragua, there is no specific record.

Notes.—*Harpyhaliaetus solitarius* and the South American *H. coronatus* (Vieillot, 1817) "may form a superspecies, though probably not" (Amadon 1982).

Genus *BUTEO* Lacépède

Buteo Lacépède, 1799, Tabl. Mamm. Ois., p. 4. Type, by tautonymy, *Falco buteo* Linnaeus.
Craxirex Gould, 1839, in Darwin, Zool. Voy. Beagle 3(6): 22. Type, by subsequent designation (G. R. Gray, 1840), *Polyborus galapagoensis* Gould.
Tachytriorchis Kaup, 1844, Class. Säugeth. Vögel, p. 123. Type, by monotypy, *Buteo pterocles* Temminck = *Buteo albicaudatus* Vieillot.

Notes.—Species of this genus are known in Old World literature under the group name Buzzard.

Buteo magnirostris (Gmelin). Roadside Hawk.

Falco magnirostris Gmelin, 1788, Syst. Nat. 1(1): 282. Based mainly on "éspervier à gros bec de Cayenne" Daubenton, Planches Enlum., pl. 464. (in Cayenna = Cayenne.)

Habitat.—Tropical Lowland Evergreen Forest Edge, Tropical Deciduous Forest, Gallery Forest, River-edge Forest, Secondary Forest, Second-growth Scrub (0–2500 m; Tropical and Subtropical zones).

Distribution.—*Resident* from Jalisco, Hidalgo, southern Nuevo León, and southern Tamaulipas south through Middle America (including Cozumel Island off Quintana Roo; Roatán, Barbareta, and Guanaja in the Bay Islands, off Caribbean Honduras; and Coiba, Taboguilla, Iguana, and the Pearl islands off Panama), and in South America from Colombia, Venezuela, and the Guianas south, west of the Andes to western Ecuador and east of the Andes to central Argentina.

Casual in southern Texas (lower Rio Grande Valley).

Notes.—A close relationship between *B. magnirostris, B. lineatus, B. ridgwayi,* and *B. platypterus* is suggested by plumage and morphology (Johnson and Peeters 1963).

Buteo lineatus (Gmelin). Red-shouldered Hawk.

Falco lineatus Gmelin, 1788, Syst. Nat. 1(1): 268. Based on the "Barred-breasted Buzzard" Latham, Gen. Synop. Birds 1(1): 56, and the "Red-shouldered Falcon" Pennant, Arct. Zool. 2: 206. (in insula Longa = Long Island, New York.)

Habitat.—Moist and riverine forest, and in eastern North America, wooded swamps, and occasionally pine woodland and mangroves; in winter, also in more open country (Tropical to Temperate zones).

Distribution.—*Breeds* from southwestern Oregon (probably), northern California south, west of the Sierran divide, to Baja California; and from eastern Nebraska, Iowa, central Minnesota, northern Wisconsin, northern Michigan, southern Ontario, southwestern Quebec, and (rarely) southern New Brunswick south to northern Tamaulipas (at least formerly), Texas, the Gulf coast, and Florida (to Florida Keys).

Winters, at least sporadically, through the breeding range, but in eastern North America primarily from eastern Kansas, central Missouri, the Ohio Valley, northwestern Pennsylvania, southern New York, and southern New England south to central Mexico.

Casual to Washington, southern Idaho (sight report), Montana, southern Saskatchewan (sight reports), and southern Manitoba, and in eastern California, western Nevada, Utah, southern Arizona, and Sinaloa. A report from Jamaica is highly questionable.

Notes.—Sibley and Monroe (1990) considered *B. lineatus* and *B. ridgwayi* to constitute a superspecies. See comments under *B. magnirostris.*

Buteo ridgwayi (Cory). Ridgway's Hawk.

> *Rupornis ridgwayi* Cory, 1883, Q. J. Boston Zool. Soc. 2: 46. (Santo Domingo = Samana, Dominican Republic.)

Habitat.—Tropical Lowland Evergreen Forest Edge (0–2000 m).

Distribution.—Resident on Hispaniola and surrounding small islands (Beata, Gonâve, île-à-Vache, Alto Velo, Grand Cayemite, and Petite Cayemite).

Notes.—See comments under *B. magnirostris and B. lineatus.*

Buteo platypterus (Vieillot). Broad-winged Hawk.

> *Falco pennsylvanicus* Wilson, 1812, Amer. Ornithol. 6: 92, pl. 54, fig. 1. (l'Amérique septentrionale = near the Schuylkill River, Pennsylvania.) [Not *Falco pennsylvanicus* Wilson, 1812, ibid., p. 13 = *Falco velox* Wilson.]
>
> *Sparvius platypterus* Vieillot, 1823, in Bonnaterre and Vieillot, Tabl. Encycl. Méth. (Ornithol.): 3(93): 1273. New name for *Falco pennsylvanicus* Wilson, preoccupied.

Habitat.—Deciduous and mixed coniferous-deciduous forest, often near edges; in migration, also in open country; in winter, forest edge, woodland.

Distribution.—*Breeds* in east-central British Columbia, central Alberta, and central Saskatchewan, and from central Manitoba, central Ontario, southern Quebec, New Brunswick, and Nova Scotia south to central (rarely) and eastern Texas, the Gulf coast, and northern Florida, and west to north-central Colorado (once) and western South Dakota (Black Hills).

Winters regularly in southern Florida (casually farther north), and mainly from Colima and Chiapas (casually from Sinaloa and southern Texas) south through Middle America and South America to central Bolivia and southern Brazil. Casual in southern portions of the breeding range.

Migrates regularly through central and eastern United States (west as far as central Montana, Wyoming, Utah, central New Mexico, and in coastal California), eastern and southern Mexico, and western Cuba, casually elsewhere in the western states west to Washington, Oregon, and Arizona.

Resident in the Antilles on Cuba and Puerto Rico, and from Antigua and Dominica south to Grenada and Tobago.

Casual north to south-coastal and interior British Columbia, northern Alberta, northern Saskatchewan, northern Ontario, and central Quebec, and to Baja California, Hispaniola (questionably), and Barbados.

Notes.—See comments under *B. magnirostris.*

Buteo brachyurus Vieillot. Short-tailed Hawk.

> *Buteo brachyurus* Vieillot, 1816, Nouv. Dict. Hist. Nat. (nouv. éd.) 4: 477. (No locality given = Cayenne.)

Habitat.—Tropical Lowland Evergreen Forest, Tropical Deciduous Forest, Gallery Forest, Pine-Oak Forest, almost always near open country (0–1200 m; Tropical and Subtropical zones).

Distribution.—*Resident* locally in peninsular Florida (from St. Marks and San Mateo south to southern Dade County, in winter mostly south of Lake Okeechobee), and from central Sonora and Tamaulipas south through Middle America (including Cozumel Island off Quintana Roo, but absent from El Salvador) and South America west of the Andes to western Ecuador and east of the Andes to northern Argentina, Paraguay, and southern Brazil.

Causal in southern and south-central Texas; sight reports from southern Arizona and Hispaniola (Dominican Republic) are unverified.

Notes.—Suggestions that Andean *B. albigula* Philippi, 1899, and *B. brachyurus* are conspecific (Rand 1960, Blake 1977) require further study.

Buteo swainsoni Bonaparte. Swainson's Hawk.

Buteo vulgaris (not Swainson, 1832) Audubon, 1837, Birds Amer. (folio) 4: pl. 372. (near the Columbia River = mouth of Walla Walla River, eastern Washington; Slipp, 1947, Auk 64: 389–400).

Buteo Swainsoni Bonaparte, 1838, Geogr. Comp. List, p. 3. New name for *Buteo vulgaris* Audubon, preoccupied.

Habitat.—Savanna, grassland, and cultivated lands with scattered trees.

Distribution.—*Breeds* locally in east-central Alaska (formerly?), Yukon, and Mackenzie, and from British Columbia, central Alberta, central Saskatchewan, southern Manitoba, western and southern Minnesota, and western Illinois south to southern California (rarely), Baja California (formerly), Sonora, Durango, Chihuahua, central and southern Texas, northwestern Arkansas (casually), and west-central Missouri.

Winters primarily on the pampas of southern South America (south to Uruguay and Argentina), irregularly north to El Salvador and southern Florida; small population winters in the Central Valley of California; casually elsewhere (documented records for Baja California, southern California, southern Texas, and southern Louisiana). Many unverified winter sight reports farther north in North America.

Migrates regularly through most of Middle America, and rarely east through the Gulf states to Florida; occasionally a common fall migrant through the Florida Keys; recorded annually at Cape May, New Jersey.

Casual in eastern North America from Indiana, northern Michigan, southern Ontario, southern Quebec, New York, and Massachusetts south to Pennsylvania and Virginia; sight reports from Nova Scotia, Maryland, and North Carolina; accidental in Norway; a report from Jamaica is highly questionable.

Buteo albicaudatus Vieillot. White-tailed Hawk.

Buteo albicaudatus Vieillot, 1816, Nouv. Dict. Hist. Nat. (nouv. éd.) 4: 477. (l'Amérique meridionale = Rio de Janeiro, Brazil.)

Habitat.—Low Seasonally Wet Grassland, Arid Lowland Scrub, Arid Montane Scrub, Second-growth Scrub, lowland pine savanna (0–2200 m; Tropical and Subtropical zones).

Distribution.—*Resident* from southern Arizona (formerly, one breeding record in 1897), Sonora, Durango, Zacatecas, and southern and southeastern Texas south locally through Middle America (including Isla Taboga off Panama, but absent from El Salvador), and in South America from Colombia, Venezuela (including the Netherlands Antilles and Margarita Island), Trinidad, and the Guianas south, east of the Andes, to central Argentina (absent from most of Amazonia).

Casual in central Texas and southwestern Louisiana; sight report for St. Vincent (in the Lesser Antilles).

Buteo albonotatus Kaup. Zone-tailed Hawk.

Buteo albonotatus "G. R. Gray" Kaup, 1847, Isis von Oken, col. 329. (No locality given = Mexico.)

Habitat.—Gallery Forest, Tropical Deciduous Forest, Pine-Oak Forest, Tropical Lowland Evergreen Forest Edge, often foraging over adjacent open country (0–2200 m; Tropical and Subtropical zones).

Distribution.—*Resident* (although partly migratory in northern part of breeding range) from southern California, northern Baja California, central Arizona, northern New Mexico, and western and central Texas south locally through Middle America (including the Pearl Islands off Panama), and in South America from Colombia, Venezuela, Trinidad, and the Guianas south, west of the Andes to western Ecuador, and east of the Andes (excluding most of Amazonia) to eastern Bolivia, Paraguay, and southeastern Brazil; also recorded in western Peru (Lima area).

Accidental in Nova Scotia and Louisiana (St. Bernard Parish); a sight report for southern Nevada.

Buteo solitarius Peale. Hawaiian Hawk.

> *Buteo solitarius* Peale, 1848, U. S. Explor. Exped. 8: 62. (Island of Hawaii.)

Habitat.—Open forest and forest edge from sea level to highlands.
Distribution.—*Resident* in small numbers on Hawaii, in the Hawaiian Islands.
Accidental on Oahu (Pearl Harbor); sight reports for Kauai and Maui.
Notes.—Also known as Io.

Buteo jamaicensis (Gmelin). Red-tailed Hawk.

> *Falco jamaicensis* Gmelin, 1788, Syst. Nat. 1(1): 266. Based on the "Cream-coloured Buzzard" Latham, Gen. Synop. Birds 1(1): 49. (in Jamaica.)

Habitat.—A wide variety of open woodland and open country with scattered trees, especially cultivated lands (Subtropical and Temperate zones).
Distribution.—*Breeds* from western and central Alaska, central Yukon, western Mackenzie, northern Saskatchewan, northern Manitoba, northern Ontario, central Quebec, New Brunswick, Prince Edward Island, and Nova Scotia south to southeastern Alaska, Baja California, Sonora, Chihuahua, Nuevo León, southern Texas, the Gulf coast, and Florida, and in the highlands of Middle America to Costa Rica and western Panama (east to Veraguas); in the Tres Marias and Socorro islands, off western Mexico; and in the northern Bahamas (Grand Bahama, Abaco, Andros), Greater Antilles, and northern Lesser Antilles (from Saba south to Nevis).

Winters from southern Canada south throughout the remainder of the breeding range, occurring also in the lowlands of Middle America.

Casual in Bermuda; an old record from England is not acceptable (B.O.U. 1974).

Notes.—The dark and variable populations breeding in western, central, and south-coastal Alaska, and in western Canada were formerly regarded as a distinct species, *B. harlani* (Audubon, 1831) [Harlan's Hawk], but are now treated as a race of *B. jamaicensis* (see Mindell 1983).

Buteo regalis (Gray). Ferruginous Hawk.

> *Archibuteo regalis* G. R. Gray, 1844, Genera Birds 1: pl. vi. (No locality given = Real del Monte, Hidalgo.)

Habitat.—Open country, primarily dry prairie, plains, sagebrush, and badlands, often in vicinity of prairie-dog (*Cynomys*) colonies; in winter, also plowed fields and other cultivated lands.
Distribution.—*Breeds* from south-central British Columbia, eastern Washington, southern Alberta, southern Saskatchewan, and southwestern Manitoba south to eastern Oregon, Nevada, northern and southeastern Arizona (formerly), central and eastern (formerly also southwestern) New Mexico, northern and north-central Texas, western Oklahoma, and western Kansas. Recorded in summer (and probably breeding) in northeastern California.

Winters primarily from the central and southern parts of the breeding range (casually north to Alberta and Saskatchewan) south to Baja California, Chihuahua, Durango, Guanajuato, Hidalgo, and Tamaulipas.

Migrates east to western Minnesota.

Casual east to Wisconsin, Illinois, Indiana, Michigan, Virginia, Missouri, Arkansas, Louisiana, Mississippi, Alabama, and Florida; a sight report for Ontario.

Buteo lagopus (Pontoppidan). Rough-legged Hawk.

Falco Lagopus Pontoppidan, 1763, Dan. Atlas 1: 616. (No locality given = Denmark.)

Habitat.—Open coniferous forest, tundra, and generally barren country, usually near cliffs for nest sites; in winter, grasslands and open cultivated areas, occasionally marshes and coastal dunes.

Distribution.—*Breeds* in North America from western and northern Alaska (also Kodiak Island, and west to Umnak in the eastern Aleutians), northern Yukon, the Arctic islands (north to Banks, Prince Patrick, Victoria, Bylot, and southwestern Baffin islands) and northern Labrador south to northern and southeastern Mackenzie, northern Manitoba, extreme northern Ontario, southeastern Quebec, and Newfoundland; and in Eurasia in the Arctic from Scandinavia east to northern Siberia, Kamchatka, and the Sea of Okhotsk.

Winters in North America from south-coastal Alaska (casually), southern Canada (southern British Columbia east to southern Quebec and Newfoundland) south to southern California, southern Arizona, southern New Mexico, panhandle Texas, Arkansas, Tennessee, and Virginia, casually to eastern and southern Texas and the Gulf coast (sight reports from northeastern Sonora, northern Chihuahua, and Florida); and in Eurasia from the British Isles, southern Scandinavia, and central Russia south to southern Europe, southern Russia, Manchuria, Ussuriland, and Japan.

Casual or accidental in the central and western Aleutians, St. Lawrence Island, Hawaiian Islands (Laysan), Bermuda, Iceland, the Faeroe Islands, southern Europe, and northern Africa; sight reports for northern Baja California and South Carolina.

Notes.—Also known as Rough-legged Buzzard.

Genus *MORPHNUS* Dumont

Morphnus Dumont, 1816, Dict. Sci. Nat. 1 (suppl.): 88. Type, by subsequent designation (Chubb, 1816), *Falco guianensis* Daudin.

Morphnus guianensis (Daudin). Crested Eagle.

Falco guianensis Daudin, 1800, Traité Ornithol. 2: 78. Based on "Petit Aigle de la Guiane" Mauduyt, Encycl. Méth., Hist. Nat. Ois. 1: 475. (Guiane = Cayenne.)

Habitat.—Tropical Lowland Evergreen Forest (0–1200 m; Tropical and lower Subtropical zones).

Distribution.—*Resident* locally in northern Guatemala (Petén), Belize, northern Honduras (San Pedro Sula, La Ceiba), Costa Rica (Cuabre and Cañas Gordas region), and Panama (both slopes, but doubtfully on Isla Coiba), and in South America, west of the Andes in Colombia, and east of the Andes from Colombia, Venezuela, and the Guianas south to central Bolivia, eastern Paraguay, northeastern Argentina (possibly), and southeastern Brazil. No definite records for Nicaragua.

Genus *HARPIA* Vieillot

Harpia Vieillot, 1816, Analyse, p. 24. Type, by monotypy, "Aigle destructeur" Buffon = *Vultur harpyja* Linnaeus.

Harpia harpyja (Linnaeus). Harpy Eagle.

Vultur Harpyja Linnaeus, 1758, Syst. Nat. (ed. 10) 1: 86. Based on "Yzquauhtli" Hernandez, Nova Plant Anim. Min. Mex. Hist., p. 34. (in Mexico.)

Habitat.—Tropical Lowland Evergreen Forest (0–900 m; Tropical Zone).

Distribution.—*Resident* locally from southern Mexico (southern Veracruz, Tabasco, and Chiapas) south through Middle America (excluding El Salvador, primarily occurring on the Caribbean slope north of Costa Rica), and in South America, west of the Andes in northern Colombia, and east of the Andes from Colombia, Venezuela, and the Guianas south to northern Argentina and southeastern Brazil.

Casual in Oaxaca.

Genus *AQUILA* Brisson

Aquila Brisson, 1760, Ornithologie 1: 28; 6: 419. Type, by tautonymy, *Aquila* Brisson = *Falco chrysaetos* Linnaeus.

Aquila chrysaetos (Linnaeus). Golden Eagle.

Falco Chrysaëtos Linnaeus, 1758, Syst. Nat. (ed. 1) 1: 88. (in Europa = Sweden.)

Habitat.—Generally open country, in prairies, tundra, open coniferous forest, desert, and barren areas, especially in hilly or mountainous regions.

Distribution.—*Breeds* in North America from northern and western Alaska east across Yukon, western and southern Mackenzie, northwestern Manitoba, northern Ontario, and northern Quebec to Labrador, and south to southern Alaska (west to Unalaska in the eastern Aleutians), northern Baja California, the highlands of northern Mexico (south to Durango, Guanajuato, and Nuevo León; possibly also in Oaxaca), western and central Texas (at least formerly), western Oklahoma, and western Kansas, and in eastern North America to central Tennessee, Pennsylvania, New York (formerly), and Maine; and in Eurasia from the British Isles, Scandinavia, northern Russia, and northern Siberia south to northern Africa, Arabia, Iran, the Himalayas, central China, Korea, and Japan.

Winters in North America from south-central Alaska (casually, the Alaska Range) and the southern portions of the Canadian provinces south throughout the breeding range elsewhere in North America, rarely or casually in the southeastern United States to the Gulf coast from Texas east to central Florida (sight reports to Florida Keys), and casually to Sonora, Sinaloa, and Hidalgo; and in Eurasia generally in the breeding range, casually south to eastern China.

Accidental in the Hawaiian Islands (Kauai, possibly an escaped or released individual that remained 17 years; 1984, Amer. Birds 38: 967).

Notes.—Stresemann and Amadon *in* Mayr and Cottrell (1979) considered *A. chrysaetos* and the Australasian *A. audax* (Latham, 1801) to constitute a superspecies.

Genus *SPIZASTUR* Gray

Spizastur G. R. Gray, 1841, List Genera Birds, ed. 2, p. 3. Type, by original designation, *S. atricapillus* (Cuv.) = *Buteo melanoleucus* Vieillot.

Spizastur melanoleucus (Vieillot). Black-and-white Hawk-Eagle.

Buteo melanoleucus Vieillot, 1816, Nouv. Dict. Hist. Nat. (nouv. éd.) 4: 482. (la Guyane = Guyana.)

Habitat.—Tropical Lowland Evergreen Forest, River-edge Forest, Montane Evergreen Forest (0–1200 m; Tropical and Subtropical zones).

Distribution.—*Resident* from western and southern Mexico (Nayarit, Oaxaca, southern Veracruz, Tabasco, Chiapas, and the Yucatan Peninsula) south through Middle America (except El Salvador), and in South America from Colombia, Venezuela, and the Guianas south, east of the Andes, to northern Argentina and southeastern Brazil; a sight report for southern Tamaulipas.

Genus *SPIZAETUS* Vieillot

Spizaëtus Vieillot, 1816, Analyse, p. 24. Type, by subsequent designation (G. R. Gray, 1840), "L'Autour huppé" Levaillant = *Falco ornatus* Daudin.

Spizaetus tyrannus (Wied). Black Hawk-Eagle.

Falco tyrannus Wied, 1820, Reise Bras. 1: 360. (Ilha do Chave, below Quartel dos Arcos, Rio Belmonte, Bahia, Brazil.)

Habitat.—Tropical Lowland Evergreen Forest, Tropical Deciduous Forest, Montane Evergreen Forest (0–2000 m; Tropical and lower Subtropical zones).

Distribution.—*Resident* from southern San Luis Potosí, Veracruz, and Guerrero south locally through Middle America (not recorded Nicaragua), and in South America from Colombia, Venezuela, Trinidad, and the Guianas south, west of the Andes to northwestern Peru and east of the Andes to northern Argentina and southeastern Brazil.

Spizaetus ornatus (Daudin). Ornate Hawk-Eagle.

Falco ornatus Daudin, 1800, Traité Ornithol. 2: 77. Based on "L'Aigle Moyen de la Guiane" Mauduyt, Encycl. Méth., Hist. Nat. Ois. 1: 475, and "L'Autour Huppé" Levaillant, Hist. Nat. Ois. Afr. 1: 76, pl. 2. (Cayenne.)

Habitat.—Tropical Lowland Evergreen Forest, Montane Evergreen Forest (0–1200 m; Tropical and Subtropical zones).

Distribution.—*Resident* from Colima, Hidalgo, and Tamaulipas south through Middle America (including Isla Coiba off Panama), and in South America from Colombia, Venezuela, Tobago, Trinidad, and the Guianas south, west of the Andes to northwestern Peru and east of the Andes to northern Argentina and southeastern Brazil.

Suborder FALCONES: Caracaras and Falcons

Family **FALCONIDAE**: Caracaras and Falcons

Notes.—The arrangement in three subfamilies rather than the four used previously (A.O.U. 1983) follows Griffiths (1994).

Subfamily MICRASTURINAE: Forest-Falcons

Genus *MICRASTUR* Gray

Brachypterus (not Kugelann, 1794, nor Latreille, 1819) Lesson, 1836, Oeuvres Compl. Buffon 7: 113. Type, by tautonymy, *Falco brachypterus* Temminck = *Sparvius semitorquatus* Vieillot.
Micrastur G. R. Gray, 1841, List Genera Birds, ed. 2, p. 6. New name for *Brachypterus* Lesson, preoccupied.

Micrastur ruficollis (Vieillot). Barred Forest-Falcon.

Sparvius ruficollis Vieillot, 1817, Nouv. Dict. Hist. Nat. (nouv. éd.) 10: 322. (l'Amérique méridionale = Rio de Janeiro, Brazil.)

Habitat.—Tropical Lowland Evergreen Forest, Montane Evergreen Forest (0–2600 m; Tropical and Subtropical zones).

Distribution.—*Resident* from Guerrero, southeastern San Luis Potosí, Hidalgo, and Veracruz south through Middle America (except Yucatán and El Salvador), and in South America west of the Andes from Colombia south to northwestern Peru, and east of the Andes in northern Venezuela, and from eastern Peru and central and eastern Brazil (south of the Amazon) south to northern Argentina and southern Brazil.

Notes.—The South American *M. gilvicollis* (Vieillot, 1817) was formerly (e.g., Blake 1977) considered conspecific with *M. ruficollis,* but see Schwartz (1972).

Micrastur mirandollei (Schlegel). Slaty-backed Forest-Falcon.

Astur mirandollei Schlegel, 1862, Mus. Hist. Nat. Pays-Bas, livr. 1, Astures, p. 27. (Surinam.)

Habitat.—Tropical Lowland Evergreen Forest (0–800 m; Tropical Zone).

Distribution.—*Resident,* primarily in the Caribbean lowlands, in Costa Rica and Panama; and in South America from central Colombia, southern Venezuela and the Guianas south, east of the Andes, to northern Bolivia and Amazonian and eastern Brazil.

Micrastur semitorquatus (Vieillot). Collared Forest-Falcon.

> *Sparvius semi-torquatus* Vieillot, 1817, Nouv. Dict. Hist. Nat. (nouv. éd.) 10: 322.
> Based on "Esparvero Faxado" Azara, Apunt. Hist. Nat. Páx. Parag. 1: 126 (no. 29).
> (Paraguay.)

Habitat.—Tropical Lowland Evergreen Forest, Tropical Deciduous Forest, Gallery Forest (0–1500 m; Tropical and Subtropical zones).

Distribution.—*Resident* from southern Sinaloa, southeastern San Luis Potosí, and southern Tamaulipas south through Middle America, and in South America from Colombia, Venezuela, and the Guianas south, west of the Andes to northwestern Peru and east of the Andes to northern Argentina and southern Brazil.

Accidental in extreme southern Texas (Bentsen-Rio Grande Valley State Park, Hidalgo County; photograph published in Amer. Birds 48: 225, 1994, and in DeBenedictis 1996).

Subfamily CARACARINAE: Caracaras

Notes.—Formerly listed as Tribe Polyborini; see note under *Caracara*.

Genus *DAPTRIUS* Vieillot

> *Daptrius* Vieillot, 1816, Analyse, p. 22. Type, by monotypy, *Daptrius ater* Vieillot.

Daptrius americanus (Boddaert). Red-throated Caracara.

> *Falco americanus* Boddaert, 1783, Table Planches Enlum., p. 25. Based on "Le Petit Aigle d'Amerique" Daubenton, Planches Enlum., pl. 417. (Cayenne.)

Habitat.—Tropical Lowland Evergreen Forest, Montane Evergreen Forest (0–1400 m; Tropical and lower Subtropical zones).

Distribution.—*Resident,* at least formerly, from southern Mexico (Veracruz, Chiapas) south through Middle America (not reported Belize or El Salvador), and in South America from Colombia, Venezuela, and the Guianas south, west of the Andes to western Ecuador and east of the Andes to central Bolivia and southern Brazil.

Notes.—Brown and Amadon (1968) and Griffiths (1994) suggested that this species should be placed in the monotypic genus *Ibycter* Vieillot.

Genus *CARACARA* Merrem

> *Caracara* Merrem, 1826, in Ersch and Gruber, Allg. Encycl. Wiss. Künste 15: 159. Type, by subsequent designation (Hellmayr and Conover, 1949, Field Mus. Nat. Hist. Publ., Zool. Ser., vol. 13, pt 1, no. 4), *Falco plancus* Miller.

Notes.—Formerly listed as *Polyborus*. The type-species of *Polyborus* Vieillot, 1816, is not identifiable; therefore, the name *Caracara* must be used (Banks and Dove 1992). See comments under *Milvago*.

Caracara plancus (Miller). Crested Caracara.

> *Falco plancus* J. F. Miller, 1777, Var. Subj. Nat. Hist., pt. 3, pl. 17. (Tierra del Fuego.)

Habitat.—Arid Lowland Scrub, Arid Montane Scrub, Low Seasonally Wet Grassland, Second-growth Scrub, lowland pine savanna (0–3000 m; Tropical and Subtropical zones, also Temperate Zone in South America).

Distribution.—*Resident* [*cheriway* group] in central and southern Florida (north to Brevard County, formerly to Enterprise and St. Augustine), Cuba, and the Isle of Pines, and from northern Baja California, southern Arizona, Sonora, Sinaloa, Zacatecas, Nuevo León, central and southern Texas, and southwestern Louisiana (Gum Cove area) south locally through Middle America (including the Tres Marias Islands off Nayarit, but not reported Belize), and throughout most of South America (including islands off Venezuela from Aruba east to Trinidad) south to northern and central Peru and northern Brazil; [*lutosus* group] formerly on Guadalupe Island, off Baja California (now extinct); and [*plancus* group] from southern Peru and central Brazil south to Tierra del Fuego and the Falkland Islands.

Casual [*cheriway* group] north to central New Mexico, southwestern Mississippi, and to islands off Panama (Taboga and Pearl) and Jamaica. Individuals reported from west to Washington, Oregon, and California, and north to Wyoming, Ontario, Pennsylvania, New York, and New Jersey are of questionable origin.

Notes.—Groups: *C. cheriway* (Jacquin, 1784) [Crested Caracara], *C. lutosus* (Ridgway, 1876) [Guadalupe Caracara], and *C. plancus* [Southern Caracara]. The Guadalupe Island forms is recognized by many authors as a distinct species. The *cheriway* group is also considered by some authors to represent a separate species, but intergradation between it and the *plancus* group has been reported near the mouth of the Amazon. (Hellmayr and Conover 1949).

Genus *MILVAGO* Spix

Milvago Spix, 1824, Avium Spec. Nov. Bras. 1: 12. Type, by monotypy, *Milvago ochrocephalus* Spix = *Polyborus chimachima* Vieillot.

Notes.—Vuilleumier (1970) recommended that this genus and *Caracara* be merged.

Milvago chimachima (Vieillot). Yellow-headed Caracara.

Polyborus chimachima Vieillot, 1816, Nouv. Dict. Hist. Nat. (nouv. éd.) 5: 259. Based on "Chimachima" Azara, Apunt. Hist. Nat. Páx. Parag. 1: 50 (no. 6). (Paraguay.)

Habitat.—Low Seasonally Wet Grassland, Pastures/Agricultural Lands, Second-growth Scrub (0–1800 m; Tropical and lower Subtropical zones).

Distribution.—*Resident* in southwestern Costa Rica (north to San José province) and Panama (including the Pearl Islands), and in South America from Colombia, Venezuela, Trinidad, and the Guianas south, mostly east of the Andes, to northern Argentina and southern Brazil.

Subfamily FALCONINAE: True Falcons and Laughing Falcons

Tribe HERPETOTHERINI: Laughing Falcons

Genus *HERPETOTHERES* Vieillot

Herpetotheres Vieillot, 1817, Nouv. Dict. Hist. Nat. (nouv. éd.) 18: 317. Type, by subsequent designation (G. R. Gray, 1840), *Falco cachinnans* Linnaeus.

Herpetotheres cachinnans (Linnaeus). Laughing Falcon.

Falco cachinnans (Rolander MS) Linnaeus, 1758, Syst. Nat. (ed. 10) 1: 90. (in America meridionali = Surinam.)

Habitat.—Tropical Lowland Evergreen Forest Edge, Gallery Forest, River-edge Forest, Tropical Deciduous Forest (0–1500 m; Tropical and Subtropical zones).

Distribution.—*Resident* from extreme southern Sonora and Tamaulipas south along both slopes of Middle America, and in South America from Colombia, Venezuela, and the Guianas south, west of the Andes to northwestern Peru and east of Andes to northern Argentina and southern Brazil.

Tribe FALCONINI: True Falcons

Genus *FALCO* Linnaeus

Falco Linnaeus, 1758, Syst. Nat. (ed. 10) 1: 88. Type, by subsequent designation (A.O.U., 1886), *Falco subbuteo* Linnaeus.

Tinnunculus Vieillot, 1808, Hist. Nat. Ois. Amer. Sept. 1 (livr. 2): 39. Type, by subsequent designation (Walden, 1872), *Falco columbarius* Linnaeus.

Hierofalco Cuvier, 1816, Règne Anim. 1: 312. Type, by monotypy, *Falco subbuteo*
Gmelin = *Falco rusticolus* Linnaeus.

Cerchneis Boie, 1826, Isis von Oken, col. 970. Type, by monotypy, *Falco rupicolus*
Daudin = *Falco tinnunculus* Linnaeus.

Hypotriorchis Boie, 1826, Isis von Oken, col. 970. Type, by original designation, *Falco
subbuteo* Linnaeus.

Aësalon Kaup, 1829, Skizz. Entw.-Ges. Eur. Thierw., pp. 40, 190. Type, by tautonymy,
Falco aesalon Tunstall = *Falco columbarius* Linnaeus.

Rhynchodon Nitzsch, 1829, Observ. Avium Art. Carot. Comm., p. 20. Type, by subsequent designation (A.O.U. Comm., 1886), *Falco peregrinus* Tunstall.

Rhynchofalco Ridgway, 1873, Proc. Boston Soc. Nat. Hist. 16: 46. Type, by original
designation, *Falco femoralis* Temminck.

Planofalco Oberholser, 1974, Bird Life Texas, p. 976. Type, by original designation,
Falco mexicanus Schlegel.

Falco tinnunculus Linnaeus. Eurasian Kestrel.

Falco Tinnunculus Linnaeus, 1758, Syst. Nat. (ed. 10) 1: 90. (in Europæ turribus, etc.
= Sweden.)

Habitat—Open country and partly open situations.

Distribution.—*Breeds* from the British Isles and northern Eurasia south to southern Africa,
India, eastern China, and Japan.

Winters from the breeding range south to the East Indies and Philippines.

Casual in Alaska (Attu and Shemya, in the Aleutians, and at sea in the central and southern
Bering Sea). Accidental in British Columbia (Alkali Lake), New Brunswick (Ft. Beausejour),
Nova Scotia (Minudie), Massachusetts (Nantasket Beach), New Jersey (Cape May Point),
the Lesser Antilles (Martinique), Greenland, Iceland, and the Faeroe Islands; sight reports
for Bermuda and French Guiana.

Notes.—Also known as European Kestrel and, in Old World literature, as the Kestrel.
See comments under *F. sparverius*.

Falco sparverius Linnaeus. American Kestrel.

Falco sparverius Linnaeus, 1758, Syst. Nat. (ed. 10) 1: 90. Based on "The Little Hawk"
Catesby, Nat. Hist. Carolina 1: 5, pl. 5. (in America = South Carolina.)

Habitat.—Open and partly open country with scattered trees, cultivated lands, and occasionally suburban areas; breeding habitat requires nest sites such as holes in trees, cliffs,
or buildings (Tropical to Temperate zones).

Distribution.—*Breeds* from western and central Alaska, southern Yukon, western (and
probably northwestern) Mackenzie, northern Alberta, northern Saskatchewan, northern Manitoba, northern Ontario, southern Quebec, New Brunswick, Prince Edward Island, Nova
Scotia, and southern Newfoundland south to southern Baja California (including Guadalupe
Island), Sinaloa, the highlands of Middle America (to central Honduras), the Gulf coast and
(at least formerly) southern Florida; in the Bahamas (north to Eleuthera) and the Antilles
(rare south of Guadeloupe); the lowland pine savanna of eastern Honduras and northeastern
Nicaragua; and through most of South America (including the Netherlands Antilles and
Trinidad, but absent from heavily forested regions such as the Amazon basin) south to Tierra
del Fuego (including the Juan Fernández Islands off Chile).

Winters from south-coastal Alaska (casually), southern British Columbia, the northern
United States, southern Manitoba (casually), southern Ontario, southwestern Quebec, and
(rarely) Nova Scotia south throughout the breeding range, including the northern Bahamas
and Cayman Islands, and Bermuda and virtually all of Middle America, the northern populations migrating as far south as Panama.

Casual or accidental in northern and southwestern Alaska, District of Franklin (Jenny
Lind Island), on the Revillagigedo Islands (Socorro Island), Barbados, the Falkland Islands,
British Isles, Denmark, the Azores, and Malta.

Notes.—Formerly known in American literature as Sparrow Hawk. Various Old World taxa, including *F. tinnunculus,* have been considered to form a superspecies with *F. sparverius* (Mayr and Short 1970; Stresemann and Amadon *in* Mayr and Cottrell 1979), but relationships are uncertain.

Falco columbarius Linnaeus. Merlin.

Falco columbarius Linnaeus, 1758, Syst. Nat. (ed. 10) 1: 90. Based on "The Pigeon-Hawk" Catesby, Nat. Hist. Carolina 1: 3, pl. 3. (in America = South Carolina.)

Habitat.—Open country from open coniferous woodland to prairie, occasionally in adjacent suburbs; in winter, open woodland, grasslands, open cultivated fields, marshes, estuaries, and seacoasts.

Distribution.—*Breeds* in North America from northwestern Alaska, northern Yukon, northwestern and central Mackenzie, southeastern Keewatin, northern Manitoba, northern Ontario, northern Quebec, Labrador, and Newfoundland south to southern Alaska, southwestern British Columbia, central Washington, eastern Oregon, Idaho, northern Utah (formerly), Colorado (at least formerly), western South Dakota, western North Dakota, northern Minnesota, Iowa (formerly), northern Wisconsin, northern Michigan, southern Ontario, northern Ohio (formerly), southern Quebec, New Brunswick, Nova Scotia, and Maine; and in Eurasia from Iceland, the Faeroe Islands, British Isles, and Scandinavia east across Russia and Siberia to the Sea of Okhotsk, and south to Lake Baikal, Mongolia, and Sakhalin.

Winters from south-coastal Alaska and southern (primarily coastal) British Columbia east across southern Canada (mostly in cities) through Alberta, Saskatchewan, Manitoba, southern Ontario, southwestern Quebec, and New Brunswick to Nova Scotia and Newfoundland, and from Montana, Colorado, western and southern Texas, the Gulf states, and Maryland (casually elsewhere north to the Canadian border) south through Middle America, Bermuda, and the West Indies to northwestern Peru, northern Colombia, northern Venezuela, and Trinidad; and in Eurasia from Iceland, the British Isles, southern Scandinavia, southern Russia, and southern Japan south to the Mediterranean region, northern Africa, Asia Minor, northern India, eastern China, and Korea.

Casual in Greenland and Spitsbergen; a sight report for the northwestern Hawaiian Islands (Midway).

Notes.—Formerly known as Pigeon Hawk.

Falco subbuteo Linnaeus. Eurasian Hobby.

Falco Subbuteo Linnaeus, 1758, Syst. Nat (ed. 10) 1: 89. (in Europa = Sweden.)

Habitat .—Woodland and partly open country.

Distribution.—*Breeds* in the Palearctic and southeastern Asia, and *Winters* south to tropical Africa and southern Asia.

Casual in Alaska in the Aleutian Islands (Attu, Agattu) and Pribilof Islands (St. George) (Gibson and Kessel 1992); an earlier report from Cordova, Alaska and a sight report from British Columbia are unsatisfactory.

Falco femoralis Temminck. Aplomado Falcon.

Falco femoralis Temminck, 1822, Planches Color., livr. 21, pl. 121 and text. (Brazil.)

Habitat.—Low Seasonally Wet Grassland, lowland pine savanna (0–4400 m; Tropical Zone, in South America to Temperate Zone).

Distribution.—*Resident* from Sinaloa (at least formerly), northeastern Chihuahua, southeastern San Luis Potosí, and Veracruz (formerly north to southeastern Arizona, southern New Mexico, and west-central and southern Texas, the last documented breeding in the United States in 1952 in New Mexico, where an apparently wild bird was also photographed in 1991 and 1992) south locally to Chiapas, the Yucatan Peninsula (at least formerly) and Belize; in the pine savanna of eastern Honduras and northeastern Nicaragua; and from western Panama south locally throughout South America (absent from much of Amazonia) to Tierra del Fuego and the Falkland Islands. Reintroduction of breeding birds is being attempted in southern Texas.

Casual in Guatemala (San Agustín), western Nicaragua, Costa Rica, and, in recent years, in the former breeding range in the southwestern United States. Reintroduced in southern Texas (T.O.S. 1995).

Falco rufigularis Daudin. Bat Falcon.

> *Falco rufigularis* Daudin, 1800, Traité Ornithol. 2: 131. Based on the "Orange-breasted Hobby" Latham, Gen. Synop. Birds (suppl.) 1: 28. (in Cayana = Cayenne.)

Habitat.—Tropical Lowland Evergreen Forest Edge, Tropical Deciduous Forest Edge, Gallery Forest, Secondary Forest (0–1600 m; Tropical and Subtropical zones).

Distribution.—*Resident* from southern Sonora, eastern Nuevo León, and Tamaulipas south along both slopes through Middle America (including Coiba, Taboga, and the Pearl islands off Panama), and in South America from Colombia, Venezuela, Tobago, Trinidad, and the Guianas south, west of the Andes to western Ecuador and east of the Andes to northern Argentina and southern Brazil.

Notes.—For use of *F. rufigularis* instead of *F. albigularis* Daudin, 1800, see Eisenmann (1966).

Falco deiroleucus Temminck. Orange-breasted Falcon.

> *Falco deiroleucus* Temminck, 1825, Planches Color., livr. 59, pl. 348. (Dans l'île Saint Francois, partie méridionale du Brésil = São Francisco Island, Santa Catarina, Brazil.)

Habitat.—Tropical Lowland Evergreen Forest (0–2000 m; Tropical and Subtropical zones).

Distribution.—*Resident* (rare and local) in southern Mexico (recorded Veracruz, Campeche), Guatemala (primarily Petén and Pacific slope), Belize, Honduras (El Hatillo), Nicaragua (Matagalpa and the northeastern lowlands), Costa Rica, and Panama (Chiriquí, Coclé, and Darién), and in South America from Colombia, Venezuela, Trinidad, and the Guianas south locally, mostly east of the Andes, to northern Argentina and southern Brazil.

Notes.—Stresemann and Amadon *in* Mayr and Cottrell (1979) suggested that *F. deiroleucus* and *F. peregrinus* constitute a superspecies.

Falco rusticolus Linnaeus. Gyrfalcon.

> *Falco rusticolus* Linnaeus, 1758, Syst. Nat. (ed. 10) 1: 88. (in Svecia = Sweden.)

Habitat.—Primarily open country in the Arctic, including tundra, from mountains to rocky seacoasts, and occasionally open coniferous forest; breeding habitat requires cliffs (occasionally trees) for nest sites.

Distribution.—*Breeds* in North America from northern Alaska, northern Yukon, and Banks, Prince Patrick, and Ellesmere islands south to central Alaska (including the Aleutians west to Umnak), northwestern British Columbia, southern Yukon, northern Mackenzie, southern Keewatin, Southampton Island, central Quebec, and northern Labrador; and in the Palearctic from Greenland, Iceland, and northern Scandinavia east across northern Russia and northern Siberia to the Chukotski Peninsula, and south to Anadyrland, Kamchatka, and Bering Island.

Winters in North America from the breeding range south irregularly to the Pribilof and Aleutian islands, southern Alaska, southern Canada, and the extreme northern United States; and in Eurasia from the breeding range south to the British Isles, western (casually central) Europe, southern Russia, Lake Baikal, Manchuria, Sakhalin, the Kuril Islands, and Japan.

Casual in winter south as far as central California, Oregon, northern Utah, northeastern Colorado, Oklahoma, Kansas, Missouri, Illinois, northern Ohio, Pennsylvania, Delaware, Virginia, and Bermuda; sight reports for Indiana and Tennessee.

Notes.—Known in Old World literature as Gyr Falcon. Stresemann and Amadon *in* Mayr and Cottrell (1979) suggested that *F. rusticolus, F. mexicanus,* and Old World *F. jugger* Gray, 1834, *F. biarmicus* Temminck, 1825, and *F. cherrug* Gray, 1834, constitute a superspecies.

Falco peregrinus Tunstall. Peregrine Falcon.

> *Falco Peregrinus* Tunstall, 1771, Ornithol. Brit., p. 1. (No locality given = Northamptonshire, England.)

Habitat.—A variety of open situations, usually near water, from tundra, marshes, and seacoasts to high mountains, more open forested regions, deserts, and urban areas; suitable breeding habitat requires cliffs for nest sites, but ledges on large buildings provide a substitute in urban areas.

Distribution.—*Breeds* in North America from northern Alaska, northern Mackenzie, Banks, Victoria, southern Melville, Somerset, and northern Baffin islands, and Labrador south to southern Baja California, the coast of Sonora, southern Arizona, New Mexico, and western and central (formerly) Texas, in the Sierra Madre Occidental and Sierra Madre Oriental of northern Mexico, and, at least formerly, Kansas, Missouri, Arkansas, northeastern Louisiana, Tennessee, northern Alabama, and northwestern Georgia; in South America in Ecuador, Peru, central and southern Argentina, and central and southern Chile; and in much of the Old World from Greenland, the British Isles, Scandinavia, northern Russia, northern Siberia and the Chukotski Peninsula south, at least locally, through Eurasia and Africa to South Africa, India, Sri Lanka, the East Indies, Australia (including Tasmania), Vanuatu, and the Fiji and Loyalty islands. Absent as a breeding bird through much of continental North America, especially in the eastern part south of the Canadian Arctic, since the 1950's; recently reestablished as a breeding bird through introductions in many parts of southern Canada and the United States.

Migrates along coasts and less commonly interior where not known to breed or to winter; migrants recorded regularly on Bermuda and at sea.

Winters in the Americas from southern Alaska (the Aleutians and Prince William Sound), the Queen Charlotte Islands, coastal British Columbia, the central and southern United States (rarely farther north) and New Brunswick south through Middle America, the West Indies, and South America to Tierra del Fuego; and in the Old World generally through the breeding range, with northernmost populations usually migrating to tropical regions.

Casual in the Hawaiian Islands, the Revillagigedo Islands, Clipperton Island, Iceland, the Faeroe Islands, and Canary Islands. Accidental on South Georgia.

Notes.—Also known in Old World literature as Peregrine. Populations from the North African desert region, Arabia, and the Middle East are sometimes (Vaurie 1965, Sibley and Monroe 1990) regarded as a distinct species, *F. pelegrinoides* Temminck, 1829 [Barbary Falcon]. The South American *F. kreyenborgi* Kleinschmidt, 1929, appears to be a color morph of *F. peregrinus* (Ellis and Grant 1983).

Falco mexicanus Schlegel. Prairie Falcon.

> *Falco mexicanus* Schlegel, 1850, Abh. Geb. Zool. Vergl. Anat. 3: 15. (Mexico = Monterrey, Nuevo León.)

Habitat.—Dry grasslands and prairies, locally alpine tundra; suitable breeding habitat usually requires cliffs for nest sites; in winter, also cultivated fields and lake shores.

Distribution.—*Breeds* from south-central British Columbia, southern Alberta, southern Saskatchewan, and western North Dakota south to Baja California, southern Arizona, southern New Mexico, Chihuahua, central Durango, northern San Luis Potosí, western and northern Texas, and (formerly) northwestern Missouri.

Winters from the breeding range in southern Canada south to Baja California, Sonora, Durango, Zacatecas, Aguascalientes, Nuevo León, and Tamaulipas.

Casual north and east to northeastern British Columbia, Manitoba (regular in southwest?), Ontario (sight report), Minnesota, Wisconsin (sight report), Michigan, Illinois, Ohio, Kentucky, Tennessee, and Mississippi, and south to Hidalgo. Accidentals reported in Alabama, Georgia, Florida, and South Carolina are of uncertain origin.

Notes.—See comments under *F. rusticolus*.

Order **GALLIFORMES**: Gallinaceous Birds

Superfamily CRACOIDEA: Megapodes, Curassows, and Allies

Family **CRACIDAE**: Curassows and Guans

Genus *ORTALIS* Merrem

Ortalida [accusative case] = *Ortalis* [nominative] Merrem, 1786, Avium Rar. Icones Descr. 2: 40. Type, by original designation, *Phasianus motmot* Linnaeus.

Ortalis vetula (Wagler). Plain Chachalaca.

Penelope vetula Wagler, 1830, Isis von Oken, col. 1112. (Mexico = near city of Veracruz, Veracruz; Miller and Griscom, Auk 38: 455, 1921.)

Habitat.—Tropical Lowland Evergreen Forest Edge, Gallery Forest, Secondary Forest, wooded residential areas (0–1850 m; Tropical Zone).

Distribution.—*Resident* on the Gulf-Caribbean slope from southern Texas (lower Rio Grande Valley) and Nuevo León south through the lowlands of eastern Mexico (including the Yucatan Peninsula and Isla Cancun), Belize, and eastern Guatemala to northern Honduras (including Isla Utila in the Bay Islands), and in the interior valleys of Chiapas, central Honduras, and north-central Nicaragua; also northwestern Costa Rica (Guanacaste).

Introduced and established on islands off the coast of Georgia (Sapelo, Blackbeard, and Little St. Simons).

Notes.—The isolated population in northwestern Costa Rica was assigned to *O. leucogastra* by A.O.U. (1983, 1985) and Sibley and Monroe (1990).

Ortalis cinereiceps Gray. Gray-headed Chachalaca.

Ortalida cinereiceps G. R. Gray, 1867, List Birds Brit. Mus., pt. 5, p. 12. (north-west coast of America = San Miguel Island, Pearl Islands, Panama.)

Habitat.—Tropical Lowland Evergreen Forest Edge, Gallery Forest, Secondary Forest (0–1100 m; Tropical Zone).

Distribution.—*Resident* in eastern Honduras (Olancho, Mosquitia), eastern and central Nicaragua, Costa Rica (except the dry northwest), Panama (including Isla del Rey in the Pearl Islands), and northwestern Colombia.

Notes.—The South American *O. garrula* (Humboldt, 1805) and *O. cinereiceps* constitute a superspecies (Sibley and Monroe 1990); they are considered by some (e.g., Blake 1977) as conspecific. The composite species may be called Chestnut-winged Chachalaca.

Ortalis ruficauda Jardine. Rufous-vented Chachalaca.

Ortalis ruficauda Jardine, 1847, Ann. Mag. Nat. Hist. (1) 20: 374. (Tobago.)

Habitat.—Tropical Deciduous Forest, Gallery Forest, Tropical Lowland Evergreen Forest Edge, Secondary Forest (0–1600 m; Tropical Zone).

Distribution.—*Resident* [*ruficrissa* group] in northeastern Colombia and extreme northwestern Venezuela; and [*ruficauda* group] in northern Venezuela (south to the Arauca and Orinoco rivers), and on Margarita Island and Tobago.

Introduced [*ruficauda* group] in the Lesser Antilles in the Grenadines (on Union and Bequia), where apparently established by the late 17th Century, but there have been no recent reports from Bequia. Early writings also alluded to its presence on St. Vincent in the late 17th Century.

Notes.—Also known as Rufous-tailed Chachalaca. Groups: *O. ruficrissa* Sclater and Salvin, 1870 [Rufous-vented Chachalaca] and *O. ruficauda* [Rufous-tipped Chachalaca].

Ortalis wagleri Gray. Rufous-bellied Chachalaca.

Ortalida wagleri G. R. Gray, 1867, List Birds Brit. Mus., pt. 5, p. 12. (California and Mexico = western Mexico.)

Habitat.—Tropical Deciduous Forest, Gallery Forest (0–2000 m; Tropical Zone).

Distribution.—*Resident* in western Mexico from southern Sonora, Sinaloa, and western Durango south to northern Jalisco.

Notes.—Also known as Wagler's Chachalaca. Treatment of *O. wagleri* as a species distinct from *O. poliocephala* follows Banks (1990a).

Ortalis poliocephala (Wagler). West Mexican Chachalaca.

Penelope poliocephala Wagler, 1830, Isis von Oken, col. 1112. (Mexico.)

Habitat.—Tropical Deciduous Forest, Tropical Lowland Evergreen Forest Edge (0–1800 m; Tropical Zone).

Distribution.—*Resident* from southern and northeastern Jalisco and Michoacán south to Morelos, western Puebla, Oaxaca, and extreme western Chiapas (vicinity of Tonalá).

Notes.—See notes under *O. wagleri.*

Ortalis leucogastra (Gould). White-bellied Chachalaca.

Penelope leucogastra Gould, 1844, Proc. Zool. Soc. London (1843), p. 105. (Mazatenango, Suchitepequez, Guatemala; Vaurie, 1968, Bull. Amer. Mus. Nat. Hist. 138: 244.)

Habitat.—Tropical Deciduous Forest, Secondary Forest, Gallery Forest (0–1050 m; Tropical Zone).

Distribution.—*Resident* in the Pacific lowlands from western Chiapas (vicinity of Tonalá) south to northwestern Nicaragua.

Notes.—Although formerly considered a race of *O. vetula,* this form may be allied to the South American *O. motmot* (Linnaeus, 1766) superspecies (Delacour and Amadon 1973). See notes under *O. vetula.*

Genus *PENELOPE* Merrem

Penelope Merrem, 1786, Avium Rar. Icones Descr. 2: 39. Type, by subsequent designation (Lesson, 1828), *Penelope marail* "Linnaeus" [= Gmelin] = *Penelope jacupema* Merrem = *Phasianus marail* Müller.

Penelope purpurascens Wagler. Crested Guan.

Penelope purpurascens Wagler, 1830, Isis von Oken, col. 1110. (Mexico = probably Veracruz.)

Habitat.—Tropical Lowland Evergreen Forest, Tropical Deciduous Forest, Gallery Forest, Montane Evergreen Forest (0–2000 m; Tropical and lower Subtropical zones).

Distribution.—*Resident* from Sinaloa and southern Tamaulipas south along both slopes of Middle America to Colombia, western Ecuador, and northern Venezuela.

Genus *CHAMAEPETES* Wagler

Chamaepetes Wagler, 1832, Isis von Oken, col. 1227. Type, by monotypy, *Ortalida goudotii* Lesson.

Chamaepetes unicolor Salvin. Black Guan.

Chamaepetes unicolor Salvin, 1867, Proc. Zool. Soc. London, p. 159. (Veragua, Panama = Calovévora, Panama.)

Habitat.—Montane Evergreen Forest (1000–3000 m; upper Tropical and Subtropical zones).

Distribution.—*Resident* in the mountains of Costa Rica (north to Cordillera de Guanacaste) and western Panama (east to Coclé).

Genus *PENELOPINA* Reichenbach

Penelopina Reichenbach, 1862, Avium Syst. Nat., Columbariae, p. 152. Type, by monotypy, *Penelope niger* Fraser.

Penelopina nigra (Fraser). Highland Guan.

Penelope niger Fraser, 1852, Proc. Zool. Soc. London (1850), p. 246, pl. 29. (No locality given = Guatemala.)

Habitat.—Montane Evergreen Forest, Tropical Deciduous Forest, Pine-Oak Forest (900–3150 m; upper Tropical and Subtropical zones).

Distribution.—*Resident* in the mountains of extreme eastern Oaxaca (Sierra Madre de Chiapas), Chiapas, Guatemala, El Salvador, Honduras, and north-central Nicaragua.

Notes.—Also known as Black Chachalaca.

Genus *OREOPHASIS* Gray

Oreophasis G. R. Gray, 1844, Genera Birds 3: [485], col. pl. 121 and pl. [121]. Type, by monotypy, *Oreophasis derbianus* Gray.

Oreophasis derbianus Gray. Horned Guan.

Oreophasis derbianus G. R. Gray, 1844, Genera Birds 3: [485], col. pl. 121 and pl. [121]. (Guatemala.)

Habitat.—Montane Evergreen Forest (1800–3100 m; Subtropical and lower Temperate zones).

Distribution.—*Resident* locally in the mountains of Chiapas and Guatemala.

Genus *CRAX* Linnaeus

Crax Linnaeus, 1758, Syst. Nat. (ed. 10) 1: 157. Type, by subsequent designation (Ridgway, 1896), *Crax rubra* Linnaeus.

Crax rubra Linnaeus. Great Curassow.

Crax rubra Linnaeus, 1758, Syst. Nat. (ed. 10) 1: 157. Based on "The Red Peruvian Hen" Albin, Nat. Hist. Birds 3: 37, pl. 40. (in America = western Ecuador.)

Habitat.—Tropical Lowland Evergreen Forest, Tropical Deciduous Forest (0–800 m; Tropical and lower Subtropical zones).

Distribution.—*Resident* from southeastern San Luis Potosí, southern Tamaulipas, Veracruz, and Oaxaca south along both slopes of Middle America (including the Yucatan Peninsula and Cozumel Island) to western Colombia and western Ecuador.

Notes.—*Crax rubra* is part of a large complex including several South American species that probably constitutes a superspecies (Delacour and Amadon 1973).

Superfamily PHASIANOIDEA: Partridges, Grouse, Turkeys, and Quail

Family **PHASIANIDAE**: Partridges, Grouse, Turkeys, and Old World Quail

Subfamily PHASIANINAE: Partridges and Pheasants

Genus *ALECTORIS* Kaup

Alectoris Kaup, 1829, Skizz. Entw.-Ges. Eur. Thierw., pp. 180, 193. Type, by monotypy, *Perdix petrosa* Auct. (not Gmelin) = *Perdix barbara* Bonnaterre.

Alectoris chukar (Gray). Chukar.

Perdix Chukar J. E. Gray, 1830, in Hardwicke, Illus. Indian Zool. 1(2): pl. 54. (India = Srinagar, Kumaon, India.)

Habitat.—Rocky hillsides, dry mountain slopes with grassy vegetation, open and flat desert with sparse grasses, and barren plateaus.

Distribution.—*Resident* in Eurasia from southeastern Europe and Asia Minor east to southern Manchuria, northern China, Turkestan, and the western Himalayas.

Introduced widely in North America and established, at least locally, from south-central British Columbia, northern Idaho, and central and eastern Montana south to southern California, southern Nevada, northern Arizona, and western Colorado; also in the Hawaiian Islands (main islands from Kauai eastward, but no longer on Oahu).

Notes.—*Alectoris chukar* was long regarded as a subspecies of *A. graeca* (Meisner, 1804) of Europe, but see Watson (1962a, 1962b). *Tetrao kakelik* Falk, 1786 has been used for this species in Russian literature but is indeterminate (Hartert 1917).

Genus *FRANCOLINUS* Stephens

Francolinus Stephens, 1819, in Shaw, Gen. Zool. 11(2): 316. Type, by tautonymy, *Francolinus vulgaris* Stephens = *Tetrao francolinus* Linnaeus.

Francolinus pondicerianus (Gmelin). Gray Francolin.

Tetrao pondicerianus Gmelin, 1789, Syst. Nat. 1(2): 760. Based on the "Pondicherry Partridge" Latham, Gen. Synop. Birds 2(2): 774. (in Coromandel = Pondicherry, India.)

Habitat.—Dry habitats, often near thickets and large lawns; in native range, dry country with scrub or grass, cultivated fields, and desert scrub.

Distribution.—*Resident* from eastern Iran east to India and Sri Lanka.

Introduced and established in the Hawaiian Islands (in 1958, presently on Oahu, Molokai, Lanai, Maui, and Hawaii) and in southern Arabia and the Andaman, Seychelles, Amirante, and Mascarene islands.

Francolinus francolinus (Linnaeus). Black Francolin.

Tetrao Francolinus Linnaeus, 1766, Syst. Nat. (ed. 12) 1: 275. (in Italia, Orienta, Africa, Asia = Cyprus.)

Habitat.—Dry grasslands and pastures; in native range, grasslands (primarily tall grass), scrubby and brushy areas, marshes and, locally, clearings in open forest.

Distribution.—*Resident* from Cyprus, Asia Minor, and the Near East east to southern Russia (Transcaucasia), northern Iran, India, and Assam.

Introduced and established in the Hawaiian Islands (in 1959, now on Kauai, Molokai, Maui, and Hawaii). Introductions into southwestern Louisiana (Calcasieu and Cameron parishes) and southern Florida (Palm Beach County) have failed.

Francolinus erckelii (Rüppell). Erckel's Francolin.

Perdix Erckelii Rüppell, 1835, Neue Wirbelth., Vögel, p. 12, pl. 6. (Taranta Mts., northeastern Ethiopia.)

Habitat.—Grasslands and open forest; in native range, scrub, brush, and open areas with scattered trees, primarily in hilly or mountainous country.

Distribution.—*Resident* in eastern Sudan (Red Sea Province), northern Ethiopia, and Eritrea.

Introduced and established in the Hawaiian Islands (in 1957, now on all main islands from Kauai eastward, except Maui).

Notes.—Crowe et al. (1992) placed this species in the genus *Pternistis* Wagler, 1832.

Genus *TETRAOGALLUS* J. E. Gray

Tetraogallus J. E. Gray, in Hardwicke, 1832, Illus. Indian Zool., 2, pt. 11, pl. 46. Type, by monotypy, *Tetraogallus nigellii* J. E. Gray = *Tetraogallus himalayensis* G. R. Gray.

Tetraogallus himalayensis G. R. Gray. Himalayan Snowcock.

Tetraogallus himalayensis G. R. Gray, 1843, Proc. Zool. Soc. London (1842), p. 105. New name for bird figured in Jardine and Selby, 1828, Ill. Orn., pl. 141, as *Lophophorus nigelli,* not *L. nigelli* Jardine and Selby 1828, op. cit., pl. 76 (Himalayas; restricted to hills north of Simla by Meinertzhagen, 1927, Ibis 3 (12th ser.), p. 629.)

Habitat.—Steep rocky slopes with sparse vegetation, alpine meadows.

Distribution.—*Resident* in south-central Eurasia in Afghanistan, Turkestan, northern India, and western China.

Introduced and established (1963 and subsequent years) in northeastern Nevada in the Ruby and East Humboldt mountains (Stiver 1984).

Genus *PERDIX* Brisson

Perdix Brisson, 1760, Ornithologie, 1, pp. 26, 219. Type, by tautonymy, *Perdix cinerea* Brisson = *Tetrao perdix* Linnaeus.

Perdix perdix (Linnaeus). Gray Partridge.

Tetrao Perdix Linnaeus, 1758, Syst. Nat. (ed. 10) 1: 160. (in Europæ agris = southern Sweden.)

Habitat.—Primarily cultivated fields and grasslands with hedgerows; in Old World, more widespread in open country.

Distribution.—*Resident* in Eurasia from the British Isles, southern Scandinavia, and northern Russia south to southern Europe, Turkey, northern Iran, Turkestan, and Mongolia.

Widely introduced in North America and established locally from southern British Columbia, central Alberta, central Saskatchewan, southern Manitoba, southern Ontario, southwestern Quebec, Prince Edward Island, and Nova Scotia south to northeastern California (formerly, never definitely established), northern Nevada, northern Utah, northern Wyoming, northeastern Nebraska, Iowa, northern Missouri, extreme northern Illinois, central Indiana (formerly), west-central Ohio (formerly), northern New York, and northern Vermont. Many populations have declined or disappeared in recent decades.

Notes.—Also known as Hungarian Partridge or Common Partridge and, in Old World literature, as the Partridge.

Genus *COTURNIX* Bonnaterre

Coturnix Bonnaterre, 1791, Tabl. Encycl. Méth., Ornithol. 1(47): pl. lxxxvii. Type, by tautonymy, "Caille" Bonnaterre = *Tetrao coturnix* Linnaeus.

Coturnix japonica Temminck & Schlegel. Japanese Quail.

Coturnix vulgaris japonica Temminck and Schlegel, 1849, in Siebold, Fauna Jpn., Aves, p. 103, pl. 61. (Japan.)

Habitat.—Grasslands, marshes, cultivated fields and pastures.

Distribution.—*Breeds* from northern Mongolia and Transbaicalia east through Amurland to Ussuriland, Sakhalin, and the Kuril Islands, and south to Manchuria, Korea, and Japan.

Winters from Transbaicalia (rarely) and central Japan south to the northern Indochina region, southern China, and the Ryukyu Islands.

Introduced and established in the Hawaiian Islands (in 1921, now on main islands from Kauai eastward, except Oahu).

Notes.—*Coturnix coturnix* (Linnaeus, 1758) and *C. japonica* constitute a superspecies (Vaurie 1965).

Genus *GALLUS* Brisson

Gallus Brisson, 1760, Ornithologie 1: 26, 166. Type, by tautonymy, *Gallus* Brisson = *Phasianus gallus* Linnaeus.

Gallus gallus (Linnaeus). Red Junglefowl.

Phasianus Gallus Linnaeus, 1758, Syst. Nat. (ed. 10) 1: 158. (in India Orientali: Pouli candor etc. = Island of Pulo Condor, off the mouth of the Mekong River.)

Habitat.—Forest undergrowth, second growth, scrub, and cultivated lands.

Distribution.—*Resident* from the Himalayas, southern China, and Hainan south to central India, Southeast Asia, Sumatra, and Java.

Introduced in the Hawaiian Islands (by early Polynesians, probably about 500 A.D.), now on Kauai, formerly on other main islands, with recent reintroductions not known to have become established except at Waimea Falls Park, on Oahu; on islands in the Bahamas (Little San Salvador), off Puerto Rico (Mona, and possibly Culebra, and in the Grenadines (Kick-'em-Jenny); and in the Philippines, and on many islands of the East Indies and Polynesia.

Genus *LOPHURA* Fleming

Lophura Fleming, 1822, Philos. Zool. 2: 230. Type, by monotypy, *Phasianus ignitus* [Shaw].

Gennaeus Wagler, 1832, Isis von Oken, col. 1228. Type, by monotypy, *Phasianus nycthemerus* Linnaeus.

Lophura leucomelanos (Latham). Kalij Pheasant.

Phasianus leucomelanos Latham, 1790, Index Ornithol. 2: 633. (India = Nepal.)

Habitat.—Dense scrub, forest undergrowth, thickets, and wooded ravines, in Hawaii in ohia–tree fern and koa forest, and on plantations.

Distribution.—*Resident* in the Himalayas from western Nepal east to northern Assam and Bhutan.

Introduced and established in the Hawaiian Islands (on Hawaii in 1962, now in the North Kona district and on the slopes of Mauna Loa and Mauna Kea).

Genus *PHASIANUS* Linnaeus

Phasianus Linnaeus, 1758, Syst. Nat. (ed. 10) 1: 158. Type, by tautonymy, *Phasianus colchicus* Linnaeus (*Phasianus,* prebinomial specific name, in synonymy).

Phasianus colchicus Linnaeus. Ring-necked Pheasant.

Phasianus colchicus Linnaeus, 1758, Syst. Nat. (ed. 10) 1: 158. (in Africa, Asia = Rion, formerly Phasis, Republic of Georgia)

Habitat.—Croplands and windbreaks, meadows, and marsh edges; in Old World, also scrubby wastes, open woodland and edges, grassy steppe, desert oases, riverside thickets, and open mountain forest.

Distribution.—*Resident* [*colchicus* group] from central Russia, Transcaucasia, Turkestan, Mongolia, and Ussuriland south to northern Iran, northern Burma, China, and Korea; and [*versicolor* group] in Japan (Honshu and Shikoku) and the Seven Islands of Izu.

Introduced and established [*colchicus* group] in the Hawaiian Islands (about 1865, now on all main islands from Kauai eastward), widely in North America from southern British Columbia (including Vancouver Island), central Alberta, central Saskatchewan, southwestern Manitoba, central Minnesota, central Wisconsin, central Michigan, southern Ontario, southwestern Quebec, New Brunswick, Prince Edward Island, and Nova Scotia south, at least locally, to southern interior California, northern Baja California, Utah, southern New Mexico, northern and southeastern Texas, northwestern Oklahoma, Kansas, northern Missouri, central Illinois, central Indiana, southern Ohio, Pennsylvania, northern Maryland, New Jersey, central Virginia, and North Carolina (Outer Banks), and in the Bahama Islands (Eleuthera, probably), Japan, New Zealand, and Europe; and [*versicolor* group] in the Hawaiian Islands (locally on Hawaii, with smaller numbers on Kauai, Lanai, and possibly Maui).

Notes.—Known in Old World literature as the Pheasant. Groups: *P. colchicus* [Ring-necked or Common Pheasant] and *P. versicolor* Vieillot, 1825 [Green or Japanese Pheasant].

Within the *colchicus* group, the Asiatic complex may be a species, *P. torquatus* Gmelin, 1789 [Ring-necked Pheasant], distinct from the more western *P. colchicus* [Common or English Pheasant]; most North American populations are from *torquatus* stock, although birds from European *colchicus* are mixed with *torquatus* in many areas.

Genus *PAVO* Linnaeus

Pavo Linnaeus, 1758, Syst. Nat. (ed. 10) 1: 156. Type, by tautonymy, *Pavo cristatus* Linnaeus (*Pavo,* prebinomial specific name, in synonymy).

Pavo cristatus Linnaeus. Common Peafowl.

Pavo cristatus Linnaeus, 1758, Syst. Nat. (ed. 10) 1: 156. (in India orientali, Zeylona = India.)

Habitat.—Open forest, forest edge, second growth, scrub, open areas with scattered trees, and cultivated lands.
Distribution.—*Resident* throughout India and on Sri Lanka.
Introduced in the Hawaiian Islands (initially in 1860, now established on Oahu, Maui, and Hawaii) and the Bahamas (Exuma); local, semi-domesticated populations also have persisted for years in various parts of the North American continent.

Subfamily TETRAONINAE: Grouse

Notes.—Sometimes regarded as a family, the Tetraonidae (e.g., A.O.U. 1957). The taxonomic arrangement is based on Ellsworth et al. (1995, 1996).

Genus *BONASA* Stephens

Bonasa Stephens, 1819, in Shaw, Gen. Zool. 11(2): 298. Type, by subsequent designation (A.O.U. Comm., 1886), *Tetrao umbellus* Linnaeus.

Bonasa umbellus (Linnaeus). Ruffed Grouse.

Tetrao umbellus Linnaeus, 1766, Syst. Nat. (ed. 12) 1: 275. Based on "The Ruffed Heath-cock or Grous" Edwards, Glean. Nat. Hist. 1: 79, pl. 248. (in Pensylvania = eastern Pennsylvania.)

Habitat.—Forest, mainly mixed deciduous-coniferous and deciduous, in both wet and relatively dry situations, from boreal forest and northern hardwood-ecotone to eastern deciduous forest and oak-savanna woodland.
Distribution.—*Resident* from central Alaska, northern Yukon, southwestern Mackenzie, northern Saskatchewan, northern Manitoba, northern Ontario, southern Quebec, southern Labrador, New Brunswick, Prince Edward Island, and Nova Scotia south to northwestern California, northeastern Oregon, central and eastern Idaho, central Utah, northwestern Colorado , western and northern Wyoming, southern Alberta, southern Saskatchewan, southern Manitoba (absent from prairie regions of three preceding provinces), northern North Dakota, central and southeastern Minnesota, Iowa, northern Illinois (at least formerly), central Indiana, Ohio, in the Appalachians to northern Georgia, western South Carolina, and western North Carolina, and to northeastern Virginia; also locally south to western South Dakota (Black Hills), northeastern Kansas, northern Arkansas, central Missouri, western Tennessee, and northeastern Alabama.
Introduced and established on Anticosti Island and in Newfoundland.

Genus *CENTROCERCUS* Swainson

Centrocercus [subgenus] Swainson, 1832, in Swainson and Richardson, Fauna Bor.-Amer. 2 (1831): 358, 496. Type, by original designation, *Tetrao urophasianus* Bonaparte.

Centrocercus urophasianus (Bonaparte). Sage Grouse.

Tetrao urophasianus Bonaparte, 1827, Zool. J. 3: 213. (Northwestern countries beyond the Mississippi, especially on the Missouri = North Dakota.)

Habitat.—Foothills, plains, rocky plateaus, and mountain slopes where sagebrush is present.

Distribution.—*Resident* locally (formerly widespread) from central Washington, Montana, southeastern Alberta, southwestern Saskatchewan, southwestern North Dakota, western South Dakota, and extreme northwestern Nebraska south to eastern California, south-central Nevada, southern Utah, and western Colorado, formerly north to southern British Columbia, south to northern New Mexico and southeast to extreme western Oklahoma.

Notes.—The isolated populations of the Gunnison Basin of Colorado represent a distinct unnamed species (Hupp and Braun 1991, Young et al. 1994).

Genus *FALCIPENNIS* Elliot

Falcipennis Elliot, 1864, Proc. Acad. Nat. Sci. Philadelphia 16: 23. Type, by monotypy, *Falcipennis hartlaubi* Elliot = *Tetrao falcipennis* Hartlaub.
Canachites Stejneger, 1885, Proc. U. S. Natl. Mus. 8: 410. Type, by original designation, *Tetrao canadensis* Linnaeus.

Notes.—*Canachites* has been considered generically distinct (Peters 1934, A.O.U. 1957, Ellsworth et al. 1995) or merged with *Dendragapus* (Short 1967, A.O.U. 1983); the latter treatment would make *Dendragapus* paraphyletic (Ellsworth et al. 1996). Yamashina (1939) recommended its merger with *Falcipennis,* as have Dickerman and Gustafson (1996).

Falcipennis canadensis (Linnaeus). Spruce Grouse.

Tetrao canadensis Linnaeus, 1758, Syst. Nat. (ed. 10) 1: 159. Based on "The Black and Spotted Heath-cock" Edwards, Nat. Hist. Birds 3: 118, pl. 118. (in Canada = Churchill, Manitoba; restricted by Todd, 1963, Birds Labrador Peninsula, p. 252.)

Habitat.—Coniferous forest, primarily spruce and pine, especially with dense understory of grasses and shrubs or regenerating burns.

Distribution.—*Resident* [*canadensis* group] from northern Alaska, northern Yukon, northern Mackenzie, southwestern Keewatin, northern Manitoba, northern Ontario, northern Quebec, and Labrador south to coastal and south-central Alaska, central British Columbia, central Alberta, central Saskatchewan, southern Manitoba, northern Minnesota, northern Wisconsin, central Michigan, southern Ontario, northern New York, northern Vermont, northern New Hampshire, and eastern Maine; and [*franklinii* group] from southeastern Alaska (west to base of the Alaska Peninsula), central British Columbia and west-central Alberta south to northern Oregon, central and southeastern Idaho, and western Montana.

Introduced and established [*canadensis* group] in Newfoundland.

Notes.—Groups: *F. canadensis* [Spruce Grouse] and *F. franklinii* (Douglas, 1829) [Franklin's Grouse]. Formerly placed in *Dendragapus* or *Canachites*.

Genus *LAGOPUS* Brisson

Lagopus Brisson, 1760, Ornithologie 1: 26, 181. Type, by tautonymy, *Lagopus* Brisson = *Tetrao lagopus* Linnaeus.

Lagopus lagopus (Linnaeus). Willow Ptarmigan.

Tetrao Lagopus Linnaeus, 1758, Syst. Nat. (ed. 10) 1: 159. (in Europæ alpinis = Swedish Lapland.)

Habitat.—Open tundra, especially in areas heavily vegetated with grasses, mosses, herbs, and shrubs, less frequently in openings in boreal coniferous forest.

Distribution.—*Breeds* [*lagopus* group] in North America across the Arctic from northern Alaska east through Banks, southern Melville, and Bathurst islands to western Baffin Island, and south to the central and eastern Aleutian Islands, southern Alaska, northwestern and east-central British Columbia, extreme west-central Alberta, central Mackenzie, southern Keewatin, northeastern Manitoba, extreme northern Ontario, the Twin Islands (in James Bay), central Quebec, Labrador, and Newfoundland; and in Eurasia from Greenland and Scandinavia east across Russia and Siberia, and south (except the British Isles) to Mongolia, Ussuriland, and Sakhalin.

Resident [*scoticus* group] in the British Isles, Orkney Islands, and Hebrides.

Winters [*lagopus* group] mostly in the breeding range, in North America wandering irregularly (or casually) south to Montana (formerly), North Dakota, Minnesota, Wisconsin, central Ontario, and Maine; and in Eurasia south to northern Europe.

Introduced [*lagopus* group] and established (in 1968, from the Newfoundland population) on Scatarie Island in Nova Scotia.

Accidental [*lagopus* group] in Nova Scotia before introduction.

Notes.—In the Old World known as Willow Grouse. Groups: *L. lagopus* [Willow Ptarmigan] and *L. scoticus* (Latham, 1789) [Red Grouse].

Lagopus mutus (Montin). Rock Ptarmigan.

> *Tetrao mutus* Montin, 1776, Phys. Sälskap. Handl. 1: 155. (Alpibus lapponicus = Sweden.)

Habitat.—Open tundra, barren and rocky slopes in Arctic and alpine areas; in winter, some movement to thickets and forest edge.

Distribution.—*Breeds* in North America from northern Alaska east through the Canadian Arctic islands to Ellesmere and Baffin islands, and south to the Aleutians, southern Alaska (including Kodiak Island), western and northern British Columbia, central Mackenzie, central Keewatin, Southampton Island, northern Quebec, northern Labrador, and Newfoundland; and in the Palearctic from Greenland, Iceland, Scotland, and Scandinavia east across northern Russia and northern Siberia to Kamchatka, and at high elevations in the Pyrenees and Alps of southern Europe, the mountain ranges of central Asia, and in the Kuril Islands and Japan (Honshu).

Winters regularly in North America from the breeding range south to southern Mackenzie, northern Saskatchewan, northern Manitoba, northwestern Ontario, and central Quebec, casually to coastal British Columbia (the Queen Charlotte Islands); and in the Palearctic primarily resident in the breeding range.

Accidental in northern Minnesota.

Notes.—Known in Old World literature as the Ptarmigan.

Lagopus leucurus (Richardson). White-tailed Ptarmigan.

> *Tetrao (Lagopus) leucurus* "Swains." Richardson, 1831, in Wilson and Bonaparte, Amer. Ornithol. (Jameson ed.) 4: 330. (Rocky Mountains, lat. 54° N.)

Habitat.—Alpine tundra, especially in rocky areas with sparse vegetation; in winter, moves slightly lower, to areas where vegetation protrudes above snow.

Distribution.—*Resident* from south-central Alaska (Alaska Range), northern Yukon, and southwestern Mackenzie south to southern Alaska (west to the Kenai Peninsula and Lake Clark), southern British Columbia (including Vancouver Island), and the Cascade Mountains of Washington, and along the Rocky Mountains (locally, mostly on alpine summits) from southeastern British Columbia and southwestern Alberta south through central southern Wyoming and Colorado to northern New Mexico.

Introduced and established in northeastern Utah (Uinta Mountains) and California (central Sierra Nevada); introduced also in northeastern Oregon (Wallowa Mountains) with unknown success.

Genus *DENDRAGAPUS* Elliot

> *Dendragapus* Elliot, 1864, Proc. Acad. Nat. Sci. Philadelphia 16: 23. Type, by subsequent designation (Baird, Brewer, and Ridgway, 1874), *Tetrao obscurus* Say.

Dendragapus obscurus (Say). Blue Grouse.

> *Tetrao obscurus* Say, 1823, in Long, Exped. Rocky Mount. 2: 14. (near Defile Creek = about 20 miles north of Colorado Springs, Colorado.)

Habitat.—Coniferous and coniferous-deciduous forest, often adjacent to open country; in winter, more restricted to dense coniferous forest [*obscurus* group]; open coniferous forest [*fuliginosus* group].

Distribution.—*Resident* [*obscurus* group] from southeastern Alaska (except coastal areas), southern Yukon, and extreme southwestern Mackenzie south through the mountains of interior British Columbia (except coastal, southwestern, and south-central areas), southwestern Alberta, eastern Washington, and the Rocky Mountains to eastern Nevada, northern and eastern Arizona (south to White Mountains), southwestern and north-central New Mexico, western and central Colorado and (formerly) western South Dakota; and [*fuliginosus* group] from coastal southeastern Alaska (north to Yakutat) and coastal British Columbia (including the Queen Charlotte and Vancouver islands) south in coastal ranges and the Cascades to northwestern California, the Sierra Nevada, and (at least formerly) to southern California (Ventura County) and extreme western Nevada.

Notes.—Groups: *D. obscurus* [Dusky Grouse] and *D. fuliginosus* (Ridgway, 1874) [Sooty Grouse].

Genus *TYMPANUCHUS* Gloger

> *Tympanuchus* Gloger, 1841, Gemein. Handb. und Hilfsb. Naturgesch., p. 396. Type, by monotypy, *Tetrao cupido* Linnaeus.
>
> *Pedioecetes* Baird, 1858, in Baird, Cassin, and Lawrence, Rep. Explor. Surv. R. R. Pac. 9: xxi, xliv. Type, by monotypy, *Tetrao phasianellus* Linnaeus.

Notes.—For comments on relationships within this genus, see Ellsworth et al. (1994).

Tympanuchus phasianellus (Linnaeus). Sharp-tailed Grouse.

> *Tetrao Phasianellus* Linnaeus, 1758, Syst. Nat. (ed. 10) 1: 160. Based on "The Long-tailed Grous from Hudson's-Bay" Edwards, Nat. Hist. Birds 3: 117, pl. 117. (in Canada = Hudson Bay.)

Habitat.—Grasslands, especially with scattered woodlands, arid sagebrush, brushy hills, oak savanna, edges of riparian woodland, muskeg, and bogs; in winter, more restricted to areas with shrub or tree cover.

Distribution.—*Resident,* at least locally, from central Alaska, central Yukon, northwestern Mackenzie, northern Saskatchewan, northern Manitoba, northern Ontario, and west-central Quebec south to eastern Washington, southern Idaho, northern Utah, southwestern, central and northeastern Colorado, western and north-central Kansas, central Nebraska, eastern South Dakota, eastern North Dakota, northern Minnesota, central Wisconsin, central Michigan, and southern Ontario; formerly occurred south to southern Oregon, northeastern California, northeastern Nevada, northeastern New Mexico, southern Iowa and northern Illinois, probably also northern Texas.

Notes.—See comments under *T. cupido.*

Tympanuchus cupido (Linnaeus). Greater Prairie-Chicken.

> *Tetrao Cupido* Linnaeus, 1758, Syst. Nat. (ed. 10) 1: 160. Based on "Le Cocq de bois d'Amérique" Catesby, Nat. Hist. Carolina 2 (app.): 1, pl. 1. (in Virginia = Pennsylvania.)

Habitat.—Tall-grass prairie, occasionally feeding in adjacent cultivated lands; formerly in eastern (fire-produced) grassland and blueberry barrens.

Distribution.—*Resident* locally and in much reduced numbers from eastern North Dakota, northwestern and central Minnesota, and northern Wisconsin south to southeastern Wyoming, northeastern Colorado, Kansas (except southwestern), northeastern Oklahoma, central Missouri, and southern Illinois; also in southeastern Texas. Formerly occurred (now extirpated or nearly so) from east-central Alberta, central Saskatchewan, southern Manitoba, and southern Ontario south, east of the Rocky Mountains, to eastern Texas, southwestern Louisiana, east-central Arkansas, central Indiana, western Kentucky, and western Ohio; and in the east from Massachusetts south to Maryland, after 1835 confined to the island of Martha's Vineyard, Massachusetts (where last reported in 1932).

Notes.—The extinct eastern population was called Heath Hen. This species and *T. pallidicinctus* constitute a superspecies and are considered to be conspecific by some authors (e.g., Johnsgard 1983); with this concept, Prairie Chicken or Pinnated Grouse may be used. *Tympanuchus cupido* and *T. phasianellus* hybridize sporadically, but occasionally they interbreed extensively on a local level (Johnsgard and Wood 1968).

Tympanuchus pallidicinctus (Ridgway). Lesser Prairie-Chicken.

Cupidonia cupido var. *pallidicinctus* Ridgeway [sic], 1873, For. Stream 1: 289. (Prairie of Texas [near lat. 32° N.].)

Habitat.—Dry short-grass prairie, often interspersed with shrubs and short trees, regularly feeding in adjacent cultivated lands.

Distribution.—Resident locally and in reduced numbers from southeastern Colorado, south-central Kansas, and western Oklahoma to extreme southeastern New Mexico and northern Texas (Panhandle), formerly north to southwestern Nebraska.

Notes.—See comments under *T. cupido.*

Subfamily MELEAGRIDINAE: Turkeys

Notes.—Sometimes regarded as a family, the Meleagrididae (e.g., A.O.U. 1957).

Genus *MELEAGRIS* Linnaeus

Meleagris Linnaeus, 1758, Syst. Nat. (ed. 10) 1: 156. Type, by tautonymy, *Meleagris gallopavo* Linnaeus (*Meleagris,* prebinomial specific name, in synonymy).
Agriocharis Chapman, 1896, Bull. Amer. Mus. Nat. Hist. 6: 287, 288. Type, by monotypy, *Meleagris ocellata* "Temminck" [= Cuvier].

Notes.—Osteological studies by Steadman (1980) have shown that the genus *Agriocharis* should not be separated from *Meleagris.*

Meleagris gallopavo Linnaeus. Wild Turkey.

Meleagris Gallopavo Linnaeus, 1758, Syst. Nat. (ed. 10) 1: 156. Based mainly on the "Wild Turkey" Catesby, Nat. Hist. Carolina 1: 44, pl. 44. (in America septentrionali = Mirador, Veracruz.)

Habitat.—Forest and open woodland, deciduous (particularly oak) or mixed deciduous-coniferous, especially with adjacent clearings or pastures (Subtropical and Temperate zones).

Distribution.—Resident locally and generally in reduced numbers (formerly widespread) from northern Arizona, New Mexico, Kansas, eastern Nebraska, southeastern South Dakota, northern Iowa, southern and eastern Wisconsin, southern Ontario (formerly), extreme southern Quebec, northern New York, southern Vermont, southern New Hampshire, and southwestern Maine south to Guerrero (at least formerly), Veracruz, southern Texas, the Gulf coast, and Florida.

Reintroduced widely through its former breeding range north of Mexico, and established locally north to southern British Columbia, Washington, Idaho, southern Alberta, southern Saskatchewan, southern Manitoba, southeastern Minnesota, northern Michigan, and southern Ontario, and in the Hawaiian Islands (initially in 1788, now on Niihau, Lanai, Maui, and Hawaii) and New Zealand.

Meleagris ocellata Cuvier. Ocellated Turkey.

Meleagris ocellata Cuvier, 1820, Mém. Mus. Hist. Nat. 6: 1, 4, pl. 1. (Gulf of Honduras = Belize.)

Habitat.—Tropical Lowland Evergreen Forest Edge, Tropical Deciduous Forest (Tropical Zone).

Distribution.—*Resident* in southeastern Mexico (Tabasco and the Yucatan Peninsula), northern Guatemala (Petén), and northern Belize.

Notes.—Formerly placed in the genus *Agriocharis.*

Subfamily NUMIDINAE: Guineafowl

Genus *NUMIDA* Linnaeus

Numida Linnaeus, 1766, Syst. Nat., ed. 12, 1, p. 273. Type, by monotypy, *Numida meleagris* Linnaeus = *Phasianus meleagris* Linnaeus.

Numida meleagris (Linnaeus). Helmeted Guineafowl.

Phasianus Meleagris Linnaeus, 1758, Syst. Nat., ed. 10, 1, p. 158 (in Africa = Nubia, upper Nile.)

Habitat.—Open woodland, cultivated lands, and grasslands.

Distribution.—*Resident* [*galeata* group] in western Africa east to western Zaire; [*meleagris* group] in Arabia and northeastern Africa south to northeastern Zaire; and [*mitrata* group] in south-central and southern Africa.

Widely domesticated throughout the world, and escaped individuals are frequently reported. Introduced and established in the Hawaiian Islands (in 1874 on Hawaii and possibly other main islands, perhaps not well established), in the West Indies (on Cuba, Isle of Pines, Hispaniola, Puerto Rico, and Barbuda), and on Ascension, Trinidad, and the Cape Verde Islands.

Notes.—The three groups are sometimes regarded as separate species, *N. galeata* Pallas, 1767 [West African Guineafowl], *N. meleagris* [Helmeted Guineafowl], and *N. mitrata* Pallas, 1767 [Tufted Guineafowl], although they all intergrade where their ranges meet (see Crowe 1978).

Family **ODONTOPHORIDAE**: New World Quail

Notes.—Formerly considered a subfamily of Phasianidae, the Odontophoridae are given family status because of evidence from skeletal (Holman 1961) and DNA-DNA hybridization studies (Sibley and Ahlquist 1990).

Genus *DENDRORTYX* Gould

Dendrortyx Gould, 1844, Monogr. Odontoph. 1: pl. [3] and text. Type, by monotypy, *Ortyx macroura* Jardine and Selby.

Dendrortyx barbatus Gould. Bearded Wood-Partridge.

Dendrortyx barbatus (Lichtenstein MS) Gould, 1846, Monogr. Odontoph. 2: pl. [2] and text. (Jalapa, Veracruz.)

Habitat.—Montane Evergreen Forest, Pine Forest (950–1550 m; Subtropical Zone).

Distribution.—Resident in eastern San Luis Potosí, eastern Hidalgo, eastern Puebla, and central Veracruz.

Dendrortyx macroura (Jardine and Selby). Long-tailed Wood-Partridge.

Ortyx macroura Jardine and Selby, 1828, Illus. Ornithol. 1: text to pl. 38 (in "Ortyx synopsis specierum"), and pl. 49 and text. (Mexico = mountains about valley of México.)

Habitat.—Montane Evergreen Forest, Pine-Oak Forest (1800–3700 m; Subtropical and Temperate zones).

Distribution.—*Resident* in the mountains of Jalisco, Michoacán, México, Distrito Federal, Morelos, Guerrero, Puebla, Veracruz, and Oaxaca.

Dendrortyx leucophrys (Gould). Buffy-crowned Wood-Partridge.

Ortyx leucophrys Gould, 1844, Proc. Zool. Soc. London (1843), p. 132. (Cobán, Guatemala.)

Habitat.—Montane Evergreen Forest, Pine-Oak Forest (1000–2900 m; upper Tropical and Subtropical zones).

Distribution.—*Resident* locally in the mountains of Chiapas (Sierra Madre de Chiapas), Guatemala, El Salvador, Honduras, north-central Nicaragua, and Costa Rica (central highlands, including Dota Mountains).

Genus *OREORTYX* Baird

Oreortyx Baird, 1858, in Baird, Cassin, and Lawrence, Rep. Explor. Surv. R. R. Pac. 9: xlv, 638, 642. Type, by monotypy, *Ortyx picta* Douglas.

Notes.—This genus may not be as closely related to *Callipepla* as its traditional placement suggests (Gutiérrez et al. 1983).

Oreortyx pictus (Douglas). Mountain Quail.

Ortyx picta Douglas, 1829, Philos. Mag. (n.s.) 5: 74. (No locality given = junction of Willamette and Santiam rivers, Linn County, Oregon; Browning, 1977, Proc. Biol. Soc. Wash. 90: 808–812.)

Habitat.—Brushy mountainsides, chaparral, pine-oak woodland, dense second-growth, and in more arid areas, sagebrush, and pinyon-juniper woodland.

Distribution.—*Resident* from southwestern British Columbia (on Vancouver Island, where introduced), western and southern Washington, and central Idaho south through the mountains of California and northern and western Nevada to northern Baja California (Sierra Juárez, Sierra San Pedro Mártir).

Genus *CALLIPEPLA* Wagler

Callipepla Wagler, 1832, Isis von Oken, col. 277. Type, by monotypy, *Callipepla strenua* Wagler = *Ortyx squamatus* Vigors.
Lophortyx Bonaparte, 1838, Geogr. Comp. List, p. 42. Type, by subsequent designation (G. R. Gray, 1840), *Tetrao californicus* Shaw.

Callipepla squamata (Vigors). Scaled Quail.

Ortyx squamatus Vigors, 1830, Zool. J. 5: 275. (Mexico.)

Habitat.—Arid Lowland Scrub, Arid Montane Scrub, Northern Temperate Grassland, Second-growth Scrub (0–2550 m; Subtropical and lower Temperate zones).

Distribution.—*Resident* from northeastern and southeastern Arizona, northern New Mexico, east-central Colorado, and southwestern Kansas south through western Oklahoma and the western half of Texas, and the interior of Mexico to northeastern Jalisco, Guanajuato, Querétaro, Hidalgo, and western Tamaulipas.

Introduced and established in central Washington (Yakima and Grant counties), eastern Nevada and Nebraska, with no or uncertain success.

Callipepla douglasii (Vigors). Elegant Quail.

Ortyx douglasii Vigors, 1829, Zool. J. 4 (1828): 354. (Monterey, error = Mazatlán, Sinaloa.)

Habitat.—Arid Lowland Scrub, Tropical Deciduous Forest (0–1550 m; Tropical Zone).
Distribution.—*Resident* from northern Sonora and southwestern Chihuahua south through Sinaloa, northwestern Durango, and Nayarit to northwestern Jalisco.

A small population present near Nogales, Arizona, from 1964 to the early 1970's apparently originated from escaped individuals.

Notes.—This and the next two species sometimes are separated from *Callipepla* in the genus *Lophortyx* (e.g., A.O.U. 1957). Also known as Douglas Quail.

Callipepla californica (Shaw). California Quail.

Tetrao californicus Shaw, 1798, in Shaw and Nodder, Naturalists' Misc. 9: text to pl. 345. (California = Monterey.)

Habitat.—Brushy, grassy, and weedy areas in both humid and arid regions, including chaparral, forest edge, riparian woodland edge, oak woodland, cultivated lands, semi-desert scrub, sagebrush, wooded suburbs, and, less frequently, pinyon-juniper woodland.

Distribution.—*Resident* from southern Oregon south through California (including Santa Catalina Island, where possibly introduced) to southern Baja California and extreme western Nevada (Fish Lake Valley).

Introduced north to southwestern British Columbia, east to western Idaho, and Utah, and in the Hawaiian Islands, New Zealand, Australia, Chile, Argentina, and Corsica, also widely elsewhere in the western United States.

Notes.—See comments under *C. douglasii* and *C. gambelii*.

Callipepla gambelii (Gambel). Gambel's Quail.

Lophortyx Gambelii "Nutt." Gambel, 1843, Proc. Acad. Nat. Sci. Philadelphia 1: 260. (Some distance west [= east] of California = southern Nevada.)

Habitat.—Deserts, primarily with brush or low trees, desert riparian woodland, also in adjacent cultivated land and suburbs (Tropical and Subtropical zones).

Distribution.—*Resident* from southeastern California, southern Nevada, southern Utah, western Colorado, and northern New Mexico south to northeastern Baja California, Sonora (including Isla Tiburón in the Gulf of California), coastal Sinaloa, extreme northern Chihuahua, and the Rio Grande Valley of western Texas.

Introduced and established in the Hawaiian Islands (in 1928, now on Lanai, Kahoolawe, and possibly Hawaii), on San Clemente Island (off California), and in west-central Idaho.

Notes.—*Callipepla gambelii* and *C. californica* constitute a superspecies (Mayr and Short 1970). See comments under *C. squamata* and *C. douglasii*.

Genus *PHILORTYX* Gould

Philortyx Gould, 1846, Monogr. Odontoph. 2: pl. 6 and text. Type, by monotypy, *Ortyx fasciatus* Gould.

Philortyx fasciatus (Gould). Banded Quail.

Ortyx fasciatus Gould, 1843, Proc. Zool. Soc. London (1842), p. 133. (California, error = Mexico.)

Habitat.—Arid Lowland Scrub, Arid Montane Scrub, Tropical Deciduous Forest, Second-growth Scrub (0–2500 m; Tropical and lower Subtropical zones.)

Distribution.—Resident in southwestern Jalisco, Colima, Michoacán, Guerrero, México, Morelos, and Puebla.

Notes.—Also known as Barred Quail.

Genus *COLINUS* Goldfuss

Colinus Goldfuss, 1820, Handb. Zool. 2: 220. Type, by monotypy, *Perdix mexicanus, Caille de la Louisiane,* Planches enlum. 149 = *Tetrao virginianus* Linnaeus.

Colinus virginianus (Linnaeus). Northern Bobwhite.

Tetrao virginianus Linnaeus, 1758, Syst. Nat. (ed. 10) 1: 161. Based on "The American Partridge" Catesby, Nat. Hist. Carolina 3: 12, pl. 12. (in America = Virginia.)

Habitat.—Brushy fields, grasslands (primarily long grass), cultivated lands, and open woodland, in both humid and semi-arid situations (Tropical to Temperate zones).

Distribution.—*Resident* from southeastern Wyoming, central South Dakota, southern Minnesota, central Wisconsin, central Michigan, extreme southern Ontario, southern New York, and Massachusetts (formerly farther north) south through the central and eastern United States (west to southeastern Wyoming, eastern Colorado, eastern New Mexico, and west-central Texas) to southern Florida, the Gulf coast, and eastern and southern Mexico, west to eastern Coahuila, western San Luis Potosí, southeastern Nayarit, eastern Jalisco, Guanajuato, México, Puebla, and northern Oaxaca, east to Tabasco, eastern Chiapas, and extreme northwestern Guatemala (Nenton-Comitán valley), and in the Pacific lowlands in Oaxaca and Chiapas; also in southeastern Arizona (formerly, extirpated late 1890's, reintroductions attempts not certainly successful) and eastern Sonora.

Introduced and established in western North America (Washington and Oregon), the Greater Antilles (Cuba, Hispaniola, Puerto Rico, and formerly on St. Croix), the Bahamas (Andros, Abaco, and New Providence), and New Zealand.

Notes.—Known in earlier literature as the Bobwhite and Common Bobwhite. *Colinus virginianus* and *C. nigrogularis* constitute a superspecies (Mayr and Short 1970).

Colinus nigrogularis (Gould). Black-throated Bobwhite.

> *Ortyx nigrogularis* Gould, 1843, Proc. Zool. Soc. London (1842), p. 181. (Mexico = Yucatán.)

Habitat.—Arid Lowland Scrub, Low Seasonally Wet Grassland, Second-growth Scrub, lowland pine savanna (Tropical Zone).

Distribution.—*Resident* in the northern and central Yucatan Peninsula (northern Campeche, Yucatán, and northern and central Quintana Roo), northern Guatemala (Petén), and Belize; and in the Mosquitia of eastern Honduras and northeastern Nicaragua.

Notes.—See comments under *C. virginianus.*

Colinus cristatus (Linnaeus). Crested Bobwhite.

> *Tetrao cristatus* Linnaeus, 1766, Syst. Nat. (ed. 12) 1: 277. Based mainly on "La Caille hupée du Mexique" Brisson, Ornithologie 1: 260, pl. 25, fig. 2. (in Mexico, Guiania, error = Curaçao.)

Habitat.—Arid Lowland Scrub, Low Seasonally Wet Grassland, Second-growth Scrub (0–1500 m; Tropical Zone, in South America to Temperate Zone).

Distribution.—*Resident* [*leucopogon* group] on the Pacific slope from western Guatemala (including the upper Motagua Valley on the Caribbean drainage) south through El Salvador, Honduras (including the Sula, Comayagua, and Quimistán valleys on the Caribbean slope) and Nicaragua to central Costa Rica; and [*cristatus* group] on the Pacific slope of southwestern Costa Rica (Golfo Dulce region) and western Panama (east to western Panamá province), and from western Colombia east through most of Venezuela (also Aruba, Curaçao, and Margarita Island) to the Guianas and eastern Brazil.

Introduced and established in the Virgin Islands (St. Thomas, now extirpated) and the Grenadines (Mustique).

Notes.—Some authors (e.g., Blake 1977) recognize the two groups as separate species, *C. leucopogon* (Lesson, 1842) [Spot-bellied Bobwhite] and *C. cristatus* [Crested Bobwhite].

Genus *ODONTOPHORUS* Vieillot

> *Odontophorus* Vieillot, 1816, Analyse, p. 51. Type, by monotypy, "Tocro" Buffon = *Tetrao gujanensis* Gmelin.

Odontophorus gujanensis (Gmelin). Marbled Wood-Quail.

> *Tetrao gujanensis* Gmelin, 1789, Syst. Nat. 1(2): 767. Based in part on the "Guiana Partridge" Latham, Gen. Synop. Birds 2(2): 776. (in Cayenna et Gujana = Cayenne.)

Habitat.—Tropical Lowland Evergreen Forest (0–900 m; Tropical and lower Subtropical zones).

Distribution.—*Resident* in southern and southwestern Costa Rica (Pacific slope from Gulf of Nicoya eastward) and Panama (Pacific slope in Chiriquí, where probably now extirpated; Caribbean lowlands from Coclé eastward; and Pacific slope from eastern Panamá province eastward), and in South America from northern Colombia, Venezuela, and the Guianas south, mostly east of the Andes, to central Bolivia and Amazonian Brazil.

Odontophorus melanotis Salvin. Black-eared Wood-Quail.

Odontophorus melanotis Salvin, 1865, Proc. Zool. Soc. London (1864), p. 586. (Tucurrique, Costa Rica.)

Habitat.—Tropical Lowland Evergreen Forest, Montane Evergreen Forest (0–1600 m; Tropical and lower Subtropical zones).

Distribution.—*Resident* locally in northern and eastern Honduras (Caribbean slope west to the Sula Valley), Nicaragua (Caribbean slope), Costa Rica (mostly Caribbean slope), and Panama (both slopes).

Notes.—The earlier merger (Peters 1934, A.O.U. 1983) of *O. melanotis* with the South American *O. erythrops* Gould, 1859 was not based on published taxonomic evidence; differences between these two forms are as least as great as those between other species pairs in the genus (Ridgely and Gwynne 1989).

Odontophorus dialeucos Wetmore. Tacarcuna Wood-Quail.

Odontophorus dialeucos Wetmore, 1963, Smithson. Misc. Collect. 145(6): 5. (1,450 meters elevation, 6 1/2 kilometers west of the summit of Cerro Malí, Serranía del Darién, Darién, Panama.)

Habitat.—Montane Evergreen Forest (1050–1450 m; Subtropical Zone).

Distribution.—Resident in eastern Panama (on Cerro Malí and Cerro Tacarcuna, at the southern end of the Serranía del Darién, in Darién).

Odontophorus leucolaemus Salvin. Black-breasted Wood-Quail.

Odontophorus leucolaemus Salvin, 1867, Proc. Zool. Soc. London, p. 161. (Cordillera de Tolé, Veraguas, Panama.)

Habitat.—Montane Evergreen Forest (700–1850 m; upper Tropical and Subtropical zones).

Distribution.—Resident in the central highlands of Costa Rica (west to Cordillera de Guanacaste) and western Panama (east to Coclé, mostly on the Caribbean drainage).

Notes.—Also known as White-throated Wood-Quail.

Odontophorus guttatus (Gould). Spotted Wood-Quail.

Ortyx guttata Gould, 1838, Proc. Zool. Soc. London (1837), p. 79. (Bay of Honduras = Belize.)

Habitat.—Montane Evergreen Forest, Tropical Lowland Evergreen Forest (0–2900 m; Tropical, Subtropical, and lower Temperate zones).

Distribution.—Resident in southern Mexico (Veracruz, northern and southeastern Oaxaca, Tabasco, Chiapas, Campeche, and Quintana Roo), northern Guatemala (Petén and the Caribbean lowlands), and Belize, and in the highlands of central Guatemala, Honduras, north-central Nicaragua, Costa Rica, and extreme western Panama (western Chiriquí).

Genus *DACTYLORTYX* Ogilvie-Grant

Dactylortyx Ogilvie-Grant, 1893, Cat. Birds Brit. Mus. 22: xiv, 99, 429. Type, by monotypy, *Ortyx thoracicus* Gambel.

Dactylortyx thoracicus (Gambel). Singing Quail.

> *Ortyx thoracicus* Gambel, 1848, Proc. Acad. Nat. Sci. Philadelphia 4: 77. (Jalapa, [Veracruz,] Mexico.)

Habitat.—Montane Evergreen Forest, Tropical Lowland Evergreen Forest, Pine-Oak Forest, Tropical Deciduous Forest (0–2600 m; Tropical and Subtropical zones).

Distribution.—*Resident* locally in southwestern Tamaulipas, southeastern San Luis Potosí, northeastern Puebla, and central Veracruz; in western Jalisco and probably central Colima; in the Yucatan Peninsula; and from southeastern Oaxaca (Sierra Madre de Chiapas) south through the mountains of Chiapas, Guatemala, and El Salvador to central Honduras.

Genus *CYRTONYX* Gould

> *Cyrtonyx* Gould, 1844, Monogr. Odontoph. 1: pl. [2], and text. Type, by monotypy, *Ortyx massena* Lesson = *Ortyx montezumae* Vigors.

Cyrtonyx montezumae (Vigors). Montezuma Quail.

> *Ortyx Montezumæ* Vigors, 1830, Zool. J. 5: 275. (Mexico.)

Habitat.—Pine-Oak Forest, Arid Montane Scrub, Northern Temperate Grassland (1100–3100 m; Subtropical, and lower Temperate zones).

Distribution.—*Resident* [*montezumae* group] from central Arizona (north to White Mountains), southern New Mexico, western (formerly central) Texas, northern Coahuila, central Nuevo León, and central Tamaulipas south in the mountains of Mexico to northern Michoacán, Distrito Federal, Puebla, and west-central Veracruz; and [*sallaei* group] on the Pacific slope of Mexico from central Michoacán south to central Oaxaca (La Cieneguilla).

Notes.—Also known as Harlequin Quail (A.O.U. 1957) or Mearns's Quail. *Cyrtonyx montezumae,* and *C. ocellatus* constitute a superspecies. (Mayr, and Short 1970) Groups: *C. montezumae* [Montezuma Quail] and *C. sallaei* Verreaux, 1859 [Salle's Quail].

Cyrtonyx ocellatus (Gould). Ocellated Quail.

> *Ortyx ocellatus* Gould, 1837, Proc. Zool. Soc. London (1836), p. 75. (No locality given = Guatemala.)

Habitat.—Pine-Oak Forest, Arid Montane Scrub, Pine Forest (750–3050 m; Subtropical Zone).

Distribution.—Resident in the mountains of southeastern Oaxaca (Sierra Madre de Chiapas), Chiapas, Guatemala, El Salvador (at least formerly), Honduras, and north-central Nicaragua.

Notes.—See comments under *C. montezumae.*

Genus *RHYNCHORTYX* Ogilvie-Grant

> *Rhynchortyx* Ogilvie-Grant, 1893, Cat. Birds Brit. Mus. 22: xv, 100, 443. Type, by monotypy, *Odontophorus spodiostethus* Salvin [= male], and *Odontophorus cinctus* Salvin [= female].

Rhynchortyx cinctus (Salvin). Tawny-faced Quail.

> *Odontophorus cinctus* Salvin, 1876, Ibis, p. 379. (Veragua = Panama.)

Habitat.—Tropical Lowland Evergreen Forest, Montane Evergreen Forest (0–1400 m; Tropical and lower Subtropical zones).

Distribution.—*Resident* locally on the Caribbean slope of northern and eastern Honduras (west to the Sula Valley), Nicaragua, and Costa Rica, on both slopes of Panama (rare west of the Canal area), and in western Colombia, and western Ecuador.

Order **GRUIFORMES**: Rails, Cranes, and Allies

Family **RALLIDAE**: Rails, Gallinules, and Coots

Notes.—The sequence and placement of genera in this family is essentially that of Olson (1973).

Genus *COTURNICOPS* Gray

Coturnicops G. R. Gray, 1855, Cat. Genera Subgenera Birds, p. 120. Type, by monotypy, *Rallus noveboracensis* Gmelin = *Fulica noveboracensis* Gmelin.

Coturnicops noveboracensis (Gmelin). Yellow Rail.

Fulica noveboracensis Gmelin, 1789, Syst. Nat. 1(2): 701. Based on the "Yellow-breasted Gallinule" Pennant, Arct. Zool. 2: 491. (in Noveboraco = New York.)

Habitat.—Shallow marshes, and wet meadows; in winter, drier fresh-water and brackish marshes, as well as dense, deep grass, and rice fields.

Distribution.—*Breeds* locally from northwestern Alberta, southern Mackenzie, central Saskatchewan, northern Manitoba, northern Ontario, central Quebec, New Brunswick, eastern Maine, and (probably) Nova Scotia south to south-central Oregon, southern Alberta, southern Saskatchewan, North Dakota, central Minnesota, central Wisconsin, northern Michigan, southern Ontario, and southern Quebec (formerly in east-central California, and to northern Illinois and central Ohio). Reported in summer in southeastern Alaska, southern British Columbia, Montana, and eastern Colorado.

Winters from coastal North Carolina south to southern Florida, west through the central, and southern Gulf states to central, and southeastern Texas and (casually) Arkansas, and (locally and casually) from Oregon south to southern California.

Resident in central Mexico (Lerma marshes in México).

Migrates through western North America (rare and irregular; recorded northeastern British Columbia, Washington, Arizona, and New Mexico), and irregularly through most of the United States east of the Rocky Mountains.

Casual in Labrador, the Bahamas (Grand Bahama), and Bermuda.

Notes.—Relationships with the Asiatic *C. exquisitus* (Swinhoe, 1873) are uncertain, but that form and *C. noveboracensis* may constitute a superspecies (Mayr and Short 1970).

Genus *MICROPYGIA* Bonaparte

Micropygia Bonaparte, 1856, C. R. Acad. Sci. Paris 43: 599. Type, by virtual monotypy, *Micropygia schomburgi* "Cabanis" = *Crex schomburgkii* Schomburgk.

Micropygia schomburgkii (Schomburgk). Ocellated Crake.

Crex Schomburgkii (Cabanis MS) Schomburgk, 1848, Reisen Brit.-Guiana 2: 245. (Our Village, on the upper Kukenaam River, Terr. Yuruari, Venezuela.)

Habitat.—Low Seasonally Wet Grassland (0–1250 m)

Distribution.—*Resident* locally in southeastern Colombia, southern Venezuela, and the Guianas, and in extreme southeastern Peru, eastern Bolivia, and central and southeastern Brazil (absent from forested Amazonia).

One record from Costa Rica (Buenos Aires, Puntarenas province, 9 March 1967; Dickerman 1968).

Genus *LATERALLUS* Gray

Laterallus G. R. Gray, 1855, Cat. Genera Subgenera Birds, p. 120. Type, by monotypy, *Rallus melanophaius* Vieillot.

Laterallus ruber (Sclater and Salvin). Ruddy Crake.

> *Corethrura rubra* Sclater and Salvin, 1860, Proc. Zool. Soc. London, p. 300. (In provincia Veræ Pacis = Cobán, Alta Verapaz, Guatemala.)

Habitat.—Freshwater Marshes (0–1500 m; Tropical and lower Subtropical zones).

Distribution.—*Resident* in lowlands from Colima and Oaxaca on the Pacific slope and Tamaulipas on the Gulf-Caribbean slope south through Middle America (including Cozumel Island off Quintana Roo) to Honduras and northern Nicaragua; a sight report for northwestern Costa Rica (Guanacaste).

Laterallus albigularis (Lawrence). White-throated Crake.

> *Corethrura albigularis* Lawrence, 1861, Ann. Lyc. Nat. Hist. N. Y. 7: 302. (Atlantic side of the Isthmus of Panama, along the line of the Panama Railroad.)

Habitat.—Freshwater Marshes (0–1600 m; Tropical and lower Subtropical zones).

Distribution.—*Resident* on the Caribbean slope of Central America from southeastern Honduras (Río Segovia) south to western Panama (Veraguas), and on the Pacific slope from Costa Rica (Gulf of Nicoya) south through Panama (including Isla Coiba) to western and northern Colombia and western Ecuador.

Notes.—*Laterallus albigularis* was formerly treated as conspecific with the South American *L. melanophaius* (Vieillot, 1819), but they are now regarded as separate species (Wetmore 1965).

Laterallus exilis (Temminck). Gray-breasted Crake.

> *Rallus exilis* Temminck, 1831, Planches Color., livr. 87, pl. 523. (No locality given = Cayenne.)

Habitat.—Freshwater Marshes, Pastures/Agricultural Lands (0–1200 m; Tropical and lower Subtropical zones).

Distribution.—*Resident* locally in Belize (Middlesex), eastern Guatemala, southeastern Honduras (Río Segovia [= Coco]), eastern Nicaragua, Costa Rica, Panama (Isla Coiba, San Blas, and the Canal area), and South America (scattered reports from Colombia, Venezuela, Trinidad, the Guianas, northern Brazil, Ecuador, eastern Peru, eastern Bolivia, and southern Paraguay).

Laterallus jamaicensis (Gmelin). Black Rail.

> *Rallus jamaicensis* Gmelin, 1789, Syst. Nat. 1(2): 718. Based on "The Least Water-Hen" Edwards, Glean. Nat. Hist. 2: 142, pl. 278, lower fig. (in Jamaica.)

Habitat.—Shallow margins of salt marshes, less frequently in wet savanna, and freshwater marshes.

Distribution.—*Breeds* locally in California (recorded from the San Francisco Bay area, and the Imperial Valley, San Luis Obispo County, formerly also San Diego County), and in the lower Colorado River valley in southeastern California and southwestern Arizona; locally in Kansas (Stafford, Finney, Franklin, Barton, and Riley counties), northern and central Illinois, and southwestern Ohio; along the Atlantic coast from New York south to southern Florida; on the Gulf coast in eastern Texas (Brazoria Refuge, possibly also Galveston) and western Florida (from St. Marks to Clearwater); in Belize and Panama (eastern Panamá province); and in western Peru, Chile, and western Argentina. Recorded in summer (and possibly breeding) in Missouri, northwestern Indiana, extreme northern Baja California, Veracruz (Tecolutla), Cuba, Jamaica, Hispaniola, and (at least formerly) Puerto Rico.

Winters along the coast of California from the breeding range north to Tomales Bay, and in the Imperial and lower Colorado River valleys; along the Gulf coast from southeastern Texas east to Florida; along the Atlantic coast north to North Carolina (casually Maryland); and in the breeding range in Belize and South America.

Casual or accidental in the Farallon Islands, Arizona, Colorado, Minnesota, Arkansas,

Missouri, the Great Lakes region, Connecticut, the Bahamas (Eleuthera), Guatemala (Dueñas), and Bermuda; sight reports from Wisconsin, Honduras, and Costa Rica

Genus *CREX* Bechstein

Crex Bechstein, 1803, Ornithol. Taschenb. Dtsch. 2: 336. Type, by tautonymy, *Crex pratensis* Bechstein = *Rallus crex* Linnaeus.

Crex crex (Linnaeus). Corn Crake.

Rallus Crex Linnaeus, 1758, Syst. Nat. (ed. 10) 1: 153. (in Europæ agris, carectis = Sweden.)

Habitat.—Grasslands, meadows, and cultivated grain fields, mostly in lowland and mountain valleys, occasionally in marshy locations.

Distribution.—*Breeds* from the Faeroe Islands, British Isles, Scandinavia, northern Russia, and central Siberia south to the northern Mediterranean region, Turkey, Iran, and Lake Baikal.

Winters from the Mediterranean region (rarely), south throughout most of Africa, Madagascar, and Arabia.

Casual on Baffin Island, along the Atlantic coast of North America (recorded, but few recent records, from Newfoundland, Nova Scotia, St. Pierre et Miquelon, Maine, Rhode Island, Connecticut, New York, New Jersey, eastern Pennsylvania, and Maryland), Bermuda, Greenland, Iceland, the eastern Atlantic islands, India, Australia, and New Zealand.

Genus *RALLUS* Linnaeus

Rallus Linnaeus, 1758, Syst. Nat. (ed. 10) 1: 153. Type, by subsequent designation (Fleming, 1821), *Rallus aquaticus* Linnaeus.

Rallus longirostris Boddaert. Clapper Rail.

Rallus longirostris Boddaert, 1783, Table Planches Enlum., p. 52. Based on "Râle à long bec, de Cayenne" Daubenton, Planches Enlum., pl. 849. (Cayenne.)

Habitat.—Salt and brackish marshes, and mangrove swamps, locally (mostly in the Imperial and lower Colorado River valleys) in fresh-water marshes (Tropical and Subtropical zones).

Distribution.—*Resident* [*obsoletus* group] locally along the Pacific coast from central California (Marin County) south to southern Baja California (including San José and Espíritu Santo islands in the southern Gulf of California), in the interior of southeastern California and southwestern and south-central Arizona (where absent in winter), and along the Pacific coast from Sonora to Nayarit; and [*longirostris* group] along the Atlantic and Gulf coasts from Connecticut south to southern Florida and west to southern Texas (Brownsville), in the West Indies (south to Antigua and in Guadeloupe), Quintana Roo (Holbox, and islands of the Chinchorro Bank, possibly also Cayo Culebra), Yucatán (Río Lagartos), Belize (Ycacos Lagoon), and western Panama (Bocas del Toro), and along both coasts of South America (including Margarita Island and Trinidad) south to northwestern Peru and southeastern Brazil. Northernmost populations tend to be partially migratory.

Wanders [*obsoletus* group] casually on the Pacific coast to the Farallon Islands, north to northern California (Humboldt Bay), and inland away from the breeding grounds; and [*longirostris* group] on the Atlantic coast north to New Brunswick, Prince Edward Island, Nova Scotia, and Newfoundland, and inland to central Nebraska (near Stapleton), central New York, Vermont, West Virginia, central Virginia, and Tennessee; also Bermuda.

Notes.—*Rallus longirostris* and *R. elegans* hybridize to a limited extent where fresh and salt marshes meet in eastern and southern United States (Meanley 1969, Bledsoe 1988a). They are considered a superspecies by Mayr and Short (1970) and are merged into a single species by Ripley (1977). See comments under *R. elegans*.

Rallus elegans Audubon. King Rail.

Rallus elegans Audubon, 1834, Birds Amer. (folio) 3: pl. 203; 1835, Ornithol. Biogr. 3: 27. (Kentucky, South Carolina, Louisiana, and north to Camden, New Jersey, and Philadelphia = Charleston, South Carolina.)

Habitat.—Fresh-water and, locally, brackish marshes, rice fields; [*tenuirostris* group] Freshwater Marshes (1550–2800 m).

Distribution.—*Breeds* [*elegans* group] locally from southern and east-central South Dakota, northern Iowa, southern Wisconsin, southern Michigan, extreme southern Ontario, central New York, Connecticut, and (rarely) Massachusetts south through eastern Wyoming, eastern Nebraska, northwestern and central Kansas, central Oklahoma, and most of the eastern United States to western and southern Texas, southern Louisiana, central Mississippi, southern Alabama, and southern Florida; in the Greater Antilles (Cuba and the Isle of Pines); [*tenuirostris* group] in the interior of Mexico from Nayarit, Jalisco, Guanajuato, and San Luis Potosí south to Guerrero, Morelos, Puebla, and Veracruz.

Winters primarily from southern Georgia, Florida, the southern portions of the Gulf states, and southern Texas south to Guerrero, Puebla and Veracruz, and in Cuba, and the Isle of Pines; occurs less frequently in winter in the central portions of the breeding range, and casually to the northern limits.

Casual or accidental in eastern Colorado, North Dakota, southern Manitoba, Minnesota, southern Ontario, southern Quebec, Maine, New Brunswick, Nova Scotia, and Newfoundland.

Notes.—The breeding population in the interior of Mexico has been treated as a race of *R. longirostris* (Friedmann et al. 1950) or as a species, *R. tenuirostris* Ridgway, 1874 [Mexican Rail] (Davis 1972). See comments under *R. longirostris*.

Rallus limicola Vieillot. Virginia Rail.

Rallus limicola Vieillot, 1819, Nouv. Dict. Hist. Nat. (nouv. éd.) 28: 558. (Etats Unis = Pennsylvania.)

Habitat.—Fresh-water and (locally) brackish marshes, mostly in cattails, reeds, and deep grasses; in winter, also salt marshes, rice fields, and locally wet fields with tall grass (Subtropical and Temperate zones).

Distribution.—*Breeds* locally in North America from southern British Columbia (including Vancouver Island), northwestern Alberta, central Saskatchewan, central Manitoba, central Ontario, southern Quebec, New Brunswick, Prince Edward Island (probably), Nova Scotia, and southwestern Newfoundland south to northwestern Baja California, southern Arizona, southern New Mexico, west-central Texas, Oklahoma (rarely), Kansas, Missouri, southern Illinois, northern Indiana, southern Ohio, western Virginia, northern Georgia, and coastal North Carolina, also in northern Alabama and northern Florida (once); in Puebla, Tlaxcala, México, central Veracruz, Chiapas, and (probably) Guatemala.

Winters in North America from southern British Columbia south to northern Baja California, and from Utah, Colorado (local), central Texas, the Gulf states, and southern New England south locally through most of Mexico to central Guatemala, casually in interior North America north to Alberta, Montana, South Dakota, southern Minnesota, southern Ontario, and New York.

Resident in western South America in southwestern Colombia and Peru.

Casual or accidental in Alaska (Prince of Wales Island), Bermuda, Cuba, and Greenland; sight reports for the Bahama Islands (Grand Bahama and Eleuthera) and Puerto Rico.

Genus *ARAMIDES* Pucheran

Aramides Pucheran, 1845, Rev. Zool. [Paris] 8: 277. Type, by subsequent designation (Sclater and Salvin, 1869), *Fulica cayennensis* Gmelin = *Fulica cajanea* Müller.

Notes.—Ripley (1977) merged this genus with the Old World *Eulabeornis* Gould, 1844.

Aramides axillaris Lawrence. Rufous-necked Wood-Rail.

> *Aramides axillaris* Lawrence, 1863, Proc. Acad. Nat. Sci. Philadelphia 15: 107. (Barranquilla, New Granada [= Colombia].)

Habitat.—Mangrove Forest, Tropical Lowland Evergreen Forest, Tropical Deciduous Forest (0–1200 m; Tropical and lower Subtropical zones).

Distribution.—*Resident* locally on the Pacific slope of central Mexico (recorded Sinaloa, Nayarit and Guerrero), in the Yucatán peninsula, Belize, El Salvador, Honduras (Guanaja and Roatán in the Bay Islands and Pacific coast of Bay of Fonseca), western Nicaragua (Volcán San Cristóbal and Volcán Mombacho), northwestern Costa Rica (Guanacaste) and Panama (on the Caribbean coast in northwestern Bocas del Toro and the Canal area and on the Pacific in southern Coclé) and along the coasts of northern South America (including Trinidad and Isla Los Roques, off northern Venezuela) south to northwestern Peru and east to Surinam.

Aramides cajanea (Müller). Gray-necked Wood-Rail.

> *Fulica Cajanea* P. L. S. Müller, 1776, Natursyst., Suppl., p. 119. Based on "Poule d'eau, de Cayenne" Daubenton, Planches Enlum., pl. 352. (Cayenne.)

Habitat.—River-edge Forest, Gallery Forest, Freshwater Marshes (0–1200 m; Tropical and lower Subtropical zones).

Distribution.—*Resident* from southern Tamaulipas and Pacific lowlands of southern Oaxaca south along both slopes of Middle America (including the Yucatán Peninsula, Cozumel Island, and the Pearl Islands off Panama), and in South America from northern Colombia, Venezuela, Trinidad, and the Guianas south, east of the Andes, to central Argentina.

Genus *AMAUROLIMNAS* Sharpe

> *Amaurolimnas* Sharpe, 1893, Bull. Brit. Ornithol. Club 1: xxviii. Type, by original designation, *A. concolor* (Gosse) = *Rallus concolor* Gosse.

Notes.—Ripley (1977) merged this genus with the Old World *Eulabeornis* Gould, 1844.

Amaurolimnas concolor (Gosse). Uniform Crake.

> *Rallus concolor* Gosse, 1847, Birds Jamaica, p. 369. (Basin Spring and the neighbourhood of the Black River, in St. Elizabeth's, Jamaica.)

Habitat.—Gallery Forest, Secondary Forest, River-edge Forest (0–1000 m; Tropical Zone).

Distribution.—*Resident* locally from southern Mexico (recorded Veracruz, Oaxaca, Tabasco and Chiapas) south through Middle America (mostly Caribbean slope, not recorded El Salvador), and in South America very locally in western Ecuador, Guyana, and from eastern Colombia and Amazonian Brazil south to northern Bolivia and southeastern Brazil; also formerly in Jamaica (last reported in 1911).

Genus *PORZANA* Vieillot

> *Porzana* Vieillot, 1816, Analyse, p. 61. Type, by tautonymy, "Marouette" Buffon = *Rallus porzana* Linnaeus.
>
> *Pennula* Dole, 1878, in Thrum, Hawaiian Almanac and Annual (1879), p. 54. Type, by monotypy, *Pennula millei* [sic] Dole = *Rallus sandwichensis* Gmelin.
>
> *Porzanula* Frohawk, 1892, Ann. Mag. Nat. Hist. (6)9: 247. Type, by monotypy, *Porzanula palmeri* Frohawk.

†*Porzana palmeri* (Frohawk). Laysan Rail.

> *Porzanula Palmeri* Frohawk, 1892, Ann. Mag. Nat. Hist. (6)9: 247. (Laysan Island, lat. 25°46' N., long. 171°49' W.)

Habitat.—Grass tussocks and scattered vegetation in sandy areas, foraging often in more open areas.

Distribution.—EXTINCT. Formerly *resident* on Laysan Island, in the Hawaiian Islands, where it disappeared between 1923 and 1936.

Introduced and established in the Midway group on Eastern Island (between 1887 and 1891, extirpated around 1944) and on Sand Island (in 1910, last reported 1943); attempted introductions elsewhere in the western Hawaiian Islands were unsuccessful.

Porzana porzana (Linnaeus). Spotted Crake.

> *Rallus Porzana* Linnaeus, 1766, Syst. Nat. (ed. 12) 1: 262. (in Europa ad ripas = France.)

Habitat.—Swamps, wet meadows, and marshes.

Distribution.—*Breeds* throughout Europe east to northern Russia and Lake Baikal, and winters south to central Africa and the Bay of Bengal, rarely to the eastern Atlantic islands and southern Africa.

Accidental in the Lesser Antilles (Marigot, St. Martin, 8 October 1956; Voous 1957) and Greenland.

Porzana carolina (Linnaeus). Sora.

> *Rallus carolinus* Linnaeus, 1758, Syst. Nat. (ed. 10) 1: 153. Based on "The Little American Water Hen" Edwards, Nat. Hist. Birds 3: 144, pl. 144, and the "Soree" Catesby, Nat. Hist. Carolina 1: 70, pl. 70. (in America septentrionali = Hudson Bay.)

Habitat.—Primarily fresh-water marshes with dense cattails, less frequently in flooded fields; in winter, also in salt-water and brackish marshes, rice fields.

Distribution.—*Breeds* from southeastern Alaska, northwestern British Columbia, southern Yukon, west-central and southwestern Mackenzie, northern Saskatchewan, northern Manitoba, northern Ontario, west-central and southern Quebec, New Brunswick, Prince Edward Island, Nova Scotia and southwestern Newfoundland south locally to northwestern Baja California (at least formerly), central Nevada, central Arizona, southern New Mexico, eastern Colorado, central Oklahoma, southwestern Tennessee, central Illinois, central Indiana, southern Ohio, West Virginia and Maryland.

Winters regularly from southern Oregon, central Arizona, northern New Mexico, southern Texas, the Gulf coast and southern Maryland south through Middle America (including Cozumel Island and Chinchorro Reef), Bermuda, the West Indies, and northern South America (including the Netherlands Antilles, Tobago and Trinidad) west of the Andes to central Peru and (rarely) east of the Andes to eastern Colombia, eastern Ecuador, Venezuela and Guyana; occasionally recorded in winter north to extreme southern Canada and the northern United States.

Casual in east-central Alaska, the Queen Charlotte Islands, southern Labrador, Greenland, the British Isles, Sweden, France, and Spain.

†*Porzana sandwichensis* (Gmelin). Hawaiian Rail.

> *Rallus sandwichensis* Gmelin, 1789, Syst. Nat. 1(2): 717. Based on the "Sandwich Rail" Latham, Gen. Synop. Birds 3(1): 236. (in insulis Sandwich = Hawaii.)

Habitat.—Open country below the forest belt, presumably in grassy areas.

Distribution.—EXTINCT. Formerly *resident* on Hawaii in the Hawaiian Islands; last specimen taken in 1864, last reported in 1884.

Porzana flaviventer (Boddaert). Yellow-breasted Crake.

> *Rallus flaviventer* Boddaert, 1783, Table Planches Enlum., p. 52. Based on "Petit Râle, de Cayenne" Daubenton, Planches Enlum., pl. 847. (Cayenne.)

Habitat.—Freshwater Marshes (0–600 m; Tropical and lower Subtropical zones).

Distribution.—Resident locally in the Greater Antilles (Cuba, Jamaica, Hispaniola, and

Puerto Rico), and from Guerrero, Veracruz, and Chiapas south through Guatemala (La Avellana), Belize, El Salvador (Lake Olomega), Nicaragua (Río San Juan) and northwestern Costa Rica (Guanacaste) to Panama (east to eastern Panamá province and on Isla Coiba) and in South America from Colombia, Venezuela, Trinidad and the Guianas south, east of the Andes, to northern Argentina, Paraguay and eastern Brazil (absent from most of Amazonia).

Genus *NEOCREX* Sclater and Salvin

Neocrex Sclater and Salvin, 1869, Proc. Zool. Soc. London (1868), p. 457. Type, by monotypy, *Porzana erythrops* Sclater.

Notes.—Merged into the genus *Porzana* by Ripley (1977).

Neocrex colombianus Bangs. Colombian Crake.

Neocrex colombianus Bangs, 1898, Proc. Biol. Soc. Wash. 12: 171. (Palomina, Santa Marta Mountains, Colombia.)

Habitat.—Low Seasonally Wet Grassland, Freshwater Marshes (0–2100 m; Tropical and Subtropical zones).

Distribution.—*Resident* on the Pacific slope of Panama (Achiote Road just beyond Canal area border in western Colón and the Tucumán marsh in eastern Panamá province), western Colombia and western Ecuador.

Notes.—Considered by Hellmayr and Conover (1942) to be conspecific with *N. erythrops,* with which it constitutes a superspecies (Sibley and Monroe 1990).

Neocrex erythrops (Sclater). Paint-billed Crake.

Porzana erythrops Sclater, 1867, Proc. Zool. Soc. London, p. 343, pl. 21. (Lima, Peru.)

Habitat.—Low Seasonally Wet Grassland, Pastures/Agricultural Lands, Freshwater Marshes (0–2600 m).

Distribution.—*Resident* on the Caribbean slope of western Panama (Bocas del Toro; Behrstock 1983); and in South America from eastern Colombia, Venezuela and the Guianas south, east of the Andes, to northwestern Argentina, Paraguay and eastern Brazil, also western Peru and the Galapagos Islands.

Accidental in Texas (near College Station, Brazos County, 17 February 1972; Arnold 1978) and Virginia (western Henrico County, 15 December 1978; Blem 1980).

Notes.—See comments under *N. colombianus.*

Genus *CYANOLIMNAS* Barbour and Peters

Cyanolimnas Barbour and Peters, 1927, Proc. N. Engl. Zool. Club 9: 95. Type, by monotypy, *Cyanolimnas cerverai* Barbour and Peters.

Cyanolimnas cerverai Barbour and Peters. Zapata Rail.

Cyanolimnas cerverai Barbour and Peters, 1927, Proc. N. Engl. Zool. Club 9: 95. (Santo Tomás, Zapata Peninsula, Cuba, Greater Antilles.)

Habitat.—Freshwater Marshes.

Distribution.—*Resident* only in the Zapata Swamp in the vicinity of Santo Tomás and north of Cochinos Bay, in western Cuba.

Genus *PARDIRALLUS* Bonaparte

Pardirallus Bonaparte, 1856, C. R. Acad. Sci. Paris 43: 599. Type, by monotypy, *Rallus variegatus* Gmelin = *Rallus maculatus* Boddaert.

Pardirallus maculatus (Boddaert). Spotted Rail.

Rallus maculatus Boddaert, 1783, Table Planches Enlum., p. 48. Based on "Le Râle tacheté, de Cayenne" Daubenton, Planches Enlum., pl. 775. (Cayenne.)

Habitat.—Freshwater Marshes (0–800 m; Tropical Zone).

Distribution.—*Resident* locally in Cuba (Havana, Matanzas and Las Villas provinces), the Isle of Pines (probably) and Hispaniola (Dominican Republic, since 1978); in Mexico, where recorded from Nayarit (San Blas and near Laguna Agua Brava), Puebla (Laguna San Felipe), Veracruz (Tecolutla and near Tlacotalpan), Guerrero (near Acapulco), Oaxaca (near Putla de Guerrero), Quintana Roo (Lake Cobá) and Chiapas (Tuxtla Gutiérrez and San Cristóbal); in Belize (Ycacos Lagoon), El Salvador (Laguna El Jocotal, Islas Trasajera), Costa Rica (Guanacaste, Turrialba and near Cartago), Panama (San Blas and eastern Panamá provinces, sight reports only); and in South America from Colombia, Venezuela, Tobago, Trinidad and the Guianas south locally, west of the Andes to northwestern Peru and east of the Andes locally to northern Argentina and southern Brazil.

Casual in Jamaica (Black River marshes) where suggested breeding in last century is without basis (Levy 1994).

Accidental in Pennsylvania (Shippingport, Beaver County), Texas (Brownwood, Brown County) and the Juan Fernández Islands (off Chile).

Genus *PORPHYRULA* Blyth

Porphyrula Blyth, 1852, Cat. Birds Mus. Asiat. Soc. (1849), p. 283. Type, by monotypy, *Porphyrula chloronotus* Blyth = *Porphyrio alleni* Thomson.

Notes.—Some authors (e.g., Urban et al. 1986) merge *Porphyrula* into the Old World genus *Porphyrio* Brisson, 1760.

Porphyrula martinica (Linnaeus). Purple Gallinule.

Fulica martinica Linnaeus, 1766, Syst. Nat. (ed. 12) 1: 259. (in Martinicæ inundatis = Martinique, West Indies.)

Habitat.—Primarily fresh-water marshes with emergent and floating vegetation (Tropical to Temperate zones).

Distribution.—*Breeds* locally in the interior of the eastern United States in southern Illinois (casually), western Tennessee and central Ohio (once), and, primarily in lowlands, on the Pacific coast from Nayarit and on the Atlantic-Gulf-Caribbean coast from (at least casually) Maryland and Delaware south through Middle America, eastern and southern Texas, the Gulf states, Florida, the Bahamas, Greater Antilles, the Cayman Islands (Grand Cayman,) and southern Lesser Antilles (Guadeloupe southward) to South America, where found virtually throughout south at least to northern Chile and northern Argentina.

Winters from Nayarit, southern Texas and Florida south throughout the remainder of the breeding range.

Casual or accidental north to central California, southern Nevada, southern Utah, southeastern Wyoming, Minnesota, Wisconsin, northern Michigan, central Ontario, southern Quebec, New Brunswick, Nova Scotia, Labrador and Newfoundland, and to the Bahamas and northern Lesser Antilles (north to Barbuda), Bermuda, the Galapagos and Falkland islands, South Georgia, Tristan da Cunha, Ascension, St. Helena, Iceland, Britain, Norway, Switzerland, the Azores, and South Africa.

Notes.—Also known as American Purple-Gallinule. *Porphyrula martinica* and the African *P. alleni* Thomson, 1842, appear to constitute a superspecies (Sibley and Monroe 1990).

Porphyrula flavirostris (Gmelin). Azure Gallinule.

Fulica flavirostris Gmelin, 1789, Syst. Nat. 1(2): 699. (Cayenne.)

Habitat.—Fresh-water marshes (0–500 m).

Distribution.—*Resident* locally in South America east of the Andes from eastern Colombia, eastern Ecuador, and northeastern Peru to central Amazonian Brazil.

Breeds in the Guianas and eastern Amazonian Brazil, and possibly elsewhere in south America east of the Andes. Breeding distribution and seasonal movements poorly known (Remsen and Parker 1990).

Winters in southeastern Peru, southwestern Brazil, eastern Bolivia, eastern Paraguay, and probably northern Argentina (and may breed locally within this area).

Accidental in high Andes of Colombia and Venezuela, the tepui region of Venezuela, southeastern Brazil, Trinidad, and New York (Fort Salonga, Suffolk County, 14 December 1986; Spencer and Kolodnicki 1988, Remsen and Parker 1990).

Genus *GALLINULA* Brisson

Gallinula Brisson, 1760, Ornithologie l: 50; 6: 2. Type, by tautonymy, *Gallinula* Brisson = *Fulica chloropus* Linnaeus.

Gallinula chloropus (Linnaeus). Common Moorhen.

Fulica Chloropus Linnaeus, 1758, Syst. Nat. (ed. 10) 1: 152. (in Europa = England.)

Habitat.—Fresh-water marshes, lakes, and ponds with tall, dense emergent vegetation (Tropical to Temperate zones).

Distribution.—*Breeds* in the Western Hemisphere locally from northern California, northern Utah, northern New Mexico, Oklahoma, Kansas, Nebraska, Iowa, southeastern Minnesota, southern Wisconsin, central Michigan, southern Ontario, southwestern Quebec, New Brunswick and Nova Scotia south, most frequently in lowlands, throughout Middle America, Clipperton Island, Bermuda, the West Indies, and most of South America (also the Galapagos Islands, Netherlands Antilles, Tobago and Trinidad) to northern Chile and northern Argentina; and in the Old World from the British Isles, Shetlands, southern Scandinavia, central Russia, southern Siberia, Sakhalin, and Japan south throughout most of Eurasia and Africa to the eastern Atlantic islands, southern Africa, the borders of the northern Indian Ocean (including Sri Lanka), the East Indies (to Sumbawa and Sulawesi), Philippines, Taiwan, and the Ryukyu, Bonin, and Volcano islands.

Winters in eastern North America primarily from South Carolina and the Gulf coast southward, elsewhere in the Americas throughout the breeding range, occasionally north to Utah, southern Ontario, and New England; and in the Old World from the British Isles, southern Scandinavia, southern Russia, and eastern China south throughout the remainder of the breeding range, casually to the Seven Islands of Izu.

Resident in the Hawaiian Islands (now on Kauai, Oahu, and Molokai, formerly on all main islands from Kauai eastward, except Lanai).

Casual north to southwestern British Columbia, eastern Oregon, southern Idaho, western Montana, Wyoming, southern Manitoba, central Ontario, eastern Quebec, New Brunswick, Nova Scotia, Newfoundland, and Greenland. Accidental in Iceland, the Faeroe Islands, Spitsbergen, and the Commander Islands.

Notes.—Also known as Common Gallinule, in New World literature as Florida Gallinule, and in Old World literature as the Moorhen.

Genus *FULICA* Linnaeus

Fulica Linnaeus, 1758, Syst. Nat. (ed. 10) 1: 152. Type, by tautonymy, *Fulica atra* Linnaeus (*Fulica,* prebinomial specific name, in synonymy).

Fulica atra Linnaeus. Eurasian Coot.

Fulica atra Linnaeus, 1758, Syst. Nat. (ed. 10) 1: 152. (in Europa = Sweden.)

Habitat.—Similar to that of *F. americana.*

Distribution.—*Breeds* from Iceland, the British Isles, and northern Eurasia south to northern Africa, India, and eastern China, also in New Guinea and Australia, and *winters* throughout the breeding range and south to the East Indies and Philippines.

Casual or accidental in Alaska (St. Paul, in the Pribilof Islands), Labrador (Tangnaivik Island in Anaktalak Bay, and Separation Point in Sandwich Bay), Newfoundland (Exploits Harbour), Quebec (Kegaska), Greenland, the Faeroes, and Northern Mariana Islands.

Notes.—Also known as European Coot and, in Old World literature, as the Coot.

Fulica alai Peale. Hawaiian Coot.

> *Fulica alai* Peale, 1848, U. S. Explor. Exped., 8, p. 224. (Hawaiian Islands.)

Habitat.—Fresh-water lakes and ponds.

Distribution.—*Resident* in the Hawaiian Islands on all main islands from Niihau eastward, except Lanai.

Notes.—Treatment as a species follows Pratt (1987).

Fulica americana Gmelin. American Coot.

> *Fulica americana* Gmelin, 1789, Syst. Nat. 1(2): 704. Based on the "Cinereous Coot" Latham, Gen. Synop. Birds 3(1): 279. (in America septentrionali = North America.)

Habitat.—Breeds on shallow fresh-water lakes, ponds, and marshes with emergent vegetation; in winter, also deep lakes, slow-moving rivers, brackish bays, and estuaries, also ponds and lakes in urban areas, often foraging on adjacent lawns.

Distribution.—*Breeds* in North America from east-central Alaska (casually), southern Yukon, southern Mackenzie, northwestern and central Saskatchewan, central Manitoba, western and southern Ontario, southwestern Quebec, southern New Brunswick, Prince Edward Island, and Nova Scotia south locally to southern Baja California, through Middle America (including Clipperton Island, at least formerly) to Nicaragua and northwestern Costa Rica (Guanacaste), and to the Gulf coast, southern Florida, Bermuda, the Bahamas, and Greater Antilles (locally east to St. John in the Virgin Islands).

Winters widely from southeastern Alaska, British Columbia, Idaho, central and eastern Colorado, northern New Mexico, Kansas, the Mississippi and Ohio valleys, Great Lakes, and southern New England south throughout Middle America, the southeastern United States, Bermuda, and West Indies (south to Grenada) to eastern Panama and (apparently) northern Colombia.

Resident in the Andes of central Colombia and northern Ecuador (at least formerly).

Casual west to the eastern Aleutians, and north to western Alaska (Seward Peninsula), Franklin District, northern Ontario, central Quebec, Labrador, Newfoundland, and western Greenland; also to islands of the western Caribbean Sea (Corn and Providencia), Iceland, the Faeroe Islands, and Ireland.

Notes.—The South American *F. ardesiaca* Tschudi, 1843, has been treated as a race of *F. americana* (e.g., Blake 1977), but see Fjeldså (1982b, 1983).

Fulica caribaea Ridgway. Caribbean Coot.

> *Fulica caribæa* Ridgway, 1884, Proc. U. S. Natl. Mus. 7: 358. (St. John, Virgin Islands.)

Habitat.—Freshwater Lakes and Ponds, Freshwater Marshes, Saltwater/Brackish Marshes (Tropical Zone).

Distribution.—*Resident* in most of the Greater Antilles (rare in Cuba, absent from the Isle of Pines and smaller islands), the Caicos Islands, most of the larger Lesser Antilles (south to Grenada and Barbados), on Trinidad (questionably on Tobago), on Curaçao, and in northwestern Venezuela.

Casual in the Cayman Islands (Cayman Brac).

Notes.—Reports from southern Florida, primarily in nonbreeding season, and locally at scattered locations throughout the United States, apparently pertain to variants of *F. americana* (Roberson and Baptista 1988, Robertson and Woolfendon 1992). The relationships of *F. americana* and *F. caribaea* are not fully understood; the latter may eventually prove to be a morph of *F. americana*. Individuals with intermediate characteristics have been reported from southern Florida, Cuba, Hispaniola, and St. Croix. Mixed pairs of *F. americana* and *F. caribaea* with young have been observed on St. John, Virgin Islands (1984, Amer. Birds 38: 252).

Family **HELIORNITHIDAE**: Sungrebes

Genus *HELIORNIS* Bonnaterre

Heliornis Bonnaterre, 1791, Tabl. Encycl. Méth., Ornithol. 1(47): lxxxiv, 64. Type, by monotypy, *Heliornis fulicarius* Bonnaterre = *Colymbus fulica* Boddaert.

Heliornis fulica (Boddaert). Sungrebe.

Colymbus fulica Boddaert, 1783, Table Planches Enlum., p. 54. Based on "Le Grebi-foulque, de Cayenne" Daubenton, Planches Enlum., pl. 893. (Cayenne.)

Habitat.—Freshwater Lakes and Ponds, Streams (Tropical Zone).
Distribution.—*Resident* from San Luis Potosí, southern Tamaulipas, central Veracruz, northern Oaxaca, Campeche, northern Chiapas, and Quintana Roo south in the Gulf-Caribbean lowlands of Central America to Costa Rica (locally also on the Pacific slope around the Gulf of Nicoya), on the Pacific slope of Chiapas and Guatemala, in Panama (both slopes), and in South America from Colombia, Venezuela, and the Guianas south, west of the Andes to western Ecuador, and east of the Andes to central Bolivia, Paraguay, and southeastern Brazil.
Accidental in Trinidad.
Notes.—Also known as American Finfoot.

Family **EURYPYGIDAE**: Sunbitterns

Genus *EURYPYGA* Illiger

Eurypyga Illiger, 1811, Prodromus, p. 257. Type, by monotypy, *Ardea helias* "Lin. Gm." [= Pallas].

Eurypyga helias (Pallas). Sunbittern.

Ardea Helias Pallas, 1781, Neue Nord. Beytr. 2: 48, pl. 3. (Brazil.)

Habitat.—River-edge Forest, Streams (0–1200 m; Tropical and lower Subtropical zones).
Distribution.—*Resident* locally on the Gulf-Caribbean slope of Guatemala, Honduras and Nicaragua, on both slopes of Costa Rica and Panama, and in South America from Colombia, Venezuela, and the Guianas south, west of the Andes to northwestern Peru, and east of the Andes to central Bolivia and Amazonian Brazil. Reports from southern Mexico (Tabasco, Chiapas) are unverified.

Family **ARAMIDAE**: Limpkins

Genus *ARAMUS* Vieillot

Aramus Vieillot, 1816, Analyse, p. 58. Type, by monotypy, "Courliri" Buffon = *Scolopax guarauna* Linnaeus.

Aramus guarauna (Linnaeus). Limpkin.

Scopolax [sic] *Guarauna* Linnaeus, 1766, Syst. Nat. (ed. 12) 1: 242. Based on "Le Courly brun d'Amérique" Brisson, Ornithologie 5: 330, and "Guarauna" Marcgrave, Hist. Nat. Bras., p. 204. (in America australi = Cayenne.)

Habitat.—Freshwater Marshes, swamps (Tropical Zone).
Distribution.—*Resident* in southeastern Georgia (rare; north to the Altamaha River), Florida (absent from the Panhandle west of Walton County), the Bahamas (Eleuthera), Greater Antilles (Cuba, the Isle of Pines, Jamaica, Hispaniola, and, at least formerly, Puerto Rico), and from Veracruz and western Colima and southeastern Oaxaca south along both slopes of Middle America and through South America (including Trinidad), west of the Andes to western Ecuador and east of the Andes to southern Bolivia, northern Argentina, and Uruguay.

Casual or accidental north to Nova Scotia, Tennessee (sight report), Maryland, North Carolina, and southeastern Mississippi, in the Florida Keys, and on Dry Tortugas; a specimen from southern Texas is of questionable origin (T.O.S. 1995).

Family **GRUIDAE**: Cranes

Subfamily GRUINAE: Typical Cranes

Genus *GRUS* Brisson

Grus Brisson, 1760, Ornithologie 5: 374. Type, by tautonymy, *Ardea grus* Linnaeus. *Limnogeranus* Sharpe, 1893, Bull. Brit. Ornithol. Club 1: xxxvii. Type, by original designation, *Limnogeranus americanus* (L.) = *Ardea americana* Linnaeus.

Notes.—The use of *Grus* Brisson, 1760, rather than *Grus* Pallas, 1766, follows Direction 55 of International Commission of Zoological Nomenclature.

Grus canadensis (Linnaeus). Sandhill Crane.

Ardea canadensis Linnaeus, 1758, Syst. Nat. (ed. 10) 1: 141. Based on "The Brown and Ash-colour'd Crane" Edwards, Nat. Hist. Birds 3: 133, pl. 133. (in America septentrionali = Hudson Bay.)

Habitat.—Low-lying tundra, marshes, swampy edges of lakes and ponds, river banks, and wet pine savanna, often foraging in adjacent grasslands and fields; in winter, migratory populations found primarily in agricultural fields and wet prairie.

Distribution.—*Breeds* from western and central Alaska, northern Yukon, northern Mackenzie, Banks Island, northern Keewatin (Boothia Peninsula), southern Devon Island, and Baffin Island south locally to St. Lawrence Island, southern Alaska (the Alaska Peninsula and Cook Inlet), northeastern California, northern Nevada, northwestern Utah, western Colorado, South Dakota (formerly), Nebraska (formerly), central Iowa, northern Illinois, southern Michigan, northeastern Indiana, northern Ohio, southern Ontario, and western Quebec; also locally in northeastern Siberia south to the Chukotski Peninsula.

Winters from south-coastal British Columbia (casually), southern Washington, Oregon, California, southern Arizona, central and northeastern New Mexico, western and southern Texas, Arkansas, the Gulf states, and southern Georgia south to northern Baja California, Sinaloa, Jalisco, México (formerly), Veracruz, and southern Florida, casually north to the Great Lakes.

Resident from southern Mississippi, southern Alabama, and southern Georgia (Okefenokee Swamp) south through Florida to Cuba and the Isle of Pines, formerly also in southeastern Texas.

Casual in the Pribilof and Aleutian islands, and in eastern North America north to New Brunswick, Prince Edward Island, and Nova Scotia. Accidental in Hawaiian Islands (Oahu), Quintana Roo (Chinchorro Reef), Bermuda, the Faeroe Islands, British Isles, and Japan (Hokkaido).

Grus grus (Linnaeus). Common Crane.

Ardea Grus Linnaeus, 1758, Syst. Nat. (ed. 10) 1: 141. (in Europæ, Africæ = Sweden.)

Habitat.—Marshes and open areas near water.

Distribution.—*Breeds* from northern Eurasia south to central Europe, Mongolia, and Manchuria, and *winters* from the Mediterranean region east to India, and in Southeast Asia.

Accidental in Alaska (Fairbanks), Alberta (Cavendish, Lethbridge, and Athabasca) and Nebraska (Phelps and Kearney counties and a sight report for Lincoln County); a sight report for New Mexico (Bitter Lake).

Notes.—Also known as European Crane and, in Old World literature, as the Crane.

Grus americana (Linnaeus). Whooping Crane.

> *Ardea americana* Linnaeus, 1758, Syst. Nat. (ed. 10) 1: 142. Based on "The Hooping Crane" Catesby, Nat. Hist. Carolina 1: 75, pl. 75, and "The Hooping-Crane from Hudson's Bay" Edwards, Nat. Hist. Birds 3: 132, pl. 132. (in America septentrionali = Hudson Bay.)

Habitat.—Open, marshy coniferous woods with shallow lakes and ponds; formerly also fresh-water marshes and wet prairies; in winter, primarily fresh-water and brackish marshes.

Distribution.—*Breeds* in south-central Mackenzie (vicinity of Wood Buffalo National Park) and adjacent northern Alberta; formerly bred from southern Mackenzie, northeastern Alberta, northern Saskatchewan, and northern Manitoba south to North Dakota, Minnesota, and Iowa, and in southeastern Texas and southwestern Louisiana.

Winters primarily near the coast of southeastern Texas (mostly in the vicinity of the Aransas National Wildlife Refuge); formerly wintered from southern Texas and the Gulf coast (east, at least casually, to Georgia and Florida), south to Jalisco, Guanajuato, and northern Tamaulipas.

Migrates primarily through the Great Plains from southern Canada and the Dakotas south to Texas; formerly ranged west to Wyoming and Colorado, and east to Ontario, Pennsylvania, and South Carolina.

Unsuccessfully introduced in Idaho (Grays Lake) through placement of eggs in nests of *G. canadensis*; these birds wintered in New Mexico.

Casual in migration recently west to central and southeastern British Columbia and eastern Colorado, and east to Minnesota (Marshall and Polk counties), Illinois (Pike County), Missouri (Mingo, Squaw Creek), and Arkansas.

Order **CHARADRIIFORMES**. Shorebirds, Gulls, Auks, and Allies

Notes.—Hypotheses for the phylogenetic relationships among the families of this order differ (e.g., Strauch 1978, Mickevich and Parenti 1980, Sibley and Ahlquist 1990, Christian et al. 1992, Ward 1992, Björklund 1994, Chu 1994, 1995); we retain a traditional arrangement until a consensus is reached concerning these relationships. See notes under Alcidae.

Suborder CHARADRII: Plovers and Allies

Family **BURHINIDAE**: Thick-knees

Genus *BURHINUS* Illiger

> *Burhinus* Illiger, 1811, Prodromus, p. 250. Type, by monotypy, *Charadrius magnirostris* Latham.

Burhinus bistriatus (Wagler). Double-striped Thick-knee.

> *Charadrius bistriatus* Wagler, 1829, Isis von Oken, col. 648. (San Matteo, Mexico = San Mateo del Mar, Oaxaca; Binford, 1989, Ornithol. Monogr. 43, p. 337.)

Habitat.—Low Seasonally Wet Grassland, Arid Lowland Scrub, Pastures/Agricultural Lands (0–800 m; Tropical Zone).

Distribution.—*Resident* in Middle America from Veracruz, Tabasco, Oaxaca, and Chiapas south through the Pacific lowlands of Central America to northwestern Costa Rica (Guanacaste); in the Greater Antilles (Hispaniola); and in South America from northern Colombia east through Venezuela (also Margarita Island) to Guyana and extreme northwestern Brazil. Now rare and local.

Accidental in Texas (King Ranch, Kleberg County, 5 December 1961; MacInnes and Chamberlain 1963), Barbados, and Curaçao (perhaps human-assisted vagrants); a record from Arizona is widely regarded as an escape.

Family **CHARADRIIDAE**: Lapwings and Plovers

Subfamily VANELLINAE: Lapwings

Notes.—See Ward (1992) for relationships of this subfamily.

Genus *VANELLUS* Brisson

Vanellus Brisson, 1760, Ornithologie 1: 48; 5: 94. Type, by tautonymy, *Vanellus* Brisson = *Tringa vanellus* Linnaeus.

Belonopterus Reichenbach, 1853, Hand. Spec. Ornithol., Die Vögel, pt. 3 (1852), p. xviii. Type, by original designation, *Tringa cajennensis* Latham = *Parra chilensis* Molina.

Vanellus vanellus (Linnaeus). Northern Lapwing.

Tringa Vanellus Linnaeus, 1758, Syst. Nat. (ed. 10) 1: 148. (in Europa, Africa = Sweden.)

Habitat.—Open fields, pastures, wet meadows, bogs, and grassy banks of ponds and lakes; in migration and winter also cultivated fields, seacoasts, and mudflats.

Distribution.—*Breeds* from the Faeroe Islands (rarely), British Isles, northern Scandinavia, northern Russia, Transbaicalia, and Ussuriland south to Morocco, the northern Mediterranean region, Black Sea, Iran, Turkestan, and northern Mongolia.

Winters from the British Isles, central Europe, southern Russia, Asia Minor, Iraq, Iran, India, Burma, China, and Japan south to Madeira, the Canary Islands, northern Africa, Southeast Asia, Taiwan, and the Ryukyu Islands.

Casual to northeastern North America from Baffin Island, Labrador, and Newfoundland south through southern Quebec, New Brunswick, Prince Edward Island, Nova Scotia, and New England to New York. Accidental in Ohio, North Carolina, South Carolina, Bermuda, the Bahamas (Hog Island), Puerto Rico, and Barbados.

Notes.—Known in Old World literature as the Lapwing.

Vanellus chilensis (Molina). Southern Lapwing.

Parra Chilensis Molina, 1782, Saggio Stor. Nat. Chili, p. 258. (Chile.)

Habitat.—Low Seasonally Wet Grassland, Pastures/Agricultural Lands, Fresh-water Marshes (0–2600 m; Tropical to Temperate zones).

Distribution.—*Resident* [*cayennensis* group] in South America from Colombia, Venezuela, and the Guianas south, east of the Andes, to southern Bolivia, northern Argentina, and Uruguay; and [*chilensis* group] in Chile and central and southern Argentina.

Rare and local visitant [*cayennensis* group] to eastern Panama (Chiriquí, eastern Panamá province, eastern San Blas, and eastern Darién); a sight report for Trinidad.

Reports of individuals of this species from southern Florida (north to Orange County) from 1959 to 1962 are apparently based on escaped birds (Robertson and Woolfenden 1992).

Notes.—Also known as Spur-winged Lapwing. Groups: *V. cayennensis* (Gmelin 1789) [Cayenne Lapwing] and *V. chilensis* [Southern Lapwing].

Subfamily CHARADRIINAE: Plovers

Genus *PLUVIALIS* Brisson

Pluvialis Brisson, 1760, Ornithologie 1: 46; 5: 42. Type, by tautonymy, *Pluvialis aurea* Brisson = *Charadrius pluvialis* Linnaeus = *Charadrius apricarius* Linnaeus.

Squatarola Cuvier, 1816, Règne Anim. 1: 467. Type, by tautonymy, *Tringa squatarola* Linnaeus.

Pluvialis squatarola (Linnaeus). Black-bellied Plover.

> *Tringa Squatarola* Linnaeus, 1758, Syst. Nat. (ed. 10) 1: 149. (in Europa = Sweden.)

Habitat.—Dry tundra ridges (breeding); mudflats, beaches, bare shores of ponds and lakes, and occasionally plowed fields (nonbreeding).

Distribution.—*Breeds* in North America from northern Alaska (Barrow eastward), north-western Mackenzie, and Banks, southern Melville, Bathurst, Devon, Bylot, and western and southern Baffin islands south to the western Alaska (Hooper Bay, Nelson Island), Yukon River, north-central Mackenzie (Cockburn Point), southern Victoria Island, northern Keewatin (Adelaide and Melville peninsulas), and Southampton and Coats islands; and in Eurasia from north-central Russia east across northern Siberia (including Kolguyev Island, southern Novaya Zemlya, the New Siberian Islands, and Wrangel Island) to the Gulf of Anadyr. Nonbreeding individuals frequently summer in the wintering range.

Winters in the Americas primarily in coastal areas from southwestern British Columbia and southern New England (rarely farther north) south along both coasts of the United States (and inland in southeastern California at the Salton Sea and in southwestern Louisiana), and Middle America, through the West Indies, and along both coasts of South America (also the Galapagos and other offshore islands) to central Chile and northern Argentina, also casually throughout the Hawaiian Islands; and in the Old World from the British Isles, southern Europe, northern India, Southeast Asia, southeastern China, southern Japan, and the Mariana (rarely) and Solomon islands south to southern Africa, islands of the Indian Ocean, the Malay Peninsula, Australia, and New Zealand.

Migrates primarily along coasts in the Northern Hemisphere from western and southern Alaska (casually the Aleutians), Labrador (casually), and Newfoundland southward, and locally through interior North America, especially the Great Salt Lake, the Mississippi and Ohio valleys, and the Great Lakes region.

Casual in the Revillagigedo Islands (Socorro Island; sight reports), Clipperton Island, and in northern Ellesmere Island, Greenland, Iceland, the Faeroe Islands, Azores, and Madeira.

Notes.—In Old World literature known as Gray Plover.

Pluvialis apricaria (Linnaeus). European Golden-Plover.

> *Charadrius apricarius* Linnaeus, 1758, Syst. Nat. (ed. 10) 1: 150. (in Oelandia, Canada = Lapland.)

Habitat.—Similar to that of *P. dominica.*

Distribution.—*Breeds* from northern Eurasia south to the British Isles, northern Europe, the Baltic states, and Taimyr Peninsula.

Winters south to northern Africa, the Caspian Sea, and eastern India, in migration regularly in Greenland.

Casual in Labrador and Newfoundland; a sight report for Alaska (Point Barrow).

Notes.—Also known as Eurasian Golden-Plover or Greater Golden-Plover and, in Old World literature, as Golden Plover.

Pluvialis dominica (Müller). American Golden-Plover.

> *Charadrius Dominicus* P.L.S. Müller, 1776, Natursyst., Suppl., p. 116. (St. Domingo = Hispaniola.)

Habitat.—Grassy tundra; where syntopic with *P. fulva,* usually in areas of higher elevation, with sparser and shorter vegetation, and more rocks (breeding); short-grass prairie, pastures, plowed fields, and less often mudflats, beaches, and bare shores of lakes (nonbreeding).

Distribution.—*Breeds* in North America from northern Alaska, northern Yukon, northern Mackenzie, and Banks, southern Melville (probably), Bathurst, Devon, and northern Baffin islands south to central Alaska (interior mountain ranges), southern Yukon, north-central British Columbia (Spatsizi Plateau), central Mackenzie, southern Keewatin, northeastern Manitoba, northern Ontario (Cape Henrietta Maria), and Southampton and southern Baffin islands.

Winters in South America from Bolivia, Uruguay, and southern Brazil south to northern Chile and northern Argentina.

Migrates in spring through Middle America and the interior of North America (from the Rockies to the Mississippi and Ohio valleys), rarely but regularly to the Pacific and Atlantic coasts, and in fall mostly from Newfoundland and Nova Scotia to New England, thence southward over the Atlantic, less commonly through the West Indies and the interior of North America.

Casual or accidental in Bermuda, Greenland, Iceland, the British Isles, continental Europe, and Australia.

Notes.—Also known as Lesser Golden-Plover. See comments under *P. fulva.*

Pluvialis fulva (Gmelin). Pacific Golden-Plover.

> *Charadrius fulvus* Gmelin, 1789, Syst. Nat. 1(2): 687. Based on the "Fulvous Plover" Latham, Gen. Synops. Birds 3: 211. (In Tahiti maritimis et uliginosis = Tahiti.)

Habitat.—Grassy tundra, usually in areas at lower elevation, in denser and taller vegetative cover than *P. dominica* (breeding); pastures, plowed fields, and less often mudflats, beaches, and bare shores of lakes (nonbreeding).

Distribution.—*Breeds* along the Bering coast of Alaska (Wales south to Kuskokwim River, including St. Lawrence, Nunivak, and Nelson islands), and in Eurasia from the Arctic coast of Siberia (Yamal Peninsula eastward) south to the Stanovoi and Koryak mountains and the Gulf of Anadyr. Nonbreeding individuals occasionally summer in the Hawaiian and Mariana islands.

Winters in the Hawaiian Islands, and in the Old World from northeastern Africa, the Red Sea, India, southern China, Taiwan, and islands of Polynesia south to the Malay Peninsula, Australia, Tasmania, New Zealand, the Tonga and Tuamotu islands, and, rarely, in south-coastal British Columbia, coastal and lowland interior California, and Guadalupe and the Revillagigedo islands.

Migrates through the Aleutian Islands, along the Pacific coast of North America in central and southern California, and in Eurasia primarily in eastern Asia and over oceanic islands of the Pacific.

Casual or accidental in northern Baja California, Clipperton Island, inland in western North America (to Alberta), and in Maine, Barbados, Chile, Greenland, Europe, the Cape Verde Islands, Mediterranean region, Africa, and Arabia.

Notes.—Also known as Asiatic Golden-Plover. Recent studies (Connors et al. 1993) confirm earlier suggestions (Connors 1983) that *P. fulva* is a species distinct from *P. dominica.*

Genus *CHARADRIUS* Linnaeus

> *Charadrius* Linnaeus, 1758, Syst. Nat. (ed. 10) 1: 150. Type, by tautonymy, *Charadrius hiaticula* Linnaeus (*Charadrius s. Hiaticula,* prebinomial specific name, in synonymy).
>
> *Eudromias* C. L. Brehm, 1830, Isis von Oken, col. 987. Type, by monotypy, *Charadrius morinellus* Linnaeus.
>
> *Eupoda* J. F. Brandt, 1845, in Tchihatchev, Voy. Sci. Altai Orient., p. 444. Type, by monotypy, *Charadrius asiaticus* Pallas.
>
> *Aegialeus* Reichenbach, 1853, Hand. Spec. Ornithol., Die Vögel, pt. 3 (1852), p. 18. Type, by original designation, *Charadrius semipalmatus* "Aud." [= Bonaparte].
>
> *Oxyechus* Reichenbach, 1853, Hand. Spec. Ornithol., Die Vögel, pt. 3 (1852), p. 18. Type, by original designation, *Charadrius vociferus* Linnaeus.
>
> *Ochthodromus* (not *Ochthedromus* Le Conte, 1848, Coleoptera) Reichenbach, 1853, Hand. Spec. Ornithol., Die Vögel, pt. 3 (1852), p. 18. Type, by original designation, *Charadrius wilsonia* Ord.
>
> *Leucopolius* Bonaparte, 1856, C. R. Acad. Sci. Paris 43: 417. Type, by tautonymy, *Charadrius niveifrons* Cuvier = *Charadrius leucopolius* Wagler = *Charadrius marginatus* Vieillot.
>
> *Podasocys* Coues, 1866, Proc. Acad. Nat. Sci. Philadelphia 18: 96. Type, by original designation, *Charadrius montanus* Townsend.

Pagolla Mathews, 1913, Birds Aust. 3: 83. New name for *Ochthodromus* Reichenbach, preoccupied.

Charadrius mongolus Pallas. Mongolian Plover.

Charadrius mongolus Pallas, 1776, Reise Versch. Prov. Russ. Reichs 3: 700. (circa lacus salsos versus Mongoliae fines = Kulussutai, probably on the Onon River, eastern Siberia.)

Habitat.—Mudflats, beaches, and shores of lakes and ponds, breeding on barren flats and steppe, along sandy and stony banks of rivers, lakes, and ponds.

Distribution.—*Breeds* in central and northeastern Eurasia from the Pamir Mountains east to the Chukotski Peninsula, Kamchatka, and the Commander Islands, and south to western China and Tibet; has bred in North America in northern and western Alaska (Brooks Range, Choris Peninsula, Goodnews Bay, Seward Peninsula).

Winters in the Old World from the Red Sea, Iran, India, Southeast Asia, southeastern China, the Philippines, and the Mariana and Caroline islands south to southern Africa, the Seychelles, Sri Lanka, Andaman Islands, Indonesia, New Guinea ,and Australia.

Migrates regularly through the Aleutians (east to Adak), islands in the Bering Sea (St. Lawrence and the Pribilofs), and coastal western Alaska, casually to northern Alaska (Barrow) and south-coastal Alaska (Cook Inlet, Valdez).

Casual in the Hawaiian Islands, Oregon, California, Ontario, New Jersey, and Louisiana; sight reports for British Columbia (Vancouver) and Alberta.

Charadrius collaris Vieillot. Collared Plover.

Charadrius collaris Vieillot, 1818, Nouv. Dict. Hist. Nat. (nouv. éd.) 27: 136. Based on "Mbatuitui Collar negro" Azara, Apunt. Hist. Nat. Páx. Parag. 3: 291 (no. 392). (Paraguay.)

Habitat.—Riverine Sand Beaches, Coastal Sand Beaches (0–800 m; Tropical Zone).

Distribution.—*Resident* primarily in coastal areas from Sinaloa and Veracruz south through Middle America (except the Yucatan Peninsula and El Salvador), and in South America from Colombia, Venezuela (including the Netherlands Antilles and Margarita Island), Tobago, Trinidad, and the Guianas south, west of the Andes to western Peru and east of the Andes to central Argentina, occasionally in central Chile.

Ranges in the non-breeding season north to the southern Lesser Antilles (Mustique in the Grenadines and Grenada, sight reports in St. Martin, St. Kitts, and Barbados), and in interior Mexico to Tlaxcala and Morelos.

Accidental in Texas (Uvalde; 9–12 May 1992, photograph; 1992, Amer. Birds 46: 501; DeBenedictis 1994b, Yovanovich 1995).

Charadrius alexandrinus Linnaeus. Snowy Plover.

Charadrius alexandrinus Linnaeus, 1758, Syst. Nat. (ed. 10) 1: 150. (ad Ægypti ex Nilo canalem = Egypt.)

Habitat.—Sandy beaches, dry mud or salt flats, and sandy shores of rivers, lakes, and ponds (Tropical to Temperate zones).

Distribution.—*Breeds* [*nivosus* group] in western and central North America along the Pacific coast from southern Washington south to southern California (including San Clemente Island), southern Baja California, and locally from interior southern Oregon, northeastern California, western Nevada, Utah, southwestern Wyoming, western Montana, southern Saskatchewan, central and southeastern Colorado, central Kansas, and north-central Oklahoma south to southeastern California, southern Arizona, southern New Mexico, and north-central Texas, on the Pacific coast of Oaxaca; in the Gulf states from Florida (south locally to Marco Island) west (absent as a breeding bird from Louisiana) to Texas and northeastern Tamaulipas; and in the southern Bahamas (north to Andros, Exuma, and San Salvador), Greater Antilles (east to the Virgin Islands), and Lesser Antilles (St. Martin, St. Kitts), and on islands off the north coast of Venezuela (Curaçao east to Margarita Island); and [*alexandrinus* group] in Eurasia from southern Sweden, central Russia, central Siberia, and Japan south to the Cape Verde Islands, northern Africa, the Red Sea, northwestern India, Sri Lanka, Java, southeastern China, and the southern Ryukyu Islands.

Winters [*nivosus* group] on islands and in coastal areas of North America from Washington, the Gulf coast, and Bahamas south to southern Mexico (casually north to southeastern New Mexico and south to Guatemala, Honduras, Costa Rica, and Panama), and the Greater Antilles, rarely in the interior valleys of California; in the breeding range in South America; and [*alexandrinus* group] in the Old World from the Mediterranean region and breeding range in Asia south to tropical Africa, Arabia, Sri Lanka, Southeast Asia, Indonesia, the Philippines, Taiwan, and the Bonin Islands.

Resident [*occidentalis* group] along the Pacific coast of South America from western Ecuador to Chile.

Casual [*nivosus* group] in central western Alaska (Seward Peninsula, photograph, probably this group), in the interior of North America north to central British Columbia (in coastal regions to the Queen Charlotte Islands), and from southern Alberta, southern Saskatchewan, and southern Ontario through much of the interior of eastern North America, especially near Great Lakes, and on the coast of South Carolina and on the Atlantic coast of Florida (Merritt Island, Florida Keys;) and [*alexandrinus* group] from Sakhalin to the Palau Islands.

Notes.—Known in Old World literature as Kentish Plover. Groups: *C. nivosus* (Cassin, 1858) [Snowy Plover], *C. occidentalis* (Cabanis, 1872) [Peruvian Plover], and *C. alexandrinus* [Kentish Plover]. *Charadrius alexandrinus,* the Australian *C. ruficapillus* Temminck, 1822, and the African *C. marginatus* Vieillot, 1818, constitute a superspecies (Vaurie 1965, Mayr and Short 1970).

Charadrius wilsonia Ord. Wilson's Plover.

Charadrius wilsonia Ord, 1814, in Wilson, Amer. Ornithol. 9: 77, pl. 73, fig. 5. (shore of Cape Island [= Cape May], New Jersey.)

Habitat.—Sandy beaches islets, tidal mudflats, occasionally slightly inland on extensive mudflats.

Distribution.—*Breeds* from central Baja California and northern Sonora south along the Pacific coast of Middle and South America to northwestern Peru (including the Pearl Islands off Panama); and from southern New Jersey (rare north of Virginia) south along the Atlantic-Gulf-Caribbean coasts of North America and Middle America (not recorded breeding south of Belize), the southeastern United States and West Indies (present south to Dominica, and on Grenada and the Grenadines) to northern South America east to northeastern Brazil (including islands off the coast of Venezuela).

Winters from Baja California and Sonora south along the Pacific coast to central Peru; and from the Gulf coast of western Louisiana and Texas, and Florida south in the Caribbean-Gulf-Atlantic region throughout the breeding range to northern South America.

Casual north to central California (Monterey, Ventura, and San Diego counties); one breeding record for the Salton Sea in southeastern California), Oklahoma (Tulsa), Arkansas, Minnesota (Duluth), and the Lake Erie region (southern Ontario, Ohio, and Pennsylvania); along the Atlantic coast to Nova Scotia; and in Bermuda, Veracruz, Barbados, and Venezuela.

Notes.—Also known as Thick-billed Plover.

Charadrius hiaticula Linnaeus. Common Ringed Plover.

Charadrius Hiaticula Linnaeus, 1758, Syst. Nat. (ed. 10) 1: 150. (in Europa & America ad ripas = Sweden.)

Habitat.—Sandy areas with scattered low vegetation, cultivated fields, short-grass areas near water, dry stream beds, and sandy, pebbly and grassy tundra (breeding); in migration and winter also mudflats, beaches, and shores of lakes, ponds, and rivers.

Distribution.—*Breeds* in North America in western Alaska (St. Lawrence and St. Matthew islands), and on Ellesmere, Bylot, and eastern Baffin islands; and in the Palearctic in Greenland, Iceland, and the Faeroe Islands, and from Scandinavia, northern Russia, and northern Siberia south to northwestern France (Bretagne), central Poland, the Chukotski Peninsula, Anadyrland, and the Sea of Okhotsk.

Winters from the British Isles, western Europe, the Mediterranean region, the Persian Gulf, western India, and Sakhalin south to the eastern Atlantic islands, southern Africa, the Maldive Islands, northern China, Japan, the Volcano Islands, and (casually) to Australia.

Casual in the Pribilof (St. Paul) and the Aleutian islands (Amchitka, Attu, Adak, Shemya), and the mainland of western Alaska (Wales and Nome region). Accidental in Nova Scotia (Seal Island), Virginia (Craney Island), and the Lesser Antilles (Barbados); sight reports for Quebec, Massachusetts, and Rhode Island.

Notes.—Also known as Ringed Plover. *Charadrius hiaticula* and *C. semipalmatus* may constitute a superspecies (Mayr and Short 1970); *C. semipalmatus* was treated as a subspecies of *C. hiaticula* by Bock (1959).

Charadrius semipalmatus Bonaparte. Semipalmated Plover.

> *Tringa hiaticula* (not *Charadrius hiaticula* Linnaeus) Ord, 1824, in Wilson, Amer. Ornithol. (Ord reprint) 7: 65. (coast of New Jersey.)
> *Charadrius semipalmatus* Bonaparte, 1825, J. Acad. Nat. Sci. Philadelphia 5: 98. New name for *Tringa hiaticula* Ord, preoccupied.

Habitat.—Sandy areas, grassy or mossy tundra, and gravelly plains (breeding); tidal mudflats, muddy beaches, tide pools in salt marshes, wet dirt fields, and bare shores of lakes and ponds (nonbreeding).

Distribution.—*Breeds* from northern Alaska, northern Yukon, northern Mackenzie, Banks, Victoria, and southern Somerset islands, northern Keewatin (Melville Peninsula), central Baffin Island, and the northern Labrador coast south to the Pribilof and Aleutian islands (west to Adak), southern Alaska (west to the Alaska Peninsula), northwestern and central British Columbia (including the Queen Charlotte Islands; also locally near Vancouver), southeastern Yukon, southern Mackenzie, northeastern Alberta, northern Saskatchewan, northern Manitoba, northern Ontario (coast of Hudson and James bays), central Quebec, and, coastally, the Gulf of St. Lawrence, southern New Brunswick, southern Nova Scotia, and Newfoundland, casually to western Washington and interior Oregon. Nonbreeding birds often summer in the wintering areas south to northwestern South America.

Winters primarily in coastal areas from south-coastal British Columbia (rarely), Washington, central Sonora, the Gulf coast, and South Carolina (casually north to New York) south through the West Indies, and along both coasts of Middle America and South America (including the Galapagos Islands, Tobago, and Trinidad) to central Chile and Argentina (Patagonia), casually in the Hawaiian Islands.

Migrates along both coasts of North America and commonly through the interior, locally in the intermountain region from Idaho and Montana to Arizona, and casually to the western Aleutians.

Casual in the Revillagigedo Islands (Socorro Island), Clipperton Island, Bermuda, Greenland, the Azores, Britain, eastern Siberia, and Johnston and Baker islands in the Pacific.

Notes.—See comments under *C. hiaticula*.

Charadrius melodus Ord. Piping Plover.

> *Charadrius melodus* Ord, 1824, in Wilson, Amer. Ornithol. (Ord reprint) 7: 71. (Great Egg Harbor, New Jersey.)

Habitat.—Sandy or alkaline shores of salty, shallow lakes, sandbars in rivers (inland), and sandy beaches from dunes to the high tide line (coastal); in winter, primarily sandy beaches and tidal mudflats; in migration, also bare shores of lakes and ponds.

Distribution.—*Breeds* locally in the interior of North America from south-central Alberta, northern Saskatchewan (once), south-central Manitoba, and central northern Minnesota (Lake of the Woods) south to north-central and northeastern Montana, North Dakota, eastern Colorado, southeastern South Dakota (Union County), central and eastern Nebraska and northern Iowa (also isolated breeding in northwestern Oklahoma); in the Great Lakes region (locally, formerly more widespread) from extreme southwestern Ontario and northern Michigan south to the southern shore of lakes Michigan, Erie, and Ontario; and in coastal areas from northern

New Brunswick, Prince Edward Island, southern Nova Scotia, southeastern Quebec (including the Magdalen Islands), and Newfoundland (including St. Pierre and Miquelon islands) south along the Atlantic coast to Virginia North Carolina, and South Carolina.

Winters primarily on the Atlantic-Gulf coast from North Carolina south to Florida and west to eastern Texas, and, less commonly, throughout the Bahamas and Greater Antilles (east to the Virgin Islands) and south to the Yucatan Peninsula.

Migrates through the interior of North America east of the Rockies (especially in the Mississippi Valley) as well as along the Atlantic coast.

Casual in east-central Washington, southern California, northwestern Sonora, Nayarit, Veracruz, central and northeastern New Mexico, the interior of Texas, Bermuda, St. Kitts (sight report), and Barbados. Accidental in southwestern Ecuador; sight reports for Oregon and southern New Mexico.

Charadrius dubius Scopoli. Little Ringed Plover.

Charadrius (dubius) Scopoli, 1786, Del Flor. Faun. Insubr., 2: 93. (Luzon, Philippines.)

Habitat.—Inland fresh-water areas.

Distribution.—*Breeds* from northern Eurasia south to the eastern Atlantic islands, northern Africa, Sri Lanka, Southeast Asia, Indonesia, New Guinea, and the Bismarck Archipelago.

Winters from southern Europe, the Caspian and Black seas, India, eastern China, and Japan south to tropical Africa and Australia.

Casual in the western Aleutian Islands (Attu, Shemya, Buldir).

Charadrius vociferus Linnaeus. Killdeer.

Charadrius vociferus Linnaeus, 1758, Syst. Nat. (ed. 10) 1: 150. (in America septentrionali = South Carolina.)

Habitat.—Fields, meadows, pastures, bare shores of lakes, ponds, and rivers, expansive lawns, occasionally nesting on adjacent gravel roads, railroad beds, and even gravel parking-lots (breeding); in winter, also in plowed and wet dirt fields, mudflats, and occasionally coastal beaches.

Distribution.—*Breeds* in North America from east-central and southeastern Alaska, southern Yukon, northwestern and southern Mackenzie, northern Saskatchewan, northern Manitoba, northern Ontario, south-central Quebec (including the Magdalen Islands), New Brunswick, Prince Edward Island, western Nova Scotia, and Newfoundland south to southern Baja California, central Mexico (recorded breeding to Guerrero and Guanajuato), Tamaulipas, the Gulf coast, and Florida Keys; in the southern Bahamas (Inagua, Caicos, and Turks islands, probably also New Providence) and the Greater Antilles (east to the Virgin Islands); and in western South America along the coast from western Ecuador to extreme northwestern Chile.

Winters from southeastern Alaska (rarely), southern British Columbia, Oregon, Idaho, the central United States from Montana east to the Ohio Valley (casually from southern Canada east of British Columbia) and New England south throughout the remainder of North America, Middle America, Bermuda, the West Indies, and northern South America (also most islands throughout these regions) to Colombia, Venezuela, and western Ecuador; also in the breeding range in Peru and Chile.

Casual in the Hawaiian (Kauai, Oahu, Maui) and Pribilof islands; north to western and northern Alaska, northern Yukon, northern Mackenzie, southern Keewatin, and central Labrador; and to Clipperton Island, Greenland, Iceland, the Faeroe Islands, British Isles, continental Europe, the Azores, and Madeira.

Charadrius montanus Townsend. Mountain Plover.

Charadrius montanus J. K. Townsend, 1837, J. Acad. Nat. Sci. Philadelphia 7: 192. (tableland of the Rocky Mountains = near Sweetwater River, Wyoming.)

Habitat.—Dry open short-grass prairie and grassland up to 2500 m, usually with areas of bare soil (breeding); short-grass plains and fields, plowed fields, and sandy deserts (non-breeding).

Distribution.—*Breeds* locally from extreme southern Alberta (Milk River), southwestern Saskatchewan, northern Montana, and southwestern North Dakota (formerly) south through Wyoming, western Nebraska, Colorado, and western Kansas to northeastern Utah, northwestern, central and southeastern New Mexico, western Texas (Davis Mountains, formerly Brewster County), and western Oklahoma (Cimarron County).

Winters locally from central (rarely northern) California, Nevada (casual), southern Arizona, and central and coastal Texas south to southern Baja California and northern Mexico (Sonora east to Tamaulipas), rarely farther south (recorded Zacatecas).

Casual north to western Washington and southeastern Alberta, and in western Missouri. Accidental in Mississippi (Grenada Lake), Alabama (Gulf Shores), Massachusetts (Chatham), Virginia (Chincoteague), and Florida; a sight report from Georgia.

Notes.—Formerly placed in the genus *Eupoda*. *Charadrius montanus* and the Old World *C. veredus* and *C. asiaticus* Pallas, 1773, appear to constitute a superspecies (Mayr and Short 1970).

Charadrius morinellus Linnaeus. Eurasian Dotterel.

> *Charadrius Morinellus* Linnaeus, 1758, Syst. Nat. (ed. 10) 1: 150. (in Europa = Sweden.)

Habitat.—Stony steppes, plains, newly plowed fields and marginal grassland (breeding); open stony or sandy areas, less frequently marshes, mudflats, and seacoasts (nonbreeding).

Distribution.—*Breeds* locally in North America in northern and western Alaska (from Barrow to the Seward Peninsula and St. Lawrence Island); and in Eurasia in the mountains of the British Isles, Scandinavia, and central Europe, and scattered across northern Russia and Siberia from the Ural Mountains to the Verkhoyansk Mountains and the Kolyma River, and in northern Mongolia.

Winters in southern Europe, North Africa, Arabia, Iraq, and Iran, casually in the Canary Islands, Madeira, Sakhalin, the Kuril Islands, and Japan.

Migrates through coastal western Alaska, casually east along the Beaufort coast of northern Alaska, and in the fall through the western Aleutians.

Accidental in the Hawaiian Islands (Kure), Washington (Ocean Shores, Westport), California (from Del Norte County south to the Farallon Islands and Point Reyes), and the Commander Islands.

Notes.—In Old World literature known as the Dotterel. Formerly placed in the genus *Eudromias*; for placement in genus *Charadrius*, see Nielson (1975) and Strauch (1978).

Family **HAEMATOPODIDAE**: Oystercatchers

Genus *HAEMATOPUS* Linnaeus

> *Hæmatopus* Linnaeus, 1758, Syst. Nat. (ed. 10) 1: 152. Type, by monotypy, *Haematopus ostralegus* Linnaeus.

Haematopus ostralegus Linnaeus. Eurasian Oystercatcher.

> *Hæmatopus Ostralegus* Linnaeus, 1758, Syst. Nat. (ed. 10) 1: 152. (in Europæ, Americæ septentrionalis littoribus marinis = Öland Island, Sweden.)

Habitat.— Sea coasts, sandy plains, river valleys, lake shores (breeding); coasts, rocky shores, mudflats, fields, and beaches (nonbreeding).

Distribution.—*Breeds* in Eurasia from Iceland, Faeroes, British Isles, and coasts of Europe to northern Russia and south to Iberian Peninsula; along coasts of Mediterranean, Adriatic, Aegean, and northern Black seas; central Russia, Turkey, and Iran; locally Kamchatka, western Siberia, China, and Korea.

Winters from Mediterranean, Red, Arabian seas, and Persian Gulf to southern Africa, Sri Lanka, and southern China. Casual in southern Greenland.

Accidental in North America: one record on Fox Island near Tors Cove, Avalon Peninsula, Newfoundland, 24–25 May 1994 (photographs; Mactavish 1994).

Haematopus palliatus Temminck. American Oystercatcher.

> *Hæmatopus palliatus* Temminck, 1820, Man. Ornithol. (ed. 2) 2: 532. (à l'Amérique méridionale = Venezuela.)

Habitat.— Rocky and sandy seacoasts and islands, tidal mudflats.

Distribution.—*Breeds* locally along the Atlantic coast from Massachusetts (Monomoy) south to Florida, and along the Gulf coast south to the Yucatan Peninsula (including Cozumel Island); in the Bahamas, Greater Antilles (but breeding not yet confirmed in Cuba), and Lesser Antilles (St. Barthélemy, from Guadeloupe to St. Lucia, and the Grenadines); along the Pacific coast from central Baja California (San Benito Islands, possibly also Los Coronados Islands in northern Baja California) and the Gulf of California south to Guerrero (also the Revillagigedo, Tres Marías, and Tres Marietas islands), along the coast of Costa Rica, and along the Pacific coast from the Bay of Panama (Pearl Islands and Los Santos) south to central Chile (Isla de Chiloé); and along the Caribbean-Atlantic coast of South America (including most islands off Venezuela, possibly also Tobago and Trinidad) south to south-central Argentina.

Winters on the Atlantic-Gulf coast from Maryland (casually from New England) south to southeastern Mexico, casually to Belize and Honduras; on the Pacific coast of North America from central Baja California south to Honduras, also in Costa Rica; and generally in the breeding range in the West Indies and along both South American coasts, casually on the Caribbean coast north to the Canal area.

Casual in California, southern Ontario, southern Quebec, Maine, Nova Scotia, and western Argentina. Accidental in interior southern California (Salton Sea); a sight report for Idaho.

Notes.—*Haematopus palliatus* and *H. bachmani,* formerly considered conspecific [American Oystercatcher], form a hybrid zone about 200 miles in width in central Baja California (Jehl 1985). Some authors (e.g., Friedmann et al. 1950, Mayr and Short 1970) considered these two forms conspecific with *H. ostralegus*; the complex constitutes a superspecies (Sibley and Monroe 1990).

Haematopus bachmani Audubon. Black Oystercatcher.

> *Hæmatopus Bachmani* Audubon, 1838, Birds Amer. (folio) 4: pl. 427, fig. 1 (1839, Ornithol. Biogr. 5: 245). (Mouth of the Columbia River = near Puget Sound; see Burns, 1934, Auk 51: 403–404.)

Habitat.—Primarily rocky seacoasts and especially islands, also occasionally on adjacent sandy beaches and mudflats.

Distribution.—*Resident* from the western Aleutians (Kiska eastward) south along the Pacific coast of North America (including most islands offshore) to central Baja California (Punta Abreojos and Isla de Natividad); also has bred on Round Island, in the southern Bering Sea.

Accidental in the Pribilof Islands; a sight report for Idaho.

Notes.—Known also as the American Black Oystercatcher. See comments under *H. palliatus.*

Family **RECURVIROSTRIDAE**: Stilts and Avocets

Genus *HIMANTOPUS* Brisson

> *Himantopus* Brisson, 1760, Ornithologie 1: 46; 5: 33. Type, by tautonymy, *Himantopus* Brisson = *Charadrius himantopus* Linnaeus.

Himantopus himantopus (Linnaeus). Black-winged Stilt.

> *Charadrius Himantopus* Linnaeus, 1758, Syst. Nat. (ed. 10) 1: 151. (in Europa australiore = southern Europe.)

Habitat.—Marshes and flooded fields.

Distribution.—*Breeds* in Eurasia and Africa; northernmost populations are migratory southward.

Accidental in Alaska (Nizki, in the Aleutian Islands, 24 May-2 June 1983, photograph; Zeillemaker et al. 1985).

Notes.—See comments under *H. mexicanus*.

Himantopus mexicanus (Müller). Black-necked Stilt.

Charadrius Mexicanus P. L. S. Müller, 1776, Natursyst., Suppl., p. 117. Based on the "L'échasse du Mexique" Brisson, Ornithologie 5: 36. (in Mexico.)

Habitat.—Shallow grassy marshes and adjacent mudflats, shallow ponds, and flooded fields; breeding habitat has bare ground for nest sites (Tropical to Temperate zones).

Distribution.—*Breeds* [*mexicanus* group] locally on the Atlantic coast from southern New Jersey (formerly), southeastern Pennsylvania, Delaware, Maryland, and Virginia south to southern Florida, in Bermuda, and the West Indies (the Bahamas south to Antigua, St. Kitts, and Montserrat), and from central (casually northern) coastal California, western Oregon, Washington, southern Alberta, southern Saskatchewan (rarely), eastern Montana, western and central Nebraska, central Kansas, north-central Oklahoma, southeastern Missouri, Arkansas, southwestern Kentucky, western Tennessee, central and coastal Texas, southern Louisiana, southern Mississippi, and southern Alabama south through Middle America and South America (including the Galapagos Islands, islands off Venezuela, and Tobago and Trinidad) to coastal and Andean Peru, eastern Ecuador, and Amazonian Brazil. Recorded in summer and probably breeding [*mexicanus* group] in North Dakota and western South Dakota.

Winters [*mexicanus* group] from northern California, Sonora, the Gulf coast, and central Florida south locally through Middle America, the West Indies, and South America to the limits of the breeding range.

Resident [*knudseni* group] in the Hawaiian Islands (main islands from Niihau eastward, except Lanai and Kahoolawe, recorded also from Midway and Nihoa); and [*melanurus* group] in southern South America from eastern Peru, Bolivia, and southeastern Brazil south to southern Chile and southern Argentina.

Casual [*mexicanus* group] north to southwestern British Columbia, southern Alberta, southern Saskatchewan, southern Manitoba, Minnesota, Wisconsin, central Michigan, southern Ontario, southern Quebec, New Brunswick, Nova Scotia, and Newfoundland, and on Bermuda.

Notes.—Groups: *H. mexicanus* [Black-necked Stilt], *H. knudseni* Stejneger, 1887 [Hawaiian Stilt], and *H. melanurus* Vieillot, 1817 [White-backed Stilt]. *Himantopus mexicanus* is sometimes considered conspecific with the Old World *H. himantopus* (e.g., Vaurie 1965, Blake 1977); all forms in the genus may constitute a superspecies (Mayr and Short 1970).

Genus *RECURVIROSTRA* Linnaeus

Recurvirostra Linnaeus, 1758, Syst. Nat. (ed. 10) 1: 151. Type, by monotypy, *Recurvirostra avosetta* Linnaeus.

Recurvirostra americana Gmelin. American Avocet.

Recurvirostra americana Gmelin, 1789, Syst. Nat. 1(2): 693. Based mainly on the "American Avoset" Pennant, Arct. Zool. 2: 502, pl. 21. (in America septentrionali et nova Hollandia = North America.)

Habitat.—Lowland marshes, mudflats, ponds, alkaline lakes, and estuaries, nesting colonially (usually) on open flats or areas with scattered tufts of grass along lakes (especially alkaline) and marshes.

Distribution.—*Breeds* from southern British Columbia, central Alberta, central Saskatchewan, southern Manitoba, western Ontario (Lake of the Woods), and western Minnesota south to northern Baja California, Arizona, southern Colorado, southern New Mexico, and Valley of México (Distrito Federal), and east to central Nebraska, central Kansas, and coastal Texas; also breeding records for Wisconsin (Dodge County), Virginia (Craney), and North Carolina (Pea Island, 1968). Formerly bred north to southern Mackenzie. Nonbreeding individuals frequently summer in the wintering range.

Winters from south-coastal British Columbia (rarely), but mostly in coastal lowlands from northern California, western Louisiana, and coastal Mississippi and Alabama south to southern Mexico, casually to Guatemala (Pacific lowlands), Belize, Honduras, Costa Rica, and Panama, also locally in Delaware and southern Florida.

Migrates primarily throughout the western half of the United States, rarely in interior and eastern North America east to northern Michigan, southern Ontario, and New England, and south to the Gulf coast and Florida.

Casual or accidental in Alaska (Valdez), Northwest Territories, southern Quebec, New Brunswick, Prince Edward Island, Nova Scotia, Bermuda, the Bahamas (Andros, San Salvador), Cuba, Jamaica, Puerto Rico, St. Croix, the Cayman Islands, Barbados, western Ecuador, and Greenland.

Suborder SCOLOPACI: Sandpipers, Jacanas, and Allies

Family **JACANIDAE**: Jacanas

Genus *JACANA* Brisson

Jacana Brisson, 1760, Ornithologie 1: 48; 5: 121. Type, by tautonymy, *Jacana* Brisson = *Parra jacana* Linnaeus.
Asarcia Sharpe, 1896, Cat. Birds Brit. Mus. 24: ix, 68, 86. Type, by monotypy, *Parra variabilis* Linnaeus = *Fulica spinosa* Linnaeus.

Jacana spinosa (Linnaeus). Northern Jacana.

Fulica spinosa Linnaeus, 1758, Syst. Nat. (ed. 10) 1: 152. Based on "The Spur-winged Water Hen" Edwards, Nat. Hist. Birds 1: 48, pl. 48. (in America australi = Panama.)

Habitat.—Freshwater Marshes; requires extensive areas of floating vegetation in breeding habitat (0–1500 m; Tropical and lower Subtropical zones).

Distribution.—*Resident* from Sinaloa, southern Texas (formerly north to Brazoria County), and Tamaulipas south along both slopes of Middle America (including Cozumel Island) to western Panama (east to Veraguas), and on the Mexican Plateau in Jalisco, Michoacán, and Guanajuato; also in the Greater Antilles (Cuba, Isle of Pines, Jamaica, and Hispaniola).

Casual in southern Arizona, western and central Texas (north to Brewster, Kerr, Gonzales, and Travis counties), and Puerto Rico; reports from Florida are unsubstantiated.

Notes.—Limited hybridization with *J. jacana* occurs in western Panama (Wetmore 1965).

Jacana jacana (Linnaeus). Wattled Jacana.

Parra Jacana Linnaeus, 1766, Syst. Nat. (ed. 12) 1: 259. Based mainly on "Jacana quarta species" Marcgrave, Hist. Nat. Bras., p. 191, and "Le Chirurgien brun" Brisson, Ornithologie 5: 125, pl. 11, fig. 1. (in America australi = Surinam.)

Habitat.—Freshwater Marshes; requires extensive areas of floating vegetation in breeding habitat (0–900 m; Tropical Zone).

Distribution.—*Resident* from western Panama (from eastern Chiriquí and Veraguas eastward) south through South America (including Trinidad) west of the Andes to northwestern Peru, and east of the Andes to central Argentina
Casual north to southwestern Costa Rica.

Notes.—See comments under *J. spinosa.*

Family **SCOLOPACIDAE**: Sandpipers, Phalaropes, and Allies

Subfamily SCOLOPACINAE: Sandpipers and Allies

Tribe TRINGINI: Tringine Sandpipers

Genus *TRINGA* Linnaeus

Tringa Linnaeus, 1758, Syst. Nat. (ed. 10) 1: 148. Type, by tautonymy, *Tringa ochropus* Linnaeus (*Tringa,* prebinomial specific name, in synonymy).

Totanus Bechstein, 1803, Ornithol. Taschenb. Dtsch. 2: 282. Type, by tautonymy, *Totanus maculatus* Bechstein = *Scolopax totanus* Linnaeus.

Glottis Koch, 1816, Syst. Baier. Zool. 1: xlii, 304. Type, by tautonymy, *Totanus glottis* Bechstein = *Scolopax nebularia* Gunnerus.

Neoglottis Ridgway, 1919, Bull. U.S. Natl. Mus. 50(8): 329. Type, by original designation, *Scolopax melanoleuca* Gmelin.

Notes.—Some authors (e.g., Vaurie 1965) have merged all the genera through *Xenus* in *Tringa*.

Tringa nebularia (Gunnerus). Common Greenshank.

Scolopax nebularia Gunnerus, 1767, in Leem, Beskr. Finm. Lapper, p. 251. (District of Trondhjem, Norway.)

Habitat.—Marshes, bogs, and wet meadows in the taiga or high moorlands (breeding); marshes, ponds, lakes, and mudflats (nonbreeding).

Distribution.—*Breeds* from Scotland and Scandinavia east across Russia and Siberia to Anadyrland, Kamchatka, and the Sea of Okhotsk, and south to Lake Baikal.

Winters from the Mediterranean region, Iraq, the Persian Gulf, eastern China, and Taiwan south to southern Africa, India, Sri Lanka, the Maldive Islands, East Indies, New Guinea, and Australia, straggling to the eastern Atlantic islands and New Zealand.

Migrates regularly in spring through the western Aleutians (Near Islands), casually as far east as the Pribilofs (St. Paul) and as far north as St. Lawrence Island.

Accidental in Quebec (Métabetchouan-St. Gédéon), Newfoundland (Conception Bay, Harbour Grace), and Nova Scotia (Cherry Hill); a sight report for New York. Audubon's record from Sandy Key, near Cape Sable, Florida, is questionable.

Notes.—Known in Old World literature as the Greenshank.

Tringa melanoleuca (Gmelin). Greater Yellowlegs.

Scolopax melanoleuca Gmelin, 1789, Syst. Nat. 1(2): 659. Based on the "Stone Snipe" Pennant, Arct. Zool. 2: 468. (auctumno in arenis littoris Labrador = Chateaux Bay, Labrador.)

Habitat.—Bogs, muskeg, ponds, lakes, open woodlands, and burns (breeding); marshes, ponds, flooded fields, rice fields, stream margins, lagoons, and coastal mudflats (nonbreeding).

Distribution.—*Breeds* from southern Alaska (the lower Kuskokwim River, and from the Alaska Peninsula eastward), southwestern Mackenzie, and central British Columbia east across the northern and central portions of the Canadian provinces to central and southern Labrador, Newfoundland, northeastern Nova Scotia (Cape Breton Island), and southern Quebec (Anticosti Island). Nonbreeding individuals sometimes summer on the wintering grounds, especially along the coasts of the United States and in the West Indies.

Winters from south-coastal British Columbia, Washington, Idaho, Utah, central New Mexico, southern Texas, the Gulf coast, and southern New England south through Middle America, the West Indies, and South America to Tierra del Fuego.

Migrates regularly through the North American continent south of the breeding range.

Casual north to northern Alaska (Barrow), southern Mackenzie, southern Keewatin, Southampton and Baffin islands, and northern Quebec, and in the Hawaiian, Pribilof (St. Paul, St. George), Aleutian (Adak, Shemya, Attu), and Galapagos islands, and in Bermuda. Accidental in Clipperton Island, Greenland, Iceland, the British Isles, the Azores, Japan, and the Marshall Islands.

Tringa flavipes (Gmelin). Lesser Yellowlegs.

Scolopax flavipes Gmelin, 1789, Syst. Nat. 1(2): 659. Based on the "Yellowshank" Pennant, Arct. Zool. 2: 468. (auctumno in Noveboraco = New York.)

Habitat.—Muskeg, bogs, open boreal forest and burns, near lakes and ponds (breeding); marshes, ponds, wet meadows, flooded fields and mudflats (nonbreeding).

Distribution.—*Breeds* from western (rarely) and central Alaska, northern Yukon, northwestern and east-central Mackenzie, southern Keewatin, northern Manitoba, northern Ontario, and extreme west-central Quebec south to northern British Columbia, south-central Alberta, central Saskatchewan, and central Manitoba, formerly sporadically south to southern Wisconsin. Nonbreeding birds occasionally are reported in summer south from the breeding range as far as Argentina.

Winters from south coastal British Columbia (rarely), southern Arizona, southern New Mexico, southern Texas, the Gulf coast, and coastal South Carolina (rarely from Long Island, New York) south through Middle America, the West Indies, and South America (also the Galapagos Islands) to Tierra del Fuego.

Migrates regularly through North America south of the breeding range and east to southern Ontario, southern Quebec, New Brunswick, and Nova Scotia, more locally through western North America.

Casual in the Hawaiian, Pribilof, and Aleutian islands, Labrador, Newfoundland, Bermuda, the Azores, and New Zealand. Accidental in Clipperton Island, Greenland, Iceland, the British Isles, continental Europe, the Azores, Zambia, South Africa, and the Marshall and Falkland islands.

Tringa stagnatilis (Bechstein). Marsh Sandpiper.

Totanus stagnatilis Bechstein, 1803, Ornithol. Taschenb. Dtsch. 2: 292, pl. 29. (Germany.)

Habitat.—Marshes and wet meadows (breeding); shores, mudflats, and estuaries (nonbreeding).

Distribution.—*Breeds* from eastern Europe east to western Siberia.

Winters from the Mediterranean region, Persian Gulf, and Southeast Asia south to southern Africa, India, the East Indies, and Australia.

Accidental in the Aleutian Islands (Buldir, 2 September 1974; Byrd et al. 1978) and Marshall Islands (Kwajalein).

Tringa totanus (Linnaeus). Common Redshank.

Scolopax Totanus Linnaeus, 1758, Syst. Nat., ed. 10, 1, p. 145. (in Europa = Sweden.)

Habitat.—Marshes and wet meadows (breeding); shores, mudlfats, and estuaries (nonbreeding).

Distribution.—*Breeds* from Iceland, Faeroe Islands, British Isles, and northern Scandinavia east across central Russia, central and southern Siberia to Amurland, Ussuriland, and Anadyrland, south to southern Europe, northern Africa (Tunisia), Turkey, southern Russia, Turkestan, northern India, Tibet, western and northern China, and Mongolia.

Winters from southern Europe across southern Asia to the Philippines and south to southern Africa and the East Indies.

Accidental in Newfoundland (Knowles 1995, Mactavish 1996). Unsatisfactory sight reports from Nova Scotia and Texas.

Notes.—Known in the Old World literature as the Redshank.

Tringa erythropus (Pallas). Spotted Redshank.

Scolopax erythropus Pallas, 1764, in Vroeg, Cat. Rais. Ois., Adumbr., p. 6. (Holland.)

Habitat.—Marshy sites in bushy tundra and edge of the taiga (breeding); marshes, ponds, wet meadows, and mudflats (nonbreeding).

Distribution.—*Breeds* from Scandinavia, northern Russia, and northern Siberia south to central Russia, central Siberia, Anadyrland, and Kamchatka.

Winters from the Mediterranean region, Persian Gulf, India, and eastern China south to equatorial Africa, Sri Lanka, and Southeast Asia.

Migrates in fall regularly through the western and central Aleutians (Attu, Alaid, Shemya, Buldir, Adak), casually as far east as the Pribilofs (St. Paul).

Casual or accidental in British Columbia, Oregon, California, Kansas, southern Ontario,

Newfoundland, Nova Scotia, Massachusetts, Connecticut, New York, New Jersey, North Carolina, and Barbados; sight reports for Nevada, Saskatchewan, Ohio, and New Jersey.

Tringa glareola Linnaeus. Wood Sandpiper.

Tringa Glareola Linnaeus, 1758, Syst. Nat. (ed. 10) 1: 149. (in Europa = Sweden.)

Habitat.—Edges of ponds in the taiga (breeding); lakes, ponds, streams, wet meadows, bogs, and shallow pools, frequently in wooded regions (nonbreeding).

Distribution.—*Breeds* in North America in the western and central Aleutian Islands (Amchitka and Attu, probably also Adak and elsewhere); and in Eurasia from Scandinavia, northern Russia, and northern Siberia south to southern Europe, Turkestan, northern Mongolia, Kamchatka, the Kuril, and Commander islands, and the Chukotski Peninsula.

Winters from the Mediterranean region, Iran, India, northern Thailand, and southern China south to southern Africa, Sri Lanka, the Malay Peninsula, East Indies, and Australia.

Migrates in spring regularly through the western and central Aleutian islands, reaching as far north as St. Lawrence Island and as far east as the Pribilofs and the mainland of western Alaska (Seward Peninsula).

Casual or accidental in the Hawaiian Islands (Kure, Midway), northern (Barrow) and mainland southwestern Alaska (Ugasik Bay), Yukon (Herschel Island, Pauline Cove), British Columbia (Queen Charlotte Islands), New York, Bermuda, Barbados, the Faeroe and eastern Atlantic islands, and on western Pacific islands.

Tringa ochropus Linnaeus. Green Sandpiper.

Tringa Ocrophus [sic] Linnaeus, 1758, Syst. Nat. (ed. 10) 1: 149. (in Europa = Sweden.)

Habitat.—Woodlands, swamps, and marshes (breeding); marshes, flooded fields, wet meadows, and mudflats (nonbreeding).

Distribution.—*Breeds* in northern Eurasia.

Winters in Africa, southern Asia, and Australia.

Casual in Alaska in the western Aleutians (Attu, Nizki, Shemya) and on St. Lawrence Island (Gibson and Kessel 1992); early records for Hudson Bay and Nova Scotia are unsatisfactory (Godfrey 1986).

Notes.—The original spelling of *"Ocrophus"* has been suppressed and the name *"ochropus"* validated by the I.C.Z.N. (1952).

Tringa solitaria Wilson. Solitary Sandpiper.

Tringa solitaria Wilson, 1813, Amer. Ornithol. 7: 53, pl. 58, fig. 3. (Pocano Mt., Pa., Kentucky, and New York = Pocono Mountains, Pennsylvania.)

Habitat.—Bogs and ponds in coniferous forest, taiga, and muskeg, nesting in trees in deserted passerine nests (breeding); freshwater ponds, stream edges, temporary pools, flooded ditches, and fields, rarely on mudflats and open marshes (nonbreeding).

Distribution.—*Breeds* through central Alaska, and from northern Yukon, western and southern Mackenzie, northern Saskatchewan, northern Manitoba, northern and central Ontario, central Quebec, and central and southern Labrador south to mainland southeastern Alaska, northeastern and central British Columbia, south-central Alberta, central Saskatchewan, southern Manitoba, and northern Minnesota; also probably in west-central Oregon (Lane County).

Winters from northern Mexico (casually north to the southern United States) and the Bahamas south through Middle America, the West Indies, and South America south to central Argentina.

Migrates through the southern portions of the breeding range and south over most of the North American continent (rare on the Pacific coast).

Casual or accidental in the Hawaiian Islands (Hawaii), western and northern Alaska (the Pribilof Islands, Hooper Bay, Griffin Point, Barrow), Clipperton Island, Bermuda, Chile (sight report), South Georgia, Greenland, Iceland, the British Isles, Sweden, France, Spain, and South Africa.

Genus *CATOPTROPHORUS* Bonaparte

Catoptrophorus Bonaparte, 1827, Ann. Lyc. Nat. Hist. N. Y. 2: 323. Type, by monotypy, *Totanus semipalmatus* Temminck = *Scolopax semipalmata* Gmelin.

Notes.—See comments under *Tringa*.

Catoptrophorus semipalmatus (Gmelin). Willet.

Scolopax semipalmata Gmelin, 1789, Syst. Nat. 1(2): 659. (in Noveboraco = New York.)

Habitat.—Marshy lake and pond margins and wet meadows in western North America; salt marshes and beaches in eastern North America (breeding); marshes, tidal mudflats, beaches, and shallow lake margins (nonbreeding).

Distribution.—*Breeds* in western North America locally from eastern Oregon, southern Idaho, central Alberta, southern Saskatchewan, and southern Manitoba south to northeastern and east-central California, western Nevada, central Utah, northern Colorado, western and northern Nebraska, and eastern South Dakota, formerly in western Minnesota and north-western Iowa; in eastern North America locally along the Atlantic-Gulf coast from southern New Brunswick, Prince Edward Island, and Nova Scotia south to southern Florida and west to southern Texas and Tamaulipas; in the West Indies, on the Bahamas, Antilles (Cuba, Beata Island off Hispaniola, Anegada and St. Croix in the Virgin Islands, Antigua, and Guadeloupe, possibly also Barbuda, St. Martin, Anguilla, and St. Kitts), and in the Cayman Islands; and on Los Roques, off northern Venezuela. Nonbreeding individuals occur sporadically in summer as far south as northern South America.

Winters from northern California (casually from southwestern British Columbia and western Washington; also regularly inland in southeastern California at the Salton Sea), the Gulf coast, and Virginia south along both coasts of Middle America (including offshore islands), the West Indies, and both coasts of South America to the Galapagos Islands, central Chile, Uruguay, and southern Brazil.

Migrates primarily through coastal areas but also irregularly through most of the interior western and central United States, regularly east to the Great Lakes, casually elsewhere in the eastern United States.

Casual north to northeastern British Columbia, southern Hudson Bay, southern Quebec, and Newfoundland. Accidental in the Hawaiian Islands (Oahu, Maui), Bermuda, Finland, France, and the Azores; a sight report for Alaska (Minto Lakes).

Genus *HETEROSCELUS* Baird

Heteroscelus Baird, 1858, in Baird, Cassin, and Lawrence, Rep. Explor. Surv. R. R. Pac. 9: xxii, xlvii, 728, 734. Type, by monotypy, *Totanus brevipes* Vieillot.

Notes.—See comments under *Tringa*.

Heteroscelus incanus (Gmelin). Wandering Tattler.

Scolopax incana Gmelin, 1789, Syst. Nat. 1(2): 658. Based on the "Ash-coloured Snipe" Latham, Gen. Synop. Birds 3(1): 154. (in insulis Eimeo et Palmerston = Eimeo [Moorea] Island, Society Group, Pacific Ocean.)

Habitat.—Mountains and hilly regions, primarily along streams and lakes in areas that are rocky, mossy, or covered with scrubby vegetation, and in damp meadows, occasionally in forest clearings away from water (breeding); rocky seacoasts and islands, jetties, and sandy beaches of oceanic islands (nonbreeding).

Distribution.—*Breeds* in North America in mountains of western, central, and south-coastal Alaska, northern, central, and southern Yukon, and northwestern British Columbia; and in Eurasia in northeastern Siberia, Anadyrland, and the Chukotski Peninsula. Nonbreeding individuals regularly occur in summer on the wintering grounds.

Winters along the Pacific coast of the Americas from northern California (rarely Oregon, Washington, and British Columbia) south regularly to the Revillagigedo Islands and Oaxaca, and locally to El Salvador, Honduras (Bay of Fonseca), Nicaragua, Costa Rica (Cocos Island), Panama (Isla Coiba, Bay of Panama, and rarely to the Caribbean coast of the Canal area), Clipperton Island, Colombia (Malpelo Island), the Galapagos Islands, Ecuador, and Peru; and in the Pacific from the Hawaiian Islands, Marianas, and Philippines south to the Fiji, Samoa, Society, and Tuamotu islands.

Migrates regularly through the Aleutian Islands and along the Pacific coast of Central America.

Casual inland in North America (recorded northwestern Mackenzie, northeastern British Columbia, Alberta, eastern Washington, eastern Oregon, central and southeastern California, northeastern Baja California, Utah, and southern Arizona), and in the Pacific from the Bonin, Volcano, and Ryukyu islands, Japan, and Taiwan south to New Guinea, Australia, and New Zealand. Accidental in Texas (Galveston), Manitoba (Churchill), southern Ontario (Windmill Point, Fort Erie), and Massachusetts (Monomoy).

Notes.—*Heteroscelus incanus* and *H. brevipes* may constitute a superspecies, although their breeding ranges overlap marginally in eastern Siberia (Mayr and Short 1970).

Heteroscelus brevipes (Vieillot). Gray-tailed Tattler.

Totanus brevipes Vieillot, 1816, Nouv. Dict. Hist. Nat. (nouv. éd.) 6: 410. (Pays inconnu = Timor.)

Habitat.—Shores of streams, lakes, and ponds in mossy or scrubby hills (breeding); rocky coasts and sandy beaches (nonbreeding).

Distribution.—*Breeds* apparently in eastern Siberian mountains from Lake Baikal to the Verkhoyansk Mountains and Anadyrland, and on the southern Taimyr Peninsula, possibly also in Kamchatka and the Kuril Islands; nest and eggs unknown.

Winters from the Malay Peninsula, Philippines, and the Caroline, Mariana, and Marshall islands south to Christmas Island (in the Indian Ocean), Java, New Guinea, Australia, and Norfolk Island.

Migrates regularly through the Aleutian (east to Unalaska) and Pribilof islands, St. Lawrence Island, and along the coasts of Japan and China, casually along the coast to northern Alaska (Barrow) and south-coastal Alaska (Middleton Island).

Accidental in the Hawaiian Islands (Midway, Kure, Oahu), Washington (Leadbetter Point), and interior California (Lancaster), and in the British Isles; a sight report for Oregon.

Notes.—Also known as Polynesian Tattler. See comments under *H. incanus*.

Genus *ACTITIS* Illiger

Actitis Illiger, 1811, Prodromus, p. 262. Type, by subsequent designation (Stejneger, 1885), *Tringa hypoleucos* Linnaeus.

Notes.—See comments under *Tringa*.

Actitis hypoleucos (Linnaeus). Common Sandpiper.

Tringa Hypoleucos Linnaeus, 1758, Syst. Nat. (ed. 10) 1: 149. (in Europa = Sweden.)

Habitat.—Streams, rivers, lakes, and ponds (breeding); streams, ponds, lakes, and sea-coasts, generally with sandy or rocky margins, less frequently in marshes (nonbreeding).

Distribution.—*Breeds* from the British Isles, Scandinavia, northern Russia, and northern Siberia south to the Mediterranean region, northern Iran, Afghanistan, the Himalayas, Mongolia, Manchuria, Ussuriland, Kamchatka, the Kuril Islands, and Japan; also in East Africa (Uganda).

Winters from southern Europe, the Mediterranean region, Iraq, eastern China, and southern Japan south to southern Africa, Madagascar, Sri Lanka, islands in the eastern Indian Ocean, Australia, New Guinea, and islands of the western Pacific.

Migrates regularly through the western Aleutians (Near Islands), casually as far east as the Pribilof Islands (St. George, St. Paul) and central Aleutians (Adak), and as far north as St. Lawrence Island (also a sight report for Nome).

Notes.—*Actitis hypoleucos* and *A. macularia* constitute a superspecies (Mayr and Short 1970).

Actitis macularia (Linnaeus). Spotted Sandpiper.

> *Tringa macularia* Linnaeus, 1766, Syst. Nat. (ed. 12) 1: 249. Based mainly on the "Spotted Tringa" Edwards, Glean. Nat. Hist. 2: 139, pl. 277. (in Europa & America septentrionali = Pennsylvania.)

Habitat.—Sandy or muddy shores of streams, rivers, lakes, ponds, and coastal saltwater (breeding); also on rocky coasts and jetties (nonbreeding).

Distribution.—*Breeds* from central Alaska, northern Yukon, northwestern and central Mackenzie, southern Keewatin, northeastern Manitoba, northern Ontario, northern Quebec, Labrador, and Newfoundland south to southern Alaska (west to the base of the Alaska Peninsula), southern California, central Arizona, southern New Mexico, central Texas, the northern portions of the Gulf states (except Louisiana and Florida), North Carolina, Virginia, and Maryland. Occasional nonbreeding individuals remain in summer on the wintering grounds.

Winters from southwestern British Columbia, western Washington, western Montana (casually), southern Arizona, southern New Mexico, southern Texas, the southern portions of the Gulf states, and coastal South Carolina south through Middle America, the West Indies, and South America (also the Galapagos Islands, and all islands off the Caribbean coast) to northern Chile, northern Argentina, and Uruguay.

Migrates regularly along both coasts and through interior North America, and on Bermuda.

Casual or accidental in the Revillagigedo Islands (Socorro Island), on Clipperton Island, in the Hawaiian Islands (Oahu, Hawaii), Tristan da Cunha, Greenland, Iceland, the British Isles (reported breeding in Scotland; Hayman et al. 1986), continental Europe, the eastern Atlantic islands, Johnston Island, and the Marshall Islands.

Notes.—See comments under *A. hypoleucos.*

Genus *XENUS* Kaup

> *Xenus* Kaup, 1829, Skizz. Entw.-Ges. Eur. Thierw., p. 115. Type, by monotypy, *Scolopax cinerea* Güldenstädt.

Notes.—See comments under *Tringa.*

Xenus cinereus (Güldenstädt). Terek Sandpiper.

> *Scolopax cinerea* Güldenstädt, 1775, Novi Comm. Acad. Sci. Petropol. 19 (1774): 473, pl. 19. (ad mare caspium, circa ostium fluvii Terek = shores of the Caspian Sea at the mouth of the Terek River.)

Habitat.—River meadows, marshes, grassy banks of streams, ponds, and lakes, especially in wooded regions; winters also on mudflats and shallow estuaries and bays.

Distribution.—*Breeds* from Finland, northern Russia, and northern Siberia south to central Russia, Lake Baikal, and Anadyrland.

Winters from the Persian Gulf, southern Red Sea, Southeast Asia, and Hainan south to South Africa (along the coast of eastern Africa), Madagascar, India, Sri Lanka, the Andaman Islands, East Indies, New Guinea, and Australia.

Migrates regularly through the western Aleutians (Attu, Agattu, Shemya, Buldir), casually reaching St. Lawrence Island and the mainland of western (Seward Peninsula) and southern Alaska (Anchorage). Casual or accidental in British Columbia (Sooke), California (Carmel River), western Europe, North Africa, and New Zealand; sight reports for northeastern Manitoba and Massachusetts.

Notes.—The name *Scolopax cinerea* Güldenstädt, 1775 is not preoccupied by *Tringa cinerea* Brünnich, 1764 [= *Calidris canutus*], even if *Xenus* is merged in *Tringa* (Monroe 1989).

Tribe NUMENIINI: Curlews

Genus *BARTRAMIA* Lesson

> *Bartramia* Lesson, 1831, Traité Ornithol. 7: 553. Type, by monotypy, *Bartramia laticauda* Lesson = *Tringa longicauda* Bechstein.

Bartramia longicauda (Bechstein). Upland Sandpiper.

> *Tringa longicauda* Bechstein, 1812, in Latham, Allg. Uebers. Vögel 4(2): 452, pl. 42. (Nordamerika = North America.)

Habitat.—Grasslands, especially prairies, dry meadows, pastures, airport margins, and (in Alaska, Yukon) open woodlands at timberline (breeding); also along shores and mudflats (nonbreeding).

Distribution.—*Breeds* locally from north-central Alaska (Brooks Range, Alaska Range, and Wrangell Mountains), northern Yukon, central and northeastern British Columbia, extreme southwestern Mackenzie, northern Alberta, central Saskatchewan, southern Manitoba, western and southern Ontario, southern Quebec, central Maine, New Brunswick, and Prince Edward Island south in the interior to eastern Washington, northeastern Oregon, Idaho, Wyoming (except northwestern), northeastern (formerly southeastern) Colorado, northern Oklahoma, north-central Texas, central Missouri, southern Illinois, northern Kentucky, southern Ohio, West Virginia, central Virginia, and Maryland.

Winters in eastern South America from Surinam and northern Brazil south to central Argentina and Uruguay.

Migrates mostly through interior North America (rarely along Pacific coast from southern Alaska to Washington, and rarely in Nova Scotia and the South Atlantic coastal region) south through Middle America (rarely northwestern Mexico), the West Indies, and most of South America (including Tobago and Trinidad) east of the Andes.

Casual or accidental in California, Arizona, eastern Quebec, Bermuda, Chile, the Falkland Islands, Tristan da Cunha, Greenland, Iceland, the British Isles, continental Europe, the Azores, and Australia.

Notes.—Also known in Old World literature as Bartram's Sandpiper; formerly known as Upland Plover.

Genus *NUMENIUS* Brisson

> *Numenius* Brisson, 1760, Ornithologie 1: 48; 5: 311. Type, by tautonymy, *Numenius* Brisson = *Scolopax arquata* Linnaeus.
> *Phæopus* Cuvier, 1816, Règne Anim. 1: 485. Type, by tautonymy, *Scolopax phæopus* Linnaeus.
> *Mesoscolopax* Sharpe, 1896, Cat. Birds Brit. Mus. 24: 371. Type, by original designation, *Numenius minutus* Gould.

Numenius minutus Gould. Little Curlew.

> *Numenius minutus* Gould, 1841, Proc. Zool. Soc. London (1840), p. 176. (New South Wales, Australia.)

Habitat.—Grassy clearings and meadows in stunted subalpine forest.

Distribution.—*Breeds* in central Siberia.

Winters from Indonesia and the Philippines south to Australia and New Zealand.

Accidental in California (Santa Maria Valley, Santa Barbara County, 16 September-14 October 1984, photograph; Lehman and Dunn 1985, also one seen there 4–20 August 1993) and Alaska (Gambell, St. Lawrence Island, 7–8 June 1989, specimen; Gibson and Kessel 1992); additional sight reports for California.

Notes.—Also known as Little Whimbrel. See comments under *N. borealis*.

Numenius borealis (Forster). Eskimo Curlew.

> *Scolopax borealis* J. R. Forster, 1772, Philos. Trans. R. Soc. London 62: 431. (Fort Albany [on James Bay], Hudson Bay.)

Habitat.—Barren tundra (breeding); grasslands, pastures, plowed fields, and, less frequently, marshes and mudflats (nonbreeding).

Distribution.—Probably extinct. *Bred* formerly in northwestern Mackenzie, possibly west to western Alaska (Norton Sound).

Wintered formerly in southern South America from south-central Brazil south through

Paraguay and Uruguay to southern Argentina, and in Chile (Isla Chiloé); last sight report in winter from Argentina (near General Lavalle, Province of Buenos Aires, 17 January 1939).

Recorded in migration in spring from Chihuahua (Lake Palomas) and regularly north from Texas and Louisiana through the Mississippi and Missouri river drainages and west of the Great Lakes and Hudson Bay to the breeding grounds; recorded in fall west of Hudson Bay and regularly from southern Labrador and the Gulf of St. Lawrence to the New England coast, casually to the Great Lakes (Illinois, Michigan, and southern Ontario), along the Atlantic coast (to South Carolina), and in Bermuda and the West Indies (recorded on Puerto Rico, Guadeloupe, Carriacou in the Grenadines, Grenada, and Barbados).

Since the mid-1950's recorded (primarily sight reports) in spring from Texas (Galveston to Rockport, 1959–1963, with photographs from Galveston in March-April 1962), Manitoba (Lake Manitoba, May 1980) and Saskatchewan (Regina, 1982), and in fall from the west coast of James Bay (1976), Massachusetts (Plymouth Beach, 1970), New Jersey (Cape May, 1959), South Carolina (Charleston area, 1956), and Florida (Port Canaveral, 1960); last recorded specimen from Barbados (4 September 1963).

Casual or accidental formerly in the Pribilofs, Colorado, Montana, Baffin Island, Tobago, Trinidad, the Falkland Islands, Greenland, Iceland, and the British Isles.

Notes.—*Numenius borealis* and *N. minutus* may constitute a superspecies (Mayr and Short 1970).

Numenius phaeopus (Linnaeus). Whimbrel.

Scolopax Phæopus Linnaeus, 1758, Syst. Nat. (ed. 10) 1: 146. (in Europa = Sweden.)

Habitat.—Tundra (breeding); beaches, rocky coasts, tidal mudflats, marshes, estuaries, flooded fields, and pastures (nonbreeding).

Distribution.—*Breeds* [*hudsonicus* group] in North America from northern Alaska, northern Yukon, and northwestern Mackenzie south to western and central Alaska (Norton Sound, Alaska Range, Susitna River highlands) and southwestern Yukon, and along the western side of Hudson Bay from southern Keewatin south to northwestern James Bay (Lake River, Ontario); and [*phaeopus* group] in Eurasia from Iceland, the Faeroe Islands, northern Scandinavia, northern Russia, and northern Siberia south to the Orkney and Shetland islands, southern Scandinavia, central Russia, central Siberia, Anadyrland, and the Sea of Okhotsk. Recorded in summer and possibly breeding [*hudsonicus* group] on Banks and Southampton islands; nonbreeding birds also may summer in the wintering range, especially along the Atlantic and Gulf coasts of the United States, in the West Indies, and along the coasts of California and western South America.

Winters [*hudsonicus* group] in the Americas in coastal areas from southern British Columbia (rarely), Washington, the Gulf coast, and South Carolina (rarely farther north) south through Middle America, the Revillagigedo Islands, the West Indies (except Cuba), and South America (also the Galapagos Islands) to southern Chile and southern Brazil (casually to extreme northern Argentina); and [*phaeopus* group] in the Old World from the Mediterranean region (occasionally the British Isles), Arabia, India, Southeast Asia, and eastern China south to southern Africa, Madagascar, islands in the Indian Ocean, Australia, New Zealand, and the Fiji and Phoenix islands.

Migrates [*hudsonicus* group] primarily along the coast from southern Alaska (from Bristol Bay eastward, most commonly in spring), around Hudson and James bays, and (in fall) from Labrador and Newfoundland southward, regularly along the Great Lakes, locally (or casually) elsewhere in interior North America from southern Canada south to Arizona, New Mexico, and the Gulf states, and in Cuba; and [*phaeopus* group] through the western Aleutians (Near Islands), rarely to the Pribilof and St. Lawrence islands, and eastern Atlantic islands.

Casual [*hudsonicus* group] in the Hawaiian Islands, Clipperton Island, Bolivia, Europe, the Azores, and New Zealand; and [*phaeopus* group] in the Hawaiian Islands, mainland Alaska (Point Barrow), along the Atlantic coast of North America from southern Labrador, Newfoundland, and Nova Scotia south to New Jersey, and on Barbados; sight reports from Washington, Oregon, California, Ohio, Ontario, Quebec, Virginia, North Carolina, southern Florida, and the Virgin Islands.

Notes.—Groups: *N. hudsonicus* Latham, 1790 [Hudsonian Curlew] and *N. phaeopus*

[Whimbrel]. The two groups are genetically strongly differentiated (Zink et al. 1995) and may constitute two different species.

Numenius tahitiensis (Gmelin). Bristle-thighed Curlew.

Scolopax tahitiensis Gmelin, 1789, Syst. Nat. 1(2): 656. Based on the "Otaheite Curlew" Latham, Gen. Synop. Birds 3(1): 122. (in Tahiti [Society Islands].)

Habitat.—Montane tundra with scattered shrubs (breeding); coastal tundra, grassy fields, tidal mudflats, and beaches (nonbreeding).

Distribution.—*Breeds* in western Alaska (near the mouth of the Yukon River and on the Seward Peninsula); nonbreeding birds occur in summer on coastal tundra from Kotzebue Sound south to Hooper Bay, and occasionally in the Hawaiian Islands.

Winters on Pacific islands from the Hawaiian (most commonly from Midway east to French Frigate Shoals) and Marshall islands south to the Fiji, Tonga, Samoa, Marquesas, and Tuamotu islands.

Migrates regularly in spring through south-coastal Alaska (Cook Inlet to Prince William Sound and Middleton Island).

Casual in western Alaska (the Pribilof and Aleutian islands) and British Columbia (Vancouver Island), and west to the Mariana and Caroline islands. Accidental in Japan.

Numenius madagascariensis (Linnaeus). Far Eastern Curlew.

Scolopax madagascariensis Linnaeus, 1766, Syst. Nat. (ed. 12) 1: 242. Based on "Le Courly de Madagascar" Brisson, Ornithologie 5: 321, pl. 28. (in Madagascar, error = Macassar, Sulawesi.)

Habitat.—Moorlands and wet meadows (breeding); mudflats, beaches, and occasionally marshes (nonbreeding).

Distribution.—*Breeds* from eastern Siberia and Kamchatka south to Transbaicalia, northern Mongolia, northern Manchuria, and Ussuriland.

Winters from Taiwan and the Philippines south to the East Indies, New Guinea, Australia, and (rarely) New Zealand.

Migrates regularly in spring through the Aleutian Islands (Attu, Adak, Shemya, Buldir, Amchitka, Nizki), casually reaching the Pribilof Islands (St. Paul, St. George).

Accidental in British Columbia (Boundary Bay, Delta).

Numenius tenuirostris Vieillot. Slender-billed Curlew.

Numenius tenuirostris Vieillot, 1817, Nouv. Dict. Hist. Nat. (nouv. éd.) 8: 302. (Egypt.)

Habitat.— Boggy areas in steppe country (breeding); mudflats, beaches, marshes, and wet fields (nonbreeding).

Distribution.—*Breeds* in southwestern Siberia.

Winters along beaches and mudflats west to the Mediterranean region, straggling to the British Isles and northwestern Africa; nearing extinction.

Accidental in Ontario (Crescent Beach, fall, "about 1925"; Beardslee and Mitchell 1965).

Numenius arquata (Linnaeus). Eurasian Curlew.

Scolopax Arquata Linnaeus, 1758, Syst. Nat. (ed. 10) 1: 145. (in Europa = Sweden.)

Habitat.—Grasslands and marshes (breeding); beaches, on mudflats and in wet meadows (nonbreeding).

Distribution.—*Breeds* from northern Eurasia south to southern Europe and the Gobi Desert region.

Winters from the southern parts of the breeding range south to southern Africa, Madagascar, the Indian Ocean, Southeast Asia, and the East Indies.

Accidental in Newfoundland (Ferryland), New York (Long Island), Massachusetts (Monomoy, Martha's Vineyard, Tuckernuck Island), and Greenland; sight reports for Nova Scotia, Florida, and the Bahama Islands (Eleuthera).

Notes.—Also known as Common Curlew and, in Old World literature, as the Curlew. *Numenius arquata* and *N. americanus* may constitute a superspecies (Mayr and Short 1970).

Numenius americanus Bechstein. Long-billed Curlew.

Numenius americanus Bechstein, 1812, in Latham, Allg. Uebers. Vögel 4(2): 432. (New York.)

Habitat.—Prairies and grassy meadows, sagebrush, generally near water or wet areas (breeding); tidal mudflats, marshes, wet fields, and wet grasslands (nonbreeding).

Distribution.—*Breeds* (at least locally) from south-central British Columbia, southern Alberta, southern Saskatchewan, and southern Manitoba (formerly) south to east-central California, central Nevada, central Utah, central New Mexico, and northern Texas, and east to southwestern North Dakota, northwestern South Dakota, north-central Nebraska, and southwestern Kansas, formerly also to North Dakota, northwestern Iowa, Wisconsin, and Illinois. Small numbers of nonbreeding individuals occasionally summer in the winter range.

Winters from southwestern British Columbia (rarely), Washington, southern Arizona (rarely), extreme northern Mexico, southern Texas, southern Louisiana, southern Alabama, and coastal South Carolina south to southern Mexico (Oaxaca, Veracruz, and the Yucatan Peninsula) and southern Florida, irregularly through northern Central America to Honduras and Costa Rica.

Casual in southern Mackenzie, Minnesota, Missouri, Arkansas, the Atlantic coast (north to New Brunswick, at least formerly), Belize, and the Greater Antilles (Cuba, Jamaica); sight reports for southeastern Alaska, eastern James Bay (Brae Island), southern Ontario, Ohio, Tennessee, the Virgin Islands. Accidental in Panama (Canal area) and northeastern Venezuela.

Notes.—See comments under *N. arquata*.

Tribe LIMOSINI: Godwits

Genus *LIMOSA* Brisson

Limosa Brisson, 1760, Ornithologie 1: 48; 5: 261. Type, by tautonymy, *Limosa* Brisson = *Scolopax limosa* Linnaeus.
Vetola Mathews, 1913, Birds Aust. 3(2): 191. Type, by original designation, *Scolopax lapponicus* Linnaeus.

Limosa limosa (Linnaeus). Black-tailed Godwit.

Scolopax Limosa Linnaeus, 1758, Syst. Nat. (ed. 10) 1: 147. (in Europa = Sweden.)

Habitat.—Marshy grasslands, wet meadows, steppe, and moorlands (breeding); marshes, flooded fields, beaches, and mudflats (nonbreeding).

Distribution.—*Breeds* in Iceland, the Faeroe Islands, southern Scandinavia, the Baltic countries, central Russia, central Siberia, and Kamchatka south to southern Europe, southern Russia, Lake Baikal, Mongolia, and the Sea of Okhotsk.

Winters in the British Isles, Mediterranean region, India, Burma, China, and the Philippines south to east-central Africa, Sri Lanka (rarely), Malaysia, the East Indies, Australia, and Tasmania.

Migrates regularly in spring through the western Aleutian Islands (casually east to Adak), casually as far east as the Pribilof (St. Paul), St. Lawrence, and Little Diomede islands, the mainland of western (Golovin), southwestern (Naknek), and south-coastal Alaska (Kodiak Island).

Casual or accidental in Newfoundland, on Miquelon Island, and in Massachusetts (Dartmouth), Pennsylvania (Philadelphia), New Jersey (Brigantine), North Carolina (Bodie Island), Florida (Merritt Island), Louisiana (Vermilion Parish); sight reports for Ontario, Quebec, Delaware, the Lesser Antilles (St. Kitts, Barbados), and South Africa.

Limosa haemastica (Linnaeus). Hudsonian Godwit.

> *Scolopax Hæmastica* Linnaeus, 1758, Syst. Nat. (ed. 10) 1: 147. Based on "The Red-breasted Godwit" Edwards, Nat. Hist. Birds 3: 138, pl. 138. (in America septentrionali = Hudson Bay.)

Habitat.—Grassy tundra near water (breeding); marshes, flooded fields, rice fields, and tidal mudflats (nonbreeding).

Distribution.—*Breeds* locally in south-coastal Alaska (Cook Inlet area) and probably also in western Alaska (Kotzebue Sound and Norton Bay); in Mackenzie (Fort Anderson, Great Slave Lake, and mouth of Mackenzie River area) and northwestern British Columbia (Chilkat Pass); and around Hudson Bay (in northeastern Manitoba and northern Ontario). Recorded in summer in central and northern Alaska, in north-central Mackenzie (Bathurst Inlet), in the interior of Southampton Island, and on Akimiski Island in James Bay.

Winters in South America on the coasts of Peru and Chile (from Isla Chiloé south to the Straits of Magellan), and from Paraguay, southern Brazil, and Uruguay south to Tierra del Fuego and the Falkland Islands, casually also in New Zealand.

Migrates in spring primarily through the interior of North America from Texas and Louisiana north to northeastern British Columbia, Alberta, Saskatchewan, and the west side of Hudson Bay, along the Pacific coast of Oaxaca, Chiapas, Guatemala, and Costa Rica, and in Tamaulipas and Veracruz; in fall mostly southeastward from James Bay to the Maritime Provinces and New England, thence by sea southward, regularly recorded on Barbados and casually on Guadeloupe.

Casual in coastal and interior western North America from British Columbia, Idaho, and Montana south to southern California, Arizona, and New Mexico, in the interior of the eastern United States, in Newfoundland, along the Atlantic coast (south to Florida and west to Mississippi, primarily in fall), in southeastern Mexico (Distrito Federal), the Bahamas (Eleuthera), Greater Antilles (recorded definitely from Cuba, Hispaniola, Puerto Rico, and the Virgin Islands), coastal Venezuela (including Curaçao), Trinidad, and Bolivia. Accidental in the Hawaiian Islands (Oahu), Britain, Denmark, South Africa, and Marshall Islands (Kwajalein); sight reports for Yucatan Peninsula and Panama.

Limosa lapponica (Linnaeus). Bar-tailed Godwit.

> *Scolopax lapponica* Linnaeus, 1758, Syst. Nat. (ed. 10) 1: 147. (in Lapponia = Lapland.)

Habitat.—Coastal tundra and sedge–dwarf shrub tundra of foothills (breeding); tidal mudlfats, less frequently marshes and flooded fields (nonbreeding).

Distribution.—*Breeds* in North America in Alaska from Wales and the Yukon River Delta east (rarely) to Point Barrow and the Sagavanirktok River Delta; and in Eurasia from northern Scandinavia east across northern Russia and northern Siberia to the Chukotski Peninsula and northern Anadyrland.

Winters from the British Isles, North Sea, Mediterranean region, Black Sea, Iraq, and the Persian Gulf south to central Africa, islands of the northern Indian Ocean and Sri Lanka, casually to the Azores, Canary Islands, southern Africa, Madagascar, the Seychelles, and Maldive Islands; and from southeastern China, Taiwan, and the Philippines south to the East Indies, western Polynesia, Australia, New Zealand, and the Chatham Islands.

Migrates through the Aleutian and Pribilof islands, along the Bering Sea coast of the Alaska Peninsula, and in the Pacific from the coast of Japan south through the islands of Polynesia to the Gilbert, Samoa, and Tonga islands, rarely along the Pacific coast from south-coastal Alaska (west to Kodiak) and British Columbia south to northern Baja California.

Casual in the Hawaiian Islands, in the Atlantic coastal region (Newfoundland, Quebec, Maine, Massachusetts, New York, New Jersey, Virginia, North Carolina, and Florida), and in Iceland and the Faeroe and Cape Verde islands. Accidental in the Virgin Islands (St. Croix) and Venezuela. Sight reports for Saskatchewan and Nova Scotia.

Limosa fedoa (Linnaeus). Marbled Godwit.

> *Scolopax Fedoa* Linnaeus, 1758, Syst. Nat. (ed. 10) 1: 146. Based on "The Greater American Godwit" Edwards, Nat. Hist. Birds 3: 137, pl. 137. (in America septentrionali = Hudson Bay.)

Habitat.—Grasslands, prairie sloughs, marshes, and ponds, locally tundra (breeding); primarily tidal mudflats and marshes (nonbreeding).

Distribution.—*Breeds* in Alaska on the Alaska Peninsula (Ugashik Bay in the vicinity of the King Salmon and Dog Salmon rivers, probably in the Cinder River area, and possibly as far south and west as Port Heiden) and from east-central Alberta, south-central Saskatchewan, and southern Manitoba, western Ontario (Rainy River, also an isolated breeding population in northern Ontario on the southwestern coast of James Bay and Akimiski Island) south to central and eastern Montana, northeastern Colorado (once), North Dakota, northeastern South Dakota, and northwestern Minnesota, formerly to central Iowa, east-central Minnesota, and southern Wisconsin. Nonbreeding birds occur in summer in the winter range.

Winters from south-coastal British Columbia (rarely), coastal Washington, western Nevada, the Gulf coast and coastal South Carolina south to Florida, and along both coasts of Middle America (irregular or local south of Mexico) to Colombia and Venezuela, rarely south to northern Chile.

Migrates primarily through interior western North America and along the California coast, regularly north on the Pacific coast to British Columbia and southeastern and south-coastal Alaska, and, primarily in fall, casually through interior eastern North America and along the Atlantic coast from southern Ontario, Quebec, New Brunswick, Prince Edward Island, Nova Scotia, and Newfoundland south to the Greater Antilles (east to Anegada in the Virgin Islands) and Grand Cayman in the Cayman Islands.

Accidental in the Hawaiian (Laysan, Hawaii) and Galapagos islands; reports from the Lesser Antilles, Tobago, and Trinidad are questionable.

Tribe ARENARIINI: Turnstones

Notes.—Formerly (A.O.U. 1957) considered a subfamily, the Arenariinae, which included the genus *Aphriza,* now regarded as related to *Calidris* (Jehl 1968a).

Genus *ARENARIA* Brisson

Arenaria Brisson, 1760, Ornithologie 1: 48; 5: 132. Type, by tautonymy, *Arenaria* Brisson = *Tringa interpres* Linnaeus.

Arenaria interpres (Linnaeus). Ruddy Turnstone.

Tringa Interpres Linnaeus, 1758, Syst. Nat. (ed. 10) 1: 148. (in Europa & America septentrionali = Gotland, Sweden.)

Habitat.—Tundra, usually near water; in winter, rocky coasts, jetties, beaches, rarely tidal mudflats; in migration, also bare lake-shores and occasionally wet dirt fields.

Distribution.—*Breeds* in North America from northern Alaska and the Canadian Arctic islands (Banks east to Ellesmere, Devon, southwestern Baffin, and Mansel islands) south to western Alaska (St. Lawrence Island and the Yukon River delta); and in the Palearctic from northern Greenland, Iceland, northern Scandinavia, Spitsbergen, Novaya Zemlya, and the New Siberian Islands south to central Greenland, the west coast of Norway, islands in the Baltic Sea, and the northern Siberian coast (east to the Bering Sea). Nonbreeding birds may be found in summer through the winter range.

Winters in the Pacific from the Hawaiian Islands southward; in North America in coastal areas from British Columbia, the Gulf coast, and southern New England (casually north to Nova Scotia) south along both coasts of Middle America (including Clipperton and the Revillagigedo Islands, off Mexico), through the West Indies, and along both coasts of South America (including the Galapagos Islands, Netherlands Antilles, Tobago, and Trinidad) to Tierra del Fuego; and in the Old World from the British Isles, southern Scandinavia, the Mediterranean region, Canary Islands, and southeastern China south to southern Africa, India, Indonesia, Australia, and New Zealand.

Migrates in North America regularly through the Aleutian and Pribilof islands, from Hudson Bay east to Labrador and Newfoundland (mostly in fall), and along the Atlantic coast from the Maritime Provinces southward, and in the Old World primarily along coastal areas between breeding and wintering ranges; in small numbers through the prairie areas of the Canadian provinces, the lower Great Lakes, and the Mississippi and Ohio valleys; rarely along the Pacific coast from southeastern Alaska south to northern and interior southeastern California (to Salton Sea); and casually elsewhere through the interior of central and western North America, and to Bermuda.

Accidental in Jan Mayen and Franz Josef Land.

Notes.—Known in Old World literature as the Turnstone.

Arenaria melanocephala (Vigors). Black Turnstone.

Strepsilas melanocephalus Vigors, 1829, Zool. J. 4 (1828): 356. (northwest coast of [North] America.)

Habitat.—Coastal salt-grass tundra (breeding); rocky seacoasts and offshore islets, jetties, less frequently in seaweed on beaches and tidal mudflats (nonbreeding).

Distribution.—*Breeds* locally along the coast of western and southern Alaska, from southern Kotzebue Sound south to the Yukon-Kuskokwim delta and the north side of the Alaska Peninsula. Nonbreeding birds may be found in summer through the wintering range.

Winters from south-coastal and southeastern Alaska (west to Kodiak) south along the Pacific coast to southern Baja California and central Sonora.

Casual in the central Aleutians (Amchitka), Pribilofs (St. Paul), and inland in central Alaska, Yukon (Watson Lake, Kluane Lake), British Columbia (Atlin, Nulki Lake), Montana (Glacier National Park), Oregon (Washington County), and California. Accidental in Wisconsin (Winnebago County); a sight report for Nayarit.

Tribe CALIDRIDINI: Calidridine Sandpipers

Genus *APHRIZA* Audubon

Aphriza Audubon, 1839, Ornithol. Biogr. 5: 249. Type, by monotypy, *Aphriza townsendi* Audubon = *Tringa virgata* Gmelin.

Notes.—*Aphriza* was formerly (A.O.U. 1957) included in the subfamily Arenariinae, but it is closely related to *Calidris* (Jehl 1968a).

Aphriza virgata (Gmelin). Surfbird.

Tringa virgata Gmelin, 1789, Syst. Nat. 1(2): 674. Based on the "Streaked Sandpiper" Latham, Gen. Synop. Birds 3(1): 180. (in sinu Sandwich = Prince William Sound, Alaska.)

Habitat.—Rocky tundra above treeline in interior mountains (breeding); primarily rocky seacoasts and islands, jetties (nonbreeding).

Distribution.—*Breeds* widely in the mountain systems of western, central, and south-coastal Alaska (including Kodiak Island) and Yukon (except southeastern part). Occasional nonbreeding individuals summer as far south as Panama, and others have been recorded in summer (and possibly breeding) in western Alaska (from Kotzebue Sound south to Hooper and Goodnews bays).

Winters along the Pacific coast from south-coastal and southeastern Alaska (west to Kodiak) south along the Pacific coast of North America, Middle America (not recorded Honduras) and South America to Tierra del Fuego.

Casual in central Alberta (Beaverhill Lake), interior California, the Gulf coast of Texas (Galveston, Port Aransas, Padre Island), and Florida (Escambia and Lee counties); a sight report for western Pennsylvania and in the Revillagigedo Islands (Socorro Island).

Genus *CALIDRIS* Merrem

Calidris Anonymous [= Merrem], 1804, Allg. Lit. Ztg. 2(168): col. 542. Type, by tautonymy, *Tringa calidris* Gmelin = *Tringa canutus* Linnaeus.

Ereunetes Illiger, 1811, Prodromus, p. 262. Type, by monotypy, *Ereunetes petrificatus* Illiger = *Tringa pusilla* Linnaeus.

Erolia Vieillot, 1816, Analyse, p. 55. Type, by monotypy, *Erolia variegata* Vieillot = *Scolopax testacea* Pallas.

Pelidna Cuvier, 1816, Règne Anim. 1: 490. Type, by subsequent designation (G. R. Gray, 1840), *Tringa cinclus* Linnaeus = *Tringa alpina* Linnaeus.

Crocethia Billberg, 1828, Synop. Faunae Scand. (ed. 2) 1(2): 132. Type, by monotypy, *Charadrius calidris* Linnaeus = *Trynga alba* Pallas.

Pisobia Billberg, 1828, Synop. Faunae Scand. (ed. 2) 1(2): 136, tab. A. Type, by subsequent designation (A.O.U. Comm., 1908), *Tringa minuta* Leisler.

Actodromas Kaup, 1829, Natürl. Syst., p. 55. Type *Tringa minuta* Leisler = *Calidris minuta* Leisler.

Arquatella Baird, 1858, in Baird, Cassin, and Lawrence, Rep. Explor. Surv. R. R. Pac. 9: 714, 717. Type, by original designation, *Tringa maritima* Brünnich.

Micropalama Baird, 1858, in Baird, Cassin, and Lawrence, Rep. Explor. Surv. R. R. Pac. 9: xxii, xlvii, 714, 726. Type, by monotypy, *Tringa himantopus* Bonaparte.

Notes.—See comments under *Eurynorhynchus.*

Calidris tenuirostris (Horsfield). Great Knot.

Totanus tenuirostris Horsfield, 1821, Trans. Linn. Soc. London 13(1): 192. (Java.)

Habitat.—Barren or stony mountain tundra (breeding); rocky seacoasts, sandy beaches, and tidal mudflats (nonbreeding).

Distribution.—*Breeds* in the mountains of northeastern Siberia from the lower Kolyma to Anadyrland, probably also from the Verkhoyansk Mountains east to the Sea of Okhotsk.

Winters from the Persian Gulf, India, and Malaysia east and south to the Philippines, East Indies, New Guinea, and Australia.

Migrates regularly along the coast of eastern Asia from Kamchatka south to Taiwan and the Ryukyu Islands, rarely in the interior of Siberia, and casually in spring through southwestern and western Alaska in the Aleutians (Shemya, Adak), Pribilofs (St. Paul), and on St. Lawrence Island and the Seward Peninsula.

Accidental in Oregon (Bandon), England, Morocco, and Arabia.

Calidris canutus (Linnaeus). Red Knot.

Tringa Canutus Linnaeus, 1758, Syst. Nat. (ed. 10) 1: 149. (in Europa = Sweden.)

Habitat.—Barren or stony tundra, but usually near water (breeding); primarily seacoasts on tidal mudflats and beaches; migrants inland usually found on extensive mudflats or bare lake-shores (nonbreeding).

Distribution.—*Breeds* in North America in northwestern and northern Alaska (Seward Peninsula and Delong Mountains, rarely at Point Barrow and Cooper Island) and the Canadian Arctic islands east to Ellesmere and south to Victoria and Southampton, probably also on the Adelaide Peninsula and Mansel Island; and in the Palearctic from northern Greenland and Spitsbergen east to the New Siberian and Wrangel islands. Nonbreeding individuals occasionally summer in the wintering range, especially on the Atlantic and Gulf coasts of the United States.

Winters in the Americas in coastal regions from southern British Columbia (rarely), Washington, the Gulf coast, and Massachusetts south to Tierra del Fuego, generally less commonly north of southern South America; and in the Old World from the British Isles, southern Europe, the Black Sea, India, Southeast Asia, and the Philippines south to central Africa, Australia, and New Zealand, casually to the Azores, South Africa, and Sri Lanka.

Migrates in North America primarily along the Atlantic coast from New Brunswick and Nova Scotia south to Florida (rarely in fall in southern Labrador and Newfoundland), through the Great Lakes region, along the Pacific coast from southern Alaska and British Columbia southward (including interior southeastern California at the Salton Sea), irregularly along the coasts of Middle America (not recorded Nicaragua) and South America (including Trinidad), locally (or casually) elsewhere through the interior of North America and through the West Indies (recorded Greater Antilles in Cuba [sight reports], the Cayman Islands, the Virgin Islands, the northern Lesser Antilles, Martinique, and Barbados); and in the Old

World generally in coastal areas through regions between the breeding and wintering ranges, casually through the eastern Atlantic islands.

Casual or accidental in the Hawaiian Islands (Kauai, Oahu), on islands in the Bering Sea, and in Bermuda, the Galapagos Islands, and Bolivia.

Calidris alba (Pallas). Sanderling.

> *Trynga alba* Pallas, 1764, in Vroeg, Cat. Raisonné Ois., Adumbr., p. 7. (de Noordsche Zeekusten = coast of the North Sea.)

Habitat.—Dry sedge, barren, or stony tundra, but generally near water (breeding); primarily sandy beaches, less frequently on mudflats, bare shores of lakes or rivers, jetties, and rocky seacoasts (nonbreeding).

Distribution.—*Breeds* in North America in northern Alaska (Barrow), and from Banks, Prince Patrick, Lougheed, and northern Ellesmere islands south to northern Mackenzie, western Victoria Island, northern Keewatin (Melville Peninsula), the northwest coast of Hudson Bay (Cape Fullerton), and Southampton and northern Baffin islands; and in the Palearctic in northern Greenland, Spitsbergen, the Taimyr Peninsula, Severnaya Zemlya, mouth of the Lena River, and the New Siberian Islands. Nonbreeding birds occur in summer in the winter range.

Winters in the Hawaiian Islands; in the Americas in the Aleutians (locally), and from southern Alaska (west to the Aleutians), the Gulf coast, and Massachusetts (casually north to Nova Scotia) south along the coasts of North America and Middle America, through the West Indies, and along the coasts of South America to Tierra del Fuego (also in interior southeastern California at the Salton Sea); in the Old World from the British Isles, Outer Hebrides, Mediterranean region, Caspian Sea, Gulf of Oman, northern India, Burma, and China south to South Africa, Madagascar, southern India, the Maldive Islands, Sri Lanka, the East Indies and Australia; and on Pacific islands from the Mariana and Marshall islands south to the Phoenix, Union, and Galapagos islands.

Migrates in North America along the Pacific coast from the Aleutians and southern Alaska, the Atlantic coast from Newfoundland, and through the interior in the prairie areas of the Canadian provinces and from the Great Lakes southward, locally elsewhere in the interior and north to Labrador.

Casual on Clipperton Island, Jan Mayen, Franz Josef Land, and New Zealand.

Calidris pusilla (Linnaeus). Semipalmated Sandpiper.

> *Tringa pusilla* Linnaeus, 1766, Syst. Nat. (ed. 12) 1: 252. Based on "La petite Alouette-de-mer de S. Domingue" Brisson, Ornithologie 5: 222, pl. 25, fig. 2. (in Domingo = Hispaniola.)

Habitat.—Open low-lying tundra, generally near water (breeding); mudflats, beaches, shores of shallow lakes and ponds, freshwater marshes, and occasionally wet meadows (nonbreeding).

Distribution.—*Breeds* from the Arctic coast of western and northern Alaska (south to Norton Bay), northern Yukon, northern Mackenzie, Canadian Arctic islands (Banks, Victoria, King William, central Baffin, and probably also Melville and Somerset islands), and northern Labrador south to western Alaska (mouth of the Yukon River), east-central Mackenzie, southeastern Keewatin, northeastern Manitoba, Southampton Island, northern Ontario (Cape Henrietta Maria), northern Quebec, and coastal Labrador; also in eastern Siberia. Nonbreeding individuals often summer in coastal North America south to the Gulf coast and Panama.

Winters from southern Florida and the Bahamas south through the West Indies (also the northern Yucatan Peninsula and possibly elsewhere along the Gulf-Caribbean coast of Middle America) and along the Caribbean-Atlantic coast of South America (including Tobago and Trinidad) to Paraguay and southern Brazil, casually to southern Argentina; and along the Pacific coast of Middle America and South America from Chiapas south to northern Chile.

Migrates primarily along the Atlantic-Gulf coast of North America from Newfoundland southward, through the interior of North America east of the Rockies, and rarely but regularly through the Pribilofs, along the Pacific coast from British Columbia south to northern Baja California, and through the interior of western North America.

Casual in the Hawaiian Islands (Oahu), Aleutian Islands, Bermuda, the Galapagos Islands, Greenland, the British Isles, continental Europe, and the Azores.

Calidris mauri (Cabanis). Western Sandpiper.

Ereunetes Mauri Cabanis, 1857, J. Ornithol. 4 (1856): 419. (Cuba.)

Habitat.—Coastal, hilly sedge–dwarf tundra, generally near water (breeding); mudflats, beaches, shores of shallow lakes and ponds, and flooded fields, in winter primarily on tidal mudflats (nonbreeding).

Distribution.—*Breeds* on islands in the Bering Sea (St. Lawrence, Nunivak) and along the coasts of western and northern Alaska (from Bristol Bay and the Kashunuk River to the Seward Peninsula and, less frequently, Point Barrow and Camden Bay), and in northeastern Siberia. Nonbreeding birds summer south at least to Panama.

Winters from the coast of Washington (rarely from southern Alaska) and North Carolina (rarely New Jersey) south along both coasts of North America and Middle America, and through the West Indies to South America (including the Netherlands Antilles and Trinidad), on the Pacific coast to northern Peru and the Atlantic coast east to Surinam, casually in western and southern Arizona and southern New Mexico.

Migrates most commonly through the Pacific region from Alaska to South America, less commonly through the interior from central British Columbia, central Alberta, southern Saskatchewan, southern (casually northeastern) Manitoba, and southern Ontario southward, regularly in small numbers (especially in fall) through the Pribilofs, along the Atlantic coast from New England (rarely Quebec, New Brunswick, and Nova Scotia) southward, and casually to the Aleutians.

Casual in the Hawaiian, Clipperton, and Galapagos islands. Accidental in the British Isles, western Europe, the Azores, Canary Islands, Madeira, Tasmania, and Japan. Sight report for the Revillagigedo Islands (Socorro Island).

Calidris ruficollis (Pallas). Red-necked Stint.

Trynga ruficollis Pallas, 1776, Reise Versch. Prov. Russ. Reichs 3: 700. (circa Lacus salsos Dauuriae campestris = Kulussutai, eastern Siberia.)

Habitat.—Marshy or mossy tundra and nearby rivers (breeding); tidal mudflats, beaches, and marshes (nonbreeding).

Distribution.—*Breeds* in North America in northern and western Alaska (Point Barrow and Seward Peninsula); and in Eurasia in northeastern Siberia (Chukotski Peninsula to Anadyrland and Koryakland). Recorded in summer (and possibly breeding) elsewhere in Alaska (Kotzebue Sound, St. Lawrence Island).

Winters from southern China south to the Andaman and Nicobar islands, East Indies, New Guinea, the Bismarck and Solomon islands, Australia, Tasmania, and New Zealand.

Migrates regularly through the western and central Aleutians, islands in the Bering Sea, and the mainland coast of northwestern and western Alaska (east rarely as far as the Colville River Delta), and casually from south-coastal and southeastern Alaska south along the Pacific coast of British Columbia (Fraser River delta), Oregon, and California.

Casual or accidental in the Hawaiian Islands, Ohio (Ashtabula), New York, Maine (Biddeford Pool), Massachusetts (Monomoy, Scituate), Connecticut (Guilford), and Delaware (Little Creek, Point Mahon). Sight reports for the Hawaiian Islands (Kure), Alberta, Nevada, Saskatchewan, Ontario, Missouri, Virginia, Peru, and South Africa.

Notes.—Also known as Rufous-necked Stint or Rufous-necked Sandpiper.

Calidris minuta (Leisler). Little Stint.

Tringa minuta Leisler, 1812, Nactr. Bechstein's Naturgesch. Dtsch., pt. 1, p. 74. (region of Hanau am Main, Germany.)

Habitat.—Mossy or wet tundra (breeding); marshes, flooded fields, and mudflats (nonbreeding).

Distribution.—*Breeds* from northern Scandinavia east to the Chukotski Peninsula.

Winters in Africa and the Indian region.

Migrates rarely (or casually) through northern Alaska (Barrow), the western Aleutians (Attu, Shemya, Buldir), the Pribilofs (St. Paul, St. George), and St. Matthews and St. Lawrence islands.

Casual or accidental in the Hawaiian Islands (Kure, Oahu), British Columbia (Richmond Delta), Oregon, California, Ontario, New York, New Brunswick, Nova Scotia, Massachusetts, North Carolina, and Bermuda. Sight reports for Tennessee, New Jersey, and Delaware.

Calidris temminckii (Leisler). Temminck's Stint.

> *Tringa Temminckii* Leisler, 1812, Nachtr. Bechstein's Naturgesch. Dtsch., pt. 1, p. 64. (region of Hanau am Main, Germany.)

Habitat.—Mossy or wet tundra, and grassy meadows in the taiga (breeding); mudflats, shallow marshes, shores of lakes and ponds, flooded fields and, rarely, tidal flats (nonbreeding).

Distribution.—*Breeds* from northern Scandinavia east across northern Russia to northern Siberia, and south to the Chukotski Peninsula and Anadyrland. Nonbreeding individuals summer south to Lake Baikal.

Winters from the Mediterranean region, Arabia, Iraq, Iran, India, southeastern China, and Taiwan south to central Africa, Sri Lanka, the Maldive Islands, Southeast Asia, and Borneo, casually in Japan and the Philippines.

Migrates casually through the Aleutians (Attu, Shemya, Buldir, Adak) and islands in the Bering Sea (St. Matthew, St. Lawrence, Pribilofs).

Accidental in British Columbia (Reifel Island, Delta) and South Africa. A sight report for northern Alaska (Wales).

Calidris subminuta (Middendorff). Long-toed Stint.

> *Tringa subminuta* Middendorff, 1853, Reise Sib. 2(2): 222. (Höhen des Westabhanges vom Stanowoi Gebirge und des Nähe des Ausflusses des Uda = Stanovoi Mountains, Siberia.)

Habitat.—Mossy or wet tundra (breeding); sandy beaches, mudflats and shores of lakes and ponds (nonbreeding).

Distribution.—*Breeds* in the Commander Islands, in Anadyrland and (probably) Kamchatka, and on Sakhalin and the northern Kuril Islands.

Winters from eastern India, southeastern China, Taiwan, and the Philippines south to Sri Lanka, the East Indies, and northern Australia.

Migrates regularly through the western Aleutians (from the Near Islands east rarely as far as Adak), casually to the Pribilofs (Otter, St. Paul, St. George), St. Lawrence Island, and western mainland Alaska (Wales).

Accidental in the northwestern Hawaiian Islands, Oregon (South Jetty, Columbia River), California (Salinas), England, and South Africa; reports from British Columbia and Connecticut require confirmation.

Calidris minutilla (Vieillot). Least Sandpiper.

> *Tringa minutilla* Vieillot, 1819, Nouv. Dict. Hist. Nat. (nouv. éd.) 34: 466. (Amérique jusqu'au delà du Canada = Halifax, Nova Scotia.)

Habitat.—Mossy or wet grassy tundra, occasionally in drier areas with scattered scrubby bushes bogs (breeding); marshes, flooded and wet fields, and shores of pools and shallow lakes, occasionally beaches and mudflats (nonbreeding).

Distribution.—*Breeds* from western Alaska (Kobuk River), northern Yukon, northern Mackenzie, southern Keewatin, Southampton Island, northern Quebec, and northern Labrador south to the Pribilofs (St. Paul), eastern Aleutians (Unalaska), Alaska Peninsula, southeastern Alaska, northwestern British Columbia (including northwestern Queen Charlotte Islands; Atlin), northern Saskatchewan, northeastern Manitoba, northern Ontario, New Brunswick (Machias Seal Island, probably), eastern Quebec (Anticosti and Magdalen islands), Nova Scotia (Sable Island), and Newfoundland, with an isolated breeding in Massachusetts (Monomoy). Nonbreeding birds summer in the wintering range, primarily in North America south to California and the Gulf coast.

Winters in the Hawaiian Islands, and from south-coastal British Columbia (rarely), Washington, southern Nevada, Utah, central New Mexico, central Texas, Oklahoma, Arkansas, the Gulf states, and North Carolina (casually north to Long Island) south through Middle America, the West Indies, and South America (also all islands off the north coast) to the Galapagos Islands, northern Chile, central Bolivia, and central Brazil.

Migrates regularly along coastal areas and through interior North America, west to the Pribilof and eastern Aleutian islands, and east to western Greenland.

Casual north to southern Victoria, Melville, and southern Baffin islands, and in Clipperton Island, Bermuda, Iceland, the British Isles, Europe, and the Azores.

Calidris fuscicollis (Vieillot). White-rumped Sandpiper.

Tringa fuscicollis Vieillot, 1819, Nouv. Dict. Hist. Nat. (nouv. éd.) 34: 461. (Paraguay.)

Habitat.—Mossy or grassy, usually low-lying, tundra near water (breeding); grassy marshes, mudflats, flooded fields, and shores of ponds and lakes (nonbreeding).

Distribution.—*Breeds* from northern Alaska, northern Yukon (possibly), northwestern Mackenzie, and Banks, Melville, Bathurst, and northern Bylot islands south to the mainland coasts of Mackenzie and Keewatin, northwestern Hudson Bay (Chesterfield Inlet), and Southampton and southern Baffin islands.

Winters extensively in South America, primarily east of the Andes, south to Cape Horn and Tierra del Fuego, casually west of the Andes to Chile.

Migrates in spring primarily through Central America, eastern Mexico (recorded Tamaulipas, Veracruz, Yucatán, and Cozumel Island) and the interior of North America from the Great Plains east to the Mississippi and Ohio valleys, less commonly on the Atlantic seaboard north to the Maritime Provinces; and in fall mostly from Hudson Bay through the interior and along the Atlantic coast from Labrador and Newfoundland south through the West Indies and northern South America (also most islands off Venezuela).

Casual on Prince Patrick Island, and in western North America from south-coastal Alaska (Copper River delta), British Columbia, and Montana south to southern California and Arizona. Casual or accidental in the Galapagos Islands, Iceland, the British Isles, continental Europe, Franz Josef Land, the Azores, South Georgia, southern Africa, and Australia; a sight report for the Pacific coast of Oaxaca.

Calidris bairdii (Coues). Baird's Sandpiper.

Actodromas Bairdii Coues, 1861, Proc. Acad. Nat. Sci. Philadelphia 13: 194. (Fort Resolution [Great Slave Lake, Mackenzie].)

Habitat.—Dry coastal and alpine tundra (breeding); grassy marshes, and dry grassy areas near lakes and ponds, dried mudflats, rarely dry pastures and prairies away from water (nonbreeding).

Distribution.—*Breeds* from western and northern Alaska (Wales and Point Barrow eastward), northern Yukon, and Banks, Melville, Ellef Ringnes, and Ellesmere islands south to central Alaska (Askinuk Mountains and Susitna River highlands), extreme northwestern British Columbia (Haines Highway), northern Mackenzie, northern Keewatin, southern Melville Peninsula, and Southampton and south-central Baffin islands; also in northwestern Greenland, on Wrangel Island, and on the Chukotski Peninsula in northeastern Siberia.

Winters in South America locally in the Andes from Ecuador to Chile and Argentina, and in lowlands from Paraguay and Uruguay south through Chile and Argentina to Tierra del Fuego.

Migrates primarily through the central interior of Canada and the central plains of the United States and, in spring only, through Venezuela, Colombia, and Middle America; less frequently (primarily juveniles) and, mostly in fall, through the Pacific region (from Alaska south to Baja California, Arizona, and central Mexico, rarely elsewhere in Middle America) and along the Atlantic coast from New England south to Florida.

Casual in the Hawaiian Islands (Laysan, Oahu), Tres Marías Islands (off Nayarit), eastern Canada (Maritime Provinces), the Outer Hebrides, Faeroe Islands, British Isles, continental Europe, the Azores, and the Kuril and Galapagos islands; sight reports for the Bahamas, the Virgin Islands, and Barbados. Accidental on South Georgia and in southern Africa and Tasmania.

Calidris melanotos (Vieillot). Pectoral Sandpiper.

Tringa melanotos Vieillot, 1819, Nouv. Dict. Hist. Nat. (nouv. éd.) 34: 462. (Paraguay.)

Habitat.—Wet, grassy coastal tundra (breeding); wet meadows, marshes, flooded fields, grassy shores of ponds and pools, and occasionally mudflats (nonbreeding).

Distribution.—*Breeds* from western and northern Alaska (Wales and Point Barrow eastward), northern Yukon, northern Mackenzie, and Banks, Victoria, Bathurst, Devon, northern Baffin, and Southampton islands south to western Alaska (Goodnews Bay), central Mackenzie, southeastern Keewatin, and (rarely) extreme northeastern Ontario (Cape Henrietta Maria); and along the Arctic coast of central and eastern Siberia from the Taimyr Peninsula eastward.

Winters in southern South America from Peru, Bolivia, and southern Brazil south to central Chile and southern Argentina, casually north to Mexico, the Gulf coast, and Florida.

Migrates chiefly through interior North America, Middle America, and northern South America, and in fall (uncommon in spring) through eastern North America (north to Labrador and Newfoundland) and the West Indies, including most islands off the north coast of South America; also regularly (mostly in fall) through the Hawaiian Islands, Pribilof and Aleutian islands (rarely), to the Pacific coast from British Columbia southward, and along the coast of eastern Asia from the Kuril Islands and Sakhalin south to Japan.

Casual north to Prince Patrick Island, and in western Greenland, Iceland, the British Isles, continental Europe, the Azores, Africa, Australia, New Zealand, and Polynesia. Accidental on Clipperton, the Galapagos Islands, and South Georgia.

Calidris acuminata (Horsfield). Sharp-tailed Sandpiper.

Totanus acuminatus Horsfield, 1821, Trans. Linn. Soc. London 13(1): 192. (Java.)

Habitat.—Grassy tundra (breeding); wet grassy areas, marshes, flooded fields, shores of lakes and ponds, and occasionally mudflats (nonbreeding).

Distribution.—*Breeds* in northern Siberia from the Indigirka to the Kolyma, probably also on the Chukotski Peninsula. Recorded rarely in summer (and possibly breeding) in western Alaska (Barrow, Kivalina).

Winters from New Guinea, New Caledonia, and the Tonga Islands south to Australia, Tasmania and (rarely) New Zealand.

Migrates regularly through the Hawaiian Islands, western Alaska (north to Cape Seppings and Kotzebue Sound), islands in the Bering Sea, the Aleutians, and east to Kodiak Island, and from eastern Siberia, Sakhalin, and Japan south through eastern China, the Philippines, East Indies (occasionally), and Ryukyu Islands; and rarely (primarily in fall) from south-coastal and southeastern Alaska south along the Pacific coast to southern California, and through Pacific islands from Johnston and the Marshall islands south to the Gilbert and Phoenix islands.

Casual elsewhere in North America, mostly in fall (recorded from northeastern British Columbia, Alberta, Saskatchewan, North Dakota, Ontario, New York, and New England south to Arizona, New Mexico, Texas, the Gulf coast, and Florida); a sight report for Quebec. Accidental on Tristan da Cunha, in the British Isles, Scandinavia, France, and northern India; an erroneous record from Vera Paz, Guatemala.

Calidris maritima (Brünnich). Purple Sandpiper.

Tringa Maritima Brünnich, 1764, Ornithol. Bor., p. 54. (E Christiansöe & Norvegia = Christiansöe, Denmark.)

Habitat.—Tundra, especially rocky ridges and barren coastal beaches(breeding); rocky seacoasts and jetties; inland migrants (rare) usually along rocky shores of large inland bodies of water (nonbreeding).

Distribution.—*Breeds* in North America from Melville, Bathurst, Devon, Bylot, and Baffin islands south to Southampton and Belcher islands, and James Bay (North Twin Island); and in the Palearctic from western and southeastern Greenland, Iceland, Spitsbergen, Bear Island, Franz Josef Land, Novaya Zemlya, and the New Siberian Islands south to the Faeroe Islands, northern Scandinavia, and northern Siberia (Taimyr Peninsula). Recorded in summer (and possibly breeding) west to Banks and Prince Patrick islands.

Winters in North America from southern New Brunswick, Prince Edward Island, Nova Scotia, and Newfoundland south along the Atlantic coast to Virginia, rarely south to Florida, and casually inland to the Great Lakes (west to Wisconsin, Illinois, and Indiana) and along the Gulf coast to southern Texas; and in the Palearctic south to northwestern Europe, rarely to the Mediterranean region.

Migrates to Prince of Wales Island, Franklin District, and in coastal areas from Labrador southward, also regularly in the fall to the eastern Great Lakes region.

Casual or accidental in northern Alaska (Point Barrow), Manitoba, Minnesota. Oklahoma and the Azores; sight reports for Saskatchewan and interior Texas.

Notes.—*Calidris maritima* and *C. ptilocnemis* constitute a superspecies (Mayr and Short 1970).

Calidris ptilocnemis (Coues). Rock Sandpiper.

> *Tringa ptilocnemis* Coues, 1873, in Elliott, Rep. Seal Islands [*in* Affairs in Alaska] (not paged). (St. George Island, Pribilof Islands.)

Habitat.—Dry grassy or mossy tundra in coastal or montane areas (breeding); rocky seacoasts and jetties (nonbreeding).

Distribution.—*Breeds* in northeastern Siberia (Chukotski Peninsula and the Commander Islands), on islands in the Bering Sea (St. Lawrence, St. Matthew, Nunivak, and the Pribilofs), in the Aleutian and Shumagin (Sanak) islands.

Winters from southern Alaska (west to the Aleutians and Alaska Peninsula) south along the Pacific coast to central (casually southern) California; and in Eurasia from the Commander Islands south to the northern Kuril Islands.

Casual in interior northwestern British Columbia; a sight report for Saskatchewan. Unsubstantiated reports from northwestern Baja California.

Notes.—See comments under *C. maritima*.

Calidris alpina (Linnaeus). Dunlin.

> *Tringa alpina* Linnaeus, 1758, Syst. Nat. (ed. 10) 1: 149. (in Lapponia = Lapland.)

Habitat.—Wet, marshy coastal tundra (breeding); mudflats, marshes, flooded fields, sandy beaches, and shores of lakes and ponds, occasionally rocky coasts, in winter primarily on tidal mudflats (nonbreeding).

Distribution.—*Breeds* in North America from northern Alaska, northern Mackenzie (Baillie Island), northeastern Keewatin, southern Somerset Island, and Baffin Island south to western and south-coastal Alaska (rarely east to Cook Inlet and Copper River delta), Southampton Island, northeastern Manitoba (Churchill), and the south coast of Hudson Bay (locally to Cape Henrietta Maria); and in the northern Palearctic from Spitsbergen, northern Norway, and Novaya Zemlya south to the British Isles, Baltic region, and Arctic coast of northern Russia. Nonbreeding individuals are sometimes recorded in summer in the winter range.

Winters in the Hawaiian Islands (in small numbers); in North America along the Pacific coast of North America from southeastern Alaska south to Baja California and Nayarit, rarely east inland to western and southern Arizona and southern New Mexico, and south to Panama; on the Atlantic-Gulf-Caribbean coast from Massachusetts (rarely north to Nova Scotia) south to Florida, west to Texas, and south to the Yucatan Peninsula; and in the Old World from the British Isles, Mediterranean and Red seas, Gulf of Aden, India, southeastern China, and Japan south to the Cape Verde Islands, northern Africa, Arabia, the Indian coast, and Taiwan.

Migrates primarily along the Bering Sea coast of Alaska, the Pacific coast from the Aleutians and southern Alaska southward, the Atlantic coast from eastern Quebec and Nova Scotia southward, and in smaller numbers through the interior of North America from southern Canada south to Arizona, New Mexico, Texas, and the Gulf coast, most frequently through the Mississippi Valley and Great Lakes region.

Casual in Newfoundland; sight reports for Belize, the West Indies (south to Barbados), French Guiana, Peru, and Argentina.

Calidris ferruginea (Pontoppidan). Curlew Sandpiper.

Tringa Ferruginea Pontoppidan, 1763, Dan. Atlas 1: 624. (Iceland and Christiansöe [Denmark].)

Habitat.—Tundra; in Alaska, primarily wet coastal tundra (breeding); mudflats, marshes, and beaches (nonbreeding).

Distribution.—*Breeds* in North America rarely in northern Alaska (Barrow); and in Eurasia in northern Siberia from the Yenisei Delta east through the Taimyr Peninsula and New Siberian Islands to Cape Baranov.

Winters from the British Isles (rarely), Mediterranean region, Iraq, India, Burma, southern Thailand, and the Philippines (rarely) south to southern Africa, Madagascar, Mauritius, Sri Lanka, the Malay Peninsula, southern Australia, Tasmania, and New Zealand.

Casual during migration in western Alaska and the Aleutian Islands, along the Pacific coast of North America from south-coastal Alaska south to southern California, in eastern North America from Quebec, New Brunswick, and Nova Scotia south to Florida and west along the Gulf coast to Texas, and in the Lesser Antilles (Grenada, Carriacou, and Barbados, sight reports from Antigua and the Virgin Islands); also scattered reports in interior North America from Washington, Alberta, Montana, Manitoba, and southern Ontario south to southeastern California, northern Utah (sight report), Kansas, Illinois, Indiana, and Ohio. Accidental in the Hawaiian Islands (Oahu), Costa Rica, Ecuador, Peru, Argentina, and the Marshall Islands (Kwajalein).

Calidris himantopus (Bonaparte). Stilt Sandpiper.

Tringa himantopus Bonaparte, 1826, Ann. Lyc. Nat. Hist. N. Y. 2: 157. (Long Branch, New Jersey.)

Habitat.—Sedge tundra near water, often near wooded borders of the taiga (breeding); mudflats, flooded fields, shallow ponds and pools, and marshes (nonbreeding).

Distribution.—*Breeds* from northern Alaska (west to Prudhoe Bay, probably rarely Colville River), northern Yukon, northern Mackenzie (Cockburn Point, Perry River), and southern Victoria Island southeast to southeastern Keewatin, northeastern Manitoba, and northern Ontario (Cape Henrietta Maria), probably also south locally in Canada to borders of the taiga.

Winters from Nayarit and Tamaulipas (irregularly also interior Mexico) and the West Indies south through Middle America and North America to northern Chile, south-central Brazil, and northern Argentina, casually north to central California (especially the Salton Sea), the Gulf coast, and Florida.

Migrates mostly through interior North America, in the fall also regularly along the Atlantic coast from New Brunswick and Nova Scotia southward (including the West Indies), and rarely in both migration periods along the Pacific coast from southeastern Alaska southward, casually through western Alaska, the Pribilof Islands, south-coastal Alaska, and British Columbia.

Casual on Bathurst Island, and in Bermuda, and the Galapagos Islands. Accidental in Iceland, the British Isles, continental Europe, and northern Australia.

Notes.—Formerly classified in the monotypic genus *Micropalama,* but morphological (Jehl 1968b) and genetic (Dittmann and Zink 1991) data support its membership in the genus *Calidris.*

Genus *EURYNORHYNCHUS* Nilsson

Eurynorhynchus Nilsson, 1821, Ornithol. Svecica 2: 29. Type, by monotypy, *Eurynorhynchus griseus* Nilsson = *Platalea pygmea* Linnaeus.

Notes.—In spite of its unusual bill morphology, great similarities exist between this monotypic genus and the genus *Calidris,* particularly in the anatomy (Burton 1971) and plumage of the downy young (Jehl 1968b). Some authors (Portenko 1972, Voous 1973) have suggested that *Eurynorhynchus* may be merged eventually into *Calidris.* Strauch (1978) found that the morphology of *Eurynorhynchus* is intermediate between *Calidris* and *Micropalama,* subsequently merged into *Calidris.* Tomkovich (1991) found behavioral differences between it and *Calidris,* but did not comment on taxonomy. Further studies are needed.

Eurynorhynchus pygmeus (Linnaeus). Spoonbill Sandpiper.

Platalea pygmea Linnaeus, 1758, Syst. Nat. (ed. 10) 1: 140. Based on *Platalea* corpore supra fusco, subtus albo Linnaeus, Mus. Adolphi Friderici 2: . . . (in Surinami, error = eastern Asia.)

Habitat.—Stone or shell banks (breeding); mudflats and beaches (nonbreeding).
Distribution.—*Breeds* in northeastern Siberia.
Winters in Southeast Asia.
Casual in northwestern Alaska (Arctic coast at Wainwright), the Aleutians (Attu, Buldir), and southwestern British Columbia (Iona Island, Richmond); sight reports for the Pribilof Islands (St. Paul) and Alberta.

Genus *LIMICOLA* Koch

Limicola C. L. Koch, 1816, Syst. Baier. Zool. 1: 316. Type, by monotypy, *Numenius pygmaeus* Bechstein = *Scolopax falcinellus* Pontoppidan.

Limicola falcinellus (Pontoppidan). Broad-billed Sandpiper.

Scolopax Falcinellus Pontoppidan, 1763, Dan. Atlas 1: 263. (No locality given = Denmark.)

Habitat.—Wet subarctic bogs and grassy sloughs (breeding); muddy ponds, marshes, wet meadows, sewage plants, tidal mudflats (nonbreeding).
Distribution.—*Breeds* in northeastern Siberia.
Winters from India and southeastern China south to the East Indies, Australia, and New Zealand.
Casual in the Aleutians (Shemya, Buldir, Adak); sight reports for Nova Scotia and South Africa.

Genus *TRYNGITES* Cabanis

Tryngites Cabanis, 1857, J. Ornithol. 4 (1856): 418. Type, by original designation, *Tringa rufescens* Vieillot = *Tringa subruficollis* Vieillot.

Tryngites subruficollis (Vieillot). Buff-breasted Sandpiper.

Tringa subruficollis Vieillot, 1819, Nouv. Dict. Hist. Nat. (nouv. éd.) 34: 465. (Paraguay.)

Habitat.—Dry areas in moist grassy tundra (breeding); dry grasslands (usually short grass), pastures, plowed fields, and, rarely, beaches (nonbreeding).
Distribution.—*Breeds* from northern Alaska (Barrow and Atkasuk eastward), northern Yukon, northwestern Mackenzie, and Banks, Melville, Bathurst, and Devon islands south to southern Victoria, Jenny Lind (in Queen Maud Gulf), and King William islands.
Winters in South America (occasionally in the northern part) in Paraguay, Uruguay, and northern Argentina.
Migrates primarily through the interior of North America (between the Rocky Mountains

and the Mississippi Valley), eastern Mexico, Central America (not recorded Belize) and northern South America east to Trinidad, Guyana, and Surinam, rarely (mostly in fall) through eastern North America from northern Ontario, southern and eastern Quebec, Nova Scotia, and Newfoundland south to southern Florida, and through the West Indies, casually in western North America from western Alaska, the Pribilof and Aleutian islands, southern Alaska, northeastern British Columbia, and Montana south to California and New Mexico.

Casual or accidental in the Hawaiian Islands (Kure, Midway, Kauai, Oahu), Labrador, Iceland, the British Isles, continental Europe, the Azores, Egypt, eastern Siberia, the Kuril Islands, Japan, and Australia; a sight report for southern Africa.

Genus *PHILOMACHUS* Merrem

Philomachus Anonymous [= Merrem], 1804, Allg. Lit. Ztg. 2(168): col. 542. Type, by monotypy, *Tringa pugnax* Linnaeus.
Machetes Cuvier, 1817, Règne Anim. 1:490. Type, by original designation, *Tringa pugnax* Linnaeus.

Philomachus pugnax (Linnaeus). Ruff.

Tringa Pugnax Linnaeus, 1758, Syst. Nat. (ed. 10) 1: 148. (in Europa minus boreali = southern Sweden.)

Habitat.—Grassy tundra, along shores of lakes and ponds, in wet meadows and marshes, and rarely in hayfields (breeding); mudflats, marshes, and flooded fields (nonbreeding).

Distribution.—*Breeds* in Eurasia from northern Scandinavia, northern Russia, and northern Siberia south to the British Isles (at least formerly), western and northern Europe, southern Russia, southern Siberia, and Anadyrland; also has nested in North America in northwestern Alaska (Point Lay). Occasional nonbreeding individuals are recorded in summer in the wintering range.

Winters from the British Isles, southern Europe, Iraq, Arabia, the Persian Gulf, southeastern China,, and Taiwan south to southern Africa, India, Sri Lanka, the East Indies, Philippines, and Australia.

Migrates regularly through the Hawaiian Islands, western and southwestern Alaska (including St. Lawrence, Pribilof, and Aleutian islands), along the east coast of North America (from Massachusetts to Florida), and to Puerto Rico, the Virgin Islands, and Lesser Antilles (mostly in fall, recorded Antigua, Guadeloupe, Barbados, St. Lucia, and Grenada).

Casual in western North America (primarily along the Pacific coast) from south-coastal Alaska and northeastern British Columbia south to southern California, northern Baja California, and Arizona; throughout most of North America east of the Rockies from southern Alberta, southern Saskatchewan, Manitoba, Minnesota, Wisconsin, Michigan, southern Ontario, Quebec, Nova Scotia, and Newfoundland south to Texas, the Gulf coast, the Bahamas and Greater Antilles; and in Guatemala (Santa Rosa), Trinidad, Greenland, Iceland, the Faeroe Islands, Johnston Island, the Marshall Islands, and New Zealand; sight reports for Costa Rica, Panama, Venezuela, and Peru.

Tribe LIMNODROMINI: Dowitchers

Genus *LIMNODROMUS* Wied

Limnodromus Wied, 1833, Beitr. Naturgesch. Bras. 4: 716. Type, by monotypy, *Scolopax noveboracensis* Gmelin = *Scolopax grisea* Gmelin.

Limnodromus griseus (Gmelin). Short-billed Dowitcher.

Scolopax grisea Gmelin, 1789, Syst. Nat. 1(2): 658. Based on the "Brown Snipe" Pennant, Arct. Zool. 2: 464. (in Noveboraci maritimis = Long Island, New York.)

Habitat.—Grassy or mossy tundra and muskegs and wet meadows (breeding); mudflats, estuaries, and (less frequently) shallow marshes, pools, ponds, flooded fields, and sandy beaches, in winter primarily tidal mudlfats (nonbreeding).

Distribution.—*Breeds* in coastal regions of southern Alaska (Bristol Bay east to the Stikine River mouth); in central Canada from southern Yukon, southern Mackenzie, and central Quebec (interior of the Ungava Peninsula) south to northwestern British Columbia, central Alberta, central Saskatchewan, northeastern Manitoba, the north coast of Ontario, and James Bay (and islands), south-central Quebec, and central Labrador. Nonbreeding individuals often summer in the wintering range.

Winters from central Washington, the Gulf coast, and coastal South Carolina south through the West Indies and along both coasts of Middle America and South America to central Peru and east-central Brazil.

Migrates regularly along the Pacific coast of North America from southeastern Alaska southward, through the interior of North America in the prairie regions of the Canadian provinces and from the Great Lakes region south through the Mississippi Valley, and along the Atlantic coast from southern Quebec, New Brunswick, Nova Scotia, and Newfoundland southward, occurring rarely elsewhere in the interior of western North America.

Casual or accidental in the Hawaiian Islands, Pribilof Islands, Bermuda, Greenland, the British Isles, continental Europe, and the Azores.

Notes.—*Limnodromus griseus* and *L. scolopaceus* were formerly considered to be a single species until Pitelka (1950) showed that they are separate species; they may constitute a superspecies (Mayr and Short 1970), but they are strongly differentiated genetically (Avise and Zink 1988).

Limnodromus scolopaceus (Say). Long-billed Dowitcher.

> *Limosa scolopacea* Say, 1823, in Long, Exped. Rocky Mount. 1: 170. (near Boyer Creek = Council Bluffs, Iowa.)

Habitat.—Grassy tundra and muskegs and wet meadows (breeding); marshes, shores of ponds and lakes, mudflats, and flooded fields, primarily in fresh-water situations (nonbreeding).

Distribution.—*Breeds* in North America in coastal western and northern Alaska (Hooper Bay, north coast), northern Yukon, and northwestern Mackenzie; and in Eurasia in northeastern Siberia on the Chukotski Peninsula and in Anadyrland.

Winters from south coastal British Columbia, Utah (rarely), southern New Mexico, central Texas, the Gulf coast, and southern Florida (casually north to Maryland and Delaware) south through Mexico (except the Yucatan Peninsula) to Guatemala, rarely to Costa Rica, and casually to Panama (Bocas del Toro, and probably Canal area).

Migrates most commonly through western North America west of the Rocky Mountains, regularly (and primarily in fall) east of the Rockies from southern Canada (Alberta east to Quebec and, rarely, New Brunswick and Nova Scotia) south to Florida, casually through the Aleutians and to the Antilles (recorded Cuba, Jamaica, the Virgin Islands, and St. Kitts), and Cayman Islands, also in the Hawaiian Islands.

A record of an individual of this species in breeding plumage taken in October in Argentina (Buenos Aires) is doubtful; sight reports from South America may pertain to *L. griseus*.

Casual on Clipperton Island, and in the British Isles and continental Europe.

Notes.—See comments under *L. griseus*.

Tribe GALLINAGINI: Snipe

Notes.—The tribe name has been formed incorrectly in the past as Gallinagoini (A.O.U. 1983) and Gallinaginini (Auk 101: 340, 1984). The appropriate root upon which the family-group name is based is "Gallinag."

Genus *LYMNOCRYPTES* Kaup

> *Lymnocryptes* Kaup, 1829, Skizz. Entw.-Ges. Eur. Thierw., p. 118. Type, by monotypy, *Scolopax gallinula* Linnaeus = *Scolopax minima* Brünnich.

Lymnocryptes minimus (Brünnich). Jack Snipe.

> *Scolopax Minima* Brünnich, 1764, Ornithol. Bor., p. 49. (E Christiansöe [Island, Denmark].)

Habitat.—Tundra (breeding); marshes and flooded fields (nonbreeding).

Distribution.—*Breeds* from northern Eurasia south to central Russia and central Siberia. *Winters* from the British Isles, southern Europe, India, and southeastern China south to central Africa, Sri Lanka, and Taiwan.

Casual in Iceland, the Faeroe Islands, Madeira, the Azores, Kuril Islands, and Japan. Accidental in Alaska (St. Paul in the Pribilof Islands, Spring 1919), California (Gridley, Butte County, 20 November 1938; Colusa, 2 December 1990), Labrador (Makkovik Bay, 24 December 1927), and Barbados (12 November 1960).

Genus *GALLINAGO* Brisson

Gallinago Brisson, 1760, Ornithologie 5: 298. Type, by tautonymy, *Gallinago* Brisson = *Scolopax gallinago* Linnaeus.

Capella Frenzel, 1801, Beschr. Vögel Eyer Wittenberg, p. 58. Type, by monotypy, *Scolopax coelestis* Frenzel = *Scolopax gallinago* Linnaeus.

Notes.—For use of *Gallinago* instead of *Capella,* see Mayr (1963).

Gallinago gallinago (Linnaeus). Common Snipe.

Scolopax Gallinago Linnaeus, 1758, Syst. Nat. (ed. 10) 1: 147. (in Europa = Sweden.)

Habitat.—Wet, grassy areas from tundra to temperate lowlands and hilly regions; in winter and migration, also wet meadows, flooded fields, bogs, marshes, and marshy banks of rivers and lakes (Temperate Zone; in migration and winter also to Tropical and Subtropical zones).

Distribution.—*Breeds* [*delicata* group] in North America from northern Alaska, northern Yukon, northwestern and central Mackenzie, southern Keewatin, northeastern Manitoba, northern Ontario, northern Quebec, and central Labrador south to southern Alaska (west to Unalaska in the Aleutians), southern California, east-central Arizona, northern New Mexico, southern Colorado, western Nebraska, northern Iowa, northeastern Illinois, northern Indiana, northern Ohio, northern West Virginia, northwestern Pennsylvania, northern New Jersey, New England, and the Maritime Provinces; and [*gallinago* group] in Eurasia from Iceland, the Faeroe, Orkney, and Shetland islands, the British Isles, Scandinavia, northern Russia, northern Siberia, and Bering Island south to southern Europe, southern Russia, the Himalayas, and Kuril Islands, and (probably) in the western Aleutians (Near Islands).

Winters [*delicata* group] in the Americas from southern (rarely) and southeastern Alaska, southern British Columbia, eastern Washington, Idaho, the central United States (from Montana, southern Minnesota, and the lower Mississippi and Ohio valleys), Pennsylvania and southern New England (casually from southern Canada) south through Middle America and the West Indies to Colombia, Venezuela, Surinam, and Ecuador; and [*gallinago* group] in the Old World from the British Isles, southern Europe, Madeira (casually), southern Russia, and Japan south to south-central Africa, Sri Lanka, the Andaman Islands, Java, and the Philippines, and (rarely) in the Hawaiian Islands.

Casual or accidental [*delicata* group] in the Hawaiian Islands, Bermuda, Greenland, and Scotland; and [*gallinago* group] in the Pribilof Islands, St. Lawrence Island, Labrador (Jack Lane's Bay), Bermuda, and Greenland.

Notes.—Known in Old World literature as the Snipe. Groups: *G. gallinago* [Common Snipe] and *G. delicata* (Ord, 1825) [Wilson's Snipe]; the close approach of the breeding ranges in the Aleutian Islands, and differences in display sounds (Thönen 1969) and external morphology (Oberholser 1921, Wetmore 1926, Tuck 1972), suggest that the two groups may be distinct species, but there appears to be no conclusive genetic evidence to support this treatment (Zink et al. 1995). The South American *G. paraguaiae* (Vieillot, 1816) and *G. andina* Taczanowski, 1875, are considered conspecific with *G. gallinago* by some authors (e.g., Blake 1977); they and the African *G. nigripennis* Bonaparte, 1839, constitute a superspecies (Mayr and Short 1970).

Gallinago stenura (Bonaparte). Pin-tailed Snipe.

Scolopax stenura (Kuhl MS) Bonaparte. 1831, Ann. Stor. Nat. Bologna 4: 335. (Sunda Archipelago.)

Habitat.—Wet meadows and marshes.

Distribution.—*Breeds* from northeastern Russia and northern Siberia south to central Russia, northern Manchuria, and the Sea of Okhotsk.

Winters from India, Southeast Asia, southeastern China, and Taiwan south to the East Indies, casually to northeastern Africa and islands in the Indian Ocean.

Accidental in the Hawaiian Islands (Kure Atoll, 13 January 1964; Clapp and Woodward 1968) and the western Aleutians (Attu, 25 May 1991; Gibson and Kessel 1992).

Tribe SCOLOPACINI: Woodcocks

Genus *SCOLOPAX* Linnaeus

Scolopax Linnaeus, 1758, Syst. Nat. (ed. 10) 1: 145. Type, by tautonymy, *Scolopax rusticola* Linnaeus (*Scolopax*, prebinomial specific name, in synonymy).

Subgenus *SCOLOPAX* Linnaeus

Scolopax rusticola Linnaeus. Eurasian Woodcock.

Scolopax Rusticola Linnaeus, 1758, Syst. Nat. (ed. 10) 1: 146. (in Europa = Sweden.)

Habitat.—Moist woodland, both deciduous and coniferous, generally with ground cover of brackens and bushes, also in bogs, heath, and moorlands.

Distribution.—*Breeds* locally from the British Isles, Scandinavia, and the area of the Arctic Circle in Russia and Siberia south to the eastern Atlantic islands, northern Mediterranean region, southern Russia, northern India, the Himalayas, Turkestan, Transcaucasia, Japan, the Seven Islands of Izu, Kuril Islands, and Sakhalin.

Winters from the British Isles, southern Europe, Iraq, Iran, India, southeastern China, and Japan south to the Cape Verde Islands, northern Africa, southern India, the Malay Peninsula, Philippines (rarely), and Ryukyu Islands.

Casual in eastern North America (recorded from Newfoundland, southwestern Quebec, New Jersey, Pennsylvania, Virginia, and Alabama, mostly in the 19th Century), and in Greenland, Iceland, the Faeroe Islands, and Spitsbergen.

Notes.—Also known as European Woodcock and, in Old World literature, as the Woodcock.

Subgenus *PHILOHELA* Gray

Philohela G. R. Gray, 1841, List Genera Birds, ed. 2, p. 90. Type, by original designation, *Scolopax minor* Gmelin.

Scolopax minor Gmelin. American Woodcock.

Scolopax minor Gmelin, 1789, Syst. Nat. 1(2): 661. Based on the "Little Woodcock" Pennant, Arct. Zool. 2: 463, pl. 19, upper fig. (in Americæ, . . . in Carolinæ, . . . in Noveboraci silvis humidis = New York.)

Habitat.—Moist woodland, primarily deciduous or mixed, thickets along streams or in boggy areas, usually with nearby wet grassy meadows and fields.

Distribution.—*Breeds* from southern Manitoba, central Ontario, southern Quebec, northern New Brunswick, Prince Edward Island, Nova Scotia, and southwestern Newfoundland south to eastern Oklahoma, east-central Texas, the Gulf states, and southern Florida, and west to central and eastern Colorado, eastern North Dakota, eastern South Dakota, eastern Nebraska, and eastern Kansas.

Winters in the southeastern United States from Oklahoma, southern Missouri, Tennessee, the northern portions of the Gulf states, and southern New England south to east-central Texas, the Gulf coast, and southern Florida, rarely wintering farther north in the breeding range.

Casual in Montana, Wyoming, New Mexico, southern Texas, Manitoba, northeastern Ontario, eastern Quebec, and Bermuda, also sight reports for Saskatchewan, Wyoming, southeastern Arizona, and eastern Mexico (Tamaulipas, Quintana Roo).

Subfamily PHALAROPODINAE: Phalaropes

Genus *PHALAROPUS* Brisson

Phalaropus Brisson, 1760, Ornithologie 1: 50; 6: 12. Type, by tautonymy, *Phalaropus* Brisson = *Tringa fulicaria* Linnaeus.

Lobipes Cuvier, 1816, Règne Anim., 1, p. 495. Type, by original designation, *Tringa hyperborea* Linnaeus = *Tringa lobata* Linnaeus.

Steganopus Vieillot, 1818, Nouv. Dict. Hist. Nat. (nouv. éd.) 24 (1817): 124. Type, by monotypy, "Chorlito tarso comprimido" Azara = *Steganopus tricolor* Vieillot.

Phalaropus tricolor (Vieillot). Wilson's Phalarope.

Steganopus tricolor Vieillot, 1819, Nouv. Dict. Hist. Nat. (nouv. éd.) 32: 136. Based on "Chorlito Tarso comprimido" Azara, Apunt. Hist. Nat. Páx. Parag. 3: 327 (no. 407). (Paraguay.)

Habitat.—Shallow fresh-water marshes and wet meadows (breeding); also on lake shores, mudflats, and salt marshes, and (rarely) along seacoasts, staging in migration on salt lakes (nonbreeding).

Distribution.—*Breeds* from coastal British Columbia (Vancouver Island), southern Yukon, northern Alberta, central Saskatchewan, central Manitoba, western and southern Ontario, extreme southern Quebec, northeastern New York, and New Brunswick south locally in the interior to east-central California, central Nevada, central Utah, east-central Arizona, northern New Mexico, northern Texas, central Kansas, western Nebraska, eastern South Dakota, northern Iowa, northern Illinois, northern Indiana (formerly), and northern Ohio, with isolated breeding in northeastern Manitoba, southwestern James Bay, and Massachusetts (Plum Island). Recorded in summer (nonbreeding) in central and south-coastal Alaska (probably has bred), central Mackenzie, northern Saskatchewan, and Nova Scotia.

Winters primarily in western and southern South America from Peru, Bolivia, Paraguay, and Uruguay south through Chile and Argentina, casually as far north as central California, Utah, central New Mexico, southern Texas, southwestern Louisiana, and Florida.

Migrates regularly through western North America (east to the Great Plains and Louisiana), Middle America (not recorded Nicaragua), Colombia, and Ecuador, and uncommonly through central and eastern North America from southern Quebec (including Anticosti Island) and New Brunswick south to Florida and the Gulf coast; recorded regularly in fall on Barbados.

Casual or accidental in the Hawaiian Islands, western and northern Alaska, Clipperton Island, elsewhere in the West Indies (recorded Great Inagua in the Bahamas, Grand Cayman, Jamaica, Puerto Rico, the Virgin Islands, Guadeloupe, and Martinique), the Galapagos and Falkland islands, South Georgia, Venezuela, Iceland, British Isles, continental Europe, the Azores, Africa, islands of the central Pacific (Johnston and Easter), Australia, New Zealand, and Antarctica; a sight report for Surinam.

Phalaropus lobatus (Linnaeus). Red-necked Phalarope.

Tringa tobata [sic] Linnaeus, 1758, Syst. Nat. (ed. 10) 1: 148 [*lobata* in Emendanda, p. 824]. Based on "The Cock Coot-footed Tringa" Edwards, Nat. Hist. Birds 3: 143, pl. 143. (in America septentrionali, Lapponia = Hudson Bay.)

Habitat.—Grass-sedge borders of ponds and lakes in tundra (breeding); in winter, primarily pelagic, most commonly at upwellings; occurring in migration on ponds, lakes, open marshes, estuaries, and bays.

Distribution.—*Breeds* in North America from northern Alaska, northern Yukon, northern Mackenzie, southern Victoria Island, central Keewatin, and Southampton and southern Baffin islands south to the Pribilof and Aleutian islands, southern Alaska, northwestern British Columbia, southern Yukon, southern Mackenzie, northern Alberta, northern Saskatchewan, northern Manitoba, northern Ontario, islands in southern James Bay, northern Quebec, and locally along the Labrador coast; and in the Palearctic from Greenland, Iceland, the northern British Isles, Faeroe and Shetland islands, and Spitsbergen east across Scandinavia, northern Russia, and northern Siberia to the Bering Sea, Kamchatka, and the Commander Islands. Nonbreeding individuals occur in summer along the coast of Newfoundland and on Miquelon Island.

Winters primarily at sea, in the Pacific from the Ryukyu Islands, central equatorial islands and central Mexico (north to Colima) south to the Lesser Sunda Islands, New Guinea, Australia (rarely), New Zealand, and southern South America, casually north to central California; in the South Atlantic off southern South America and Africa, casually north to the Azores; and in the Indian Ocean from East Africa east to Malaya.

Migrates regularly through the North Pacific and North Atlantic oceans along North American and Eurasian coasts, also regularly through interior California, northern Utah (mainly Great Salt Lake), and western Europe; less commonly but regularly through interior western North America from British Columbia and the prairie regions of Alberta, Saskatchewan, and Manitoba south to Arizona, New Mexico, and western Texas; rarely or irregularly through interior central and eastern North America and Middle America south to Distrito Federal, southern Texas, the Gulf coast, and Florida; and casually through Middle America (not recorded Belize), Cuba, and Bermuda; sight reports from Jamaica, Puerto Rico, and the Bahamas (New Providence).

Accidental in the Hawaiian Islands (Laysan, Kauai, Oahu).

Notes.—Dittmann and Zink (1991) confirmed that this species and *P. fulicaria* are more closely related to each other than either is to *P. tricolor.*

Phalaropus fulicaria (Linnaeus). Red Phalarope.

> *Tringa Fulicaria* Linnaeus, 1758, Syst. Nat. (ed. 10) 1: 148. Based on "The Red Coot-footed Tringa" Edwards, Nat Hist. Birds 3: 142, pl. 142. (in America = Hudson Bay.)

Habitat.—Wet coastal tundra (breeding); in winter, primarily pelagic, most commonly at upwellings; occurring in migration on bays and estuaries, less frequently on ponds, lakes, and marshes.

Distribution.—*Breeds* in North America from western Alaska (Yukon delta and St. Lawrence Island) east across northern Alaska, northern Yukon, northern Mackenzie, and Banks, Melville, Ellesmere, Bylot, Dundas, and northern Baffin islands, and south to eastern Keewatin, Southampton, and Mansel islands, and northern Labrador (probably); and in the Palearctic from Greenland and Iceland east through Arctic islands (Spitsbergen, Bear, Novaya Zemlya, and New Siberian) to northern Siberia. Nonbreeding individuals summer off the coasts of California and Newfoundland.

Winters at sea off the Hawaiian Islands, off the Pacific coast of South America from Colombia and Ecuador south to Chile (also regularly off California, Mexico, and in the Gulf of Mexico and Atlantic Ocean from Florida southward); in the South Atlantic off Patagonia and the Falkland Islands, and off western Africa; and in the western Pacific from Japan south, at least casually to New Zealand.

Migrates regularly through the Aleutians and along both coasts of North America (recorded south to Baja California, Guerrero, Oaxaca, Texas, the Gulf coast, and Florida), rarely or casually through the interior from Mexico north; also through the North Atlantic, western Mediterranean Sea, western Europe, and the Pacific Ocean off Japan.

Casual in Guatemala and Cuba; sight reports from Barbados. Accidental in India, the Philippines, and Antarctica.

Notes.—See under *P. lobatus.*

Family **GLAREOLIDAE**: Coursers and Pratincoles

Subfamily GLAREOLINAE: Pratincoles

Genus *GLAREOLA* Brisson

> *Glareola* Brisson, 1760, Ornithologie 1: 48; 5: 141. Type, by tautonymy, *Glareola* Brisson = *Hirundo pratincola* Linnaeus.

Glareola maldivarum Forster. Oriental Pratincole.

Glareola (Pratincola) Maldivarum J. R. Forster, 1795, Faunula Indica, ed. 2, p. 11. (open sea, in the latitude of the Maldivia [= Maldive] Isles.)

Habitat.—Grassy steppe.

Distribution.—*Breeds* in eastern Asia from Mongolia and southern Siberia south to Pakistan, India, Sri Lanka, the Andaman Islands and eastern China, and *winters* from southern Asia and the Philippines south to northern Australia, in migration casually east to Japan and the Kuril Islands.

Accidental in Alaska (Attu in the Aleutians, 19–20 May 1985, and St. Lawrence Island, 5 June 1986; Gibson and Kessel 1992).

Family **LARIDAE**: Skuas, Gulls, Terns, and Skimmers

Subfamily STERCORARIINAE: Skuas and Jaegers

Notes.—We follow Sibley and Monroe (1990) for sequence of genera and species.

Genus *CATHARACTA* Brünnich

Catharacta Brünnich, 1764, Ornithol. Bor., p. 32. Type, by subsequent designation (Reichenbach, 1852), *Catharacta skua* Brünnich.

Megalestris Bonaparte, 1856, C. R. Acad. Sci. Paris 43: 643. Type, by monotypy, *Larus catarractes* Linnaeus = *Catharacta skua* Brünnich.

Catharacta skua Brünnich. Great Skua.

Catharacta skua Brünnich, 1764, Ornithol. Bor., p. 33. (E. Feroa Islandia = Iceland.)

Habitat.—Coastal islands with low vegetation, usually near seabird colonies; in Old World, also moors or pastures near the sea, occasionally sandy flats in estuaries (breeding); pelagic, mainly over continental shelf (nonbreeding).

Distribution.—*Breeds* [*skua* group] in Iceland, and the Faeroe, Shetland and Orkney islands; [*antarctica* group] in the Falkland Islands and along the coast of southern Argentina; and [*lonnbergi* group] widely on southern oceanic islands such as the South Shetlands, Deception, South Orkneys, South Georgia, Bouvet, Prince Edwards, Crozets, Kerguelen, Heard, Macquarie, Auckland, Campbell and Antipodes. Nonbreeding birds [*skua* group] have been recorded in summer from Franklin District (Barrow Straits, Lancaster Sound, Baffin Bay), southern Labrador, Newfoundland, Nova Scotia, Massachusetts (Georges Bank), Greenland, Jan Mayen, Spitsbergen and the northern European coast.

Winters at sea [*skua* group] in the eastern North Atlantic, from lat. 60° N. south to the Tropic of Cancer, regularly on the Newfoundland Banks and off the coast from Nova Scotia to New Jersey, and rarely to the Canary Islands and Mediterranean region; [*antarctica* group] primarily in the South Atlantic and along eastern South America from Brazil to the Straits of Magellan; and [*lonnbergi* group] in southern oceans, most regularly off Australia.

Accidental [*skua* group] in Belize (Ambergris Cay), Guyana, Novaya Zemlya and continental Europe; and [*lonnbergi* group] off Îles des Saintes (near Guadeloupe, Lesser Antilles, recovery of bird banded in South Shetlands, although there is some doubt about the identity of this individual; Devillers 1978). Reports of *C. s. antarctica* and *C. s. lonnbergi* off the west coast of North America all pertain to *C. maccormicki* (see Devillers 1978), and those from Barbados and off Haiti and Puerto Rico may pertain to species other than *C. skua*.

Notes.—Also known as Brown Skua. Groups: *C. antarctica* (Lesson, 1831) [Falkland Skua], *C. lonnbergi* Mathews, 1912 [Southern Skua], and *C. skua* [Northern Skua]. *Catharacta (skua) antarctica* and *C. chilensis* (Bonaparte, 1856) exhibit limited hybridization in areas where both breed on the coast of Argentina (Devillers 1978) and have been considered conspecific by earlier authors. Although many authors previously treated *C. maccormicki* as a race of *C. skua*, *C. (s.) lonnbergi* and *C. maccormicki* breed sympatrically with limited hybridization on some sub-Antarctic islands (Parmelee 1988).

Catharacta maccormicki (Saunders). South Polar Skua.

Stercorarius maccormicki Saunders, 1893, Bull. Brit. Ornithol. Club 3: 12. (Possession Island, Victoria Land, lat. 71°14′ S., long. 171°15′ W.)

Habitat.—Pelagic Waters; breeds on barren promontories and islands, usually near seabird colonies.

Distribution.—*Breeds* on the South Shetland Islands, and along the coast of Antarctica.

Ranges at sea regularly to the North Pacific, occurring in the northern spring, summer and fall from the Gulf of Alaska south to Mexico (occasional reports of skuas off Panama probably pertain to this species), in Hawaiian waters (at least casually), and off Japan; and to the North Atlantic (north to New England, Newfoundland and Greenland). It is likely that most skua reports in the central North Atlantic in the northern summer pertain to this species (Devillers 1977a).

Accidental in North Dakota (Lake Oahe); a sight report for northern Alaska.

Notes.—See comments under *C. skua.*

Genus *STERCORARIUS* Brisson

Stercorarius Brisson, 1760, Ornithologie 1: 56; 6: 149. Type, by tautonymy, Stercorarius Brisson = *Larus parasiticus* Pallas.

Coprotheres Reichenbach, 1853, Handb. Spec. Ornithol., Die Vögel, pt. 3 (1852), p. v. Type, by original designation, *Lestris pomarinus* Temminck.

Stercorarius pomarinus (Temminck). Pomarine Jaeger.

Lestris pomarinus Temminck, 1815, Man. Ornithol. (ed. 1, 1814): 514. (les régions du cercle arctique; de passage accidentel sur les côtes de Hollande et de France = Arctic regions of Europe.)

Habitat.—Coastal marshy or mossy tundra (breeding); primarily pelagic, casually on large inland bodies of water (nonbreeding).

Distribution.—*Breeds* in North America in western and northern Alaska (south to Hooper Bay) east across the Canadian Arctic islands (north to Melville, Bathurst, Devon, Bylot and Baffin islands), and south to northern Mackenzie, Southampton Island and northwestern Quebec; and in the Palearctic in western Greenland, Spitsbergen, Bear Island, Novaya Zemlya, and in northern Russia and northern Siberia from the Taimyr Peninsula to Anadyrland. Nonbreeding birds occur in summer off Alaska and British Columbia (Bering Sea and Aleutians south to Queen Charlotte Islands) and California, in central Canada (south to northern Alberta and Hudson Bay), and in the Atlantic from Labrador and Newfoundland south to New England; also off Scandinavia.

Winters primarily at sea in the Pacific near the Hawaiian Islands (primarily off Oahu), from northern California south to Peru and the Galapagos Islands, and off eastern Australia; and in the Gulf-Caribbean-Atlantic region north to the Gulf coast and Florida (possibly to North Carolina), and off the coasts of northeastern South America (Colombia to Guyana) and Africa.

Migrates regularly off both coasts of North America and along the Gulf coast (west to Texas and south to the Yucatan Peninsula); not recorded off the Caribbean coast of Middle America between southern Mexico and Costa Rica.

Casual in the interior of North America (from southern Canada south to southeastern California, Arizona, New Mexico, Coahuila and the Gulf states, frequently recorded in the Great Lakes region, especially on Lake Ontario), and in central Europe, Japan, New Zealand and Antarctica.

Notes.—Also known as Pomarine Skua or Pomatorhine Skua in the Old World. Cohen et al. (1997) presented evidence that *S. pomarinus* might be more closely related to the skuas (*Catharacta*) than to the other two species of *Stercorarius*.

Stercorarius parasiticus (Linnaeus). Parasitic Jaeger.

Larus parasiticus Linnaeus, 1758, Syst. Nat. (ed. 10) 1: 136. (intra tropicum Cancri, Europæ, Americæ, Asiæ = coast of Sweden.)

Habitat.—Barren and dwarf-shrub coastal tundra and coastal marshes (breeding); mostly pelagic, primarily over continental shelf, regularly near shore; migrants inland (rare) on large bodies of water (nonbreeding).

Distribution.—*Breeds* in North America from western and northern Alaska, northern Yukon, northwestern Mackenzie, and Banks, southern Melville, Cornwallis, southern Ellesmere and Baffin islands south to the Aleutians, Alaska Peninsula, Kodiak Island, central Mackenzie, southern Keewatin, northeastern Manitoba, Southampton Island, extreme northern Ontario, northern Quebec and northern Labrador; and in the Palearctic from Greenland, Jan Mayen, Spitsbergen, Bear Island and Franz Josef Land south to Iceland, the northern British Isles, northern Scandinavia, northern Russia, Novaya Zemlya, northern Siberia, the Commander Islands, Kamchatka and the Sea of Okhotsk. Nonbreeding birds occur in summer off the Pacific coast of North America south to California, off the Atlantic coast to Newfoundland, and in the interior to southern Canada; also along the northern coasts of Europe.

Winters mostly in offshore areas in the Pacific from central California to southern Chile, and west to eastern Australia and New Zealand; in the Atlantic from Maine and the British Isles south to Brazil, eastern Argentina, the west coast of Africa, and the Mediterranean region, occurring west in the Gulf-Caribbean area to Texas; and in the Indian Ocean in the Persian Gulf and Arabian Sea.

Migrates regularly along the Pacific coast of North America, and Atlantic coast from North Carolina to Florida, the Bahamas, Cuba and the Virgin Islands, less abundantly through the interior of North America (most frequently recorded in the Great Lakes region) south to southern California (Salton Sea), Arizona, Coahuila, Texas, the Gulf Coast, the Lesser Antilles and Grenadines, and casually along both coasts of Middle America.

A sight report off the Hawaiian Islands.

Notes.—Known in Old World literature as Arctic Skua.

Stercorarius longicaudus Vieillot. Long-tailed Jaeger.

Stercorarius longicaudus Vieillot, 1819, Nouv. Dict. Hist. Nat. (nouv. éd.) 32: 157. (le nord de l'Europe, de l'Asie et de l'Amérique = northern Europe.)

Habitat.—Open or alpine tundra, flats with sparse vegetation, less common in coastal tundra (breeding); pelagic, casually along seacoasts and on inland waters (nonbreeding).

Distribution.—*Breeds* in North America in western Alaska (including St. Matthew, St. Lawrence and Nunivak islands), and from northern Alaska, northern Yukon, northern Mackenzie, northern Keewatin and throughout the Canadian Arctic islands south to central Alaska (Brooks Range, Alaska Range, Susitna River highlands), southwestern Yukon, southern Keewatin, Southampton Island and northern Quebec; and in the Palearctic from Greenland, Iceland, Jan Mayen, Spitsbergen, Bear Island and Novaya Zemlya south to northern Scandinavia, northern Russia, northern Siberia, Anadyrland, Kamchatka and the Sea of Okhotsk. Nonbreeding birds occur rarely in summer south to the Aleutian Islands, south-coastal Alaska, southern Mackenzie and southern Hudson Bay.

Winters mostly at sea in the Pacific off southern South America, and in the South Atlantic south to Argentina (more commonly in the southern areas).

Migrates primarily well offshore, along the Pacific coast from the western Aleutians and southeastern Alaska to Middle America (recorded south to Costa Rica) and the Atlantic coast from Newfoundland to Florida, also rarely in the Hawaiian Islands and through the interior of North America (mostly in the Great Lakes region and from central British Columbia and the prairie regions of the Canadian provinces, the Great Plains states and Mississippi Valley south, casually through the western states), along the Gulf coast (Texas to Florida) and through the West Indies (recorded Cuba, Martinique and Barbados, and off Cayman Brac and Haiti); also off the coasts of Europe and Africa, casually in the Mediterranean region.

Accidental in New Zealand and South Georgia.

Notes.—In Old World literature known as Long-tailed Skua.

Subfamily LARINAE: Gulls

Genus *LARUS* Linnaeus

Larus Linnaeus, 1758, Syst. Nat. (ed. 10) 1: 136. Type, by subsequent designation (Selby, 1840), *Larus marinus* Linnaeus.

Hydrocoloeus Kaup, 1829, Skizz. Entw.-Ges. Eur. Thierw., pp. 113, 196. Type, by subsequent designation (G. R. Gray, 1841), *Larus minutus* Pallas.

Chroicocephalus Eyton, 1836. Cat. Brit. Birds, p. 53. Type, by original designation, *Larus capistratus* Temminck = *Larus ridibundus* Linnaeus.

Blasipus Bruch, 1853, J. Ornithol. 1: 108. Type, by original designation, *Larus modestus* Tschudi.

Microlarus Oberholser, 1974, Bird Life Texas, p. 982. Type, by original designation, *Sterna philadelphia* Ord.

Notes.—See comments under *Xema*.

Larus atricilla Linnaeus. Laughing Gull.

Larus Atricilla Linnaeus, 1758, Syst. Nat. (ed. 10) 1: 136. Based on the "Laughing Gull" Catesby, Nat. Hist. Carolina 1: 89, pl. 89. (in America = Bahamas.)

Habitat.—Beaches, estuaries, bays, inshore coastal waters; nests on sandy islands with scattered patches of tall grass and brush (breeding); also to cultivated fields, rarely on large inland bodies of water (nonbreeding).

Distribution.—*Breeds* on the Pacific coast of western Mexico from the head of the Gulf of California (formerly at the Salton Sea, southern California) and northwestern Sonora south to Colima; and in the Atlantic-Gulf-Caribbean region from southern New Brunswick and southern Nova Scotia (at least formerly) south locally along the coast to Florida and west to southern Texas, through the West Indies to islands off the north coast of Venezuela (Las Aves east to Tobago and Trinidad) and to French Guiana, and on islands off Campeche (Cayo Arcas) and Yucatán (Alacrán reef). Nonbreeding birds occur in summer regularly in southeastern California (Salton Sea), on the Great Lakes (especially Erie and Michigan), along the Gulf-Caribbean coast of Middle America, and along the west coast of Mexico.

Winters along the Pacific coast from Mexico (including the Revillagigedo islands) south to northern Peru (casually north to central California, and to the Galapagos Islands); and from the Gulf coast and North Carolina (casually north to southeastern New York) south throughout the Gulf-Caribbean region to the coast of South America (Colombia east to the Amazon delta).

Casual in the Hawaiian Islands; on the Pacific coast north to Washington; in the Revillagigedo Islands (Socorro Island; sight reports); Clipperton Island; in interior North America from southeastern Oregon, north-central California, southern Nevada, Arizona, New Mexico, western Montana, eastern Colorado, North Dakota, James Bay, and West Virginia southward; to the interior lakes of Middle America; and north to Newfoundland and Greenland. Accidental in Chile, the Marshall Islands, Samoa, Iceland, the British Isles, and continental Europe; sight reports for southeastern Alaska (Ketchikan), Saskatchewan and Manitoba.

Larus pipixcan Wagler. Franklin's Gull.

Larus Pipixcan Wagler, 1831, Isis von Oken, col. 515. (Advena est, neque educat stagnis Mexicanis Prolem = Mexico.)

Habitat.—Extensive fresh-water marshes in prairie, foraging also in nearby fields (breeding); beaches, bays, estuaries, lakes, rivers, marshes, ponds, and agricultural fields (nonbreeding).

Distribution.—*Breeds* from northwestern British Columbia (Kotcho Lake), central and eastern Alberta, central Saskatchewan, southern Manitoba and northwestern Minnesota south locally to east-central Oregon, northeastern California (once), southern Idaho, northwestern Utah, northwestern Wyoming and northeastern South Dakota, formerly northwestern Iowa (once). Nonbreeding birds occur in summer north to northeastern British Columbia and northeastern Manitoba, and south to southern California, northern New Mexico, southeastern Wyoming, Kansas, central Iowa, and the Great Lakes (especially Lake Michigan).

Winters primarily along the Pacific coast of South America south to southern Chile (also the Galapagos Islands), less commonly from Mexico southward, and (rarely) on high Andean lakes in Peru and Bolivia; also casually north to central coastal California and peninsular Florida.

Migrates regularly through western North America from southern British Columbia and the Rocky Mountains south (east to western Arkansas and coastal Louisiana) to southern California, through Mexico (casually to the Yucatan Peninsula), and along the Atlantic coast from southern Quebec, New Brunswick, Nova Scotia and Newfoundland, rarely to the Great Lakes region and the Mississippi and Ohio valleys, south to Florida and west on the Gulf coast to Louisiana.

Casual in southern Alaska (from Ugasik Bay east to Ketchikan, and on St. Paul Island in the Pribilofs), the Hawaiian Islands, and Europe. Accidental in the Revillagigedo Islands (Socorro Island), northern Baffin Island, Bermuda, the Antilles (Puerto Rico and St. Barthélemy), Amazonian Peru, Tristan da Cunha, and Iceland, the Faeroe Islands, the British Isles, continental Europe, the Azores, South Africa, and the Marshall and Truk islands; sight reports for northeastern Manitoba, Clipperton Island, and French Guiana.

Larus minutus Pallas. Little Gull.

> *Larus minutus* Pallas, 1776, Reise Versch. Prov. Russ. Reichs 3: 702. (Circa alueos majorum Sibiriae fluminum = Berezovo, Tobolsk, Siberia.)

Habitat.—Grassy marshes and lakes (breeding); beaches, bays, estuaries, rivers, lakes, ponds, marshes, and flooded fields (nonbreeding).

Distribution.—*Breeds* locally in North America in Manitoba (Churchill, 1981), southern Minnesota (Jackson County, 1986), northern Wisconsin (Manitowoc and Brown counties), northern Michigan (Delta County, to 1980), Ontario and southern Quebec (Montreal area, 1982); and in Eurasia from southern Scandinavia and northwestern Russia south to northern Europe, south-central Russia, central Siberia and Lake Baikal.

Winters in North America on the Great Lakes (especially Erie and Ontario), and along the Atlantic coast from Newfoundland to Virginia; and in the Old World from Iceland, the Faeroe Islands, British Isles, southern Scandinavia and the Baltic coast south to the Mediterranean, Black and Caspian seas, probably also in eastern China.

Migrates primarily through central Europe and western Asia.

Casual along the Atlantic coast south to Florida and in Bermuda; on the Arctic coast of Yukon; in the interior from southern Yukon, northeastern British Columbia, Alberta, Saskatchewan, northern Manitoba, Minnesota and the Great Lakes states south to New Mexico, central Texas, Kansas, Arkansas and the Gulf states (from Texas east to western Florida); and along the Pacific coast from southern British Columbia south to southern California; and in Colombia, Sierra Leone and Kenya. Sight reports for south-coastal Alaska, Idaho, Veracruz, and Puerto Rico.

Larus ridibundus Linnaeus. Black-headed Gull.

> *Larus ridibundus* Linnaeus, 1766, Syst. Nat. (ed. 12) 1: 225. (in Mari Europæo = England.)

Habitat.—Lakes, rivers, bogs, moors, grasslands, and coastal marshes; in winter, also seacoasts, estuaries, and bays.

Distribution.—*Breeds* from western Greenland, Iceland, the Faeroe Islands, central Scandinavia, northern Russia, and northern Siberia south to the Mediterranean Sea, central Russia, central Siberia, northwestern Mongolia and Kamchatka; also in Newfoundland, Quebec (Magdalen Islands), Maine (Petit Manan), and Massachusetts (Monomoy, 1984). Nonbreeding birds occur north to Jan Mayen Island and northern Scandinavia, occasionally south in the wintering regions.

Winters (and summers occasionally) in North America along the Atlantic coast from Labrador, Newfoundland, New Brunswick and Nova Scotia south to New York (Long Island), casually to Mississippi and Florida, and on lakes Erie and Ontario; and in the Old World from the southern part of the breeding range south to the eastern Atlantic islands, central Africa, the Persian Gulf, northern India, Malay Peninsula, eastern China, Taiwan and the Philippines.

Migrates regularly through the western and central Aleutians, regularly as far east as the Pribilofs and as far north as St. Lawrence Island, and casually as far as the Alaskan mainland coast of the Bering Sea (Port Moller, Safety Sound, Nome) and the Chukchi Sea (Kukpowruk River mouth).

Casual or accidental in the Hawaiian Islands (Midway, Oahu), in central Alaska (Yarger Lake), along the Pacific coast of North America from south-coastal Alaska to southern California, and in northeastern Colorado, Minnesota, Wisconsin, Illinois, Indiana, Tennessee, Kentucky, Maryland, Virginia, Kansas, Missouri, Arkansas, Texas, Veracruz, the Antilles (Puerto Rico, the Virgin Islands, and many of the Lesser Antilles) and Guam; sight reports from Wyoming, Manitoba (Churchill), Nebraska, Iowa, Alabama, Cuba, Trinidad, Surinam, and French Guiana.

Notes.—Also known as Common Black-headed Gull. The South American *L. maculipennis* Lichtenstein, 1823 [Brown-hooded Gull] was considered conspecific with *L. ridibundus* by Hellmayr and Conover (1948).

Larus philadelphia (Ord). Bonaparte's Gull.

> *Sterna Philadelphia* Ord, 1815, in Guthrie, Geogr. (ed. 2, Amer.) 2: 319. (No locality given = near Philadelphia, Pennsylvania.)

Habitat.—Open coniferous woodland near ponds and lakes (breeding); seacoasts, bays, estuaries, mudflats, marshes, rivers, lakes, ponds, and flooded fields (nonbreeding).

Distribution.—*Breeds* from western and central Alaska, central southern Yukon, northwestern and central Mackenzie and northern Manitoba south to the base of the Alaska Peninsula, south-coastal and (rarely) southeastern Alaska, central British Columbia, southwestern (rarely) and central Alberta, central Saskatchewan, southern Manitoba, central Ontario, Wisconsin, and south-central Quebec. Nonbreeding birds occur in summer south in coastal areas to California and New England, and in southeastern California (Salton Sea) and the interior to the Great Lakes (where formerly bred).

Winters from south-coastal British Columbia (casually from south-coastal Alaska) south along the Pacific coast to southern Baja California, Sonora and Sinaloa; in the interior from interior California (rarely), southern Arizona, central New Mexico, Kansas and the Great Lakes (primarily Erie and Ontario) south to Chihuahua (rarely to Jalisco and Guanajuato) and through the Ohio and lower Mississippi valleys to the Gulf coast from southern Texas east to Florida; on the Atlantic coast from Massachusetts south to Florida, and in Bermuda, the Bahamas and Greater Antilles (Cuba, Hispaniola, Puerto Rico).

Migrates most commonly through North America from the Rockies east to the Appalachians, but locally or sporadically elsewhere throughout the continent from southern Canada and Newfoundland southward.

Casual or accidental in the Hawaiian Islands, Lesser Antilles (Martinique, Barbados), Greenland, the British Isles, continental Europe, the Azores, and Japan; sight reports from the Yucatan Peninsula and Costa Rica.

Larus heermanni Cassin. Heermann's Gull.

> *Larus Heermanni* Cassin, 1852, Proc. Acad. Nat. Sci. Philadelphia 6: 187. (San Diego, California.)

Habitat.—Coastal Waters, Coastal Sand Beaches; nests on flat rocky islets or isolated coasts.

Distribution.—*Breeds* on islets off the Pacific coast of Baja California (Isla Benito del Centro in the San Benito Islands, and Isla San Roque), in the Gulf of California (George, Raza, Salsipuedes, Ildefonso and Monserrate islands), locally on islets off Mexico south to Isla Isabela (off Nayarit), and elsewhere along the coast of Sinaloa; isolated breeding reports in coastal California (San Luis Obispo County, 1980, Alcatraz Island 1979–1981). Nonbreeding individuals often spend the breeding season in the postbreeding range.

Ranges after the breeding season north coastally to southern British Columbia and south to the Pacific coast of Guatemala (at least casually).

Casual or accidental in southeastern Alaska (Ketchikan), the Revillagigedo Islands (Socorro Island), eastern Oregon, interior California, western Nevada (Pyramid Lake), Utah, southern Arizona, Wyoming, southern New Mexico, Oklahoma (Tulsa), Texas (Reagan and Nueces counties), Michigan (Lake St. Clair), and Ohio (Lorain); sight report for Costa Rica.

Larus modestus Tschudi. Gray Gull.

> *Larus modestus* Tschudi, 1843, Arch. Naturgesch. 9: 389. (in Oceani pacifici littoribus = Lurín, south of Lima, Peru.)

Habitat.—Interior Deserts (breeding); Coastal Waters (nonbreeding).

Distribution.—*Breeds* in Chile and *ranges* in nonbreeding season along the Pacific coast of South America from Ecuador to central Chile.

Accidental off Costa Rica (Cocos Island, 22 May 1925; Slud 1967) and off Colombia (Gorgona Island); sight reports for Panama (Pacific entrance to Canal, and south of Isla Otoque in the Bay of Panama). A bird photographed in Cameron Parish, Louisiana, 19 December 1987 (1988, Amer. Birds 42: 277) may not be a natural vagrant.

Larus belcheri Vigors. Band-tailed Gull.

> *Larus belcheri* Vigors, 1829, Zool. J. 4 (1828): 358. (No locality given = Peru.)

Habitat.—Coastal Waters; in winter also in bays and estuaries.

Distribution.—*Breeds* along the Pacific coast of South America in Peru and northwestern Chile.

Casual in Panama (Pacific coast of Canal area, several sight reports, one adult photographed (Ridgely and Gwynne 1989).

Also Florida (near Pensacola, September 1968, weakened individual caught, photographed and kept in captivity for more than a decade; Marco Island, 6 June 1970, adult photographed; Cape Romano, 11 November 1974–29 January 1975, photographed; and near Marco, January–11 February 1976, adult photographed).

Notes.—We follow Devillers (1977b) in recognizing *L. belcheri* and *L. atlanticus* Olrog, 1958 [Olrog's Gull] of the Atlantic coast of South America as separate species. Photographs of birds in nonbreeding plumage (Pensacola and Cape Romano individuals) have been identified as the Pacific *L. belcheri,* suggesting the possibility that Florida birds are escaped captives or man-assisted vagrants; other reports and photographs of birds in breeding plumage cannot be identified to group. Also known as Belcher's Gull.

Larus crassirostris Vieillot. Black-tailed Gull.

> *Larus crassirostris* Vieillot, 1818, Nouv. Dict. Hist. Nat. (nouv. éd.) 21: 508. (Nagasaki, Japan.)

Habitat.—Small, rocky, coastal islands (breeding); coastal waters (nonbreeding).

Distribution.—*Breeds* from southern Sakhalin, Ussuriland and the Kuril Islands south through Japan to eastern China and Korea, and *winters* along coasts from Japan and Korea south to eastern China, Taiwan and the Ryukyu Islands.

Casual or accidental in Alaska (St. Lawrence Island, off Buldir in the western Aleutians, Homer and Ketchikan), coastal British Columbia (Queen Charlotte Islands), southern California (San Diego Bay, 16–18 November 1954, specimen; Monroe 1955), Belize (Dangriga, March 1988), and Maryland (Sandy Point, photograph; 1984, Amer. Birds 38: 1006–1007); sight reports for Attu and Amchitka in the Aleutians, and for southern Manitoba, Rhode Island, and Virginia.

Larus canus Linnaeus. Mew Gull.

> *Larus canus* Linnaeus, 1758, Syst. Nat. (ed. 10) 1: 136. (in Europa = Sweden.)

Habitat.—Rocky or sandy coasts or inland along large lakes, rivers, marshes and other wetlands (breeding); rocky seacoasts, estuaries, beaches, and bays (nonbreeding).

Distribution.—*Breeds* [*brachyrhynchus* group] in North America from western and central Alaska (Brooks Range and Kotzebue Sound), central Yukon, and northwestern and southern Mackenzie south to the Alaska Peninsula, south-coastal and southeastern Alaska, coastal and northern British Columbia (including the Queen Charlotte and Vancouver islands) and northern Alberta, also in northeastern Manitoba (Churchill); [*canus* group] in Eurasia from the Faeroe Islands, British Isles, Scandinavia and northern Russia east to central Siberia (Lena River), and south to central Europe, the Black and Caspian seas, Lake Baikal, northern Mongolia and southwestern Siberia; and [*kamtschatschensis* group] in Siberia west to the Lena River and south to Anadyrland, the Sea of Okhotsk, Kamchatka, the Kuril Islands and Sakhalin. Nonbreeding birds [*brachyrhynchus* group] occur in summer north to the northern coast of Alaska and northern Keewatin, and south to California, central Alberta and central Saskatchewan.

Winters [*brachyrhynchus* group] in North America from southern Alaska (west to the central Aleutians) south along the Pacific coast to northern Baja California, casually (or rarely) inland to southern British Columbia, eastern Washington, eastern Oregon, interior California, Nevada, Utah and Arizona, and rarely to the Atlantic coast from New Brunswick, Nova Scotia and Newfoundland south to Massachusetts (sight reports farther south); [*canus* group] in the Old World from the breeding range south to the Mediterranean region, northern Africa, Iraq, the Persian Gulf and Afghanistan; and [*kamtschatschensis* group] in Southeast Asia, coastal China, Taiwan, Japan, and islands south of Japan.

Migrates [*brachyrhynchus* group] regularly through interior British Columbia and northern Yukon.

Casual or accidental [*brachyrhynchus* group] in the western Hawaiian Islands (Kure), and in continental North America from Idaho, Montana, North Dakota, Minnesota, Wisconsin, Illinois, Michigan, southern Ontario, southern Quebec, New York and southern New England south to southern New Mexico, Texas, Illinois, Ohio and Delaware (sight reports to Iowa, Indiana, Pennsylvania, and Florida); [*canus* group] in Nova Scotia (winter 1988–1989, photograph; 1989, Amer. Birds 43: 279), Greenland, Iceland, Spitsbergen, Bear Island, and the eastern Atlantic and Commander islands; and [*kamtschatschensis* group] in the western Aleutians (Attu, Shemya) and the Pribilofs (St. Paul). Other reports of the *canus* group from eastern North America are unsubstantiated; all specimens from this region are *brachyrhynchus*.

Notes.—Also known as Common Gull or Short-billed Gull. Groups: *L. brachyrhynchus* Richardson, 1831 [Short-billed Gull], *L. canus* [Mew Gull], and *L. kamtschatschensis* Bonaparte, 1857 [Kamchatka Gull].

Larus delawarensis Ord. Ring-billed Gull.

Larus Delawarensis Ord, 1815, in Guthrie, Geogr. (ed. 2, Amer.) 2: 319. (Delaware River, below Philadelphia, Pennsylvania.)

Habitat.—Lakes, marshes, rivers, nesting on rocky, grassy and sandy islets, isolated shores, or occasionally in marshes (breeding); seacoasts, bays, estuaries, rivers, lakes, ponds, irrigated and plowed fields, and parks and garbage dumps in urban areas (nonbreeding).

Distribution.—*Breeds* from central interior British Columbia, western and central Washington, northeastern Alberta, northwestern and central Saskatchewan, north-central Manitoba, northern Ontario, southern Quebec, Prince Edward Island, southern Labrador and northeastern Newfoundland south to northeastern California (Honey Lake), northwestern Nevada, northwestern Utah, south-central Colorado (formerly), Wyoming, northeastern South Dakota (Waubay Lake), east-central Minnesota, eastern Wisconsin, northern Illinois southern Michigan, southern Ontario, northern Ohio (Lucas County), central New York (Lake Oneida), central New Hampshire and New Brunswick. Nonbreeding individuals occur in summer north to south-coastal Alaska, southern Yukon, southern Mackenzie, and southeastern Keewatin, and south through the wintering range.

Winters in the Hawaiian Islands, and from southern British Columbia, the northern United States, southern Ontario, southern Quebec and the Gulf of St. Lawrence south along the Pacific coast to southern Mexico (including the Revillagigedo Islands), in the interior to central Mexico, on the Gulf coast south to the Yucatan Peninsula (and east to Florida) and on the Atlantic coast to Florida, Bermuda, the Bahamas, the Greater Antilles (east to the Virgin Islands), and the Cayman Islands.

Casual or accidental in interior Alaska, Guatemala, El Salvador, Costa Rica (Chomes), Panama, the Lesser Antilles (south to Barbados), Colombia, Ecuador, the Galapagos Islands, Amazonian Brazil, and to Japan, Iceland, Greenland, the British Isles, continental Europe, Spitsbergen. the Canary Islands and Morocco; a sight report from Caribbean Honduras.

Larus californicus Lawrence. California Gull.

> *Larus Californicus* Lawrence, 1854, Ann. Lyc. Nat. Hist. N. Y. 6: 79. (near Stockton, California.)

Habitat.—Lakes and marshes, foraging also in nearby agricultural fields; nests on open sandy or gravelly areas on islands or along shores of lakes and ponds (breeding); rocky seacoasts, beaches, bays, estuaries, mudflats, marshes, irrigated fields, lakes, ponds, agricultural lands, and in urban areas in garbage dumps (nonbreeding).

Distribution.—*Breeds* from southern interior British Columbia, Idaho and southwestern Montana south to south-central Washington, south-central and southeastern Oregon, northern California, western Nevada, northern Utah and central and eastern Colorado, and from southern Mackenzie south through Alberta, Saskatchewan and Manitoba to central Montana, east-central North Dakota and northeastern South Dakota. Occurs in summer and fall (nonbreeding) in southeastern Alaska (from the Stikine River south), rarely as far north and west as south-coastal Alaska (Anchorage), throughout California, and south to northern New Mexico.

Winters from southwestern and south-central British Columbia, eastern Idaho, Montana and eastern Colorado south throughout the western United States, most commonly along the Pacific coast, to southern Baja California, the Pacific coast of Mexico (to Colima and in the Revillagigedo Islands), and locally the interior of Mexico (to México).

Casual or accidental in the Hawaiian Islands and Revillagigedos (Socorro Island), in eastern North America from northeastern Manitoba, Minnesota, the Great Lakes, Quebec, New York and New Brunswick south to the Gulf coast of Texas, southwestern Louisiana and western Florida, and in Guerrero. Reports from Guatemala are erroneous.

Notes.—The species listed from *L. californicus* through *L. fuscus* are closely interrelated; this complex poses one of the most complicated problems in ornithological systematics today.

Larus argentatus Pontoppidan. Herring Gull.

> *Larus Argentatus* Pontoppidan, 1763, Dan. Atlas 1: 622. (No locality given = Christiansöe, Denmark.)

Habitat.—Wide variety of habitats near water, nesting on rocky or sandy coasts, on tundra, on islands in larger lakes and rivers, and on cliffs (breeding); seacoasts, beaches, bays, estuaries, lakes, rivers, ocean over continental shelf, and garbage dumps in urban areas (nonbreeding).

Distribution.—*Breeds* in North America from northern Alaska, northern Yukon, northern Mackenzie, central Keewatin, Southampton and western Baffin islands, northern Quebec and northern Labrador south to south-coastal and southeastern Alaska, south-central British Columbia, central Alberta, central Saskatchewan, southeastern Wyoming, southern Manitoba, northern Minnesota, northern Wisconsin, northeastern Illinois, northeastern Indiana, northern Ohio, southern Ontario, northern New York, and along the Atlantic coast to northeastern South Carolina, also isolated breeding in southern Alabama (Gaillard Island), southern Louisiana (Chandeleur Islands) and southern Texas (Cameron County); and in the Palearctic from Greenland (occasionally), Iceland, the Faeroe Islands, British Isles, Scandinavia and northern Europe across northern Russia and northern Siberia to Kamchatka, the Chukotski Peninsula, Anadyrland and the Sea of Okhotsk, and south locally to Italy. Nonbreeding birds summer south through much of the wintering range, especially in coastal areas.

Winters in the Hawaiian Islands (rarely); from the Aleutian Islands, southern Alaska, the Great Lakes region and Newfoundland south (mostly at sea and along coasts, large rivers and lakes, uncommonly through the western and central interior) through North America, Middle America (including the Revillagigedo Islands, but rare south of Mexico), Bermuda, and the West Indies to Panama and Barbados; and in the Old World mostly in the breeding range south to central Europe, the Mediterranean region, Black and Caspian seas, Gulf of Aden, Persian Gulf, India, central China, Taiwan, and the Ryukyu and Bonin islands.

Sight reports for the Revillagigedo Islands (Socorro Island) and northern South America.

Notes.—For comments on relationships or hybridization, see notes under *L. californicus, L. cachinnans, L. thayeri, L. fuscus, L. glaucescens, L. hyperboreus,* and *L. marinus.*

Larus cachinnans Pallas. Yellow-legged Gull.

> *Larus cachinnans* Pallas, 1811, Zoogr. Rosso-Asiat. 2: 318. (Caspian Sea.)

Habitat.— Seacoasts, lakes, and rivers.

Distribution—*Breeds* from the eastern Atlantic islands, southern Europe and northern Africa east to central Asia, and *winters* south to northeastern Africa and the Persian Gulf.

Casual in Maryland (Sandy Point) and District of Columbia (photographs; Wilds and Czaplak 1994). Accidental in Quebec (Fatima, Madeleine Islands, 16 August 1973; specimen #60750 in Canadian Museum of Nature) and Newfoundland (St. John's, photograph; 1995, Nat. Audubon. Soc. Field Notes 49: 122).

Notes.—*L. cachinnans* is a species distinct from *L. argentatus* (Marion et al. 1985, Yésou 1991). The specimen from Quebec was reported as a probable hybrid between *L. argentatus* and *L. fuscus* (Gosselin et al. 1986) but has been re-identified as *L. cachinnans* (Wilds and Czaplak 1994).

Larus thayeri Brooks. Thayer's Gull.

> *Larus thayeri* Brooks, 1915, Bull. Mus. Comp. Zool. Harv. 59: 373. (Buchanan Bay, Ellesmere Land.)

Habitat.—Arctic coasts and tundra, nesting on cliffs facing sounds (breeding); seacoasts, estuaries, and bays, less commonly on large inland lakes and rivers and garbage dumps (nonbreeding).

Distribution.—*Breeds* from Banks, southern Melville, Cornwallis, Axel Heiberg and central Ellesmere islands south to southern Victoria Island, northern Keewatin, northern Southampton and northern Baffin islands, and on northwestern Greenland. Nonbreeding birds sometimes summer in the wintering range.

Winters primarily on the Pacific coast from southern British Columbia south to central Baja California, less commonly in south-coastal and southeastern Alaska, the Gulf of St. Lawrence, and sparingly on the southern Great Lakes, rarely in the interior south to southern California, southern Arizona, southern New Mexico, and the Gulf coast from Texas east to Florida, and casually on the Atlantic coast south to Florida.

Casual in Newfoundland.

Notes.—*L. thayeri* was formerly (A.O.U. 1957) regarded as a race of *L. argentatus,* but it is now generally regarded as a distinct species. However, it is treated as a subspecies of *L. glaucoides* by Godfrey (1986). Recent studies suggest that *L. thayeri* and *L. glaucoides kumlieni* interbreed on Baffin and Southampton islands (Gaston and Decker 1985, Snell 1989). Relationships of these populations require further study. See comments under *L. californicus* and *L. glaucoides.*

Larus glaucoides Meyer. Iceland Gull.

> *Larus glaucoides* "Temm." Meyer, 1822, in Meyer and Wolf, Zusatz. Berich. Taschenb. Dtsch. Vögelkd., p. 197. (Meere der arktischen Zone, z. B. in Island, zuweilen im Herbst an den Küsten der Ost- und Nordsee = Iceland.)

Habitat.—Arctic coasts, nesting on steep cliffs and ledges facing sounds and fjords (breeding); primarily coastal waters, less commonly on ocean over continental shelf, rarely on large inland bodies of water (nonbreeding).

Distribution.—*Breeds* [*kumlieni* group] on southern Baffin Island (Foxe Peninsula and

Home Bay southward) and in northwestern Quebec (Erik Cove, Digges Island); and [*glaucoides* group] in the Palearctic in Greenland and Jan Mayen.

Winters [*kumlieni* group] in North America from Newfoundland and the Gulf of St. Lawrence south on the Atlantic coast to Virginia and Bermuda, and inland to the Great Lakes (especially lakes Erie and Ontario, rarely farther west); and [*glaucoides* group] in the Palearctic from Iceland, the Faeroe Islands and Scandinavia south, at least rarely, to the British Isles, northern Europe and the Baltic region.

Casual [*kumlieni* group] in interior North America (recorded from Montana, Nebraska, Iowa and Indiana) and Bermuda; sight reports west to Alaska, and south, east of the Great Plains, to the Gulf states. Accidental [*kumlieni* group] in British Columbia, Texas, Georgia and Florida.

Notes.—Reports of individuals of the *glaucoides* group in North America in winter remain to be verified. The *kumlieni* group might be regarded as a distinct species, *L. kumlieni* Brewster, 1883 [Kumlien's Gull]. See comments under *L. thayeri.*

Larus fuscus Linnaeus. Lesser Black-backed Gull.

Larus fuscus Linnaeus, 1758, Syst. Nat. (ed. 10) 1: 136. (in Europa = Sweden.)

Habitat.— Tundra, along sandy or rocky coasts, and on islands in lakes and larger rivers (breeding); coastal regions, bays, estuaries, inland on lakes and rivers, and garbage dumps in urban areas (nonbreeding).

Distribution.—*Breeds* from Greenland (occasionally), Iceland, the Faeroe Islands, northern Scandinavia, northern Russia and northern Siberia (east to the Taimyr Peninsula) south to the British Isles and France. Nonbreeding birds sometimes summer in the wintering range.

Winters from the British Isles, southern Scandinavia and the Baltic Sea south to central Africa, the Red Sea, Persian Gulf and India; also in small numbers (but increasing) in North America from the Great Lakes region, Labrador, southeastern Quebec, Newfoundland and Nova Scotia and Bermuda south to the Gulf coast (west to Missouri, Oklahoma, Texas and northern Tamaulipas) and Florida.

Casual in Alaska, northwestern Mackenzie, Victoria Island, British Columbia, Saskatchewan, Manitoba, California, eastern Colorado, Minnesota, Puerto Rico, and St. Croix (Virgin Islands). Accidental in Panama; sight reports for Utah, North Dakota, Nebraska, Trinidad, and French Guiana. A report from Australia is erroneous.

Notes.—*L. argentatus* and *L. fuscus* are widely sympatric with only local hybridization (Brown 1967).

Larus schistisagus Stejneger. Slaty-backed Gull.

Larus schistisagus Stejneger, 1884, Auk 1: 231. (Bering Island and Petropaulski, Kamtschatka = Bering Island, Commander Islands.)

Habitat.— Rocky seacoasts, on cliffs and rocky islands, nesting occasionally on flat sandy shores with bushes (breeding); coastal waters (nonbreeding).

Distribution.—*Breeds* from the Gulf of Anadyr and the western Bering Sea coast south through Kamchatka and the Kuril Islands to Sakhalin and Japan. Nested in 1996 on Bering Sea coast of Alaska (1996, N.A.S. Field Notes 50:984). Reported breeding at Harrowby Bay, northwestern Mackenzie, has been seriously questioned (Höhn 1958).

Winters from the Bering Sea and Kamchatka south to Japan, the Seven Islands of Izu, Volcano and Ryukyu islands, and the coast of eastern China. Occurs throughout the year (nonbreeding) on coasts of western and southwestern Alaska (from the Bering Strait south to the Pribilof and Aleutian islands), rarely (in summer) as far north as Barrow and east as Prudhoe Bay.

Casual in south-coastal (Kodiak, Homer, Anchorage) and southeastern Alaska (Juneau, Ketchikan). Accidental in the Hawaiian Islands (Kure, Sand Island), British Columbia (Vancouver Island), southern Saskatchewan, Washington, Oregon, Missouri, Illinois, Indiana, southern Texas, Quebec, and the Niagara River in Ontario and New York; sight reports for Yukon, Iowa, and Ohio.

Notes.—See comments under *L. glaucescens.*

Larus livens Dwight. Yellow-footed Gull.

> *Larus occidentalis livens* Dwight, 1919, Proc. Biol. Soc. Wash. 32: 11. (San Jose Island, Lower [= Baja] California.)

Habitat.—Coastal Waters, Coastal Sand Beaches; nests on islands; during post-breeding dispersal, also inland along shores of Salton Sea, California.

Distribution.—*Breeds* in the Gulf of California from George Island and Consag Rock south to Espíritu Santo and San Pedro Nolasco islands.

Migrates to southern interior California (Salton Sea).

Winters in the Gulf of California and along the coast of Sonora, rarely in southern interior California (Salton Sea), and casually north to coastal southern California (San Diego County) and southern Nevada.

Casual south to Oaxaca (sight report).

Notes.—This species was formerly (A.O.U. 1957) considered conspecific with *L. occidentalis,* but differences in morphology, habitat, behavior, and vocalizations (Hand 1981, Weber 1981) indicate that it should be treated as a species.

Larus occidentalis Audubon. Western Gull.

> *Larus occidentalis* Audubon, 1839, Ornithol. Biogr. 5: 320. (Cape Disappointment [Washington].)

Habitat.—Coastal waters, nesting on rocky islands and coastal cliffs (breeding); beaches, rocky coasts, bays, estuaries, ocean over continental shelf, and garbage dumps in urban areas (nonbreeding).

Distribution.—*Breeds* along the Pacific coast from southwestern British Columbia south to west-central Baja California (Isla Asunción) and Guadalupe Island.

Winters from south-coastal British Columbia south to southern Baja California, casually to interior Oregon and southern California, and to the coast of Sonora.

Accidental in Alaska, southern Yukon, Idaho, Nevada, Arizona, northern New Mexico, western and coastal Texas, and Guerrero; sight reports for the Hawaiian Islands and Oaxaca.

Notes.—See comments under *L. glaucescens* and *L. livens.*

Larus glaucescens Naumann. Glaucous-winged Gull.

> *Larus glaucescens* J. F. Naumann, 1840, Naturgesch. Vögel Dtsch. 10: 351. (Nord-Amerika = North America.)

Habitat.—Rocky seacoasts and other coastal waters, nesting on flats and grassy slopes of islands, cliffs (breeding); beaches, rocky coasts, bays, estuaries, ocean over continental shelf, and garbage dumps in urban areas (nonbreeding).

Distribution.—*Breeds* in North America from the southern Bering Sea (including the Pribilof and Aleutian islands), and southern and southeastern Alaska south along the Pacific coast to western Washington and northwestern Oregon; and in the Commander Islands. Nonbreeding birds often summer in the wintering range.

Winters in North America from the southern Bering Sea and southern Alaska south along the Pacific coast to southern Baja California and the Gulf of California, rarely in the interior in Utah; and in Asia from Bering Island to Kamchatka, the Kuril Islands and Japan.

Casual or accidental in the Hawaiian Islands, and in interior western North America from Yukon, Alberta, Saskatchewan and southern Manitoba south to southwestern Arizona, southwestern New Mexico, central and northeastern Colorado, North Dakota, Minnesota, Wisconsin, Illinois, Nebraska and Oklahoma, and the Revillagigedo Islands.

Notes.—Frequent hybridization between *L. glaucescens* and *L. occidentalis* occurs in mixed colonies from northern Washington to southern Oregon, but mating is assortative (Hoffman et al. 1978) and gene flow is constrained (Bell 1996). Hybridization also occurs between *L. glaucescens* and *L. argentatus,* at least on a limited basis, in south-coastal and southeastern Alaska (Williamson and Peyton 1963, Patten and Weisbrod 1974), and between

L. glaucescens and *L. schistisagus* in Kamchatka (Firsova and Levada 1982, as cited *in* Bell 1996).

Larus hyperboreus Gunnerus. Glaucous Gull.

Larus hyperboreus Gunnerus, 1767, in Leem, Beskr. Finm. Lapper, p. 226 (note). (Northern Norway.)

Habitat.—Sea cliffs, rocky coasts, or borders of tundra lakes (breeding); estuaries, bays beaches, less commonly on ocean over continental shelf, along large inland bodies of water, and garbage dumps (nonbreeding).

Distribution.—*Breeds* in North America on Arctic coasts and islands from western and northern Alaska (south to Hooper Bay, and St. Lawrence, St. Matthew, Hall and, at least formerly, the Pribilof islands), northern Yukon, northern Mackenzie, and Banks, Prince Patrick, Ellef Ringnes and northern Ellesmere islands south to northern Keewatin, northern Quebec, northern Labrador (south to Hopedale), and to Southampton, Coats, Belcher and southern Baffin islands; and in the Palearctic from northern Greenland, Iceland, Jan Mayen, Spitsbergen, Bear Island and Franz Josef Land east across northern Russia and northern Siberia (including Novaya Zemlya and the New Siberian Islands) to Anadyrland. Nonbreeding individuals occasionally summer in the wintering range.

Winters in North America from the southern Chukchi Sea (rarely) and Bering Sea south through the Pacific region to northern Baja California, and on the Atlantic-Gulf coasts from Labrador south to Florida and (rarely) west to Texas, and inland to the Great Lakes; and in the Palearctic from the breeding range south to the British Isles, northern Europe, and central Siberia, casually to the Mediterranean, Black, and Caspian seas.

Casual in the Hawaiian Islands; in coastal Sonora; in the interior of North America from southern Canada (where more regular in occurrence) south to California, Nevada, Utah, southern Arizona, and New Mexico; and in Bermuda and the eastern Atlantic islands.

Notes.—Reports of extensive hybridization between *L. hyperboreus* and *L. argentatus* in Iceland (Ingolfsson 1987) have been questioned (see Ingolfsson 1993, Snell 1993). *Larus hyperboreus* hybridizes to an uncertain degree with *L. glaucescens* in the eastern Bering Sea region (Strang 1977).

Larus marinus Linnaeus. Great Black-backed Gull.

Larus marinus Linnaeus, 1758, Syst. Nat. (ed. 10) 1: 136. (in Europa = Gotland, Sweden.)

Habitat.—Rocky coasts and islands, occasionally on inland lakes (breeding); estuaries, beaches, bays, rocky coasts, garbage dumps in urban areas, less commonly on large inland bodies of water and on ocean over continental shelf (nonbreeding).

Distribution.—*Breeds* in North America along the Atlantic coast from northern Quebec, northern Labrador and Newfoundland south to the St. Lawrence River, Anticosti Island, and (along the coast) to North Carolina, also in southern Ontario (Lake Huron and northern Lake Ontario), New York (Lake Oneida, casually) and northern Vermont (Lake Champlain); and in the Palearctic from Greenland, Iceland, the Faeroe Islands, Shetlands, Spitsbergen, Bear Island, northern Scandinavia and northern Russia south to the British Isles, northern Europe and central Russia. Nonbreeding individuals occasionally summer north to southern Baffin Island, west to Hudson Bay, and south through the wintering range.

Winters in North America along the Atlantic coast from Newfoundland south to Florida, in Bermuda, inland on the Great Lakes, and rarely on the Gulf coast of Florida (casually west to southern Texas); also in Eurasia from Iceland, the Faeroe Islands, British Isles, Scandinavia, and northern Europe south to the Mediterranean, Black and Caspian seas, casually to the eastern Atlantic islands.

Casual west to British Columbia, Alberta (sight report), Saskatchewan (sight reports) Manitoba, Montana, north-central and eastern Colorado and Nebraska, and south to the Bahamas (Abaco, San Salvador) and Antilles (Cuba, Hispaniola, Mona Island, Puerto Rico, St. Barthélemy and Barbados); a sight report for Belize.

Genus *XEMA* Leach

Xema Leach, 1819, in Ross, Voy. Discovery, app. 2, p. lvii. Type, by monotypy, *Larus sabini* Sabine.

Notes.—The genus *Xema* is merged in *Larus* by some authors (e.g., Vaurie 1965, Cramp and Simmons 1983).

Xema sabini (Sabine). Sabine's Gull.

Larus Sabini J. Sabine, 1819, Trans. Linn. Soc. London 12: 522, pl. 29. (Sabine Islands near Melville Bay, west coast of Greenland.)

Habitat.—Coastal wet meadows and salt-grass flats in tundra (breeding); primarily pelagic, mainly over continental shelf, casually along coasts or in inland lakes (nonbreeding).

Distribution.—*Breeds* in North America from northern and coastal western Alaska (south to Bristol Bay), northwestern Mackenzie, and Banks, Victoria, Bathurst, northwestern Devon and Bylot islands south locally to King William, southern Southampton and southwestern Baffin islands, and northern Keewatin; and in the Palearctic in northern Greenland and Spitsbergen, and from the New Siberian Islands and northern Siberia south to the Taimyr Peninsula and Lena Delta. Nonbreeding birds occur in summer to northern Ellesmere Island, central Alberta, Saskatchewan, Manitoba, northern Ontario, and northeastern Quebec, casually at sea south to wintering areas.

Winters at sea in the eastern Pacific from southern Baja California (at least irregularly) and Panama south to central Chile; and, less commonly, in the Atlantic (primarily tropical areas, rarely the North Atlantic).

Migrates regularly through the Pacific region (mostly coastal) of North America from Alaska to Costa Rica; along Hudson Bay (Churchill) and the Atlantic coast (from Labrador to New England, irregularly to Florida); and around Iceland and the coasts of Europe.

Casual through the interior of North America (mostly in migration) from Idaho, Alberta, Montana, North Dakota and the Great Lakes south to southeastern California, Arizona, New Mexico, Texas, the Gulf coast, Yucatan Peninsula and Cuba; in Caribbean Panama (Canal area); and to Japan and the North Sea.

Genus *RISSA* Stephens

Rissa Stephens, 1826, in Shaw, Gen. Zool. 13(1): 180. Type, by monotypy, *Rissa brunnichii* Stephens = *Larus tridactylus* Linnaeus.

Rissa tridactyla (Linnaeus). Black-legged Kittiwake.

Larus tridactylus Linnaeus, 1758, Syst. Nat. (ed. 10) 1: 136. (in Europa septentrionali = Great Britain.)

Habitat.—Rocky seacoasts and islands, occasionally on ledges of buildings in Old World (breeding); primarily pelagic, also pack ice, sometimes along seacoasts, bays, and estuaries, casually on large inland bodies of water (nonbreeding).

Distribution.—*Breeds* in Alaska along the Chukchi and Bering seacoasts and on Bering Sea islands from Cape Lisburne and the Diomede Islands south to the Aleutians, and east along the Pacific coast to Glacier Bay and Dixon Harbor; in northeastern North America from eastern Somerset, Prince Leopold, Bylot and Cobourg islands south locally through northern and central Baffin Island, Labrador (probably) and Newfoundland to southeastern Quebec, New Brunswick and Nova Scotia; and in the Palearctic from Greenland, Iceland, the Faeroe Islands, Jan Mayen, Spitsbergen, Franz Josef Land, Novaya Zemlya, and the New Siberian, Bennet and Wrangel islands south to the British Isles, northern Europe, the northern Russian coast, Sakhalin, Kamchatka, and the Kuril and Commander islands. Nonbreeding birds occur in summer along the Arctic coast and islands of Alaska and Canada, rarely south along the Pacific coast to California.

Winters along the Pacific coast of North America from the southern Bering Sea and southern Alaska south (irregularly) to Baja California, casually to Nayarit (San Blas); in the Great Lakes region; along the Atlantic coast (mostly offshore) from Newfoundland, Nova

Scotia and the Gulf of St. Lawrence south to Florida, less frequently to Bermuda; and in the Old World from the breeding range south to northwestern Africa, the Mediterranean region and Japan, casually to the Cape Verde Islands, West Africa, and the Baltic Sea.

Casual in the Hawaiian Islands (Kure east to Laysan, and on Oahu); in the interior of North America from Alberta, Saskatchewan, Manitoba and Minnesota south to southeastern California, Arizona, New Mexico and the Gulf coast (Texas east to western Florida); and in the Bahamas (Andros, Great Abaco, Berry Islands) and Greater Antilles (Cuba, off Jamaica, Virgin Islands). Accidental in South Africa; sight reports for Peru and the Lesser Antilles (St. Lucia).

Rissa brevirostris (Bruch). Red-legged Kittiwake.

Larus (Rissa) brevirostris "Brandt" Bruch, 1853, J. Ornithol. 1: 103. (Nord-Westküste von Amerika = Northwestern America.)

Habitat.—Steep cliffs on islands (breeding); primarily pelagic, mostly beyond continental shelf, and pack ice (nonbreeding).

Distribution.—*Breeds* in Alaska in the Pribilof (St. George, St. Paul), Aleutian (Buldir, Bogoslof, Fire Islands) and Commander islands.

Winters in the extreme northern Pacific Ocean, occurring east to the Gulf of Alaska (Kodiak and Middleton islands).

Casual or accidental on St. Lawrence Island, in east-central Alaska (near junction of Kandik and Yukon rivers), west-central Yukon (Forty Mile), coastal British Columbia, coastal Washington, northwestern Oregon, southern California, and Nevada (near Las Vegas); a sight report for southwestern Washington.

Genus *RHODOSTETHIA* MacGillivray

Rhodostethia MacGillivray, 1842, Man. Brit. Ornithol. 2: 252. Type, by original designation, *Larus rossii* Richardson = *Larus roseus* MacGillivray.

Rhodostethia rosea (MacGillivray). Ross's Gull.

Larus roseus MacGillivray, 1824, Mem. Wernerian Nat. Hist. Soc. 5: 249. (Alagnak, Melville Peninsula, Canada.)

Habitat.—Arctic coasts, river deltas, and marshy tundra (breeding); mostly pelagic in Arctic waters, often around pack ice, rarely in coastal waters (nonbreeding).

Distribution.—*Breeds* in northern Siberia from the Kolyma Delta to Aby, Malaya (on the Alazeya River), Sredne Kolymsk and the Chaun River, and along the lower Indigirka River and on the southern Taimyr Peninsula; also on Cheyne Island (east of Bathurst Island, 1976 and 1978), in northeastern Manitoba (Churchill, since 1980), and once in west-central Greenland (Disko Bay).

Winter range unknown, probably pelagic in open Arctic waters.

Migrates along the Arctic coast of Alaska (primarily at Point Barrow), rarely to St. Lawrence Island, and casually in the Pribilofs and Aleutians (Alaid); also recorded in migration on the Boothia and Melville peninsulas, on Cornwallis and eastern Baffin islands, in Keewatin (McConnell River), and in Greenland and the Arctic islands of the Old World, casually to the Faeroe Islands, British Isles and continental Europe.

Casual or accidental in southwestern British Columbia, Oregon, Colorado, North Dakota, Nebraska, Minnesota, Missouri, Illinois, Ontario, Newfoundland, Nova Scotia, Massachusetts, Connecticut, off New Jersey, Maryland, and Japan; sight reports for Alberta, Saskatchewan, Quebec, New York, and Tennessee.

Genus *PAGOPHILA* Kaup

Pagophila Kaup, 1829, Skizz. Entw.-Ges. Eur. Thierw., pp. 69, 196. Type, by monotypy, *Larus eburneus* Phipps.

Pagophila eburnea (Phipps). Ivory Gull.

> *Larus Eburneus* Phipps, 1774, Voy. North Pole, App., p. 187. (Spitsbergen.)

Habitat.—Associated with the Arctic ice pack and drift ice; nests on steep cliffs or low rocky islets near ice or snow.

Distribution.—*Breeds* in Arctic North America on Seymour, southeastern Ellesmere, Devon, northern Baffin and, at least formerly, Prince Patrick, the Polynia and Meighen islands; and in the Palearctic in northern Greenland, Spitsbergen, Franz Josef Land, northern Novaya Zemlya and North Land.

Winters in North America primarily over drift ice south to the southern Bering Sea (Pribilof Islands), northern Canada (east to Labrador and Newfoundland), rarely along the Atlantic coast from eastern Quebec and Nova Scotia south (rarely) to New Jersey, and casually south to south-coastal and southeastern Alaska and south-coastal and central British Columbia and the Great Lakes; and in the Palearctic from southern Greenland, Iceland, the Faeroe Islands, Scandinavia, northern Russia and northern Siberia south to the Commander Islands, casually to the British Isles and continental Europe.

Casual or accidental in southern California, southern Alberta, central Saskatchewan, Manitoba, Montana, northeastern Colorado, Minnesota, Iowa, Wisconsin, Michigan, Illinois, Tennessee, southwestern Quebec and central New York; sight reports for Washington and North Carolina.

Subfamily STERNINAE: Terns

Genus *STERNA* Linnaeus

> *Sterna* Linnaeus, 1758, Syst. Nat. (ed. 10) 1: 137. Type, by tautonymy, *Sterna hirundo* Linnaeus (*Sterna,* prebinomial specific name, in synonymy).
>
> *Thalasseus* Boie, 1822, Isis von Oken, col. 563. Type, by subsequent designation (Wagler, 1832), *"Th. cantiacus"* = *Sterna cantiaca* Gmelin = *Sterna sandvicensis* Latham.
>
> *Sternula* Boie, 1822, Isis von Oken, col. 563. Type, by monotypy, *Sterna minuta* Linnaeus = *Sterna albifrons* Pallas.
>
> *Hydroprogne* Kaup, 1829, Skizz. Entw.-Ges. Eur. Thierw., p. 91. Type, by subsequent designation (G. R. Gray, 1846), *Sterna caspia* Pallas.
>
> *Gelochelidon* C. L. Brehm, 1830, Isis von Oken, col. 994. Type, by monotypy, *Gelochelidon meridionalis* Brehm = *Sterna nilotica* Gmelin.

Sterna nilotica Gmelin. Gull-billed Tern.

> *Sterna nilotica* Gmelin, 1789, Syst. Nat. 1(2): 606. Based on the "Egyptian Tern" Latham, Gen. Synop. Birds 3(2): 356. (in Aegypto = Egypt.)

Habitat.—Salt marshes, estuaries, lagoons and plowed fields, less frequently along rivers, around lakes and in fresh-water marshes.

Distribution.—*Breeds* locally in western North America in southern California (San Diego Bay, Salton Sea), and on the coasts of Sonora (Bahía de Tobarí) and Sinaloa, Montague Island (Baja California), and elsewhere in the Gulf of California; in eastern North America along the Atlantic-Gulf coast from New York (Long Island) south to Florida (also inland) and west to southern Texas (also inland), probably also to Tamaulipas and Veracruz, and in the Bahamas (Harbour Island, Long Island, Great Inagua) and Virgin Islands (Anegada, probably Sombrero, formerly Cockroach Cay); in South America in southwestern Ecuador, and from central Brazil south to northern Argentina; and in the Old World from northern Europe, central Russia, southern Mongolia, and eastern China south to northwestern Africa, Asia Minor, Iran, India, Sri Lanka, and southern China, also in Australia.

Winters in the Americas in coastal areas from Nayarit, the Gulf coast and southern Florida south through Middle America and the West Indies to Peru on the Pacific coast and northern Argentina on the Atlantic coast; and in the Old World from tropical Africa, the Persian Gulf, India, Southeast Asia, eastern China and the Philippines south to southern Africa, Java and Borneo, also in Australia and Tasmania.

Casual or accidental in the Hawaiian Islands (Oahu, Molokai, Maui), north to coastal central California (to Santa Barbara County) and Arizona (lower Colorado River), and in New Brunswick, Nova Scotia, Kentucky and Bermuda.

Notes.—Often placed in the monotypic genus *Gelochelidon.*

Sterna caspia Pallas. Caspian Tern.

Sterna caspia Pallas, 1770, Novi Comm. Acad. Sci. Petropol. 14: 582, pl. 22. (Mare Caspium = Caspian Sea, southern Russia.)

Habitat.—Seacoasts, bays, estuaries, lakes, marshes, and rivers.

Distribution.—*Breeds* locally in western North America in south-coastal Alaska (Copper River Delta), and from south-coastal and central interior British Columbia, coastal and eastern Washington, eastern Oregon, southern Idaho, western and central Montana and northwestern Wyoming south (mostly in the interior) to southern California (San Diego Bay, southern end of Salton Sea) and western Nevada (Lahontan Reservoir); in western Mexico in northern Baja California and on the coast of Sinaloa (Isla Larición); in the interior of North America from northeastern Alberta, southern Mackenzie, central Saskatchewan, north-central Manitoba and central James Bay south to Montana, Wyoming, North Dakota (McLean County), northeastern Wisconsin, central Michigan, southern Ontario, northwestern Pennsylvania (formerly) and northeastern New York; at scattered localities along the Atlantic coast in Labrador (Lake Melville), Newfoundland, southeastern Quebec (Fog Island, Natashquam, Magdalen Islands), New Jersey (Barnegat), Virginia (Metomkin and formerly Cobbs islands), North Carolina (Oregon Inlet), South Carolina (Cape Romain) and Florida (rarely); along the Gulf coast from Texas east to Florida (Tampa Bay); and in the Old World from southern Scandinavia, northern Europe, southern Russia, the Black and Caspian seas, northern Mongolia, Ussuriland and eastern China south to the Mediterranean region, Persian Gulf, Sri Lanka, Australia, and New Zealand; along the coasts of Africa and in the interior at Lake Rudolph. Nonbreeding birds often summer in the James Bay and Great Lakes regions, in Colorado, and along both coasts of the United States, less frequently south in Middle America to Costa Rica.

Winters in the Americas primarily in coastal areas from central California (also Salton Sea) south to Baja California and Oaxaca, and from North Carolina south along the Atlantic-Gulf coasts to eastern Mexico, less frequently along both coasts and on inland lakes of Middle America (not recorded El Salvador) to northern Colombia and Venezuela, and rarely to the Bahamas, Greater Antilles (east to the Virgin Islands), and Cayman Islands; and in the Old World from the breeding range south to tropical Africa, the Persian Gulf, India and (rarely) Southeast Asia.

Migrates in North America primarily along coasts from southeastern Alaska (rarely), British Columbia and Nova Scotia southward, along the Great Lakes, and less frequently along large rivers in the interior.

Casual in the Hawaiian Islands (Oahu, Maui, Hawaii); in the interior of western North America north to east-central Alaska and west-central Yukon, and south to New Mexico; and in the Old World north to the Faeroe Islands, British Isles and Japan; accidental in Bermuda; a sight report from French Guiana.

Notes.—Often placed in the monotypic genus *Hydroprogne.*

Sterna maxima Boddaert. Royal Tern.

Sterna maxima Boddaert, 1783, Table Planches Enlum., p. 58. Based on the "Hirondelle de Mer de Cayenne" Daubenton, Planches Enlum., pl. 988. (Cayenne.)

Habitat.—Seacoasts, lagoons, and estuaries, also ocean over continental shelf.

Distribution.—*Breeds* locally on the Pacific coast in southern California (north to Orange County), Baja California (locally), along the coast of Sonora and Sinaloa, and in the Tres Marías Islands (erroneously reported from Isla Isabela); in the Atlantic-Gulf-Caribbean region from New Jersey and the Gulf coast (west to southern Texas) south through the West Indies to islands off the north coast of Venezuela (Netherlands Antilles east to Los Roques, and Trinidad) and French Guiana, and in Yucatán (Cayo Arcas and Alacrán Reef); in South America on the coast of northern Argentina; and in West Africa (islands off Mauritania).

Nonbreeding individuals occur in summer in coastal areas in the Americas north to central California and Maine, and south throughout the wintering range (rarely on the Pacific coast south of Mexico).

Winters from central California, the Gulf coast and North Carolina south along both coasts of the Americas to Peru, Uruguay and Argentina; and on the west coast of Africa from Morocco to Angola, casually to southern Africa.

Casual north on the Pacific coast to northern California, and on the Atlantic coast to New Brunswick, Nova Scotia and Newfoundland. Accidental in the interior in southern California (Salton Sea), Wisconsin (Manitowoc), Illinois (Chicago and Lake Calumet), Ontario (Kingsville), New York (Rochester), Ohio (Lorain), Oklahoma, Arkansas and eastern Tennessee, also in the British Isles, Norway, Spain, Gibraltar, and Mozambique; a sight report from interior Mexico (Distrito Federal).

Notes.—This and the following three species are often placed in the genus *Thalasseus*. Mayr and Short (1970) considered *S. maxima* and *S. bergii* to constitute a superspecies.

Sterna bergii Lichtenstein. Great Crested Tern.

Sterna Bergii Lichtenstein, 1823, Verz. Doubl., p. 80. (Cape of Good Hope.)

Habitat.—Coastal and pelagic waters.

Distribution.—*Breeds* from the southern African and Indian Ocean regions east to the western Pacific and Australian regions, and *ranges* at sea in the Indian and western Pacific oceans.

Accidental in the Hawaiian Islands on Oahu (21 October 1988-March 1989, photograph, Amer. Birds 43: 27; Pyle 1990) and French Frigate Shoals (August 1991).

Notes.—See comments under *S. maxima*.

Sterna elegans Gambel. Elegant Tern.

Sterna elegans Gambel, 1849, Proc. Acad. Nat. Sci. Philadelphia 4 (1848): 129. (Mazatlan [Sinaloa], Pacific coast of Mexico.)

Habitat.—Coastal Waters, occasionally ocean far from land.

Distribution.—*Breeds* along the Pacific coast from southern California (Bolsa Chica, Orange County; San Diego Bay) south to central Baja California (locally), and from the Gulf of California (Rasa and Montague islands; formerly more widespread) south along the coast of Sonora and Sinaloa.

Winters along the Pacific coast from Guatemala south to central Chile (most commonly from Ecuador south, rare north of Panama).

Wanders north in summer regularly to central (rarely northern) California, and casually to Oregon and southwestern British Columbia. Casual in Arizona and inland in California; accidental in Virginia, Texas (Lake Balmorhea), French Guiana, Ireland and France.

Notes.—See comments under *S. maxima* and *S. sandvicensis*.

Sterna sandvicensis Latham. Sandwich Tern.

Sterna Sandvicensis Latham, 1787, Gen. Synop. Birds (suppl.) 1: 296. (Sandwich, Kent, England.)

Habitat.—Seacoasts, bays, estuaries, and mudflats, occasionally ocean far from land.

Distribution.—*Breeds* [*sandvicensis* group] locally on the Atlantic coast of North America in Virginia (Fisherman's Island), North Carolina (Oregon Inlet), South Carolina and Florida (Nassau Sound), along the Gulf coast from southern Texas east to southern Mississippi (between Petit Bois and Horn islands), Alabama and Florida, in the Bahamas, off southern Cuba (Cayo Los Ballenatos), on islets in the Virgin Islands (off Culebra, St. Thomas and Anegada), in the Lesser Antilles (St. Barthélemy), off Yucatán (Cayo Arcas, Alacrán Reef), off Belize, on Curaçao and Trinidad, and in the Old World from the British Isles and southern Scandinavia south to the Mediterranean, Black and Caspian seas; and [*eurygnatha* group] in Puerto Rico (Culebra Island), the Virgin Islands (St. Thomas, paired with *sandvicensis*), on islands off the coast of Venezuela (Netherlands Antilles, Las Aves, Los Roques, and on

Soldado Rock off northern Trinidad, the latter colony sometimes assigned to the *sandvicensis* group) and French Guiana, and along the coast of Brazil (north to Espírito Santo) and southern Argentina. Nonbreeding individuals [*sandvicensis* group] occur in summer throughout the wintering range, most commonly in the Atlantic-Gulf-Caribbean region.

Winters [*sandvicensis* group] along the Pacific coast from Oaxaca to Ecuador and Peru, in the Atlantic-Gulf-Caribbean region from Florida (casually from Virginia) and the Gulf coast south throughout the West Indies, casually along coasts to southern Brazil and Uruguay, and in the Old World generally from the southern portions of the breeding range south to the eastern Atlantic islands, southern Africa, the Persian Gulf and India; and [*eurygnatha* group] from the islands off Venezuela (including Tobago and Trinidad) and the Colombian coast south along the Atlantic coast to northern Argentina.

Casual or accidental [*sandvicensis* group] in the Hawaiian Islands (Oahu); north to southern California (to Los Angeles County), Minnesota, southern Ontario, New Brunswick and Nova Scotia; sight reports from Illinois, Michigan, Newfoundland, Bermuda, the northern Lesser Antilles (St. Martin), Ecuador, Peru, and Chile, and [*eurygnatha* group] for North Carolina (sight report, Cape Hatteras), Puerto Rico and the Virgin Islands (where breeding in 1982, paired with one of the *sandvicensis* group).

Notes.—The two groups are often regarded as separate species, *S. sandvicensis* [Sandwich or Cabot's Tern] and *S. eurygnatha* Saunders, 1876 [Cayenne Tern], but limited interbreeding occurs (Junge and Voous 1955, Voous 1983, Buckley and Buckley 1984, Norton 1984). Mayr and Short (1970) considered *S. sandvicensis, S elegans, S. bernsteini* Schlegel, 1863, and *S. bengalensis* Lesson, 1831, to constitute a superspecies. See comments under *S. maxima*.

Sterna dougallii Montagu. Roseate Tern.

Sterna Dougallii Montagu, 1813, Suppl. Ornithol. Dict., [not paged], see under Tern, Roseate (with plate). (The Cumbrey Islands in Firth of Clyde [Scotland].)

Habitat.—Coastal waters, bays, estuaries, nesting on sandy beaches, open bare ground, grassy areas and under tumbled boulders, primarily on islands (breeding); mostly pelagic, rarely along seacoasts, bays and estuaries (nonbreeding).

Distribution.—*Breeds* locally along the Atlantic coast of North America from Quebec (Magdalen Islands), Maine and Nova Scotia south to North Carolina (Core Bank); in the Florida Keys, Bahamas, Cuba (several cays), Jamaica (Pedro Cays), Hispaniola (Beata Island, Cayos de los Pájaros), Puerto Rico, the Virgin Islands, Lesser Antilles and islands off Venezuela (Netherlands Antilles, Las Aves and Los Roques); off Belize and Caribbean Honduras (on Sandy Cay near Utila in the Bay Islands); in Bermuda (formerly); and in the Old World locally from the British Isles and northern Europe south to the eastern Atlantic islands and southern South Africa, and from Sri Lanka and the Andaman Islands south in the Indian Ocean along the east coast of Africa and to the Seychelles and western Australia, and in the Pacific Ocean from China and the Ryukyu Islands south to the Philippines, Solomon Islands, New Caledonia, and northern and eastern Australia. Breeding populations in the Northern Hemisphere show serious declines in recent years.

Winters in the Americas primarily in the eastern Caribbean from the West Indies southward, ranging along the Atlantic coast of South America to the Guianas, casually to eastern Brazil; and in the Old World from the eastern Atlantic islands and northern Africa south through the breeding range, and in the Indian and Pacific ocean areas near the breeding grounds.

Migrates primarily at sea off the Atlantic coast of North America south to Florida; also off western Europe and in the western Mediterranean region.

Casual along the Gulf of Florida, and in central and southern Europe. Accidental in Indiana (Miller), interior El Salvador (La Palma), on Corn Island (off Nicaragua), and on Gorgona Island (off Pacific coast of Colombia, recovery of a bird banded on Long Island, New York). An old report from the Pacific coast of Oaxaca is questionable.

Sterna hirundo Linnaeus. Common Tern.

Sterna Hirundo Linnaeus, 1758, Syst. Nat. (ed. 10) 1: 137. (in Europa = Sweden.)

Habitat.—Seacoasts, estuaries, bays, lakes, rivers and marshes; in winter, primarily coastal waters, beaches.

Distribution.—*Breeds* in the interior of North America from northern Alberta, south-central Mackenzie, northern Saskatchewan, northwestern and central Manitoba, northern Ontario (including southern James Bay), southern Quebec, southern Labrador, Newfoundland and Nova Scotia south to Montana, North Dakota, northeastern South Dakota, central Minnesota, northeastern Illinois, northwestern Indiana (formerly), southern Michigan, northern Ohio, northwestern Pennsylvania (Presque Isle), central and northern New York, and northwestern Vermont, and locally along the Atlantic coast to North Carolina (to Wrightsville Beach) and South Carolina (Deveaux Beach); locally on the Gulf coast in Texas (Port Isabel to Galveston Bay), Louisiana, Mississippi (between Petit Bois and Horn islands) and western Florida (St. George Island); in Bermuda, the Greater Antilles (islets off Hispaniola east to the Virgin Islands), Dominica and the Netherlands Antilles; and in the Old World from the British Isles, northern Europe, northern Russia and northern Siberia south to the eastern Atlantic islands, Mediterranean region, Black and Caspian seas, Asia Minor, the Middle East, northern India, Tibet, Anadyrland and Kamchatka. Nonbreeding individuals occur in summer on James Bay, throughout the Great Lakes region, along the Atlantic-Gulf coast (west to southern Texas), on the Pacific Coast of southern California, south in Middle America to Costa Rica, and throughout the West Indies.

Winters in the Americas from southern California (casually) and Baja California (rarely) south along the Pacific coast of Middle America and South America to Peru, and from Florida and the Gulf coast (rarely) south through the West Indies and along the Caribbean-Atlantic coast of Middle America and South America to northern Argentina; and in the Old World from the southern portions of the breeding range south to southern Africa, Madagascar, Sri Lanka, the Malay Peninsula, New Guinea, the Solomon Islands and Australia.

Migrates regularly in the western Aleutians (rarely east to the Pribilofs and north to St. Lawrence Island), along the Pacific coast from Alaska southward, in interior North America in southeastern California (Salton Sea), the Mississippi and Ohio valleys, and along the Atlantic-Gulf-Caribbean coast, uncommonly elsewhere in North America (reported north to Yukon, and south to Arizona and New Mexico).

Casual or accidental in the Hawaiian Islands (main islands from Kauai eastward), Clipperton Island (sight report), Labrador, and interior South America (Ecuador, Bolivia).

Sterna paradisaea Pontoppidan. Arctic Tern.

Sterna Paradisæa Pontoppidan, 1763, Dan. Atlas 1: 622. (Christiansöe, Denmark.)

Habitat.—Rocky or grass-covered coasts and islands, tundra, and sometimes along inland lakes and rivers (breeding); mostly pelagic, rarely in coastal bays and estuaries (nonbreeding).

Distribution.—*Breeds* in North America from northern Alaska, northern Yukon, northern Mackenzie, Banks, Bathurst and northern Ellesmere islands, Labrador and Newfoundland south to the Aleutian Islands, south-coastal and southeastern Alaska, southern Yukon, northwestern British Columbia, southern Mackenzie, northwestern Saskatchewan, northern Manitoba, extreme northern Ontario (islands in James Bay), central Quebec, New Brunswick and, along the Atlantic coast, locally to Maine and Massachusetts, also in Washington (Everett, since 1977); and in the Palearctic from Greenland, Iceland, the British Isles, southern Scandinavia, northern Russia and northern Siberia south to northern Europe, Anadyrland, the Commander Islands, and Gulf of Shelekhova.

Winters primarily in the Southern Hemisphere in subantarctic and Antarctic waters of the Pacific, Atlantic and Indian oceans, from off central Chile, central Argentina and South Africa to the Weddell Sea and (rarely) Antarctic continent.

Migrates primarily well at sea, along the Pacific coast from Alaska to southern California, and off South America from Colombia to Chile; on the southbound migration, most North American birds cross the Atlantic at 50–60° N and move south along the coasts of Europe and Africa. A few cross from western Africa back to southern Argentina and continue south. Others move south from westernmost Africa or follow the African coast. Only northbound migrants are normally seen in the west Atlantic from Brazil north.

Casual or accidental in the Hawaiian Islands, south-central British Columbia, interior California, southern Nevada, northern and central Alberta, Idaho, eastern Colorado, Arizona, New Mexico, southern Saskatchewan, Manitoba, Minnesota, Illinois, Indiana, the Great Lakes region, Ottawa River, inland New York (Cayuga Lake), Georgia (Okefenokee Swamp),

Louisiana, Cuba, the Virgin Islands, Bolivia (sight report), the Black Sea, and New Zealand; a sight report from western Maryland.

Sterna forsteri Nuttall. Forster's Tern.

Sterna hirundo (not Linnaeus) Richardson, 1832, in Swainson and Richardson, Fauna Bor.-Amer. 2 (1831): 412. (on the banks of the Saskatchewan [River] = about 10–50 miles west of Cumberland House, Saskatchewan.)
Sterna Forsteri Nuttall, 1834, Man. Ornithol. U. S. Can. (ed. 1) 2: 274. New name for *Sterna hirundo* Richardson, preoccupied.

Habitat.—Fresh-water and salt marshes; in migration and winter, also seacoasts, bays, estuaries, rivers, and lakes.

Distribution.—*Breeds* in the interior of North America from southeastern British Columbia (Creston), central Alberta, central Saskatchewan, central Manitoba and southern Ontario south through east-central Washington and eastern and south-central Oregon to northern Baja California, western Nevada, south-central Idaho, north-central Utah, northern and eastern Colorado, eastern New Mexico, central Kansas, western Nebraska, northern Iowa, northeastern Illinois, northwestern Indiana (formerly) and eastern Michigan; along the Atlantic coast from southern New York (Long Island, casually) and Massachusetts (Plum Island) south locally to South Carolina and, formerly, South Carolina (Bulls Bay); and along the Gulf coast from northern Tamaulipas and Texas east to southern Louisiana and southern Alabama (Gaillard Island).

Winters from northern California, Baja California, southwestern Arizona, southern New Mexico, Texas, the Gulf coast, Virginia and Bermuda (casually farther north) south (mostly along coasts) to Guatemala, casually to Panama; and in the Bahamas and Greater Antilles (east to Puerto Rico; sight reports from the Virgin Islands).

Migrates primarily through interior North America, and on the Pacific coast (north to southern British Columbia) and Atlantic coast (north to New Brunswick and Nova Scotia); a sight report for southern Quebec. Birds from Atlantic coast breeding populations apparently disperse northward, at least to New England, prior to fall migration.

Casual in northeastern British Columbia, the Cayman Islands, Iceland, the British Isles, the Netherlands, and at sea several hundred miles east of Pernambuco, Brazil.

Sterna albifrons Pallas. Little Tern.

Sterna albifrons Pallas, 1764, in Vroeg, Cat. Adumbr., p. 6. (Maasland, Netherlands.)

Habitat.—Beaches, rivers, and lakes.

Distribution.—*Breeds* in northern Eurasia from the British Isles, southern Scandinavia, central Russia, southeastern Siberia, Korea and Japan south to West Africa, the Mediterranean region, the Middle East, southern Asia, Indonesia and Australia, and *winters* in the more tropical parts of the breeding range.

Casual in the Hawaiian Islands (Tern Island, Midway, and, probably, French Frigate Shoals; Clapp 1989, Conant et al. 1991).

Notes.—See notes under *S. antillarum.*

Sterna antillarum (Lesson). Least Tern.

Sternula antillarum Lesson, 1847, Oeuvres Compl. Buffon 20: 256. (Guadeloupe, West Indies.)

Habitat.—Sandy or gravelly beaches and islands along shallow coasts, rivers, and lakes; nests also on flat rooftops of buildings; in winter, seacoasts, beaches, bays, estuaries, and lagoons.

Distribution.—*Breeds* along the Pacific coast from central California (San Francisco Bay) south to southern Baja California and Chiapas; in the interior of North America locally along the Colorado, Red, Arkansas, Missouri, Mississippi and Ohio river systems from northeastern Montana, western North Dakota, central and southeastern South Dakota, western Iowa, southeastern Missouri, southern Illinois, southwestern Indiana and central Kentucky south to southeastern Colorado, east-central New Mexico, central and northeastern Texas, central and northeastern Louisiana, western Mississippi, and western Tennessee; along the Atlantic-Gulf coast from Maine (Scarborough) south to Florida (including Florida Keys) and west to Tamaulipas; in the Atlantic-Caribbean region in Bermuda (at least formerly), throughout the Bahamas and Greater Antilles, in the Lesser Antilles (St. Martin, St. Kitts, Antigua, Guadeloupe), on the Yucatan Peninsula (including Isla Cancun), off Belize (Grassy Cay), in Honduras (on Sandy Cay near Utila Island, and at Puerto Caxinas), and on islands off Venezuela (Netherlands Antilles, Los Roques and Margarita), possibly also Trinidad. Non-breeding birds casually occur in summer north to eastern Wyoming, central Colorado, Minnesota, southern Wisconsin, northeastern Illinois and central Michigan, southern Ontario and Ohio, and south through the wintering range.

Winters in South America along the Pacific coast south to Peru (casually north to Nayarit), and along the Atlantic coast from Colombia east to eastern Brazil.

Migrates throughout the Gulf-Caribbean region (including the Lesser Antilles and Trinidad), and along both coasts of Middle America.

Casual or accidental in the Hawaiian Islands, on the Pacific coast north to Washington, in southeastern California, southern Arizona, Peru and Argentina, and north to eastern Montana, Saskatchewan, southern Manitoba, Minnesota, Newfoundland, New Brunswick and Nova Scotia; a sight report for Idaho.

Notes.—*S. antillarum* has been considered conspecific with *S. albifrons,* but see Massey (1976). The two species, in addition to *S. superciliaris* and *S. lorata* Philippi and Landbeck, 1861 of South America, and *S. saundersi* Hume, 1877 of the northwestern Indian Ocean region, appear to constitute a superspecies (Sibley and Monroe 1990). *S. nereis* (Gould, 1843) of Australia and *S. baleanarum* (Strickland, 1852) of southern Africa may be included.

Sterna superciliaris Vieillot. Yellow-billed Tern.

> *Sterna superciliaris* Vieillot, 1819, Nouv. Dict. Hist. Nat. (nouv. éd.) 32: 176. Based on "Hatí Ceja blanca" Azara, Apunt. Hist. Nat. Páx. Parag., 3, p. 377 (no. 415). (Paraguay.)

Habitat.—Rivers and lakes.

Distribution.—*Breeds* in South America east of the Andes from Colombia, Venezuela and the Guianas south to central Bolivia, Paraguay, northeastern Argentina and Uruguay, and *winters* in the breeding range, wandering to coastal areas, Tobago and Trinidad.

Accidental in Panama (Coco Solo, Canal area, 17–20 October 1977; Ridgely 1981: 366).

Notes.—See comments under *S. antillarum.*

Sterna aleutica Baird. Aleutian Tern.

> *Sterna aleutica* Baird, 1869, Trans. Chicago Acad. Sci. 1: 321. (Kadiak = Kodiak Island, Alaska.)

Habitat.—Coastal waters, nesting on grassy or mossy flats, on small offshore islands and coastal spits, around lagoons or near river mouths, and foraging mainly offshore (breeding); pelagic (nonbreeding).

Distribution.—*Breeds* in Alaska from the Chukchi Sea coast (from Tasaychek Lagoon east to Cape Krusenstern and Kotzebue Sound) south along the western coast to the Aleutians (west to Attu) and Alaska Peninsula, and east along the southern coast (including Kodiak Island) to Glacier Bay; and in Asia on the east coast of Kamchatka and Sakhalin.

Winters at sea, range unknown, although recently reported from the Philippines in May and Hong Kong (August–October).

Casual in the Pribilof and Commander islands, on St. Lawrence Island, and in Japan. Accidental in British Columbia (Queen Charlotte Islands) and Great Britain.

Sterna lunata Peale. Gray-backed Tern.

> *Sterna lunata* Peale, 1848, U. S. Explor. Exped. 8: 277. (Vincennes Island, Paumotu Group = Kauehi Island, Tuamotu Islands.)

Habitat.—Coastal waters, nesting on sandy beaches or bare ground on islands (breeding); mostly pelagic (nonbreeding).

Distribution.—*Breeds* from the northwestern Hawaiian Islands (from Kure east to Kaula and Moku Manu off Oahu), Wake Island and the Marianas (Guguan) south to the Phoenix, Fiji, Line, and Tuamotu islands.

Winters at sea in the central Pacific Ocean, wandering casually to Clipperton Island and the Moluccas.

Sterna anaethetus Scopoli. Bridled Tern.

> *Sterna (Anaethetus)* Scopoli, 1786, Del. Flor. Faun. Insubr., fasc. 2, p. 92. (in Guinea = Panay, Philippine Islands.)

Habitat.—Coastal waters, nesting on islands usually in rocky areas or on coral, occasionally on sand, but generally in crevices, on ledges, or partially concealed (breeding); Pelagic Waters (nonbreeding).

Distribution.—*Breeds* in the Pacific Ocean (mostly on islets) in Nayarit (Isla Isabela, San Blas), Guerrero (near Zihuetanejo, White Friar Rocks), northwestern Costa Rica (Nicoya and Osa peninsulas) and southwestern Ecuador (Isla Pelado), possibly also Honduras (Los Farallones) and Panama (Frailes del Sur, off the Azuero Peninsula), and from Taiwan and the Palau Islands south to Indonesia, New Guinea and Australia; in the Atlantic-Caribbean region in the Florida Keys (Pelican Shoals), Bahamas, Cuba (many small cays), the Cayman Islands (Grand Cayman), Jamaica (Morant and Pedro cays, and off Port Royal), Hispaniola (Navassa, Seven Brothers and Beata islands), Puerto Rico (Mona and Desecheo islands), the Virgin Islands, Lesser Antilles, off the Yucatan Peninsula (Cancun and Cozumel islands), Belize and Venezuela (Las Aves and Los Roques, formerly on Aruba and off Tobago); off Mauritania, and on islands in the Gulf of Guinea; the Red Sea and Persian Gulf; and in the Indian Ocean from off western India south to the Seychelles, Mauritius, and the Laccadive and Maldive islands.

Ranges at sea in the Pacific off Middle and South America from Nayarit south to Ecuador, and widely in the western Pacific from the breeding range north to Japan, Marcus Islands, and the Volcano and Ryukyu islands; in the Atlantic-Caribbean region widely in the West Indies, north along the Atlantic coast (most abundantly after storms) from Florida to North Carolina (casually to Maine), along the Gulf coast from Florida west to Texas, and rarely along the north coast of Venezuela; and in the Indian Ocean from India and Sri Lanka south in the breeding range, and to the east coast of Africa.

Casual in Bermuda. Accidental in Caribbean Costa Rica and Newfoundland, and in the British Isles, Denmark, France, and at Cape Horn; a sight report for Arkansas.

Notes.—Mayr and Short (1970) considered *S. anaethetus* and *S. fuscata* to constitute a superspecies.

Sterna fuscata Linnaeus. Sooty Tern.

> *Sterna fuscata* Linnaeus, 1766, Syst. Nat. (ed. 12) 1: 228. Based mainly on "L'Hirondelle-de-mer brune" Brisson, Ornithologie 6: 220, pl. 21, fig. 2. (in Insula Domincensi = Hispaniola.)

Habitat.—Nests on islands on sandy beaches, bare ground or coral, most often with scattered grasses or herbs present, less commonly on rocky ledges; generally forages offshore; Pelagic Waters (nonbreeding).

Distribution.—*Breeds* in the Pacific from the Hawaiian Islands (Kure east to Kaula, and Moku Manu and Manana off Oahu), on islands off western Mexico (Alijos Rocks, Clipperton, Revillagigedo, Tres Marías, and Isabela), and the Ryukyu, Bonin, Marcus and Wake islands south to the Australian region, Micronesia, central Polynesia and Tuamotu islands, also in the Galapagos Islands (Culpepper), and on San Felix off Chile; in the Atlantic-Gulf-Caribbean region on small islands along the Gulf coast of Texas (Matagorda Bay to Cameron County), Louisiana (Chandeleur Islands) and the Yucatan Peninsula (Alacrán reef, Isla Cancun, and formerly Isla Mujeres and Cayos Arcas), in North Carolina (Morgan Island, 1978), South Carolina (Bird Key, Cape Romaine), and Florida (Dry Tortugas, occasionally elsewhere), throughout the Bahamas, off Cuba, Jamaica, Hispaniola and Puerto Rico (Monito and Culebra islands), in the Virgin Islands and Lesser Antilles, off Belize and probably also Honduras (Isla Roatán), off the north coast of Venezuela (Islas de Aves, islets off Tobago and Trinidad, and formerly Margarita), French Guiana and Brazil (Rocas Reef, Fernando de Noronha, Trindade, Martin Vas), and in the tropical Atlantic (Ascension, and islets off St. Helena and Príncipe); and in the Indian Ocean from the Mascarene, Seychelles, Laccadive, Maldive and Andaman islands to western Australia.

Ranges at sea widely in the Pacific, throughout the Hawaiian Islands, off the west coast of Middle America from Sinaloa to Panama; and widely in the tropical and subtropical Pacific, throughout most of the Caribbean-Gulf region, regularly from Texas east to Florida (especially after storms) and casually north along the Atlantic coast to New England and Nova Scotia, also to Bermuda, along the coast of South America east to the Guianas, to the British Isles, continental Europe and the Azores, and off the coast of western Africa; and widely throughout the tropical and subtropical Indian Ocean.

Casual inland after storms in the Atlantic states north to New York, and to western Texas, Arkansas, Wisconsin, Tennessee and West Virginia, and in California and at Lago de Nicaragua; sight reports for southern Ontario.

Notes.—See comments under *S. anaethetus.*

Genus *PHAETUSA* Wagler

Phaetusa Wagler, 1832, Isis von Oken, col. 1224. Type, by monotypy, *Sterna magni-rostris* Lichtenstein = *Sterna simplex* Gmelin.

Phaetusa simplex (Gmelin). Large-billed Tern.

Sterna simplex Gmelin, 1789, Syst. Nat. 1(2): 606. Based on the "Simple Tern" Latham, Gen. Synop. Birds 3(2): 355. (in Cayenna = Cayenne.)

Habitat.—Rivers and lakes; in nonbreeding season, also seacoasts.

Distribution.—*Breeds* in South America in western Ecuador (at least formerly), and from Colombia, Venezuela (including Margarita Island), Trinidad and the Guianas south, east of the Andes, to central Argentina, and *ranges* to seacoasts in the nonbreeding season.

Casual in Panama (Coco Solo, Canal area, and vicinity; and near El Rincón, Herrera). Accidental in Bermuda, Cuba (Nipe Bay) and Aruba, also records (of individuals whose origin has been questioned) for Illinois (photograph, Lake Calumet, Chicago), Ohio (sight report, Evans Lake, near Youngstown) and New Jersey (photographs, Kearny Marsh).

Genus *CHLIDONIAS* Rafinesque

Chlidonias Rafinesque, 1822, Ky. Gazette (new ser.) 1(8): 3, col. 5. Type, by monotypy, *Sterna melanops* Rafinesque = *Sterna surinamensis* Gmelin = *Sterna nigra* Linnaeus.
Hydrochelidon Boie, 1822, Isis von Oken, col. 563. Type, by subsequent designation (G. R. Gray 1841), *Sterna nigra* Linnaeus.

Chlidonias leucopterus (Temminck). White-winged Tern.

Sterna leucoptera Temminck, 1815, Man. Ornithol. (ed. 1, 1814), p. 483. (les bords de la Méditerranée, etc. = Mediterranean Sea.)

Habitat.—Marshes (breeding); coasts, rivers and lakes (nonbreeding).

Distribution.—*Breeds* from eastern Europe east to southern Siberia, Sakhalin and Manchuria, and *winters* from tropical Africa, India, Southeast Asia and eastern China south to southern Africa, Madagascar, Sri Lanka, the East Indies, New Guinea, Australia and, rarely, New Zealand, migrating through Europe, Korea and Japan.

Casual or accidental in Alaska (Nizki Island in the Aleutians, Homer), Manitoba, Wisconsin, Ontario, Quebec (Saint-Gédéon; bred successfully, paired with *C. niger* and raised young), New Brunswick, Vermont, Massachusetts, New York, New Jersey, Delaware, Virginia, the Bahamas (Great Inagua), Virgin Islands (St. Croix), Barbados, Guam, the northern Marianas, and Palau; sight reports for Indiana and Georgia.

Notes.—Also known as White-winged Black Tern.

Chlidonias hybridus (Pallas). Whiskered Tern.

> *Sterna hybrida* Pallas, 1811, Zoogr. Rosso-Asiat. 2: 338. (circa Jaïcum seu Rhymnum, australem Volgam et ad Sarpae lacus = Southern Volga and Sarpa Lake, southeastern Russia.)

Habitat.—Marshes, lagoons, rivers and lakes (breeding); coasts, rivers and lakes (non-breeding).

Distribution.—*Breeds* from southern Europe, southern Russia and southern Siberia south to South Africa and Australia, and *winters* in Africa, and from southern Asia to Australia.

Accidental in New Jersey (Cape May) and Delaware (Delaware Bay, same individual, 29 June-6 September 1993, photograph; VIREO; published photograph, DeBenedictis 1994b), and in Barbados (16–23 April, 1994, photograph; 1995, Nat. Audubon Soc. Field Notes 49: 204).

Notes.—Also known as Marsh Tern.

Chlidonias niger (Linnaeus). Black Tern.

> *Sterna nigra* Linnaeus, 1758, Syst. Nat. (ed. 10) 1: 137. (in Europa = near Uppsala, Sweden.)

Habitat.—Extensive marshes, sloughs and wet meadows, primarily fresh-water (breeding); pelagic, as well as along seacoasts, bays, estuaries, lagoons, lakes and rivers (non-breeding).

Distribution.—*Breeds* in North America from central and northeastern British Columbia, northern Alberta, south-central Mackenzie, northwestern Saskatchewan, northern Manitoba, northern Ontario, southern Quebec, southern New Brunswick and central Nova Scotia south locally to south-central California, northern Nevada, northern Utah, central and eastern Colorado, Nebraska, Missouri (formerly), central Illinois, Kentucky (formerly), northern Ohio, Pennsylvania, western New York, northwestern Vermont and Maine (one old record from Fort Yukon, east-central Alaska); and in the Old World from Iceland, northern Europe, north-central Russia and central Siberia south to the Mediterranean Sea, Asia Minor, Turkestan, and the Caspian and Aral seas. Nonbreeding birds occur in summer south on the Pacific coast to Panama, in the interior to Arizona and New Mexico, and in eastern North America to the Gulf coast, where abundant.

Winters on the west coast of the Americas from Jalisco (casually north to California) south to Peru, and on the northern coast of South America from Colombia to Surinam; and in the Old World primarily in tropical Africa south to Angola and Tanzania, casually to Madeira and northern China.

Migrates through the interior of North America south of the breeding range; along both coasts and through the interior of Middle America; along the Atlantic coast from Nova Scotia south to Florida and the West Indies (rarely south to Barbados); and often far at sea.

Casual in the Hawaiian Islands, Alaska, Yukon, Clipperton Island, Bermuda, Chile, and northern Argentina.

Genus *LAROSTERNA* Blyth

> *Larosterna* Blyth, 1852, Cat. Birds Mus. Asiat. Soc. (1849), p. 293. Type, by monotypy, *Sterna inca* Lesson.

Larosterna inca (Lesson). Inca Tern.

> *Sterna Inca* Lesson, 1827, Voy. Coquille, Zool., Atlas, livr. 3, pl. 47. (Lima, Peru.)

Habitat.—Coastal Waters; nests on islands

Distribution.—*Breeds* in Peru and Chile, and *ranges* along the Pacific coast of South America.

Casual off the Pacific coast of Panama (Bay of Panama), where present in moderate numbers, 31 May-27 June 1983 (maximum of 65 individuals), in apparent association with a major "El Niño Southern Oscillation" (Reed 1988; photograph).

Genus *ANOUS* Stephens

> *Anoüs* Stephens, 1826, in Shaw, Gen. Zool. 13(1): 139. Type, by subsequent designation (G. R. Gray, 1840), *Anoüs niger* Stephens = *Sterna stolida* Linnaeus.
> *Megalopterus* Boie, 1826, Isis von Oken, col. 980. Type, by monotypy, *Sterna tenui-rostris* Temminck.

Anous stolidus (Linnaeus). Brown Noddy.

> *Sterna stolida* Linnaeus, 1758, Syst. Nat. (ed. 10) 1: 137. Based mainly on Hirundo marina minor, capite albo Sloane, Voy. Jamaica 1: 31, pl. 6, fig. 2, and "The Noddy" Catesby, Nat. Hist. Carolina 1: 88, pl. 88. (in Americæ Pelago = West Indies.)

Habitat.—Pelagic Waters; nests on islands on bare ground, rock ledges, sandy beaches or in trees.

Distribution.—*Breeds* in the Pacific Ocean from the Hawaiian (from Kure east to Kaula, Lehua off Niihau, and Moku Manu and Manana off Oahu), Ryukyu and Bonin islands south to northern Australia, Norfolk Island and the Tuamotu Archipelago, and islands off western Mexico (Revillagigedo, Tres Marías, Tres Marietas, and Isabela; possibly Las Rocas Potosí) south to Costa Rica (Cocos Island, possibly also on the Santa Elena Peninsula) and Colombia (Octavia Rocks, Gorgona Island); in the Atlantic-Gulf-Caribbean region from the Bahamas and Florida Keys (Dry Tortugas) south through most of the Antilles to islands off the coasts of the Yucatan Peninsula (Alacrán reef), Belize, Isla San Andrés, Venezuela (Las Aves east to Margarita, Tobago and Trinidad), and French Guiana; and in the Atlantic Ocean on Trindade, Ascension, St. Helena, Tristan da Cunha and Gough, also islands in the Gulf of Guinea; and in the Indian Ocean region from the Red Sea, Gulf of Aden and Laccadive Islands south to Madagascar and the Seychelles.

Winters at sea, generally in the vicinity of the breeding grounds, ranging casually (mostly after storms) in the Atlantic-Gulf-Caribbean region north to New Jersey and south to the coasts of Middle America (Caribbean coast and islands off El Salvador and Honduras, and both coasts of Panama).

Casual in Bermuda. Accidental in Massachusetts, Rhode Island, Louisiana and Texas, also in Norway and Germany.

Notes.—Also known as Noddy Tern or Common Noddy.

Anous minutus Boie. Black Noddy.

> *Anous minutus* Boie, 1844, Isis von Oken, col. 188. (New Holland = Raine Island, Australia.)

Habitat.—Pelagic Water; nests on islands in trees or on rock ledges.

Distribution.—*Breeds* in the tropical Pacific Ocean from the Hawaiian Islands (throughout), and Marcus and Wake islands south to New Guinea, northeastern Australia and the Tuamotu Archipelago, also off the coast of Middle America on Clipperton Island, and on Cocos Island (off Costa Rica); in the Caribbean region off Belize (formerly on Southwest Cay in Glover's Reef, no recent records), in the Lesser Antilles (Sombrero off Anguilla), and off Venezuela (Los Roques, Aruba since 1992, and possibly Las Aves); and in the tropical South Atlantic from St. Paul's Rocks and Fernando de Noronha to St. Helena and (formerly) Inaccessible Island. Summers in small numbers (since 1960) in the Florida Keys (Dry Tortugas).

Winters at sea in the vicinity of the breeding grounds.

Casual in Isla Cancun, Anguilla, and the Netherlands Antilles (Bonaire); sight reports from Honduras (Isla Utila) and the Bahamas. Accidental on the central coast of Texas (Nueces County).

Notes.—Some authors (e.g., Vaurie 1965) treat *A. tenuirostris* (Temminck, 1823) of the Indian Ocean as conspecific with *A. minutus;* they constitute a superspecies. With a single species concept, White-capped Noddy is the appropriate English name.

Genus *PROCELSTERNA* Lafresnaye

Procelsterna [subgenus] Lafresnaye, 1842, Mag. Zool. [Paris] (2)4 (Ois.): pl. 29, p. 1. Type, by monotypy, *Procelsterna tereticollis* Lafresnaye = *Sterna cerulea* Bennett.

Procelsterna cerulea (Bennett). Blue-gray Noddy.

Sterna cerulea F. D. Bennett, 1840, Narr. Whaling Voy. 2: 248. (Christmas Island, Pacific Ocean.)

Habitat.—Pelagic Waters; nests in recesses and shallow cavities on rocky islands, and in the open on sandy islets.

Distribution.—*Breeds* in the tropical Pacific Ocean from the Hawaiian Islands (Gardner Pinnacles, French Frigate Shoals, Necker, Nihoa and Kaula) and Johnston Atoll south to southwestern Micronesia and Polynesia, and east to San Ambrosio and Easter islands.

Winters at sea in the general vicinity of the breeding grounds.

Notes.—Also known as Gray Ternlet. *Procelsterna cerulea* and the southwestern Pacific *P. albivitta* Bonaparte, 1856 constitute a superspecies; they are considered one species by Sibley and Monroe (1993).

Genus *GYGIS* Wagler

Gygis Wagler, 1832, Isis von Oken, col. 1223. Type, by monotypy, *Sterna candida* Gmelin = *Sterna alba* Sparrman.

Gygis alba (Sparrman). Common White-Tern.

Sterna alba Sparrman, 1786, Mus. Carlson., fasc. 1, pl. 11. (in India orientali, ad promontorium Bonae Spet Insulasquae maris pacifici = Ascension Island.)

Habitat.—Pelagic Waters; nests on islands on bare limbs or crotches in branches of trees (no nest), less commonly on rocky ledges or coral, sometimes in old nests of *Anous minutus* and on various man-made structures.

Distribution.—*Breeds* [*alba* group] in the tropical South Atlantic on Fernando de Noronha, Trindade, Martin Vas Rocks, Ascension and St. Helena; on islands in the tropical Pacific Ocean [*candida* group] from the Hawaiian (Kure east to Kaula, and on Oahu), Carolina and Marshall islands south to Norfolk, Kermadec, Tonga and Society islands, also on Clipperton Island and Cocos Island (off Costa Rica), in the Galapagos Islands, and on Easter and Sala-y-Gomez islands, and in the Indian Ocean in the Seychelles; and [*microrhyncha* group] on the larger Marquesas Islands and Kiribati.

Ranges at sea generally near the breeding range.

Accidental [*candida* group] in the Revillagigedo Islands (Oneal Rock near Socorro, erroneously reported breeding); and [*alba* group] on Bermuda (7–9 December 1972; photograph of individual referable to this group) and Tobago.

Notes.—Also known as White Noddy, White Tern, or Fairy Tern, the latter name now restricted to *Sterna nereis* (Gould, 1843) of the southwest Pacific. Groups: *G. alba* (Sparrman, 1786) [Atlantic White-Tern], *G. candida* (Gmelin, 1789) [Pacific White-Tern], and *G. microrhyncha* Saunders 1876 [Little White-Tern]. The latter is given species rank by Pratt et al. (1987) and Sibley and Monroe (1990), although some hybridization occurs in the Marquesas Islands and Kiribati (Holyoak and Thibault 1976).

Subfamily RYNCHOPINAE: Skimmers

Genus *RYNCHOPS* Linnaeus

Rynchops Linnaeus, 1758, Syst. Nat. (ed. 10) 1: 138. Type, by subsequent designation (G. R. Gray, 1840), *Rynchops nigra* Linnaeus.

Rynchops niger Linnaeus. Black Skimmer.

Rynchops nigra Linnaeus, 1758, Syst. Nat. (ed. 10) 1: 138. Based mainly on the "Cut Water" Catesby, Nat. Hist. Carolina 1: 90, pl. 90. (in America = coast of South Carolina.)

Habitat.—Primarily near coasts on sandy beaches, shell banks, coastal islands, tropical rivers, and locally, gravelly rooftops, occasionally inland in flooded farmlands; in migration and winter, also bays, estuaries, lagoons and mudflats (Tropical to Temperate zones).

Distribution.—*Breeds* in western North America in southern California (north to Orange County and the Salton Sea; since 1994 also in San Francisco Bay), possibly also in Baja California, and along the Pacific coast of Sonora, Sinaloa, Nayarit, and Oaxaca; and locally on the Atlantic-Gulf coast from southern Massachusetts, Connecticut (Bluff Island), New York (Long Island) and New Jersey south to southern Florida (Miami area), and from western Florida (south to the Tampa Bay region) along the Gulf coast to Texas and south to the Yucatan Peninsula; and in South America south along the Pacific coast to western Ecuador and in the Caribbean-Atlantic drainage, in the middle reaches of large rivers (Orinoco, Cauca, Amazon, Paraná) to northern Argentina.

Winters from southwestern California, Sonora, the Gulf coast, and Florida (rarely from North Carolina) south along the coasts of Cuba (rare but regular), Middle America and South America (including Margarita Island and Trinidad) to central Argentina. Postbreeding individuals wander rarely north to central California and (usually following storms) to Prince Edward Island, New Brunswick, Nova Scotia and Newfoundland.

Casual inland in coastal states, on the Mexican Plateau, and to Arizona, New Mexico, Kansas, Oklahoma, Arkansas, Tennessee, Indiana, western and southern Ontario and southern Quebec, also to Bermuda, the Bahamas (Bimini, Great Inagua), the Cayman Islands, Hispaniola (off the coast), the Virgin Islands, Guadeloupe, and Grenada.

Family **ALCIDAE**: Auks, Murres, and Puffins

Notes.—The position of the auks and their relatives with respect to other groups in the Charadriiformes has been subject to considerable controversy. Opinions have ranged from considering them as a subfamily of the Laridae (Sibley and Ahlquist 1990) to the sister group to the rest of the Charadriiformes (Mickevich and Parenti 1980, Björklund 1994). They are here accorded family rank, but conclusions concerning their position within the order must await further studies. See Strauch (1985), Moum et al. (1994), and Friesen et al. (1996) for phylogenetic hypotheses, generally concordant, concerning relationships among tribes, genera, and species.

Tribe ALCINI: Dovekies, Murres, and Auks

Genus *ALLE* Link

Plautus Gunnerus, 1761, Trondheimske Selks. Skr. 1: 263, pl. 6. Type, by monotypy, Plotus eller Plautus columbarius Gunnerus = *Alca alle* Linnaeus. (Unavailable name; see Wetmore and Watson 1969, Bull. Brit. Ornithol. Club, 89, pp. 6–7.)
Alle Link, 1806, Beschr. Naturh. Samml. Univ. Rostock 1: 46. Type, by monotypy, *Alle nigricans* Link = *Alca alle* Linnaeus.

Alle alle (Linnaeus). Dovekie.

Alca Alle Linnaeus, 1758, Syst. Nat. (ed. 10) 1: 131. (in Europæ, Americæ arcticæ oceano. Restricted to Greenland by Vaurie [1965: 504].)

Habitat.—Mostly pelagic; nests in crevices on steep coastal cliffs.

Distribution.—*Breeds* on eastern Baffin Island, and in the Palearctic in Greenland, Iceland, Jan Mayen, Spitsbergen, Bear Island, Franz Josef Land, Novaya Zemlya and North Land; also probably islands in the Bering Sea (St. Lawrence and Little Diomede), and possibly on eastern Ellesmere Island. Nonbreeding birds occur in summer along the Atlantic coast to Maine.

Winters offshore from the breeding range south to Southampton Island, Ungava Bay, the Gulf of St. Lawrence and Bay of Fundy (irregularly along the Atlantic coast as far as North Carolina), and in the eastern Atlantic to the Canary Islands, Azores, France and the Baltic Sea, also casually south to southern Florida, Cuba, the Bahamas (Grand Bahama), Bermuda, Madeira and the western Mediterranean Sea.

Casual along the Arctic coast of Alaska (Point Barrow) and Canada, Melville Island and Keewatin, on islands in the southern Bering Sea (St. Matthew, St. George, St. Paul), and in the interior of northeastern North America west to central Manitoba, Minnesota, Wisconsin, Michigan, Ontario and New York; also in the British Isles and interior of Europe. Accidental in western Florida (Bay County); sight reports for the Aleutian Islands (near Unimak) and Illinois.

Notes.—Also known as Little Auk.

Genus *URIA* Brisson

Uria Brisson, 1760, Ornithologie 1: 52; 6: 70. Type, by tautonymy, *Uria* Brisson = *Colymbus aalge* Pontoppidan.

Uria aalge (Pontoppidan). Common Murre.

Colymbus aalge Pontoppidan, 1763, Dan. Atlas 1: 621, pl. 26. (Island = Iceland.)

Habitat.—Pelagic and along rocky seacoasts; nests in coastal cliff ledges.

Distribution.—*Breeds* in North America along the Pacific coast from western Alaska (Cape Lisburne, Kotzebue Sound, Diomede Islands) south through Norton Sound and the Bering Sea (St. Matthew, Nunivak and the Pribilof islands) to the Aleutians, and from south-coastal Alaska to central California (including the Farallon Islands, and south to Monterey County, formerly Santa Barbara County); in eastern North America from Labrador (locally east from Nunarsuk Island) and southeastern Quebec (north shore of Gulf of St. Lawrence, Anticosti and Bonaventure islands, and Bird Rocks) south to Newfoundland and Nova Scotia (at least formerly); and in the Palearctic from Greenland and Iceland east to Norway, and south to northern France and central Norway, and from the Commander Islands and Kamchatka south to southern Sakhalin, eastern Korea and Japan.

Winters primarily offshore in areas near the breeding grounds, in the Pacific south regularly to southern California and (rarely) northern Baja California; in eastern North America south to Massachusetts, casually as far as Virginia (Back Bay); and in the Palearctic to northern Europe.

A sight report for Sinaloa.

Notes.—Also known as Thin-billed Murre and, in Old World literature, as the Guillemot.

Uria lomvia (Linnaeus). Thick-billed Murre.

Alca Lomvia Linnaeus, 1758, Syst. Nat. (ed. 10) 1: 130. (in Europa boreali = Greenland.)

Habitat.—Mostly pelagic; nests in steep, coastal cliffs.

Distribution.—*Breeds* in western North America from northern Alaska (Cape Lisburne, Kotzebue Sound, Diomede Islands) south through the Pribilofs to the Aleutians and to British Columbia (Triangle Island), east to Kodiak, Middleton and St. Lazaria islands, and in north-western Mackenzie (Cape Parry); in eastern North America from Prince Leopold, Cobourg, Bylot and eastern Baffin islands south to northern Hudson Bay (Coats Island and Chesterfield Inlet), northern Quebec (Ungava Bay to Cape Chidley), Labrador, the Gulf of St. Lawrence and Newfoundland (Bird Rock), formerly to Maine (Penobscot Bay); and in the Palearctic from Greenland, Iceland, Jan Mayen, Spitsbergen, Novaya Zemlya, northern Russia and northern Siberia south to the Chukotski Peninsula, Kamchatka, and the Commander and Kuril islands.

Winters primarily offshore from the breeding grounds, in western North America south to southeastern Alaska, casually to central California (Monterey Bay); in eastern North America south along the Atlantic coast to New Jersey, casually south to Florida and inland to the Great Lakes region (recorded from Michigan, Ontario and Quebec south to Iowa, Indiana, Ohio and Pennsylvania); and in the Palearctic south to northern Europe and Japan.

Notes.—Also known as Brunnich's Murre and, in Old World literature, as Brunnich's Guillemot.

Genus *ALCA* Linnaeus

Alca Linnaeus, 1758, Syst. Nat. (ed. 10) 1: 130. Type, by tautonymy, *Alca torda* Linnaeus (*Alca,* prebinomial specific name, in synonymy).

Alca torda Linnaeus. Razorbill.

Alca Torda Linnaeus, 1758, Syst. Nat. (ed. 10) 1: 130. (in Europæ borealis oceano = Stora Karlsö, Baltic Sea.)

Habitat.—Mostly pelagic; nests in coastal cliffs and on rocky shores and islands.

Distribution.—*Breeds* in North America from extreme southeastern Baffin Island and the coast of Labrador south to southeastern Quebec (north shore of Gulf of St. Lawrence, Cape Whittle, Bird Rocks, and Anticosti, Bonaventure, Magdalen and Pèlerins islands), eastern Newfoundland, southern New Brunswick (Grand Manan, Machias Seal Island), eastern Maine (Matinicus Rock) and Nova Scotia; and in the Palearctic from Greenland east to the British Isles, Bear I., Scandinavia and northern Russia. Recorded in summer (and possibly breeding) on Digges Island, off northwestern Quebec.

Winters offshore from the breeding grounds in North America south to New York (Long Island), casually to South Carolina and Florida (including the Gulf coast) and inland to southern Ontario; and in the Palearctic from southern Scandinavia and the Baltic Sea south to the western Mediterranean Sea.

Accidental in central New York (Seneca County).

Notes.—Also known as Razor-billed Auk.

Genus *PINGUINUS* Bonnaterre

Plautus (not Gunnerus) Brünnich, 1771, Zool. Fund., p. 78. Type, by monotypy, "Brillefuglen" = *Alca impennis* Linnaeus.
Pinguinus Bonnaterre, 1791, Tabl. Encycl. Méth., Ornithol., livr. 47, pp. lxxxiii, 28. Type, by subsequent designation (Ogilvie-Grant, 1898), *Alca impennis* Linnaeus.

†*Pinguinus impennis* (Linnaeus). Great Auk.

Alca impennis Linnaeus, 1758, Syst. Nat. (ed. 10) 1: 130. (in Europa arctica = Norwegian Sea.)

Habitat.—Mostly at sea; nested on low coastal rocky islands.

Distribution.—EXTINCT. Formerly *bred* in the Gulf of St. Lawrence (Bird Rocks), Newfoundland (Funk Island), Greenland, Iceland and the Outer Hebrides (St. Kilda), possibly in the Faeroe Islands and on Lundy, doubtfully on the Isle of Man.

Wintered from the breeding grounds south to Maine and Massachusetts, casually to South Carolina; and to the British Isles, France, Spain, Denmark and Scandinavia.

Last verified record: two taken in Iceland on 3 June 1844.

Notes.—Strauch (1985)'s analysis of primarily morphological characters indicated that *Pinguinus* should be merged into *Alca.*

Tribe CEPHINI: Guillemots

Genus *CEPPHUS* Pallas

Cepphus Pallas, 1769, Spic. Zool. 1(5): 33. Type, by monotypy, *Cepphus lacteolus* Pallas = *Alca grylle* Linnaeus.

Cepphus grylle (Linnaeus). Black Guillemot.

> *Alca Grylle* Linnaeus, 1758, Syst. Nat. (ed. 10) 1: 130. (in Europæ borealis oceano = Gotland, Sweden.)

Habitat.—Mostly coastal; nests in holes under rocks (rarely in ground) on rocky islands, in crevices in base of coastal cliffs, and (in Alaska) in or under beach flotsam.

Distribution.—*Breeds* in northern Alaska (along the Chukchi and Beaufort seacoasts from Cape Thompson east at least to Barter Island, possibly also on St. Lawrence Island in the Bering Sea) and northern Yukon (Herschel Island); in eastern North America from Ellesmere, Devon, Somerset, Bylot and eastern Baffin islands south to the Melville Peninsula, Southampton Island, northern Ontario (Cape Henrietta Maria), the eastern shore of Hudson and James bays, Newfoundland, shores and islands of the eastern St. Lawrence River (Pèlerins Islands), Gulf of St. Lawrence, New Brunswick, Maine and southern Nova Scotia; and in the northern Palearctic from Greenland, Iceland, Jan Mayen, Spitsbergen, Bear I., Franz Josef Land and Novaya Zemlya east to the New Siberian, Wrangel and Herald islands, and south to the British Isles, Scandinavia, and the coast of northern Russia and northern Siberia. Recorded in summer west to Banks Island and northern Keewatin.

Winters from the breeding grounds south in the Bering Sea ice front to the Pribilof Islands, and in eastern North America to New England, rarely New York (Long Island) and New Jersey; and in the Palearctic to northern Europe.

Casual or accidental inland to Alberta, Saskatchewan (sight report), Mackenzie, Manitoba, southern Ontario, northeastern Ohio, eastern Pennsylvania (Delaware River near Chester) and New York, and south to South Carolina.

Notes.—*C. grylle* and *C. columba,* and possibly also Asiatic *C. carbo* Pallas, 1811 (Mayr and Short 1970), constitute a superspecies (Sibley and Monroe 1990).

Cepphus columba Pallas. Pigeon Guillemot.

> *Cepphus Columba* Pallas, 1811, Zoogr. Rosso-Asiat. 2: 348. (in oceano arctico pariterque circa Camtschatcam et in omni freto inter Sibiriam et Americam = Kamchatka and Bering Strait.)

Habitat.—Mostly coastal; nests in crevices in coastal cliffs, excavated holes in banks or among rocks along shores also under docks and piers.

Distribution.—*Breeds* [*columba* group] in western North America from northern Alaska (Cape Lisburne and Cape Thompson) south through Norton Sound, Cape Newenham and Cape Peirce, and the Bering Sea islands (Diomede, St. Lawrence, St. Matthew, Hall, Nunivak) to the Aleutians, and south along the Pacific coast to southern California (to Santa Barbara Island, and on the mainland to northern Santa Barbara County); and in eastern Siberia from the Chukotski Peninsula south to Kamchatka and the Commander Islands. Nonbreeding individuals [*columba* group] occur in summer elsewhere in the Bering Sea (Pribilof Islands) and in Baja California.

Winters [*columba* group] offshore near the breeding grounds, in North America from the Pribilof and Aleutian islands south to central California (casually to San Diego County), and in Eurasia south to northern Japan.

Resident (*snowi* group) in the Kuril Islands.

Notes.—Groups: *C. columba* [Pigeon Guillemot] and *C. snowi* Stejneger, 1897 [Kuril Guillemot]. See comments under *C. grylle.*

Tribe BRACHYRAMPHINI: Brachyramphine Murrelets

Genus *BRACHYRAMPHUS* Brandt

Brachyramphus M. Brandt, 1837, Bull. Sci. Acad. Imp. Sci. St.-Petersbourg 2(22): col. 346. Type, by subsequent designation (G. R. Gray, 1840), *Colymbus marmoratus* Gmelin.

Brachyramphus perdix (Pallas). Long-billed Murrelet.

Cepphus Perdix Pallas, Zoogr. Rosso-Asiat., 2, 1811, p. 351, pl. 80. (Bering Sea and Sea of Okhotsk.)

Habitat.—Oceanic, most numerous on near-shore waters and bays. Nests on masses of lichens in coniferous trees and (probably) on the ground.

Distribution.—*Breeds* in eastern Asia, along the western shores of the Sea of Okhotsk from the Penzhina Delta south to Olga Bay, on both coasts of Sakhalin Island, and from the southern Kurile Islands (Urup, Iterup) to northeastern Hokkaido (Mt. Mokoto), and on the east coast of Kamchatka. (The report of nesting on the Commander Islands is not considered valid by recent Russian authors.)

Winters south along both coasts of Japan, regularly to northern Honshu and rarely or casually to southern Korea and Amami-oshima in the Ryu-kyu Islands.

Casual in interior North America: Alaska (Denali National Park), California (Mono Lake, 4 specimens), Montana, Colorado, Arkansas, Indiana, Ohio, Quebec, St. Lawrence River (Ontario/New York). Massachusetts, North Carolina, South Carolina, and Florida; accidental in coastal California (Humboldt Bay); also sight reports for this or *B. marmoratus* from Saskatchewan, Iowa, and Indiana (Lake Michigan); see summary in Sealy et al. (1991).

Notes.—Treated as a species by Ridgway (1919) and AOU (1931), but subsequently (e.g.. AOU 1957) generally considered a subspecies of *B. marmoratus*. Molecular data (Friesen et al. 1996) indicate that *B. brevirostris* may be more closely related to *B. marmoratus* than is *B. perdix*; other molecular data (Zink et al. 1995) also show a degree of differentiation between *perdix* and *marmoratus* comparable to that between well-differentiated species. Also known as Asiatic Murrelet.

Brachyramphus marmoratus (Gmelin). Marbled Murrelet.

Colymbus marmoratus Gmelin, 1789, Syst. Nat. 1(2): 583. Based on the "Marbled Guillemot" Pennant, Arct. Zool. 2: 517, pl. 22, right fig. (in America occidentali et Camtschatca = Prince William Sound, Alaska.)

Habitat.—Mostly coastal; nests on large horizontal branches in coniferous trees near coasts, occasionally on islands on open barren ground.

Distribution.—*Breeds* definitely in southern Alaska (Kenai Peninsula, Barren Islands, Baranof Island), coastal British Columbia (including lakes near the coast, Campbell et al. 1990), western Washington and central California (Santa Cruz County). Occurs in summer and probably breeds in North America from southern Alaska (the Aleutians, Alaska Peninsula and south-coastal region) south to central California.

Winters offshore near the breeding grounds from southern Alaska (casually the Aleutians and Pribilofs) south to central California, casually to northern Baja California.

Notes.—See comments under *B. perdix*.

Brachyramphus brevirostris (Vigors). Kittlitz's Murrelet.

Uria brevirostris Vigors, 1829, Zool. J. 4 (1828): 357. (San Blas [Mexico], error = North Pacific.)

Habitat.—Mostly coastal, showing preference for ice-filled waters (Kessel 1989); nests in coastal cliffs, and barren ground, rock ledges and talus above timberline in coastal mountains. Generally near snowfields.

Distribution.—*Breeds* in Alaska from Point Hope south to the Aleutians and east to Glacier Bay, and along the north shore of the Chukotski Peninsula.

Winters generally offshore from the Aleutians east to Glacier Bay.

Casual in the Kuril Islands. Accidental in British Columbia (Victoria), Washington (San Juan Island) and southern California (La Jolla).

Notes.—See comments under *B. perdix.*

Tribe SYNTHLIBORAMPHINI: Synthliboramphine Murrelets

Genus *SYNTHLIBORAMPHUS* Brandt

Synthliboramphus M. Brandt, 1837, Bull. Sci. Acad. Imp. Sci. St.-Petersbourg 2(22): col. 347. Type, by subsequent designation (G. R. Gray, 1840), *Alca antiqua* Gmelin.
Endomychura Oberholser, 1899, Proc. Acad. Nat. Sci. Philadelphia 51: 201. Type, by original designation, *Brachyramphus hypoleucus* Xántus de Vesey.

Notes.—Strauch (1985) merged *Endomychura* into *Synthliboramphus* (cf. Moum et al. 1994), and placed *Synthliboramphus* in the Cepphini.

Synthliboramphus hypoleucus (Xántus de Vesey). Xantus's Murrelet.

Brachyramphus hypoleucus Xántus de Vesey, 1860, Proc. Acad. Nat. Sci. Philadelphia 11 (1859): 299. (Cape St. Lucas, Lower California = 14 miles off the coast of Cape San Lucas, Baja California.)

Habitat.—Coastal Waters, Pelagic Waters; nests on islands on the ground, in crevices beneath large rocks, or under dense clumps of vegetation.

Distribution.—*Breeds* on islands off southern California (San Miguel, Santa Cruz, Anacapa, Santa Barbara, San Clemente, and, formerly, Santa Catalina) and western Baja California (Los Coronados, Todos Santos, Natividad, San Benito and Guadalupe). On large islands (e.g., San Miguel, Santa Cruz, San Clemente, Guadalupe) confined largely or entirely to offshore rocks (Drost and Lewis 1995).

Winters primarily from northern California (rarely) south to southern Baja California, casually farther north (recorded from off the coasts of Oregon, Washington, and southern British Columbia).

Notes.—There is some evidence that *S. hypoleucus* [Xantus's Murrelet] and the form *S. scrippsi* (Green and Arnold, 1939) [Scripps's Murrelet], here considered a subspecies of *hypoleucus,* breed in the San Benito Islands and on Santa Barbara Island with but limited hybridization; thus there may be two species within this complex (Jehl and Bond 1975). *Synthliboramphus hypoleucus* and *S. craveri* were formerly considered conspecific, but both apparently breed in the San Benito Islands with very little hybridization (Jehl and Bond 1975). *Synthliboramphus hypoleucus* and *S. craveri* constitute a superspecies (Mayr and Short 1970). These two species were formerly placed in the genus *Endomychura.*

Synthliboramphus craveri (Salvadori). Craveri's Murrelet.

Uria Craveri Salvadori, 1865, Atti Soc. Ital. Sci. Nat., Mus. Civ. Stor. Nat. Milano 8: 387. (Golfo della California, Lat. 27° 50′ 12″ Long. 110° 10′ 45″ = Isla Natividad, Baja California; Violani and Boano, 1990, Riv. Piem. St. Nat. 11: 155–162.)

Habitat.—Coastal Waters, Pelagic Waters; nests in rock crevices on islands.

Distribution.—*Breeds* on most islands in the Gulf of California (north to Consag Rock), and probably north along the west coast of Baja California to Magdalena Bay and the San Benito Islands.

Winters at sea in the Gulf of California and to the coast of Sonora (possibly farther south off western Mexico).

Wanders after the breeding season along the Pacific coast of Baja California and California north (uncommonly) to Monterey Bay and south to Nayarit; a sight report for central California (Farallon Islands).

A record from Oregon is erroneous.

Notes.—Olson (1996) pointed out that the singular possessive form of the English name of this species is technically incorrect because the species was evidently named for the Craveri brothers. See comments under *S. hypoleucus.*

Synthliboramphus antiquus (Gmelin). Ancient Murrelet.

> *Alca antiqua* Gmelin, 1789, Syst. Nat. 1(2): 554. Based on the "Antient Auk" Pennant, Arct. Zool. 2: 512. (in mari inter Camtschatcam, insulas Kuriles et Americam intermedio = Bering Sea.)

Habitat.—Mostly pelagic; nests along rocky seacoasts in crevices, under rocks, and in burrows in the ground.

Distribution.—*Breeds* in western North America from southern Alaska (the Aleutian, Sanak and Kodiak islands) south to British Columbia (Queen Charlotte Islands), casually to northwestern Washington (Carroll Island); and in eastern Asia from the Commander Islands and Kamchatka south to Amurland, Sakhalin, northern Japan (Hokkaido and Honshu), Korea and Dagelet Island.

Winters primarily offshore in North America from the Aleutian Islands south to central (rarely southern) California; and in Asia from the Commander Islands south to Taiwan and the Ryukyu Islands. Post-breeding dispersal reported north through Bering Straits to Chukchi Sea (Kessel 1989).

Casual in Baja California and in the interior of western and central North America in southern Yukon, and from southern British Columbia, Alberta, Idaho, Montana, southern Manitoba, the Great Lakes region and southern Quebec south to southeastern California, Nevada, Utah, northern New Mexico, central Colorado, Nebraska, Louisiana, central Illinois, northwestern Indiana, northern Ohio and Pennsylvania.

Accidental in the British Isles.

Notes.—*S. antiquus* and the Japanese *S. wumizusume* (Temminck, 1835) [Japanese or Temminck's Murrelet] constitute a superspecies (Sibley and Monroe 1990).

Tribe AETHIINI: Auklets

Genus *PTYCHORAMPHUS* Brandt

> *Ptychoramphus* M. Brandt, 1837, Bull. Sci. Acad. Imp. Sci. St.-Petersbourg 2(22): col. 347. Type, by monotypy, *Uria aleutica* Pallas.

Ptychoramphus aleuticus (Pallas). Cassin's Auklet.

> *Uria Aleutica* Pallas, 1811, Zoogr., Rosso-Asiat. 2: 370. (Russia ad Oceanum orientalem = North Pacific Ocean.)

Habitat.—Mostly pelagic; nests on islands in burrows in the ground.

Distribution.—*Breeds* locally on coastal islands from southern Alaska (west to Buldir in the Aleutians) south to southern Baja California (including Asunción, San Roque and Guadalupe islands).

Winters along the Pacific coast from southern British Columbia (Vancouver Island), rarely from southeastern Alaska, south to southern Baja California.

Accidental in the Hawaiian Islands (Oahu).

Genus *AETHIA* Merrem

> *Aethia* Merrem, 1788, Vers. Grundr. Allg. Ges. Nat. Eintheil. Vögel 1 (Tentamen Nat. Syst. Avium): 7, 13, 20. Type, by monotypy, *Alca cristatella* Pallas.
> *Cyclorrhynchus* Kaup, 1829, Skizz. Entw.-Ges. Eur. Thierw., p. 155. Type, by monotypy, *Alca psittacula* Pallas.

Notes.—See Strauch (1985), Moum et al. (1994), and Friesen et al. (1996) for merger of *Cyclorrhynchus* into *Aethia.*

Aethia psittacula (Pallas). Parakeet Auklet.

> *Alca psittacula* Pallas, 1769, Spic. Zool 1(5): 13, pl. ii; pl. v, figs. 4–6. (in mari Kamtschatkam . . . et circa insulas partim versus Iaponiam partim versus Americam septentrionalem sparsas = Kamchatka.)

Habitat.—Mostly pelagic; nests along rocky seacoasts in cliff crevices, among boulders on beaches, and on rocky slopes with dense vegetation.

Distribution.—*Breeds* in western Alaska from the Diomede Islands, Fairway Rock, Sledge Island and Norton Sound south through the Bering Sea (St. Lawrence, St. Matthew and the Pribilof islands) to the Aleutians, and east to islands in Prince William Sound; and in eastern Siberia along the Gulf of Anadyr and in the Commander Islands.

Winters at sea in the North Pacific from the Pribilof and Aleutian islands south well offshore rarely to central (casually to southern) California, and in Asia south to Sakhalin and the Kuril Islands, rarely to Japan.

Casual in the Hawaiian Islands (Kure, Midway) and northern Alaska (Point Barrow). Accidental in Sweden.

Aethia pusilla (Pallas). Least Auklet.

> *Uria pusilla* Pallas, 1811, Zoogr. Rosso-Asiat. 2: 373. (circa Camtschatcam = Kamchatka.)

Habitat.—Mostly pelagic; nests on talus slopes and beach rock rubble, occasionally in small crevices in coastal cliffs.

Distribution.—*Breeds* in western Alaska from the Diomede Islands south through islands of the Bering Sea (including the Pribilofs) to the Aleutian, Shumagin and Semidi islands; and in eastern Siberia along the Chukotski Peninsula and the Commander Islands south to the central Kuril Islands (Jones 1993).

Winters in the southern Bering Sea, at sea off the Aleutians, and from the coast of eastern Siberia south to Kamchatka, Sakhalin, the Kuril Islands and northern Japan.

Casual north to northern Alaska (Point Barrow) and east to northern Mackenzie (Kittigazuit). Accidental in California (San Mateo County).

Aethia pygmaea (Gmelin). Whiskered Auklet.

> *Alca pygmaea* Gmelin, 1789, Syst. Nat. 1(2): 555. Based on the "Pygmy Auk" Pennant, Arct. Zool. 2: 513. (circa insulam avium, inter Asiam septentrionalem et Americam = St. Matthew Island; Feinstein, 1959, Auk 76: 60–67.)

Habitat.—Mostly pelagic; nests in crevices in talus slopes, among boulders along beaches, and on lava flows on high slopes.

Distribution.—*Breeds* in southwestern Alaska in the Aleutians (east at least to Unimak Pass and west to Buldir, possibly also in the Near Islands), and in the Commander and central Kuril islands.

Winters at sea off the Aleutians, and from the Commander Islands and Kamchatka south to the Kuril Islands and Japan.

Casual north in the Bering Sea to St. Lawrence Island and Bristol Bay, and south to Japan.

Aethia cristatella (Pallas). Crested Auklet.

> *Alca cristatella* Pallas, 1769, Spic. Zool. 1(5): 18, pl. iii; pl. v, figs. 7–9. (Ultimarum versus Japoniam maxime incola et circa insulam Matmey = Hokkaido to Kamchatka.)

Habitat.—Mostly pelagic; nests on talus slopes and beach boulder rubble, occasionally in crevices in cliffs.

Distribution.—*Breeds* in western Alaska on Bering Sea islands (from the Diomedes south, including King, St. Lawrence and St. Matthew, to the Pribilofs), and in the Aleutians east at least to the Shumagin and Semidi islands, but not in the Near Islands); and in eastern Siberia from the Chukotski Peninsula south to Sakhalin and the central Kuril Islands. Nonbreeding birds occur in summer north to northern Alaska (Wainwright and Barrow), and to Wrangel and Herald islands, off northern Siberia.

Winters in open waters of the Bering Sea and around the Aleutians, east to the vicinity of Kodiak, and in Asiatic waters near breeding areas, straggling south to Japan.

Accidental inland in Alaska (Nulato), in British Columbia (Vancouver Island), in California (Marin County), and in the North Atlantic off the northeastern coast of Iceland; sight reports for coastal Oregon and Baja California.

Tribe FRATERCULINI: Puffins

Genus *CERORHINCA* Bonaparte

Cerorhinca Bonaparte, 1828, Ann. Lyc. Nat. Hist. N. Y. 2: 427. Type, by monotypy, *Cerorhinca occidentalis* Bonaparte = *Alca monocerata* Pallas.

Cerorhinca monocerata (Pallas). Rhinoceros Auklet.

Alca monocerata Pallas, 1811, Zoogr. Rosso-Asiat. 2: 362. (circa promontorium S. Eliae Americae et ad littora insulae Kadiak = Cape St. Elias, Alaska.)

Habitat.—Mostly pelagic; nests on islands in ground burrows.

Distribution.—*Breeds* on islands along the Pacific coast of North America from south-coastal and southeastern Alaska (Barren, Middleton, St. Lazaria and Forrester islands) south to southern California (to Santa Barbara County, off San Miguel Island); and in eastern Asia from southern Sakhalin and the southern Kuril Islands south to Korea and Japan. Nonbreeding birds occur in summer south casually to southern California (San Pedro).

Winters off the Pacific coast of North America from southern British Columbia (casually from southern Alaska) south to Baja California (Santa Margarita Island); and in Asia in the southern part of the breeding range.

Casual in the Aleutian and Commander islands.

Notes.—Also known as Horn-billed Puffin.

Genus *FRATERCULA* Brisson

Fratercula Brisson, 1760, Ornithologie 1: 52; 6: 81. Type, by tautonymy, *Fratercula* Brisson = *Alca arctica* Linnaeus.

Lunda Pallas, 1811, Zoogr. Rosso-Asiat. 2: 363. Type, by subsequent designation (G. R. Gray, 1840), *Alca cirrhata* Pallas.

Fratercula arctica (Linnaeus). Atlantic Puffin.

Alca arctica Linnaeus, 1758, Syst. Nat. (ed. 10) 1: 130. (in Europæ borealis oceano = northern Norway.)

Habitat.—Primarily pelagic; nests on rocky island slopes and seacoasts, usually in burrows, rarely in cliff crevices.

Distribution.—*Breeds* in eastern North America from Labrador (north to Nain) south in coastal areas to southeastern Quebec (Mingan, Anticosti, Bonaventure and Magdalen islands, and Gaspé Peninsula), Newfoundland, southwestern New Brunswick (Machias Seal Island) and eastern Maine (Seal Island and Matinicus Rock), also on Digges Island off northwestern Quebec; and in the Palearctic from Greenland, Iceland, the Faeroe Islands, Spitsbergen, Bear Island and Novaya Zemlya south to the British Isles, northern Europe, southern Scandinavia and the coast of northern Russia.

Winters in the North Atlantic off North America from Labrador south to Massachusetts, casually to New Jersey, Maryland and Virginia; and in Eurasia from the breeding range south to the eastern Atlantic islands, northwestern Africa, the western Mediterranean region, and southern Europe.

Casual or accidental in Ohio (Toledo area), Ontario (Ottawa; Cochrane), southwestern Quebec (Lake St. Peter), Vermont (Rutland) and Florida (Martin County).

Notes.—Also known as Common Puffin and, in Old World literature, as the Puffin. *Fratercula arctica* and *F. corniculata* constitute a superspecies (Mayr and Short 1970).

Fratercula corniculata (Naumann). Horned Puffin.

Mormon corniculata Naumann, 1821, Isis von Oken, col. 782. (Kamchatka.)

Habitat.—Mostly pelagic; nests on rocky islands in cliff crevices and among boulders, rarely in ground burrows.

Distribution.—*Breeds* on islands and along coasts of the Chukchi and Bering seas from the Diomede Islands and Cape Lisburne south to the Aleutian Islands, and along the Pacific coast of western North America from the Alaska Peninsula and south-coastal Alaska south to British Columbia (Queen Charlotte Islands, and probably elsewhere along the coast); and in Asia from northeastern Siberia (Kolyuchin Bay) south to the Commander Islands, Kamchatka, Sakhalin, and the northern Kuril Islands. Nonbreeding birds occur in late spring and summer south along the Pacific coast of North America to southern California, and north in Siberia to Wrangel and Herald islands.

Winters from the Bering Sea and Aleutians south, at least casually, to the northwestern Hawaiian Islands (from Kure east to Laysan), and off North America (rarely) to southern California; and in Asia from northeastern Siberia south to Japan.

Accidental in Mackenzie (Basil Bay); a sight report for Baja California.

Notes.—See comments under *F. arctica.*

Fratercula cirrhata (Pallas). Tufted Puffin.

Alca cirrhata Pallas, 1769, Spic. Zool. 1(5): 7, pl. i; pl. v, figs. 1–3. (in Mari inter Kamtschatcam et Americam Archipelagumque Kurilum = Bering Sea.)

Habitat.—Primarily pelagic; nests on islands and coastal slopes in ground burrows, sometimes under boulders and piles of rocks, occasionally under dense vegetation.

Distribution.—*Breeds* along the Pacific coast of North America from the Diomede Islands and Cape Thompson south through islands of the Bering Sea (including the Pribilofs) to the Aleutians, east to the Alaska Peninsula, Kodiak Island, and southeastern Alaska, and south to southern California (to Santa Barbara County, off San Miguel Island); and in eastern Asia from the Kolyuchin Islands and East Cape south to Kamchatka, the Commander and Kuril islands, Sea of Okhotsk, Sakhalin, and northern Japan.

Winters offshore from southern Alaska and Kamchatka south through the breeding range to central (rarely southern) California and southern Japan.

Accidental in the Hawaiian Islands (Laysan) and Maine.

Notes.—Formerly placed in the monotypic genus *Lunda.*

Family **Incertae Sedis**
Family **PTEROCLIDIDAE**: Sandgrouse

Notes.—The relationships of the Pteroclididae are so controversial that we leave them *incertae sedis*. Maclean (1967, 1969) and Fjeldså (1976) placed them in the Charadriiformes, a position supported by recent molecular analyses (Sibley and Ahlquist 1990). Others (Olson 1970, Strauch 1978) retain them in their traditional position in the Columbiformes.

Genus *PTEROCLES* Temminck

Pterocles Temminck, 1815, Pig. Gall. 3: 238, 712. Type, by subsequent designation (G. R. Gray, 1840), *Tetrao alchata* Linnaeus.

Pterocles exustus Temminck. Chestnut-bellied Sandgrouse.

Pterocles exustus Temminck, 1825, Planches Color., livr. 60, pls. 354, 360. (west coast of Africa, Egypt and Nubia = Senegal.)

Habitat.—Dry keawe scrub forest, rocky grasslands, and pastures at low and moderate elevations; in native range, deserts and arid scrub.

Distribution.—*Resident* across northern Africa (south of the Sahara) from Senegal east to Somalia and Kenya, and from Arabia and Syria east to Baluchistan and India.

Introduced and established in the Hawaiian Islands (North Kona district of Hawaii, since 1961).

Order **COLUMBIFORMES**: Pigeons and Doves

Family **COLUMBIDAE**: Pigeons and Doves

Genus *COLUMBA* Linnaeus

Columba Linnaeus, 1758, Syst. Nat. (ed. 10) 1: 162. Type, by subsequent designation (Vigors, 1825), *Columba oenas* Linnaeus.

Patagioenas Reichenbach, 1853, Handb. Spec. Ornithol., Die Vögel, pt. 3 (1852), p. xxv. Type, by monotypy, *Columba leucocephala* Linnaeus.

Lithoenas Reichenbach, 1853, Handb. Spec. Ornithol., Die Vögel, pt. 3 (1852), p. xxv. Type, by monotypy, *Columba livia* "Linnaeus" = Gmelin.

Chloroenas Reichenbach, 1853, Handb. Spec. Ornithol., Die Vögel, pt. 3 (1852), p. xxv. Type, by monotypy, *Columba monilis* Vigors = *Columba fasciata* Say.

Lepidoenas Reichenbach, 1853, Handb. Spec. Ornithol., Die Vögel, pt. 3 (1852), p. xxv. Type, by monotypy, *Columba speciosa* Gmelin.

Ænoenas [subgenus] Salvadori, 1893, Cat. Birds Brit. Mus. 21: 248. Type, by subsequent designation (Ridgway, 1916), *Columba nigrirostris* Sclater.

Notes.—For modern usage of *Patagioenas* and *Oenoenas* as genera distinct from *Columba*, see Johnston (1962); for contrary opinion, see Corbin (1968).

Columba livia Gmelin. Rock Dove.

Columba domestica ß *livia* Gmelin, 1789, Syst. Nat. 1(2): 769. (No locality given = southern Europe.)

Habitat.—In the wild state along rocky seacoasts or inland in gorges, river valleys, caves, and desert oases, nesting on cliff ledges or in holes and fissures; feral birds in the Western Hemisphere occasionally in natural habitats, more abundantly near human settlement, especially in cities.

Distribution.—*Resident* in Eurasia from the Faeroe Islands, southern Scandinavia, Russia, western Siberia, Manchuria, and northern China south through the British Isles, western Europe, and the Mediterranean region to the eastern Atlantic islands, northern Africa, Arabia, Iran, India, Sri Lanka, and Burma.

Introduced and established widely throughout the world, including the Hawaiian Islands, most of North America (from the central parts of the Canadian provinces south), in the Revillagigedo Islands (Socorro Island), and the West Indies.

Notes.—Also known as Rock Pigeon or Domestic Pigeon; established, feral populations are sometimes called Feral Pigeon or Common Pigeon. Oberholser (1974) used the name *Lithoenas domestica*; see Banks and Browning (1995).

Columba cayennensis Bonnaterre. Pale-vented Pigeon.

Columba cayennensis Bonnaterre, 1792, Tabl. Encycl. Méth., Ornithol. 1(51): 234. Based on "Le Pigeon Ramier de Cayenne" Holandre, Abrege Hist. Nat. 2: 214. (Cayenne.)

Habitat.—Gallery Forest, River-edge Forest, Edge of Tropical Lowland Forest, and Secondary Forest, lowland pine savanna (0–800 m; Tropical Zone, in South America to Temperate Zone).

Distribution.—*Resident* from extreme southeastern Veracruz, Tabasco, the Yucatan Peninsula, and northern Chiapas south on the Gulf-Caribbean slope to Nicaragua, on both slopes of Costa Rica and Panama, and in South America from Colombia, Venezuela, Tobago,

Trinidad, and the Guianas south, west of the Andes to western Ecuador and east of the Andes to northern Argentina and southeastern Brazil.

Notes.—Also known as Rufous Pigeon.

Columba speciosa Gmelin. Scaled Pigeon.

Columba speciosa Gmelin, 1789, Syst. Nat. 1(2): 783. Based primarily on "Pigeon ramier, de Cayenne" Daubenton, Planches Enlum., pl. 213. (in Cayenna = Cayenne.)

Habitat.—Tropical Lowland Evergreen Forest, Montane Evergreen Forest, Gallery Forest, lowland pine savanna (0–1400 m; Tropical and lower Subtropical zones).

Distribution.—*Resident* from southern Veracruz and northern Oaxaca south on the Gulf-Caribbean slope of Middle America to Nicaragua, on both slopes of Costa Rica (absent from dry northwest) and Panama, and in South America from Colombia, Venezuela, Trinidad, and the Guianas south, west of the Andes to northwestern Peru, and east of the Andes (excluding most of Amazonia) to northern Argentina and southeastern Brazil.

Columba squamosa Bonnaterre. Scaly-naped Pigeon.

Columba squamosa Bonnaterre, 1792, Tabl. Encycl. Méth., Ornithol. 1, 1(51): 234. Based on "Le Pigeon Ramier de la Guadeloupe" Holandre, Abrege Hist. Nat. 2: 214. (Guadeloupe.)

Habitat.—Montane Evergreen Forest, Tropical Lowland Evergreen Forest (0–2500 m).

Distribution.—*Resident* in the Greater Antilles (rare on Jamaica), Lesser Antilles (not recorded Anguilla, St. Barthélemy or Désirade), and islands off the north coast of Venezuela (Curaçao, Bonaire, Los Testigos, and Los Frailes, formerly also Aruba).

Casual in southern Florida (Key West).

Notes.—Also known as Red-necked Pigeon.

Columba leucocephala Linnaeus. White-crowned Pigeon.

Columba leucocephala Linnaeus, 1758, Syst. Nat. (ed. 10) 1: 164. Based mainly on "The White-crown'd Pigeon" Catesby, Nat. Hist. Carolina 1: 25, pl. 25. (in America septentrionali = Bahama Islands.)

Habitat.—Mangrove Forest, Tropical Deciduous Forest, Tropical Lowland Evergreen Forest (0–2000 m).

Distribution.—*Breeds* in southern Florida (mangrove islets in the Florida Keys from Elliot to Marquesas keys, and throughout Florida Bay), Bahamas, Antilles (south to Barbuda and Antigua), Cayman Islands, islands of the western Caribbean Sea (Cozumel off Quintana Roo, cays off Belize, the Bay and Hog islands off Honduras, Providencia and Corn islands), and Caribbean Panama (Swan Cay, Escudo de Veraguas, and coast of Bocas del Toro, also San Blas Islands). Individuals from Florida Bay commonly forage on the mainland (southern Dade and Monroe counties).

Winters throughout most of the breeding range, regularly in southern peninsular Florida, the Florida Keys, and northern Bahamas, ranging in Middle America to coastal areas (recorded Quintana Roo, Belize, Honduras, and western Panama), and in the Lesser Antilles south to St. Lucia.

Casual on the mainland of southern Florida (north to Fort Pierce region); a sight report for southern Texas. A report from Oaxaca (Salina Cruz) is questionable (Binford 1989).

Columba flavirostris Wagler. Red-billed Pigeon.

Columba flavirostris Wagler, 1831, Isis von Oken, col. 519. (Mexico = Veracruz.)

Habitat.—Tropical Deciduous Forest, Gallery Forest (0–2100 m; Tropical and lower Subtropical zones).

Distribution.—*Resident* from central Sonora, southern Chihuahua, Durango, San Luis Potosí, Nuevo León, and southern Texas south through Middle America (including the Tres

Marías Islands, but absent from most of Caribbean slope from Honduras south) to central Costa Rica; northernmost populations are migratory southward.

Notes.—*C. flavirostris* and *C. inornata* appear to constitute a superspecies (Mayr and Short 1970).

Columba inornata Vigors. Plain Pigeon.

> *Columba inornata* Vigors, 1827, Zool. J. 3: 446. (near Havana, Cuba.)

Habitat.—Tropical Lowland Evergreen Forest, Montane Evergreen Forest, Secondary Forest (0–2000 m).

Distribution.—*Resident* on Cuba, the Isle of Pines, Hispaniola (including Tortue Island), Jamaica, and Puerto Rico (where presently confined to vicinity of Cidra, west-central Puerto Rico).

Notes.—See comments under *C. flavirostris.*

Columba fasciata Say. Band-tailed Pigeon.

> *Columba fasciata* Say, 1823, in Long, Exped. Rocky Mount. 2: 10 (note). (small tributary of the Platte = Plum Creek, near Castle Rock, Douglas County, Colorado.)

Habitat.—Temperate and mountain forests, primarily in oaks, less commonly in coniferous forest, and locally in lowlands, foraging also in cultivated areas; increasingly common in wooded suburbs in Pacific coastal region (Subtropical and Temperate zones).

Distribution.—*Breeds* [*fasciata* group] from southwestern British Columbia south (primarily in mountains) through Washington, Oregon, California, and western Nevada to southern Baja California; from southern Nevada, Arizona, central Utah, north-central Colorado, New Mexico, and western Texas south through the mountains of Mexico, Guatemala, El Salvador, and Honduras to (at least formerly) north-central Nicaragua. Regular in summer (and probably breeding) north to southeastern Alaska (as far north as Mitkof Island and the Stikine River) and west-central British Columbia.

Winters [*fasciata* group] from western Washington, central California, central Arizona, central New Mexico (rarely), and western Texas southward through the breeding range, occurring widely in Mexico in foothills at lower elevations than in the breeding season, regularly north to southwestern British Columbia, rarely west to islands off the coast of California, and east to Nevada.

Resident [*albilinea* group] in the mountains of Costa Rica and western Panama (east to eastern Veraguas); and in South America in the mountains from Venezuela, Trinidad, and Colombia south to northwestern Argentina.

Casual [*fasciata* group] in western and northern Alaska (near Nome, upper Ikpikpuk River), and from Idaho, Montana, central Alberta, southern Saskatchewan, southern Manitoba, western and southern Ontario, New Hampshire, New Brunswick, Maine, and Nova Scotia south to Wyoming, western Missouri, Oklahoma, western Texas, Louisiana, Mississippi, Alabama, and Florida.

Notes.—Groups: *C. fasciata* [Band-tailed Pigeon] and *C. albilinea* Bonaparte, 1854 [White-necked Pigeon]. *Columba fasciata, C. caribaea,* and the South American *C. araucana* Lesson, 1827, may constitute a superspecies (Mayr and Short 1970).

Columba caribaea Jacquin. Ring-tailed Pigeon.

> *Columba (caribæa)* Jacquin, 1784, Beytr. Ges. Vögel, p. 30. Based on "Pigeon à queue annelée de la Jamaique" Brisson, Ornithologie 1: 138. (Karibäische Inseln = Jamaica.)

Habitat.—Tropical Lowland Evergreen Forest, Montane Evergreen Forest (0–1500 m.)
Distribution.—*Resident* on Jamaica.
Notes.—See comments under *C. fasciata.*

Columba subvinacea (Lawrence). Ruddy Pigeon.

> *Chloroenas subvinacea* Lawrence, 1868, Ann. Lyc. Nat. Hist. N. Y. 9: 135. (Dota, Costa Rica.)

Habitat.—Tropical Lowland Evergreen Forest, River-edge Forest, Montane Evergreen Forest (0–1800 m; Tropical and Subtropical zones).

Distribution.—*Resident* [*subvinacea* group] in the mountains of Costa Rica and western Panama (east to Veraguas), and from northern and eastern Colombia, Venezuela, and the Guianas south, east of the Andes, to central Bolivia and Amazonian Brazil; and [*berlepschi* group] in eastern Panama (eastern Panamá province, San Blas, and eastern Darién) and western Colombia south to northwestern Peru.

Notes.—Wetmore (1968) suggested that the two groups represent distinct species, *C. subvinacea* [Ruddy Pigeon] and *C. berlepschi* Hartert, 1898 [Berlepsch's Pigeon]. See notes under *C. nigrirostris.*

Columba nigrirostris Sclater. Short-billed Pigeon.

Columba nigrirostris Sclater, 1859, Proc. Zool. Soc. London, p. 390. (In statu Oaxaca reipubl. Mexicanæ = probably Playa Vicente, Veracruz; Binford, 1989, Ornithol. Monogr. 43, p. 337.)

Habitat.—Tropical Lowland Evergreen Forest, Montane Evergreen Forest (0–1500 m; Tropical and lower Subtropical zones).

Distribution.—*Resident* from southern Veracruz, northern Oaxaca, Tabasco, eastern Chiapas, and southern Quintana Roo south on the Gulf-Caribbean slope of Central America to Costa Rica (including southwestern portion on the Pacific slope), Panama (both slopes), and northwestern Colombia (Chocó).

Notes.—Wetmore (1968) considered the unique type of *C. chiriquensis* (Ridgway, 1915) to be an immature *C. nigrirostris,* although Johnston (1962) considered it to be an example of *C. subvinacea. Columba nigrirostris* and *C. goodsoni* Hartert, 1902, appear to constitute a superspecies (Johnston 1962).

Genus *STREPTOPELIA* Bonaparte

Streptopelia Bonaparte, 1855, C. R. Acad. Sci. Paris 40: 17. Type, by subsequent designation (G. R. Gray, 1855), *Columba risoria* Linnaeus.

Streptopelia orientalis (Latham). Oriental Turtle-Dove.

Columba orientalis Latham, 1790, Index Ornithol., 2: 606. (China.)

Habitat.—Open forest and savanna.

Distribution.—*Breeds* in Asia from the Ural Mountains east to the Sea of Okhotsk and Japan, and south to southern Asia, and *winters* in the southern part of the breeding range.

Casual in Alaska in the Pribilof Islands (St. Paul, 23 June-18 July 1984, photograph; Gibson and Kessel 1992), at sea about 50 miles from the Pribilof Islands (individual came aboard a fishing vessel, about 20–26 July 1986, photograph; Gibson and Kessel 1992), and in the Aleutian Islands (Attu, 20 May-12 June 1989, photograph; 1989, Amer. Birds 43: 525; DeBenedictis 1991; Attu, 21 May—3 June 1996, Nat. Aud. Soc. Field Notes 50: 320). A report from British Columbia (Vancouver Island) may be an escape from captivity.

Notes.—Also known as Rufous Turtle-Dove.

Streptopelia risoria (Linnaeus). Ringed Turtle-Dove.

Columba risoria Linnaeus, 1758, Syst. Nat. (ed. 10) 1: 165. (in India.)

Habitat.—Feral populations occur in open woodland and parks around human habitation; related species in the wild state inhabit arid country with trees and shrubs, often near human habitation.

Distribution.—Origin and native country uncertain; long domesticated and in captivity worldwide.

Introduced and established in west-central Florida (Pinellas County), the Bahamas (New Providence), Puerto Rico, and apparently also in eastern Texas (Houston region) and Alabama (Montgomery). Other North American populations (e.g., in Los Angeles) have failed to become established.

Notes.—Also known as Barbary Dove. This widely domesticated and locally introduced form is now deemed to be derived from the African *S. roseogrisea* (Sundevall, 1957) [African Collared-Dove] rather than *S. decaocto* (Goodwin 1983). Surviving North American populations may now be entirely human-supported and totally human-dependent. There is controversy whether the name *risoria* can be applied to any wild population at all (Sibley and Monroe 1990).

Streptopelia turtur (Linnaeus). European Turtle-Dove.

> *Columba Turtur* Linnaeus, 1758, Syst. Nat., ed. 10, 1, p. 164. (in India, error = England.)

Habitat.—Open woodland, scrub, plains, and gardens.

Distribution.—*Breeds* from the British Isles and Europe south to northern Africa and southwestern Asia, and *winters* south to southwestern Africa.

Accidental in southern Florida (Lower Matecumbe Key, 9–11 April 1990, photograph; Hoffman et al. 1990). Some consider the origin of this individual uncertain; see DeBenedictis (1994b).

Streptopelia decaocto (Frivaldszky). Eurasian Collared-Dove.

> *Columba risoria* L. var. *decaocto* Frivaldszky, 1838, K. Magyar Tudos Társág Evkönyvi 3(3) (1834–36): 183, pl. 8. (Turkey.)

Habitat.—Suburbs, parks, and farm groves; in Old World, a variety of habitats from open woodland to scrub and desert, as well as around human habitation.

Distribution.—Western Palearctic from the British Isles, southern Scandinavia, and western Russia south to southern Europe, Egypt, and southern Asia east to Burma and Sri Lanka; European populations represent a relatively recent expansion and may be the result of introductions.

Introduced and established in the Bahama Islands (New Providence, 1974), whence it has spread to other northern islands in the Bahamas (Grand Bahama, Abaco, Bimini, Eleuthera, Andros), to Cuba, to the Lesser Antilles (Montserrat, St. Kitts, Dominica, Guadeloupe), and to southern Florida (late 1970's, now common to abundant from the Tampa and Palm Beach areas south to Key West, breeding locally west to Destin in the Panhandle); also established locally in coastal Georgia, South Carolina, and southeastern Louisiana, occurring casually north to North Carolina (nesting 1995) and Pennsylvania, and west to southwestern Louisiana, Arkansas, and central and northwestern Texas (origin uncertain); a small population in southeastern Colorado is of uncertain origin. Also apparently spreading in Caribbean, with recent populations discovered in Cuba, Montserrat, and Dominica. Also introduced in Japan.

Notes.—For a discussion of the history of *S. decaocto* in North America, see Smith (1987). For distribution in West Indies, see Barre et al. (1996). *Streptopelia decaocto* and *S. bitorquata* (Temminck) 1810, of Indonesia and the Philippines, appear to constitute a superspecies (Goodwin 1983).

Streptopelia chinensis (Scopoli). Spotted Dove.

> *Columba (chinensis)* Scopoli, 1786, Del Flor. Faun. Insubr., fasc. 2, p. 94. (China = Canton.)

Habitat.—Primarily suburban areas and cultivated lands around human habitation with groves of trees.

Distribution.—*Resident* from eastern Afghanistan, the Himalayas, and eastern China south to Sri Lanka, the Malay Peninsula, East Indies, and Philippines.

Introduced and established in the Hawaiian Islands (main islands from Kauai eastward); in southern California (primarily from Santa Barbara, where now rare, and Bakersfield south to San Diego and the Coachella Valley) and (probably) extreme northwestern Baja California (Tijuana area), casually to Imperial Valley; and in Mauritius, Sulawesi, Australia, New Zealand, and various islands of Polynesia. A small population may persist on St. Croix, Virgin Islands (introduced in 1964).

Genus *GEOPELIA* Swainson

Geopelia Swainson, 1837, Class. Birds 2: 348. Type, by monotypy, *Geopelia lineata* Mus. Carl. pl. 67 = *Columba striata* Linnaeus.

Geopelia striata (Linnaeus). Zebra Dove.

Columba striata Linnaeus, 1766, Syst. Nat. (ed. 12) 1: 282. Based on "La Tourterelle rayée des Indes" Brisson, Ornithologie 1: 109, and "The Transverse Striped or Barred Dove" Edwards 1: 16, pl. 16. (in India orientali = Java.)

Habitat.—Open country with trees and shrubby growth, parks, gardens, and cultivated areas, especially near human habitation.

Distribution.—*Resident* from the Malay Peninsula and Philippines south to the East Indies.

Introduced and established in the Hawaiian Islands (in 1922, now on all main islands from Kauai eastward).

Notes.—Also known as Barred Dove. *Geopelia placida* Gould, 1844 [Peaceful Dove] of Australia and *G. maugeus* (Temminck, 1811) [Barred Dove] of the Lesser Sunda Islands are often merged with *G. striata* (see Christidis and Boles 1994).

Genus *ZENAIDA* Bonaparte

Zenaida Bonaparte, 1838, Geogr. Comp. List, p. 41. Type, by tautonymy, *Zenaida amabilis* Bonaparte = *Columba zenaida* Bonaparte = *Columba aurita* Temminck.

Zenaidura Bonaparte, 1855, C. R. Acad. Sci. Paris 40: 96. Type, by original designation, *Columba carolinensis* Linnaeus = *Columba macroura* Linnaeus.

Melopelia Bonaparte, 1855, C. R. Acad. Sci. Paris 40: 98. Type, by subsequent designation (G. R. Gray, 1855), *Columba meloda* Tschudi = *Columba asiatica* Linnaeus.

Zenaida asiatica (Linnaeus). White-winged Dove.

Columba asiatica Linnaeus, 1758, Syst. Nat. (ed. 10) 1: 163. Based on "The Brown Indian Dove" Edwards, Nat. Hist. Birds 2: 76, pl. 76. (in Indiis = Jamaica.)

Habitat.—Tropical Deciduous Forest, Gallery Forest, Riparian Thickets, Second-growth Scrub, Arid Lowland Scrub (0–2500 m; Tropical and Subtropical zones).

Distribution.—*Breeds* [*asiatica* group] in southeastern California, southern Nevada, and extreme southwestern Utah.

Resident [*asiatica* group] from central Arizona, central New Mexico, northern Chihuahua, western and central Texas, and (locally) southern Louisiana and southern Alabama south to Baja California, through most of Middle America (including Isla Tiburón off Sonora, the Tres Marías Islands off Nayarit, and Cozumel and Holbox islands off Quintana Roo) to Honduras, locally in the Pacific lowlands to northwestern Costa Rica (Guanacaste), in mangrove swamps of western Panama around the shores of Golfo de Parita from Herrera (lower Río Parita) to Coclé (Río Pocrí and Río Antón), in the southern Bahamas (north to Great Exuma and Long Island) and Greater Antilles (east to Puerto Rico), and on islands in the western Caribbean (Providencia, San Andrés); and [*meloda* group] along the Pacific coast of South America from southwestern Ecuador to northern Chile.

Winters [*asiatica* group] south to Costa Rica and islands in the Caribbean Sea.

Introduced [*asiatica* group] in central and southern Florida.

Casual [*asiatica* group] in northwestern North America north to southeastern Alaska (Skagway), British Columbia, Montana, and Colorado, in eastern North America from Minnesota, northern Ontario, New Brunswick, Maine, and Nova Scotia south to northern Texas, central Louisiana, and northern Florida, in the northern Bahamas (Grand Bahama, Acklin's Island), and in the Virgin Islands (St. Croix, St. John).

Notes.—Groups: *Z. asiatica* [White-winged Dove] and *Z. meloda* (Tschudi, 1843) [Pacific Dove].

Zenaida aurita (Temminck). Zenaida Dove.

Columba Aurita Temminck, 1809, Les Pigeons, livr. 6, Les Colombes, p. 60, pl. 25. (Martinique.)

Habitat.—Tropical Deciduous Forest, Arid Lowland Scrub, Second-growth Scrub (0–600 m; Tropical Zone).

Distribution.—*Resident* in the Florida Keys (formerly), Bahamas, Greater Antilles (east to Virgin Islands), Cayman Islands and Lesser Antilles; and along the north coast of the Yucatan Peninsula (Yucatán, Quintana Roo), including on Holbox, Cancun, Mujeres, and Cozumel islands. A specimen from Belize is of dubious authenticity (Barlow et al. 1969).

Casual in southern Florida (from Key West to Key Largo, with sight reports north to Osceola County).

Zenaida auriculata (Des Murs). Eared Dove.

Peristera auriculata Des Murs, 1847, in Gay, Hist. Fis. Pol. Chile, Zool. 1: 381, pl. 6. (central provinces of Chile.)

Habitat.—Second-growth Scrub, Arid Lowland Scrub, Arid Montane Scrub (0–3400 m; Tropical to Temperate zones).

Distribution.—*Resident* in the southern Lesser Antilles on Grenada and the Grenadines; and throughout most of South America from Colombia, Venezuela (including islands from the Netherlands Antilles east to Tobago and Trinidad) and the Guianas south to Tierra del Fuego.

Casual on St. Lucia and Martinique; accidental in the Falkland Islands and on South Georgia. An individual photographed in Panama (Coco Solo, Canal area) may have been an escape from captivity; also a sight report from Tocumen, Panamá Prov.

Notes.—*Z. auriculata* and *Z. macroura* constitute a superspecies (Mayr and Short 1970).

Zenaida macroura (Linnaeus). Mourning Dove.

Columba macroura Linnaeus, 1758, Syst. Nat. (ed. 10) 1: 164. Based mainly on "The Long-tailed Dove" Edwards, Nat. Hist. Birds 1: 15, pl. 15. (in Canada, error = Cuba.)

Habitat.—Cultivated lands with scattered trees and bushes, open woodland, suburbs, and arid and desert country (generally near water) (Tropical to Temperate zones).

Distribution.—*Breeds* from central British Columbia (including Vancouver Island), central Alberta, central Saskatchewan, southern Manitoba, northern Minnesota, northern Wisconsin, northern Michigan, central Ontario, southern Quebec, Maine, New Brunswick, Prince Edward Island and Nova Scotia south to southern Baja California, Sonora (in Pacific lowlands), in the interior mountains and Central Plateau of Mexico to Oaxaca and Puebla, and to northern Tamaulipas (in the Caribbean lowlands), Texas, the Gulf coast, and southern Florida; in Bermuda, the Bahama Islands, and Greater Antilles (east to Puerto Rico and Culebra and Vieques islands); in Guadalupe, the Revillagigedo and Tres Marías islands off western Mexico; and in western Nicaragua, Costa Rica, and western Panama (east to western Panamá province), probably also elsewhere in northern Central America.

Winters primarily from northern California east across the central United States to Iowa, southern Michigan, southern Ontario, southwestern Quebec, New York, and New England (uncommonly to the northern limits of the breeding range), and south throughout the breeding range and over most of Middle America to central Panama.

Casual north to western and central Alaska (almost annually), southern Yukon, southern Mackenzie, northern Manitoba, northern Ontario, central Quebec, Labrador, Newfoundland, and Greenland, and to the Cayman Islands. Accidental on Clipperton Island, Colombia, and the British Isles.

Introduced and established in the Hawaiian Islands (on Hawaii in 1963, presently a small population in the North Kona region).

Notes.—See comments under *Z. auriculata* and *Z. graysoni*.

Zenaida graysoni (Lawrence). Socorro Dove.

Zenaidura graysoni (Baird MS) Lawrence, 1871, Ann. Lyc. Nat. Hist. N. Y. 10: 17.
(Socorro Island, Mexico.)

Habitat.—Arid Lowland Scrub.

Distribution.—Formerly *resident* on Socorro Island, in the Revillagigedo Islands, off
western Mexico; several recent searches (1988–1991) found only *Z. macroura* (a new invader
to Socorro) and confirm the extirpation in the wild of *Z. graysoni,* although there are still
living birds in captivity at this time.

Notes.—Although considered by many authors as conspecific with *Z. macroura,* differences in morphology, vocalizations, and behavior support the maintenance of specific status
for *Z. graysoni* (Baptista et al. 1983).

Genus *ECTOPISTES* Swainson

Ectopistes Swainson, 1827, Zool. J. 3: 362. Type, by subsequent designation (Swainson,
1837), *Columba migratoria* Linnaeus.

†*Ectopistes migratorius* (Linnaeus). Passenger Pigeon.

Columba migratoria Linnaeus, 1766, Syst. Nat. (ed. 12) 1: 285. Based mainly on "The
Pigeon of Passage" Catesby, Nat. Hist. Carolina 1: 23, pl. 23. (in America septentrionali = South Carolina.)

Habitat.—Forest, foraging in open country and cultivated lands adjacent to forest.

Distribution.—EXTINCT. *Bred* formerly from central Montana, east-central Saskatche-
wan, southern Manitoba, Minnesota, Wisconsin, Michigan, central Ontario, southern Quebec,
New Brunswick, Prince Edward Island, and Nova Scotia south to eastern Kansas, Oklahoma,
Mississippi, and Georgia.

Wintered from Arkansas, southeastern Missouri, Tennessee, and North Carolina south to
Texas, the Gulf coast, and northern Florida, occasionally north to Indiana, southern Pennsylvania, and Connecticut.

Casual or accidental to Nevada, Idaho, Wyoming, British Columbia, Mackenzie, Alberta,
northern Saskatchewan, northern Manitoba, Baffin Bay, northern Quebec, Labrador, Prince
Edward Island, Bermuda, Cuba (Havana market), and Mexico (recorded Puebla, Veracruz,
and Tabasco); also in Scotland, Ireland, and France, although the European individuals may
have been escapes from captivity. Last specimen obtained in the wild taken at Sargento,
Pike County, Ohio, on 24 March 1900; last living individual died in captivity in the Cincinnati
Zoological Gardens, Cincinnati, Ohio, on 1 September 1914.

Notes.—Oberholser (1974) used the name *E. canadensis* (Linnaeus), but see Banks and
Browning (1995).

Genus *COLUMBINA* Spix

Columbina Spix, 1825, Avium Spec. Nov. Bras. 2: 57. Type, by subsequent designation
(G. R. Gray, 1841), *Columbina strepitans* Spix = *Columba picui* Temminck.

Columbigallina Boie, 1826, Isis von Oken, col. 977. Type, by monotypy, *Columba
passerina* Linnaeus.

Chamæpelia Swainson, 1827, Zool. J. 3: 361. Type, by subsequent designation (G. R.
Gray, 1841), *Columba passerina* Linnaeus.

Scardafella Bonaparte, 1855, C. R. Acad. Sci. Paris 40: 24. Type, by original designation, *Columba squamosa* Temminck (not Bonnaterre) = *Columba squammata* Lesson.

Columbina inca (Lesson). Inca Dove.

Chamæpelia inca Lesson, 1847, Descr. Mamm. Ois., p. 211. (Mexico [probably west
coast].)

Habitat.—Second-growth Scrub, Riparian Thickets, Arid Lowland Scrub, Arid Montane
Scrub (0–2400 m; Tropical, less frequently Subtropical zones).

Distribution.—*Resident* from southeastern California, northeastern Baja California, southern Nevada, central Arizona, southern New Mexico, central Texas, and western Louisiana south through Mexico (except the Yucatan Peninsula and the remainder of Baja California), Guatemala (rare in Petén and Caribbean lowlands), El Salvador, Honduras (Pacific lowlands and arid interior valleys), and Nicaragua (Pacific lowlands) to northwestern Costa Rica (Guanacaste and highlands to vicinity of San José); and, at least formerly, in the Florida Keys (Key West), where now apparently extirpated.

Wanders regularly to eastern and southwestern California (Inyo, Los Angeles, and Kern counties), and casually to southern Utah, north-central and southeastern Colorado, North Dakota, Nebraska, Kansas, northwestern Missouri, Oklahoma, Arkansas, and northeastern Louisiana. Accidental in Ontario. The origin of the Key West breeding populations may have been escaped cage-birds.

Notes.—Often placed in the genus *Scardafella,* but see Johnston (1961). *Columbina inca* is sometimes merged with *C. squammata* (Lesson, 1831) of South American (Hellmayr and Conover 1942, Mayr and Short 1970).

Columbina passerina (Linnaeus). Common Ground-Dove.

> *Columba passerina* Linnaeus, 1758, Syst. Nat. (ed. 10) 1: 165. Based mainly on "The Ground Dove" Catesby, Nat. Hist. Carolina 1: 26, pl. 26. (in America inter tropicos = South Carolina.)

Habitat.—Arid Lowland Scrub, Arid Montane Scrub, Second-growth Scrub, Pastures/ Agricultural Lands, lowland pine savanna (0–2300 m; Tropical and Subtropical zones).

Distribution.—*Resident* from southern California (north to Santa Barbara County), central Arizona, southwestern New Mexico, central Texas, the Gulf coast, South Carolina, Bermuda, and the Bahamas south through Mexico (including Socorro Island in the Revillagigedos, Tres Marías and Tres Marietas islands off Nayarit, and islands off the Yucatan Peninsula, but rare in the central highlands), the Antilles, and Central America (mostly in the highlands and arid interior, but also in the Caribbean lowland savanna, and in the Bay Islands off Honduras) to central Costa Rica (Guanacaste and the arid central highlands); in western Panama (Azuero Peninsula); and in northern South America from Colombia, Venezuela (including islands from the Netherlands Antilles east to Trinidad), and the Guianas south to Ecuador and eastern Brazil. Northwestern populations are partly migratory.

Wanders casually north to central California, southern Nevada, Utah, Wyoming, Nebraska, Iowa, Wisconsin, northern Michigan, central Ontario, Pennsylvania, New York, Massachusetts, and Nova Scotia.

Notes.—Also known as Scaly-breasted Ground-Dove. Oberholser (1974) used the generic name *Columbigallina.*

Columbina minuta (Linnaeus). Plain-breasted Ground-Dove.

> *Columba minuta* Linnaeus, 1766, Syst. Nat. (ed. 12) 1: 285. Based on "La petite Tourterelle brun d'Amérique" Brisson, Ornithologie 1: 116, pl. 8, fig. 2. (in America = Cayenne.)

Habitat.—Arid Lowland Scrub, Low Seasonally Wet Grassland, Arid Montane Scrub, Second-growth Scrub (0–1400 m; Tropical and Subtropical zones).

Distribution.—*Resident* on the Gulf-Caribbean slope of Middle America in southern Mexico (southern Veracruz, northern Oaxaca, Tabasco, Chiapas, and southwest Campeche, presumably also Morelos), Belize, Guatemala, and, locally, north-central and northeastern Nicaragua (probably also in eastern Honduras) and extreme northeastern Costa Rica; along the Pacific coast of Middle America locally from Jalisco, Guerrero, and southwestern Oaxaca south to Costa Rica (not recorded Honduras or Pacific lowlands of Nicaragua, but present in the central highlands of Nicaragua) and Panama (east to eastern Panamá province, also recorded on Caribbean slope in Canal area); and disjunctly in South America in northern Colombia, Venezuela, Trinidad, the Guianas, Peru, eastern and central Brazil, eastern Bolivia, and northern Paraguay.

Columbina talpacoti (Temminck). Ruddy Ground-Dove.

Columba talpacoti Temminck, 1810, Les Pigeons, livr. 12/13, Les Colombi-Gallines, p. 22. (l'Amérique méridionale = Brazil.)

Habitat.—Second-growth Scrub, Riparian Thickets, Arid Lowland Scrub (0–1200 m; Tropical, less frequently Subtropical zones).

Distribution.—*Resident* from southern Sonora, eastern San Luis Potosí, and Tamaulipas south through Middle America (including Cozumel and Cancun islands off Quintana Roo, and Coiba and Pearl islands off Panama), and in South America from Colombia, Venezuela (including Margarita Island), Tobago, Trinidad, and the Guianas south, east of the Andes, to northern Argentina and northern Uruguay.

Ranges north rarely to southern California (north to Santa Barbara and Inyo counties), southern Arizona, and western and southern Texas, casually to southern Nevada, southwestern New Mexico, southern Baja California (sight reports), and Chile.

Notes.—*C. talpacoti* and *C. buckleyi* (Sclater and Salvin, 1877) of western Ecuador and northwestern Peru, form a superspecies (Goodwin 1983). Oberholser (1974) used the generic name *Columbigallina*.

Genus *CLARAVIS* Oberholser

Peristera (not Rafinesque, 1815) Swainson, 1827, Zool. J. 3: 360. Type, by original designation, *Columba cinerea* Temminck = *Peristera pretiosa* Ferrari-Perez.
Claravis Oberholser, 1899, Proc. Acad. Nat. Sci. Philadelphia 51: 203. New name for *Peristera* Swainson, preoccupied.

Claravis pretiosa (Ferrari-Perez). Blue Ground-Dove.

Columba cinerea (not Scopoli, 1786) Temminck, 1811, Les Pigeons, livr. 14/15, Les Colombes, p. 126, pl. 58. (au Brésil = Brazil.)
Peristera pretiosa Ferrari-Perez, 1886, Proc. U. S. Natl. Mus. 9: 175. New name for *Columba cinerea* Temminck, preoccupied.

Habitat.—Tropical Lowland Evergreen Forest Edge, Secondary Forest, River-edge Forest, Gallery Forest (0–1200 m; Tropical and lower Subtropical zones).

Distribution.—*Resident* from Chiapas on the Pacific slope, and from southeastern San Luis Potosí, Hidalgo, and southern Tamaulipas on the Gulf-Caribbean slope south through Middle America, and in South America from Colombia, Venezuela, Trinidad, and the Guianas south, west of the Andes to northwestern Peru, and east of the Andes to northern Argentina, Paraguay, and southeastern Brazil.

Claravis mondetoura (Bonaparte). Maroon-chested Ground-Dove.

Peristera mondetoura Bonaparte, 1856, C. R. Acad. Sci. Paris 42: 765. (Caracas, Venezuela.)

Habitat.—Montane Evergreen Forest, especially with heavy undergrowth or bamboo (900–3000 m; Subtropical Zone).

Distribution.—*Resident* locally in the mountains of Veracruz, Chiapas, Guatemala, El Salvador, Honduras, Costa Rica, and western Panama (Chiriquí); and in the Andes of South America from Colombia and northwestern Venezuela south to northern Bolivia.

Notes.—*C. mondetoura* and *C. godefrida* (Temminck, 1811), of eastern South America, constitute a superspecies (Goodwin 1983).

Genus *LEPTOTILA* Swainson

Leptotila Swainson, 1837, Class. Birds 2: 349. Type, by monotypy, *P[eristera]. rufaxilla* Nat. Lib. v. pl. 24 = *Columba jamaicensis* Linnaeus.

Leptotila verreauxi Bonaparte. White-tipped Dove.

Leptotila verreauxi Bonaparte, 1855, C. R. Acad. Sci. Paris 40: 99. (de la Nouvelle-Grenade = Colombia.)

Habitat.—Tropical Deciduous Forest, Gallery Forest, Secondary Forest, River-edge Forest, Tropical Lowland Evergreen Forest Edge (0–2800 m; Tropical to lower Temperate zones).

Distribution.—*Resident* [*verreauxi* group] from central Sonora, southwestern Chihuahua, southeastern San Luis Potosí, Nuevo León, and southern Texas (lower Rio Grande Valley north to central Texas coast) south through Middle America (including the Tres Marías Islands off Nayarit, and the Pearl Islands and many other small islands off Panama), and in South America from Colombia, Venezuela (including islands from the Netherlands Antilles east to Tobago and Trinidad), and the Guianas south, west of the Andes, to northern Peru; and [*brasiliensis* group] from eastern Peru, eastern Bolivia, and Brazil south to northern Argentina and Uruguay.

Notes.—Also known as White-fronted Dove. Groups: *L. verreauxi* [White-tipped Dove] and *L. brasiliensis* (Bonaparte, 1856) [Brazilian Dove]. *Leptotila verreauxi* and the South American *L. megalura* Sclater and Salvin, 1879, appear to constitute a superspecies (Goodwin 1983).

Leptotila rufaxilla (Richard and Bernard). Gray-fronted Dove.

Columba Rufaxilla Richard and Bernard, 1792, Actes Soc. Hist. Nat. Paris 1: 118. (Cayenne.)

Habitat.—Tropical Lowland Evergreen Forest Edge, Secondary Forest (0–1000 m; Tropical and lower Subtropical zones);

Distribution.—*Resident* [*plumbeiceps* group] from southern Tamaulipas, southeastern San Luis Potosí, southern Veracruz, and northern Oaxaca south on the Gulf-Caribbean slope (except Yucatán) through Belize, northern Guatemala, Honduras, Nicaragua (also Pacific slope in southwest), and Costa Rica (both slopes) to western Panama (western Bocas del Toro), and in the Western Andes and Cauca Valley of Colombia; [*battyi* group] in western Panama (Azuero Peninsula in southern Veraguas and western Herrera, and Cébaco and Coiba islands); and [*rufaxilla* group] in South America from eastern Colombia, Venezuela, Trinidad, and the Guianas south, east of the Andes, to central Bolivia, Paraguay, northeastern Argentina, and southern Brazil.

Notes.—Various groups in this species are often (Goodwin 1983) considered distinct species, *L. plumbeiceps* Sclater and Salvin, 1868 [Gray-headed Dove], which includes *battyi* (along with *L. wellsi*), and *L. rufaxilla* [Gray-fronted Dove]. Wetmore (1968) recognized *L. battyi* Rothschild, 1901 [Brown-backed Dove] as a distinct species, and Howell and Webb (1995) recognized *L. plumbeiceps* as a species. *Leptotila rufaxilla, L. wellsi,* and *L. jamaicensis* appear to constitute a superspecies (Goodwin 1983). See comments under *L. wellsi.*

Leptotila wellsi (Lawrence). Grenada Dove.

Engyptila wellsi Lawrence, 1884, Auk, 1, p. 180. (Fontenoy, St. Georges, Grenada.)

Habitat.—Tropical Deciduous Forest.

Distribution.—*Resident* on the southwestern peninsula of Grenada, where surviving in small numbers; formerly more widely distributed on Grenada and on offshore islands (Glover's, Green). Not definitely known from Tobago or St. Vincent although sometimes listed for those islands.

Notes.—Formerly (A.O.U. 1983) included with *L. rufaxilla,* from which it differs in vocalizations, plumage, and soft part colors (Blockstein and Hardy 1989). See comments under *L. rufaxilla.*

Leptotila jamaicensis (Linnaeus). Caribbean Dove.

Columba jamaicensis Linnaeus, 1766, Syst. Nat. (ed. 12) 1: 283. Based on *Columba minor ventre candido* Sloane, Voy. Jamaica 2: 303, pl. 262, fig. 1, and "Le Pigeon de la Jamaïque" Brisson, Ornithologie 1: 134. (in Jamaica.)

Habitat.—Tropical Deciduous Forest, Tropical Lowland Evergreen Forest Edge, Secondary Forest.

Distribution.—*Resident* on Jamaica, Grand Cayman Island, the northern Yucatan Peninsula (including Holbox, Mujeres, Cancun, and Cozumel islands), on islands off Belize (Ambergris Cay) and Honduras (Roatán and Barbareta in the Bay Islands, and Little Hog Island), and on Isla San Andrés in the western Caribbean Sea.

Introduced and established in the Bahamas (New Providence).

Notes.—Also known as White-bellied Dove. See comments under *L. rufaxilla.*

Leptotila cassini Lawrence. Gray-chested Dove.

Leptotila cassini Lawrence, 1867, Proc. Acad. Nat. Sci. Philadelphia 19: 94. (Line of the Panama Railroad, New Granada = Atlantic slope, Canal area.)

Habitat.—Tropical Lowland Evergreen Forest Edge, Secondary Forest (0–1400 m; Tropical and lower Subtropical zones).

Distribution.—*Resident* on the Gulf-Caribbean slope of Middle America from eastern Tabasco and northern Chiapas south through Belize, northern Guatemala, Honduras, and Nicaragua, and on both slopes from Costa Rica through Panama to northern Colombia.

Notes.—Also known as Cassin's Dove.

Genus *GEOTRYGON* Gosse

Geotrygon Gosse, 1847, Birds Jamaica, p. 316 (footnote). Type, by subsequent designation (Reichenbach, 1853), *Columba cristata* Latham [= Gmelin, not Temminck] = *Geotrygon sylvatica* Gosse = *Columbigallina versicolor* Lafresnaye.

Oreopeleia Reichenbach, 1853, Handb. Spec. Ornithol., Die Vögel, pt. 3 (1852), p. xxv. Type, by original designation, *"Columba martinicana"* Brisson = *Columba martinica* Linnaeus = *Columba montana* Linnaeus.

Geotrygon veraguensis Lawrence. Olive-backed Quail-Dove.

Geotrygon veraguensis Lawrence, 1867, Ann. Lyc. Nat. Hist. N. Y. 8: 349. (Veragua [Panama].)

Habitat.—Tropical Lowland Evergreen Forest (0–900 m; Tropical Zone).

Distribution.—*Resident* in the Caribbean lowlands of Costa Rica and Panama (also on Pacific slope in eastern Panamá province and Darién), and in western Colombia and northwestern Ecuador.

Notes.—Also known as Veraguas Quail-Dove.

Geotrygon chrysia Bonaparte. Key West Quail-Dove.

Geotrygon chrysia Bonaparte, 1855, C. R. Acad. Sci. Paris 40: 100. (Floride = Florida.)

Habitat.—Tropical Deciduous Forest (0–500 m).

Distribution.—*Resident* in the Bahamas (Grand Bahama, Great Abaco, Andros, New Providence, Eleuthera, San Salvador, Long Island, and North Caicos), Cuba, the Isle of Pines, Hispaniola (including Gonâve, Tortue, and Catalina islands), Puerto Rico (possibly also Mona Island).

Casual in southern Florida (the Florida Keys, and southern mainland, mostly near coasts). Formerly reported as common and breeding at Key West (Howell 1932).

Notes.—*G. chrysia* and *G. mystacea* constitute a superspecies (Goodwin 1983).

Geotrygon mystacea (Temminck). Bridled Quail-Dove.

Columba mystacea Temminck, 1811, Les Pigeons, livr. 14/15, Les Colombes, p. 124, pl. 56. (l'Amerique = probably Lesser Antilles.)

Habitat.—Tropical Deciduous Forest, Tropical Lowland Evergreen Forest (0–700 m).

Distribution.—*Resident* in eastern Puerto Rico (locally), the Virgin Islands (except Anegada), and Lesser Antilles (from Saba and Barbuda south to St. Lucia).

Notes.—See comments under *G. chrysia.*

Geotrygon albifacies Sclater. White-faced Quail-Dove.

> *Geotrygon albifacies* Sclater, 1858, Proc. Zool. Soc. London, p. 98. (environs of Jalapa, [Veracruz,] Southern Mexico.)

Habitat.—Montane Evergreen Forest (1200–2700 m; Subtropical Zone).
Distribution.—*Resident* in the mountains of southeastern San Luis Potosí, Hidalgo, Veracruz, Guerrero, Oaxaca, Chiapas, Guatemala, El Salvador, Honduras, and north-central Nicaragua.
Notes.—*G. albifacies* and *G. chiriquensis* are often (Goodwin 1983) considered as conspecific with the South American *G. linearis* (Prévost, 1843), but retention of three species constituting a superspecies complex seems more satisfactory. If all are combined into a single species, *G. linearis,* the name White-faced Quail-Dove is still appropriate.

Geotrygon chiriquensis Sclater. Chiriqui Quail-Dove.

> *Geotrygon chiriquensis* Sclater, 1856, Proc. Zool. Soc. London, p. 143. (vicinity of the Town of David in the Province of Chiriqui in the State of Panama.)

Habitat.—Montane Evergreen Forest (600–3100 m; upper Tropical and Subtropical zones).
Distribution.—*Resident* in the mountains of Costa Rica and western Panama (Chiriquí and Veraguas).
Notes.—See comments under *G. albifacies.*

Geotrygon carrikeri Wetmore. Tuxtla Quail-Dove.

> *Geotrygon lawrenceii carrikeri* Wetmore, 1941, Proc. Biol. Soc. Wash. 54, p. 205. (Volcán San Martín, Sierra de Tuxtla, Veracruz, Mexico, 3000–4000 feet elev.)

Habitat.—Montane Evergreen Forest (350–1500 m; upper Tropical and lower Subtropical zones).
Distribution.—*Resident* in southeastern Veracruz (Sierra de los Tuxtlas).
Notes.—Formerly treated as a subspecies of *G. lawrencii,* but see Peterson (1993); cf. Howell and Webb (1995).

Geotrygon lawrencii Salvin. Purplish-backed Quail-Dove.

> *Geotrygon lawrencii* Salvin, 1874, Ibis, p. 329. (Calóbre, Veraguas, Panama.)

Habitat.—Montane Evergreen Forest (400–1050 m; upper Tropical and lower Subtropical zones).
Distribution.—*Resident* in the mountains of Costa Rica and Panama (east to Darién).
Notes.—*Geotrygon lawrencii, G. costaricensis,* and *G. goldmani* are closely related, but degree of relationship is uncertain; *G. lawrencii* and *G. costaricensis* are reportedly sympatric in Costa Rica, and *G. lawrencii* and *G. goldmani* overlap in eastern Panama.

Geotrygon costaricensis Lawrence. Buff-fronted Quail-Dove.

> *Geotrygon costaricensis* Lawrence, 1868, Ann. Lyc. Nat. Hist. N. Y. 9: 136. (Costa Rica = Las Cruces de la Candelaria, Costa Rica.)

Habitat.—Montane Evergreen Forest (1000–3000 m; Subtropical and Temperate zones).
Distribution.—*Resident* in the mountains of Costa Rica and western Panama (east to Veraguas).
Notes.—Also known as Costa Rican Quail-Dove. See comments under *G. lawrencii.*

Geotrygon goldmani Nelson. Russet-crowned Quail-Dove.

> *Geotrygon goldmani* Nelson, 1912, Smithson. Misc. Collect. 60(3): 2. (Mount Pirri, at 5,000 feet altitude, head of Rio Limon, eastern Panama.)

Habitat.—Montane Evergreen Forest (750–1600 m; upper Tropical and lower Subtropical zones).

Distribution.—*Resident* in the mountains of eastern Panama (eastern Panamá province and Darién) and extreme northwestern Colombia (Juradó).

Notes.—Also known as Goldman's Quail-Dove. See comments under *G. lawrencii*.

Geotrygon caniceps (Gundlach). Gray-headed Quail-Dove.

Columba caniceps Gundlach, 1852, J. Boston Soc. Nat. Hist. 6: 315. (Cuba.)

Habitat.—Tropical Lowland Evergreen Forest (Cuba) and Montane Evergreen Forest (Hispaniola) (0–1800 m).

Distribution.—*Resident* in the lowlands of Cuba and in the mountains of Hispaniola (Dominican Republic, not known from Haiti).

Notes.—Also known as Moustached Quail-Dove.

Geotrygon versicolor (Lafresnaye). Crested Quail-Dove.

Columbigallina versicolor Lafresnaye, 1846, Rev. Zool. [Paris] 9: 321. (Jamaïque = Jamaica.)

Habitat.—Montane Evergreen Forest (100–1800 m).

Distribution.—*Resident* in the mountains of Jamaica.

Geotrygon violacea (Temminck). Violaceous Quail-Dove.

Columba violacea Temminck, 1809, Les Pigeons, livr. 7, Les Colombes, p. 67, pl. 29. (le Nouveau Monde = Rio de Janeiro, Brazil.)

Habitat.—Tropical Lowland Evergreen Forest, Secondary Forest (0–1600 m; Tropical and lower Subtropical zones).

Distribution.—*Resident* in eastern Nicaragua (Caribbean lowlands), Costa Rica (humid Caribbean lowlands and foothills, also in semiarid Guanacaste lowlands on Pacific slope), and Panama (from Colón eastward), and in South America from northern Colombia, Venezuela, and Surinam south, east of the Andes, to Bolivia, northeastern Argentina, eastern Paraguay, and eastern Brazil.

Geotrygon montana (Linnaeus). Ruddy Quail-Dove.

Columba montana Linnaeus, 1758, Syst. Nat. (ed. 10) 1: 163. Based mainly on "The Mountain Partridge" Sloane, Voy. Jamaica 2: 304, pl. 261, fig. 1. (in Jamaica.)

Habitat.—Tropical Lowland Evergreen Forest, Montane Evergreen Forest, Tropical Deciduous Forest (0–1400 m; Tropical and lower Subtropical, locally to lower Temperate zones).

Distribution.—*Resident* [*montana* group] in the Greater Antilles, on Grenada (in the Lesser Antilles), from southern Sinaloa, Puebla, and southern Tamaulipas south along both slopes of Middle America to Panama (including Isla Coiba and Isla San José in the Pearl Islands), and in South America from Colombia, Venezuela, Trinidad, and the Guianas south, west of the Andes to western Ecuador and east of the Andes to northeastern Argentina, northern Paraguay, and southeastern Brazil; and [*martinica* group] in the Lesser Antilles (from Guadeloupe and Dominica south to St. Vincent). Some (many?) populations evidently undergo seasonal movements.

Casual [*montana* group] in southern Texas (Bentsen-Rio Grande State Park, 2–6 March 1996), southern Florida (Florida Keys, Dry Tortugas), and the Virgin Islands.

Notes.—Groups: *G. montana* [Ruddy Quail-Dove] and *G. martinica* (Linnaeus, 1758) [Martinique Quail-Dove].

Genus *STARNOENAS* Bonaparte.

Starnœnas Bonaparte, 1838, Geogr. Comp. List, p. 41. Type, by monotypy, *Columba cyanocephala* Linnaeus.

Starnoenas cyanocephala (Linnaeus). Blue-headed Quail-Dove.

> *Columba cyanocephala* Linnaeus, 1758, Syst. Nat. (ed. 10) 1: 163. Based on "The Turtle-Dove from Jamaica" Albin, Nat. Hist. Birds 2: 45, pl. 49. (in America = Jamaica.)

Habitat.—Tropical Lowland Evergreen Forest, Tropical Deciduous Forest.
Distribution.—*Resident* on Cuba.

Recorded from the Isle of Pines (one specimen, 1909) and Jamaica (apparently through attempted introduction). Specimens and reports from southern Florida are not sufficiently documented to constitute evidence of occurrence (Robertson and Woolfendon 1992).

Order **PSITTACIFORMES**: Parrots

Notes.—The Psittaciformes are sometimes divided into several families.

Family **PSITTACIDAE**: Lories, Parakeets, Macaws, and Parrots

Notes.—Individuals of many parrot species occur as escapes from captivity, especially in Florida (Robertson and Woolfenden 1992, Stevenson and Anderson 1994) and southern California (Johnston and Garrett 1994).

Subfamily PLATYCERCINAE: Australian Parakeets and Rosellas

Genus *MELOPSITTACUS* Gould

> *Melopsittacus* Gould, 1840, Birds Aust., pt. 1, pl. [10] (= 5, pl. 44 of bound volume). Type, by monotypy, *Psittacus undulatus* Shaw.

Melopsittacus undulatus (Shaw). Budgerigar.

> *Psittacus undulatus* Shaw, 1805, in Shaw and Nodder, Naturalists' Misc. 16: pl. 673. (New Holland = New South Wales, Australia.)

Habitat.—Suburbs with adjacent grassy open areas, such as beaches; in Australia, open woodland and scrubby areas, especially in semi-arid habitats, suburban areas, and parks.
Distribution.—*Resident* (though nomadic) through most of the interior of Australia, rarely ranging to coastal areas.

Introduced and established in west-central Florida (Charlotte to Citrus counties); escaped cage birds may be seen almost anywhere in North America. There is no evidence of establishment in Puerto Rico as previously reported.
Notes.—Also known as Shell Parakeet or Budgerygah.

Subfamily PSITTACINAE: Typical Parrots

Genus *PSITTACULA* Cuvier

> *Psittacula* Cuvier, 1800, Leçons Anat. Comp. 1: table at end. Type, by subsequent designation (Mathews, 1917), *Psittacus alexandri* Linnaeus.

Psittacula krameri (Scopoli). Rose-ringed Parakeet.

> *Psittacus krameri* Scopoli, 1769, Annus I, Hist.-Nat., p. 31. (No locality given = Senegal.)

Habitat.—Suburbs; in Africa, open woodland, savanna, cultivated lands, and areas around human habitation.
Distribution.—*Resident* in North Africa from Senegal east (south of the Sahara) to Eritrea, Ethiopia and Sudan; and in southern Asia from Afghanistan, India and Nepal south to Sri Lanka and Burma.

Introduced and established in small numbers in southern Florida (locally in Dade, Collier, and Dixie counties, since 1960's), Egypt, the Near East, Zanzibar, Mauritius, Singapore, Hong Kong and Macao; small introduced groups have also persisted in the Hawaiian Islands (on Oahu since 1971, breeding reported on Hawaii in 1981, probably breeding also on Kauai) and Virginia (Hampton, since 1973).

Subfamily ARINAE: New World Parakeets, Macaws, and Parrots

Genus *PYRRHURA* Bonaparte

Pyrrhura Bonaparte, 1856, Naumannia 6: Consp. Gen. Psittacorum, gen. 14. Type, by subsequent designation (Salvadori, 1891), *Psittacus vittatus* Shaw [not Boddaert] = *Psittacus frontalis* Vieillot.

Pyrrhura picta (Müller). Painted Parakeet.

Psittacus pictus P. L. S. Müller, 1776, Natursyst., Suppl., pl. 75. (Cayenne.)

Habitat.—Tropical Lowland Evergreen Forest (0–1200 m; Tropical Zone).

Distribution.—*Resident* in western Panama (Azuero Peninsula); and in South America from northern Colombia, southern Venezuela and the Guianas south, east of the Andes, to central Peru and Amazonian Brazil.

Notes.—The populations in Panama and northern Colombia may be subspecies of the South American *P. leucotis* (Kuhl, 1820) rather than *P. picta* (Ridgely and Gwynne 1989). *Pyrrhura picta* and *P. leucotis* constitute a superspecies (Delgado 1985, Sibley and Monroe 1990) and may even be conspecific (G. Smith 1982).

Pyrrhura hoffmanni (Cabanis). Sulphur-winged Parakeet.

Conurus hoffmanni Cabanis, 1861, Sitzungber. Ges. Naturforsch. Freunde Berlin, 13 November. (Costa Rica.)

Habitat.—Montane Evergreen Forest, Secondary Forest (1200–3000 m; Subtropical, rarely Tropical zones).

Distribution.—*Resident* in the mountains of Costa Rica (from Cordillera de Talamanca and Dota Mountains southward, including to Volcán Irazú) and western Panama (Chiriquí, Bocas del Toro and Veraguas, occurring also in the lowlands of the latter two).

Notes.—Also known as Hoffmann's Conure.

Genus *MYIOPSITTA* Bonaparte

Myiopsitta Bonaparte, 1854, Rev. Mag. Zool. (2)6: 150. Type, by subsequent designation (G. R. Gray, 1855), *Psittacus monachus* Boddaert.

Myiopsitta monachus (Boddaert). Monk Parakeet.

Psittacus monachus Boddaert, 1783, Table Planches Enlum., p. 48. Based on Daubenton, Planches Enlum., pl. 768. (No locality given = Montevideo, Uruguay.)

Habitat.—Primarily urban parks and suburbs; in South America, open woodland, savanna, arid scrubland, riverine forest, cultivated lands and orchards, especially around human habitation (Tropical and Subtropical zones).

Distribution.—*Resident* from central Bolivia, Paraguay and southern Brazil south to central Argentina.

Introduced and established in the eastern United States from Illinois, Michigan, southern Quebec, southern New York, Connecticut and Rhode Island south to New Jersey, with individual reports west and south to California, Oregon, Idaho, Oklahoma, Kentucky, and Virginia (control measures in progress in several localities); and in Texas, Florida, the Bahama Islands (Eleuthera), the Cayman Islands (Grand Cayman), Puerto Rico, the Dominican Republic, and Guadeloupe.

Genus *CONUROPSIS* Salvadori

Conuropsis Salvadori, 1891, Cat. Birds Brit. Mus. 20: xiii, 146, 203. Type, by original designation, *Psittacus carolinensis* Linnaeus.

†*Conuropsis carolinensis* (Linnaeus). Carolina Parakeet.

Psittacus carolinensis Linnaeus, 1758, Syst. Nat. (ed. 10) 1: 97. Based on the "Parrot of Carolina" Catesby, Nat. Hist. Carolina 1: 11, pl. 11. (in Carolina, Virginia = South Carolina.)

Habitat.—Riverine forest, cypress swamps and deciduous woodland, foraging in open situations including cultivated lands and gardens.

Distribution.—EXTINCT. Formerly ranged from eastern Nebraska (reports from the Dakotas questionable), Iowa, southeastern Wisconsin, Ohio, Pennsylvania and New Jersey south to southern Oklahoma, the Gulf states (from Texas eastward) and south-central Florida. Last known living individual died in the Cincinnati Zoo, 21 February 1918, although there are questionable sight reports for Florida in 1926 and South Carolina in 1936.

Genus *ARATINGA* Spix

Aratinga Spix, 1824, Avium Spec. Nov. Bras. 1: 29. Type, by subsequent designation (G. R. Gray, 1855), *Psittacus luteus* Boddaert = *Psittacus solstitialis* Linnaeus.

Notes.—Members of *Aratinga* and other related genera are sometimes referred to by the group name Conure.

Aratinga holochlora (Sclater). Green Parakeet.

Conurus holochlorus Sclater, 1859, Ann. Mag. Nat. Hist. (3)4: 224. (Jalapa, Vera Cruz, Mexico.)

Habitat.—[*holochlora* group] Tropical Lowland Evergreen Forest, Tropical Deciduous Forest, Secondary Forest, Pine-Oak Forest (0–2200 m; Tropical and Subtropical zones); [*brevipes* group] Tropical Deciduous Forest (0–1000 m); and [*rubritorquis* group] Pine-Oak Forest, Pine Forest, Tropical Deciduous Forest (800–2600 m; Subtropical Zone).

Distribution.—*Resident* [*holochlora* group] in southwestern Chihuahua and northeastern Sinaloa, wandering to southern Sonora, and from southern Nuevo León and Tamaulipas south to Veracruz, with disjunct populations in southeastern Oaxaca and Chiapas; [*brevipes* group] on Socorro Island, in the Revillagigedos; and [*rubritorquis* group] in the highlands of central and eastern Guatemala, El Salvador, Honduras and northern Nicaragua.

Reports from southern Florida are based on escaped cage-birds; established in southern Texas in lower Rio Grande Valley, probably from introduced individuals.

Notes.—Groups: *A. holochlora* [Green Parakeet]; *A. brevipes* Lawrence, 1871 [Socorro Parakeet]; and *A. rubritorquis* (Sclater, 1887) [Red-throated Parakeet]. Howell and Webb (1995) treated the three groups as separate species. *Aratinga holochlora* and *A. strenua* constitute a superspecies; they are sometimes considered conspecific (e.g., Forshaw 1973), but differences are retained in areas of close approach.

Aratinga strenua (Ridgway). Pacific Parakeet.

Conurus holochlorus strenuus Ridgway, 1915, Proc. Biol. Soc. Wash. 28: 106. (Ometepe, Nicaragua.)

Habitat.—Tropical Deciduous Forest, Gallery Forest, Tropical Lowland Evergreen Forest, Secondary Forest (0–1300 m Tropical, less frequently Subtropical zones).

Distribution.—*Resident* on the Pacific slope of Middle America from southeastern Oaxaca and Chiapas south to southwestern Nicaragua.

Notes.—See comments under *A. holochlora*.

Aratinga finschi (Salvin). Crimson-fronted Parakeet.

> *Conurus finschi* Salvin, 1871, Ibis, p. 91, pl. 4. (Bugaba, Chiriqui, Veragua [= Panama].)

Habitat.—Tropical Lowland Evergreen Forest Edge, Secondary Forest (0–1600 m; Tropical and Subtropical zones).

Distribution.—*Resident* in southeastern Nicaragua (Caribbean lowlands), Costa Rica (primarily Caribbean slope and Golfo Dulce lowlands on Pacific slope, wandering elsewhere on latter in dry season on cordilleras Guanacaste and Central), and western Panama (Caribbean slope in western Bocas del Toro and western Chiriquí, and Pacific lowlands in western Veraguas and Herrera).

Reports from southern Florida are based on escaped cage-birds (Stevenson and Anderson 1994).

Notes.—*A. finschi* and the South American *A. leucophthalmus* (P. L. S. Müller, 1776) constitute a superspecies (Sibley and Monroe 1990).

Aratinga chloroptera (de Souancé). Hispaniolan Parakeet.

> *Psittacara chloroptera* de Souancé, 1856, Rev. Mag. Zool. (2)8: 59. (Saint-Domingue = Hispaniola.)

Habitat.—Montane Evergreen Forest, Tropical Lowland Evergreen Forest (0–2000 m).

Distribution.—*Resident* on Hispaniola, on Mona Island (formerly, last individual taken in 1892), and probably also on Puerto Rico (based on hearsay evidence, but certainly not there after 1883).

Reports from southern Florida are based on escaped cage-birds (Stevenson and Anderson 1994).

Notes.—*A. chloroptera* and *A. euops* constitute a superspecies (Sibley and Monroe 1990).

Aratinga euops (Wagler). Cuban Parakeet.

> *Sittace euops* Wagler, 1832, Abh. Math. Phys. Kl. Bayr. Akad. Wiss. 1: 638, pl. 24, fig. 2. (Cuba.)

Habitat.—Tropical Lowland Evergreen Forest, Tropical Deciduous Forest (0–800 m).

Distribution.—*Resident* on Cuba (widespread, most common in remote forested areas) and the Isle of Pines (apparently surviving in small numbers).

Notes.—See comments under *A. chloroptera*.

Aratinga nana (Vigors). Olive-throated Parakeet.

> *Psittacara nana* Vigors, 1830, Zool. J. 5: 273. (Jamaica.)

Habitat.—Tropical Lowland Evergreen Forest Edge, Gallery Forest, Secondary Forest (0–800 m; Tropical and lower Subtropical zones).

Distribution.—*Resident* [*astec* group] on the Gulf-Caribbean slope of Middle America from southern Tamaulipas and Veracruz south (including Holbox Island, off Quintana Roo) to extreme western Panama (western Bocas del Toro); and [*nana* group] on Jamaica.

Notes.—Groups: *A. astec* (de Souancé, 1875) [Aztec Parakeet] and *A. nana* [Jamaican Parakeet]. Howell and Webb (1995) treated the groups as species.

Aratinga canicularis (Linnaeus). Orange-fronted Parakeet.

> *Psittacus canicularis* Linnaeus, 1758, Syst. Nat. (ed. 10) 1: 98. Based mainly on "The Red and Blue-headed Parakeet" Edwards, Nat. Hist. Birds 4: 176, pl. 176. (in America = northwestern Costa Rica.)

Habitat.—Tropical Deciduous Forest, Gallery Forest, Secondary Forest (0–1500 m; Tropical and lower Subtropical zones).

Distribution.—*Resident* on the Pacific slope of Middle America from central Sinaloa and western Durango south to northwestern Costa Rica (to the Gulf of Nicoya and San José region), also in the arid Comayagua Valley on the Caribbean slope of Honduras.

Introduced in Puerto Rico; reports from southern Florida are based on escaped cage-birds (Stevenson and Anderson 1994).

Notes.—*A. canicularis* and the South American *A. aurea* (Gmelin, 1788) may constitute a superspecies (Sibley and Monroe 1990).

Aratinga pertinax (Linnaeus). Brown-throated Parakeet.

> *Psittacus pertinax* Linnaeus, 1758, Syst. Nat. (ed. 10) 1: 98. Based mainly on "The Brown-throated Parrakeet" Edwards, Nat. Hist. Birds 4: 177, pl. 177. (in Indiis = Curaçao.)

Habitat.—Tropical Deciduous Forest, Arid Lowland Scrub, Second-growth Scrub, Tropical Lowland Evergreen Forest Edge (0–1200 m; Tropical Zone).

Distribution.—*Resident* [*ocularis* group] in western Panama (Pacific slope from western Chiriquí to eastern Panamá province, ranging to Caribbean slope in the Canal area); and [*pertinax* group] along the north coast of South America (including islands from the Netherlands Antilles east to Margarita) from northern Colombia east to the Guianas and northern Brazil.

Introduced and established (before 1860) [*pertinax* group] on St. Thomas, in the Virgin Islands (from the population on Curaçao), then spreading to Culebra Island, Tortola, and Puerto Rico. These populations disappeared between 1975 and 1982 (Wiley 1993).

Reports from southern Florida are based on escaped cage-birds (Stevenson and Anderson 1994).

Notes.—Known on St. Thomas as the Caribbean Parakeet. Groups: *A. ocularis* (Sclater and Salvin, 1865) [Veraguas Parakeet] and *A. pertinax* [Brown-throated Parakeet]. *Aratinga pertinax* and South American *A. cactorum* (Kuhl, 1820), may constitute a superspecies (Sibley and Monroe 1990).

Genus *ARA* Lacépède

> *Ara* Lacépède, 1799, Tabl. Mamm. Ois., p. 1. Type, by subsequent designation (Ridgway, 1916), *Psittacus macao* Linnaeus.

Ara severa (Linnaeus). Chestnut-fronted Macaw.

> *Psittacus severus* Linnaeus, 1758, Syst. Nat. (ed. 10) 1: 97. Based on *Psittacus severus* Linnaeus, Mus. Adolphi Friderici 1: 13. (in Indiis = Amazon River.)

Habitat.—River-edge Forest, Gallery Forest, Tropical Lowland Evergreen Forest Edge (0–800 m; Tropical and lower Subtropical zones).

Distribution.—*Resident* from eastern Panama (Darién, possibly ranging, at least formerly, west to the Canal area), Colombia, Venezuela and the Guianas south, east of the Andes, to central Bolivia and Amazonian and central Brazil.

Breeding has been reported in Florida (Miami), but there is no evidence for establishment (Stevenson and Anderson 1994).

Ara militaris (Linnaeus). Military Macaw.

> *Psittacus militaris* Linnaeus, 1766, Syst. Nat. (ed. 12) 1: 139. (No locality given = Colombia.)

Habitat.—Montane Evergreen Forest, Tropical Deciduous Forest, Pine-Oak Forest, Tropical Lowland Evergreen Forest (450–2600 m; Tropical, less commonly Subtropical and lower Temperate zones).

Distribution.—*Resident* in Mexico from southeastern Sonora, southwestern Chihuahua and Sinaloa south to Guerrero (formerly), Oaxaca and Chiapas, also (at least formerly) in eastern Nuevo León, southern Tamaulipas and southeastern San Luis Potosí; and in South America in a series of isolated populations in northern Venezuela, Colombia (east and south of the range of *A. ambigua*), eastern Ecuador, eastern Peru, eastern Bolivia, and northwestern Argentina.

Reports from southern Florida are based on escaped cage-birds (Stevenson and Anderson 1994).

Notes.—*A. militaris* and *A. ambigua* may constitute a superspecies (Sibley and Monroe 1990) and may even be conspecific (Fjeldså et al. 1987).

Ara ambigua (Bechstein). Great Green Macaw.

> *Psittacus ambiguus* Bechstein, 1811, in Latham, Allg. Uebers. Vögel 4(1): 65. Based on "Le Grand Ara Militaire" Levaillant, Hist. Nat. Perr. 1: 15, pl. 6. (South America = northwestern Colombia.)

Habitat.—Tropical Lowland Evergreen Forest (0–700 m; Tropical and Subtropical zones).

Distribution.—*Resident* on the Caribbean slope of eastern Honduras (Olancho, Mosquitia), Nicaragua (also Pacific slope) and Costa Rica, locally on both slopes of Panama, and in northwestern Colombia, with an isolated population in western Ecuador. Now much reduced and local throughout its Central American range.

Notes.—Also known as Green Macaw or Buffon's Macaw. See comments under *A. militaris*.

Ara chloropterus Gray. Red-and-green Macaw.

> *Macrocercus macao* (not *Psittacus macao* Linnaeus) Vieillot, 1816, Nouv. Dict. Hist Nat. (nouv. éd.) 2: 262. (British Guiana.)
> *Ara chloropterus* G. R. Gray, 1859, List Birds Brit. Mus., pt. 3(2), p. 26. New name for *Macrocercus macao* Vieillot, preoccupied.

Habitat.—Tropical Lowland Evergreen Forest, Montane Evergreen Forest (0–1400 m; Tropical and lower Subtropical zones).

Distribution.—*Resident* in eastern Panama (San Blas and Darién, probably also eastern Panamá province), and in South America from northern and eastern Colombia, Venezuela and the Guianas south, east of the Andes, to northern Argentina and southeastern Brazil.

Notes.—Also known as Green-winged Macaw and Red-blue-and-green Macaw.

Ara macao (Linnaeus). Scarlet Macaw.

> *Psittacus Macao* Linnaeus, 1758, Syst. Nat. (ed. 10) 1: 96. Based mainly on "The Red and Blue Maccaw" Edwards, Nat. Hist. Birds 4: 158, pl. 158. (in America meridionali = Pernambuco, eastern Brazil.)

Habitat.—Tropical Lowland Evergreen Forest, Tropical Deciduous Forest, Gallery Forest, lowland pine savanna (0–900 m; Tropical and lower Subtropical zones.)

Distribution.—*Resident* locally from eastern Chiapas and (at least formerly), southern Campeche (formerly north to southern Tamaulipas) south along the Gulf-Caribbean slope of Middle America to Honduras, on both slopes of Nicaragua, Costa Rica and Panama (including Isla Coiba), and in South America from Colombia, Venezuela, Trinidad and the Guianas south, east of the Andes, to central Bolivia and Amazonian Brazil. Extirpated from most of its Middle American range.

Reports from southern Florida are based on escaped cage-birds (Stevenson and Anderson 1994).

†*Ara tricolor* Bechstein. Cuban Macaw.

> *Ara tricolor* Bechstein, 1811, in Latham, Allg. Uebers. Vögel 4(1): 64, pl. 1. Based on "L'Ara tricolor" Levaillant, Hist. Nat. Perr. 1: 13, pl. 5. (South America, error = Cuba.)
> *Ara cubensis* Wetherbee, 1985, Carib. J. Sci. 21: 174. (Cuba.)

Habitat.—Forest edge and open country with scattered trees, especially palms.

Distribution.—EXTINCT. Formerly resident on Cuba (except Oriente Province), possibly also the Isle of Pines; last specimen taken in the Ciénaga de Zapata in 1864.

Notes.—For continued use of *A. tricolor* for the Cuban birds, *contra* Wetherbee (1985), see Walters (1995).

Ara ararauna (Linnaeus). Blue-and-yellow Macaw.

Psittacus Ararauna Linnaeus, 1758, Syst. Nat. (ed. 10) 1: 96. Based mainly on "The Blue and Yellow Maccaw" Edwards, Nat. Hist. Birds 4: 159, pl. 159. (in America meridionali = Pernambuco, eastern Brazil.)

Habitat.—Gallery Forest, River-edge Forest, Tropical Lowland Evergreen Forest (0–700 m; Tropical Zone).

Distribution.—*Resident* from eastern Panama (Pacific slope in eastern Panamá province and Darién), Colombia, southern Venezuela, Trinidad and the Guianas south, east of the Andes, to central Bolivia, Paraguay, and central and eastern Brazil.

Introduced birds, presumably escapees, breed in Puerto Rico (Perez-Rivera 1996). Reports from southern Florida are based on escaped cage-birds (Stevenson and Anderson 1994).

Genus *RHYNCHOPSITTA* Bonaparte

Rhynchopsitta Bonaparte, 1854, Rev. Mag. Zool. (2) 6: 149. Type, by monotypy, *Macrocercus pachyrhynchus* Swainson.

Rhynchopsitta pachyrhyncha (Swainson). Thick-billed Parrot.

Macrocercus pachyrhynchus Swainson, 1827, Philos. Mag. (n.s.) 1: 439. (Table land, Mexico.)

Habitat.—Pine Forest, Pine-Oak Forest (1500–3400 m; Subtropical and Temperate zones).
Distribution.—*Breeds* in the mountains of Chihuahua and Durango, probably elsewhere in the Sierra Madre Occidental of central and northern Mexico.

Wanders widely, recorded from central Sonora south to Jalisco and Michoacán, formerly recorded north to south-central and southeastern Arizona (Chiricahua, Dragoon, Galiuro and Patagonia mountains) and, possibly, southwestern New Mexico (unverified reports from the Animas Mountains), and east to México (Popocatépetl) and central Veracruz (Cofre de Perote and Jalapa).

Recently introduced in southeastern Arizona, ranging north to Mogollon Rim.

Notes.—Often considered conspecific with *R. terrisi,* but see Hardy (1967); they constitute a superspecies (Sibley and Monroe 1990).

Rhynchopsitta terrisi Moore. Maroon-fronted Parrot.

Rhynchopsitta terrisi Moore, 1947, Proc. Biol. Soc. Wash. 60: 27. (Sierra Potosí, about 7500 feet, Nuevo León, Mexico.)

Habitat.—Pine Forest, Pine-Oak Forest (1500–2800 m; upper Subtropical and Temperate zones).
Distribution.—*Resident* in the Sierra Madre Oriental of southeastern Coahuila, Nuevo León and western Tamaulipas.

Reports from southern Florida are based on escaped cage-birds.

Notes.—See comments under *R. pachyrhyncha.*

Genus *BOLBORHYNCHUS* Bonaparte

Bolborhynchus Bonaparte, 1857, Rem. Observ. Blanchard, Psittacides, p. 6. Type, by subsequent designation (Richmond, 1915), *Myiopsitta catharina* Bonaparte = *Psittacula lineola* Cassin.

Bolborhynchus lineola (Cassin). Barred Parakeet.

Psittacula lineola Cassin, 1853, Proc. Acad. Nat. Sci. Philadelphia 6: 372. (vicinity of the National bridge, Mexico = Puerto Nacional, Veracruz.)

Habitat.—Montane Evergreen Forest, often where bamboo is seeding (800–3300 m; Subtropical, less commonly Temperate or upper Tropical, zones).
Distribution.—*Resident* locally in the highlands of Middle America from northern Oa-

xaca, Veracruz and Chiapas south through Guatemala, Honduras, Nicaragua and Costa Rica to western Panama (Chiriquí, Bocas del Toro and Veraguas); and in the Andes of South America from Colombia and northwestern Venezuela south to central Peru.

Genus *FORPUS* Boie

Forpus Boie, 1858, J. Ornithol. 6: 363. Type, by subsequent designation (Hellmayr, 1929), *Psittacus passerinus* Linnaeus.

Forpus passerinus (Linnaeus). Green-rumped Parrotlet.

Psittacus passerinus Linnaeus, 1758, Syst. Nat. (ed. 10) 1: 103. Based on *Psittacus minimus* Linnaeus, Mus. Adolphi Friderici 1: 14. (in America = Surinam.)

Habitat.—Tropical Deciduous Forest, Gallery Forest, Tropical Lowland Evergreen Forest Edge, Secondary Forest (0–900 m; Tropical and Subtropical zones).

Distribution.—*Resident* in northeastern Colombia, northern Venezuela, Trinidad, the Guianas and Brazil south to the Amazon basin; also recorded from Curaçao, where possibly introduced.

Introduced and established on Jamaica (common) and Barbados (rare and apparently decreasing); attempted introduction on Martinique was unsuccessful.

Notes.—Also known as Guianan Parrotlet. *Forpus passerinus* and *F. xanthopterygius* constitute a superspecies (Sibley and Monroe 1990).

Forpus cyanopygius (de Souancé). Mexican Parrotlet.

Psittacula cyanopygia de Souancé, 1856, Rev. Mag. Zool. (2)8: 157. (No locality given = northwestern Mexico.)

Habitat.—Tropical Deciduous Forest, Secondary Forest (0–1300 m; Tropical and lower Subtropical zones).

Distribution.—*Resident* in southern Sonora, Sinaloa, western Durango, Zacatecas, Nayarit (including the Tres Marías Islands), Jalisco, and Colima.

Notes.—Also known as Blue-rumped Parrotlet.

Forpus conspicillatus (Lafresnaye). Spectacled Parrotlet.

Psittacula conspicillata Lafresnaye, 1848, Rev. Zool. [Paris] 11: 172. (in Colombia aut Mexico = Honda, upper Magdalena River, Tolima, Colombia.)

Habitat.—Tropical Deciduous Forest, Secondary Forest, Tropical Lowland Evergreen Forest Edge (0–1800 m; Tropical and lower Subtropical zones).

Distribution.—*Resident* in eastern Panama (eastern Panamá province and eastern Darién), Colombia, and southwestern Venezuela.

Genus *BROTOGERIS* Vigors

Brotogeris Vigors, 1825, Zool. J. 2: 400. Type, by original designation, *Psittacus pyrrhopterus* Latham.

Brotogeris jugularis (Müller). Orange-chinned Parakeet.

Psittacus jugularis P. L. S. Müller, 1776, Natursyst., Suppl., p. 80. Based on "Petit Perruche à gorge jaune d'Amerique" Daubenton, Planches Enlum., pl. 190, fig. 1. (in America = Bonda, Santa Marta, Colombia.)

Habitat.—Tropical Deciduous Forest, Tropical Lowland Evergreen Forest Edge, Gallery Forest, Secondary Forest (0–1200 m; Tropical and lower Subtropical zones).

Distribution.—*Resident* in southwestern Mexico (Pacific lowlands of southeastern Oaxaca and Chiapas), Guatemala (Pacific lowlands), El Salvador, Honduras (Pacific lowlands and arid interior valleys), Nicaragua (Pacific drainage, and locally in cleared areas on Caribbean slope), Costa Rica (Pacific lowlands and humid Caribbean region south at least to Limón),

Panama (both slopes, including Coiba and Taboga islands), northern Colombia and northern Venezuela. Reports from Guerrero are open to question.

Reports from southern Florida are based on escaped cage-birds (Stevenson and Anderson 1994).

Notes.—Also known as Tovi Parakeet.

Brotogeris versicolurus (Müller). White-winged Parakeet.

> *Psittacus versicolurus* P. L. S. Müller, 1776, Natursyst., Suppl., p. 75. (No locality given = Cayenne.)

Habitat.—Suburbs and parks; in South America, open woodland, scrubland and open areas with scattered trees, less frequently in dense forest, in both arid and humid situations (Tropical and lower Subtropical zones).

Distribution.—*Resident* from eastern Colombia, eastern Ecuador, and northeastern Peru east through the Amazon Basin to French Guiana and the Belém area of Pará, Brazil.

Introduced and established in southern California, west-central and southeastern Florida, Puerto Rico, and western Peru (Lima).

Notes.—Populations in Florida (Smith and Smith 1993) and southern California (Johnston and Garrett 1994) are being replaced *by B. chiriri* (Vieillot, 1817) [Yellow-chevroned Parakeet], formerly considered conspecific with *versicolurus* but separated on the basis of morphological differences and near sympatry in Pará, Brazil (Pinto and Camargo 1957). See Appendix.

Genus *TOUIT* Gray

> *Touit* G. R. Gray, 1855, Cat. Genera Subgenera Birds, p. 89. Type, by original designation, *Psittacus huetii* Temminck.

Touit costaricensis (Cory). Red-fronted Parrotlet.

> *Urochroma costaricensis* Cory, 1913, Field Mus. Nat. Hist. Publ., Ornithol. Ser. 1: 283. (vicinity of Puerto Limón, Costa Rica.)

Habitat.—Montane Evergreen Forest (500–1000 m; Tropical and Subtropical zones).

Distribution.—*Resident* in Costa Rica (Turrialba to Puerto Limón, and Cordillera de Talamanca) and western and central Panama (Chiriquí, Bocas del Toro, Coclé).

Notes.—*T. costaricensis* and *T. dilectissima* have been considered conspecific, but see Wetmore (1968); they constitute a superspecies (Sibley and Monroe 1990).

Touit dilectissima (Sclater and Salvin). Blue-fronted Parrotlet.

> *Urochroma dilectissima* Sclater and Salvin, 1871, Proc. Zool. Soc. London (1870), p. 788, pl. 47. (south of Mérida, Venezuela.)

Habitat.—Montane Evergreen Forest, Tropical Lowland Evergreen Forest (800–1700 m; Tropical and lower Subtropical zones).

Distribution.—*Resident* in eastern Panama (eastern Panamá province and Darién), northern and western Colombia, northwestern Venezuela and western Ecuador.

Notes.—See comments under *T. costaricensis*.

Genus *PIONOPSITTA* Bonaparte

> *Pionopsitta* Bonaparte, 1854, Rev. Mag. Zool. (2) 6: 152. Type, by monotypy, *Psittacus pileatus* Scopoli.

Pionopsitta pyrilia (Bonaparte). Saffron-headed Parrot.

> *Psittacula pyrilia* Bonaparte, 1853, C. R. Acad. Sci. Paris 37: 807, note. (Riohacha = Sierra Negra, southeast of Fonseca [Guajira Prov.], Colombia; Dugand, 1948, Caldasia 5: 183.)

Habitat.—Tropical Lowland Evergreen Forest, Montane Evergreen Forest (0–1000 m; Tropical and lower Subtropical zones).

Distribution.—*Resident* in extreme eastern Panama (eastern Darién), northern Colombia, and western Venezuela.

Pionopsitta haematotis (Sclater and Salvin). Brown-hooded Parrot.

> *Pionus hæmatotis* Sclater and Salvin, 1860, Proc. Zool. Soc. London, p. 300. (In prov. Veræ Pacis regione calida = Vera Paz, Guatemala.)

Habitat.—Tropical Lowland Evergreen Forest, Montane Evergreen Forest (0–1200 m; Tropical and Subtropical zones).

Distribution.—*Resident* on the Gulf-Caribbean slope from southern Veracruz, northern Oaxaca, northern Chiapas, southern Campeche and southern Quintana Roo south to Nicaragua, on both slopes of Costa Rica and Panama, and from western Colombia to western Ecuador.

Notes.—*P. haematotis* and *P. pulchra* Berlepsch, 1897, of northern South America, constitute a superspecies (Sibley and Monroe 1990).

Genus *PIONUS* Wagler

> *Pionus* Wagler, 1832, Abh. Math. Phys. Kl. Bayr. Akad. Wiss. 1: 497. Type, by subsequent designation (G. R. Gray, 1840), *Psittacus menstruus* Linnaeus.

Pionus menstruus (Linnaeus). Blue-headed Parrot.

> *Psittacus menstruus* Linnaeus, 1766, Syst. Nat. (ed. 12) 1: 148. Based mainly on "The Blue-headed Parrot" Edwards, Glean. Nat. Hist. 3: 226, pl. 314. (in Surinamo = Surinam.)

Habitat.—River-edge Forest, Gallery Forest, Tropical Lowland Evergreen Forest Edge, Secondary Forest, lowland pine savanna (0–1200 m; Tropical and lower Subtropical zones).

Distribution.—*Resident* in eastern Costa Rica (from Río Pacuare on the Caribbean slope eastward and, rarely, in the Golfo Dulce region on the Pacific) and Panama (both slopes, including Coiba and the Pearl islands), and in South America from Colombia, Venezuela, Trinidad and the Guianas south, west of the Andes to western Ecuador and east of the Andes to central Bolivia, and Amazonian and southeastern Brazil.

Pionus senilis (Spix). White-crowned Parrot.

> *Psittacus senilis* Spix, 1824, Avium Spec. Nov. Bras. 1: 42, pl. 31, fig. 1. (No locality given = Veracruz, Mexico.)

Habitat.—Montane Evergreen Forest, Tropical Lowland Evergreen Forest, Secondary Forest (0–1600 m; Tropical and Subtropical zones).

Distribution.—*Resident* on the Gulf-Caribbean slope of Middle America from southeastern San Luis Potosí and southern Tamaulipas south through eastern Mexico (including southern Campeche and southern Quintana Roo) and Central America to Costa Rica (both slopes) and western Panama (western Chiriquí and western Bocas del Toro).

Reports from southern Florida are based on escaped cage-birds (Stevenson and Anderson 1994).

Genus *AMAZONA* Lesson

> *Amazona* Lesson, 1830, Traité Ornithol., livr. 3, p. 189. Type, by subsequent designation (Salvadori, 1891), *C. farinosa* = *Psittacus farinosus* Boddaert.

Notes.—Members of the genus *Amazona* are sometimes referred to under the group name Amazon.

Amazona albifrons (Sparrman). White-fronted Parrot.

> *Psittacus albifrons* Sparrman, 1788, Mus. Carlson., fasc. 3, pl. 52. Based on the "White-crowned Parrot" Latham, Gen. Synop. Birds 1(1): 281. (No locality given = southwestern Mexico.)

Habitat.—Tropical Deciduous Forest, Tropical Lowland Evergreen Forest, Secondary Forest (0–1800 m; Tropical and Subtropical zones).

Distribution.—*Resident* from southern Sonora, Sinaloa, western Durango and southeastern Veracruz south on the Gulf-Caribbean slope of Middle America (including the Yucatan Peninsula) to Honduras and on the Pacific slope to northwestern Costa Rica (Guanacaste).

Introduced and breeding in Puerto Rico (Mayaguez area) but establishment uncertain. Reports from southern Florida are based on escaped cage-birds (Stevenson and Anderson 1994).

Amazona xantholora (Gray). Yellow-lored Parrot.

> *Psittacus albifrons* (not Sparrman) Kuhl, 1820, Consp. Psittacorum, p. 80. (No locality given.)
>
> *Chrysotis xantholora* G. R. Gray, 1859, List Birds Brit. Mus., pt. 3(2), p. 83. New name for *Psittacus albifrons* "Latham" [= Kuhl], preoccupied. (Honduras = probably Belize.)

Habitat.—Tropical Deciduous Forest, Secondary Forest (Tropical Zone).

Distribution.—*Resident* throughout the Yucatan Peninsula (including Cozumel Island), in Belize, and (formerly) on Isla Roatán (in the Bay Islands, Honduras).

Amazona leucocephala (Linnaeus). Cuban Parrot.

> *Psittacus leucocephalus* Linnaeus, 1758, Syst. Nat. (ed. 10) 1: 100. Based mainly on "The White-headed Parrot" Edwards, Nat. Hist. Birds 4: 166, pl. 166. (in America = eastern Cuba.)

Habitat.—Tropical Lowland Evergreen Forest, Montane Evergreen Forest, Tropical Deciduous Forest (0–800 m).

Distribution.—*Resident* in the Bahamas (Great Inagua and Abaco, formerly also on Long, Crooked, Acklin, and Fortune islands), Cuba, the Isle of Pines, and the Cayman Islands (Grand Cayman and Cayman Brac, formerly also Little Cayman).

Notes.—Sibley and Monroe (1990) considered *A. leucocephala, A. collaria,* and *A. ventralis* to constitute a superspecies.

Amazona collaria (Linnaeus). Yellow-billed Parrot.

> *Psittacus collarius* Linnaeus, 1758, Syst. Nat. (ed. 10) 1: 102. Based on *Psittacus* minor, collo miniaceo Sloane, Voy. Jamaica 2: 297. (in America = Jamaica.)

Habitat.—Montane Evergreen Forest, Tropical Lowland Evergreen Forest (0–1200 m).
Distribution.—*Resident* on Jamaica.

Amazona ventralis (Müller). Hispaniolan Parrot.

> *Psittacus ventralis* P. L. S. Müller, 1776, Natursyst., Suppl., p. 79. Based on "Perroquet à ventre pourpre, de la Martinique" Daubenton, Planches Enlum., pl. 548. (Martinique, error = Hispaniola.)

Habitat.—Montane Evergreen Forest, Tropical Lowland Evergreen Forest (0–1500 m).
Distribution.—*Resident* on Hispaniola (including Gonâve, Grand Cayemite, Beata and Saona islands).

Introduced and established on Puerto Rico and in the Virgin Islands (St. Croix and St. Thomas).

Reports from southern Florida are based on escaped cage-birds (Stevenson and Anderson 1994).

Amazona vittata (Boddaert). Puerto Rican Parrot.

Psittacus vittatus Boddaert, 1783, Table Planches Enlum., p. 49. Based on "Perroquet de St. Domingue" Daubenton, Planches Enlum., pl. 792. (Santo Domingo, error = Puerto Rico.)

Habitat.—Montane Evergreen Forest (0–900 m).
Distribution.—*Resident* on Puerto Rico (a small population surviving in the Luquillo National Forest and vicinity), and formerly also Culebra Island.

Amazona agilis (Linnaeus). Black-billed Parrot.

Psittacus agilis Linnaeus, 1758, Syst. Nat. (ed. 10) 1: 99. Based on "The Little Green Parrot" Edwards, Nat. Hist. Birds 4: 168, pl. 168. (in America = Jamaica.)

Habitat.—Montane Evergreen Forest, Tropical Lowland Evergreen Forest (500–1600 m).
Distribution.—*Resident* at higher elevations in western Jamaica (absent from Blue and John Crow mountains in eastern Jamaica).

Amazona viridigenalis (Cassin). Red-crowned Parrot.

Chrysotis viridigenalis Cassin, 1853, Proc. Acad. Nat. Sci. Philadelphia 6: 371. (South America, error = northeastern Mexico.)

Habitat.—Tropical Lowland Evergreen Forest, Gallery Forest, Pine-Oak Forest (0–1200 m; Tropical and lower Subtropical zones).
Distribution.—*Resident* in eastern Nuevo León, Tamaulipas, San Luis Potosí and extreme northeastern Veracruz.
A breeding population in southern Texas (lower Rio Grande Valley, recorded northwest to Falcon Dam) is most likely established from escapes from captivity, but a wild origin for some of the individuals cannot be ruled out. Introduced and established in southern Florida (Dade and Monroe counties), and Puerto Rico; a small group has also persisted since 1970 in the Hawaiian Islands (on Oahu).
Notes.—Also known as Green-cheeked Parrot. *Amazona viridigenalis* and *A. finschi* are closely related and, along with South American *A. tucumana* (Cabanis), 1885, and *A. pretrei* (Temminck), 1830, appear to constitute a superspecies (Sibley and Monroe 1990).

Amazona finschi (Sclater). Lilac-crowned Parrot.

Chrysotis finschi Sclater, 1864, Proc. Zool. Soc. London, p. 298. (Mexico = Tehuantepec City, Oaxaca; Binford, 1989, Ornithol. Monogr. 43, p. 337.)

Habitat.—Pine-Oak Forest, Tropical Lowland Evergreen Forests, Tropical Deciduous Forests (0–2200 m; Tropical and Subtropical zones).
Distribution.—*Resident* on the Pacific slope of western Mexico from southeastern Sonora and southwestern Chihuahua south to Oaxaca (the Isthmus of Tehuantepec).
Reports from southern Florida are based on escaped cage-birds.
Notes.—See comments under *A. viridigenalis*.

Amazona autumnalis (Linnaeus). Red-lored Parrot.

Psittacus autumnalis Linnaeus, 1758, Syst. Nat. (ed. 10) 1: 102. Based on "The Lesser Green Parrot" Edwards, Nat. Hist. Birds 4: 164, pl. 164. (in America = southern Mexico.)

Habitat.—Edge of Tropical Lowland Forests, Tropical Deciduous Forest, Gallery Forest, Secondary Forest (0–1100 m; Tropical and lower Subtropical zones).
Distribution.—*Resident* [*autumnalis* group] from Tamaulipas and southeastern San Luis Potosí south on the Gulf-Caribbean slope (including southern Campeche, but absent from

the remainder of the Yucatan Peninsula) to Honduras (including the Bay Islands); most Nicaraguan birds are intermediate between this and the following group; [*salvini* group] in eastern Nicaragua and on Isla Ometepe in Lago de Nicaragua, on both slopes of Costa Rica (on the Pacific mainly in the southwestern region) and Panama (including Coiba and the Pearl islands), and in South America in northern and western Colombia, western Ecuador and northwestern Venezuela; and [*diadema* group] in the upper Amazon basin of Brazil.

Reports from southern Florida are based on escaped cage-birds (Stevenson and Anderson 1994).

Notes.—Also known as Yellow-cheeked Parrot. Groups: *A. autumnalis* [Yellow-cheeked Parrot], *A. salvini* (Salvadori, 1891) [Salvin's Parrot], and *A. diadema* (Spix, 1824) [Diademed Parrot].

Amazona farinosa (Boddaert). Mealy Parrot.

> *Psittacus farinosus* Boddaert, 1783, Table Planches Enlum., p. 52. Based on "Le Perroquet Meunier de Cayenne" Daubenton, Planches Enlum., pl. 861. (Cayenne.)

Habitat.—Tropical Lowland Evergreen Forest (0–1200 m; Tropical and lower Subtropical zones).

Distribution.—*Resident* from southern Veracruz, northern Oaxaca and southern Campeche south on the Gulf-Caribbean slope (except the remainder of the Yucatan Peninsula) to Nicaragua (including north-central highlands), on both slopes of Costa Rica and Panama (including Isla Coiba and other islets), and in South America from Colombia and Venezuela south, west of the Andes to western Ecuador and east of the Andes to central Bolivia and central Brazil.

Reports from southern Florida are based on escaped cage-birds (Stevenson and Anderson 1994).

Notes.—Also known as Blue-crowned Parrot.

Amazona oratrix Ridgway. Yellow-headed Parrot.

> *Chrysotis levaillantii* (not *Amazona levaillantii* Lesson, 1831) G. R. Gray, 1859, List Birds Brit. Mus., pt. 3(2), p. 79. ([probably Santo Domingo] Petapa, Oaxaca; Binford, 1989, Ornithol. Monogr. 43, p. 337.)
>
> *Amazona oratrix* Ridgway, 1887, Man. N. Amer. Birds, p. 587. New name for *Chrysotis levaillantii* Gray, preoccupied.

Habitat.—Tropical Deciduous Forest, Gallery Forest, Tropical Lowland Evergreen Forest (0–700 m; Tropical Zone).

Distribution.—*Resident* on the Pacific slope of Mexico (including Tres Marias Islands) from Colima to Oaxaca (the Isthmus of Tehuantepec); on the Gulf slope of northeastern Mexico from southern Nuevo León and Tamaulipas south to Veracruz and Tabasco; and in Belize; a sight report from northeastern Guatemala.

Introduced and possibly established in Puerto Rico and southern Florida (Dade County).

Notes.—Although *A. oratrix* and *A. auropalliata* are frequently considered conspecific with *A. ochrocephala,* the close approach of *A. oratrix* and *A. auropalliata* in Pacific Oaxaca without evidence of interbreeding (Binford 1989), and the presence of both *A. auropalliata* and *A. ochrocephala* in Caribbean Honduras, suggest that the best treatment would be as allospecies of a superspecies complex (Monroe and Howell 1966). Losada and Howell (1996), however, suggested that species limits should be re-evaluated because of misunderstanding of plumage variation in Caribbean lowland populations. With a single species, Yellow-headed Parrot is the appropriate name.

Amazona auropalliata (Lesson). Yellow-naped Parrot.

> *Psittacus (amazona)* [sic] *auro-palliatus* Lesson, 1842, Rev. Zool. [Paris] 5: 135. (Realejo, centre Amérique [= Nicaragua].)

Habitat.—Tropical Deciduous Forest, Gallery Forest, Secondary Forest, lowland pine savanna (0–600 m; Tropical Zone).

Distribution.—*Resident* on the Pacific slope of Middle America from extreme south-eastern Oaxaca south to northwestern Costa Rica (Guanacaste); in the Sula Valley of northern Honduras (where possibly introduced); in the Bay Islands off Caribbean Honduras (Roatán, Barbareta and Guanaja); and the Mosquitia in eastern Honduras and northeastern Nicaragua.

Reports from southern Florida are based on escaped cage-birds (Stevenson and Anderson 1994).

Notes.—See comments under *A. oratrix*.

Amazona ochrocephala (Gmelin). Yellow-crowned Parrot.

> *Psittacus ochrocephalus* Gmelin, 1788, Syst. Nat. 1(1): 339. Based in part on "Le Perroquet Amazone du Brésil" Brisson, Ornithologie 4: 272, pl. 26, fig. 1. (in America australi = Venezuela.)

Habitat.—River-edge Forest, Gallery Forest, Tropical Deciduous Forest (0–850 m; Tropical and lower Subtropical zones).

Distribution.—*Resident* in the Sula Valley of northern Honduras (at least formerly, where present since at least mid-19th Century, apparently a native population); and from Panama (including Coiba and the Pearl islands), Colombia, Venezuela, Trinidad (probably), and the Guianas south, east of the Andes, to central Bolivia and Amazonian Brazil.

Introduced and established on Puerto Rico; reports from southern Florida are based on escaped cage-birds (Stevenson and Anderson 1994).

Notes.—See comments under *A. oratrix*.

Amazona arausiaca (Müller). Red-necked Parrot.

> *Psittacus arausiacus* P. L. S. Müller, 1766, Natursyst., Suppl., p. 79. Based on the "Blue-faced Green Parrot" Edwards, Glean. Nat. Hist. 1: 43, pl. 230. (Dominica.)

Habitat.—Tropical Lowland Evergreen Forest, Montane Evergreen Forest (0–1200 m).

Distribution.—*Resident* on Dominica, in the Lesser Antilles, surviving in reduced numbers.

Notes.—Species of *Amazona* may also have been present on Martinique and Guadeloupe, for which names have been proposed although no specimens exist (see Appendix).

Amazona versicolor (Müller). St. Lucia Parrot.

> *Psittacus versicolor* P. L. S. Müller, 1776, Natursyst., Suppl., p. 78. Based on "Perroquet, de la Havane" Daubenton, Planches Enlum., pl. 360. (Havana, error = St. Lucia.)

Habitat.—Tropical Lowland Evergreen Forest (0–1000 m).

Distribution.—*Resident* on St. Lucia, in the Lesser Antilles, where surviving in much reduced numbers.

Notes.—See comments under *A. arausiaca*.

Amazona guildingii (Vigors). St. Vincent Parrot.

> *Psittacus Guildingii* Vigors, 1837, Proc. Zool. Soc. London (1836), p. 80. (St. Vincent [Lesser Antilles].)

Habitat.—Montane Evergreen Forest, Tropical Lowland Evergreen Forest (0–1000 m).

Distribution.—*Resident* on St. Vincent, in the Lesser Antilles.

Amazona imperialis Richmond. Imperial Parrot.

> *Psittacus augustus* (not Shaw, 1792) Vigors, 1837, Proc. Zool. Soc. London (1836), p. 80. (South America, error = Dominica.)
> *Amazona imperialis* (Ridgway MS) Richmond, 1899, Auk 16: 186 (in text). New name for *Psittacus augustus* Vigors, preoccupied.

Habitat.—Montane Evergreen Forest (500–1400 m).

Distribution.—*Resident* on Dominica, in the Lesser Antilles, where surviving in small numbers.

Order CUCULIFORMES: Cuckoos and Allies

Family CUCULIDAE: Cuckoos, Roadrunners, and Anis

Notes.—Sibley and Ahlquist (1990) treated each of the subfamilies at the family level. Hughes (1996) proposed a realignment of the some genera on the basis of behavioral and skeletal characters.

Subfamily CUCULINAE: Old World Cuckoos

Genus *CUCULUS* Linnaeus

Cuculus Linnaeus, 1758, Syst. Nat. (ed. 10) 1: 110. Type, by tautonymy, *Cuculus canorus* Linnaeus (*Cuculus,* prebinomial specific name, in synonymy).

Cuculus canorus Linnaeus. Common Cuckoo.

Cuculus canorus Linnaeus, 1758, Syst. Nat. (ed. 10) 1: 110. (in Europa = Sweden.)

Habitat.—Open woodland, forest edge and clearings, taiga, open country with scattered trees and, occasionally, treeless regions with bushy growth.

Distribution.—*Breeds* from the British Isles, Scandinavia, northern Russia and northern Siberia south to northern Africa, the Mediterranean region, Asia Minor, the Himalayas, Burma, Southeast Asia and eastern China.

Winters in Africa, India, Southeast Asia, the East Indies, New Guinea and the Philippines, casually to the eastern Atlantic islands, Sri Lanka, and the Bonin, Molucca and Palau islands in the western Pacific.

Migrates through the Mediterranean region, Arabia, Taiwan, the Ryukyu Islands, Japan and the Kuril Islands to Kamchatka and Anadyrland, ranging casually to the Commander Islands and western and central Aleutian Islands (from Attu to Adak), occasionally reaching the Pribilof Islands (St. Paul) islands, St. Lawrence Island, and the mainland of western Alaska (Tutakoke River mouth and Seward Peninsula, near Nome), casually also to Iceland and the Faeroe Islands.

Accidental in Massachusetts (Martha's Vineyard), the Lesser Antilles (Barbados), and Greenland.

Notes.—Known in Old World literature as the Cuckoo. *Cuculus canorus* and the African *C. gularis* Stephens, 1815, constitute a superspecies (Cramp 1985).

Cuculus saturatus Blyth. Oriental Cuckoo.

Cuculus saturatus (Hodgson MS) Blyth, 1843, J. Asiat. Soc. Bengal 12: 942. (Nepal.)

Habitat.—Forested regions, primarily coniferous, less frequently deciduous woodland or mixed coniferous-deciduous areas, locally in montane forest.

Distribution.—*Breeds* [*saturatus* group] from central Russia, central Siberia, Anadyrland and Kamchatka south to the Himalayas, northern Burma, southern China, Taiwan and Japan.

Resident [*lepidus* group] in southeast Asia and western Indonesia.

Winters [*saturatus* group] from the Malay Peninsula and Philippines south through Indonesia and New Guinea to northern and eastern Australia and Lord Howe Island.

Wanders [*saturatus* group] casually to the western Aleutian Islands (Attu, Rat Islands), the Pribilof Islands (St. Paul), St. Lawrence Island, and (once) to the western Alaskan mainland (Cape Prince of Wales).

Notes.—Also known as Himalayan Cuckoo. Groups: *C. saturatus* [Oriental Cuckoo] and *C. lepidus* Müller, 1845 [Sunda Cuckoo].

Subfamily COCCYZINAE: New World Cuckoos

Genus *COCCYZUS* Vieillot

Coccyzus Vieillot, 1816, Analyse, p. 28. Type, by monotypy, "Coucou de la Caroline" Buffon = *Cuculus americanus* Linnaeus.

Coccyzus erythropthalmus (Wilson). Black-billed Cuckoo.

Cuculus erythropthalma [sic] Wilson, 1811, Amer. Ornithol. 4: 16, pl. 28, fig. 2. (No locality given = probably near Philadelphia, Pennsylvania.)

Habitat.—Forest edge and open woodland, both deciduous and coniferous, with dense deciduous thickets (breeding); scrub (arid or humid) as well as forest, although most frequently in lowland humid regions (nonbreeding).

Distribution.—*Breeds* from east-central and southeastern Alberta, southern Saskatchewan, southern Manitoba, northern Minnesota, central Ontario, southwestern Quebec, New Brunswick, Prince Edward Island and Nova Scotia south, at least locally, to Montana (rarely in west), southeastern Wyoming, eastern Colorado, Nebraska, Kansas, north-central Oklahoma, north-central Texas (once successfully in southern Texas), northern Arkansas (rare), Tennessee, northern Alabama, and the Carolinas.

Winters in South America (including Trinidad) from northern Colombia and northern Venezuela south to central Bolivia (limits of winter range poorly known).

Migrates regularly through the southeastern United States, Bermuda, Mexico (primarily from Guerrero, Guanajuato and Tamaulipas southward, mostly in Gulf-Caribbean lowlands, including Cozumel Island) and Middle America (not recorded El Salvador); and casually west to the Pacific region from southeastern British Columbia south to southern California, Arizona, Sinaloa and New Mexico, and through the Bahamas (Grand Bahama, New Providence) and the Antilles (recorded Cuba, the Isle of Pines, Jamaica, Puerto Rico and Barbuda).

Casual or accidental in Newfoundland, Paraguay, northern Argentina, Greenland, Iceland, the British Isles, continental Europe, and the Azores.

Coccyzus americanus (Linnaeus). Yellow-billed Cuckoo.

Cuculus americanus Linnaeus, 1758, Syst. Nat. (ed. 10) 1: 111. Based on "The Cuckoo of Carolina" Catesby, Nat. Hist. Carolina 1: 9, pl. 9. (in Carolina = South Carolina.)

Habitat.—Open woodland, especially where undergrowth is thick, parks and riparian woodland (breeding); forest, woodland, and scrub (nonbreeding).

Distribution.—*Breeds* from interior California (formerly north to western Washington), southern Idaho, Wyoming, southeastern Montana, the Dakotas, southern Manitoba (rarely), Minnesota, southern Ontario, southwestern Quebec and southern New Brunswick (probably) south to southern Baja California, southern Arizona, Chihuahua, Coahuila, Nuevo León, Tamaulipas, sporadically farther south in Mexico (recorded breeding in Zacatecas and Yucatán) the Gulf coast, the Florida Keys and the Greater Antilles (Cuba, Jamaica, Hispaniola, Gonâve Island, Puerto Rico, and St. Croix in the Virgin Islands), probably also in the Bahamas (Great Inagua) and Lesser Antilles (St. Kitts). In recent years, western distribution has contracted.

Winters from northern South America (also Tobago and Trinidad) south to northern Argentina, casually north to the southern United States.

Migrates regularly through the southern United States, Middle America, Bermuda, and the West Indies; regular in fall in Nova Scotia.

Casual or accidental north to southeastern Alaska (Ketchikan), southwestern British Columbia, central Alberta, southern Saskatchewan, southern Manitoba, Labrador, and Newfoundland, and on Clipperton Island, Greenland, Iceland, the British Isles, continental Europe and the Azores.

Notes.—*C. americanus* and *C. euleri* may form a superspecies (Mayr and Short 1970).

Coccyzus euleri Cabanis. Pearly-breasted Cuckoo.

Coccygus [sic] *Euleri* Cabanis, 1873, J. Ornithol. 21: 72. (Cantagallo, Rio de Janeiro, Brazil.)

Habitat.—Tropical Lowland Evergreen Forest, Gallery Forest, River-edge Forest (0–900 m).

Distribution.—*Breeds* in southern South America presumably from eastern Brazil south to northern Argentina, and *winters* (possibly also locally breeding) in northern South America in Colombia, Venezuela and the Guianas.

Accidental in the northern Lesser Antilles (Sombrero Island, 1863) and Bolivia.

Notes.—Although *C. julieni* Lawrence, 1864 has priority over *C. euleri* (Banks 1988a), the former has been suppressed for purposes of priority by the I.C.Z.N. (1992). See comments under *C. americanus*.

Coccyzus minor (Gmelin). Mangrove Cuckoo.

> *Cuculus minor* Gmelin, 1788, Syst. Nat. 1(1): 411. Based mainly on "Petit Vieillard" Buffon, Hist. Nat. Ois. 6: 401, and the "Mangrove Cuckoo" Latham, Gen. Synop. Birds 1(2): 537. (in Cayenna = Cayenne.)

Habitat.—Tropical Deciduous Forest, Gallery Forest, Mangrove Forest, Secondary Forest (0–1250 m; Tropical and, rarely, Subtropical zones).

Distribution.—*Resident* from Sinaloa and Tamaulipas south on both slopes of Middle America (including Holbox, Mujeres and Cozumel islands off the Yucatan Peninsula, and the Bay Islands off Honduras) to western Panama (Veraguas, Bocas del Toro); and from southern Florida (Tampa Bay and Miami areas southward in coastal areas, including the Florida Keys) and the Bahamas south throughout the Antilles (not recorded Isle of Pines) and islands in the western Caribbean Sea (Cayman, Swan, Providencia and San Andrés) to Venezuela (including islands from the Netherlands Antilles and Trinidad), the Guianas and northern Brazil.

Casual north to southeastern Texas (Port Bolivar, sight reports elsewhere) in northern and peninsular Florida (including the interior), and south to central Panama (Canal area and the Pearl Islands).

Notes.—Sibley and Monroe (1990) treated *C. minor* and *C. ferrugineus* as a superspecies.

Coccyzus ferrugineus Gould. Cocos Cuckoo.

> *Coccyzus ferrugineus* Gould, 1843, Proc. Zool. Soc. London, p. 105. (Cocos Island.)

Habitat.—Tropical Lowland Evergreen Forest.

Distribution.—*Resident* on Cocos Island, off Costa Rica.

Notes.—See comments under *C. minor*.

Coccyzus melacoryphus Vieillot. Dark-billed Cuckoo.

> *Coccyzus melacoryphus* Vieillot, 1817, Nouv. Dict. Hist. Nat. 8: 271. (Paraguay.)

Habitat.—Tropical Deciduous Forest, Gallery Forest, Secondary Forest, River-edge Forest, Tropical Lowland Evergreen Forest (0–1200 m).

Distribution.—*Resident* in South America (including Trinidad and the Galapagos Islands), the more southerly populations migratory northward in winter.

Accidental on Clipperton Island (13 August 1958; Stager 1964), in Grenada (Levera Pond, 26 May 1963; Schwartz and Klinikowski 1965), and in Panama (Tocumen, eastern Panamá province, 26 January 1980; Ridgely and Gwynne 1989). A specimen record from southern Texas is under review.

Genus *SAUROTHERA* Vieillot

> *Saurothera* Vieillot, 1816, Analyse, p. 28. Type, by monotypy, "Coucou à long bec" Buffon = *Cuculus vetula* Linnaeus.

Saurothera merlini d'Orbigny. Great Lizard-Cuckoo.

> *Saurothera merlini* d'Orbigny, 1839, in La Sagra, Hist. Fis. Pol. Nat. Cuba, Ois., p. 152 [p. 115 in Spanish edition], pl. 25. (Cuba.)

Habitat.—Tropical Lowland Evergreen Forest, Tropical Deciduous Forest, Secondary Forest (0–1200 m).

Distribution.—*Resident* in the northern Bahamas (Andros, New Providence and Eleuthera), Cuba (including Cayo Santa Maria and Cayo Coco), and the Isle of Pines.

Saurothera vetula (Linnaeus). Jamaican Lizard-Cuckoo.

> *Cuculus Vetula* Linnaeus, 1758, Syst. Nat. (ed. 10) 1: 111. Based mainly on *Cuculus major* Sloane, Voy. Jamaica 2: 312, pl. 258. (in Jamaica.)

Habitat.—Tropical Lowland Evergreen Forest, Tropical Deciduous Forest (0–1200 m).
Distribution.—*Resident* on Jamaica.
Notes.—*S. vetula, S. vieilloti,* and *S. longirostris* have been treated as conspecific (e.g., Peters 1940); they constitute a superspecies (Sibley and Monroe 1990).

Saurothera longirostris (Hermann). Hispaniolan Lizard-Cuckoo.

> *Cuculus longirostris* Hermann, 1783, Tabula Affinit. Anim., p. 186. (Hispaniola.)

Habitat.—Tropical Lowland Evergreen Forest, Tropical Deciduous Forest (0–2000 m).
Distribution.—*Resident* on Hispaniola (including Tortue, Saona and Gonâve islands).
Notes.—See comments under *S. vetula.*

Saurothera vieilloti Bonaparte. Puerto Rican Lizard-Cuckoo.

> *Saurothera vetula* (not Linnaeus, 1758) Vieillot, 1819, Nouv. Dict. Hist. Nat. (nouv. éd.) 32: 348. (Porto Rico = Puerto Rico.)
> *Saurothera vieilloti* Bonaparte, 1850, Consp. Gen. Avium 1(1): 97. New name for *Saurothera vetula* Vieillot, preoccupied.

Habitat.—Tropical Lowland Evergreen Forest, Tropical Deciduous Forest (0–800 m).
Distribution.—*Resident* on Puerto Rico and (formerly) Vieques Island, possibly at one time on St. Thomas in the Virgin Islands.
Notes.—See comments under *S. vetula.*

Genus *HYETORNIS* Sclater

> *Ptiloleptis* (not *Ptiloleptus* Swainson, 1837, emended to *Ptiloleptis* by G. R. Gray, 1849) Bonaparte, 1854, Ateneo Ital. 2: 121. Type, by monotypy, *Cuculus pluvialis* Gmelin.
> *Hyetornis* Sclater, 1862, Cat. Collect. Amer. Birds, pp. xiii, 321. New name for *Ptiloleptis* Bonaparte, preoccupied.

Notes.—*Hyetornis* was merged with *Piaya* by Peters (1940).

Hyetornis rufigularis (Hartlaub). Bay-breasted Cuckoo.

> *Coccyzus rufigularis* "Herz. c. Württemb." Hartlaub, 1852, Naumannia 2: 55. (Mountain forests of Spanish Santo Domingo = Dominican Republic.)

Habitat.—Tropical Deciduous Forest, Tropical Lowland Evergreen Forest (0–900 m).
Distribution.—*Resident* on Hispaniola (primarily the Dominican Republic, rare in Haiti) and Gonâve Island.

Hyetornis pluvialis (Gmelin). Chestnut-bellied Cuckoo.

> *Cuculus pluvialis* Gmelin, 1788, Syst. Nat. 1(1): 411. Based in part on the "Old man or rainbird" Sloane, Voy. Jamaica 2: 321, pl. 258, fig. 1. (in Jamaica.)

Habitat.—Tropical Lowland Evergreen Forest, Secondary Forest (0–1500 m).
Distribution.—*Resident* on Jamaica.

Genus *PIAYA* Lesson

> *Piaya* Lesson, 1830, Traité Ornithol., livr. 2, p. 139. Type, by original designation, *Cuculus cayanus* Gmelin [= Linnaeus].

Piaya cayana (Linnaeus). Squirrel Cuckoo.

> *Cuculus cayanus* Linnaeus, 1766, Syst. Nat. (ed. 12) 1: 170. Based on "Le Coucou de Cayenne" Brisson, Ornithologie 4: 122, pl. 8, fig. 2. (in Cayana = Cayenne.)

Habitat.—Tropical Lowland Evergreen Forest, Tropical Deciduous Forest, Secondary Forest, Gallery Forest, River-edge Forest (0–2500 m; Tropical and Subtropical zones).

Distribution.—*Resident* from southern Sonora, southwestern Chihuahua, southeastern San Luis Potosí and southern Tamaulipas south through Middle America (including the Yucatan Peninsula, casually Isla Cancun, but doubtfully recorded from Holbox and Mujeres islands), and in South America from Colombia, Venezuela, Trinidad, and the Guianas south, west of the Andes to northwestern Peru and east of the Andes to southern Bolivia, northern Argentina, and Uruguay.

Piaya minuta (Vieillot). Little Cuckoo.

Coccyzus minutus Vieillot, 1817, Nouv. Dict. Hist. Nat. (nouv. éd.) 8: 275. Based in part on "Le petit Coucou de Cayenne" Brisson, Ornithologie 4: 124, pl. 16, fig. 2. (No locality given = Cayenne.)

Habitat.—Tropical Lowland Evergreen Forest Edge, Secondary Forest, Second-growth Scrub (0–900; Tropical Zone).

Distribution.—*Resident* from eastern Panama (from Canal area and eastern Panamá province eastward), Colombia, Venezuela, Trinidad and the Guianas south, east of the Andes, to central Bolivia and Amazonian and south-central Brazil.

Subfamily NEOMORPHINAE: Ground-Cuckoos and Roadrunners

Genus *TAPERA* Thunberg

Tapera Thunberg, 1819, Göteborgs Kungl. Vetensk. Vitterhets-Samh. Handl. 3: 1. Type, by monotypy, *Tapera brasiliensis* Thunberg = *Cuculus naevius* Linnaeus.

Tapera naevia (Linnaeus). Striped Cuckoo.

Cuculus nævius Linnaeus, 1766, Syst. Nat. (ed. 12) 1: 170. Based on "Le Coucou tacheté de Cayenne" Brisson, Ornithologie 4: 127, pl. 9, fig. 1. (in Cayania = Cayenne.)

Habitat.—Second-growth Scrub, Low Seasonally Wet Grassland, Riparian Thickets (0–1500 m; Tropical and lower Subtropical zones).

Distribution.—*Resident* from central Veracruz, northern Oaxaca, Tabasco, Chiapas and southern Quintana Roo south along both slopes of Middle America, and in South America from Colombia, Venezuela (including Margarita Island), Trinidad and the Guianas south, west of the Andes to northwestern Peru, and east of the Andes to northern Argentina and southern Brazil.

Genus *DROMOCOCCYX* Wied

Dromococcyx Wied, 1832, Beitr. Naturgesch. Bras. 4(1): 351. Type, by monotypy, *Macropus phasianellus* Spix.

Dromococcyx phasianellus (Spix). Pheasant Cuckoo.

Macropus phasianellus Spix, 1824, Avium Spec. Nov. Bras. 1: 53, pl. 42. (forest of Rio Tonantins, Amazon Valley, Brazil.)

Habitat.—Tropical Lowland Evergreen Forest, River-edge Forest, Tropical Deciduous Forest (0–1600 m; Tropical Zone.)

Distribution.—*Resident* on both slopes of Middle America from Guerrero, Puebla, Oaxaca, southeastern Veracruz, Chiapas and the Yucatan Peninsula south to Panama, and in South America from Colombia, Venezuela and the Guianas south, east of the Andes, to central Bolivia, Paraguay, northeastern Argentina, and southeastern Brazil.

Genus *MOROCOCCYX* Sclater

Morococcyx Sclater, 1862, Cat. Collect. Amer. Birds, p. 322. Type, by monotypy, *Coccyzus erythropyga* Lesson.

Morococcyx erythropygus (Lesson). Lesser Ground-Cuckoo.

> *Coccyzus erythropyga* Lesson, 1842, Rev. Zool. [Paris] 5: 210. (San-Carlos, Centre Amérique = La Unión, El Salvador.)

Habitat.—Arid Lowland Scrub, Tropical Deciduous Forest Edge, Second-growth Scrub (0–1500 m; Tropical Zone).

Distribution.—*Resident* on the Pacific slope of western Mexico from southern Sinaloa south to northwestern Costa Rica (Río Grande de Tárcoles), occurring also in the arid interior valleys on the Caribbean slope of Guatemala (Motagua) and Honduras (Quimistán, Sula, Comayagua, Aguán).

Genus *GEOCOCCYX* Wagler

> *Geococcyx* Wagler, 1831, Isis von Oken, col. 524. Type, by monotypy, *Geococcyx variegata* Wagler = *Saurothera californiana* Lesson.

Geococcyx velox (Wagner). Lesser Roadrunner.

> *Cuculus velox* A. Wagner, 1836, Gelehrte Anz., München 3: col. 96. (Mexico = outskirts of Mexico City.)

Habitat.—Arid Lowland Scrub, Arid Montane Scrub, Pine Forest (0–2800 m; Tropical and Subtropical zones).

Distribution.—*Resident* in western Mexico from extreme southern Sonora south to Chiapas (Tuxtla Guttiérez), and in the interior of Middle America from eastern Nayarit, Jalisco, Michoacán, México, Morelos, Puebla, west-central Veracruz and Oaxaca south through Central America to central Nicaragua; an isolated population in Yucatán and northern Campeche.

Geococcyx californianus (Lesson). Greater Roadrunner.

> *Saurothera Californiana* Lesson, 1829, Oeuvres Compl. Buffon 6: 420. (Californie = San Diego, California.)

Habitat.—Desert scrub, chaparral, edges of cultivated lands, and arid open situations with scattered brush, locally in cedar glades and pine-oak woodland (Tropical and Subtropical zones).

Distribution.—*Resident* from north-central California, western and central Nevada, southern Utah, southern Colorado, southern Kansas, central and eastern Oklahoma, southwestern Missouri, central and western Arkansas and western and north-central Louisiana south to southern Baja California, Sinaloa, Durango, Zacatecas, northeastern Jalisco, eastern Michoacán, México, Puebla, Veracruz, northern Tamaulipas and the Gulf coast of Texas.

Notes.—Often called the Roadrunner in American literature.

Genus *NEOMORPHUS* Gloger

> *Neomorphus* Gloger, 1827, in Froriep, Notizen 16: col. 278, note. Type, by original designation, *Coccyzus geoffroyi* Temminck.

Neomorphus geoffroyi (Temminck). Rufous-vented Ground-Cuckoo.

> *Coccyzus geoffroyi* Temminck, 1820, Planches Color., livr. 2, pl. 7. (No locality given = Pará, Brazil.)

Habitat.—Tropical Lowland Evergreen Forest (0–1200 m; Tropical and lower Subtropical zones).

Distribution.—*Resident* locally in Nicaragua (Caribbean slope), Costa Rica (primarily Caribbean slope, on Pacific drainage in Cordillera de Guanacaste), and Panama (both slopes), and in South America from Colombia south, east of the Andes, to central Bolivia and Amazonian Brazil.

Notes.— Sibley and Monroe (1990) considered *N. geoffroyi* and Amazonian *N. squamiger* Todd, 1925 [Scaled Ground-Cuckoo] to constitute a superspecies.

Subfamily CROTOPHAGINAE: Anis

Genus *CROTOPHAGA* Linnaeus

Crotophaga Linnaeus, 1758, Syst. Nat. (ed. 10) 1: 105. Type, by monotypy, *Crotophaga ani* Linnaeus.

Crotophaga major Gmelin. Greater Ani.

Crotophaga major Gmelin, 1788, Syst. Nat. 1(1): 363. Based in part on "Le grand Bout-de-petun" Brisson, Ornithologie 4: 180, pl. 18, fig. 2, and Daubenton, Planches Enlum., pl. 102, fig. 1. (in Cayenna = Cayenne.)

Habitat.—River-edge Forest, Gallery Forest, Freshwater Marshes (0–800 m; Tropical Zone, locally to Temperate Zone).

Distribution.—*Resident* from eastern Panama (on the Caribbean slope from western Colón eastward, on the Pacific from the Canal area eastward), Colombia, Venezuela, Trinidad and the Guianas south, west of the Andes to western Ecuador and east of the Andes virtually throughout to northern Argentina. Two specimens taken along the Río Tamesí, southern Tamaulipas, may represent a resident population in northeastern Mexico (Olson 1978), but subsequent searches for the species have failed.

Crotophaga ani Linnaeus. Smooth-billed Ani.

Crotophaga Ani Linnaeus, 1758, Syst. Nat. (ed. 10) 1: 105. Based mainly on the "Razor-billed Blackbird" Catesby, Nat. Hist. Carolina 2 (app.): 3, pl. 3, and Sloane, Voy. Jamaica 2: 298, pl. 256, fig. 1. (in America, Africa = Jamaica.)

Habitat.—Second-growth Scrub, Agricultural Pastures/Cropland (0–2000 m; Tropical and lower Subtropical zones).

Distribution.—*Resident* in central and southern Florida (Tampa Bay and Merritt Island region southward, mainly from Lake Okeechobee area to Dade County); from the Bahamas south throughout the Antilles (including the Cayman Islands); on islands off Quintana Roo (Cozumel), Belize (Ambergris Cay), Honduras (Swan and Bay islands) and Nicaragua (Corn, Providencia and San Andrés); and in southwestern Costa Rica (Pacific slope north to the Gulf of Nicoya region) and Panama (both slopes, including Coiba and the Pearl islands), and in South America from Colombia, Venezuela (including Margarita Island), Tobago, Trinidad and the Guianas south, west of the Andes to western Ecuador and east of the Andes to northern Argentina.

Casual north to North Carolina, in northern Florida, and to the mainland of Honduras (Trujillo region, where possibly breeding). Accidental in Ohio. Reports from Louisiana, Indiana, and New Jersey are questionable.

Crotophaga sulcirostris Swainson. Groove-billed Ani.

Crotophaga sulcirostris Swainson, 1827, Philos. Mag. (n.s.) 1: 440. (Table land. Temiscaltepec = Temascaltepec, México.)

Habitat.—Second-growth Scrub, Riparian Thickets (0–2300 m; Tropical and Subtropical zones).

Distribution.—*Resident* in southern Baja California (Cape district, formerly, with one recent report of a vagrant); from southern Sonora, central and southern (casually western, north-central and southeastern) Texas and southern Louisiana (rarely, one breeding record, Plaquemines Parish) south along both slopes of Middle America (including Mujeres, Holbox and Cozumel islands off Quintana Roo) and along both coasts of South America to extreme northern Chile and Guyana (also the Netherlands Antilles); and in northwestern Argentina.

Wanders regularly east along the Gulf coast to peninsular Florida, and casually northward to southern California, southern Nevada, northern Arizona, central New Mexico, Colorado, South Dakota, Minnesota, Wisconsin, Michigan, southern Ontario, Ohio, and Maryland. Accidental in the Revillagigedo Islands (Socorro Island; sight reports). Reports from Trinidad are erroneous (ffrench 1991).

Order STRIGIFORMES: Owls

Family TYTONIDAE: Barn Owls

Genus *TYTO* Billberg

Tyto Billberg, 1828, Synop. Faunae Scand. (ed. 2) 1(2): tab. A. Type, by monotypy, *Strix flammea* auct. = *Strix alba* Scopoli.

Tyto alba (Scopoli). Barn Owl.

> *Strix alba* Scopoli, 1769, Annus I, Hist.-Nat., p. 21. (Ex Foro Juli = Friuli, northern Italy.)

Habitat.—Open and partly open country in a wide variety of situations, often around human habitation; nests in buildings, caves, crevices on cliffs, burrows and hollow trees, rarely in trees with dense foliage, such as palms (Tropical to Temperate zones).

Distribution.—*Resident* in the Americas from southwestern and south-central British Columbia, western Washington, Oregon, southern Idaho, Montana, North Dakota, Iowa, southern Wisconsin, southern Michigan (formerly), extreme southern Ontario, southern Quebec, New York, southern Vermont and Massachusetts south through the United States and Middle America (including many islands around Baja California and in the Gulf of California, the Tres Marías Islands, Bay Islands off Honduras, and Pearl Islands off Panama), Bermuda, the Bahamas, Greater Antilles (except Puerto Rico and the Virgin Islands) and Lesser Antilles (Dominica, St. Vincent, Grenada and the Grenadines), and in South America in the Galapagos Islands (Santa Cruz, Isabela, James, San Cristóbal and Fernandina) and from Colombia and Venezuela (including islands of the Netherlands Antilles, Tobago and Trinidad) south to Tierra del Fuego; and in the Old World from the British Isles, Baltic countries, southern Russia and southern Siberia south throughout most of Eurasia and Africa to southern Africa, Madagascar, the Malay Peninsula, the East Indies (except Sumatra, Borneo and the Philippines) and Australia, and east in the western Pacific to the Society Islands. Northernmost populations in North America are partially migratory, wintering south to southern Mexico and the West Indies.

Wanders casually north to northeastern British Columbia, southern Saskatchewan, southern Manitoba, northern Minnesota, New Brunswick, Newfoundland and Nova Scotia; a record from Alaska is erroneous.

Introduced and established in the Hawaiian Islands (in 1958, now on all main islands from Kauai eastward) and on Lord Howe Island.

Notes.—Also known as Common Barn-Owl. *Tyto alba* and the closely related *T. glaucops* are regarded as species because sympatry occurs on Hispaniola.

Tyto glaucops (Kaup). Ashy-faced Owl.

> *Strix glaucops* Kaup, 1853, in Jardine, Contrib. Ornithol. (1852), p. 118. (Jamaica, error = Hispaniola.)

Habitat.—Arid Lowland Scrub, Arid Montane Scrub, Second-growth Scrub, nesting in limestone caves and sinkholes, and often foraging around old buildings and ruins (0–2000 m).

Distribution.—*Resident* on Hispaniola.

Notes.—Also known as Hispaniolan Barn-Owl or Ashy-faced Barn-Owl. See comments under *T. alba*.

Family STRIGIDAE: Typical Owls

Genus *OTUS* Pennant

Otus Pennant, 1769, Indian Zool., p. 3. Type, by monotypy, *Otus bakkamoena* Pennant.
Gymnasio Bonaparte, 1854, Rev. Mag. Zool. (2)6: 543. Type, by monotypy, *Strix nudipes* Daudin.

Gymnoglaux Cabanis, 1855, J. Ornithol. 3: 466. Type, by monotypy, *Noctua nudipes*
Lembeye (not *Strix nudipes* Daudin) = *Gymnoglaux lawrencii* Sclater and Salvin.

Otus flammeolus (Kaup). Flammulated Owl.

Scops (Megascops) flammeola "Licht." Kaup, 1853, in Jardine, Contrib. Ornithol.
(1852), p. 111. (Mexico.)

Habitat.—Montane forest, primarily open ponderosa pine association, occasionally aspen;
in migration, wooded areas in lowlands and mountains (upper Subtropical and Temperate
zones).

Distribution.—*Breeds* locally from south-central British Columbia (Kamloops, Pentic-
ton), central Washington, eastern Oregon, southern Idaho, western Montana and north-central
Colorado south to south-central California (Palomar Mountain), southern Arizona, southern
New Mexico and western Texas (Guadalupe, Chisos, and, probably, Davis mountains); also
in Coahuila, Tamaulipas, Nuevo León, México (Chimalpa), and Veracruz (Las Vigas). A
report of one heard in Oaxaca requires confirmation (Binford 1989).

Winters from central Mexico (Sinaloa, Jalisco, Michoacán and Distrito Federal) south in
the highlands to Guatemala and El Salvador, casually north to southern California.

Migrates east to central Montana, central Colorado, eastern New Mexico and western
Texas.

Casual or accidental in Wyoming, southeastern Texas (Galveston, Port Aransas), Louisiana
(Baton Rouge), Alabama (Shelby County), Florida (Redington Beach) and the Gulf of Mexico
(ca. 75 miles southeast of Galveston, Texas).

Notes.—Also known as Flammulated Screech-Owl. The Eurasian *O. scops* (Linnaeus,
1758) and *O. flammeolus* differ in vocalizations and are separate species (Marshall 1978);
Mayr and Short (1970) considered them to represent a superspecies. Marshall and King (in
Monroe and Sibley 1993) considered *O. flammeolus* as probably related to *O. brucei* (Hume,
1873) [Pallid Scops-Owl].

Otus sunia (Hodgson). Oriental Scops-Owl.

Scops sunia Hodgson, 1836, Asiat. Res. 19: 175. (Nepal.)

Habitat.—Forest and woodland.

Distribution.—*Breeds* from the northern limit of trees in northeastern Asia and the large
islands of Japan south to northern China and Korea. *Winters* from southeastern China and
Japan south to Southeast Asia.

Accidental in Alaska in the Aleutian Islands on Buldir (5 June 1977) and Amchitka (late
June 1979).

Notes.—*O. sunia* and other Old World forms are sometimes merged in the Eurasian *O.
scops* (Linnaeus, 1758), but studies of vocalizations and behavior confirm their status as
species (Marshall 1967, 1978). See comments under *O. flammeolus*.

Otus kennicottii (Elliot). Western Screech-Owl.

Scops Kennicottii Elliot, 1867, Proc. Acad. Nat. Sci. Philadelphia 19: 99. (Sitka, Alaska.)

Habitat.—Woodland, especially oak and riparian woodland, and giant cacti (Subtropical
and Temperate zones).

Distribution.—*Resident* [*kennicottii* group] from south-coastal (west to Cordova) and
southeastern Alaska, coastal and south-central British Columbia, northern Idaho, western
and south-central Montana, northwestern Wyoming (Wind River Mountains), southeastern
Colorado, and extreme western Oklahoma south to southern Baja California, central Sonora,
in the Mexican highlands through central and eastern Chihuahua and Coahuila as far as the
Distrito Federal, and to south-central Texas (east to Kerr County); and [*vinaceus* group] in
southern Sonora, western Chihuahua and northern Sinaloa.

Casual [*kennicottii* group] in Alberta and Kansas (Morton Co.).

Notes.—Also known as Kennicott's Screech-Owl. Groups: *O. kennicottii* [Western
Screech-Owl) and *O. vinaceus* (Brewster, 1888) [Vinaceous Screech-Owl]. Relationships of

North and Middle American *Otus* are discussed in Marshall (1967), in which the four groups of *O. asio* are recognized on the basis of vocalizations and behavior as "incipient species"; these groups are now considered to be allospecies of a superspecies. Long-distance dispersal apparently accounts for overlap and rare mixed pairs in marginally poor habitat along the Arkansas River in southeastern Colorado and the Rio Grande in Texas. If these four species (*O. kennicottii* and the following three species) are treated as a single species, then *O. asio* and Common Screech-Owl are the appropriate scientific and English names, respectively. Intergradation of *O. k. cardonensis* Huey, 1926 and *O. k. xantusi* (Brewster, 1902) in Baja California is uncertain. The latter form may represent *O. cooperi* because of vocal similarities. Miller and Miller (1951) discussed the relationship of *O. kennicottii* and *O. vinaceus,* the latter formerly treated as a separate species. Because they are similar in voice and intergrade, they are regarded as conspecific.

Otus asio (Linnaeus). Eastern Screech-Owl.

Strix Asio Linnaeus, 1758, Syst. Nat. (ed. 10) 1: 92. Based on "The Little Owl" Catesby, Nat. Hist. Carolina 1: 7, pl. 7. (in America = South Carolina.)

Habitat.—Open woodland, deciduous forest, open mixed deciduous-coniferous woodland, parklands, residential areas, and riparian woodland in drier regions.

Distribution.—*Resident* from southern Saskatchewan, southern Manitoba, central Minnesota, north-central Michigan, southern Ontario, southwestern Quebec and Maine (formerly) south through the eastern United States to Coahuila, central Nuevo León, eastern San Luis Potosí, southern Tamaulipas, southern Texas, the Gulf coast and southern Florida (upper Florida Keys), and west to central Montana, northern and eastern Wyoming, eastern Colorado, Kansas, western Oklahoma, and west-central Texas. Recorded in summer (and probably breeding) in central Alberta.

Casual in Nova Scotia (Indian Lake); sight reports from New Brunswick.

Notes.—Also known as the Screech Owl. See comments under *O. kennicottii.*

Otus seductus Moore. Balsas Screech-Owl.

Otus vinaceus seductus Moore, 1941, Proc. Biol. Soc. Wash. 54: 156. (5 miles northeast of Apatzingán, Michoacán, altitude 1000 feet.)

Habitat.—Tropical Deciduous Forest, mesquite (0–1200 m; Tropical and lower Subtropical zones).

Distribution.—*Resident* in Colima, southern Jalisco, the Río Balsas drainage of Michoacán, and western Guerrero.

Notes.—See comments under *O. kennicottii.*

Otus cooperi (Ridgway). Pacific Screech-Owl.

Scops cooperi Ridgway, 1878, Proc. U. S. Natl. Mus. 1: 116. (Santa Ana, Costa Rica.)

Habitat.—Tropical Deciduous Forest, Gallery Forest, Secondary Forest, Mangrove Forest, Tropical Lowland Evergreen Forest Edge (0–950 m; Tropical and Subtropical zones).

Distribution.—*Resident* along the Pacific coast of Middle America from Oaxaca (west to Puerto Angel region and Rancho Las Animas) south to northwestern Costa Rica (Guanacaste region).

Notes.—Also known as Cooper's Screech-Owl. See comments under *O. kennicottii.*

Otus trichopsis (Wagler). Whiskered Screech-Owl.

Scops trichopsis Wagler, 1832, Isis von Oken, col. 276. (Mexico = mountains of southwestern Puebla.)

Habitat.—Pine Forest, Pine-Oak Forest, (600–2950 m; Subtropical and lower Temperate zones).

Distribution.—*Resident* from southeastern Arizona, northeastern Sonora, southwestern New Mexico, Chihuahua, Coahuila, Nuevo León and Tamaulipas south through the mountains of Mexico (west to Sinaloa, Nayarit, Jalisco, Michoacán and Guerrero, and east to west-central Veracruz), Guatemala, El Salvador and Honduras to northern Nicaragua.

Notes.—Also known as Whiskered Owl or Spotted Screech-Owl.

Otus choliba (Vieillot). Tropical Screech-Owl.

> *Strix choliba* Vieillot, 1817, Nouv. Dict. Hist. Nat. (nouv. éd.) 7: 39. Based on "Chóliba" Azara, Apunt. Hist. Nat. Páx. Parag. 2: 218 (no. 48). (Paraguay.)

Habitat.—Secondary Forest, Tropical Lowland Evergreen Forest Edge, River-edge Forest, Gallery Forest (0–2800 m; Tropical and Subtropical zones).

Distribution.—*Resident* from central Costa Rica (San José region) south through Panama (including the Pearl Islands), and in South America from Colombia and Venezuela (including Margarita Island), Trinidad and the Guianas south, east of the Andes, to northern Argentina and Paraguay; erroneously reported from Honduras.

Otus barbarus (Sclater and Salvin). Bearded Screech-Owl.

> *Scops barbarus* Sclater and Salvin, 1868, Proc. Zool. Soc. London, p. 56. (Verapaz, Guatemala.)

Habitat.—Pine Forest, Montane Evergreen Forest (1400–2200 m; Subtropical and Temperate zones).

Distribution.—*Resident* in the mountains of Chiapas and northern Guatemala.

Notes.—Also known as Santa Barbara Screech-Owl or Bridled Screech-Owl.

Otus guatemalae (Sharpe). Vermiculated Screech-Owl.

> *Scops brasilianus* Subsp. ß. *Scops guatemalæ* Sharpe, 1875, Cat. Birds Brit. Mus. 2: ix, 112, pl. 9. (Central America, from Veraguas northwards to Mexico = Guatemala.)

Habitat.—Tropical Lowland Evergreen Forest, Montane Evergreen Forest, Secondary Forest, Tropical Deciduous Forest, Pine-Oak Forest (0–1800 m; Tropical and Subtropical zones).

Distribution.—*Resident* [*guatemalae* group] from southeastern Sonora and southern Tamaulipas south on both slopes of Mexico to Chiapas and the Yucatan Peninsula (including Cozumel Island), and thence south through Guatemala, Belize and Honduras to north-central Nicaragua; and [*vermiculatus* group] locally from northeastern Costa Rica and Panama and south locally to western Colombia.

Notes.—Includes *O. guatemalae* [Middle American Screech-Owl] and *O. vermiculatus* (Ridgway, 1887) [Vermiculated Screech-Owl], sometimes treated as separate species because of vocal differences (Sibley and Monroe 1990, Marshall et al. 1991). Marshall et al. (1991) proposed that populations of *vermiculatus* from northern South America, excluding those from western Colombia, be merged into *O. atricapillus* of South America, a treatment followed by Monroe and Sibley (1993), but see König (1994) and Heidrich et al. (1995a).

Otus clarkii Kelso and Kelso. Bare-shanked Screech-Owl.

> *Otus clarkii* L. and E. H. Kelso, 1935, Biol. Leaflet, no. 5, [not paged]. (Calobre, Panama.)

Habitat.—Montane Evergreen Forest (900–3300 m; Subtropical and lower Temperate zones).

Distribution.—*Resident* in the mountains of Costa Rica (Cordillera Central eastward), Panama (recorded from western Chiriquí, Veraguas and eastern Darién) and extreme northwestern Colombia.

Notes.—Also known as Bare-legged Screech-Owl. Once called *Otus nudipes* in the literature, based on *Bubo nudipes* Vieillot, 1807, but the latter name is now regarded as a *nomen dubium*; furthermore, with the following species placed in *Otus, Bubo nudipes* is also a junior secondary homonym of *Strix nudipes*.

Otus nudipes (Daudin). Puerto Rican Screech-Owl.

> *Strix nudipes* Daudin, 1800, Traité Ornithol. 2: 199. (Porto Rico and Cayenne = Puerto Rico.)

Habitat.—Tropical Lowland Evergreen Forest, Tropical Deciduous Forest (0–900 m).

Distribution.—*Resident* on Puerto Rico (including Vieques and Culebra islands) and, very local or extirpated, in the Virgin Islands (St. Thomas, St. John, Tortola, Virgin Gorda and St. Croix).

Notes.—Also known as Puerto Rican Bare-legged Owl.

Otus lawrencii (Sclater and Salvin). Cuban Screech-Owl.

> *Gymnoglaux lawrencii* Sclater and Salvin, 1868, Proc. Zool. Soc. London, p. 327, pl. 29. (Cuba = Remedios, Cuba.)

Habitat.—Tropical Lowland Evergreen Forest, Tropical Deciduous Forest; nests in holes in coconut palms and limestone cliffs.

Distribution.—*Resident* on Cuba, Cayo Romano, and the Isle of Pines.

Notes.—Formerly placed in monotypic genus *Gymnoglaux* and known as Bare-legged Owl.

Genus *LOPHOSTRIX* Lesson

> *Lophostrix* Lesson, 1836, Oeuvres Compl. Buffon 7: 261. Type, by monotypy, *Strix griseata* Latham = *Strix cristata* Daudin.

Lophostrix cristata (Daudin). Crested Owl.

> *Strix cristata* Daudin, 1800, Traité Ornithol. 2: 307. Based on "La Chouette à aigrette blanche" Levaillant, Ois. Afr. 1: 43. (Guiana.)

Habitat.—Tropical Lowland Evergreen Forest, Montane Evergreen Forest (0–1000 m) (Tropical and lower Subtropical zones).

Distribution.—*Resident* on both slopes of Middle America from southern Veracruz, northern and southeastern Oaxaca, and Chiapas) south to Panama, and in South America from Colombia, western Venezuela and the Guianas south, west of the Andes to western Ecuador and east of the Andes to central Bolivia and Amazonian Brazil.

Genus *PULSATRIX* Kaup

> *Pulsatrix* Kaup, 1848, Isis von Oken, col. 771. Type, by monotypy, *Strix torquata* Daudin = *Strix perspicillata* Latham.

Pulsatrix perspicillata (Latham). Spectacled Owl.

> *Strix perspicillata* Latham, 1790, Index Ornithol. 1: 58. Based on the "Spectacle Owl" Latham, Gen. Synop. Birds (suppl.) 1: 50, pl. 107. (in Cayana = Cayenne.)

Habitat.—River-edge Forest, Tropical Lowland Evergreen Forest, Gallery Forest, Secondary Forest, Tropical Deciduous Forest (0–1000 m; Tropical and lower Subtropical zones).

Distribution.—*Resident* on both slopes of Middle America from southern Veracruz, northern and southeastern Oaxaca, and Chiapas south to Panama, and in South America from Colombia, Venezuela, Trinidad and the Guianas south, west of the Andes to western Ecuador and east of the Andes to northwestern Argentina, Paraguay and southeastern Brazil.

Genus *BUBO* Duméril

> *Bubo* Duméril, 1806, Zool. Anal., p. 34. Type, by tautonymy, *Strix bubo* Linnaeus.

Bubo virginianus (Gmelin). Great Horned Owl.

> *Strix virginiana* Gmelin, 1788, Syst. Nat. 1(1): 287. Based mainly on the "Virginia Eared Owl" Latham, Gen. Synop. Birds 1(1): 119. (in omni America, etc. = Virginia.)

Habitat.—A wide variety of forested habitats, moist or arid, deciduous or evergreen lowland forest to open temperate woodland, including second-growth forest, swamps, orchards, parklands, riverine forest, brushy hillsides and semi-desert (Tropical to Alpine zones, most commonly Subtropical and Temperate zones).

Distribution.—*Breeds* from western and central Alaska, central Yukon, northwestern and southern Mackenzie, southern Keewatin, northern Manitoba, northern Ontario, northern Quebec, northern Labrador and Newfoundland south throughout the Americas (except the West Indies, most islands, and most of Amazonia) to Tierra del Fuego.

Winters generally throughout the breeding range, with the northernmost populations being partially migratory, wintering south to southern Canada and the northern United States.

Genus *NYCTEA* Stephens

Nyctea Stephens, 1826, in Shaw, Gen. Zool. 13(2): 62. Type, by tautonymy, *Strix erminea* Shaw = *Strix nyctea* Linnaeus = *Strix scandiaca* Linnaeus.

Nyctea scandiaca (Linnaeus). Snowy Owl.

Strix scandiaca Linnaeus, 1758, Syst. Nat. (ed. 10) 1: 92. (in Alpibus Lapponiæ = Lapland.)

Habitat.—Tundra, primarily where mounds, hillocks, or rocks are present; in winter and migration, occurring also in open country such as prairie, marshes, fields, pastures, and sandy beaches.

Distribution.—*Breeds* in North America in the western Aleutians (Attu, Buldir), on Hall Island (in the Bering Sea), and from northern Alaska, northern Yukon (Herschel Island), and Banks, Prince Patrick and northern Ellesmere islands south to coastal western Alaska (to Hooper Bay), northern Mackenzie, southern Keewatin, northeastern Manitoba (Churchill), Southampton and Belcher islands, northern Quebec and northern Labrador; and in the Palearctic in northern Greenland, and from northern Scandinavia, northern Russia, southern Novaya Zemlya and northern Siberia south to the British Isles (rarely), southern Scandinavia, the limits of tundra in Eurasia, and the Commander Islands.

Winters irregularly from the breeding range in North America south to southern Canada, North Dakota, Minnesota, northern Illinois, northern Michigan, and New York, casually or sporadically to central California (Monterey County), southern Nevada, Utah, Colorado, Oklahoma, central and southeastern Texas, the Gulf states and Georgia (sight reports from central Florida); and in Eurasia south to Iceland, the British Isles, northern continental Europe, central Russia, northern China and Sakhalin.

Casual or accidental in Bermuda, the Azores, Mediterranean region, Iran, northwestern India, and Japan.

Genus *SURNIA* Duméril

Surnia Duméril, 1806, Zool. Anal., p. 34. Type, by subsequent designation (G. R. Gray, 1840), *Strix funerea* Gmelin = *Strix ulula* Linnaeus.

Surnia ulula (Linnaeus). Northern Hawk Owl.

Strix Ulula Linnaeus, 1758, Syst. Nat. (ed. 10) 1: 93. (in Europa = Sweden.)

Habitat.—Open coniferous or mixed coniferous-deciduous forest, forest edge and clearings, forest burns, dense tamarack, bogs, scrubby second-growth woodland and muskeg.

Distribution.—*Breeds* in North America from the limit of trees in western and central Alaska, central Yukon, northwestern and central Mackenzie, southern Keewatin, northern Manitoba, northern Ontario, northern Quebec, central Labrador and Newfoundland south to south-coastal Alaska (Kodiak Island), central British Columbia, northwestern Montana, west-central Alberta, central Saskatchewan, southern Manitoba, northern Minnesota, northern Wisconsin, southeastern Ontario, northern Michigan (once, Isle Royale, 1905), southern Quebec, and New Brunswick (breeding sporadic along southern limits of range); and in

Eurasia from northern Scandinavia, northern Russia and northern Siberia south to central Russia, northern Mongolia, northern Manchuria, and Sakhalin.

Winters from the breeding range southward, in North America irregularly to southern Canada and northern Minnesota, casually to Oregon, Idaho, Montana, Wyoming, Nebraska, Iowa, central Illinois, southern Michigan, northern Ohio and Pennsylvania; and in Eurasia to the British Isles, continental Europe and southern Russia.

Notes.—Known widely as the Hawk Owl.

Genus *GLAUCIDIUM* Boie

Glaucidium Boie, 1826, Isis von Oken, col. 970. Type, by subsequent designation (G. R. Gray, 1840), *Strix passerina* Linnaeus.

Glaucidium gnoma Wagler. Northern Pygmy-Owl.

Glaucidium Gnoma Wagler, 1832, Isis von Oken, col. 275. (Mexico.)

Habitat.—Open forest and woodlands, in coniferous, hardwood, mixed and pine-oak woodland (Subtropical and Temperate zones).

Distribution.—*Resident* [*californicum* group] from southern Alaska (recorded west to Yakutat), British Columbia (including Vancouver Island), west-central Alberta and western and central Montana south, mostly in mountainous regions, to southern California (Laguna Mountains), southern Arizona, and southern New Mexico (perhaps northern Mexico); [*gnoma* group] the interior of Mexico, Guatemala, and central Honduras; and [*hoskinsii* group] in the Cape district of southern Baja California.

Casual [*californicum* group] in northwestern Wyoming and western Texas.

Notes.—Heidrich et al. (1995b) considered *G. californicum* Sclater, 1857 [Northern Pygmy-Owl], and *G. gnoma* [Mexican Pygmy-Owl] to represent separate species based on genetic and vocal differences (as anticipated by Sibley and Monroe [1990] and Monroe and Sibley [1993]). König (1991) and Heidrich et al. (1995b) proposed, based on vocalizations, that the populations of Costa Rica and Panama traditionally assigned to *G. jardinii* belong with *G. gnoma*.

Glaucidium jardinii (Bonaparte). Andean Pygmy-Owl.

Phalænopsis jardinii Bonaparte, 1855, C. R. Acad. Sci. Paris 41: 654. (Andes of Quito, Ecuador.)

Habitat.—Montane Evergreen Forest (2000–3400 m; Subtropical and Temperate zones).

Distribution.—*Resident* in the mountains of central Costa Rica and Panama (recorded Chiriquí and Veraguas); and in the Andes of South America from Colombia and western Venezuela south to northern Argentina.

Notes.—Also known as Mountain Pygmy-Owl. See comments under *G. gnoma*. König (1991) described the population from Peru to Argentina as a separate species, *G. bolivianum* [Yungas Pygmy-Owl], based on vocal differences.

Glaucidium griseiceps Sharp. Central American Pygmy-Owl.

Glaucidium griseiceps Sharp, 1875, Ibis 1875, p. 41. (Veragua [Panama] and Chisec and Choctum [Guatemala] = tropical lowlands [Coban] of Alta Vera Paz, Guatemala.)

Habitat.—Humid Evergreen Forest (0–1300 m; Tropical to lower Subtropical zones).

Distribution.—Resident on the Gulf-Caribbean slope of Middle America from southeastern Veracruz and northern Oaxaca south (not recorded Yucatan Peninsula or Nicaragua) to northwestern Colombia (also disjunct records on Pacific slope of Guatemala, in eastern Panama province, Canal area, and Darién, and north-northwest of Alto Tambo, Prov. Esmeraldas, Ecuador).

Notes.—*Glaucidium griseiceps, G. sanchezi, G. palmarum* and three South American forms (*G. minutissimum* [Wied, 1830], *G. parkeri* Robbins and Howell, 1995, and *G. hardyi* Vielliard, 1989) were formerly treated as conspecific, under *G. minutissimum* [Least Pygmy-Owl]. Howell and Robbins (1995) and Robbins and Howell (1995) summarized data on vocalizations, morphology, coloration, and habitat distribution, which support the treatment of these six forms as species; see Vielliard (1989) and König (1991) for additional data on South American forms.

Glaucidium sanchezi Lowery and Newman. Tamaulipas Pygmy-Owl.

> *Glaucidium minutissimum sanchezi* Lowery and Newman, 1949, Occas. Papers Louisiana State University Museum of Zoology 22:1–4. (Llano de Garzas, near Cerro Coneja, San Luis Potosí, Mexico.)

Habitat.—Humid Evergreen Forest (900–2100 m; lower Subtropical to upper Subtropical zones).

Distribution.—Resident on the Gulf-Caribbean slope of Mexico in southern Tamaulipas and eastern San Luis Potosí.

Notes.—See comments under *G. griseiceps*.

Glaucidium palmarum Nelson. Colima Pygmy-Owl.

> *Glaucidium palmarum* Nelson, 1901, Auk 18:46. (Arroyo de Juan Sanchez, Territory of Tepic, Mexico.)

Habitat.—Tropical Deciduous Forest, Pine-Oak Forest (0–1500 m; lower Subtropical to upper Subtropical zones.)

Distribution.—Resident on the Pacific slope of Mexico from central Sonora to south-central Oaxaca (foothills inland of Puerto Angel) and in the Balsas drainage of southern Morelos and northern Guerrero.

Notes.—See comments under *G. griseiceps*.

Glaucidium brasilianum (Gmelin). Ferruginous Pygmy-Owl.

> *Strix brasiliana* Gmelin, 1788, Syst. Nat. 1(1): 289. Based on "Le Hibou de Brésil" Brisson, Ornithologie, 1, p. 499. (in Brasilia = Ceará, Brazil.)

Habitat.—Arid Lowland Scrub, Arid Montane Scrub, Second-growth Scrub, Tropical Deciduous Forest, Tropical Lowland Evergreen Forest Edge, Secondary Forest, lowland pine savanna, giant cacti (0–2000 m; Tropical and lower Subtropical zones).

Distribution.—*Resident* from south-central Arizona (formerly north to Phoenix area), Sonora (at least formerly), Chihuahua, Coahuila, Nuevo León and southern Texas (north to Starr and Kenedy counties) south through Mexico (including Isla Cancun off Quintana Roo), Belize, Guatemala, El Salvador, Honduras, Nicaragua, Costa Rica (Pacific slope, very rare on Caribbean drainage) and Panama (Pacific slope east to western Panamá province), and in South America from the coastal lowlands of Colombia, Venezuela (including Margarita Island), Trinidad and the Guianas south, east of the Andes to central Argentina.

Notes.—Also known as Ferruginous Owl. *Glaucidium nanum* (King, 1827) [Austral Pygmy-Owl] has been treated as conspecific (e.g.. Marín et al. 1989) with *G. brasilianum,* but vocal differences support recognition as a species (König 1991); they constitute a superspecies (Mayr and Short 1970). König (1991) described the population of northwestern Peru as a separate species, *G. peruanum* [Peruvian Pygmy-Owl], based primarily on vocal differences; this treatment was followed by Monroe and Sibley (1993).

Glaucidium siju (d'Orbigny). Cuban Pygmy-Owl.

> *Noctua siju* d'Orbigny, 1839, in La Sagra, Hist. Fis. Pol. Nat. Cuba, Ois., p. 41, pl. 3. (Cuba.)

Habitat.—Tropical Lowland Evergreen Forest, Tropical Deciduous Forest, Pine Forest, Secondary Forest (0–1500 m).

Distribution.—*Resident* on Cuba, Cayo Coco (Archipelago Sabana-Camagüey), and the Isle of Pines.

Genus *MICRATHENE* Coues

Micrathene Coues, 1866, Proc. Acad. Nat. Sci. Philadelphia 18: 51. Type, by original designation, *Athene whitneyi* Cooper.

Micropallas Coues, 1889, Auk 6: 71. New name for *Micrathene* Coues, thought to be preoccupied.

Micrathene whitneyi (Cooper). Elf Owl.

Athene whitneyi Cooper, 1861, Proc. Calif. Acad. Sci. (1)2: 118. (Fort Mojave, latitude 35° [N.], Colorado Valley [Arizona].)

Habitat.—Arid Lowland Scrub, Gallery Forest, Pine-Oak Forest (0–2100 m; Tropical and lower Subtropical zones).

Distribution.—*Breeds* from extreme southern Nevada (Colorado River, opposite Fort Mohave, Arizona, at least formerly), extreme southeastern California (lower Colorado River Valley, formerly west to central Riverside County), central Arizona, southwestern New Mexico, western and southern Texas, Coahuila and Nuevo León south to Sonora (including Isla Tiburón), Guanajuato and Puebla, probably elsewhere in central Mexico; also in southern Baja California (Cape district) and formerly in the Revillagigedo Islands (Socorro).

Winters from southern Sinaloa, Michoacán, Morelos and southern Texas south to Guerrero, Puebla and northwestern Oaxaca, certainly also elsewhere in central Mexico; resident on Socorro Island and in Baja California, where recorded north to lat. 28° 10′ N., possibly only as a vagrant.

Accidental in eastern New Mexico.

Genus *ATHENE* Boie

Athene Boie, 1822, Isis von Oken, col. 549. Type, by subsequent designation, (G. R. Gray, 1841), *A. noctua* (Retz.) Boie, Pl. enl. 439. *Str. passerina* Auct. = *Strix noctua* Scopoli.

Speotyto Gloger, 1841, Gemein. Handb.-und-Hilfsb., p. 226. Type, by monotypy, *Strix cunicularia* Molina.

Notes.—Although karyotypic and molecular studies suggest generic status for *Speotyto* (Schmutz et al. 1989. Sibley and Ahlquist 1990), we follow Amadon and Bull (1988) in merging *Speotyto* into *Athene*.

Athene cunicularia (Molina). Burrowing Owl.

Strix Cunicularia Molina, 1782, Saggio Stor. Nat. Chili, p. 263. (Chili = Chile.)

Habitat.—Northern Temperate Grassland, Arid Lowland Scrub, Arid Montane Scrub, tropical grasslands (0–4000 m; Tropical to Alpine zones).

Distribution.—*Breeds* from southern interior British Columbia, southern Alberta, central Saskatchewan (formerly) and southern Manitoba south through eastern Washington (formerly), central Oregon and California (including the Channel islands, formerly the Farallon Islands) to Baja California (including many coastal islands, and on Guadalupe Island), east locally to western Minnesota, northwestern Iowa, northwestern Missouri, Oklahoma and western Texas, and south to central Mexico (including Isla Clarión in the Revillagigedo group, but southern limits of the breeding range in the interior in Mexico not known); in Florida (north to Madison and Duval counties), the Bahamas, Cuba (western Pinar del Rio, northern Matanzas, southern Ciego de Avila, Cayo Coco, and near Guantánamo), Isle of Pines (Los Indios), Hispaniola (including Gonâve and Beata islands) and, at least formerly, the northern Lesser Antilles (St. Kitts, Nevis, Antigua, Redonda, and Marie Galante); and locally in South America from Colombia and Venezuela (including Margarita Island) south to northern Tierra del Fuego.

Winters in North America and Middle America in general through the breeding range, except for the northern portions in the Great Basin and Great Plains regions, and regularly south to southern Mexico, Guatemala and El Salvador (at least formerly), casually to Honduras (Monte Redondo), Costa Rica (Los Cuadros on Volcán Irazú) and Panama (Divalá in

Chiriquí); and through the breeding range in the West Indies and South America, casually to Cuba.

Casual north and east in eastern North America to Wisconsin, Michigan, western and southern Ontario, southern Quebec, Maine, New York, Massachusetts, Virginia and North Carolina, and in the Gulf states east to Alabama and northwestern Florida; a sight report for New Brunswick.

Genus *CICCABA* Wagler

Ciccaba Wagler, 1832, Isis von Oken, col. 1222. Type, by monotypy, *Ciccaba huhula* = *Strix huhula* Daudin.

Notes.—*Ciccaba* is often merged in *Strix*. If *Ciccaba* is recognized as a genus, it appears to be polyphyletic, according to morphological studies (Voous 1964, Norberg 1977) and genetic data (Sibley and Ahlquist 1990).

Ciccaba virgata (Cassin). Mottled Owl.

Syrnium virgatum Cassin, 1849, Proc. Acad. Nat. Sci. Philadelphia 4 (1848): 124. (South America = Bogotá, Colombia.)

Habitat.—Tropical Lowland Evergreen Forest, Montane Evergreen Forest, Tropical Deciduous Forest, Gallery Forest (0–2200 m; Tropical and Subtropical zones).

Distribution.—*Resident* from southern Sonora, southwestern Chihuahua, Sinaloa, Nayarit, Jalisco, Guanajuato, San Luis Potosí, central Nuevo León, and Tamaulipas south through Middle America (including the Yucatan Peninsula), and in South America from Colombia, Venezuela, Trinidad, and the Guianas south, west of the Andes to western Ecuador and east of the Andes to central Bolivia, Paraguay, and northeastern Argentina.

Accidental in southern Texas (Feb. 1983 in Hidalgo County; Lasley et al. 1988).

Notes.—Also known as Mottled Wood-Owl.

Ciccaba nigrolineata Sclater. Black-and-white Owl.

Ciccaba nigrolineata Sclater, 1859, Proc. Zool. Soc. London, p. 131. (In Mexico Meridionali = state of Oaxaca; Binford, 1989, Ornithol. Monogr. 43, p. 338.)

Habitat.—Tropical Lowland Evergreen Forest, Gallery Forest, Tropical Deciduous Forest, Montane Evergreen Forest (0–1500 m; Tropical and lower Subtropical zones).

Distribution.—*Resident* on both slopes of Middle America from southeastern San Luis Potosí, Veracruz, northern and southeastern Oaxaca, Chiapas, and Quintana Roo south locally to Panama, and in South America from Colombia east to northwestern Venezuela and south, west of the Andes, to western Ecuador and northwestern Peru.

Notes.—*C. nigrolineata* and the South American *C. huhula* Daudin, 1800, constitute a superspecies (Sibley and Monroe 1990).

Genus *STRIX* Linnaeus

Strix Linnaeus, 1758, Syst. Nat. (ed. 10) 1: 92. Type, by tautonymy, *Strix stridula* Linnaeus (*Strix,* prebinomial specific name, in synonymy) = *Strix aluco* Linnaeus.

Notes.—See comments under *Ciccaba*.

Strix occidentalis (Xántus de Vesey). Spotted Owl.

Syrnium occidentale Xántus de Vesey, 1860, Proc. Acad. Nat. Sci. Philadelphia 11 (1859): 193. (Fort Tejon, California.)

Habitat.—Dense mature coniferous forest (primarily Douglas fir), especially in shaded, steep-walled canyons (Temperate Zone).

Distribution.—*Resident* [*occidentalis* group] in the mountains and in humid coastal forest from extreme southwestern British Columbia (north to Atka Lake, east to Manning Provincial Park) south through western Washington and western Oregon to south-central California

(Laguna Mountains) and, probably, northern Baja California (Sierra San Pedro Mártir); and [*lucida* group] in the Rocky Mountain region from southern Utah and central Colorado south through the mountains of Arizona, New Mexico, extreme western Texas (Guadalupe Mountains), northern Sonora, Chihuahua, Coahuila and Nuevo León to Jalisco, Michoacán and Guanajuato.

Notes.—The two groups, *S. occidentalis* [California Spotted-Owl] and *S. lucida* (Nelson, 1903) [Mexican Spotted-Owl], are genetically distinct to a degree reflecting long isolation (Barrowclough and Gutiérrez 1990). Several hybrids have occurred between *S. occidentalis* and *S. varia* (Hamer et al. 1994), which may form a superspecies (Mayr and Short 1970).

Strix varia Barton. Barred Owl.

Strix varius Barton, 1799, Fragm. Nat. Hist. Pa., p. 11. (Philadelphia, Pennsylvania.)

Habitat.—Dense woodland and forest (coniferous or hardwood), swamps, wooded river valleys, and cabbage palm-live oak hammocks, especially where bordering streams, marshes, and meadows (Subtropical and Temperate zones).

Distribution.—*Resident* from southeastern Alaska (from Skagway to Ketchikan), southern (including Vancouver Island) and eastern British Columbia south to northwestern California, Oregon and western Montana, east across central Alberta, and central Saskatchewan, and from southern Manitoba, central Ontario, southern Quebec, New Brunswick, Prince Edward Island and Nova Scotia, central and southern Texas, the Gulf coast and southern Florida, and west to eastern North Dakota, southeastern South Dakota (formerly), eastern Nebraska, central Kansas and western Oklahoma; and in the Central Plateau of Mexico from Durango south to Guerrero (Mount Teotepec) and Oaxaca (La Parada and Cerro San Felipe), and east to San Luis Potosí, Puebla, and Veracruz. Some Mexican populations are widely disjunct.

Northernmost populations are partially migratory, individuals occasionally ranging to the Gulf coast.

Accidental in Wyoming.

Notes.—*S. varia* and *S. fulvescens* are possibly conspecific, based on similar appearance and voice (Hardy et al. 1988). See comments under *S. occidentalis*.

Strix fulvescens (Sclater and Salvin). Fulvous Owl.

Syrnium fulvescens Sclater and Salvin, 1868, Proc. Zool. Soc. London, p. 58. (Guatemala.)

Habitat.—Montane Evergreen Forest, Pine-Oak Forest (1200–3100 m; Subtropical and lower Temperate zones).

Distribution.—*Resident* in the mountains of Chiapas, Guatemala, El Salvador, and Honduras; records from Oaxaca are erroneous.

Notes.—See comments under *S. varia*.

Strix nebulosa Forster. Great Gray Owl.

Strix nebulosa J. R. Forster, 1772, Philos. Trans. R. Soc. London 62: 424. (Severn River [northwestern Ontario].)

Habitat.—Dense coniferous and hardwood forest, especially pine, spruce, paper birch and poplar, with adjacent meadows, bogs, or clearings; in migration and winter also in second growth, especially near water, foraging in wet meadows.

Distribution.—*Breeds* in North America from central Alaska, northern Yukon, northwestern and central Mackenzie, northern Manitoba, northern Ontario and west-central Quebec south locally in the interior to the mountains of north-central Washington, south-central Oregon, California (southern Sierra Nevada), northern Idaho, western Montana, western Wyoming, southwestern and central Alberta, central Saskatchewan, southern Manitoba, northern Minnesota, northern Wisconsin, northern Michigan (casually) and south-central Ontario; and in Eurasia from northern Scandinavia, northern Russia and northern Siberia south to central Russia, northern Mongolia, northern Manchuria, Amurland and Sakhalin. Recorded in summer (and possibly breeding) in southern Quebec.

Winters generally through the breeding range, in central and eastern North America wandering south irregularly to northern Utah, southern Montana, North Dakota, southern Minnesota, southern Wisconsin, northern Michigan, southern Ontario and central New York, casually as far as coastal northern California, southern Idaho, Nebraska, Iowa, Indiana, Ohio, and from southern and eastern Quebec, New Brunswick, and Nova Scotia south to Pennsylvania and New Jersey.

Genus *ASIO* Brisson

Asio Brisson, 1760, Ornithologie 1: 28, 477. Type, by tautonymy, *Asio* Brisson = *Strix otus* Linnaeus.

Asio otus (Linnaeus). Long-eared Owl.

Strix Otus Linnaeus, 1758, Syst. Nat. (ed. 10) 1: 92. (in Europa = Sweden.)

Habitat.—Riparian woodland and coniferous or mixed coniferous-deciduous forest, especially near water, usually with adjacent fields or meadows.

Distribution.—*Breeds* in North America from south-coastal and south-central British Columbia, southwestern Mackenzie, northern Saskatchewan, northern Manitoba, northern Ontario, southern Quebec, New Brunswick, Prince Edward Island and Nova Scotia south locally to northwestern Baja California (lat. 30° N.), southern Arizona (rarely), southern New Mexico, western (formerly central) Texas, Coahuila, central Oklahoma, Arkansas (formerly), Missouri, central Illinois, southern Indiana, central Ohio, Pennsylvania (also in the mountains to western Virginia), New York and New England (formerly to central Maryland); and in Eurasia from the British Isles, Scandinavia, northern Russia and northern Siberia south to the Azores, Canary Islands, northwestern Africa, southern Europe, Asia Minor, Iran, the Himalayas, Manchuria, Taiwan, and Korea.

Winters in North America from southern Canada south to northern Baja California (casually to Los Coronados, Cedros and Tiburón islands), Guerrero, Oaxaca, Puebla, San Luis Potosí, southern Texas, the Gulf coast and Georgia, casually to Florida, Bermuda and Cuba; and in the Old World from the breeding range south to northern Africa, Iraq, India, and southern China.

Casual or accidental in southeastern Alaska (Skagway, Taku River), Yukon (Dempster Highway) and Labrador (Red Bay).

Asio stygius (Wagler). Stygian Owl.

Nyctalops stygius Wagler, 1832, Isis von Oken, col. 1222. (Brazil or South Africa = Minas Gerais, Brazil.)

Habitat.—Montane Evergreen Forest, Pine-Oak Forest, Pine Forest, Tropical Lowland Evergreen Forest, Tropical Deciduous Forest (0–3100 m; Tropical to Temperate zones).

Distribution.—*Resident* locally in Middle America in northeastern Sinaloa, southwestern Chihuahua, northwestern Durango, Jalisco, Guerrero (Omilteme), Veracruz (Mirador), Chiapas (Volcán Tacaná), Guatemala (Cobán), Belize, and north-central Nicaragua; in the Greater Antilles (Cuba, the Isle of Pines, Hispaniola and Gonâve Island); and locally in South America in Colombia, western Venezuela, Ecuador, Brazil, Paraguay, and northern Argentina. Recorded also (and possibly resident) on Cozumel Island, Quintana Roo.

Asio flammeus (Pontoppidan). Short-eared Owl.

Strix flammea Pontoppidan, 1763, Dan. Atlas 1: 617, pl. 25. (Sweden.)

Habitat.—Open country, including prairie, meadows, tundra, moorlands, marshes, savanna, in the Hawaiian Islands also around towns; in winter, primarily in open country with tall grass.

Distribution.—*Breeds* in the Hawaiian Islands (main islands from Kauai eastward), and on Pohnpei in the Caroline Islands; in North America from northern Alaska, northern Yukon, northern Mackenzie, central Keewatin, southern Baffin Island (probably), northern Quebec, northern Labrador and Newfoundland south to the eastern Aleutian Islands (west to Unalaska), southern Alaska, central (casually southern) California, northern Nevada, Utah, northeastern Colorado, Kansas, Missouri, southern Illinois, western Kentucky, southern Indiana, central Ohio, Pennsylvania, New Jersey and northern (formerly coastal) Virginia; in the Greater Antilles (Cuba, Cayo Coco, Hispaniola, Puerto Rico); in South America from Colombia, Venezuela and the Guianas south to Tierra del Fuego (including the Galapagos, Juan Fernández and Falkland islands); and in Eurasia from Iceland, the British Isles, Scandinavia, northern Russia and northern Siberia south to southern Europe, Afghanistan, Transbaicalia, northern Mongolia, northern Manchuria, Anadyrland, Sakhalin, the northern Kuril Islands and Kamchatka.

Winters generally in the breeding range, in the Hawaiian Islands ranging casually to the western islands (Kure, Midway, and casually east to French Frigate Shoals); in North America and Middle America mostly from southern Canada south to southern Baja California (casually to Los Coronados Islands and Isla Tiburón), Oaxaca, Puebla, Veracruz, the Gulf coast, southern Florida, and the Greater Antilles and Cayman Islands; and in the Old World south to northwestern Africa, the Mediterranean region, northeastern Africa, Asia Minor, Sri Lanka, the Malay Peninsula, southern China and Japan, casually to the Azores, eastern Atlantic islands, Borneo, the Philippines and Ryukyu Islands.

Casual or accidental in the Revillagigedo Islands (Clarión), Guatemala (Volcán de Agua), Bahamas (Grand Turk), the Virgin Islands (St. Thomas, Guana, possibly St. John), Lesser Antilles (St. Barthélemy), Bermuda, and Greenland.

Genus *PSEUDOSCOPS* Kaup

Pseudoscops Kaup, 1848, Isis von Oken, col. 769. Type, by monotypy, *Ephialtes grammicus* Gosse.

Rhinoptynx Kaup, 1851, Arch. Naturgesch. 17: 107. Type, by subsequent designation (Sharpe, 1875), *Otus mexicanus* Cuv. = *Bubo clamator* Vieillot.

Pseudoscops clamator (Vieillot). Striped Owl.

Bubo Clamator Vieillot, 1808, Hist. Nat. Ois. Amer. Sept. 1 (livr. 4): pl. 20. (depuis Caienne jusq'à la Baie d'Hudson = Cayenne.)

Habitat.—Low Seasonally Wet Grassland, Second-growth Scrub (0–1400 m; Tropical Zone).

Distribution.—*Resident* locally on the Gulf-Caribbean slope in northern Oaxaca, southern Veracruz, southern Belize, Guatemala, Honduras and Nicaragua, on the Pacific slope in El Salvador, on both slopes of Costa Rica and Panama, and in South America from eastern Colombia, Venezuela (also Tobago) and the Guianas south, west of the Andes to western Ecuador and east of the Andes (excluding much of Amazonia) to northern Argentina and Uruguay.

Notes.—Frequently placed either in *Asio* or in the monotypic genus *Rhinoptynx,* but see Olson (1995).

Pseudoscops grammicus (Gosse). Jamaican Owl.

Ephialtes grammicus Gosse, 1847, Birds Jamaica, p. 19 (footnote). (Bluefields Mountains and Tait-Shafton, Jamaica = Tait-Shafton.)

Habitat.—Tropical Lowland Evergreen Forest, Secondary Forest (0–600 m).
Distribution.—*Resident* on Jamaica.

Genus *AEGOLIUS* Kaup

Aegolius Kaup, 1829, Skizz. Entw.-Ges. Eur. Thierw., p. 34. Type, by monotypy, *Strix tengmalmi* Gmelin = *Strix funereus* Linnaeus.

Aegolius funereus (Linnaeus). Boreal Owl.

Strix funereus Linnaeus, 1758, Syst. Nat. (ed. 10) 1: 93. (in Europa = Sweden.)

Habitat.—Dense coniferous forest, mixed coniferous-hardwood forest, and thickets of alder, aspen or stunted spruce, muskeg, most commonly in proximity to open grassy situations.

Distribution.—*Breeds* in North America to tree line from central Alaska, central Yukon, southern Mackenzie, northern Saskatchewan, northern Manitoba, northern Ontario, central Quebec, Labrador and Newfoundland (probably) south to southern Alaska (Kodiak Island), northern and interior British Columbia, eastern Washington, northeastern Oregon, central Idaho, western Montana, northwestern and southern Wyoming, western Colorado, northern New Mexico, central Saskatchewan, southern Manitoba, northern Minnesota, western and central Ontario, southern Quebec (Magdalen Islands) and New Brunswick (Grand Manan); and in Eurasia from northern Scandinavia, northern Russia and northern Siberia south to the mountains of southern Europe, the western Himalayas, western China, Sakhalin and Kamchatka.

Winters generally in the breeding range, in North America south irregularly (or casually) to southern British Columbia, central Montana, North Dakota, eastern South Dakota, southern Minnesota, central Wisconsin, southern Michigan, southern Ontario, New York and New England, casually to southern Oregon, Nebraska, northern Illinois, Pennsylvania, and New Jersey; and in Eurasia to southern Europe, Ussuriland, the Kuril Islands, and Japan.

Accidental in the Pribilofs (St. Paul).

Notes.—Known in Old World literature as Tengmalm's Owl.

Aegolius acadicus (Gmelin). Northern Saw-whet Owl.

Strix acadica Gmelin, 1788, Syst. Nat. 1(1): 296. Based on the "Acadian Owl" Latham, Gen. Synop. Birds 1(1): 149, pl. 5, fig. 2. (in America septentrionali = Nova Scotia.)

Habitat.—Dense coniferous or mixed coniferous-hardwood forest, cedar groves, alder thickets and tamarack bogs; in migration and winter, also in dense second growth, brushy areas, arid scrub and open buildings.

Distribution.—*Breeds* from southern Alaska (west to the base of the Alaska Peninsula), southern and northeastern British Columbia (including the Queen Charlotte Islands), central Alberta, central Saskatchewan, central Manitoba, central Ontario, southern Quebec (possibly also Anticosti Island), northern New Brunswick, Prince Edward Island and Nova Scotia south to the mountains of south-central California (also on Santa Cruz and Santa Catalina islands) and presumably northern Baja California (sight reports, Sierra San Pedro Martír), locally in the highlands of Mexico from Tamaulipas and Coahuila to Oaxaca (Cerro San Felipe), and to extreme western Texas, central Oklahoma, central Missouri (formerly), central Illinois, central Indiana, central Ohio, West Virginia, Virginia, western Maryland, and New York (Long Island); also in the mountains and adjacent lowlands of eastern Tennessee and western North Carolina.

Winters generally throughout the breeding range, south irregularly or casually to desert regions of southern California and southern Arizona, to the Gulf coast (eastern Texas eastward), and through the Atlantic states to northeastern (possibly southern) Florida.

Casual or accidental on islands in the Bering Sea (St. Lawrence Island, and St. Paul in the Pribilofs), Newfoundland and Bermuda.

Notes.—*A. acadicus* and *A. ridgwayi* are closely related and may be conspecific [Saw-whet Owl]; they constitute a superspecies (Binford 1989, Hardy et al. 1989).

Aegolius ridgwayi (Alfaro). Unspotted Saw-whet Owl.

Cryptoglaux ridgwayi Alfaro, 1905, Proc. Biol. Soc. Wash. 18: 217. (Cerro de la Candelaria, near Escasú, Costa Rica.)

Habitat.—Montane Evergreen Forest, Pine-Oak Forest (2300–3300 m; Subtropical and lower Temperate zones).

Distribution.—*Resident* locally in Chiapas, Guatemala (Sacapulas, Quetzaltenango and Soloma), El Salvador (Los Esesmiles, at least formerly), Costa Rica (Volcán Irazú, and Candelaria and Dota mountains) and western Panama (Volcán Barú, in western Chiriquí).

Notes.—See comments under *A. acadicus*.

Order **CAPRIMULGIFORMES**: Goatsuckers, Oilbirds, and Allies

Family **CAPRIMULGIDAE**: Goatsuckers

Subfamily CHORDEILINAE: Nighthawks

Genus *LUROCALIS* Cassin

Lurocalis Cassin, 1851, Proc. Acad. Nat. Sci. Philadelphia 5: 189. Type, by subsequent designation (G. R. Gray, 1855), *Caprimulgus nattereri* Temminck = *Caprimulgus semitorquatus* Gmelin.

Lurocalis semitorquatus (Gmelin). Short-tailed Nighthawk.

Caprimulgus semitorquatus Gmelin, 1789, Syst. Nat. 1(2): 1031. Based on the "White-collared Goatsucker" Latham, Gen. Synop. Birds 2(2): 599. (in Cayenna = Cayenne.)

Habitat.—Tropical Lowland Evergreen Forest, River-edge Forest (0–1700 m; Tropical and lower Subtropical zones).

Distribution.—*Resident* [*semitorquatus* group] from eastern Chiapas, Guatemala, northern Honduras and northeastern Nicaragua (Río Banbana) south through Costa Rica (entire Caribbean slope, and Pacific southwest) and Panama (both slopes, including Isla Cébaco), and in South America in northern Colombia, Venezuela (except western), Trinidad, the Guianas and extreme northwestern Brazil; and [*nattereri* group] in the lowlands of South America from eastern Ecuador and Amazonian and eastern Brazil south to northern Bolivia and northern Argentina.

Notes.—Also known as Semicollared Nighthawk. Groups: *L. semitorquatus* [Short-tailed Nighthawk] and *L. nattereri* (Temminck, 1822) [Chestnut-banded Nighthawk]. The two groups were treated by Hardy et al. (1989) as separate species based on vocalizations, but no comprehensive analysis of vocalizations has been published. *Lurocalis rufiventris* Taczanowski [Rufous-bellied Nighthawk] of the Andes of South America, is now usually regarded as a species distinct from *L. semitorquatus* (Parker et al. 1991, Monroe and Sibley 1993) based on strong differences in vocalizations and plumage (e.g., see Fjeldså and Krabbe 1990).

Genus *CHORDEILES* Swainson

Chordeiles [subgenus] Swainson, 1832, in Swainson and Richardson, Fauna Bor.-Amer. 2 (1831): 337, 496. Type, by original designation, *Caprimulgus virginianus* Gmelin = *Caprimulgus minor* Forster.

Chordeiles acutipennis (Hermann). Lesser Nighthawk.

Caprimulgus acutipennis Hermann, 1783, Tabula Affinit. Anim., p. 230. Based mainly on "Crapaud-volant ou Tette-chevre de la Guiane" Daubenton, Planches Enlum., pl. 732. (Cayenne.)

Habitat.—Open country, desert regions, scrub, savanna and cultivated areas, primarily in arid habitats (Tropical to lower Temperate zones).

Distribution.—*Breeds* from central interior California, southern Nevada, extreme southwestern Utah, central Arizona, central New Mexico and south-central Texas south to southern Baja California, and through the lowlands of both slopes of Mexico (including the Yucatan Peninsula and Cozumel Island) to Guatemala, also locally in Honduras (arid interior valleys on Caribbean drainage), Nicaragua (Tipitapa), Costa Rica (Pacific slope of Guanacaste, and Puerto Cortés area) and Panama (Coclé and western Panamá province); and in South America from Colombia, Venezuela (including Margarita Island), Tobago, Trinidad and the Guianas south locally to Paraguay and southern Brazil.

Winters from southern California (casually), Baja California, southwestern Arizona (casually), central Sinaloa, Durango and Veracruz south through Middle America and South America to the limits of the breeding range; also casually to Chile.

Migrates regularly through Middle America (including the Bay Islands off Honduras), most commonly on the Pacific slope. In North America, ranges casually east along the Gulf coast to Alabama.

Casual or accidental in Alaska (specimen from Noatak River mouth), Colorado, northeastern New Mexico, Oklahoma (Boise City), Ontario (Point Pelee), Florida (Pensacola area and Dry Tortugas), and Bermuda.

Notes.—Also known as Trilling Nighthawk.

Chordeiles minor (Forster). Common Nighthawk.

> *Caprimulgus minor* J. R. Forster, 1771, Cat. Anim. N. Amer., p. 13. Based on "The Whip-poor Will" Catesby, Nat. Hist. Carolina 2 (app.): 16. (No locality given = South Carolina.)

Habitat.—A wide variety of open and semi-open situations, especially in savanna, grasslands, fields, and around human habitation, including cities and towns; frequently nests on flat gravel roofs of buildings (Tropical to Temperate zones).

Distribution.—*Breeds* from southern Yukon, southern Mackenzie, northern Saskatchewan, northern Manitoba, northern Ontario, central Quebec, southern Labrador and Nova Scotia south to southern California (San Bernardino Mountains), southern Nevada, southern Arizona, northeastern Sonora, Chihuahua, Texas, Tamaulipas, the Gulf coast and southern Florida, and south locally through the Gulf and Caribbean slopes of Mexico (excluding the Yucatan Peninsula) to Chiapas, in the pine savanna of Belize and the Mosquitia of eastern Honduras and Nicaragua, and in Costa Rica and Panama (east to eastern Panamá province).

Winters in South America south to northern Argentina.

Migrates through Middle America and the West Indies, including most islands in the Caribbean Sea and those off Venezuela, and, (in fall) in southeastern Alaska.

Casual or accidental in the Hawaiian Islands (French Frigate Shoals); north to south-coastal, central and northern Alaska, northern Yukon, Melville Island, coastal Labrador, Newfoundland and Greenland; Clipperton Island, Bermuda, and Europe; and at sea near the Azores.

Notes.—Also known as Booming Nighthawk. *Chordeiles minor* and *C. gundlachii* are often treated as conspecific, despite differences in vocalizations (but see McAtee 1947, Eisenmann 1962a, Stevenson et al. 1983, Hardy et al. 1988); they probably constitute a superspecies (Sibley and Monroe 1990).

Chordeiles gundlachii Lawrence. Antillean Nighthawk.

> *Chordeiles gundlachii* Lawrence, 1857, Ann. Lyc. Nat. Hist. N. Y. 6: 165. (Cuba.)

Habitat.—Second-growth Scrub, Arid Lowland Scrub (0–600 m).

Distribution.—*Breeds* in the Florida Keys, the Bahamas, Greater Antilles (east to the Virgin Islands, including small cays off Cuba, Gonâve and Tortue) and Cayman Islands; also on the southern Florida mainland (identified by call).

Winters presumably in South America.

Casual in summer in Louisiana (New Orleans) and in migration in the Swan Islands (western Caribbean Sea).

Notes.—See comments under *C. minor*.

Subfamily CAPRIMULGINAE: Nightjars

Genus *NYCTIDROMUS* Gould

> *Nyctidromus* Gould, 1838, Icones Avium, pt. 2, pl. [12] and text. Type, by monotypy, *Nyctidromus derbyanus* Gould = *Caprimulgus albicollis* Gmelin.

Nyctidromus albicollis (Gmelin). Common Pauraque.

> *Caprimulgus albicollis* Gmelin, 1789, Syst. Nat. 1(2): 1030. Based on the "White-throated Goatsucker" Latham, Gen. Synop. Birds 2(2): 596. (in Cayenna = Cayenne.)

Habitat.—Tropical Lowland Evergreen Forest Edge, Secondary Forest, Gallery Forest, Tropical Deciduous Forest, lowland pine savanna (0–1700 m; Tropical and Subtropical zones).

Distribution.—*Resident* from southern Sonora, Sinaloa, southern Texas (McMullen and Refugio counties, casually north to Zavala, Frio and De Witt counties), Nuevo León and Tamaulipas south along both slopes of Middle America (including the Tres Marias, Mujeres and Cozumel islands off Mexico, and the Pearl Islands off Panama), and in South America from Colombia, Venezuela, Trinidad and the Guianas south, west of the Andes to northwestern Peru and east of the Andes to northern Argentina and southern Brazil.

Notes.—Also known as the Pauraque.

Genus *PHALAENOPTILUS* Ridgway

Phalænoptilus Ridgway, 1880, Proc. U. S. Natl. Mus. 3: 5. Type, by original designation, *Caprimulgus nuttallii* Audubon.

Phalaenoptilus nuttallii (Audubon). Common Poorwill.

Caprimulgus Nuttallii Audubon, 1844, Birds Amer. (octavo ed.) 7: 350, pl. 495. (upper Missouri = between Fort Pierre and mouth of the Cheyenne River, South Dakota.)

Habitat.—Rocky and gravelly terrain in sparse scrubland, broken chaparral, and openings in woodland and forest.

Distribution.—*Breeds* from southern interior British Columbia, Montana, extreme southwestern Saskatchewan, central North Dakota, southwestern (and formerly also southeastern) South Dakota and Nebraska south through eastern Washington, central and eastern Oregon and California to southern Baja California, southern Sonora, Durango, Jalisco, Guanajuato and Coahuila, and east to eastern Kansas, western Oklahoma and central Texas.

Winters in southern parts of the breeding range in California and Arizona (probably also farther east), sometimes in a torpid condition, and south to the limits of the breeding range in Mexico.

Casual or accidental in southwestern British Columbia, southern Manitoba (Treesbank), northwestern Ontario (near Moosonee), Minnesota (Swift County), and eastern Oklahoma (Tulsa).

Genus *SIPHONORHIS* Sclater

Siphonorhis Sclater, 1861, Proc. Zool. Soc. London, p. 77. Type, by original designation, *Caprimulgus americanus* Linnaeus.

†*Siphonorhis americanus* (Linnaeus). Jamaican Pauraque.

Caprimulgus americanus Linnaeus, 1758, Syst. Nat. (ed. 10) 1: 193. Based on the "Small wood owl" Sloane, Voy. Jamaica 2: 296, pl. 255, fig. 1. (in America calidiore = Jamaica.)

Habitat.—Tropical Deciduous Forest, Arid Lowland Scrub.

Distribution.—EXTINCT. Formerly *resident* on Jamaica; last collected near Spanishtown in September 1859 (specimen USNM).

Notes.—*S. americanus* and *S. brewsteri* are closely related and constitute a superspecies (Sibley and Monroe 1990). Called Jamaican Poorwill by Sibley and Monroe (1990).

Siphonorhis brewsteri (Chapman). Least Pauraque.

Microsiphonorhis brewsteri Chapman, 1917, Bull. Amer. Mus. Nat. Hist. 37: 329. (Túbano, Province of Azua, Dominican Republic.)

Habitat.—Tropical Deciduous Forest, Arid Lowland Scrub (0–900 m).

Distribution.—*Resident* locally on Hispaniola (including Gonâve Island).

Notes.—See comments under *S. americanus*. Called Least Poorwill by Sibley and Monroe (1990).

Genus *NYCTIPHRYNUS* Bonaparte

Nyctiphrynus Bonaparte, 1857, Riv. Contemp. 9: 215. Type, by subsequent designation (Oberholser, 1914), *Caprimulgus ocellatus* Tschudi.

Otophanes Brewster, 1888, Auk 5: 88. Type, by original designation, *Otophanes mcleodii* Brewster.

Nyctagreus Nelson, 1901, Proc. Biol. Soc. Wash. 14: 171. Type, by original designation, *Caprimulgus yucatanicus* Hartert.

Nyctiphrynus mcleodii (Brewster). Eared Poorwill.

Otophanes mcleodii Brewster, 1888, Auk 5: 89. (Sierra Madre of Chihuahua, Mexico.)

Habitat.—Pine-Oak Forest, Tropical Deciduous Forest (1100–1800 m; upper Tropical and lower Subtropical zones).

Distribution.—*Resident* locally in Chihuahua (including near the Sonora-Chihuahua border), eastern Sinaloa, Jalisco, Colima, Guerrero and Oaxaca (Sierra de Miahuatlán).

Notes.—This and the following two species are often placed in the genus *Otophanes* (Friedmann et al. 1950).

Nyctiphrynus yucatanicus (Hartert). Yucatan Poorwill.

Caprimulgus yucatanicus Hartert, 1892, Cat. Birds Brit. Mus. 16: xv, 525, 575. (Tizimin, Yucatan.)

Habitat.—Tropical Deciduous Forest, Arid Lowland Scrub (Tropical Zone).

Distribution.—*Resident* in the Yucatan Peninsula, northern Guatemala (Petén) and Belize.

Notes.—See comments under *N. mcleodii.*

Nyctiphrynus ocellatus (Tschudi). Ocellated Poorwill.

Caprimulgus ocellatus Tschudi, 1844, Arch. Naturgesch. 10: 268. (Republica Peruana = Peru.)

Habitat.—Tropical Lowland Evergreen Forest, Secondary Forest, lowland pine savanna (0–1350 m; Tropical Zone).

Distribution.—*Resident* (presumably) in northern Nicaragua (single specimen from Peña Blanca, Jinotega); northern Costa Rica (Brasilia), and in South America east of the Andes from southeastern Colombia, eastern Ecuador, and Amazonian Brazil south to Paraguay and northeastern Argentina. A sight report for Panama (Canal area) requires confirmation.

Notes.—See comments under *N. mcleodii.*

Genus *CAPRIMULGUS* Linnaeus

Caprimulgus Linnaeus, 1758, Syst. Nat. (ed. 10) 1: 193. Type, by tautonymy, *Caprimulgus europaeus* Linnaeus (*Caprimulgus,* prebinomial specific name, in synonymy).

Antrostomus Bonaparte, 1838, Geogr. Comp. List, p. 8. Type, by subsequent designation (G. R. Gray, 1840), *Caprimulgus carolinensis* Gmelin.

Antiurus Ridgway, 1912, Proc. Biol. Soc. Wash. 25: 98. Type, by original designation, *Stenopsis maculicaudus* Lawrence.

Setochalcis Oberholser, 1914, Bull. U. S. Natl. Mus., no. 86, p. 11. Type, by original designation, *Caprimulgus vociferus* Wilson.

Caprimulgus carolinensis Gmelin. Chuck-will's-widow.

Caprimulgus carolinensis Gmelin, 1789, Syst. Nat. 1(2): 1028. Based mainly on "The Goat Sucker of Carolina" Catesby, Nat. Hist. Carolina 1: 8, pl. 8. (in Virginia et Carolina = South Carolina.)

Habitat.—Deciduous forest, pine-oak association and live-oak groves; in migration and winter also in open woodland, scrub, and Tropical Evergreen Forest.

Distribution.—*Breeds* from eastern Kansas, southern and eastern Iowa, central Illinois, northwestern and central Indiana, extreme southern Ontario, southern Ohio, central West Virginia, Maryland, New Jersey and southern New York (Long Island) and (probably) Massachusetts (Martha's Vineyard) south to eastern Oklahoma, south-central and southeastern Texas, the Gulf coast and southern Florida. Recorded sporadically in summer north to southeastern South Dakota, southern Minnesota, Wisconsin, southern Michigan and Pennsylvania.

Winters from southeastern Texas (rare), southern Louisiana (rare), and coastal Alabama (rare) south through Middle America (reported on the Gulf-Caribbean slope of Mexico and Belize and on both slopes south of Mexico) to Colombia, and from central Florida and the Bahamas south through the Greater Antilles to the northern Lesser Antilles (Saba, St. Martin, Barbuda).

Casual or accidental in California, Nevada, eastern New Mexico, southern Quebec, northern New York, Maine, New Brunswick, Nova Scotia, Newfoundland, the Cayman Islands and Netherlands Antilles (Bonaire), and Venezuela.

Notes.—*C. carolinensis* and *C. rufus* constitute a superspecies (Mayr and Short 1970).

Caprimulgus rufus Boddaert. Rufous Nightjar.

> *Caprimulgus rufus* Boddaert, 1783, Table Planches Enlum., p. 46. Based on "Crapaud-Volant ou Tette-Chèvre de Cayenne" Daubenton, Planches Enlum., pl. 735. (Cayenne.)

Habitat.—Tropical Deciduous Forest, Secondary Forest, Gallery Forest (0–1800 m; Tropical and lower Subtropical zones).

Distribution.—*Resident* [*minimus* group] in southeastern Costa Rica, Panama (primarily the Pacific slope, including Isla Coiba), northern Colombia, western and northern Venezuela and Trinidad; [*rufus* group] in South America from Colombia, southern Venezuela and the Guianas south, east of the Andes to northern Argentina, Paraguay and southern Brazil; and [*otiosus* group] in the Lesser Antilles (St. Lucia); erroneously reported from northern Venezuela.

Notes.—Groups: *C. minimus* Griscom and Greenway, 1937 [Ruddy Nightjar], *C. rufus* [Rufous Nightjar], and *C. otiosus* (Bangs, 1911) [St. Lucia Nightjar]. We follow Robbins and Parker (1997a) in treating *C. otiosus* as a subspecies of *C. rufus*. See comments under *C. carolinensis*.

Caprimulgus cubanensis (Lawrence). Greater Antillean Nightjar.

> *Antrostomus Cubanensis* Lawrence, 1860, Ann. Lyc. Nat. Hist. N. Y. 7: 260. (Cienaga de Zapata, and on the coast of Manzanillo, Cuba.)

Habitat.—Tropical Lowland Evergreen Forest, Pine Forest (0–2000 m).

Distribution.—*Resident* [*cubanensis* group] in Cuba and the Isle of Pines; and [*ekmani* group] in Hispaniola.

Notes.—Differences in vocalizations (Hardy et al. 1988) suggest that the two groups may represent separate species, *C. cubanensis* [Cuban Nightjar] and *C. ekmani* (Lönnberg, 1929) [Hispaniolan Nightjar].

Caprimulgus salvini Hartert. Tawny-collared Nightjar.

> *Caprimulgus salvini* Hartert, 1892, Ibis, p. 287. New name for *Antrostomus macromystax* Baird, Brewer and Ridgway, preoccupied.

Habitat.—Tropical Deciduous Forest (Tropical Zone).

Distribution.—*Breeds* from Nuevo León and southern Tamaulipas south through eastern San Luis Potosí and Veracruz to northern Oaxaca (winter only) and Chiapas (probably resident throughout most of this range north of Oaxaca).

Recorded from Nicaragua (Matagalpa); probably represents a vagrant.

Notes.—Without explanation, Peters (1940) considered *C. salvini* to be conspecific with *C. sericocaudatus* (Cassin, 1849) [Silky-tailed Nightjar]. See notes under *C. badius*.

Caprimulgus badius (Bangs and Peck). Yucatan Nightjar.

> *Antrostomus badius* Bangs and Peck, 1908, Proc. Biol. Soc. Washington, 21, p. 44. (Toledo District, British Honduras = Belize.)

Habitat.—Tropical Deciduous Forest (Tropical Zone).

Distribution.—*Breeds* in the Yucatan Peninsula (including Cozumel Island).

Recorded in *winter* in Belize (including Half Moon Cay) and northern Honduras.

Notes.—Formerly considered conspecific with *C. salvini* and with the South American *C. sericocaudatus* (Cassin, 1849) [Silky-tailed Nightjar]. The three taxa are apparently closely related but have distinctive vocalizations (Hardy and Straneck 1989).

Caprimulgus ridgwayi (Nelson). Buff-collared Nightjar.

Antrostomus ridgwayi Nelson, 1897, Auk 14: 50. (Tlalkisala, Guerrero, Mexico.)

Habitat.—Tropical Deciduous Forest, Arid Montane Scrub, Arid Lowland Scrub, Pine-Oak Forest (0–2000 m; Tropical and Subtropical zones).

Distribution.—*Resident* from southern Arizona, southern Sonora, Sinaloa and Durango south through western Mexico and the southern portions of the Central Plateau to Morelos, Oaxaca and Chiapas; disjunctly on the Caribbean slope in central Veracruz; and in the Motagua Valley of Guatemala, the interior of Honduras, and central Nicaragua. Casual in summer elsewhere in southeastern Arizona and extreme southwestern New Mexico (Guadalupe Canyon). Northernmost populations are migratory southward.

A specimen record from California (Ventura Co.) is under review.

Notes.—Also known as Ridgway's Whip-poor-will.

Caprimulgus vociferus Wilson. Whip-poor-will.

Caprimulgus vociferus Wilson, 1812, Amer. Ornithol. 5: 71, pl. 41, figs. 1–3. (Pennsylvania = Philadelphia.)

Habitat.—Forest and open woodland, both arid and humid, from lowland moist and deciduous forest to montane forest and pine-oak association, breeding in the tropics primarily in open montane forest (Tropical to Temperate zones).

Distribution.—*Breeds* [*arizonae* group] in southern California (probably, in San Gabriel, San Bernardino, San Jacinto and Clark mountains), and from southern Nevada, northern Arizona, central New Mexico and extreme western Texas south through the highlands of Mexico, Guatemala and El Salvador to Honduras, also (probably) in southern Baja California; and [*vociferus* group] from south-central Saskatchewan, southern Manitoba, central Ontario, southern Quebec, central New Brunswick and Nova Scotia south, east of the Great Plains (west to eastern North Dakota, southeastern South Dakota, eastern Nebraska, eastern Kansas and Oklahoma) to extreme northeastern Texas, Arkansas, northern Mississippi, north-central Alabama, central Georgia, South Carolina, east-central North Carolina and Virginia.

Winters [*arizonae* group] in central Mexico; and [*vociferus* group] from northern Mexico (Sonora eastward), southern Texas, the Gulf coast and east-central South Carolina (casually farther north, on the Atlantic coast to New Jersey) south through Middle America to Costa Rica, casually to southern California, western Panama (western Chiriquí) and Cuba.

Casual [*arizonae* group] in central northern California, southern Alberta, southwestern Saskatchewan, northwestern Montana (calls only) and central Colorado; and [*vociferus* group] in eastern Colorado (probably) and central eastern Quebec. Accidental [*vociferus* group] in southeastern Alaska (Kupreanof Island).

Notes.—The two groups differ in egg pigmentation (Phillips et al. 1964) and in vocalizations (Hardy et al. 1988) and may represent separate species, *C. arizonae* (Brewster, 1881) [Western Whip-poor-will] and *C. vociferus* [Eastern Whip-poor-will]. *Caprimulgus vociferus* and *C. noctitherus* constitute a superspecies (Mayr and Short 1970).

Caprimulgus noctitherus (Wetmore). Puerto Rican Nightjar.

Setochalcis noctitherus Wetmore, 1919, Proc. Biol. Soc. Wash. 32: 235. (Bayamón, Puerto Rico.)

Habitat.—Tropical Deciduous Forest.

Distribution.—*Resident* on Puerto Rico, where now restricted to the southwestern portion of the island.

Notes.—Also known as Puerto Rican Whip-poor-will. Reynard (1962) documented vocal differences between this form and *C. vociferus* that support their treatment as separate species. See also comments under *C. vociferus*.

Caprimulgus saturatus (Salvin). Dusky Nightjar.

Antrostomus saturatus Salvin, 1870, Proc. Zool. Soc. London, p. 203. (Volcán de Chiriquí, Panama.)

Habitat.—Montane Evergreen Forest (1500–3100 m; Subtropical and Temperate zones).
Distribution.—*Resident* in the central highlands of Costa Rica, and in western Panama (vicinity of Volcán Barú, western Chiriquí).

Caprimulgus cayennensis Gmelin. White-tailed Nightjar.

Caprimulgus cayennensis Gmelin, 1789, Syst. Nat. 1(2): 1031. Based mainly on "Engoulevent de Cayenne" Buffon, Hist. Nat. Ois. 6: 545, and the "White-necked Goatsucker" Latham, Gen. Synop. Birds 2(2): 599. (in Cayennae cultis = Cayenne.)

Habitat.—Low Seasonally Wet Grassland, Second-growth Scrub (0–1000 m; Tropical and Subtropical zones).
Distribution.—*Resident* in the Lesser Antilles (Martinique, where possibly extirpated); and in Costa Rica and Panama, and in South America from northern Colombia, Venezuela (including islands from the Netherlands Antilles to Tobago and Trinidad) and the Guianas south locally to northern Ecuador and northern Brazil.
Accidental in Puerto Rico (sight report).
Notes.—*C. cayennensis* and *C. candicans* appear to constitute a superspecies (Sibley and Monroe 1990).

Caprimulgus maculicaudus (Lawrence). Spot-tailed Nightjar.

Stenopsis maculicaudus Lawrence, 1862, Ann. Lyc. Nat. Hist. N. Y. 7: 459. (Para [Brazil].)

Habitat.—Low Seasonally Wet Grassland, lowland pine savanna (0–1500 m; Tropical Zone).
Distribution.—*Breeds* locally in the Gulf-Caribbean lowlands of southern Mexico (southern Veracruz, northern Oaxaca), in the Mosquitia of northeastern Nicaragua (probably also eastern Honduras), and in South America from eastern Colombia, Venezuela and the Guianas south locally, east of the Andes, to central Bolivia and southeastern Brazil.
Apparently at least partly migratory from the Middle American breeding grounds, as there are few records during the nonbreeding season; recorded also from central Honduras (Lake Yojoa), probably as a transient. Presumably resident in the South American portion of the breeding range.

Caprimulgus indicus Latham. Jungle Nightjar.

Caprimulgus indicus Latham, 1790, Index Ornithol. 2: 588. Based on the "Indian Goatsucker" Latham, Gen. Synop. Birds (suppl.) 1: 196. (in India.)

Habitat & Distribution.—*Breeds* in open woodland and forest from Manchuria and Japan south to India, Sri Lanka and eastern China, and *winters* in a variety of woodland and partly open habitats from the Himalayas, eastern China and Japan south to the East Indies and New Guinea.
Casual in the Kuril Islands and Sakhalin. Accidental in Alaska (Buldir Island in the Aleutians, 31 May 1977; Day et al. 1979).
Notes.—Also known as Gray Nightjar.

Family **NYCTIBIIDAE**: Potoos

Genus *NYCTIBIUS* Vieillot

Nyctibius Vieillot, 1816, Analyse, p. 38. Type, by monotypy, "Grand Engoulevent de Cayenne" Buffon = *Caprimulgus grandis* Gmelin.

Nyctibius grandis (Gmelin). Great Potoo.

> *Caprimulgus grandis* Gmelin, 1789, Syst. Nat. 1(2): 1029. Based mainly on "Le grand Tette-chévre tacheté du Brésil" Brisson, Ornithologie, 2, 485, and the "Grand Goatsucker" Latham, Gen. Synop. Birds, 2 (2), 590. (in Cayenna = Cayenne.)

Habitat.—Tropical Lowland Evergreen Forest, Gallery Forest (Tropical Zone).

Distribution.—*Resident* locally in eastern Chiapas, Guatemala (Polochic and Salinas rivers), eastern Honduras (Olancho), Nicaragua (San Emilio), Costa Rica and Panama (Caribbean lowlands throughout, and Pacific lowlands in eastern Panamá province and Darién), and in South America from Colombia, Venezuela and the Guianas south, east of the Andes, to central Bolivia and southeastern Brazil.

Nyctibius griseus (Gmelin). Common Potoo.

> *Caprimulgus griseus* Gmelin, 1789, Syst. Nat. 1(2): p. 1029. (in Cayenna = Cayenne.)

Habitat.—Tropical Lowland Evergreen Forest Edge, Secondary Forest, Gallery Forest, Montane Evergreen Forest Edge, River-edge Forest, lowland pine savanna (0–1800 m; Tropical and lower Subtropical zones).

Distribution.—*Resident* from southwestern Costa Rica and eastern Nicaragua (recorded also in northwestern Nicaragua) south to Panama, and in South America from Colombia, Venezuela, (also Trinidad and Tobago) and the Guianas south, west of the Andes to western Ecuador and east of the Andes to Bolivia, northern Argentina and Uruguay.

Notes.—Despite a lack of abrupt morphological change, dramatic differences in vocalizations indicate that specific status is warranted for this species and *N. jamaicensis*. (Davis 1978, Hardy et al. 1988, Stiles and Skutch 1989).

Nyctibius jamaicensis (Gmelin). Northern Potoo.

> *Caprimulgus jamaicensis* Gmelin, 1789, Syst. Nat. 1(2): p. 1029. (Jamaica.)

Habitat.—Open woodland, sometimes near human settlement (Subtropical and Tropical zones)

Distribution.—*Resident* from southern Sinaloa, southern San Luis Potosí and southern Tamaulipas south along both slopes of Middle America to Caribbean slope of eastern Honduras (including Isla Roatán in the Bay Islands) and Pacific slope of Central Costa Rica, and in the Greater Antilles (Jamaica, Hispaniola and Gonâve Island).

Notes.—Formerly treated as conspecific with *N. griseus*; see note under that species. They constitute a superspecies.

Family **STEATORNITHIDAE**: Oilbirds

Genus *STEATORNIS* Humboldt

> *Steatornis* Humboldt, 1814, in Humboldt and Bonpland, Voy. Inter. Amer. 1: 416. Type, by monotypy, "Guacharo" = *Steatornis caripensis* Humboldt.

Steatornis caripensis Humboldt. Oilbird.

> *Steatornis caripensis* Humboldt, 1817, Bull. Sci. Soc. Philom. Paris, p. 52. (caverns of Caripe, Cumaná, Venezuela.)

Habitat.—Tropical Lowland Evergreen Forest, Montane Evergreen Forest; nests and roosts in caves; forages at night for fruits in open woodland (0–2200 m).

Distribution.—*Resident* in Colombia, Venezuela, Trinidad and the Guianas, and in the Andes locally south to central Bolivia.

Casual (although probably resident) in Panama (Canal area, eastern Panamá province, eastern Darién). Accidental in Costa Rica (Cerro de la Muerte).

Order **APODIFORMES**: Swifts and Hummingbirds

Family **APODIDAE**: Swifts

Subfamily CYPSELOIDINAE: Cypseloidine Swifts

Genus *CYPSELOIDES* Streubel

Cypseloides Streubel, 1848, Isis von Oken, col. 366. Type, by subsequent designation (Sclater, 1865), *Hemiprocne fumigata* Streubel.

Cypseloides niger (Gmelin). Black Swift.

> *Hirundo nigra* Gmelin, 1789, Syst. Nat. 1(2): 1025. Based on "Le Martinet de S. Domingue" Brisson, Ornithologie 2: 514, pl. 46, fig. 3. (in insulae S. Dominici et Cayennae = Hispaniola.)

Habitat.—Primarily montane areas (except in the most northern part of the range), foraging over both forest and open areas; nests in crevices or shallow caves in steep rock faces and canyons, usually near or behind waterfalls (occasionally in sea caves) (Subtropical and Temperate zones).

Distribution.—*Breeds* locally from southeastern Alaska (north to the Stikine River), south-central British Columbia, and southwestern Alberta south through the Pacific states to southern California, and from Idaho, northwestern Montana, western and central Colorado, central Utah, southeastern Arizona, north-central New Mexico, Chihuahua, Durango, Nayarit, Hidalgo, and Veracruz south through southern Mexico, Guatemala, and Honduras to Costa Rica (not recorded Nicaragua); and in the Antilles (Cuba, Jamaica, Hispaniola, Puerto Rico, Montserrat, Guadeloupe, Dominica, Martinique, St. Lucia, and St. Vincent).

Migrates through western North America through California, Arizona, New Mexico, and Mexico (including Baja California, with records at sea in the Pacific off Chiapas and Guatemala) to Costa Rica and northwestern Colombia, and through the Lesser Antilles to Trinidad and Guyana.

Winters (presumably) in South America, but distribution unknown (Stiles and Negret 1994).

Migrates in western North America through California, Arizona, New Mexico, and Mexico (including Baja California, with records at sea in the Pacific off Chiapas and Guatemala), and to the Virgin Islands and Lesser Antilles.

Casual in south-coastal Alaska (Wooded Islands); sight report for Panama (Chiriquí). Sight reports for Florida and Texas are questionable.

Notes.—Formerly placed in the monotypic genus *Nephoecetes* Baird, 1858. Mayr and Short (1970) considered *C. niger* and South American *C. lemosi* Eisenmann and Lehmann, 1962, and *C. fumigatus* (Streubel, 1848) to constitute a superspecies.

Cypseloides storeri Navarro et al. White-fronted Swift.

> *Cypseloides storeri* Navarro et al., 1992, Wilson Bull. 104: 56. (Puerto del Gallo, Tlacotepec, Guerrero, Mexico.)

Habitat.—Montane Evergreen Forest; generally near waterfalls (1500–2500 m; Subtropical Zone).

Distribution.—Known from five specimens from the mountains of Jalisco (Autlán), Michoacán (Tacámbaro), and Guerrero (Sierra de Atoyac).

Notes—Howell and Webb (1995) treated *storeri* as a subspecies of *C. cryptus*.

Cypseloides cryptus Zimmer. White-chinned Swift.

> *Cypseloides cryptus* Zimmer, 1945, Auk 62: 588. (Inca Mine, Río Tavara, Perú.)

Habitat.—Montane Evergreen Forest, Tropical Lowland Evergreen Forest, Tropical Lowland Evergreen Forest Edge (0–3000 m; Tropical and Subtropical zones).

Distribution.—*Breeds* in western and central Costa Rica (Cordillera de Guanacaste, Tres Ríos, Rara Avis), and presumably in South America (recorded Colombia, Venezuela, Guyana, Ecuador, and Peru); recorded locally from the Caribbean slope of Belize, Honduras (San Esteban), Nicaragua (El Recreo), and Panama (San Blas and Isla Coiba).
Notes—See comments under *C. storeri.*

Cypseloides cherriei Ridgway. Spot-fronted Swift.

> *Cypseloides cherriei* Ridgway, 1893, Proc. U. S. Natl. Mus. 16: 44. (Volcán de Irazú, Costa Rica.)

Habitat.—Montane Evergreen Forest; nests on rock ledges near waterfalls (900–1100 m; Subtropical Zone).
Distribution.—Known only from Costa Rica (Volcán de Irazú, and Puntarenas province), Colombia (Santander), Venezuela (Aragua, where nesting has been verified), and northwestern Ecuador.

Genus *STREPTOPROCNE* Oberholser

> *Streptoprocne* Oberholser, 1906, Proc. Biol. Soc. Wash. 19: 69. Type, by original designation, *Hirundo zonaris* Shaw.
> *Semicollum* [subgenus] Brooke, 1970, Durban Mus. Novit. 9: 16. Type, by original designation, *Acanthylis semicollaris* de Saussure.

Streptoprocne rutila (Vieillot). Chestnut-collared Swift.

> *Hirundo rutila* Vieillot, 1817, Nouv. Dict. Hist. Nat. (nouv. éd.) 14: 528. (No locality given = Trinidad.)

Habitat.—Montane Evergreen Forest, Secondary Forest, Second-growth Scrub; nests on rock faces near or behind waterfalls (occasionally in sea caves) (800–2800 m; Tropical and Subtropical zones).
Distribution.—*Resident* from eastern Sinaloa, Durango, Zacatecas, Hidalgo, and Veracruz south through Middle America (not reported Nicaragua), and in South America from Colombia, Venezuela, Trinidad, Guyana, and French Guiana (probably) south in the Andes to central Bolivia. Possibly migratory in part, especially the northern Middle American populations. A sight report for southwestern Chihuahua.
Notes.—Formerly placed in the genus *Chaetura* or *Cypseloides,* but see Marín and Stiles (1992), who showed that *rutila* and its close allies share numerous characters with *Streptoprocne,* especially in reproductive and nesting traits.

Streptoprocne zonaris (Shaw). White-collared Swift.

> *Hirundo zonaris* Shaw, 1796, in J. F. Miller, Cimelia Phys., p. 100, pl. 55. (No locality given = Chapada, Mato Grosso, Brazil.)

Habitat.—Montane Evergreen Forest, Tropical Lowland Evergreen Forest, Secondary Forest, Second-growth Scrub, Pine Forest; nests on cliffs near or behind waterfalls (0–3600 m; Tropical to Temperate zones).
Distribution.—*Resident* from Guerrero, San Luis Potosí, and Tamaulipas south through Middle America (including Isla Coiba off Panama), and in South America from Colombia, Venezuela, Trinidad, and the Guianas south to northwestern Argentina, and central and southeastern Brazil; and in the Greater Antilles (Cuba, Jamaica, Hispaniola, Tortue Island, and possibly also the Isle of Pines).
Wanders irregularly north in the Lesser Antilles to Grenada and the Grenadines. Accidental in Texas (Freeport Rockport, Padre Island), northwestern Florida (Perdido Key), and the northern Lesser Antilles (Saba); sight reports from northwestern California, Michigan (Iosco Co.), Sinaloa, Colima, Jalisco, Vieques Island (off Puerto Rico), and St. Kitts.
Notes.—In the West Indies, also known as Antillean Cloud Swift.

Streptoprocne semicollaris (Saussure). White-naped Swift.

> *Acanthylis semicollaris* Saussure, 1859, Rev. Mag. Zool. (2)11: 118. (les grandes forêts, du Mexique = San Joaquin, near City of Mexico.)

Habitat.—Pine-Oak Forest, Tropical Deciduous Forest, Second-growth Scrub; nests on ledges in caves (800–3400 m; Tropical to lower Temperate zones).

Distribution.—*Resident* in northern and central Mexico (recorded Sinaloa, Chihuahua, Durango, Nayarit, México, Distrito Federal, Morelos, and Guerrero). Accidental in Chiapas.

Subfamily CHAETURINAE: Chaeturine Swifts

Genus *CHAETURA* Stephens

> *Chætura* Stephens, 1826, in Shaw, Gen. Zool. 13(2): 76. Type, by subsequent designation (Swainson, 1829), *Chaetura pelasgia* [sic] = *Hirundo pelagica* Linnaeus.

Chaetura pelagica (Linnaeus). Chimney Swift.

> *Hirundo pelagica* Linnaeus, 1758, Syst. Nat. (ed. 10) 1: 192. Based on "The American Swallow" Catesby, Nat. Hist. Carolina 2 (app.): 8, pl. 8. (in America = South Carolina.)

Habitat.—Open situations and woodland, especially around human habitation; now nests and roosts primarily in chimneys, originally on cliffs or in hollow trees.

Distribution.—*Breeds* in eastern North America east of the Rocky Mountains from east-central Saskatchewan, southern Manitoba, central Ontario, southern Quebec, New Brunswick, Prince Edward Island, Nova Scotia, and Newfoundland (probably) south to eastern New Mexico (probably), south-central and southern Texas, the Gulf coast, and southern Florida, and west to southeastern Wyoming and eastern Colorado, with one confirmed breeding record for southern California (Ventura, 1977); recorded in summer (and probably breeding) elsewhere in central and southern California, and in Arizona.

Winters in western Peru, northern Chile, and in the upper Amazon basin of eastern Peru and northwestern Brazil.

Migrates regularly through the lowlands of eastern Mexico, the Caribbean slope of Middle America (including Cozumel Island, the Bay Islands off Honduras, and Taboga Island off Panama, casually on the Pacific slope of eastern Panama), Colombia, and western Venezuela, casually west to Montana, Utah, California (primarily southern portion), Arizona, and New Mexico, and through the Bahamas, Greater Antilles (recorded Cuba, Jamaica, Hispaniola, Tortue Island, and the Virgin Islands), and the Swan and Cayman islands.

Casual or accidental in Alaska (St. George Island in the Pribilofs), Bermuda, Greenland, and the British Isles; sight reports from Alberta are questionable.

Notes.—*Chaetura pelagica, C. vauxi,* and *C. chapmani* may constitute a superspecies (Mayr and Short 1970).

Chaetura vauxi (Townsend). Vaux's Swift.

> *Cypcelus* [sic] *Vauxi* J. K. Townsend, 1839, Narr. Journey Rocky Mount., etc., p. 348. (Columbia River = Fort Vancouver, Washington.)

Habitat.—Breeds primarily in mature coniferous and mixed forest, foraging and migrating also over open country; Tropical Lowland Evergreen Forest, Montane Evergreen Forest, Tropical Deciduous Forest, Secondary Forest, Second-growth Scrub (Tropical to Temperate zones).

Distribution.—*Breeds* [*vauxi* group] in western North America from southeastern Alaska (north to Haines and Skagway), southern British Columbia, northern Idaho, and western Montana south to central California (Santa Cruz County, probably Monterey County), and in southwestern Tamaulipas, southeastern San Luis Potosí, and Hidalgo. Recorded in summer (and probably breeding) [group uncertain] through much of central and southeastern Mexico.

Winters [*vauxi* group] from central Mexico (rarely from northern California) south throughout the breeding range in Middle America, and in Venezuela,

Migrates [*vauxi* group] east of the breeding range from Idaho, Nevada, and Utah (rarely) south through the southwestern United States, Baja California, and western Mexico.

Resident [*richmondi* group] from Jalisco, Veracruz, and Chiapas south to Panama (including Coiba and the Pearl islands) and northern Venezuela (Lara to Monagas); and [*gaumeri* group] on the Yucatan Peninsula (including Cozumel Island).

Casual [*vauxi* group] in southern Louisiana and western Florida (sight reports).

Notes.—The three groups have often been treated as separate species, *C. vauxi* [Vaux's Swift], *C. richmondi* Ridgway, 1910 [Dusky-backed Swift], and *C. gaumeri* Lawrence, 1882 [Yucatan Swift]. See comments under *C. pelagica.*

Chaetura chapmani Hellmayr. Chapman's Swift.

> *Chætura chapmani* Hellmayr, 1907, Bull. Br. Ornithol. Club 19: 62. (Caparo, Trinidad.)

Habitat.—Tropical Lowland Evergreen Forest, Secondary Forest, Second-growth Scrub (0–1500 m; Tropical to lower Temperate zones)

Distribution.—*Resident* from eastern Colombia, Venezuela, Trinidad, and the Guianas south locally to southwestern and northeastern Brazil, the southernmost population migratory northward.

Ranges casually to (and possibly resident in) central Panama (Gatun, Canal area, 11 July 1911, and Mandinga, San Blas, 30 January 1957).

Notes.—Also known as Dark-breasted Swift. See comments under *C. pelagica.*

Chaetura brachyura (Jardine). Short-tailed Swift.

> *Acanthylis brachyura* Jardine, 1846, Ann. Mag. Nat. Hist. (1) 18: 120. (Tobago.)

Habitat.—Secondary Forest, Tropical Lowland Evergreen Forest Edge, Tropical Deciduous Forest, Second-growth Scrub (0–1050 m; Tropical Zone).

Distribution.—*Resident* in the Lesser Antilles (St. Vincent, the population apparently partly migratory), and from Panama (eastern Colón, Canal area, and Darién), Colombia, Venezuela, Tobago, Trinidad, and the Guianas south, east of the Andes to northern Bolivia and central Brazil; also west of the Andes in southwestern Ecuador and northwestern Peru.

Accidental in the Virgin Islands (St. Croix). Reports from Grenada are regarded as doubtful.

Chaetura andrei Berlepsch and Hartert. Ashy-tailed Swift.

> *Chaetura andrei* Berlepsch and Hartert, 1902, Novit. Zool. 9: 91. (Caicara, Orinoco River, Venezuela.)

Habitat.—Tropical Lowland Evergreen Forest Edge, Secondary Forest, Second-growth Scrub (0–1600 m).

Distribution.—*Breeds* in Venezuela, and from eastern Brazil south to Paraguay, northern Argentina, and southern Brazil, *ranging* in winter from the breeding range north, at least casually, to Venezuela and Colombia.

Accidental in Panama (Juan Díaz, western Panamá province, 4 August 1923; Rogers 1939).

Notes.—Also known as Andre's Swift. Although the nominate form may be a subspecies of *C. vauxi,* the subspecies *C. a. meridionalis,* the form recorded in Panama, may be a separate species, *C. meridionalis* Hellmayr, 1907 [Sick's Swift] (Marín 1997).

Chaetura spinicauda (Temminck). Band-rumped Swift.

> *Cypselus spinicaudus* Temminck, 1839, Planches Color., livr. 102, Tabl. Méth., p. 57. Based on "Hirondelle à queue pointue de Cayenne" Daubenton, Planches Enlum., pl. 726, fig. 1. (Cayenne.)

Habitat.—Tropical Lowland Evergreen Forest Edge, Secondary Forest (0–1000 m; Tropical and lower Subtropical zones).

Distribution.—*Resident* in southwestern Costa Rica (El General, Térraba, and Golfo Dulce regions) and Panama, and in South America from Colombia, Venezuela, Trinidad, and the Guianas south, west of the Andes to western Ecuador, and east of the Andes to Amazonian Brazil.

Chaetura cinereiventris Sclater. Gray-rumped Swift.

Chætura cinereiventris Sclater, 1862, Cat. Collect. Amer. Birds, p. 283. (Bahia, Brazil.)

Habitat.—Tropical Lowland Evergreen Forest, Montane Evergreen Forest, River-edge Forest, Secondary Forest (0–1800 m; Tropical and Subtropical zones).

Distribution.—*Resident* [*sclateri* group] in the Lesser Antilles (Grenada), from the Caribbean slope of Nicaragua and Costa Rica south to western Panama (western Bocas del Toro), and in South America from Colombia, Venezuela, Trinidad, and the Guianas south, at least locally, west of the Andes to western Ecuador, and east of the Andes to northern Bolivia and Amazonian Brazil; and [*cinereiventris* group] in northeastern Argentina and southeastern Brazil.

Notes.—Groups: *C. sclateri* Pelzeln, 1916 [Ash-rumped Swift] and *C. cinereiventris* [Gray-rumped Swift]. *Chaetura cinereiventris* and *C. martinica* constitute a superspecies (Sibley and Monroe 1990).

Chaetura martinica (Hermann). Lesser Antillean Swift.

Hirundo martinica Hermann, 1783, Tabula Affinit. Anim., p. 229. (Martinique, West Indies.)

Habitat.—Tropical Lowland Evergreen Forest, Secondary Forest (0–1000 m).

Distribution.—*Resident* in the Lesser Antilles (Guadeloupe, Dominica, Martinique, St. Lucia, and St. Vincent); doubtfully recorded from Nevis (sight report). Reports from Trinidad are erroneous, being based on specimens actually taken on Dominica.

Notes.—See comments under *C. cinereiventris*.

Genus *HIRUNDAPUS* Hodgson

Hirund-apus Hodgson, 1837, J. Asiat. Soc. Bengal 5 (1836): 780. Type, by original designation, *Cypselus (Chaetura) nudipes* Hodgson.

Hirundapus caudacutus (Latham). White-throated Needletail.

Hirundo caudacuta Latham, 1802, Index Ornithol., suppl. (1801), p. 57. (Nova Hollandia = New South Wales, Australia.)

Habitat.—Montane forest; nests in hollow trees; in migration and winter in forested and open regions.

Distribution.—*Breeds* in the Himalayas and from Siberia south to Mongolia, Manchuria, Korea, and Japan, and *winters* from India and Taiwan south to Australia and Tasmania.

Casual in the western Aleutians (Attu, Shemya), Europe, the Shetland Islands, and New Zealand.

Notes.—Also known as White-throated Needle-tailed Swift.

Genus **AERODRAMUS** Oberholser

Aerodramus Oberholser, 1906, Proc. Acad. Nat. Sci. Philadelphia 58: 179, 182. Type, by original designation, *Collocalia innominata* Hume = *Hirundo fuciphaga* Thunberg.

Notes.—We follow Lee et al. (1996) in maintaining the genus *Aerodramus*; see also Browning (1993).

Aerodramus bartschi (Mearns). Guam Swiftlet.

> *Collocalia bartschi* Mearns, 1909, Proc. U. S. Nat. Mus., 36, p. 476. (Guam.)

Habitat.—Steep valleys on tropical islands; nests in caves or behind waterfalls.

Distribution.—*Resident* on the island of Guam, at least formerly, and in the northern Mariana Islands (Saipan, Tinian, Agiguan, formerly Rota). Introduced (in 1962) and established in Hawaii (Halava Valley, Oahu, breeding in 1989).

Notes.—Formerly (A.O.U. 1983) treated as part of the species *A. vanikorensis,* but Browning (1993) has shown that the species in the A.O.U. area is distinct, and has presented evidence that the species is established where introduced in Hawaii.

Subfamily APODINAE: Apodine Swifts

Genus *APUS* Scopoli

> *Apus* Scopoli, 1777, Introd. Hist. Nat., p. 483. Type, by tautonymy, *Hirundo apus* Linnaeus.
> *Tachymarptis* Roberts, 1922, Ann. Transvaal Mus., 8, p. 216. Type, by original designation, *Hirundo melba* Linnaeus.

Apus apus (Linnaeus). Common Swift.

> *Hirundo Apus* Linnaeus, 1758, Syst. Nat. (ed. 10) 1: 192. (in Europæ altis = Sweden.)

Habitat.—Nests in tree cavities and in cliffs.

Distribution.—*Breeds* from northern Eurasia south to northern Africa, Arabia, Iraq, the Himalayas, and northeastern China, and *winters* in the southern half of Africa.

Accidental in Alaska (St. Paul Island, in the Pribilofs, 28 June 1950; Kenyon and Phillips 1965); a sight report from Barbados is questionable.

Notes.—Known in Old World literature as the Swift.

Apus pacificus (Latham). Fork-tailed Swift.

> *Hirundo pacifica* Latham, 1802, Index Ornithol., suppl., (1801) p. lviii. (Nova Hollandia = New South Wales, Australia.)

Habitat.—A wide variety of habitats from seacoasts to mountains, generally nesting in colonies on cliffs, and in caves, buildings or tree cavities.

Distribution.—*Breeds* from eastern Siberia and Kamchatka south to northern India, the Malay Peninsula, and southern China.

Winters from the Himalayas and Malay Peninsula south to New Guinea, Australia, and New Zealand.

Ranges casually (primarily in summer and fall) to the Pribilof (St. George, St. Paul) and western Aleutian (Attu, Agattu, Shemya) islands; a sight report from Middleton Island in the Gulf of Alaska.

Accidental in the Seychelles and Marshall Islands.

Notes.—Also known as White-rumped Swift, a name now generally restricted to the African species *A. caffer* (Lichtenstein, 1823).

Apus melba (Linnaeus). Alpine Swift.

> *Hirundo Melba* Linnaeus, 1758, Syst. Nat. (ed. 10) 1: 192. (ad fretum Herculeam = Gibraltar.)

Habitat.—Nests on cliffs and buildings.

Distribution.—*Breeds* from southern Europe and India south to southern Africa, Madagascar, and Sri Lanka, and *winters* generally throughout the breeding range, the northernmost populations being partly migratory.

Accidental in the Lesser Antilles (Barbados, September 1955, after a hurricane; Bond 1959: 11) and Puerto Rico (9 July 1987, photograph; 1987, Amer. Birds 41: 1492); a sight report for St. Lucia.

Notes.—Sometimes placed in the genus *Tachymarptis* (Sibley and Monroe 1990).

Genus *AERONAUTES* Hartert

Aëronautes Hartert, 1892, Cat. Birds Br. Mus. 16: xiii, 436, 459. Type, by monotypy, *Cypselus melanoleucus* Baird = *Acanthylis saxatalis* Woodhouse.

Aeronautes saxatalis (Woodhouse). White-throated Swift.

Acanthylis saxatalis Woodhouse, 1853, in Sitgreaves, Rep. Exped. Zuni Colo. Rivers, p. 64. (Inscription Rock, New Mexico.)

Habitat.—Primarily mountainous country, especially near cliffs and canyons, foraging over forest and open situations; nests in cliffs, occasionally in buildings and on seacliffs (Subtropical and Temperate zones).

Distribution.—*Breeds* from extreme south-central British Columbia, Idaho, Montana, and southwestern South Dakota south through the Pacific and southwestern states (including the Channel Islands off California) to southern Baja California (a questionable sight record of nesting on Guadalupe Island in 1892, unreported there since 1922), east to western Nebraska, northeastern and central New Mexico, and western Texas (to Val Verde County), and south through the interior of Mexico to Guatemala, El Salvador, and Honduras.

Winters from central California, central Arizona, and, rarely, southern New Mexico (casually farther north) south to the limits of the breeding range in Middle America.

Casual in Kansas and eastern and southern Texas. Accidental in coastal British Columbia, Missouri (Cape Giraudeau), Arkansas (Hot Springs), and Michigan; sight reports for North Dakota and the Dominican Republic.

Genus *PANYPTILA* Cabanis

Panyptila Cabanis, 1847, Arch. Naturgesch. 13: 345. Type, by original designation, *Hirundo cayennensis* Gmelin.

Panyptila cayennensis (Gmelin). Lesser Swallow-tailed Swift.

Hirundo cayennensis Gmelin, 1789, Syst. Nat. 1(2): 1024. Based on "Le Martinet à collier blanc" Buffon, Hist. Nat. Ois. 6: 671, and "Martinet à collier de Cayenne" Daubenton, Planches Enlum., pl. 725, fig. 2. (in Cayenna = Cayenne.)

Habitat.—Tropical Lowland Evergreen Forest, Secondary Forest (0–1200 m; Tropical Zone).

Distribution.—*Resident* from southern Veracruz, northern Oaxaca, and Chiapas (both slopes) south locally on the Caribbean slope of Belize, Guatemala (also Pacific slope), Honduras, and Nicaragua, in Costa Rica (Caribbean slope, and Golfo Dulce region on the Pacific), and Panama (both slopes), and in South America from Colombia, Venezuela, Tobago, Trinidad, and the Guianas south, west of the Andes to northwestern Peru, and east of the Andes to northern Bolivia and east-central Brazil.

Notes.—Also known as Cayenne Swift.

Panyptila sanctihieronymi Salvin. Great Swallow-tailed Swift.

Panyptila sancti-hieronymi Salvin, 1863, Proc. Zool. Soc. London, p. 190, pl. 23. (San Geronimo, [Baja] Verapaz, Guatemala.)

Habitat.—Montane Evergreen Forest, Pine Forest, Secondary Forest, Arid Montane Scrub (900–1850 m; Subtropical and Temperate zones).

Distribution.—*Resident* in the highlands and Pacific slope of Nayarit, Jalisco, Colima, Michoacán, México, Guerrero, Oaxaca, Chiapas, Guatemala, and Honduras.

Casual in north-central Nicaragua (El Corozo, Nueva Segovia); sight reports for Costa Rica.

Notes.—Also known as Geronimo Swift.

Genus *TACHORNIS* Gosse

Tachornis Gosse, 1847, Birds Jamaica, p. 58 (footnote). Type, by monotypy, *Tachornis phoenicobia* Gosse.

Tachornis phoenicobia Gosse. Antillean Palm-Swift.

Tachornis phœnicobia Gosse, 1847, Birds Jamaica, p. 58 (footnote). (Jamaica.)

Habitat.—Low Seasonally Wet Grassland, Second-growth Scrub; nests in colonies in palm trees.

Distribution.—*Resident* on Cuba, the Isle of Pines, Hispaniola (including Saona and Beata islands, and île-à-Vache), and Jamaica.

Accidental in the Florida Keys (Key West), July–August 1972 (Robertson and Woolfenden 1992); a sight report for Puerto Rico.

Family **TROCHILIDAE**: Hummingbirds

Notes.—For recognition of subfamilies, see Bleiweiss et al. (1994).

Subfamily PHAETHORNITHINAE: Hermits

Genus *GLAUCIS* Boie

Glaucis Boie, 1831, Isis von Oken, col. 545. Type, by subsequent designation (G. R. Gray, 1840), *G. braziliensis* (Lath.) = *Trochilus hirsutus* Gmelin.

Notes.—Gill and Gerwin (1989), based on allozyme data, recommended the merger of *Threnetes* into *Glaucis*.

Glaucis aenea Lawrence. Bronzy Hermit.

Glaucis æneus Lawrence, 1868, Proc. Acad. Nat. Sci. Philadelphia 19 (1867): 232. (Costa Rica.)

Habitat.—Tropical Lowland Evergreen Forest, Secondary Forest (0–800 m; Tropical Zone).

Distribution.—*Resident* from the Caribbean slope of Nicaragua south through Costa Rica (both slopes) to western Panama (Bocas del Toro, Chiriquí, western Veraguas); and the Pacific lowlands of Colombia and northwestern Ecuador.

Notes.—*Glaucis aenea* and *G. hirsuta* are closely related and constitute a superspecies (Sibley and Monroe 1990).

Glaucis hirsuta (Gmelin). Rufous-breasted Hermit.

Trochilus hirsutus Gmelin, 1788, Syst. Nat. 1(1): 490. Based in part on "Le Colibry du Brésil" Brisson, Ornithologie 3: 670. (in Brasilia = northeastern Brazil.)

Habitat.—Tropical Lowland Evergreen Forest, Secondary Forest, River-edge Forest (0–1100 m; Tropical Zone).

Distribution.—*Resident* from central and eastern Panama (from Coclé and western Panamá province eastward), eastern Colombia, Venezuela, Trinidad, Tobago, and the Guianas south, east of the Andes, to central Bolivia and central Brazil; and in the Lesser Antilles on Grenada.

Notes.—See comments under *G. aenea*.

Genus *THRENETES* Gould

Threnetes Gould, 1852, Monogr. Trochil., pt. 4, pl. [14 and 15]. Type, by subsequent designation (G. R. Gray, 1855), *Trochilus leucurus* Linnaeus.

Notes.—See note under *Glaucis*.

Threnetes ruckeri (Bourcier). Band-tailed Barbthroat.

> *Trochilus Ruckeri* Bourcier, 1847, Proc. Zool. Soc. London, p. 46. (No locality given = Esmeraldas, Ecuador.)

Habitat.—Tropical Lowland Evergreen Forest, Secondary Forest (0–1050 m; Tropical Zone).

Distribution.—*Resident* on the Caribbean slope of southern Belize, eastern Guatemala, Honduras, and Nicaragua, and in Costa Rica (both slopes, except dry northwest), Panama, Colombia, western Venezuela, and western Ecuador.

Notes.—*Threnetes ruckeri* and the South American *T. leucurus* (Linnaeus, 1766) constitute a superspecies.

Genus *PHAETHORNIS* Swainson

> *Phæthornis* Swainson, 1827, Philos. Mag.(n.s.) 1: 441. Type, by original designation, "*Troch. superciliosus* of Authors" = *Trochilus superciliosus* Linnaeus.
> *Pygmornis* Bonaparte, 1854, Rev. Mag. Zool. (2)6: 250. Type, by monotypy, *Trochilus intermedius* Lesson = *Trochilus longuemareus* Lesson.

Phaethornis guy (Lesson). Green Hermit.

> *Trochilus Guy* Lesson, 1833, Les Trochil., p. 119, Index, p. xiv. (Brazil, error = Venezuela.)

Habitat.—Montane Evergreen Forest (800–2000 m, locally to 350 m; upper Tropical and Subtropical zones).

Distribution.—*Resident* in the mountains of Costa Rica, Panama, and South America from Colombia, northern Venezuela, and Trinidad south on western slope of the Andes to western Colombia and on eastern slope to southern Peru.

Phaethornis superciliosus (Linnaeus). Long-tailed Hermit.

> *Trochilus superciliosus* Linnaeus, 1766, Syst. Nat. (ed. 12) 1: 189. Based on "Le Colibry a longue queue de Cayenne" Brisson, Ornithologie 3: 686, pl. 35, fig. 5. (in Cayania = Cayenne.)

Habitat.—Tropical Lowland Evergreen Forest, Montane Evergreen Forest, Tropical Deciduous Forest (0–1400 m; Tropical and lower Subtropical zones).

Distribution.—*Resident* [*griseoventer* group] in western Mexico from west-central Nayarit (near Tepic and San Blas) south to Jalisco (Sierra de Autlán, Mineral San Sebastian) and Colima (Cerro Grande); [*mexicanus* group] in Guerrero and western Oaxaca; [*longirostris* group] on the Gulf-Caribbean slope from Veracruz, Tabasco, northern Oaxaca, and Chiapas (Arroyo de la Playas, Palenque) south through Central America to Nicaragua, on both slopes of Costa Rica and Panama, and in northern Colombia and northwestern Venezuela; [*baroni* group] in South America west of the Andes in western Ecuador and northwestern Peru; and [*superciliosus* group] in South America east of the Andes from northern Colombia and southern Venezuela south to central Bolivia and Amazonian Brazil.

Notes.—Groups: *P. griseoventer* Phillips, 1962 [Jalisco Hermit], *P. mexicanus* Hartert, 1897 [Hartert's Hermit], *P. longirostris* DeLattre, 1843 [Long-tailed Hermit], *P. baroni* Hartert, 1897 [Baron's Hermit], and *P. superciliosus* [Rusty-breasted Hermit]. At least the three northern groups should probably be treated as species; Howell and Webb (1995) treated *griseoventer* and *mexicanus* together as a species under the latter name. Hinckelmann (1996) recognized all Central American populations as *P. longirostris,* distinct from *superciliosus* and *baroni.*

Phaethornis anthophilus (Bourcier). Pale-bellied Hermit.

> *Trochilus anthophilus* Bourcier, 1843, Rev. Zool. [Paris] 6: 71. (la vallée supérieure de la Madeleine, région tempérée, la Colombie = upper Magdalena Valley, Colombia.)

Habitat.—Tropical Lowland Evergreen Forest, Secondary Forest (0–900 m; Tropical and lower Subtropical zones).

Distribution.—*Resident* from eastern Panama (eastern San Blas, eastern Panamá province) east through northern Colombia to northern Venezuela.

Phaethornis longuemareus (Lesson). Little Hermit.

> *Trochilus Longuemareus* Lesson, 1832, Les Trochil., p. 15; 1833, p. 160, pl. 2, 62. (Cayenne.)

Habitat.—Tropical Lowland Evergreen Forest, Secondary Forest (0–1200 m; Tropical and lower Subtropical zones).

Distribution.—*Resident* [*adolphi* group] on the Gulf-Caribbean slope of Middle America from Veracruz, northern Oaxaca, Tabasco, Chiapas, Campeche, and Quintana Roo south through Belize and eastern Guatemala to Honduras, on both slopes in Nicaragua (rare on Pacific slope), Costa Rica (rare in dry northwest), and Panama, and in western Colombia and western Ecuador; and [*longuemareus* group] in South America from northern Colombia, Venezuela, and Trinidad south, east of the Andes, to central Peru and Amazonian Brazil.

Notes.—The groups perhaps should be recognized as distinct species, *P. adolphi* Gould, 1857 [Boucard's Hermit] and *P. longuemareus* [Little Hermit]. These forms belong to a well defined group of small species (Gill and Gerwin 1989) that may be recognizable at the generic level as *Pygmornis* Bonaparte, 1854 (as treated by Howell and Webb 1995).

Genus *EUTOXERES* Reichenbach

> *Eutoxeres* Reichenbach, 1849, Avium Syst. Nat., pl. XL [generic description only]; species added, Gould, 1851, Monogr. Trochil., pt. 2, pl. [5 and 6]. Type, by subsequent designation (G. R. Gray, 1855), *Trochilus aquila* "Lodd." = Bourcier.

Eutoxeres aquila (Bourcier). White-tipped Sicklebill.

> *Trochilus Aquila* (Loddiges MS) Bourcier, 1847, Proc. Zool. Soc. London, p. 42. (Nouvelle Grenade, les environs de Bogota = vicinity of Bogotá, Colombia.)

Habitat.—Humid Montane, Tropical Lowland Evergreen Forest (0–2100 m; upper Tropical and lower Subtropical zones).

Distribution.—*Resident* from central Costa Rica south locally through Panama, and in South America on western slope of the Andes from western Colombia south to western Ecuador and on eastern slope from Colombia south to northern Peru.

Subfamily TROCHILINAE: Typical Hummingbirds

Genus *ANDRODON* Gould

> *Androdon* Gould, 1863, Ann. Mag. Nat. Hist. (3)12: 247. Type, by monotypy, *Androdon aequatorialis* Gould.

Androdon aequatorialis Gould. Tooth-billed Hummingbird.

> *Androdon æquatorialis* Gould, 1863, Ann. Mag. Nat. Hist. (3) 12: 247. (Ecuador.)

Habitat.—Montane Evergreen Forest, Tropical Lowland Evergreen Forest (750–1550 m; Tropical and Subtropical zones).

Distribution.—*Resident* from eastern Panama (eastern Darién) and Colombia (east to Magdalena Valley) south along the Pacific coast to northwestern Ecuador.

Genus *DORYFERA* Gould

> *Doryfera* Gould, 1847, Proc. Zool. Soc. London, p. 95. Type, by subsequent designation (G. R. Gray, 1855), *Trochilus ludovicae* Bourcier and Mulsant.
> *Helianthea* α *Hemistephania* Reichenbach, 1854, J. Ornithol. 1 (Beil. zu Extrah.): 12. Type, by monotypy, *Trochilus ludovicæ* Bourcier and Mulsant.

Doryfera ludovicae (Bourcier and Mulsant). Green-fronted Lancebill.

> *Trochilus ludovicæ* Bourcier and Mulsant, 1847, Ann. Sci. Phys. Nat. Agric. Ind. Soc. R., etc., Lyon 10: [136]. (Colombia = Buena Vista, 4500 feet, Eastern Andes above Villavicencio, Colombia.)

Habitat.—Montane Evergreen Forest, usually associated with rushing streams and waterfalls (750–2800 m; Subtropical Zone).

Distribution.—*Resident* in the highlands of central Costa Rica (primarily the Caribbean slope of the Cordillera Central), Panama (Chiriquí, Veraguas, eastern Darién), and in the Andes of South America from Colombia and western Venezuela south to northern Bolivia.

Genus *PHAEOCHROA* Gould

> *Phæochroa* Gould, 1861, Introd. Trochil., p. 54. Type, by subsequent designation (Elliot, 1879), *Trochilus cuvierii* DeLattre and Bourcier.

Phaeochroa cuvierii (DeLattre and Bourcier). Scaly-breasted Hummingbird.

> *Trochilus Cuvierii* DeLattre and Bourcier, 1846, Rev. Zool. [Paris] 9: 310. (isthme de Panama et Teleman, Amérique centrale.)

Habitat.—Secondary Forest, Second-growth Scrub, Tropical Lowland Evergreen Forest (0–1200 m; Tropical Zone).

Distribution.—*Resident* [*roberti* group] on the Caribbean slope from eastern Chiapas, northern Guatemala, and Belize south to northeastern Costa Rica (Puerto Viejo de Sarapiquí); and [*cuvierii* group] from central Costa Rica (primarily on the Pacific slope) south through Panama (both slopes) to northern Colombia.

Notes.—Groups: *P. roberti* (Salvin, 1861) [Robert's Hummingbird] and *P. cuvierii* [Cuvier's Hummingbird].

Genus *CAMPYLOPTERUS* Swainson

> *Campylopterus* Swainson, 1827, Zool. J. 3: 358. Type, by subsequent designation (G. R. Gray, 1840), *C. latipennis* (Lath.) = *Trochilus largipennis* Boddaert.
>
> *Pampa* Reichenbach, 1854, J. Ornithol. 1 (Beil. zu Beitr.): 11. Type, by monotypy, *P. campyloptera* Reichenbach = *Ornismya pampa* Lesson = *Trochilus curvipennis* Deppe.

Campylopterus curvipennis (Deppe). Wedge-tailed Sabrewing.

> *Trochilus curvipennis* "Lichtenst[ein]." W. Deppe, 1830, Preis.-Verz. Säugeth. Vögel, etc., Mex., p. 1, no. 32. (Mexico.)

Habitat.—Tropical Lowland Evergreen Forest, Secondary Forest (0–1400 m; Tropical and lower Subtropical zones).

Distribution.—*Resident* [*curvipennis* group] on the Gulf-Caribbean slope from southeastern San Luis Potos' and southern Tamaulipas south through Veracruz and northeastern Puebla to northern Oaxaca; and [*pampa* group] in the Yucatan Peninsula, Tabasco, northeastern Chiapas, Guatemala (Péten and Alta Verapaz), Belize, and eastern Honduras (Olancho).

Notes.—Also known as Curve-winged Sabrewing. Groups: *C. curvipennis* [Curve-winged Sabrewing] and *C. pampa* (Lesson, 1832) [Wedge-tailed Sabrewing]. *Campylopterus curvipennis* and *C. excellens* may be conspecific; they constitute a superspecies (Sibley and Monroe 1990). Further study of this complex is needed.

Campylopterus excellens (Wetmore). Long-tailed Sabrewing.

> *Pampa pampa excellens* Wetmore, 1941, Proc. Biol. Soc. Wash. 54: 207. (Volcán san Martín, 3300 feet, Tuxtla Mountains, Vera Cruz, México.)

Habitat.—Tropical Lowland Evergreen Forest, Montane Evergreen Forest (0–1050 m; Tropical and lower Subtropical zones).

Distribution.—*Resident* in southern Veracruz (Sierra de los Tuxtlas and Jesús Carranza) and northwestern Chiapas.

Notes.—Recognition of *C. excellens* as a distinct species follows Lowery and Dalquest (1951). See comments under *C. curvipennis*.

Campylopterus rufus Lesson. Rufous Sabrewing.

> *Campylopterus rufus* Lesson, 1840, Rev. Zool. [Paris] 3: 73. (No locality given = Guatemala.)

Habitat.—Montane Evergreen Forest, Secondary Forest (950–2000 m; upper Tropical and Subtropical zones).

Distribution.—*Resident* in southeastern Oaxaca (Sierra Madre de Chiapas), Chiapas, central Guatemala, and El Salvador. Records from Oaxaca west of the Isthmus of Tehuantepec are doubtful (Binford 1989).

Campylopterus hemileucurus (Deppe). Violet Sabrewing.

> *Trochilus hemileucurus* "Lichtenst[ein]." W. Deppe, 1830, Preis.-Verz. Säugeth. Vögel, etc., Mex., p. 1, no. 33. (Mexico.)

Habitat.—Montane Evergreen Forest (900–2400 m; upper Tropical and Subtropical, occasionally lower Tropical zones).

Distribution.—*Resident* in the foothills and highlands of Middle America from southern Mexico (Guerrero, Veracruz, Oaxaca, Tabasco, and Chiapas) and Belize south to western Panama (Chiriquí, Veraguas, Herrera, Los Santos), ranging in nonbreeding season to lower elevations, occasionally to sea level.

Genus *FLORISUGA* Bonaparte

> *Florisuga* Bonaparte, March 1850, Consp. Gen. Avium 1(1): 73. Type, by subsequent designation (Bonaparte, April 1850), *Trochilus mellivorus* Linnaeus.

Florisuga mellivora (Linnaeus). White-necked Jacobin.

> *Trochilus mellivorus* Linnaeus, 1758, Syst. Nat. (ed. 10) 1: 121. Based on "The White-belly'd Humming Bird" Edwards, Nat. Hist. Birds 1: 35, pl. 35, upper fig. (in India, error = Surinam.)

Habitat.—Tropical Lowland Evergreen Forest, Secondary Forest, Tropical Deciduous Forest (0–900 m; Tropical and, locally, lower Subtropical zones).

Distribution.—*Resident* on the Gulf-Caribbean slope of Middle America from southern Veracruz and northern Oaxaca south through Chiapas, northern Guatemala, and Belize to Honduras, on both slopes of Nicaragua, Costa Rica (rare in dry northwest), and Panama, and in South America from Colombia, Venezuela, Trinidad, Tobago, and the Guianas south, west of the Andes to western Ecuador and east of the Andes to central Bolivia and Amazonian Brazil.

Accidental in the southern Lesser Antilles (Carriacou) and Netherlands Antilles (Aruba, Curaçao).

Genus *COLIBRI* Spix

> *Colibri* Spix, 1824, Avium Spec. Nov. Bras. 1: 80. Type, by subsequent designation (G. R. Gray, 1855), *Trochilus serrirostris* Vieillot.

Colibri delphinae (Lesson). Brown Violet-ear.

> *Ornismya Delphinæ* Lesson, 1839, Rev. Zool. [Paris] 2: 44. (No locality given = Santa Fé de Bogotá, Colombia.)

Habitat.—Montane Evergreen Forest, Secondary Forest, Tropical Lowland Evergreen Forest (600–2500 m; Upper Tropical and Subtropical zones).

Distribution.—*Resident* locally in foothills on the Caribbean slope of Middle America from southern Belize and eastern Guatemala south to Costa Rica and Panama (locally in highlands on both slopes), and locally in South America from Colombia, Venezuela, Trinidad, and the Guianas south, on the western slope of the Andes to northwestern Ecuador and on the eastern slope to central Bolivia, also widely scattered records in northern and eastern Brazil.

Colibri thalassinus (Swainson). Green Violet-ear.

> *Trochilus thalassinus* Swainson, 1827, Philos. Mag. (n.s.) 1: 441. (Temiscaltipec, Mexico = Temascaltepec, México.)

Habitat.—Secondary Forest, Second-growth Scrub (1400–3000 m; upper Tropical and Subtropical zones, in South America also Temperate Zone).

Distribution.—*Resident* [*thalassinus* group] from Jalisco, Guanajuato, San Luis Potosí, and Veracruz south through the highlands of southern Mexico and Belize to Guatemala, El Salvador, Honduras, and northwestern Nicaragua; and [*cyanotus* group] in the mountains of Costa Rica and western Panama (Chiriquí, Veraguas); and in montane South America from Colombia and northern Venezuela south in Western Andes to western Ecuador and in Eastern Andes to central Bolivia.

Ranges [*thalassinus* group] rarely north to Texas, casually to Arkansas (four records).

Accidental [*thalassinus* group] in Ontario, Michigan, Missouri, Alabama, and North Carolina (Asheville); sight reports for southern Baja California and Yucatán. Reports from California are not adequately documented.

Notes.—Groups: *C. thalassinus* [Green Violet-ear] and *C. cyanotus* Bourcier, 1843 [Mountain Violet-ear].

Genus *ANTHRACOTHORAX* Boie

> *Anthracothorax* Boie, 1831, Isis von Oken, col. 545. Type, by subsequent designation (Elliot, 1879), *Trochilus violicauda* Boddaert = *Trochilus viridigula* Boddaert.

Anthracothorax prevostii (Lesson). Green-breasted Mango.

> *Trochilus prevostii* Lesson, 1832, Hist. Nat. Colibris, livr. 13, p. 87, pl. 24. (No locality given = Veracruz, Mexico; Cory, 1918, Field Mus. Nat. Hist. Zool. Ser. 13.)

Habitat.—Secondary Forest, Gallery Forest, (0–1000 m; Tropical Zone).

Distribution.—*Resident* [*prevostii* group] from San Luis Potosí and southern Tamaulipas south to northern Oaxaca, Veracruz, and Chiapas, and along both slopes of Middle America (including the Yucatan Peninsula and larger islands offshore, Hunting Cay off Belize, the Bay Islands off Honduras, and on Providencia and San Andrés islands in the Caribbean Sea off Nicaragua) to central Costa Rica and northwestern Panama (Bocas del Toro), also in central and northeastern Colombia and northern Venezuela; and [*iridescens* group] in the arid Pacific lowlands from western Ecuador south to northwestern Peru. Northeasternmost populations in Mexico are migratory to southern Mexico.

Accidental [*prevostii* group] in southern Texas (Corpus Christi; 6–27 Jan. 1992; 1992, Amer. Birds 46: 289; photograph in DeBenedictis 1994b).

Notes.—Also known as Prevost's Mango. The *iridescens* group may be a species, *A. iridescens* (Gould, 1861) [Ecuadorian Mango], or (e.g., Hilty and Brown 1986) a subspecies of *A. nigricollis* (Sibley and Monroe 1990). *Anthracothorax nigricollis, A. veraguensis,* and *A. prevostii* are closely related and constitute a superspecies.

Anthracothorax nigricollis (Vieillot). Black-throated Mango.

> *Trochilus nigricollis* Vieillot, 1817, Nouv. Dict. Hist. Nat. (nouv. éd.) 7: 349. (Brazil.)

Habitat.—Secondary Forest, Gallery Forest, Tropical Lowland Evergreen Forest Edge, Second-growth Scrub (0–1000 m; Tropical and lower Subtropical zones).

Distribution.—*Resident* in central and eastern Panama (from the Canal area eastward), and in South America from Colombia, Venezuela, Tobago, Trinidad, and the Guianas south, east of the Andes, to central Bolivia, Paraguay, and northeastern Argentina.

Notes.—See comments under *A. prevostii.*

Anthracothorax veraguensis Reichenbach. Veraguan Mango.

Anthracothorax veraguensis Reichenbach, 1855, Trochil. Enum., p. 9, pl. 794, fig. 4848. (Veragua, designated as David, Chiriquí, by Wetmore, 1968, Smiths. Misc. Coll. 150, pt. 2, p. 292.)

Habitat.—Secondary Forest, Gallery Forest (Tropical Zone).

Distribution.—*Resident* in the Pacific lowlands of western Panama (possibly also southwestern Costa Rica) from Chiriquí east to southern Coclé, and on the Caribbean slope in Bocas del Toro and the Canal area.

Notes.—Formerly treated as a subspecies of *A. prevostii,* but see Olson (1993a). See comments under *A. prevostii.*

Anthracothorax dominicus (Linnaeus). Antillean Mango.

Trochilus dominicus Linnaeus, 1766, Syst. Nat. (ed. 12) 1: 191. Based on "Le Colibry de S. Domingue" Brisson, Ornithologie 3: 672, pl. 35, fig. 4. (in Dominica = Hispaniola.)

Habitat.—Tropical Lowland Evergreen Forest, Tropical Deciduous Forest, Secondary Forest (0–1500 m).

Distribution.—*Resident* on Hispaniola (including Gonâve, Tortue, and Beata islands, and île-à-Vache), central and western Puerto Rico (including Vieques, Culebra, and Culebrita islands), and the Virgin Islands (Anegada, formerly on St. Thomas and St. John).

Anthracothorax viridis (Audebert and Vieillot). Green Mango.

Trochilus viridis Audebert and Vieillot, 1801, Ois. Dorés 1: 34, pl. 15. (îles de l'Amérique Septentrionale = Puerto Rico.)

Habitat.—Tropical Lowland Evergreen Forest, Secondary Forest (0–900 m).

Distribution.—*Resident* on Puerto Rico. Accidental in the Virgin Islands (St. Thomas).

Anthracothorax mango (Linnaeus). Jamaican Mango.

Trochilus Mango Linnaeus, 1758, Syst. Nat. (ed. 10) 1: 121. Based on Mellivora mango Albin, Nat. Hist. Birds 2: 45, pl. 49, fig. 1. (in Jamaica.)

Habitat.—Tropical Lowland Evergreen Forest, Secondary Forest.

Distribution.—*Resident* on Jamaica.

Genus *EULAMPIS* Boie

Eulampis Boie, 1831, Isis von Oken, col. 547. Type, by subsequent designation (G. R. Gray, 1840), *E. aurata* (Audebert) i.e. Gmelin = *Trochilus jugularis* Linnaeus.

Anthracothorax γ *Sericotes* Reichenbach, 1854, J. Ornithol. 1 (Beil. zu Extrah.): 11. Type, by subsequent designation (G. R. Gray, 1855), *Trochilus holosericeus* Linnaeus.

Eulampis jugularis (Linnaeus). Purple-throated Carib.

Trochilus jugularis Linnaeus, 1766, Syst. Nat. (ed. 12) 1: 190. Based on the "Redbreasted Humming-bird" Edwards, Glean. Nat. Hist. 2: 118, pl. 266, fig. 1. (in Cayenna, Surinamo, error = Lesser Antilles.)

Habitat.—Tropical Lowland Evergreen Forest, Secondary Forest (0–1100 m).

Distribution.—*Resident* in the Lesser Antilles (Saba, St. Eustatius, St. Kitts, Nevis, Montserrat, Antigua, Guadeloupe, Dominica, Martinique, St. Lucia, and St. Vincent).

Casual in the Virgin Islands (St. Croix, St. John), Barbuda, Désirade, îles des Saintes, and Bequia; sight reports for Barbados and Grenada.

Notes.—Also known as Garnet-throated Hummingbird, a name now restricted to *Lamprolaima rhami.*

Eulampis holosericeus (Linnaeus). Green-throated Carib.

> *Trochilus holosericeus* Linnaeus, 1758, Syst. Nat. (ed. 10) 1: 120. Based on "The Black-belly'd Green Humming Bird" Edwards, Nat. Hist. Birds 1: 36, pl. 36. (in America = Lesser Antilles.)

Habitat.—Second-growth Scrub, Secondary Forest (0–900 m).

Distribution.—*Resident* in Puerto Rico (primarily eastern), the Virgin Islands, and Lesser Antilles (south to St. Vincent, Barbados, the northern Grenadines, and Grenada).

Accidental on Tobago (specimen, USNM).

Notes.—Also known as Emerald-throated Hummingbird. Formerly placed in the monotypic genus *Sericotes.*

Genus *CHRYSOLAMPIS* Boie

> *Chrysolampis* Boie, 1831, Isis von Oken, col. 546. Type, by subsequent designation (G. R. Gray, 1840), *Trochilus "moschita"* [= *mosquitus*] Linnaeus.

Chrysolampis mosquitus (Linnaeus). Ruby-topaz Hummingbird.

> *Trochilus Mosquitus* Linnaeus, 1758, Syst. Nat. (ed. 10) 1: 120. Based on Trochilus rectricibus æqualibus ferrugineis Linnaeus, Mus. Adolphi Friderici 2: [?]. (in Indiis, error = Surinam.)

Habitat.—Gallery Forest, Tropical Deciduous Forest, Low Seasonally Wet Grassland (0–1300 m).

Distribution.—*Resident* from Colombia, Venezuela (including islands from the Netherlands Antilles east to Tobago and Trinidad), and the Guianas south to extreme eastern Bolivia and southeastern Brazil (generally absent from Amazonia).

Accidental in Panama (El Real, Darién, 27 January 1985, photograph in VIREO; Braun and Wolf 1987). A sight report for Grenada.

Genus *ORTHORHYNCUS* Lacépède

> *Orthorhyncus* Lacépède, 1799, Tabl. Mamm. Ois., p. 9. Type, by subsequent designation (G. R. Gray, 1840), *Trochilus cristatus* Linnaeus.

Orthorhyncus cristatus (Linnaeus). Antillean Crested Hummingbird.

> *Trochilus cristatus* Linnaeus, 1758, Syst. Nat. (ed. 10) 1: 121. Based on "The Crested Humming Bird" Edwards, Nat. Hist. Birds 1: 37, pl. 37. (in America = Barbados, Lesser Antilles.)

Habitat.—Second-growth Scrub, Secondary Forest, Tropical Lowland Evergreen Forest (0–1000 m).

Distribution.—*Resident* in Puerto Rico (including on Vieques and Culebra islands), the Virgin Islands, and Lesser Antilles south to Grenada.

A specimen obtained in Texas (Galveston Island, February 1967; Pulich 1968) is of questionable origin (DeBenedictis 1992, T.O.S. 1995).

Genus *KLAIS* Reichenbach

> *Basilinna* ß *Klais* Reichenbach, 1854, J. Ornithol. 1 (Beil. zu Extrah.): 13. Type, by monotypy, *Trochilus guimeti* Bourcier.

Klais guimeti (Bourcier). Violet-headed Hummingbird.

Trochilus Guimeti Bourcier, 1843, Rev. Zool. [Paris] 6: 72. (à Caracas, capitale de Vénezuéla, la Colombie = Caracas, Venezuela.)

Habitat.—Montane Evergreen Forest, Tropical Lowland Evergreen Forest, Secondary Forest (300–1400 m; upper Tropical and Subtropical zones, rarely lower Tropical Zone).
Distribution.—*Resident* on the Caribbean slope of eastern Honduras (west to the Sula Valley) and Nicaragua, in Costa Rica (Caribbean slope and the Pacific southwest) and Panama (both slopes), and in South America from eastern Colombia and western and northern Venezuela south to central Bolivia and extreme western Brazil.

Genus *ABEILLIA* Bonaparte

Abeillia Bonaparte, 1850, Consp. Gen. Avium 1(1): 79. Type, by original designation, *Abeillia typica* Bonaparte = *Ornismya abeillei* Lesson and DeLattre.

Abeillia abeillei (DeLattre and Lesson). Emerald-chinned Hummingbird.

Ornismya Abeillei DeLattre and Lesson, *in* Lesson and DeLattre, 1839, Rev. Zool. [Paris] 2: 16. (Jalapa [Veracruz].)

Habitat.—Montane Evergreen Forest, Secondary Forest (1000–1850 m; Tropical and Subtropical zones).
Distribution.—*Resident* in the highlands from Veracruz, southeastern Oaxaca (Sierra Madre de Chiapas), and Chiapas south through the highlands of Guatemala, El Salvador, and western Honduras to north-central Nicaragua.

Genus *LOPHORNIS* Lesson

Lophornis Lesson, 1829, Hist. Nat. Ois.-Mouches, p. xxxvii. Type, by subsequent designation (G. R. Gray, 1840), *L. ornata* (L.) Less. Ois. M., pl. 41 = *Trochilus ornatus* Boddaert.
Paphosia Mulsant and J. and E. Verreaux, 1866, Mém. Soc. Imp. Sci. Nat. Cherbourg 12: 219. Type, by monotypy, *Ornismya helenae* DeLattre.

Lophornis brachylopha Moore. Short-crested Coquette.

Lophornis delattrei brachylopha Moore, 1949, Proc. Biol. Soc. Wash. 62: 103. (San Vicente de Benitez, altitude 1500 feet, Guerrero, México.)

Habitat.—Montane Evergreen Forest (500–1350 m; .
Distribution.—*Resident* locally in the Sierra Madre del Sur of Guerrero.
Notes.—Banks (1990b) provided rationale for treating *L. brachylopha* as a species distinct from *L. delattrei*.

Lophornis delattrei (Lesson). Rufous-crested Coquette.

Ornismya (Lophorinus) De Lattrei Lesson, 1839, Rev. Zool. [Paris] 2: 19. (No locality given = Peru.)

Habitat.—Secondary Forest, Tropical Lowland Evergreen Forest, Montane Evergreen Forest Edge (0–2000 m; Tropical and Subtropical zones).
Distribution.—*Resident* locally in central Costa Rica (San José region, known from four specimens; unrecorded since 1906) and Panama (throughout, but most frequent in central Panama); and the upper Magdalena Valley of Colombia and along the base of the Eastern Andes from northern Colombia to central Bolivia.

Lophornis helenae (DeLattre). Black-crested Coquette.

Ornismya Helenæ DeLattre, 1843, Rev. Zool. [Paris] 6: 133. (Vera-Pax, propte, Petinck in republica Guatimala = Vera Paz, Guatemala.)

Habitat.—Montane Evergreen Forest, Tropical Lowland Evergreen Forest, Secondary Forest (300–1450 m; Tropical and lower Subtropical zones).

Distribution.—*Resident* on the Gulf-Caribbean slope of Middle America from Veracruz, northern Oaxaca, and Chiapas (also Pacific slope) south to central Costa Rica (on Caribbean slope, vagrant to the vicinity of San José and the Pacific slope).

Reports from southern Texas are erroneous (T.O.S. 1995).

Notes.—This species and the following are often placed in the genus *Paphosia*.

Lophornis adorabilis Salvin. White-crested Coquette.

Lophornis adorabilis Salvin, 1870, Proc. Zool. Soc. London, p. 207. (Bugaba, Chiriquí, Panama.)

Habitat.—Tropical Lowland Evergreen Forest Edge, Secondary Forest, Second-growth Scrub (300–1200 m; upper Tropical and Subtropical zones).

Distribution.—*Resident* in central and southwestern Costa Rica (north to the Cordillera Central) and extreme western Panama (western Chiriquí); a report from Isla Cébaco, Panama, is considered doubtful.

Notes.—Also known as Adorable Coquette. See comments under *L. helenae*.

Genus *DISCOSURA* Bonaparte

Discosura Bonaparte, 1850, Consp. Gen. Avium. 1(1): 84. Type, by subsequent designation (G. R. Gray, 1855), *Trochilus longicaudus* Gmelin.
Popelairia Reichenbach, 1854, J. Ornithol. 1 (Beil. zu Extrah.): 12. Type, by monotypy, *Popelairia tricholopha* Reichenbach = *Trochilus popelairii* Du Bus de Gisignies.

Discosura conversii (Bourcier and Mulsant). Green Thorntail.

Trochilus Conversii Bourcier and Mulsant, 1846, Ann. Sci. Phys. Nat. Agric. Ind. Soc. R., etc., Lyon 9: 313, pl. [9]. (Bogotá, Colombia.)

Habitat.—Montane Evergreen Forest, Tropical Lowland Evergreen Forest Edge (700–1400 m; upper Tropical and Subtropical zones).

Distribution.—*Resident* in Costa Rica (Caribbean slope north to the Cordillera Central), locally in Panama (recorded eastern Chiriquí, Veraguas, Coclé, the Canal area, eastern Panamá province, and eastern Darién), and on the Pacific slope of western Colombia and western Ecuador.

Notes.—Often placed in the genus *Popelairia* Reichenbach, 1854 (e.g., Sibley and Monroe 1990).

Genus *CHLOROSTILBON* Gould

Chlorostilbon Gould, 1853, Monogr. Trochil., pt. 5, pl. [14] and text. Type, by monotypy, *Chlorostilbon prasinus* Gould (not other authors) = *Trochilus pucherani* Bourcier = *Ornismya aureo-ventris* d'Orbigny and Lafresnaye.
Chlorestes δ *Riccordia* Reichenbach, 1854, J. Ornithol. 1 (Beil. zu Extrah.): 8. Type, by subsequent designation (G. R. Gray, 1855), *Riccordia ramondii* Reichenbach = *Ornismya ricordii* Gervais.

Chlorostilbon auriceps (Gould). Golden-crowned Emerald.

Trochilus auriceps Gould, 1852, Jardine's Contr. Orn., p. 137. (Mexico.)

Habitat.—Second-growth Scrub, Secondary Forest, Tropical Deciduous Forest Edge (0–1800 m; Tropical and Subtropical zones).

Distribution.—*Resident* on the Pacific slope from Sinaloa south to southern Oaxaca (Waiat), and inland to southern Morelos.

Notes.—Formerly considered a subspecies of *C. canivetii,* but see Howell (1993). See comments under *C. canivetii.*

Chlorostilbon forficatus Ridgway. Cozumel Emerald.

Chlorostilbon forficatus Ridgway, 1885, Descr. New Species Birds, Cozumel Is., p. 3 (Cozumel Island, Yucatan.)

Habitat.—Second-growth Scrub, Secondary Forest (Tropical Zone).
Distribution.—*Resident* on Cozumel Island, rarely on Isla Mujeres, Quintana Roo, Mexico. Historical reports from Isla Holbox are unreliable.
Notes.—Formerly considered a subspecies of *C. canivetii,* but see Howell (1993). See comments under *C. canivetii.*

Chlorostilbon canivetii (Lesson). Canivet's Emerald.

Ornismya canivetii Lesson, 1832, Hist. Nat. Colibris, livr. 13, p. 174, pl. 37, 38. (Brésil, error = Jalapa, Veracruz.)

Habitat.—Tropical Deciduous Forest Edge, Second-growth Scrub, Secondary Forest, Tropical Lowland Evergreen Forest Edge (0–1900 m; Tropical and Subtropical zones).
Distribution.—*Resident* on the Gulf-Caribbean slope from San Luis Potosí and southern Tamaulipas south through northern and southeastern Oaxaca to northern Guatemala and Belize (including Holbox Island off the Yucatan peninsula, and the Bay and Hog islands off Honduras), and on both slopes of Middle America from southeastern Chiapas, western and southern Guatemala, El Salvador, and Honduras south to Nicaragua and northern Costa Rica (primarily Guanacaste, but also to central plateau region).
Notes.—This species formerly included *C. auriceps* and *C. forficatus*; the complex was known as Fork-tailed Emerald. It presently incudes *C. osberti* Gould, 1860, and *C. salvini* Cabanis and Heine, 1860, which Howell (1993) recommended combining as a species, *C. salvini* [Salvin's Emerald]. The expanded *C. canivetii* sometimes (Eisenmann 1955) includes *C. assimilis,* and that complex along with several South American forms has been merged (Meyer de Schauensee 1966) under the comprehensive name *C. mellisugus* (Linnaeus, 1758), Blue-tailed Emerald. See Stiles (1996a).

Chlorostilbon assimilis Lawrence. Garden Emerald.

Chlorostilbon assimilis Lawrence, 1861, Ann. Lyc. Nat. Hist. N. Y. 7: 292. (Atlantic side of the Isthmus of Panama, along the line of the Panama Railroad.)

Habitat.—Tropical Lowland Evergreen Forest Edge, Second-growth Scrub, Secondary Forest (0–800 m; Tropical and lower Subtropical zones).
Distribution.—*Resident* in southwestern Costa Rica (north to the Térraba region) and Panama (Pacific slope east to western Darién, including Coiba, Pearl, and many smaller islands), also Caribbean slope in Bocas del Toro and Canal area.
Notes.—Also known as Allied Emerald. See comments under *C. canivetii.*

Chlorostilbon ricordii (Gervais). Cuban Emerald.

Ornismya Ricordii Gervais, 1835, Mag. Zool. [Paris] 5: cl. 2, pl. 41, 42. (Santiago de Cuba = Santiago, Cuba.)

Habitat.—Tropical Lowland Evergreen Forest, Secondary Forest, Pine Forest (0–1200 m).
Distribution.—Resident in the Bahamas (Abaco, including offshore cays, Grand Bahama, Andros, and Green Cay), and on Cuba (including offshore cays) and the Isle of Pines.
Sight reports from southern and east-central Florida are unsubstantiated (DeBenedictis 1991, Robertson and Woolfenden 1992).

Chlorostilbon bracei (Lawrence). Brace's Emerald.

Sporadinus Bracei Lawrence, 1877, Ann. N. Y. Acad. Sci. 1: 50. (New Providence, Bahama Islands.)

Habitat.—Unknown.

Distribution.—EXTINCT; formerly *resident* on New Providence Island in the Bahamas (Abaco, where known from the type specimen only, although fossils from the type locality are probably referable to this species).

Notes.—For recognition of this form as a species, see Graves and Olson (1987).

Chlorostilbon swainsonii (Lesson). Hispaniolan Emerald.

Ornismya Swainsonii Lesson, 1829, Hist. Nat., Ois.-Mouches, p. "xvij" [= xvii]; 1830, p. 197, pl. 70. (le Brésil, error = Hispaniola.)

Habitat.—Montane Evergreen Forest, Tropical Lowland Evergreen Forest, Secondary Forest, Second-growth Scrub (0–2400 m).

Distribution.—*Resident* on Hispaniola; reports from Gonâve Island are unsubstantiated.

Chlorostilbon maugaeus (Audebert and Vieillot). Puerto Rican Emerald.

Trochilus Maugæus Audebert and Vieillot, 1801, Ois. Dorés 1: 77, 79, pl. 37, 38. (Puerto Rico.)

Habitat.—Montane Evergreen Forest, Tropical Lowland Evergreen Forest, Tropical Deciduous Forest, Secondary Forest, Second-growth Scrub (0–1000 m)

Distribution.—*Resident* on Puerto Rico.

Genus *CYNANTHUS* Swainson

Cynanthus Swainson, 1827, Philos. Mag. (n.s.) 1: 441. Type, by subsequent designation (Stone, 1907), *Cynanthus latirostris* Swainson.

Phæoptila Gould, 1861, Monogr. Trochil., pt. 5, text to pl. 340. Type, by original designation, *Cyanomyia sordida* Gould.

Cynanthus sordidus (Gould). Dusky Hummingbird.

Cyanomyia (?) *sordida* Gould, 1859, Ann. Mag. Nat. Hist. (3)4: 97. ([state of] Oaxaca, Mexico; Binford, 1989, Ornithol. Monogr. 43, p. 338.)

Habitat.—Arid Montane Scrub, Gallery Forest (900–2250 m; Subtropical and lower Temperate zones).

Distribution.—*Resident* from eastern Michoacán, México, and Morelos south to Oaxaca and Puebla.

Cynanthus latirostris Swainson. Broad-billed Hummingbird.

Cynanthus latirostris Swainson, 1827, Philos. Mag. (n.s.) 1: 441. (Tableland of Mexico = valley of México, near Mexico City.)

Habitat.—Tropical Deciduous Forest, Gallery Forest (0–2100 m; Tropical and lower Subtropical zones).

Distribution.—*Breeds* [*latirostris* group] from western Sonora, southeastern Arizona, southwestern New Mexico (Guadalupe Canyon), northern Chihuahua, western Texas (Brewster County, casually), and Tamaulipas south through Mexico (including the Tres Marias Islands) to northern Veracruz, Hidalgo, and Puebla.

Winters [*latirostris* group] from central Sonora, Chihuahua, and Tamaulipas south through the breeding range, casually north to southern Arizona.

Resident [*doubledayi* group] in the Pacific lowlands of southern Guerrero, southern Oaxaca, and western Chiapas.

Casual [*latirostris* group] north to Baja California, California (to Sonoma County), Utah, central Arizona, central and eastern Texas, and southern Louisiana; sight reports to southern Nevada and central New Mexico. Accidental in southern Ontario, Michigan, and Illinois; a sight report for South Carolina.

Notes.—Groups: *C. latirostris* [Broad-billed Hummingbird] and *C. doubledayi* (Bourcier, 1847) [Doubleday's Hummingbird]. Howell and Webb (1995) suggested that the two groups should be treated as species.

Genus *CYANOPHAIA* Reichenbach

Cyanophaia Reichenbach, 1854, J. Ornithol. 1 (Beil. zu Extrah.): 10. Type, by subsequent designation (G. R. Gray, 1855), *Trochilus bicolor* "Linn." [= Gmelin].

Cyanophaia bicolor (Gmelin). Blue-headed Hummingbird.

Trochilus bicolor Gmelin, 1788, Syst. Nat. 1(1): 496. Based in part on "Saphir-émer-
aude" Buffon, Hist. Nat. Ois. 6: 26, and the "Sapphire and Emerald Humming-bird"
Latham, Gen. Synop. Birds 1(2): 775. (in Guadeloupe, error = Dominica.)

Habitat.—Tropical Lowland Evergreen Forest, Secondary Forest (0–900 m).
Distribution.—*Resident* on Dominica and Martinique, in the Lesser Antilles.

Genus *THALURANIA* Gould

Thalurania Gould, 1848, Proc. Zool. Soc. London, p. 13. Type, by subsequent designation (G. R. Gray, 1855), *Trochilus furcatus* Gmelin.

Thalurania ridgwayi Nelson. Mexican Woodnymph.

Thalurania ridgwayi Nelson, 1900, Auk, 17, p. 262. (San Sebastian, Jalisco, México.)

Habitat.—Montane Evergreen Forest, Tropical Lowland Evergreen Forest, Secondary
Forest (200–2100 m).
Distribution.—Pacific slope of Nayarit, western Jalisco, and Colima.
Notes.—Escalante-Pliego and Peterson (1992) provided reasons for treating *T. ridgwayi*
and *T. fannyi* as species distinct from *T. colombica*.

Thalurania colombica (Bourcier). Violet-crowned Woodnymph.

Ornismya Colombica Bourcier, 1843, Rev. Zool. [Paris], 6, p. 2. (in Colombie = San
Agustín, Magdalena Valley, Colombia.)

Habitat.—Tropical Lowland Evergreen Forest, Secondary Forest, Montane Evergreen
Forest, Tropical Deciduous Forest (0–1900 m).
Distribution.—Lowlands [*townsendi* group] of Caribbean slope from Guatemala and Be-
lize south to Costa Rica and western and central Panama (east to Canal area and eastern
Panamá province); lowlands to 1900 m [*colombica* group] of northern Colombia and western
Venezuela.
Notes.—Groups: *T. townsendi* Ridgway, 1888 [Violet-crowned Woodnymph], and *T. col-
ombica* [Colombian Woodnymph]. See *Thalurania ridgwayi*.

Thalurania fannyi (DeLattre and Bourcier). Green-crowned Woodnymph.

Trochilus Fannyi DeLattre and Bourcier, 1846, Rev. Zool. [Paris], 9, p. 310. (Río Dagua,
near Buenaventura, Colombia.)

Habitat.—Tropical Deciduous Forest (0–800 m).
Distribution.—[*fannyi* group] eastern Panama (eastern Colón, Darién, and eastern San
Blas) and northwestern Colombia; and [*hypochlora* group] Pacific slope of southwestern
Colombia south to northwestern Peru.
Notes.—Groups: *T. fannyi* [Green-crowned Woodnymph], and *T. hypochlora* Gould 1871
[Emerald-bellied Woodnymph]. See *Thalurania ridgwayi*.

Genus *PANTERPE* Cabanis and Heine

Panterpe Cabanis and Heine, 1860, Mus. Heineanum 3: 43 (footnote). Type, by original
designation, *Panterpe insignis* Cabanis and Heine.

Panterpe insignis Cabanis and Heine. Fiery-throated Hummingbird.

> *Panterpe insignis* Cabanis and Heine, 1860, Mus. Heineanum 3: 43 (footnote). (Costa Rica.)

Habitat.—Montane Evergreen Forest Edge, Second-growth Scrub, Paramo Grassland (1400–3100 m; Subtropical and Temperate zones).
Distribution.—*Resident* in Costa Rica (cordilleras de Talamanca and Central) and western Panama (western Chiriquí and western Bocas del Toro).

Genus *DAMOPHILA* Reichenbach

> *Damophila* Reichenbach, 1854, J. Ornithol. 1 (Beil. zu Extrah.): 7. Type, by subsequent designation (Elliot, 1879), *T. julie* Bourcier = *Ornismyia julie* Bourcier.

Damophila julie (Bourcier). Violet-bellied Hummingbird.

> *Ornismyia Julie* Bourcier, 1842, Rev. Zool. [Paris] 5: 373. (Tunja en Colombie = Tunja, Colombia.)

Habitat.—Tropical Lowland Evergreen Forest Edge, Secondary Forest, Tropical Deciduous Forest (0–900 m; Tropical Zone).
Distribution.—*Resident* in central and eastern Panama (from northern Coclé and the Canal area eastward), western Colombia, and western Ecuador; specimens reported from "Costa Rica" are probably mislabeled (Stiles and Skutch 1989).

Genus *LEPIDOPYGA* Reichenbach

> *Agyrtria* γ *Lepidopyga* Reichenbach, 1855, Trochil. Enum., p. 7. Type, by subsequent designation (Ridgway, 1911), *Trochilus goudoti* Bourcier.

Lepidopyga coeruleogularis (Gould). Sapphire-throated Hummingbird.

> *Trochilus (———?) cæruleogularis* Gould, 1851, Proc. Zool. Soc. London (1850), p. 163. (Near David, on the north side of the Cordillera, Veragua [Chiriquí, Panama].)

Habitat.—Tropical Lowland Evergreen Forest Edge, Secondary Forest, Second-growth Scrub (0–700 m; Tropical Zone).
Distribution.—*Resident* in Panama (the Pacific lowlands from western Chiriquí eastward, including Isla Coiba, and the Caribbean lowlands in the Canal area and San Blas) and northern Colombia; an old specimen from "Costa Rica" is probably mislabeled, but there is a sight report from Costa Rica (Stiles and Skutch 1989).

Genus *HYLOCHARIS* Boie

> *Hylocharis* Boie, 1831, Isis von Oken, col. 546. Type, by subsequent designation (G. R. Gray, 1840), *H. sapphirina* (Gm.) Boie = *Trochilus sapphirinus* Gmelin.
> *Basilinna* Boie, 1831, Isis von Oken, col. 546. Type, by subsequent designation (G. R. Gray, 1855), *Trochilus leucotis* Vieillot.

Hylocharis grayi (DeLattre and Bourcier). Blue-headed Sapphire.

> *Trochilus Grayi* DeLattre and Bourcier, 1846, Rev. Zool. [Paris] 9: 307. (Popayán, Nouvelle-Grenade [= Colombia].)

Habitat.—Tropical Lowland Evergreen Forest Edge, Secondary Forest, Mangrove Forest (0–2000 m; Tropical and lower Subtropical zones).
Distribution.—*Resident* from extreme eastern Panama (near Jaque in southern Darién) south through western and central Colombia to northwestern Ecuador.

Hylocharis eliciae (Bourcier and Mulsant). Blue-throated Goldentail.

> *Trochilus Eliciæ* Bourcier and Mulsant, 1846, Ann. Sci. Phys. Nat. Agric. Ind. Soc. R., etc., Lyon 9: 314. (No locality given.)

Habitat.—Tropical Lowland Evergreen Forest, Gallery Forest, Secondary Forest (0–1100 m; Tropical and lower Subtropical zones).

Distribution.—*Resident* from Veracruz, Oaxaca, and Chiapas south along both slopes of Central America to Panama (including Isla Coiba) and northwestern Colombia (northwestern Chocó).

Hylocharis leucotis (Vieillot). White-eared Hummingbird.

> *Trochilus leucotis* Vieillot, 1818, Nouv. Dict. Hist. Nat. (nouv. éd.) 23: 428. (au Brésil, error = Orizaba, Veracruz.)

Habitat.—Pine Forest, Pine-Oak Forest (900–3100 m; Subtropical and Temperate zones).

Distribution.—*Resident* from southern Arizona, Sonora, Chihuahua, Coahuila, Nuevo León, and Tamaulipas south through the highlands of Mexico, Guatemala, El Salvador, and Honduras to north-central Nicaragua. Recorded irregularly in summer (and probably breeding) in the mountains of southwestern New Mexico (Animas Mountains) and western Texas (Big Bend, Guadalupe Mountains); northernmost populations are migratory southward.

Casual in southern Texas. Accidental in Mississippi.

Notes.—*Hylocharis leucotis* and *H. xantusii* may constitute a superspecies (Mayr and Short 1970). Howell and Webb (1995) placed these two species in the genus *Basilinna*.

Hylocharis xantusii (Lawrence). Xantus's Hummingbird.

> *Amazilia Xantusii* Lawrence, 1860, Ann. Lyc. Nat. Hist. N. Y. 7: 109. (Cape St. Lucas, South California = San Nicolás, 10 miles northeast of Cape San Lucas, Baja California.)

Habitat.—Arid Lowland Scrub, Arid Montane Scrub (0–1900 m; Tropical to Temperate zones).

Distribution.—*Resident* in southern Baja California, casually north to lat. 29° N., including islands in the Gulf of California north to Isla San José.

Accidental in California (Ventura, Anza-Borrego Desert); see Hainebach (1992).

Notes.—See comments under *H. leucotis*.

Genus *GOLDMANIA* Nelson

> *Goldmania* Nelson, 1911, Smithson. Misc. Collect. 56(21): 1. Type, by original designation, *Goldmania violiceps* Nelson.

Goldmania violiceps Nelson. Violet-capped Hummingbird.

> *Goldmania violiceps* Nelson, 1911, Smithson. Misc. Collect. 56(21): 1. (Cerro Azul, 3000 feet, northwest of Chepo, Panama.)

Habitat.—Tropical Lowland Evergreen Forest (600–1000 m; Subtropical Zone).

Distribution.—*Resident* in eastern Panama (eastern Colón, eastern Panamá province and eastern Darién) and extreme northwestern Colombia.

Genus *GOETHALSIA* Nelson

> *Goethalsia* Nelson, 1912, Smithson. Misc. Collect. 60(3): 6. Type, by original designation, *Goethalsia bella* Nelson.

Goethalsia bella Nelson. Rufous-cheeked Hummingbird.

> *Goethalsia bella* Nelson, 1912, Smithson. Misc. Collect. 60(3): 7. (Cana, at 2,000 feet altitude, eastern Panama.)

Habitat.—Montane Evergreen Forest (600–150 m; upper Tropical and Subtropical zones).

Distribution.—*Resident* in extreme eastern Panama (cerros Pirre and Sapo in eastern Darién) and adjacent northwestern Colombia (Alturas del Nique in Chocó).

Notes.—Also known as Pirre Hummingbird.

Genus *TROCHILUS* Linnaeus

Trochilus Linnaeus, 1758, Syst. Nat. (ed. 10) 1: 119. Type, by subsequent designation (G. R. Gray, 1840), *Trochilus polytmus* Linnaeus.

Trochilus polytmus Linnaeus. Streamertail.

Trochilus Polytmus Linnaeus, 1758, Syst. Nat. (ed. 10) 1: 120. Based mainly on *Polytmus* viridans aureo varie splendens, etc. Brown, Jamaica, p. 145, and the "Long-tailed Black-cap Humming Bird" Edwards, Nat. Hist. Birds 1: 34, pl. 34. (in America = Jamaica.)

Habitat.—Montane Evergreen Forest, Tropical Lowland Evergreen Forest, Secondary Forest (0–1500 m).

Distribution.—*Resident* [*polytmus* group] in western and central Jamaica (west of the Morant River); and [*scitulus* group] in eastern Jamaica (John Crow Mountains, and east of the Morant River).

Notes.—The two groups differ in bill color, display, and vocalizations, with an apparent narrow hybrid zone between them; some authors suggest that these be recognized as distinct species, *T. polytmus* [Western Streamertail] and *T. scitulus* (Brewster and Bangs, 1901) [Eastern Streamertail]. For discussions, see Schuchmann (1978) and Gill et al. (1973).

Genus *AMAZILIA* Lesson

Amazilia Lesson, 1843, Echo Monde Savant (2)7: col. 757. Type, by subsequent designation (Stone, 1918), *Ornismia cinnamomea* Less[on] (= *O. rutila* DeLattre) = *Ornismya rutila* DeLattre.

Saucerottia Bonaparte, 1850, Consp. Gen. Avium 1(1): 77. Type, by original designation, *Saucerottia typica* Bonaparte = *Trochilus saucerrottei* DeLattre and Bourcier.

Polyerata Heine, 1863, J. Ornithol. 11: 194. Type, by monotypy, *Trochilus amabilis* Gould.

Amazilia candida (Bourcier and Mulsant). White-bellied Emerald.

Trochilus candidus Bourcier and Mulsant, 1846, Ann. Sci. Phys. Nat. Agric. Ind. Soc. R., etc., Lyon 9: 326. (Cobán, Alta Verapaz, Guatemala.)

Habitat.—Tropical Lowland Evergreen Forest, Tropical Deciduous Forest (0–1600 m; Tropical and lower Subtropical zones).

Distribution.—*Resident* (mostly) from southeastern San Luis Potosí and northern Veracruz south along the Gulf-Caribbean slope of Middle America (including the Yucatan Peninsula, also Pacific lowlands of Chiapas and Guatemala) to Honduras, and Nicaragua, where also in north-central highlands, and, probably only as a vagrant, Costa Rica (south to Osa Peninsula). There are winter records for the Pacific slope of Oaxaca (Binford 1989).

Amazilia luciae (Lawrence). Honduran Emerald.

Thaumatias Luciæ Lawrence, 1867, Proc. Acad. Nat. Sci. Philadelphia 19: 233. (Honduras.)

Habitat.—Tropical Deciduous Forest (Tropical Zone).

Distribution.—*Resident* in Honduras (Caribbean lowlands from Cofradía east to Catacamas).

Amazilia amabilis (Gould). Blue-chested Hummingbird.

Trochilus (———?) amabilis Gould, 1853, Proc. Zool. Soc. London (1851), p. 115. (New Grenada = Colombia.)

Habitat.—Tropical Lowland Evergreen Forest Edge, Secondary Forest (Tropical and lower Subtropical zones).

Distribution.—*Resident* on the Caribbean slope of Nicaragua and Costa Rica, and in

Panama (Caribbean slope throughout, and Pacific slope from eastern Panamá province eastward), Colombia (east to the Magdalena Valley, and south along the Pacific coast) and western Ecuador.

Notes.—*Amazilia amabilis* and *A. decora* constitute a superspecies (Sibley and Monroe 1990).

Amazilia decora (Salvin). Charming Hummingbird.

Polyerata decora Salvin, 1891, Ann. Mag. Nat. Hist. (6)7: 377. (western slopes of the Volcano of Chiriqui [Panama].)

Habitat.—Tropical Lowland Evergreen Forest Edge, Secondary Forest (Tropical and lower Subtropical zones).

Distribution.—*Resident* on the Pacific slope of southwestern Costa Rica (El General-Térraba-Golfo Dulce region) and extreme western Panama (western Chiriquí).

Notes.—See comments under *A. amabilis*.

Amazilia boucardi (Mulsant). Mangrove Hummingbird.

Arena Boucardi Mulsant, 1877, Descr. Esp. Nouv. Trochil., p. 6. (Punta Arenas, Costa Rica.)

Habitat.—Mangrove Forest (Tropical Zone).

Distribution.—*Resident* on the Pacific coast of Costa Rica (Gulf of Nicoya to Golfo Dulce region).

Notes.—Also known as Boucard's Hummingbird.

Amazilia cyanocephala (Lesson). Azure-crowned Hummingbird.

Ornismya cyanocephalus Lesson, 1829, Hist. Nat. Ois.-Mouches, p. xlv. (Le Brésil, error = Veracruz, Veracruz.)

Habitat.—[*cyanocephala* group] Pine-Oak Forest, Pine Forest, Montane Evergreen Forest (600–1800 m); [*chlorostephana* group] lowland pine savanna (100 m); (Tropical and Subtropical zones).

Distribution.—*Breeds* [*cyanocephala* group] from southern Tamaulipas south, primarily in the foothills, through Veracruz, northern and southeastern Oaxaca, Chiapas, southern Quintana Roo, central and eastern Guatemala, Belize, El Salvador, and Honduras to north-central Nicaragua.

Resident [*chlorostephana* group] in Honduras and northeastern Nicaragua.

Winters [*cyanocephala* group] generally in the breeding range, occurring also in lowland habitats (recorded San Luis Potosí and Quintana Roo).

Notes.—Also known as Red-billed Azurecrown. Groups: *A. cyanocephala* [Azure-crowned Hummingbird] and *A. chlorostephana* Howell, 1965 [Mosquitia Hummingbird]. *Amazilia microrhyncha* (Elliot, 1876) [Small-billed Azurecrown], is now regarded as being based on an aberrant specimen of *A. cyanocephala* (Monroe 1968).

Amazilia cyanifrons (Bourcier). Indigo-capped Hummingbird.

Trochilus cyanifrons Bourcier, 1843, Rev. Zool. [Paris] 6: 100. (Ybagué, Nouvelle-Grenade = Ibague, Colombia.)

Habitat.—Secondary Forest, Montane Evergreen Forest Edge, Tropical Lowland Evergreen Forest Edge (400–2000 m; Tropical and Subtropical zones).

Distribution.—*Resident* in northern Colombia (Atlántico and the Magdalena Valley to Norte de Santander); one specimen known from northwestern Costa Rica (Volcán Miravalles).

Notes.—Also known as Blue-fronted Hummingbird. This form is known from Middle America only from the single specimen taken in Costa Rica and described as a new species, *A. alfaroana* Underwood, 1896. The type closely resembles *A. cyanifrons* and does not appear to be a hybrid between any Middle American species of *Amazilia*. The unique specimen of *alfaroana* is tentatively considered to represent a subspecies of *A. cyanifrons* (Stiles and Skutch 1989); its status can be clarified only by additional data.

Amazilia beryllina (Deppe). Berylline Hummingbird.

Trochilus beryllinus "Lichtenst[ein]." W. Deppe, 1830, Preis.-Verz. Sšugeth. Všgel, etc., Mex., p. 1. (México = Temascaltepec, México.)

Habitat.—Pine-Oak Forest, Pine Forest, Tropical Deciduous Forest, Secondary Forest (0–3100 m; Tropical and Subtropical zones).

Distribution.—*Resident* from southeastern Arizona (Huachuca Mountains), Sonora, and southern Chihuahua south through western Mexico (east to Durango, Guanajuato, Tlaxcala, Puebla, and west-central Veracruz), Guatemala, and El Salvador to central Honduras.

Accidental in southwestern New Mexico (Guadalupe Canyon); a sight report for western Texas.

Notes.—Hybridization between *A. beryllina* and *A. cyanura* had been reported from south-central Guatemala (Patulul) and El Salvador, but verification of hybridization is lacking (Howell and Webb 1995). *Amazilia sumichrasti* Salvin, 1891, is based on an individual of *A. beryllina* taken at Santa Efigenia, Oaxaca (Friedmann et al. 1950).

Amazilia cyanura Gould. Blue-tailed Hummingbird.

Amazilia cyanura Gould, 1859, Monogr. Trochil., pt. 18, pl. [12] and text. (Realejo, Nicaragua.)

Habitat.—Secondary Forest, Tropical Deciduous Forest, Tropical Lowland Evergreen Forest Edge (0–1500 m; Tropical and lower Subtropical zones).

Distribution.—*Resident* on the Pacific slope from central Chiapas to western Nicaragua (also locally on the Caribbean slope of Honduras).

Casual in Costa Rica (near San José and Finca La Selva), possibly a rare and local resident.

Notes.—*Amazilia cyanura* and *A. saucerrottei* appear to constitute a superspecies (Sibley and Monroe 1990). See comments under *A. beryllina.*

Amazilia saucerrottei (DeLattre and Bourcier). Steely-vented Hummingbird.

Trochilus Saucerrottei DeLattre and Bourcier, 1846, Rev. Zool. [Paris] 9: 311. (Caly, Nouvelle-Grenade = Cali, Colombia.)

Habitat.—Tropical Lowland Evergreen Forest Edge, Gallery Forest, Secondary Forest, Second-growth Scrub (0–2000 m; Tropical to Temperate zones).

Distribution.—*Resident* in Middle America from western and southern Nicaragua south to southern Costa Rica (primarily on the Pacific slope and in the central plateau, south to the Dota region); and in South America in Colombia and northwestern Venezuela.

Casual in Caribbean Costa Rica (Carrillo).

Notes.—Also known as Blue-vented Hummingbird. See comments under *A. cyanura.*

Amazilia edward (DeLattre and Bourcier). Snowy-bellied Hummingbird.

Trochilus Edward DeLattre and Bourcier, 1846, Rev. Zool. [Paris] 9: 308. (isthme de Panama.)

Habitat.—Tropical Lowland Evergreen Forest Edge, Montane Evergreen Forest Edge, Secondary Forest (0–1800 m; Tropical and Subtropical zones).

Distribution.—*Resident* [*niveoventer* group] in southwestern Costa Rica (El General-Térraba-Golfo Dulce region) and western Panama (east to western Coclé and the Azuero Peninsula, including Isla Coiba); and [*edward* group] in central and eastern Panama (from eastern Coclé and western Panamá east to Darién, primarily on the Pacific slope, and including the Pearl, Taboga, Taboguilla, and Uravá islands).

Notes.—Also known as Snowy-breasted Hummingbird. The two groups, *A. niveoventer* (Gould, 1851) [Snowy-bellied Hummingbird] and *A. edward* [Edward's Hummingbird], intergrade in central Panama (Wetmore 1968).

Amazilia tzacatl (De la Llave). Rufous-tailed Hummingbird.

Trochilus Tzacatl De la Llave, 1833, Registro Trimestre 2(5): 48. (México.)

Habitat.—Tropical Lowland Evergreen Forest Edge, Secondary Forest, Tropical Deciduous Forest (0–1800 m; Tropical and lower Subtropical zones).

Distribution.—*Resident* [*tzacatl* group] from southern Tamaulipas south in the Gulf-Caribbean lowlands to northern Oaxaca, Chiapas, the Yucatan Peninsula, Guatemala, Belize, Honduras, and Nicaragua, and on both slopes of Costa Rica (rare in the arid northwest) and Panama (including many islands off the Pacific coast), and in South America from Colombia (including Gorgona Island) east to northwestern Venezuela and south to western Ecuador; and [*handleyi* group] on Isla Escudo de Veraguas, off the Caribbean coast of western Panama.

Reports [*tzacatl* group] from southern Texas (Brownsville) are questionable (DeBenedictis 1992), as are those from the Pacific slope of Guatemala.

Notes.—Also known as Rieffer's Hummingbird. The two groups are regarded by Wetmore (1968) as distinct species, *A. tzacatl* [Rufous-tailed Hummingbird] and *A. handleyi* Wetmore, 1963 [Escudo Hummingbird].

Amazilia yucatanensis (Cabot). Buff-bellied Hummingbird.

Trochilus yucatanensis Cabot, 1845, Proc. Boston Soc. Nat. Hist. 2: 74. (Yucatán.)

Habitat.—Tropical Deciduous Forest, Gallery Forest, Secondary Forest, Tropical Lowland Evergreen Forest Edge (0–1250 m; Tropical Zone).

Distribution.—*Resident* from Coahuila, Nuevo León, and southern Texas (north to Corpus Christi) south in the Gulf-Caribbean lowlands (including the Yucatan Peninsula) to northern Guatemala (Petén) and Belize.

Winters regularly in southeastern Texas, southern Louisiana, southern Mississippi, and northwestern Florida. Casual or accidental in Arkansas, southern Alabama, and southeastern Florida.

Notes.—Also known as Fawn-breasted Hummingbird or Yucatan Hummingbird. A specimen from Honduras referred to this species (Monroe 1968) is apparently a hybrid *A. rutila* x *A. tzacatl* (Howell and Webb 1995). Mayr and Short (1970) considered *A. yucatanensis* and *A. rutila* to constitute a superspecies.

Amazilia rutila (DeLattre). Cinnamon Hummingbird.

Ornismya cinnamomea (not *Ornismya cinnamomeus* Gervais, 1835) Lesson, 1842, Rev. Zool. [Paris] 5: 175. (Acapulco [Guerrero].)
Ornismya rutila DeLattre, 1843, Echo Monde Savant (2)7: col. 1069. New name for *Ornismya cinnamomea* Lesson, preoccupied.

Habitat.—Tropical Deciduous Forest, Secondary Forest, Gallery Forest, Arid Lowland Scrub (0–1250 m; Tropical and lower Subtropical zones).

Distribution.—*Resident* on the Pacific slope of Middle America (including the Tres Marías Islands) from central Sinaloa south to central Costa Rica; and on the Caribbean slope on the Yucatan Peninsula (including Holbox, Contoy, Mujeres, and Cancun islands, and Cayo Culebra), in Belize (including offshore cays), in the arid interior valleys of Guatemala and Honduras, and in the Mosquitia of eastern Honduras and northeastern Nicaragua.

Accidental in southern Arizona (Patagonia; 21–23 July 1992; 1992, Amer. Birds 46: 1161; photograph in DeBenedictis 1994b) and southwestern New Mexico (Santa Teresa, Doña Ana County, 18–23 Sept. 1993; 1994, Amer. Birds 48: 138, photo p. 160).

Notes.—See comments under *A. yucatanensis*.

Amazilia violiceps (Gould). Violet-crowned Hummingbird.

Cyanomyia violiceps Gould, 1859, Ann. Mag. Nat. Hist. (3)4: 97. ([state of] Oaxaca, South Mexico; Binford, 1989, Ornithol. Monogr. 43, p. 338–339.)

Habitat.—Tropical Deciduous Forest, Gallery Forest, Secondary Forest; in United States, primarily in riparian woodland of cottonwoods and sycamores with dense understory (0–2200 m; Subtropical and lower Temperate zones).

Distribution.—*Resident* from northern Sonora, southeastern Arizona (Huachuca and Chiricahua mountains), southwestern New Mexico (Guadalupe Canyon), and western Chihuahua south to Guerrero and (at least seasonally) northwestern Oaxaca. Northernmost populations are migratory southward.

Casual or accidental in central southern California (Sonoma, Los Angeles, and Ventura counties), central Arizona, southern New Mexico, western Texas (El Paso), and Veracruz; a sight report from Baja California.

Notes.—The name *A. verticalis* (W. Deppe, 1830), often used for this species, has been relegated to the synonymy of *A. cyanocephala* (see Phillips 1965). *Amazilia violiceps* and *A. viridifrons* are sometimes considered conspecific, but apparent sympatry in Guerrero and Oaxaca without intergradation seems to support their status as full species (Binford 1989).

Amazilia viridifrons (Elliot). Green-fronted Hummingbird.

> *Cyanomyia viridifrons* Elliot, 1871, Ann. Mag. Nat. Hist. (4)8: 267. (Putla [de Guerrero, Oaxaca], Mexico; Binford, 1989, Ornithol. Monogr. 43, p. 339.)

Habitat.—Tropical Deciduous Forest, Arid Lowland Scrub, Arid Montane Scrub, Tropical Lowland Evergreen Forest Edge (0–1550 m; Tropical and lower Temperate zones).

Distribution.—*Resident* [*viridifrons* group] on the Pacific slope of southern Mexico from central Guerrero south to western Oaxaca, and in eastern Oaxaca and western Chiapas (east to Tonalá and Ocozocoautla); [*wagneri* group] in southern Oaxaca.

Notes.—Groups: *A. viridifrons* [Green-fronted Hummingbird] and *A. wagneri* Phillips, 1965 [Cinnamon-sided Hummingbird]. The form *wagneri* may represent a distinct species (Howell 1993, Howell and Webb 1995). See comments under *A. violiceps*.

Genus *EUPHERUSA* Gould

> *Eupherusa* Gould, 1857, Monogr. Trochil., pt. 14, pl. [12] and text. Type, by monotypy, *Ornismya eximia* DeLattre.

Eupherusa eximia (DeLattre). Stripe-tailed Hummingbird.

> *Ornismya eximia* DeLattre, 1843, Echo Monde Savant (2)7: col. 1069. (Guatemala = Cobán, Alta Verapaz, Guatemala.)

Habitat.—Tropical Lowland Evergreen Forest, Secondary Forest, Montane Evergreen Forest (800–2000 m; Tropical and Subtropical zones).

Distribution.—*Resident* in the highlands of Middle America from Puebla, Veracruz, northern and southeastern Oaxaca, and Chiapas south through eastern Guatemala, Belize, and Honduras to north-central Nicaragua, and in the interior highlands of Costa Rica and western Panama (east to Veraguas).

Winters to lower elevations.

Eupherusa cyanophrys Rowley and Orr. Blue-capped Hummingbird.

> *Eupherusa cyanophrys* Rowley and Orr, 1964, Condor 66: 82. (11 miles south of [San Pedro] Juchatengo, 4700 feet, Oaxaca, México.)

Habitat.—Montane Evergreen Forest, Tropical Deciduous Forest (1200–2600 m; Subtropical Zone).

Distribution.—*Resident* in southern Oaxaca (Sierra de Miahuatlán).

Eupherusa poliocerca Elliot. White-tailed Hummingbird.

> *Eupherusa poliocerca* Elliot, 1871, Ann. Mag. Nat. Hist. (4)8: 266. (Putla [de Guerrero, Oaxaca], Mexico; Binford, 1989, Ornithol. Monogr. 43, p. 339.)

Habitat.—Tropical Deciduous Forest, Montane Evergreen Forest (900–1400 m; Subtropical Zone).

Distribution.—*Resident* in the Sierra Madre del Sur of Guerrero and western Oaxaca. Reports of this species from Puebla (Friedmann et al. 1950) are questionable.

Eupherusa nigriventris Lawrence. Black-bellied Hummingbird.

Eupherusa nigriventris Lawrence, 1868, Proc. Acad. Nat. Sci. Philadelphia 19 (1867): 232. (Costa Rica.)

Habitat.—Montane Evergreen Forest (900–2000 m; Subtropical Zone).
Distribution.—*Resident* in Costa Rica (primarily central highlands) and western Panama (east to Veraguas, mostly on the Caribbean slope).

Genus *ELVIRA* Mulsant, Verreaux and Verreaux

Elvira Mulsant, and J. and E. Verreaux, 1866, Mém. Soc. Imp. Sci. Nat. Cherbourg 12: 176. Type, by monotypy, *Trochilus (Thaumatias) chionura* Gould.

Elvira chionura (Gould). White-tailed Emerald.

Trochilus (Thaumatias?) chionura Gould, 1851, Proc. Zool. Soc. London (1850), p. 162. (Chiriqui near David, province of Veragua, at an altitude of from 2000 to 3000 feet [Chiriquí, Panama].)

Habitat.—Montane Evergreen Forest (900–2000 m; Subtropical Zone).
Distribution.—*Resident* in the highlands of southwestern Costa Rica (north to the Dota Mountains) and western Panama (Chiriquí, Veraguas, and eastern Coclé).

Elvira cupreiceps (Lawrence). Coppery-headed Emerald.

Eupherusa cupreiceps Lawrence, 1866, Ann. Lyc. Nat. Hist. N. Y. 8: 348. (Barranca, Costa Rica.)

Habitat.—Montane Evergreen Forest (700–1500 m; Subtropical Zone).
Distribution.—*Resident* in the highlands of Costa Rica (primarily on the Caribbean slope of the Cordillera Central, and in the cordilleras de Tilarán and Guanacaste).

Genus *MICROCHERA* Gould

Microchera Gould, 1858, Monogr. Trochil., pt. 16, pl. [12] and text. Type, by original designation, *Mellisuga albo-coronata* Lawrence.

Microchera albocoronata (Lawrence). Snowcap.

Mellisuga albo-coronata Lawrence, 1855, Ann. Lyc. Nat. Hist. N. Y. 6 . . . 137, pl. 4. (Belen, Veraguas, New Grenada [= Panama].)

Habitat.—Tropical Lowland Evergreen Forest Edge, Montane Evergreen Forest Edge (300–1000 m; Tropical and lower Subtropical zones).
Distribution.—*Resident* on the Caribbean slope of eastern Honduras (Olancho, sight reports), Nicaragua, Costa Rica, and western Panama (Veraguas, western Colón, Coclé, and western Panamá province).

Genus *CHALYBURA* Reichenbach

Agyrtria δ *Chalybura* Reichenbach, 1854, J. Ornithol. 1 (Beil. zu Extrah.): 10. Type, by subsequent designation (Elliot, 1879), *Trochilus buffonii* Lesson.

Chalybura buffonii (Lesson). White-vented Plumeleteer.

Trochilus Buffonii Lesson, 1832, Les Trochil., p. 31, pl. 5. (Brazil, error = Bogotá region, Colombia.)

Habitat.—Tropical Lowland Evergreen Forest, Tropical Deciduous Forest, Secondary Forest (0–900 m; Tropical Zone).

Distribution.—*Resident* [*buffonii* group] in Panama (from western Panamá province on the Pacific slope to the Canal area in the Caribbean lowlands eastward), western and northern Colombia, and western and northern Venezuela (east to Miranda and Guárico); [*caeruleogaster* group] in southeastern Colombia (from western Arauca to Meta); and [*intermedia* group] in southwestern Ecuador and northwestern Peru.

Notes.—Groups: *C. buffonii* [White-vented Plumeleteer], *C. intermedia* E. and C. Hartert, 1894 [Ecuadorian Plumeleteer], and *C. caeruleogaster* (Gould, 1847) [Blue-bellied Plumeleteer].

Chalybura urochrysia (Gould). Bronze-tailed Plumeleteer.

Hypuroptila urochrysia Gould, 1861, Monogr. Trochil., pt. 22, pl. [7] and text. (neighborhood of Panamá, error = western Colombia.)

Habitat.—Tropical Lowland Evergreen Forest (0–900 m; Tropical Zone).

Distribution.—*Resident* [*melanorrhoa* group] on the Caribbean slope of extreme eastern Honduras (Gracias a Dios), Nicaragua, and Costa Rica; and [*urochrysia* group] from Panama (locally on both slopes) and western Colombia south to northwestern Ecuador.

Notes.—The two groups have been recognized as full species, *C. melanorrhoa* Salvin, 1865 [Black-vented Plumeleteer] and *C. urochrysia* [Bronze-tailed Plumeleteer], but free interbreeding occurs in northwestern Panama (Eisenmann and Howell 1962).

Genus *LAMPORNIS* Swainson

Lampornis Swainson, 1827, Philos. Mag. (n.s.) 1: 442. Type, by monotypy, *Lampornis amethystinus* Swainson.

Lampornis viridipallens (Bourcier and Mulsant). Green-throated Mountain-gem.

Trochilus Viridi-pallens Bourcier and Mulsant, 1846, Ann. Sci. Phys. Nat. Agric. Ind. Soc. R., etc., Lyon 9: 321. (Cobán, Alta Verapaz, Guatemala.)

Habitat.—Montane Evergreen Forest, Pine-Oak Forest (1200–3100 m; Subtropical and lower Temperate zones).

Distribution.—*Resident* in the highlands of extreme southeastern Oaxaca (Sierra Madre de Chiapas), Chiapas, Guatemala, El Salvador, and western Honduras (west of the Comayagua-Ulúa river valley).

Notes.—*Lampornis viridipallens* and *L. sybillae* constitute a superspecies (Monroe 1963a, Sibley and Monroe 1990).

Lampornis sybillae (Salvin and Godman). Green-breasted Mountain-gem.

Delattria sybillæ Salvin and Godman, 1892, Ibis, p. 327. (Matagalpa, Nicaragua.)

Habitat.—Montane Evergreen Forest, Pine-Oak Forest (100–2400 m; Subtropical and lower Temperate zones).

Distribution.—*Resident* in the highlands of eastern Honduras (east of the Comayagua-Ulúa river valley) and north-central Nicaragua.

Notes.—For treatment of *L. sybillae* as a separate species from *L. viridipallens,* see Monroe (1963a). See comments under *L. viridipallens.*

Lampornis amethystinus Swainson. Amethyst-throated Hummingbird.

Lampornis amethystinus Swainson, 1827, Philos. Mag. (n.s.) 1: 442. (Temiscaltipec [= Temascaltepec] and Real del Monte, [México,] Mexico.)

Habitat.—Pine-Oak Forest, Montane Evergreen Forest (900–3400 m; Subtropical and lower Temperate zones).

Distribution.—*Resident* from southern Nayarit, Jalisco, southeastern San Luis Potosí, and southern Tamaulipas south through the highlands of southern Mexico, Guatemala, and El Salvador to central Honduras.

Notes.—Populations irregularly distributed from Michoacán to Oaxaca consisting of blu-ish-throated rather than pink-throated males may represent a species, *L. margaritae* (Salvin and Godman, 1889) [Margaret's Hummingbird], distinct from *L. amethystinus* (Binford 1989).

Lampornis clemenciae (Lesson). Blue-throated Hummingbird.

Ornismya Clemenciae Lesson, 1829, Hist. Nat. Ois.-Mouches, p. xlv; 1830, p. 216, pl. 80. (le Mexique = Mexico.)

Habitat.—Pine-Oak Forest, Pine Forest, Montane Evergreen Forest Edge, in migration also visiting flowers in open situations and gardens; in United States, breeds primarily in moist, wooded canyons (1500–3400 m; Subtropical and lower Temperate zones).

Distribution.—*Breeds* from northern Sonora, southeastern Arizona, Chihuahua, and west-ern Texas south through Coahuila, Durango, and western Mexico to Oaxaca and (possibly) Chiapas. Recorded (mostly in summer) in southwestern and central Colorado.

Winters from southern Sonora (casually southeastern Arizona) and Chihuahua south through the breeding range in Mexico.

Migrates casually east to New Mexico and southern Texas (Rockport and Corpus Christi area southward).

Accidental in south-central California (a female mated to either *Calypte anna* or *Archil-ochus alexandri* raised young in 1977 and 1978 at Three Rivers, Tulare County; Baldridge et al. 1983) and Louisiana (Baton Rouge, Slidell).

Lampornis hemileucus (Salvin). White-bellied Mountain-gem.

Oreopyra hemileuca Salvin, 1865, Proc. Zool. Soc. London (1864), p. 584. (Turrialba and Tucurruquí, Costa Rica.)

Habitat.—Montane Evergreen Forest (700–1400 m; Subtropical Zone).
Distribution.—*Resident* in Costa Rica (in the Tilarán, Central, and Talamanca cordilleras) and western Panama (recorded Chiriquí and Veraguas).

Lampornis calolaema (Salvin). Purple-throated Mountain-gem.

Oreopyra calolæma Salvin, 1865, Proc. Zool. Soc. London (1864), p. 584. (Volcán de Cartago = Volcán de Irazú, Costa Rica.)

Habitat.—Montane Evergreen Forest, Secondary Forest (800–3200 m; Subtropical and lower Temperate zones).

Distribution.—*Resident* in the highlands of western Nicaragua (Volcán Mombacho and Volcán Maderas, Isla de Ometepe in Lago de Nicaragua) and western and central Costa Rica (from the Cordillera de Guanacaste south to the Dota region and the northern tip of the Cordillera de Talamanca); also in west-central Panama (Chiriquí west to the Fortuna area, Veraguas, and western Coclé).

Notes.—Relationships within the *L. calolaema-castaneoventris* complex are not well un-derstood. It has been suggested by some authors (e.g., Ridgely and Gwynne 1989) that the purple-throated males *(calolaema)* and white-throated males *(castaneoventris)* are morphs of the same species; some introgression occurs in areas where both types are found, although they tend to maintain their distinctness (Stiles and Skutch 1989). Until the matter is resolved, it seems best to treat the forms as separate species with limited hybridization in the areas of sympatry. If the entire complex is regarded as a single species, as advocated by Wetmore (1968), the name Variable Mountain-gem may be used. See comments under *L. castaneov-entris*.

Lampornis castaneoventris (Gould). White-throated Mountain-gem.

Trochilus (——?) *castaneoventris* Gould, 1851, Proc. Zool. Soc. London (1850), p. 163. (Cordillera of Chiriqui, at an altitude of 6000 feet [Panama].)

Habitat.—[*cinereicauda* group] Montane Evergreen Forest, Secondary Forest (1800–

3100 m; Subtropical and lower Temperate zones); [*castaneoventris* group] Montane Evergreen Forest, Secondary Forest (1250–3150 m; Subtropical and lower Temperate zones).

Distribution.—*Resident* [*cinereicauda* group] in the highlands of southern Costa Rica (north to the Cordillera de Talamanca); and [*castaneoventris* group] western Panama (Volcán de Chiriquí region of western Chiriquí east to Boquete).

Notes.—The two groups are sometimes regarded as distinct species, *L. castaneoventris* [White-throated Mountain-gem] and *L. cinereicauda* (Lawrence, 1867) [Gray-tailed Mountain-gem], but see Ridgely (1981); Stiles and Skutch (1989) treated these two and *L. calolaema* as allospecies. See comments under *L. calolaema*.

Genus *LAMPROLAIMA* Reichenbach

Heliodoxa δ *Lamprolaima* Reichenbach, 1854, J. Ornithol. 1 (Beil. zu Extrah.): 9. Type, by subsequent designation (G. R. Gray, 1855), *Ornismya rhami* Lesson.

Lamprolaima rhami (Lesson). Garnet-throated Hummingbird.

Ornismya Rhami Lesson, 1839, Rev. Zool. [Paris] 1: 315. (Mexico.)

Habitat.—Montane Evergreen Forest, Pine-Oak Forest (110–3100 m; Subtropical and lower Temperate zones).

Distribution.—*Resident* from Guerrero and western Veracruz south through Oaxaca, Chiapas, Guatemala, and El Salvador to Honduras.

Genus *HELIODOXA* Gould

Heliodoxa Gould, 1850, Proc. Zool. Soc. London (1849), p. 95. Type, by subsequent designation (Bonaparte, 1850), *Trochilus leadbeateri* Bourcier.

Heliodoxa jacula Gould. Green-crowned Brilliant.

Heliodoxa jacula Gould, 1850, Proc. Zool. Soc. London (1849), p. 96. (Santa Fé de Bogota [Colombia].)

Habitat.—Montane Evergreen Forest, Tropical Lowland Evergreen Forest (500–2150 m; Subtropical Zone).

Distribution.—*Resident* from Costa Rica (north to the Cordillera Central, primarily on Caribbean slope) south locally through Panama and northern Colombia to western Ecuador.

Genus *EUGENES* Gould

Eugenes Gould, 1856, Monogr. Trochil., pt. 12, pl. [7] and text. Type, by monotypy, *Trochilus fulgens* Swainson.

Eugenes fulgens (Swainson). Magnificent Hummingbird.

Trochilus fulgens Swainson, 1827, Philos. Mag. (n.s.) 1: 441. (Temiscaltipec, Mexico = Temascaltepec, México.)

Habitat.—Pine-Oak Forest, Pine Forest, Montane Evergreen Forest (1300–3300 m; Subtropical and Temperate zones).

Distribution.—*Breeds* [*fulgens* group] in north-central Colorado (once), and from southeastern Arizona, southwestern (and probably also north-central) New Mexico, and western Texas (Culberson, Jeff Davis, and Brewster counties) south through the highlands of Mexico, Guatemala, western El Salvador, and Honduras to north-central Nicaragua; recorded in summer (and probably breeding) elsewhere in southwestern and central Colorado.

Winters [*fulgens* group] from Sonora and Chihuahua south through the breeding range in Middle America, casually in southern Arizona and southern New Mexico.

Resident [*spectabilis* group] in the mountains from central Costa Rica to western Panama (western Chiriquí).

Casual [*fulgens* group] north to southern Utah, northern New Mexico, northeastern Kansas, and south-central Texas; sight reports from Wyoming and eastern Texas. Accidental in Minnesota, Georgia, and Florida.

Notes.—Also known as Rivoli's Hummingbird. Groups: *E. fulgens* [Magnificent or Rivoli's Hummingbird] and *E. spectabilis* (Lawrence, 1867) [Admirable Hummingbird].

Genus *HAPLOPHAEDIA* Simon

Haplophædia Simon, 1918, Not. Travaux Sci., p. 39. Type, by monotypy, *Trochilus aureliae* Bourcier and Mulsant.

Haplophaedia aureliae (Bourcier and Mulsant). Greenish Puffleg.

Trochilus Aureliæ Bourcier and Mulsant, 1846, Ann. Sci. Phys. Nat. Agric. Ind. Soc. R., etc., Lyon 9: 315, pl. 10. (Bogotá, Colombia.)

Habitat.—Montane Evergreen Forest, Secondary Forest (1400–2500 m; upper Tropical and Subtropical zones).

Distribution.—*Resident* in eastern Panama (in eastern Darién on cerros Pirre, Malí, and Tacarcuna); and in the Andes of South America from Colombia south to northern Bolivia.

Genus *HELIOTHRYX* Boie

Heliothryx Boie, 1831, Isis von Oken, col. 547. Type, by subsequent designation (G. R. Gray, 1840), *H. aurita* (L.) = *Trochilus auritus* Gmelin.

Heliothryx barroti (Bourcier). Purple-crowned Fairy.

Trochilus Barroti Bourcier, 1843, Rev. Zool. [Paris] 6: 72. (Carthagène = Cartagena, Colombia.)

Habitat.—Tropical Lowland Evergreen Forest, Secondary Forest (0–1300 m; Tropical and lower Subtropical zones).

Distribution.—*Resident* on the Gulf-Caribbean slope from Tabasco and northern Chiapas south through eastern Guatemala, Belize, and Honduras to Nicaragua, on both slopes of Costa Rica (except the arid northwest) and Panama, and from northern Colombia south, west of the Andes, to southwestern Ecuador.

Notes.—*Heliothryx barroti* and *H. aurita* (Gmelin, 1788), of South America, constitute a superspecies (Sibley and Monroe 1990).

Genus *HELIOMASTER* Bonaparte

Heliomaster Bonaparte, March 1850, Consp. Gen. Avium 1(1): 70. Type, by subsequent designation (Bonaparte, April 1850), *Orn. angel.* = *Ornismya angelae* Lesson = *Trochilus furcifer* Shaw.

Heliomaster longirostris (Audebert and Vieillot). Long-billed Starthroat.

Trochilus longirostris Audebert and Vieillot, 1801, Ois. Dorés 1: 107, pl. 59. (West Indies = Trinidad.)

Habitat.—Tropical Lowland Evergreen Forest Edge, Tropical Deciduous Forest, Gallery Forest, Secondary Forest (0–1500 m; Tropical and Subtropical zones).

Distribution.—*Resident* on both slopes of Middle America from Guerrero and Veracruz south (exclusive of the Yucatan Peninsula) through Middle America (rare on Pacific slope from Honduras to northwestern Costa Rica), and in South America from Colombia, Venezuela, Trinidad, and the Guianas south, west of the Andes to northwestern Peru and east of the Andes to central Bolivia and central Brazil.

Heliomaster constantii (DeLattre). Plain-capped Starthroat.

Ornismya Constantii DeLattre, 1843, Echo Monde Savant (2)7: col. 1069, in text. (Guatemala.)

Habitat.—Tropical Deciduous Forest, Gallery Forest, Arid Lowland Scrub (0–1250 m; Tropical Zone).

Distribution.—*Resident* on the Pacific slope of Middle America from southern Sonora south to Costa Rica (primarily the Guanacaste region in the northwest, rarely in the El General-Térraba region in the southwest).

Casual in southeastern Arizona (north to Phoenix); a sight report for southwestern New Mexico.

Notes.—Also known as Constant's Starthroat.

Genus *CALLIPHLOX* Boie

Calliphlox Boie, 1831, Isis von Oken, col. 544. Type, by subsequent designation (G. R. Gray, 1855), *Trochilus amethystinus* Gm. = Boddaert.

Philodice Mulsant, and J. and E. Verreaux, 1866, Mém. Soc. Imp. Sci. Nat. Cherbourg 12: 230. Type, by monotypy, *Trochilus mitchellii* Bourcier.

Calliphlox evelynae (Bourcier). Bahama Woodstar.

Trochilus Evelynæ Bourcier, 1847, Proc. Zool. Soc. London, p. 44. (Nassau, New Providence [Bahamas].)

Habitat.—Secondary Forest, Second-growth Scrub, Tropical Lowland Evergreen Forest Edge.

Distribution.—*Resident* throughout the Bahama Islands.

Casual in southern Florida (Lantana, Homestead, Miami area).

Notes.—Often treated in the genus *Philodice*.

Calliphlox bryantae (Lawrence). Magenta-throated Woodstar.

Doricha bryantæ Lawrence, 1867, Ann. Lyc. Nat. Hist. N. Y. 8: 483. (Costa Rica.)

Habitat.—Montane Evergreen Forest Edge, Secondary Forest, Second-growth Scrub (700–1900 m; Subtropical and lower Temperate zones).

Distribution.—*Resident* in the highlands of Costa Rica (from the Cordillera de Guanacaste to the central plateau near San José, the Dota Mountains, and Cerro de Talamanca), and western Panama (Chiriquí and Veraguas).

Notes.—Also known as Costa Rican Woodstar. Frequently placed in the genus *Philodice*.

Calliphlox mitchellii (Bourcier). Purple-throated Woodstar.

Trochilus Mitchellii Bourcier, 1847, Proc. Zool. Soc. London, p. 47. (Zimapán [, Colombia].)

Habitat.—Montane Evergreen Forest, Second-growth Scrub (1000–1900 m; Subtropical and lower Temperate zones).

Distribution.—*Resident* in western Colombia and western Ecuador.

Presumably resident in eastern Panama (Cana region, Cerro Pirre, eastern Darién), where known from two female specimens: 13 April 1938 (Wetmore 1968; reported as *Acestrura heliodor*) and 11 August 1982 (Robbins et al. 1985).

Notes.—For a full discussion of these two specimens, see Robbins et al. (1985). This species is sometimes placed in the genus *Philodice* (e.g., Hilty and Brown 1986).

Genus *DORICHA* Reichenbach

Calliphlox ß *Doricha* Reichenbach, 1854, J. Ornithol. 1 (Beil. zu Extrah.): 12. Type, by monotypy, *Trochilus enicurus* Vieillot.

Notes.—Merged with *Calothorax* by Howell and Webb (1995).

Doricha enicura (Vieillot). Slender Sheartail.

Trochilus enicurus Vieillot, 1818, Nouv. Dict. Hist. Nat. (nouv. éd.) 23: 429. (Brazil, error = Guatemala.)

Habitat.—Montane Evergreen Forest Edge, Second-growth Scrub (1000–2100 m; Subtropical Zone).

Distribution.—*Resident* in the highlands of Chiapas, Guatemala, El Salvador, and western Honduras (east to La Paz).

Doricha eliza (DeLattre and Lesson). Mexican Sheartail.

> *Trochilus Eliza* DeLattre and Lesson, *in* Lesson and DeLattre, 1839, Rev. Zool. [Paris] 2: 20. (Pas du Taureau, entra la Vera Cruz et Jalapa = Paso del Toro, Veracruz.)

Habitat.—Arid Lowland Scrub (Tropical Zone).

Distribution.—*Resident* in two disjunct areas of southeastern Mexico (in central Veracruz, and the coastal scrub of the Yucatan Peninsula, including Holbox Island; a sight record for Isla Cancun).

Genus *TILMATURA* Reichenbach

> *Tilmatura* Reichenbach, 1855, Trochil. Enum., p. 5. Type, by monotypy, *Trochilus lepidus* Reichenbach = *Ornismya dupontii* Lesson.

Tilmatura dupontii (Lesson). Sparkling-tailed Hummingbird.

> *Ornismya dupontii* Lesson, 1832, Hist. Nat. Colibris, livr. 13, p. 100, pl. 1. (México.)

Habitat.—Pine-Oak Forest, Montane Evergreen Forest Edge, Second-growth Scrub (900–2500 m; Subtropical and lower Temperate zones).

Distribution.—*Resident* in the highlands from Sinaloa, Jalisco, Colima, Michoacán, México, Morelos, and western Veracruz south through Guerrero, Oaxaca, Chiapas, Guatemala, El Salvador, and Honduras to north-central Nicaragua.

Notes.—Placed in the genus *Philodice* by Howell and Webb (1995).

Genus *CALOTHORAX* Gray

> *Calothorax* G. R. Gray, 1840, List Genera Birds, p. 13. Type, by original designation, *C. cyanopogon* (Lesson) = *Cynanthus lucifer* Swainson.

Calothorax lucifer (Swainson). Lucifer Hummingbird.

> *Cynanthus Lucifer* Swainson, 1827, Philos. Mag. (n.s.) 1: 442. (Temiscaltipec, Mexico = Temascaltepec, México.)

Habitat.—Arid Montane Scrub; in United States, primarily on steep desert slopes with agave, sotol, and ocotillo adjacent to brushy washes with nectar-producing plants such as havard penstemon, and woolly paintbrush (1550–2750 m; upper Tropical and Subtropical zones).

Distribution.—*Breeds* from southern Arizona (Cochise County), southwestern New Mexico (Peloncillo Mountains), western Texas (Brewster County), and Nuevo León south in the highlands of Mexico to Valley of México, possibly to Morelos and Puebla.

Winters from northern Mexico south to the limits of the breeding range, casually to western Veracruz, Oaxaca, and (questionably) Chiapas.

Casual elsewhere in southern Arizona and southern New Mexico, and in southern Texas (east to Hays, Bee, and Aransas counties).

Notes.—*Calothorax lucifer* and *C. pulcher* appear to constitute a superspecies (Sibley and Monroe 1990).

Calothorax pulcher Gould. Beautiful Hummingbird.

> *Calothorax pulcher* Gould, 1859, Ann. Mag. Nat. Hist. (3)4: 97. ([state of] Oaxaca, in Western Mexico; Binford, 1989, Ornithol. Monogr. 43, p. 339.)

Habitat.—Arid Montane Scrub (1000–2250 m; Subtropical and lower Temperate zones).

Distribution.—*Resident* from eastern Guerrero and southern Puebla south to central Oaxaca (west of the Isthmus of Tehuantepec); reports from Chiapas are questionable.

Notes.—See comments under *C. lucifer.*

Genus *ARCHILOCHUS* Reichenbach

Selasphorus ß *Archilochus* Reichenbach, 1854, J. Ornithol. 1 (Beil. zu Extrah.): 13. Type, by monotypy, *Trochilus alexandri* Bourcier [= Bourcier and Mulsant].

Notes.—See comments under *Calypte* and *Stellula.*

Archilochus colubris (Linnaeus). Ruby-throated Hummingbird.

Trochilus Colubris Linnaeus, 1758, Syst. Nat. (ed. 10) 1: 120. Based mainly on "The Hummingbird" Catesby, Nat. Hist. Carolina 1: 65, pl. 65. (in America, imprimis septentrionali = South Carolina.)

Habitat.—Deciduous or mixed woodland, second growth, parks, and open situations with scattered trees, foraging also in meadows and gardens; in migration and winter, a wide variety of woodland and open habitats.

Distribution.—*Breeds* from central Alberta, central Saskatchewan, southern Manitoba, central Ontario, southern Quebec, New Brunswick, Prince Edward Island, Nova Scotia, and Newfoundland south, east of the Rocky Mountains, to southern Texas, the Gulf coast, and southern Florida, and west to the eastern Dakotas, central Nebraska, central Kansas, central Oklahoma, and central Texas.

Winters from on Pacific slope of Mexico from southern Sinaloa south, and in interior and Caribbean slope from southern Veracruz, the Yucatan Peninsula, and Oaxaca, south through Middle America (including Cozumel and Holbox islands) to central Costa Rica (south of Nicaragua most commonly on the Pacific slope), casually to western Panama (Chiriquí and western Panamá province); also small numbers from southeastern Texas and southern Louisiana along Gulf Coast to northwestern Florida, and also in southern Florida; casual in western Cuba.

Migrates through southern Texas and northeastern and north-central Mexico; regular in Cuba, especially in spring.

Casual north to southwestern British Columbia, northern Manitoba, northern Ontario, Labrador, and Newfoundland, and in California (east-central and the Farallon Islands), eastern New Mexico, the northern Bahamas (Grand Bahama, New Providence), and Bermuda; sight reports from southeastern Colorado and southern Baja California. Reports from Grand Cayman, Jamaica, Hispaniola, and Puerto Rico are questionable. Accidental in Alaska (St. Michael).

Notes.—Although the breeding ranges of *A. colubris* and *A. alexandri* overlap slightly in central Texas, it seems best to regard these species as constituting a superspecies (Mayr and Short 1970).

Archilochus alexandri (Bourcier and Mulsant). Black-chinned Hummingbird.

Trochilus Alexandri Bourcier and Mulsant, 1846, Ann. Sci. Phys. Nat. Agric. Ind. Soc. R., etc., Lyon 9: 330. (Sierra Madre [Occidental], Mexico.)

Habitat.—Open woodland, scrub, desert washes, riparian woodland, chaparral, parks, and gardens, most frequently in arid regions.

Distribution.—*Breeds* from south-central British Columbia, Washington, central Idaho, and northwestern Montana south to northern Baja California, northern Sonora, northern Chihuahua, northern Coahuila (probably), and southern Texas, and east to southwestern Wyoming, southeastern Colorado, southwestern Oklahoma, and central Texas (to Dallas, Navarro, and Hidalgo counties).

Winters from primarily along Pacific slope from southern Sonora (casually southern California) south to Michoacán and Morelos, and also small numbers in southeastern Texas east along the Gulf coast to northwestern Florida; casually also in Georgia and South Carolina.

Migrates through much of northern Mexico south of the breeding range from eastern Baja California and Sonora to western Tamaulipas, south to limit of winter range.

Casual in south-coastal British Columbia, southern Alberta, Wyoming, Kansas, Arkansas, North Carolina, and southern Florida, also in southern Baja California and Veracruz. Accidental in southern Ontario, Massachusetts, and Tennessee; sight reports for southern Saskatchewan and Nova Scotia.

Notes.—See comments under *A. colubris.*

Genus *MELLISUGA* Brisson

Mellisuga Brisson, 1760, Ornithologie 1: 40; 3: 694. Type, by tautonymy, *Mellisuga* Brisson = *Trochilus minimus* Linnaeus.

Mellisuga minima (Linnaeus). Vervain Hummingbird.

Trochilus minimus Linnaeus, 1758, Syst. Nat. (ed. 10) 1: 121. Based on "The Least Humming-bird" Edwards, Nat. Hist. Birds 2: 105, pl. 105. (in America = Jamaica.)

Habitat.—Second-growth Scrub, Tropical Lowland Evergreen Forest Edge (0–2400 m).
Distribution.—*Resident* on Jamaica and Hispaniola (including Gonâve, Tortue, Saona, and Catalina islands, and Île-à-Vache).
A sight report in Puerto Rico.

Mellisuga helenae (Lembeye). Bee Hummingbird.

Orthorhynchus helenæ (Gundlach MS) Lembeye, 1850, Aves Isla Cuba, p. 70, pl. 10, fig. 2. (Cárdenas, Cuba.)

Habitat.—Second-growth Scrub, Montane Evergreen Forest Edge, Pine Forest Edge, Tropical Lowland Evergreen Forest Edge, Secondary Forest (0–1200 m).
Distribution.—*Resident* on Cuba and the Isle of Pines.

Genus *CALYPTE* Gould

Calypte Gould, 1856, Monogr. Trochil., pt. 11, pl. [5–7] and text. Type, by subsequent designation (Baird, Brewer, and Ridgway, 1875), *Ornismya costae* Bourcier.

Notes.—Merged with *Archilochus* by Howell and Webb (1995).

Calypte anna (Lesson). Anna's Hummingbird.

Ornismya Anna Lesson, 1829, Hist. Nat. Ois.-Mouches, p. "xxxj" [= xxxi]; 1830, p. 205, pl. 74. (La Californie = San Francisco, California.)

Habitat.—Open woodland, chaparral, scrubby areas, and partly open situations, foraging also in gardens and meadows; ascends to montane regions in summer postbreeding season.
Distribution.—*Breeds* in southwestern British Columbia (including Vancouver Island), western Washington, western Oregon, California (west of the Sierra Nevada from Humboldt, Shasta, and Tehama counties southward), northwestern Baja California, and southern Arizona (north to Phoenix and Superior). Recorded in summer (and probably breeding) in southern New Mexico and western Texas (Davis Mountains).
Winters from central British Columbia south to central Baja California, and east to Utah (casually), southern Arizona, central New Mexico, northern Sonora, and northern Chihuahua, casually north to south-coastal Alaska, central British Columbia, and western Montana, and east to central New Mexico, northern Coahuila, and east-central and southeastern Texas, southern Louisiana, southern Mississippi, and southern Alabama.
Casual or accidental in southern Alberta, Saskatchewan, Minnesota, Wisconsin, Montana, Wyoming, Colorado, Kansas, Oklahoma, Missouri, Arkansas, Tennessee, Florida (Tallahassee), and Georgia.

Calypte costae (Bourcier). Costa's Hummingbird.

Ornismya Costae Bourcier, 1839, Rev. Zool. [Paris] 2: 294. (la Californie = Magdalena Bay, Baja California.)

Habitat.—Desert and semi-desert, especially in washes, and arid brushy foothills and chaparral; in migration and winter, also adjacent mountains and in open meadows and gardens.

Distribution.—*Breeds* from central California (north to Monterey, Stanislaus, and Inyo counties), southern Nevada, and southwestern Utah south to southern Baja California (including the Channel Islands off California, and islands off the coast of Baja California), Sonora (including Tiburón and San Esteban islands), southern Arizona, and (probably) southwestern New Mexico; there is an isolated breeding attempt (eggs laid, nest destroyed) for southern Oregon.

Winters from southern California and southern Arizona south to Sinaloa and Nayarit, casually north to southwestern British Columbia, Oregon, and central Nevada, and east to central and southern Texas (Hays and Kleberg counties).

Accidental in south-coastal Alaska (Anchorage); a sight report for southern Alberta.

Genus *STELLULA* Gould

Stellula Gould, 1861, Introd. Trochil., p. 90. Type, by monotypy, *Trochilus calliope* Gould.

Notes.—Merged with *Archilochus* by Howell and Webb (1995).

Stellula calliope (Gould). Calliope Hummingbird.

Trochilus (Calothorax) Calliope Gould, 1847, Proc. Zool. Soc. London, p. 11. (Mexico = Real del Monte, Hidalgo.)

Habitat.—Open shrubby montane forest, mountain meadows, second-growth, and willow and alder thickets; in migration and winter, also chaparral, lowland brushy areas, deserts, and semi-desert regions.

Distribution.—*Breeds* in the mountains from central interior British Columbia (also Vancouver Island) and west-central Alberta south through Washington, Oregon, Nevada, and California to northern Baja California (Sierra San Pedro Mártir), and east to western Montana, western Wyoming, and Utah.

Winters from southern Sinaloa south to Michoacán, Guerrero, and Oaxaca, and east to Aguascalientes, Guanajuato, and Distrito Federal; casual, but increasingly regular, along Gulf Coast in southeastern Texas, southern Louisiana, southern Mississippi, southern Alabama, and northwestern Florida; one December record from western Texas (El Paso).

Migrates regularly through the southwestern United States, northern Baja California, and northwestern Mexico, and casually east to southwestern Saskatchewan, South Dakota, western Nebraska, Kansas, and western Texas.

Casual north to northeastern British Columbia. Accidental in Minnesota, Kansas, and North Carolina. Sight reports for southeastern Alaska and western Oklahoma.

Genus *ATTHIS* Reichenbach

Trochilus δ *Atthis* Reichenbach, 1854, J. Ornithol. 1 (Beil. zu Extrah.): 12. Type, by subsequent designation (G. R. Gray, 1855), *Ornismya heloisa* Lesson and DeLattre.

Notes.—Merged with *Selasphorus* by Howell and Webb (1995).

Atthis heloisa (DeLattre and Lesson). Bumblebee Hummingbird.

Ornysmia Heloisa DeLattre and Lesson, *in* Lesson and DeLattre, 1839, Rev. Zool. [Paris] 2: 15. (Jalapa et Quatepu = Coátepec, Veracruz.)

Habitat.—Pine-Oak Forest, Montane Evergreen Forest Edge (1025–3800 m; Subtropical and lower Temperate zones).

Distribution.—*Resident* in the highlands from southwestern Chihuahua, southeastern Sinaloa, Nayarit, Jalisco, Guanajuato, San Luis Potosí, Nuevo León, and southern Tamaulipas south to Oaxaca (west of the Isthmus of Tehuantepec) and western Veracruz.

Accidental in Arizona (Huachuca Mountains).

Notes.—Also known as Heloise's Hummingbird. *Atthis heloisa* and *A. ellioti* constitute a superspecies (Sibley and Monroe 1990).

Atthis ellioti Ridgway. Wine-throated Hummingbird.

Atthis ellioti Ridgway, 1878, Proc. U. S. Natl. Mus. 1: 8, 9, and fig. (Volcán de Fuego, Guatemala.)

Habitat.—Pine-Oak Forest, Montane Evergreen Forest Edge, Second-growth Scrub (900–2650 m; Subtropical and Temperate zones).

Distribution.—*Resident* in the highlands of Chiapas, Guatemala, El Salvador, and Honduras.

Notes.—See comments under *A. heloisa.*

Genus *SELASPHORUS* Swainson

Selasphorus Swainson, 1832, in Swainson and Richardson, Fauna Bor.-Amer. 2 (1831): 324, 496. Type, by subsequent designation (G. R. Gray, 1840), *Trochilus rufus* Gmelin.

Platurornis Oberholser, 1974, Bird Life Texas, p. 986. Type, by original designation, *Selasphorus platycercus = Trochilus platycercus* Swainson.

Notes.—See comments under *Atthis.*

Selasphorus platycercus (Swainson). Broad-tailed Hummingbird.

Trochilus platycercus Swainson, 1827, Philos. Mag. (n.s.) 1: 441. (No locality given = Mexico.)

Habitat.—Open woodland, especially pine, pine-oak, and pinyon-juniper, brushy hillsides, montane scrub, and thickets; in migration and winter also open situations in lowlands where flowering shrubs are present (Subtropical and Temperate zones).

Distribution.—*Breeds* in the mountains from north-central Idaho (Latah County), southwestern Montana, and northern Wyoming south to southeastern California, northeastern Sonora, Guanajuato, México, Distrito Federal, Hidalgo, Nuevo León, and western Texas (east to Bandera County); and in eastern Chiapas and Guatemala (rare in eastern mountains).

Winters from the highlands of northern Mexico south to western Veracruz and Oaxaca (west of the Isthmus of Tehuantepec), in the breeding range in Chiapas and Guatemala, and rarely but regularly to coastal Texas and southern Louisiana, casually to southern Mississippi, southern Alabama, Georgia, and also southern Arizona.

Migrates casually east to Nebraska, central Kansas, and eastern and southeastern Texas, and west to Oregon and coastal California.

Casual, primarily in summer, north to Oregon and Montana, and in fall in Kansas and Arkansas; sight reports for British Columbia and western Florida.

Selasphorus rufus (Gmelin). Rufous Hummingbird.

Trochilus rufus Gmelin, 1788, Syst. Nat. 1(1): 497. Based mainly on the "Ruffed Honeysucker" Pennant, Arct. Zool. 2: 290. (in sinu Americae Natka = Nootka Sound, Vancouver Island, British Columbia.)

Habitat.—Coniferous forest edge, second growth, thickets, and brushy hillsides, foraging in adjacent scrubby areas and meadows; in winter, primarily pine-oak woodland; in migration, primarily lowlands in spring but montane meadows in fall.

Distribution.—*Breeds* from southern Alaska (west to Prince William Sound), southern Yukon, western and southern British Columbia (including the Queen Charlotte Islands), west-central Alberta, and western Montana south, primarily in the mountains, to northwestern California (Humboldt County), eastern Oregon, central Idaho, and western Wyoming.

Winters primarily from Sinaloa and Chihuahua south to Oaxaca, México, Distrito Federal, and western Veracruz. Also over much of the Gulf Coast region from central and eastern Texas to northwestern Florida, casually northward (usually unsuccessfully) through much of the eastern United States. Also casually to rarely in British Columbia and coastal southern California.

Migrates regularly through the southwestern United States, Baja California, and northern and central Mexico, casually east to eastern Alberta, Saskatchewan, Manitoba, South Dakota, Nebraska, Kansas, Missouri, and Oklahoma. Casual east across interior eastern North America (recorded from Minnesota, Wisconsin, Michigan, southern Ontario, and northern New York south to Missouri, Kentucky, and Tennessee), and along the Atlantic coast (north to Nova Scotia), some attempting to winter. Accidental on Big Diomede Island and Grand Bahama. Some of these eastern records may pertain to *S. sasin.*

Notes.—*Selasphorus rufus* and *S. sasin* constitute a superspecies (Mayr and Short 1970).

Selasphorus sasin (Lesson). Allen's Hummingbird.

Ornismya Sasin Lesson, 1829, Hist. Nat. Ois.-Mouches, p. xxx; 1830, p. 190, pl. 66, 67. (La Californie, la côte N.-O. d'Amérique = San Francisco, California.)

Habitat.—Chaparral, open oak woodland, riparian woodland, residential areas; in winter, montane woodland.

Distribution.—*Breeds* from southwestern Oregon south through coastal California to Ventura County.

Winters mostly in central Mexico south to Distrito Federal, perhaps north to Aguascalientes and Guanajuato, also casually along Gulf Coast in southeastern Texas, southern Louisiana, Mississippi, Alabama, and Georgia.

Migrates through southern California and northern Baja California (including Los Coronados and Cedros islands), most of northwestern and north-central Mexico, and east, at least casually, to southern Arizona and southern New Mexico.

Resident in the Channel Islands (off southern California), and in coastal southern California (Los Angeles County, probably also Orange County).

Accidental in Washington (Seattle), eastern Kansas, Massachusetts (Nantucket), and southwestern Texas; reports from Florida do not eliminate *S. rufus.*

Notes.—See comments under *S. rufus.*

Selasphorus flammula Salvin. Volcano Hummingbird.

Selasphorus flammula Salvin, 1865, Proc. Zool. Soc. London (1864), p. 586. (Volcán de Cartago [= Irazú], Costa Rica.)

Habitat.—Paramo Grassland, Second-growth Scrub, Montane Evergreen Forest Edge, Secondary Forest (1850–2400 m; upper Subtropical and Temperate zones).

Distribution.—*Resident* in the highlands of Costa Rica (Cordillera Central south along the Cordillera de Talamanca) and western Panama (Volcán Barú in western Chiriquí).

Notes.—There has been much confusion regarding the status and distribution of the forms of this species. As presently understood (Stiles 1983a), the mauve-gorgeted race *flammula* breeds on the Irazú-Turrialba massifs in central Costa Rica; *S. torridus* Salvin, 1870 [Heliotrope-throated Hummingbird], based on dull-gorgeted males, breeds the length of the Cordillera de Talamanca and is now considered a subspecies of *flammula* (formerly it was considered but a color morph). The red-gorgeted form *S. simoni* Carriker, 1910 [Cerise-throated Hummingbird], breeds on Volcán Poás and Volcán Barba of the northern Cordillera Central and (formerly?) the Cerros de Escazú south of San José; *simoni* is divergent in morphology (but not in displays) and was previously considered a species related to *S. ardens,* but it appears to be but a distinct subspecies of *flammula* (Stiles 1983a). If any of the preceding are regarded as specifically distinct, then Rose-throated Hummingbird would be the appropriate English name for *S. flammula.* See comments under *S. ardens.*

Selasphorus ardens Salvin. Glow-throated Hummingbird.

> *Selasphorus ardens* Salvin, 1870, Proc. Zool. Soc. London, p. 209. (Calovévora and
> Castilla, Panama.)

Habitat.—Second-growth Scrub, Montane Evergreen Forest Edge, Secondary Forest
(750–1800 m; Subtropical Zone).
Distribution.—*Resident* in the mountains of western Panama in eastern Chiriquí (Cerro
Flores) and Veraguas (Santa Fé, Castillo, and Calovévora).
Notes.—This species has been considered closely related to *S. flammula* on the basis of
gorget color and measurements, but in wing and tail morphology (and presumably displays)
it is more similar to *S. scintilla,* with which it may constitute a superspecies (Stiles 1983a).
See comments under *S. flammula.*

Selasphorus scintilla (Gould). Scintillant Hummingbird.

> *Trochilus (Selosphorus) scintilla* Gould, 1851, Proc. Zool. Soc. London (1850), p. 162.
> (Volcano of Chiriqui, at an altitude of 9000 feet [Panama].)

Habitat.—Second-growth Scrub, Montane Evergreen Forest Edge, Secondary Forest
(900–2100 m; Subtropical and lower Temperate zones).
Distribution.—*Resident* in the mountains of central Costa Rica (Cordillera Central south
along the Pacific slope of the Cordillera de Talamanca, and north, at least casually, to the
Cordillera de Tilarán) and western Panama (western Chiriquí).
Notes.—See comments under *S. ardens.*

Order **TROGONIFORMES**: Trogons

Family **TROGONIDAE**: Trogons

Subfamily TROGONINAE: Trogons

Genus *PRIOTELUS* Gray

> *Temnurus* (not Lesson, 1831) Swainson, 1837, Class. Birds 2: 337. Type, by monotypy,
> *T. albicollis* Pl. col. 326 = *Trogon temnurus* Temminck.
> *Priotelus* G. R. Gray, 1840, List Genera Birds, p. 10. New name for *Temnurus* Swainson,
> preoccupied.
> *Temnotrogon* Bonaparte, 1854, Ateneo Ital. 2: 129. Type, by monotypy, *Trogon ro-*
> *seigaster* Vieillot.

Priotelus temnurus (Temminck). Cuban Trogon.

> *Trogon temnurus* Temminck, 1825, Planches Color., livr. 55, pl. 326. (Havana, Cuba.)

Habitat.—Tropical Lowland Evergreen Forest, Tropical Deciduous Forest, Pine Forest,
Secondary Forest (0–2000 m).
Distribution.—*Resident* on Cuba and the Isle of Pines.

Priotelus roseigaster (Vieillot). Hispaniolan Trogon.

> *Trogon roseigaster* Vieillot, 1817, Nouv. Dict. Hist. Nat. (nouv. éd.) 8: 314. (Santo
> Domingo and México = Hispaniola.)

Habitat.—Montane Evergreen Forest, Pine Forest (0–3000 m).
Distribution.—*Resident* on Hispaniola.
Notes.—Often placed in the monotypic genus *Temnotrogon.*

Genus *TROGON* Brisson

> *Trogon* Brisson, 1760, Ornithologie 1: 42; 4: 164. Type, by subsequent designation
> (Stone, 1907), *Trogon viridis* Linnaeus.

Curucujus Bonaparte, 1854, Ateneo Ital. 2: no. 8. Type, by subsequent designation (G. R. Gray, 1855), *"Trogon curucui* Linn." = *Trogon melanurus* Swainson.

Trogonurus Bonaparte, Ateneo Ital. 2: no. 8. Type, by subsequent designation (G. R. Gray, 1855), *Trogon collaris* Vieillot.

Microtrogon (not Bertoni, 1901) Goeldi, 1908, Bol. Mus. Goeldi, 5: 92. Type, by monotypy, *Trogon ramoniana* Deville and Des Murs.

Chrysotrogon Ridgway, 1911, Bull. U. S. Natl. Mus. 50(5): 784. New name for *Microtrogon* Goeldi, preoccupied.

Trogon melanocephalus Gould. Black-headed Trogon.

Trogon melanocephala Gould, 1836, Monogr. Trogonidae, ed. 1, pt. 2, pl. [6] and text. (State of Tamaulipas, Mexico.)

Habitat.—Tropical Lowland Evergreen Forest, Tropical Deciduous Forest, Gallery Forest, Secondary Forest (0–1000 m; Tropical and lower Subtropical zones, mostly below 600 m).

Distribution.—*Resident* from southern Tamaulipas (formerly?) and southern Veracruz (and possibly eastern San Luis Potosí) south on the Gulf-Caribbean slope (including the Yucatan Peninsula) to northeastern Costa Rica, and on the Pacific slope from El Salvador south to northwestern Costa Rica.

Notes.—Formerly considered conspecific (e.g., Peters 1945), *T. melanocephalus* and *T. citreolus* constitute a superspecies (Sibley and Monroe 1990).

Trogon citreolus Gould. Citreoline Trogon.

Trogon citreolus Gould, 1835, Proc. Zool. Soc. London, p. 30. (No locality given = Colima.)

Habitat.—Tropical Deciduous Forest, Gallery Forest, Secondary Forest (0–1000 m; Tropical and lower Subtropical zones).

Distribution.—*Resident* on the Pacific slope from southern Sinaloa to western Chiapas.

Notes.—See comments under *T. melanocephalus.*

Trogon viridis Linnaeus. White-tailed Trogon.

Trogon viridis Linnaeus, 1766, Syst. Nat. (ed. 12) 1: 167. Based on "Le Couroucou verd de Cayenne" Brisson, Ornithologie 4: 168, pl. 17, fig. 1. (in Cayania = Cayenne.)

Habitat.—Tropical Lowland Evergreen Forest (0–1300 m; Tropical and lower Subtropical zones).

Distribution.—*Resident* in Panama (west on the Caribbean slope nearly to the Costa Rican border, and on the Pacific to eastern Panamá province), and in South America from Colombia, Venezuela, Trinidad, and the Guianas south, west of the Andes to western Ecuador and east of the Andes to northern Bolivia and south-central Brazil.

Notes.—Formerly considered conspecific (e.g., Peters 1945), *T. viridis* and *T. bairdii* constitute a superspecies (Sibley and Monroe 1990).

Trogon bairdii Lawrence. Baird's Trogon.

Trogon bairdii Lawrence, 1868, Ann. Lyc. Nat. Hist. N. Y. 9: 119. (San Mateo, Costa Rica.)

Habitat.—Tropical Lowland Evergreen Forest (0–1250 m; Tropical and lower Subtropical zones).

Distribution.—*Resident* on the Pacific slope of southwestern Costa Rica (north to the region around Río Grande de Tárcoles) and western Panama (western Chiriquí).

Notes.—See comments under *T. viridis.*

Trogon violaceus Gmelin. Violaceous Trogon.

Trogon violaceus Gmelin, 1788, Syst. Nat. 1(1): 404. Based mainly on "Couroucou à chaperon violet" Buffon, Hist. Nat. Ois. 6: 294, and the "Violet-headed Curucui" Latham, Gen. Synop. Birds 1(2): 491. (No locality given = Surinam.)

Habitat.—Tropical Lowland Evergreen Forest, Secondary Forest, Tropical Deciduous Forest (0–1800 m; Tropical and lower Subtropical zones).

Distribution.—*Resident* [*caligatus* group] from southeastern San Luis Potosí, Puebla, Veracruz, and Oaxaca south along both slopes of Middle America (including the Yucatan Peninsula) to Panama, western and northern Colombia, northwestern Venezuela, and western Ecuador; and [*violaceus* group] from eastern Colombia, southern Venezuela, Trinidad, and the Guianas south, east of the Andes, to northern Bolivia and Amazonian Brazil.

Notes.—Groups: *T. caligatus* Gould, 1838 [Gartered Trogon] and *T. violaceus* [Violaceous Trogon].

Trogon mexicanus Swainson. Mountain Trogon.

Trogon Mexicanus Swainson, 1827, Philos. Mag. (n.s.) 1: 440. (Temiscaltipec, Mexico = Temascaltepec, México.)

Habitat.—Pine-Oak Forest, Pine Forest, Montane Evergreen Forest (1200–3500 m; Subtropical and Temperate zones).

Distribution.—*Resident* from eastern Sinaloa, southern Chihuahua, Durango, Zacatecas, San Luis Potosí and southern Tamaulipas south through the mountains of Mexico and Guatemala to El Salvador and central Honduras.

Notes.—Also known as Mexican Trogon.

Trogon elegans Gould. Elegant Trogon.

Trogon elegans Gould, 1834, Proc. Zool. Soc. London, p. 26. (apud Guatimala, in Mexico = Guatemala.)

Habitat.—Tropical Deciduous Forest, Pine-Oak Forest; in United States, primarily sycamore riparian woodland adjacent to pine-oak woodland (0–2500 m; Tropical to lower Temperate zones).

Distribution.—*Resident* [*ambiguus* group] from Sonora, southeastern Arizona, southwestern New Mexico (rarely), Chihuahua, Durango, Zacatecas, Nuevo León, and Tamaulipas south through Mexico (including María Madre and María Magdalena in the Tres Marias Islands) to Guerrero, Veracruz, and Oaxaca (west of the Isthmus of Tehuantepec); and [*elegans* group] in southern and eastern Guatemala (Motagua Valley and Pacific lowlands), El Salvador, Honduras (interior valleys and Pacific lowlands), Nicaragua (Pacific slope), and northwestern Costa Rica (Guanacaste). Northernmost populations [*ambiguus* group] are mostly migratory, the species being casual in the southwestern United States in winter.

Casual [*ambiguus* group] in south-central Arizona (west to Phoenix area) and southern Texas (Big Bend and lower Rio Grande Valley).

Notes.—Groups: *T. ambiguus* Gould, 1835 [Coppery-tailed Trogon] and *T. elegans* [Elegant Trogon].

Trogon collaris Vieillot. Collared Trogon.

Trogon collaris Vieillot, 1817, Nouv. Dict. Hist. Nat. (nouv. éd.) 8: 320. (Cayenne.)

Habitat.—Tropical Lowland Evergreen Forest, Montane Evergreen Forest, River-edge Forest, Tropical Deciduous Forest (0–2500 m; Tropical and Subtropical zones).

Distribution.—*Resident* [*puella* group] from Guerrero, Hidalgo, southeastern San Luis Potosí, Veracruz, and northern Oaxaca south along both slopes of Middle America including the Yucatan Peninsula (not recorded Pacific slope of Nicaragua) to Panama (western Chiriquí, western Bocas del Toro, and Darién); and [*collaris* group] in extreme eastern Panama (Cerro Pirre in eastern Darién), and in South America from Colombia, Venezuela, Tobago, Trinidad, and the Guianas south, west of the Andes to southwestern Ecuador and east of the Andes to central Bolivia and Amazonian and southeastern Brazil.

Notes.—Groups: *T. puella* Gould, 1845 [Bar-tailed Trogon] and *T. collaris* [Collared Trogon]. See comments under *T. aurantiiventris*.

Trogon aurantiiventris Gould. Orange-bellied Trogon.

Trogon aurantiiventris Gould, 1856, Proc. Zool. Soc. London, p. 107. (near David, Veragua [= Chiriquí, Panama].)

Habitat.—Montane Evergreen Forest, Secondary Forest (600–2100 m; Subtropical and lower Temperate zones).

Distribution.—*Resident* in the mountains of Costa Rica and western and central Panama (east to western Panamá province).

Notes.—Probably a localized color morph of *T. collaris* (Stiles and Skutch 1989; see also Wetmore 1968).

Trogon rufus Gmelin. Black-throated Trogon.

Trogon rufus Gmelin, 1788, Syst. Nat. 1(1): 404. Based mainly on "Couroucou à queue rousse de Cayenne" Buffon, Hist. Nat. Ois. 6: 293, and Daubenton, Planches Enlum., pl. 736. (in Cayenna = Cayenne.)

Habitat.—Tropical Lowland Evergreen Forest, Secondary Forest (0–1000 m; Tropical Zone).

Distribution.—*Resident* on the Caribbean slope of Honduras (east of the Sula Valley) and Nicaragua, on both slopes of Costa Rica (except the dry northwest) and Panama, and in South America from Colombia, Venezuela, and the Guianas south, west of the Andes to western Ecuador and east of the Andes to central Peru, Amazonian and southeastern Brazil, extreme northeastern Argentina, and eastern Paraguay.

Notes.—Also known as Graceful Trogon.

Trogon melanurus Swainson. Black-tailed Trogon.

Trogon melanurus Swainson, 1838 (January), Animals in Menageries, *in* Lardner, Cabinet Cyclopedia 98: 329. (Demerara [Guyana].)

Habitat.—Tropical Lowland Evergreen Forest, River-edge Forest, Mangrove Forest (0–1000 m; Tropical Zone).

Distribution.—*Resident* [*macroura* group] in central and eastern Panama (the Canal area eastward), northern Colombia, and northwestern Venezuela; and [*melanurus* group] from eastern Colombia, southern Venezuela, and the Guianas south, east of the Andes to central Bolivia and Amazonian Brazil, and west of the Andes in western Ecuador and northwestern Peru.

Notes.—Groups: *T. macroura* Gould, 1838 (March) [Large-tailed Trogon] and *T. melanurus* [Black-tailed Trogon].

Trogon massena Gould. Slaty-tailed Trogon.

Trogon massena Gould, 1838, Monogr. Trogonidae, ed. 1, pt. 3, pl. [4] and text. (México.)

Habitat.—Tropical Lowland Evergreen Forest, Secondary Forest (0–1200 m; Tropical and lower Subtropical zones).

Distribution.—*Resident* [*massena* group] on the Gulf-Caribbean slope of southern Veracruz, Oaxaca, Tabasco, Chiapas, southern Campeche, southern Quintana Roo, Belize, Guatemala, and Honduras, and on both slopes of Nicaragua, Costa Rica (absent from the dry northwest), and Panama; and [*australis* group] on the Pacific slope of Colombia and northwestern Ecuador.

Notes.—Also known as Massena Trogon. Groups: *T. massena* [Massena Trogon] and *T. australis* (Chapman, 1915) [Chapman's Trogon].

Trogon clathratus Salvin. Lattice-tailed Trogon.

Trogon clathratus Salvin, 1866, Proc. Zool. Soc. London, p. 75. (Santa Fé de Veragua, Panamá = Calovévora, Veraguas, Panama.)

Habitat.—Tropical Lowland Evergreen Forest (100–1100 m; Tropical and lower Subtropical zones).

Distribution.—*Resident* on the Caribbean slope of Costa Rica (recorded from Río San Juan on the Nicaragua-Costa Rica border) and Panama (Bocas del Toro, Veraguas, and Coclé, locally also on the Pacific slope in Chiriquí and Veraguas).

Genus *EUPTILOTIS* Gould

Euptilotis (not *Euptilotus* Reichenbach, 1850) Gould, 1858, Monogr. Trogonidae, ed. 2, pt. 1, pl. 4 and text. Type, by original designation, *Trogon neoxenus* Gould.
Leptuas Cabanis and Heine, 1863, Mus. Heineanum 4(1): 185, 206. Type, by monotypy, *Trogon neoxenus* Gould.

Euptilotis neoxenus (Gould). Eared Trogon.

Trogon neoxenus Gould, 1838, Monogr. Trogonidae, ed. 1, pt. 3, pl. [10] and text. (Mexico.)

Habitat.—Pine Forest, Pine-Oak Forest (1800–3100 m; Temperate Zone).

Distribution.—*Resident* in the mountains of southern Arizona (Ramsey Canyon, rarely), northwestern Chihuahua, Sinaloa, Durango, Zacatecas, Nayarit, Jalisco, and Michoacán.

Recorded casually elsewhere in southern Arizona (Huachuca and Chiricahua mountains) and Sonora; a sight report for southwestern New Mexico (Animas Mountains).

Notes.—Also known as Eared Quetzal.

Genus *PHAROMACHRUS* de la Llave

Pharomachrus de la Llave, 1832, Registro Trimestre 1: 48. Type, by monotypy, *Pharomachrus mocinno* de la Llave.

Pharomachrus auriceps (Gould). Golden-headed Quetzal.

Trogon (Calurus) auriceps Gould, 1842, Ann. Mag., Nat. Hist. (1)9: 238. (the Cordillerian Andes.)

Habitat.—Montane Evergreen Forest (1200–1500 m; upper Tropical Zone).

Distribution.—*Resident* in eastern Panama (Cerro Pirre in eastern Darién); and in South America in the Andes from Colombia and northwestern Venezuela south to northern Bolivia.

Notes.—Sibley and Monroe (1990) considered *P. auriceps* and Amazonian *P. pavoninus* (Spix, 1824) to constitute a superspecies; they were considered conspecific by Peters (1945).

Pharomachrus mocinno de la Llave. Resplendent Quetzal.

Pharomachrus Mocinno de la Llave, 1832, Registro Trimestre 1: 48. (Guatemala and Chiapas.)

Habitat.—Montane Evergreen Forest (1300–3000 m; Subtropical and lower Temperate zones).

Distribution.—*Resident* in the mountains of southeastern Oaxaca (Sierra Madre de Chiapas), Chiapas, Guatemala, El Salvador, Honduras, north-central Nicaragua, Costa Rica (except the Cordillera de Guanacaste), and western Panama (east to Veraguas, at least formerly).

Notes.—Sibley and Monroe (1990) considered *P. mocinno* and the Andean *P. antisianus* (d'Orbigny, 1837) to constitute a superspecies; they were considered conspecific by Peters (1945). For use of "*mocinno*" instead of the emended "*mocino*," see Eisenmann (1959a).

Order UPUPIFORMES: Hoopoes and Allies

Family UPUPIDAE: Hoopoes

Genus *UPUPA* Linnaeus

Upupa Linnaeus, 1758, Syst. Nat. (ed. 10) 1: 117. Type, by tautonymy, *Upupa epops* Linnaeus (*Upupa,* prebinomial specific name, in synonymy).

Upupa epops Linnaeus. Eurasian Hoopoe.

Upupa Epops Linnaeus, 1758, Syst. Nat. (ed. 10) 1: 117. (in Europæ sylvis = Sweden.)

Habitat.—A variety of open and partly open situations.
Distribution.—*Breeds* from northern Eurasia south to southern Africa, Madagascar, India, and Southeast Asia, and *winters* from southern Europe, India, and southern China south through the remainder of the breeding range.
Accidental in western Alaska (Old Chevak, Yukon-Kuskokwim Delta, 2–3 September 1975; Dau and Paniyak 1977).

Order CORACIIFORMES: Rollers, Motmots, Kingfishers, and Allies

Suborder ALCEDINES: Todies, Motmots, and Kingfishers

Superfamily TODOIDEA: Todies and Motmots

Family TODIDAE: Todies

Genus *TODUS* Brisson

Todus Brisson, 1760, Ornithologie 1: 44; 4: 528. Type, by tautonymy, *Alcedo todus* Linnaeus.

Todus multicolor Gould. Cuban Tody.

Todus multicolor Gould, 1837, Icones Avium, pt. 1, pl. [12] and text. (No locality given = western Cuba.)

Habitat.—Arid Lowland Scrub, Arid Montane Scrub, Tropical Deciduous Forest, Tropical Lowland Evergreen Forest, Montane Evergreen Forest, Pine Forest (0–2400 m)
Distribution.—*Resident* on Cuba and the Isle of Pines.

Todus subulatus Gray. Broad-billed Tody.

Todus subulatus "Gould" G. R. Gray, 1847, Genera Birds 1: pl. 22. (No locality given.)

Habitat.—Tropical Deciduous Forest, Arid Lowland Scrub, Secondary Forest, Tropical Lowland Evergreen Forest Edge, Second-growth Scrub (0–1700 m).
Distribution.—*Resident* on Hispaniola (including Gonâve Island).
Notes.—Also known as Hispaniolan Tody.

Todus angustirostris Lafresnaye. Narrow-billed Tody.

Todus angustirostris Lafresnaye, 1851, Rev. Mag. Zool. (2)3: 478. (in Sancti-Dominicensis insulâ = Hispaniola.)

Habitat.—Montane Evergreen Forest, Secondary Forest (900–2400 m).
Distribution.—*Resident* in the mountains of Hispaniola (locally also at low elevations in the Dominican Republic).

Todus todus (Linnaeus). Jamaican Tody.

> *Alcedo Todus* Linnaeus, 1758, Syst. Nat. (ed. 10) 1: 116. Based mainly on "The Green Sparrow, or Green Humming Bird" Edwards, Nat. Hist. Birds 3: 121, pl. 121, upper fig. (in America = Jamaica.)

Habitat.—Tropical Lowland Evergreen Forest, Tropical Deciduous Forest, Secondary Forest, Mangrove Forest (0–1800 m).
Distribution.—*Resident* on Jamaica.

Todus mexicanus Lesson. Puerto Rican Tody.

> *Todus mexicanus* Lesson, 1838, Ann. Sci. Nat. (Zool.) (2)9: 167, note 1. (Mexico, particularly Tampico, error = Puerto Rico.)

Habitat.—Montane Evergreen Forest, Tropical Lowland Evergreen Forest, Tropical Deciduous Forest, Secondary Forest, Second-growth Scrub (0–1000 m).
Distribution.—*Resident* on Puerto Rico.

Family MOMOTIDAE: Motmots

Genus *HYLOMANES* Lichtenstein

> *Hylomanes* Lichtenstein, 1839, Abh. Phys. Kl. Akad. Wiss. Berlin (1838), p. 449, pl. 4. Type, by monotypy, *Hylomanes momotula* Lichtenstein.

Hylomanes momotula Lichtenstein. Tody Motmot.

> *Hylomanes momotula* Lichtenstein, 1839, Abh. Phys. Kl. Akad. Wiss. Berlin (1838), p. 449, pl. 4. (Valle Real, Mexico = Valle Nacional, Oaxaca; Binford, 1990, Wilson Bull. 102: 151.)

Habitat.—Tropical Lowland Evergreen Forest, Montane Evergreen Forest (0–1500 m; Tropical and lower Subtropical zones).
Distribution.—*Resident* from southern Veracruz and northern Oaxaca south on the Gulf-Caribbean slope (including the Yucatan Peninsula) to Nicaragua (recorded only at Peña Blanca, depto. Jinotega), locally on the Pacific slope of Chiapas, Guatemala, and El Salvador (El Imposible), and in Costa Rica (most frequently on the Pacific slope of Cordillera de Guanacaste), Panama (local, recorded Veraguas, Colón, eastern Panamá province, eastern San Blas, and Darién), and western Colombia.

Genus *ASPATHA* Sharpe

> *Aspatha* Sharpe, 1892, Cat. Birds Br. Mus. 17: x, 313, 331. Type, by monotypy, *Prionites gularis* Lafresnaye.

Aspatha gularis (Lafresnaye). Blue-throated Motmot.

> *Prionites gularis* Lafresnaye, 1840, Rev. Zool. [Paris] 3: 130. (Guatimala = Guatemala.)

Habitat.—Montane Evergreen Forest, Pine-Oak Forest (1500–3100 m; Subtropical and lower Temperate zones).
Distribution.—*Resident* in the mountains of southeastern Oaxaca (Sierra Madre de Chiapas), Chiapas, Guatemala, El Salvador, and Honduras.

Genus *MOMOTUS* Brisson

> *Momotus* Brisson, 1760, Ornithologie 1: 44; 4: 465. Type, by tautonymy, *Momotus* Brisson = *Ramphastos momota* Linnaeus.

Momotus mexicanus Swainson. Russet-crowned Motmot.

> *Momotus Mexicanus* Swainson, 1827, Philos. Mag. (n.s.) 1: 442. (Temiscaltipec, Mexico = Temascaltepec, México.)

Habitat.—Tropical Deciduous Forest, Gallery Forest, Secondary Forest (0–1900 m; Tropical and lower Subtropical zones).

Distribution.—*Resident* in western and interior Mexico from southern Sonora, southwestern Chihuahua, Durango, and Zacatecas south to Morelos, western Puebla, Oaxaca, and Chiapas; and in the interior of Guatemala (upper Motagua Valley).

Momotus momota (Linnaeus). Blue-crowned Motmot.

Ramphastos Momota Linnaeus, 1766, Syst. Nat. (ed. 12) 1: 152. (in America meridionali = Cayenne.)

Habitat.—Tropical Lowland Evergreen Forest, Montane Evergreen Forest, Secondary Forest, Gallery Forest, Tropical Deciduous Forest, River-edge Forest (0–1600 m; Tropical and Subtropical zones).

Distribution.—*Resident* [*coeruliceps* group] in Nuevo León, Tamaulipas, San Luis Potosí and northern Veracruz; [*lessonii* group] from southern Veracruz and northern and southeastern Oaxaca south along both slopes of Middle America (including the Yucatan Peninsula) to western Panama; [*subrufescens* group] in eastern Panama, northern Colombia, and northern Venezuela; [*momota* group] in South America from eastern Colombia, southern Venezuela (also Tobago and Trinidad), and the Guianas south, west of the Andes to northwestern Peru and east of the Andes to northern Argentina, Paraguay, and south-central Brazil; and [*aequatorialis* group] on the east slope of the Andes from Colombia south to northern Bolivia.

Notes.—Throughout the extensive range of this species, various morphologically, and possibly vocally (Ridgely and Gwynne 1989), distinct groups exist, which may represent distinct species: *M. coeruliceps* (Gould, 1836) [Blue-crowned Motmot], *M. lessonii* Lesson, 1842 [Lesson's Motmot], *M. subrufescens* Sclater, 1853 [Tawny-bellied Motmot], *M. momota* [Blue-diademed Motmot], and *M. aequatorialis* Gould, 1858 [Highland Motmot]. Each of these groups was treated as a separate species by Ridgway (1914) and Cory (1918), and Fjeldså and Krabbe (1990) treated *aequatorialis* as a species.

Genus *BARYPHTHENGUS* Cabanis and Heine

Baryphthengus Cabanis and Heine, 1859, Mus. Heineanum 2: 114. Type, by subsequent designation (Sharpe, 1892), *Baryphonus ruficapillus* Vieillot.

Baryphthengus martii (Vieillot). Rufous Motmot.

Prionites martii Spix, 1824, Av. Bras. 1: 64. (near Pará, Brazil.)

Habitat.—Tropical Lowland Evergreen Forest (0–1400 m; Tropical and lower Subtropical zones).

Distribution.—*Resident* on the Caribbean slope of northeastern Honduras (Gracias a Dios), Nicaragua, and Costa Rica, on both slopes of Panama, and in South America from Colombia south, west of the Andes to western Ecuador and east of the Andes south to central Bolivia and Amazonian Brazil.

Notes.—Wetmore (1968) and Ridgely and Gwynne (1989) treated *B. martii* as a separate species from *B. ruficapillus* (Vieillot, 1818) [Rufous-capped Motmot] of southeastern South America, partly because they thought that *ruficapillus* never acquires racquet tail tips, in contrast to *martii*; evidently, they did not realize that Amazonian *martii* also lacks racquet tail tips. Nevertheless, Sick's (1984, 1993) descriptions of the vocal differences between *ruficapillus* and *martii* strongly suggest that they should be treated as separate species, the treatment followed here (contra A.O.U. 1983).

Genus *ELECTRON* Gistel

Crypticus (not Latreille, 1817) Swainson, 1837, Class. Birds 2: 338. Type, by monotypy, *C. platyrhynchus* Ill. of Orn. iii. pl. 106 = *Momotus platyrhynchus* Leadbeater.

Electron Gistel, 1848, Naturgesch. Thierr. Höhere Schulen, p. viii. New name for *Crypticus* Swainson, preoccupied.

Electron carinatum (Du Bus de Gisignies). Keel-billed Motmot.

> *Prionites carinatus* Du Bus de Gisignies, 1847, Bull. Acad. R. Sci. Lett. Beaux-Arts Belg., 14, p. 108. (Guatemala.)

Habitat.—Tropical Lowland Evergreen Forest, Montane Evergreen Forest (0–1500 m; Tropical and Subtropical zones).

Distribution.—*Resident* locally on the Caribbean slope from southeastern Mexico (Veracruz, Tabasco, and Oaxaca) south through Central America to northeastern Costa Rica.

Electron platyrhynchum (Leadbeater). Broad-billed Motmot.

> *Momotus platyrhynchus* Leadbeater, 1829, Trans. Linn. Soc. London 16: 92. (Brazil, error = western Ecuador.)

Habitat.—Tropical Lowland Evergreen Forest (0–1500 m; Tropical and Subtropical zones).

Distribution.—*Resident* [*platyrhynchum* group] in eastern Honduras (Lancetilla, Olancho), Nicaragua (Caribbean slope), Costa Rica (mostly Caribbean slope, locally on Pacific drainage), Panama (both slopes), western Colombia, and western Ecuador; and [*pyrrholaemum* group] in South America from southeastern Colombia south, east of the Andes, to east-central Bolivia, and central Brazil.

Notes.—Groups: *E. platyrhynchum* [Broad-billed Motmot] and *E. pyrrholaemum* (Berlepsch and Stolzmann, 1902) [Plain-tailed Motmot].

Genus *EUMOMOTA* Sclater

> *Eumomota* Sclater, 1858, Proc. Zool. Soc. London (1857), p. 257. Type, by monotypy, *Prionites superciliaris* Jardine and Selby = *Pyronites superciliosus* Sandbach.

Eumomota superciliosa (Sandbach). Turquoise-browed Motmot.

> *Pyronites superciliosus* Sandbach, 1837, Athenaeum, no. 517, p. 698. (México = Campeche.)

Habitat.—Tropical Deciduous Forest, Gallery Forest, Secondary Forest (0–1400 m; Tropical Zone).

Distribution.—*Resident* in the Gulf-Caribbean lowlands of southeastern Mexico (from eastern Tabasco through the Yucatan Peninsula, formerly from southern Veracruz); in the Pacific lowlands of Middle America from Oaxaca (vagrant only) and Chiapas south to central Costa Rica (south to Quepos); and in the interior valleys of Guatemala (Motagua and Río Negro drainages) and Honduras (locally spreading to Caribbean lowlands).

Superfamily ALCEDINOIDEA: Kingfishers

Family **ALCEDINIDAE**: Kingfishers

Subfamily CERYLINAE: Typical Kingfishers

Genus *CERYLE* Boie

> *Ceryle* Boie, 1828, Isis von Oken, col. 316. Type, by subsequent designation (G. R. Gray, 1840), *C. rudis* (Gm.) = *Alcedo rudis* Linnaeus.

Subgenus *MEGACERYLE* Kaup

> *Megaceryle* Kaup, 1848, Verh. Naturhist. Ver. Grossherz. Hessen 2: 68. Type, by subsequent designation (Sharpe, 1871), *Alcedo guttata* Vigors = *Ceryle guttulata* Stejneger.
> *Streptoceryle* Bonaparte, 1854, Ateneo Ital. 2: 320. Type, by subsequent designation (G. R. Gray, 1855), *Alcedo torquata* Linnaeus.

Ceryle torquata (Linnaeus). Ringed Kingfisher.

Alcedo torquata Linnaeus, 1766, Syst. Nat. (ed. 12) 1: 180. Based mainly on "Le Martin-pescheur hupé du Mexique" Brisson, Ornithologie 4: 518, pl. 41, fig. 1. (in Martinica, Mexico = Mexico.)

Habitat.—Rivers, Freshwater Lakes and Ponds, Coastal Waters, Mangrove Forest (0–2000 m; Tropical to lower Temperate zones).

Distribution.—*Resident* from southern Sinaloa, Nuevo León, southern Texas (lower Rio Grande Valley west to Val Verde County), and Tamaulipas south along both slopes of Middle America (including islands off the Pacific coast from the Tres Marias south to the Pearl islands), and throughout most of South America from Colombia, Venezuela (including Margarita Island), Trinidad, and the Guianas south to Tierra del Fuego; and in the Lesser Antilles (Guadeloupe, Dominica, and Martinique, doubtfully recorded from Grenada and St. Kitts).

Casual in western Texas (Big Bend), and north to central and southeastern Texas (Travis, Kerr, and Fort Bend counties); a sight report from Puerto Rico.

Ceryle alcyon (Linnaeus). Belted Kingfisher.

Alcedo Alcyon Linnaeus, 1758, Syst. Nat. (ed. 10) 1: 115. Based mainly on the "Kingfisher" Catesby, Nat. Hist. Carolina 1: 69, pl. 69. (in America = South Carolina.)

Habitat.—Mainly wooded rivers, streams, and lakes; in nonbreeding season more widespread, i.e., shorelines of bodies of water wherever trees, rocks, or manmade objects provide suitable hunting perches, including along coasts, watercourses in open country, or marshes.

Distribution.—*Breeds* from western and central Alaska, central Yukon, British Columbia (including the Queen Charlotte and Vancouver islands), western and south-central Mackenzie, northern Saskatchewan, central (and probably northern) Manitoba, northern Ontario, central Quebec, east-central Labrador, and Newfoundland south to southern California, southern Arizona, southern New Mexico, southern Texas, the Gulf coast, and central Florida.

Winters from south-coastal and southeastern Alaska, southern British Columbia, western and central Montana, Wyoming, Nebraska, southern Minnesota, the southern Great Lakes region, New York, and New England (casually north to the Maritime Provinces) south throughout the continental United States, Middle America (including offshore islands from western Mexico to Cocos and the Pearl islands), the West Indies, and Bermuda to northern South America (recorded Colombia, Venezuela, Guyana, and most islands off Venezuela) and the Galapagos Islands.

Casual in the Hawaiian Islands, the eastern Aleutians, northern Alaska (Point Barrow), Clipperton Island, Greenland, Iceland, the British Isles, continental Europe, and the Azores.

Genus *CHLOROCERYLE* Kaup

Chloroceryle [subgenus] Kaup, 1848, Verh. Naturhist. Ver. Grossherz. Hessen 2: 68. Type, by subsequent designation (Sharpe, 1871), *Alcedo superciliosa* Linnaeus = *Alcedo aenea* Pallas.

Chloroceryle amazona (Latham). Amazon Kingfisher.

Alcedo amazona Latham, 1790, Index Ornithol. 1: 257. Based on the "Amazonian Kingfisher" Latham, Gen. Synop. Birds (suppl.) 1: 116. (in Cayana = Cayenne.)

Habitat.—Rivers, Freshwater Lakes and Ponds (0–1200 m; Tropical and lower Subtropical zones).

Distribution.—*Resident* from southern Sinaloa, southeastern San Luis Potosí and southern Tamaulipas south along both slopes of Middle America (except Campeche and Yucatán), and in South America west of the Andes in western Colombia, and east of the Andes from Colombia, Venezuela, Trinidad, and the Guianas south to northern Argentina and Uruguay.

Ranges north in winter to southern Sinaloa.

Chloroceryle americana (Gmelin). Green Kingfisher.

> *Alcedo americana* Gmelin, 1788, Syst. Nat. 1(1): 451. Based on "Martin-pescheur du Brésil" Brisson, Ornithologie 4: 510, and "Martin-pecheur vert et blanc de Cayenne" Daubenton, Planches Enlum., pl. 591. (in Cayenna = Cayenne.)

Habitat.—Streams, Freshwater Lakes and Ponds, Rivers (0–2100 m; Tropical and Subtropical zones).

Distribution.—*Resident* from southern Arizona, Sonora, Chihuahua, northern Coahuila, and central Texas south, primarily in the lowlands, along both slopes of Middle America (including Isla Coiba, Isla Cébaco, and other small islands off Panama), and in South America from Colombia, Venezuela (also Tobago and Trinidad), and the Guianas south, west of the Andes to northern Chile and east of the Andes to central Argentina.

Casual north to north-central and eastern Texas.

Chloroceryle inda (Linnaeus). Green-and-rufous Kingfisher.

> *Alcedo inda* Linnaeus, 1766, Syst. Nat. (ed. 12) 1: 179. Based on the "Spotted King's-fisher" Edwards, Glean. Nat. Hist. 3: 262, pl. 335. (in India occidentali, error = Guyana.)

Habitat.—Streams, Freshwater Lakes and Ponds (Tropical Zone; mostly below 200 m).

Distribution.—*Resident* locally on the Caribbean slope of southeastern Nicaragua, Costa Rica, and Panama, locally on the Pacific slope of Panama (from Panamá province east, including the Pearl Islands), and in South America from Colombia, Venezuela, and the Guianas south, west of the Andes to western Ecuador and east of the Andes to central Bolivia and central and southeastern Brazil.

Chloroceryle aenea (Pallas). American Pygmy Kingfisher.

> *Alcedo (aenea)* Pallas, 1764, in Vroeg, Cat. Raisonné Ois., Adumbr., p. 1, no. 54. (Surinam.)

Habitat.—Streams, Freshwater Lakes and Ponds (Tropical Zone; 0–750 m).

Distribution.—*Resident* from southeastern San Luis Potosí, Veracruz, northern Oaxaca, northern and southeastern Chiapas, and the Yucatan Peninsula south in the lowlands of both slopes of Middle America (including Cozumel Island off Quintana Roo, the Bay Islands off Honduras, and Isla Coiba off Panama), and in South America from Colombia, Venezuela, Trinidad, and the Guianas south, west of the Andes to western Ecuador and east of the Andes to central Bolivia and central and southeastern Brazil.

Order **PICIFORMES**: Puffbirds, Jacamars, Toucans, Woodpeckers, and Allies

Notes.—For relationships within the Order, see Beecher (1953), Simpson and Cracraft (1981), Swierczewski and Raikow (1981), Olson (1983), Raikow and Cracraft (1983), Avise and Aquadro (1987), Lanyon and Zink (1987), Brom (1990), Sibley and Ahlquist (1990), and Harshman (1994).

Suborder GALBULI: Puffbirds and Jacamars

Family **BUCCONIDAE**: Puffbirds

Genus *NYSTALUS* Cabanis and Heine

> *Nystalus* Cabanis and Heine, 1863, Mus. Heineanum 4(1): 139. Type, by subsequent designation (Sclater, 1882), *Alcedo maculata* Gmelin.

Nystalus radiatus (Sclater). Barred Puffbird.

> *Bucco radiatus* Sclater, 1854, Proc. Zool. Soc. London (1853), p. 122, pl. 50–51. (in Nova Grenada = Magdalena Valley, Colombia.)

Habitat.—Tropical Lowland Evergreen Forest Edge, Secondary Forest (0–900 m; Tropical and lower Subtropical zones).

Distribution.—*Resident* from Panama (west to Coclé and western Panamá province, possibly to Veraguas) and northern Colombia south through western Colombia to western Ecuador.

Notes.—The genus *Nystalus* was merged into *Bucco* Brisson, 1760 by A.O.U. (1983) but see A.O.U. (1993).

Genus *NOTHARCHUS* Cabanis and Heine

Notharchus Cabanis and Heine, 1863, Mus. Heineanum 4(1): 146, 149. Type, by subsequent designation (Sclater, 1882), *Bucco hyperrhynchus* Sclater = *Bucco macrorhynchos* Gmelin.

Notharchus macrorhynchos (Gmelin). White-necked Puffbird.

Bucco macrorhynchos Gmelin, 1788, Syst. Nat., 1(1): 406. Based in part on "Le plus grand Barbu à gros bec de Cayenne" Daubenton, Planches Enlum., pl. 689. (in Cayenna = Cayenne.)

Habitat.—Tropical Lowland Evergreen Forest, Secondary Forest (0–900 m; Tropical and lower Subtropical zones).

Distribution.—*Resident* [*macrorhynchos* group] from southern Mexico (west-central Veracruz, Oaxaca, Chiapas, southern Campeche, and Quintana Roo) south along both slopes of Middle America, and in South America from Colombia, Venezuela, and the Guianas south, west of the Andes to western Ecuador and east of the Andes to central Bolivia and Amazonian Brazil; and [*swainsonii* group] in Paraguay, northeastern Argentina, and southeastern Brazil.

Notes.—This and the following two species were placed in the genus *Bucco* by A.O.U. (1983) but see A.O.U. (1993). Groups: *N. macrorhynchos* [White-necked Puffbird] and *N. swainsonii* (Gray, 1846) [Buff-bellied Puffbird].

Notharchus pectoralis (Gray). Black-breasted Puffbird.

Bucco pectoralis G. R. Gray, 1846, Genera Birds 1: pl. 26. (No locality given; Valley of the lower Magdalena River, Colombia, suggested by Cory [1919].)

Habitat.—Tropical Lowland Evergreen Forest, Secondary Forest (0–1000 m; Tropical Zone).

Distribution.—*Resident* in eastern Panama (west to the Canal area, mostly on the Pacific drainage), and in South America from northern Colombia south, west of the Andes, to northwestern Ecuador.

Notes.—See comments under *N. macrorhynchos*.

Notharchus tectus (Boddaert). Pied Puffbird.

Bucco tectus Boddaert, 1783, Table Planches Enlum., p. 43. Based on "Barbu à plastron noir" Daubenton, Planches Enlum., pl. 688, fig. 2. (Cayenne.)

Habitat.—Tropical Lowland Evergreen Forest Edge, Secondary Forest (0–1000 m; Tropical Zone).

Distribution.—*Resident* on the Caribbean slope of Costa Rica (from Río Sarapiquí drainage southward), in Panama (throughout the Caribbean slope, on the Pacific known from eastern Panamá province and Darién), and in South America from Colombia, southern Venezuela, and the Guianas south, east of the Andes, to eastern Peru, extreme east-central Bolivia, and Amazonian Brazil, also west of the Andes in northwestern Ecuador.

Notes.—See comments under *N. macrorhynchos*.

Genus *MALACOPTILA* Gray

Malacoptila G. R. Gray, 1841, List Genera Birds, ed. 2, p. 13. Type, by subsequent designation (G. R. Gray, 1846), *Bucco fuscus* Gmelin.

Malacoptila panamensis Lafresnaye. White-whiskered Puffbird.

Malacoptila panamensis Lafresnaye, 1847, Rev. Zool. [Paris] 10: 79. (Panamá.)

Habitat.—Tropical Lowland Evergreen Forest, Secondary Forest (0–1250 m; Tropical and lower Subtropical zones).

Distribution.—*Resident* on the Gulf-Caribbean slope of Middle America from Tabasco and Chiapas south to Nicaragua, on both slopes of Costa Rica (absent from the drier portions of Guanacaste in the northwest) and Panama, and in South America from northern Colombia south, west of the Andes, to northwestern Ecuador.

Genus *MICROMONACHA* Sclater

Micromonacha Sclater, 1881, Monogr. Jacamars Puff-birds, pt. 5, p. 131, pl. 44. Type, by monotypy, *Bucco lanceolata* Deville.

Micromonacha lanceolata (Deville). Lanceolated Monklet.

Bucco lanceolata Deville, 1849, Rev. Mag. Zool. (2)1: 56. (Pampa del Sacramento, misión de Sarayacu [upper Amazon].)

Habitat.—Montane Evergreen Forest, Tropical Lowland Evergreen Forest (300–2100 m; Tropical and Subtropical zones).

Distribution.—*Resident* locally in Costa Rica (northern slope of Cordillera Central, Caribbean slope of Cordillera de Talamanca), Panama (one record from Caribbean slope of western Veraguas), western Colombia, and western Ecuador; also in South America east of the Andes in eastern Colombia, eastern Ecuador, eastern Peru, northern Bolivia, and western Amazonian Brazil.

Genus *NONNULA* Sclater

Nonnula Sclater, 1854, Proc. Zool. Soc. London (1853), p. 124. Type, by original designation, *Bucco rubecula* Spix.

Nonnula ruficapilla (Tschudi). Gray-cheeked Nunlet.

Lypornix ruficapilla Tschudi, 1844, Arch. Naturgesch. 10: 300. (Republica Peruana = Vitoc Valley, Peru.)

Habitat.—Tropical Lowland Evergreen Forest Edge, Secondary Forest (0–1000 m; Tropical Zone).

Distribution.—*Resident* [*frontalis* group] in central and eastern Panama (west to northern Coclé and the Canal area) and northern Colombia; and [*ruficapilla* group] in eastern Peru, eastern Bolivia, and western Brazil.

Notes.—The two groups are often regarded as distinct species, *N. frontalis* (Sclater, 1854) [Gray-cheeked Nunlet] and *N. ruficapilla* [Rufous-capped Nunlet] (Peters 1948, Wetmore 1968). Meyer de Schauensee (1970) treated the two as conspecific.

Genus *MONASA* Vieillot

Monasa Vieillot, 1816, Analyse, p. 27. Type, by monotypy, "Coucou noir de Cayenne" Buffon = *Cuculus ater* Boddaert.

Monasa morphoeus (Hahn and Küster). White-fronted Nunbird.

Bucco Morphæus "Wagler" Hahn and Küster, 1823, Vögel Asien, Afr., etc., lief. 14, pl. 2 and text. (Brazil.)

Habitat.—Tropical Lowland Evergreen Forest, Montane Evergreen Forest (0–1100 m; Tropical Zone).

Distribution.—*Resident* [*grandior* group] in the Caribbean lowlands of eastern Honduras (Olancho), Nicaragua, Costa Rica, and western Panama (western Bocas del Toro); [*pallescens* group] in eastern Panama (both slopes, west to western Colón) and northern and western Colombia; and [*morphoeus* group] from southeastern Colombia and southwestern Venezuela south, east of the Andes, to central Bolivia and central and southeastern Brazil.

Notes.—Groups: *M. grandior* Sclater and Salvin, 1868 [Costa Rican Nunbird]; *M. pallescens* Cassin, 1850 [Pale-winged Nunbird]; and *M. morphoeus* [White-fronted Nunbird].

Family **GALBULIDAE**: Jacamars

Genus **BRACHYGALBA** Bonaparte

Brachygalba Bonaparte, 1854, Ateneo Ital. 2: 129. Type, by subsequent designation (G. R. Gray, 1855), *Galbula albigularis* Spix.

Brachygalba salmoni Sclater and Salvin. Dusky-backed Jacamar.

Brachygalba salmoni Sclater and Salvin, 1879, Proc. Zool. Soc. London, p. 535. (Río Neche [= Nechí], Antioquia, Colombia.)

Habitat.—Tropical Lowland Evergreen Forest Edge, Tropical Second-growth Edge (0–600 m; Tropical Zone).

Distribution.—*Resident* in extreme eastern Panama (eastern Darién) and northwestern Colombia.

Notes.—*Brachygalba salmoni* and three South American species, *B. albogularis* (Spix, 1824), *B. goeringi* Sclater and Salvin, 1869, and *B. lugubris* (Swainson, 1838), may constitute a superspecies (Haffer 1967, 1974).

Genus **GALBULA** Brisson

Galbula Brisson, 1760, Ornithologie 1: 42; 4: 86. Type, by tautonymy, *Galbula* Brisson = *Alcedo galbula* Linnaeus.

Galbula ruficauda Cuvier. Rufous-tailed Jacamar.

Galbula ruficauda Cuvier, 1816, Règne Anim. 1: 420. Based on Levaillant, Hist. Nat. Ois. Paradis Rolliers 2: pl. 50. (Guiana.)

Habitat.—Tropical Lowland Evergreen Forest Edge, Gallery Forest, Tropical Deciduous Forest, River-edge Forest (0–1300 m; Tropical and lower Subtropical zones).

Distribution.—*Resident* [*melanogenia* group] from southern Veracruz, northern Oaxaca, and southern Campeche south on the Gulf-Caribbean slope of Middle America (except the Yucatan Peninsula) to Nicaragua, on both slopes of Costa Rica (except the dry northwest) and western Panama (western Chiriquí and western Bocas del Toro), and in eastern Panama (Darién), western Colombia, and northwestern Ecuador; and [*ruficauda* group] from eastern Panama (eastern Panamá province and eastern Darién), northern Colombia, Venezuela, Tobago, Trinidad, and the Guianas south to eastern Colombia, and from Amazonian Brazil south to southern Bolivia, northeastern Argentina, Paraguay, and southeastern Brazil.

Notes.—The two groups were formerly treated as separate species, *G. melanogenia* Sclater, 1853 [Black-chinned Jacamar], and *G. ruficauda* [Rufous-tailed Jacamar](Haffer 1967); however, intergradation between the two occurs in eastern Panama and northwestern Colombia (Wetmore 1968). *Galbula ruficauda* appears to be part of a large superspecies including the following South American allospecies (Haffer 1974): *G. galbula* (Linnaeus, 1766), *G. tombacea* Spix, 1824, *G. cyanescens* Deville, 1849, and *G. pastazae* Taczanowski and Berlepsch, 1885.

Genus **JACAMEROPS** Lesson

Jacamerops Lesson, 1830, Traité Ornithol., livr. 3, p. 234. Type, by monotypy, *Alcedo grandis* Gmelin = *Alcedo aurea* Müller.

Jacamerops aurea (Müller). Great Jacamar.

> *Alcedo aurea* P. L. S. Müller, 1776, Natursyst., Suppl., p. 94. Based on the "Long-tailed Kingfisher" Vosmaer, Beschr. Missch. Amer. Langst. Ys-Vogel. (Berbice, British Guiana.)

Habitat.—Tropical Lowland Evergreen Forest (0–1100 m; Tropical Zone).

Distribution.—*Resident* in Costa Rica (Caribbean slope west to the Sarapiquí region) and Panama (both slopes), and in South America from Colombia, Venezuela, and the Guianas south, west of the Andes to northwestern Ecuador and east of the Andes to central Bolivia and Amazonian Brazil.

Suborder PICI: Toucans, New World Barbets, Barbets, and Woodpeckers

Family **RAMPHASTIDAE**: New World Barbets and Toucans

Notes.—Comparative anatomy, skeletal morphology, and molecular genetics indicate that the Capitonidae should be treated as a subfamily of the Ramphastidae, separate from the Old World barbets (Burton 1984, Prum 1988, Sibley and Ahlquist 1990, and Lanyon and Hall 1994).

Subfamily CAPITONINAE: New World Barbets

Genus *CAPITO* Vieillot

> *Capito* Vieillot, 1816, Analyse, p. 27. Type, by monotypy, "Tamatia à tête et gorge rouges" Buffon = *Bucco niger* P. L. S. Müller.

Capito maculicoronatus Lawrence. Spot-crowned Barbet.

> *Capito maculicoronatus* Lawrence, 1861, Ann. Lyc. Nat. Hist. N. Y. 7: 300. (Atlantic side of the Isthmus of Panama, along the line of the Panama Railroad = Canal Zone.)

Habitat.—Tropical Lowland Evergreen Forest, Secondary Forest (0–1000 m; Tropical Zone).

Distribution.—*Resident* in Panama (west to northern Coclé on the Caribbean slope and to eastern Panamá province on the Pacific) and western Colombia.

Notes.—*Capito maculicoronatus* and the South American *C. squamatus* Salvin, 1876, may constitute a superspecies (Sibley and Monroe 1990).

Genus *EUBUCCO* Bonaparte

> *Eubucco* Bonaparte, 1850, Consp. Gen. Avium 1(1): 142. Type, by subsequent designation (G. R. Gray, 1855), *Capito richardsoni* G. R. Gray.

Eubucco bourcierii (Lafresnaye). Red-headed Barbet.

> *Micropogon Bourcierii* Lafresnaye, 1845, Rev. Zool. [Paris] 8: 179. (Bogotá, Colombia.)

Habitat.—Montane Evergreen Forest, Secondary Forest (900–2400 m; upper Tropical and Subtropical zones).

Distribution.—*Resident* in the highlands of Costa Rica (north to the Cordillera Central) and Panama (recorded east to Veraguas, in San Blas, and in eastern Darién); and in South America in the Andes from Colombia and western Venezuela south to northern Peru.

Subfamily SEMNORNITHINAE: Toucan-Barbets

Genus *SEMNORNIS* Richmond

> *Tetragonops* Anonymous [= Jardine] (not Gerstäcker, Feb./Mch. 1855, Coleoptera) Oct. 1855, Edinburgh New Philos. J. (n.s.) 2: 404. Type, by monotypy, *Tetragonops ramphastinus* Jardine.

Pan (not Oken, 1816, Mammalia) Richmond, 1899, Auk 16: 77. New name for *Tetragonops* Jardine, preoccupied.

Semnornis Richmond, 1900, Auk 17: 179. New name for *Pan* Richmond, preoccupied.

Notes.—This genus may be more closely related to toucans than to barbets (Prum 1988, Remsen et al. 1993).

Semnornis frantzii (Sclater). Prong-billed Barbet.

Tetragonops frantzii Sclater, 1864, Ibis, p. 371, pl. 10. (in int. reipubl. Costa Rica = near San José, Costa Rica.)

Habitat.—Montane Evergreen Forest (1200–2450 m; Subtropical and lower Temperate zones).

Distribution.—*Resident* in the mountains of Costa Rica (north to the Cordillera de Tilarán, and primarily on the Caribbean slope) and western Panama (east to Veraguas).

Subfamily RAMPHASTINAE: Toucans

Genus *AULACORHYNCHUS* Gould

Aulacorhynchus Gould, 1835, Proc. Zool. Soc. London (1834), p. 147. Type, by subsequent designation (G. R. Gray, 1840), *A. sulcatus* (Swains.) = *Pteroglossus sulcatus* Swainson.

Aulacorhynchus prasinus (Gould). Emerald Toucanet.

Pteroglossus prasinus "Licht." Gould, 1834, Proc. Zool. Soc. London, p. 78. (México = "Valle Real, Veracruz" [= Valle Nacional, Oaxaca; Binford, 1990, Wilson Bull. 102: 150–154].)

Habitat.—Montane Evergreen Forest, Tropical Lowland Evergreen Forest (0–3000 m; upper Tropical to lower Temperate zones).

Distribution.—*Resident* in the highlands of Middle America from southeastern San Luis Potosí, Hidalgo, Puebla, Veracruz, Guerrero, Oaxaca, Chiapas, and Quintana Roo south through Central America to north-central Nicaragua, also in highlands of Costa Rica and Panama; and in foothills of the Andes of South America from Colombia and western Venezuela south to central Bolivia (also in lowlands of southern Peru and northern Bolivia).

Notes.—Formerly, *A. caeruleogularis* (Gould, 1854) was treated as a separate species (Ridgway 1914, Cory 1919), but most authors consider it now to be conspecific with *A. prasinus* (Peters 1948, Haffer 1974, Ridgely 1976, Stiles and Skutch 1989).

Genus *PTEROGLOSSUS* Illiger

Pteroglossus Illiger, 1811, Prodromus, p. 202. Type, by subsequent designation (G. R. Gray, 1840), *Ramphastos aracari* Linnaeus.

Pteroglossus torquatus (Gmelin). Collared Aracari.

Ramphastos torquatus Gmelin, 1788, Syst. Nat. 1(1): 354. Based in part on "Le Toucan à collier du Mexique" Brisson, Ornithologie 4: 421, and the "Collared Toucan" Latham, Gen. Synop. Birds 1(1): 330. (in novae Hispaniae maritimis = Veracruz.)

Habitat.—Tropical Lowland Evergreen Forest, Secondary Forest (0–1200 m; Tropical and lower Subtropical zones).

Distribution.—*Resident* [*torquatus* group] from Veracruz, Oaxaca, Chiapas, and the Yucatan Peninsula south along both slopes of Middle America (except the Pacific slope in Costa Rica and Panama from the Gulf of Nicoya east to western Panamá province), northern Colombia, and western and northern Venezuela; and [*sanguineus* group] in extreme eastern Panama (eastern Darién), western Colombia, and northwestern Ecuador.

Notes.—*Pteroglossus torquatus, P. frantzii,* and the South American *P. erythropygius*

Gould, 1843, and *P. pleuricinctus* Gould, 1836, appear to constitute a superspecies (Haffer 1974). *Pteroglossus torquatus* and *P. frantzii* are closely related and were formerly considered conspecific, but Slud (1964) and most subsequent works have considered them as separate species. The two groups *P. torquatus* [Collared Aracari], and *P. sanguineus* Gould, 1854 [Stripe-billed Aracari], show limited interbreeding in a narrow zone in eastern Panama and northwestern Colombia and were considered conspecific by Haffer (1974); however, they are treated as separate species by many recent authors (e.g., Hilty and Brown 1986, Sibley and Monroe 1990).

Pteroglossus frantzii Cabanis. Fiery-billed Aracari.

> *Pteroglossus Frantzii* Cabanis, 1861, Sitzungsber. Ges. Naturforsch. Freunde Berlin, 13 November. (Costa Rica = Aguacate, Costa Rica.)

Habitat.—Tropical Lowland Evergreen Forest, Secondary Forest (0–1500 m; Tropical and lower Subtropical zones).
Distribution.—*Resident* on the Pacific slope of Costa Rica (west to the Gulf of Nicoya) and western Panama (east to Veraguas).
Notes.—See comments under *P. torquatus.*

Genus *SELENIDERA* Gould

> *Selenidera* Gould, 1837, Icones Avium, pt. 1, pl. [7] and text. Type, by subsequent designation (G. R. Gray, 1840), *S. gouldii* (Natt.) = *Pteroglossus gouldii* Natterer.

Selenidera spectabilis Cassin. Yellow-eared Toucanet.

> *Selenidera spectabilis* Cassin, 1858, Proc. Acad. Nat. Sci. Philadelphia 9: 214. (Cucuyos de Veragua, Panamá.)

Habitat.—Tropical Lowland Evergreen Forest, Montane Evergreen Forest (0–1500 m; Tropical and lower Subtropical zones).
Distribution.—*Resident* on the Caribbean slope of Honduras (west to the Sula Valley), Nicaragua, Costa Rica, and Panama, and locally in Pacific slope foothills from Costa Rica (Guanacaste) and Panama south to western Colombia and northwestern Ecuador.
Notes.—All six species in the genus, which includes the South American forms *S. maculirostris* (Lichtenstein, 1823), *S. gouldii* (Natterer, 1837), *S. reinwardtii* (Wagler, 1827), *S. nattereri* (Gould, 1835), and *S. culik* (Wagler, 1827), appear to constitute a superspecies (Haffer 1974).

Genus *RAMPHASTOS* Linnaeus

> *Ramphastos* Linnaeus, 1758, Syst. Nat. (ed. 10) 1: 103. Type, by subsequent designation (Vigors, 1826), *Ramphastos erythrorhynchus* Gmelin = *Ramphastos tucanus* Linnaeus.

Ramphastos sulfuratus Lesson. Keel-billed Toucan.

> *Ramphastos sulfuratus* Lesson, 1830, Traité Ornithol., 3: 173. (le Mexique = Mexico.)

Habitat.—Tropical Lowland Evergreen Forest, Secondary Forest, Montane Evergreen Forest (0–1600 m; Tropical and lower Subtropical zones).
Distribution.—*Resident* on the Gulf-Caribbean slope from southeastern San Luis Potosí, Puebla, Veracruz, northern Oaxaca, Tabasco, Chiapas, and the Yucatan Peninsula south to Honduras, on both slopes (although locally distributed on the Pacific) of Nicaragua, Costa Rica, and Panama, and in northern Colombia and northwestern Venezuela.
Notes.—*Ramphastos sulfuratus* and the South American species *R. brevis*, Meyer deSchauensee, 1945, *R. citreolaemus* Gould, 1844, *R. culminatus* Gould, 1833, *R. dicolorus* Linnaeus, 1776, and *R. vitellinus* Lichtenstein, 1823, appear to constitute a superspecies (Haffer 1974).

Ramphastos swainsonii Gould. Chestnut-mandibled Toucan.

> *Ramphastos Swainsonii* Gould, 1833, Proc. Zool. Soc. London, p. 69. (in montosis Columbiæ = mountains of Colombia.)

Habitat.—Tropical Lowland Evergreen Forest, Montane Evergreen Forest (0–2000 m; Tropical and lower Subtropical zones).

Distribution.—*Resident* in eastern Honduras (Olancho, Mosquitia), Nicaragua (Caribbean slope), Costa Rica (absent from dry northwest and most of central plateau), Panama (absent from Pacific slope from eastern Chiriquí east to western Panamá province), western and northern Colombia, and western Ecuador.

Notes.—*Ramphastos swainsonii* and the South American *R. ambiguus* Swainson, 1823, are closely related and constitute a superspecies [Yellow-breasted Toucan]; these two allospecies plus the South American *R. tucanus* Linnaeus, 1758, and *R. cuvieri* Wagler, 1827, may constitute a larger superspecies (Haffer 1974).

Family **PICIDAE**: Woodpeckers and Allies

Subfamily JYNGINAE: Wrynecks

Genus *JYNX* Linnaeus

> *Jynx* Linnaeus, 1758, Syst. Nat. (ed. 10) 1: 112. Type, by monotypy, *Jynx torquilla* Linnaeus.

Jynx torquilla Linnaeus. Eurasian Wryneck.

> *Jynx Torquilla* Linnaeus, 1758, Syst. Nat. (ed. 10) 1: 112. (in Europa = Sweden.)

Habitat.—Open woodland and second growth.

Distribution.—*Breeds* from northern Eurasia south to northwestern Africa, the Mediterranean region and central Asia, and *winters* from central Eurasia south to northern tropical Africa, India, Southeast Asia, southern China, and southern Japan.

Accidental in Alaska (Wales, 8 September 1945; Bailey 1947) and Taiwan.

Notes.—Known in Old World literature as the Wryneck.

Subfamily PICUMNINAE: Piculets

Tribe PICUMNINI: Typical Piculets

Genus *PICUMNUS* Temminck

> *Picumnus* Temminck, 1825, Planches Color., livr. 62, text to pl. 371. Type, by subsequent designation (G. R. Gray, 1840), *Picus minutissimus* (Gm.) = *Picumnus buffoni* Lafresnaye = *Picus exilis* Lichtenstein.

Picumnus olivaceus Lafresnaye. Olivaceous Piculet.

> *Picumnus olivaceus* Lafresnaye, 1845, Rev. Zool. [Paris] 8: 7. (Bogotá, Colombia.)

Habitat.—Tropical Lowland Evergreen Forest Edge, Secondary Forest, Tropical Deciduous Forest (0–2300 m; Tropical and Subtropical zones).

Distribution.—*Resident* locally on the Caribbean slope of eastern Guatemala, Honduras, and southern Nicaragua, in southwestern Costa Rica (north to the Gulf of Nicoya), and Panama (Pacific slope from Chiriquí to Los Santos, and both slopes from Canal area eastward), and in northern South America from Colombia east to northwestern Venezuela and south to northwestern Peru.

Tribe NESOCTITINI: Antillean Piculets

Genus *NESOCTITES* Hargitt

Nesoctites Hargitt, 1890, Cat. Birds Br. Mus. 18: xv, 8, 552. Type, by original designation, *Picumnus micromegas* Sundevall.

Nesoctites micromegas (Sundevall). Antillean Piculet.

Picumnus micromegas Sundevall, 1866, Consp. Avium Picinarum, p. 95. (Brazil, error = Hispaniola.)

Habitat.—Tropical Deciduous Forest, Tropical Lowland Evergreen Forest, Arid Lowland Scrub (0–1800 m).
Distribution.—*Resident* on Hispaniola (including Gonâve Island).

Subfamily PICINAE: Woodpeckers

Genus *MELANERPES* Swainson

Notes.—Pending a revision of the group, the classification of Peters (1948) and Short (1982) has been followed; for details see Selander and Giller (1959, 1963), Goodge (1972), Olson (1972), and Short (1974).

Melanerpes Swainson, 1832, in Swainson and Richardson, Fauna Bor.-Amer. 2 (1831): 300, 303, 310, 316. Type, by monotypy, *Picus erythrocephalus* Linnaeus.
Centurus Swainson, 1837, Class. Birds, 2, p. 310. Type, by subsequent designation (G. R. Gray, 1840), *C. carolinus* (L.) = *Picus carolinus* Linnaeus.
Tripsurus Swainson, 1837, Class. Birds 2: 311. Type, by monotypy, *T. flavifrons* Spix, pl. 52 = *Picus flavifrons* Vieillot.
Asyndesmus Coues, 1866, Proc. Acad. Nat. Sci. Philadelphia 17: 55. Type, by original designation, *Picus torquatus* Wilson = *Picus lewis* Gray.
Balanosphyra Ridgway, 1911, Proc. Biol. Soc. Wash. 24: 34. Type, by original designation, *Picus formicivorus* Swainson.
Chryserpes W. Miller, 1915, Bull. Amer. Mus. Nat. Hist. 34: 517. Type, by original designation, *Picus striatus* Müller.

Melanerpes lewis (Gray). Lewis's Woodpecker.

Picus torquatus (not Boddaert, 1783) Wilson, 1811, Amer. Ornithol. 3: 31, pl. 20, fig. 3. (No locality given = Clearwater River, about two miles north of Kamiah, Idaho County, Idaho.)
Picus Lewis "Drap[iez]." G. R. Gray, 1849, Genera Birds 3 (app.): 22. New name for *Picus torquatus* Wilson, preoccupied.

Habitat.—Open forest and woodland, often logged or burned, including oak and coniferous (primarily ponderosa pine), open riparian woodland with tall cottonwoods, orchards, less commonly in pinyon-juniper.
Distribution.—*Breeds* from southern British Columbia (also Vancouver Island), south-central Alberta, Montana, southwestern South Dakota, and northwestern Nebraska south to south-central California (San Luis Obispo and Kern counties), central Arizona, southern New Mexico, southern Colorado, and extreme western Oklahoma.
Winters from southern British Columbia, southern Idaho, western Montana, and northern Colorado south irregularly to northern Baja California, Sonora (including Isla Tiburón), northern Chihuahua, southern New Mexico, and western Texas.
Casual north and east to northern Alberta, central and southern Saskatchewan, Manitoba, Ontario, Minnesota, Iowa, Wisconsin, Missouri, Arkansas, and central Texas. Accidental in Newfoundland, Massachusetts, Rhode Island, and Virginia; sight reports for Coahuila.

Melanerpes herminieri (Lesson). Guadeloupe Woodpecker.

> *Picus Herminieri* Lesson, 1830, Traité Ornithol., livr. 3, p. 228. (l'Amérique du nord, error = Guadeloupe, Lesser Antilles.)

Habitat.—Tropical Lowland Evergreen Forest, Secondary Forest, Mangrove Forest (0–700 m).

Distribution.—*Resident* on Guadeloupe, in the Lesser Antilles.

Melanerpes portoricensis (Daudin). Puerto Rican Woodpecker.

> *Picus portoricensis* Daudin, 1803, Ann. Mus. Hist. Nat. [Paris] 2: 286, pl. 51. (Puerto Rico.)

Habitat.—Tropical Lowland Evergreen Forest, Tropical Deciduous Forest, Secondary Forest (0–1000 m).

Distribution.—*Resident* on Puerto Rico (including Vieques Island), formerly also in the Virgin Islands on St. Thomas.

Melanerpes erythrocephalus (Linnaeus). Red-headed Woodpecker.

> *Picus erythrocephalus* Linnaeus, 1758, Syst. Nat. (ed. 10) 1: 113. Based on "The Red-headed Wood-pecker" Catesby, Nat. Hist. Carolina 1: 20, pl. 20. (in America = South Carolina.)

Habitat.—Open woodland (especially with beech or oak), open situations with scattered tall trees, open pine woods, parks, and suburbs.

Distribution.—*Breeds* from southern Saskatchewan (locally), southern Manitoba, western and southern Ontario, southwestern Quebec (rarely), New England (rarely), and southern New Brunswick (formerly) south to central Texas, the Gulf coast, and Florida (except the southernmost portion), extending west to central Montana, eastern Wyoming, eastern Colorado, and central New Mexico. Occurs in summer (and probably breeds) in southern Alberta.

Winters regularly through the southern two-thirds of the breeding range, rarely or casually north to the limits of the breeding range.

Casual or accidental north to southern British Columbia, southern Alberta, south-central Saskatchewan, New Brunswick, Prince Edward Island, and Nova Scotia, and in Idaho, Nevada, northeastern Utah, California, Arizona, and the Florida Keys (Dry Tortugas); a sight report for southeastern Oregon.

Melanerpes formicivorus (Swainson). Acorn Woodpecker.

> *Picus formicivorus* Swainson, 1827, Philos. Mag. (n.s.) 1: 439. (Temiscaltipec, Mexico = Temascaltepec, México.)

Habitat.—Oaks, either in unmixed open woodland or mixed with conifers (Subtropical to Temperate, locally also in Tropical zones).

Distribution.—*Resident* (mostly west of the Cascades and Sierra Nevada) from central southern Washington, northwestern Oregon south through California (including Santa Catalina and Santa Cruz islands, and locally east of the Sierra Nevada in Lassen County) to southern Baja California; from southern Utah, northern Arizona, northern New Mexico, western and central Texas, Nuevo León, and southwestern Tamaulipas south mostly through the highlands of Middle America (including also lowland southeastern Mexico, Belize, and the Mosquitia of eastern Honduras and northeastern Nicaragua) to extreme western Panama (western Chiriquí); and in South America in the Andes of Colombia.

Casual in Colorado (possibly breeding near Durango) and western Wyoming.

Melanerpes chrysauchen Salvin. Golden-naped Woodpecker.

> *Melanerpes chrysauchen* Salvin, 1870, Proc. Zool. Soc. London, p. 213. (Bogaba, [Chiriquí,] Panamá.)

Habitat.—Tropical Lowland Evergreen Forest Edge, Secondary Forest (0–1550 m; Tropical and lower Subtropical zones).

Distribution.—*Resident* [*chrysauchen* group] in southwestern Costa Rica (west to the Gulf of Nicoya) and western Panama (Pacific slope of Chiriquí and Veraguas); and [*pulcher* group] in northern Colombia (Magdalena Valley).

Notes.—Groups: *M. chrysauchen* [Golden-naped Woodpecker] and *M. pulcher* Sclater, 1870 [Beautiful Woodpecker]. *Melanerpes chrysauchen, M. pucherani,* and the South American *M. flavifrons* (Vieillot, 1818) and *M. cruentatus* (Boddaert, 1783) appear to constitute a superspecies (Short 1974, 1982); this complex is sometimes placed in the genus *Tripsurus* but Selander and Giller (1963) placed it in *Centurus*.

Melanerpes pucherani (Malherbe). Black-cheeked Woodpecker.

Zebrapicus Pucherani Malherbe, 1849, Rev. Mag. Zool. (2)1: 542. (Tobago, error = Colombia.)

Habitat.—Tropical Lowland Evergreen Forest, Secondary Forest (0–1000 m; Tropical and lower Subtropical zones).

Distribution.—*Resident* from the Gulf-Caribbean slope of southern Veracruz, northern Oaxaca, Tabasco, and Chiapas south to Costa Rica (where also rare and local on the Pacific drainage in the northwest), and in Panama (Caribbean slope throughout and on the Pacific from Veraguas eastward), Colombia (the Pacific slope and lower Cauca Valley), and western Ecuador (Pacific lowlands and foothills).

Notes.—Also known as Pucheran's Woodpecker. See comments under *M. chrysauchen*.

Melanerpes striatus (Müller). Hispaniolan Woodpecker.

Picas [sic] *striatus* P. L. S. Müller, 1776, Natursyst., Suppl., p. 91. (Santo Domingo.)

Habitat.—Tropical Lowland Evergreen Forest, Secondary Forest, Tropical Deciduous Forest, Mangrove Forest (0–2400 m).

Distribution.—*Resident* on Hispaniola.

Notes.—Sometimes placed in the monotypic genus *Chryserpes* (Olson 1972).

Melanerpes radiolatus (Wagler). Jamaican Woodpecker.

Picus radiolatus Wagler, 1827, Syst. Avium. 1 (Genus Picus): sp. 39. (Jamaica.)

Habitat.—Tropical Lowland Evergreen Forest, Secondary Forest (0–1800 m).

Distribution.—*Resident* on Jamaica.

Notes.—*Melanerpes radiolatus* and all following species of *Melanerpes* are sometimes placed in the genus *Centurus* (Selander and Giller 1963).

Melanerpes chrysogenys (Vigors). Golden-cheeked Woodpecker.

Picus chrysogenys Vigors, 1839, in Beechey, Zool. Voy. "Blossom", p. 24. (No locality given = either Mazatlán, Sinaloa, or San Blas or Tepic, Nayarit, Mexico.)

Habitat.—Tropical Deciduous Forest, Gallery Forest, Secondary Forest (0–1500 m; Tropical and lower Subtropical zones).

Distribution.—*Resident* from Sinaloa south in the Pacific lowlands to Oaxaca (east to Bahía Santa Cruz), and in the interior of western Mexico to eastern Michoacán, northern Guerrero, Morelos, and extreme southwestern Puebla.

Notes.—See comments under *M. radiolatus*.

Melanerpes hypopolius (Wagler). Gray-breasted Woodpecker.

Picus hypopolius Wagler, 1829, Isis von Oken, col. 514. (México = Tehuacán and Tecuapán, Puebla, Mexico.)

Habitat.—Arid Montane Scrub, Gallery Forest (900–2450 m; Tropical and Subtropical zones).

Distribution.—*Resident* from northwestern Guerrero and Puebla south in the interior of Mexico to central Oaxaca (east to vicinity of San Pedro Totolapan).

Notes.—Although sometimes considered conspecific with *M. uropygialis* (e.g., Peters 1948), Selander and Giller (1963) provided evidence for treating *M. hypopolius* as a distinct species. See comments under *M. radiolatus*.

Melanerpes pygmaeus (Ridgway). Red-vented Woodpecker.

Centurus rubriventris pygmæus Ridgway, 1885, Proc. U. S. Natl. Mus. 8: 576. (Cozumel Island.)

Habitat.—Arid Lowland Scrub, Tropical Deciduous Forest (Tropical Zone).

Distribution.—*Resident* on the Yucatan Peninsula (including Cozumel Island), in northeastern Belize (south to the vicinity of Belize City), and on Guanaja Island (in the Bay Islands, off Honduras).

Notes.—Also known as Yucatan Woodpecker. *Melanerpes pygmaeus* and *M. rubricapillus* constitute a superspecies (Short 1982). See comments under *M. radiolatus*.

Melanerpes rubricapillus (Cabanis). Red-crowned Woodpecker.

Centurus rubricapillus Cabanis, 1862, J. Ornithol. 10: 328. (Barranquilla, Colombia.)

Habitat.—Tropical Lowland Evergreen Forest Edge, Secondary Forest, Gallery Forest, Tropical Deciduous Forest, Mangrove Forest (0–1800 m; Tropical and lower Subtropical zones).

Distribution.—*Resident* from southwestern Costa Rica (Cordillera de Talamanca southward) south and east through Panama (both slopes, including Isla Coiba, the Pearl Islands, and other small islets off the Pacific coast), northern Colombia, and northern Venezuela (also islands of Margarita, Patos, and Tobago) to Guyana and Surinam.

Notes.—See comments under *M. pygmaeus* and *M. radiolatus*.

Melanerpes uropygialis (Baird). Gila Woodpecker.

Centurus uropygialis Baird, 1854, Proc. Acad. Nat. Sci. Philadelphia 7: 120. (Bill Williams Fork of Colorado River, New Mexico [= Arizona].)

Habitat.—Arid Lowland Scrub, Arid Montane Scrub, Tropical Deciduous Forest, Gallery Forest, Second-growth Scrub, Secondary Forest (0–1550 m; Tropical and lower Subtropical zones).

Distribution.—*Resident* from southeastern California (Imperial and lower Colorado River valleys), extreme southern Nevada (opposite Fort Mohave, Arizona), central Arizona, and southwestern New Mexico south through Baja California, Sonora (including Isla Tiburón), southwestern Chihuahua, Sinaloa, Durango, Nayarit, and Zacatecas to Jalisco and Aguascalientes.

Notes.—See comments under *M. radiolatus, M. hypopolius,* and *M. aurifrons*.

Melanerpes hoffmannii (Cabanis). Hoffmann's Woodpecker.

Centurus Hoffmannii Cabanis, 1862, J. Ornithol. 10: 322. (Costa Rica.)

Habitat.—Tropical Deciduous Forest, Secondary Forest, Second-growth Scrub (0–2050 m; Tropical and lower Subtropical zones).

Distribution.—*Resident* in the Pacific lowlands of southern Honduras (Río Pespire southeastward) and Nicaragua, and in Costa Rica in the arid northwest (Guanacaste) and central plateau (Cordillera Central area, locally on the Caribbean drainage).

Notes.—Hybridizes locally with *M. aurifrons* along the Río Pespire in southern Honduras (Monroe 1968, Short 1982). See comments under *M. radiolatus* and *M. aurifrons*.

Melanerpes aurifrons (Wagler). Golden-fronted Woodpecker.

Picus aurifrons "Lichtenst." Wagler, 1829, Isis von Oken, col. 512. (México = Ismiquilpam, Hidalgo.)

Habitat.—Arid Lowland Scrub, Arid Montane Scrub, Gallery Forest, Tropical Lowland Evergreen Forest Edge, Secondary Forest, Tropical Deciduous Forest, Pine Forest (0–2400 m; Tropical and Subtropical zones).

Distribution.—*Resident* from southwestern Oklahoma and north-central Texas south through central Texas (west to the Big Bend region), Mexico (west to central Chihuahua, eastern Durango, Zacatecas, southwestern Jalisco, and Michoacán, and including Cozumel Island), Guatemala, Belize (including Turneffe Islands), El Salvador, and Honduras (including Utila, Roatán, and Barbareta islands in the Bay Islands, but absent from northeastern Honduras and from the Pacific lowlands east of the Río Pespire) to north-central Nicaragua.

Accidental in Michigan (Cheboygan) and Florida (Pensacola), although these birds may have been xanthic individuals of *M. carolinus* as described by Gerber (1986); sight reports for southeastern New Mexico.

Notes.—Hybridizes locally with *M. uropygialis* in western Mexico (Selander and Giller 1963) and with *M. carolinus* in central Texas (J. Smith 1987). *Melanerpes aurifrons, M. carolinus, M. hoffmannii, M. uropygialis,* and *M. superciliaris* appear to constitute a superspecies (Short 1982). See comments under *M. radiolatus* and *M. hoffmannii.*

Melanerpes carolinus (Linnaeus). Red-bellied Woodpecker.

Picus carolinus Linnaeus, 1758, Syst. Nat. (ed. 10) 1: 113. Based on the "Red-bellied Wood-pecker" Catesby, Nat. Hist. Carolina 1: 19, pl. 19. (in America septentrionali = South Carolina.)

Habitat.—Open woodland (primarily deciduous, less commonly coniferous), riverine forest, swamps, parks, and suburbs.

Distribution.—*Resident* from south-central and southeastern North Dakota, eastern South Dakota, central Minnesota, central Wisconsin, central Michigan, southern Ontario, central New York, and Massachusetts south to central Texas, the Gulf coast, and southern Florida (including the Florida Keys), and west to Iowa, central Nebraska, northeastern Colorado, western Kansas, western Oklahoma, and north-central Texas.

Casual north to Idaho, southern Saskatchewan, northeastern Montana, southeastern Wyoming, southern Manitoba, central Ontario, southern Quebec, New Brunswick, and Nova Scotia, and west to southeastern Colorado and eastern New Mexico.

Notes.—See comments under *M. radiolatus* and *M. aurifrons.*

Melanerpes superciliaris (Temminck). West Indian Woodpecker.

Picus superciliaris Temminck, 1827, Planches Color., livr. 73, pl. 433. (Cuba.)

Habitat.—Tropical Lowland Evergreen Forest Edge, Tropical Deciduous Forest, Secondary Forest, Mangrove Forest (0–2000 m).

Distribution.—*Resident* [*superciliaris* group] in the Bahamas (Grand Bahama, Abaco, and San Salvador), Cuba (including offshore cays) and the Isle of Pines; and [*caymanensis* group] Grand Cayman.

Notes.—Also known as Great Red-bellied Woodpecker, West Indian Red-bellied Woodpecker, or Bahama Woodpecker. Groups: *M. superciliaris* [West Indian Woodpecker] and *M. caymanensis* (Cory, 1886) [Cayman Woodpecker]. See comments under *M. radiolatus, M. aurifrons, and M. carolinus.*

Genus *SPHYRAPICUS* Baird

Sphyrapicus Baird, 1858, in Baird, Cassin, and Lawrence, Rep. Explor. Surv. R. R. Pac. 9: xviii, xxviii, 80, 101. Type, by original designation, *Picus varius* Linnaeus.

Sphyrapicus thyroideus (Cassin). Williamson's Sapsucker.

Picus thyroideus Cassin, 1852, Proc. Acad. Nat. Sci. Philadelphia 5 (1851): 349. (California = Georgetown, about twelve miles from Sutter's Mill, El Dorado County, California.)

Habitat.—Montane coniferous forest, primarily fir and pine, also locally in aspen; in migration and winter, primarily pine and pine-oak woodland.

Distribution.—*Breeds* from extreme south-central British Columbia, Idaho, western Montana, and Wyoming south in the mountains to northern and east-central California (also locally in mountains of southern California from Mt. Pinos to Mt. San Jacinto), northern Baja California (Sierra San Pedro Mártir), central Arizona, and southern New Mexico.

Winters from California, Arizona, New Mexico, and western Texas (rarely farther north) south to northern Baja California and Michoacán, and east to Chihuahua, Durango, and Zacatecas.

Casual or accidental east to southern Alberta, southern Saskatchewan, South Dakota, north-central Minnesota, eastern Nebraska, Oklahoma (Cimarron County), central Texas, and southwestern Louisiana (Cameron); sight reports from Kansas, Illinois, and east-central and southeastern Texas.

Sphyrapicus varius (Linnaeus). Yellow-bellied Sapsucker.

Picus varius Linnaeus, 1766, Syst. Nat. (ed. 12) 1: 176. Based mainly on "The yellow belly'd Wood-pecker" Catesby, Nat. Hist. Carolina 1: 21, pl. 21. (in America septentrionali = South Carolina.)

Habitat.—Deciduous or mixed deciduous-coniferous forest; in migration and winter, also a variety of forest and open woodland habitats, orchards, parks, and wooded suburbs.

Distribution.—*Breeds* from extreme east-central Alaska, southwestern Yukon, southwestern Mackenzie, northern Saskatchewan, central Manitoba, northern Ontario, south-central Quebec (including Anticosti Island), southern Labrador, and central Newfoundland south to northeastern British Columbia, south-central Alberta, central and southeastern Saskatchewan, north-central and eastern North Dakota, eastern South Dakota, northern Iowa, northeastern Missouri (formerly), central Illinois, northern Indiana, northern Ohio, western Pennsylvania, northwestern Connecticut, western Massachusetts, and New Hampshire, and locally in the Appalachians south to eastern Tennessee and western North Carolina.

Winters from Missouri, Illinois, Indiana, the Ohio Valley, and southern New England (rarely farther north) south through Texas, the southeastern United States, Middle America (except northwestern Mexico north of Sinaloa and west of Coahuila), the Bahamas, the Cayman Islands, and the Antilles (south to Dominica, but rare east of Hispaniola and in the Lesser Antilles) to central Panama (east to the Canal area) and the Netherlands Antilles, rarely in California.

Casual or accidental in western North America from south-coastal Alaska, Montana, and Colorado south to Arizona and New Mexico, and in the Revillagigedo Islands (Socorro), Bermuda, Greenland, Iceland, and the British Isles; sight reports for northern Baja California.

Notes.—Formerly *S. nuchalis* was considered conspecific with *S. varius,* with or without inclusion also of *S. ruber.* Limited and localized hybridization occurs among the three species (Howell 1952); changes since Howell's work have been reported by Scott et al. (1976). *Sphyrapicus varius, S. nuchalis,* and *S. ruber* constitute a superspecies (Mayr and Short 1970).

Sphyrapicus nuchalis Baird. Red-naped Sapsucker.

Sphyrapicus varius var. *nuchalis* Baird, 1858, in Baird, Cassin, and Lawrence, Rep. Explor. Surv. R. R. Pac. 9: xxviii, 103. (Mimbres River, New Mexico.)

Habitat.—Coniferous forest, especially where mixed with aspen, montane riparian woodland; in migration and winter, also a variety of forest and open woodland habitats, orchards, parks, and wooded suburbs.

Distribution.—*Breeds* in the Rocky Mountain region from central and southeastern British Columbia, west-central and southeastern Alberta, southwestern Saskatchewan (Cypress Hills), western and central Montana, and southwestern South Dakota (Black Hills) south, east of the Cascades and Sierra Nevada, to east-central California, southern Nevada, central Arizona, southern New Mexico, and extreme western Texas (Davis and Guadalupe mountains), and east to southwestern South Dakota.

Winters from southern California (casually from Oregon), southern Nevada, southern (casually northern) Utah, and central New Mexico south to southern Baja California, Jalisco, Durango, Coahuila, and Nuevo León.

Casual or accidental in southwestern British Columbia, Kansas, western Nebraska, Oklahoma, southeastern Louisiana, Guatemala, and Honduras. Many extralimital records lack sufficient documentation.

Notes.—Although formerly considered conspecific with *S. varius,* this form is a separate species (Johnson and Zink 1983, Johnson and Johnson 1985) that is genetically more closely related to *S. ruber* than to *S. varius* (Cicero and Johnson 1995). See comments under *S. varius.*

Sphyrapicus ruber (Gmelin). Red-breasted Sapsucker.

> *Picus ruber* Gmelin, 1788, Syst. Nat. 1(1): 429. Based on the "Red-breasted Woodpecker" Latham, Gen. Synop. Birds 1(2): 562. (in Cayenna, error = Nootka Sound, Vancouver Island.)

Habitat.—Aspen-pine association, coniferous forest, including humid coastal lowlands; in migration and winter, also open woodland and parks.

Distribution.—*Breeds* from southeastern Alaska, and coastal and central interior British Columbia (including the Queen Charlotte and Vancouver islands) south, west of the Cascades, to central coastal California (Marin County), in the Sierra Nevada and interior mountains to south-central California (Laguna Mountains), extreme western Nevada (Lake Tahoe region), and (locally) southern Nevada. Recorded in summer (and possibly breeding) in western Arizona (Mohave County).

Winters throughout the breeding range (rarely in interior British Columbia) and south through most of California (west of the deserts) to northern Baja California.

Casual in south-coastal and east-central Alaska (west to Kodiak and Middleton islands, and at Tok), Alberta, extreme southwestern Utah and southern Arizona.

Notes.—See comments under *S. varius* and *S. nuchalis.*

Genus *XIPHIDIOPICUS* Bonaparte

> *Xiphidiopicus* Bonaparte, 1854, Ateneo Ital. 2: 126. Type, by monotypy, *Picus percussus* Temminck.

Xiphidiopicus percussus (Temminck). Cuban Green Woodpecker.

> *Picus percussus* Temminck, 1826, Planches Color., livr. 66, pl. 390, 424. (Cuba.)

Habitat.—Tropical Lowland Evergreen Forest, Tropical Deciduous Forest, Secondary Forest (0–2000 m).

Distribution.—*Resident* on Cuba (including many cays) and the Isle of Pines.

Genus *DENDROCOPOS* Koch

> *Dendrocopos* C. L. Koch, 1816, Syst. Baier. Zool. 1: xxvii, 72, pl. 1A, fig. a. Type, by subsequent designation (Hargitt, 1890), *D. major* = *Picus major* Linnaeus.

Notes.—Frequently merged in *Picoides,* but treatment of most Old World forms in *Dendrocopos* seems warranted (Ouellet 1977, Shields 1982).

Dendrocopos major (Linnaeus). Great Spotted Woodpecker.

> *Picus major* Linnaeus, 1758, Syst. Nat. (ed. 10) 1: 114. (in Europa = Sweden.)

Habitat.—Forests and woodland.

Distribution.—*Resident* in Eurasia from the British Isles and Scandinavia east to eastern Siberia, and south to northwestern Africa, the Mediterranean region and southern Asia.

Accidental in the Aleutian Islands (Attu, 9 and 31 October 1985, 27 April 1986, specimen; Wagner 1989; also 21–22 May 1996; Nat. Aud. Soc. Field Notes 50: 320, 1996).

Genus *PICOIDES* Lacépède

Picoïdes Lacépède, 1799, Tabl. Mamm. Ois., p. 7. Type, by subsequent designation (G. R. Gray 1840), *Picus tridactylus* Linnaeus.

Dryobates Boie, 1826, Isis von Oken, p. 977. Type, by monotypy, *Picus pubescens* Linnaeus.

Phrenopicus Bonaparte, 1854, Ateneo Ital. 2: 123. Type, by subsequent designation (G. R. Gray 1855), *Picus querulus* Wilson = *Picus borealis* Vieillot.

Xenopicus Baird, 1858, *in* Baird, Cassin, and Lawrence, Rep. Explor. Surv. R. R. Pac. 9: xviii, xxviii, 83, 96. Type, by monotypy, *Leuconerpes albolarvatus* Cassin.

Picoides scalaris (Wagler). Ladder-backed Woodpecker.

Picus scalaris Wagler, 1829, Isis von Oken 22: col. 511. (México; restricted to central Veracruz by Oberholser, 1911, Proc. U. S. Nat. Mus. 41: 142.)

Habitat.—Arid Lowland Scrub, Arid Montane Scrub, Gallery Forest, Pine-Oak Forest, Tropical Deciduous Forest, lowland pine savanna (0–2600 m; Tropical to Temperate zones).

Distribution.—*Resident* from southern interior and southeastern California (north to Los Angeles, Kern, and southern Inyo counties), southern Nevada, southwestern Utah, north-central New Mexico, southeastern Colorado, southwestern Kansas, western Oklahoma, and Texas (except eastern) south through the southwestern United States and most of Mexico (including Baja California, islands in the Gulf of California, the Tres Marias Islands, and Holbox, Cancun, and Cozumel islands off Quintana Roo) to Chiapas, the Yucatan Peninsula, and Belize; and locally in central Guatemala, Honduras (interior valleys, Pacific lowlands, and presumably the Mosquitia in the northeast), and northeastern Nicaragua (Mosquitia).

Notes.—*Picoides scalaris* is closely related to *P. nuttallii*; they constitute a superspecies (Short 1968, 1982).

Picoides nuttallii (Gambel). Nuttall's Woodpecker.

Picus Nuttalii [sic] Gambel, 1843, Proc. Acad. Nat. Sci. Philadelphia 1: 259. (near the Pueblo de los Angelos [sic], Upper California = Los Angeles, California.)

Habitat.—Oak, pine-oak, and riparian (especially willow-cottonwood) woodland.

Distribution.—*Resident* from northern California south, west of the deserts and the Sierra divide (also in the Owens Valley), to northwestern Baja California.

Casual or accidental in southern Oregon, western Nevada, and southeastern California (Salton Sea; a specimen from Arizona (Phoenix) is probably mislabeled.

Notes.— See comments under *P. scalaris*.

Picoides pubescens (Linnaeus). Downy Woodpecker.

Picus pubescens Linnaeus, 1766, Syst. Nat. (ed. 12) 1: 175. Based on the smallest Spotted Woodpecker, *Picus varius minimus* Catesby, Nat. Hist. Carolina 1: 21. (in America septentrionali = South Carolina.)

Habitat.—Deciduous and mixed deciduous-coniferous woodland, riparian woodland, second growth, parks, orchards, and suburbs.

Distribution.—*Breeds* from western and central Alaska, southern Yukon, southwestern Mackenzie, northern Alberta, northern Saskatchewan, northern Manitoba, northern Ontario, south-central Quebec (including Anticosti Island), and Newfoundland south to southern California (except the southeastern deserts), central Arizona, southern New Mexico, central Texas, the Gulf coast, and southern Florida (except the Florida Keys).

Winters throughout the breeding range.

Casual on the Queen Charlotte Islands (British Columbia) and in southeastern Arizona; a sight report for northern Baja California.

Picoides villosus (Linnaeus). Hairy Woodpecker.

Picus villosus Linnaeus, 1766, Syst. Nat. (ed. 12) 1: 175. Based on "The Hairy Woodpecker" Catesby, Nat. Hist. Carolina 1: 19, pl. 19. (in America septentrionali = New Jersey.)

Habitat.—Deciduous or coniferous forest, open woodland, swamps, well-wooded towns and parks, and open situations with scattered trees, and in Middle America in Pine-Oak Forest and Montane Evergreen Forest (Subtropical and Temperate zones).

Distribution.—*Resident* from western and central Alaska, central Yukon, southwestern and south-central Mackenzie, northern Saskatchewan, northern Manitoba, northern Ontario, southern Quebec (including Anticosti Island), central western Labrador, and Newfoundland south throughout most of North America (including the Queen Charlotte and Vancouver islands) to northern Baja California (Sierra San Pedro Mártir), east-central California (to Clark Mountain), Arizona (except southwestern), through the highlands of Middle America (except Belize) to western Panama (Chiriquí and Bocas del Toro), and to the Gulf coast, southern Florida (except the Florida Keys), and the Bahamas (Grand Bahama, Mores Island, Abaco, New Providence, and Andros).

Winters generally throughout the breeding range, with the more northern populations partially migratory southward.

A sight report for Mona Island (off Puerto Rico).

Picoides stricklandi (Malherbe). Strickland's Woodpecker.

Picus (Leuconotopicus) Stricklandi Malherbe, 1845, Rev. Zool., p. 373. (du Mexique = Mount Orizaba massif; restricted by Moore, 1946, Proc. Biol. Soc. Wash. 59: 103–106.)

Habitat.—Pine-Oak Forest, primarily in oak [*arizonae* group] or pine [*stricklandi* group] (1250–4200 m; upper Subtropical and Temperate zones).

Distribution.—*Resident* [*arizonae* group] from southern Arizona and southwestern New Mexico (Peloncillo and Animas mountains) south in the Sierra Madre Occidental to Jalisco and northern and east-central Michoacán; and [*stricklandi* group] in eastern Michoacán, México, Distrito Federal, Morelos, Puebla, and west-central Veracruz.

Notes.—The groups have been considered (e.g., Davis 1965, Ligon 1968) as separate species, *P. arizonae* (Hargitt, 1886) [Arizona Woodpecker] and *P. stricklandi* [Strickland's Woodpecker], but we follow Short (1982) in treating them as conspecific. Also known as Brown-backed Woodpecker, but this name is properly restricted to the African *Dendrocopos obsoletus* (Wagler, 1829).

Picoides borealis (Vieillot). Red-cockaded Woodpecker.

Picus borealis Vieillot, 1809, Hist. Nat. Ois. Amer. Sept., 2 (1808), livr. 21, p. 66, pl. 122. (dans le nord des états-Unis, error = southern United States.)

Habitat.—Open mature pine woodland with grassy or sparse understory, rarely in deciduous woodland near pine or in mixed woodland.

Distribution.—*Resident* locally from southeastern Oklahoma, southern Missouri (formerly), southern (formerly northern) Arkansas, northern Mississippi, northern Alabama, northern Georgia, southeastern Virginia, and southern Maryland (Dorchester County, formerly) south to eastern Texas, the Gulf coast, and southern Florida, and north in the Cumberland Plateau through eastern Tennessee to eastern Kentucky (Daniel Boone National Forest). Recorded in summer (and possibly breeding) in central Maryland (Anne Arundel County).

Accidental in Ohio, Pennsylvania, and New Jersey.

Picoides albolarvatus (Cassin). White-headed Woodpecker.

Leuconerpes albolarvatus Cassin, 1850, Proc. Acad. Nat. Sci. Philadelphia 5: 106. (near Sutter's Mill, California = Oregon Canyon, near Georgetown, 12 miles from Sutter's Mill.)

Habitat.—Montane coniferous forest, primarily pines with large cones, occasionally fir.

Distribution.—*Resident* from southern interior British Columbia (Thompson-Okanagan region), north-central Washington, and northern Idaho south through Oregon (east of the Cascades) to south-central California (to mountains of San Diego County; absent from the humid coastal coniferous forest) and west-central Nevada.

Casual in the coastal and desert lowlands of California, western Montana, and northwestern Wyoming.

Picoides tridactylus (Linnaeus). Three-toed Woodpecker.

Picus tridactylus Linnaeus, 1758, Syst. Nat (ed. 10) 1: 114. (in Svecia ad Alpes Lapponicas, Dalekarlicas . . . = mountains of Sweden.)

Habitat.—Coniferous forest (primarily spruce), less frequently mixed coniferous-deciduous forest, occasionally in willow thickets along streams; favors areas with many large dead trees, such as burns and areas with outbreaks of wood-boring insects.

Distribution.—*Resident* in North America from northern Alaska, northern Yukon, northwestern and central Mackenzie, northern Saskatchewan, northern Manitoba, northern Ontario, north-central Quebec, north-central Labrador, and Newfoundland south to western and southern Alaska, southern Oregon, eastern Nevada, central Arizona, southern New Mexico, and southwestern South Dakota (Black Hills), and to southwestern and central Alberta, central Saskatchewan, southern Manitoba, northeastern Minnesota, northern Michigan, central Ontario, northern New York, northern Vermont, northern New Hampshire, northern Maine, northern New Brunswick, southern Quebec (including Anticosti Island), and (rarely) Nova Scotia; and in Eurasia south of the tree line from Scandinavia and Siberia to mountains of southern Europe (locally), western China, northern Mongolia, northern Korea, and Japan.

Wanders casually or irregularly north to southwestern Keewatin, and south to northwestern Nebraska, southern Minnesota, southern Wisconsin, southern Michigan, southern Ontario, Pennsylvania, Delaware, Rhode Island, Massachusetts, and Nova Scotia; sight reports for northeastern California, Iowa, and Prince Edward Island.

Notes.—Also known as the Northern Three-toed Woodpecker. Marked genetic differences exist between North American and Asian populations in spite of minor morphological differences (Zink et al. 1995).

Picoides arcticus (Swainson). Black-backed Woodpecker.

Picus (Apternus) arcticus Swainson, 1832, *in* Swainson and Richardson, Fauna Bor.-Amer. 2 (1831): 313. (near the sources of the Athabasca River, lat. "57°" [= 54° N.], on the eastern declivity of the Rocky Mountains.)

Habitat.—Coniferous forest (primarily spruce and fir), especially windfalls and burned areas with standing dead trees, less frequently in mixed coniferous-deciduous forest; in winter rarely in deciduous woodland.

Distribution.—*Resident,* often locally, from western and central Alaska, southern Yukon, west-central and southern Mackenzie, northern Saskatchewan, northern Manitoba, northern Ontario, central Quebec, central Labrador, and Newfoundland south to interior British Columbia, through the Cascade, Siskiyou, and Warner mountains, and Sierra Nevada of Washington, Oregon, and California (south to Tulare County) and west-central Nevada, through Montana to northern Wyoming and southwestern South Dakota, and to southwestern and central Alberta, central Saskatchewan, central and southeastern Manitoba, northern Minnesota, northern Wisconsin, central Michigan, southeastern Ontario, northern New York, northern Vermont, northern New Hampshire, and northern Maine.

Wanders irregularly south in winter to Iowa, central Illinois, northern Indiana, Ohio, Pennsylvania, West Virginia, New Jersey, and Delaware.

Notes.—Also known as Arctic Three-toed Woodpecker, Black-backed Three-toed Woodpecker, or Arctic Woodpecker.

Genus *VENILIORNIS* Bonaparte

Veniliornis Bonaparte, 1854, Ateneo Ital. 2: 125. Type by subsequent designation (G. R. Gray, 1855), *Picus sanguineus* Lichtenstein.

Veniliornis fumigatus (d'Orbigny). Smoky-brown Woodpecker.

> *Picus fumigatus* d'Orbigny, 1840, Voy. Amer. Mérid. 4: Ois., livr. 51, pl. 65, fig. 1; 1847, livr. 89, p. 380. (Province of Corrientes, Argentina in lat. 28° S., and Santa Cruz de la Sierra and Province of Chiquitos in Bolivia = Yungas, Bolivia.)

Habitat.—Montane Evergreen Forest, Tropical Lowland Evergreen Forest, Secondary Forest (0–4000 m; Tropical and Subtropical zones).

Distribution.—*Resident* in Nayarit, Jalisco, Guerrero, México, Hidalgo, southeastern San Luis Potosí, southern Tamaulipas, northern Oaxaca, northern and southeastern Chiapas, and north-central Yucatan Peninsula, along both slopes of Middle America (no records from the Pacific slope of Nicaragua) to western Panama (east to Veraguas); and from extreme eastern Panama (eastern Darién) east through Colombia to northern Venezuela, and south along the western slope of the Andes to north-central Peru and the eastern slope to northwestern Argentina.

Veniliornis kirkii (Malherbe). Red-rumped Woodpecker.

> *Picus (Chloropicus) Kirkii* Malherbe, 1845, Rev. Zool. [Paris] 8: 400. (Tobago.)

Habitat.—Tropical Lowland Evergreen Forest, Tropical Deciduous Forest, Montane Evergreen Forest (0–1900 m; Tropical and Subtropical zones).

Distribution.—*Resident* locally in southwestern Costa Rica (lower Térraba valley) and Panama (recorded western Chiriquí, Veraguas, eastern Panamá province, Isla Coiba, eastern San Blas, and eastern Darién), and in South America from northern Colombia east to northern Venezuela, Tobago, and Trinidad, and south, west of the Andes, to northwestern Ecuador.

Notes.—*Veniliornis kirkii* and the South American *V. affinis* (Swainson, 1821), *V. maculifrons* (Spix, 1824), and *V. cassini* (Malherbe, 1861) may constitute a superspecies (Short 1982).

Genus *PICULUS* Spix

> *Piculus* Spix, 1824, Avium Spec. Nov. Bras. 1: [3] of index. Type, by subsequent designation (Oberholser, 1923), *Piculus macrocephalus* Spix = *Picus chrysochloros* Vieillot.

Piculus simplex (Salvin). Rufous-winged Woodpecker.

> *Chloronerpes simplex* Salvin, 1870, Proc., Zool. Soc. London, p. 212. (Bugaba, Chiriquí.)

Habitat.—Tropical Lowland Evergreen Forest Secondary Forest (0–900 m; Tropical and lower Subtropical zones).

Distribution.—*Resident* on the Caribbean slope of Honduras (east of the Sula Valley) and Nicaragua, in Costa Rica (Caribbean slope and Pacific southwest) and, at least formerly, in western Panama (east to Veraguas).

Notes.—See notes under *P. callopterus.*

Piculus callopterus (Lawrence). Stripe-cheeked Woodpecker.

> *Picus callopterus* Lawrence, 1862, Ann. Lyc. Nat. Hist. New York. 7, p. 476. (Atlantic side, line of the Panama Railroad = Caribbean slope, Canal Zone, Panama.)

Habitat.—Tropical Lowland Evergreen Forest (0–1400 m; Tropical Zone).

Distribution.—*Resident* on both slopes of Panama from Veraguas on the Caribbean slope and from eastern Panamá province on the Pacific east to Darién.

Notes.—Formerly included, along with *P. simplex,* in the South American *P. leucolaemus* (Natterer and Malherbe, 1845), but now generally recognized as distinct (e.g., Hilty and Brown 1986, Ridgely and Gwynne 1989).

Piculus chrysochloros (Vieillot). Golden-green Woodpecker.

Picus chrysochloros Vieillot, 1818, Nouv. Dict. Hist. Nat. (nouv. éd.) 26: 98. Based on "Carpintero Verde dorado" Azara, Apunt. Hist. Nat. Páx. Parag. 2: 318 (no. 256). (Paraguay and Brazil.)

Habitat.—Tropical Lowland Evergreen Forest, Gallery Forest, Tropical Deciduous Forest (0–650m; Tropical Zone).

Distribution.—*Resident* from eastern Panama (eastern Panamá province and eastern Darién) east across northern Colombia and northwestern and southern Venezuela to the Guianas, and south, east of the Andes, to northeastern Peru, thence east across Brazil (generally south of the Río Negro and the Amazon) and south to central Bolivia, north-central Argentina, Paraguay, and southeastern Brazil.

Notes.—*Piculus chrysochloros* and the South American *P. aurulentus* (Temminck, 1823) may constitute a superspecies (Short 1982).

Piculus rubiginosus (Swainson). Golden-olive Woodpecker.

Picus rubiginosus Swainson, 1820, Zool. Illus. (1)1(3): pl. 14 and text. ("Spanish Main" = Caracas, Venezuela.)

Habitat.—Montane Evergreen Forest, Tropical Lowland Evergreen Forest, Tropical Deciduous Forest, Secondary Forest, Pine-Oak Forest, lowland pine savanna (0–2200 m; Tropical and Subtropical zones).

Distribution.—*Resident* [*aeruginosus* group] from central Nuevo León and Tamaulipas south through eastern San Luis Potosí to northeastern Puebla and northern Veracruz (reports from Guerrero and Oaxaca are erroneous); and [*rubiginosus* group] from northern and southeastern Oaxaca, eastern Veracruz, Tabasco, Chiapas, and the Yucatan Peninsula south along both slopes of Middle America, and in South America from Colombia east through Venezuela, Tobago, Trinidad to the Guianas and south, west of the Andes to northwestern Peru and on the eastern slope of the Andes to northwestern Argentina.

Notes.—Groups: *P. aeruginosus* (Malherbe, 1862) [Bronze-winged Woodpecker] and *P. rubiginosus* [Golden-olive Woodpecker]. *Piculus rubiginosus* and *P. auricularis* may constitute a superspecies (Short 1982, Baptista 1978).

Piculus auricularis (Salvin and Godman). Gray-crowned Woodpecker.

Chloronerpes auricularis Salvin and Godman, 1889, Ibis, p. 381. (Xautipa, Sierra Madre del Sur in the State of Guerrero, Mexico.)

Habitat.—Pine-Oak Forest, Montane Evergreen Forest (900–2000 m; upper Tropical and Subtropical zones).

Distribution.—*Resident* on the Pacific slope from southeastern Sonora south to Oaxaca (west of the Isthmus of Tehuantepec).

Notes.—See comments under *P. rubiginosus*.

Genus *COLAPTES* Vigors

Colaptes Vigors, 1825, Trans. Linn. Soc. London 14: 457 (note). Type, by original designation, *Cuculus auratus* Linnaeus.

Chrysoptilus Swainson, 1832, in Swainson and Richardson, Fauna Bor.-Amer. 2 (1831): 300. Type, by subsequent designation (G. R. Gray, 1840), *C. cayanensis* (Gm.) Swainson, pl. enl. 613 = *Picus punctigula* Boddaert.

Nesoceleus Sclater and Salvin, 1873, Nomencl. Avium Neotrop., pp. 101, 155. Type, by original designation, *Colaptes fernandinae* Vigors.

Colaptes punctigula (Boddaert). Spot-breasted Woodpecker.

Picus punctigula Boddaert, 1783, Table Planches Enlum., p. 37. Based on Daubenton, Planches Enlum., pl. 613. (Cayenne.)

Habitat.—River-edge Forest, Secondary Forest, Mangrove Forest (0–1500 m; Tropical Zone).

Distribution.—*Resident* in Panama (locally on the Pacific slope from eastern Panamá province east to Darién), and in South America from northern Colombia, Venezuela, and the Guianas south, east of the Andes, to central Bolivia, and western and central Amazonian Brazil.

Notes.—*Chrysoptilus punctigula* and the South American *C. melanochloros* (Gmelin, 1788) may constitute a superspecies (Short 1982). This species is often placed in the genus *Chrysoptilus*.

Colaptes auratus (Linnaeus). Northern Flicker.

Cuculus auratus Linnaeus, 1758, Syst. Nat. (ed. 10) 1: 112. Based on "The Golden-winged Wood-pecker" Catesby, Nat. Hist. Carolina 1: 18, pl. 18. (in Carolina = South Carolina.)

Habitat.—Open woodland, both deciduous and coniferous, open situations with scattered trees and snags, riparian woodland, pine-oak association, and parks (Subtropical and Temperate zones).

Distribution.—*Breeds* [*auratus* group] from western and central Alaska, northern Yukon, northwestern and southern Mackenzie, northern Manitoba, northern Ontario, north-central Quebec, south-central Labrador, and Newfoundland south through central and eastern British Columbia, west-central and southwestern Alberta, eastern Montana, and eastern North America (east of the Rocky Mountains) to central and eastern Texas, the Gulf coast, and southern Florida (including the upper Florida Keys); and [*cafer* group] from southeastern Alaska, coastal and southern British Columbia (including the Queen Charlotte and Vancouver islands), west-central and southern Alberta, and southwestern Saskatchewan south (from the western edge of the Great Plains westward) to northern Baja California (formerly also on Guadalupe Island), southern Arizona, southern New Mexico, and western Texas, and in the interior highlands of Mexico to west-central Veracruz and Oaxaca (west of the Isthmus of Tehuantepec).

Winters [*auratus* group] from southern Canada (rarely to the northern limits of the breeding range) south through the remainder of the breeding range to southern Texas, the Gulf coast, and southern Florida (including the Florida Keys), rarely to the Pacific states from Washington south to California, Arizona, and New Mexico; and [*cafer* group] generally throughout the breeding range and east to eastern Kansas, eastern Oklahoma, and eastern and southern Texas, the northern populations being largely migratory.

Resident [*chrysocaulosus* group] on Cuba (including Cayo Coco and Cayo Romano), the Isle of Pines, and Cayman Islands (Grand Cayman); and [*mexicanoides* group] in the highlands of Middle America from Chiapas south through Guatemala, El Salvador, and Honduras to north-central Nicaragua.

Casual [*auratus* group] north to the Arctic and Bering coasts of Alaska, islands in the Bering Sea (St. George in the Pribilofs, and Nunivak), and northern Quebec, and south to northern Mexico; and [*cafer* group] east to northern Alberta, southern Keewatin, Manitoba, Minnesota, Iowa, Missouri, and Arkansas. Accidental [*auratus* group] in the British Isles and Denmark; and [*cafer* group] in Pennsylvania, New Jersey, and Florida.

Notes.—Also known as Common Flicker. The two northern groups were formerly treated as separate species, *C. auratus* [Yellow-shafted Flicker] and *C. cafer* [Red-shafted Flicker] (Short 1965a, 1965b, 1982, Johnson 1969, Bock 1971, Moore and Buchanan 1985, Moore and Koenig 1986, Grudzien et al. 1987, Moore 1987, Moore et al. 1991, Moore and Price 1993); the other two groups, which are isolates, have usually been treated as races of one of the preceding, *mexicanoides* [Guatemalan Flicker] and *chrysocaulosus* [Cuban Flicker] (Short 1965b) in *C. cafer* and *C. auratus*, respectively (Short 1967a). See comments under *C. chrysoides*.

Colaptes chrysoides (Malherbe). Gilded Flicker.

Geopicus (Colaptes) chrysoïdes Malherbe, 1852, Rev. et Mag. Zool., ser 2, 4, p. 553. (l'Amérique; restricted to Cape San Lucas, Baja California, by Anthony, 1895, Auk, 12, p. 347.)

Habitat.—Stands of giant cactus (saguaro), Joshua tree, and riparian groves of cotton-woods and tree willows in warm desert lowlands and foothills.

Distribution.—from southeastern California (at least formerly), extreme northeastern Baja California (Colorado River) and central Arizona south to southern Baja California and through Sonora (including Isla Tiburón) to northern Sinaloa.

Notes.—Formerly merged with *C. auratus*. Interbreeding between *C. chrysoides* and *C. auratus* is extremely limited, especially compared to the massive, free interbreeding between the *auratus* subspecies-group and the *cafer* group in the Great Plains. In Arizona, *auratus* and *chrysoides* hybridize at a few sites, but most populations consist of pure parental types with no evidence of gene flow between them. Major differences exist between the two species in size, color, habitat, and clutch size despite their parapatric distributions (Johnson 1969, Koenig 1984).

Colaptes fernandinae Vigors. Fernandina's Flicker.

Colaptes Fernandinæ Vigors, 1827, Zool. J. 3: 445. (near Habana, Cuba.)

Habitat.—Low Seasonally Wet Grassland and Tropical Lowland Evergreen Forest Edge.

Distribution.—*Resident* locally in Cuba, primarily in the Zapata Swamp area. Formerly more widespread

Notes.—Also known as Fernandina's Woodpecker.

Genus *CELEUS* Boie

Celeus Boie, 1831, Isis von Oken, col. 542. Type, by subsequent designation (G. R. Gray, 1840), *C. flavescens* (Gm.) = *Picus flavescens* Gmelin.

Celeus loricatus (Reichenbach). Cinnamon Woodpecker.

Meiglyptes loricatus Reichenbach, 1854, Handb. Spec. Ornithol., cont. xii, Scansoriae C. Picinae, p. 405, pl. DCLXXXI, fig. 4495, 4496. (Peru.)

Habitat.—Tropical Lowland Evergreen Forest (0–800 m; Tropical Zone).

Distribution.—*Resident* on the Caribbean slope of Nicaragua (one record, Eden) and Costa Rica, and from Panama (Caribbean slope throughout, and Pacific slope from the Canal area eastward) east through northern Colombia to the Magdalena Valley, and south along the Pacific coast to northwestern Ecuador.

Celeus castaneus (Wagler). Chestnut-colored Woodpecker.

Picus castaneus Wagler, 1829, Isis von Oken, col. 515. (No locality given = "Valle Real, Veracruz" [= Valle Nacional, Oaxaca; Binford, 1990, Wilson Bull. 102: 151].)

Habitat.—Tropical Lowland Evergreen Forest (0–750 m; Tropical and lower Subtropical zones).

Distribution.—Resident on the Gulf-Caribbean slope from southern Mexico (southern Veracruz, northern Oaxaca, Tabasco, Chiapas, and the Yucatan Peninsula) south to extreme western Panama (western Bocas del Toro).

Notes.—*Celeus castaneus* and the South American *C. elegans* (P. L. S. Müller, 1776), *C. lugubris* (Malherbe, 1851), and *C. flavescens* (Gmelin, 1788) may constitute a superspecies (Short 1972, 1982), but this treatment has been questioned (Koenig 1984).

Genus *DRYOCOPUS* Boie

Dryocopus Boie, 1826, Isis von Oken, col. 977. Type, by monotypy, *Picus martius* Linnaeus.

Hylatomus Baird, 1858, in Baird, Cassin, and Lawrence, Rep. Explor. Surv. R. R. Pac. 9: xxviii, 107. Type, by monotypy, *Picus pileatus* Linnaeus.

Dryocopus lineatus (Linnaeus). Lineated Woodpecker.

Picus lineatus Linnaeus, 1766, Syst. Nat. (ed. 12) 1: 174. Based on "Le Pic noir hupé de Cayenne" Brisson, Ornithologie 4: 31, pl. 1, fig. 2. (in Cayana = Cayenne.)

Habitat.—River-edge Forest, Gallery Forest, Secondary Forest, Tropical Lowland Evergreen Forest Edge, Tropical Deciduous Forest, Montane Evergreen Forest Edge, lowland pine savanna (0–1550 m; Tropical and lower Subtropical zones).

Distribution.—Resident from southern Sonora, southeastern Nuevo León, and central Tamaulipas south along both slopes of Middle America (including the Yucatan Peninsula and Isla Cancun), and in South America from Colombia, Venezuela, Trinidad, and the Guianas south, west of the Andes to northwestern Peru and east of the Andes to northern Argentina, Paraguay, and southern Brazil.

Notes.—*Dryocopus lineatus, D. pileatus,* and the South American *D. schulzi* (Cabanis, 1883) may constitute a superspecies (Mayr and Short 1970, Short 1982)

Dryocopus pileatus (Linnaeus). Pileated Woodpecker.

> *Picus pileatus* Linnaeus, 1758, Syst. Nat. (ed. 10) 1: 113. Based mainly on "The larger red-crested Wood-pecker" Catesby, Nat. Hist. Carolina 1: 17, pl. 17. (in America = South Carolina.)

Habitat.—Deciduous and coniferous forest and woodland, swamps, also second growth and (locally) parks and wooded suburbs where tall trees present.

Distribution.—*Resident* from south-coastal and central interior British Columbia (including Vancouver Island), southwestern Mackenzie, northern Alberta, northwestern and central Saskatchewan, central Manitoba, central Ontario, southern Quebec (including Gaspé Peninsula), New Brunswick, Prince Edward Island (formerly), and Nova Scotia south in the western North America through Washington and Oregon to northern and central California (the coast range to Santa Cruz County, and the Sierra Nevada to Kern County), through Alberta to south-central Idaho, western Montana, and Wyoming, and south in central and eastern North America (west to the eastern Dakotas, Iowa, Missouri, eastern Kansas, and central Oklahoma) to central and eastern Texas, the Gulf coast, and southern Florida (Key Largo).

Casual in southeastern Alberta, northwestern Wyoming, and eastern Nebraska; sight reports from east-central Alaska, coastal southern California, and southwestern New Mexico.

Notes.—See comments under *D. lineatus.*

Genus *CAMPEPHILUS* Gray

> *Campephilus* G. R. Gray, 1840, List Genera Birds, p. 54. Type, by original designation, *Picus principalis* Linnaeus.
> *Phlæoceastes* Cabanis, 1862, J. Ornithol. 10: 175, 176. Type, by original designation, *Ph. robustus* (Ill. Licht.) = *Picus robustus* Lichtenstein.

Campephilus haematogaster (Tschudi). Crimson-bellied Woodpecker.

> *Picus hæmatogaster* Tschudi, 1844, Arch. Naturgesch. 10: 302. (Republica Peruana = Peru.)

Habitat.—Montane Evergreen Forest, Tropical Lowland Evergreen Forest (0–2200 m; Tropical and lower Subtropical zones, in South America also to upper Subtropical Zone).

Distribution.—*Resident* [*splendens* group] in Panama (from Bocas del Toro on the Caribbean and eastern Panamá province on the Pacific slopes) and northwestern Colombia south to western Ecuador; and [*haematogaster* group] in South America, on the eastern slope of the Andes, from eastern Colombia south to central Peru.

Notes.—Groups: *C. splendens* Hargitt, 1889 [Splendid Woodpecker] and *C. haematogaster* [Crimson-bellied Woodpecker].

Campephilus melanoleucos (Gmelin). Crimson-crested Woodpecker.

> *Picus melanoleucos* Gmelin, 1788, Syst. Nat. 1(1): 426. Based on the "Buff-crested Woodpecker" Latham, Gen. Synop. Birds 1(2): 558, pl. 25. (in Surinamo = Surinam.)

Habitat.—River-edge Forest, Tropical Lowland Evergreen Forest Edge, Gallery Forest, Secondary Forest (0–2500 m; Tropical and Subtropical, occasionally lower Temperate zones).

Distribution.—*Resident* in Panama (from central Bocas del Toro and eastern Chiriquí eastward), and in South America from Colombia, Venezuela, Trinidad, and the Guianas south, east of the Andes, to northern Argentina, Paraguay, and southeastern Brazil.

Notes.—*Campephilus melanoleucos, C. guatemalensis,* and the South American *C. gayaquilensis* (Lesson, 1845) may constitute a superspecies (Short 1982).

Campephilus guatemalensis (Hartlaub). Pale-billed Woodpecker.

Picus guatemalensis Hartlaub, 1844, Rev. Zool. [Paris] 7: 214. (Guatemala.)

Habitat.—Tropical Lowland Evergreen Forest Edge, Gallery Forest, Secondary Forest, Tropical Deciduous Forest (0–1550 m; Tropical and lower Subtropical zones, locally or occasionally to upper Subtropical Zone).

Distribution.—Resident from southern Sonora, San Luis Potosí and southern Tamaulipas south along both slopes of Middle America to extreme western Panama (western Bocas del Toro and western Chiriquí).

Notes.—Also known as Flint-billed Woodpecker. See comments under *C. melanoleucos.*

Campephilus principalis (Linnaeus). Ivory-billed Woodpecker.

Picus principalis Linnaeus, 1758, Syst. Nat. (ed. 10) 1: 113. Based on "The Largest White-bill Woodpecker" Catesby, Nat. Hist. Carolina 1: 16, pl. 16. (in America septentrionali = South Carolina.)

Habitat.—[*principalis* group] Largely mature lowland deciduous forest, especially swamps, and less frequently in pines; [*bairdii* group] in both montane and lower forest (pine and deciduous). More recently both groups reported from secondary deciduous woodland and partially cleared pinelands.

Distribution.—*Resident* formerly [*principalis* group] from eastern Texas, southeastern Oklahoma, eastern Arkansas, eastern Missouri, southern Illinois, Kentucky, and southeastern North Carolina south to the Gulf coast and southern Florida; and [*bairdii* group] formerly Cuba.

Nearing extinction, if not already extinct, with unverified reports in recent years [*principalis* group] from eastern Texas (Big Thicket region), Louisiana (Atchafalaya basin), South Carolina, southern Georgia, central Florida; although recently rediscovered [*bairdii* group] in eastern Cuba (Sierra de Moa), probably now extinct (Lammertink and Estrada 1995).

Notes.—Groups: *C. principalis* [Northern Ivory-billed Woodpecker] and *C. bairdii* Cassin, 1863 [Cuban Ivory-billed Woodpecker]. *Campephilus principalis* and *C. imperialis* may constitute a superspecies (Short 1982).

Campephilus imperialis (Gould). Imperial Woodpecker.

Picus imperialis Gould, 1832, Proc. Zool. Soc. London, Comm. Sci. Corresp. 2: 140. (California, error = Jalisco.)

Habitat.—Pine Forest, Pine-Oak Forest (2200–3150 m; upper Subtropical and Temperate zones).

Distribution.—*Resident* formerly from northeastern Sonora and western Chihuahua south through the Sierra Madre Occidental to western and western Durango, west-central Zacatecas (possibly), northeastern Nayarit (once), central Jalisco, and northern Michoacán.

Unreported since 1956–1957 (sight reports) and possibly extinct, but some may survive in remote areas of Chihuahua and western Durango.

Notes.—See comments under *C. principalis.*

Order **PASSERIFORMES**: Passerine Birds

Suborder TYRANNI: Suboscines

Family **FURNARIIDAE**: Ovenbirds

Notes.—See comments under Dendrocolaptidae.

Genus *SYNALLAXIS* Vieillot

Synallaxis Vieillot, 1818, Nouv. Dict. Hist. Nat. (nouv. éd.) 24 (1817): 117 (generic characters only); 1819, 32: 310 (species added). Type, by subsequent designation (G. R. Gray, 1840), *Synallaxis ruficapilla* Vieillot.

Synallaxis albescens Temminck. Pale-breasted Spinetail.

Synallaxis albescens Temminck, 1823, Planches Color., livr. 38, pl. 227, fig. 2. (Brazil = Cimeterio do Lambari, near Sorocaba, São Paulo.)

Habitat.—Second-growth Scrub, Pastures/Agricultural Lands (0–1500 m; Tropical and lower Subtropical zones).

Distribution.—*Resident* locally in southwestern Costa Rica (Térraba region and Osa Peninsula), on the Pacific slope of Panama (Chiriquí east to eastern Panamá province), and in South America from northern Colombia east through Venezuela (including Margarita Island) and Trinidad to the Guianas and south, east of the Andes (except forested Amazonia), to central Argentina and southeastern Brazil.

Synallaxis brachyura Lafresnaye. Slaty Spinetail.

Synnallaxis [sic] *brachyurus* Lafresnaye, 1843, Rev. Zool. [Paris] 6: 290. (de Colombie = Bogotá, Colombia.)

Habitat.—Second-growth Scrub, Riparian Thickets, Montane Evergreen Forest Edge, Tropical Lowland Evergreen Forest Edge (0–2000 m; Tropical Zone).

Distribution.—*Resident* on the Caribbean slope of Honduras (east of the Sula Valley) and Nicaragua, and locally on both slopes of Costa Rica (absent from dry northwest) and Panama (east to Darién), to western Colombia and the Magdalena Valley, western Ecuador, and extreme northwestern Peru.

Synallaxis erythrothorax Sclater. Rufous-breasted Spinetail.

Synallaxis erythrothorax Sclater, 1855, Proc. Zool. Soc. London, p. 75, pl. 86. (in America Centrali: Coban et Honduras = Honduras.)

Habitat.—Secondary Forest, Second-growth Scrub (0–1000 m; Tropical Zone).

Distribution.—*Resident* in the Gulf-Caribbean lowlands from Veracruz, northern Oaxaca, Tabasco, northern Chiapas, and the Yucatan Peninsula south through Guatemala and Belize to northern Honduras (east to Tela and south to Lake Yojoa); and in the Pacific lowlands from southwestern Chiapas south through Guatemala to El Salvador.

Genus *CRANIOLEUCA* Reichenbach

Cranioleuca Reichenbach, 1853, Handb. Spec. Ornithol., cont. x, Scansoriae A. Sittinae, p. 167. Type, by monotypy, *Synallaxis albiceps* d'Orbigny and Lafresnaye.
Acrorchilus Ridgway, 1909, Proc. Biol. Soc. Wash. 22: 71. Type, by original designation, *Synallaxis erythrops* Sclater.

Notes.—Vaurie (1980) merged *Cranioleuca* into *Certhiaxis* Lesson, 1844.

Cranioleuca erythrops (Sclater). Red-faced Spinetail.

Synallaxis erythrops Sclater, 1860, Proc. Zool. Soc. London, p. 66. (In rep. Equatoriana = Pallatanga, Ecuador.)

Habitat.—Montane Evergreen Forest (700–2300 m; Subtropical and lower Temperate zones).

Distribution.—*Resident* in the highlands of Costa Rica (from the central highlands southward), Panama (recorded Chiriquí, Veraguas, and eastern Darién), and the western slope of the Western Andes in Colombia and Ecuador, western slope of the Central Andes of Colombia, and the coastal mountains of southwestern Ecuador.

Cranioleuca vulpina (Pelzeln). Rusty-backed Spinetail.

Synallaxis vulpina "Natterer" Pelzeln, 1856, Sitzungsb. K. Akad. Wiss. Wien, Math.-Naturwiss. Kl., 20, p. 162. (Brazil = Engeho do Gama, Rio Guaporé, Mato Grosso.)

Habitat.—Tropical Deciduous Forest (on Isla Coiba); in South America in reedbeds, tangled undergrowth, brushy areas and savanna, often near watercourses (Tropical Zone).

Distribution.—*Resident* [*dissita* group] on Isla Coiba, Panama; and [*vulpina* group] in South America from eastern Colombia and Venezuela south, east of the Andes, to northern Bolivia, and central Brazil.

Notes.—The two widely disjunct groups likely represent distinct species, *C. vulpina* [Rusty-backed Spinetail] and *C. dissita* Wetmore, 1957 [Coiba Spinetail], and were treated as separate species by Ridgely and Gwynne (1989) and Ridgely and Tudor (1994).

Genus *XENERPESTES* Berlepsch

Xenerpestes Berlepsch, 1886, Ibis, pp. 53, 54. Type, by monotypy, *Xenerpestes minlosi* Berlepsch.

Notes.—The relationships of this peculiar genus are uncertain.

Xenerpestes minlosi Berlepsch. Double-banded Graytail.

Xenerpestes minlosi Berlepsch, 1886, Ibis, pp. 53, 54, pl. 4. (near Bucaramanga, Colombia.)

Habitat.—Montane Evergreen Forest, Tropical Lowland Evergreen Forest (0–1000 m; Tropical Zone).

Distribution.—*Resident* in eastern Panama (Darién; one sight report from eastern Panamá province), and western and northern Colombia.

Notes.—Also known as Double-banded Softtail.

Genus *PREMNOPLEX* Cherrie

Premnoplex Cherrie, 1891, Proc. U. S. Natl. Mus. 14: 339. Type, by original designation, *Margarornis brunnescens* "Lawr." = Sclater.

Notes.—Vaurie (1980) merged *Premnoplex* into *Margarornis*.

Premnoplex brunnescens (Sclater). Spotted Barbtail.

Margarornis brunnescens Sclater, 1856, Proc. Zool. Soc. London, p. 27, pl. 116. (Bogota [Colombia].)

Habitat.—Montane Evergreen Forest (600–2500 m; Subtropical and lower Temperate zones).

Distribution.—*Resident* in the highlands of Costa Rica (north to the Cordillera de Tilarán) and western Panama (recorded Chiriquí, Bocas del Toro, Veraguas, western Panamá province, western San Blas, and Darién), and in South America in the mountains of northern Venezuela (east to Miranda) and in the Andes of Colombia, on the western slope south to southern Ecuador, and on the eastern slope south to central Bolivia.

Notes.—*Premnoplex tatei* (Chapman, 1925) [White-throated Barbtail], of northeastern Venezuela (west to Anzoátegui), and *P. brunnescens* probably constitute a superspecies; they were treated as conspecific by Peters (1951) and Vaurie (1980).

Genus *MARGARORNIS* Reichenbach

Margarornis Reichenbach, 1853, Handb. Spec. Ornithol., cont. x, Scansoriae A. Sittinae, pp. 146, 179. Type, by subsequent designation (G. R. Gray, 1855), *Sittasomus perlatus* Lesson.

Notes.—See comments under *Premnoplex*.

Margarornis bellulus Nelson. Beautiful Treerunner.

> *Margarornis bellulus* Nelson, 1912, Smithson. Misc. Collect. 60(3): 12. (Mount Pirri, at 4500 feet altitude, near head of Rio Limon, eastern Panama.)

Habitat.—Montane Evergreen Forest, Elfin Forest (1350–1600 m; Subtropical Zone).
Distribution.—*Resident* in eastern Panama (Cerro Pirre and Cerro Mali, eastern Darién).
Notes.—*Margornis bellulus* and the South American *M. squamiger* (d'Orbigny and Lafresnaye, 1838) [Pearled Treerunner] constitute a superspecies. Some authors (e.g., Vaurie 1980) treat *bellulus* as a subspecies of *squamiger,* and others question whether *bellulus* should be maintained as a species. In the absence of an analysis, particularly of vocalizations, we reluctantly maintain the traditional treatment of *bellulus* as a species.

Margarornis rubiginosus Lawrence. Ruddy Treerunner.

> *Margarornis rubiginosa* Lawrence, 1865, Ann. Lyc. Nat. Hist. N. Y. 8: 128. (San Jose, Costa Rica.)

Habitat.—Montane Evergreen Forest (1200–3000 m; Subtropical and Temperate zones).
Distribution.—*Resident* in the highlands of Costa Rica (north to Cordillera de Guanacaste) and western Panama (eastern Chiriquí and Veraguas).

Genus *PSEUDOCOLAPTES* Reichenbach

> *Pseudocolaptes* Reichenbach, 1853, Handb. Spec. Ornithol., cont. x, Scansoriae A. Sittinae, pp. 148, 209. Type, by subsequent designation (G. R. Gray, 1855), *Anabates auritus* "Lichtenstein" [= Tschudi] = *Anabates boissonneautii* Lafresnaye.

Pseudocolaptes lawrencii Ridgway. Buffy Tuftedcheek.

> *Pseudocolaptes lawrencii* Ridgway, 1878, Proc. U. S. Natl. Mus. 1: 253, 254. (La Palma and Navarro, 3500–5000 feet, Costa Rica.)

Habitat.—Montane Evergreen Forest; epiphyte-laden forest (1200–3100 m; Subtropical and Temperate zones).
Distribution.—*Resident* [*lawrencii* group] in the highlands of Costa Rica (from the central highlands southward) and western Panama (Chiriquí, western Bocas del Toro, and Veraguas), and [*johnsoni* group] in the Western Andes of Colombia and Ecuador.
Notes.—Groups: *P. lawrencii* [Buffy Tuftedcheek] and *P. johnsoni* Lönnberg and Rendahl, 1922 [Pacific Tuftedcheek]. *Pseudocolaptes lawrencii* and the South American *P. boissonneautii* (Lafresnaye, 1840) constitute a superspecies, and *johnsoni* may merit species rank (Robbins and Ridgely 1990, Ridgely and Tudor 1994).

Genus *HYLOCTISTES* Ridgway

> *Hyloctistes* Ridgway, 1909, Proc. Biol. Soc. Wash. 22: 72. Type, by original designation, *Philydor virgatus* Lawrence.

Notes.—See comments under *Philydor.*

Hyloctistes subulatus (Spix). Striped Woodhaunter.

> *Sphenura subulata* Spix, 1824, Avium Spec. Nov. Bras. 1: 26, pl. 36, fig. 1. (No locality given = Rio Solimões, Brazil.)

Habitat.—Tropical Lowland Evergreen Forest, Montane Evergreen Forest (0–1300 m; Tropical Zone).
Distribution.—*Resident* in eastern Nicaragua (Caribbean lowlands), Costa Rica (absent from dry northwest), Panama (locally throughout), and in South America from Colombia and southern Venezuela south, west of the Andes to western Ecuador and east of the Andes to northern Bolivia and central Amazonian Brazil.

Notes.—Ridgely and Tudor (1994) suggested that Central American and trans-Andean populations might be a separate species from cis-Andean populations based on vocal differences.

Genus *SYNDACTYLA* Reichenbach

Syndactyla Reichenbach, 1853, Handb. Spec. Ornithol., cont. x, Scansoriae A. Sittinae, p. 171. Type, by monotypy, *Xenops rufosuperciliatus* Lafresnaye.
Xenicopsis Cabanis and Heine, 1859, Mus. Heineanum 2: 32. Type, by original designation, *Xenops rufosuperciliatus* Lafresnaye.
Xenoctistes Hellmayr, 1925, Field Mus. Nat. Hist. Publ (Zool. Ser.) 13(4): 188. New name for *Syndactyla* Reichenbach.

Notes.—See comments under *Philydor*.

Syndactyla subalaris (Sclater). Lineated Foliage-gleaner.

Anabates subalaris Sclater, 1859, Proc. Zool. Soc. London, p. 141. (Pallatanga, Ecuador.)

Habitat.—Montane Evergreen Forest (600–2300 m; Subtropical Zone).
Distribution.—*Resident* in Costa Rica (central highlands southward) and western Panama (locally, recorded Chiriquí, Veraguas, and Darién), and in South America from Colombia and northwestern Venezuela south in the Andes on the western slope to southern Ecuador and on the eastern slope to central Peru.

Genus *ANABACERTHIA* Lafresnaye

Anabacerthia Lafresnaye, 1842, Dict. Univ. Hist. Nat. 1 (1840): 412. Type, by monotypy, *Anabacerthia striaticollis* Lafresnaye.
Xenicopsoides [subgenus] Cory, 1919, Auk 36: 273. Type, by original designation, *Anabazenops variegaticeps* Sclater.

Notes.—See comments under *Philydor*.

Anabacerthia variegaticeps (Sclater). Scaly-throated Foliage-gleaner.

Anabazenops variegaticeps Sclater, 1857, Proc. Zool. Soc. London (1856), p. 289. (Cordova [= Córdoba] in the State of Vera Cruz, Southern Mexico.)

Habitat.—Montane Evergreen Forest, Tropical Lowland Evergreen Forest (400–2500 m; upper Tropical and Subtropical zones).
Distribution.—*Resident* [*variegaticeps* group] locally in the highlands of Guerrero, western Veracruz, Oaxaca, Chiapas, Guatemala, southern Belize, El Salvador, Honduras, Costa Rica, and western Panama (western Chiriquí); and [*temporalis* group] on the west slope of the Western Andes in Colombia and Ecuador.
Notes.—Also known as Spectacled Foliage-gleaner; see Remsen (1997) for use of Scaly-throated Foliage-gleaner. Groups: *A. variegaticeps* [Scaly-throated Foliage-gleaner] and *A. temporalis* (Sclater, 1859) [Spot-breasted Foliage-gleaner]. *Anabacerthia variegaticeps* and the South American *A. striaticollis* Lafresnaye, 1842, constitute a superspecies; they have been treated as conspecific by some authors (Cory and Hellmayr 1925, Peters 1951).

Genus *PHILYDOR* Spix

Philydor Spix, 1824, Avium Spec. Nov. Bras. 1: 73. Type, by subsequent designation (G. R. Gray, 1855), *Anabates atricapillus* Wied.

Notes.—Vaurie (1980) merged the genera *Hyloctistes, Syndactyla,* and *Anabacerthia* into *Philydor*.

Philydor fuscipennis (Salvin). Slaty-winged Foliage-gleaner.

Philydor fuscipennis Salvin 1866, Proc. Zool. Soc. London (1865), p. 72 (Santiago de Veragua, Panama.)

Habitat.—Tropical Lowland Evergreen Forest, Montane Evergreen Forest (0–1050 m; Tropical Zone).

Distribution.—*Resident* [*fuscipennis* group] in Panama (Veraguas, Coclé, eastern Colón, Canal area); and [*erythronotus* group] in eastern Panama (west to San Blas and eastern Panamá province), western and central Colombia, and western Ecuador.

Notes.—Groups: *P. fuscipennis* [Dusky-winged Foliage-gleaner] and *P. erythronotus* Sclater and Salvin, 1873 [Rufous-backed Foliage-gleaner]. Although *fuscipennis* and *erythronotus* were treated as species by Cory and Hellmayr (1925), Zimmer (1935) considered them subspecies of *P. erythrocercus* (Pelzeln, 1859) [Rufous-rumped Foliage-gleaner] because of similarities in plumage and measurements. That treatment has been followed by most authors (e.g., Peters 1951, Vaurie 1980, A.O.U. 1983). However, Hilty and Brown (1986) and Ridgely and Gwynne (1989) treated *fuscipennis* (including *erythronotus*) as a separate species, suggesting a closer relationship to *P. pyrrhodes* than to *erythrocercus* because of behavioral and ecological similarities. That treatment was followed by Sibley and Monroe (1990) and Ridgely and Tudor (1994). We return to the earlier treatment of *fuscipennis* as a species although we consider the situation unresolved by a true analysis of data.

Philydor rufus (Vieillot). Buff-fronted Foliage-gleaner.

Dendrocopus rufus Vieillot, 1818, Nouv. Dict. Hist. Nat. (nouv. éd.) 26: 119. (Brazil = Rio de Janeiro.)

Habitat.—Montane Evergreen Forest (800–2500 m; upper Tropical and Subtropical zones).

Distribution.—*Resident* in Costa Rica (primarily the central highlands and Dota Mountains) and western Panama (western Chiriquí and Bocas del Toro), and disjunctly in South America in the coastal mountains of northern Venezuela, the tepui region of southern Venezuela, and locally in the foothills of the Andes on the west slope to southern Ecuador and on the east slope to central Bolivia, ranging into the lowlands in southeastern Peru, also in south-central and southeastern Brazil, eastern Paraguay, and northeastern Argentina.

Genus *AUTOMOLUS* Reichenbach

Automolus Reichenbach, 1853, Handb. Spec. Ornithol., cont. x, Scansoriae A. Sittinae, pp. 146, 173. Type, by monotypy, *Sphenura sulphurascens* Lichtenstein = *Anabates leucophthalmus* Wied.

Automolus ochrolaemus (Tschudi). Buff-throated Foliage-gleaner.

Anabates ochrolæmus Tschudi, 1844, Arch. Naturgesch. 10: 295. (Republica Peruana = Peru.)

Habitat.—Tropical Lowland Evergreen Forest (0–1400 m; Tropical and lower Subtropical zones).

Distribution.—*Resident* on the Gulf-Caribbean slope of Oaxaca, Veracruz, Tabasco, Chiapas, Guatemala, Belize, Honduras, and Nicaragua, on both slopes of Costa Rica (absent from dry northwest) and Panama, and in South America west of the Andes from northern Colombia to western Ecuador, and east of the Andes from central Colombia, central Venezuela, and the Guianas south to central Bolivia and Amazonian Brazil.

Automolus rubiginosus (Sclater). Ruddy Foliage-gleaner.

Anabates rubiginosus Sclater, 1857, Proc. Zool. Soc. London (1856), p. 288. (Cordova [= Córdoba] in the State of Vera Cruz, Southern Mexico.)

Habitat.—Montane Evergreen Forest, Tropical Lowland Evergreen Forest (500–2500 m; Subtropical and upper Tropical zones, in South America in Tropical Zone).

Distribution.—*Resident* in the highlands of Mexico (recorded Guerrero, southeastern San Luis Potosí, Hidalgo, Puebla, Veracruz, Oaxaca, and Chiapas), Guatemala, El Salvador, Honduras, north-central Nicaragua, southwestern Costa Rica (Coto Brus Valley), and Panama (recorded Chiriquí, western San Blas, and eastern Darién); and in South America west of the Andes in Colombia and Ecuador, and east of the Andes in southern Venezuela, the Guianas, and northeastern Brazil, and along the base of the Eastern Andes locally from Colombia to northern Bolivia.

Notes.—This species may consist of several separate species. Ridgway (1911), for example, recognized four species within Middle America alone. Descriptions of call notes from different parts of the Neotropics (Ridgely and Tudor 1994, Howell and Webb 1995) also suggest that more than one species is involved.

Genus *THRIPADECTES* Sclater

Thripadectes Sclater, 1862, Cat. Collect. Amer. Birds, p. 157. Type, by monotypy, *Anabates flammulatus* Eyton.

Rhopoctites Ridgway, 1909, Proc. Biol. Soc. Wash. 17: 72. Type, by original designation, *Philydor rufobrunneus* Lawrence.

Thripadectes rufobrunneus (Lawrence). Streak-breasted Treehunter.

Philydor rufobrunneus Lawrence, 1865, Ann. Lyc. Nat. Hist. N. Y. 8: 127. (San Jose, Costa Rica.)

Habitat.—Montane Evergreen Forest, especially in deep ravines (700–3000 m; upper Tropical, Subtropical and Temperate zones).

Distribution.—*Resident* in the highlands of Costa Rica (primarily on the Caribbean slope, also on the Pacific slope in the Dota Mountains and Cordillera de Talamanca) and western Panama (Chiriquí, Bocas del Toro, and Veraguas).

Genus *XENOPS* Illiger

Xenops Illiger, 1811, Prodromus, p. 213. Type, by monotypy, *Xenops genibarbis* Illiger = *Turdus minutus* Sparrman.

Xenops minutus (Sparrman). Plain Xenops.

Turdus minutus Sparrman, 1788, Mus. Carlson., fasc. 3, pl. 68.

Habitat.—Tropical Lowland Evergreen Forest, River-edge Forest (0–1500 m; Tropical and lower Subtropical zones).

Distribution.—*Resident* on the Gulf-Caribbean slope of Middle America from southern Mexico (southern Veracruz, northern Oaxaca, Tabasco, Chiapas, Campeche, and Quintana Roo) south to Nicaragua, on both slopes of Costa Rica (rare in dry northwest) and Panama, and in South America from Colombia, Venezuela, and the Guianas south, west of the Andes to northwestern Peru and east of the Andes to central Bolivia and Amazonian Brazil, and southeastern Brazil, eastern Paraguay, and northeastern Argentina.

Xenops rutilans Temminck. Streaked Xenops.

Xenops rutilans Temminck, 1821, Planches Color., livr. 12, pl. 72, fig. 2. (Brazil.)

Habitat.—Montane Evergreen Forest (540–1800 m; Subtropical Zone, in South America also Tropical Zone).

Distribution.—Resident in the highlands of Costa Rica (central highlands southward) and Panama (western Chiriquí and eastern Darién); and in South America in Trinidad, northern Venezuela, Andean foothills from northern Colombia to northwestern Argentina (ranging locally into lowlands, especially western Ecuador and northwestern Peru), and in lowlands of eastern Bolivia and Amazonian Brazil south of the Amazon to Paraguay, northeastern Argentina, and southeastern Brazil.

Genus *SCLERURUS* Swainson

Sclerurus Swainson, 1827, Zool. J. 3,: 356. Type, by subsequent designation (Cabanis, 1847), *Thamnophilus caudacutus* Vieillot.

Notes.—Members of this genus were formerly known by the group name Leafscraper.

Sclerurus mexicanus Sclater. Tawny-throated Leaftosser.

Sclerurus mexicanus Sclater, 1857, Proc. Zool. Soc. London (1856), p. 290. (Cordova [= Córdoba] in the State of Vera Cruz, Southern Mexico.)

Habitat.—Montane Evergreen Forest, Tropical Lowland Evergreen Forest (0–1850 m; Subtropical and Tropical zones).

Distribution.—*Resident* locally in Hidalgo, eastern Puebla, Veracruz, northern and southeastern Oaxaca, Chiapas, Guatemala, Honduras, Costa Rica, and Panama, and in South America from northern Colombia and northwestern Venezuela south, west of the Andes to western Ecuador, and east of the Andes to central Bolivia and southwestern Amazonian Brazil, and in Trinidad and Tobago, eastern Venezuela, the Guianas, and eastern Amazonian Brazil, and in coastal eastern Brazil.

Sclerurus albigularis Sclater and Salvin. Gray-throated Leaftosser.

Sclerurus albigularis Sclater and Salvin, 1869, Proc. Zool. Soc. London (1868), pp. 627, 630. (Venezuela = Cumbre de Valencia.)

Habitat.—Montane Evergreen Forest, Tropical Lowland Evergreen Forest (600–2100 m; upper Tropical and Subtropical zones).

Distribution.—*Resident* in Costa Rica (cordilleras de Guanacaste, de Tilarán and Central) and western Panama (western Chiriquí); and in South America in northeastern Colombia, northern Venezuela, Tobago, and Trinidad, in eastern Andean foothills from central Colombia south to central Bolivia, and in Amazonian lowlands of eastern Peru (Ucayali), extreme eastern Bolivia (Santa Cruz), and western Brazil (Rondônia)

Sclerurus guatemalensis (Hartlaub). Scaly-throated Leaftosser.

Tinactor guatemalensis Hartlaub, 1844, Rev. Zool. [Paris] 7: 370. (No locality given = Guatemala.)

Habitat.—Tropical Lowland Evergreen Forest, Montane Evergreen Forest (0–1250 m; Tropical, rarely lower Subtropical zones).

Distribution.—*Resident* on the Gulf-Caribbean slope from southern Mexico (southeastern Veracruz, Tabasco, Oaxaca, Chiapas, southern Campeche, and southern Quintana Roo) south to Nicaragua, both slopes of Costa Rica (absent from dry northwest), Panama, Colombia (east to the Magdalena Valley and south to the Baudó mountains), and western Ecuador.

Genus *LOCHMIAS* Swainson

Lochmias Swainson, 1827, Zool. J. 3: 355. Type, by subsequent designation (Swainson, 1836), *Lochmias squamulata* Swainson = *Myiothera nematura* Lichtenstein.

Lochmias nematura (Lichtenstein). Sharp-tailed Streamcreeper.

Myiothera nematura Lichtenstein, 1823, Verz. Doubl. Zool. Mus. Berlin, p. 43. (São Paulo, Brazil.)

Habitat.—Montane Evergreen Forest; stream edges (900–1580 m; upper Tropical and Subtropical zones).

Distribution.—Locally in eastern Panama (eastern Darién), in the mountains of northern and extreme southern Venezuela, and from the Andes of Colombia south on the eastern slope to northwestern Argentina; and in lowlands of south-central and southeastern Brazil, eastern Paraguay, northeastern Argentina, and Uruguay .

Notes.—Also known as Streamside Lochmias.

Family **DENDROCOLAPTIDAE**: Woodcreepers

Notes.—Sometimes treated as the subfamily Dendrocolaptinae of the Furnariidae (e.g., Sibley and Monroe 1990), but see Clench (1995). Monophyly of the Dendrocolaptidae is supported by genetic (Sibley and Ahlquist 1990) and morphological characters (Feduccia

1973, Raikow 1994, Clench 1995). Raikow (1994) found that anatomical characters support the monophyly of genera in the A.O.U. Check-list area except *Deconychura*. The group name Woodhewer was formerly used for members of this family.

Genus *DENDROCINCLA* Gray

Dendrocincla G. R. Gray, 1840, List Genera Birds, p. 18. Type, by original designation, *D. turdinus* (Licht.) = *Dendrocopus fuliginosus* Vieillot.

Dendrocincla fuliginosa (Vieillot). Plain-brown Woodcreeper.

Dendrocopus fuliginosus Vieillot, 1818, Nouv. Dict. Hist. Nat. (nouv. éd.) 26: 117. Based on Levaillant, Hist. Nat. Promerops, pl. 28. (Cayenne.)

Habitat.—Tropical Lowland Evergreen Forest (0–1200 m; Tropical and lower Subtropical zones).

Distribution.—*Resident* [*meruloides* group] from southeastern Honduras (Olancho), Nicaragua, and Costa Rica (locally also on Pacific drainage in northwest), on both slopes of Panama, and in South America from Colombia, Venezuela (except southeastern), Tobago, and Trinidad south, west of the Andes to western Ecuador and east of the Andes to Bolivia and western Amazonian Brazil; [*fuliginosa* group] in southeastern Venezuela, the Guianas, and central Amazonian Brazil; [*atrirostris* group] in northern and eastern Bolivia and extreme southwestern Brazil (Rondônia); and [*turdina* group] in eastern and southeastern Brazil, eastern Paraguay, and northeastern Argentina.

Notes.—Groups: *D. turdina* (Lichtenstein, 1820) [Plain-winged Woodcreeper], *D. meruloides* (Lafresnaye, 1851) [Plain-brown Woodcreeper], *D. fuliginosa* [Line-throated Woodcreeper], and *D. atrirostris* (d'Orbigny and Lafresnaye, 1838) [d'Orbigny's Woodcreeper]. Willis (1983a) treated *turdina* of southeastern South America as a separate species based on calls and plumage. This treatment was followed by Sibley and Monroe (1990) and Ridgely and Tudor (1994). Because no analysis of the complex variation in this group of taxa has been published, especially with respect to vocal characters, we think that, although probably correct, acceptance of this taxonomy is premature..

Dendrocincla anabatina Sclater. Tawny-winged Woodcreeper.

Dendrocincla anabatina Sclater, 1859, Proc. Zool. Soc. London, p. 54, pl. 150. (Omoa, Honduras.)

Habitat.—Tropical Lowland Evergreen Forest, Mangrove Forest (0–1500 m; Tropical and lower Subtropical zones).

Distribution.—*Resident* on the Gulf-Caribbean slope from southeastern Mexico (southeastern Veracruz, northern Oaxaca, Tabasco, Chiapas, and the Yucatan Peninsula) south to Nicaragua; and on the Pacific slope of southwestern Costa Rica (north to the Gulf of Nicoya) and extreme western Panama (western Chiriquí).

Dendrocincla homochroa (Sclater). Ruddy Woodcreeper.

Dendromanes homochrous Sclater, 1859, Proc. Zool. Soc. London, p. 382. (In statu Oaxacensi reipubl. Mexicanae . . . Teotalcingo = Teotalcingo, Oaxaca; Binford, 1989, Ornithol. Monogr. 43, p. 340.)

Habitat.—Tropical Lowland Evergreen Forest, Montane Evergreen Forest, Tropical Deciduous Forest (0–1500 m; mainly upper Tropical and Subtropical zones).

Distribution.—*Resident* locally on both slopes from northern and southeastern Oaxaca, Chiapas, and the Yucatan Peninsula (including Cozumel and Mujeres islands) south through Middle America to eastern Panama and northwestern Colombia (Chocó); also locally in extreme northern Colombia and northwestern Venezuela

Genus *SITTASOMUS* Swainson

Sittasomus Swainson, 1827, Zool. J. 3: 355. Type, by original designation, *Dendrocolaptes sylviellus* Temminck = *Dendrocopus griseicapillus* Vieillot.

Sittasomus griseicapillus (Vieillot). Olivaceous Woodcreeper.

> *Dendrocopus griseicapillus* Vieillot, 1818, Nouv. Dict. Hist. Nat. (nouv. éd.) 26: 119.
> Based on "Trepadore palido y roxo" Azara, Apunt. Hist. Nat. Páx. Parag. 2: 282
> (no. 244). (Paraguay = Concepción del Paraguay.)

Habitat.—Tropical Lowland Evergreen Forest, River-edge Forest, Montane Evergreen
Forest, Secondary Forest, Tropical Deciduous Forest (0–2000 m; Tropical and Subtropical
zones).

Distribution.—*Resident* [*griseicapillus* group] from Jalisco, San Luis Potosí and southern
Tamaulipas south along both slopes of Middle America to Panama (where local, primarily
on the Pacific drainage), and in South America from Colombia, Venezuela (also Tobago),
and the Guianas south, east of the Andes, to northern Argentina and central Brazil; [*aequatorialis* group] western Ecuador and northwestern Peru; [*reiseri* group] northeastern
Brazil; and [*sylviellus* group] southeastern Brazil, eastern Paraguay, and northeastern Argentina.

Notes.—Groups: *S. griseicapillus* [Grayish Woodcreeper], *S. aequatorialis* Ridgway, 1891
[Pacific Woodcreeper], *S. reiseri* Hellmayr, 1917 [Reiser's Woodcreeper], and *S. sylviellus*
(Temminck, 1821) [Olivaceous Woodcreeper]. Vocal differences among groups, as well as
marked plumage differences, suggest that this species actually consists of several species
(Hardy et al. 1991, Ridgely and Tudor 1994, Parker et al. 1995).

Genus *DECONYCHURA* Cherrie

> *Deconychura* Cherrie, 1891, Proc. U. S. Natl. Mus. 14: 338. Type, by original desig-
> nation, *Deconychura typica* Cherrie = *Dendrocincla longicauda* Pelzeln.

Deconychura longicauda (Pelzeln). Long-tailed Woodcreeper.

> *Dendrocincla longicauda* "Natterer" Pelzeln, 1868, Ornithol. Bras. 1: 42, 60. (Borba,
> Marabitanas, Barre do Rio Negro = Manaus, Brazil.)

Habitat.—Tropical Lowland Evergreen Forest (0–1300 m; Tropical and lower Subtropical
zones).

Distribution.—*Resident* [*typica* group] locally in southeastern Honduras (Olancho), Costa
Rica (Caribbean slope of Cordillera Central, and southwestern region from the Gulf of Nicoya
southward) to Panama (Chiriquí, and from eastern Panamá province east through Darién)
and northern Colombia, and [*longicauda* group] in South America from southeastern Colombia, southern Venezuela, and the Guianas south to northern Bolivia and Amazonian
Brazil.

Notes.—Groups: *D. typica* Cherrie, 1891 [Cherrie's Woodcreeper] and *D. longicauda*
[Long-tailed Woodcreeper]. Vocal differences between Middle American and South American populations east of the Andes (see Hardy et al. 1991) suggest that at least two species
are involved (Ridgely and Tudor 1994).

Genus *GLYPHORYNCHUS* Wied

> *Glyphorynchus* Wied, 1831, Beitr. Naturgesch. Bras. 3(2): 1149. Type, by monotypy,
> *Glyphorynchus ruficaudus* Wied = *Dendrocolaptes cuneatus* Lichtenstein = *Neops*
> *spirurus* Vieillot.

Notes.—This genus has been misspelled frequently in the literature as "*Glyphorhynchus*"
(e.g., Meyer de Schauensee 1966).

Glyphorynchus spirurus (Vieillot). Wedge-billed Woodcreeper.

> *Neops spirurus* Vieillot, 1819, Nouv. Dict. Hist. Nat. (nouv. éd.) 31: 338. Based on
> Levaillant, Hist. Nat. Promerops, pl. 31, fig. 1. (South America = Cayenne.)

Habitat.—Tropical Lowland Evergreen Forest, Montane Evergreen Forest (0–1500 m;
Tropical and lower Subtropical zones).

Distribution.—*Resident* on the Gulf-Caribbean slope of Middle America from Veracruz, northern Oaxaca, and Chiapas south to Nicaragua, in Costa Rica (primarily Caribbean slope, less commonly in the Pacific southwest) and Panama (mostly Caribbean slope, locally on Pacific), and in South America west of the Andes in western Colombia and Ecuador, and east of the Andes from Colombia, Venezuela, and the Guianas south to central Bolivia and Amazonian Brazil, and in coastal eastern Brazil.

Genus *XIPHOCOLAPTES* Lesson

Xiphocolaptes Lesson, 1840, Rev. Zool. [Paris] 3: 269. Type, by subsequent designation (G. R. Gray, 1855), *Dendrocopus albicollis* Vieillot.

Xiphocolaptes promeropirhynchus (Lesson). Strong-billed Woodcreeper.

Dendrocolaptes promeropirhynchus Lesson, 1840, Rev. Zool. [Paris] 3: 270. (No locality given = Bogotá, Colombia.)

Habitat.—Montane Evergreen Forest, Pine-Oak Forest (700–3100 m; Subtropical and lower Temperate zones, occasionally to Tropical Zone).

Distribution.—*Resident* [*promeropirhynchus* group] in the highlands of Guerrero, and from southeastern San Luis Potosí, Hidalgo, and Veracruz south through northern Oaxaca, Chiapas, and northern Central America to north-central Nicaragua, locally in Costa Rica (Caribbean slope of cordilleras Central and Talamanca) and western Panama (Chiriquí and Veraguas), and in South America from northern Colombia east across northern Venezuela to Guyana, and south in the Andes to northern Bolivia; and [*orenocensis* group] in South America, east of the Andes, from southeastern Venezuela south to central Bolivia and Amazonian Brazil.

Notes.—Groups: *X. promeropirhynchus* [Strong-billed Woodcreeper] and *X. orenocensis* Berlepsch and Hartert, 1902 [Great-billed Woodcreeper]. Cory and Hellmayr (1925) treated the two groups as separate species, and Ridgely and Tudor (1994) suspected that this treatment was correct. Sibley and Monroe (1990) considered *X. promeropirhynchus* and the South American *X. albicollis* (Vieillot, 1818) to constitute a superspecies.

Genus *DENDROCOLAPTES* Hermann

Dendrocolaptes Hermann, 1804, Observ. Zool., p. 135. Type, by subsequent designation (G. R. Gray, 1840), *D. cayanensis* (Gm.), Pl. enl. 621 = *Picus certhia* Boddaert.

Dendrocolaptes sanctithomae (Lafresnaye). Northern Barred-Woodcreeper.

Dendrocops Sancti-Thomae Lafresnaye, 1852, Rev. et Mag. Zool. (2) 4, p. 466. ("In Sancti-Thomae Insula," error = Santo Tomás, near Omoa, Honduras.)

Habitat.—Tropical Lowland Evergreen Forest, Tropical Deciduous Forest (0–1300 m; Tropical and lower Subtropical zones).

Distribution.—*Resident* from Veracruz, northern Oaxaca, Tabasco, Chiapas, southern Campeche, northeastern Yucatán, and Quintana Roo south primarily on the Gulf-Caribbean slope (locally also on the Pacific slope of Guerrero, Oaxaca, and Central America) to Costa Rica (Caribbean slope and Pacific southwest, rare in dry northwest), Panama (absent from dry Pacific region), western and northern Colombia, western Venezuela, and northwestern Ecuador.

Notes.—*D. sanctithomae* was previously treated as a subspecies of *D. certhia* (Boddaert, 1783) [Amazonian Barred-Woodcreeper], but they differ in behavior and voice (Willis 1992) and plumage (Marantz 1997).

Dendrocolaptes picumnus Lichtenstein. Black-banded Woodcreeper.

Dendrocolaptes Picumnus Lichtenstein, 1820, Abh. Phys. Kl. Akad. Wiss. Berlin (1818–19), p. 202. Based on Levaillant, Hist. Nat. Promerops, pl. 26. (Cayenne.)

Habitat.—Tropical Lowland Evergreen Forest, Montane Evergreen Forest (Subtropical and lower Temperate zones, 900–3000 m; in South America to Tropical Zone).

Distribution.—*Resident* [*picumnus* group] in the highlands of Middle America from Chiapas south through Guatemala and Honduras, and locally in Costa Rica (primarily Cordillera Central, Cordillera Talamanca, and the Dota Mountains) and western Panama (western Chiriquí and Veraguas), and in South America from southeastern Colombia, southern Venezuela, and the Guianas south, primarily east of the Andes, to northern Bolivia and northern Amazonian Brazil; [*multistrigatus* group] highlands of Colombia and northern and western Venezuela; [*transfasciatus* group] in central Amazonian Brazil; and [*pallescens* group] in eastern Bolivia, southwestern Brazil, Paraguay, and northwestern Argentina.

Notes.—Groups: *D. multistrigatus* Eyton, 1851 [Cordilleran Woodcreeper], *D. picumnus* [Black-banded Woodcreeper], *D. transfasciatus* Todd, 1925 [Cross-barred Woodcreeper], and *D. pallescens* Pelzeln, 1868 [Pale-billed Woodcreeper]. *D. picumnus* and the South American *D. platyrostris* Spix, 1824, constitute a superspecies (Sibley and Monroe 1990, Marantz 1997); Willis (1982) considered *D. platyrostris* to be a subspecies of *picumnus*.

Genus *XIPHORHYNCHUS* Swainson

Xiphorhynchus Swainson, June 1827, Philos. Mag. (n.s.) 1: 440. Type, by subsequent designation (Oberholser, 1905), *Xiphorhynchus flavigaster* Swainson.
Dendroplex Swainson, Dec. 1827, Zool. J. 3: 354. Type, by subsequent designation (Swainson, 1837), "*D. guttatus* Spix, 1, 91, f. 1" = *Dendrocolaptes ocellatus* Spix.

Xiphorhynchus picus (Gmelin). Straight-billed Woodcreeper.

Oriolus Picus Gmelin, 1788, Syst. Nat. 1(1): 384. Based on "Talapiot" Daubenton, Planches Enlum., pl. 605, and the "Climbing Oriole" Latham, Gen. Synop. Birds 1(2): 453. (in Gujanae = Cayenne.)

Habitat.—Mangrove Forest, Secondary Forest (0–300 m; Tropical Zone).
Distribution.—*Resident* in Panama (on the Pacific slope from the Azuero Peninsula eastward, locally on the Caribbean slope in the Canal area), and in South America from northern Colombia east to Venezuela (including Margarita Island), Trinidad, and the Guianas, and south, east of the Andes, to central Bolivia and Amazonian and coastal eastern Brazil.

Xiphorhynchus susurrans (Jardine). Cocoa Woodcreeper.

Dendrocolaptes susurrans Jardine, 1847, Ann. and Mag. Nat. Hist. 19, p. 81. (Tobago.)

Habitat.— Tropical Lowland Evergreen Forest, River-edge Forest, Secondary Forest, Mangrove Forest (0–900 m; Tropical and lower Subtropical zones).
Distribution.—*Resident* on the Caribbean slope of eastern Guatemala (lower Río Motagua valley), Honduras, and Nicaragua, on both slopes of Costa Rica and Panama, and in South America from northern Colombia east to northern Venezuela, Tobago, and Trinidad.

Notes.—Formerly (A.O.U. 1983) treated as a subspecies of *X. guttatus* (Lichtenstein, 1822) [Buff-throated Woodcreeper]. Willis (1983b) considered the two as separate species based on song and body size differences; this treatment was followed by Ridgely and Tudor (1994). Although no quantitative, geographically comprehensive analysis has been published, no rationale was provided by Peters (1951) for the treatment of these taxa as one species.

Xiphorhynchus flavigaster Swainson. Ivory-billed Woodcreeper.

Xiphorhynchus flavigaster Swainson, 1827, Philos. Mag. (n.s.) 1: 440. (Temiscaltipec, Mexico = Temascaltepec, México.)

Habitat.—Tropical Lowland Evergreen Forest, Montane Evergreen Forest, Tropical Deciduous Forest, Secondary Forest, Pine-Oak Forest (0–2400 m; Tropical and Subtropical zones).
Distribution.—*Resident* on both slopes of Middle America from central and southern Sinaloa, western Durango, southeastern San Luis Potosí and southern Tamaulipas south to Honduras, then largely confined to the Pacific slope in Nicaragua and northwestern Costa Rica (south to the Nicoya Peninsula).

Notes.—The unique type of *Xiphorhynchus striatigularis* (Richmond, 1900) [Stripe-throated Woodcreeper], from Tamaulipas, is regarded as an aberrant individual of *X. flavigaster* (Winker 1995).

Xiphorhynchus lachrymosus (Lawrence). Black-striped Woodcreeper.

Dendrornis lachrymosus Lawrence, 1862, Ann. Lyc. Nat. Hist. N. Y. 7: 467. (Atlantic side of the Isthmus of Panama, along the line of the Panama Railroad = Lion Hill, Canal Zone.)

Habitat.—Tropical Lowland Evergreen Forest, Mangrove Forest (0–1200 m; Tropical and lower Subtropical zones).

Distribution.—*Resident* from eastern Nicaragua south through Costa Rica (except dry northwest) and Panama (more widespread on Caribbean coast) to western Colombia and northwestern Ecuador.

Xiphorhynchus erythropygius (Sclater). Spotted Woodcreeper.

Dendrornis erythropygia Sclater, 1859, Proc. Zool. Soc. London, p. 366. (In Stat. Veræ Crucis et Oaxaca reipubl. Mexicanæ = Jalapa, Veracruz.)

Habitat.—Montane Evergreen Forest, Tropical Lowland Evergreen Forest (100–2200 m; Subtropical and lower Temperate zones, from Nicaragua southward also in Tropical Zone).

Distribution.—*Resident* [*erythropygius* group] in the highlands from Guerrero, Oaxaca, southeastern San Luis Potosí, Hidalgo, Veracruz, and Chiapas south through northern Central America to north-central Nicaragua; and [*aequatorialis* group] in lowlands as well as highlands from eastern Nicaragua south through Costa Rica, Panama, and western Colombia to western Ecuador.

Notes.—Groups: *X. erythropygius* [Spotted Woodcreeper] and *X. aequatorialis* (Berlepsch and Taczanowski, 1884) [Spot-throated Woodcreeper]. Because *X. triangularis* (Lafresnaye, 1842) is very similar in plumage to *X. erythropygius,* they have been regarded as conspecific by some authors (e.g., Cory and Hellmayr 1925); however, they are separated by elevation in the Western Andes of Colombia and Ecuador, with *X. triangularis* occurring at higher elevations (Wetmore 1972, Hilty and Brown 1986), and no hybrids between the two taxa are known; they constitute a superspecies (Fjeldså and Krabbe 1990, Sibley and Monroe 1990).

Genus *LEPIDOCOLAPTES* Reichenbach

Lepidocolaptes Reichenbach, 1853, Handb. Spec. Ornithol., cont. x, Scansoriae A. Sittinae, p. 183. Type, by subsequent designation (G. R. Gray, 1855), *Dendrocolaptes squamatus* Lichtenstein.

Lepidocolaptes leucogaster (Swainson). White-striped Woodcreeper.

Xiphorhynchus leucogaster Swainson, 1827, Philos. Mag. (n.s.) 1: 440. (Temiscaltipec, Mexico = Temascaltepec, México.)

Habitat.—Pine-Oak Forest, Pine Forest, Tropical Deciduous Forest (900–3500 m; Tropical to Temperate zones).

Distribution.—*Resident* from southeastern Sonora, southern Chihuahua, Durango, Zacatecas, and western San Luis Potosí south to Oaxaca (west of Isthmus of Tehuantepec), Puebla, and western Veracruz.

Lepidocolaptes souleyetii (Des Murs). Streak-headed Woodcreeper.

Dendrocolaptes Souleyetii (Lafresnaye MS) Des Murs, 1849, Iconogr. Ornithol., livr. 12, pl. 70 and text. (Perú = Payta, Peru.)

Habitat.—Tropical Deciduous Forest, Gallery Forest, Tropical Lowland Evergreen Forest, Secondary Forest (0–1500 m; Tropical and lower Subtropical zones).

Distribution.—*Resident* from Guerrero, Oaxaca, Veracruz, Tabasco, Chiapas, and southern Campeche south through Central America, and in South America in northern and eastern Colombia, northern Venezuela, and Trinidad (locally also in southeastern Venezuela and northern Brazil), and west of the Andes from southwestern Colombia to northwestern Peru.

Lepidocolaptes affinis (Lafresnaye). Spot-crowned Woodcreeper.

Dendrocolaptes affinis Lafresnaye, 1839, Rev. Zool. [Paris] 2: 100. (Mexico.)

Habitat.—Montane Evergreen Forest, Secondary Forest (1000–3100 m; Subtropical and Temperate zones).

Distribution.—*Resident* [*affinis* group] in the highlands from Guerrero, México, Hidalgo, southeastern San Luis Potosí and southwestern Tamaulipas south through Middle America (except the Yucatan Peninsula and Belize) to northern Nicaragua, Costa Rica, and western Panama (Chiriquí); and [*lacrymiger* group] in South America from the mountains of Colombia and northern Venezuela south in the Andes on the western slope to southern Ecuador and on the eastern slope to central Bolivia.

Notes.—Although most recent authors have treated South American populations of *L. lacrymiger* (Des Murs, 1849) [Montane Woodcreeper] as conspecific with *L. affinis,* Cory and Hellmayr (1925), Eisenmann (1955), and Ridgely and Tudor (1994) treated South American populations as a species, separate from *L. affinis* [Spot-crowned Woodcreeper]. The plumage patterns of the two groups differ strongly, more so than do those of some other pairs of woodcreepers with similar distributions (e.g., *Xiphorhynchus erythropygius* and *X. triangularis*). Although Ridgely and Tudor (1994) stated that the vocalizations of the two groups differ strongly, no analysis of these characters has been published.

Genus *CAMPYLORHAMPHUS* Bertoni

Campylorhamphus Bertoni, 1901, An. Cien. Parag., ser. 1, no. 1, p. 70. Type, by monotypy, *Campylorhamphus longirostris* Bertoni = *Dendrocopus falcularius* Vieillot.

Campylorhamphus trochilirostris (Lichtenstein). Red-billed Scythebill.

Dendrocolaptes trochilirostris Lichtenstein, 1820, Abh. Phys. Kl. Akad. Wiss. Berlin (1818–19), p. 207, pl. 3. (Brazil = Bahia, Brazil.)

Habitat.—Tropical Lowland Evergreen Forest, Montane Evergreen Forest, Tropical Deciduous Forest (0–1050 m; Tropical and Subtropical zones).

Distribution.—*Resident* in eastern Panama (from northern Coclé and eastern Panamá province eastward), and in South America from Colombia, Venezuela, and the Guianas south, west of the Andes to northwestern Peru and east of the Andes to northern Argentina, Paraguay, and central and eastern Brazil.

Notes.—Peters (1951) considered *C. falcularius* (Vieillot, 1823) of southeastern South America to be a subspecies of *C. trochilirostris*; Sibley and Monroe (1990) considered *C. falcularius* and *C. trochilirostris* to form a superspecies.

Campylorhamphus pusillus (Sclater). Brown-billed Scythebill.

Xiphorhynchus pusillus Sclater, 1860, Proc. Zool. Soc. London, p. 278, footnote. (In Nov. Granada int. = Bogotá, Colombia.)

Habitat.—Montane Evergreen Forest, Tropical Lowland Evergreen Forest (600–17000 m; upper Tropical to Subtropical zones).

Distribution.—*Resident* locally in Costa Rica (Caribbean slope of highlands from Cordillera de Tilarán southward, and in lowlands of Pacific southwest) and Panama (Chiriquí, Veraguas, eastern Panamá province, eastern Darién), and in South America mainly in the Andes locally from northern Colombia and western Venezuela south to extreme northern Peru.

Family **THAMNOPHILIDAE**: Antbirds

Notes.—We follow Sibley and Monroe (1990), Harshman (1994), and Ridgely and Tudor (1994) in treating the antbirds as a separate family from the antthrushes and antpittas (Formicariidae).

Genus *CYMBILAIMUS* Gray

Cymbilaimus G. R. Gray, 1840, List Genera Birds, p. 36. Type, by original designation, *C. lineatus* (Leach) = *Lanius lineatus* Leach.

Cymbilaimus lineatus (Leach). Fasciated Antshrike.

Lanius lineatus Leach, 1814, Zool. Misc. 1: 20, pl. 6. (Berbice, British Guiana.)

Habitat.—Tropical Lowland Evergreen Forest; primarily dense vine tangles at mid-levels at forest edge (0–1200 m; Tropical and lower Subtropical zones).

Distribution.—*Resident* on the Caribbean slope of extreme southeastern Honduras (Olancho), Nicaragua, and Costa Rica, throughout Panama (except the Azuero Peninsula), and in South America from Colombia, Venezuela, and the Guianas south, west of the Andes to northwestern Ecuador, and east of the Andes to central Bolivia and Amazonian Brazil.

Genus *TARABA* Lesson

Taraba Lesson, 1831, Traité Ornithol., livr. 5 (1830), p. 375. Type, by subsequent designation (Sherborn, 1931), *Tamnophilus* [sic] *magnus* Wied = *Thamnophilus major* Vieillot.

Taraba major (Vieillot). Great Antshrike.

Thamnophilus major Vieillot, 1816, Nouv. Dict. Hist. Nat. (nouv. éd.) 3: 313. Based on "Batara major" Azara, Apunt. Hist. Nat. Páx. Parag 2: 192 (no. 211). (Paraguay.)

Habitat.—Tropical Lowland Evergreen Forest Edge, Secondary Forest, Gallery Forest, Riparian Thickets, Second-growth Scrub; primarily in very dense vegetation (0–1400 m; Tropical, rarely Subtropical zones).

Distribution.—*Resident* from southern Veracruz, northern Oaxaca, Tabasco, and Chiapas south on the Gulf-Caribbean slope through northern Central America to Nicaragua, on both slopes of Costa Rica (rare in dry northwest) and Panama, and in South America from Colombia, Venezuela, Trinidad, and the Guianas south, west of the Andes to northwestern Peru and east of the Andes to northern Argentina, Paraguay, and south-central Brazil.

Genus *THAMNOPHILUS* Vieillot

Thamnophilus Vieillot, 1816, Analyse, p. 40. Type, by subsequent designation (Swainson, 1824), *Lanius doliatus* Linnaeus.
Erionotus Cabanis and Heine, 1859, Mus. Heineanum 2: 15. Type, by original designation, *Thamnophilus caerulescens* Vieillot.
Abalius Cabanis, 1861, J. Ornithol. 9: 242. Type, by original designation, *Thamnophilus punctatus* Sclater = *Thamnophilus bridgesi* Sclater

Thamnophilus doliatus (Linnaeus). Barred Antshrike.

Lanius doliatus Linnaeus, 1764, Mus. Adolphi Friderici 2 (Prodr.): 12. (No locality given = Surinam.)

Habitat.—Second-growth Scrub, Riparian Thickets, (Isla Coiba only) Tropical Deciduous Forest (0–2000 m; Tropical Zone).

Distribution.—*Resident* [*doliatus* group] from southeastern San Luis Potosí, southern Tamaulipas, Veracruz, eastern Puebla, and northern and southeastern Oaxaca south on both slopes of Middle America (including the Yucatan Peninsula) to Panama (including Isla Coiba and the Pearl Islands), and in South America from northern and eastern Colombia, Venezuela (including Margarita Island), Tobago, Trinidad, and the Guianas south, east of the Andes, to northern Argentina and southern Brazil; and [*zarumae* group] in southwestern Ecuador and northwestern Peru.

Notes.—Groups: *T. doliatus* [Barred Antshrike] and *T. zarumae* Chapman, 1921 [Chapman's Antshrike].

Thamnophilus nigriceps Sclater. Black Antshrike.

Thamnophilus nigriceps Sclater, 1869, Proc. Zool. Soc. London (1868), p. 571. (Bogotá, Colombia, error = probably Barranquilla.)

Habitat.—Tropical Lowland Evergreen Forest Edge, Secondary Forest (0–600 m; Tropical Zone).

Distribution.—*Resident* in eastern Panama (eastern Panamá province and Darién) and northern and north-central Colombia (east to the Santa Marta Mountains).

Notes.—*Thamnophilus nigriceps* and *T. praecox* Zimmer, 1937, of eastern Ecuador, constitute a superspecies and may be conspecific (Ridgely and Tudor 1994).

Thamnophilus bridgesi Sclater. Black-hooded Antshrike.

Thamnophilus bridgesi Sclater, 1856, Proc. Zool. Soc. London, p. 141. (river David, in the vicinity of the Town of David in the Province of Chiriqui in the State of Panama.)

Habitat.—Tropical Lowland Evergreen Forest Edge, Gallery Forest, Secondary Forest, Mangrove Forest (0–1150 m; Tropical and lower Subtropical zones).

Distribution.—*Resident* on the Pacific slope of southwestern Costa Rica (locally north to southern Guanacaste) and western Panama (east to the Azuero Peninsula).

Thamnophilus atrinucha Salvin and Godman. Western Slaty-Antshrike.

Thamnophilus atrinucha Salvin and Godman, 1892, Biol. Centrali-Amer., Aves, 2, p. 200. (Central America = Panamá.)

Habitat.—Tropical Deciduous Forest, Secondary Forest, Tropical Lowland Evergreen Forest Edge, Gallery Forest (0–1500 m; Tropical and lower Subtropical zones).

Distribution.—*Resident* on the Caribbean slope from southern Belize and eastern Guatemala south to Costa Rica, and in Panama (entire Caribbean slope, and Pacific slope from Coclé eastward), western Colombia (including Gorgona Island), and western Ecuador; and in northern Colombia in Cauca and Magdalena valleys.

Notes.—We follow Isler et al. (1997) in considering *atrinucha* as one of several species-level taxa, all differing in voice and plumage, that have been treated as subspecies of *T. punctatus* (Shaw, 1809).

Genus *XENORNIS* Chapman

Xenornis Chapman, 1924, Amer. Mus. Novit., no. 123, p. 1. Type, by original designation, *Xenornis setifrons* Chapman.

Xenornis setifrons Chapman. Spiny-faced Antshrike.

Xenornis setifrons Chapman, 1924, Amer. Mus. Novit., no. 123, p. 1. (Tacarcuna, 2050 feet, eastern Panama.)

Habitat.—Tropical Lowland Evergreen Forest (0–600 m; upper Tropical zone).

Distribution.—*Resident* in eastern Panama in San Blas and eastern Darién (Cerro Tacarcuna foothills), and in northwestern Colombia in Chocó (Río Baudó).

Notes.—Also known as Speckled Antshrike, Speckle-breasted Antshrike, or Gray-faced Antbird (but see Remsen 1997). Appears to be the ecological counterpart of, if not closely related to, South American species of the genus *Thamnomanes* (Whitney and Rosenberg 1993).

Genus *THAMNISTES* Sclater and Salvin

Thamnistes Sclater and Salvin, 1860, Proc. Zool. Soc. London, p. 299. Type, by original designation, *Thamnistes anabatinus* Sclater and Salvin.

Thamnistes anabatinus Sclater and Salvin. Russet Antshrike.

Thamnistes anabatinus Sclater and Salvin, 1860, Proc. Zool. Soc. London, p. 299. (In prov. Veræ Pacis regionale calida = Choctum, Alta Verapaz, Guatemala.)

Habitat.—Montane Evergreen Forest, Tropical Lowland Evergreen Forest (0–1700 m; upper Tropical and Subtropical zones).

Distribution.—*Resident* [*anabatinus* group] on the Gulf-Caribbean slope from Oaxaca, Tabasco, and Chiapas south through northern Central America to Nicaragua, on both slopes of Costa Rica (absent from dry northwest) and Panama, and in Colombia, Venezuela, and Ecuador; and [*rufescens* group] in Andean foothills of Peru and Bolivia.

Notes.—Also known as Tawny Antshrike. Groups: *T. anabatinus* [Russet Antshrike] and *T. rufescens* Cabanis, 1873 [Peruvian Antshrike].

Genus *DYSITHAMNUS* Cabanis

Dysithamnus Cabanis, 1847, Arch. Naturgesch. 13: 223. Type, by subsequent designation (G. R. Gray, 1855), *Myothera strictothorax* [sic] Temminck.

Dysithamnus mentalis (Temminck). Plain Antvireo.

Myothera mentalis Temminck, 1823, Planches Color., livr. 30, pl. 179, fig. 3. (Brazil = Curytiba, Paraná, Brazil.)

Habitat.—Montane Evergreen Forest, Tropical Lowland Evergreen Forest (0–2500 m; Tropical and Subtropical zones). Elevational range shifts from lowlands at northern edge of range (e.g., 0–350 in Guatemala), to foothills in middle portion of range (e.g., 400–1200 m in Honduras), to foothill and lower montane forests at southern end (e.g., 700–2200 m, in Costa Rica).

Distribution.—*Resident* in Middle America locally from eastern Tabasco, Campeche, northern Guatemala, and Belize south, mostly on the Caribbean slope, through Honduras and Costa Rica (not recorded Nicaragua) to Panama (throughout on both slopes), and in South America west of the Andes to northwestern Peru, in lowlands of northern Colombia, Venezuela, Tobago, and Trinidad, along the eastern slope of the Andes to east-central Bolivia, in the tepuis of Venezuela, and in lowlands from central eastern Bolivia and central Brazil south to Paraguay and northeastern Argentina.

Dysithamnus striaticeps Lawrence. Streak-crowned Antvireo.

Dysithamnus striaticeps Lawrence, 1865, Ann. Lyc. Nat. Hist. N. Y. 8: 130. (Angostura, Costa Rica.)

Habitat.— Tropical Lowland Evergreen Forest (0–800 m; Tropical and lower Subtropical zones).

Distribution.—*Resident* on the Caribbean slope of extreme southeastern Honduras (Arenal), Nicaragua, and Costa Rica, occurring locally also on the Pacific slope along the Cordillera de Guanacaste in northwestern Costa Rica.

A report from western Panama (Río Sixaola) is erroneous, being based on a specimen of *D. puncticeps.*

Notes.—*Dysithamnus striaticeps* and *D. puncticeps* are closely related and appear to constitute a superspecies.

Dysithamnus puncticeps Salvin. Spot-crowned Antvireo.

Dysithamnus puncticeps Salvin, 1866, Proc. Zool. Soc. London, p. 72. (Veragua, Caribbean lowlands of Panamá.)

Habitat.—Tropical Lowland Evergreen Forest (0–800 m; Tropical Zone).

Distribution.—*Resident* in extreme southeastern Costa Rica (Caribbean lowlands), Panama (entire Caribbean lowlands, and the Pacific lowlands in Darién), northern and western Colombia, and northwestern Ecuador.

Notes.—See comments under *D. striaticeps*.

Genus *MYRMOTHERULA* Sclater

Myrmotherula Sclater, 1858, Proc. Zool. Soc. London, p. 234. Type, by subsequent designation (Sclater, 1890), *M[uscicapa]. pygmaea* Gmelin = *Muscicapa brachyura* Hermann.

Myrmopagis Ridgway, 1909, Proc. Biol. Soc. Wash. 22: 69. Type, by original designation, *Myrmothera axillaris* Vieillot.

Notes.—Hackett and Rosenberg (1990) presented evidence that this genus is not a monophyletic group.

Myrmotherula brachyura (Hermann). Pygmy Antwren.

Muscic[apae] brachyurae [nom. pl.] Hermann, 1783, Tabula Affinit. Anim., p. 229. Based on "Le petit Gobe-mouche tacheté, de Cayenne" Buffon, Hist. Nat. Ois. 4: 554, and Daubenton, Planches Enlum., pl. 831, fig. 2. (Cayenne.)

Habitat.—Tropical Lowland Evergreen Forest Edge, Secondary Forest (0–600 m; Tropical Zone).

Distribution.—*Resident* [*ignota* group] in central and eastern Panama (Canal area eastward on both slopes), and western Colombia; and [*brachyura* group] in South America from eastern Colombia, southern Venezuela, and the Guianas south, east of the Andes, to central Bolivia and Amazonian Brazil.

Notes.—The two groups are distinctive and may prove to be separate species (Hilty and Brown 1986), *M. ignota* Griscom, 1929 [Griscom's Antwren] and *M. brachyura* [Pygmy Antwren]. Meyer de Schauensee (1966) suggested that *ignota* may be more closely related to *M. obscura* Zimmer, 1932 [Short-billed Antwren] than to *M. brachyura*.

Myrmotherula surinamensis (Gmelin). Streaked Antwren.

Sitta surinamensis Gmelin, 1788, Syst. Nat. 1(1): 442. Based on the "Surinam Nuthatch" Latham, Gen. Synop. Birds 1(2): 654, pl. 28. (in Surinamo = Surinam.)

Habitat.—River-edge Forest, Tropical Lowland Evergreen Forest Edge, Secondary Forest (0–600 m; Tropical Zone).

Distribution.—*Resident* from Panama (entire Caribbean slope, and Pacific drainage west to western Panamá province) east across Colombia and southern Venezuela to the Guianas, and south, west of the Andes to western Ecuador and east of the Andes to northern Bolivia and Amazonian Brazil.

Notes.—Groups: *M. pacifica* [Pacific Streaked-Antwren] and *M. surinamensis* [Amazonian Streaked-Antwren] (Ridgely and Tudor 1994).

Myrmotherula fulviventris Lawrence. Checker-throated Antwren.

Myrmetherula [sic] *fulviventris* Lawrence, 1862, Ann. Lyc. Nat. Hist. N. Y. 7: 468. (on the Atlantic side of the Isthmus of Panama, along the line of the Panama Railroad = Lion Hill, Canal Zone.)

Habitat.—Tropical Lowland Evergreen Forest (0–1100 m; Tropical and lower Subtropical zones).

Distribution.—*Resident* on the Caribbean slope of eastern Honduras (Olancho, Gracias a Dios), Nicaragua, and Costa Rica, in Panama (both slopes, the Pacific from Veraguas eastward), and in South America from central and western Colombia south to southwestern Ecuador.

Myrmotherula axillaris (Vieillot). White-flanked Antwren.

>*Myrmothera axillaris* Vieillot, 1817, Nouv. Dict. Hist. Nat. (nouv. éd.) 12: 113. ("La Guyane" = Cayenne.)

Habitat.—Tropical Lowland Evergreen Forest, River-edge Forest, Secondary Forest (0–1100 m; Tropical Zone).

Distribution.—*Resident* on the Caribbean slope of southern Mexico (Chiapas; one record), northeastern Honduras (Gracias a Dios), Nicaragua, and Costa Rica, in Panama (both slopes, the Pacific from western Panamá province eastward), and in South America from Colombia, Venezuela, Trinidad, and the Guianas south, west of the Andes to western Ecuador and east of the Andes to central Bolivia and Amazonian and southeastern Brazil.

A single specimen from Chiapas, Mexico, presumably represents a previously undetected population there (Marín 1993).

Myrmotherula schisticolor (Lawrence). Slaty Antwren.

>*Formicivora schisticolor* Lawrence, 1865, Ann. Lyc. Nat. Hist. N. Y. 8: 172. (Turrialba, Costa Rica.)

Habitat.—Montane Evergreen Forest, Tropical Lowland Evergreen Forest (600–2200 m; Tropical and Subtropical zones).

Distribution.—*Resident* from Chiapas south through Guatemala, Belize, and Honduras to north-central Nicaragua; in lowlands and foothills of eastern Nicaragua, Costa Rica, and Panama, and in South America in the Andes from Colombia and northern Venezuela south to southern Peru.

Genus *HERPSILOCHMUS* Cabanis

>*Herpsilochmus* Cabanis, 1847, Arch. Naturgesch 12: 224. Type, by subsequent designation (G. R. Gray, 1855), *Myiothera pileata* Lichtenstein.

Herpsilochmus rufimarginatus (Temminck). Rufous-winged Antwren.

>*Myiothera rufimarginata* Temminck, 1822, Planches Color., livr. 22, pl. 132, figs. 1–2. (Brazil = Rio de Janeiro.)

Habitat.—Tropical Lowland Evergreen Forest, Montane Evergreen Forest; primarily dense vine tangles at forest edge (0–1050 m; Tropical and lower Subtropical zones).

Distribution.—*Resident* locally in eastern Panama (recorded in eastern Panamá province and Darién), and in South America, west of the Andes from northern Colombia to northwestern Ecuador, in foothills of Eastern Andes from Venezuela to central Bolivia, and locally in lowlands east of Andes, mainly in southern Venezuela, eastern Bolivia, and southwestern, eastern, and southeastern Brazil.

Genus *MICRORHOPIAS* Sclater

>*Microrhopias* Sclater, 1862, Cat. Collect. Amer. Birds, p. 182. Type, by subsequent designation (Sclater, 1890), *F. quixensis* = *Thamnophilus quixensis* Cornalia.

Microrhopias quixensis (Cornalia). Dot-winged Antwren.

>*Thamnophilus quixensis* Cornalia, 1849, Vertebr. Synop. Mus. Mediolanense Osculati, pp. 6, 12. (eastern Ecuador.)

Habitat.—Tropical Lowland Evergreen Forest, Tropical Second-growth Forest (0–1100 m; Tropical Zone).

Distribution.—*Resident* [*boucardi* group] on the Gulf-Caribbean slope from southern Veracruz, northern Oaxaca, Tabasco, Chiapas, southern Campeche, and southern Quintana Roo south through northern Central America to Nicaragua, on both slopes of Costa Rica (absent from the dry northwest) and Panama (mainly Caribbean slope), and in western Colombia and western Ecuador; and [*quixensis* group] in South America, east of the Andes, in southeastern Colombia, Peru, Amazonian Brazil (mainly south of Amazon), the Guianas, and northern Bolivia.

Notes.—Groups: *M. boucardi* (Sclater, 1858) [Boucard's Antwren] and *M. quixensis* [Amazonian Antwren]; there may be other recognizable groups within the latter (Meyer de Schauensee 1966).

Genus *FORMICIVORA* Swainson

Formicivora Swainson, 1824, Zool. J. 1: 301 (in text). Type, by subsequent designation (G. R. Gray, 1840), *Formicivora nigricollis* Swainson = *Turdus griseus* Boddaert.
Neorhopias Hellmayr, 1920, Anz. Ornithol. Ges. Bayern 3: 20. Type, by original designation, *Formicivora iheringi* Hellmayr.

Formicivora grisea (Boddaert). White-fringed Antwren.

Turdus griseus [sic] Boddaert, 1783, Table Planches Enlum., p. 39. Based on "Le Grisin, de Cayenne" Daubenton, Planches Enlum., pl. 643, fig. 1. (Cayenne.)

Habitat.—Tropical Deciduous Forest, Secondary Forest (0–200 m; Tropical Zone).
Distribution.—*Resident* in the Pearl Islands, off Pacific Panama; and in South America in northern Colombia, northern Venezuela (also Margarita and Chacachacare islands, and Tobago) and the Guianas, Amazonian Brazil, and extreme eastern Bolivia; and southeastern Brazil.
Notes.—Also known as Black-breasted Antwren.

Genus *TERENURA* Cabanis and Heine

Terenura Cabanis and Heine, 1859, Mus. Heineanum 2: 11. Type, by monotypy, *Myiothera maculata* Wied.

Terenura callinota (Sclater). Rufous-rumped Antwren.

Formicivora callinota Sclater, 1855, Proc. Zool. Soc. London, p. 89, pl. 96. (Santa Fé di Bogota [Colombia].)

Habitat.—Montane Evergreen Forest (750–1200 m; Subtropical Zone).
Distribution.—*Resident* (*callinota* group) locally in the highlands of Costa Rica (Caribbean slope of Cordillera Central) and Panama (recorded Chiriquí, Bocas del Toro, Veraguas, and eastern Darién), and in South America in Guyana (Acary Mountains) and Surinam, and in the Andes from Colombia south on the western slope to southern Ecuador and on the eastern slope to southern Peru; and (*venezuelana* group) in northwestern Venezuela (Sierra de Perijá).
Notes.—Groups: *T. callinota* [Rufous-rumped Antwren] and *T. venezuelana* Phelps and Phelps 1954 [Perija Antwren]. *Terenura callinota* probably forms a superspecies with South American *T. spodioptila* Sclater and Salvin, 1881 [Ash-winged Antwren], *T. humeralis* Sclater and Salvin [Chestnut-shouldered Antwren], 1881, and *T. sharpei* Berlepsch, 1901 [Yellow-rumped Antwren].

Genus *CERCOMACRA* Sclater

Cercomacra Sclater, 1858, Proc. Zool. Soc. London, p. 244. Type, by subsequent designation (Sclater, 1890), *Cercomacra caerulescens* Sclater = *Cercomacra brasiliana* Hellmayr.

Cercomacra tyrannina (Sclater). Dusky Antbird.

Pyriglena tyrannina Sclater, 1855, Proc. Zool. Soc. London, p. 90, pl. 98. (Santa Fé di Bogota [Colombia].)

Habitat.—Tropical Lowland Evergreen Forest Edge, Montane Evergreen Forest Edge, Secondary Forest (0–1800 m; Tropical and lower Subtropical zones).
Distribution.—*Resident* on the Gulf-Caribbean slope from southeastern Veracruz, north-

ern Oaxaca, Tabasco, Chiapas, southern Campeche, and southern Quintana Roo south on the Gulf-Caribbean slope to Honduras, on both slopes of Nicaragua (also in Pacific southwest), Costa Rica (rare in Pacific northwest), and Panama, and in South America from Colombia, Venezuela, and the Guianas south, west of the Andes to western Ecuador and east of the Andes to northern Amazonian and eastern Brazil.

Notes.—Also known as Tyrannine Antbird.

Cercomacra nigricans Sclater. Jet Antbird.

> *Cercomacra nigricans* Sclater, 1858, Proc. Zool. Soc. London, p. 245. (New Grenada, S. Martha; Bogota = Santa Marta, Colombia.)

Habitat.—Tropical Lowland Evergreen Forest Edge; often near streams (0–1500 m; Tropical Zone).

Distribution.—*Resident* in Panama (on the Caribbean slope from western Colón east to western San Blas, on the Pacific from Veraguas east to Darién, and in the Pearl Islands), and in South America, west of the Andes south to southwestern Ecuador and in northern and eastern Colombia and northern Venezuela.

Genus *GYMNOCICHLA* Sclater

> *Gymnocichla* Sclater, 1858, Proc. Zool. Soc. London, p. 274. Type, by monotypy, *Myiothera nudiceps* Cassin.

Notes.—Ridgely and Tudor (1994) suggested that this genus should be merged into *Myrmeciza*.

Gymnocichla nudiceps (Cassin). Bare-crowned Antbird.

> *Myiothera nudiceps* Cassin, 1850, Proc. Acad. Nat. Sci. Philadelphia 5: 106, pl. 6. (Panama.)

Habitat.—Tropical Lowland Evergreen Forest Edge (Tropical and lower Subtropical zones). 0–200 m in north (Guatemala, Honduras) to 0–1200 m in south (Costa Rica, Panama).

Distribution.—*Resident* on the Caribbean slope of eastern Guatemala, Belize, Honduras, and Nicaragua, on both slopes of Costa Rica (absent from dry northwest) and Panama, and in northern Colombia.

Genus *MYRMECIZA* Gray

> *Myrmeciza* G. R. Gray, 1841, List Genera Birds, ed. 2, p. 34. Type, by original designation, *Drymophila longipes* Swainson.

Myrmeciza longipes (Swainson). White-bellied Antbird.

> *Drymophila longipes* Swainson, 1825, Zool. J. 2: 152. ("some part of Brazil," error = Trinidad.)

Habitat.—Tropical Deciduous Forest, Tropical Lowland Evergreen Forest, Gallery Forest (0–1700 m; Tropical Zone).

Distribution.—*Resident* in central and eastern Panama (from Coclé to Darién on the Pacific slope, and mainly near the Río Chagres on the Caribbean slope), and in South America east across northern Colombia to Venezuela, Trinidad, and Guyana, and northern Brazil (north of the Amazon).

Myrmeciza exsul Sclater. Chestnut-backed Antbird.

> *Myrmeciza exsul* Sclater, 1858, Proc. Zool. Soc. London, p. 540. (Panamá and Nicaragua.)

Habitat.—Tropical Lowland Evergreen Forest, Tropical Second-growth Forest; especially in dense thickets along streams, tree-fall gaps, bamboo (0–900 m; Tropical and lower Subtropical zones).

Distribution.—*Resident* [*exsul* group] in Nicaragua (Caribbean slope), Costa Rica (absent from dry northwest), Panama (both slopes, except southeastern Darién); and [*maculifer* group] in extreme eastern Panama (southeastern Darién), northern and western Colombia, and western Ecuador.

Notes.—Groups: *M. exsul* [Chestnut-backed Antbird] and *M. maculifer* (Hellmayr, 1906) [Wing-spotted Antbird]; intergradation between the two reportedly occurs in eastern Panamá province and western Darién (Sibley and Monroe 1990).

Myrmeciza laemosticta Salvin. Dull-mantled Antbird.

Myrmeciza læmosticta Salvin, 1865, Proc. Zool. Soc. London (1864), p. 582. (Tucur-riquí, Costa Rica.)

Habitat.—Tropical Lowland Evergreen Forest; especially near streams and in shady ra-vines (300–1200 m; Tropical and lower Subtropical zones).

Distribution.—*Resident* in Costa Rica (Caribbean slope, from the Cordillera de Guana-caste southward) and Panama (mainly on Caribbean slope, locally on Pacific slope), and in South America from northern Colombia east to northwestern Venezuela.

Notes.—Robbins and Ridgely (1991) provided evidence for elevation of the taxon *ni-gricauda* to species rank. This form, found in the Pacific lowlands of Colombia and north-western Ecuador, was treated (A.O.U. 1983) as conspecific with *M. laemosticta.* Therefore, the South American distribution of the latter extends only from northern Colombia east to extreme western Venezuela.

Myrmeciza immaculata (Lafresnaye). Immaculate Antbird.

Thamnophilus immaculatus Lafresnaye, 1845, Rev. Zool. [Paris] 8: 340. (Bogotá, Co-lombia.)

Habitat.—Tropical Lowland Evergreen Forest (300–1700 m; upper Tropical and Sub-tropical zones).

Distribution.—*Resident* on the Caribbean slope of Costa Rica (Cordillera de Talamanca, Cordillera Central, and Dota Mountains), Panama (recorded Bocas del Toro, Chiriquí, Ver-aguas, and eastern Darién), and in South America from northern Colombia and northwestern Venezuela south, west of the Andes to southwestern Ecuador and east of the Andes to central Colombia.

Genus *HYLOPHYLAX* Ridgway

Hylophylax Ridgway, 1909, Proc. Biol. Soc. Wash. 22: 70. Type, by original designation, *Conopophaga naevioides* Lafresnaye.

Hylophylax naevioides (Lafresnaye). Spotted Antbird.

Conopophaga nævioides Lafresnaye, 1847, Rev. Zool. [Paris] 10: 69. (No locality given = Panama.)

Habitat.—Tropical Lowland Evergreen Forest (0–900 m; Tropical and lower Subtropical zones).

Distribution.—*Resident* in eastern Honduras (west to La Ceiba), eastern Nicaragua, Costa Rica (primarily Caribbean slope), Panama (both slopes), northern and western Colombia, and western Ecuador.

Notes.—*Hylophylax naevioides* and the South American *H. naevia* (Gmelin, 1789), found east of the Andes, probably constitute a superspecies.

Genus *MYRMORNIS* Hermann

Myrmornis Hermann, 1783, Tabula Affinit. Anim., pp. 180, 210, 235. Type, by sub-sequent designation (Hellmayr, 1924), "Fourmilier proprement dit" Buffon = *For-micarius torquatus* Boddaert.

Rhopoterpe Cabanis, 1847, Arch. Naturgesch. 13: 227, 337. Type, by original designation, *Turdus formicivorus* Gmelin = *Formicarius torquatus* Boddaert.

Myrmornis torquata (Boddaert). Wing-banded Antbird.

Formicarius torquatus Boddaert, 1783, Table Planches Enlum., p. 43. Based on Daubenton, Planches Enlum., pl. 700, fig. 1. (Cayenne.)

Habitat.—Tropical Lowland Evergreen Forest (0–1200 m; Tropical Zone).

Distribution.—*Resident* [*stictoptera* group] locally in eastern Nicaragua (Caribbean lowlands), Panama (Caribbean slope in the Canal area and San Blas; Pacific slope in eastern Panamá province and Darién), and northern and western Colombia; and [*torquata* group] in South America east of the Andes from eastern Colombia, southern Venezuela, and the Guianas south locally to northeastern Peru and Amazonian Brazil.

Notes.—Also known as Wing-banded Antpitta or Wing-banded Antthrush. Groups: *M. stictoptera* (Salvin, 1893) [Buff-banded Antbird] and *M. torquata* [Wing-banded Antbird].

Genus *GYMNOPITHYS* Bonaparte

Gymnopithys Bonaparte, 1857, Bull. Soc. Linn. Normandie 2: 35. Type, by monotypy, *Gymnopithys pectoralis* "Schiff, ex Lath." = *Turdus pectoralis* Latham = *Turdus rufigula* Boddaert.

Anoplops Cabanis and Heine, 1859, Mus. Heineanum 2: 9. Type, by original designation, *Turdus rufigula* Boddaert.

Gymnopithys leucaspis (Sclater). Bicolored Antbird.

Myrmeciza leucaspis Sclater, 1855, Proc. Zool. Soc. London (1854), p. 253, pl. 70. (In Peruvia Chamicurros; in Nova Grenada; at Rio Negro, Cobati = Villavicencio, Colombia.)

Habitat.—Tropical Lowland Evergreen Forest (0–1500 m; Tropical Zone).

Distribution.—*Resident* [*bicolor* group] in northern and eastern Honduras (west to the Sula Valley), Nicaragua (Caribbean lowlands), Costa Rica (absent from dry northwest), Panama (both slopes), north-central and western Colombia, and western Ecuador; and [*leucaspis* group] in South America east of the Andes in eastern Colombia, eastern Ecuador, northeastern Peru, and northwestern Brazil (east to Rio Negro).

Notes.—Some authors (e.g., Hilty and Brown 1986, Wetmore 1972, Sibley and Monroe 1990) recognize the two groups as distinct species, *G. bicolor* (Lawrence, 1863) [Bicolored Antbird] and *G. leucaspis* [White-cheeked Antbird]. This is based on Willis' (1967) opinion that if South American *G. rufigula* [Rufous-throated Antbird] is ranked at the species level, then *bicolor* and *leucaspis* must also be ranked as species. Willis (1967), however, found no differences in ecology or vocalizations between *bicolor* and *leucaspis,* and Hackett (1993) found only weak genetic differentiation between them, despite their disjunct distributions; see also Zimmer (1937) and Ridgely and Tudor (1994).

Genus *PHAENOSTICTUS* Ridgway

Phænostictus Ridgway, 1909, Proc. Biol. Soc. Wash. 22: 70. Type, by original designation, *Phlegopsis macleannani* [sic] Lawrence.

Phaenostictus mcleannani (Lawrence). Ocellated Antbird.

Phlogopsis MeLeannani [sic] Lawrence, 1860, Ann. Lyc. Nat. Hist. N. Y. 7: 285. (Isthmus of Panama, Lion Hill, Canal Zone.)

Habitat.—Tropical Lowland Evergreen Forest (0–1200 m; Tropical and lower Subtropical zones).

Distribution.—*Resident* in eastern Honduras (Olancho, Gracias a Dios), eastern Nicaragua (Caribbean slope), Costa Rica (primarily Caribbean slope), Panama (both slopes, but local west of eastern Panamá province on Pacific), north-central and western Colombia, and northwestern Ecuador.

Family **FORMICARIIDAE**: Antthrushes and Antpittas

Notes.—See comments under Thamnophilidae.

Genus *FORMICARIUS* Boddaert

Formicarius Boddaert, 1783, Table Planches Enlum., pp. 43, 44, 50. Type, by subsequent designation (G. R. Gray, 1840), *Formicarius cayanensis* Boddaert = *Formicarius colma* Boddaert.

Formicarius analis (d'Orbigny and Lafresnaye). Black-faced Antthrush.

Myothera analis d'Orbigny and Lafresnaye, 1837, Mag. Zool. [Paris] 7(2): pl. 77–79, p. 14. (Yuracares et Chiquitos, Bolivia.)

Habitat.—Tropical Lowland Evergreen Forest, River-edge Forest (0–1500 m; Tropical and Subtropical zones).

Distribution.—*Resident* [*moniliger* group] on the Gulf-Caribbean slope from southern Veracruz, northern Oaxaca, Tabasco, Chiapas, and eastern and southern Yucatan Peninsula south to northern Honduras; [*hoffmanni* group] on the Caribbean slope of eastern Honduras (Olancho) and Nicaragua, on both slopes of Costa Rica (rare in dry northwest) and Panama, and Colombia (except southeastern), northern Venezuela, and Trinidad; and [*analis* group] in South America from southeastern Colombia, southern Venezuela, and the Guianas south, east of the Andes, to central Bolivia and Amazonian Brazil.

Notes.—Groups: *F. moniliger* Sclater, 1857 [Mexican Antthrush], *F. hoffmanni* (Cabanis, 1861) [Hoffmann's Antthrush], and *F. analis* [Black-faced Antthrush]. The *moniliger* and *hoffmanni* groups differ in voice, plumage, and elevational distribution, and probably deserve to be considered as distinct species (Howell 1994). The relationships among populations farther south, including those in South America, are complex (Howell 1994, Ridgely and Tudor 1994).

Formicarius nigricapillus Ridgway. Black-headed Antthrush.

Formicarius nigricapillus Ridgway, 1893, Proc. U. S. Natl. Mus. 16: 670, 675. (Buena Vista, Costa Rica.)

Habitat.—Montane Evergreen Forest, Tropical Lowland Evergreen Forest (400–1500 m; upper Tropical and lower Subtropical zones).

Distribution.—*Resident* locally in Costa Rica (primarily on the Caribbean slope of the Guanacaste, Central and Talamanca cordilleras) and Panama (mainly Caribbean slope), and along the Pacific slope of northwestern South America south to western Ecuador.

Formicarius rufipectus Salvin. Rufous-breasted Antthrush.

Formicarius rufipectus Salvin, 1866, Proc. Zool. Soc. London, p. 73, pl. 8. (Santiago de Veraguas, Panamá.)

Habitat.—Montane Evergreen Forest; especially *Heliconia* thickets (750–1500 m; upper Tropical to lower Temperate zones).

Distribution.—*Resident* locally in the highlands of Costa Rica (Caribbean slope of Cordillera Tilarán south), Panama (Bocas del Toro, Chiriquí, Veraguas, eastern Darién), and in South America on the western slope of the Andes from Colombia to southern Ecuador and the eastern slope (locally) in northwestern Venezuela and from northern Ecuador to southern Peru.

Genus *PITTASOMA* Cassin

Pittasoma Cassin, 1860, Proc. Acad. Nat. Sci. Philadelphia 12: 189. Type, by monotypy, *Pittasoma michleri* Cassin.

Pittasoma michleri Cassin. Black-crowned Antpitta.

> *Pittasoma Michleri* Cassin, 1860, Proc. Acad. Nat. Sci. Philadelphia 12: 189. (River Truando, New Grenada [= Colombia].)

Habitat.—Tropical Lowland Evergreen Forest (300–1000 m; Tropical and lower Subtropical zones).

Distribution.—*Resident* locally in Costa Rica (Caribbean slope from the Cordillera Tilarán southeastward), Panama (both slopes, but only locally on Pacific slope), and extreme northwestern Colombia (Chocó).

Genus *GRALLARIA* Vieillot

> *Grallaria* Vieillot, 1816, Analyse, p. 43. Type, by monotypy, "Roi des Fourmilliers" Buffon = *Formicarius varius* Boddaert.

Notes.—See comments under *Hylopezus.*

Grallaria guatimalensis Prévost and Des Murs. Scaled Antpitta.

> *Grallaria guatimalensis* Prévost and Des Murs, 1846, Voy. Venus, Atlas, Zool., Ois. (1842), pl. 4. (Guatemala.)

Habitat.—Montane Evergreen Forest, Tropical Lowland Evergreen Forest (575–3000 m; upper Tropical to lower Temperate zones).

Distribution.—*Resident* in the highlands and on the Gulf-Caribbean slope from Jalisco, Guerrero, Michoacán, México, Morelos, Hidalgo, Veracruz, and Tabasco south through Oaxaca, Chiapas, and northern Central America (except Belize) to north-central Nicaragua; in the highlands of Costa Rica (primarily on Caribbean drainage) and Panama (recorded Bocas del Toro, Chiriquí, Veraguas, and eastern Darién); and in Trinidad, South America in southern Venezuela and adjacent northern Brazil (Tepui region), and from northern Colombia south, on the western slope of the Andes to northwestern Peru and on the eastern slope to northern Bolivia.

Genus *HYLOPEZUS* Ridgway

> *Hylopezus* Ridgway, 1909, Proc. Biol. Soc. Wash. 22: 71. Type, by original designation, *Grallaria perspicillata* Lawrence.

Notes.—For recognition of this genus as distinct from *Grallaria,* see Lowery and O'Neill (1969).

Hylopezus perspicillatus (Lawrence). Streak-chested Antpitta.

> *Grallaria perspicillata* Lawrence, 1861, Ann. Lyc. Nat. Hist. N. Y. 7: 303. (New Grenada, Isthmus of Panama.)

Habitat.—Tropical Lowland Evergreen Forest (0–1250 m; Tropical and lower Subtropical zones).

Distribution.—*Resident* on the Caribbean slope in northeastern Honduras (Gracias a Dios), Nicaragua (Caribbean slope), Costa Rica (absent from dry northwest), Panama (more local on Pacific slope), north-central and western Colombia, and western Ecuador.

Notes.—Also known as Spectacled Antpitta.

Hylopezus dives (Salvin). Thicket Antpitta.

> *Grallaria dives* Salvin, 1864 (1865), Proc. Zool. Soc. London, p. 582. (Tucurriquí, Costa Rica.)

Habitat.—Tropical Lowland Evergreen Forest Edge, Secondary Forest; especially in very dense undergrowth (0–900 m; Tropical and lower Subtropical zones).

Distribution.—*Resident* on the Caribbean slope of northeastern Honduras (Olancho), Nicaragua, and Costa Rica, and in Panama (locally in Bocas del Toro and eastern Darién) and western Colombia.

Notes.—We follow Ridgely and Gwynne (1989) and Ridgely and Tudor (1994) in treating

H. dives as a separate species from *H. fulviventris* [White-lored Antpitta], but not in using the translation of the latter's scientific name for the English name of the former.

Genus *GRALLARICULA* Sclater

> *Grallaricula* Sclater, 1858, Proc. Zool. Soc. London, p. 283. Type, by subsequent designation (Sclater, 1890), *Grallaria flavirostris* Sclater.

Grallaricula flavirostris (Sclater). Ochre-breasted Antpitta.

> *Grallaria flavirostris* Sclater, 1858, Proc. Zool. Soc. London, p. 68. (Rio Napo in the Republic of Ecuador.)

Habitat.—Montane Evergreen Forest; especially in tree-fall gaps (750–1850 m; upper Tropical and Subtropical zones).

Distribution.—*Resident* locally in the highlands of Costa Rica (in the Dota Mountains and on the Caribbean slope of the Cordillera Central) and Panama (Chiriquí, Bocas del Toro, Veraguas, and eastern Darién), and in South America in the Andes from Colombia south, on the western slope to southern Ecuador and on the eastern slope to northern Bolivia.

Family **RHINOCRYPTIDAE**: Tapaculos

Genus *SCYTALOPUS* Gould

> *Scytalopus* Gould, 1837, Proc. Zool. Soc. London (1836), p. 89. Type, by subsequent designation (G. R. Gray, 1840), *Sylvia magellanicus* (Lath.) = *Motacilla magellanica* Gmelin.

Scytalopus panamensis Chapman. Tacarcuna Tapaculo.

> *Scytalopus panamensis* Chapman, 1915, Auk 32: 420. (Tacarcuna, 3,600 ft., eastern Panama.)

Habitat.—Montane Evergreen Forest (1020–1380 m; Subtropical Zone).
Distribution.—*Resident* in extreme eastern Panama (Cerro Tacarcuna and Cerro Malí, eastern Darién).
Notes.—See comments under *S. chocoensis*.

Scytalopus chocoensis Krabbe and Schulenberg. Choco Tapaculo.

> *Scytalopus chocoensis* Krabbe and Schulenberg, 1997, Ornithol. Monogr., no. 48, p. 75. (El Placer, ca. 670 m, prov. Esmeraldas, Ecuador.)

Habitat.—Montane Evergreen Forest (1340–1465 m; Subtropical Zone).
Distribution.—*Resident* in extreme eastern Panama (Cerro Pirre, eastern Darién), and in the Western Andes from Colombia south to northwestern Ecuador.
Notes.—Populations of this species were formerly treated under *Scytalopus vicinior* Zimmer, 1939 or *S. panamensis vicinior,* but Krabbe and Schulenberg (1997) found that *chocoensis* differs from *vicinior* in voice, measurements, and elevational distribution.

Scytalopus argentifrons Ridgway. Silvery-fronted Tapaculo.

> *Scytalopus argentifrons* Ridgway, 1891, Proc. U. S. Natl. Mus. 14: 475. (Volcan de Irazú, Costa Rica.)

Habitat.—Montane Evergreen Forest; especially in dense, shady undergrowth along streams (1000–3100 m; Subtropical and lower Temperate zones).
Distribution.—*Resident* in the highlands of [*argentifrons* group] Costa Rica (northwest to Cordillera de Guanacaste); and [*chiriquensis* group] western Panama (Chiriquí, Bocas del Toro, and Veraguas).
Notes.—Groups: *S. argentifrons* [Silvery-fronted Tapaculo] and *S. chiriquensis* Griscom, 1924 [Chiriqui Tapaculo]; see Wetmore (1972) for treatment as one species.

Superfamily TYRANNOIDEA: Tyrant Flycatchers, Cotingas, Manakins, and Allies

Family **TYRANNIDAE**: Tyrant Flycatchers

Notes.— Limits of the families and subfamilies in this superfamily are difficult to define. Sequence and placement of genera here are modified from those of Traylor (*in* Traylor 1979b), principally on the basis of morphological studies by W.E. Lanyon (1984, 1985, 1986, 1988a, 1988b), Prum and Lanyon (1989), Prum (1990, 1992), and McKitrick (1985). Many of the assemblages recognized here also are corroborated by DNA hybridization data of Sibley and Ahlquist (1990). However, we follow Lanyon (1988a) in not recognizing Sibley and Ahlquist's "Pipromorphinae" because of conflicts with morphological data and the absence of key genera from the DNA studies.

Subfamily ELAENIINAE: Tyrannulets, Elaenias and Allies

Genus *ORNITHION* Hartlaub

Ornithion Hartlaub, 1853, J. Ornithol. 1: 35. Type, by monotypy, *Ornithion inerme* Hartlaub.
Microtriccus Ridgway, 1905, Proc. Biol. Soc. Wash. 18: 210. Type, by original designation, *Tyrannulus semiflavus* Sclater and Salvin.

Ornithion semiflavum (Sclater and Salvin). Yellow-bellied Tyrannulet.

Tyrannulus semiflavus Sclater and Salvin, 1860, Proc. Zool. Soc. London, p. 300. (In prov. Veræ Pacis regione calida = Choctum, Alta Verapaz, Guatemala.)

Habitat.—Tropical Lowland Evergreen Forest Edge, Secondary Forest (0–1250 m; Tropical Zone).
Distribution.—*Resident* in the Gulf-Caribbean lowlands of Middle America from northern Oaxaca, southern Veracruz, Tabasco, and northern Chiapas south to Nicaragua, and in Costa Rica (primarily Pacific slope southward, locally on Caribbean slope in Alajuela province).
Notes.—*O. semiflavum* and *O. brunneicapillum* are closely related and have been considered conspecific, but they are vocally distinct and apparently sympatric in northern Costa Rica (Stiles and Skutch 1989: 339); they constitute a superspecies.

Ornithion brunneicapillum (Lawrence). Brown-capped Tyrannulet.

Tyrannulus brunneicapillus Lawrence, 1862, Ibis, p. 12. (Isthmus of Panama = Lion Hill, Canal Zone.)

Habitat.—Tropical Lowland Evergreen Forest, Secondary Forest (0–900 m; Tropical and lower Subtropical zones).
Distribution.—*Resident* in Costa Rica (Caribbean slope north to Alajuela province) and Panama (Caribbean slope throughout, Pacific from Canal area eastward), and in South America from northern Colombia south to western Ecuador and east to northern Venezuela.
Notes.—See comments under *O. semiflavum*.

Genus *CAMPTOSTOMA* Sclater

Camptostoma Sclater, 1857, Proc. Zool. Soc. London, p. 203. Type, by monotypy, *Camptostoma imberbe* Sclater.

Camptostoma imberbe Sclater. Northern Beardless-Tyrannulet.

Camptostoma imberbe Sclater, 1857, Proc. Zool. Soc. London, p. 203. (In vicinitate urbis S[an]. Andres Tuxtla, [Veracruz,] in rep. Mexicana.)

Habitat.—Gallery Forest, Secondary Forest, Riparian Thickets (0–2100 m; Tropical and Subtropical zones).

Distribution.—*Breeds* from southeastern Arizona, southwestern New Mexico (Guadalupe Canyon), Durango, Zacatecas, Nuevo León, and southern Texas (north to Kenedy County) south along both slopes of Middle America (including Cozumel Island) to Nicaragua (primarily Pacific slope, also San Francisco on Río San Juan), and northern Costa Rica (primarily Guanacaste, locally on the Caribbean slope in the Río Frío region).

Winters from northern Mexico (casually southern Arizona) south throughout the remainder of the breeding range.

Migrates through the Tres Marias Islands, off Nayarit, where possibly also breeding.

Notes.—Also known as Northern Beardless Flycatcher. *C. imberbe* and *C. obsoletum* are closely related and have been considered conspecific, but both breed sympatrically in the Tempisque region of Costa Rica (Stiles and Skutch 1989: 337); they constitute a superspecies.

Camptostoma obsoletum (Temminck). Southern Beardless-Tyrannulet.

Muscicapa obsoleta (Natterer MS) Temminck, 1824, Planches Color., livr. 46, pl. 275, fig. l. (Brazil = Curitiba, Paraná, Brazil.)

Habitat.—Secondary Forest, Gallery Forest, Riparian Thickets, Second-growth Scrub (0–1500 m; Tropical and lower Subtropical zones).

Distribution.—*Resident* in southwestern Costa Rica (Pacific slope north to the Tempisque Valley) and Panama (Pacific slope throughout, including Coiba, Cébaco, and the Pearl islands, locally on the Caribbean slope in Colón, Canal area, and San Blas), and in South America from Colombia, Venezuela, Trinidad, and the Guianas south, west of the Andes to central Peru, and east of the Andes throughout to central Argentina, Uruguay, and southern Brazil.

Notes.—Also known as Southern Beardless Flycatcher. See comments under *C. imberbe*.

Genus *PHAEOMYIAS* Berlepsch

Phaeomyias Berlepsch, 1902, Novit. Zool. 9: 41. Type, by subsequent designation (Chubb, 1921), *"P. imcompta"* = *Elainea incomta* Cabanis and Heine = *Platyrhynchus murinus* Spix.

Phaeomyias murina (Spix). Mouse-colored Tyrannulet.

Platyrhynchus murinus Spix, 1825, Avium Spec. Nov. Bras. 2: 14, pl. 16, fig. 2. (Brazil = Rio São Francisco, northern Bahia.)

Habitat.—Arid Lowland Scrub, Tropical Deciduous Forest, Second-growth Scrub, Gallery Forest (0–1750 m; Tropical and lower Subtropical zones).

Distribution.—*Resident* in western and central Panama (Pacific slope from Chiriquí east to eastern Panamá province), and in South America from Colombia, Venezuela (including Monos Island), Trinidad and the Guianas south, west of the Andes to northwestern Peru and east of the Andes to eastern Peru, northern and eastern Bolivia, northwestern Argentina, Paraguay, and central and eastern Brazil.

Genus *NESOTRICCUS* Townsend

Nesotriccus C. H. Townsend, 1895, Bull. Mus. Comp. Zool. Harv. 27: 124. Type, by original designation, *Nesotriccus ridgwayi* Townsend.

Nesotriccus ridgwayi Townsend. Cocos Flycatcher.

Nesotriccus Ridgwayi C. H. Townsend, 1895, Bull. Mus. Comp. Zool. Harv. 27: 124. (Cocos Island.)

Habitat.—Tropical Lowland Evergreen Forest (0–500 m; Tropical Zone).
Distribution.—*Resident* on Cocos Island, off Costa Rica.

Genus *CAPSIEMPIS* Cabanis and Heine

Capsiempis Cabanis and Heine, 1859, Mus. Heineanum 2: 56. Type, by original designation, *Muscicapa flaveola* Lichtenstein.

Capsiempis flaveola (Lichtenstein). Yellow Tyrannulet.

Muscicapa flaveola Lichtenstein, 1823, Verz. Doubl. Zool. Mus. Berlin, p. 56. (Bahia, Brazil.)

Habitat.—Tropical Lowland Evergreen Forest Edge, Secondary Forest, Tropical Deciduous Forest, Gallery Forest, often associated with bamboo (0–1250 m; Tropical Zone).

Distribution.—*Resident* in Nicaragua (Caribbean slope north to Río Escondido), Costa Rica (Caribbean slope and Pacific southwest) and Panama (locally east to eastern Colón and eastern Panamá province, also Isla Coiba), and in South America west of the Andes in western Ecuador, and east of the Andes locally from southeastern Colombia, Venezuela, and the Guianas south to southeastern Peru, northern and eastern Bolivia, central and southeastern Brazil, Paraguay, and extreme northeastern Argentina.

Genus *TYRANNULUS* Vieillot

Tyrannulus Vieillot, 1816, Analyse, p. 31. Type, by monotypy, "Roitelet-Mésange" Buffon = *Sylvia elata* Latham.

Tyrannulus elatus (Latham). Yellow-crowned Tyrannulet.

Sylvia elata Latham, 1790, Index Ornithol. 2: 549. Based on "Le Roitelet Mesange" Buffon, Hist. Nat. Ois. 5: 375, and "Mesange huppée de Cayenne" Daubenton, Planches Enlum., pl. 708, fig. 2. (in Cayanæ uliginosis = Cayenne.)

Habitat.—River-edge Forest, Tropical Lowland Evergreen Forest, Secondary Forest (0–1200 m; Tropical Zone).

Distribution.—*Resident* in southwestern Costa Rica (Golfo Dulce region) and Panama (Pacific slope throughout, Caribbean slope from Coclé eastward), and in South America from Colombia, Venezuela, and the Guianas south, west of the Andes to western Ecuador and east of the Andes to eastern Peru, northern Bolivia, and Amazonian Brazil.

Genus *MYIOPAGIS* Salvin and Godman

Myiopagis Salvin and Godman, 1888, Biol. Cent.-Am. (Aves) 2: 26. Type, by original designation, *Elainea placens* Sclater = *Sylvia viridicata* Vieillot.

Myiopagis gaimardii (d'Orbigny). Forest Elaenia.

Muscicapara Gaimardii d'Orbigny, 1840, Voy. Am. Mérid. 4 (Ois.)(3): 326. (Yuracares, Bolivia.)

Habitat.—Tropical Lowland Evergreen Forest, Gallery Forest, Secondary Forest (0–1000 m; Tropical Zone).

Distribution.—*Resident* from central Panama (west on the Caribbean slope to Coclé, on Pacific slope to the Canal area) east across northern Colombia, Venezuela (including Chacachacare Island), and Trinidad to the Guianas, and south, east of the Andes, to eastern Peru, northern Bolivia, and Amazonian and central Brazil.

Myiopagis caniceps (Swainson). Gray Elaenia.

Tyrannula caniceps Swainson, 1835, Ornithol. Drawings, pt. 4, pl. 49. (Brazil = Santo Amaro, Reconcavo de Baía, Brazil.)

Habitat.—Tropical Lowland Evergreen Forest (0–900 m; Tropical and Lower Subtropical zones).

Distribution.—*Resident* locally in central and eastern Panama (Canal area, eastern Darién), western Colombia, and western Ecuador; also in northwestern Venezuela, and from southeastern Colombia and southern Venezuela south, east of the Andes, to eastern Peru, Paraguay, extreme northeastern Argentina, and central and eastern Brazil.

Myiopagis cotta (Gosse). Jamaican Elaenia.

Elania [sic] *cotta* Gosse, 1849, Ann. Mag. Nat. Hist. (2)3: 257. (Jamaica.)

Habitat.—Tropical Lowland Evergreen Forest, Montane Evergreen Forest, Secondary Forest (0–1400 m; Tropical and Subtropical zones).

Distribution.—*Resident* on Jamaica.

Notes.— Known as Jamaican Yellow-crowned Elaenia in Bond (1971).

Myiopagis viridicata (Vieillot). Greenish Elaenia.

Sylvia viridicata Vieillot, 1817, Nouv. Dict. Hist. Nat. (nouv. éd.) 11: 171. Based on "Contramaestre Pardo verdoso corona amarilla" Azara, Apunt. Hist. Nat. Páx. Parag. 2: 57 (no. 156). (Paraguay.)

Habitat.—Tropical Lowland Evergreen Forest, Tropical Deciduous Forest, Gallery Forest, Secondary Forest (0–1700 m; Tropical and Lower Subtropical zones).

Distribution.—*Resident* from Sinaloa, Durango, southeastern San Luis Potosí and southern Tamaulipas south along both slopes of Mexico (including the Yucatan Peninsula, and Tres Marias and Cozumel islands, but a record from Isla Mujeres is unverified) and Central America (throughout, including Utila in the Bay Islands off Honduras, but in Costa Rica confined primarily to the Pacific slope) to Panama (Pacific slope throughout, including Coiba and the Pearl islands, locally on the Caribbean slope in Colón and the Canal area), and in South America from western Colombia south, west of the Andes, to western Ecuador (including Puna Island), and locally from Venezuela and southeastern Colombia south, east of the Andes, to southeastern Peru, central Bolivia, northern Argentina, Paraguay, and south-central and eastern Brazil.

Accidental in Texas (High Island; 1984, Amer. Birds 38:934).

Genus *ELAENIA* Sundevall

Elænia Sundevall, 1836, Vetensk.-Akad. Handl. (1835), p. 89. Type, by subsequent designation (G. R. Gray, 1855), *Muscicapa pagana* Lichtenstein = *Pipra flavogaster* Thunberg.

Elaenia martinica (Linnaeus). Caribbean Elaenia.

Muscicapa martinica Linnaeus, 1766, Syst. Nat. (ed. 12) 1: 325. Based on "Le Gobe-mouche hupé de la Martinique" Brisson, Ornithologie 2: 362, pl. 36, fig. 2. (in Martinica = Martinique.)

Habitat.—Tropical Lowland Evergreen Forest, Tropical Deciduous Forest, Secondary Forest (0–700 m; Tropical Zone).

Distribution.—*Resident* [*martinica* group] in the Cayman, Providencia and San Andrés islands in the Caribbean Sea, on islands off the Yucatan Peninsula (Cozumel, Mujeres and Cayo Culebra, probably also Holbox) and Belize (Ambergris Cay), and from Puerto Rico (including Vieques, Culebra and Culebrita islands), and the Virgin Islands south through the Lesser Antilles to Grenada (apparently absent from the Grenadines) and the Netherlands Antilles; and [*chinchorroensis* group] Banco Chinchorro (off Quintana Roo), and (formerly) Half Moon Cay, and Glover's Reef (off Belize).

Ranges in winter [*martinica* group] to the Yucatan Peninsula.

Casual [*chinchorroensis* group] on the mainland of Belize (Belize City); a report from northwestern Florida (near Pensacola), based on photographs (not definitive) and descriptions of vocalizations, very likely pertains to this species [*martinica* group].

Notes.—Groups: *E. martinica* [Caribbean Elaenia] and *E. chinchorroensis* Griscom, 1926 [Chinchorro Elaenia].

Elaenia flavogaster (Thunberg). Yellow-bellied Elaenia.

Pipra flavogaster Thunberg, 1822, Mém. Acad. Imp. Sci. St. Pétersbourg, 8, pp. 283, 286. (Brazil = probably Rio de Janeiro.)

Habitat.—Second-growth Scrub, Riparian Thickets, Secondary Forest (0–1700 m; Tropical and Subtropical zones).

Distribution.—*Resident* from central Veracruz, northern Oaxaca and Chiapas south along both slopes of Middle America (including the Yucatan Peninsula, islas Mujeres and Holbox off Quintana Roo, Ambergris Cay off Belize, and the Pearl, Taboga, Coiba and smaller islands off Panama), and in South America from Colombia, Venezuela (also Margarita and Patos islands), and the Guianas south, west of the Andes to northwestern Peru, and east of the Andes (absent from southeastern Colombia, eastern Ecuador and central Amazonian Brazil) to southeastern Peru, northern and eastern Bolivia, northwestern and northeastern Argentina, Paraguay, and southern Brazil; also the southern Lesser Antilles (Grenada, the Grenadines and St. Vincent), Tobago and Trinidad. Populations north of the Isthmus of Tehuantepec migrate southward in winter.

Elaenia chiriquensis Lawrence. Lesser Elaenia.

Elainea Chiriquensis Lawrence, 1867, Ann. Lyc. Nat. Hist. N. Y. 8: 176. (near David, Chiriqui, New Granada [= Panama].)

Habitat.— Second-growth Scrub (0–1800 m; Tropical and Subtropical zones).

Distribution.—*Resident* in northern (Volcan Miravalles), central (Cartago and Paraiso), and southwestern Costa Rica (El General-Térraba and Coto Brus valleys), in Panama (Caribbean slope in Colón and the Canal area, Pacific slope from Chiriquí east to eastern Panamá province, and on Coiba, Cébaco and the Pearl islands), and in South America from Colombia, Venezuela, and the Guianas south, west of the Andes locally to northwestern Ecuador, and east of the Andes to eastern Peru, central and eastern Bolivia, northern Argentina, eastern Paraguay, and central and southeastern Brazil.

Accidental on Bonaire, in the Netherlands Antilles. Rare in Costa Rica between September and January, suggesting migration to Panama or South America (Stiles and Skutch 1989).

Elaenia frantzii Lawrence. Mountain Elaenia.

Elainea frantzii Lawrence, 1867, Ann. Lyc. Nat. Hist. N. Y. 8: 172. (San Jose, Costa Rica.)

Habitat.—Montane Evergreen Forest, Secondary Forest (900–3600 m; Subtropical and Temperate zones).

Distribution.—*Resident* in the mountains of central Guatemala, northern and western El Salvador, Honduras, north-central and southwestern Nicaragua, Costa Rica, western Panama (Chiriquí, Veraguas and western Herrera), Colombia, and western and northern Venezuela.

Elaenia fallax Sclater. Greater Antillean Elaenia.

Elainea fallax Sclater, 1861, Proc. Zool. Soc. London, p. 76 (footnote). (Jamaica.)

Habitat.—Montane Evergreen Forest, Pine Forest, upper elevations of Tropical Lowland Evergreen Forest (500–2000 m; Subtropical Zone).

Distribution.—*Resident* on Jamaica (primarily in Blue Mountains, less frequently in hills of St. Ann and Trelawny) and Hispaniola (high elevations).

Genus *SERPOPHAGA* Gould

Serpophaga Gould, 1839, in Darwin, Zool. Voy. Beagle 3(9): 49. Type, by subsequent designation (G. R. Gray, 1855), *Serpophaga albocoronatus* [sic] Gould = *Sylvia subcristata* Vieillot.

Serpophaga cinerea (Tschudi). Torrent Tyrannulet.

> *Leptopogon cinereus* Tschudi, 1844, Arch. Naturgesch. 10: 276. (Republica Peruana = vicinity of Tarma, depto. Junín, Peru.)

Habitat.—Along rocky torrents in humid montane regions (750–2000 m, to 3200 m in South America; Subtropical Zone).

Distribution.—*Resident* in the highlands of Costa Rica (Cordillera de Tilarán southward) and western Panama (east to Veraguas); and in South America in the Andes from Colombia and northwestern Venezuela south to Peru and northern Bolivia.

Genus *MIONECTES* Cabanis

> *Mionectes* Cabanis, 1844, Arch. Naturgesch. 10: 275. Type, by original designation, *M. poliocephalus* Tsch[udi]. = *Muscicapa striaticollis* d'Orbigny and Lafresnaye.
> *Pipromorpha* G. R. Gray, 1855, Cat. Genera Subgenera Birds, p. 146. Type, by monotypy, *Muscicapa oleagina* [sic] Lichtenstein.

Mionectes olivaceus Lawrence. Olive-striped Flycatcher.

> *Mionectes olivaceus* Lawrence, 1868, Ann. Lyc. Nat. Hist. N. Y. 9: 111. (Barranca and Dota, Costa Rica = Barranca, Costa Rica.)

Habitat.—Tropical Lowland Evergreen Forest, Montane Evergreen Forest, Secondary Forest (0–1800 m; Tropical and Subtropical zones).

Distribution.—*Resident* in Costa Rica (on both slopes of highlands, most descend below 1200 m during nonbreeding season) and Panama (both slopes), and in South America from Colombia, northern Venezuela, and Trinidad south, west of the Andes to southwestern Ecuador, and east of the Andes to northern Bolivia.

Mionectes oleagineus (Lichtenstein). Ochre-bellied Flycatcher.

> *Muscicapa oleaginea* Lichtenstein, 1823, Verz. Doubl. Zool. Mus. Berlin, p. 55. (Bahía, Brazil.)

Habitat.—Tropical Lowland Evergreen Forest, River-edge Forest, Secondary Forest (0–1200 m; Tropical and lower Subtropical zones).

Distribution.—*Resident* from eastern Puebla, central Veracruz, northern Oaxaca, Tabasco, Chiapas and the Yucatan Peninsula (including Isla Mujeres, probably vagrant only) south along both slopes of Central America to Panama (including Coiba, Cébaco and the Pearl islands), and in South America from Colombia, Venezuela, Tobago, Trinidad and the Guianas south, west of the Andes to western Ecuador and east of the Andes to eastern Peru, Bolivia, and Amazonian and extreme eastern Brazil.

Notes.—Formerly placed in the genus *Pipromorpha*.

Genus *LEPTOPOGON* Cabanis

> *Leptopogon* Cabanis, 1844, Arch. Naturgesch 10: 275. Type, by subsequent designation (G. R. Gray, 1855), *Leptopogon superciliaris* Tsch[udi].

Leptopogon amaurocephalus Tschudi. Sepia-capped Flycatcher.

> *Leptopogon amaurocephalus* (Cabanis MS) Tschudi, 1846, Unters. Fauna Peru, lief. 6, Ornithol., p. 162 (footnote). (São Paulo, Brazil.)

Habitat.—Tropical Lowland Evergreen Forest, Secondary Forest (0–1300 m; Tropical and lower Subtropical zones).

Distribution.—*Resident* on the Gulf-Caribbean slope of Middle America from northern Oaxaca, southern Veracruz, Tabasco, Chiapas, southern Campeche and southern Quintana Roo south to Nicaragua, on both slopes of Costa Rica (rare, mainly in northern foothills south to Cordillera Central, also in Terraba and Coto Brus region of southern Pacific slope), and in western and central Panama (Pacific slope east to eastern Panamá province, including

Isla Coiba, several records from the Caribbean slope in the Canal area); in South America from northern and eastern Colombia east across Venezuela to French Guiana, and northeastern Brazil, and from eastern Ecuador, eastern Peru and southern Amazonian Brazil south to central Bolivia, northern and northeastern Argentina, and Paraguay.

Leptopogon superciliaris Tschudi. Slaty-capped Flycatcher.

> *Leptopogon superciliaris* Tschudi, 1844, Arch. Naturgesch. 10: 275. (Republica Peruana = Montaña de Vitoc, Peru.)

Habitat.—Montane Evergreen Forest (600–2100 m; upper Tropical and Subtropical zones).

Distribution.—*Resident* in the highlands of Costa Rica (Caribbean slope from Cordillera de Tilarán southward, and Pacific slope on Cordillera de Tilamanca and coastal ranges) and Panama (western Chiriquí east to western Cocle, and in eastern Darién), and in South America from the Andes of Colombia east across northern Venezuela to Trinidad, south on the western Andean slope to northwestern Peru, and on the eastern slope to eastern Peru and northern Bolivia; a record from extreme southern Venezuela (Amazonas) was from a misidentified specimen.

Genus *PHYLLOSCARTES* Cabanis and Heine

> *Phylloscartes* Cabanis and Heine, 1859, Mus. Heineanum 2: 52. Type, by monotypy, *Muscicapa ventralis* Temminck.

Phylloscartes flavovirens (Lawrence). Yellow-green Tyrannulet.

> *Leptopogon flavovirens* Lawrence, 1862, Ann. Lyc. Nat. Hist. N. Y. 7: 472. (Atlantic side of the Isthmus of Panama, along the line of the Panama Railroad = Atlantic slope, Canal Zone.)

Habitat.—Tropical Lowland Evergreen Forest (0–500 m; Tropical Zone).

Distribution.—*Resident* locally in Panama (Pacific lowlands from the Canal area east to eastern Darién, Caribbean slope in the Canal area).

Phylloscartes superciliaris (Sclater and Salvin). Rufous-browed Tyrannulet.

> *Leptotriccus superciliaris* Sclater and Salvin, 1869, Proc. Zool. Soc. London (1868), p. 389. (Chitrá, Veragua, Panama.)

Habitat.—Montane Evergreen Forest (600–1200 m, to 1700 in South America; Subtropical Zone).

Distribution.—*Resident* locally in Costa Rica (Cordillera de Guanacaste south at least to Cordillera Central), Panama (Bocas del Toro and Chiriquí east to Cocle, and in eastern Darién), Colombia (Rio Virolin), northwestern Venezuela (Sierra de Perija), southeastern Ecuador (Cordillera de Cutucu, Cordillera del Condor), and extreme northern Peru (Cordillera del Condor).

Genus *PHYLLOMYIAS* Cabanis and Heine

> *Phyllomyias* Cabanis and Heine, 1859, Mus. Heineanum 2: 57. Type, by subsequent designation (Sclater, 1888), *"P. brevirostris"* = *Platyrhynchus brevirostris* Spix = *Pipra fasciata* Thunberg.
>
> *Tyranniscus* Cabanis and Heine, 1859, Mus. Heineanum 2: 57. Type, by monotypy, *Tyrannulus nigricapillus* [sic] Lafresnaye.
>
> *Acrochordopus* Berlepsch and Hellmayr, 1905, J. Ornithol. 53: 26. Type, by monotypy, *Phyllomyias subviridis* Pelzeln = *Phyllomyias burmeisteri* Cabanis and Heine.

Phyllomyias burmeisteri Cabanis and Heine. Rough-legged Tyrannulet.

> *Phyllomyias Burmeisteri* Cabanis and Heine, 1859, Mus. Heineanum 2: 57. (Brasilien = Rio de Janeiro, Brazil.)

Habitat.—Montane Evergreen Forest (900–1850 m; upper Tropical and Subtropical zones).

Distribution.—*Resident* [*zeledoni* group] in the highlands of central Costa Rica (Caribbean slope from Cordillera de Tilarán southward, and Pacific slope of Cordillera de Talamanca) and western Panama (Chiriquí); [*leucogonys* group] locally in the mountains from eastern Colombia and northern Venezuela south along the eastern slope of the Andes to southeastern Peru; and [*burmeisteri* group] in eastern Bolivia and northwestern Argentina, and from eastern Paraguay across extreme northeastern Argentina to southeastern Brazil.

Notes.—The *zeledoni* and *leucogonys* groups are treated by many authors together as a separate species, *P. zeledoni* (Lawrence, 1869) [White-fronted Tyrannulet] (e.g., Wetmore 1972, Ridgley and Tudor 1994), but careful study is lacking. Formerly treated in the genus *Acrochordopus* but merged into *Phyllomyias* by Traylor (1977).

Phyllomyias griseiceps (Sclater and Salvin). Sooty-headed Tyrannulet.

> *Tyranniscus griseiceps* Sclater and Salvin, 1871, Proc. Zool. Soc. London (1870), pp. 841, 843. (Babahoyo and Pallatanga, Ecuador, and Lake of Valencia, Venezuela = Babahoyo, Ecuador.)

Habitat.—Tropical Lowland Evergreen Forest Edge, Tropical Deciduous Forest, Secondary Forest (0–1300 m; Tropical Zone).

Distribution.—*Resident* locally in extreme eastern Panama (eastern Darién, also a single report from eastern Panamá province), and in South America from Colombia and Venezuela south, west of the Andes to western Ecuador, and east of the Andes to central Peru, and locally along the lower Amazon River in Brazil.

Notes.— Also known as Crested Tyrannulet (e.g., Wetmore 1972).

Genus *ZIMMERIUS* Traylor

> *Zimmerius* Traylor, 1977, Bull. Mus. Comp. Zool. Harv. 148: 147. Type, by original designation, *Tyrannulus chrysops* Sclater = *Elaenia viridiflavus* Tschudi.

Zimmerius vilissimus (Sclater and Salvin). Paltry Tyrannulet.

> *Elainia vilissima* Sclater and Salvin, 1859, Ibis, p. 122, pl. 4, fig. 1. (Central America = Cobán, Alta Verapaz, Guatemala.)

Habitat.—Montane Evergreen Forest, Tropical Lowland Evergreen Forest, Secondary Forest (0–3000 m; Tropical to lower Temperate zones).

Distribution.—*Resident* [*vilissimus* group] in the highlands of eastern Chiapas, Guatemala (rare in Petén) and central El Salvador (Sierra de Balsamo); and [*parvus* group] in the lowlands of Honduras, Nicaragua (except Pacific slope), Costa Rica (throughout, except dry northwest), Panama and northwestern Colombia; and [*improbus* group] northeastern Colombia and northern Venezuela.

Notes.—Formerly placed in the genus *Tyranniscus* Cabanis and Heine, 1859. The two Middle American groups, *Z. vilissimus* [Paltry Tyrannulet] and *Z. parvus* (Lawrence, 1862) [Mistletoe Tyrannulet] differ in habitat (especially elevation) and in size, and may represent distinct species. Sibley and Monroe (1990) and Ridgley and Tudor (1994) recognize *Z. improbus* (Sclater and Salvin, 1871) [Venezuelan Tyrannulet], of the highlands of northeastern Colombia and northern Venezuela, as a distinct species.

Genus *SUBLEGATUS* Sclater and Salvin

> *Sublegatus* Sclater and Salvin, 1869, Proc. Zool. Soc. London (1868), p. 923. Type, by monotypy, *Sublegatus glaber* Sclater and Salvin = *Elainea arenarum* Salvin.

Sublegatus arenarum (Salvin). Northern Scrub-Flycatcher.

> *Elainea arenarum* Salvin, 1863, Proc. Zool. Soc. London, p. 190. (Punta Arenas, Costa Rica.)

Habitat.—Tropical Deciduous Forest, Gallery Forest, Mangrove Forest, Arid Lowland Scrub (0–250 m; Tropical Zone).

Distribution.—*Resident* [*arenarum* group] in the Pacific lowlands of south-central Costa Rica (around Gulf of Nicoya) and Panama (including Coiba, Cébaco, Taboga and the Pearl islands); and [*glaber* group] in South America from northern Colombia eastward through northern Venezuela (including islands from Netherlands Antilles east to Trinidad) to French Guiana.

Notes.— Species limits confusing. We follow Traylor (1982) in excluding the wide-ranging interior South American form *S. modestus* (Wied, 1831) [Southern Scrub-Flycatcher] from this species. The two groups recognized here may constitute two species: *S. arenarum* [Northern Scrub-Flycatcher], and *S. glaber* Sclater and Salvin, 1868 [Smooth Scrub-Flycatcher]. Ridgley and Tudor (1994) also treated the Amazonian form, *S. obscurior* Todd, 1920, as a distinct species [Amazonian Scrub-Flycatcher].

Genus *PSEUDOTRICCUS* Taczanowski and Berlepsch

Pseudotriccus Taczanowski and Berlepsch, 1885, Proc. Zool. Soc. London, p. 88. Type, by monotypy, *Pseudotriccus pelzelni* Taczanowski and Berlepsch.

Pseudotriccus pelzelni Taczanowski and Berlepsch. Bronze-olive Pygmy-Tyrant.

Pseudotriccus pelzelni Taczanowski and Berlepsch, 1885, Proc. Zool. Soc. London, p. 88. (Machay and [Hacienda] Mapoto, Tungurahua, Ecuador.)

Habitat.—Montane Evergreen Forest (700–2000 m; Subtropical, less frequently upper Tropical zones).

Distribution.—*Resident* in the highlands of extreme eastern Panama (cerros Pirre and Tacarcuna, eastern Darién), and in South America from Colombia south, in the western Andes to southwestern Ecuador, and in the eastern Andes to central Peru.

Subfamily PLATYRINCHINAE: Tody-Tyrants and Flatbills

Genus *MYIORNIS* Bertoni

Myiornis Bertoni, 1901, Aves Nuev. Parag., p. 129. Type, by monotypy, *Euscarthmus minutus* Bertoni = *Platyrhynchos auricularis* Vieillot.
Perissotriccus Oberholser, 1902, Proc. U. S. Natl. Mus. 25: 64. Type, by original designation, *Todirostrum ecaudatum* Lafresnaye and d'Orbigny.

Notes.—This genus was merged with *Hemitriccus* Cabanis and Heine, 1859, by W. E. Lanyon (1988b), on the basis of syringeal characters. We retain the genus because of the unique external morphology and flight behavior of its species (Traylor and Fitzpatrick 1982).

Myiornis atricapillus (Lawrence). Black-capped Pygmy-Tyrant.

Orchilus atricapillus Lawrence, 1875, Ibis, p. 385. (Angostura and Volcan de Irazu, Costa Rica = Talamanca, Costa Rica.)

Habitat.—Tropical Lowland Evergreen Forest (0–700 m; Tropical Zone).

Distribution.—*Resident* in Costa Rica (Caribbean lowlands), Panama (Caribbean slope, locally also on Pacific slope in eastern Panamá province and eastern Darién), western Colombia, and western Ecuador.

Notes.—*M. atricapillus* and the South American *M. ecaudatus* (Lafresnaye and d'Orbigny, 1837) are closely related and constitute a superspecies.

Genus *LOPHOTRICCUS* Berlepsch

Lophotriccus Berlepsch, 1884, Proc. Zool. Soc. London (1883), p. 533. Type, by subsequent designation (Sharpe, 1884), *Lophotriccus squamicristatus* (Lafr.) = *Todirostrum squamaecrista* Lafresnaye = *Euscarthmus pileatus* Tschudi.

Atalotriccus Ridgway, 1905, Proc. Biol. Soc. Wash. 18: 208. Type, by original designation, *Colopterus pilaris* Cabanis.

Lophotriccus pileatus (Tschudi). Scale-crested Pygmy-Tyrant.

Euscarthmus pileatus Tschudi, 1844, Arch. Naturgesch. 10: 273. (Republica Peruana = valley of Vitoc, depto. Junín, Peru.)

Habitat.—Montane Evergreen Forest, Tropical Lowland Evergreen Forest (750–1700 m; to 2100 m in South America; upper Tropical and Subtropical zones).

Distribution.—*Resident* in the foothills and highlands on both slopes of Costa Rica and Panama, and in South America from Colombia and northern Venezuela south, in the western Andes to western Ecuador, and in the eastern Andes to southeastern Peru.

Sight report exists for eastern Honduras.

Lophotriccus pilaris (Cabanis). Pale-eyed Pygmy-Tyrant.

Colopterus pilaris Cabanis, 1847, Arch. Naturgesch. 13: 253, pl. 5, fig. 4. (environs of Cartagena, Bolívar, Colombia.)

Habitat.—Tropical Deciduous Forest, Tropical Lowland Evergreen Forest (0–800 m; Tropical, occasionally lower Subtropical zones).

Distribution.—*Resident* on the Pacific slope of western and central Panama (western Chiriquí east to eastern Panamá province), and in South America in northern Colombia, northern Venezuela, and Guyana.

Notes. – Formerly placed in the monotypic genus *Atalotriccus,* which was merged with *Lophotriccus* by Lanyon (1988b).

Genus *ONCOSTOMA* Sclater

Oncostoma Sclater, 1862, Cat. Collect. Amer. Birds, p. 208. Type, by monotypy, *Todirostrum cinereigulare* Sclater.

Oncostoma cinereigulare (Sclater). Northern Bentbill.

Todirostrum cinereigulare Sclater, 1857, Proc. Zool. Soc. London (1856), p. 295. (Cordova [= Córdoba] in the State of Vera Cruz, Southern Mexico.)

Habitat.—Tropical Lowland Evergreen Forest Edge, Tropical Deciduous Forest, Secondary Forest (0–1200 m; Tropical Zone).

Distribution.—*Resident* from southern Veracruz and northern and southeastern Oaxaca south along both slopes of Middle America (including the Yucatan Peninsula) to western Panama (western Bocas del Toro and western Chiriquí; an old specimen from "Canal Zone" is probably mislabeled).

Notes.—*O. cinereigulare* and *O. olivaceum* constitute a superspecies. With treatment as a single species, the English name would be Bentbill.

Oncostoma olivaceum (Lawrence). Southern Bentbill.

Todirostrum olivaceum Lawrence, 1862, Ibis, p. 12. (Isthmus of Panama = Lion Hill, Canal Zone.)

Habitat.—Tropical Lowland Evergreen Forest Edge, Secondary Forest (0–1000 m; Tropical Zone).

Distribution.—*Resident* in eastern Panama (west on the Caribbean slope to Coclé and west on the Pacific slope to the Canal area) and northern Colombia.

Notes.—See comments under *O. cinereigulare.*

Genus *POECILOTRICCUS* Berlepsch

Poecilotriccus Berlepsch,1884, Journ. Orn., 32, p. 298. Type by monotypy *Todirostrum lenzi* Berlepsch = *Todirhamphus ruficeps* Kaup.

Poecilotriccus sylvia (Desmarest). Slate-headed Tody-Flycatcher.

> *Todus sylvia* Desmarest, 1806, Hist. Nat. Tangaras, Manakins, Todiers, livr. 10, pl. 71. (No locality given = probably Cayenne.)

Habitat.—Tropical Lowland Evergreen Forest Edge, Tropical Deciduous Forest, Gallery Forest, Secondary Forest, Second-growth Scrub (0–1100 m; Tropical and lower Subtropical zones).

Distribution.—*Resident* on the Gulf-Caribbean slope of Middle America from southern Veracruz, northern Oaxaca, Tabasco, northern Chiapas, southern Campeche and Quintana Roo south through northern Central America to Honduras, on both slopes of Nicaragua, Costa Rica (most common on Pacific slope from Gulf of Nicoya southward), and Panama (Pacific slope east to eastern Panamá province, on Caribbean slope east to the Canal area), and in South America from northern Colombia locally across northwestern and southern Venezuela, and Guyana to French Guiana, and in extreme northern and northeastern Brazil.

Notes. Long placed in the genus *Todirostrum,* but transferred to *Poecilotriccus* by Lanyon (1988b).

Genus *TODIROSTRUM* Lesson

> *Todirostrum* Lesson, 1831, Traité Ornithol., livr. 5 (1830), p. 384. Type, by subsequent designation (G. R. Gray, 1840), *T. cinereum = Todus cinereus* Linnaeus.

Todirostrum cinereum (Linnaeus). Common Tody-Flycatcher.

> *Todus cinereus* Linnaeus, 1766, Syst. Nat. (ed. 12) 1: 178. Based on "The Grey and Yellow Flycatcher" Edwards, Glean. Nat. Hist. 2: 110, pl. 262, fig. 1. (in Surinamo = Surinam.)

Habitat.—Tropical Lowland Evergreen Forest Edge, Secondary Forest, Gallery Forest, Montane Evergreen Forest Edge, Tropical Deciduous Forest Edge (0–1500 m; Tropical and lower Subtropical zones).

Distribution.—*Resident* on both slopes of Middle America from central Veracruz, northern Oaxaca, Tabasco, northern and southeastern Chiapas, and the Yucatan Peninsula (a specimen from Isla Mujeres is suspect) south to Panama (including Isla Coiba), and in South America from Colombia, Venezuela and the Guianas south, west of the Andes to northwestern Peru, and east of the Andes to eastern Peru, northern and eastern Bolivia, and southern Brazil.

Notes.—*T. cinereum* and the distinct form from northwestern Venezuela, *T. viridanum* Hellmayr, 1927, constitute a superspecies (Sibley and Monroe 1990).

Todirostrum nigriceps Sclater. Black-headed Tody-Flycatcher.

> *Todirostrum nigriceps* Sclater, 1855, Proc. Zool. Soc. London, p. 66, pl. 84, fig. 1. (Santa Martha in Nov. Grenada = Sierra Nevada de Santa Marta, Colombia.)

Habitat.—Tropical Lowland Evergreen Forest (0–1100 m; Tropical Zone).

Distribution.—*Resident* in Costa Rica (primarily Caribbean lowlands, locally on Pacific drainage of Cordillera de Guanacaste) and Panama (Caribbean slope generally throughout, Pacific slope from the Canal area eastward), and in South America in northern and eastern Andean Colombia, northwestern Venezuela, and western Ecuador.

Notes.—*T. nigriceps* and the South American *T. chrysocrotaphum* Strickland, 1850 [Yellow-browed Tody-Flycatcher] constitute a superspecies.

Genus *CNIPODECTES* Sclater and Salvin

> *Cnipodectes* Sclater and Salvin, 1873, Proc. Zool. Soc. London, p. 281. Type, by monotypy, *Cyclorhynchus subbrunneus* Sclater.

Cnipodectes subbrunneus (Sclater). Brownish Flycatcher.

> *Cyclorhynchus subbrunneus* Sclater, 1860, Proc. Zool. Soc. London, p. 282. (In rep. Equator = Babahoyo, Los Ríos, Ecuador.)

Habitat.—Tropical Lowland Evergreen Forest (0–1200 m; Tropical Zone).

Distribution.—*Resident* in Panama (eastward from the Valiente Peninsula, Bocas del Toro, on the Caribbean slope, and from the Canal area on the Pacific slope), and in South America from Colombia south, west of the Andes to western Ecuador, and east of the Andes to northeastern Peru and western Brazil.

Notes.— Also known as Brownish Twistwing (Ridgely and Tudor 1994).

Genus *RHYNCHOCYCLUS* Cabanis and Heine

Cyclorhynchus (not *Cyclorrhynchus* Kaup, 1829) Sundevall, 1836, Vetensk.-Akad. Handl. (1835), p. 83. Type, by monotypy, *Platyrhynchus olivaceus* Temminck. *Nomen oblitum.*

Rhynchocyclus Cabanis and Heine, 1859, Mus. Heineanum 2: 56. New name for *Cyclorhynchus* Sundevall.

Rhynchocyclus brevirostris (Cabanis). Eye-ringed Flatbill.

Cyclorhynchus brevirostris Cabanis, 1847, Arch. Naturgesch. 13: 249. (Xalapa, Mexico = Jalapa, Veracruz.)

Habitat.—Tropical Lowland Evergreen Forest, Montane Evergreen Forest (0–1800, rarely to 2100 m; Tropical and Subtropical zones).

Distribution.—*Resident* on both slopes of Middle America from Guerrero, Puebla, central Veracruz, Chiapas and the Yucatan Peninsula (north to central Campeche and northern Quintana Roo) south to Nicaragua (not recorded Pacific slope of Guatemala or Nicaragua), both slopes of Costa Rica (locally on northern cordilleras) and Panama (locally on both slopes to Darién).

Notes.—*R. brevirostris* and *R. pacificus* (Chapman, 1914), of northwestern South America, constitute a superspecies.

Rhynchocyclus olivaceus (Temminck). Olivaceous Flatbill.

Platyrhynchos olivaceus Temminck, 1820, Planches Color., livr. 2, pl. 12, fig. 1. (Brésil = Rio de Janeiro, Brazil.)

Habitat.—Tropical Lowland Evergreen Forest, River-edge Forest (0–600 m, to 1000 m in South America; Tropical Zone).

Distribution.—*Resident* in Panama (on Caribbean slope west to western Colón, on Pacific slope west to the Canal area, one old record from "Veragua" in western Panama), and in South America from northern Colombia, Venezuela and the Guianas south, east of the Andes, to eastern Peru, northern Bolivia, and Amazonian and southeastern Brazil.

Genus *TOLMOMYIAS* Hellmayr

Tolmomyias Hellmayr, 1927, Field Mus. Nat. Hist. Publ. (Zool. Ser) 13(5): 273. Type, by original designation, *Platyrhynchus sulphurescens* Spix.

Tolmomyias sulphurescens (Spix). Yellow-olive Flycatcher.

Platyrhynchus sulphurescens Spix, 1825, Avium Spec. Nov. Bras. 2: 10, pl. 12, fig. 1. (Rio de Janeiro and Piauí, Brazil = Rio de Janeiro.)

Habitat.—Tropical Lowland Evergreen Forest, Montane Evergreen Forest, Tropical Deciduous Forest, River-edge Forest, Gallery Forest, Secondary Forest (0–1650 m, to 2100 m in South America; Tropical and Subtropical zones).

Distribution.— *Resident* from northern and southeastern Oaxaca and central Veracruz south through Middle America (both slopes, including the Yucatan Peninsula) to eastern Panama, and in South America from Colombia, Venezuela, Trinidad and the Guianas south, west of the Andes to northwestern Peru, and east of the Andes to northern Argentina and southern Brazil (not recorded Uruguay).

Notes.— Considerable geographic variation in plumage and vocalizations suggest that this widespread taxon contains more than one species.

Tolmomyias assimilis (Pelzeln). Yellow-margined Flycatcher.

Rhynchocyclus assimilis Pelzeln, 1868, Ornithol. Bras. 2: 110, 181. (Engenho do Gama, S. Vicente, Borba, Rio Negro, and Barra do Rio Negro, n. Brazil = Borba, Rio Madeira.)

Habitat.—Tropical Lowland Evergreen Forest (0–1000 m; Tropical and Subtropical zones).

Distribution.—*Resident* in Costa Rica (Caribbean slope throughout) and Panama (both slopes, but seemingly absent on the Pacific slope between western Chiriquí and the Canal area), and in South America from Colombia, southern Venezuela and the Guianas south, west of the Andes to western Ecuador, and east of the Andes to eastern Peru, northern Bolivia, and Amazonian Brazil.

Genus *PLATYRINCHUS* Desmarest

Platyrinchus Desmarest, 1805, Hist. Nat. Tangaras, Manakins, Todiers, livr. 4, p. [2] of text to pl. [72]. Type, by tautonymy, *Platyrinchus fuscus* Desmarest = *Todus platyrhynchos* Gmelin.

Platyrinchus cancrominus Sclater and Salvin. Stub-tailed Spadebill.

Platyrhynchus cancrominus Sclater and Salvin, 1860, Proc. Zool. Soc. London, p. 299. (In prov. Veræ Pacis regione calida, et in Mexico Merid. statu Veræ Crucis = Choctum, Alta Verapaz, Guatemala.)

Habitat.—Tropical Lowland Evergreen Forest, Tropical Deciduous Forest, Gallery Forest (0–1500 m; Tropical and lower Subtropical zones).

Distribution.—*Resident* from southern Veracruz, northern and southeastern Oaxaca, Tabasco, Chiapas, Campeche and Quintana Roo south along both slopes of Central America to Nicaragua, in northwestern Costa Rica (Pacific slope south to Parrita), and in Panama (known only from numerous islands off Bocas del Torro, and from one specimen on the nearby mainland).

Notes.—*P. cancrominus* and *P. mystaceus* are closely related, and constitute a superspecies. Olson (1993a) discussed the apparently relict population of *cancrominus* in Panama.

Platyrinchus mystaceus Vieillot. White-throated Spadebill.

Platyrhynchus mystaceus Vieillot, 1818, Nouv. Dict. Hist. Nat. (nouv. éd.) 27: 14. Based on "Tachuri Bigotillos" Azara, Apunt. Hist. Nat. Páx. Parag. 2: 93 (no. 173). (Paraguay = San Ignacio Guazú, southern Paraguay.)

Habitat.—Montane Evergreen Forest, Tropical Lowland Evergreen Forest (700–2150 m, rarely to sea level; upper Tropical and Subtropical zones).

Distribution.—*Resident* [*albogularis* group] in Costa Rica (Caribbean slope throughout, and Pacific slope of central highlands from the Dota Mountains eastward) and highlands of Panama, and in South America from Colombia, Venezuela, Tobago, Trinidad, the Guianas and adjacent northern Brazil south, west of the Andes to northwestern Peru, and on eastern Andean slopes to northern Bolivia; and [*mystaceus* group] in southern and eastern Brazil, eastern Paraguay, and extreme northeastern Argentina.

Notes.—The two groups differ considerably from one another ecologically and in plumage and soft-part coloration, and have been treated as separate species (e.g., Olson 1993a): *P. albogularis* Sclater, 1860 [White-throated Spadebill] and *P. mystaceus* [Yellow-crested Spadebill]. See comments under *P. cancrominus*.

Platyrinchus coronatus Sclater. Golden-crowned Spadebill.

Platyrhynchus coronatus (Verreaux MS) Sclater, 1858, Proc. Zool. Soc. London, p. 71. (Rio Napo in the Republic of Ecuador.)

Habitat.—Tropical Lowland Evergreen Forest (0–1200 m; Tropical and lower Subtropical zones).

Distribution.—*Resident* on the Caribbean slope of Honduras (west to the Sula Valley) and Nicaragua, in Costa Rica (Caribbean slope, southern Pacific slope, and in northern Pacific on the Cordillera de Guanacaste) and Panama (both slopes, but rare and local on Pacific slope), and in South America west of the Andes in western Colombia and western Ecuador, and east of the Andes from southeastern Colombia, southern Venezuela, and the Guianas south to eastern Peru, northern Bolivia, and Amazonian Brazil.

Genus *ONYCHORHYNCHUS* Fischer von Waldheim

Onychorhynchus Fischer von Waldheim, 1810, Descr. Obj. Rares Mus. Hist. Nat. Univ. Imp. Moscou 1: 1, pl. 1. Type, by monotypy, *Todus regius* "Linn. Gmel." = *Muscicapa coronata* Müller.

Onychorhynchus coronatus (Müller). Royal Flycatcher.

Muscicapa coronata P. L. S. Müller, 1776, Natursyst., Suppl., p. 168. Based on Daubenton, Planches Enlum., pl. 289. (Cayenne.)

Habitat.—Tropical Lowland Evergreen Forest (0–1100 m; Tropical and lower Subtropical zones).

Distribution.—*Resident* [*mexicanus* group] from southern Veracruz and northern and southeastern Oaxaca south along both slopes of Middle America (including the Yucatan Peninsula north to northern Campeche and northern Quintana Roo), most common on the Gulf-Caribbean slope south through Nicaragua to northern Costa Rica (east to Rio Frio region), and on the Pacific slope in Costa Rica and Panama west of Azuero Peninsula, to northern Colombia and northwestern Venezuela; [*occidentalis* group] in South America west of the Andes in western Ecuador and northwestern Peru; [*coronatus* group] in South America east of the Andes from eastern Colombia, southern Venezuela, and the Guianas south to northern Bolivia and Amazonian Brazil; and [*swainsoni* group] in southeastern Brazil.

Notes.—Groups may represent separate species: *O. mexicanus* (Sclater, 1857) [Northern Royal-Flycatcher], *O. occidentalis* (Sclater, 1860) [Western Royal-Flycatcher], *O. coronatus* [Amazonian Royal-Flycatcher] and *O. swainsoni* (Pelzeln, 1858) [Swainson's Royal-Flycatcher].

Subfamily FLUVICOLINAE: Fluvicoline Flycatchers

Genus *TERENOTRICCUS* Ridgway

Terenotriccus Ridgway, 1905, Proc. Biol. Soc. Wash. 18: 207. Type, by original designation, *Myiobius fulvigularis* Salvin and Godman = *Myiobius erythrurus* Cabanis.

Notes.—Mobely and Prum (1995) followed Lanyon (1988c) in merging the monotypic genus *Terenotriccus* into *Myiobius,* but we consider the numerous structural, behavioral, and plumage differences between *T. erythrurus* and the otherwise homogeneous *Myiobius* species to be recognizable at the generic level.

Terenotriccus erythrurus (Cabanis). Ruddy-tailed Flycatcher.

Myiobius erythrurus Cabanis, 1847, Arch. Naturgesch. 13: 249, pl. 5, fig. 1. (Guiana, Cayenne = Cayenne.)

Habitat.—Tropical Lowland Evergreen Forest (0–1200 m; Tropical and lower Subtropical zones).

Distribution.—*Resident* on the Gulf-Caribbean slope of Chiapas, Tabasco, southern Campeche, Guatemala, southern Belize, Honduras and Nicaragua, on both slopes of Costa Rica (absent from the dry northwest) and Panama, and in South America from northern Colombia, Venezuela and the Guianas south, west of the Andes to western Ecuador, and east of the Andes to eastern Peru, northern Bolivia, and Amazonian and central Brazil.

Genus *MYIOBIUS* Darwin

Tyrannula (not *Tyrannulus* Vieillot, 1816) Swainson, 1827, Zool. J. 3: 358. Type, by monotypy, *Muscicapa barbata* Gmelin.
Myiobius (Gray MS) Darwin, 1839, Zool. Voy. Beagle 3(9): 46. New name for *Tyrannula* Swainson, preoccupied.

Myiobius villosus Sclater. Tawny-breasted Flycatcher.

Myiobius villosus Sclater, 1860, Proc. Zool. Soc. London, p. 93. (in rep. Ecuat., part. = Nanegal, Pichincha, Ecuador.)

Habitat.—Montane Evergreen Forest (1200–1440 m in Panama, 800–2100 m in South America; upper Tropical and Subtropical zones).
Distribution.—*Resident* from extreme eastern Panama (two specimens from Cerro Tacarcuna in eastern Darién), Colombia and northwestern Venezuela south, in the western Andes to northwestern Ecuador, and in the eastern Andes to eastern Peru and northern Bolivia.

Myiobius sulphureipygius (Sclater). Sulphur-rumped Flycatcher.

Tyrannula sulphureipygia Sclater, 1857, Proc. Zool. Soc. London (1856), p. 296. (Cordova [= Córdoba] in the State of Vera Cruz, Southern Mexico.)

Habitat.—Tropical Lowland Evergreen Forest, Gallery Forest, Secondary Forest (0–1200 m; Tropical and lower Subtropical zones).
Distribution.—*Resident* from southern Veracruz, northern Oaxaca, Tabasco, northern Chiapas, southern Campeche and Quintana Roo south on the Caribbean slope of northern Central America to Nicaragua, both slopes of Costa Rica (south of Carara on the Pacific slope) and Panama (local on Pacific slope), and in South America in the Pacific lowlands of western Colombia and western Ecuador.
Notes.—*M. sulphureipygius* and the South American *M. barbatus* (Gmelin, 1789) were treated as conspecific by Sibley and Monroe (1990) and Ridgely and Tudor (1994). We treat the two as members of a superspecies.

Myiobius atricaudus Lawrence. Black-tailed Flycatcher.

Myiobius atricaudus Lawrence, 1863, Ibis, p. 183. (Isthmus of Panama = Lion Hill, Canal Zone.)

Habitat.—Tropical Lowland Evergreen Forest, Gallery Forest, Secondary Forest (0–1400 m; Tropical Zone).
Distribution.—*Resident* [*atricaudus* group] in Costa Rica (local on the Pacific slope south of the Tempisque Basin), Panama (both slopes, but local in the west and absent between Azuero Peninsula and western Panama province), northern and western Colombia, western Ecuador, and extreme northwestern Peru; also in South America east of the Andes in eastern Venezuela, and from southeastern Ecuador and eastern Peru east through Amazonian and eastern Brazil; and [*ridgwayi* group] in southeastern Brazil.
Notes.—Groups: *M. atricaudus* [Black-tailed Flycatcher] and *M. ridgwayi* Berlepsch, 1888 [Buff-rumped Flycatcher].

Genus *MYIOPHOBUS* Reichenbach

Myiophobus Reichenbach, 1850, Avium Syst. Nat., pl. 67. Type, by subsequent designation (G. R. Gray, 1855), *Muscicapa ferruginea* Swainson = *Muscicapa fasciata* Müller.

Myiophobus fasciatus (Müller). Bran-colored Flycatcher.

Muscicapa fasciata P. L. S. Müller, 1776, Natursyst., Suppl., p. 172. Based on Daubenton, Planches Enlum., pl. 574, fig. 3. (Cayenne.)

Habitat.—Second-growth Scrub, Riparian Thickets, River-edge Forest (0–1200 m, to 2000 m in South America; Tropical and lower Subtropical zones).

Distribution.—*Resident* [*fasciatus* group] in southwestern Costa Rica (El General-Térraba region), western and central Panama (Pacific slope east to eastern Panamá province, Caribbean slope in the Canal area and adjacent Colón, and in the Pearl Islands), and in South America from northern Colombia south, west of the Andes to northwestern Peru, and east of the Andes in northern Venezuela (including Chacachacare Island), Trinidad and the Guianas, and from central and eastern Peru east across central and eastern Brazil (but absent from much of the Amazon basin), thence southward through Paraguay and Uruguay to central Argentina; and [*rufescens* group] western Peru south from La Libertad to northern Chile.

Notes.—Groups: *M. fasciatus* [Bran-colored Flycatcher] and *M. rufescens* (Salvadori, 1864) [Rufescent Flycatcher].

Genus *LATHROTRICCUS* Lanyon and Lanyon

Lathrotriccus Lanyon and Lanyon, 1986, Auk 103: 347. Type, by original designation, *Empidochanes euleri* Cabanis.

Notes.—For evidence that the species *euleri* should not be placed in the genus *Empidonax,* see Zink and Johnson (1984). For recognition of *Lathrotriccus* for *euleri,* and its placement within the Tyrannidae, see Lanyon and Lanyon (1986) and Lanyon (1986).

Lathrotriccus euleri (Cabanis). Euler's Flycatcher.

Empidochanes Euleri Cabanis, 1868, J. Ornithol. 16: 195. (Cantagallo, Rio de Janeiro, Brazil.)

Habitat.—Tropical Lowland Evergreen Forest, Montane Evergreen Forest, Secondary Forest (0–1350 m in South America; Tropical and lower Subtropical zones).

Distribution.—*Resident* [*flaviventris* group] in the southern Lesser Antilles (on Grenada, where possibly extirpated), and in South America from eastern Colombia across northern Venezuela and Trinidad to Surinam, and south, east of the Andes, to Bolivia and Amazonian Brazil; and [*euleri* group] in South America in southeastern Bolivia, eastern and southeastern Brazil, Paraguay, northern Argentina and Uruguay. Southernmost breeding populations [*euleri* group] migrate northward to Peru, Colombia and Venezuela.

Notes.—Secies limits within this form are not clear, and at least two species may be involved. Groups: *L. flaviventris* (Lawrence, 1887) [Lawrence's Flycatcher], and *L. euleri* [Euler's Flycatcher]. With treatment of *euleri* in *Lathrotriccus, Blacicus flaviventris* Lawrence, 1887 is no longer preoccupied by *Tyrannula flaviventris* Baird, 1843 [= *Empidonax flaviventris*], and the name *flaviventris* antedates *L. lawrencei* (Allen, 1889).

Genus *APHANOTRICCUS* Ridgway

Aphanotriccus Ridgway, 1905, Proc. Biol. Soc. Wash. 18: 207. Type, by original designation, *Myiobius capitalis* Salvin.

Prædo Nelson, 1912, Smithson. Misc. Collect. 60(3): 14. Type, by original designation, *Praedo audax* Nelson.

Aphanotriccus capitalis (Salvin). Tawny-chested Flycatcher.

Myiobius capitalis Salvin, 1865, Proc. Zool. Soc. London (1864), p. 583. (Tucurrique, Costa Rica.)

Habitat.—Tropical Lowland Evergreen Forest, Secondary Forest (0–1000 m; upper Tropical and Subtropical zones).

Distribution.—*Resident* on the Caribbean slope of eastern Nicaragua and northern Costa Rica south to Turrialba and Puerto Limón.

Aphanotriccus audax (Nelson). Black-billed Flycatcher.

Prædo audax Nelson, 1912, Smithson. Misc. Collect. 60(3): 15. (Cana, at 2,000 feet altitude, eastern Panamá.)

Habitat.—Tropical Lowland Evergreen Forest (0–600 m; Tropical Zone).

Distribution.—*Resident* locally in eastern Panama (near Puerto San Antonio and Majé in eastern Panamá province, and near Cana and on Cerro Pirre in eastern Darién), and locally in northwestern and northern Colombia.

Genus *XENOTRICCUS* Dwight and Griscom

Xenotriccus Dwight and Griscom, 1927, Amer. Mus. Novit., no. 254, p. 1. Type, by original designation, *Xenotriccus callizonus* Dwight and Griscom.
Aechmolophus Zimmer, 1938, Auk 55: 663. Type, by original designation, *Aechmolophus mexicanus* Zimmer.

Xenotriccus callizonus Dwight and Griscom. Belted Flycatcher.

Xenotriccus callizonus Dwight and Griscom, 1927, Amer. Mus. Novit., no. 254, p. 2. (Panajachel, 5,500 ft., Lake Atitlán, Guatemala.)

Habitat.—Tropical Deciduous Forest, especially with oaks (1200–2000 m; Subtropical Zone.)

Distribution.—*Resident* locally in Chiapas (El Sumidero, Ocozocoautla, Chichimá), Guatemala (Lake Atitlán, Baja Verapaz), and El Salvador (south to El Encinal).

Xenotriccus mexicanus (Zimmer). Pileated Flycatcher.

Aechmolophus mexicanus Zimmer, 1938, Auk 55: 664. (Cuernavaca, altitude 5000 feet, [Guerrero,] Mexico.)

Habitat.—Arid Montane Scrub, especially mesquite or oak-thorn (900–2000 m; upper Tropical and Subtropical zones).

Distribution.—*Resident* from eastern Michoacán south through the interior of Guerrero, Morelos and southwestern Puebla to central Oaxaca (west of the Isthmus of Tehuantepec).

Notes.—Formerly placed in the monotypic genus *Aechmolophus,* which was merged with *Xenotriccus* by Traylor (1977).

Genus *MITREPHANES* Coues

Mitrephorus (not Schönherr, 1837) Sclater, 1859, Proc. Zool. Soc. London, p. 44. Type, by subsequent designation (Sclater, 1888), *Mitrephorus phaeocercus* Sclater.
Mitrephanes Coues, 1882, Bull. Nuttall Ornithol. Club 7: 55. New name for *Mitrephorus* Sclater, preoccupied.

Mitrephanes phaeocercus (Sclater). Tufted Flycatcher.

Mitrephorus phæocercus Sclater, 1859, Proc. Zool. Soc. London, p. 44. (In Mexico merid. et in Guatemala = Córdoba, Veracruz.)

Habitat.—Montane Evergreen Forest, Pine-Oak Forest, Montane Evergreen Forest Edge (600–3600 m; upper Tropical to lower Temperate zones).

Distribution.—*Resident* [*phaeocercus* group] in the highlands from northeastern Sonora, western Chihuahua, Sinaloa, Durango, western Zacatecas, southeastern San Luis Potosí and southern Tamaulipas south through Mexico, Guatemala, El Salvador and Honduras to north-central Nicaragua, both slopes of Costa Rica south locally through Panama (Bocas del Toro, Chiriquí, Veraguas, Coclé and eastern Darién), and western Colombia to northwestern Ecuador; and [*olivaceus* group] in South America from northern Peru south along the Andes to northern Bolivia.

Accidental in Texas (Big Bend; Zimmer and Bryan 1993; DeBenedictis 1994a).

Notes.— Many authors, including Wetmore (1972), Sibley and Monroe (1990) and Ridgely and Tudor (1994), treat the two groups as separate species: *M. olivaceus* Berlepsch and Stolzmann, 1894 [Olive Tufted-Flycatcher] and *M. phaeocercus* (Sclater, 1859) [Common Tufted-Flycatcher].

Genus *CONTOPUS* Cabanis

Syrichta (not *Syrichtus* Boisduval, 1833) Bonaparte, 1854, Ann. Sci. Nat. (4)1: 133. Type, by monotypy, *Tyrannula ardosiaca* Lafresnaye. *Nomen nudum.*

Contopus Cabanis, 1855, J. Ornithol. 3: 479. Type, by original designation, *Muscicapa virens* Linnaeus.

Blacicus Cabanis, 1855, J. Ornithol. 3: 480. Type, by original designation, *Muscipeta caribaea* d'Orbigny.

Syrichtha Bonaparte, 1857, Bull. Soc. Linn. Normandie 2: 36. Type, by monotypy, *Syrichtha curtipes* Bonaparte ex Swainson = *Platyrhynchus cinereus* Spix.

Myiochanes Cabanis and Heine, 1859, Mus. Heineanum 2: 71. New name for *Syrichtha* Bonaparte.

Syrichta G. R. Gray, 1869, Handl. Genera Spec. Birds 1: 362. Type, by original designation, *Tyrannula ardosiaca* Lafresnaye = *Tyrannus fumigatus* d'Orbigny and Lafresnaye.

Nuttallornis Ridgway, 1887, Man. N. Amer. Birds, p. 337. Type, by monotypy, *C. borealis* (Swainson) = *Tyrannus borealis* Swainson.

Contopus cooperi (Nuttall). Olive-sided Flycatcher.

Muscicapa cooperi Nuttall, 1831, Man. Ornithol. U. S. and Canada, p. 282. (Mount Auburn, near Boston, Massachusetts.)

Tyrannus borealis Swainson, 1832, in Swainson and Richardson, Fauna Bor.-Amer. 2 (1831): 141, pl. 35. (Cumberland House [= Carlton House], lat. 54°, banks of the Saskatchewan [Canada].)

Habitat.— Taiga, subalpine coniferous forest, spruce bogs, burns, and mixed coniferous-deciduous forest with standing dead trees; in migration and winter in a variety of forest habitats, especially with emergent dead limbs.

Distribution.—*Breeds* from western and central Alaska, central Yukon, west-central and southern Mackenzie, northern Saskatchewan, north-central Manitoba, northern Ontario, south-central Quebec, south-central Labrador and central Newfoundland south along humid coast to central California, and in interior mountains to northern Baja California (Sierra San Pedro Mártir), southern Nevada, northern Arizona, southern New Mexico and western Texas, and, east of the Rocky Mountains, to central Saskatchewan, southern Manitoba, northern Minnesota, northern Wisconsin, northern Michigan, southern Ontario, northeastern Ohio (formerly) and western Massachusetts, also locally in the Appalachians south through New York, Pennsylvania, eastern West Virginia, and southwestern Virginia to eastern Tennessee and western North Carolina.

Winters mainly in mountains of South America from Colombia, Venezuela and Trinidad south through Ecuador and Peru to Bolivia and southeastern Brazil, rarely in Middle America as far north as southern Mexico in Jalisco, Oaxaca and Chiapas; casual in southern California.

Migrates regularly through most of the western United States and Middle America, less commonly throughout eastern United States south to the Gulf coast, and casually along the southern Atlantic coast to peninsular Florida.

Casual or accidental in northern Alaska (Point Barrow), St. Lawrence Island in the Bering Sea, Greenland, Bermuda, the Netherlands Antilles, Surinam, and Amazonian Brazil.

Notes.—Formerly placed in the monotypic genus *Nuttallornis.* For the use of *cooperi* rather than *borealis,* see Banks and Browning (1995: 636).

Contopus pertinax Cabanis and Heine. Greater Pewee.

Contopus pertinax (Lichtenstein MS) Cabanis and Heine, 1859, Mus. Heineanum 2: 72. (Xalapa = Jalapa, Veracruz.)

Habitat.—Pine Forest, Pine-Oak Forest, Montane Evergreen Forest (900–3400 m; Subtropical and Temperate zones).

Distribution.—*Breeds* from central Arizona, southwestern New Mexico, central Chihuahua, southern Coahuila, central Nuevo León, and southern Tamaulipas south in the highlands of Mexico and northern Central America (including Belize) to north-central Nicaragua.

Winters from northern Mexico (casually southern Arizona and southern Texas) south through the breeding range in Middle America.

Migrates casually through western and south-central Texas.

Casual (primarily in winter) in central coastal and southern California (north to Alameda County); a record from Colorado is erroneous.

Notes.— Formerly known as Coues's Flycatcher. *C. pertinax, C. lugubris* and the South American *C. fumigatus* (Lafresnaye and d'Orbigny, 1837) are closely related and constitute a superspecies. *C. pertinax* is sometimes replaced with *C. musicus* (Swainson), based on *Tyrannula musica* Swainson, 1827, a name generally regarded as unidentifiable (see Banks and Browning 1995: 636).

Contopus lugubris Lawrence. Dark Pewee.

> *Contopus lugubris* Lawrence, 1865, Ann. Lyc. Nat. Hist. N. Y. 8: 134. (Barranca, Costa Rica.)

Habitat.—Montane Evergreen Forest, Montane Evergreen Forest Edge, Secondary Forest (1200–2200 m; Subtropical zone).

Distribution.—*Resident* in the mountains of Costa Rica (from the Cordillera de Tilarán southward) and extreme western Panama (western and central Chiriquí).

Notes.—See comments under *C. pertinax*.

Contopus ochraceus Sclater and Salvin. Ochraceous Pewee.

> *Contopus ochraceus* Sclater and Salvin, 1869, Proc. Zool. Soc. London, p. 419. (Costa Rica.)

Habitat.—Montane Evergreen Forest (2100–3000 m; Temperate Zone).

Distribution.—*Resident* locally at high elevations in Costa Rica (Irazú and Turrialba volcanoes, and Cordillera de Talamanca) and extreme western Panama in Chiriquí (one nineteenth century specimen known from "Chiriquí", plus sight records and photographs from Cerro Punta).

Contopus sordidulus Sclater. Western Wood-Pewee.

> *Contopus sordidulus* Sclater, 1859, Proc. Zool. Soc. London, p. 43. (In Mexico meridionali et Guatemala = Orizaba, Veracruz.)

Habitat.— Coniferous or mixed coniferous-deciduous forest, riparian woodland (Subtropical and Temperate zones, in nonbreeding season also Tropical Zone).

Distribution.—*Breeds* from east-central Alaska, southern Yukon, southern Mackenzie, northern Alberta, northwestern and central Saskatchewan, south-central Manitoba, and northwestern Minnesota (Roseau County) south to southern Baja California, and in the interior highlands of Mexico and Guatemala to Honduras and (possibly) north-central Nicaragua, and east to central North Dakota, western South Dakota, western Nebraska, western Kansas, western Texas, and southern Tamaulipas. Breeding reports from Costa Rica and Panama are unverified; one from Colombia is erroneous (pertaining to *C. cinereus*).

Winters in forested mountains from Colombia and Venezuela south to Peru and Bolivia, and (possibly) northern Argentina, casually north to Costa Rica. One record (specimen) for southern Texas.

Migrates regularly east to western Kansas, and south through Middle America, occurring in lowlands on both slopes as well as in highlands.

Casual or accidental in northern Alaska (Point Barrow, Umiat), central Ontario, Massachusetts, Maryland, southern and southeastern Texas, southwestern Louisiana, Mississippi, Florida (one verified record, following late spring hurricane), Cuba and Jamaica, with reports of vagrants (based on identification by call) from Iowa, Wisconsin, Illinois, Indiana and southern Ontario; a report from Belize is considered uncertain.

Notes.— See comments under *C. virens*. This species was formerly known as *C. richardsonii*, based on *Tyrannula richardsonii* Swainson, 1832, now regarded as a synonym of *Sayornis phoebe* (see Phillips and Parkes 1955). Called Western Pewee in Howell and Webb (1995).

Contopus virens (Linnaeus). Eastern Wood-Pewee.

> *Muscicapa virens* Linnaeus, 1766, Syst. Nat. (ed. 12) 1: 327. Based on "Le Gobemouche cendré de la Caroline" Brisson, Ornithologie 2: 368. (in Carolina ad ripas = South Carolina.)

Habitat.— Deciduous or mixed deciduous-coniferous forest, forest edge, open woodland, and parks; in migration and winter, a variety of open forest and forest edge habitats.

Distribution.—*Breeds* from southeastern Saskatchewan, southern Manitoba, central Ontario, southern Quebec, northern Maine, New Brunswick, Prince Edward Island and Nova Scotia (including Cape Breton Island) south to Texas, the Gulf coast and central Florida, and west to central North Dakota, eastern South Dakota, western Nebraska, eastern Kansas, central Oklahoma, and south-central Texas.

Winters from Colombia and Venezuela south to Bolivia and western Brazil, casually north to Costa Rica.

Migrates through the eastern United States, Gulf-Caribbean lowlands of Mexico, and along both slopes from southeastern Oaxaca, Chiapas, Guatemala and Belize south through Middle America (more abundantly on the Caribbean slope, including most offshore islands), casually through the western Bahamas (New Providence, Grand Bahama, Eleuthera, Mayaguana), western Cuba, the Isle of Pines, Jamaica, Cayman Islands, and islands of the western Caribbean (Swan, Providencia and San Andrés islands, and Albuquerque Cay).

Casual or accidental off Labrador (200 miles at sea), and in Clipperton Island, California, Arizona, eastern Montana, eastern Wyoming, eastern Colorado, New Mexico, Newfoundland, St. Pierre et Miquelon, Bermuda and Barbados.

Notes.—*C. virens, C. sordidulus*, and *C. cinereus* constitute a superspecies (Sibley and Monroe 1990).

Contopus cinereus (Spix). Tropical Pewee.

> *Platyrhynchus cinereus* Spix, 1825, Avium Spec. Nov. Bras. 2: 11, pl. 13, fig. 2. ("in sylvis flum. Amazonum," error = Rio de Janeiro, Brazil.)

Habitat.—Tropical Lowland Evergreen Forest Edge, Montane Evergreen Forest Edge, Tropical Deciduous Forest, Gallery Forest, Secondary Forest (0–1500 m, to 2200 m in South America; Tropical and lower Subtropical zones, locally in South America to lower Temperate Zone).

Distribution.—*Resident* [*brachytarsus* group] from northern Oaxaca, southern Veracruz, southern Chiapas, and southwestern Guatemala south along both slopes of Middle America (including the entire Yucatan Peninsula, Cozumel and Cancun islands) to Panama (including Isla Coiba); and [*cinereus* group] in South America from northern Colombia, northern Venezuela, Trinidad and the Guianas south in the Andes to Peru, locally in arid southwestern Ecuador, extreme southern Venezuela, and adjacent northern Brazil, and from central and eastern Brazil south to eastern Bolivia, northern and northeastern Argentina, Paraguay and southern Brazil. Populations in southern Mexico migrate southward in the winter.

Notes.—Groups: *C. brachytarsus* (Sclater, 1859) [Short-legged Pewee] and *C. cinereus* [Tropical Pewee].

Contopus caribaeus (d'Orbigny). Cuban Pewee.

> *Muscipeta caribaea* d'Orbigny, 1839, *in* La Sagra, Hist. Fis. Pol. Nat. Cuba, Ois., p. 92. (Cuba = Holguín, Oriente Prov., Cuba.)

Habitat.—Tropical Lowland Evergreen Forest, Tropical Deciduous Forest, Pine Forest, Secondary Forest (0–1000 m; Tropical and Upper Tropical Zone).

Distribution.—*Resident* in the northern Bahama Islands (Grand Bahama, Abaco, New Providence, Eleuthera and Cat islands) and Cuba (including cays off the coast of both Cuba and the Isle of Pines).

Notes.—*C. pallidus, C. hispaniolensis* and *C. caribaeus* formerly were considered a single species, *C. caribaeus* [Greater Antillean Pewee], but differ in vocalization, plumage, and measurements (Reynard et al. 1993). They are treated here as members of a superspecies.

Contopus pallidus (Gosse). Jamaican Pewee.

Myiobius pallidus Gosse, 1847, Birds Jamaica, p. 166. (Jamaica.)

Habitat.—Tropical Lowland Evergreen Forest, Montane Evergreen Forest, Secondary Forest (0–1000 m; Tropical and Upper Tropical Zone).
Distribution.—*Resident* in Jamaica
Notes.—See notes under *C. caribaeus.*

Contopus hispaniolensis (Bryant). Hispaniolan Pewee.

Tyrannula carriboea [sic] var. *hispaniolensis* Bryant, 1867, Proc. Bost. Soc. Nat. Hist., 11, p. 91. (Santo Domingo = mountains near Port-au-Prince, Republic of Haiti, Hispaniola; Deignan, 1961, U. S. Nat. Mus. Bull. 221, p. 283.)

Habitat.—Tropical Lowland Evergreen Forest, Tropical Deciduous Forest, Montane Evergeen Forest, Pine Forest, Secondary Forest (0–2000 m; Tropical and Subtropical zones).
Distribution.—*Resident* on Hispaniola (including Gonâve Island).
Accidental on Mona Island (off Puerto Rico); a sight report for the Caicos Islands.
Notes.—See notes under *C. caribaeus.*

Contopus latirostris (Verreaux). Lesser Antillean Pewee.

Myiobius latirostris Verreaux, 1866, Bull. Nouv. Arch. Mus. Hist. Nat. [Paris] 2: 22, pl. 3, fig. 2. (Sainte Lucie, dans la Nouvelle Grenade = St. Lucia, in the Lesser Antilles.)

Habitat.—Tropical Lowland Evergreen Forest, Montane Evergreen Forest, Tropical Deciduous Forest (0–900 m; Tropical Zone).
Distribution.—*Resident* on Puerto Rico (primarily western and central portions) and in the northern Lesser Antilles (St. Lucia, Martinique, Dominica, and Guadeloupe).

Genus *EMPIDONAX* Cabanis

Empidonax Cabanis. 1855, J. Ornithol. 3: 480. Type, by monotypy, *Empidonax pusillus* Cabanis = *Platyrhynchos virescens* Vieillot.

Empidonax flaviventris (Baird and Baird). Yellow-bellied Flycatcher.

Tyrannula flaviventris W. M. and S. F. Baird, 1843, Proc. Acad. Nat. Sci. Philadelphia 1: 283. ([near Carlisle,] Cumberland Co., Pa.)

Habitat.— Breeds in boreal coniferous forest, especially spruce bogs, but also fir, jack pine and tamarack; winters in Tropical Lowland Evergreen Forest, Tropical Deciduous Forest, and forest edges.
Distribution.—*Breeds* from central and northeastern British Columbia, west-central and southern Mackenzie, northern Saskatchewan, northern Manitoba, northern Ontario, central Quebec, south-central Labrador, and Newfoundland south to central Alberta, central Saskatchewan, northern Minnesota, northern Wisconsin, northern Michigan, southern Ontario, northeastern Pennsylvania, north-central New York, New Brunswick, Prince Edward Island and Nova Scotia, with isolated breeding also in West Virginia, and western Virginia (Mt. Rogers, at least formerly).
Winters in Middle America from southern Tamaulipas, southeastern San Luis Potosí and Puebla on the Gulf-Caribbean slope and southern Oaxaca on the Pacific slope south to western Panama (casually east to the Canal area and Darién).

Migrates regularly through the eastern United States west to the central Great Plains and central Texas, uncommonly through the Gulf and South Atlantic states from South Carolina and Florida to eastern Louisiana, and casually through eastern New Mexico and western Texas.

Casual in east-central Alaska, California and Montana. Accidental in Arizona (Tucson), Nayarit (San Blas), Cuba and Greenland; a sight report from the Bahama Islands (Eleuthera).

Empidonax virescens (Vieillot). Acadian Flycatcher.

Muscicapa querula (not Vieillot, 1807) Wilson, 1810, Amer. Ornithol. 2: 77, pl. 13, fig. 3. (No locality given = near Philadelphia, Pennsylvania.)

Platyrhynchos virescens Vieillot, 1818, Nouv. Dict. Hist. Nat. (nouv. éd.) 27: 22. New name for *Muscicapa querula* Wilson, preoccupied.

Habitat.—Breeds in humid deciduous forest; northerly populations prefer moist ravines, often with hemlocks; winters in Tropical Lowland Evergreen Forest Edge, Secondary Forest, and Tropical Deciduous Forest.

Distribution.—*Breeds* from southeastern South Dakota, southern and eastern Iowa, southeastern Minnesota, southern Wisconsin, southern Michigan, extreme southern Ontario, northeastern Pennsylvania, central New York, Massachusetts, Vermont, and (probably) southern New Hampshire south to central and southern Texas (west to Tom Greene County), the Gulf coast and central Florida, and west to eastern Nebraska, central Kansas, and central Oklahoma.

Winters on the Caribbean slope of Nicaragua, on both slopes (more commonly on the Caribbean) of Costa Rica and Panama (including Taboguilla and the Pearl islands), and in northern and western Colombia, northwestern Venezuela, and western Ecuador.

Migrates regularly (but uncommonly recorded) on the Gulf-Caribbean slope of Middle America from northeastern Mexico south to Costa Rica, casually west to western South Dakota (at least formerly) and western Nebraska, and through the Bahamas (recorded from Grand Bahama, New Providence, Eleuthera and Cay Lobos), and western Cuba.

Casual or accidental in southeastern British Columbia, Arizona, North Dakota, Quebec and New Brunswick.

Empidonax alnorum Brewster. Alder Flycatcher.

Empidonax traillii alnorum Brewster, 1895, Auk 12: 161. (Upton, Maine.)

Habitat.— Breeds in damp, brushy thickets, alder swamps, open second growth, forested swamps, and brushy margins of lakes and streams; winters in Riparian Thickets, Second Growth Forest, and Second Growth Scrub.

Distribution.—*Breeds* from central Alaska, central Yukon, northwestern and southern Mackenzie, northern Alberta, northern Saskatchewan, northern Manitoba, northern Ontario, central and eastern Quebec, southern Labrador and southern Newfoundland south to southern Alaska, south-central British Columbia, southern Alberta, southern Saskatchewan, northern North Dakota, south-central Minnesota, central Wisconsin, southern Michigan, southern Ontario, northern Ohio, western Maryland, eastern Pennsylvania, northern New Jersey and Connecticut; and in the Appalachians south to eastern Tennessee, western Virginia and western North Carolina. Recorded in summer (and possibly breeding) in northern Indiana.

Winters apparently exclusively in South America, where definitely recorded on the basis of call in eastern Ecuador, eastern Peru and northern and eastern Bolivia; individuals of the "traillii complex" reported in South America from Colombia and northwestern Venezuela south, east of the Andes, to eastern Peru, Bolivia and northern Argentina probably belong to this species.

Migrates through the eastern United States, west to central Montana (casually to south-central Oregon and eastern Colorado), and through Middle America (mostly Caribbean slope, reported from southern Mexico, where found on both slopes, southward); few records of the complex exist for the West Indies.

Casual or accidental in northern Alaska, California, Cuba, the Isles of Pines (possibly referable to *E. traillii*) and Bermuda.

Notes.—Formerly recognized as a single species, *E. traillii* [Traill's Flycatcher], *E. alnorum* and *E. traillii* are closely related and nearly indistinguishable morphologically, but differ in vocalizations, ecology (Stein 1958, 1963), and winter distribution.

Empidonax traillii (Audubon). Willow Flycatcher.

> *Muscicapa Traillii* Audubon, 1828, Birds Amer. (folio) 1: pl. 45 (1831, Ornithol. Biogr. 1: 236). (woods along the prairie lands of the Arkansas River = Fort of Arkansas [Arkansas Post], Arkansas.)

Habitat.— Breeds in moist, brushy thickets, open second growth, and riparian woodland, especially with willow and buttonbush; winters in Tropical Lowland Evergreen Forest Edge, Second Growth Forest, and Second Growth Scrub.

Distribution.—*Breeds* from central British Columbia, southern Alberta, southern Saskatchewan, southwestern Manitoba, northern North Dakota, western and southern Minnesota, central Wisconsin, Michigan, southern Ontario, southwestern Quebec, central Maine, New Brunswick, Prince Edward Island and Nova Scotia (possibly) south to southern California (local, formerly widespread), northern Baja California and northern Sonora (at least formerly), southern Arizona (locally), southern New Mexico, northeastern Oklahoma, Arkansas (rarely), northeastern Louisiana, central Tennessee, northern Georgia, western South Carolina, western North Carolina, and central and eastern Virginia.

Winters in Middle America from Nayarit and southwestern Oaxaca south to Panama and possibly extreme northwestern Colombia.

Migrates widely through the southern United States, presumably occurring as a regular migrant through Middle America south to the limits of the wintering range.

Casual north to western, south-coastal and southeastern Alaska, and to central Ontario.

Notes.—Sometimes treated as *E. brewsteri* Oberholser, 1918, but *traillii* clearly pertains to this species and has priority (Eisenmann 1970). See comments under *E. alnorum*.

Empidonax albigularis Sclater and Salvin. White-throated Flycatcher.

> *Empidonax albigularis* Sclater and Salvin, 1859, Ibis, p. 122. (Dueñas [Sacatepéquez, Guatemala].)

Habitat.—Breeds in Riparian Thickets and Second-growth Scrub (900–1800 m; Subtropical and lower Temperate zones, in winter also to Tropical Zone); winters mainly in marshes with scrubby edges.

Distribution.—*Breeds* in the highlands from southwestern Chihuahua, Durango, Zacatecas, San Luis Potosí and southern Tamaulipas south through interior Mexico, Guatemala, El Salvador, and Honduras to north-central Nicaragua; and in central Costa Rica (vicinity of Cartago) and western Panama (Chiriquí).

Winters from Jalisco, Guanajuato and Hidalgo south through the breeding range, descending mostly to lowlands (recorded near sea level in Nayarit, Colima, Veracruz, Oaxaca, Campeche, Belize, Guatemala and Honduras), casually to Costa Rica and central Panama (recorded Bocas del Toro and the Canal area).

Empidonax minimus (Baird and Baird). Least Flycatcher.

> *Tyrannula minima* W. M. and S. F. Baird, 1843, Proc. Acad. Nat. Sci. Philadelphia 1: 284. ([near Carlisle,] Cumberland Co., Pa.)

Habitat.—Breeds in open deciduous woodland, poplar stands, forest edge, and parks; winters in Tropical Lowland Evergreen Forest Edge, Tropical Deciduous Forest, Arid Lowland Scrub, and Arid Montane Scrub.

Distribution.—*Breeds* from southern Yukon, west-central and southern Mackenzie, northern Alberta, northern Saskatchewan, north-central Manitoba, northern Ontario, southern Quebec, New Brunswick, Prince Edward Island, and Nova Scotia south to western Washington, eastern Oregon, northeastern California, Montana, northeastern Colorado, central and southeastern South Dakota, eastern Nebraska (formerly), Missouri, central Illinois, northern Indiana, central Ohio, Pennsylvania, central New Jersey, and in the Appalachians, through

West Virginia, western Maryland, western Virginia, eastern Tennessee, and western North Carolina to northwestern Georgia. Recorded in summer (and possibly breeding) in east-central and southeastern Alaska, northern Utah, and eastern Kentucky.

Winters from southern Sonora (at least casually) and southern Tamaulipas south along both slopes of Middle America to Honduras and northern Nicaragua, casually to Costa Rica and central Panama (east to the Canal area); also casually in central and southern California, southern Texas, southern Louisiana, and southern Florida.

Migrates commonly through the south-central United States from the Rockies east to the Mississippi Valley and Gulf states, and through most of Mexico (except the northwestern portion), casually, primarily in the fall, from southwestern British Columbia south through California (including the Farallon Islands), southern Nevada, Arizona, Baja California and Sonora, and in the southeastern United States.

Casual in south-coastal Alaska (Anchorage, Middleton Island), Newfoundland and St. Pierre et Miquelon; accidental in Cuba and the Cayman Islands (Grand Cayman).

Notes.—For comments on the preferable use of the name *E. minimus* over *E. pusillus* (Swainson, 1827), see Banks and Browning (1995: 637).

Empidonax hammondii (Xántus de Vesey). Hammond's Flycatcher.

> *Tyrannula hammondii* Xántus de Vesey, 1858, Proc. Acad. Nat. Sci. Philadelphia, 10, p. 117. (Fort Tejon, California.)

Habitat.—Breeds primarily in dense fir forest and associated coniferous woodland; winters primarily in Pine-oak Forest, Pine Forest, and Arid Montane Scrub.

Distribution.—*Breeds* from east-central Alaska, southern Yukon, northeastern British Columbia, southwestern Alberta, western and south-central Montana, and northwestern Wyoming south to southeastern Alaska, and through British Columbia and the Pacific states to east-central California (south to Tulare County), east-central Nevada, central Utah, north-eastern Arizona, western Colorado, and north-central New Mexico.

Winters from southeastern Arizona (casually central and southern California), south-western New Mexico, western Chihuahua, southern Coahuila, central Nuevo León and central Tamaulipas south through the highlands of Mexico, Guatemala and El Salvador to Honduras, and (probably) north-central Nicaragua; reports from Peru are unfounded.

Migrates regularly through the southwestern United States (east to western Texas) and northern Mexico, casually east to western Nebraska, west-central Kansas, western Oklahoma and central Texas.

Casual on the Queen Charlotte Islands, and in northern Alaska, central Texas, Louisiana, southern Alabama, Michigan, Pennsylvania, Massachusetts, Maryland and Delaware; a photograph from Panama (western Chiriquí), although not absolutely definitive, is probably of this species.

Empidonax wrightii Baird. Gray Flycatcher.

> *Empidonax wrightii* Baird, 1858, in Baird, Cassin and Lawrence, Rep. Explor. Surv. R. R. Pac., 9, p. 200 (in text). (El Paso, Texas.)

Habitat.—Breeds in arid habitats, especially sagebrush, pinyon-juniper woodland and, less frequently, open pine-oak association; winters in Arid Lowland Scrub, Arid Montane Scrub, and Riparian Thickets.

Distribution.—*Breeds* from extreme southern British Columbia, central and eastern Washington, eastern Oregon, south-central Idaho, southern Wyoming and central Colorado south to south-central California (San Bernardino County), southern Nevada, central Arizona, southern New Mexico, and western Texas (Davis Mountains).

Winters from southern California (rarely), central Arizona, southern Coahuila, western Texas and central Tamaulipas south to southern Baja California, Jalisco, northern Michoacán, Mexico, Puebla and northwestern Oaxaca.

Migrates regularly through the southwestern United States east to eastern New Mexico (casually to southwestern Kansas), and through northern Mexico.

Casual in northern Wyoming, western Washington, western Oregon and central Texas. Accidental in Ontario (Toronto), Ohio (Lucas County), and Massachusetts (Littleton).

Notes.—Formerly known as *E. griseus* Brewster, 1889. See comments under *E. ober-holseri*. For comments on the preferable use of the name *E. wrightii* over *E. obscurus* (Swainson, 1827), see Banks and Browning (1995: 636).

Empidonax oberholseri Phillips. Dusky Flycatcher.

> *Empidonax oberholseri* Phillips, 1939, Auk 56: 311. (Hart Prairie, San Francisco Mountain, Arizona.)

Habitat.— Breeds in aspen groves, willow thickets, scrub, open coniferous and mixed coniferous-deciduous forest, and mountain chaparral; winters in similar habitats, also Pine-oak Forest and Gallery Forest.

Distribution.—*Breeds* from southwestern Yukon south through northeastern and central British Columbia to north-central Washington, thence eastward through south-central Alberta to southwestern Saskatchewan, and south (except in coastal areas of Washington and Oregon) to mountains of southern California, northern Baja California (probably), southern Nevada, southwestern Utah, central Arizona, and central and northeastern New Mexico, and east to eastern Montana, western South Dakota (Black Hills), and central Colorado.

Winters from southern California (casually), southern Arizona, southwestern New Mexico, Sonora, northwestern Durango, southern Coahuila, western Texas, central Nuevo León and central Tamaulipas south, mostly in the highlands, to Guerrero and Oaxaca; a report from northwestern Guatemala is unverified.

Migrates regularly through the southwestern United States (east to southwestern Kansas and western Texas), casually through the coastal areas of Washington and Oregon, to northern Baja California, and east to central and southern Texas.

Accidental in northern and southeastern Alaska (Icy Cape, Sergief Island), southern Ontario and Pennsylvania (Kutztown); a sight report for Delaware.

Notes.—Formerly known as *E. wrightii* [Wright's Flycatcher]; all records of *E. wrightii* prior to 1939 and most prior to 1957 pertain to *E. oberholseri* (Johnson 1963).

Empidonax affinis (Swainson). Pine Flycatcher.

> *Empidonax affinis* Swainson, 1827, Philos. Mag. (n.s.) 1: 367. (Maritime parts of Mexico = Temascaltepec, México.)

Habitat.—Pine Forest, Pine-Oak Forest (1600–3500 m; Subtropical and Temperate zones).

Distribution.—*Resident* from northern Sinaloa, central Chihuahua, southern Coahuila, Zacatecas and San Luis Potosí south in the Mexican highlands to central Oaxaca, Puebla and west-central Veracruz, also (apparently resident) in Chiapas, and Guatemala.

Notes.— Vocal differences on either side of the Isthmus of Tehuantepec suggest that two species may be involved (Howell and Webb 1995: 500).

Empidonax difficilis Baird. Pacific-slope Flycatcher.

> *Empidonax difficilis* Baird, 1858, in Baird, Cassin and Lawrence, Rep. Explor. Surv. R. R. Pac. 9: xxx, 198 (in text). (west coast of United States, Fort Steilacoom, Shoalwater Bay, Washington, Fort Tejon, California = Fort Steilacoom, Washington.)

Habitat.—Breeds in humid coniferous forest (mostly coastal), pine-oak forest, and dense second-growth woodland; winters in Montane Evergreen Forest, Gallery Forest, Tropical Deciduous Forest, and Tropical Lowland Evergreen Forest.

Distribution.—*Breeds* [*difficilis* group] from southeastern Alaska and central British Columbia (including the Queen Charlotte and Vancouver islands) south to southwestern California (generally west of the Sierra Nevada), and the mountains of northern Baja California; and in southern Baja California (Victoria Mountains in the Sierra de la Laguna); and [*insulicola* group] in the Channel Islands, off southern California.

Winters [*difficilis* group] from southern California (rarely), southern Baja California, and northwestern Mexico (casually north to northern California) south to the Isthmus of Tehuantepec (Oaxaca); winter range of the *insulicola* group is unknown.

Migrates through Arizona, western and southern New Mexico, and western Texas.

Casual [*difficilis* group] in southern Louisiana and accidental [*difficilis* group] in Pennsylvania (southern Lancaster County).

Notes.—*E. difficilis* and *E. occidentalis* until recently were considered conspecific [Western Flycatcher], but they differ in vocalizations and allozymes and are sympatric in the Siskiyou region of northern California (Johnson 1980, Johnson and Marten 1988, Johnson 1994). The form *insulicola* Oberholser, 1897 [Channel Islands Flycatcher] may also be a distinct species but is currently regarded as a race of *difficilis*. *E. difficilis, E. occidentalis* and *E. flavescens* are all closely related and constitute a superspecies.

Empidonax occidentalis Nelson. Cordilleran Flycatcher.

Empidonax bairdi occidentalis Nelson, 1897, Auk 14: 53. (Pluma, Oaxaca, Mexico = Pluma Hidalgo, Oaxaca; Binford, 1989, Ornithol. Monogr. 43, p. 341.)

Habitat.—Breeds in humid coniferous forest, dense second-growth woodland, and pine-oak forest (1000–3500 m; Subtropical and Temperate zones); winters in Pine-oak Forest, Montane Evergreen Forest, Gallery Forest, Deciduous Forest, and Tropical Lowland Evergreen Forest Edge.

Distribution.—*Breeds* from west-central Alberta, northern Idaho, central Montana, Wyoming and western South Dakota south to northeastern California, central Nevada, and central and southeastern Arizona, in the mountains of Mexico to central Oaxaca (west of the Isthmus of Tehuantepec), Puebla and west-central Veracruz, and east to northwestern Nebraska, central Colorado, central New Mexico, and western Texas.

Winters in the mountains of Mexico south to Oaxaca; reports from Chiapas, Guatemala and Honduras are based on *E. flavescens*.

Migrates casually through eastern New Mexico, southwestern Kansas, South Dakota, and the Tres Marias Islands (off Nayarit).

Notes.—See comments under *E. difficilis*.

Empidonax flavescens Lawrence. Yellowish Flycatcher.

Empidonax flavescens Lawrence, 1865, Ann. Lyc. Nat. Hist. N. Y. 8: 133. (Barranca, Costa Rica.)

Habitat.—Montane Evergreen Forest, Pine-Oak Forest (900–3000 m; Subtropical and Temperate zones).

Distribution.—*Resident* in the highlands of southeastern Veracruz (Sierra de los Tuxtlas), southeastern Oaxaca (Sierra Madre de Chiapas), Guatemala, El Salvador, Honduras, north-central Nicaragua, Costa Rica, and western Panama (Chiriquí and Veraguas).

Notes.—See comments under *E. difficilis*.

Empidonax fulvifrons (Giraud). Buff-breasted Flycatcher.

Muscicapa fulvifrons Giraud, 1841, Descr. Sixteen New Spec. N. Amer. Birds, pl. 4, fig. 2. (Texas, error = Miquiahuana, Tamaulipas.)

Habitat.—Pine-Oak Forest, Pine Forest, Tropical Deciduous Forest, Arid Montane Scrub (1000–3500 m, descends to 600 m in winter; Subtropical and lower Temperate zones, in winter casually to Tropical Zone).

Distribution.—*Breeds* from east-central and southeastern Arizona (formerly north to Prescott and the White Mountains), west-central and southwestern New Mexico (formerly), northeastern Sonora, Chihuahua, Durango, Zacatecas, San Luis Potosí, and western Nuevo León south locally through the highlands of Mexico, Guatemala, and El Salvador to central Honduras.

Winters from Sonora and Chihuahua south through the breeding range, occurring also in adjacent lowlands.

Empidonax atriceps Salvin. Black-capped Flycatcher.

Empidonax atriceps Salvin, 1870, Proc. Zool. Soc. London, p. 198. (Volcán de Chiriquí, Panama.)

Habitat.—Montane Evergreen Forest, Secondary Forest (2100–3300 m; upper Subtropical and Temperate zones).

Distribution.—*Resident* in the mountains of Costa Rica (Cordillera Central, Dota Mountains and Cordillera de Talamanca) and western Panama (western Chiriquí and adjacent Bocas del Toro).

Genus *SAYORNIS* Bonaparte

Sayornis Bonaparte, 1854, C. R. Acad. Sci. Paris 38: 657. Type, by monotypy, *Sayornis nigricans* Bonaparte = *Tyrannula nigricans* Swainson.

Sayornis nigricans (Swainson). Black Phoebe.

Tyrannula nigricans Swainson, 1827, Philos. Mag. (n.s.) 1: 367. (Table land of Mexico = Valley of Mexico.)

Habitat.—Usually along streams or lake margins in open to wooded country; nests in rocky canyon walls, in coastal cliffs, and under bridges or on other man-made structures (Tropical to Temperate zones).

Distribution.—*Breeds* [*nigricans* group] from southwestern Oregon, California, southern Nevada, southern Utah, northern Arizona, southeastern Colorado, central New Mexico, and western and west-central Texas (east to Crockett, Val Verde and Uvalde counties) south to southern Baja California and, mostly in the highlands, through Middle America (except the Yucatan Peninsula) to western Panama (Chiriquí, Bocas del Toro); and [*latirostris* group] in highlands from central and eastern Panama (west to eastern Colón and eastern Panamá province) east to northern Venezuela, and south in the Andes from Colombia to northwestern Argentina.

Partially migratory, northern populations [*nigricans* group] wandering after the breeding season and tropical ones [*nigricans* and *latirostris* groups] descending locally to lower elevations.

Casual [*nigricans* group] north to southern British Columbia (Vancouver) and western Washington, and east to southeastern Texas and Florida; sight reports for Idaho and Minnesota.

Notes.—Groups: *S. nigricans* [Black Phoebe] and *S. latirostris* (Cabanis and Heine, 1859) [White-winged Phoebe].

Sayornis phoebe (Latham). Eastern Phoebe.

Muscicapa Phoebe Latham, 1790, Index Ornithol. 2: 489. Based on the "Dusky Flycatcher" Pennant, Arct. Zool. 2: 389, and the "Phoebe Flycatcher" Latham, Gen. Synop. Birds (suppl.) 1: 173. (in America septentrionali, Noveboraco = New York.)

Habitat.—Breeds in open deciduous woodland and farmland with scattered trees; nests on cliffs, under bridges and eaves, and sometimes inside buildings. Winters in a variety of open forest habitats.

Distribution.—*Breeds* from northeastern British Columbia, west-central and southern Mackenzie, northern Saskatchewan, northern Manitoba, western and central Ontario, southwestern Quebec, central New Brunswick and southern Nova Scotia south to southern Alberta, northeastern Wyoming, southwestern South Dakota, southeastern Colorado, northeastern New Mexico, central and northeastern Texas, northwestern Louisiana, Arkansas, southwestern Tennessee, northeastern Mississippi, central Alabama, northwestern Florida, northern Georgia, and western and northeastern South Carolina.

Winters from California (rarely), southeastern Arizona, southern New Mexico, central Texas, Arkansas, Tennessee, and Virginia (casually from Oklahoma, southern Missouri, the Ohio Valley, southern Ontario and New England) south to southern Florida, northern Oaxaca, and southern Veracruz.

Casual in northern Alaska, west to the Pacific region from southeastern Alaska, southwestern Yukon, southern British Columbia and Montana south to Baja California, and to Quintana Roo, Florida keys, Cuba, the Bahamas (Grand Bahama, Bimini, Eleuthera) and

Bermuda; accidental in the British Isles; sight reports for Sonora, Sinaloa, Newfoundland, and St. Pierre et Miquelon.

Sayornis saya (Bonaparte). Say's Phoebe.

> *Muscicapa saya* Bonaparte, 1825, Amer. Ornithol. 1: 20, pl. 11, fig. 3. (Arkansaw River, about twenty miles from the Rocky Mountains = near Pueblo, Colorado.)

Habitat.—Breeds in arid scrub and desert; nests frequently on cliffs and in abandoned mine and ranch buildings; winters in similar habitats, and in more humid open country.

Distribution.—*Breeds* from western and northern Alaska, northern Yukon, northwestern and central Mackenzie, central Alberta, central Saskatchewan and southwestern Manitoba south to southern California (absent or very rare west of the coastal ranges from southern Alaska to central California), northern Baja California, Michoacán, Guanajuato, Hidalgo, and northwestern Oaxaca (possibly), and east to North Dakota, central South Dakota, north-western Iowa, east-central Nebraska, central Kansas, western Oklahoma, western and north-ern Texas, Nuevo León, and San Luis Potosí.

Winters from southern Oregon, California, southern Utah, central (rarely northern) New Mexico and central Texas south (including islands off southern California) to southern Baja California and Veracruz.

Migrates rarely through the coastal areas of southeastern Alaska, British Columbia, Washington and Oregon, and casually east to western Minnesota, western Iowa, western Missouri, Arkansas and eastern Texas.

Casual or accidental in south-coastal Alaska and the Queen Charlotte Islands; east across the northern United States (south to Illinois and Tennessee), central and southern Ontario, and southern Quebec to Newfoundland, Nova Scotia, New Brunswick, New England, Pennsylvania and New Jersey; east along the Gulf states to east-central Florida and Georgia; and in Chiapas.

Genus *PYROCEPHALUS* Gould

> *Pyrocephalus* Gould, 1839, in Darwin, Zool. Voy. Beagle 3(9): 44. Type, by subsequent designation (G. R. Gray, 1840), "*P. coronatus* (L) Gould" = *Pyrocephalus major* Pelzeln = *Muscicapa rubinus* Boddaert.

Pyrocephalus rubinus (Boddaert). Vermilion Flycatcher.

> *Muscicapa rubinus* Boddaert, 1783, Table Planches Enlum., p. 42. Based on Daubenton, Planches Enlum., pl. 675, fig. 2. (riviere des Amazones = Teffé, Brazil.)

Habitat.— Open country, often near water; Pastures and Agricultural Lands, Riparian Thickets, Second-growth Scrub, Gallery Forest Edge, Tropical Deciduous Forest Edge, and lowland pine savanna (0–2600 m; Tropical to Temperate zones).

Distribution.—*Breeds* [*rubinus* group] from southern California (north to Santa Barbara and Kern counties), southern Nevada, extreme southwestern Utah, northern Arizona, central (rarely northeastern) New Mexico, northeastern Colorado (once), western Oklahoma, and western and central Texas south through Mexico (including Baja California and the Yucatan Peninsula) to northern Guatemala (Petén) and Belize, in the Mosquitia of eastern Honduras and northeastern Nicaragua, and in South America from northern Colombia east across northern Venezuela to Guyana and south, west of the Andes, to extreme northern Chile, and east of the Andes in north-central Brazil, and from eastern Bolivia and east-central Brazil south to central Argentina and Uruguay.

Winters [*rubinus* group] from southern California, southern Nevada, northern Arizona, southern New Mexico, central Texas, southern Arkansas (rarely) and the Gulf coast (east to southern Florida) south through the breeding range in Middle America, casually to central Guatemala and northern Honduras; and in South America, where more northern populations are essentially resident while the southern ones migrate northward, east of the Andes, to eastern Peru, eastern Colombia, and Amazonian Brazil.

Resident [*nanus* group] in the Galapagos Islands.

Casual [*rubinus* group] in North America north and east to west-central Washington, Wyoming, South Dakota, northern Minnesota, Wisconsin, southern Ontario, New York (including Long Island), Pennsylvania, West Virginia, Maryland, Kentucky, Tennessee and Georgia, also in Panama (western Panamá province and the Canal area); sight reports for Oregon, North Dakota, northern Michigan and Nova Scotia.

Notes.—Groups: *P. rubinus* [Vermilion Flycatcher] and *P. nanus* Gould, 1839 [Galapagos Flycatcher].

Genus *FLUVICOLA* Swainson

Fluvicola Swainson, 1827, Zool. J. 3: 172. Type, by subsequent designation (Swainson, 1831), *Fluvicola cursoria* Swainson = *Lanius nengeta* Linnaeus.

Fluvicola pica (Boddaert). Pied Water-Tyrant.

Muscicapa Pica Boddaert, 1783, Table Planches Enlum., p. 42. Based on Daubenton, Planches Enlum., pl. 675, fig. 1. (Cayenne.)

Habitat.—Freshwater Marshes, Riparian Thickets (0–1000 m; Tropical Zone).

Distribution.—*Resident* [*pica* group] locally in Panama (eastern Panamá province and Canal area), and in South America from northern and eastern Colombia east across northern and central Venezuela to Trinidad and extreme northern Brazil; and [*albiventer* group]from eastern Bolivia east to eastern Brazil, and south to central Argentina and Uruguay; *migrant* [*albiventer* group] in austral winter north to eastern Peru and western Amazonian Brazil.

Notes.— The two groups, *F. pica* and the South American *F. albiventer* (Spix, 1825) [Black-backed Water-Tyrant] were treated as separate species by Sibley and Monroe (1990) and Ridgely and Tudor (1994).

Genus *COLONIA* Gray

Colonia J. E. Gray, 1827, in Cuvier and Griffith, Anim. Kingdom 6: 336. Type, by monotypy, *Muscicapa colonus* Vieillot.

Colonia colonus (Vieillot). Long-tailed Tyrant.

Muscicapa colonus Vieillot, 1818, Nouv. Dict. Hist. Nat. (nouv. éd.) 21: 448. Based on "Suiriri El Colón" Azara, Apunt. Hist. Nat. Páx. Parag. 2: 114 (no. 180). (Paraguay.)

Habitat.—Tropical Lowland Evergreen Forest Edge, Montane Evergreen Forest Edge, Secondary Forest (0–900 m, to 1800 m in South America; Tropical and lower Subtropical zones).

Distribution.—*Resident* on the Caribbean slope of northeastern Honduras (Olancho, Gracias a Dios), Nicaragua and Costa Rica, on both slopes of Panama (local on Pacific slope), and in South America from Colombia, southern Venezuela and the Guianas south, west of the Andes to western Ecuador, and east of the Andes to eastern Peru, central Bolivia, Paraguay, extreme northeastern Argentina and southern Brazil (absent from central Amazonia).

Genus *MACHETORNIS* Gray

Chrysolophus (not Gray, 1834) Swainson, 1837, Class. Birds 2: 225. Type, by monotypy, *C. ambulans* Spix, II, pl. 23 = *Tyrannus rixosus* Vieillot.
Machetornis G. R. Gray, 1841, List. Gen. Birds, ed. 2, p. 41. New name for *Chrysolophus* Swainson.

Machetornis rixosus (Vieillot). Cattle Tyrant.

Tyrannus rixosus Vieillot, 1819, Nouv. Dict. Hist. Nat. (nouv. éd.) 35, p. 85. Based on "Suiriri" Azara, Apunt. Hist. Nat. Páx. Parag. 2, p. 148 (no. 197). (Paraguay.)

Habitat.—Pastures/Agricultural Lands, Second-growth Scrub (0–1000 m in South America, Tropical Zone).

Distribution.—*Resident* in northern and eastern Colombia and northern Venezuela, and from central Bolivia, Paraguay and central Brazil south to northern Argentina and Uruguay, with the southernmost populations migratory northward in winter.

Accidental in Panama near Colón, Panamá (16 September 1991, D. Engleman, photographs deposited in VIREO) and at Cana, Darién (sight report, 18 June 1981; Ridgely and Gwynne 1989: 307).

Subfamily TYRANNINAE: Tyrannine Flycatchers

Genus *ATTILA* Lesson

Attila Lesson, 1831, Traité Ornithol., livr. 5 (1830), p. 360. Type, by monotypy, *Attila brasiliensis* Lesson = *Muscicapa spadicea* Gmelin.

Notes.—The genus *Attila* was formerly placed in the Cotingidae, but cranial and syringeal morphology confirm its position within the Tyrannidae and suggest a close relationship to the genus *Myiarchus* (Lanyon 1985).

Attila spadiceus (Gmelin). Bright-rumped Attila.

Muscicapa spadicea Gmelin, 1789, Syst. Nat. 1(2): 937. Based on the "Yellow-rumped Flycatcher" Latham, Gen. Synop. Birds 2(1): 354. (in Cayenna = Cayenne.)

Habitat.—Tropical Lowland Evergreen Forest, Tropical Deciduous Forest, Montane Evergreen Forest (0–1850 m; Tropical and lower Subtropical zones).

Distribution.—*Resident* from extreme southern Sonora, Sinaloa, western Durango, Nayarit, Jalisco, Colima, Michoacán, México and southern Veracruz south along both slopes of Middle America to Panama (including the Yucatan Peninsula, Cozumel and other islands off Quintana Roo, and Coiba and Parida islands off Panama), and in South America from Colombia, Venezuela, Trinidad and the Guianas south, west of the Andes to western Ecuador, and east of the Andes to eastern Peru, northern and eastern Bolivia, and Amazonian and southeastern Brazil.

Genus *SIRYSTES* Cabanis and Heine

Sirystes Cabanis and Heine, 1859, Mus. Heineanum 2: 75. Type, by monotypy, *Muscicapa sibilator* Vieillot.

Notes.— Relationships of this genus to *Rhytipterna* and the *Myiarchus* assemblage are discussed in Lanyon and Fitzpatrick (1983) and Lanyon (1985).

Sirystes sibilator (Vieillot). Sirystes.

Muscicapa sibilator Vieillot, 1818, Nouv. Dict. Hist. Nat. (nouv. éd.) 21: 457. Based on "Suiriri Pitador" Azara, Apunt. Hist. Nat. Páx. Parag. 2: 135 (no. 191). (Paraguay.)

Habitat.—Tropical Lowland Evergreen Forest, Gallery Forest (0–1250 m; Tropical and lower Subtropical zones).

Distribution.—*Resident* [*albogriseus* group] in Panama (eastern Panama province, and from the Canal area eastward; early specimens from "Veragua" may be mislabeled), and in South America in northwestern Colombia, western Ecuador, and east of the Andes from southeastern Colombia, western Venezuela, and Surinam south to northern Bolivia and southern Amazonian Brazil; and [*sibilator* group] from central and eastern Brazil south to eastern Paraguay and northeastern Argentina.

Notes.—Groups: *S. albogriseus* (Lawrence, 1863) [White-rumped Sirystes] and *S. sibilator* [Sibilant Sirystes].

Genus *RHYTIPTERNA* Reichenbach

Rhytipterna Reichenbach, 1850, Avium Syst. Nat., pl. 65. Type, by subsequent designation (G. R. Gray, 1855), *Tyrannus calcaratus* Swainson = *Muscicapa simplex* Lichtenstein.

Notes.—See comments under *Attila* and *Sirystes*.

Rhytipterna holerythra (Sclater and Salvin). Rufous Mourner.

Lipaugus holerythra Sclater and Salvin, 1861, Proc. Zool. Soc. London (1860), p. 300. (Choctum, Vera Paz, Guatemala.)

Habitat.—Tropical Lowland Evergreen Forest, Secondary Forest (0–1200 m; Tropical and lower Subtropical zones).

Distribution.—*Resident* from southeastern Veracruz, northern Oaxaca and Chiapas south on the Caribbean slope of northern Central America to Nicaragua, on both slopes of Costa Rica (absent from dry northwest) and Panama (more widespread on Caribbean slope), and in northern and western Colombia, and northwestern Ecuador.

Genus *MYIARCHUS* Cabanis

Myiarchus Cabanis, 1844, Arch. Naturgesch. 10: 272. Type, by subsequent designation (G. R. Gray, 1855), *Muscicapa ferox* Gmelin.
Hylonax Ridgway, 1905, Proc. Biol. Soc. Wash. 18: 210. Type, by original designation, *Myiarchus validus* Cabanis.

Notes.—We follow Lanyon (1967, 1978; literature summarized in Lanyon 1985) for specific and generic limits in *Myiarchus* and its relatives.

Myiarchus yucatanensis Lawrence. Yucatan Flycatcher.

Myiarchus yucatanensis Lawrence, 1871, Proc. Acad. Nat. Sci. Philadelphia 22: 235. (Yucatan = Merida, Yucatán.)

Habitat.—Tropical Deciduous Forest, Secondary Forest (0–250 m; Tropical Zone).

Distribution.—*Resident* on the Yucatan Peninsula (Campeche, Yucatán, and Quintana Roo), Cozumel Island, northern Guatemala (Petén), and northern Belize (Gallon Jug, Ambergris Cay).

Myiarchus barbirostris (Swainson). Sad Flycatcher.

Tyrannula barbirostris Swainson, 1827, Philos. Mag. (n. s.) 1: 367. (Mexico, error = Jamaica.)

Habitat.—Tropical Lowland Evergreen Forest, Montane Evergreen Forest, Secondary Forest (0–2000 m).

Distribution.—*Resident* on Jamaica.

Notes.—See comments under *M. tuberculifer*.

Myiarchus tuberculifer (d'Orbigny and Lafresnaye). Dusky-capped Flycatcher.

Tyrannus tuberculifer d'Orbigny and Lafresnaye, 1837, Mag. Zool. [Paris] 7(2): pl. 77–79, p. 43. (Guarayos, [Santa Cruz], Bolivia.)

Habitat.—Montane Evergreen Forest, Tropical Lowland Evergreen Forest, Tropical Deciduous Forest, Pine-Oak Forest, Secondary Forest (0–3400 m; Tropical and Subtropical zones).

Distribution.—*Breeds* [*tuberculifer* group] from southeastern Arizona, southwestern New Mexico, northern Sonora, Chihuahua, Coahuila, western Texas (possibly), central Nuevo León and central Tamaulipas south along both slopes of Middle America (including the Tres Marias Islands off Nayarit, the Yucatan Peninsula and Cozumel Island, and most islands off the Pacific coast of Panama), and in South America from Colombia, Venezuela, Trinidad and the Guianas south, west of the Andes to southern Ecuador, and east of the Andes to northern Bolivia and Amazonian and southeastern Brazil.

Winters [*tuberculifer* group] from southern Sonora, Durango, southern Nuevo León and southern Tamaulipas south through the breeding range; the populations in the southwestern United States, extreme northern Mexico, and the Yucatan Peninsula migrate southward in winter; southernmost populations in South America range somewhat northward in austral winter.

Resident [*atriceps* group] along eastern slope of the Andes from southern Ecuador south through Peru and Bolivia to northwestern Argentina.

Casual or accidental [*tuberculifer* group] in California (north to Humboldt County), central Arizona (north to Gila County and west to Yuma County), southeastern Colorado, Baja California (Sierra Laguna), and on Isla Isabela (off Nayarit).

Notes.—Also known as Olivaceous Flycatcher. Groups: *M. tuberculifer* [Dusky-capped Flycatcher] and *M. atriceps* Cabanis, 1883 [Dark-capped Flycatcher]. *M. tuberculifer* and *M. barbirostris* are closely related and constitute a superspecies.

Myiarchus panamensis Lawrence. Panama Flycatcher.

Myiarchus panamensis Lawrence, 1860, Ann. Lyc. Nat. Hist. N. Y. 7: 284. (Isthmus of Panama.)

Habitat.—Tropical Deciduous Forest, Gallery Forest, Secondary Forest, Mangrove Forest, Arid Lowland Scrub (0–1400 m; Tropical and lower Subtropical zones).

Distribution.—*Resident* in Costa Rica (Pacific coast only, from the Gulf of Nicoya southward, primarily in mangroves), Panama (both slopes, including Coiba, Taboga and the Pearl islands), northern and northwestern Colombia, and northwestern Venezuela.

Notes.—Closely related to the widespread South American *M. ferox* (Gmelin, 1789), from which it differs primarily in vocalizations. *M. panamensis* and *M. ferox* constitute a superspecies.

Myiarchus cinerascens (Lawrence). Ash-throated Flycatcher.

Tyrannula cinerascens Lawrence, 1851, Ann. Lyc. Nat. Hist. N. Y. 5: 121. (Western Texas.)

Habitat.—Breeds in desert scrub, pinyon-juniper and oak woodland, chaparral, thorn scrub, and riparian woodland; winters in similar habitats, also open deciduous woodland.

Distribution.—*Breeds* from northwestern Oregon, eastern Washington, southern Idaho, southern Wyoming, western and southern Colorado, western Kansas, western Oklahoma, and northern and central Texas south to southern Baja California, southern Sonora, and in the Mexican highlands to northern Jalisco, northern Michoacán (at least formerly), northern Guanajuato, southern San Luis Potosí, and southern Tamaulipas.

Winters from southern California (rarely), central Arizona, Chihuahua, Nuevo León and southern Tamaulipas (casually farther north in the breeding range) south throughout most of western and interior Mexico and interior Guatemala, and on the Pacific slope to Honduras, casually to Nicaragua and northern Costa Rica (San Carlos).

Casual north to southern British Columbia and Montana; east to Minnesota, Illinois, West Virginia and the northeastern Atlantic region (recorded southern Ontario, New York, Massachusetts, and New Brunswick south to Maryland and South Carolina; sight reports for Quebec, Maine, Tennessee, Virginia, North Carolina and Bermuda); and southeast along the Gulf coast to southern Alabama and Florida.

Notes.—*M. cinerascens* and *M. nuttingi* constitute a superspecies.

Myiarchus nuttingi Ridgway. Nutting's Flycatcher.

Myiarchus nuttingi Ridgway, 1883, in Nutting, Proc. U. S. Natl. Mus. 5 (1882): 394. ([Hacienda] La Palma[, Golfo] de Nicoya, W[estern]. Costa Rica.)

Habitat.—Tropical Deciduous Forest, Gallery Forest, Arid Lowland Scrub, Second-growth Scrub (0–1800 m; Tropical and lower Subtropical zones).

Distribution.—*Resident* from central Sonora and southwestern Chihuahua south along the Pacific slope of Mexico (also through the interior in México, Morelos and Puebla, and to the Gulf drainage in southern San Luis Potosí and Hidalgo), and in the Pacific lowlands and interior valleys of Guatemala, El Salvador, Honduras, Nicaragua, and northwestern Costa Rica (arid zone, south to Canas).

Casual in Arizona (Roosevelt Lake, Elgin); a report from Baja California pertains to *M. cinerascens*.

Notes.—Also known as Pale-throated Flycatcher. See comments under *M. cinerascens*.

Myiarchus crinitus (Linnaeus). Great Crested Flycatcher.

Turdus crinitus Linnaeus, 1758, Syst. Nat. (ed. 10) 1: 170. Based on "The Crested Fly-catcher" Catesby, Nat. Hist. Carolina 1: 52, pl. 52. (in America = South Carolina.)

Habitat.—Breeds in deciduous and evergreen broadleaf forest, including open woodland, parks and orchards; winters in lowland forest and woodland.

Distribution.—*Breeds* from east-central Alberta, central and southeastern Saskatchewan, southern Manitoba, western and southern Ontario, southwestern Quebec, northern Maine, central New Brunswick, Prince Edward Island, and southern Nova Scotia south to north-eastern Coahuila (probably), central and southeastern Texas, the Gulf coast and the Florida Keys, and west to central North Dakota, eastern South Dakota, northeastern Colorado, western Kansas, and west-central Oklahoma.

Winters in central and southern Florida, and from southern Veracruz, southwestern Oaxaca and the Yucatan Peninsula south along both slopes of Middle America (more commonly on the Gulf-Caribbean) to Colombia and northern Venezuela.

Migrates through eastern New Mexico (rarely) and eastern Mexico (west at least to Nuevo León and Guanajuato), casually west to Montana, Wyoming, Colorado and Arizona.

Casual or accidental in south-central Alaska (Middleton Island), northern Mackenzie (Coppermine), California (primarily coastal areas), southern Arizona (Huachuca Mountains), Montana, Newfoundland and Cuba; sight reports from the Bahamas (New Providence, Eleuthera), Puerto Rico and Ecuador (Napo).

Myiarchus tyrannulus (Müller). Brown-crested Flycatcher.

Muscicapa tyrannulus P. L. S. Müller, 1776, Natursyst., Suppl., p. 169. Based on Daubenton, Planches Enlum., pl. 571, fig. 1. (Cayenne.)

Habitat.—Tropical Deciduous Forest, Gallery Forest, Secondary Forest, Arid Lowland Scrub, Mangrove Forest (0–1700 m; Tropical and lower Subtropical zones).

Distribution.—*Breeds* [*magister* group] from southeastern California (north to San Bernardino and Kern counties), extreme southern Nevada, extreme southwestern Utah, Arizona and southwestern New Mexico south along the Pacific slope of Mexico (including the Tres Marias Islands) to Oaxaca (west of the Isthmus of Tehuantepec), and east to western Durango, Zacatecas, Morelos and southwestern Puebla, and from eastern Coahuila and southern Texas (north to Bexar County) south on the Gulf-Caribbean slope (including the Yucatan Peninsula and Cozumel and Cancun islands) to northern Honduras (also the Bay Islands), thence across the Sula Valley of Honduras to the Pacific lowlands of El Salvador and Honduras.

Winters [*magister* group] from northern Mexico south through the breeding range (wandering outside this range in Mexico and Guatemala), and casually in southern Florida.

Resident [*brachyurus* group] on the Pacific slope of Nicaragua (including Isla Ometepe in Lago de Nicaragua) and northwestern Costa Rica; and [*tyrannulus* group] in South America from northern Colombia, Venezuela (including islands from Aruba east to Tobago and Trinidad) and the Guianas southeast to the lower Amazon basin and eastern Brazil, thence south and west across central and southeastern Brazil to southeastern Peru, Bolivia and northern Argentina.

Casual or accidental [*magister* group] in British Columbia (Vancouver), coastal California (north to the Farallon Islands), coastal Texas and southern Louisiana.

Notes.—Also known as Wied's Crested Flycatcher. The Middle American group may represent a species, *M. magister* Ridgway, 1884 [Wied's Flycatcher], distinct from the South American *M. tyrannulus* [Brown-crested Flycatcher]; populations from the Pacific slope of northern Central America have sometimes been regarded as a species, *M. brachyurus* Ridgway, 1887 [Ometepe Flycatcher], but intergradation with *tyrannulus* occurs in El Salvador and Honduras. The Lesser Antillean *M. nugator* and *M. tyrannulus* [sensu lato] constitute a superspecies.

Myiarchus nugator Riley. Grenada Flycatcher.

> *Myiarchus oberi nugator* Riley, 1904, Smithson. Misc. Collect. 47: 275. (Grenada, West Indies.)

Habitat.—Tropical Lowland Evergreen Forest, Secondary Forest (0–900 m; Tropical Zone).

Distribution.—*Resident* in the southern Lesser Antilles (Grenada, the Grenadines, and St. Vincent).

Notes.—See comments under *M. tyrannulus.*

Myiarchus validus Cabanis. Rufous-tailed Flycatcher.

> *Myiarchus validus* Cabanis, 1847, Arch. Naturgesch. 13: 351. ("one of the West Indian islands" = Jamaica.)

Habitat.—Tropical Lowland Evergreen Forest, Montane Evergreen Forest, Secondary Forest (0–2000 m; Tropical and Subtropical zones).

Distribution.—*Resident* on Jamaica.

Myiarchus sagrae (Gundlach). La Sagra's Flycatcher.

> *Muscicapa sagræ* Gundlach, 1852, J. Boston Soc. Nat. Hist. 6: 313. (Cuba.)

Habitat.—Tropical Lowland Evergreen Forest, Secondary Forest, Pine Forest, Mangrove Forest (0–1500 m; Tropical and lower Subtropical zones).

Distribution.—*Resident* in the Bahama Islands (common throughout the northern islands, irregularly in the southern ones, absent from Turks and Caicos), and on Cuba (including offshore cays), the Isle of Pines, and Grand Cayman.

Casual in southern Florida (north to Boca Raton), accidental in Alabama (Oroville, Dallas County).

Notes.— *M. stolidus, M. sagrae, M. antillarum* and *M. oberi* constitute a superspecies.

Myiarchus stolidus (Gosse). Stolid Flycatcher.

> *Myiobius stolidus* Gosse, 1847, Birds Jamaica, p. 168 (footnote). (Jamaica.)

Habitat.—Tropical Deciduous Forest, Secondary Forest, Tropical Lowland Evergreen Forest Edge, Mangrove Forest (0–1800 m; Tropical Zone).

Distribution.—*Resident* on Jamaica and Hispaniola (including Gonâve, Tortue, Grande Cayemite and Beata islands).

Notes.—See comments under *M. sagrae.*

Myiarchus antillarum (Bryant). Puerto Rican Flycatcher.

> *Tyrannus antillarum* Bryant, 1866, Proc. Boston Soc. Nat. Hist. 10: 249. (Porto Rico.)

Habitat.—Tropical Deciduous Forest, Arid Lowland Scrub, Mangrove Forest, Tropical Lowland Evergreen Forest (0–800 m; Tropical Zone).

Distribution.—*Resident* on Puerto Rico (including Vieques and Culebra islands), and in the Virgin Islands (St. Thomas, St. John, Tortola and Virgin Gorda).

Notes.— See comments under *M. sagrae.*

Myiarchus oberi Lawrence. Lesser Antillean Flycatcher.

> *Myiarchus oberi* Lawrence, 1878, Ann. N. Y. Acad. Sci. 1 (1877): 48. (Dominica.)

Habitat.—Tropical Lowland Evergreen Forest (0–900 m; Tropical Zone).

Distribution.—*Resident* in the Lesser Antilles (St. Kitts, Nevis, Barbuda, Guadeloupe, Dominica, Martinique and St. Lucia).

Notes.— See comments under *M. sagrae.*

Genus *DELTARHYNCHUS* Ridgway

Deltarhynchus Ridgway, 1893, Proc. U. S. Natl. Mus. 16: 606. Type, by original designation, *Myiarchus flammulatus* Lawrence.

Notes.— See comments under *Myiarchus*.

Deltarhynchus flammulatus (Lawrence). Flammulated Flycatcher.

Myiarchus flammulatus Lawrence, 1875, Ann. Lyc. Nat. Hist. N. Y. 11: 71. ([Rancho de] Cacoprieto, Tehuantepec [= Oaxaca], Mexico.)

Habitat.—Tropical Deciduous Forest (0–1400 m; Tropical Zone).
Distribution.—*Resident* in the Pacific lowlands of Mexico from Sinaloa south to western Chiapas.

Genus *PITANGUS* Swainson

Pitangus Swainson, 1827, Zool. J. 3: 165. Type, by original designation, *Tyrannus sulphuratus* Vieillot = *Lanius sulphuratus* Linnaeus.
Philohydor Lanyon, 1984, Amer. Mus. Novit., no. 2797. p. 23. Type, by original designation, *Lanius lictor* Lichtenstein.

Pitangus lictor (Lichtenstein). Lesser Kiskadee.

Lanius Lictor Lichtenstein, 1823, Verz. Doubl. Zool. Mus. Berlin, p. 49. (Pará [= Belém], Brazil.)

Habitat.—Riparian Thickets, Freshwater Marshes (Tropical Zone).
Distribution.—*Resident* in eastern Panama (west to the Canal area), and in South America from Colombia, Venezuela, and the Guianas south, east of the Andes, to eastern Peru, northern Bolivia, and southern Brazil.
Notes.— Placed in a new, monotypic genus, *Philohydor,* by Lanyon (1984) on the basis of differences in the syrinx and nest structure between *lictor* and *P. sulphuratus.* Lanyon showed that the two species are closely related, however, and we recognize their close relationship by maintaining them in a single genus.

Pitangus sulphuratus (Linnaeus). Great Kiskadee.

Lanius sulphuratus Linnaeus, 1766, Syst. Nat. (ed. 12) 1: 137. Based on "La Piegriesche jaune de Cayenne" Brisson, Ornithologie 2: 176, pl. 16, fig. 4. (in Cayania = Cayenne.)

Habitat.—Secondary Forest, Riparian Thickets, Gallery Forest, Second-growth Scrub, most common near water (0–1600 m; Tropical and lower Subtropical zones).
Distribution.—*Resident* from southern Sonora, Sinaloa, Durango, Zacatecas, Nuevo León and southern Texas (north to Webb County and the Corpus Christi area) south along both slopes of Middle America (including the Yucatan Peninsula and Isla Cancun), and in South America from Colombia, Venezuela, Trinidad and the Guianas south, east of the Andes, to central Argentina.
Introduced and established (from Trinidad stock) on Bermuda.
Casual north to southern Arizona, southeastern New Mexico, west-central, central and southeastern Texas, western Oklahoma and southern Louisiana, also in Chile; sight reports for Baja California and New Jersey, which may be escaped individuals; a bird remaining from 1957 to 1959 in northern California is regarded as an escape; the single Florida record (Fort Lauderdale, winter of 1960–61) was photographed, but its origin was suspect.
Notes.—Also known as Kiskadee Flycatcher.

Genus *MEGARYNCHUS* Thunberg

Megarynchus Thunberg, 1824, Dissert. Megaryncho Schaerstrom, p. 2. Type, by subsequent designation (Heine, 1859), *Lanius pitangua* Linnaeus.

Notes.— This genus is often misspelled; "*Megarhynchus*" is incorrect.

Megarynchus pitangua (Linnaeus). Boat-billed Flycatcher.

Lanius Pitangva [sic] Linnaeus, 1766, Syst. Nat. (ed. 12) 1: 136. Based in part on "La Tyran du Brésil" Brisson, Ornithologie 2: 401, pl. 36, fig. 5. (in Brasilia = Rio de Janeiro, Brazil.)

Habitat.—Tropical Lowland Evergreen Forest Edge, Secondary Forest, Gallery Forest Edge, Tropical Deciduous Forest, River-edge Forest (0–1850 m; Tropical and Subtropical zones).

Distribution.—*Resident* from southern Sinaloa, southeastern San Luis Potosí and southern Tamaulipas south along both slopes of Middle America (including the Yucatan Peninsula and Isla Cébaco, off Panama), and in South America west of the Andes to northwestern Peru, and east of the Andes in Colombia, Venezuela, Trinidad and the Guianas south to eastern Bolivia, Paraguay, northeastern Argentina and southern Brazil.

Casual on Isla Cancun, off Quintana Roo.

Genus *MYIOZETETES* Sclater

Myiozetetes Sclater, 1859, Proc. Zool. Soc. London, p. 46. Type, by original designation, *Elainia cayennensis* Auct. = *Muscicapa cayanensis* Linnaeus.

Myiozetetes cayanensis (Linnaeus). Rusty-margined Flycatcher.

Muscicapa cayanensis Linnaeus, 1766, Syst. Nat. (ed. 12) 1: 327. Based on "Le Gobemouche de Cayenne" Brisson, Ornithologie, 2, p. 404, pl. 38, fig. 4. (in Cayana = Cayenne.)

Habitat.—Second-growth Scrub, Tropical Lowland Evergreen Forest Edge, Secondary Forest, usually near water (0–1500 m; Tropical and lower Subtropical zones).

Distribution.—*Resident* in Panama (west on the Caribbean slope to the Canal area, and on the Pacific to eastern Chiriquí), and in South America from Colombia, Venezuela and the Guianas south, west of the Andes to southwestern Ecuador, and east of the Andes across eastern and southern Amazonian Brazil to eastern Bolivia and central and southeastern Brazil.

Myiozetetes similis (Spix). Social Flycatcher.

Muscicapa similis Spix, 1825, Avium Spec. Nov. Bras. 2: 18. (Amazon Valley = mouth of the Rio Madeira, Brazil.)

Habitat.—Tropical Lowland Evergreen Forest Edge, Tropical Deciduous Forest Edge, Gallery Forest, Secondary Forest; abundant around settlements (0–1800 m; Tropical and lower Subtropical zones).

Distribution.—*Resident* [*texensis* group] from southern Sonora, Sinaloa, western Durango, Zacatecas, southeastern San Luis Potosí and southern Tamaulipas south along both slopes of Middle America (including the Yucatan Peninsula and Isla Cancun) to Costa Rica (except southwestern portion); and [*similis* group] from southwestern Costa Rica (Golfo Dulce region southward) to central Panama (east to eastern Colón and eastern Panamá province), and in South America from Colombia and Venezuela south, west of the Andes to northwestern Peru and east of the Andes to eastern Peru, northern Bolivia, eastern Paraguay, extreme northeastern Argentina and southern Brazil; the southernmost populations in South America migrate northward in nonbreeding season.

Notes.— The two groups differ somewhat in vocalizations and may be distinct species, *M. texensis* (Giraud, 1841) [Vermilion-crowned Flycatcher] and *M. similis* [Social Flycatcher].

Myiozetetes granadensis Lawrence. Gray-capped Flycatcher.

Myiozetetes granadensis Lawrence, 1862, Ibis, p. 11. (Isthmus of Panama = Lion Hill, Canal Zone.)

Habitat.—River-edge Forest, Tropical Lowland Evergreen Forest Edge, Secondary Forest (0–1650 m; Tropical and lower Subtropical zones).

Distribution.—*Resident* on the Caribbean slope of eastern Honduras (Olancho, Gracias a Dios) and Nicaragua, on both slopes of Costa Rica (on Pacific slope south of the Central Highlands) and Panama (more commonly on the Caribbean), and in South America west of the Andes from northern Colombia south to northwestern Ecuador and northwestern Peru, and east of the Andes from southern Colombia, and southern Venezuela south to eastern Peru, northern Bolivia, and western Amazonian Brazil.

Genus *CONOPIAS* Cabanis and Heine

Conopias Cabanis and Heine, 1859, Mus. Heineanum 2: 62. Type, by monotypy, *Tyrannula superciliosa* Swainson = *Muscicapa trivirgata* Wied.
Coryphotriccus Ridgway, 1906, Proc. Biol. Soc. Wash. 19: 115. Type, by original designation, *Pitangus albovitattus* Lawrence.

Conopias albovittata (Lawrence). White-ringed Flycatcher.

Pitangus albovittatus Lawrence, 1862, Ibis, p. 11. (Isthmus of Panama = Canal Zone.)

Habitat.—Tropical Lowland Evergreen Forest, Secondary Forest (0–1000 m; Tropical and lower Subtropical zones).

Distribution.—*Resident* [*albovittata* group] in eastern Honduras (Olancho, Gracias a Dios), Costa Rica (Caribbean slope), central and eastern Panama (west to the Canal area and eastern Panamá province), western Colombia and northwestern Ecuador; and [*parva* group] in South America locally east of the Andes in southeastern Colombia, eastern Ecuador, northeastern Peru, southern Venezuela, the Guianas, and northern and western Amazonian Brazil.

Notes.— Called *C. parva* by Traylor (*in* Traylor 1979b), but *albovittata* has priority; this also overlooked by other authors (e.g. Wetmore 1972) who placed this species in the genus *Coryphotriccus* Ridgway, 1906. *Coryphotriccus* was merged into *Conopias* without comment by Traylor (1977) and by Lanyon (1984). The groups, *C. albovittata* [White-ringed Flycatcher] and *C. parva* (Pelzeln, 1868) [Yellow-throated Flycatcher], are recognized as two species by Sibley and Monroe (1990) and Ridgely and Tudor (1994).

Genus *MYIODYNASTES* Bonaparte

Myiodynastes Bonaparte, 1857, Bull. Soc. Linn. Normandie 2: 35. Type, by monotypy, *Myiodynastes audax* Bp. ex Gm. = *Muscicapa audax* Gmelin = *Muscicapa maculata* Müller.

Myiodynastes hemichrysus (Cabanis). Golden-bellied Flycatcher.

Hypermitres hemichrysus Cabanis, 1862, J. Ornithol. 9 (1861): 247. (Los Frailes, Costa Rica.)

Habitat.—Montane Evergreen Forest (700–1850 m; upper Tropical and Subtropical zones).

Distribution.—*Resident* on both slopes in the highlands of Costa Rica (from Cordillera de Guanacaste southward, more common on Caribbean slope) and western Panama (east to Veraguas).

Notes.—*M. hemichrysus* and *M. chrysocephalus* constitute a superspecies.

Myiodynastes chrysocephalus (Tschudi). Golden-crowned Flycatcher.

Scaphorhynchus chrysocephalus Tschudi, 1844, Arch. Naturgesch. 10: 272. (Republica Peruana = Chanchamayo, depto. de Junín, Peru.)

Habitat.—Montane Evergreen Forest, Secondary Forest (800–2400 m; upper Tropical and Subtropical zones).

Distribution.—*Resident* in extreme eastern Panama (cerros Pirre, Tacarcuna, and Malí in eastern Darién), and in South America from Colombia and northern Venezuela south, in the western Andes to western Ecuador, and in the eastern Andes to eastern Peru and northern Bolivia (also a sight report in northern Argentina).

Notes.—See comments under *M. hemichrysus.*

Myiodynastes maculatus (Müller). Streaked Flycatcher.

Muscicapa maculata P. L. S. Müller, 1776, Natursyst., Suppl., p. 169. Based on "Gobe-mouche tachetée de Cayenne" Daubenton, Planches Enlum., pl. 453, fig. 2. (Cayenne.)

Habitat.—Tropical Lowland Evergreen Forest Edge, Secondary Forest, Gallery Forest, River-edge Forest (0–1500 m; Tropical and lower Subtropical zones).

Distribution.—*Breeds* [*maculatus* group] on the Gulf-Caribbean slope from southern San Luis Potosí, southern Tamaulipas, Puebla, northern Oaxaca, the Yucatan Peninsula (except the northwest), northern Guatemala, and Belize to northern Honduras, and in Costa Rica (Pacific slope from Gulf of Nicoya southward) and Panama (both slopes, and Coiba, Cébaco and the Pearl islands), and in South America from Colombia, Venezuela (including Margarita Island), Tobago, Trinidad and the Guianas south, west of the Andes to northwestern Peru, and east of the Andes to northeastern Peru and Amazonian Brazil; and [*solitarius* group] in central Bolivia, central and southern Brazil, Paraguay, Uruguay, and northern Argentina.

Winters [*maculatus* group] from northern Costa Rica and Panama south through the breeding range in South America to Peru, Bolivia and southern Brazil; the southernmost breeding populations [*solitarius* group] migrate north to northern South America.

Accidental [*solitarius* group] in Chile.

Notes.— Groups: *M. maculatus* [Streaked Flycatcher] and *M. solitarius* (Vieillot, 1819) [Solitary Flycatcher].

Myiodynastes luteiventris Sclater. Sulphur-bellied Flycatcher.

Myiodynastes luteiventris Sclater, 1859, Proc. Zool. Soc. London, p. 42. (In Mexico merid., Guatemala, et America centrali = Orizaba, Veracruz.)

Habitat.—Tropical Deciduous Forest, Gallery Forest, Tropical Lowland Evergreen Forest Edge (0–1850 m; Tropical and Subtropical zones).

Distribution.—*Breeds* from southeastern Arizona, eastern Sonora, western Chihuahua, Nuevo León and Tamaulipas south along both slopes of Middle America (including the Yucatan Peninsula) to central Costa Rica (south to the Central Valley and Reventazon drainage).

Winters in South America east of the Andes from eastern Ecuador to northern Bolivia and (probably) extreme western Amazonian Brazil.

Migrates regularly through all of Middle America and northern and eastern Colombia.

Casual north to southern California (north to Santa Barbara County), central Arizona, southwestern New Mexico, western and southern Texas, and the Gulf coast of Texas, Louisiana, and Alabama. Accidental in Ontario and New Brunswick.

Genus *LEGATUS* Sclater

Legatus Sclater, 1859, Proc. Zool. Soc. London, p. 46. Type, by original designation, *Legatus albicollis* (Vieillot) = *Tyrannus albicollis* Vieillot = *Platyrhynchos leucophaius* Vieillot.

Legatus leucophaius (Vieillot). Piratic Flycatcher.

Platyrhynchos leucophaius Vieillot, 1818, Nouv. Dict. Hist. Nat. (nouv. éd.) 27: 11. (l'Amérique méridionale = Cayenne.)

Habitat.—Tropical Lowland Evergreen Forest Edge, Gallery Forest, Secondary Forest (0–1500 m; Tropical and lower Subtropical zones).

Distribution.—*Breeds* on the Gulf-Caribbean slope of Middle America from southern

San Luis Potosí, Veracruz, Puebla, northern Oaxaca, Tabasco, Chiapas (also Pacific slope) and southern Quintana Roo south to Nicaragua, on both slopes of Costa Rica and Panama, and in South America from Colombia, Venezuela, Trinidad and the Guianas south, west of the Andes to western Ecuador, and east of the Andes to northern Argentina, Paraguay and southern Brazil.

Winters generally throughout the breeding range in South America, recorded only casually anywhere in Middle America between October and March. Movements of populations within South America are poorly understood.

Possibly accidental in southern Florida (Dry Tortugas; see *Empidonomus varius*).

Genus *EMPIDONOMUS* Cabanis and Heine

Empidonomus Cabanis and Heine, 1859, Mus. Heineanum 2: 76. Type, by monotypy, *Muscicapa varia* Vieillot.

Empidonomus varius (Vieillot). Variegated Flycatcher.

Muscicapa varia Vieillot, 1818, Nouv. Dict. Hist. Nat. (nouv. éd.) 21: 458. Based on "Suiriri Chorreado debaxo" Azara, Apunt. Hist. Nat. Páx. Parag. 2: 125 (no. 187). (Paraguay.)

Habitat.—Tropical Deciduous Forest Edge, Tropical Lowland Evergreen Forest Edge, Gallery Forest, Secondary Forest (0–1200 m; Tropical Zone).

Distribution.—*Resident* throughout most of South America east of the Andes, the southernmost populations migrating northward in winter as far as the northern South American coast and Trinidad.

Accidental in Maine (Biddeford Pool, 5–11 November 1977, photograph; Abbott and Finch 1978), Tennessee (Reelfoot Lake, May 1983, photograph; Nicholson and Steadman 1988: 3), and southern Florida (Garden Key, Dry Tortugas, 15 March 1991; Bradbury 1992); the Florida record is debated, and may represent *Legatus leucophaius*.

Genus *TYRANNUS* Lacépède

Tyrannus Lacépède, 1799, Tabl. Mamm. Ois., p. 5. Type, by tautonymy, *Lanius tyrannus* Linnaeus.

Muscivora Lacépède, 1799, Tabl. Mamm. Ois., p. 5. Type, by subsequent designation (Fischer, 1831), *Muscicapa forficata* Gmelin.

Tolmarchus Ridgway, 1905, Proc. Biol. Soc. Wash. 18: 209. Type, by original designation, *Pitangus taylori* Sclater = *Tyrannus caudifasciatus* d'Orbigny.

Tyrannus melancholicus Vieillot. Tropical Kingbird.

Tyrannus melancholicus Vieillot, 1819, Nouv. Dict. Hist. Nat. (nouv. éd.) 35: 84. Based on "Suirirí-guazú" Azara, Apunt. Hist. Nat. Páx. Parag. 2: 152 (no. 198). (Paraguay.)

Habitat.—Secondary Forest, Second-growth Scrub, River-edge Forest Edge, Tropical Lowland Evergreen Forest Edge; common around settlements with scattered trees (0–1800 m, to 2200 m in winter; Tropical and Subtropical zones).

Distribution.—*Breeds* from southeastern (rarely central) Arizona, Sonora, eastern San Luis Potosí and rarely southern Texas (Brownsville) south on both slopes of Middle America (including the Tres Marias Islands, Yucatan Peninsula, and most islands off the Middle American coast), and in South America from Colombia, Venezuela (also Netherlands Antilles east to Tobago, Trinidad and probably Grenada), and the Guianas south, west of the Andes to central Peru, and east of the Andes to central Argentina.

Winters from Baja California, Sonora, and northeastern Mexico (north at least to central Tamaulipas) south through the Middle American and South American breeding range; southernmost populations in South America migrate north to Amazonia.

Casual (mostly in fall and winter) along the Pacific coast from southern British Columbia (including Vancouver Island) south through California, and in Cuba; accidental in Maine (Scarborough), Connecticut (New Haven), North Carolina (Fairfield) and Louisiana. Sight reports or photographic records for southern Nevada, southwestern New Mexico, the Gulf coast east to southern Florida, the Florida Keys, Quebec, Nova Scotia and Massachusetts cannot be verified as to species, and may represent *T. couchii*.

Notes.—Populations in Arizona and western Mexico (south to Guerrero) were formerly regarded as a separate species, *T. occidentalis* Hartert and Goodson, 1917 [West Mexican Kingbird]. *T. melancholicus* and *T. couchii* long were believed to be conspecific, but these forms are widely sympatric (possibly with limited hybridization) in eastern and southern Mexico (Traylor 1979a).

Tyrannus couchii Baird. Couch's Kingbird.

> *Tyrannus couchii* Baird, 1858, in Baird, Cassin and Lawrence, Rep. Explor. Surv. R. R. Pac. 9: xxx, 170, 175. (Northeastern Mexico to Rio Grande = New Leon and San Diego, [Nuevo León,] Mexico.)

Habitat.—Gallery Forest, Tropical Deciduous Forest, Secondary Forest, Riparian Thickets (0–800 m; Tropical and lower Subtropical zones).

Distribution.—*Resident* from southern Texas (north to Val Verde, Webb, Jim Wells and southern Nueces counties), Nuevo León and Tamaulipas south on the Gulf-Caribbean slope of eastern and southeastern Mexico (including the Yucatan Peninsula and most islands off the coast) to northern Guatemala (Petén) and Belize. Populations in southern Texas and northern Mexico migrate casually southward, but seasonal movements within central and southern Mexico unclear.

Casual in central New Mexico, central and southeastern Texas, Louisiana, and Florida.

Notes.—See comments under *T. melancholicus*.

Tyrannus vociferans Swainson. Cassin's Kingbird.

> *Tyrannus vociferans* Swainson, 1826, Q. J. Sci. Lit. Arts R. Inst. 20: 273. (Temascáltepec, México.)

Habitat.—Breeds in dry savanna, scrub, riparian woodland, and pinyon-juniper-oak woodland; winters in similar habitats, and in highland pine-oak woodland (0–2500 m; Tropical and Subtropical zones).

Distribution.—*Breeds* from central California, southern Nevada, northern Arizona, southern Utah, central and eastern Wyoming, southeastern Montana, southwestern South Dakota, northwestern Nebraska (probably), extreme western Oklahoma, and western Texas south to northwestern Baja California, and through the Mexican highlands to Michoacán, Oaxaca, Puebla, and central Tamaulipas.

Winters from central California (irregularly), southern Baja California, southern Arizona (casually) and northern Mexico south to central Guatemala, casually to Honduras (Comayagüela).

Migrates casually east to western South Dakota, southwestern Kansas, Arkansas and southwestern Louisiana.

Accidental in Oregon, northern California, Ontario, Massachusetts and Florida; sight reports for Idaho, Arkansas, Wisconsin and Virginia.

Tyrannus crassirostris Swainson. Thick-billed Kingbird.

> *Tyrannus crassirostris* Swainson, 1826, Q. J. Sci. Lit. Arts R. Inst. 20: 273. (Mexico = Acapulco, Guerrero.)

Habitat.—Gallery Forest, Tropical Deciduous Forest Edge (0–1850 m; Tropical and lower Subtropical zones).

Distribution.—*Breeds* from southeastern Arizona (Patagonia, Guadalupe Mountains), southwestern New Mexico (Guadalupe Canyon), Sonora, southwestern Chihuahua, western Texas (Big Bend), Sinaloa, and western Durango south to Guerrero, México, Morelos, southern Puebla and western Oaxaca.

Winters from Sonora south through the breeding range to Chiapas, casually to south-central Guatemala (Escuintla).

Casual or accidental in southwestern British Columbia (Vancouver Island), California (north to San Francisco), Baja California and south-central and southern Arizona (north to Pinal County); a sight report for central Colorado (Jefferson County).

Tyrannus verticalis Say. Western Kingbird.

Tyrannus verticalis Say, 1823, in Long, Exped. Rocky Mount. 2: 60. (Ash River, near Rocky Mts. = near La Junta, Colorado.)

Habitat.—Breeds in open country with scattered trees, especially savanna and agricultural lands. Winters in similar habitats, also Tropical Deciduous Forest and Second Growth Scrub, often flocking at fruiting trees (0–1800 m).

Distribution.—*Breeds* from western Washington, southern interior British Columbia, southern Alberta, southern Saskatchewan, southern Manitoba, and western Minnesota south to northern Baja California, Sonora, northwestern Chihuahua, southern New Mexico, and southern and south-central Texas, rarely or sporadically eastward to east-central Minnesota, southern Wisconsin, Illinois, southern Michigan, western and southern Ontario, western Missouri, and southwestern Louisiana.

Winters from Guerrero and southern Mexico (except the Yucatan Peninsula) south, primarily along the Pacific slope, through Middle America (except Belize and northern Guatemala) to central and southwestern Costa Rica, and in small numbers along the Atlantic and Gulf coasts from South Carolina to southern Florida and west to southern Louisiana.

Migrates regularly in small numbers (chiefly in fall) through northeastern North America from the Great Lakes region, southern Quebec, New Brunswick and Nova Scotia south to North Carolina, casually in the Bahamas, Swan Islands (western Caribbean Sea) and Cuba (sight report).

Casual in summer north to central Alaska and the northern portions of the Canadian provinces (east to Ontario and Newfoundland). Accidental on Bathurst Island. In winter, casual north to central California, northern Mexico and southern Texas; a sight report for central Panama.

Tyrannus tyrannus (Linnaeus). Eastern Kingbird.

Lanius Tyrannus Linnaeus, 1758, Syst. Nat. (ed. 10) 1: 94. Based mainly on "The Tyrant" Catesby, Nat. Hist. Carolina 1: 55, pl. 55. (in America septentrionali = South Carolina.)

Habitat.—Breeds in open country with scattered trees and shrubs, including cultivated land with hedgerows; winters in tropical forest and forest-edge habitats, where large flocks visit fruiting trees.

Distribution.—*Breeds* from southwestern and northeastern British Columbia (including Vancouver Island), southern Mackenzie, northern Saskatchewan, central Manitoba, central (casually northern) Ontario, southern Quebec, New Brunswick, Prince Edward Island, Nova Scotia, and southwestern Newfoundland south to western Washington, Oregon (east of the Cascades), northeastern California (casually), northern Nevada (at least formerly), northern Utah, Colorado, northwestern and central New Mexico, west-central and eastern Texas, the Gulf coast, and southern Florida. Occurs rarely in summer (and possibly has bred) in southeastern Alaska.

Winters primarily in western Amazonia, from eastern Ecuador and eastern Peru to western Brazil, but moves southward casually through winter to northern Chile and northern Argentina.

Migrates through northeastern Mexico, and from Oaxaca (Isthmus of Tehuantepec) and the Yucatan Peninsula south on both slopes of Middle America (including most islands) to northwestern South America, rarely through California, and casually to southern Baja California, Arizona, Chihuahua, Clipperton Island, Bermuda, the Bahamas, Cuba, the Isle of Pines, the Cayman Islands, Puerto Rico, and the Swan, Providencia and San Andrés islands in the Caribbean Sea.

Casual north to northern and western Alaska (including Nunivak and the Pribilof islands), southern Yukon, the northern Hudson Bay region, central Quebec, Labrador, Newfoundland

and southern Greenland, and in South America to eastern Venezuela, Guyana, Surinam, central Brazil, and northeastern Argentina. Accidental on South Georgia Island.

Tyrannus dominicensis (Gmelin). Gray Kingbird.

Lanius Tyrannus β *dominicensis* Gmelin, 1788, Syst. Nat. 1(1): 302. Based largely on "Le Tyran de S. Domingue" Brisson, Ornithologie 2: 394, pl. 38, fig. 2. (in insula S. Dominici et Jamaica = Hispaniola.)

Habitat.—Tropical Lowland Evergreen Forest Edge, Secondary Forest, Mangrove Forest, Second-growth Scrub (0–900 m; Tropical and lower Subtropical zones).

Distribution.—*Breeds* along the Atlantic and Gulf coasts from South Carolina (formerly) south to the Florida Keys, and west to southern Alabama and islands off the coast of Mississippi; rare but increasing as a breeder in interior Florida peninsula; throughout the West Indies, and on islands off South America from the Netherlands Antilles east to Tobago and Trinidad; and locally in northern Colombia, and northern Venezuela.

Winters from Hispaniola and Puerto Rico (casually from southern Florida) south through the Lesser Antilles and on islands off northern Venezuela, and from central Panama east across Colombia and Venezuela to the Guianas, and extreme northern Brazil.

Migrates throughout the West Indies, and rarely but regularly through the Swan Islands, islands off the Yucatan Peninsula and Belize, and along the Caribbean coast of Nicaragua and Costa Rica.

Casual along the Atlantic coast north to Massachusetts (sight reports to New Brunswick and Nova Scotia), west along the Gulf coast to southeastern Texas. Accidental in British Columbia (Vancouver Island), southern Wisconsin, Michigan, southern Ontario, central New York and Bermuda.

Tyrannus caudifasciatus d'Orbigny. Loggerhead Kingbird.

Tyrannus caudifasciatus d'Orbigny, 1839, in La Sagra, Hist. Fis. Pol. Nat. Cuba, Ois., p. 70 [p. 82 in French ed.], pl. 12. (Cuba.)

Habitat.—Tropical Lowland Evergreen Forest, Pine Forest (0–2000 m; Tropical and Subtropical zones).

Distribution.—*Resident* in the northern Bahama Islands (Grand Bahama, Abaco, Andros and New Providence) and Greater Antilles (east to Puerto Rico, including Vieques and the Cayman islands).

Casual winter visitant to southern Florida (Monroe and Dade counties, also sight reports for Merritt and Hypoluxo islands); a sight report for the central Bahamas (Long Island).

Notes.—Formerly placed in the monotypic genus *Tolmarchus.*

Tyrannus cubensis Richmond. Giant Kingbird.

Tyrannus magnirostris (not Swainson, 1831) d'Orbigny, 1839, in La Sagra, Hist. Fis. Pol. Nat. Cuba, Ois., p. 69 [p. 80 in French ed.], pl. 13. (Cuba.)
Tyrannus cubensis Richmond, 1898, Auk 15: 330. New name for *Tyrannus magnirostris* d'Orbigny, preoccupied.

Habitat.—Pine Forest (0–1100 m; Tropical and Subtropical zones)

Distribution.—*Resident* on Cuba and the Isle of Pines, formerly in the southern Bahamas (Great Inagua and Caicos islands).

A nineteenth century record from Isla Mujeres (off Quintana Roo) is questionable.

Tyrannus forficatus (Gmelin). Scissor-tailed Flycatcher.

Muscicapa forficata Gmelin, 1789, Syst. Nat. 1(2): 931. Based mainly on the "Swallow-tailed Flycatcher" Latham, Gen. Synop. Birds 2(1): 356. (in nova Hispania = Mexico.)

Habitat.—Breeds in open country, especially dry grasslands, cultivated lands, scrub and savanna; winters in similar habitats, but often roosts in large flocks in trees in marshes, mangroves, and towns.

Distribution.—*Breeds* from eastern New Mexico, southeastern Colorado, southern Nebraska, central Missouri, central Arkansas, and western Louisiana south to northern Nuevo León and southern Texas; also isolated breeding reports from southeastern California (San Bernardino County), central Iowa (Ames), southwestern Indiana (Daviess County), Mississippi (three locations), central Tennessee (Murfreesboro), northwestern Alabama (Florence), Georgia (Cartersville) and South Carolina (Laurens County).

Winters in central and southern Florida, and in Middle America from southern Veracruz and Oaxaca south (primarily on the Pacific slope) to central Costa Rica, rarely to western Panama (east to the Canal area); casual in winter north to central California and southern Louisiana.

Migrates through most of Mexico (mainly in the east, rare or absent in the northwest and Baja California) and sparingly along the Gulf coast from Louisiana to southern Florida.

Casual throughout most of North America outside the breeding range from central British Columbia, Alberta, Saskatchewan, Manitoba, Minnesota, Wisconsin, northern Michigan, central Ontario, central Quebec, New Brunswick, and Nova Scotia south to Baja California, Arizona, the Gulf states, Bahamas (Grand Bahama, San Salvador, Great Abaco), Cuba and Puerto Rico; sight reports for southeastern Alaska.

Notes.—This and the following species were formerly placed in the genus *Muscivora*.

Tyrannus savana Vieillot. Fork-tailed Flycatcher.

> *Muscivora Tyrannus* (not *Lanius tyrannus* Linnaeus, 1758) Linnaeus, 1766, Syst. Nat. (ed. 12) 1: 325. Based on "Le Tyran a queue fourchue" Brisson, Ornithologie 2: 395, pl. 39, fig. 3. (in Canada, Surinamo = SurinAmer.)
> *Tyrannus savana* Vieillot, 1808, Hist. Nat. Ois. Amer. Sept. 1 (livr. 8): 72, pl. 43. New name for *Muscivora tyrannus* Linnaeus, preoccupied.

Habitat.—Low, Seasonally Wet Grassland, Second-growth Scrub, Pastures/Agricultural Lands, and lowland pine savanna (0–1600 m, to 2400 in nonbreeding season; Tropical and Subtropical zones).

Distribution.—*Resident* (but nomadic) locally, mostly on the Gulf-Caribbean slope of Middle America from Veracruz and Tabasco (possibly also northern Oaxaca, northern Chiapas, Campeche and Quintana Roo), central Belize, northern and central Guatemala, and central Honduras south to central Panama (eastern Panamá province and the Canal area). Also breeds in South America in northern and central Colombia and northern Venezuela, and locally from Surinam, eastern Amazonia and central Brazil, and eastern Bolivia south to southern Argentina and Uruguay, and in the Falkland Islands.

Winters widely in South America from Colombia, Venezuela (including Curaçao), Tobago, Trinidad and the Guianas south, east of the Andes, to Peru, Bolivia, northern Argentina and southern Brazil; and casually in the southern Lesser Antilles (Barbados, Grenada and the Grenadines).

Patterns of migration and local movement across entire range, including within Middle America, are poorly understood.

Casual in North America north to California, Idaho, Minnesota, Wisconsin, Michigan, central Ontario, southern Quebec, New Brunswick and Nova Scotia (with most reports from the east); also in central and southern Texas, Florida, Bermuda, Cuba, and, in the Lesser Antilles, in St. Martin and St. Lucia (sight report), and elsewhere in Panama (Taboga and Coiba islands, and San Blas); a sight report from southern Alabama.

Notes.—Formerly known as *Muscivora tyrannus* (Linnaeus, 1766). One New Jersey specimen (possibly mislabeled) has been referred to the race breeding in Venezuela and Colombia, *T. s. sanctaemartae* (Zimmer, 1937); all other specimens taken north of Mexico, as well as those in the southern Lesser Antilles, have been referred to *T. s. savana,* the subspecies breeding in southern South America, whereas photographs of two individuals from southern Texas have been identified as the Middle American race, *T. s. monachus* Hartlaub, 1844.

Genera *INCERTAE SEDIS*

Notes.— The seven genera to follow have presented taxonomic challenges for more than a century. Allozyme and DNA hybridization data suggest that the enigmatic genus *Sapayoa* is an outgroup to all other Tyrannoidea (S. M. Lanyon 1985, Sibley and Ahlquist 1990), whereas syringeal characters suggest that *Sapayoa* is allied as a sister group to, or within, the Tyrannidae (Prum 1990). Summarizing numerous morphological characters, Prum and Lanyon (1989) hypothesized that *Schiffornis, Laniocera,* and *Pachyramphus,* along with three South American genera, constitute a monophyletic assemblage. This "Schiffornis group" appears to be allied to *Piprites, Lipaugus,* and *Tityra,* but cannot be placed within the otherwise rather well-defined, monophyletic assemblages here referred to as the families Tyrannidae, Cotingidae, and Pipridae (see also Prum 1990). We list these seven genera as a group, *incertae sedis,* to acknowledge that they are unequivocally tyrannoid but of uncertain affinity within the superfamily.

Genus *SAPAYOA* Hartert

> *Sapayoa* Hartert, 1903, Novit. Zool. 10: 117. Type, by original designation, *Sapayoa aenigma* Hartert.

Sapayoa aenigma Hartert. Sapayoa.

> *Sapayoa aenigma* Hartert, 1903, Novit. Zool. 10: 117. (Río Sapayo [= Sapallo Grande], prov. Esmeraldas, Ecuador.)

Habitat.—Tropical Lowland Evergreen Forest (0–1350 m; Tropical and lower Subtropical zones).

Distribution.—*Resident* on the Pacific slope of eastern Panama (west to the Canal area), western Colombia (upper Sinú valley, Córdoba), and northwestern Ecuador (Esmeraldas).

Notes.—Formerly known as Broad-billed Manakin; called Broad-billed Sapayoa by Sibley and Monroe (1990) and Ridgely and Tudor (1994).

Genus *SCHIFFORNIS* Bonaparte

> *Schiffornis* Bonaparte, 1854, Ateneo Ital. 2: 314. Type, by monotypy, *Muscicapa turdina* Wied.
>
> *Heteropelma* "Schiff" (not Wesmaël, 1849) Bonaparte, 1854, Consp. Voluc. Anisod., p. 4. Type, by monotypy, *Muscicapa turdina* Wied.
>
> *Scotothorus* Oberholser, 1899, Proc. Acad. Nat. Sci. Philadelphia 51: 208. New name for *Heteropelma* Bonaparte, preoccupied.

Schiffornis turdinus (Wied). Thrush-like Schiffornis.

> *Muscicapa turdina* Wied, 1831, Beitr. Naturgesch. Bras. 3(2): 817. (eastern Brazil = Bahia.)

Habitat.—Tropical Lowland Evergreen Forest, Montane Evergreen Forest (0–1500 m; Tropical and lower Subtropical zones).

Distribution.—*Resident* [*veraepacis* group] on the Gulf-Caribbean slope of Middle America from southern Veracruz, northern Oaxaca, Tabasco, northern Chiapas, Campeche and Quintana Roo south to Nicaragua, and on both slopes of Costa Rica (absent from the dry northwest) and Panama (east to Coclé and western Panamá province, and on Cerro Tacarcuna and Cerro Pirre in eastern Darién); and [*turdinus* group] in central and eastern Panama (west to the Canal area), and in South America from Colombia, southern Venezuela and the Guianas south, west of the Andes to western Ecuador, and east of the Andes to northern Bolivia and central and southeastern Brazil.

Notes.—Groups: *S. veraepacis* (Sclater and Salvin, 1860) [Brown Schiffornis] and *S. turdinus* [Thrush-like Schiffornis]. Vocal and plumage differences exist between these groups, including between the highland and lowland forms that approach one another in eastern Panama. Similar differences also exist between highland and lowland forms in South America. It is certain that two or more species are involved, but the complex requires careful study across its entire range, including attention to the relationships of these groups to the form *S. virescens* from southeastern Brazil. We choose to retain the groups under a single name until the taxonomy and biogeography of the complex are clarified.

Genus *PIPRITES* Cabanis

> *Piprites* Cabanis, 1847, Arch. Naturgesch. 13: 234. Type, by monotypy, *Pipra pileata* Temminck.

Piprites griseiceps Salvin. Gray-headed Piprites.

> *Piprites griseiceps* Salvin, 1865, Proc. Zool. Soc. London (1864), p. 583. (Tucurruque [= Tucurriquí], Costa Rica.)

Habitat.—Tropical Lowland Evergreen Forest (0–800 m; Tropical Zone).
Distribution.—*Resident* on the Caribbean slope of eastern Guatemala (near Izabal), eastern Honduras (Olancho), Nicaragua and Costa Rica (south to Suretka).
Notes.— *P. griseiceps* and *P. chloris* (Temminck, 1822) [Wing-barred Piprites], a widespread polytypic species in South America, constitute a superspecies.

Genus *LIPAUGUS* Boie

> *Lipangus* [typo. error = *Lipaugus*] Boie, 1828, Isis von Oken, col. 318. Type, by subsequent designation (G. R. Gray, 1840), *Muscicapa plumbea* Licht. = *Muscicapa vociferans* Wied.

Lipaugus unirufus Sclater. Rufous Piha.

> *Lipaugus unirufus* Sclater, 1859, Proc. Zool. Soc. London, p. 385. (Playa Vicente, Oaxaca, Mexico, and Coban, Vera Paz, Guatemala = Playa Vicente, Veracruz; Binford, 1989, Ornithol. Monogr. 43, p. 341–342.)

Habitat.—Tropical Lowland Evergreen Forest (0–1200 m; Tropical Zone).
Distribution.—*Resident* from southern Veracruz, northern Oaxaca, Tabasco and Chiapas south on the Caribbean slope of Central America to Nicaragua, on both slopes of Costa Rica (absent from dry northwest) and Panama (more common on Caribbean slope), and in western Colombia and northwestern Ecuador.

Genus *LANIOCERA* Lesson

> *Laniocera* Lesson, 1840, Rev. Zool. [Paris] 3: 353. Type, by monotypy, *Laniocera sanguinaria* Lesson = *Ampelis hypopyrra* Vieillot.

Laniocera rufescens (Sclater). Speckled Mourner.

> *Lipaugus rufescens* Sclater, 1858, Proc. Zool. Soc. London (1857), p. 276. (In rep. Guatimalensi prope urbem Coban = northern Alta Verapaz, Guatemala.)

Habitat.—Tropical Lowland Evergreen Forest (0–750 m, to 1350 m in eastern Panama and South America; Tropical Zone).
Distribution.—*Resident* locally on the Gulf-Caribbean slope from southern Mexico (northern Oaxaca, Chiapas) south through Central America to Costa Rica (also Gulfo Dulce region on Pacific slope, north to Quepos) and Panama (Caribbean slope throughout, and rarely on Pacific slope from the Canal area eastward), and in northern and western Colombia and northwestern Ecuador.
Notes.—*L. rufescens* and the South American *L. hypopyrra* (Vieillot, 1817) [Cinereous Mourner] constitute a superspecies.

Genus *PACHYRAMPHUS* Gray

> *Pachyramphus* G. R. Gray, 1840, List Genera Birds, p. 31. Type, by original designation, *Psaris cuvierii* Swainson = *Tityra viridis* Vieillot.

Platypsaris [subgenus] Sclater, 1857, Proc. Zool. Soc. London, p. 72. Type, by subsequent designation (Sclater, 1888), *Pachyrhynchus aglaiae* Lafresnaye.

Pachyramphus versicolor (Hartlaub). Barred Becard.

Vireo versicolor Hartlaub, 1843, Rev. Zool. [Paris] 6: 289. (du la Nouvelle-Grenade = Bogotá, Colombia.)

Habitat.—Montane Evergreen Forest, Elfin Forest (1500–3000 m; Subtropical and lower Temperate zones).

Distribution.—*Resident* in the mountains of Costa Rica (Cordillera Central, Cordillera de Talamanca, Dota Mountains, rare in Cordillera de Tilaran), western Panama (western Chiriquí), and in South America from Colombia and northwestern Venezuela south, in the western Andes to northwestern Peru, and in the eastern Andes to northern Bolivia.

Pachyramphus rufus (Boddaert). Cinereous Becard.

Muscicapa rufa Boddaert, 1783, Table Planches Enlum., p. 27. Based on "Le Gobemouche roux, de Cayenne" Daubenton, Planches Enlum., pl. 453, fig. 1. (Cayenne.)

Habitat.—River-edge Forest, Gallery Forest, Secondary Forest, Tropical Lowland Evergreen Forest Edge (0–1500 m; Tropical and lower Subtropical zones).

Distribution.—*Resident* locally in central and eastern Panama (from the Canal area, at least formerly, and eastern Panamá province and Darién, also a doubtful record from "Veragua"), and in South America from central and northern Colombia east across northern Venezuela to the Guianas, and south, east of the Andes, to northeastern Peru, thence eastward across Amazonian Brazil to Pará (including Marajó and Mexiana islands).

Notes.—*P. rufus* and *P. spodiurus* Sclater, 1860 [Slaty Becard], of western Ecuador and northwestern Peru, constitute a superspecies.

Pachyramphus cinnamomeus Lawrence. Cinnamon Becard.

Pachyramphus cinnamomeus Lawrence, 1861, Ann. Lyc. Nat. Hist. N. Y. 7: 295. (on the Atlantic side of the Isthmus of Panama, along the line of Panama Railroad = Lion Hill, Canal Zone.)

Habitat.—Tropical Lowland Evergreen Forest and edge, Secondary Forest (0–750, to 1200 m in eastern Panama and South America; Tropical and lower Subtropical zones).

Distribution.—*Resident* on the Gulf-Caribbean slope of Middle America from northeastern Oaxaca, Tabasco and Chiapas south to Nicaragua, on both slopes of Costa Rica (absent from the dry northwest) and Panama (more commonly on the Caribbean slope), and in South America west of the Andes south to southwestern Ecuador, and in northern Colombia and northwestern Venezuela.

Notes.—*P. cinnamomeus* and the South American *P. castaneus* (Jardine and Selby, 1827) constitute a superspecies.

Pachyramphus polychopterus (Vieillot). White-winged Becard.

Platyrhynchus polychopterus Vieillot, 1818, Nouv. Dict. Hist. Nat. (nouv. éd.) 27: 10. (Nouvelle-Hollande, error = Bahía, Brazil.)

Habitat.—Tropical Lowland Evergreen Forest Edge, River-edge Forest, Gallery Forest, Secondary Forest (0–1200 m, to 1800 m in South America; Tropical and lower Subtropical zones).

Distribution.—*Resident* on the Caribbean slope of eastern Guatemala, southern Belize and Honduras, on both slopes of Nicaragua, Costa Rica (less common in the dry northwest) and Panama, and in South America from Colombia, Venezuela, Tobago, Trinidad and the Guianas south, mostly east of the Andes, to eastern Peru, northern and eastern Bolivia, northern Argentina, Uruguay and southern Brazil. Southernmost populations in South America move northward in nonbreeding season. Reported but not verified from extreme southeastern Mexico (Chiapas).

Pachyramphus albogriseus Sclater. Black-and-white Becard.

Pachyrhamphus albo-griseus Sclater, 1857, Proc. Zool. Soc. London, p. 78. (New Grenada, Bogota = Bogotá, Colombia.)

Habitat.—Montane Evergreen Forest, Tropical Deciduous Forest (800–2100 m; 500–3000 m in South America; Tropical and Subtropical zones).

Distribution.—*Resident* in Costa Rica (mainly on Caribbean slope from Cordillera de Tilarán southward) and western Panama (Chiriquí and Veraguas, records elsewhere are unverified); and locally in South America in northern Colombia and northern Venezuela, and on both slopes of the Andes from extreme southern Colombia south, west of the Andes to northwestern Peru, and east of the Andes to central Peru. The old record of this species from Nicaragua pertains to *P. polychopterus.*

Pachyramphus major (Cabanis). Gray-collared Becard.

Bathmidurus major Cabanis, 1847, Arch. Naturgesch. 13: 246. (Xalapa [= Jalapa], Vera Cruz, Mexico.)

Habitat.—Montane Evergreen Forest, Pine-Oak Forest, Tropical Deciduous Forest, Tropical Lowland Evergreen Forest Edge (0–2500 m; Subtropical Zone, and Tropical Zone in drier habitats).

Distribution.—*Resident* from southern Sonora, Sinaloa, western Durango, San Luis Potosí, Nuevo León and Tamaulipas south through the interior highlands of central and southern Mexico, and on both slopes of Middle America (including the Yucatan Peninsula) to El Salvador, Honduras, and north-central Nicaragua. Appears to descend to lower elevations in winter.

Pachyramphus aglaiae (Lafresnaye). Rose-throated Becard.

Platyrhynchus Aglaiæ Lafresnaye, 1839, Rev. Zool. [Paris] 2: 98. (Mexico = Jalapa, Veracruz.)

Habitat.—Gallery Forest, Tropical Deciduous Forest, Tropical Lowland Evergreen Forest Edge (0–1250 m, locally to 2700 m; Tropical and Subtropical zones).

Distribution.—*Breeds* from southeastern Arizona (locally), northeastern Sonora, western Chihuahua, northeastern Coahuila, Nuevo León and southern Texas (Cameron and Hidalgo counties) south along both slopes of Middle America (including the Tres Marias Islands and Yucatan Peninsula) to Costa Rica, where primarily in the dry northwest south to the Gulf of Nicoya; records from the Caribbean slope are probably migrants; sight reports for southwestern New Mexico and western Panama (Chiriquí) presumably are vagrants.

Winters from northern Mexico south throughout the remainder of the breeding range.

Notes.—*P. aglaiae, P. homochrous, P. niger,* and two South American species, *P. validus* (Lichtenstein, 1823) [= *P. rufus* (Vieillot, 1816)] and *P. minor* (Lesson, 1830), were placed in the genus *Platypsaris* until the generic merger by Snow (1973).

Pachyramphus homochrous Sclater. One-colored Becard.

Pachyramphus homochrous Sclater, 1859, Proc. Zool. Soc. London, p. 142. (Pallatanga, Ecuador.)

Habitat.—Tropical Lowland Evergreen Forest, Tropical Deciduous Forest, Gallery Forest, Secondary Forest (0–900 m; Tropical Zone).

Distribution.—*Resident* locally from central Panama (the Caribbean slope in the Canal area, both slopes of eastern Panamá province, and in the Pacific lowlands of Darién) east across northern Colombia to northwestern Venezuela and south, west of the Andes, to northwestern Peru.

Notes.—See comments under *P. aglaiae.*

Pachyramphus niger (Gmelin). Jamaican Becard.

Lanius niger Gmelin, 1788, Syst. Nat. 1(1): 301. Based on the "Black Shrike" Latham, Gen. Synop. Birds 1(2): 187. (in Jamaica.)

Habitat.—Tropical Lowland Evergreen Forest, Montane Evergreen Forest (0–1800 m; Tropical and lower Subtropical zones).
Distribution.—*Resident* on Jamaica.
Notes.—See comments under *P. aglaiae*.

Genus *TITYRA* Vieillot

Tityra Vieillot, 1816, Analyse, p. 39. Type, by monotypy, "Bécarde" Buffon = *Lanius cayanus* Linnaeus.
Erator [subgenus] Kaup, 1852, Proc. Zool. Soc. London (1851), p. 47. Type, by subsequent designation (G. R. Gray, 1855), *Lanius inquisitor* Lichtenstein.

Tityra semifasciata (Spix). Masked Tityra.

Pachyrhynchus semifasciatus Spix, 1825, Avium Spec. Nov. Bras. 2: 32, pl. 44, fig. 2. (Pará, Brazil.)

Habitat.—Tropical Lowland Evergreen Forest, Montane Evergreen Forest, Secondary Forest (0–1200 m, locally to 2500 m; Tropical and lower Subtropical zones).
Distribution.—*Resident* from southern Sonora, Sinaloa, western Durango, southern Tamaulipas and San Luis Potosí south along both slopes of Middle America (including the Yucatan Peninsula) to Panama (including Cébaco and Coiba islands), and in South America from northern Colombia, northern Venezuela, and Trinidad south, west of the Andes to western Ecuador, and east of the Andes from southeastern Colombia and eastern Ecuador south to northern Bolivia, thence eastward over southern Amazonian Brazil to Amapa, Pará, and northern Maranhão, and in French Guiana.
Accidental in southern Texas (Bentsen-Rio Grande State Park, Hidalgo County; T.O.S. 1995).

Tityra inquisitor (Lichtenstein). Black-crowned Tityra.

Lanius inquisitor (Olfers MS) Lichtenstein, 1823, Verz. Doubl. Zool. Mus. Berlin, p. 50. (São Paulo, Brazil.)

Habitat.—Tropical Lowland Evergreen Forest, Secondary Forest (0–1200 m; Tropical and lower Subtropical zones).
Distribution.—*Resident* on the Gulf-Caribbean slope of Middle America from southeastern San Luis Potosí, Veracruz, eastern Puebla, northern Oaxaca, Tabasco, Chiapas and the Yucatan Peninsula south to Nicaragua, on both slopes of Costa Rica and Panama, and in South America from Colombia, Venezuela and the Guianas south, west of the Andes to western Ecuador, and east of the Andes to eastern Peru, northern and eastern Bolivia, eastern Paraguay, northeastern Argentina, and southern Brazil.
Notes.—Formerly placed in the genus *Erator*.

Family **COTINGIDAE**: Cotingas

Genus *COTINGA* Brisson

Cotinga Brisson, 1760, Ornithologie 2: 339. Type, by tautonymy, *Cotinga* Brisson = *Ampelis cotinga* Linnaeus.

Cotinga amabilis Gould. Lovely Cotinga.

Cotinga amabilis Gould, 1857, Proc. Zool. Soc. London, p. 64, pl. 123. (Guatemala = northern Alta Verapaz, Guatemala.)

Habitat.—Tropical Lowland Evergreen Forest, Secondary Forest (0–1700 m; Tropical Zone).

Distribution.—*Resident* from southern Veracruz, northern Oaxaca and northern Chiapas south along the Caribbean slope through northern Guatemala, southern Belize, northern Honduras and Nicaragua to southeastern Costa Rica; a sight report from western Panama (Bocas del Toro); may move seasonally.

Notes.—*C. amabilis, C. ridgwayi* and *C. nattererii* constitute a superspecies.

Cotinga ridgwayi Ridgway. Turquoise Cotinga.

Cotinga ridgwayi (Zeledón MS) Ridgway, 1887, Proc. U. S. Natl. Mus. 10: 1, pl. 6, fig. 3. (Pozo Azul, Costa Rica.)

Habitat.—Tropical Lowland Evergreen Forest, Secondary Forest (0–1400 m; Tropical Zone).

Distribution.—*Resident* on the Pacific slope from southwestern Costa Rica (south end of Gulf of Nicoya) south to western Panama in western Chiriquí (Bugaba, El Volcán).

Notes.—See comments under *C. amabilis.*

Cotinga nattererii (Boissonneau). Blue Cotinga.

Ampelis Nattererii Boissonneau, 1840, Rev. Zool. [Paris] 3: 2. (Santa-Fé de Bogota [Colombia].)

Habitat.—Tropical Lowland Evergreen Forest, Secondary Forest (0–1250 m; Tropical Zone).

Distribution.—*Resident* on both slopes of Panama from western Colon and the Canal area east through Darién and San Blas, and in South America in northern and western Colombia south to northwestern Ecuador, and in northwestern Venezuela.

Notes.— See comments under *C. amabilis.*

Genus *CARPODECTES* Salvin

Carpodectes Salvin, 1865, Proc. Zool. Soc. London (1864), p. 583. Type, by original designation, *Carpodectes nitidus* Salvin.

Carpodectes hopkei Berlepsch. Black-tipped Cotinga.

Carpodectes hopkei Berlepsch, 1897, Ornithol. Monatsber. 5: 174. (San José, Rio Dagua, Colombia.)

Habitat.—Tropical Lowland Evergreen Forest (0–900 m; Tropical Zone).

Distribution.—*Resident* in extreme eastern Panama (eastern Darién), and in South America west of the Andes from northwestern Colombia south to northwestern Ecuador. May move seasonally.

Notes.—The three allopatric forms of *Carpodectes (hopkei, antoniae,* and *nitidus)* were treated as conspecific by Hellmayr (1929), but as separate species by Ridgway (1907) and by most recent authors (e.g., Wetmore 1972, Snow *in* Traylor 1979b, Snow 1982). We consider these forms as members of a superspecies.

Carpodectes antoniae Ridgway. Yellow-billed Cotinga.

Carpodectes antoniæ (Zeledón MS) Ridgway, 1884, Ibis, p. 27, pl. 2. (Pirris, Southwestern Costa Rica.)

Habitat.—Tropical Lowland Evergreen Forest, Mangrove Forest (0–800 m; Tropical Zone, near sea level).

Distribution.—*Resident* and local in the Pacific coastal forests of southwestern Costa Rica from the southern Golfo de Nicoya region (Pigres) south to the Osa Peninsula, and rare in extreme western Panama in western Chiriquí (Pedregal, Puerto Armuelles), possibly east as far as Coclé (Aguadulce; specimen lost). Appears to move seasonally in Costa Rica.

Notes.—Also known as Antonia's Cotinga. See notes under *C. hopkei*.

Carpodectes nitidus Salvin. Snowy Cotinga.

> *Carpodectes nitidus* Salvin, 1865, Proc. Zool. Soc. London (1864), p. 583, pl. "36" [= 35]. (Tucurique [= Tucurriqui], Costa Rica.)

Habitat.—Tropical Lowland Evergreen Forest, Secondary Forest (0–750 m; Tropical Zone).

Distribution.—*Resident* in the Gulf-Caribbean lowlands from northern Honduras (La Ceiba) south through Nicaragua and Costa Rica to extreme western Panama (western Bocas del Toro). Appears to move seasonally in Costa Rica.

Notes.—See notes under *C. hopkei*.

Genus *QUERULA* Vieillot

> *Querula* Vieillot, 1816, Analyse, p. 37. Type, by monotypy, "Piauhau" Buffon = *Muscicapa purpurata* Müller.

Querula purpurata (Müller). Purple-throated Fruitcrow.

> *Muscicapa purpurata* P. L. S. Müller, 1776, Natursyst., Suppl., p. 169. Based on "Gobe-Mouche noir à gorge pourpre de Cayenne" Daubenton, Planches Enlum., pl. 381. (Cayenne.)

Habitat.—Tropical Lowland Evergreen Forest (0- 600 m; to 1050 m in South America; Tropical Zone).

Distribution.—*Resident* in Costa Rica (entire Caribbean lowlands) and Panama (entire Caribbean slope, and Pacific slope from Canal area eastward), and in South America from northern Colombia south, west of the Andes to northwestern Ecuador, and east of the Andes from eastern Colombia, southern Venezuela, and the Guianas south to northern Bolivia and Amazonian Brazil.

Genus *CEPHALOPTERUS* Geoffroy Saint-Hilaire

> *Cephalopterus* Geoffroy Saint-Hilaire, 1809, Ann. Mus. Hist. Nat. [Paris] 13: 235, 238. Type, by original designation, *Cephalopterus ornatus* Geoffroy Saint-Hilaire.

Cephalopterus glabricollis Gould. Bare-necked Umbrellabird.

> *Cephalopterus glabricollis* Gould, 1851, Proc. Zool. Soc. London (1850), p. 92, pl. 20. (Cordillera de Chiriqué in Veragua, at an elevation of 8000 feet [Panama].)

Habitat.—Montane Evergreen Forest, Tropical Lowland Evergreen Forest (breeds 800–2500 m; 0–500 in nonbreeding season; Subtropical Zone, seasonally to Tropical Zone).

Distribution.—*Resident* in Caribbean slope of Costa Rica (from Cordillera de Guanacaste southward) and western Panama (highlands of Chiriquí, Bocas del Toro, and Veraguas); descends to the Caribbean lowlands in nonbreeding season.

Notes.—*C. glabricollis* and the South American *C. penduliger* Sclater, 1859 [Long-wattled Umbrellabird] were treated as races of *C. ornatus* Geoffroy Saint-Hilaire, 1809 [Amazonian Umbrellabird] by Hellmayr (1929). Most authors before and since have recognized three allopatric species (e.g., Ridgway 1907, Wetmore 1972, Snow *in* Traylor 1979b, Snow 1982). The three constitute a superspecies.

Genus *PROCNIAS* Illiger

> *Procnias* Illiger, 1811, Prodromus, p. 228. Type, by subsequent designation (G. R. Gray, 1840), *P. variegatus* (L.) Ill. = *Ampelis variegata* Gmelin = *Ampelis averano* Hermann.

Procnias tricarunculata (Verreaux and Verreaux). Three-wattled Bellbird.

> *Casmarhynchus tricarunculatus* J. and E. Verreaux, 1853, Rev. Mag. Zool. (2)5: 193. (Bocos del toro (Nouvelle-Grenade) = Bocas del Toro, western Panama.)

Habitat.—Montane Evergreen Forest, Tropical Lowland Evergreen Forest (breeds 900–2300 m; 0–3000 m during nonbreeding seasons; Subtropical Zone, seasonally to sea level).

Distribution.—*Breeds* in the highlands of Nicaragua (including Isla de Ometepe in Lago de Nicaragua), Costa Rica (Cordillera de Guanacaste and Peninsula de Nicoya south through the Cordillera de Talamanca) and western Panama (Bocas del Toro, Chiriquí and Veraguas, possibly also to the Azuero Peninsula); highly mobile while not breeding, both ascending and descending to adjacent forested habitats, especially the Caribbean lowlands (also Pacific lowlands in Panama, and ranging east rarely to the Canal area). Casual in eastern Honduras (Olancho).

Family **PIPRIDAE**: Manakins

Notes.—Based on an exhaustive phylogenetic analysis of syringeal characters, Prum (1992) proposed new generic limits within the Pipridae, and discussed the evolution of manakin social behavior based on his proposed phylogeny (Prum 1990, 1994). The biggest changes from existing classifications involved creation of two new genera for certain species within the genus *Pipra,* which Prum concluded to be polyphyletic. Studies are under way to test Prum's phylogenetic hypotheses based on other characters, especially using biochemical techniques. For the present we continue to recognize the traditional generic limits of Snow (1975), excluding those removed to a position *Incertae Sedis*, above, but acknowledge the likelihood that some, perhaps all, of Prum's proposed changes will prevail. Prum's alternative treatments are provided under the respective species below.

Genus *CHLOROPIPO* Cabanis and Heine

> *Chloropipo* Cabanis and Heine, 1859, Mus. Heineanum 2: 90 (note 2). Type, by original designation, *Chloropipo flavicollis* Cabanis and Heine = *Pipra flavicapilla* Sclater.

Chloropipo holochlora Sclater. Green Manakin.

> *Chloropipo holochlora* Sclater, 1888, Cat. Birds Br. Mus. 14: xvi, 281, 287. (Colombia and Amazonia = Bogotá, Colombia.)

Habitat.—Tropical Lowland Evergreen Forest (600–1300 m; upper Tropical and lower Subtropical zones).

Distribution.—*Resident* in eastern Panama (eastern San Blas and eastern Darién), and in South America south, west of the Andes to western Ecuador, and east of the Andes to eastern Peru.

Notes.—Merged into the genus *Xenopipo* Cabanis, 1847 by Prum (1992).

Genus *MANACUS* Brisson

> *Manacus* Brisson, 1760, Ornithologie 4: 442. Type, by tautonymy, *Manacus* Brisson = *Pipra manacus* Linnaeus.

Manacus candei (Parzudaki). White-collared Manakin.

> *Pipra Candei* Parzudaki, 1841, Rev. Zool. [Paris] 4: 306. (à Truxillo, dans la baie de Honduras = Trujillo, Honduras.)

Habitat.—Tropical Lowland Evergreen Forest Edge, Secondary Forest (0–950 m; Tropical Zone).

Distribution.—*Resident* on the Gulf-Caribbean slope of Middle America from southern Veracruz, northern Oaxaca, Tabasco, Chiapas, southern Campeche, southern Quintana Roo, and Belize south to western Panama (Bocas del Toro).

Notes.—Traylor (1979b), treated this and all other forms in the genus *Manacus* as subspecies of *M. manacus* (Linnaeus, 1766), citing Haffer's (1967) summary of limited hybridization between parapatric forms as evidence for incomplete speciation. Eisenmann (*in litt.,* cited by Haffer) speculated that *M. candei* has intergraded with *M. vitellinus* in northwestern Panama, causing an intermediate population to occur there (*M. [v.] cerritus* Peters, 1927 [Almirante Manakin]). We treat *M. candei* and all other well-differentiated, allopatric or parapatric forms (*M. aurantiacus, M. vitellinus, M. manacus*) as members of a superspecies. If *candei* is merged with *vitellinus,* Collared Manakin may be used for the species; if these forms are merged into *M. manacus,* Bearded Manakin applies to the single widespread species. See comments under *M. aurantiacus.*

Manacus aurantiacus (Salvin). Orange-collared Manakin.

> *Chiromachæris aurantiaca* Salvin, 1870, Proc. Zool. Soc. London, p. 200. (Mina de Chorcha and Bugaba, Chiriquí, Panama.)

Habitat.—Tropical Lowland Evergreen Forest Edge, Secondary Forest (0–1400 m; Tropical and lower Subtropical zones).

Distribution.—*Resident* [*aurantiacus* group] on Pacific slope of southern Costa Rica (entrance of the Gulf de Nicoya) and western Panama (east to the Azuero Peninsula); and [*viridiventris* group] in western and northern Colombia and northwestern Ecuador.

Notes.—Groups: *M. aurantiacus* [Orange-collared Manakin] and *M. viridiventris* Griscom, 1929 [Greenish-bellied Manakin]. *M. aurantiacus* often is merged with *M. vitellinus,* its closest relative within the superspecies. No evidence of contact or intergradation exists between the two in western Panama, however. Because of differences in size, plumage, and leg color, *M. aurantiacus* is recognizable at the same level as *vitellinus.* See notes under *M. candei.*

Manacus vitellinus (Gould). Golden-collared Manakin.

> *Pipra vitellina* Gould, 1843, Proc. Zool. Soc. London, p. 103. (Panamá = Panama City, Panama.)

Habitat.—Tropical Lowland Evergreen Forest Edge, Secondary Forest (0–1200 m; Tropical Zone).

Distribution.—*Resident* in Panama (the entire Caribbean lowlands, including Bastimentos and Escuelo de Veraguas islands, and the Pacific coast from eastern Veraguas eastward), and in northwestern Colombia.

Notes.—See comments under *M. aurantiacus* and *M. candei.*

Genus *CORAPIPO* Bonaparte

> *Corapipo* Bonaparte, 1854, Ateneo Ital. 2: 316. Type, by monotypy, *Pipra gutturalis* Linnaeus.

Corapipo altera Hellmayr. White-ruffed Manakin.

> *Corapipo leucorrhoa altera* Hellmayr, 1906, Bull. Br. Ornithol. Club 16: 84. (Carrillo, Costa Rica.)

Habitat.—Montane Evergreen Forest, Tropical Lowland Evergreen Forest (0–1500 m, breeds above 400 m; Tropical and lower Subtropical zones).

Distribution.—*Resident* in foothills and highlands from eastern Honduras (Olancho) south through eastern Nicaragua, Costa Rica and Panama to northwestern Colombia (west of the Atrato Valley and south to the Serranía de Baudó).

Notes.—Snow *in* Traylor (1979b) follows many previous authors in merging *C. altera* with the South American *C. leucorrhoa* (Sclater, 1863) [White-bibbed Manakin]. Conspicuously different wing formulae of these two forms, presumably reflecting differences in display, prompt other authors (e.g. Wetmore 1972) to recognize both as species. Together with *C. gutturalis* (Linnaeus, 1766) [White-throated Manakin] of northern South America, *C. altera* and *C. leucorrhoa* constitute a superspecies.

Genus *CHIROXIPHIA* Cabanis

Chiroxiphia Cabanis, 1847, Arch. Naturgesch. 13: 235. Type, by subsequent designation (G. R. Gray, 1855), *Pipra caudata* Shaw and Nodder.

Chiroprion Bonaparte, 1854, Consp. Voluc. Anisod., p. 5. Type, by original designation, *Pipra pareola* Linnaeus.

Notes.—The genus *Chiroxiphia* consists of five similar, entirely allopatric forms. Four of them, namely, *C. linearis, C. lanceolata, C. pareola* (Linnaeus, 1766) [Blue-backed Manakin], and *C. boliviana* Allen, 1889 [Yungas Manakin; see Parker and Remsen 1987], differ from one another only slightly in plumage ornamentation and display behavior; these four forms constitute a superspecies.

Chiroxiphia lanceolata (Wagler). Lance-tailed Manakin.

Pipra lanceolata Wagler, 1830, Isis von Oken, col. 931. (Guiane sive Cajenna, error = Cerro Turumiquire, Sucre, Venezuela.)

Habitat.—Tropical Deciduous Forest, Gallery Forest, Tropical Lowland Evergreen Forest (0–1500 m; Tropical and lower Subtropical zones).

Distribution.—*Resident* in extreme southwestern Costa Rica (Golfo Dulce region and Cañas Gordas), on the Pacific slope of Panama east to western Darién (locally also on the Caribbean slope in the Canal area, and on Cébaco and Coiba islands), and in South America in northern Colombia (east of the Río Sinú), and northern Venezuela north of the Orinoco River east to Sucre (including Margarita Island) and south to Santander.

Chiroxiphia linearis (Bonaparte). Long-tailed Manakin.

Pipra linearis Bonaparte, 1838, Proc. Zool. Soc. London (1837), p. 113. (Mexico = Santa Efigenia, Oaxaca.)

Habitat.—Tropical Deciduous Forest, Gallery Forest, Secondary Forest (0–1500 m; Tropical Zone)

Distribution.—*Resident* on the Pacific slope from Oaxaca (west to Chivela) south to northwestern Costa Rica (east to the Dota Mountains), and on the Caribbean slope of Costa Rica from Ochomogo to (formerly?) Juan Vinas.

Genus *PIPRA* Linnaeus

Pipra Linnaeus, 1764, Mus. Adolphi Friderici 2 (Prodr.): 32. Type, by subsequent designation (G. R. Gray, 1840), *Parus aureola* Linnaeus.

Notes.—Prum (1992) concluded from syringeal characters that the genus *Pipra,* as here construed, is polyphyletic. See comments under *Pipra pipra* and *Pipra coronata.*

Pipra pipra (Linnaeus). White-crowned Manakin.

Parus Pipra Linnaeus, 1758, Syst. Nat. (ed. 10) 1: 190. Based mainly on the "Cacototl" Seba, Thes. 2: 102, pl. 96, fig. 5. (in Indiis, error = Surinam.)

Dixphia Reichenbach, 1850, Avium Syst. Nat., pl. 63. Type, by subsequent designation (G. R. Gray, 1855), *Pipra leucocilla* Linnaeus = *Pipra pipra* Linnaeus.

Lepidothrix Bonaparte, 1854, Consp. Voluc. Anisod., p. 6. Type, by subsequent designation (G. R. Gray, 1855), *Pipra cyanocapilla* Wagl. = *Pipra cyanocapilla* Hahn = *Pipra coronata* Spix.

Habitat.—Tropical Lowland Evergreen Forest, Montane Evergreen Forest (475 to 1500 m; in South America, also sea level to 600 m; upper Tropical and lower Subtropical zones).

Distribution.—*Resident* [*anthracina* group] locally in the highlands of central Costa Rica (primarily on Caribbean slope of Cordillera Talamanca and Cordillera Central) and western Panama (eastern Chiriquí, both slopes of Veraguas, and the Caribbean slope of Coclé); and [*pipra* group] in South America from northern Colombia, southern Venezuela, and the Guianas south to central Peru and Amazonian and coastal southeastern Brazil.

Notes.— Placed in the monotypic genus *Dixiphia* by Prum (1992). Groups: *P. anthracina* Ridgway, 1906 [Zeledon's Manakin] and *P. pipra* [White-crowned Manakin]. Several species probably are involved in this complex, as highland and lowland forms approach one another in eastern Peru, and vocal differences exist among several forms.

Pipra coronata Spix. Blue-crowned Manakin.

> *Pipra coronata* Spix, 1825, Avium Spec. Nov. Bras. 2: 5, pl. 7, fig. 1. (ad pagum St. Pauli in sylviis fl. Solimoëns = São Paulo de Olivença, Rio Solimões, Brazil.)

Habitat.—Tropical Lowland Evergreen Forest, Secondary Forest (0–1350 m; Tropical and lower Subtropical zones).

Distribution.—*Resident* [*velutina* group] locally in Costa Rica (northwest to the Gulf of Nicoya on the Pacific slope, and in the Sixaola region in the southeast), adjacent western Panama (western Chiriquí, Bocas del Toro, northern Veraguas), eastern Panama (both slopes from the Canal area eastward), western and northern Colombia, and northwestern Ecuador; [*coronata* group] in South America from southeastern Colombia and southern Venezuela south, east of the Andes, to northern Peru and extreme western Amazonian Brazil; and [*exquisita* group] in central and southern Peru, northern Bolivia, and western and central Amazonian Brazil.

Notes.—Placed in the genus *Lepidothrix* by Prum (1992). Groups: *P. velutina* Berlepsch, 1883 [Velvety Manakin], *P. coronata* [Blue-crowned Manakin], and *P. exquisita* Hellmayr, 1905 [Exquisite Manakin].

Pipra erythrocephala (Linnaeus). Golden-headed Manakin.

> *Parus erythrocephalus* Linnaeus, 1758, Syst. Nat. (ed. 10) 1: 191. Based on *Parus auricapillus* Klein, Hist. Avium, p. 86, and "The Golden-headed Black Titmouse" Edwards, Nat. Hist. Birds 1: 21, pl. 21, lower fig. (in America australi = Surinam.)

Habitat.—Tropical Lowland Evergreen Forest (0–1200 m; Tropical and lower Subtropical zones).

Distribution.—*Resident* in eastern Panama (from eastern San Blas and eastern Panamá province eastward), and in South America from northwestern and northern Colombia, Venezuela, Trinidad, and the Guianas south to northeastern Peru and Amazonian Brazil north of the Amazon.

Notes.—*P. erythrocephala, P. mentalis,* and *P. rubrocapilla* Temminck, 1821 [Red-headed Manakin] constitute a superspecies; *erythrocephala* and *mentalis* overlap narrowly on the Pacific slope of Panama (e.g., near Maje), and a hybrid has been reported (Ridgely and Tudor 1989).

Pipra mentalis Sclater. Red-capped Manakin.

> *Pipra mentalis* Sclater, 1857, Proc. Zool. Soc. London (1856), p. 299, pl. 121. (Cordova [= Córdoba] in the State of Vera Cruz, Southern Mexico.)

Habitat.—Tropical Lowland Evergreen Forest (0–1050 m; Tropical Zone).

Distribution.—*Resident* on the Gulf-Caribbean slope of Middle America from southern Veracruz, Oaxaca, Tabasco, Chiapas and the Yucatan Peninsula (except the northwest) south to Nicaragua, on both slopes of Costa Rica (absent from the dry northwest), and Panama (east on the Caribbean slope to western San Blas, and on the Pacific to eastern Panamá province), and in South America west of the Andes in western Colombia and northwestern Ecuador.

Notes.—Also known as Yellow-thighed Manakin. See comments under *P. erythrocephala.*

Family **OXYRUNCIDAE**: Sharpbills

Notes.— *Oxyruncus cristatus* has a unique mosaic of conflicting characters that prohibit classifying it as a member of any of the larger tyrannoid families. Sibley et al. (1984) and Sibley and Ahlquist (1990) placed it within the Cotingidae based on DNA-DNA hybridization data. S.M. Lanyon (1985; a coauther of Sibley et al., 1984) later questioned this conclusion, and also provided allozyme data suggesting that *Oxyruncus* clustered with tyrant flycatchers, tityras, and becards. Prum (1990) found syringeal similarities with the becards, but excluded it from the well-defined "Schiffornis group" to which becards belong (Prum and Lanyon 1989) on other, compelling morphological grounds. Prum recommended *incertae sedis* status. Presumably, *Oxyruncus* was an early offshoot during the radiation of the Tyrannoidea, and we acknowledge its uniqueness by retaining its family status.

Genus *OXYRUNCUS* Temminck

Oxyruncus Temminck, 1820, Man. Ornithol. (ed. 2) 1: lxxx [generic characters only, no type species indicated]. Type, by monotypy, *Oxyrhyncus cristatus* Swainson.

Oxyruncus cristatus Swainson. Sharpbill.

Oxyrhyncus [sic] *cristatus* Swainson, 1821, Zool. Illus. (1)1(9): pl. 49. (Brazil.)

Habitat.—Montane Evergreen Forest, Tropical Lowland Evergreen Forest (700–1400 m; 0–1800 m in South America; Subtropical Zone, in South America also Tropical Zone).

Distribution.—*Resident* (with disjunct distribution) in Costa Rica (mainly Caribbean slope, from Cordillera de Guanacaste south, and, perhaps formerly, in Dota Mountains), Panama (recorded Bocas del Toro, western Chiriquí, Veraguas and the cerros of eastern Darién), and in South America locally in southern Venezuela, Guyana, Surinam, eastern Peru, northwestern Bolivia, eastern Amazonian and southeastern Brazil, and eastern Paraguay.

Suborder PASSERI: Oscines

Notes.—See Sibley and Ahlquist (1990) and Sheldon and Gill (1996) for hypotheses on relationships among families in this Suborder. The arrangement of families here follows Sibley and Ahlquist (1990) in recognizing the close relationships of the Meliphagidae, Laniidae, Vireonidae, and Monarchidae to the Corvidae, i.e., the parvorder Corvida of Sibley and Ahlquist (1990); see also A.O.U. (1997).

Family **MELIPHAGIDAE**: Honeyeaters

Genus *MOHO* Lesson

Moho Lesson, 1830, Traité Ornithol., p. 302. Type, by monotypy, *Merops fasciculatus* Latham = *Gracula nobilis* Merrem.

Moho braccatus Cassin. Kauai Oo.

Mohoa [sic] *braccata* Cassin, 1855, Proc. Acad. Nat. Sci. Philadelphia 7: 440. (Sandwich Islands = Kauai, Hawaiian Islands.)

Habitat.—Thick, undisturbed native forest.

Distribution.—*Resident* on Kauai, in the Hawaiian Islands (possibly extinct, the last known male surviving at least to 1988 in the Alakai Swamp region).

Notes.—Known also as the Ooaa.

†*Moho apicalis* Gould. Oahu Oo.

Moho apicalis Gould, 1860, Proc. Zool. Soc. London, p. 381. (Owhyhee = Oahu, Hawaiian Islands.)

Habitat.—Presumably forest.

Distribution.—EXTINCT. Formerly resident on Oahu, in the Hawaiian Islands (disappeared in a short period after 1837).

Notes.—*Moho apicalis, M. bishopi,* and *M. nobilis* may constitute a superspecies.

†*Moho bishopi* (Rothschild). Bishop's Oo.

Acrulocercus bishopi Rothschild, 1893, Bull. Br. Ornithol. Club 1: 41. (Island of Molokai.)

Habitat.—Forest, primarily ohia.

Distribution.—EXTINCT. Formerly resident on Molokai, in the Hawaiian Islands (last reported in 1904). Reports of oos on Maui from 1901 to 1981 may refer to this species (Sabo 1982).

Notes.—Also known as Molokai Oo. See comments under *M. apicalis.*

†*Moho nobilis* (Merrem). Hawaii Oo.

Gracula nobilis Merrem, 1786, Avium Rar. Icones Descr. 1(1): 7, pl. 2. (Insulæ San-
duicenses = island of Hawaii.)

Habitat.—Heavy forest.
Distribution.—EXTINCT. Formerly resident on Hawaii, in the Hawaiian Islands (last
definite record in 1898; one reported heard in 1934).
Notes.—See comments under *M. apicalis.*

Genus *CHAETOPTILA* Sclater

Chaetoptila Sclater, 1871, Ibis, p. 358. Type, by original designation, *Entomyza angustipluma* Cassin [= Peale].

†*Chaetoptila angustipluma* (Peale). Kioea.

Entomiza? angustipluma Peale, 1848, U. S. Explor. Exped. 8: 147. (Hawaii.)

Habitat.—Forest.
Distribution.—EXTINCT. Formerly resident on Hawaii, in the Hawaiian Islands (last
reported in 1859).

Family **LANIIDAE**: Shrikes

Genus *LANIUS* Linnaeus

Lanius Linnaeus, 1758, Syst. Nat. (ed. 10) 1: 93. Type, by subsequent designation
(Swainson, 1824), *Lanius excubitor* Linnaeus.

Lanius cristatus Linnaeus. Brown Shrike.

Lanius cristatus Linnaeus, 1758, Syst. Nat. (ed. 10) 1: 93. (in Benghala = Bengal.)

Habitat.—Deciduous and coniferous woodland.
Distribution.—*Breeds* from northern Siberia south to Mongolia, Manchuria, and Japan.
Winters from India east to eastern China, and south to southeastern Asia and the East Indies.
Casual or accidental in the western Aleutians (Attu, Shemya), on St. Lawrence Island, in
south-coastal Alaska (Anchorage), and in California (Farallon Islands, and Olema marsh,
Marin County).
Notes.—Also known as Red-tailed Shrike. Sibley and Monroe (1990) considered *L. cris-
tatus* to form a superspecies with *L. collurio* Linnaeus, 1758 [Red-backed Shrike] and *L.
isabellinus* Ehrenberg, 1833 [Rufous-tailed Shrike].

Lanius ludovicianus Linnaeus. Loggerhead Shrike.

Lanius ludovicianus Linnaeus, 1766, Syst. Nat. (ed. 12) 1: 134. Based on "La Pie-
grieche de la Louisiane" Brisson, Ornithologie 2: 162, pl. 15, fig. 2. (in Ludovicia
= Louisiana.)

Habitat.—Open country with scattered trees and shrubs, agricultural fields, savanna, desert
scrub, and, occasionally, open woodland; habitat always has fences, low trees, brush, or
other hunting perches with at least some bare ground or very short grass (Tropical to
Temperate zones).
Distribution.—*Breeds* from California (except the northwestern portion, but including
the Channel Islands), eastern Oregon, eastern Washington, central Alberta, central Saskatchewan, southern Manitoba, Minnesota (except northeastern), southern Ontario, southwestern
Quebec, and Pennsylvania (formerly from central New York, central Maine, southwestern
New Brunswick, and Nova Scotia) south to southern Baja California (including Cedros

Island), through central Mexico (not in coastal lowlands) to central Oaxaca and Veracruz, and to the Gulf coast and southern Florida; in recent years scarce and local in the northeastern part of the breeding range.

Winters from central Washington, eastern Oregon, California, southern Nevada, Utah, southern Colorado, southern Kansas, central Missouri, Illinois, central Ohio, and Virginia (casually north to the Canadian border) south to the southern limits of the breeding range, rarely to Chiapas.

Casual from southern British Columbia south (west of the Cascades) to southwestern Oregon, and in northwestern Guatemala and the Bahama Islands (Andros). Accidental on Bermuda.

Notes.—See comments under *L. excubitor.*

Lanius excubitor Linnaeus. Northern Shrike.

Lanius Excubitor Linnaeus, 1758, Syst. Nat. (ed. 10) 1: 94. (in Europa = Sweden.)

Habitat.—Open deciduous or coniferous woodland, taiga, thickets, bogs, and scrub; in migration and winter, also open situations with scattered trees, savanna, semi-desert, and cultivated lands.

Distribution.—*Breeds* [*excubitor* group] in North America from western and northern Alaska, northern Yukon, northwestern and southern Mackenzie, and southwestern Keewatin south to southern Alaska (west to the Alaska Peninsula), northwestern British Columbia, northern Alberta, northern Manitoba, northern Ontario, northern and central Quebec, and southern Labrador, and in the Old World from northern Scandinavia, northern Russia, and northern Siberia south to central Europe, central Russia, central Asia, and the Kuril Islands; and [*meridionalis* group] from southern Europe, the Canary Islands, and northern Africa (north of the Sahara) east to India.

Winters [*excubitor* group] in North America from central Alaska and the southern portions of the breeding range in Canada, Minnesota, and northwestern Wisconsin south (irregularly) to northern California, central Nevada, northern Arizona, central New Mexico, northern Texas, northwestern Oklahoma, Kansas, central Missouri, northern Illinois, central Indiana, northern Ohio, Pennsylvania, and New Jersey, casually to the central Aleutians, south to the southern parts of California, Arizona, and New Mexico, to northern Texas, northern Tennessee, North Carolina, and Bermuda, and in Eurasia throughout the breeding range, the northern populations being mostly migratory; and [*meridionalis* group] generally within the breeding range, but eastern populations winter south to northern India and west to northeastern Africa.

Resident [*leucopygos* group] across north-central Africa in the southern portions of the Sahara.

Notes.—Also known as Great Gray Shrike. Groups: *L. excubitor* [Northern Shrike], *L. meridionalis* Temminck, 1820 [Southern Gray Shrike], and *L. leucopygos* Ehrenberg, 1833 [Saharan Shrike]. *Lanius excubitor* and *L. ludovicianus,* along with the Asiatic *L. sphenocercus* Cabanis, 1873 [Chinese Gray Shrike], constitute a superspecies (Mayr and Short 1970).

Family **VIREONIDAE**: Vireos

Notes.—The systematic position of the Vireonidae has always been controversial; see Sibley and Ahlquist (1982b) for a review. We follow Johnson et al. (1988), Sibley and Ahlquist (1990), and Sheldon and Gill (1996) in placing the vireos within the "Corvida" assemblage. There seems to be no evidence for their traditional placement within the nine-primaried oscines (e.g., see Raikow 1978). For relationships within the Vireonidae and lack of justification for subfamilies and subgenera in this family, see Johnson et al. (1988). The formerly recognized subfamilies Vireolaniinae and Cyclarhininae have often been given family status, but see Zimmer (1942), Barlow and James (1975), Raikow (1978), Orenstein and Barlow (1981), and Sibley and Ahlquist (1982a) for reasons for their inclusion within the Vireonidae.

Genus *VIREO* Vieillot

Vireo Vieillot, 1808, Hist. Nat. Ois. Amer. Sept. 1 (1807): 83. Type, by subsequent designation (Gadow, 1883), *Vireo musicus* Vieillot = *Muscicapa noveboracensis* Gmelin = *Tanagra grisea* Boddaert.

Vireosylva Bonaparte, 1838, Geogr. Comp. List, p. 26. Type, by subsequent designation (G. R. Gray, 1841), *Muscicapa olivacea* Linnaeus.

Neochloe Sclater, 1858, Proc. Zool. Soc. London (1857), p. 213. Type, by monotypy, *Neochloe brevipennis* Sclater.

Lanivireo Baird, 1858, in Baird, Cassin, and Lawrence, Rep. Explor. Surv. R. R. Pac. 9: xix, "xxxxv" [= xxxv], 329. Type, by original designation, *Vireo flavifrons* Vieillot.

Solivireo Oberholser, 1974, Bird Life Tex., p. 997. Type, by original designation, *Muscicapa solitaria* Wilson.

Melodivireo Oberholser, 1974, Bird Life Tex., p. 998. Type, by original designation, *Muscicapa gilva* Vieillot.

Vireo brevipennis (Sclater). Slaty Vireo.

Neochloe brevipennis Sclater, 1858, Proc. Zool. Soc. London (1857), p. 213. (Orizaba, [Veracruz,] Southern Mexico.)

Habitat.—Arid Montane Scrub, Pine-Oak Forest (1200-2100 m; Subtropical and lower Temperate zones).

Distribution.—*Resident* in the highlands of southern Jalisco, Colima, Guerrero, Morelos, Oaxaca, and western Veracruz.

Notes.—Sometimes placed in the monotypic genus *Neochloe*.

Vireo griseus (Boddaert). White-eyed Vireo.

Tanagra grisea Boddaert, 1783, Table Planches Enlum., p. 45. Based on "Tanagra olive, de la Louisiane" Daubenton, Planches Enlum., pl. 714, fig. 1. (Louisiana = New Orleans.)

Habitat.—Dense undergrowth at deciduous forest edge and treefalls; more widespread in migration and winter, but primarily in dense thickets (Tropical to lower Temperate zones).

Distribution.—*Breeds* [*griseus* group] from central Iowa, southeastern Minnesota (rarely), southern Wisconsin, southern Michigan, extreme southern Ontario, southern New York, and southern Massachusetts south to eastern San Luis Potosí, northern Hidalgo, extreme northern Veracruz, Tamaulipas, southern Texas, the Gulf coast, southern Florida (including the Florida Keys), and Bermuda, and west to eastern Nebraska (formerly), eastern Kansas, central Oklahoma, west-central Texas, and Coahuila; and [*perquisitor* group] in northeastern Puebla and north-central Veracruz.

Winters [*griseus* group] from central Texas, the Gulf states, extreme southeastern Virginia (Dismal Swamp), the Bahama Islands (east to San Salvador), and Bermuda south along the Gulf-Caribbean slope of Mexico (including the Yucatan Peninsula, also on the Pacific slope in southeastern Oaxaca), Belize, Guatemala, Honduras, and (rarely) northern Nicaragua, on Cuba and the Isle of Pines, and in the Cayman and Swan islands; and [*perquisitor* group] presumably in the breeding range.

Casual [*griseus* group] north to North Dakota, southern Manitoba, southern Minnesota, northern Michigan, southern Quebec, Maine, and Nova Scotia, west to California, Utah, Arizona, Colorado, southern New Mexico, Chihuahua, and south to Costa Rica, Panama, Puerto Rico (including Mona Island), and the Virgin Islands (St. John); a sight report for the Revillagigedo Islands (Socorro).

Notes.—Although *V. griseus* [White-eyed Vireo] and *V. perquisitor* Nelson, 1900 [Veracruz Vireo] were regarded by Eisenmann (1955) as distinct species, they are similar in many respects. Species and superspecies boundaries in the "white-eyed vireo" complex (all species from *V. griseus* through *V. nanus*) are poorly understood and their accurate definition awaits further research.

Vireo crassirostris (Bryant). Thick-billed Vireo.

Lanivireo crassirostris Bryant, 1859, Proc. Boston Soc. Nat. Hist. 7: 112. (New Providence, Bahama Islands.)

Habitat.—Tropical Deciduous Forest, Arid Lowland Scrub, Mangrove Forest.

Distribution.—*Resident* [*crassirostris* group] in the Bahamas (virtually throughout, even small islands), northern cays off Cuban mainland, including Cayo Coco and Cayo Paredones (rare winter resident), Cayman Islands, and Tortue Island (off Hispaniola); and [*approximans* group] on Providencia and adjacent Santa Catalina islands (in the western Caribbean Sea).

Casual [*crassirostris* group] in southern Florida (Hypoluxo Island, Lantana, Dry Tortugas, and Flamingo).

Notes.—Groups: *V. crassirostris* [Thick-billed Vireo] and *V. approximans* Ridgway, 1884 [Old Providence Vireo]. See comments under *V. griseus* and *V. pallens.*

Vireo pallens Salvin. Mangrove Vireo.

Vireo pallens Salvin, 1863, Proc. Zool. Soc. London, p. 188. (Realejo, Nicaragua, and Punta Arenas, Costa Rica = Punta Arenas, Costa Rica.)

Habitat.—Tropical Deciduous Forest, Mangrove Forest, Arid Lowland Scrub (Tropical Zone).

Distribution.—*Resident* [*pallens* group] along the Pacific coast from southwestern Sonora south to Nayarit, and from Oaxaca south to Costa Rica (to the Gulf of Nicoya); and [*semiflavus* group] on the Gulf-Caribbean coast and many islands from the Yucatan Peninsula (including Holbox and Mujeres islands) and eastern Guatemala (Petén) south through Belize (including Soldier Cay) and Honduras (including the Bay Islands) to Nicaragua (Bluefields area).

Notes.—Groups: *V. pallens* [Mangrove Vireo] and *V. semiflavus* Salvin, 1863 [Maya Vireo]. Considered by Hellmayr (1935) to be conspecific with *V. griseus.* Mayr and Short (1970) considered *V. pallens* and *V. griseus* to constitute a superspecies. Sibley and Monroe (1990) considered *V. pallens, V. bairdi, V. gundlachii, V. crassirostris,* and *V. caribaeus* to be members of a superspecies. See comments under *V. griseus.*

Vireo bairdi Ridgway. Cozumel Vireo.

Vireo bairdi Ridgway, 1885, Proc. Biol. Soc. Wash. 3: 22. (Cozumel Island, Yucatan.)

Habitat.—Tropical Deciduous Forest, Secondary Forest (Tropical Zone).
Distribution.—*Resident* on Cozumel Island, off Quintana Roo.
Notes.—See comments under *V. griseus* and *V. pallens.*

Vireo caribaeus Bond and Meyer de Schauensee. St. Andrew Vireo.

Vireo caribaeus Bond and Meyer de Schauensee, 1942, Not. Nat., Acad. Nat. Sci. Philadelphia, no. 96, p. 1. (St. Andrew's [= San Andrés] Island, Colombia.)

Habitat.—Tropical Deciduous Forest, Mangrove Forest, Arid Lowland Scrub.
Distribution.—*Resident* on Isla San Andrés, in the western Caribbean Sea.
Notes.—Sometimes regarded as a race of *V. pallens* or *V. modestus;* for a discussion of relationships, see Barlow and Nash (1985). See comments under *V. griseus* and *V. pallens.*

Vireo modestus Sclater. Jamaican Vireo.

Vireo modestus Sclater, 1861, Proc. Zool. Soc. London (1860), p. 462. (In ins. Jamaica.)

Habitat.—Tropical Deciduous Forest, Tropical Lowland Evergreen Forest, Secondary Forest, Montane Evergreen Forest (0-1500 m).
Distribution.—*Resident* on Jamaica.
Notes.—Also known as Jamaican White-eyed Vireo. See comments under *V. griseus* and *V. caribaeus.*

Vireo gundlachii Lembeye. Cuban Vireo.

> *Vireo gundlachii* Lembeye, 1850, Aves Isla Cuba, p. 29, pl. 5, fig. 1. (Cuba = Cienfuegos, Cuba.)

Habitat.—Tropical Lowland Evergreen Forest, Tropical Deciduous Forest, Arid Lowland Scrub, Secondary Forest (0-700 m).
Distribution.—*Resident* on Cuba (including many cays) and the Isle of Pines.
Notes.—See comments under *V. griseus* and *V. pallens.*

Vireo latimeri Baird. Puerto Rican Vireo.

> *Vireo latimeri* Baird, 1866, Rev. Amer. Birds 1: 364. (north side of Puerto Rico.)

Habitat.—Tropical Deciduous Forest, Tropical Lowland Evergreen Forest, Secondary Forest, Arid Lowland Scrub (0-900 m).
Distribution.—*Resident* on Puerto Rico (except the eastern portion).
Notes.—See comments under *V. griseus.*

Vireo nanus (Lawrence). Flat-billed Vireo.

> *Empidonax nanus* Lawrence, 1875, Ibis, p. 386. (St. Domingo = Dominican Republic.)

Habitat.—Tropical Deciduous Forest (0-1200 m).
Distribution.—*Resident* on Hispaniola (including Gonâve Island).
Notes.—See comments under *V. griseus.*

Vireo bellii Audubon. Bell's Vireo.

> *Vireo bellii* Audubon, 1844, Birds Amer. (octavo ed.) 7: 333, pl. 485. (short distance below Black Snake Hills = near St. Joseph, Missouri.)

Habitat.—Dense brush, willow thickets, mesquite, streamside thickets, and scrub oak; in arid regions usually near water; in migration and winter, primarily in dense scrub (Tropical, Subtropical, and Temperate zones).
Distribution.—*Breeds* from coastal southern and interior California (north to Santa Barbara and Inyo counties, now scarce and local; formerly also in the interior to Tehama County), southern Nevada, southwestern Utah, northwestern and east-central Arizona, southern New Mexico, northeastern Colorado, Nebraska, South Dakota, western North Dakota, southeastern Minnesota, southern Wisconsin, northeastern Illinois, northwestern and central Indiana, and southwestern Michigan south to northern Baja California, southern Sonora, southern Durango, Zacatecas, southern Tamaulipas, southern and eastern Texas, north-central Louisiana, Arkansas, southwestern Tennessee, southwestern Kentucky, southern Indiana. and western Ohio.

Winters from southern Baja California and southern Sonora (casually north to central California, southern Arizona, southern Texas, Louisiana, and southern Florida) south, primarily on the Pacific slope and in the interior of Middle America, to Honduras, casually to north-central Nicaragua.

Migrates regularly through northern Mexico, casually (mostly in fall) through the Gulf states east to Florida.

Casual or accidental north to Montana, Wyoming, and southern Ontario, and east to New York (Long Island), New Hampshire, New Jersey, and South Carolina.

Vireo atricapillus Woodhouse. Black-capped Vireo.

> *Vireo atricapilla* Woodhouse, 1852, Proc. Acad. Nat. Sci. Philadelphia 6: 60. (Rio San Pedro, 208 miles from San Antonio, on road to El Paso del Norte, Texas = Devils River, near Juno, Val Verde County, Texas; Sexton and Tomer, 1990, Bull. Texas Ornithol. Soc. 23: 2-5.)

Habitat.—Dense low thickets and scrub oak, with many openings, and mostly on rocky hillsides; in winter, also semi-arid tropical scrub.

Distribution.—*Breeds* from south-central Kansas (Comanche County, formerly) south through west-central Oklahoma and western and central Texas (east to Dallas, Waco, Austin, and San Antonio areas, and west to Abilene, San Angelo, and Big Bend) to central Coahuila.

Winters from Sinaloa and Durango south to southern Oaxaca.

Migrates through western and southern Texas and central Mexico (east to México and Tamaulipas).

Casual north to eastern Nebraska and northeastern Kansas. Accidental in Arizona (Tucson) and southern Ontario (Long Point). A sight report from Mississippi is questionable.

Notes.—Sibley and Monroe (1990) considered *V. atricapillus* and *V. nelsoni* to constitute a superspecies.

Vireo nelsoni Bond. Dwarf Vireo.

> *Vireo nanus* (not *Empidonax nanus* Lawrence) Nelson, 1898, Proc. Biol. Soc. Wash. 12: 59. (Querendaro, Michoacan, Mexico.)
> *Vireo nelsoni* Bond, 1936, Auk 53: 458. New name for *Vireo nanus* Nelson, preoccupied.

Habitat.—Arid Montane Scrub (1500-2400 m; Subtropical Zone, to lower Temperate Zone in winter).

Distribution.—*Breeds* locally in the highlands from Guanajuato and Michoacán to northern Oaxaca (west of the Isthmus of Tehuantepec).

Winters presumably mostly in the breeding range (ascending in migration to higher elevations); a report from Sinaloa is questionable.

Vireo vicinior Coues. Gray Vireo.

> *Vireo vicinior* Coues, 1866, Proc. Acad. Nat. Sci. Philadelphia 18: 75. (Fort Whipple, Arizona.)

Habitat.—Dry oak-juniper and pinyon-juniper woodlands, dry chaparral, and thorn scrub; in migration and winter, also desert and arid scrub.

Distribution.—*Breeds* locally from southern California (north to Inyo County), southern Nevada, southern Utah, western and southeastern Colorado, and northwestern and central New Mexico south to northwestern Baja California, central and southeastern Arizona, southern New Mexico, western Texas (east to Kinney, Colorado, and Kerr counties), and northwestern Coahuila (Sierra del Carmen).

Winters locally in central and in southern Baja California, southwestern Arizona (rarely), Sonora (including Tiburón and San Esteban islands), and (rarely) western Texas (Big Bend region).

Migrates through Baja California and Durango.

Casual to the Channel Islands off California. Accidental in Oklahoma (Cimmaron County), Wisconsin (Sheboygan County), and San Luis Potosí. Sight reports from Texas Panhandle are unsubstantiated.

Vireo osburni (Sclater). Blue Mountain Vireo.

> *Laletes osburni* Sclater, 1861, Proc. Zool. Soc. London, p. 72, pl. 14, fig. 2. (Freeman's Hall, Trelawny Parish, Jamaica.)

Habitat.—Montane Evergreen Forest, Tropical Lowland Evergreen Forest, Secondary Forest (600-2000 m; Tropical and Subtropical zones).

Distribution.—*Resident* in the hills and mountains of Jamaica (most commonly in the Blue Mountains).

Vireo flavifrons Vieillot. Yellow-throated Vireo.

> *Vireo flavifrons* Vieillot, 1808, Hist. Nat. Ois. Amer. Sept. 1 (livr. 9): 85, pl. 54. (États Unis = eastern United States.)

Habitat.—Primarily tall open deciduous forest and woodland, tall riparian woodland, and, less frequently, mixed deciduous-coniferous woodland with tall trees; in migration and winter, a variety of wooded habitats.

Distribution.—*Breeds* from southeastern Saskatchewan, southern Manitoba, Minnesota, northern Wisconsin, northern Michigan, southern Ontario, southwestern Quebec, northern New Hampshire, and southwestern Maine south to eastern Texas, the Gulf coast, and central Florida, and west to central North Dakota, eastern South Dakota, eastern Nebraska, eastern Kansas, eastern Oklahoma, and west-central Texas.

Winters from northern and south-central Oaxaca and southern Veracruz south along both slopes of Middle America (including the Yucatan Peninsula and Cozumel Island), and from extreme southern Florida through the Bahama Islands, Cuba, the Isle of Pines, and the Cayman Islands to central Colombia and northern Venezuela, casually in southern California and the Virgin Islands (St. Thomas, St. John). No documented winter records in the eastern United States north of southern Florida

Migrates regularly through eastern North America east of the Rockies, Bermuda (rare), and eastern Mexico, casually through western North America from northern California, Nevada, eastern Colorado, and western Texas southward.

Casual or accidental north to central Saskatchewan, western Ontario, Nova Scotia, and Newfoundland. Accidental in the Lesser Antilles (St. Vincent, Barbados), Tobago, Chacachacare Island (off Trinidad), and the British Isles; sight reports for Idaho and Nayarit.

Vireo plumbeus Coues. Plumbeous Vireo.

> *Vireo plumbeus* Coues, 1866, Proc. Acad. Nat. Sci. Philadelphia 18: 74. (Fort Whipple, Arizona.)

Habitat.—Open yellow pine forest, pine-oak association, oak scrub, pinyon-juniper woodland, and riparian woodland; in migration and winter, a variety of wooded habitats (Subtropical and Temperate zones).

Distribution.—*Breeds* from west-central Nevada, extreme south-central Idaho, northeastern Utah, central and southeastern Montana, southwestern South Dakota, and northwestern Nebraska south through the western United States (from mountains of east-central California east of crest of Sierra Nevada and southern California) east to western Texas and Mexico to Belize, Guatemala, El Salvador, and Honduras.

Winters from the southwestern United States and northwestern Mexico south to Honduras.

Migrates through the Great Basin, Utah, Wyoming, western and central Colorado, New Mexico, and northern and central Mexico.

Casual or accidental in south-central Oregon (Harney County), northwestern Nevada, eastern Colorado, and southwestern Louisiana. Sight records from eastern North America are unsubstantiated.

Notes.—*Vireo solitarius*, *V. cassinii*, and *V. plumbeus* were formerly regarded as subspecies of *V. solitarius* [Solitary Vireo]; they constitute a superspecies (Sibley and Monroe 1990). Specific status of the three forms is based upon differences in morphology, coloration, vocalizations (Borror 1972, James 1981), and genetics (Murray et al. 1994, Johnson 1995). Assignment of populations from Central America to *V. plumbeus* is tentative.

Vireo cassinii Xantus de Vesey. Cassin's Vireo.

> *Vireo cassinii* Xantus de Vesey, 1858, Proc. Acad. Nat. Sci. Philadelphia, 10: 117 (Fort Tejon, California.)

Habitat—Open coniferous or mixed coniferous-deciduous woodland, pine-oak association, oak woodland; in migration and winter, a variety of wooded habitats (Temperate Zone).

Distribution—*Breeds* from southern British Columbia (including Vancouver Island), southwestern Alberta, and western Montana south to central Idaho and east-central Oregon, through northern California and extreme west-central Nevada, thence west of the axis of the Sierra Nevada to the coastal slopes of the mountains of southern California and northern Baja California (Sierra San Pedro Martír) and in the Cape district of southern Baja California.

Winters from the southwestern United States (rare) and northwestern Mexico south to Guatemala. Casual in northwestern California.

Migrates through the Pacific coastal states, Idaho, western Montana, the Great Basin, Utah, Arizona, and eastward in the Rocky Mountain region through Colorado, New Mexico, and western Texas.

Casual or accidental in southeastern Alaska, Oklahoma (Cimmaron County), New York, and New Jersey.

Notes.—See comments under *V. plumbeus.*

Vireo solitarius (Wilson). Blue-headed Vireo.

Muscicapa solitaria Wilson, 1810, Amer. Ornithol. 2: 143, pl. 17, fig. 6. (Bartram's woods, near Philadelphia [Pennsylvania].)

Habitat.—Open coniferous or mixed coniferous-deciduous woodland; in migration and winter, a variety of wooded habitats, but favors tall woodland with live oaks and pines (Temperate Zone).

Distribution.—*Breeds* from northeastern British Columbia and Alberta (except southwestern part), southwestern Mackenzie, northern and southeastern Alberta, northern Saskatchewan, central Manitoba, northern Ontario, southern Quebec, New Brunswick, Prince Edward Island, Nova Scotia, and southwestern Newfoundland south to north-central North Dakota (probably), north-central and northeastern Minnesota, northern Wisconsin, south-central Indiana, south-central Ohio, eastern Pennsylvania, northern New Jersey, and Massachusetts, and south in the Appalachians and Piedmont region to eastern Tennessee, northeastern Alabama, central Georgia, northwestern South Carolina, central North Carolina, and central Virginia.

Winters from central Texas, southern Arkansas, the northern portions of the Gulf states, and southern Virginia south to southern Florida, Cuba, the Isle of Pines, and (probably) Jamaica, and through eastern and southern Mexico and Central America (mostly Gulf-Caribbean slope) to Costa Rica.

Migrates through the central and eastern United States, mostly east of the Rockies (rarely eastern New Mexico and western Texas) and casually through Bermuda and the northern Bahama Islands.

Casual or accidental in California, southern Arizona, eastern Colorado, and Greenland. Sight reports from Panama.

Notes.—See comments under *V. plumbeus.*

Vireo carmioli Baird. Yellow-winged Vireo.

Vireo carmioli Baird, 1866, Rev. Amer. Birds 1: 356. (Dota [= Santa María de Dota], San José, Costa Rica.)

Habitat.—Montane Evergreen Forest (2000-3300 m; upper Subtropical and Temperate zones).

Distribution.—*Resident* in the mountains of Costa Rica (Cordillera Central, Dota Mountains, and Cordillera de Talamanca) and western Panama (western Chiriquí).

Notes.—Genetic evidence supports a sister relationship between *V. carmioli* and *V. huttoni* (Johnson et al. 1988). Also known as Carmiol's Vireo.

Vireo huttoni Cassin. Hutton's Vireo.

Vireo Huttoni Cassin, 1851, Proc. Acad. Nat. Sci. Philadelphia 5: 150. (Monterey and Georgetown, California = Monterey, California.)

Habitat.—Pine-oak association, oak woodland, riparian woodland, and locally in tall chaparral and dense undergrowth at edge of humid coniferous forest (Subtropical and Temperate zones).

Distribution.—*Resident* from southwestern British Columbia (including Vancouver Island) south through western Washington, western Oregon, and California (west of the Sierra Nevada divide, including the Channel Islands) to northwestern Baja California; in the Cape district of southern Baja California; from central Arizona, southwestern New Mexico, and western Texas (also casually in Real County) south through the highlands of Mexico to central and southern Oaxaca; and from Chiapas to western Guatemala.

Casual in the desert region of southeastern California and southwestern Arizona; a sight report for eastern Oregon.

Notes.—An allozyme study (Cicero and Johnson 1992) showed a pronounced difference between populations in California and Arizona. See comments under *V. carmioli.*

Vireo hypochryseus Sclater. Golden Vireo.

Vireo hypochryseus Sclater, 1863, Proc. Zool. Soc. London (1862), p. 369, pl. 46. (Mexico.)

Habitat.—Tropical Deciduous Forest, Gallery Forest (0-2000 m; Tropical Zone).

Distribution.—*Resident* on the Pacific slope of Mexico from southern Sonora south to Oaxaca (west of the Isthmus of Tehuantepec); in interior from Jalisco to Morelos; also in the Tres Marias Islands, off Nayarit.

Vireo gilvus (Vieillot). Warbling Vireo.

Muscicapa gilva Vieillot, 1808, Hist. Nat. Ois. Amer. Sept. 1 (livr. 6): 65, pl. 34. (État de New-Yorck = New York.)

Habitat.—Open deciduous and mixed deciduous-coniferous woodland, riparian forest and thickets (commonly in association with cottonwoods, aspen, and tree willows; often near water), pine-oak association, orchards, and parks; in migration and winter, a variety of wooded habitats (Subtropical and Temperate zones).

Distribution.—*Breeds* [*swainsonii* group] from southeastern Alaska, northern British Columbia, west-central and southwestern Mackenzie, northern and southeastern Alberta, southwestern Saskatchewan, central Wyoming, southwestern South Dakota, and western Nebraska south to northern Baja California (also in the Victoria Mountains of southern Baja California), southern Nevada, central and southeastern Arizona, the highlands of Mexico (Sierra Madre Occidental to México, Morelos, and central Oaxaca), southern New Mexico, and western Texas; and [*gilvus* group] from central Alberta, central Saskatchewan, southern Manitoba, western and southern Ontario, extreme southwestern Quebec, Maine, New Brunswick, and southern Nova Scotia (probably) south to southeastern Texas (casually), southern Louisiana (formerly), central Mississippi, northern Alabama, southeastern Tennessee, western North Carolina, central South Carolina, and Virginia, and west to southeastern Montana, northern and eastern North Dakota, eastern South Dakota, eastern Nebraska, Kansas, and southeastern Colorado.

Winters [*swainsonii* group] in Mexico (mostly Pacific slope and interior) from southern Sonora south to Oaxaca, and east to Hidalgo and southeastern Veracruz, casually north to southern California and southern Arizona; and [*gilvus* group] from Oaxaca (rarely), southern Veracruz, and Chiapas south through Guatemala to El Salvador, rarely to Honduras and Nicaragua. Accidental in Bermuda (late December).

Migrates [*swainsonii* group] through southwestern Canada and the western United States; and [*gilvus* group] regularly through the south-central United States and eastern Mexico, rarely (or casually) through the southeastern states east to southern Florida and Bermuda.

Casual [*swainsonii* group] in south-coastal Alaska (Anchorage, Middleton Island), southern Louisiana, and northern Florida; and [*gilvus* group] in Nova Scotia (Seal Island), Newfoundland (Great Codroy), and western Cuba. A sight report [group uncertain] from northeastern Costa Rica.

Notes.—The two groups differ morphologically, vocally, genetically, and ecologically, and possibly represent distinct species, *V. swainsonii* Baird, 1858 [Western Warbling-Vireo] and *V. gilvus* [Eastern Warbling-Vireo] (J. C. Barlow, pers. comm.); they were treated as species by Sibley and Monroe (1990) and Phillips (1991). Relationships between *V. gilvus* and *V. leucophrys* remain uncertain; some authors (e.g, Blake *in* Paynter 1968, Mayr and Short 1970) treat them as conspecific; herein they are treated as sister species (Johnson et al. 1988) that form a superspecies (Sibley and Monroe 1990).

Vireo leucophrys (Lafresnaye). Brown-capped Vireo.

Hylophilus leucophrys Lafresnaye, 1844, Rev. Zool. [Paris] 7: 81. (Colombie = Colombia.)

Habitat.—Montane Evergreen Forest, Secondary Forest (1200-2600 m; Subtropical and Temperate zones).

Distribution.—*Resident* locally in the highlands from eastern San Luis Potosí and southern Tamaulipas south through Hidalgo and Puebla to Veracruz; from southeastern Oaxaca through Chiapas and Guatemala to Honduras; and in the mountains of Costa Rica and western Panama (east to Veraguas), and from eastern Panama (Darién), Colombia, and northern Venezuela south in the Andes to central Bolivia.

Notes.—See comments under *V. gilvus.*

Vireo philadelphicus (Cassin). Philadelphia Vireo.

Vireosylvia philadelphica Cassin, 1851, Proc. Acad. Nat. Sci. Philadelphia 5: 153. (Bingham's woods, near Philadelphia, Pennsylvania.)

Habitat.—Open deciduous or mixed deciduous-coniferous woodland, forest edge, second growth, and alder and willow thickets, especially near streams; in migration and winter, a variety of wooded habitats.

Distribution.—*Breeds* from northeastern British Columbia, northern Alberta, northwestern Saskatchewan, central Manitoba, northern Ontario, south-central Quebec, New Brunswick, and southwestern Newfoundland (not known to breed in Nova Scotia) south to south-central Alberta, central Saskatchewan, southern Manitoba, north-central North Dakota, northeastern Minnesota, northern Michigan, southern Ontario, northern New York, southern Quebec, Prince Edward Island, and northern New England.

Winters from Chiapas (rarely north to southern Veracruz and the Yucatan Peninsula) south to the western highlands of Panama, rarely to northern Colombia. Casual in coastal southern California, and accidental in southern Louisiana.

Migrates primarily east of the Rockies and west of the Appalachians, rarely through California in fall (casually in spring in central and southern regions of the state), and less commonly through the southeastern United States south to the Gulf coast, southern Florida, and Cuba.

Casual in east-central and south-coastal Alaska (Eagle, Middleton Island), southwestern British Columbia, eastern Washington, eastern Oregon, Montana, Wyoming, eastern Colorado, Arizona, southern New Mexico, western Texas, Nova Scotia, Bermuda, the Bahama Islands (Abaco, Eleuthera, New Providence), Jamaica, Guerrero, and northwestern Oaxaca; accidental in the British Isles; a sight report for northern Baja California.

Vireo olivaceus (Linnaeus). Red-eyed Vireo.

Muscicapa olivacea Linnaeus, 1766, Syst. Nat. (ed. 12) 1: 327. Based mainly on "The Red Ey'd Flycatcher" Catesby, Nat. Hist. Carolina 1: 54, pl. 54. (in America septentrionali = South Carolina.)

Habitat.—[*olivaceus* group] Deciduous and mixed coniferous forest, second-growth woodland, riparian woodland; in migration and winter, a variety of open forest, woodland, and scrub habitats; [*chivi* group] Tropical Lowland Evergreen Forest, Secondary Forest, Tropical Deciduous Forest, Gallery Forest (0-1500 m; Tropical and Subtropical zones.)

Distribution.—*Breeds* [*olivaceus* group] from southeastern Alaska (probably), southwestern and northeastern British Columbia (including Vancouver Island), west-central and southwestern Mackenzie, northern Alberta, northwestern and central Saskatchewan, north-central Manitoba, northern Ontario, south-central Quebec (including Anticosti and Magdalen islands), New Brunswick, Prince Edward Island, Nova Scotia, and southern Newfoundland south to northern Oregon, northern Idaho, Montana, Wyoming, eastern Colorado, western Oklahoma, northeastern Coahuila (probably), south-central (Edwards Plateau) and eastern Texas (south to Nueces River), the Gulf coast, and southern Florida; and [*chivi* group] in South America from Colombia, Venezuela (including Margarita Island), Tobago, Trinidad, and the Guianas south, west of the Andes to northwestern Peru and east of the Andes to central Argentina.

Winters [*olivaceus* group] in South America east of the Andes in the Amazon basin of eastern Colombia, southern Venezuela, eastern Ecuador, eastern Peru, and western Brazil; and [*chivi* group] in the northern part of the breeding range south to the Amazon basin.

Migrates [*olivaceus* group] through eastern North America (east of the Rockies), the Gulf-Caribbean slope of Mexico, Bermuda, the Bahama Islands, the Greater Antilles, the Cayman Islands, along both slopes of Middle America (from Chiapas southward) and northern South America, rarely but regularly through California (more frequent in fall), rarely elsewhere in western North America south of the breeding range.

Casual or accidental [*olivaceus* group] in central and south-coastal Alaska (Fairbanks, Anchorage, Middleton Island), Chile, Greenland, Iceland, the British Isles (almost annually), the Netherlands, Germany, France, and Malta; sight reports for southern Yukon and northern Baja California.

Notes.—The two groups are sometimes regarded as separate species because of a wide hiatus in distribution, but recent biochemical studies (Johnson and Zink 1985) indicate that *chivi* (Vieillot, 1817) [Chivi Vireo] and *olivaceus* [Red-eyed Vireo] are closely related and presumably conspecific, whereas *V. flavoviridis* is distinct at the species level; the approach of the breeding ranges (with no suggestion of any intergradation) of the *chivi* group and *flavoviridis* in eastern Panama and northwestern Colombia also supports recognition of *flavoviridis* at the species level. The resident population on Fernando de Noronha, formerly considered to be conspecific with the *chivi* group, is recognized as a species, *V. gracilirostris* Sharpe, 1890, by Olson (1994). *Vireo olivaceus, V. gracilirostris, V. flavoviridis, V. altiloquus,* and *V. magister* are also closely related and may constitute a superspecies (Blake *in* Paynter 1968, Mayr and Short 1970, Sibley and Monroe 1990).

Vireo flavoviridis (Cassin). Yellow-green Vireo.

Vireosylvia flavoviridis Cassin, 1851, Proc. Acad. Nat. Sci. Philadelphia 5: 162, pl. 11. (Panama and San Juan de Nicaragua = San Juan del Sur, Nicaragua.)

Habitat.—Secondary Forest, Tropical Deciduous Forest, Gallery Forest, Tropical Lowland Evergreen Forest Edge (0-1700 m; Tropical and Subtropical zones).

Distribution.—*Breeds* from central Sonora, northern Nuevo León (to Sierra Picachos, Sierra de los Lampazos), and (rarely) southern Texas (lower Rio Grande Valley) south along both slopes of Middle America (including the Tres Marias Islands, off Nayarit) to Costa Rica and Panama (Pacific slope east to eastern Panamá province, including Coiba and the Pearl islands).

Winters in South America in the western Amazon Basin from eastern Ecuador south to central Bolivia.

Migrates through Middle America (including islas Providencia and San Andrés) and Colombia. Recorded annually in fall in California.

Casual or accidental in southern Arizona, southeastern New Mexico, southwestern, central and southeastern Texas, southwestern Louisiana, Bermuda, Florida, the Lesser Antilles (Barbados), and Venezuela.

Notes.—See comments under *V. olivaceus.*

Vireo altiloquus (Vieillot). Black-whiskered Vireo.

Muscicapa altiloqua Vieillot, 1808, Hist. Nat. Ois. Amer. Sept. 1 (livr. 7): 67, pl. 38. (Jamaica, Saine-Domingue, etc. = St. Thomas, Virgin Islands.)

Habitat.—Tropical Deciduous Forest, Tropical Lowland Evergreen Forest, Secondary Forest, Mangrove Forest (0-900 m).

Distribution.—*Breeds* in central and southern Florida (Cedar Keys and New Smyrna Beach southward, mainly coastal), the Bahama Islands, throughout the Greater and Lesser Antilles (where permanent resident), Little Cayman, and Cayman Brac in the Cayman Islands, islands of the western Caribbean Sea (Providencia and San Andrés), and islands off the north coast of Venezuela (Netherlands Antilles east to Margarita Island).

Winters apparently in South America from eastern Colombia, Venezuela, and the Guianas south, east of the Andes, to northeastern Peru and Amazonian Brazil (but many of these records within this range may pertain to transients), rarely on Hispaniola, Puerto Rico, and in the northern Lesser Antilles and Providencia and San Andrés islands.

Migrates (mostly in spring) along the Gulf coast from western Florida to southeastern

Louisiana (where summer reports suggest possible breeding), on Trinidad, and casually on the Caribbean slope of Panama.

Casual in Texas, southwestern Louisiana, North Carolina, Virginia, Bermuda, Belize, Costa Rica, and Tobago; a sight report for Quintana Roo. An old record from Honduras is without basis (Monroe 1968).

Notes.—See comments under *V. olivaceus.*

Vireo magister (Lawrence). Yucatan Vireo.

> *Vireosylvia magister* (Baird MS) Lawrence, 1871, Ann. Lyc. Nat. Hist. N. Y. 10: 20. (Belize, Br. Honduras.)

Habitat.—Tropical Deciduous Forest, Secondary Forest, Mangrove Forest (Tropical Zone).

Distribution.—*Resident* in the Cayman Islands (Grand Cayman), on the Yucatan Peninsula (including Mujeres and Cozumel islands) south to Belize (including small cays offshore), and on the Bay and Hog islands off the Caribbean coast of Honduras.

Accidental in southeastern Texas (photos, 29 April - 27 May 1984, Bolivar Peninsula; Morgan et al. 1985).

Notes.—See comments under *V. olivaceus.* Also known as Belize Vireo.

Genus *HYLOPHILUS* Temminck

> *Hylophilus* Temminck, 1822, Planches Color., livr. 29, pl. 173. Type, by subsequent designation (G. R. Gray, 1840), *Hylophilus poicilotis* Temminck.

Notes.—This genus may be paraphyletic (Johnson et al. 1988).

Hylophilus flavipes Lafresnaye. Scrub Greenlet.

> *Hylophilus flavipes* Lafresnaye, 1845, Rev. Zool. [Paris] 8: 342. ("Bogotá," Colombia.)

Habitat.—Tropical Deciduous Forest, Gallery Forest, Secondary Forest, Mangrove Forest (0-1000 m; Tropical Zone).

Distribution.—*Resident* [*viridiflavus* group] on the Pacific slope of southwestern Costa Rica (north to Gulf of Nicoya area) to central Panama (also Isla Coiba, and the Caribbean slope in the Canal area); and [*flavipes* group] in South America from northern and eastern Colombia east through Venezuela (also Margarita Island and Tobago).

Notes.—Groups: *H. viridiflavus* Lawrence, 1861 [Yellow-green Greenlet] and *H. flavipes* [Scrub Greenlet]. *Hylophilus flavipes* and *H. olivaceus* Tschudi, 1844 [Olivaceous Greenlet], of eastern Ecuador and Peru, may constitute a superspecies (Sibley and Monroe 1990).

Hylophilus ochraceiceps Sclater. Tawny-crowned Greenlet.

> *Hylophilus ochraceiceps* Sclater, 1859, Proc. Zool. Soc. London, p. 375. In statu Oaxaca reipubl. Mexicanae . . . Playa Vicente = Playa Vicente, Veracruz; Binford, 1989, Ornithol. Monogr. 43, p. 344.)

Habitat.—Tropical Lowland Evergreen Forest (0-1200 m; Tropical and lower Subtropical zones).

Distribution.—*Resident* [*ochraceiceps* group] from northeastern Oaxaca and southern Veracruz south on the Gulf-Caribbean slope (except Yucatán) to Nicaragua, on both slopes of Costa Rica (absent from the dry northwest) and Panama, and in South America from Colombia, Venezuela, and the Guianas south, west of the Andes to western Ecuador and east of the Andes to central Bolivia and Amazonian Brazil (north of the Amazon); and [*rubrifrons* group] in Amazonian Brazil south of the Amazon.

Notes.—Groups: *H. ochraceiceps* [Tawny-crowned Greenlet] and *H. rubrifrons* Sclater and Salvin 1867 [Red-fronted Greenlet].

Hylophilus aurantiifrons Lawrence. Golden-fronted Greenlet.

> *Hylophilus aurantiifrons* Lawrence, 1861, Ann. Lyc. Nat. Hist. N. Y. 7: 324. (Atlantic slope, along the line of the Panama Railroad = Canal Zone.)

Habitat.—Tropical Deciduous Forest, Gallery Forest, Secondary Forest, Tropical Lowland Evergreen Forest Edge (0-1300 m; Tropical Zone).

Distribution.—*Resident* from eastern Panama (west to western Panamá province on the Pacific slope, and in the Canal area on the Caribbean slope) east across northern Colombia to northern Venezuela and Trinidad.

Notes.—Sibley and Monroe (1990) considered *H. aurantiifrons* and South American *H. semibrunneus* Lafresnaye, 1845 [Rufous-naped Greenlet], to constitute a superspecies.

Hylophilus decurtatus (Bonaparte). Lesser Greenlet

> *Sylvicola decurtata* Bonaparte, 1838, Proc. Zool. Soc. London (1837), p. 118. (Guatamala = Pacific slope, Ixtapa to Antigua, Guatemala.)

Habitat.—Tropical Lowland Evergreen Forest, Tropical Deciduous Forest, Gallery Forest, Secondary Forest (0-1400 m; Tropical Zone).

Distribution.—*Resident* [*decurtatus* group] from southeastern San Luis Potosí, Veracruz, northeastern Puebla, northern and southeastern Oaxaca, Chiapas, and northern Quintana Roo south along both slopes of Middle America (except Yucatán) to central Panama (east to the Canal area); and [*minor* group] from eastern Panama (west to the Canal area) south through northern and western Colombia to western Ecuador.

Notes.—Although the two groups are often recognized as separate species, *H. decurtatus* [Gray-headed Greenlet] and *H. minor* Berlepsch and Taczanowski, 1884 [Lesser Greenlet], they intergrade through eastern Panamá province and the Canal area (Wetmore et al. 1984).

Genus *VIREOLANIUS* Bonaparte

> *Vireolanius* (Du Bus de Gisignies MS) Bonaparte, 1850, Consp. Gen. Avium 1(2): 330. Type, by monotypy, *Vireolanius melitophrys* Bonaparte.
>
> *Smaragdolanius* Griscom, 1930, Amer. Mus. Novit., no. 438, p. 3. Type, by original designation, *Vireolanius pulchellus* Sclater and Salvin.

Vireolanius melitophrys Bonaparte. Chestnut-sided Shrike-Vireo.

> *Vireolanius melitophrys* (Du Bus de Gisignies MS) Bonaparte, 1850, Consp. Gen. Avium 1(2): 330. (Mexico = Jico, near Jalapa, Veracruz.)

Habitat.—Montane Evergreen Forest, Pine-Oak Forest (1350-3000 m; Subtropical and lower Temperate zones).

Distribution.—*Resident* in the highlands from Jalisco, southeastern San Luis Potosí and Veracruz south to western Guatemala.

Vireolanius pulchellus Sclater and Salvin. Green Shrike-Vireo.

> *Vireolanius pulchellus* Sclater and Salvin, 1859, Ibis, p. 12. (Guatemala.)

Habitat.—Tropical Lowland Evergreen Forest (0-1000 m; Tropical and lower Subtropical zones).

Distribution.—*Resident* on the Gulf-Caribbean slope of Middle America from southern Veracruz, northern Oaxaca, and Chiapas south to Nicaragua, on the Pacific slope of Chiapas, Guatemala, and El Salvador, on both slopes of Costa Rica (except the dry northwest), and mainly on the Caribbean slope of Panama (east to western San Blas and eastern Panamá province).

Notes.—*Vireolanius pulchellus* and *V. eximius* constitute a superspecies (Sibley and Monroe 1990) and are perhaps conspecific (Hellmayr 1935). These two species are frequently placed in the genus *Smaragdolanius* (Eisenmann 1955).

Vireolanius eximius Baird. Yellow-browed Shrike-Vireo.

> *Vireolanius eximius* Baird, 1866, Rev. Amer. Birds 1: 398. ("Bogotá," Colombia.)

Habitat.—Tropical Lowland Evergreen Forest, Montane Evergreen Forest (0-1500 m; Tropical and lower Subtropical zones).

Distribution.—*Resident* in extreme eastern Panama (eastern Darién), northern Colombia and western Venezuela.

Notes.—See comments under *V. pulchellus*.

Genus *CYCLARHIS* Swainson

Cyclarhis Swainson, 1824, Zool. J. 1: 294. Type, by monotypy, *Tanagra gujanensis* Gmelin.

Cyclarhis gujanensis (Gmelin). Rufous-browed Peppershrike.

Tanagra gujanensis Gmelin, 1789, Syst. Nat. 1(2): 893. Based on "Verderoux" Buffon, Hist. Nat. Ois. 5: 27. (in Gujanae silvis ingentibus = French Guiana.)

Habitat.—Tropical Lowland Evergreen Forest Edge, Gallery Forest, Secondary Forest, Montane Evergreen Forest Edge (0-2800 m; Tropical and Subtropical zones).

Distribution.—*Resident* [*gujanensis* group] from southeastern San Luis Potosí, southern Tamaulipas, Veracruz, Hidalgo, Puebla, northern Oaxaca, and Chiapas south on both slopes of Middle America (including the Yucatan Peninsula, and Cancun and Cozumel islands) to Panama (including Isla Coiba), and in South America from northern and eastern Colombia, Venezuela (including Margarita Island), Trinidad, and the Guianas south, east of the Andes, to northwestern Argentina and southern Brazil; [*virenticeps* group] in western Ecuador and northwestern Peru; [*viridis* group] in north-central Argentina and northern Paraguay and [*ochrocephala* group] southeastern Brazil, southern Paraguay, Uruguay, and northeastern Argentina.

Notes.—Groups: *C. gujanensis* [Rufous-browed Peppershrike], *C. virenticeps* Sclater, 1860 [Yellow-backed Peppershrike], *C. viridis* (Vieillot, 1822) [Chaco Peppershrike], and *C. ochrocephala* Tschudi, 1845 [Ochre-crowned Peppershrike].

Family **CORVIDAE**: Crows and Jays

Notes.—For information on relationships among genera, see Peters (1962), Hardy (1969), Mayr and Short (1970), Goodwin (1976), Sibley and Ahlquist (1990), Sibley and Monroe (1990) and Espinosa de los Monteros (1997).

Genus *PERISOREUS* Bonaparte

Perisoreus Bonaparte, 1831, G. Arcad. Sci. Lett. Arti [Rome] 49: 42. Type, by subsequent designation (G. R. Gray, 1840), *Corvus canadensis* Linnaeus.

Perisoreus canadensis (Linnaeus). Gray Jay.

Corvus canadensis Linnaeus, 1766, Syst. Nat. (ed. 12) 1: 158. Based on "Le Geay brun de Canada" Brisson, Ornithologie 2: 54, pl. 4, fig. 2. (in Canada = Quebec.)

Habitat.—Coniferous and mixed coniferous-deciduous forest (primarily spruce), including open and partly open woodland and around bogs.

Distribution.—*Resident* [*canadensis* group] (partly migratory in northern parts of breeding range) from northern Alaska, northern Yukon, northern Mackenzie, southwestern Keewatin, northern Manitoba, northern Ontario, northern Quebec, northern Labrador, and Newfoundland south to southern Alaska (west to the Alaska Peninsula, but absent from humid coastal forests of south-coastal and southeastern Alaska), British Columbia (except southwestern), eastern Washington, northeastern and east-central Oregon, Idaho, Utah, east-central Arizona (White Mountains), north-central New Mexico, central Colorado, and southwestern South Dakota (Black Hills), and (east of the Rocky Mountains) to central Saskatchewan, southern Manitoba, northern Minnesota, northern Wisconsin, northern Michigan, southern Ontario, northern New York, northern New England, New Brunswick, and Nova Scotia; and [*obscurus* group] in the coastal ranges and Cascades from southwestern British Columbia (including Vancouver Island) south through western and central Washington and western and central Oregon to northern California (to Trinity, Siskiyou, and Modoc counties).

Wanders [*canadensis* group] north of breeding range, and south in winter irregularly to northwestern Nebraska, central Minnesota, southeastern Wisconsin, central Michigan, southern Pennsylvania, central New York, Connecticut, and Massachusetts.

Notes.—The two groups may be separate species, *P. canadensis* [Canada Jay] and *P. obscurus* Ridgway, 1873 [Oregon Jay] (Phillips 1986). *Perisoreus canadensis* and the Old World *P. infaustus* (Linnaeus, 1758) [Siberian Jay] and *P. internigrans* (Thayer and Bangs, 1912) [Sichuan Jay] may constitute a superspecies (Mayr and Short 1970).

Genus *CYANOCITTA* Strickland

Cyanocitta Strickland, 1845, Ann. Mag. Nat. Hist. (1)15: 260, 261. Type, by original designation, *Corvus cristatus* Linnaeus.

Cyanocitta stelleri (Gmelin). Steller's Jay.

Corvus Stelleri Gmelin, 1788, Syst. Nat. 1(1): 370. Based on "Steller's Crow" Latham, Gen. Synop. Birds 1(1): 387. (in sinu Natka Americae borealis = Nootka Sound, Vancouver Island, British Columbia.)

Habitat.—Primarily coniferous and mixed coniferous-deciduous forest, including humid coniferous forest in northwestern North America and arid pine-oak association in the Middle American highlands (upper Subtropical and Temperate zones).

Distribution.—*Resident* from south-coastal and southeastern Alaska (west to the Kenai Peninsula), coastal and central British Columbia (including the Queen Charlotte and Vancouver islands), southwestern Alberta, western Montana, Wyoming, and Colorado south to southern California, Arizona, through the highlands of Middle America (except Belize) to north-central Nicaragua, and east to east-central Colorado, central New Mexico, and western Texas (Davis and Guadalupe mountains).

Casual north to northern British Columbia, east to west-central and southern Saskatchewan, southwestern South Dakota, northwestern Nebraska, southwestern Kansas, western Oklahoma, and central Texas, and south to extreme northwestern Baja California. Accidental in southern Quebec (Cap Rouge); a sight report for Vermont.

Notes.—*Cyanocitta stelleri* and *C. cristata* hybridize occasionally in central Colorado; they may constitute a superspecies (Mayr and Short 1970).

Cyanocitta cristata (Linnaeus). Blue Jay.

Corvus cristatus Linnaeus, 1758, Syst. Nat. (ed. 10) 1: 106. Based on "The Blew Jay" Catesby, Nat. Hist. Carolina 1: 15, pl. 15. (in America septentrionali = South Carolina.)

Habitat.—Primarily forest (deciduous or mixed deciduous-coniferous), open woodland, parks, and residential areas, especially where oaks and beech are common.

Distribution.—*Resident* from east-central British Columbia, northern Alberta, central Saskatchewan, central Manitoba, central Ontario, southern Quebec, New Brunswick, Prince Edward Island, Nova Scotia, and Newfoundland south to central and southeastern Texas, the Gulf coast, and southern Florida (including the upper Florida Keys), and west to Montana, northern and eastern Wyoming, eastern Colorado, and east-central New Mexico.

Northern populations are partly (and variably) migratory to the southern parts of the breeding range, and irregular or casual west to southern British Columbia, western Washington, western and central Oregon, California (mostly northern), west-central Nevada, Idaho, Utah, Montana, Arizona, and western New Mexico.

Accidental on Bermuda.

Notes.—See comments under *C. stelleri*.

Genus *CALOCITTA* Gray

Calocitta G. R. Gray, 1841, List Genera Birds, ed. 2, p. 50. Type, by original designation, *Pica bullockii* Wagler = *Pica formosa* Swainson.

Calocitta colliei (Vigors). Black-throated Magpie-Jay.

Pica colliei Vigors, 1829, Zool. J. 4 (1828): 353, pl. 12. (San Blas, Nayarit, Mexico.)

Habitat.—Tropical Deciduous Forest, Gallery Forest, Secondary Forest (0-1100 m; Tropical and lower Subtropical zones).

Distribution.—*Resident* on the Pacific slope from southern Sonora and western Chihuahua south to Nayarit, Jalisco, and (possibly) northern Colima.

A report from southeastern Arizona (Douglas) is almost certainly based on an escaped individual.

Notes.—*Calocitta colliei* and *C. formosa* constitute a superspecies (Sibley and Monroe 1990), and have been considered conspecific (e.g., Phillips 1986). If treated as a single species, Magpie Jay is the appropriate English name.

Calocitta formosa (Swainson). White-throated Magpie-Jay.

Pica formosa Swainson, 1827, Philos. Mag. (n.s.) 1: 437. (Temiscaltipec, Mexico = Temascaltepec, México.)

Habitat.—Tropical Deciduous Forest, Gallery Forest, Secondary Forest (0-1250 m; Tropical and lower Subtropical zones).

Distribution.—*Resident* on the Pacific slope from Colima, Michoacán, and western Puebla south to northwestern Costa Rica (Gulf of Nicoya region), also in arid interior valleys on the Gulf-Caribbean drainage in Chiapas, Guatemala (Motagua Valley), and Honduras.

Notes.—See comments under *C. colliei*.

Genus *CYANOCORAX* Boie

Cyanocorax Boie, 1826, Isis von Oken, col. 975. Type, by monotypy, *Corvus pileatus* Temminck = *Pica chrysops* Vieillot.

Psilorhinus Rüppell, 1837, Mus. Senckenb. 2(2): 188. Type, by monotypy, *Psilorhinus mexicanus* Rüppell = *Pica morio* Wagler.

Cissilopha Bonaparte, 1850, Consp. Gen. Avium 1(2): 380. Type, by monotypy, *Garrulus sanblasianus* Lafresnaye = *Pica san-blasiana* Lafresnaye.

Xanthoura Bonaparte, 1850, Consp. Gen. Avium 1(2): 380. Type, by subsequent designation (G. R. Gray, 1855), *Corvus peruvianus* Gmelin = *Corvus yncas* Boddaert.

Cyanocorax dickeyi Moore. Tufted Jay.

Cyanocorax dickeyi Moore, 1935, Auk 52: 275, pl. 13. (Rancho Batel, 5 miles N.E. of Santa Lucia, altitude 5200 ft., Sinaloa, Mexico.)

Habitat.—Montane Evergreen Forest, Pine-Oak Forest (1500-2200 m; Subtropical and Temperate zones).

Distribution.—*Resident* in the mountains of southeastern Sinaloa, northeastern Nayarit, and southwestern Durango.

Cyanocorax affinis Pelzeln. Black-chested Jay.

Cyanocorax affinis Pelzeln, 1856, Sitzungsber. K. Akad. Wiss. Wien, Math.-Naturwiss. Kl., 20, p. 164. (Bogotá, Colombia.)

Habitat.—Tropical Lowland Evergreen Forest Edge, Secondary Forest, Tropical Deciduous Forest, Gallery Forest (0-1500 m; Tropical and lower Subtropical zones).

Distribution.—*Resident* in southeastern Costa Rica (Sixaola region), Panama (both slopes), northern and eastern Colombia, and northwestern Venezuela.

Cyanocorax yncas (Boddaert). Green Jay.

Corvus yncas Boddaert, 1783, Table Planches Enlum., p. 38. Based on Daubenton, Planches Enlum., pl. 625. (Peru = Chilpes, depto. de Junín.)

Habitat.—Montane Evergreen Forest, Tropical Deciduous Forest, Secondary Forest (0-2800 m; Tropical and Subtropical zones).

Distribution.—*Resident* [*luxuosus* group] from Nayarit, Nuevo León, and southern Texas south in Middle America on the Pacific slope to western Guatemala, and on the Gulf-Caribbean slope to Belize, eastern Guatemala, and north-central Honduras (to the Tela region and Valle del Aguán); and [*yncas* group] in South America from northern Colombia and northern Venezuela south, primarily on east slope of the Andes, to central Bolivia.

Casual [*luxuosus* group] north to southeastern Texas (College Station).

Notes.—Groups: *C. luxuosus* (Lesson, 1839) [Green Jay] and *C. yncas* [Inca Jay].

Cyanocorax morio (Wagler). Brown Jay.

Pica morio Wagler, 1829, Isis von Oken, col. 751. (Mexico = Alvarado, Veracruz.)

Habitat.—Gallery Forest, Secondary Forest, Tropical Deciduous Forest, Tropical Lowland Evergreen Forest Edge (0-1500 m; Tropical to lower Temperate zones).

Distribution.—*Resident* from extreme southern Texas (Starr County), Nuevo León, and Tamaulipas south on the Gulf-Caribbean slope of Middle America to western Panama (recorded Bocas del Toro and western Colón), locally also on the Pacific drainage in central Costa Rica.

Notes.—Two distinct color morphs were formerly regarded as separate species (Miller et al. 1957), *C. morio* [Plain-tipped Brown-Jay] and *C. mexicanus* (Rüppell, 1837) [White-tipped Brown-Jay], the former occurring south to Tabasco, the latter north to central Veracruz.

Cyanocorax melanocyaneus (Hartlaub). Bushy-crested Jay.

Garrulus (Cyanocorax) melanocyaneus Hartlaub, 1844, Rev. Zool. [Paris] 7: 215. (Guatemala.)

Habitat.—Montane Evergreen Forest, Pine-Oak Forest, Secondary Forest (600-2400 m; Subtropical and lower Temperate zones, occasionally Tropical Zone).

Distribution.—*Resident* in the highlands (rarely lowlands) of Guatemala, El Salvador, Honduras, and western Nicaragua.

Notes.—Also known as Hartlaub's Jay. *Cyanocorax melanocyaneus* is closely allied to the *C. sanblasianus-yucatanicus* complex; a reasonable treatment might be to consider these three species and *C. beecheii* as a superspecies.

Cyanocorax sanblasianus (Lafresnaye). San Blas Jay.

Pica San-Blasiana Lafresnaye, 1842, Mag. Zool. [Paris] sér. 2, 4 (Ois.), pl. 28, p. 1 and plate. (à Acapulco et à San Blas sur la côte ouest du Mexique = Acapulco, Guerrero.)

Habitat.—Tropical Deciduous Forest (0-1200 m; Tropical and lower Subtropical zones).

Distribution.—*Resident* on the Pacific slope from Nayarit south to central coastal Guerrero.

A flock of eight individuals recorded in Arizona (1937-1939, Tucson) is generally regarded as an escaped group because this species is entirely sedentary as far as is known.

Notes.—Also known as Black-and-blue Jay. *Cyanocorax sanblasianus* and *C. yucatanicus* constitute a superspecies (Sibley and Monroe 1990). See comments under *C. melanocyaneus*.

Cyanocorax yucatanicus (Dubois). Yucatan Jay.

Cyanocitta yucatanica Dubois, 1875, Bull. Acad. R. Sci. Lett. Beaux-Arts Belg. (2)40: 797. (Yucatan.)

Habitat.—Tropical Deciduous Forest, Secondary Forest (Tropical Zone).

Distribution.—*Resident* in Tabasco, northern Chiapas, the Yucatan Peninsula, northern Guatemala (Petén), and northern Belize.

Notes.—See comments under *C. melanocyaneus* and *C. sanblasianus*.

Cyanocorax beecheii (Vigors). Purplish-backed Jay.

Pica Beecheii Vigors, 1829, Zool. J. 4 (1828): 353. (Montereale = Mazatlán, Sinaloa, or San Blas, Nayarit.)

Habitat.—Tropical Deciduous Forest (0-700 m; Tropical and lower Subtropical zones).
Distribution.—*Resident* on the Pacific slope from southern Sonora to northern Nayarit. Records from California and western Texas are regarded as escaped cage-birds.
Notes.—Also known as Beechey's Jay. See comments under *C. melanocyaneus.*

Genus *CYANOLYCA* Cabanis

Cyanolyca Cabanis, 1851, Mus. Heineanum 1: 233. Type, by subsequent designation (G. R. Gray, 1855), *Cyanocorax armillatus* G. R. Gray = *Garrulus viridi-cyanus* Lafresnaye and d'Orbigny.

Cyanolyca cucullata (Ridgway). Azure-hooded Jay.

Cyanocorax cucullatus Ridgway, 1885, Proc. U. S. Natl. Mus. 8: 23. (Navarro, Costa Rica.)

Habitat.—Montane Evergreen Forest (800-2100 m; Subtropical and lower Temperate zones).
Distribution.—*Resident* locally in the mountains, primarily on the Gulf-Caribbean slope, in eastern Mexico (southeastern San Luis Potosí, Hidalgo, Veracruz, Puebla, northern and southeastern Oaxaca, and interior Chiapas), Guatemala, western Honduras (east to the Sula Valley), Costa Rica, and western Panama (east to Veraguas).
Notes.—*Cyanolyca cucullata* and the South American *C. pulchra* (Lawrence, 1876) appear to constitute a superspecies (Sibley and Monroe 1990).

Cyanolyca pumilo (Strickland). Black-throated Jay.

Cyanocorax pumilo Strickland, 1849, in Jardine, Contrib. Ornithol., p. 122 (in text). (Guatemala = mountains above Antigua, depto. Sacatepéquez.)

Habitat.—Montane Evergreen Forest, Pine-Oak Forest (1900-3000 m; Subtropical and lower Temperate zones).
Distribution.—*Resident* in the mountains of Chiapas, Guatemala, northern El Salvador (at least formerly), and Honduras; reports from Belize and Nicaragua are unsatisfactory.
Notes.—Also known as Strickland's Jay.

Cyanolyca nana (Du Bus de Gisignies). Dwarf Jay.

Cyanocorax nanus Du Bus de Gisignies, 1847, Bull. Acad. R. Sci. Lett. Beaux-Arts Belg. 14: 103. (Le Mexique = Mexico.)

Habitat.—Pine-Oak Forest, Pine Forest (1600-3200 m; upper Subtropical and Temperate zones).
Distribution.—*Resident,* at least formerly, in the mountains of Veracruz, Puebla, and Oaxaca, now possibly restricted to the latter state; reports from México are open to question.

Cyanolyca argentigula (Lawrence). Silvery-throated Jay.

Cyanocitta argentigula Lawrence, 1875, Ann. Lyc. Nat. Hist. N. Y. 11: 88. (Talamanca, Costa Rica = near Pico Blanco, above Sipurio, Costa Rica.)

Habitat.—Montane Evergreen Forest (2000-3200 m; Subtropical and lower Temperate zones).
Distribution.—*Resident* in the mountains of Costa Rica (Cordillera Central on slopes of Irazú and Turrialba volcanoes, and the Cordillera de Talamanca) and western Panama (western Chiriquí).

Cyanolyca mirabilis Nelson. White-throated Jay.

> *Cyanolyca mirabilis* Nelson, 1903, Proc. Biol. Soc. Wash. 16: 154. (Omilteme [= Omiltemi], Guerrero.)

Habitat.—Pine-Oak Forest, Montane Evergreen Forest (1800-3500 m; upper Subtropical and Temperate zones).

Distribution.—*Resident* in the mountains of Guerrero (Sierra Madre del Sur) and Oaxaca (Sierra de Miahuatlán and Sierra de Yucuyacua).

Notes.—Also known as Omiltemi Jay.

Genus *APHELOCOMA* Cabanis

> *Aphelocoma* Cabanis, 1851, Mus. Heineanum 1: 221. Type, by subsequent designation (Baird, 1858), *Garrulus californicus* Vigors.
>
> *Sieberocitta* [subgenus] Coues, 1903, Key N. Amer. Birds (ed. 5) 1: 497. Type, by original designation, *Cyanocitta ultramarina arizonae* Ridgway = *Corvus ultramarinus* Bonaparte.

Aphelocoma coerulescens (Bosc). Florida Scrub-Jay.

> *Corvus coerulescens* Bosc, 1795, Bull. Sci. Soc. Philom. Paris 1 (1791-1799): 87. (in Amer. Septentrional. = Florida.)

Habitat.—Oak scrub with widely scattered pines, especially where low-growing and periodically burned.

Distribution.—*Resident* locally in the Florida peninsula, especially on central and coastal sand ridges; formerly more widespread throughout the peninsula north of the Everglades (north to Gilchrist, Clay, and Duval counties).

Notes.—*Aphelocoma coerulescens, A. californica,* and *A. insularis* were previously treated as a single species, *A. coerulescens* [Scrub Jay], following Hellmayr (1934) and Pitelka (1945, 1951). Species-level differentiation of the widely disjunct *coerulescens* and the Santa Cruz Island endemic *insularis* is confirmed by genetic, morphologic, behavioral, and fossil data (Peterson 1992, Pitelka 1951, Woolfenden and Fitzpatrick 1984, Haemig 1989, Emslie 1996).

Aphelocoma insularis Henshaw. Island Scrub-Jay.

> *Aphelocoma insularis* Henshaw, 1886, Auk 3: 452. (Santa Cruz Island, California.)

Habitat.—Open oak woodland.

Distribution.—*Resident* on Santa Cruz Island in the Channel Islands, California.

Notes.—Also known as Santa Cruz Jay. See notes under *A. coerulescens.*

Aphelocoma californica (Vigors). Western Scrub-Jay.

> *Garrulus Californicus* Vigors, 1839, Zool. Voy. "Blossom," p. 21, pl. 5. (Monterey, California.)

Habitat.—Scrub (especially oak, pinyon, and juniper), brush, chaparral, pine-oak association; also gardens, orchards, riparian woodland, mangroves (southern Baja California), and tropical deciduous forest (southern Mexico) (Subtropical and Temperate zones, upper Tropical Zone in southern Mexico).

Distribution.—*Resident* [*californica* group] from southwestern Washington south through western and central Oregon, California (except eastern mountains), and northwestern and west-central Nevada to southern Baja California; [*woodhouseii* group] from southeastern Oregon, southern Idaho, southern Wyoming, western and southern Colorado, and extreme western Oklahoma south to eastern California (from White Mountains to Providence Mountains), southern Arizona, in the Mexican highlands to northeastern Sonora, Jalisco, central Guanajuato, México, Distrito Federal, and Hidalgo, and east to western and central Texas; and [*sumichrasti* group] from Tlaxcala south to Oaxaca (west of the Isthmus of Tehuantepec), Puebla, and west-central Veracruz.

Casual [group uncertain] in southwestern British Columbia (Langley); and [*californica* group] in eastern Washington, and [*woodhouseii* group] in southeastern California, southern Manitoba, northern Wyoming, Illinois, central Kansas, and the Texas Panhandle.

Notes.—See notes under *A. coerulescens.* Genetic and behavioral data (Peterson 1991, 1992, Peterson and Burt 1992) suggest that the three groups may be separate species: *A. californica* [California Scrub-Jay], *A. woodhouseii* (Baird, 1858) [Woodhouse's Scrub-Jay], and *A. sumichrasti* (Baird and Ridgway, 1874) [Sumichrast's Scrub-Jay].

Aphelocoma ultramarina (Bonaparte). Mexican Jay.

> *Corvus ultramarinus* Bonaparte, 1825, J. Acad. Nat. Sci. Philadelphia 4: 387. (No locality given = Temascáltepec, México.)

Habitat.—Pine-Oak Forest, Gallery Forest, Pine Forest (1200-3400 m; Subtropical and Temperate zones).

Distribution.—*Resident* [*ultramarina* group] from central Arizona and southwestern New Mexico south to Colima, northern Michoacán, México, northern Morelos, Puebla and west-central Veracruz, and [*couchii* group] from western Texas (Brewster County), northern Chihuahua, and northern Coahuila south through west-central Nuevo León, western Tamaulipas, and San Luis Potosí to western Jalisco (Aguas Calientes, Ceretaras), and Hidalgo.

A record of a specimen, evidently now lost, supposedly collected in 1906 in southern Kansas (Keith 1940) requires verification.

Notes.—Also known as Gray-breasted Jay and Arizona Jay. Isozyme analyses suggest that the two groups treated together constitute a paraphyletic species (Peterson 1992). The *ultramarina* group, *A. ultramarina* (Bonaparte, 1825) [Ultramarine Jay] exhibits delayed maturation in bill color, whereas the *couchii* group, *A. couchii* (Baird, 1858) [Couch's Jay] does not, but a broad intermediate area exists where the groups meet in central Mexico (Peterson 1991). Differences in vocal and social behavior also exist between northerly populations of the two groups (Brown and Horvath 1989), but many populations remain unstudied. The *couchii* group is hypothesized to have arisen through hybridization with *A. californica* (Brown and Li 1995), but evidence remains weak. Although suggestive, these studies are insufficient to merit recognition of two species and to delineate which populations would belong to each.

Aphelocoma unicolor (Du Bus de Gisignies). Unicolored Jay.

> *Cyanocorax unicolor* Du Bus de Gisignies, 1847, Bull. Acad. R. Sci. Lett. Beaux-Arts Belg. 14(2): 103. (le Mexique = San Cristóbal [= Ciudad de Las Casas], Chiapas.)

Habitat.—Pine-Oak Forest, Montane Evergreen Forest, Pine Forest (1300-3300 m; Subtropical and lower Temperate zones).

Distribution.—*Resident* locally in mountains of south-central Guerrero (Sierra Madre del Sur), México (formerly), Hidalgo, western Puebla, Oaxaca (Sierra de Juárez and Sierra de Zempoaltepec), Chiapas, Guatemala, northern El Salvador, and Honduras.

Genus *GYMNORHINUS* Wied

> *Gymnorhinus* Wied, 1841, Reise N.-Amer. 2: 21. Type, by monotypy, *Gymnorhinus cyanocephalus* Wied.

Gymnorhinus cyanocephalus Wied. Pinyon Jay.

> *Gymnorhinus cyanocephalus* Wied, 1841, Reise N.-Amer. 2: 22. (am Maria-River = between the Marias and Yellowstone rivers, Montana.)

Habitat.—Pinyon-juniper woodland; in nonbreeding season also scrub oak and sagebrush.

Distribution.—*Breeds* from central Oregon, southern Idaho, central Montana, western South Dakota, and northwestern Nebraska south through California (primarily the eastern and southern mountains) to northern Baja California (Sierra Juárez and Sierra San Pedro Mártir), southern Nevada, northwestern and east-central Arizona, central (probably also southern) New Mexico and western Oklahoma.

Winters throughout the breeding range and irregularly from northwestern Oregon, southern Washington, northern Idaho, and central Montana south to southeastern California, southeastern Arizona, northern Chihuahua, and western and central Texas, and east to western Nebraska and western Kansas, casually to North Dakota and to coastal California (including the Channel Islands).

Casual in Iowa; a sight report for southwestern Saskatchewan.

Notes.—Hardy (1969) did not consider the genus *Gymnorhinus* to be part of the New World jays but instead closer to the genus *Nucifraga*. Ligon (1974) treated *Gymnorhinus* as a specialized, early offshoot of the New World jays.

Genus *NUCIFRAGA* Brisson

Nucifraga Brisson, 1760, Ornithologie 1: 30; 2: 58. Type, by tautonymy, *Nucifraga* Brisson = *Corvus caryocatactes* Linnaeus.

Nucifraga columbiana (Wilson). Clark's Nutcracker.

Corvus columbianus Wilson, 1811, Amer. Ornithol. 3: xv, 29, pl. 20, fig. 2. (shores of the Columbia = Clearwater River, about two miles north of Kamiah, Idaho County, Idaho.)

Habitat.—Open coniferous forest, forest edge, and clearings, exposed ridges, primarily at high elevations of mountains, ranging to lower limits of alpine tundra; in winter also irregularly in lowlands.

Distribution.—*Resident* from south-central British Columbia, southwestern Alberta, western and central Montana, western and southeastern Wyoming, and southwestern South Dakota south through the mountains of central and eastern Washington, eastern Oregon, central and eastern California, and Nevada, and in the Rockies to east-central Arizona and southern New Mexico; isolated populations in northern Baja California (Sierra San Pedro Mártir) and southern Nuevo León (Cerro Potosí).

Wanders irregularly north to western, central and southeastern Alaska, southern Yukon, central Alberta, central Saskatchewan, and southern Manitoba, west to coastal Oregon and coastal central (casually southern) California (including the Channel Islands), and south to southeastern California (casual), southern Arizona, northern Sonora (Sierra de la Madera), and western Texas, and east to southwestern South Dakota, Nebraska, and Kansas.

Casual or accidental east to Minnesota, Iowa, Wisconsin, western Ontario, Pennsylvania, Missouri, Arkansas, west-central Louisiana, central and northern Texas, and Guadalupe Island; a sight report for Michigan.

Genus *PICA* Brisson

Pica Brisson, 1760, Ornithologie 1: 20; 2: 35. Type, by tautonymy, *Pica* Brisson = *Corvus pica* Linnaeus.

Pica pica (Linnaeus). Black-billed Magpie.

Corvus Pica Linnaeus, 1758, Syst. Nat. (ed. 10) 1: 106. (in Europa = Uppsala, Sweden.)

Habitat.—Open country with scattered trees, riparian and open woodland, forest edge, and farmlands, in either arid or humid habitats.

Distribution.—*Resident* in North America from south-coastal Alaska (west to the Alaska Peninsula and Shumagin Islands), southern Yukon, northern Alberta, central Saskatchewan, central Manitoba, extreme southwestern Ontario, and northern Minnesota south (absent from coastal areas and regions west of the Cascade and Sierra Nevada ranges from southeastern Alaska southward) to northeastern and east-central California (to Inyo County), south-central Nevada, Utah, extreme northeastern Arizona (Apache County, formerly more widespread), northern New Mexico, western (casually northeastern) Oklahoma, central Kansas, and Nebraska (except southeastern); and in the Old World from the British Isles, Scandinavia, northern Russia, and central Siberia south to the Mediterranean region, northwestern Africa, the Near East, Iran, the Himalayas, Southeast Asia, eastern China, Taiwan, and Japan.

Wanders casually or irregularly from northern (Umiat) and west-central Alaska, central Yukon, southern Mackenzie, southern Keewatin, northern Saskatchewan, northern Manitoba, central Ontario, and southern Quebec, and south to southwestern British Columbia, western Washington, western Oregon, northwestern and west-central California (southern California reports probably pertain to escaped individuals), southern Nevada, northern Arizona, southern New Mexico, western Texas, northern Missouri, and western Iowa; accidental on Banks Island. Also occurs casually or accidentally farther east, but no doubt many records pertain to escaped individuals; recorded from Wisconsin, Michigan, southern Ontario, southern Quebec, and New Brunswick south to Illinois, Indiana, Ohio, West Virginia (breeding reported in the Canaan Valley), and Pennsylvania (breeding reported in Pittsburgh area), also in Florida (breeding reported in Collier County).

Notes.—Known in Old World literature as the Magpie. *Pica pica* and *P. nuttalli* are closely related and constitute a superspecies (Mayr and Short 1970); they are considered conspecific by Phillips (1986). North American populations differ morphologically from Eurasian populations (Vaurie 1959), and genetic data suggest that more than one species may exist (Zink et al. 1995).

Pica nuttalli (Audubon). Yellow-billed Magpie.

Corvus Nutalli [sic] Audubon, 1837, Birds Amer. (folio) 4: pl. 362, fig. 1. (Upper California, around the village of Sta. Barbara.)

Habitat.—Open oak woodland interspersed with grasslands or cultivated lands, open riparian woodland, and savanna.

Distribution.—*Resident* in California in the Sacramento and San Joaquin valleys (from Shasta County south to Kern County), and in valleys of the coast ranges from San Francisco Bay south to Santa Barbara County (formerly to Ventura County).

Casual north to near the Oregon border in northern California (Siskiyou County).

Notes.—See comments under *P. pica* and Verbeek (1972).

Genus *CORVUS* Linnaeus

Corvus Linnaeus, 1758, Syst. Nat. (ed. 10) 1: 105. Type, by tautonymy, *Corvus corax* Linnaeus (*Corvus,* prebinomial specific name, in synonymy).

Corvus monedula Linnaeus. Eurasian Jackdaw.

Corvus Monedula Linnaeus, 1758, Syst. Nat. (ed. 10) 1: 105. (in Europa = Sweden.)

Habitat.— Open woodland and around towns.

Distribution.—*Resident* throughout most of the Palearctic.

Casual (beginning in 1983) in northeastern North America in southern Ontario, southeastern Quebec, Nova Scotia, Miquelon Island, Massachusetts, Connecticut, and Rhode Island (P. W. Smith 1985); also in Pennsylvania (Lewisburg), where a pair was apparently breeding (1985, Amer. Birds 39: 300, 913). Many (if not all) North American records may be the result of ship-assisted individuals.

Notes.—Known in Old World literature as the Jackdaw.

Corvus brachyrhynchos Brehm. American Crow.

Corvus brachyrhynchos C. L. Brehm, 1822, Beitr. Vögelkd. 2: 56. (Nordlichen Amerika = Boston, Massachusetts.)

Habitat.—Open forest and woodland for nesting and roosting, increasing in urban and suburban areas, open and partly open country for foraging, including agricultural lands, urban areas, orchards, and tidal flats; restricted mostly to riparian woodland and adjacent areas in arid regions.

Distribution.—*Breeds* from extreme southeastern Alaska (east of *C. caurinus*), north-central British Columbia, southwestern Mackenzie, northern Saskatchewan, northern Manitoba, northern Ontario, south-central Quebec, and Newfoundland south (except in Pacific coastal areas south to northwestern Washington) to extreme northwestern Baja California (to lat. 32° S.), central Arizona, southern New Mexico, central and southeastern Texas, the Gulf coast, and southern Florida (except the Florida Keys).

Winters from southern Canada (British Columbia east to Newfoundland) south throughout the breeding range, occasionally to the Florida Keys, and casually to southern Arizona.

Introduced and established on Bermuda.

Casual in eastern Keewatin, northwestern Sonora and western Chihuahua.

Notes.—Also known as Common Crow. *Corvus brachyrhynchos* and *C. caurinus* are closely related and may be conspecific (Johnston 1961, Phillips 1986); they constitute a superspecies. Although a few authors consider *C. brachyrhynchos* and the Old World *C. corone* to be closely related (or even conspecific) (Meise 1928, Dorst 1947, Dement'ev and Gladkov 1954), the relationships of the latter appear to be with other Old World species (Goodwin 1976). Mayr and Short (1970) considered *C. brachyrhynchos* and *C. nasicus* to constitute a superspecies, but see Goodwin (1976).

Corvus caurinus Baird. Northwestern Crow.

> *Corvus caurinus* Baird, 1858, in Baird, Cassin, and Lawrence, Rep. Explor. Surv. R. R. Pac. 9: xliii, 559, 569. (Washington Territory and northwestern coast = Fort Steilacoom, Washington.)

Habitat.—Coastal tidelands near coniferous woodland or forest edge, foraging also in adjacent croplands and around human habitation.

Distribution.—*Resident* along the Pacific coast from south-coastal and southeastern Alaska (west to Kodiak Island) south through western British Columbia (including the Queen Charlotte and Vancouver islands) to northwestern Washington (Puget Sound area).

Reports from northwestern Oregon (Portland area) are questionable.

Notes.—See comments under *C. brachyrhynchos.*

Corvus palmarum Württemberg. Palm Crow.

> *Corvus palmarum* Württemberg, 1835, Erste Reise N. Amer.: 68. (vicinity of Cibao Mountains, Dominican Republic.)

Habitat.—Pine Forest, Tropical Lowland Evergreen Forest (0-2000 m).

Distribution.—*Resident* on Cuba (locally in Pinar del Río and Camagüey provinces, formerly more widespread) and Hispaniola (mostly in the mountains).

Notes.—See comments under *C. sinaloae.*

Corvus nasicus Temminck. Cuban Crow.

> *Corvus nasicus* Temminck, 1826, Planches Color., livr. 70: 413. (Cuba.)

Habitat.—Tropical Lowland Evergreen Forest, Secondary Forest, Pine Forest (0-1500 m).

Distribution.—*Resident* on Cuba (including the Isle of Pines) and in the southern Bahama Islands (Providenciales, North Caicos, and Grand Caicos).

Notes.—*Corvus nasicus, C. jamaicensis,* and *C. leucognaphalus* are closely related and may constitute a superspecies (Johnston 1961, Goodwin 1976). See comments under *C. brachyrhynchos.*

Corvus leucognaphalus Daudin. White-necked Crow.

> *Corvus leucognaphalus* Daudin, 1800, Traité Ornithol. 2: 231. (Puerto Rico.)

Habitat.—Pine Forest, Secondary Forest, Mangrove Forest (0-1500 m).

Distribution.—*Resident* on Hispaniola and, formerly, Puerto Rico (where extirpated, not recorded since 1963).

Casual on Gonâve and Saona islands.

Notes.—See comments under *C. nasicus.* Appears to be more closely related to ravens than crows (Rea, *in* Phillips 1986).

Corvus jamaicensis Gmelin. Jamaican Crow.

> *Corvus jamaicensis* Gmelin, 1788, Syst. Nat. 1(1): 367. Based largely on the "Chattering Crow" Latham, Gen. Synop. Birds 1(1): 377. (in Jamaicae montanis = Jamaica.)

Habitat.—Tropical Lowland Evergreen Forest, Secondary Forest, Montane Evergreen Forest (0-1200 m).
Distribution.—*Resident* on Jamaica.
Notes.—See comments under *C. nasicus*.

Corvus imparatus Peters. Tamaulipas Crow.

> *Corvus imparatus* Peters, 1929, Proc. Biol. Soc. Washington 42: 123. New name for *Corvus mexicanus* Auct. (not Gmelin) [= *Quiscalus mexicanus*]. (Rio La Cruz, Tamaulipas, Mexico.)

Habitat.—Pastures/Agricultural Lands, Tropical Deciduous Forest, Secondary Forest, Pastures/Agricultural Lands (0-900 m; Tropical Zone).
Distribution.—*Resident* on the Gulf coast from Nuevo León, Tamaulipas, and southern Texas (Brownsville) south to San Luis Potosí and northern Veracruz.
Regular postbreeding vagrant in southern Texas north to Starr and Kenedy counties.
Notes.—See comments under *C. sinaloae*. Formerly known as Mexican Crow.

Corvus sinaloae Davis. Sinaloa Crow.

> *Corvus sinaloae* Davis, 1958, Wilson Bull. 70: 163. (Escunapa [= Escuinapa], Sinaloa, Mexico.)

Habitat.—Gallery Forest, Tropical Deciduous Forest, Secondary Forest, Pastures/Agricultural Lands (0-700 m; Tropical Zone).
Distribution.—*Resident* on the Pacific coast of Mexico from southern Sonora south to southwestern Nayarit.
Notes.—Differs from *C. imparatus* in vocalizations and appears to represent a distinct species (Davis 1958, Webber and Hardy 1985, Hardy 1990a, 1990b); they constitute a superspecies [Mexican Crow], which may or may not also include *C. ossifragus* (Mayr and Short 1970) and *C. palmarum* (Mayr and Short 1970; but see Goodwin 1976).

Corvus ossifragus Wilson. Fish Crow.

> *Corvus ossifragus* Wilson, 1812, Amer. Ornithol. 5: 27, pl. 37, fig. 2. (Great Egg-Harbor = Beasley's Point, New Jersey.)

Habitat.—Beaches, bays, inlets, lagoons, swamps, and, less frequently, deciduous or coniferous woodland, in inland situations primarily in bald-cypress swamps and along major watercourses, locally also in urban and suburban areas.
Distribution.—*Resident* locally from New York (northwest to Ithaca) and Massachusetts south along the Atlantic-Gulf coast to southern Florida, and west to southern Texas; inland along major river systems to northwestern Louisiana, eastern Oklahoma, southeastern Kansas, southeastern Missouri, southern Illinois, southwestern Kentucky, western Tennessee, central Georgia, western South Carolina, northwestern North Carolina, central Virginia, central Maryland, extreme eastern West Virginia, and central Pennsylvania.
Casual in southern Maine (Portland); sight reports for southwestern Indiana, southern Ontario, and Nova Scotia.
Notes.—See comments under *C. brachyrhynchos* and *C. sinaloae*.

Corvus hawaiiensis Peale. Hawaiian Crow.

> *Corvus hawaiiensis* Peale, 1848, U. S. Explor. Exped. 8: 106. (a few miles inland from the village of Kaawaloa, Hawaii.)

Habitat.—Upland forest and forest edge, and grazed lands.

Distribution.—*Resident* in the Hawaiian Islands on Hawaii, where now very much reduced in numbers and restricted to Hualalai and southwestern slopes of Mauna Kea.

Notes.—Also known as Alala. For use of the name *hawaiiensis* see Banks (1983)

Corvus cryptoleucus Couch. Chihuahuan Raven.

> *Corvus cryptoleucus* Couch, 1854, Proc. Acad. Nat. Sci. Philadelphia 7: 66. (State of Tamaulipas, Mexico = Charco Escondido, Tamaulipas.)

Habitat.—Northern Temperate Grassland, Arid Lowland Scrub, Arid Montane Scrub (0-2400 m; Tropical and Subtropical zones).

Distribution.—*Resident* (mostly) from northern Sonora, south-central and southeastern Arizona, central and northeastern New Mexico and southeastern (formerly northeastern) Colorado south to Michoacán, Guanajuato, Querétaro, San Luis Potosí and Tamaulipas, and east to western Kansas, western Oklahoma, and central and southern Texas. Northeastern populations, especially those in Kansas, are migratory southward in winter.

Notes.—Also known as White-necked Raven, a name now restricted to the African *C. albicollis* Latham, 1790. See comments under *C. corax*.

Corvus corax Linnaeus. Common Raven.

> *Corvus Corax* Linnaeus, 1758, Syst. Nat. (ed. 10) 1: 105. (in Europa = Sweden.)

Habitat.—A wide variety of situations from lowlands to mountains, open country to forested regions, and humid regions to desert, but most frequently in mountainous or hilly areas, especially in vicinity of cliffs, a preferred nesting site (Tropical to Temperate zones).

Distribution.—*Resident* in North America from western and northern Alaska (including islands in the Bering Sea) and northern Canada (throughout, including Arctic islands north to Prince Patrick and southern Ellesmere) south to the Aleutians (west to Attu), California (including the Channel Islands), southern Baja California (including the Revillagigedo Islands, and islands in the Gulf of California), through Mexico and the highlands of Guatemala, El Salvador, and Honduras to north-central Nicaragua, east to the eastern edge of the Rockies, extreme western Oklahoma, and western and central Texas, and, east of the Rockies, south to central and eastern Montana, central Saskatchewan, southern Manitoba, northern Minnesota, northern Wisconsin, central Michigan, southern Ontario, New York, northern Connecticut, western Massachusetts, southeastern Maine, New Brunswick, Nova Scotia, and Newfoundland, also locally in the Appalachians of western Pennsylvania, West Virginia, western Maryland, eastern Kentucky, western Virginia, eastern Tennessee, western North Carolina, northwestern South Carolina, and northwestern Georgia; formerly bred locally south to northern Arkansas and northeastern Alabama; and in the Palearctic from Greenland, Iceland, and Scandinavia east across the Arctic coasts to northern Siberia, and south to the Canary Islands, northwestern Africa, the Mediterranean region, Near East, Iran, the Himalayas, Manchuria, and Japan.

Wanders sporadically or casually south throughout the Great Plains and to the southern shores of the Great Lakes, New Jersey, and southern New England, also to lower elevations in the Appalachians in central (formerly coastal) Virginia and western South Carolina.

Notes.—Also known as Northern Raven or Holarctic Raven, and, in Old World literature, as the Raven. Mayr and Short (1970) suggested that *Corvus corax* and the Old World *C. ruficollis* Lesson, 1830 [Brown-necked Raven], constitute a superspecies.

Family **MONARCHIDAE**: Monarchs

Genus *CHASIEMPIS* Cabanis

> *Chasiempis* Cabanis, 1847, Arch. Naturgesch. 13: 207. Type, by monotypy, *Muscicapa sandvichensis* Latham = *Muscicapa sandwichensis* Gmelin.

Chasiempis sandwichensis (Gmelin). Elepaio.

> *Muscicapa sandwichensis* Gmelin, 1789, Syst. Nat. 1(2): 945. Based on the "Sandwich Fly-catcher" Latham, Gen. Synop. Birds 2(1): 344. (in insulis Sandwich = Hawaii.)

Turdus sandwichensis Gmelin, 1789, Syst. Nat. 1(2): 813. Based on the "Sandwich Thrush" Latham, Gen. Synop. Birds 2(1): 39. Subjective synonym of *Muscicapa sandwichensis* Gmelin, 1789; see Olson (1989).

Habitat.—Forested areas, especially in regions of high rainfall.
Distribution.—*Resident* in the Hawaiian Islands (Kauai, Oahu, and Hawaii).

Family **ALAUDIDAE**: Larks

Notes.—Placement of the Alaudidae here in the linear sequence is based largely on historical inertia, not data. Sibley and Ahlquist's (1990) DNA-DNA hybridization suggest that the Alaudidae are a basal group in a lineage (superfamily Passeroidea) that includes the families Peucedramidae through Estrildidae in our current linear sequence. Sheldon and Gill (1996), however, found that the Alaudidae are best retained near their traditional place in linear sequences.

Genus *ALAUDA* Linnaeus

Alauda Linnaeus, 1758, Syst. Nat. (ed. 10) 1: 165. Type, by subsequent designation (Selby, 1825), *Alauda arvensis* Linnaeus.

Alauda arvensis Linnaeus. Sky Lark.

Alauda arvensis Linnaeus, 1758, Syst. Nat. (ed. 10) 1: 165. (in Europæ apricis = Uppsala, Sweden.)

Habitat.—Fields with tall grass; in Palearctic region, open country, grasslands, tundra, marshy and sandy areas, and large clearings.
Distribution.—*Breeds* [*arvensis* group] from the British Isles, Scandinavia, northern Russia, and northern Siberia south to northwestern Africa, the northern Mediterranean region, Asia Minor, northern China, and Korea, and (once) on the Pribilof Islands (1995; St. Paul Is.); and [*japonica* group] in Japan.

Winters [*arvensis* group] from the breeding range (except the northern portions) south to northern Africa, the Persian Gulf and eastern China; and [*japonica* group] in the Ryukyu Islands.

Migrates [*arvensis* group] regularly through the western Aleutians (Near Islands), and casually as far east as the Pribilofs (St. George, where possibly has bred) and as far north as St. Lawrence Island.

Introduced and established [*arvensis* group] in the Hawaiian Islands (main islands from Niihau eastward), British Columbia (southern Vancouver Island, with recent spread to San Juan Island, Washington), New York (Brooklyn in 1887, where extirpated by 1913), Australia, and New Zealand; and [*japonica* group] in the Hawaiian Islands (in 1934). Birds introduced elsewhere in North America did not become established.

Accidental [*arvensis* group] in the northwestern Hawaiian Islands (Kure), Bermuda, Madeira, and the Canary Islands. An individual, which was photographed and extensively studied, wintered for seven successive years (1978–1985) at Point Reyes, California; this bird [*arvensis* group] was probably one of the Asiatic races (Morlan and Erickson 1983).

Notes.—Also known as European Skylark, Eurasian Skylark, or Common Skylark, and, in Old World literature, as the Skylark. North American introductions, those in the Hawaiian Islands (with one exception), and the vagrant individual reported from Bermuda pertain to the European race, *A. a. arvensis;* transients through Alaska, the report from Kure, and probably the California individual, are referable to the Siberian *A. a. pekinensis* Swinhoe, 1863, a subspecies of the *arvensis* group. One Hawaiian introduction (in 1934) was of the Japanese form [*japonica* group], the relationships of which are uncertain; it may be a full species, *A. japonica* Temminck and Schlegel, 1848 [Japanese Skylark], a subspecies of the Asiatic species *A. gulgula* Franklin, 1831, or, as here regarded, a subspecies of *A. arvensis.*

Genus *EREMOPHILA* Boie

Eremophila Boie, 1828, Isis von Oken, col. 322. Type, by subsequent designation (Sharpe, 1874), *O. alpestris* = *Alauda alpestris* Linnaeus.

Otocoris Bonaparte, 1838, Nuovi Ann. Sci. Nat. Bologna 2: 407. Type, by monotypy, *Phileremos cornutus* Bonaparte = *Alauda cornuta* Wilson = *Alauda alpestris* Linnaeus.

Eremophila alpestris (Linnaeus). Horned Lark.

Alauda alpestris Linnaeus, 1758, Syst. Nat. (ed. 10) 1: 166. Based mainly on "The Lark" Catesby, Nat. Hist. Carolina 1: 32, pl. 32. (in America septentrionali = coast of South Carolina.)

Habitat.—Short-grass prairies, tundra, sandy regions, desert playas, grazed pastures, stubble fields, and open cultivated areas; favors habitats with at least some areas of bare soil (Tropical [locally], Subtropical, Temperate, and Boreal zones).

Distribution.—*Breeds* [*alpestris* group] in North America from western and northern Alaska, the Arctic coast of northern Canada, Banks, Prince Patrick, Devon, and northern Baffin islands, northern Quebec, northern Labrador, and Newfoundland south to southern Baja California (including many islands), central Sonora, in the Central Plateau region of Mexico to western Veracruz and Oaxaca (to sea level in the Isthmus of Tehuantepec), and to the Gulf coast (from northwestern Tamaulipas to southeastern Texas, formerly to southwestern Louisiana), northern Louisiana, southern Missouri, southern Tennessee, northwestern Mississippi, northern Alabama, and South Carolina; and in Eurasia from the Arctic coast south to extreme northern Africa, Asia Minor, the Himalayas, and Japan.

Winters [*alpestris* group] in North America from southern Canada (British Columbia east to Newfoundland) south throughout the breeding range, and, locally or irregularly, to the Gulf coast and southern Florida; in Colombia; and in Eurasia in the breeding range except for the more northern portions.

Resident [*alpestris* group] in the Eastern Andes of Colombia (near Bogotá); and [*teleschowi* group] in west-central China.

Accidental [*alpestris* group] in Greenland, Iceland, the western Aleutians (Shemya), and Bermuda.

Notes.—Known in the Old World as Shore Lark. Groups: *E. alpestris* [Horned Lark] and *E. teleschowi* (Przewalski, 1887) [Przewalski's Lark]. *Eremophila alpestris* and the North African *E. bilopha* (Temminck, 1823) [Temminck's Lark] may constitute a superspecies (Mayr and Short 1970).

Family **HIRUNDINIDAE**: Swallows

Subfamily HIRUNDININAE: Typical Swallows

Genus *PROGNE* Boie

Progne Boie, 1826, Isis von Oken, col. 971. Type, by monotypy, *Hirundo purpurea* "Gm. Wils. pl. 39, fig. 2" = *Hirundo subis* Linnaeus.

Phæoprogne Baird, 1865, Rev. Amer. Birds 1: 272, 283. Type, by subsequent designation (Sharpe, 1885), *Hirundo tapera* Linnaeus.

Notes.—Molecular data (Sheldon and Winkler 1993) indicate that *Phaeoprogne* should not be separated from *Progne*.

Progne subis (Linnaeus). Purple Martin.

Hirundo subis Linnaeus, 1758, Syst. Nat. (ed. 10) 1: 192. Based on "The Great American Martin" Edwards, Nat. Hist. Birds 3: 120, pl. 120. (ad sinum Hudsonis = Hudson Bay.)

Habitat.—In eastern North America, restricted to areas with artificial nest boxes, largely in towns, farmlands, and other open areas, nesting also in manmade structures; in western North America, locally in open pine and pine-oak associations, and saguaro desert (Subtropical and Temperate zones; in winter also Tropical Zone).

Distribution.—*Breeds* locally from southwestern British Columbia (southern Vancouver Island), western Washington, western Oregon, and eastern Idaho south to southern Baja California, Isla Tiburón (off Sonora), northern Arizona, central Utah, western Colorado, New Mexico, and western Texas), and in the Mexican highlands to Michoacán, Guanajuato, and San Luis Potosí; and from central Alberta, central Saskatchewan, southern Manitoba, western and southern Ontario, southern Quebec, southern New Brunswick, and central Nova Scotia south (east of the Rockies) to southern Texas, the Gulf coast, and southern Florida (except the Florida Keys).

Winters, presumably, mainly in Amazonia and south-central Brazil, but winter range not well known; records from elsewhere in South America, if valid, may refer to migrants only. No documented winter records for anywhere in North America or Middle America.

Migrates regularly through Middle America (both slopes, rarely on the Pacific slope south of Nicaragua) and the Florida Keys, and casually through the Bahamas, Cuba, and Grand Cayman.

Casual north to the Pribilof Islands (St. Paul), western and northern Alaska, central Yukon, central Ontario, Prince Edward Island, Newfoundland, Clipperton Island, and Cocos Island. Accidental in Bermuda and the British Isles.

Notes.—Species limits in this complex are uncertain. *Progne subis, P. cryptoleuca, P. dominicensis, P. sinaloae,* and *P. chalybea,* along with the South American *P. modesta* complex (including *P. elegans*) [Southern Martin], constitute a superspecies (Peters *in* Mayr and Greenway 1960, Mayr and Short 1970). See comments under these other species.

Progne cryptoleuca Baird. Cuban Martin.

> *Progne cryptoleuca* Baird, 1865, Rev. Amer. Birds 1: 277. (Cuba and Florida Keys? = Remedios, Cuba.)

Habitat.—Arid Lowland Scrub, Pastures/Agricultural Lands, Second-growth Scrub, Pine Forest (0–1500 m).

Distribution.—*Breeds* on Cuba, including the Isle of Pines.

Winter range unknown. Three specimens taken at Quiriguá and one from Gualán, in the Caribbean lowlands of Guatemala, and reported as *P. cryptoleuca* are referable to *P. chalybea*; another individual from Belize is referable to *P. subis*; possibly in Brazil.

Migrates through Jamaica and Curaçao.

A sight report for the Bahama Islands (Eleuthera).

Notes.—Variously treated as a full species, a race of *P. dominicensis* (Peters *in* Mayr and Greenway 1960, Phillips 1986), or a race of *P. subis* (Mayr and Short 1970); see further comments under these species.

Progne dominicensis (Gmelin). Caribbean Martin.

> *Hirundo dominicensis* Gmelin, 1789, Syst. Nat. 1(2): 1025. Based on "L'Hirondelle de S. Domingue" Brisson, Ornithologie 2: 493, and "Hirondelle d'Amerique" Daubenton, Planches Enlum., pl. 545, fig. 1. (in insula S. Dominici = Hispaniola.)

Habitat.—Second-growth Scrub, Pastures/Agricultural Lands (0–1500 m).

Distribution.—*Breeds* in the Greater Antilles (from Jamaica and Hispaniola eastward, absent from Cuba and the Isle of Pines), Lesser Antilles, Tobago, and Curaçao.

Winter range unknown, but presumably in South America (no West Indian records in November or December).

Casual or accidental in the Bahamas (Mayaguana, Great Inagua, and Grand Turk), the Cayman Islands, and on Cozumel Island.

Notes.—*Progne dominicensis* and *P. sinaloae* are often considered conspecific (Phillips 1986) [Snowy-bellied Martin]. See comments under *P. subis*.

Progne sinaloae Nelson. Sinaloa Martin.

> *Progne sinaloæ* Nelson, 1898, Proc. Biol. Soc. Wash. 12: 59. (Plomosas, Sinaloa.)

Habitat.—Pine-Oak Forest (1100–2800 m; Subtropical and lower Temperate zones).

Distribution.—*Breeds* in the Sierra Madre Occidental of western Mexico from central Sonora and southwestern Chihuahua south through Sinaloa, northern Nayarit, and northwestern Jalisco to central Michoacán.

Winter range unknown, but presumably in South America.

Casual in northern Guatemala (Petén). Accidental in Bermuda.

Notes.—See comments under *P. subis* and *P. dominicensis.*

Progne chalybea (Gmelin). Gray-breasted Martin.

Hirundo chalybea Gmelin, 1789, Syst. Nat. 1(2): 1026. Based mostly on "L'Hirondelle de Cayenne" Brisson, Ornithologie 2: 495, pl. 46, fig. 1. (in Cayenna = Cayenne.)

Habitat.—Second-growth Scrub, Pastures/Agricultural Lands (0–1700 m; Tropical and Subtropical zones).

Distribution.—*Breeds* from Nayarit, northeastern Coahuila, Nuevo León, and Tamaulipas south along both slopes of Middle America (including Isla Coiba off Panama), and in South America from Colombia, Venezuela, Trinidad, and the Guianas south, west of the Andes to northwestern Peru and east of the Andes to central Argentina and southern Brazil.

Winters from Nayarit and Belize south along both slopes of Middle America and South America to northern Bolivia and central Brazil (southernmost breeding populations also migratory, ranging north as far as Venezuela and Amazonian Brazil).

Casual in southern Texas (Rio Grande City, Hidalgo County) and Tobago.

Notes.—See comments under *P. subis.*

Progne elegans Baird. Southern Martin.

Progne elegans Baird, 1865, Rev. Amer. Birds 1: 275, note. (Rio Bermejo, Argentina.)

Habitat.—Second-growth Scrub, Low Seasonally Wet Grassland, (0–500 m; Tropical Zone).

Distribution.—*Breeds* from eastern Bolivia, Paraguay, and Uruguay south to central Argentina.

Winters north to eastern Peru, Colombia, and Amazonian Brazil, possibly eastern Panama (Puerto Olbadía, San Blas; summer sight reports of dark martins in eastern Panamá province and the Canal area may pertain to this species).

Accidental in southern Florida (Key West) and the Falkland Islands.

Notes.—Resident South American species *P. modesta* Gould, 1838, from the Galapagos Islands, and *P. murphyi* Chapman, 1925, from the coast of Peru and Chile, may be conspecific with *P. elegans* (as *P. modesta* [Southern Martin]) (Eisenmann 1959b, Mayr and Short 1970, Short 1975). See comments under *P. subis.*

Progne tapera (Linnaeus). Brown-chested Martin.

Hirundo Tapera Linnaeus, 1766, Syst. Nat. (ed. 12) 1: 345. Based on "L'Hirondelle d'Amérique" Brisson, Ornithologie 2: 502, pl. 45, fig. 3. (in America = Pernambuco, eastern Brazil.)

Habitat.—Low Seasonally Wet Grassland, Pastures/Agricultural Lands, Rivers; in migration and winter in a wide variety of open and partly open situations in lowland areas (Tropical Zone).

Distribution.—*Breeds* from northern Colombia, Venezuela, and the Guianas south, east of the Andes, to northern Argentina and southern Brazil; also west of the Andes in southwestern Ecuador and northwestern Peru.

Winters from southern Bolivia and southern Brazil northward to northern South America and Panama (both slopes, irregularly westward to western Bocas del Toro and western Chiriquí); a sight report from central Costa Rica.

Accidental in Massachusetts (specimen, Monomoy; Petersen et al. 1986); a sight report for Florida.

Notes.—Formerly placed in the monotypic genus *Phaeoprogne,* but genetic data (Sheldon and Winkler 1993) support earlier treatments (e.g., Peters *in* Mayr and Greenway 1960) that merged *Phaeoprogne* into *Progne*.

Genus *TACHYCINETA* Cabanis

Tachycineta Cabanis, 1850, Mus. Heineanum 1: 48. Type, by original designation, *Hirundo thalassina* Swainson.

Callichelidon (Bryant MS) Baird, 1865, Rev. Amer. Birds 1: 271 [in key, as *"Callochelidon"*], 303. Type, by original designation, *Hirundo cyaneoviridis* Bryant.

Kalochelidon [subgenus] H. Bryant, 1867, Proc. Boston Soc. Nat. Hist. 11 (1866): 95. Type, by monotypy, *Hirundo euchrysea* var. *dominicensis* Bryant = *Hirundo sclateri* Cory = *Hirundo euchrysea* Gosse.

Iridoprocne [subgenus] Coues, 1878, Birds Colo. Valley, p. 412. Type, by original designation, *Hirundo bicolor* Vieillot.

Lamprochelidon Ridgway, 1903, Proc. Biol. Soc. Wash. 16: 106. Type, by original designation, *Hirundo euchrysea* Gosse.

Leucochelidon [subgenus] Brooke, 1974, Durban Mus. Novit. 10: 135. Type, by original designation, *Petrochelidon meyeni* Cabanis = *Hirundo leucopyga* Meyen.

Tachycineta bicolor (Vieillot). Tree Swallow.

Hirundo bicolor Vieillot, 1808, Hist. Nat. Ois. Amer. Sept. 1 (1807) (livr. 6): 61, pl. 31. (Centre des États-Unis = New York.)

Habitat.—Open situations usually near water, including streams, lakes, ponds, marshes, and coastal regions; in migration and winter, may forage over any habitat, but favors marshes and lakes.

Distribution.—*Breeds* from western and central Alaska, northern Yukon, northwestern and southern Mackenzie, northern Saskatchewan, northern Manitoba, northern Ontario, north-central Quebec, central Labrador, and Newfoundland south to southwestern Alaska (Cold Bay), along the Pacific coast to southern California, central Nevada, northern Arizona, northern (rarely southwestern) New Mexico, southwestern, south-central, and northeastern Texas, northeastern Louisiana (casual), Mississippi (casual), northern Alabama, northern Georgia, southern Tennessee, and western North Carolina, generally sporadic or irregular as a breeder east of the Rocky Mountain states and south of the upper Mississippi and Ohio valleys, or along the Atlantic coast south of North Carolina. Nonbreeding individuals occur in summer in northern Alaska.

Winters from northern California, southwestern Arizona, northern Mexico, southern Texas, the Gulf coast, and the Atlantic coast from southern New Jersey (casually farther north) south along the Pacific coast of Mexico at least to southern Baja California and Colima, in the interior and along the Gulf-Caribbean coast of Middle America to western Panama and on the northern coast of South America, and to southern Florida (also irregularly the Florida Keys), the northern Bahamas, Greater Antilles, Cayman Islands, and Swan Islands.

Casual or accidental on Wrangel and St. Lawrence islands, in the Pribilof and Aleutian islands, on the Arctic islands (Seymour and Banks islands), in Keewatin and on Boothia Peninsula), and on Clipperton Island (sight report), in Bermuda, southwestern Colombia, Greenland, and the British Isles.

Tachycineta albilinea (Lawrence). Mangrove Swallow.

Petrochelidon albilinea Lawrence, 1863, Ann. Lyc. Nat. Hist. N. Y. 8: 2. (on the Atlantic side of the Isthmus of Panama, along the line of Panama Railroad = Canal Zone.)

Habitat.—Mangrove Forest, Freshwater Lakes and Ponds, Rivers, Pastures/Agricultural Lands (Tropical Zone).

Distribution.—*Resident* from central Sonora, southeastern San Luis Potosí and southern Tamaulipas south along both slopes of Middle America (including the Yucatan Peninsula and most islands nearby) to eastern Panama (east on the Caribbean coast to eastern Colón, and on the Pacific to eastern Darién, including Isla Coiba).

Tachycineta euchrysea (Gosse). Golden Swallow.

Hirundo euchrysea Gosse, 1847, Birds Jamaica, p. 68 (footnote). (higher mountains in the very centre of Jamaica, as in Manchester, and St. Ann's.)

Habitat.—Pine Forest, Montane Evergreen Forest (0–2000 m).
Distribution.—*Resident* locally on Jamaica (where very rare) and Hispaniola.

Tachycineta thalassina (Swainson). Violet-green Swallow.

Hirundo thalassinus Swainson, 1827, Philos. Mag. (n.s.) 1: 366. (Real del Monte, [Hidalgo,] Mexico.)

Habitat.—Open coniferous, deciduous, or mixed and woodland, primarily in highlands, but also locally in deserts and prairies near suitable nest sites (holes in trees, crevices in canyons); in migration and winter, may be found anywhere but favors marshes, rivers, and lakes.
Distribution.—*Breeds* from central Alaska, northern Yukon, extreme southwestern Mackenzie, northern British Columbia, west-central Alberta, extreme southwestern Saskatchewan, Montana, western North Dakota, western South Dakota, northwestern Nebraska, and western Kansas (once) south to southern Alaska (west to the Alaska Peninsula), southern Baja California, coastal Sonora, in the Mexican highlands to Jalisco, Veracruz, and (possibly) Oaxaca, and to western Texas.

Winters from central coastal and southern (casually northwestern) California, central Arizona (casually), southern Sonora, Sinaloa, southern Chihuahua, southern Coahuila, Querétaro, and Puebla south in the interior of Middle America to Honduras, casually or irregularly to Costa Rica, western Panama (Chiriquí and western Panamá province).

Casual or accidental in the Aleutian Islands (Shemya, Unalaska), east to Manitoba, western Ontario, Ohio, central Texas, New Jersey, Zacatecas, Yucatán, and south to northern Colombia; sight reports from Minnesota, Missouri, Nova Scotia, New Hampshire, and Oklahoma.

Tachycineta cyaneoviridis (Bryant). Bahama Swallow.

Hirundo cyaneoviridis H. Bryant, 1859, Proc. Boston Soc. Nat. Hist. 7: 111. (Nassau [New Providence, Bahamas].)

Habitat.—Pine Forest.
Distribution.—*Breeds* on the northern Bahama Islands (Grand Bahama, Great Abaco, Andros, and New Providence).

Winters, at least sparingly, throughout the Bahama Islands and in eastern Cuba.

Migrates irregularly through southern Florida and the lower Florida Keys (including Dry Tortugas).

Genus *PYGOCHELIDON* Baird

Pygochelidon Baird, 1865, Rev. Amer. Birds 1: 270, 306. Type, by original designation, *Hirundo cyanoleuca* Vieillot.

Pygochelidon cyanoleuca (Vieillot). Blue-and-white Swallow.

Hirundo cyanoleuca Vieillot, 1817, Nouv. Dict. Hist. Nat. (nouv. éd.) 14: 509. Based on "Golondrina Timoneles negros" Azara, Apunt. Hist. Nat. Páx. Parag. 2: 508 (no. 303). (Paraguay.)

Habitat.—Second-growth Scrub, Pastures/Agricultural Lands (0–3600 m; Tropical to Temperate zones, mostly Subtropical Zone in Middle America).
Distribution.—*Breeds* [*patagonica* group] from central Chile and central (possibly north-central) Argentina south to Tierra del Fuego. Resident (disjunctly) in coastal Peru.

Winters [*patagonica* group] from northern Chile and northern Argentina north regularly to northern South America and central Panama (west to the Canal area), casually to Nicaragua, Guatemala (sight report), and Chiapas.

Resident [*cyanoleuca* group] in the foothills and highlands of Costa Rica (northwest to the Cordillera de Guanacaste) and western Panama (Chiriquí, Veraguas, and western Panamá province); and in South America from Colombia, Venezuela, Trinidad, and the Guianas south (except in central Amazonia) to northwestern Argentina, Paraguay, Uruguay, and southern Brazil.

Notes.—Groups: *P. cyanoleuca* [Blue-and-white Swallow] and *P. patagonica* (d'Orbigny and Lafresnaye, 1837) [Patagonian Swallow]. This species is sometimes treated in the genus *Notiochelidon* Baird, 1865 (Peters *in* Mayr and Greenway 1960, Meyer de Schauensee 1966) or in the South American genus *Atticora* Boie, 1844 (Phillips 1986), but genetic data support its placement in the genus *Pygochelidon* (Sheldon and Winkler 1993).

Genus *NOTIOCHELIDON* Baird

Notiochelidon Baird, 1865, Rev. Amer. Birds 1: 270, 306. Type, by original designation, *Atticora pileata* Gould.

Notiochelidon pileata (Gould). Black-capped Swallow.

Atticora pileata Gould, 1858, Proc. Zool. Soc. London, p. 355. (Guatemala.)

Habitat.—Pine-Oak Forest, Montane Evergreen Forest, Secondary Forest (1600–3100 m; Subtropical and Temperate zones).

Distribution.—*Resident* in the mountains of Chiapas, Guatemala, northern El Salvador, and western Honduras (probably breeding).

Notes.—Also known as Coban Swallow. This species is sometimes treated in the genus *Atticora* (Phillips 1986).

Genus *NEOCHELIDON* Sclater

Microchelidon (not Reichenbach, 1853) Sclater, 1862, Cat. Collect. Amer. Birds, p. 39. Type, by monotypy, *Petrochelidon tibialis* Cassin.
Neochelidon Sclater, 1862, Cat. Collect. Amer. Birds, p. [xvi]. New name for *Microchelidon* Sclater, preoccupied.

Neochelidon tibialis (Cassin). White-thighed Swallow.

Petrochelidon ? tibialis Cassin, 1853, Proc. Acad. Nat. Sci. Philadelphia 6: 370. (probably Brazil = Rio de Janeiro, Brazil.)

Habitat.—Tropical Lowland Evergreen Forest Edge (0–1200 m; Tropical Zone).

Distribution.—*Resident* in Panama (west to Coclé, the Canal area and western Panamá province), and in South America locally from Colombia, southern Venezuela, and Surinam south, west of the Andes to western Ecuador and east of the Andes to northern Bolivia, Amazonia, and southeastern Brazil.

Genus *STELGIDOPTERYX* Baird

Stelgidopteryx [subgenus] Baird, 1858, in Baird, Cassin, and Lawrence, Rep. Explor. Surv. R. R. Pac. 9: xxxiv, 312. Type, by monotypy, *Hirundo serripennis* Audubon.

Stelgidopteryx serripennis (Audubon). Northern Rough-winged Swallow.

Hirundo serripennis Audubon, 1838, Ornithol. Biogr., 4, p. 593. (Charleston, South Carolina.)

Habitat.—Open and partly open situations, especially along or near watercourses with steep banks, and roadside cuts (for its nest burrows; also locally [*ridgwayi* group] in caves and old buildings); in migration and winter, forages primarily over open country and wetlands.

Distribution.—*Breeds* [*serripennis* group] from mainland southeastern Alaska, central British Columbia, central Alberta, central Saskatchewan, southern Manitoba, western and southern Ontario, southern Quebec, southwestern New Brunswick, and southwestern Nova Scotia south to southern Baja California, and through Middle America (except the Yucatan Peninsula) to Costa Rica, and to southern Texas, the Gulf coast, and south-central and southwestern Florida.

Winters [*serripennis* group] from southern California, southern Arizona, northern Mexico, southern Texas, southern Louisiana, coastal Alabama, and southern Florida (casually north to central California and South Carolina) south through the breeding range in Mexico and Central America, and lowlands to Panama; breeding populations from the lowlands and central interior of Mexico southward are generally sedentary. Whether individuals seen in winter months in the United States are winter residents or late/early migrants is unknown.

Migrates [*serripennis* group] through the northwestern Bahama Islands, Cuba, Jamaica, and the Cayman and Swan islands, ranging irregularly (or casually) to southwestern and south-coastal Alaska, Prince Edward Island, Newfoundland, southern Veracruz, and Tabasco.

Resident [*ridgwayi* group] in the Yucatan Peninsula (west to southern Veracruz), Belize, and northern Guatemala.

Casual or accidental [*serripennis* group] in northern Alaska (Barrow) and southern Yukon; sight reports from the Revillagigedo (Socorro), northern Bahama, and Virgin islands (St. John, St. Croix).

Notes.—Phillips (1986) treated the two groups as distinct species, *S. serripennis* [Northern Rough-winged Swallow] and *S. ridgwayi* Nelson, 1901 [Ridgway's Rough-winged Swallow]. *Stelgidopteryx serripennis* and *S. ruficollis* were formerly considered conspecific [Rough-winged Swallow], but sympatric breeding has been discovered in Costa Rica (Stiles 1981).

Stelgidopteryx ruficollis (Vieillot). Southern Rough-winged Swallow.

Hirundo ruficollis Vieillot, 1817, Nouv. Dict. Hist. Nat. (nouv. éd.) 14: 523. (Brazil.)

Habitat.—Second-growth Scrub, Pastures/Agricultural Lands, Rivers, Streams; nests in burrows (0–2000 m; Tropical to Temperate zones).

Distribution.—*Resident* in the lowlands from eastern Honduras (Olancho) south through Nicaragua (Caribbean slope), Costa Rica (both slopes, on the Pacific northwest to the Gulf of Nicoya) and Panama, and in South America from Colombia, Venezuela, Trinidad, and the Guianas south, west of the Andes to northwestern Peru and east of the Andes to central Argentina.

Notes.—See comments under *S. serripennis*.

Genus *RIPARIA* Forster

Riparia T. Forster, 1817, Synop. Cat. Br. Birds, p. 17. Type, by monotypy, *Riparia europaea* Forster = *Hirundo riparia* Linnaeus.

Riparia riparia (Linnaeus). Bank Swallow.

Hirundo riparia Linnaeus, 1758, Syst. Nat. (ed. 10) 1: 192. (in Europæ collibus arenosis abruptis = Sweden.)

Habitat.—Open and partly open situations, near vertical river banks that provide nest-sites (burrows); in migration and winter, forages primarily over wetlands and fields.

Distribution.—*Breeds* in North America from western and central Alaska, northern Yukon, northwestern and south-central Mackenzie, northern Saskatchewan, northern Manitoba, northern Ontario, south-central Quebec, southern Labrador, and southwestern Newfoundland south to southern Alaska (west to the eastern Aleutians), central (formerly southern) California (but rare west of the coast ranges from British Columbia to Oregon), western Nevada, Utah, northern New Mexico, Kansas, northeastern Oklahoma, Arkansas (formerly), Tennessee, northern Alabama, central West Virginia, eastern Virginia, and (casually) northwestern North Carolina and south-central South Carolina; also disjunctly in central New Mexico, south-central Texas, northern Tamaulipas, and northern Nuevo León; and in Eurasia from the Hebrides, Orkneys, northern Scandinavia, northern Russia, and Siberia south to the Mediterranean region, Palestine, Iran, Afghanistan, northern India, southeastern China, and Japan.

Winters largely in South America, but limits of winter range (versus areas where only a transient) not studied. Some winter records for central and eastern Panama (casually, locally north to southern California; numerous December sight reports from southern United States and western Mexico require confirmation), but evidently mainly a transient in northern South America (Colombia, Venezuela, the Guianas). Ranges south to northern Argentina and Paraguay, and northern Chile. Also in the Old World from the Mediterranean region, Near East, northern India, and eastern China south to tropical and eastern Africa, Madagascar, Arabia, southern India, Southeast Asia, Borneo, and the Philippines.

Migrates in the Americas widely through the southern United States, Middle America, the West Indies (rare in the Lesser Antilles), and northern South America (including the Netherlands Antilles east to Tobago and Trinidad); and in the Old World through the eastern Atlantic islands in addition to the region between breeding and wintering ranges.

Casual or accidental in western Aleutian and Commander islands, in northern Alaska (Barrow), on Jenny Lind, Victoria, and Melville islands, and on Clipperton Island (sight reports), Bermuda, and Barbados.

Notes.—Known in Old World literature as Sand Martin.

Genus *PETROCHELIDON* Cabanis

Petrochelidon Cabanis, 1850, Mus. Heineanum 1: 47. Type, by subsequent designation (G. R. Gray, 1855), *Hirundo melanogaster* Swainson = *Hirundo pyrrhonota* Vieillot.

Petrochelidon pyrrhonota Vieillot. Cliff Swallow.

Hirundo pyrrhonota Vieillot, 1817, Nouv. Dict. Hist. Nat. (nouv. éd.) 14: 519. (Paraguay.)

Habitat.—Open country, less frequently partly open situations, most frequently in the vicinity of water; requires cliffs, bridges, dams, buildings, culverts, or occasionally caves for nest sites; in migration and winter, widespread over open country and wetlands.

Distribution.—*Breeds* from western and central Alaska, northern Yukon, northern Mackenzie, central Keewatin, northern Manitoba, northern Ontario, southern Quebec (including Anticosti Island), New Brunswick, Prince Edward Island, and Nova Scotia south to south-coastal Alaska, northern Baja California, central Oaxaca, Veracruz, the Gulf coast (east to southern Alabama), northern Georgia, central South Carolina, also in the Lake Okeechobee region of southern Florida (1975–1982).

Winters in South America from Paraguay, and central and southeastern Brazil south to central Argentina, casually north to southern California.

Migrates regularly through the southeastern United States, northern Middle America and western South America north of the winter range, rarely through the northwestern Bahama Islands, Cuba, the Cayman Islands, and the Virgin Islands.

Casual or accidental on Wrangel Island, and in northern Alaska, the Aleutians, St. Lawrence Island, northern Manitoba, Newfoundland, Clipperton Island (sight report), St. Kitts (sight report), and Barbados, and in Chile, Tierra del Fuego, southern Greenland, and the British Isles.

Notes.—Mayr and Short (1970) considered *P. pyrrhonota* and *P. fulva* to constitute a superspecies, but their breeding distributions overlap broadly in Mexico.

Petrochelidon fulva Vieillot. Cave Swallow.

Hirundo fulva Vieillot, 1808, Hist. Nat. Ois. Amer. Sept. 1 (1807, livr. 11): 62, pl. 32. (Saint-Domingue = Hispaniola.)

Habitat.—Northern Temperate Grassland, Pastures/Agricultural Lands, Second-growth Scrub, Arid Lowland Scrub; nests in caves, sinkholes, culverts, and beneath bridges (0–1500 m).

Distribution.—*Breeds* [*pelodoma* group] from northern Arizona, southeastern New Mexico (Carlsbad Caverns), and Texas (except northern) south to southern Chihuahua, eastern Durango, Zacatecas, San Luis Potosí and western Tamaulipas; and [*fulva* group] in central Chiapas, the Yucatan Peninsula, southern Florida, and from the Greater Antilles east to

Puerto Rico (including Gonâve, Tortue, and Vieques islands, and Île-à-Vache). Breeding ranges [*pelodoma* group] in the south-central United States are expanding rapidly northward.

Winter range of northern populations unknown, except there is a sizable and increasing winter population in southern Texas and northern Mexico [*pelodoma* group]; breeding populations [*fulva* group] in southern Mexico and the Greater Antilles are essentially resident, with vagrants recorded regularly in southern (casually northern) Florida, along the eastern Gulf coast, and casually north along the Atlantic coast to Nova Scotia (Seal Island, Sable Island).

Casual or accidental [*pelodoma* group] in southeastern California, elsewhere in Arizona, southeastern Louisiana, Nebraska, and Baja California; and [*fulva* group] in Bermuda and the Cayman and Virgin islands. An old specimen record from Costa Rica has been questioned; sight reports from Panama (eastern Panamá province) and Ontario.

Notes.—The two groups, *P. pelodoma* Brooke, 1974, Cave Swallow], and *P. fulva* [Cinnamon-throated Swallow], may represent separate species (Smith et al. 1988). The name *P. pallida* (Nelson, 1902), formerly used for *pelodoma,* is preoccupied. *Petrochelidon fulva* and the closely related *P. rufocollaris* Peale, 1848 [Chestnut-collared Swallow], of southwestern Ecuador and western Peru, constitute a superspecies (Sibley and Monroe 1990); they have usually been treated as conspecific (e.g., Peters *in* Mayr and Greenway 1960, Mayr and Short 1970, A.O.U. 1983). See comments under *P. pyrrhonota.*

Genus *HIRUNDO* Linnaeus

Hirundo Linnaeus, 1758, Syst. Nat. (ed. 10) 1: 191. Type, by subsequent designation (G. R. Gray, 1840), *Hirundo rustica* Linnaeus.

Hirundo rustica Linnaeus. Barn Swallow.

Hirundo rustica Linnaeus, 1758, Syst. Nat. (ed. 10) 1: 191. (in Europæ domibus intra tectum = Sweden.)

Habitat.—Open situations, less frequently in partly open habitats, frequently near water; nests in sheltered areas in buildings, under bridges, or in caves.

Distribution.—*Breeds* [*erythrogaster* group] in North America from south-coastal and southeastern (formerly southwestern) Alaska, southern Yukon, central-western Mackenzie, northern Saskatchewan, northern Manitoba, northern Ontario, south-central Quebec, and southern Newfoundland south to extreme northwestern Baja California, Jalisco, Colima, Michoacán, México, Distrito Federal, southern Nuevo Léon (disjunctly in Chiapas), the Gulf coast, north-central (casually southern) Florida, and southern North Carolina (casually southeastern Georgia), and in northeastern Argentina (Buenos Aires); and [*rustica* group] in Eurasia from Iceland, the British Isles, Faeroe Islands, Scandinavia, northern Russia, and northern Siberia south to the Mediterranean region, northern Africa, the Near East, Arabia, Iran, the Himalayas, China, Taiwan, and Japan.

Winters [*erythrogaster* group] in the Americas from the Pacific slope of central Mexico and western Panama (casually north to central California, the southwestern United States, northern Mexico, and southern Florida), Puerto Rico, and the Lesser Antilles south throughout South America to Tierra del Fuego; and [*rustica* group] in the Old World south to tropical Africa, the East Indies, northern Australia, and Micronesia; late fall records until December and early spring migrants complicate delineation of winter range.

Migrates [*erythrogaster* group] through Middle America, the West Indies, and islands of the eastern Atlantic and western Pacific oceans and along continental coasts, as well as throughout continental areas between the breeding and wintering ranges; and [*rustica* group] casually through the western Aleutians, Pribilofs, St. Lawrence Island, and on the coast of mainland Alaska from Barrow to the Yukon Delta.

Casual or accidental [*erythrogaster* group] in the western Hawaiian Islands (also on Hawaii); north to northern Alaska, to St. Lawrence, Pribilof, Aleutian, Banks, Victoria, Cornwallis, and Mansel islands, and to northern Mackenzie, southern Keewatin, and southern Labrador; Revillagigedo Islands and Clipperton Island (sight reports), southern Greenland, the Falkland Islands, South Georgia, and Tristan da Cunha.

Notes.—Groups: *H. erythrogaster* Boddaert, 1783 [Barn Swallow] and *H. rustica* [European Swallow]. Genetic data suggest that two or more species may be involved and that North American and Siberian populations may be sister taxa (Zink et al. 1995). *Hirundo rustica* may form a superspecies with several Old World taxa (*H. lucida* Hartlaub, 1858; *H. aethiopica* Blanford, 1869; *H. angolensis* Barboza du Bocage, 1868; *H. albigularis* Strickland, 1849; *H. dumicola* Jerdon, 1844; *H. tahitica* Gmelin, 1789; and *H. neoxena* Gould, 1843) (Sibley and Monroe 1990).

Genus *DELICHON* Horsfield and Moore

Delichon "Hodgs." Horsfield and Moore, 1854, Cat. Birds Mus. Hon. E. India Co. 1 (1856): 384. Type, by monotypy, *Delichon nipalensis* Horsfield and Moore.

Delichon urbica (Linnaeus). Common House-Martin.

Hirundo urbica Linnaeus, 1758, Syst. Nat. (ed. 10) 1: 192. (in Europa = Sweden.)

Habitat.—Human settlements, farmland, towns, nesting in colonies on buildings, cliffs, and bridges.

Distribution.—*Breeds* widely through most of Eurasia south to northern Africa, the Himalayas, and China.

Winters south to southern Africa, India, and southeast Asia.

Casual in Greenland, Iceland, and the eastern Atlantic islands. Accidental in Alaska (Nome, and St. Paul in the Pribilofs, 6–7 and 12 June 1974; Hall and Cardiff 1978), St. Pierre et Miquelon (26–31 May 1989; 1989, Amer. Birds 43: 446) and in Bermuda (Devonshire Parish, 9 August 1957; Wingate 1958); additional sight reports for Alaska.

Notes.—Known in Old World literature as the House Martin.

Family **PARIDAE**: Chickadees and Titmice

Notes.—We follow Slikas et al. (1996) for generic-level taxonomy and linear sequence of species. Sheldon and Gill (1996) provided molecular evidence for why the Paridae may not be closely related to some families (Aegithalidae, Certhiidae, and Sittidae) placed close to them in traditional classifications. See comments under *Auriparus* and Aegithalidae.

Genus *POECILE* Kaup

Poecile Kaup, 1829, Skizz. Entw. Nat. Syst., p. 92. Type, by original designation, *Parus palustris* Linnaeus.

Poecile carolinensis (Audubon). Carolina Chickadee.

Parus carolinensis Audubon, 1834, Ornithol. Biogr. 2: 341. (Charleston in South Carolina [and] not far from New Orleans = Charleston, South Carolina.)

Habitat.—Deciduous, mixed, and pine woodland, and parks and suburbs.

Distribution.—*Resident* from southern Kansas, central Missouri, central Illinois, central Indiana, northern Ohio, southern Pennsylvania, and central New Jersey south to central and southeastern Texas, the Gulf coast, and central peninsular Florida.

Wanders casually northward to northern Illinois, southeastern Michigan (formerly), and southern Ontario.

Notes.—See comments under *P. atricapillus*.

Poecile atricapillus (Linnaeus). Black-capped Chickadee.

Parus atricapillus Linnaeus, 1766, Syst. Nat. (ed. 12) 1: 341. Based on "La Mésange a teste noire de Canada" Brisson, Ornithologie 3: 553, pl. 29, fig. 1. (in Canada = Quebec City, Quebec.)

Habitat.—Deciduous or mixed deciduous-coniferous woodland, riparian woodland (especially cottonwood-willow in western portion of range), and parks and suburbs.

Distribution.—*Resident* from western and central Alaska, southern Yukon, southwestern

Mackenzie, northern Saskatchewan, north-central Manitoba, northern Ontario, south-central Quebec (including Anticosti Island), and Newfoundland south to southern Alaska (west to the Alaska Peninsula, and the Shumagin and Kodiak islands), northwestern California, southern Oregon, northeastern Nevada, southeastern Utah, central New Mexico, southern Kansas, southwestern and central Missouri, central Illinois, northern Indiana, northern Ohio, southern Pennsylvania, and northern New Jersey, and in the Appalachians at higher and western Virginia to eastern Tennessee and western North Carolina.

Wanders irregularly south in winter to northern Arizona, south-central New Mexico, Oklahoma, southeastern Missouri, eastern Virginia, and Maryland.

Casual in Alaska on Nunivak Island, Wales, and Point Barrow.

Notes.—*Poecile atricapillus* and *P. carolinensis* hybridize on a limited basis in the zone of contact in the midwestern states (Kansas east to Ohio) (Rising 1968, Braun and Robbins 1986) and in the southern Appalachians (Rising 1968, 1983a; Johnston 1971, Tanner 1952), and have been viewed as conspecific (Braun and Robbins 1986, Robbins et al. 1986). Mayr and Short (1970) considered the two to represent a superspecies. However, *P. atricapillus* is genetically closer to *P. sclateri* and *P. gambeli* than to *P. carolinensis* (Gill et al. 1989). The Old World *P. montanus* Conrad von Baldenstein, 1827 [Willow Tit], may also belong in this superspecies (Vaurie and Snow 1957, Vaurie 1959, Desfayes 1964, Mayr and Short 1970), but see Gill et al. (1989).

Poecile gambeli (Ridgway). Mountain Chickadee.

> *Parus montanus* (not Conrad von Baldenstein, 1827) Gambel, 1843, Proc. Acad. Nat. Sci. Philadelphia 1: 259. (about a-day's journey [west] from Santa Fe, New Mexico.)
> *Parus gambeli* Ridgway, 1886, A.O.U. Check-list North Amer. Birds, ed. 1: 335. New name for *Parus montanus* Gambel, preoccupied.

Habitat.—Montane coniferous forest, primarily pine, spruce-fir, and locally pinyon-juniper and desert riparian woodland, also aspen; in nonbreeding season, also pine-oak association, riparian woodland, and suburbs (locally).

Distribution.—*Resident* from northwestern and central British Columbia, west-central Alberta, central Montana south (except for most of the coast ranges) to northern Baja California (Sierra Juárez and Sierra San Pedro Mártir), southern California, southern Nevada, central and southeastern Arizona (except mountains along the Mexican border), southern New Mexico, and extreme western Texas (Davis and Guadalupe mountains). Recorded in summer (and possibly breeding) in southeastern Alaska (Warm Pass Valley) and southern Yukon.

Casual (mostly in winter) elsewhere in southeastern Alaska, southwestern British Columbia, Washington, Oregon, and California, and east to southwestern Saskatchewan, southwestern South Dakota, southwestern Kansas, and the Panhandles of northern Texas and western Oklahoma.

Notes.—See comments under *P. atricapillus*.

Poecile sclateri (Kleinschmidt). Mexican Chickadee.

> *Parus meridionalis* (not Lilljeborg, 1852) Sclater, 1857, Proc. Zool. Soc. London (1856), p. 293. (El Jacale in the State of Vera Cruz [or Puebla], Southern Mexico.)
> *Parus sclateri* Kleinschmidt, 1897, J. Ornithol. 45: 133. New name for *Parus meridionalis* Sclater, preoccupied.

Habitat.—Pine Forest, Pine-Oak Forest, spruce and fir forest (1500–3900 m; Subtropical and Temperate zones).

Distribution.—*Resident* from northeastern Sonora, extreme southeastern Arizona (Chiricahua Mountains), southwestern New Mexico (Animas Mountains, casually Peloncillo Mountains), and Chihuahua south through mountains of western and southern Mexico to central Oaxaca (west of the Isthmus of Tehuantepec) and western Veracruz. Also southern Coahuila and west-central Nuevo Leon. Some movement to lower elevations in winter in northern portions of range.

Notes.—See comments under *P. atricapillus*.

Poecile rufescens (Townsend). Chestnut-backed Chickadee.

> *Parus rufescens* J. K. Townsend, 1837, J. Acad. Nat. Sci. Philadelphia 7: 190. (forests of the Columbia River = Fort Vancouver, Washington.)

Habitat.—Coniferous and mixed coniferous-deciduous forest, primarily in humid regions; in southern and drier portions of range, also in pine forest, oak woodland, pine-oak woodland, and locally in riparian woodland.

Distribution.—*Resident* from south-coastal and southeastern Alaska (west to the Prince William Sound region), western and south-central British Columbia (including the Queen Charlotte and Vancouver islands), northern Idaho, and northwestern Montana south through the coast ranges to southern California (San Luis Obispo and Santa Barbara counties), and through the interior ranges to central California (Mariposa County).

Wanders inland to northern British Columbia. Casual in southern California (Ventura County) and southwestern Alberta.

Notes.—See comments under *P. cinctus.*

Poecile hudsonicus (Forster). Boreal Chickadee.

> *Parus Hudsonicus* J. R. Forster, 1772, Philos. Trans. R. Soc. London 62: 408, 430. (Severn River [west coast of Hudson Bay, Canada].)

Habitat.—Boreal coniferous (primarily spruce) and mixed coniferous-deciduous woodland, ranging rarely to deciduous woodland.

Distribution.—*Resident* from western and central Alaska, northern Yukon, northwestern and southeastern Mackenzie, northern Ontario, northern Quebec, northern Labrador, and Newfoundland south to southern Alaska (west to the Alaska Peninsula), British Columbia (east of the coast ranges), north-central and northeastern Washington, northwestern Montana, southwestern and central Alberta, central Saskatchewan, southern Manitoba, northern Minnesota, northern Wisconsin, northern Michigan, southern Ontario (south to Algonquin Park), northern New York, northern Vermont, northern New Hampshire, New Brunswick, central Maine, and Nova Scotia.

Wanders irregularly after the breeding season north to southwestern Keewatin, and south to southwestern British Columbia, South Dakota, Iowa, northern Illinois, Indiana, Ohio, West Virginia, northern Virginia, Maryland, Delaware, and New Jersey.

Notes.—Also known as Brown-capped Chickadee. *Poecile hudsonicus* and *P. rufescens* are each other's closest relatives (Gill et al. 1989, Slikas et al. 1996). See also comments under *P. cinctus.*

Poecile cinctus (Boddaert). Grey-headed Chickadee.

> *Parus cinctus* Boddaert, 1783, Table Planches Enlum., p. 44. Based on "Mésange de Sibérie" Daubenton, Planches Enlum., pl. 708, fig. 3. (Sibérie = Siberia.)

Habitat.—Patches of boreal coniferous forest, primarily spruce, most commonly in stream basins, also locally in willow and aspen thickets.

Distribution.—*Resident* from northern Alaska east across northern Yukon (Old Crow) to northwestern Mackenzie (Aklavik, Fort Anderson), and south locally to western and central Alaska (Nulato, central Alaska Range); and in Eurasia from Scandinavia, northern Russia, and northern Siberia south to northern Mongolia, Transbaicalia, northern Amurland, Kamchatka, and Anadyrland.

Notes.—Also known as Siberian Tit or Siberian Chickadee. *Poecile cinctus, P. hudsonicus,* and *P. rufescens* may constitute a superspecies (Mayr and Short 1970, Sibley and Monroe 1990).

Genus *BAEOLOPHUS* Cabanis

> *Baeolophus* Cabanis, 1850, Mus. Heineanum 1: 91. Type, by monotypy, *Parus bicolor* Linnaeus.

Baeolophus wollweberi (Bonaparte). Bridled Titmouse.

Lophophanes wollweberi Bonaparte, 1850, C. R. Acad. Sci. Paris 31: 478. (en Mexico Zacatecas = Zacatecas, Zacatecas.)

Habitat.—Pine-Oak Forest, Gallery Forest (1200–2700 m; Subtropical and lower Temperate zones).

Distribution.—*Resident* from north-central Sonora, central and southeastern Arizona (north to the Mogollon Plateau), southwestern and south-central New Mexico, northwestern and central Chihuahua, northern Durango, Zacatecas, central Nuevo León, and western Tamaulipas south in the Mexican highlands to central Oaxaca (west of the Isthmus of Tehuantepec) and western Veracruz. Some movement to lower elevations in winter in northern portions of range.

Accidental in central Arizona (Bill Williams Delta).

Notes.—*Baeolophus wollweberi* and the other crested North American titmice represent a different lineage and are distantly related to other parids (Gill et al. 1989, Sheldon and Gill 1996).

Baeolophus inornatus (Gambel). Oak Titmouse.

Parus inornatus Gambel, 1845, Proc. Acad. Nat. Sci. Philadelphia 2: 265. (Upper California = near Monterey, California.)

Habitat—Oak and pine-oak woodland, arborescent chaparral, oak-riparian associations.

Distribution.—*Resident* from southwestern Oregon south (west of the Sierra Nevada) to southern Baja California (absent from most of central Baja California).

Notes.—*Baeolophus griseus* was formerly considered conspecific with *B. inornatus,* with the name Plain Titmouse, but they are genetically distinct at a level equivalent to that in other species-pairs in the genus (Gill and Slikas 1992, Cicero 1996), and they differ in voice, morphology, coloration, and ecology (Cicero 1996). *Baeolophus inornatus* and *B. griseus* constitute a superspecies. See comments under *B. wollweberi.*

Baeolophus griseus (Ridgway). Juniper Titmouse.

Lophophanes inornatus griseus Ridgway, 1882, Proc. U.S. Nat. Mus. 5: 344. (Middle Province of United States = Iron City, Utah.)

Parus inornatus ridgwayi Richmond, 1902, Proc. Biol. Soc. Wash. 15: 155. New name for *Lophophanes inornatus griseus* Ridgway, 1882, preoccupied in *Parus.*

Habitat—Primarily pinyon-juniper woodland.

Distribution.—*Resident* from southeastern Oregon, northeastern Nevada, southeastern Idaho, southern Wyoming, central Colorado, and extreme western Oklahoma south (east of the Sierra Nevada) to southeastern California, central and southeastern Arizona, extreme northeastern Sonora, southern New Mexico, and extreme western Texas (El Paso to Guadalupe Mountains).

Notes.—See comments under *B. wollweberi.*

Baeolophus bicolor (Linnaeus). Tufted Titmouse.

Parus bicolor Linnaeus, 1766, Syst. Nat. (ed. 12) 1: 340. Based on "The Crested Titmouse" Catesby, Nat. Hist. Carolina 1: 57, pl. 57. (in America septentrionali = South Carolina.)

Habitat.—[*bicolor* group] Forest, woodland, from deciduous and mixed deciduous-coniferous woodland in the northeast to oak-juniper scrub, mesquite, and riparian woodland in the southwest, also in parks and suburbs where tall trees present; [*atricristatus* group] Tropical Deciduous Forest, Secondary Forest, Gallery Forest (0–2300 m).

Distribution.—*Resident* [*bicolor* group] from northeastern Nebraska, central and eastern Iowa, southeastern Minnesota, southern Wisconsin, central Michigan, southern Ontario, northern Ohio, northwestern Pennsylvania, central New York, central Vermont, central New Hampshire, and central Maine south to eastern Texas (formerly to San Angelo, San Antonio, and Corpus Christi areas), the Gulf coast, and southern Florida, and west to central Kansas and west-central Oklahoma; and [*atricristatus* group] from southwestern Oklahoma and western and northern Texas (north to Randall and Armstrong counties, and east to Grimes, Lavaca, and Calhoun counties) south through central Coahuila, Nuevo León, Tamaulipas, and eastern San Luis Potosí to central-eastern Hidalgo and central Veracruz, also disjunctly in southern Veracruz (Sierra de los Tuxtlas).

Wanders [*bicolor* group] irregularly northward to South Dakota, central Minnesota, southern Quebec, Rhode Island, and New Brunswick.

Accidental [*atricristatus* group] in Massachusetts (Weymouth); a sight report from North Dakota.

Notes.—Groups: *B. bicolor* [Tufted Titmouse] and *B. atricristatus* Cassin, 1850 [Black-crested Titmouse]. Although the two groups are genetically distinct (Braun et al. 1984, Avise and Zink 1988, Sheldon et al. 1992), they interbreed freely in a narrow zone through east-central Texas (Dixon 1989, 1990). See comments under *B. wollweberi*.

Family **REMIZIDAE**: Penduline Tits and Verdins

Genus *AURIPARUS* Baird

Auriparus Baird, 1864, Rev. Amer. Birds 1: 85. Type, by original designation, *Aegithalus flaviceps* Sundevall.

Notes.—*Auriparus* is considered close to the Polioptilinae by Sibley and Monroe (1990), but see Sheldon and Gill (1996) for molecular data that confirm relationships to the Paridae.

Auriparus flaviceps (Sundevall). Verdin.

Aegithalus flaviceps Sundevall, 1850, Kongl. Svensk. Vet.-Akad. Forh. 7: 129 (note). (e Sitka in America bor. occid., vel e California = probably near Loreto, lat. 26° N., Baja California.)

Habitat.—Arid Lowland Scrub, Arid Montane Scrub, Gallery Forest; locally in residential areas of desert towns (0–2375 m).

Distribution.—*Resident* from northeastern Baja California, southeastern California (north to northeastern Los Angeles, Kern, and Inyo counties), southern Nevada, southwestern Utah, northwestern Arizona, southern New Mexico, southwestern Oklahoma (Jackson County), and central Texas (east to Callahan, Williamson, and Calhoun counties) south to southern Baja California (including Magdalena, Margarita, and many Gulf coastal islands), Jalisco, Guanajuato, Querétaro, Hidalgo, and Tamaulipas.

Casual in southwestern California (northern San Diego County) and southwestern Oklahoma (Jackson County).

Family **AEGITHALIDAE**: Long-tailed Tits and Bushtits

Notes.—This family is probably more closely related to the Sylviidae and relatives (Sheldon and Gill 1996) than to the Remizidae and Paridae, where traditionally placed.

Genus *PSALTRIPARUS* Bonaparte

Psaltriparus Bonaparte, 1850, C. R. Acad. Sci. Paris 31: 478. Type, by monotypy, *Psaltriparus personatus* Bonaparte = *Parus melanotis* Hartlaub = *Parus minimus* Townsend.

Notes.—Phillips (1986) merged *Psaltriparus* into *Aegithalos*.

Psaltriparus minimus (Townsend). Bushtit.

Parus minimus J. K. Townsend, 1837, J. Acad. Nat. Sci. Philadelphia 7: 190. (forests of Columbia River = probably near Fort Vancouver, Washington.)

Habitat.—Woodland and scrub (especially oak), pinyon-juniper, chaparral, and pine-oak association, wooded suburbs; in winter, also locally in riparian woodland (Subtropical and Temperate zones).

Distribution.—*Resident* [*minimus* group] from extreme southwestern British Columbia (southeastern Vancouver Island and lower Fraser River Valley), central Washington, and western and south-central Oregon south through California (west of the Sierra Nevada) to southern Baja California (absent from most of central Baja California); [*plumbeus* group] from southeastern Oregon, southwestern Idaho, northern Nevada, north-central Utah, south-western Wyoming, north-central Colorado, western Oklahoma (Kenton), and central Texas (east to Bosque and Travis counties) south to eastern California, central and southeastern Arizona, central Sonora, southern New Mexico, and central Texas; and [*melanotis* group] from northeastern Sonora, extreme southwestern New Mexico, and western Texas south through the highlands of Mexico to central Guatemala. Some movement to lower elevations in winter in northern portions of range.

Casual [*plumbeus* group] in central Kansas (Hays).

Notes.—Populations of the *melanotis* group were formerly regarded as a species, *P. melanotis* (Hartlaub, 1844) [Black-eared Bushtit], distinct from the other populations in the species, *P. minimus* [Common Bushtit]; that the difference in the two groups is primarily a case of polymorphism is now well established (Raitt 1967).

Family **SITTIDAE**: Nuthatches

Notes.—See comments under Paridae and Troglodytidae.

Subfamily SITTINAE: Nuthatches

Genus *SITTA* Linnaeus

Sitta Linnaeus, 1758, Syst. Nat. (ed. 10) 1: 115. Type, by monotypy, *Sitta europaea* Linnaeus.

Sitta canadensis Linnaeus. Red-breasted Nuthatch.

Sitta canadensis Linnaeus, 1766, Syst. Nat. (ed. 12) 1: 177. Based on "Le Torchepot de Canada" Brisson, Ornithologie 3: 592, pl. 29, fig. 4. (in Canada.)

Habitat.—Mature coniferous (mostly spruce and fir) and mixed coniferous-deciduous forest; in migration and winter, also deciduous forest, open woodland, parks, and riparian woodland, but prefers conifers wherever available.

Distribution.—*Breeds* from south-coastal and southeastern Alaska (west to the Kenai Peninsula and Kodiak Island), southern Yukon, southwestern Mackenzie, northwestern Sas-katchewan, central Manitoba, northern Ontario, south-central Quebec, southern Labrador, and Newfoundland south (mostly in mountains) to southern California, central and south-eastern Arizona, and southern New Mexico, east of the Rockies to northwestern and north-central Nebraska, North Dakota, north-central and eastern Minnesota, northern Illinois, south-ern Michigan, southern Ontario, northern Ohio, in the Appalachians to eastern Tennessee and western North Carolina, and to southeastern Pennsylvania, north-central Maryland, Delaware, southern New Jersey, and southern New York (including Long Island); also on Guadalupe Island, off Baja California (at least formerly). Isolated cases of breeding have been reported from Kansas (Geary and Sedgwick counties), Oklahoma (Ponce City), Iowa (Des Moines), Missouri (Kansas City), and Indiana (Terre Haute).

Winters throughout most of the breeding range except at higher latitudes and elevations, and an irruptive migrant south in some years to northern Baja California, southern Arizona, southern New Mexico, southern Texas, the Gulf coast, and central Florida.

Casual north to western and central Alaska and northern Manitoba, and to Revillagigedo Islands (Socorro) and Bermuda; accidental in Iceland and the British Isles; sight reports for Sinaloa and Nuevo León.

Notes.—*Sitta canadensis* and the Asiatic *S. villosa* Verreaux, 1865 [Snowy-browed Nut-hatch], appear to constitute a superspecies (Mayr and Short 1970); possibly they are con-specific. The treatment by some authors (e.g., Mayr and Short 1970, Sibley and Monroe

1990) of *S. canadensis* and the Old World *S. whiteheadi* Sharpe, 1884 [Corsican Nuthatch], *S. ledanti* Vieilliard, 1976 [Kabylie Nuthatch], *S. kreuperi* Pelzeln, 1863 [Krueper's Nuthatch], and *S. yunnanensis* Ogilvie-Grant, 1900 [Yunnan Nuthatch], as closely related has been questioned because of differences in nesting behavior and their fragmented distribution (Voous 1977).

Sitta carolinensis Latham. White-breasted Nuthatch.

> *Sitta carolinensis* Latham, 1790, Index Ornithol. 1: 262. Based mainly on "Le Torchepot de la Caroline" Brisson, Ornithologie 3: 596. (in America, Jamaica; Europæa minor = South Carolina.)

Habitat.—Mature deciduous (especially oak) and mixed forest and woodland, riparian woodland, Ponderosa pine woodland, (locally) pinyon-juniper woodland (upper Subtropical and Temperate zones).

Distribution.—*Resident* from southwestern and eastern Washington, southern interior and northeastern British Columbia, central Alberta, central and eastern Montana, southern Saskatchewan (rarely), southern Manitoba, south-central Ontario, southern Quebec, New Brunswick, Prince Edward Island, and Nova Scotia south to southern Baja California (absent from most of central Baja California), southern Nevada, central and southeastern Arizona, in the highlands of Mexico to central Oaxaca (west of the Isthmus of Tehuantepec), Puebla, and central Veracruz, and to western and east-central Texas, northern Louisiana, central Mississippi, central and southeastern Alabama, and northern and central (at least formerly) Florida; absent in breeding season from most of the Great Plains from southern Alberta south through the western portions of the plains states to northern and west-central Texas. Some northern birds may migrate south.

Casual in southwestern and central British Columbia and on Vancouver Island, and in the Great Plains region, southern Texas, and southern Florida.

Notes.—Vocal, morphological, and ecological differences among Pacific coast, interior montane, and eastern populations merit further investigation with respect to species limits. A few authors regard *S. carolinensis* and the Old World *S. leucopsis* Gould, 1850 to be closely related, but see Mayr and Short (1970).

Sitta pygmaea Vigors. Pygmy Nuthatch.

> *Sitta pygmaea* Vigors, 1839, in Beechey, Zool. Voy. "Blossom," p. 25, pl. 4. (Monterey, [California.])

Habitat.—Yellow pine forest and woodland in interior, Monterey pine woodland on coast; less frequently bristlecone pine and pinyon-juniper.

Distribution.—*Resident* from southern interior British Columbia, northern Idaho, western Montana, central Wyoming, southwestern South Dakota, and northwestern Nebraska south to California (south in the coastal ranges locally to San Luis Obispo County and in interior ranges to the Laguna and New York mountains), northern Baja California (Sierra Juárez and Sierra San Pedro Mártir), southern Nevada, central and southeastern Arizona, in the mountains of Mexico to Michoacán, México, Morelos, Puebla, and west-central Veracruz, and to central New Mexico and extreme western Texas (Davis and Guadalupe mountains); also in southeastern Coahuila and southwestern Nuevo León.

Casual to southwestern British Columbia (including southern Vancouver Island), western Washington, central Montana, western North Dakota, western South Dakota, central Iowa, eastern Kansas, northern and northeastern Texas, and western Oklahoma.

Notes.—*Sitta pygmaea* and *S. pusilla* are closely related and constitute a superspecies (Sibley and Monroe 1990). Although Norris (1958) found numerous differences in the biology of the two taxa, including vocalizations, Phillips et al. (1964) and Mayr and Short (1970) considered them conspecific.

Sitta pusilla Latham. Brown-headed Nuthatch.

> *Sitta pusilla* Latham, 1790, Index Ornithol. 1: 263. Based largely on "Le petit Torchepot de la Caroline" Brisson, Ornithologie 3: 598. (in Carolina, Jamaica = South Carolina.)

Habitat.—Open pine forest and pine-oak woodland.

Distribution.—*Resident* from southeastern Oklahoma, central Arkansas, southern and eastern Tennessee, western North Carolina, south-central and eastern Virginia, southern Maryland, and southern Delaware south to the Houston area of Texas, the Gulf coast, and southern Florida; also in the northern Bahama Islands (Grand Bahama).

Casual or accidental north to Missouri (Ink, St. Louis), Wisconsin (Milwaukee), New York (Elmira), and New Jersey (Haddonfield).

Notes.—See comments under *S. pygmaea.*

Family **CERTHIIDAE**: Creepers

Notes.—See comments under Troglodytidae and Polioptilinae.

Subfamily CERTHIINAE: Northern Creepers

Genus *CERTHIA* Linnaeus

Certhia Linnaeus, 1758, Syst. Nat. (ed. 10) 1: 118. Type, by tautonymy, *Certhia familiaris* Linnaeus (*Certhia,* prebinomial specific name, in synonymy).

Certhia americana Bonaparte. Brown Creeper.

Certhia familiaris (not Linnaeus, 1758) Audubon, 1838, Birds Amer. (folio) 4: 419. (North America.)

Certhia Americana Bonaparte, 1838, Geogr. Comp. List, p. 11. New name for *Certhia familiaris* Audubon, preoccupied.

Habitat.—Mature coniferous and deciduous forest, the latter more frequently in northern or montane habitats, locally in lowland situations, and in Middle America primarily in montane pine or pine-oak association; in migration and winter more widespread, but almost always where tall trees are present (Subtropical and Temperate zones).

Distribution.—*Breeds* from south-central Alaska, north-central British Columbia (including the Queen Charlotte and Vancouver islands), central Alberta, central Saskatchewan, central Manitoba, northern Ontario (rarely to Sutton Lake), south-central Quebec (including Anticosti Island), and Newfoundland south to southern California (to mountains of San Diego County), southern Nevada, central and southeastern Arizona, in the mountains of Middle America through Mexico to north-central Nicaragua, to extreme western Texas (Guadalupe Mountains; summer report from Davis Mountains), west-central and southeastern Nebraska, southern Iowa, southeastern Missouri, southern Illinois, southern Michigan, southern Ontario, central Ohio, West Virginia, in the Appalachians to eastern Tennessee and western North Carolina, and to the lowlands of Virginia, Maryland, and Delaware. Recorded in summer (and possibly breeding) north to southern Yukon, northern Saskatchewan, and northern Manitoba, and south to north-central Tennessee, western Kentucky, and southwestern Indiana.

Winters from southern coastal Alaska and southern Canada south throughout the most of the United States to southern Texas, the Gulf coast, and northern Florida (casually farther south), and in the lowlands of the western United States and extreme northern Mexico (casually to central Sonora and central Tamaulipas). Populations on the Queen Charlotte Islands and in the mountains from southeastern Arizona and southwestern New Mexico south to Nicaragua are largely or entirely resident.

A sight report for Baja California.

Notes.—*Certhia americana* was formerly regarded as conspecific with the Eurasian *C. familiaris* Linnaeus, 1758 (Vaurie 1957a, Greenway *in* Paynter 1967); however, studies of vocalizations indicate that they should be treated as separate species and that *C. americana,* at least the western North American populations, may be more closely related to another Old World species, *C. brachydactyla* C. L. Brehm, 1820, than to *C. familiaris* (Thielcke 1962, Baptista and Johnson 1982).

Family **TROGLODYTIDAE**: Wrens

Notes.—See Sibley and Ahlquist (1990) and Sheldon and Gill (1996) for possible relationships of the Troglodytidae to the Certhiidae, Polioptilinae, and Sittidae.

Genus *DONACOBIUS* Swainson

Donacobius Swainson, 1832, Zool. Illus. (2)2: text to pl. 72. Type, by monotypy, *Donacobius vociferans* Swainson = *Turdus atricapilla* Linnaeus.

Notes.—Formerly placed in the Mimidae, but studies indicate that this genus is properly placed in the Troglodytidae (see Wetmore et al. 1984; see also Miller 1964), probably closest to *Campylorhynchus* (Kiltie and Fitzpatrick 1984).

Donacobius atricapillus (Linnaeus). Black-capped Donacobius.

Turdus atricapilla Linnaeus, 1766, Syst. Nat. (ed. 12) 1: 295. Based on "Le Merle á teste [= tête] noire du Cap de Bonne Espérance" Brisson, Ornithologie 6 (suppl.): 47, pl. 3, fig. 2. (ad Cap. b. spei, error = eastern Brazil.)

Habitat.—Freshwater Marshes (500–600 m; Tropical Zone).
Distribution.—*Resident* in eastern Panama (lower Río Tuira and around El Real, in eastern Darién) and northern Colombia (south to the Río Atrato and east to the Santa Marta lowlands), and in South America east of the Andes from southeastern Colombia, Venezuela, and the Guianas south to central Bolivia, Paraguay, northeastern Argentina, and south-central Brazil.
Notes.—Also known as Black-capped Mockingthrush.

Genus *CAMPYLORHYNCHUS* Spix

Campylorhynchus Spix, 1824, Avium Spec. Nov. Bras. 1: 77. Type, by subsequent designation (G. R. Gray, 1840), *C. variegatus* (Gm.) = *Opetiorhynchus turdinus* Wied.

Notes.—For an alternative arrangement, see the phylogeny of Selander (1964: 219).

Campylorhynchus albobrunneus (Lawrence). White-headed Wren.

Heleodytes albo-brunneus Lawrence, 1862, Ibis, p. 10. (line of the Panama Railroad, near the summit of the Atlantic slope, Isthmus of Panama = Canal Zone.)

Habitat.—Tropical Lowland Evergreen Forest Edge, Secondary Forest (0–1200 m; Tropical Zone).
Distribution.—*Resident* locally in Panama (west to western Colón in the Caribbean lowlands, and to the Canal area on the Pacific slope; one old record from "Veraguas") and western Colombia (west of the Andes).
Notes.—Also known as White-headed Cactus-Wren. *Campylorhynchus albobrunneus* is sometimes (e.g., Paynter *in* Mayr and Greenway 1960, Meyer de Schauensee 1966) considered conspecific with the South American *C. turdinus* (Wied, 1821), a species widely distributed east of the Andes, but relationships are evidently with *C. zonatus*; the basis for this conclusion is a highly variable, apparently intermediate population of *C. albobrunneus* in southwestern Colombia, which may represent hybridization with *C. zonatus* (Haffer 1967).

Campylorhynchus zonatus (Lesson). Band-backed Wren.

Picolaptes zonatus Lesson, 1832, Cent. Zool., p. 210, pl. 70. (la Californie, error = Orizaba, Veracruz.)

Habitat.—Pine-Oak Forest, Montane Evergreen Forest Edge, Tropical Lowland Evergreen Forest Edge, Arid Montane Scrub (0–3000 m; Tropical to Subtropical zones).
Distribution.—*Resident* from northern Veracruz, northern Puebla, northern and southeastern Oaxaca, Tabasco, Chiapas, and southern Campeche south along both slopes of Central America (mainly in highlands, absent from Pacific lowlands) to western Panama (east to

central Bocas del Toro and the Pacific slope of Veraguas); in northern Colombia; and in northwestern Ecuador.

Notes.—Also known as Banded Cactus-Wren and Band-backed Cactus-Wren. Selander (1964) considered *C. zonatus, C. megalopterus,* and two South American species, *C. nuchalis* Cabanis, 1847 [Stripe-backed Wren] and *C. fasciatus* (Swainson, 1837) [Fasciated Wren], to constitute a superspecies. Sibley and Monroe (1990), however, considered *C. zonatus, C. albobrunneus, C. nuchalis,* and *C. fasciatus* to constitute a superspecies, and pointed out that *C. zonatus* and *C. megalopterus* were sympatric. See comments under *C. albobrunneus.*

Campylorhynchus megalopterus Lafresnaye. Gray-barred Wren.

> *Campylorhynchus megalopterus* Lafresnaye, 1845, Rev. Zool. [Paris] 8: 339. (Mexique = Mexico.)

Habitat.—Pine Forest, Pine-Oak Forest (2000–3200 m; Temperate Zone).

Distribution.—*Resident* in the mountains of Mexico from southern Jalisco east through Michoacán, México, Morelos, and western Puebla to southwestern Veracruz, and thence southeast to Oaxaca (Mount Zempoaltepec).

Notes.—Also known as Gray Cactus-Wren. Selander (1964) suggested that the subspecies *C. m. nelsoni* might be a separate species. See comments under *C. zonatus.*

Campylorhynchus chiapensis Salvin and Godman. Giant Wren.

> *Campylorhynchus chiapensis* Salvin and Godman, 1891, Ibis, p. 609. (Tonala, State of Chiapas, Mexico.)

Habitat.—Tropical Lowland Evergreen Forest Edge, Second-growth Scrub, Secondary Forest (0–500 m; Tropical Zone).

Distribution.—*Resident* in the Pacific lowlands of Chiapas (Tonalá to Escuintla).

Notes.—Also known as Chiapas Wren and Chiapas Cactus-Wren. *Campylorhynchus chiapensis* and the South American *C. griseus* (Swainson, 1837) constitute a superspecies (Sibley and Monroe 1990); they have been frequently treated as conspecific (e.g., Paynter *in* Mayr and Greenway 1960).

Campylorhynchus rufinucha (Lesson). Rufous-naped Wren.

> *Picolaptes rufinucha* Lesson, 1838, Ann. Sci. Nat. (Zool.) (2) 9: 168. (Vera-Cruz, Mexico.)

Habitat.—Tropical Deciduous Forest, Gallery Forest, Secondary Forest, Arid Lowland Scrub (0–1500 m; Tropical Zone).

Distribution.—*Resident* [*humilis* group] in the Pacific lowlands of Mexico from Colima to extreme western Chiapas; [*rufinucha* group] in central Veracruz; and [*capistratus* group] from Chiapas south in the Pacific lowlands to northwestern Costa Rica (Guanacaste), and locally in interior valleys on the Gulf-Caribbean drainage in Guatemala (Motagua Valley) and Honduras (Sula Valley).

Notes.—Also known as Rufous-naped Cactus-Wren. Groups: *C. humilis* Sclater, 1856 [Sclater's Wren], *C. rufinucha* [Rufous-naped Wren], and *C. capistratus* (Lesson, 1842) [Rufous-backed Wren]; *humilis* and *capistratus* intergrade in the Tonalá region of Chiapas (Selander 1964, 1965).

Campylorhynchus gularis Sclater. Spotted Wren

> *Campylorhynchus gularis* Sclater, 1861, Proc. Zool. Soc. London (1860), p. 462. (in Mexico = Bolaños, Jalisco.)

Habitat.—Pine-Oak Forest, Tropical Deciduous Forest, Arid Montane Scrub (450–2500 m; upper Tropical and Subtropical zones).

Distribution.—*Resident* on the Pacific slope from southeastern Sonora and southwestern

Chihuahua south to Michoacán and southeastern México, and on the Gulf slope from southwestern Tamaulipas to central Hidalgo.

Notes.—Also known as Spotted Cactus-Wren. Hellmayr (1934), Griscom (1934), van Rossem (1934), and Blake (1953) considered *C. gularis* as conspecific with *C. jocosus,* but see van Rossem (1938) and Selander (1964).

Campylorhynchus jocosus Sclater. Boucard's Wren.

> *Campylorhynchus jocosus* Sclater, 1859, Proc. Zool. Soc. London, p. 371. (In statu Oaxaca reipubl. Mexicanae . . . at Oaxaca = Oaxaca City, Oaxaca; Binford, 1989, Ornithol. Monogr. 43, p. 342.)

Habitat.—Arid Montane Scrub, locally in Pine-Oak Forest (1000–2400 m; upper Tropical to Subtropical zones).

Distribution.—*Resident* in the highlands from Guerrero, southern Morelos, and southern Puebla south to central Oaxaca (west of the Isthmus of Tehuantepec).

Notes.—Also known as Boucard's Cactus-Wren. Mayr and Short (1970) and Sibley and Monroe (1990) followed Selander (1964) in considering *C. jocosus, C. yucatanicus,* and *C. brunneicapillus* to constitute a superspecies; *C. gularis* presumably should be included also (Phillips 1986).

Campylorhynchus yucatanicus (Hellmayr). Yucatan Wren.

> *Heleodytes brunneicapillus yucatanicus* Hellmayr, 1934, Field Mus. Nat. Hist. Publ. (Zool. Ser.) 13(7): 150. (Río Lagartos, Yucatán, Mexico.)

Habitat.—Arid Lowland Scrub, primarily with *Opuntia* (0–50 m; Tropical Zone).

Distribution.—*Resident* along the northern coast of the Yucatan Peninsula (Yucatán).

Notes.—Also known as Yucatan Cactus-Wren. *Campylorhynchus yucatanicus* and *C. brunneicapillus* have been treated as conspecific (Hellmayr 1934). See comments under *C. jocosus.*

Campylorhynchus brunneicapillus (Lafresnaye). Cactus Wren.

> *Picolaptes brunneicapillus* Lafresnaye, 1835, Mag. Zool. [Paris] 5(2): pl. 47. (Californie, error = coast region of southern Sonora.)

Habitat.—Arid Lowland Scrub, Arid Montane Scrub (0–2375 m; Tropical to Subtropical zones).

Distribution.—*Resident* from southern California (north to Ventura and Inyo counties), southern Nevada, extreme southwestern Utah, central Arizona, central New Mexico, and central and southern Texas south to southern Baja California, the Pacific lowlands to northwestern Sinaloa (including Isla Tiburón, off Sonora), in the Mexican highlands to northern Michoacán, northern México, and Hidalgo, and to southwestern, central and northeastern Tamaulipas.

Casual north to east-central California (Mono County).

Notes.—Also known as Northern Cactus-Wren. See comments under *C. jocosus* and *C. yucatanicus.*

Genus *SALPINCTES* Cabanis

> *Salpinctes* Cabanis, 1847, Arch. Naturgesch. 13: 323. Type, by subsequent designation (G. R. Gray, 1855), *Troglodytes obsoleta* Say.

Notes.—See comments under *Catherpes.*

Salpinctes obsoletus (Say). Rock Wren.

> *Troglodytes obsoleta* Say, 1823, in Long, Exped. Rocky Mount. 2: 4 (note). (Northern part of Douglas Co., Colorado, near junction of Plum Creek with South Platte River.)

Habitat.—Primarily in arid or semi-arid areas with exposed rocks, canyons, and cliffs, usually with some brushy vegetation, also locally around man-made concrete or stone structures and gravel pits (Subtropical and Temperate zones).

Distribution.—*Breeds* from southern British Columbia (including southern Vancouver Island), western Washington, southern Alberta, central Saskatchewan, northern Manitoba (once), western North Dakota, and western South Dakota south mostly east of the coast ranges in Oregon and northern California) to southern Baja California (including most coastal islands, Guadalupe Island, and, formerly, San Benedicto in the Revillagigedo Islands), in the highlands of Middle America to northwestern Costa Rica (restricted to Pacific slope volcanic peaks in El Salvador, Nicaragua, and northwestern Costa Rica); and east locally to western Nebraska, western Kansas, western Oklahoma, central and southern Texas, and southwestern Tamaulipas, also once in northern Manitoba (Churchill); possibly also Iowa, and one breeding attempt in northern Minnesota.

Winters from northern California, southern Nevada, central Utah, northern New Mexico, and north-central Texas south through the southern portions of the breeding range, wandering to lower elevations, casually wintering north to Oregon, Montana, and Wyoming.

Casual in summer north to northeastern British Columbia, northwestern Mackenzie, northern Alberta and northern Manitoba (Churchill), and in migration and winter west of the coast ranges (from southern British Columbia to northern California), and east to eastern Nebraska, eastern Kansas, central Oklahoma, and eastern Texas. Casual or accidental from Minnesota, western and southern Ontario, New York, Massachusetts, and Nova Scotia, south to Louisiana, Alabama, western Florida, and Virginia.

Genus *CATHERPES* Baird

Catherpes Baird, 1858, in Baird, Cassin and Lawrence, Rep. Explor. Surv. R. R. Pac. 9: xix, xxxvi, 354, 356. Type, by original designation, *Thryothorus mexicanus* Swainson.

Notes.—Sometimes merged with *Salpinctes* (Paynter *in* Mayr and Greenway 1960), but see Hardy and Delaney (1987). See comments under *Hylorchilus*.

Catherpes mexicanus (Swainson). Canyon Wren.

Thryothorus Mexicanus Swainson, 1829, Zool. Illus. (2)1(3): pl. 11 and text. (Real del Monte [Hidalgo], Mexico.)

Habitat.—Cliffs, steep-sided canyons, rocky outcrops and boulder piles, usually in arid regions (Tropical, Subtropical, and locally in Temperate zones).

Distribution.—*Resident* from eastern Washington, southern interior British Columbia, west-central Idaho, and Montana (except northeastern) south (mostly east of the Cascades and coast ranges in Oregon and California, but including coastal areas south of Santa Cruz County) to southern Baja California (including Ildefonso and Espíritu Santo islands, and Isla Tiburón off Sonora), southern Arizona, in the Mexican highlands to Oaxaca, central Chiapas, and western Veracruz; and east locally to southwestern South Dakota, western Oklahoma, and the Trans-Pecos and Edwards Plateau of Texas (to McLennan and Travis counties). Some dispersal in winter to lowlands.

Casual on Santa Cruz Island (off southern California), Los Coronados Islands (off northern Baja California), and northern Texas. Accidental in Nebraska and Kansas.

Genus *HYLORCHILUS* Nelson

Hylorchilus Nelson, 1897, Auk 14: 71. Type, by original designation, *Catherpes sumichrasti* Lawrence.

Notes.—Sometimes merged with *Catherpes,* the presumed sister genus to *Hylorchilus* (Hardy and Delaney 1987 and references therein); see Atkinson et al. (1993). See also comments under *Microcerculus.*

Hylorchilus sumichrasti (Lawrence). Sumichrast's Wren.

Catherpes sumichrasti Lawrence, 1871, Proc. Acad. Nat. Sci. Philadelphia 22: 233. (Mato Bejuco, Vera Cruz.)

Habitat.—Rocky, limestone outcroppings in Tropical Lowland Evergreen Forest (75–950 m; Tropical Zone).

Distribution.—*Resident* locally in the lowlands of west-central Veracruz (Motzorongo, Amatlán, Presidio) and extreme north-central Oaxaca (Temascal).

Notes.—When considered conspecific with *H. navai,* known as Slender-billed Wren. See notes under *H. navai.*

Hylorchilus navai Crossin and Ely. Nava's Wren.

Hylorchilus sumichrasti navai Crossin and Ely, 1973, Condor 75: 137. (26 km. N of Ocozocoautla (elevation 2500 ft.), state of Chiapas, Mexico.)

Habitat.—Limestone outcroppings in humid evergreen forest (75–800 m; Tropical Zone).

Distribution.—*Resident* in southeastern Veracruz (Uxpanapa) and western Chiapas (El Ocote region).

Notes.—Also known as Crossin's Wren. Formerly considered a subspecies of *H. sumichrasti* but considered a separate species on the basis of vocal and morphological differences (Atkinson et al. 1993).

Genus *THRYOTHORUS* Vieillot

Thriothorus [sic] Vieillot, 1816, Analyse, pp. 45, 70 (corrected to *Thryothorus*). Type, by monotypy, "Troglodyte des roseaux" Vieillot, Ois. Amér. Sept. = *Troglodytes arundinaceus* Vieillot = *Sylvia ludoviciana* Latham.

Thryothorus spadix (Bangs). Sooty-headed Wren.

Pheugopedius spadix Bangs, 1910, Proc. Biol. Soc. Wash. 23: 74. (Naranjito, Río Dagua, Valle, Colombia.)

Habitat.—Montane Evergreen Forest, Tropical Lowland Evergreen Forest (400–1800 m; upper Tropical and lower Subtropical zones).

Distribution.—*Resident* in extreme eastern Panama (eastern Darién) and western Colombia.

Notes.—*Thryothorus spadix* and *T. atrogularis* were formerly considered conspecific (e.g., Hellmayr 1934 and Paynter *in* Mayr and Greenway 1960), but see Wetmore et al. (1984); they constitute a superspecies (Sibley and Monroe 1990).

Thryothorus atrogularis Salvin. Black-throated Wren.

Thryothorus atrogularis Salvin, 1865, Proc. Zool. Soc. London (1864), p. 580. (Tucurrique, Costa Rica.)

Habitat.—Tropical Lowland Evergreen Forest Edge, Secondary Forest (0–1100 m; Tropical and lower Subtropical zones).

Distribution.—*Resident* on the Caribbean slope from central Nicaragua (north to Río Escondido) south through Costa Rica to extreme western Panama (western Bocas del Toro).

Notes.—See comments under *T. spadix.*

Thryothorus fasciatoventris Lafresnaye. Black-bellied Wren.

Thriothorus [sic] *fasciato-ventris* Lafresnaye, 1845, Rev. Zool. [Paris] 8: 337. ("Bogotá," Colombia.)

Habitat.—Tropical Lowland Evergreen Forest Edge, Secondary Forest, Second-growth Scrub (0–1000 m; Tropical Zone).

Distribution.—*Resident* on the Pacific slope from Costa Rica (northwest to the Gulf of Nicoya) to western Panama (Chiriquí, one old record from "Veragua"), and on both slopes from central Panama (Canal area) east to northern Colombia.

Thryothorus nigricapillus Sclater. Bay Wren.

Thryothorus nigricapillus Sclater, 1861, Proc. Zool. Soc. London (1860), p. 84. (Nanegal [alt. ca. 4,000 ft.], Pichincha, Ecuador.)

Habitat.—Tropical Lowland Evergreen Forest Edge, Second-growth Scrub, Secondary Forest (0–1400 m; Tropical and lower Subtropical zones).

Distribution.—*Resident* [*castaneus* group] on the Caribbean slope of eastern Nicaragua, Costa Rica, and Panama (including Isla Escudo de Veraguas, off Bocas del Toro), and on the Pacific slope of Panama from Veraguas east to central Darién; and [*nigricapillus* group] in extreme eastern Panama (eastern Darién), western Colombia, and western Ecuador.

Notes.—Groups: *T. castaneus* Lawrence, 1861 [Bay Wren], and *T. nigricapillus* [Black-capped Wren]. *Thryothorus nigricapillus* and *T. semibadius* constitute a superspecies (Sibley and Monroe 1990); some authors (e.g., Hellmayr 1934 and Paynter *in* Mayr and Greenway 1960) consider them conspecific, but see Slud (1964) and Wetmore et al. (1984).

Thryothorus semibadius Salvin. Riverside Wren.

Thryothorus semibadius Salvin, 1870, Proc. Zool. Soc. London, p. 181. (Bugaba, Chiriquí, Panama.)

Habitat.—Tropical Lowland Evergreen Forest Edge (0–1200 m; Tropical Zone).

Distribution.—*Resident* in the Pacific lowlands of southwestern Costa Rica (El General-Térraba region north to Rio Grande de Tarcoles) and extreme western Panama (western Chiriquí).

Notes.—Also known as Salvin's Wren. See comments under *T. nigricapillus.*

Thryothorus leucopogon (Salvadori and Festa). Stripe-throated Wren.

Thryophilus leucopogon Salvadori and Festa, 1899, Bull. Mus. Zool. Anat. Comp. Torino 14(357): 6. (Río Peripa, Pichincha, Ecuador.)

Habitat.—Tropical Lowland Evergreen Forest Edge (0–750 m; Tropical Zone).

Distribution.—*Resident* in eastern Panama (from western San Blas to eastern Darién), western Colombia, and northwestern Ecuador.

Notes.—*Thryothorus leucopogon* and *T. thoracicus* constitute a superspecies (Sibley and Monroe 1990). Hellmayr (1934) and Paynter *in* Mayr and Greenway (1960) considered them conspecific, but see Wetmore et al. (1984).

Thryothorus thoracicus Salvin. Stripe-breasted Wren.

Thryothorus thoracicus Salvin, 1865, Proc. Zool. Soc. London (1864), p. 580. (Tucurrique, Costa Rica.)

Habitat.—Tropical Lowland Evergreen Forest Edge, Secondary Forest (0–1000 m; Tropical and lower Subtropical zones).

Distribution.—*Resident* on the Caribbean slope of Nicaragua, Costa Rica (locally also on the Pacific slope of the Cordillera de Guanacaste), and western Panama (sight reports east to Coclé and the Canal area, also sight reports locally in the Pacific foothills of Veraguas).

Notes.—See comments under *T. leucopogon.*

Thryothorus rutilus Vieillot. Rufous-breasted Wren.

Thryothorus rutilus Vieillot, 1819, Nouv. Dict. Hist. Nat. (nouv. éd.) 34: 55. (l'Amérique septentrionale = Trinidad.)

Habitat.—Tropical Lowland Evergreen Forest Edge, Secondary Forest (0–1700 m; Tropical and lower Subtropical zones).

Distribution.—*Resident* on the Pacific slope of Costa Rica (west to the Gulf of Nicoya) and western Panama (east to eastern Panamá province, also on the Caribbean slope of eastern Colón and the Canal area); and in South America in northern and eastern Colombia, northern Venezuela, Tobago, and Trinidad.

Notes.—*Thryothorus rutilus* and *T. maculipectus,* along with the South American *T. sclateri,* Taczanowski, 1879 [Speckle-breasted Wren], were formerly (Hellmayr 1934) regarded as conspecific [Speckled Wren]; they constitute a superspecies (Sibley and Monroe 1990). Paynter (*in* Mayr and Greenway 1960) included *sclateri* conspecific with *T. rutilus,* but considered *T. maculipectus* to be a separate species, whereas Meyer de Schauensee (1966) considered *sclateri* conspecific with *T. maculipectus,* but considered *T. rutilus* to be a separate species. In the absence of a thorough analysis, we follow Wetmore et al. (1984) and Ridgely and Tudor (1989) in keeping all three as separate species.

Thryothorus maculipectus Lafresnaye. Spot-breasted Wren.

> *Thriothorus* [sic] *maculipectus* Lafresnaye, 1845, Rev. Zool. [Paris] 8: 338. (Mexique = Veracruz.)

Habitat.—Tropical Lowland Evergreen Forest Edge, Secondary Forest, Tropical Deciduous Forest (0–1300 m; Tropical Zone).

Distribution.—*Resident* from eastern Nuevo León, southeastern San Luis Potosí, and central Tamaulipas south in the Gulf-Caribbean lowlands of Middle America (including the Yucatan Peninsula and Isla Cancun) to northeastern Costa Rica, and on the Pacific slope in southeastern Oaxaca, Chiapas, Guatemala, and El Salvador.

Notes.—See, comments under *T. rutilus* and *T. felix.*

Thryothorus rufalbus Lafresnaye. Rufous-and-white Wren.

> *Thryothorus rufalbus* Lafresnaye, 1845, Rev. Zool. [Paris] 8: 337. (Mexique, error = Guatemala.)

Habitat.—Tropical Lowland Evergreen Forest Edge, Montane Evergreen Forest Edge, Tropical Deciduous Forest, Gallery Forest, Secondary Forest (0–1800 m; Tropical and lower Subtropical zones).

Distribution.—*Resident* on the Pacific slope of Middle America from southwestern Chiapas south to western Panama (east to eastern Panamá province), locally also on the Caribbean slope in Guatemala, Honduras, Costa Rica, and central Panama (Canal area); and in northern and eastern Colombia, and western and northern Venezuela.

Notes.—The Colombian *T. nicefori* Meyer de Schauensee, 1946 [Niceforo's Wren], and *T. rufalbus* constitute a superspecies (Sibley and Monroe 1990); they might be conspecific (Paynter *in* Mayr and Greenway 1960).

Thryothorus sinaloa (Baird). Sinaloa Wren.

> *Thryophilus sinaloa* Baird, 1864, Rev. Amer. Birds 1: 122, 130. (Mazatlán, Sinaloa, Mexico.)

Habitat.—Tropical Deciduous Forest, Gallery Forest, Mangrove Forest (0–2100 m; Tropical and Subtropical zones).

Distribution.—*Resident* on the Pacific slope from southeastern Sonora and southwestern Chihuahua south through western Durango and coastal states to extreme western Oaxaca (Putla de Guerrero region).

Notes.—Also known as Bar-vented Wren. This species and *T. rufalbus* may be each other's closest relatives (Paynter *in* Mayr and Greenway 1960)

Thryothorus pleurostictus Sclater. Banded Wren.

> *Thryothorus pleurostictus* Sclater, 1860, Ibis, p. 30. (in prov. Verae Pacis, Guatemala = Gualán, Zacapa, Guatemala.)

Habitat.—Tropical Deciduous Forest, Arid Lowland Scrub (0–1750 m; Tropical and Subtropical zones).

Distribution.—*Resident* on the Pacific slope of Middle America from Michoacán, the southwestern portion of México, Morelos, and western Puebla south to northwestern Costa Rica (Guanacaste region, locally also on the Pacific slope of the central plateau).

Thryothorus ludovicianus (Latham). Carolina Wren.

> *Sylvia ludoviciana* Latham, 1790, Index Ornithol. 2: 548. Based on "Roitelet de la Louisiane" Daubenton, Planches Enlum., pl. 730, fig. 1. (in Louisiana = along the Mississippi River at New Orleans.)

Habitat.—[*ludovicianus* group] Deciduous woodland, mostly in undergrowth and thickets, and in wooded parks and residential areas with undergrowth; [*albinucha* group] Tropical Deciduous Forest, Gallery Forest, Secondary Forest (0–2200 m; Tropical and Subtropical zones, and, north of Mexico, Temperate Zone).

Distribution.—*Resident* [*ludovicianus* group] from eastern Nebraska, northern Iowa, southern Wisconsin, southern Michigan, southern Ontario, extreme southwestern Quebec, northern New York, southern Vermont, southern New Hampshire, and southern Maine south to eastern Mexico (eastern Coahuila, Nuevo León, eastern San Luis Potosí and Tamaulipas), the Gulf coast (including islands off the coast of Mississippi and northwestern Florida), and southern Florida (to Key Largo), and west to northeastern Colorado, central Kansas, west-central and southwestern Oklahoma, and central Texas; and [*albinucha* group] in southeastern Mexico (Tabasco and the Yucatan Peninsula), northern Guatemala (Petén), and Belize, and locally in the interior of Guatemala (Sacapulas) and northwestern Nicaragua. Disappears [*ludovicianus* group] from northern portions of the breeding range following severe winters.

Wanders casually [*ludovicianus* group] west and north to central New Mexico, eastern Colorado, eastern Wyoming, North Dakota, South Dakota, southern Alberta, southern Manitoba, Minnesota, northern Michigan, New Brunswick, southeastern Quebec (Magdalen Islands), and Nova Scotia (sight reports), and south to Key West, Florida.

Notes.—Groups: *T. ludovicianus* [Carolina Wren] and *T. albinucha* (Cabot, 1847) [Cabot's Wren]. Phillips (1986) not only treated *albinucha* as a species but also questioned whether *albinucha* belonged in the genus *Thryothorus*; however, see Griscom (1932), Lowery and Berrett (1963), and Cardiff and Remsen (1994).

Thryothorus felix Sclater. Happy Wren.

> *Thryothorus felix* Sclater, 1859, Proc. Zool. Soc. London, p. 371. (In statu Oaxaca, reipubl. Mexicanae . . . Juquila = Santa Catarina Juquila, Oaxaca; Binford, 1989, Ornithol. Monogr. 43, p. 342–343.)

Habitat.—Tropical Deciduous Forest, Gallery Forest, Secondary Forest, Arid Lowland Scrub (0–2000 m; Tropical and lower Subtropical zones).

Distribution.—*Resident* on the Pacific slope from southern Sonora, Sinaloa, and western Durango south to México, Morelos, western Puebla, and central Oaxaca (east to the Puerto Angel region); also in the Tres Marias Islands (María Madre and María Magdalena).

Notes.—Phillips (1986) considered *T. felix* possibly conspecific with *T. maculipectus.*

Thryothorus leucotis Lafresnaye. Buff-breasted Wren.

> *Thryothorus leucotis* Lafresnaye, 1845, Rev. Zool. [Paris] 8: 338. (in Colombia aut Mexico = Honda, Río Magdalena, Tolima, Colombia.)

Habitat.—Second-growth Scrub, River-Edge Forest, Mangrove Forest (0–300 m; Tropical Zone).

Distribution.—*Resident* in eastern Panama (west to the Canal area, and including the Pearl Islands), and in South America from northern Colombia, Venezuela, and the Guianas south, east of the Andes, to central Peru and Amazonian and central Brazil.

Notes.—*Thryothorus leucotis, T. modestus,* and the South American *T. superciliaris* (Lawrence, 1869) [Superciliated Wren], *T. guarayanus* (Lafresnaye and d'Orbigny, 1837) [Fawn-breasted Wren], and *T. longirostris* Vieillot, 1818 [Gray Wren], constitute a superspecies (Sibley and Monroe 1990). Species limits in this complex are uncertain (see Ridgely and Tudor 1989).

Thryothorus modestus Cabanis. Plain Wren.

Thryothorus modestus Cabanis, 1861, J. Ornithol. 8 (1860): 409. (San Jose, Costa Rica.)

Habitat.—Tropical Deciduous Forest, Tropical Lowland Evergreen Forest Edge, Second-growth Scrub (0–2000 m; Tropical and Subtropical zones).

Distribution.—*Resident* [*modestus* group] on the Pacific slope of Middle America from extreme southeastern Oaxaca (Sierra Madre de Chiapas) south to Costa Rica (locally also on the Caribbean slope in Chiapas, Guatemala, southern Belize, and Honduras, and in the Mosquitia of northeastern Honduras) and Panama, where occurring on both slopes (except the extreme northwestern portion) east to eastern Colón and eastern Panamá province; and [*zeledoni* group] on the Caribbean slope from southeastern Nicaragua south to extreme northwestern Panama (western Bocas del Toro).

Notes.—Groups: *T. modestus* [Plain Wren] and *T. zeledoni* (Ridgway, 1878) [Canebrake Wren]. See comments under *T. leucotis*.

Genus *THRYOMANES* Sclater

Thryomanes Sclater, 1862, Cat. Collect. Amer. Birds, p. 22. Type, by monotypy, *Troglodytes bewickii* Audubon.

Thryomanes bewickii (Audubon). Bewick's Wren.

Troglodytes Bewickii Audubon, 1827, Birds Amer. (folio) 1: pl. 18 (1831, Ornithol. Biogr. 1: 96). (Five miles from St. Francisville, Louisiana.)

Habitat.—Brushy areas, thickets, and scrub in open country, riparian woodland, and chaparral; in eastern portion of range, primarily in brushy edges of woodland (Subtropical and Temperate zones).

Distribution.—*Breeds* from southwestern British Columbia (including southeastern Vancouver Island), southeastern Washington, west-central and southern Nevada, northern Utah, southern Wyoming, extreme western and southern Colorado, Kansas, southeastern Nebraska (formerly), southeastern Iowa, southern Wisconsin, southern Michigan, southern Ontario (formerly), northern Ohio, central Pennsylvania, and southeastern New York (once) south to southern Baja California (including some islands off the coast of southern California south, formerly, to Guadalupe Island, where extirpated between 1892 and 1906), northern Sonora, in the Mexican highlands to central Oaxaca, western Puebla, and west-central Veracruz, and to southern Tamaulipas, central Texas, northern Arkansas, the northern portions of the Gulf states, central Georgia, and central South Carolina; in recent years scarce in or extirpated from much of the eastern portion of its breeding range.

Winters from the northern limits of the breeding range (west of the Rockies), southeastern Colorado, southern Kansas, southern Missouri, the lower Ohio Valley, Tennessee, and North Carolina south to the limits of the breeding range in Mexico, the Gulf coast, and northern Florida.

Casual north to Idaho (one nesting record), Montana, South Dakota, southern Minnesota, central New York, and northern New England; a sight report for North Dakota.

Notes.—See comments under *T. sissonii*.

Thryomanes sissonii (Grayson). Socorro Wren.

Thryothorus sissonii Grayson, 1868, Calif. Farmer J. Useful Sci. 29: 7. (Isla Socorro, Islas de Revillagigedo, Colima, Mexico.)
Troglodytes insularis Lawrence, 1871, Ann. Lyc. Nat. Hist. New York 10: 3. (Socorro Island, Mexico.)

Habitat.—Tropical Deciduous Forest, Arid Lowland Scrub (0–1050 m).

Distribution.—*Resident* on Socorro Island, in the Revillagigedo Islands, off western Mexico.

Notes.— Mayr and Short (1970) considered *Thryomanes sissonii* and *T. bewickii* to constitute a superspecies and suggested that they might be conspecific. This species may be better placed in *Troglodytes,* based on voice, behavior, and plumage (Howell and Webb

1995), but no analysis has been published. Phillips (1986) used the specific name *insularis* Lawrence and placed the species in *Troglodytes*; see Banks and Browning (1995) for comments on nomenclature.

Genus *FERMINIA* Barbour

Ferminia Barbour, 1926, Proc. N. Engl. Zool. Club 9: 74. Type, by original designation, *Ferminia cerverai* Barbour.

Ferminia cerverai Barbour. Zapata Wren.

Ferminia cerverai Barbour, 1926, Proc. New Engl. Zool. Club 9: 74. (Santo Tomás, Ciénaga de Zapata, Las Villas, Cuba.)

Habitat.—Freshwater Marshes.
Distribution.—*Resident* in the Ciénaga de Zapata in the vicinity of Santo Tomás, western Cuba.

Genus *TROGLODYTES* Vieillot

Troglodytes Vieillot, 1809, Hist. Nat. Ois. Amer. Sept. 2 (1808, livr. 18): 52. Type, by subsequent designation (Baird, 1858), *Troglodytes aedon* Vieillot.
Nannus Billberg, 1828, Synop. Faunae Scand. (ed. 2) 1(2): 57, tab. A. Type, by monotypy, *Motacilla troglodytes* Linnaeus.

Troglodytes aedon Vieillot. House Wren.

Troglodytes aëdon Vieillot, 1809, Hist. Nat. Ois. Amer. Sept. 2 (1808, livr. 18): 52, pl. 107. (No locality given = New York City.)

Habitat.—[*aedon* group] Thickets and scrub in partly open situations, open woodland (especially aspen), farmlands, chaparral, riparian woodland, and around human habitations; in winter, primarily scrub, weedy and brushy fields; [*brunneicollis* and *musculus* group] Second-growth Scrub, Arid Lowland Scrub, Arid Montane Scrub, Semihumid/Humid Montane Scrub; [*martinicensis* group] Tropical Lowland Evergreen Forest, Tropical Deciduous Forest, Secondary Forest, Second-growth Scrub; [*beani* group] Tropical Deciduous Forest, Second-growth Scrub, Secondary Forest (0–4600 m; Tropical to Temperate zones).

Distribution.—*Breeds* [*aedon* group] from southern and northeastern British Columbia (including Vancouver Island), northern Alberta, central Saskatchewan, southern Manitoba, central Ontario, southern Quebec, Maine, and western New Brunswick (formerly) south to northern Baja California, southern California, southern Nevada, central and southeastern Arizona, southern New Mexico, western and northern Texas, northwestern Arkansas, southern Tennessee, northern Alabama, northeastern Georgia, western South Carolina, and eastern North Carolina; and [*brunneicollis* group] from northern Sonora, southeastern Arizona (Huachuca and Santa Rita mountains), central Chihuahua, northern Coahuila, central Nuevo León and southwestern Tamaulipas south in the mountains of Mexico to central Oaxaca (west of the Isthmus of Tehuantepec) and west-central Veracruz.

Winters [*aedon* group] from central California, southern Nevada, northern Arizona, southern New Mexico, southern Oklahoma, northern Arkansas, the northern portions of the Gulf states, and coastal Maryland (casually farther north) south to southern Baja California, throughout Mexico to Oaxaca and Veracruz, and to the Gulf coast and southern Florida (including the Florida Keys); casually in early winter farther north to southern British Columbia, Kansas, Ohio, southern Ontario, and New York; and [*brunneicollis* group] from northern Mexico south throughout the remainder of the breeding range.

Resident [*musculus* group] from north-central Oaxaca, southern Veracruz (Sierra de Los Tuxtlas), Tabasco, Chiapas, and the Yucatan Peninsula (including Isla Cancun) south through Middle America (scarce or absent from arid Pacific lowlands, but present on Coiba and the Pearl islands off Panama), and in virtually all of South America from Colombia, Venezuela, Tobago, Trinidad, and the Guianas south to Tierra del Fuego (also the Falkland Islands); [*martinicensis* group] in the Lesser Antilles on Guadeloupe (no recent records, possibly extirpated), Dominica, St. Lucia (surviving in small numbers in the northeastern coastal lowlands), St. Vincent, and Grenada (vocalizations suggest Grenada birds may be part of *musculus* group), formerly also on Martinique; and [*beani* group] on Cozumel Island, off Quintana Roo.

Casual or accidental [*aedon* group] north to northern British Columbia, northern Manitoba, Prince Edward Island, Nova Scotia, and Newfoundland, and to western Cuba (near Havana) and the Bahama Islands (South Bimini, New Providence, Exuma).

Notes.—The International Commission for Zoological Nomenclature has been asked (Bull. Zool. Nomenclature 53: 187–190, 1996) to conserve the widely used specific name *aedon* despite the fact that *T. domesticus* (Wilson, 1808) has priority; see Banks and Browning (1995). Species limits within this complex are not well understood. Groups: *T. aedon* [Northern House-Wren], *T. brunneicollis* Sclater, 1858 [Brown-throated Wren], *T. musculus* Naumann, 1823 [Southern House-Wren], *T. martinicensis* (Sclater, 1866) [Antillean House-Wren], and *T. beani* Ridgway, 1885 [Cozumel Wren]. *Troglodytes aedon* and *T. brunneicollis* intergrade through intermediate breeding populations in southern Arizona (Marshall 1956, Phillips et al. 1964, Lanyon 1960), but intergradation between *brunneicollis* and *musculus* in an area of close approach in north-central Oaxaca has not been definitely established (Monroe 1968, Binford 1989). *Troglodytes beani* appears to be part of the Antillean *T. martinicensis* complex. Many or all of the distinctive Caribbean subspecies included within the *martinicensis* group may each warrant species status. Brumfield and Capparella (1996) suggested that the *musculus* group and probably the *brunneicollis* group are specifically distinct from *aedon,* but study of parapatric populations is needed to resolve species limits in this complex. See comments under *T. ochraceus.*

Troglodytes tanneri Townsend. Clarion Wren.

Troglodytes tanneri C. H. Townsend, 1890, Proc. U. S. Natl. Mus. 13: 133. (Isla Clarión, Islas de Revillagigedo, Colima, Mexico.)

Habitat.—Arid Lowland Scrub.

Distribution.—*Resident* on Isla Clarión, in the Revillagigedo Islands, off western Mexico.

Notes.—Paynter *in* Mayr and Greenway (1960) treated this species as a subspecies of *T. aedon.* See Howell and Webb (1995) for maintaining this taxon as a distinct species.

Troglodytes rufociliatus Sharpe. Rufous-browed Wren.

Troglodytes brunneicollis Subsp. α. *Troglodytes rufociliatus* Sharpe, 1882, Cat. Birds Br. Mus. 6 (1881): xii, 262. (Upper Chirostemon Forest, alt. 10,000 ft., Volcan de Fuego, [Sacatepéquez,] Guatemala.)

Habitat.—Montane Evergreen Forest, Pine-Oak Forest (1700–3500 m; Subtropical and Temperate zones).

Distribution.—*Resident* in the mountains of Chiapas, Guatemala, El Salvador, Honduras, and north-central Nicaragua.

Notes.—See comments under *T. ochraceus.*

Troglodytes ochraceus Ridgway. Ochraceous Wren.

Troglodytes (?) *ochraceus* Ridgway, 1882, Proc. U. S. Natl. Mus. 4 (1881): 334. (Volcán Irazú, Cartago, Costa Rica.)

Habitat.—Montane Evergreen Forest (750–2500 m, rarely to 3000 m; Subtropical to Temperate zones).

Distribution.—*Resident* in the mountains of Costa Rica (north to Cordillera de Tilarán) and Panama (Chiriquí, Veraguas, and eastern Darién; sight reports from Cerro Campana in western Panamá province).

Notes.—*Troglodytes ochraceus, T. rufociliatus,* the Colombian *T. monticola* Bangs, 1899 [Santa Marta Wren], the Andean *T. solstitialis* Sclater, 1859 [Mountain Wren], and *T. rufulus,* Cabanis, 1849 [Tepui Wren] of the tepui region of northern South America are closely related and constitute a superspecies (Sibley and Monroe 1990). Paynter *in* Mayr and Greenway

(1960) treated the first four as conspecific and as forming a superspecies with *T. rufulus.* See Stiles and Skutch (1989) for reasons for treating *T. ochraceus* and *T. solstitialis* as separate species. Phillips (1986) considered, probably correctly, that the form in eastern Darién *(festinus)* is a subspecies of *T. solstitialis,* which he merged with *ochraceus.*

Troglodytes troglodytes (Linnaeus). Winter Wren.

> *Motacilla Troglodytes* Linnaeus, 1758, Syst. Nat. (ed. 10) 1: 188. (in Europa = Sweden.)

Habitat.—Coniferous forest (especially spruce and fir) and mixed forests, primarily with dense understory and near water, and in open areas with low cover along rocky coasts, cliffs, islands or high mountain regions, including moors and steppes; in migration and winter also in deciduous forest and woodland with dense undergrowth and tree-falls, dense hedgerows, and brushy fields.

Distribution.—*Breeds* [*hiemalis* group] in North America from coastal southern and southeastern Alaska (including the Pribilof Islands, and throughout most of the Aleutians), coastal and central British Columbia (including Queen Charlotte and Vancouver islands), northern Alberta, central Saskatchewan, central Manitoba, northern Ontario, central Quebec, extreme southern Labrador, and Newfoundland south to central California (San Luis Obispo County, and the western slope of the central Sierra Nevada), northeastern Oregon, central Idaho, northern Utah, western Montana, southwestern Alberta, southeastern Manitoba, north-central and northeastern Minnesota, southern Wisconsin, central Michigan, southern Ontario, northeastern Ohio, in the Appalachians through eastern West Virginia, western Maryland, western Virginia, eastern Tennessee, and western North Carolina to northeastern Georgia, and to northern Pennsylvania, northern New Jersey, and southeastern New York; and [*troglodytes* group] in the Palearctic from Iceland, the Faeroe Islands, Shetlands, British Isles, northern Scandinavia, northern Russia, and central Siberia south to northwestern Africa, the Mediterranean region, Near East, Iran, northern India, central China, and Japan. Recorded [*hiemalis* group] in summer (and probably breeding) in southern Yukon, south-central Mackenzie, and northern Indiana.

Winters [*hiemalis* group] in North America from southern Alaska (including the Pribilof and Aleutian islands), coastal and central British Columbia, southwestern Alberta, western Montana, eastern Colorado, southern Nebraska, southern Minnesota, eastern Iowa, southern Michigan, southern Ontario, central New York, and Massachusetts (casually farther north to southern Quebec and Newfoundland) south to southern California, central and southeastern Arizona, southern New Mexico, Nuevo Leon (casual in Coahuila), southern Texas, the Gulf coast, and central (perhaps casually southern) Florida; and [*troglodytes* group] in the Old World generally throughout the breeding range, although the extreme northern populations usually migrate southward.

Accidental [*hiemalis* group] in northern Alaska (Point Barrow).

Notes.—Known in Old World literature as the Wren. Groups: *T. hiemalis* Vieillot, 1819 [Winter Wren] and *T. troglodytes* [Northern Wren].

Genus *CISTOTHORUS* Cabanis

> *Cistothorus* Cabanis, 1850, Mus. Heineanum 1: 77. Type, by subsequent designation (G. R. Gray, 1855), *Troglodytes stellaris* Naumann = *Sylvia platensis* Latham.
>
> *Telmatodytes* Cabanis, 1850, Mus. Heineanum 1: 78. Type, by subsequent designation (Baird, 1858), *Certhia palustris* Wilson.

Cistothorus platensis (Latham). Sedge Wren.

> *Sylvia platensis* Latham, 1790, Index Ornithol. 2: 548. Based on "Le Roitelet de Buenos-Ayres" Daubenton, Planches Enlum., pl. 730, fig. 2. (in Bonaria = Buenos Aires, Argentina.)

Habitat.—Grassy marshes, sedge meadows, wet fields with tall grass and some bushes, locally in North America in dry, cultivated grain fields; in winter and migration, also in rice fields; in South America in dry grasslands (Tropical to Alpine zones).

Distribution.—*Breeds* [*stellaris* group] in North America from east-central Alberta, central Saskatchewan, southern Manitoba, western and southern Ontario, extreme southwestern Quebec, central Maine, and southeastern New Brunswick (probably) south to northwestern and east-central Arkansas, southern Illinois, central Kentucky, west-central West Virginia, and southeastern Virginia, and west to northeastern Montana, eastern South Dakota, eastern Nebraska, eastern Kansas, and northeastern Oklahoma.

Winters [*stellaris* group] in North America from western Tennessee and Maryland (casually farther north) south to southern New Mexico, western and southern Texas, San Luis Potosí, Tamaulipas, the Gulf coast region, and southern Florida.

Resident [*stellaris* group] locally in Middle America in Durango, San Luis Potosí, Michoacán (Lake Pátzcuaro region), southern Veracruz, Distrito Federal, Chiapas, Guatemala (central highlands), northern El Salvador, Honduras (Siguatepeque, and the Mosquitia pine savanna), north-central and northeastern Nicaragua, Costa Rica (vicinity of Cartago), and western Panama (western Chiriquí); [*platensis* group] in South America locally in the Andes from northern Colombia south to Argentina and Chile, and in lowlands of southern South America in Argentina, Chile, Tierra del Fuego, and the Falkland Islands; and [*polyglottus* group] in the Santa Marta Mountains, Perijá Mountains, and the Coastal Range and eastern tepui region of Venezuela and Guyana, and in the eastern lowlands locally in northeastern Colombia, southeastern Peru, northern Bolivia, and southeastern Brazil, and locally in Andes in depto. Puno, Peru. The *platensis* and *polyglottus* groups intergrade in southeastern Brazil and Paraguay (Traylor 1988).

Casual [*stellaris* group] in California, Montana, southeastern Wyoming, and Colorado.

Notes.—Also known as Short-billed Marsh-Wren. Groups: *C. stellaris* (J. F. Naumann, 1823) [Sedge Wren], *C. platensis* [Western Grass-Wren], and *C. polyglottus* [Eastern Grass-Wren]; see Traylor (1988). *Cistothorus platensis* and two species with restricted ranges in the high Andes of Venezuela and Colombia, *C. meridae* Hellmayr, 1907 [Paramo Wren or Merida Wren], and *C. apolinari* Chapman, 1914 [Apolinar's Wren], respectively, constitute a superspecies (Mayr and Short 1970).

Cistothorus palustris (Wilson). Marsh Wren.

Certhia palustris Wilson, 1810, Amer. Ornithol. 2: 58, pl. 12, fig. 4. (Borders of the Schuylkill or Delaware [rivers, Philadelphia, Pennsylvania].)

Habitat.—Fresh-water and brackish marshes in cattails, tule, bulrush, and reeds; in winter and migration, also in rice fields, low dense growth bordering wetlands, and salt marsh.

Distribution.—*Breeds* [*paludicola* group] from southwestern and eastern British Columbia, northern Alberta, central Saskatchewan, and north-central Manitoba south to southern California, northeastern Baja California, northwestern Sonora, southwestern Arizona, southern Nevada, southern Utah, northwestern and north-central New Mexico, and extreme western Texas; and [*palustris* group] from southeastern Saskatchewan, southern Manitoba, western and southern Ontario, southwestern Quebec, southern Maine southeastern New Brunswick, and Nova Scotia south to extreme western and southern Texas, the Gulf coast (east to the Tampa Bay region, formerly farther south along the Gulf coast of peninsular Florida), and east-central Florida (St. John's River, formerly to New Smyrna Beach), generally very local in distribution in the interior of North America; also locally in México (Río Toluca).

Winters [*paludicola* group] from the breeding range south to southern Baja California, southwestern Oaxaca, Veracruz, and southern Texas; and [*palustris* group] from southern New England and the southeastern United States (mostly in coastal areas, casually north to South Dakota, central Illinois, and the Great Lakes region) south to southeastern Texas, the Gulf coast, and southern Florida.

Accidental [*palustris* group] in Greenland.

Notes.—Also known as Long-billed Marsh-Wren. The two groups are distinct vocally and morphologically, and they may constitute separate species, *C. paludicola* (Baird, 1864) [Western Marsh-Wren] and *C. palustris* [Eastern Marsh-Wren] (D. E. Kroodsma and Canady 1985, D. E. Kroodsma 1988, 1989).

Genus *UROPSILA* Sclater and Salvin

Uropsila Sclater and Salvin, 1873, Nomencl. Avium Neotrop., pp. 7, 155. Type, by original designation, *Troglodytes leucogastra* Gould.

Uropsila leucogastra (Gould). White-bellied Wren.

Troglodytes leucogastra Gould, 1837, Proc. Zool. Soc. London (1836), p. 89. (Tamaulipas, Mexico.)

Habitat.—Tropical Lowland Evergreen Forest, Secondary Forest, Secondary Forest (0–500 m; Tropical Zone).

Distribution.—*Resident* in the Pacific lowlands from southwestern Jalisco to central Guerrero (Acapulco); on the Gulf-Caribbean slope from southeastern San Luis Potosí and southern Tamaulipas south through Veracruz, northeastern Puebla, northern Oaxaca, Tabasco, northern Chiapas, and the Yucatan Peninsula to northern Guatemala (Petén) and Belize; and locally in north-central Honduras (Coyoles).

Genus *THRYORCHILUS* Oberholser

Thryorchilus Oberholser, 1904, Proc. U. S. Natl. Mus. 27: 198. Type, by original designation, *Troglodytes browni* Bangs.

Thryorchilus browni (Bangs). Timberline Wren.

Troglodytes browni Bangs, 1902, Proc. N. Engl. Zool. Club 3: 53. (Volcán de Chiriquí, alt. 10,000 ft., Chiriquí, Panama.)

Habitat.—Elfin Forest, Montane Evergreen Forest Edge (2700–3600 m, locally at 2200 m; Temperate Zone).

Distribution.—*Resident* in the high mountains of Costa Rica (Cordillera de Talamanca, and on the Irazú-Turrialba massif in the Cordillera Central) and western Panama (Volcán Barú in western Chiriquí).

Notes.—The relationships of this species remain uncertain; it may best be included in the genus *Troglodytes* (e.g., Paynter *in* Mayr and Greenway [1960], Wetmore et al. [1984], Phillips [1986]) or have affinities with *Henicorhina* (Sibley and Monroe 1990). Stiles and Skutch (1989) favored the latter because of similarities in song, behavior, and voice. Also known as Irazú Wren.

Genus *HENICORHINA* Sclater and Salvin

Heterorhina (not Westwood, 1845) Baird, 1864, Rev. Amer. Birds 1: 115. Type, by original designation, *Scytalopus prostheleucus* Sclater = *Cyphorhinus leucosticta* Cabanis.

Henicorhina Sclater and Salvin, 1868, Proc. Zool. Soc. London, p. 170. New name for *Heterorhina* Baird, preoccupied.

Henicorhina leucosticta (Cabanis). White-breasted Wood-Wren.

Cyphorhinus leucosticta Cabanis, 1847, Arch. Naturgesch. 13: 206. (Guiana and Mexico = Guiana.)

Habitat.—Tropical Lowland Evergreen Forest, Montane Evergreen Forest (0–1850 m; Tropical and lower Subtropical zones).

Distribution.—*Resident* [*prostheleuca* group] from southeastern San Luis Potosí, Hidalgo, and northern Veracruz south on the Gulf-Caribbean slope of Middle America (including the Yucatan Peninsula, and locally also on the Pacific slope in southeastern Oaxaca, southern Chiapas, and southern Guatemala) to Nicaragua, the Caribbean slope of Costa Rica, and northeastern Panama; [*pittieri* group] southwestern Costa Rica and Panama (except northeast), to northwestern Colombia, including Cauca Valley, south along Pacific coast to northwestern Ecuador; and [*leucosticta* group] in South America from eastern Colombia, southern Venezuela, and the Guianas south to northeastern Peru and northern Brazil.

Notes.—Groups: *H. prostheleuca* (Sclater, 1857] [Sclater's Wood-Wren], *H. pittieri* Cherrie, 1893 [Cherrie's Wood-Wren], and *H. leucosticta* (Cabanis, 1847) [Black-capped Wood-Wren]. The Middle American groups may deserve recognition as species separate from South America *leucosticta* (Winker et al. 1996). Although Hellmayr (1934) provided no rationale for combining the groups into a single species, Sibley and Monroe (1990) did not distinguish the former species as groups. *Henicorhina leucosticta* and *H. leucophrys* are elevational representatives of one another and may constitute a superspecies despite local sympatry (but see Sibley and Monroe 1990).

Henicorhina leucophrys (Tschudi). Gray-breasted Wood-Wren.

> *Troglodytes leucophrys* Tschudi, 1844, Arch. Naturgesch. 10: 282. (Republica Peruana = Peru.)

Habitat.—Montane Evergreen Forest (600–3000 m; Subtropical and Temperate zones).
Distribution.—*Resident* in the highlands from southwestern Jalisco, western Michoacán, Guerrero, southeastern San Luis Potosí, northeastern Hidalgo, and Puebla south through Oaxaca, Chiapas, and Guatemala to El Salvador and Honduras; in Costa Rica and Panama (recorded Chiriquí, Veraguas, western Panamá province, and eastern Darién); and in South America in the Andes of Venezuela and Colombia, south on the western slope to northern Ecuador, and on the eastern slope to central Bolivia.
Notes.—See comments under *H. leucosticta*.

Genus *MICROCERCULUS* Sclater

> *Microcerculus* Sclater, 1862, Cat. Collect. Amer. Birds, p. 19. Type, by subsequent designation (Baird, 1864), *Turdus bambla* Boddaert = *Formicarius bambla* Boddaert.

Notes.—Possibly more closely related to *Hylorchilus* (Hardy and Delaney 1987).

Microcerculus philomela (Salvin). Nightingale Wren.

> *Cyphorhinus philomela* Salvin, 1861, Proc. Zool. Soc. London, p. 202. (Alta Vera Paz, Guatemala.)

Habitat.—Tropical Lowland Evergreen Forest (0–1400 m; Tropical and Subtropical zones).
Distribution.—*Resident* from northern Chiapas south through the Gulf-Caribbean lowlands of Guatemala, southern Belize, and Honduras to Nicaragua and central Costa Rica (just north of Volcán Turrialba).
Notes.—Also known as Dark-throated Nightingale-Wren or Northern Nightingale-Wren. Although formerly regarded as conspecific with *M. marginatus,* this form is now regarded as a distinct species (Stiles 1983b).

Microcerculus marginatus (Sclater). Scaly-breasted Wren.

> *Heterocnemis marginatus* Sclater, 1855, Proc. Zool. Soc. London, p. 37, pl. 6. (Santa Fé di Bogota [Colombia].)

Habitat.—Tropical Lowland Evergreen Forest (0–1700 m; Tropical and Subtropical zones).
Distribution.—*Resident* [*luscinia* group] from central Costa Rica (south of Volcán de Turrialba) south through Panama (foothills and Caribbean slope throughout, in Pacific lowlands west to eastern Panamá province); [*taeniatus* group] in western Colombia and western Ecuador; and [*marginatus* group] in South America east of the Andes from northern Venezuela and eastern Colombia south to central Bolivia and Amazonian Brazil.
Notes.—Groups: *M. luscinia* Salvin, 1866 [Whistling Wren], *M. taeniatus* Salvin, 1881 [Scaly Nightingale-Wren], and *M. marginatus* [Southern Nightingale-Wren]. Vocal differences among populations merit further study (Ridgely and Tudor 1989). See *M. philomela*.

Genus *CYPHORHINUS* Cabanis

Cyphorhinus Cabanis, 1844, Arch. Naturgesch. 10: 282. Type, by monotypy, *Cyphorhinus thoracicus* Tschudi.

Cyphorhinus phaeocephalus Sclater. Song Wren.

Cyphorhinus phæocephalus Sclater, 1860, Proc. Zool. Soc. London, p. 291. (In rep. Equator. Occ. = Esmeraldas, Esmeraldas, Ecuador.)

Habitat.—Tropical Lowland Evergreen Forest (0–1000 m; Tropical and lower Subtropical zones).

Distribution.—*Resident* on the Caribbean slope of northeastern Honduras (Gracias a Dios) and Nicaragua, on both slopes of Costa Rica (Caribbean slope throughout, and on the Pacific slope of Cordillera de Guanacaste and in the Pacific southwest) and Panama (Caribbean slope throughout, Pacific slope west to western Panamá province), and in western Colombia and western Ecuador.

Notes.—*Cyphorhinus phaeocephalus* and the South American *C. arada* (Hermann, 1783) [Musician Wren] constitute a superspecies (Sibley and Monroe 1990). They have been frequently considered as conspecific, e.g., by Paynter *in* Mayr and Greenway (1960), who proposed that the combined species formed a superspecies with Andean *C. thoracicus* Tschudi, 1844. See also Ridgely and Tudor (1989).

Family **CINCLIDAE**: Dippers

Notes.—Sibley (1970) and Sibley and Ahlquist (1990) found evidence that the Cinclidae are more closely related to the Bombycillidae, Muscicapinae, and Turdinae than is indicated by their traditional placement near the Troglodytidae.

Genus *CINCLUS* Borkhausen

Cinclus Borkhausen, 1797, Dtsch. Fauna 1: 300. Type, by monotypy, *Cinclus hydrophilus* Borkhausen = *Sturnus cinclus* Linnaeus.

Cinclus mexicanus Swainson. American Dipper.

Cinclus Mexicanus Swainson, 1827, Philos. Mag. (n.s.) 1: 368. (Mexico = Temascaltepec, México.)

Habitat.—Montane streams, primarily swift-flowing and rocky, less frequently along mountain ponds and lakes; in winter occasionally to rocky seacoasts (Subtropical and Temperate zones).

Distribution.—*Resident* from western and northeastern Alaska (Sadlerochit Springs), north-central Yukon, west-central Alberta, western Montana, and southwestern South Dakota south to the Aleutian Islands (Unalaska, Unimak), southern California, southern Nevada, north-central and eastern Arizona, southern New Mexico, and in the mountains of northern Middle America through Mexico, Guatemala, and Honduras to north-central Nicaragua; also in the mountains of Costa Rica and western Panama (Chiriquí and Veraguas).

Casual in southern Mackenzie, southwestern Saskatchewan, the Channel Islands (off southern California), southeastern California (Mojave Desert), western Nebraska, and western Texas. Accidental in northeastern Minnesota (Cook County).

Notes.—Also known as North American Dipper.

Family **PYCNONOTIDAE**: Bulbuls

Notes.—Molecular data (Sheldon and Gill 1996) indicate that the Pycnonotidae are more closely related to the Timaliidae, Sylviini, and other groups than is reflected in traditional classifications.

Genus *PYCNONOTUS* Boie

Brachypus (not Meyer, 1814) Swainson, 1824, Zool. J. 1: 305. Type, by subsequent designation (Rand and Deignan, 1960), "Le Curouge" Levaillant = *Turdus cafer* Linnaeus.

Pycnonotus "Kuhl" Boie, 1826, Isis von Oken, col. 973. Type, by monotypy, *Turdus capensis* Linnaeus.

Pycnonotus cafer (Linnaeus). Red-vented Bulbul.

Turdus cafer Linnaeus, 1766, Syst. Nat. (ed. 12) 1: 295. Based on "Le Merle dupé du Cap de Bonne Espérance" Brisson, Ornithologie 2: 257, pl. 20, fig. 2. (ad Cap. b. spei, error = Ceylon.)

Habitat.—Scrub, brushy areas, second growth, urban residential areas, and now in the Hawaiian Islands penetrating into native forest.

Distribution.—*Resident* from Pakistan and the Himalayas south through India to Sri Lanka, central Burma, and western Yunnan.

Introduced and established in the Hawaiian Islands (Oahu), and in the Fiji, Tonga, Samoa, and Society islands.

Notes.—Two other species, *P. leucogenys* (J. E. Gray, 1835) [Himalayan Bulbul] and *P. aurigaster* (Vieillot, 1818) [Sooty-headed Bulbul] form zones of hybridization with *P. cafer* in some areas of sympatry; see Sibley and Monroe (1990), who also considered *P. cafer* to form a superspecies with 10 other species of *Pycnonotus*.

Pycnonotus jocosus (Linnaeus). Red-whiskered Bulbul.

Lanius jocosus Linnaeus, 1758, Syst. Nat. (ed. 10) 1: 95. (in China = Canton, Kwang-tung, China.)

Habitat.—Suburbs and parks; in native range, forest edge and clearings, second-growth woodland, brushy areas, cultivated lands, villages, and suburban residential areas.

Distribution.—*Resident* from India and southern China south to southern Laos and Cambodia; also in the Andaman Islands.

Introduced and established in the Hawaiian Islands (in 1967, on Oahu), Florida (Dade County), Mauritius, Australia (New South Wales), and the Nicobar Islands.

Family **REGULIDAE**: Kinglets

Notes.—Some authors have treated the genus *Regulus* as a subfamily of the Sylviidae (Voous 1977, A.O.U. 1957) or of an expanded Muscicapidae (Mayr and Amadon 1951, Morony et al. 1975, A.O.U. 1983), but others have treated it as a family (Wetmore 1930, 1960, Stepanyan 1990). Molecular data support ranking this group as a family of uncertain affinities (Sibley and Ahlquist 1990, Harshman 1994, Sheldon and Gill 1996); we retain it close to its traditional placement in linear sequences pending resolution of its relationships.

Genus *REGULUS* Cuvier

Regulus Cuvier, 1800, Leçons Anat. Comp. 1: table ii. Type, by monotypy, "Roitelets" = *Motacilla regulus* Linnaeus.

Orchilus Morris, 1837, in Wood, Naturalist 2: 124. Type, by subsequent designation (Oberholser, 1974), *Orchilus cristatus* Wood = *Motacilla regulus* Linnaeus.

Notes.—Molecular data (Sibley and Ahlquist 1985, Ingold et al. 1988) indicate that *R. satrapa* and *R. calendula* are not closely related.

Subgenus *REGULUS* Cuvier

Regulus satrapa Lichtenstein. Golden-crowned Kinglet.

Regulus satrapa Lichtenstein, 1823, Verz. Doubl. Zool. Mus. Berlin, p. 35. (Amer. sept. = North America.)

Habitat.—Coniferous forest and woodland (especially spruce, fir, hemlock); in migration and winter, also deciduous woodland, pine plantations, and parks with conifers or evergreen oaks.

Distribution.—*Breeds* from southern Alaska (west to the base of the Alaska Peninsula), southern Yukon, northern Alberta, northern Saskatchewan, northern Manitoba, northern Ontario, south-central Quebec (including Anticosti Island), New Brunswick, Prince Edward Island, Nova Scotia, and Newfoundland south in the coastal and interior mountains to south-central California (to the San Bernardino and San Jacinto mountains), extreme western and northeastern Nevada (absent from central region), southern Utah, central and southeastern Arizona, southern New Mexico, in the highlands through Mexico to western Guatemala, and east of the Rockies to central eastern Alberta, central Saskatchewan (probably), southern Manitoba, northern Minnesota, northern Wisconsin, southern Michigan, northern Ohio, southern Ontario, New York, in the mountains to eastern Tennessee and western North Carolina, and to southeastern Pennsylvania, north-central Maryland, northern New Jersey, central Massachusetts, and southern Maine; also isolated breeding reported from southwestern South Dakota (Black Hills), northern Illinois, and Indiana (Indianapolis).

Winters from south-coastal Alaska (Kodiak Island) and southern Canada (British Columbia, southern Saskatchewan, southern Manitoba, southern Ontario, southern Quebec, New Brunswick, and Newfoundland) south to northern Baja California, through the breeding range to Guatemala (rarely to lowland regions in Mexico), and to central Tamaulipas, the Gulf coast, and northern (casually central) Florida.

Causal in Bermuda.

Notes.—Reported hybridization of *R. satrapa* and *R. calendula* (Cockrum 1952, Gray 1958) is erroneous. See *Regalus cuvieri* in Appendix.

Subgenus *CORTHYLIO* Cabanis

Corthylio Cabanis, 1853, J. Ornithol. 1: 83. Type, by subsequent designation (Baird, Brewer and Ridgway, 1874), *Motacilla calendula* Linnaeus.

Regulus calendula (Linnaeus). Ruby-crowned Kinglet.

Motacilla Calendula Linnaeus, 1766, Syst. Nat. (ed. 12) 1: 337. Based on "The Ruby-crowned Wren" Edwards, Glean. Nat. Hist. 1: 95, pl. 254, fig. 2. (in Pensylvania = Philadelphia.)

Habitat.—Coniferous forest, mixed coniferous-deciduous woodland, and muskeg; in migration and winter also deciduous forest, open woodland, riparian woodland, brush, dense second-growth, and wooded suburbs and parks (especially in evergreen oaks).

Distribution.—*Breeds* from northwestern and north-central Alaska, north-central Yukon, northwestern and southern Mackenzie, northern Saskatchewan, northern Manitoba, northern Ontario, northern Quebec, Labrador, and Newfoundland south to southern Alaska (west to the base of the Alaska Peninsula), in the mountains to south-central and eastern California (San Bernardino and White mountains), central and southern Arizona, southern New Mexico, east-central Colorado, and southwestern South Dakota (Black Hills), and east of the Rockies to central-eastern Alberta, central Saskatchewan, southern Manitoba, northeastern Minnesota, northern Wisconsin, northern Michigan, southern Ontario (locally), northern New York, southern Quebec, northern Maine, and Nova Scotia; also resident (at least formerly) on Guadalupe Island, off Baja California.

Winters from southwestern British Columbia, Idaho, Utah, northern New Mexico, southeastern Nebraska, Kansas, Illinois, southern Michigan, southern Ontario, and New Jersey (casually farther north) south to southern Baja California, throughout most of Mexico to western Guatemala, and to southern Texas, the Gulf coast, and southern Florida (including the Florida Keys), casually to western Cuba, Bahama Islands, and Bermuda.

Accidental in Greenland, Iceland, and Great Britain.

Notes.—See comments under *R. satrapa*.

Family **SYLVIIDAE**: Old World Warblers and Gnatcatchers

Notes.—Sibley and Ahlquist (1990) presented data (DNA-DNA hybridization) that suggest that the family Muscicapidae, as constituted in A.O.U. (1983) and elsewhere, is polyphyletic, with the Polioptilinae more closely related to the Troglodytidae, and the Sylviinae more closely related to the Timaliidae, Pycnonotidae, and Zosteropidae, than they are to the Muscicapidae and Turdidae.

Subfamily SYLVIINAE: Old World Warblers

Genus *CETTIA* Bonaparte

Cettia Bonaparte, 1834, Iconogr. Fauna Ital. 1: text to pl. 29. Type, by original designation, *Sylvia cetti* Marmora [= Temminck].

Cettia diphone (Kittlitz). Japanese Bush-Warbler.

Sylvia diphone Kittlitz, 1830, Mém. Acad. Imp. Sci. St-Pétersbourg 1 (1831): 27, pl. 14. (Bonin Islands.)

Habitat.—Dense brush and undergrowth, tall grass, and bamboo scrub, in the Hawaiian Islands also in upper native forest, particularly on steep slopes.

Distribution.—*Resident* in Sakhalin, the Kuril Islands, Japan, and the Ryukyu, Bonin, and Volcano islands. Northernmost populations are migratory south to the Japanese islands.

Introduced and established in the Hawaiian Islands (in 1929, now widespread on Oahu, recently established on Kauai, Molokai, Lanai, and Maui).

Notes.—*Cettia diphone* and *C. canturians* (Swinhoe, 1860) [Manchurian Bush-Warbler or Chinese Bush-Warbler], of eastern Asia, may be conspecific (Orenstein and Pratt 1983) or may constitute a superspecies (Sibley and Monroe 1990).

Genus *LOCUSTELLA* Kaup

Locustella Kaup, 1829, Skizz. Entw.-Ges. Eur. Thierw., p. 115. Type, by monotypy, *Sylvia locustella* Latham = *Motacilla naevia* Boddaert.

Locustella ochotensis (Middendorff). Middendorff's Grasshopper-Warbler.

Sylvia (Locustella) Ochotensis Middendorff, 1853, Reise Sib. 2(2): 185, pl. 16, fig. 7. (Uds' Kój Ostrog = Idskoe, Khabarovsk, Sea of Okhotsk.)

Habitat—Dense grassy and bushy areas.

Distribution.—*Breeds* from Kamchatka and Sakhalin south to Japan.

Winters in the Philippines and Greater Sunda Islands.

Casual in Alaska, primarily in fall (Nunivak and St. Lawrence islands, St. Paul in the Pribilofs, and Attu and Buldir in the Aleutians), and in the Commander Islands.

Notes.—Also known as Middendorff's Warbler. *L. ochotensis, L. pleskei* (Taczanowski, 1889) [Pleske's Warbler] of Korea and Kyushu, and the eastern Eurasian *L. certhiola* (Pallas, 1811) [Pallas's Warbler] may constitute a superspecies (Sibley and Monroe 1990).

Locustella lanceolata (Temminck). Lanceolated Warbler.

Sylvia lanceolata Temminck, 1840, Man. Ornithol (ed. 2) 4: 614. ("Mayence," error = Russia.)

Habitat.—Marshes and wet meadows.

Distribution.—*Breeds* from eastern Russia to eastern Siberia and south to northern China, Korea, and Japan.

Winters in southeastern Asia and the East Indies.

Accidental in Alaska (Attu, in the Aleutian Islands, 4 June-15 July 1984, at least 25 birds; Tobish 1985) and California (Farallon Islands, 11 Sept. 1995; Hickey et al. 1996).

Genus *ACROCEPHALUS* Naumann and Naumann

Acrocephalus J. A. and J. F. Naumann, 1811, Naturgesch. Land-Wasser-Vögel Dtsch., suppl., pt. 4: 199. Type, by subsequent designation (G. R. Gray, 1840), *Turdus arundinaceus* Linnaeus.

Acrocephalus familiaris (Rothschild). Millerbird.

Tatare familiaris Rothschild, 1892, Ann. Mag. Nat. Hist. (ser. 6)10: 109. (Laysan Island, Sandwich Group.)

Habitat.—Dense low vegetation and grass.
Distribution.—*Resident* in the northwestern Hawaiian Islands [*kingi* group] on Nihoa; and [*familiaris* group] formerly on Laysan, where extirpated between 1913 and 1923.
Notes.—Groups: *A. kingi* Wetmore, 1924 [Nihoa Millerbird] and *A. familiaris* [Laysan Millerbird].

Genus *PHYLLOSCOPUS* Boie

Phylloscopus Boie, 1826, Isis von Oken, col. 972. Type, by monotypy, *Sylvia trochilus* Latham = *Motacilla trochilus* Linnaeus.

Phylloscopus sibilatrix (Bechstein). Wood Warbler.

Motacilla Sibilatrix Bechstein, 1792, Kurzefasste Gemeinützige In-Auslandes 1: 544, note. (mountains of Thuringia.)

Habitat.—Forest and woodland.
Distribution.—*Breeds* throughout much of Europe and Russia.
Winters in tropical Africa and Asia Minor, casually to the Canary Islands and Madeira.
Accidental in Alaska (Shemya Island, in the Aleutians, 9 October 1978; Gibson 1981) and Japan.

Phylloscopus fuscatus (Blyth). Dusky Warbler.

Phillopneuste fuscata Blyth, 1842, J. Asiat. Soc. Bengal 11: 113. (Calcutta, India.)

Habitat.—Bushes and scrub in hilly or mountainous areas.
Distribution.—*Breeds* from Anadyrland and the Sea of Okhotsk south to Mongolia and the eastern Himalayas.
Winters from India east to Southeast Asia and southern China.
Casual in Alaska (Shemya and Attu in the Aleutians, at sea in the Bering Sea, also two sight reports from St. Lawrence Island). Accidental in California (Farallon Islands, Hayward); a sight report from Baja California.

Phylloscopus borealis (Blasius). Arctic Warbler.

Phyllopneuste borealis Blasius, 1858, Naumannia 8: 313. (ochotzkischen Meere = Sea of Okhotsk.)

Habitat.—Dense deciduous (willow, dwarf birch, alder) riparian thickets; in Eurasia, also open coniferous or mixed coniferous-deciduous forest.
Distribution.—*Breeds* in western and central Alaska from the Noatak River and western and central Brooks Range south to southwestern Alaska, the base of the Alaska Peninsula, the Alaska Range, and Susitna River highlands; and in Eurasia from Finland, northern Russia, and northern Siberia south to central Russia, Mongolia, Amurland, Ussuriland, Japan, and Kamchatka. Recorded in summer north to Barrow, and on St. Lawrence and St. Matthew islands, and east to northern Mackenzie (Prince Patrick Island).
Winters from Southeast Asia and southeastern China south to the East Indies, Philippines, and Moluccas.
Migrates through eastern Asia and the Commander Islands, casually the Aleutians.
Accidental in California (Monterey County, Oceano). A sight report from Baja California.

Notes.—Also known as Arctic Willow-Warbler. Specimens representing Asiatic breeding populations have been taken in migration in the Aleutians (Attu, Shemya, and Amchitka).

Subfamily POLIOPTILINAE: Gnatcatchers and Gnatwrens

Notes.—Molecular data (Sheldon and Gill 1996) strongly suggest that this group is not closely related to the Sylviidae, where traditionally placed, or even the Regulidae, but rather that it is closely related to the Certhiidae and Troglodytidae (as previously suggested by Sibley and Ahlquist 1990).

Tribe RAMPHOCAENINI: Gnatwrens

Notes.—For relationships with Polioptilini, see Rand and Traylor (1953). See comments under Polioptilini and Sylviidae.

Genus *MICROBATES* Sclater and Salvin

Microbates Sclater and Salvin, 1873, Nomencl. Avium Neotrop.: 72, 155. Type, by original designation, *Microbates torquatus* Sclater and Salvin = *Rhamphocaenus collaris* Pelzeln.

Microbates cinereiventris (Sclater). Tawny-faced Gnatwren.

Ramphocaenus cinereiventris Sclater, 1855, Proc. Zool. Soc. London, p. 76, pl. 87. (in rep. Novæ Grenadæ, Pasto = Buenaventura, Colombia.)

Habitat.—Tropical Lowland Evergreen Forest (0–1200 m; Tropical and lower Subtropical zones).

Distribution.—*Resident* on the Caribbean slope of southeastern Nicaragua and Costa Rica, on both slopes of Panama (more widespread on the Caribbean), and in South America from Colombia south, west of the Andes to southwestern Ecuador and east of the Andes to southeastern Peru.

Notes.—Also known as Half-collared Gnatwren.

Genus *RAMPHOCAENUS* Vieillot

Ramphocænus Vieillot, 1819, Nouv. Dict. Hist. Nat. (nouv. éd.) 29: 5. Type, by monotypy, *Ramphocaenus melanurus* Vieillot.

Ramphocaenus melanurus Vieillot. Long-billed Gnatwren.

Ramphocænus melanurus Vieillot, 1819, Nouv. Dict. Hist. Nat. (nouv. éd.) 29: 6. (Brésil = Rio de Janeiro, Brazil.)

Habitat.—Tropical Lowland Evergreen Forest Edge, Secondary Forest (0–1500 m; Tropical and lower Subtropical zones).

Distribution.—*Resident* [*rufiventris* group] from northern Oaxaca, southern Veracruz, Tabasco, and northern and southeastern Chiapas south along both slopes of Middle America (including the Yucatan Peninsula), and in South America in western Colombia, western Ecuador, and northwestern Peru; and [*melanurus* group] in South America from northern and eastern Colombia, Venezuela, and the Guianas south, east of the Andes, to central Bolivia and central and southeastern Brazil.

Notes.—Groups: *R. rufiventris* (Bonaparte, 1838) [Long-billed Gnatwren] and *R. melanurus* [Black-tailed Gnatwren].

Tribe POLIOPTILINI: Gnatcatchers

Notes.—For relationships with Ramphocaenini, see Rand and Traylor (1953).

Genus *POLIOPTILA* Sclater

Polioptila Sclater, 1855, Proc. Zool. Soc. London, p. 11. Type, by subsequent designation (Baird, 1864), *Motacilla caerulea* Linnaeus.

Polioptila caerulea (Linnaeus). Blue-gray Gnatcatcher.

> *Motacilla cærulea* Linnaeus, 1766, Syst. Nat. (ed. 12) 1: 337. Based on the "Little Blue-grey Flycatcher" Edwards, Glean. Nat. Hist. 2: 194, pl. 302. (in Pensylvania = Philadelphia.)

Habitat.—Deciduous forest, oak woodland, pine-oak woodland, riparian woodland, brushy washes, pinyon-juniper woodland, scrub, and chaparral; in winter, primarily dense second-growth, dense brush, woodland (especially riparian), and acacia scrub (Tropical to lower Temperate zones).

Distribution.—*Breeds* from southern Oregon, southern Idaho (casually), Montana (Pryor Mountains), southwestern Wyoming, Colorado (except northeastern), eastern Nebraska, southeastern South Dakota, central Minnesota, central Wisconsin, central Michigan, southern Ontario, southwestern Quebec, New York, central Vermont, southern New Hampshire, and southern Maine south to southern Baja California, locally throughout most of Mexico (including the Yucatan Peninsula and Cozumel Island) to southern Chiapas, Belize, and (probably) western Guatemala, and to southeastern Texas, the Gulf coast, southern Florida, and the Bahama Islands (south to Grand Turk).

Winters from central California, southern Nevada, western and central Arizona, west-central Colorado (rarely), central Texas, the southern portions of the Gulf states, and on the Atlantic coast from southern Virginia south throughout Mexico to Guatemala and Honduras, and to the Bahamas, the western Greater Antilles (Cuba, the Isle of Pines), and Cayman Islands. Casual in winter (early winter only?) north to northern California, southern Utah, northern Texas, and along the Atlantic Coast to New England.

Casual north to southwestern British Columbia, southern Alberta, Montana, southern Manitoba, New Brunswick, Prince Edward Island, and Nova Scotia; a sight report for southern Saskatchewan.

Polioptila lembeyei (Gundlach). Cuban Gnatcatcher.

> *Culicivora lembeyei* Gundlach, 1858, Ann. Lyc. Nat. Hist. N. Y. 6: 273. (Eastern part of Cuba.)

Habitat.—Arid Lowland Scrub (0–200 m).

Distribution.—*Resident* in Cuba (central and eastern Camagüey and Las Villas provinces east to the Guantánamo region, also on Cayo Coco and probably Cayo Romano, off Camagüey).

Polioptila californica Brewster. California Gnatcatcher.

> *Polioptila californica* Brewster, 1881, Bull. Nuttall Ornithol. Club 6: 103. (Riverside, San Bernardino [= Riverside] Co., California.)

Habitat.—Coastal sage scrub (in California), thorn forest, desert brush, and scrub.

Distribution.—*Resident* from southwestern California (north to Los Angeles County, formerly to Ventura County) and northwestern Baja California south locally to southern Baja California (including Santa Margarita and Espíritu Santo islands).

Notes.—For discussion of the recognition of this species as distinct from *P. melanura,* see Atwood (1988).

Polioptila melanura Lawrence. Black-tailed Gnatcatcher.

> *Polioptila melanura* Lawrence, 1857, Ann. Lyc. Nat. Hist. N. Y. 6: 168. (Texas, California = Rio Grande Valley, Texas.)

Habitat.—Arid Lowland Scrub, Arid Montane Scrub (0–2100 m; Tropical and Subtropical zones).

Distribution.—*Resident* from northeastern (and possibly east-central) Baja California, southeastern California (north to southern Inyo County), southern Nevada, southwestern Utah, western and central Arizona, southwestern Colorado (possibly), southwestern (rarely central) New Mexico, and western and southern Texas (Rio Grande Valley) south to southern

Sonora (including Isla Tiburón), southern Durango, Jalisco, Guanajuato, San Luis Potosí and Tamaulipas.

A sight report for western Texas.

Notes.—Also known as Plumbeous Gnatcatcher. See *P. californica.*

Polioptila nigriceps Baird. Black-capped Gnatcatcher.

Polioptila nigriceps Baird, 1864, Rev. Amer. Birds 1: 69. (Mazatlán, Sinaloa, Mexico.)

Habitat.—Gallery Forest, Tropical Deciduous Forest, Arid Lowland Scrub (0–1200 m; Tropical and lower Subtropical zones).

Distribution.—*Breeds* from extreme southern Arizona (Nogales area, Santa Rita Mountains, at least irregularly or formerly), southern Sonora, and southwestern Chihuahua south through Sinaloa, western Durango, Nayarit, and Jalisco to Colima.

Winters throughout breeding range except for Arizona.

Notes.—Although sometimes considered conspecific with *P. albiloris* (Paynter *in* Mayr and Paynter 1964), *P. nigriceps* differs in morphology and vocalizations, and shows no approach to *albiloris* in the region of geographic proximity in western Mexico.

Polioptila albiloris Sclater and Salvin. White-lored Gnatcatcher.

Polioptila albiloris Sclater and Salvin, 1860, Proc. Zool. Soc. London, p. 298. (In rep. Guatimalensi in valle fl. Motagua = Motagua Valley, Zacapa, Guatemala.)

Habitat.—Tropical Deciduous Forest, Arid Lowland Scrub, Arid Montane Scrub, Gallery Forest (0–1900 m; Tropical and Subtropical zones).

Distribution.—*Resident* in the Pacific lowlands and arid interior valleys from southern Michoacán, northern Guerrero, Oaxaca, western Puebla, and Chiapas south through Central America to northwestern Costa Rica (south to the Gulf of Nicoya region); also disjunctly on the Yucatan Peninsula (questionably recorded also from Cozumel Island).

Notes.—Although closely related to *P. plumbea, P. albiloris* differs in appearance, voice, and habitat, and it occurs sympatrically with *plumbea* at several locations. See comments under *P. nigriceps.*

Polioptila plumbea (Gmelin). Tropical Gnatcatcher.

Todus plumbeus Gmelin, 1788, Syst. Nat. 1(1): 444. Based on the "Plumbeous Tody" Latham, Gen. Synop. Birds 1(2): 661. (in Surinamo = Surinam.)

Habitat.—Tropical Deciduous Forest, Tropical Lowland Evergreen Forest Edge, Gallery Forest, Secondary Forest, Arid Lowland Scrub, Arid Montane Scrub (0–1500 m; Tropical and lower Subtropical zones).

Distribution.—*Resident* [*bilineata* group] on the Gulf-Caribbean slope of southern Veracruz, northern Oaxaca (Isthmus of Tehuantepec), Campeche, Quintana Roo, Guatemala, Belize, Honduras, and Nicaragua, on both slopes of Costa Rica (uncommon in the dry northwest) and Panama (including Isla Coiba, also sight reports from the Pearl Islands), and in South America, west of the Andes, from Colombia to central Peru; [*plumbea* group] in South America from central and eastern Colombia, Venezuela (also Margarita Island), and the Guianas south, east of the Andes, to eastern Peru and Amazonian and eastern Brazil; and [*maior* group] in northern Peru (upper Marañón valley).

Notes.—Groups: *P. bilineata* (Bonaparte, 1850) [White-browed Gnatcatcher], *P. plumbea* [Tropical Gnatcatcher], and *P. maior* Hellmayr, 1900 [Maranon Gnatcatcher]; see Ridgely and Tudor (1989). The relationship of *P. plumbea* to the southwestern South American *P. lactea* Sharpe, 1885, is uncertain. See comments under *P. albiloris.*

Polioptila schistaceigula Hartert. Slate-throated Gnatcatcher.

Polioptila schistaceigula Hartert, 1898, Bull. Br. Ornithol. Club 7: 30. (Cachabi [= Cachaví], 500 ft., [Esmeraldas,] North Ecuador.)

Habitat.—Tropical Lowland Evergreen Forest (0–1000 m; Tropical Zone).

Distribution.—*Resident* from eastern Panama (recorded in eastern Panamá province above Madden Lake, and in eastern Darién on cerros Quía and Pirre) south through northern and western Colombia (also in Cundinamarca east of the Andes) to northwestern Ecuador.

Notes.—The relationship of *P. schistaceigula* with the northeastern South American *P. guianensis* Todd, 1920, is uncertain; Paynter *in* Mayr and Paynter (1964) suggested that they might be conspecific.

Family MUSCICAPIDAE: Old World Flycatchers

Notes.—See comments under Sylviidae.

Genus *FICEDULA* Brisson

Ficedula Brisson, 1760, Ornithologie 3: 369. Type, by tautonymy, *Ficedula* Brisson = *Ficedula hypoleuca* Pallas.

Notes.—Formerly merged in *Muscicapa,* but see Vaurie (1953).

Ficedula narcissina (Temminck). Narcissus Flycatcher.

Muscicapa narcissina Temminck, 1835, Planches Color., livr. 97, pl. 577, fig. 1. (Japan.)

Habitat.—Mountain forest, generally near water.

Distribution.—*Breeds* in southeastern Siberia (Ussuriland), Sakhalin, the southern Kuril Islands, Japan, and the Ryukyu Islands.

Winters in southeastern Asia, the Greater Sunda Islands, and Philippines.

Accidental in Alaska (Attu, in the Aleutian Islands, 20–21 May 1989, specimen; Gibson and Kessel 1992).

Ficedula mugimaki (Temminck). Mugimaki Flycatcher.

Muscicapa Mugimaki Temminck, 1835, Planches Color., livr. 97, p. 577, fig. 2. (Japan.)

Habitat.—Coniferous forest.

Distribution.—*Breeds* in southeastern Siberia and northeastern China.

Winters in southeastern Asia and Indonesia.

Accidental in the Aleutian Islands (Shemya, 24 May 1985, photographs; 1985, Amer. Birds 39: 339).

Ficedula parva (Bechstein). Red-breasted Flycatcher.

Muscicapa parva Bechstein, 1792, Kurzefasste Gemeinützige In-Auslandes 1: 531, note. (Thüringerwalde = Germany.)

Habitat.—Undergrowth of mixed deciduous-coniferous woodland.

Distribution.—*Breeds* from central Europe, Russia, and Siberia south to northern Iran, the northern Himalayas, northern Mongolia, Anadyrland, and Kamchatka.

Winters in India and Sri Lanka, migrating through western Asia and China.

Casual in Alaska in the western Aleutians (Attu, Shemya) and St. Lawrence Island.

Notes.—Also known as Red-throated Flycatcher. Includes the Himalayan form, sometimes regarded as a distinct species, *F. subrubra* (Hartert and Steinbacher 1934, Sibley and Monroe 1990).

Genus *MUSCICAPA* Brisson

Muscicapa Brisson, 1760, Ornithologie 1: 32. Type, by tautonymy, *Muscicapa* Brisson = *Motacilla striata* Pallas.

Notes.—See comments under *Ficedula.*

Muscicapa sibirica Gmelin. Siberian Flycatcher.

Muscicapa sibirica Gmelin, 1789, Syst. Nat. 1(2): 936. Based on the "Dun Fly-catcher" Pennant, Arct. Zool. 2: 390, and Latham, Gen. Synop. Birds 2(1): 351. (Circa lacum Baical, et in orientali Sibiria ad Camtschatcam usque = near Lake Baikal.)

Habitat.—Open forest of mountains and taiga.
Distribution.—*Breeds* from central and eastern Siberia south to the Himalayas, northern China, Japan, Kamchatka, and the Kuril Islands.
Winters south to northern India, southeastern Asia, Indonesia, and the Philippines.
Casual in the western Aleutians (Attu, Shemya, Buldir). Accidental in Bermuda (Sandy's Parish, 29 September 1980; Wingate 1983).
Notes.—Also known as Sooty Flycatcher, a name now generally restricted to the African *M. infuscata* (Cassin, 1855) [= *Artomyias fuliginosa* J. & E. Verreaux, 1855].

Muscicapa griseisticta (Swinhoe). Gray-spotted Flycatcher.

Hemichelidon griseisticta Swinhoe, 1861, Ibis, p. 330. (Amoy and Takoo, eastern China.)

Habitat.—Open forest of the taiga (breeding); wooded areas and scrub (nonbreeding).
Distribution.—*Breeds* from eastern Siberia and Kamchatka south to eastern Manchuria, Ussuriland, Sakhalin, and the Kuril Islands.
Winters from eastern China, Taiwan, and the Philippines south to Sulawesi, New Guinea, and islands of this general region.
Migrates through northern China, Japan, and the Ryukyu Islands, casually as far north and east as the Commander Islands and western Aleutians (Attu, Agattu, Shemya, Buldir, Amchitka).

Muscicapa dauurica Pallas. Asian Brown Flycatcher.

Muscicapa Grisola var. *Dauurica* Pallas, 1811, Zoogr. Rosso-Asiat. 1: 461. (Onon River, Dauria, Siberia.)
Muscicapa latirostris Raffles, 1822, Trans. Linn. Soc. London 13(2): 312. (Sumatra.)

Habitat.—Forest and woodland.
Distribution.—*Breeds* [*dauurica* group] in eastern Asia from southern and eastern Siberia south to northern India, northern China, and Japan, and *winters* in southeastern Asia, Sumatra, Borneo, the Lesser Sunda Islands (Sumba), and Philippines; and *resident* [*williamsoni* group] in Southeast Asia.
Accidental [*dauurica* group] in the Aleutian Islands (Attu, 25 May 1985, specimen; Gibson and Kessel 1992).
Notes.—Also known as Brown Flycatcher or Gray-breasted Flycatcher. Groups: *M. dauurica* [Asian Brown Flycatcher] and *M. williamsoni* Deignan, 1957 [Brown-streaked Flycatcher]. For use of *M. dauurica* instead of *M. latirostris,* see Watson *in* Mayr and Cottrell (1986) and Banks and Browning (1995).

Family **TURDIDAE**: Thrushes

Notes.—See comments under Sylviidae.

Genus *LUSCINIA* Forster

Luscinia T. Forster, 1817, Synop. Cat. Br. Birds, p. 14. Type, by monotypy, *Sylvia luscinia* Forster = *Luscinia megarhynchos* Brehm.

Notes.—*Luscinia* is sometimes merged with the Old World genus *Erithacus* Cuvier, 1800.

Luscinia calliope (Pallas). Siberian Rubythroat.

Motacilla Calliope Pallas, 1776, Reise Versch. Prov. Russ. Reichs 3: 697. (a Jenisea usque ad Lenam = between the Yenisei and Lena rivers.)

Habitat.—Thickets, bogs, and regenerating burns in mixed or coniferous open forest and taiga, subalpine scrub; in winter, scrub and second-growth.

Distribution.—*Breeds* from Siberia (the Urals east to Anadyrland and Kamchatka) south to Mongolia, Transbaicalia, Amurland, Sakhalin, Japan, and the Kuril Islands.

Winters from India, Southeast Asia, and southern China south to Malaya, the Philippines, and Taiwan.

Migrates through eastern China, Korea, Japan, the Ryukyu and Commander islands and western Aleutians (rare but regular in the Near Islands, casually east to Amchitka), casually east to the Pribilofs (St. Paul) and north to St. Lawrence Island.

Accidental in southern Ontario (Hornby). Casual in western Europe.

Luscinia svecica (Linnaeus). Bluethroat.

Motacilla svecica Linnaeus, 1758, Syst. Nat. (ed. 10) 1: 187. (in Europæ alpinis = Sweden and Lapland.)

Habitat.—Low dense thickets (willow and dwarf birch) in tundra, especially near water; in Eurasia, a variety of brushy habitats; in winter, marshes, swamp edges, reedbeds, and brush near water.

Distribution.—*Breeds* from northern Scandinavia, northern Russia, northern Siberia, and western and northern Alaska (from the Seward Peninsula north and east to the northern foothills of the eastern Brooks Range) south to western and central Europe, Iran, Turkestan, the northern Himalayas, and Manchuria.

Winters in northern Africa (from Morocco east to northeastern Africa), the Near East, India, and Southeast Asia.

Migrates through western Alaska (St. Lawrence Island, and casually on the mainland south to St. Michael), the British Isles, western and southern Europe, and southwestern and eastern Asia.

Casual in the western Aleutians (Attu) and Yukon.

Luscinia cyane (Pallas). Siberian Blue Robin.

Motacilla Cyane Pallas, 1776, Reise Versch. Prov. Russ. Reichs 3: 697. (Dauria, between the Onon and the Argus [southeastern Transbaicalia].)

Habitat.—Coniferous or mixed forest (spruce, fir, birch, aspen) with dense canopy and sparse undergrowth; in winter, tropical forest and second growth.

Distribution.—*Breeds* in eastern Asia from southern Siberia south to northeastern China and Japan, and *winters* in southeastern Asia, Indonesia, and the Philippines.

Accidental in the Aleutian Islands (Attu, 21 May 1985; Gibson and Kessel 1992).

Genus *TARSIGER* Hodgson

Tarsiger Hodgson, 1845, Proc. Zool. Soc. London, p. 28. Type, by monotypy, *Tarsiger chrysaeus* Hodgson.

Notes.—This genus is sometimes merged with *Erithacus* (e.g., Morony et al. 1975).

Tarsiger cyanurus (Pallas). Red-flanked Bluetail.

Motacilla Cyanurus Pallas, 1773, Reise Versch. Prov. Russ. Reichs 2: 709. (Yenisei.)

Habitat.—Taiga, moist coniferous and mixed forest; in winter, forest undergrowth and second growth.

Distribution.—*Breeds* in from Siberia south to northern China, Japan, and the Commander Islands, and *winters* in southeastern Asia.

Casual in spring in Alaska in the western Aleutians (Attu) and Pribilofs (St. Paul); a sight report from Hooper Bay. Accidental in California (Farallon Islands).

Notes.—Also known as Orange-flanked Bush-Robin.

Genus *COPSYCHUS* Wagler

Copsychus Wagler, 1827, Syst. Avium 1 (note to genus *Gracula*): 306. Type, by subsequent designation (G. R. Gray, 1840), *Gracula saularis* Linnaeus.

Copsychus malabaricus (Scopoli). White-rumped Shama.

Muscicapa (malabarica) Scopoli, 1786, Del. Flor. Faun. Insubr., fasc. 2, p. 96. (Mahé, Malabar.)

Habitat.—Forest and second growth.

Distribution.—*Resident* from India, Southeast Asia, and southwestern China south to Sri Lanka, the Andaman and Greater Sunda islands, and Hainan.

Introduced and established in the Hawaiian Islands (in 1931, now on Kauai and Oahu).

Notes.—Also known as Shama Thrush.

Genus *OENANTHE* Vieillot

Oenanthe Vieillot, 1816, Analyse, p. 43. Type, by monotypy, "Motteux" Buffon = *Turdus leucurus* Gmelin.

Oenanthe oenanthe (Linnaeus). Northern Wheatear.

Motacilla Oenanthe Linnaeus, 1758, Syst. Nat. (ed. 10) 1: 186. (in Europæ apricis lapidosis = Sweden.)

Habitat.—Dry, rocky tundra; in Eurasia, a variety of open country, tundra, steppe, and desert; in migration and winter, fields and meadows with rocks, debris, fences, or other low perches.

Distribution.—*Breeds* [*oenanthe* group] in North America from northern Alaska, northern Yukon, and northwestern Mackenzie south to western and south-coastal Alaska (to the Kenai Peninsula) and southern Yukon, and from central Ellesmere Island south to the Boothia Peninsula (possibly), southeastern Keewatin, White Island, eastern and southern Baffin Island, Coats Island, northern Quebec, and Labrador; and in the Palearctic from Greenland, Jan Mayen, Iceland, the British Isles, northern Scandinavia, northern Russia (including Novaya Zemlya), and northern Siberia south to the northern Mediterranean region, Asia Minor, the northwestern Himalayas, Turkestan, Mongolia, and Manchuria.

Winters [*oenanthe* group] from northern Africa, Arabia, India, Mongolia, and northern China south to southern Africa (at least casually), and rarely to eastern China and the Philippines.

Resident [*seebohmi* group] in northern Africa in Morocco and northern Algeria.

Migrates [*oenanthe* group] regularly through western Alaska and islands in the Bering Sea, casually the Pribilofs and Aleutians.

Casual or accidental [*oenanthe* group] along the Pacific coast in Alaska (Middleton Island, Juneau), southern British Columbia, Oregon (Malheur), and northern and central California; in southern Alberta and Arizona (Marana); and in northeastern North America from Ontario, New York, southern Quebec, New Brunswick, Nova Scotia, and Newfoundland south to Illinois, Indiana, Ohio, New Jersey, Pennsylvania, Maryland, and North Carolina; and in Arkansas (Lake Millwood), Louisiana, Alabama (Fort Morgan, Montgomery), Florida (south to Collier County), Yucatán, Quintana Roo, Bermuda, Cuba (Santiago de Cuba), Barbados, and the Netherlands Antilles; sight reports for northeastern and southern Manitoba, Minnesota, the Bahama Islands, and Puerto Rico. A report for Colorado is erroneous.

Notes.—Also known as the Wheatear. Groups: *O. oenanthe* [Northern Wheatear] and *O. seebohmi* (Dixon, 1882) [Black-throated Wheatear].

Genus *SAXICOLA* Bechstein

Saxicola Bechstein, 1802, Ornithol. Taschenb. Dtsch. 1: 216. Type, by subsequent designation (Swainson, 1827), *Motacilla rubicola* Linnaeus = *Motacilla torquata* Linnaeus.

Saxicola torquata (Linnaeus). Stonechat.

Motacilla torquata Linnaeus, 1766, Syst. Nat. (ed. 12) 1: 328. (Cape of Good Hope.)

Habitat.—Open country with scattered bushes and rocks, open scrub, brushy hillsides, marsh edges, and meadows.

Distribution.—*Breeds* [*torquata* group] in Europe and Africa east to the Black Sea and Iran, and [*maura* group] in northern and central Asia.

Winters [*torguata* group] in most of breeding range, and [*maura* group] to southern Asia and northeastern Africa.

Casual [*maura* group] in Alaska (St. Lawrence Island, Galena, Middleton Island). Accidental in New Brunswick (Grand Manan Island).

Notes.—Groups: *S. torquata* [Common Stonechat] and *S. maura* (Pallas) 1773 [Siberian Stonechat].

Genus *SIALIA* Swainson

Sialia Swainson, 1827, Philos. Mag. (n.s.) 1: 369. Type, by monotypy, *Sialia azurea* Swainson = *Motacilla sialis* Linnaeus.

Sialia sialis (Linnaeus). Eastern Bluebird.

Motacilla Sialis Linnaeus, 1758, Syst. Nat. (ed. 10) 1: 187. Based mainly on "The Blew Bird" Catesby, Nat. Hist. Carolina 1: 47, pl. 47. (in Bermudis & America calidiore = South Carolina.)

Habitat.—Open deciduous, mixed, and pine woodland, and agricultural areas with scattered trees (Tropical to Temperate zones).

Distribution.—*Breeds* from southern Saskatchewan, southern (casually northwestern) Manitoba, central Ontario, south-central Quebec, New Brunswick, Prince Edward Island, and southwestern Nova Scotia south through central and eastern North America and the highlands of Mexico, Guatemala, El Salvador, and Honduras to north-central Nicaragua (also in the lowland pine savanna of northeastern Honduras and northern Nicaragua), to southern Tamaulipas, southern Texas, the Gulf coast, and southern Florida, and west to eastern Montana, eastern Wyoming, northeastern Colorado, western Kansas, Oklahoma, Texas (except the High Plains and Trans-Pecos), and southeastern and (casually) southwestern New Mexico; also in southeastern Arizona (Nogales and Patagonia east to Huachuca and Chiricahua mountains), and in Bermuda.

Winters from the middle portions of the eastern United States (casually north to the northern states, southern Ontario, southern Quebec, and New England) south throughout the breeding range west to southeastern Arizona, and casually to the lowlands of eastern Mexico (Veracruz, Yucatán, Quintana Roo) and western Cuba; most populations from the Gulf states southward are resident.

Casual north to southeastern Utah, southern Alberta, north-central and southern Quebec (including Anticosti Island), and Prince Edward Island; a sight report for the Virgin Islands (St. John).

Sialia mexicana Swainson. Western Bluebird.

Sialia Mexicana Swainson, 1832, in Swainson and Richardson, Fauna Bor.-Amer. 2 (1831): 202. (table land of Mexico.)

Habitat.—Open pine, deciduous and mixed woodland, savanna, and riparian woodland; in winter, more widespread, including pinyon-juniper woodland, desert washes, and agricultural fields (Subtropical and Temperate zones).

Distribution.—*Breeds* from southern British Columbia (including southeastern Vancouver Island), southern Alberta, central-western Saskatchewan, western Montana, and north-central Colorado south through the mountains to northern Baja California (Sierra Juárez and Sierra San Pedro Mártir), western and southern Nevada, southern Utah, western and (rarely) southeastern Arizona, and northeastern Sonora (absent from central Idaho south to eastern Nevada, central Utah, western Colorado, and northern New Mexico), in the highlands of Mexico to

Michoacán, México, Morelos, Puebla, and west-central Veracruz, and east to southwestern Tamaulipas, Nuevo León, western (Trans-Pecos) Texas, and central New Mexico.

Winters from southern Oregon and western Montana south throughout the breeding range (including to lowland areas), to islands off California (Santa Catalina and San Clemente, at least casually) and Baja California (Todos Santos), and to southeastern California, and east to central Texas.

Casual in Oklahoma (Kenton); sight reports from North Dakota and Kansas.

Sialia currucoides (Bechstein). Mountain Bluebird.

> *Motacilla* s. *Sylvia Currucoides* (Borkhausen MS) Bechstein, 1798, in Latham, Allg. Uebers. Vögel 3(2): 546, pl. 121. (Virginien = western America.)

Habitat.—Coniferous woodland, aspen woodland, subalpine meadows, sagebrush, and montane grassland with scattered trees, and pinyon-juniper woodland; in migration and winter, also grasslands, open brushy areas, and agricultural lands.

Distribution.—*Breeds* from east-central Alaska (Delta, Eagle, Chisana), southern Yukon, north-central Alberta, northwestern (once) and central Saskatchewan, northern Manitoba, and northwestern Minnesota south in the mountains (eastern slopes of coast ranges, and in the Sierra Nevada and Rocky Mountains) to south-central and eastern California (to San Bernardino and New York mountains), central and southeastern Nevada, northern and eastern Arizona, and southern New Mexico, and east to northeastern North Dakota, western South Dakota, western Nebraska, and central Oklahoma (Cleveland County). Recorded in summer (and possibly breeding) in southern Mackenzie.

Winters from southern British Columbia (rarely) and western Montana south to northern Baja California (including islands off California and Baja California south to Guadalupe Island), Sinaloa, Michoacán, Guanajuato, Nuevo León, and southern Texas, and east, at least casually, to western Nebraska, eastern Kansas, western Oklahoma, and central Texas.

Casual in western, northern and south-coastal Alaska (Nunivak Island, Point Barrow, Middleton Island) and northern Manitoba (Churchill); east from Minnesota, Ontario, southern Quebec, New York, Vermont, Massachusetts, New Brunswick, and Nova Scotia south to Iowa, Arkansas, Kentucky, Indiana, Pennsylvania, and Maryland; and in the Gulf region from central coastal Texas to Louisiana and Mississippi.

Genus *MYADESTES* Swainson

> *Myadestes* Swainson, 1838, Flycatchers, Ornithol. 10, *in* Jardine, Naturalists' Libr. 21: 132. Type, by monotypy, *Myidestes* [sic] *genibarbis* Swainson.
> *Phaeornis* Sclater, 1859, Ibis, p. 327. Type, by monotypy, *Taenioptera obscura* = *Muscicapa obscura* Gmelin.

Notes.—For the merger of *Phaeornis* into *Myadestes,* see Pratt (1982).

Myadestes townsendi (Audubon). Townsend's Solitaire.

> *Ptilogony's* [sic] *Townsendi* Audubon, 1838, Birds Amer. (folio) 4: pl. 419, fig. 2 (1839, Ornithol. Biogr. 5: 206). (Columbia River = Astoria, Oregon.)

Habitat.—Open montane and subalpine coniferous woodland, burns, especially where exposed slopes and dirt banks provide nest sites; in winter, primarily pinyon-juniper woodland, also chaparral, desert, and riparian woodland (especially where juniper present).

Distribution.—*Breeds* from east-central, south-coastal and southeastern Alaska, north-central Yukon, and west-central and southwestern Mackenzie, southern Alberta, and southwestern Saskatchewan, south to south-central California (to Santa Rosa and San Jacinto mountains), northwestern and east-central Arizona, and southern New Mexico to Durango, Jalisco, and Zacatecas; also in southwestern South Dakota, and northwestern Nebraska.

Winters from southern British Columbia (casually north to Alaska), southern Alberta, Montana, and central North Dakota south to northern Baja California, Sonora, the southern limits of the breeding range in Mexico, and east to western Missouri, western Oklahoma, western Texas, Nuevo León, and Coahuila.

Casual on Guadalupe Island (off Baja California), in central Texas and Arkansas, and east to southern Manitoba, Minnesota, Iowa, Wisconsin, Illinois, Michigan, Ontario, Ohio, Quebec, New York, New Jersey, and New Brunswick to Newfoundland, Nova Scotia, and New England; sight reports for Indiana and Pennsylvania.

Myadestes occidentalis Stejneger. Brown-backed Solitaire.

> *Myadestes obscurus* Lafresnaye, 1839, Rev. Zool. [Paris] 2: 98. (Mexico = probably Veracruz.) Preoccupied by *Muscicapa obscura* Gmelin [= *Myadestes obscurus* (Gmelin)].
>
> *Myadestes obscurus* var. *occidentalis* Stejneger, 1882, Proc. U. S. Natl. Mus. 4: 371. (Tonila, Jalisco.)

Habitat.—Pine-Oak Forest, Montane Evergreen Forest, Tropical Lowland Evergreen Forest (900–3050 m; Subtropical Zone).

Distribution.—*Resident* from southeastern Sonora, southern Chihuahua, Sinaloa, Durango, Nayarit (including the Tres Marias Islands), Jalisco, Guanajuato, San Luis Potosí, central Nuevo León, and southern Tamaulipas south through the mountains of Mexico, Guatemala, Belize, and El Salvador to central Honduras (east to the Comayagua Valley).

Notes.—The merger of *Phaeornis* into *Myadestes* forced the change in the name of this species from *M. obscurus* Lafresnaye to *M. occidentalis* because *M. obscurus* (Gmelin) has priority (Pratt 1982).

Myadestes elisabeth (Lembeye). Cuban Solitaire.

> *Muscicapa elisabeth* Lembeye, 1850, Aves Isla Cuba, p. 39, pl. 5, fig. 3. (Cuba.)

Habitat.—Pine Forest, Tropical Lowland Evergreen Forest (0–2000 m).

Distribution.—*Resident* in the mountains of western Cuba (Pinar del Río province) and eastern Cuba (Oriente province), and (formerly) on the Isle of Pines (vicinity of Ciénaga de Lanier, now extirpated).

Myadestes genibarbis Swainson. Rufous-throated Solitaire.

> *Myidestes* [sic] *genibarbis* Swainson, 1838, Flycatchers, Ornithol. 10, *in* Jardine, Naturalists' Libr. 21: 134, pl. 13. (Africa or India, error = Martinique.)

Habitat.—Tropical Lowland Evergreen Forest, Montane Evergreen Forest (0–1800 m).

Distribution.—*Resident* [*genibarbis* group] on Jamaica and Hispaniola, and in the Lesser Antilles (Dominica, Martinique, St. Lucia); and [*sibilans* group] in the southern Lesser Antilles (St. Vincent).

Notes.—Groups: *M. genibarbis* [Rufous-throated Solitaire] and *M. sibilans* Lawrence, 1878 [St. Vincent Solitaire].

Myadestes melanops Salvin. Black-faced Solitaire.

> *Myiadestes melanops* Salvin, 1865, Proc. Zool. Soc. London (1864), p. 580, pl. 36. (Tucurrique, Costa Rica.)

Habitat.—Montane Evergreen Forest (750–2800 m) (upper Tropical and Subtropical zones).

Distribution.—*Resident* in the mountains of Costa Rica (more commonly on the Caribbean slope) and western Panama (east on both slopes to Veraguas; sight reports from western Coclé).

Winters also to lower elevations (regularly to 450 m, and occasionally to 100 m) in Costa Rica.

Notes.—*Myadestes melanops, M. coloratus,* and the Andean *M. ralloides* (d'Orbigny, 1840) [Andean Solitaire] constitute a superspecies (Sibley and Monroe 1990); they were treated as conspecific by Ripley *in* Mayr and Paynter (1964).

Myadestes coloratus Nelson. Varied Solitaire.

> *Myadestes coloratus* Nelson, 1912, Smithson. Misc. Collect. 60(3): 23. (Mount Pirri, at 5,000 feet altitude, near head of Rio Limon, eastern Panama.)

Habitat.—Montane Evergreen Forest (800–2200 m; upper Tropical and Subtropical zones).

Distribution.—*Resident* in extreme eastern Panama (Cerro Tacarcuna, Cerro Pirre, Altos de Nique, and Cerro Quía, in eastern Darién) and extreme northwestern Colombia.

Notes.—See comments under *M. melanops.*

Myadestes unicolor Sclater. Slate-colored Solitaire.

> *Myiadestes unicolor* Sclater, 1857, Proc. Zool. Soc. London (1856), p. 299. (Cordova [= Córdoba] in the State of Vera Cruz, Southern Mexico.)

Habitat.—Montane Evergreen Forest, Pine-Oak Forest (900–1500 m; upper Tropical and Subtropical zones, reaching lower Tropical Zone in winter).

Distribution.—*Resident* (some winter downslope movement) in the mountains from southeastern San Luis Potosí, Hidalgo, Puebla, northern and southeastern Oaxaca, and Veracruz south through Chiapas, Guatemala, northern El Salvador, and Honduras to north-central Nicaragua.

Myadestes myadestinus (Stejneger). Kamao.

> *Phaeornis myadestina* Stejneger, 1887, Proc. U. S. Natl. Mus. 10: 90. (Kauai Island, Hawaiian Archipelago.)

Habitat.—Forest.

Distribution.—*Resident* (possibly extinct; not seen since Hurricane Iniki in 1992) in the Hawaiian Islands on Kauai.

Notes.—This and the following three species were formerly (e.g., Ripley *in* Mayr and Paynter 1964) recognized as a single species (*Phaeornis obscurus,* [Hawaiian Thrush]), but differences in vocalizations and morphology among the living forms indicate that three or four species existed in the complex; they collectively constitute a superspecies (Pratt 1982).

†*Myadestes woahensis* (Bloxam). Amaui.

> *Turdus woahensis* Bloxam *in* Wilson and Evans, 1899, Aves Hawaiienses, introd., p. xiii. (Oahu.)

Habitat.—Forest.

Distribution.—EXTINCT. Formerly *resident* in the Hawaiian Islands on Oahu.

Notes.—Pratt (1982) considered this form, for which the specimens were then thought to have been lost, to be of uncertain validity. Olson (1996) has recently located the two specimens on which the type description was almost certainly based and regards them as representing, at best, a subspecies of *M. lanaiensis.* He also showed why the traditional citation, "*Phaeornis oahensis* Wilson and Evans, 1899 . . ." should be replaced as indicated above. See comments under *M. myadestinus.*

Myadestes lanaiensis (Wilson). Olomao.

> *Phaeornis lanaiensis* Wilson, 1891, Ann. Mag. Nat. Hist. (6)7: 460. (Lanai.)

Habitat.—Forest.

Distribution.—*Resident* (possibly extinct) in the Hawaiian Islands on Molokai (not seen since mid-1980s) and (formerly) Lanai.

Notes.—See comments under *M. myadestinus* and *M. woahensis.*

Myadestes obscurus (Gmelin). Omao.

> *Muscicapa obscura* Gmelin, 1789, Syst. Nat. 1(2): 945. Based on the "Dusky Flycatcher" Latham, Gen. Synop. Birds 2(1): 344. (in insulis Sandwich = island of Hawaii.)

Habitat.—Forest, usually dense, native koa/ohia forest, more common at higher elevations, where also found disjunctly in subalpine or alpine scrub.
Distribution.—*Resident* in the Hawaiian Islands on Hawaii.
Notes.—See comments under *M. myadestinus.*

Myadestes palmeri Rothschild. Puaiohi.

Phaeornis palmeri Rothschild, 1893, Avifauna Laysan, p. 67. (Halemanu, Kauai.)

Habitat.—Ravines in dense ohia forest.
Distribution.—*Resident* in the Hawaiian Islands on Kauai, where surviving in small numbers in the Alakai Swamp region.
Notes.—Also known as Small Kauai Thrush.

Genus CATHARUS Bonaparte

Catharus Bonaparte, 1850, Consp. Gen. Avium 1(2): 278. Type, by monotypy, *Turdus immaculatus* Bonaparte = *Turdus aurantiirostris* Hartlaub.

Notes.—See comments under *Hylocichla.*

Catharus gracilirostris Salvin. Black-billed Nightingale-Thrush.

Catharus gracilirostris Salvin, 1865, Proc. Zool. Soc. London (1864), p. 580. (Volcán de Cartago, Costa Rica.)

Habitat.— Montane Evergreen Forest, Elfin Forest, Second-growth Scrub (1800–3500 m; upper Subtropical and Temperate zones).
Distribution.—*Resident* in the mountains of Costa Rica (Cordillera Central and Cordillera de Talamanca) and extreme western Panama (Chiriquí).

Catharus aurantiirostris (Hartlaub). Orange-billed Nightingale-Thrush.

Turdus aurantiirostris Hartlaub, 1850, Rev. Mag. Zool. (2)1: 158. (Venezuela = Caracas.)

Habitat.—Montane Evergreen Forest Edge, Tropical Lowland Evergreen Forest Edge, Secondary Forest, Pine-Oak Forest, Tropical Deciduous Forest (400–2300 m; upper Tropical and Subtropical zones).
Distribution.—*Resident* [*aurantiirostris* group] from Sinaloa, southwestern Chihuahua, Durango, Nayarit, Jalisco, Guanajuato, southeastern San Luis Potosí and southwestern Tamaulipas south through Middle America (except the Yucatan Peninsula and Belize) to central Costa Rica (Pacific slope south to near Panama border), and in northern Colombia, northern Venezuela, and Trinidad; and [*griseiceps* group] in southwestern Costa Rica, western Panama (Chiriquí, Veraguas, western Coclé, and Azuero Peninsula), and western Colombia.
Ranges in winter mostly to lower elevations.
Notes.—Groups: *C. aurantiirostris* [Orange-billed Nightingale-Thrush] and *C. griseiceps* Salvin, 1866 [Gray-headed Nightingale-Thrush].

Catharus fuscater (Lafresnaye). Slaty-backed Nightingale-Thrush.

Myioturdus fuscater Lafresnaye, 1845, Rev. Zool. [Paris] 8: 341. (Bogotá, Colombia.)

Habitat.—Montane Evergreen Forest (800–2300 m; Subtropical Zone).
Distribution.—*Resident* [*hellmayri* group] in the mountains of Costa Rica (primarily on the Caribbean slope) and western Panama (Chiriquí, Bocas del Toro, and Veraguas); and [*fuscater* group] in eastern Panama (eastern Panamá province, eastern Darién), and in the Andes of South America from northern Colombia and northwestern Venezuela south locally on the western slope (evidently absent from much of Colombia) to southwestern Ecuador and on the eastern slope to northern Bolivia.
Notes.—Groups: *C. hellmayri* Berlepsch, 1902 [Black-backed Nightingale-Thrush] and *C. fuscater* [Slaty-backed Nightingale-Thrush].

Catharus occidentalis Sclater. Russet Nightingale-Thrush.

> *Catharus occidentalis* Sclater, 1859, Proc. Zool. Soc. London, p. 323. (Western Mexico, Oaxaca, Totontepec = Totontepec, Oaxaca.)

Habitat.—Pine-Oak Forest, Montane Evergreen Forest (1500–3700 m; Subtropical and lower Temperate zones).

Distribution.—*Resident* from western Chihuahua, eastern Sinaloa, Durango, Nayarit, Michoacán, Guanajuato, eastern Coahuila, southern Nuevo León, southwestern Tamaulipas, and eastern San Luis Potosí south to west-central Veracruz and central Oaxaca (east to Mount Zempoaltepec and the Río Molino areas).

Notes.—See comments under *C. frantzii*. The northwestern Mexican populations were formerly (A.O.U. 1983) recognized as a group, *C. olivascens* Nelson, 1899.

Catharus frantzii Cabanis. Ruddy-capped Nightingale-Thrush.

> *Catharus Frantzii* Cabanis, 1861, J. Ornithol. 8 (1860): 323. (Volcán de Irazú, Costa Rica.)

Habitat.—Montane Evergreen Forest, Pine-Oak Forest (1200–3100 m; Subtropical and lower Temperate zones).

Distribution.—*Resident* in the mountains from western Jalisco, Michoacán, southeastern San Luis Potosí and Hidalgo south through Middle America (except the Yucatan Peninsula and Belize) to western Panama (western Chiriquí).

Notes.—Formerly regarded as a race of *C. occidentalis* (e.g., Ripley *in* Mayr and Paynter 1964), but the two species are quite distinct and widely sympatric in central Mexico (Rowley and Orr 1964).

Catharus mexicanus (Bonaparte). Black-headed Nightingale-Thrush.

> *Malacocychla mexicana* Bonaparte, 1856, C. R. Acad. Sci. Paris 43: 998. (Jalapa, Veracruz, Mexico.)

Habitat.—Montane Evergreen Forest, Tropical Lowland Evergreen Forest (600–1800 m; Tropical and Subtropical zones).

Distribution.—*Resident* in Tamaulipas, Hidalgo, Veracruz, México, Puebla, northern and southeastern Oaxaca, Chiapas, eastern Guatemala, Honduras, Nicaragua (north-central highlands, and locally in Caribbean lowlands), Costa Rica, and western Panama (east to Veraguas).

Catharus dryas (Gould). Spotted Nightingale-Thrush.

> *Malacocichla dryas* Gould, 1855, Proc. Zool. Soc. London (1854), p. 285, pl. 75. (Guatemala.)

Habitat.—Montane Evergreen Forest (700–2300 m; upper Tropical and Subtropical zones).

Distribution.—*Resident* in the mountains of southeastern Oaxaca (Sierra Madre de Chiapas), Chiapas, Guatemala, El Salvador, and Honduras (east to the Tegucigalpa region); and in South America in the Western Andes of Ecuador and in the Eastern Andes from northwestern Venezuela and northern Colombia south to northern Argentina.

Catharus fuscescens (Stephens). Veery.

> *Turdus Fuscescens* Stephens, 1817, in Shaw's Gen. Zool. 10(1): 182. (Pensylvania.)

Habitat.—Poplar, aspen, or swampy forest, especially in more open areas with shrubby understory, also in second growth, willow or alder thickets near water; in migration, primarily deciduous forest and woodland with dense undergrowth.

Distribution.—*Breeds* from southern interior (rarely southwestern) British Columbia, central Alberta, central Saskatchewan, southern Manitoba, central Ontario, south-central Quebec (including Magdalen and possibly also Anticosti islands), New Brunswick, Prince

Edward Island, Nova Scotia, and southwestern Newfoundland south to central Oregon, northeastern Nevada, northern Utah, south-central Colorado, northeastern South Dakota, Iowa, central Illinois, north-central Indiana, and central Ohio, in the mountains through West Virginia, western and central Maryland, eastern Kentucky, western and central Virginia, eastern Tennessee, and western North Carolina to northwestern Georgia, and in the Atlantic region to eastern Pennsylvania, central New Jersey, the Maryland Piedmont, and the District of Columbia; also in east-central Arizona (rarely in Springerville area) and (probably) northern New Mexico.

Winters in south-central Brazil (Pará, Mato Grosso) and perhaps southeastern Brazil. One December specimen from Louisiana, an early January record (photograph) from Connecticut, and a December sight record for Ontario; otherwise, no documented winter records for Northern Hemisphere.

Migrates primarily through the southeastern United States west to the Rocky Mountains, eastern New Mexico, and central and southern Texas, and through eastern Mexico (recorded Veracruz, Chiapas, Yucatán, Cayos Arcas off Campeche, and Cozumel Island off Quintana Roo), northern Guatemala (Tikal), northern Honduras (Bay Islands), Costa Rica (Caribbean lowlands and San José, mainly in fall), Panama (rare but regular in fall in Caribbean lowlands, casually on Pacific slope), islands of the western Caribbean Sea (Providencia, San Andrés), Cuba, the Cayman Islands, Jamaica, the Bahamas, Colombia, Venezuela, Guyana, and northern Brazil.

Casual or accidental in extreme southeastern Alaska (Hyder), California, Arizona (elsewhere), eastern Peru, central Bolivia, Chile, the British Isles, and Sweden; a sight report for the Virgin Islands (St. John) and St. Kitts.

Notes.—*Catharus fuscescens* and the following four species were formerly included in the genus *Hylocichla* (e.g., Hellmayr 1934, A.O.U. 1957).

Catharus minimus (Lafresnaye). Gray-cheeked Thrush.

> *Turdus minimus* Lafresnaye, 1848, Rev. Zool. [Paris] 11, p. 5. (ad Bogotam, in Nova-Granada = Bogotá, Colombia.)

Habitat.—Stunted boreal coniferous forest (primarily spruce), tall scrub in taiga, willow-alder scrub in tundra; in migration and winter, a variety of wooded habitats, primarily broadleaf forest and woodland.

Distribution.—*Breeds* from northeastern Siberia (Chukotski Peninsula and Anadyrland), northern Alaska, northern Yukon, northern Mackenzie, southern Keewatin, northern Quebec, Labrador, and Newfoundland south to southern Alaska (west to the Alaska Peninsula and Kodiak Island, possibly also on St. Lawrence Island in the Bering Sea), northwestern British Columbia, southern Mackenzie, northern Alberta (probably), northeastern Saskatchewan, northern Manitoba, extreme northern Ontario, central Quebec, Newfoundland, and St. Pierre and Miquelon.

Winters rarely in Panama, primarily on the Caribbean slope, and in South America east of the Andes in Colombia, Venezuela, Trinidad, Guyana, and northwestern Brazil. Limits of winter distribution in South America poorly known. Casual in Costa Rica. One December specimen record for Ontario; other winter reports from North America are unsubstantiated.

Migrates primarily through eastern North America west to eastern Montana, the Great Plains and central Texas (casually to Wyoming and eastern Colorado), the Bahamas, and Greater Antilles, less frequently through the Swan Islands and southern Central America (Costa Rica and Panama, most commonly in fall), and rarely through southern Mexico (recorded Tabasco, Chiapas, Campeche, and Cozumel Island off Quintana Roo), Guatemala (Petén), Belize (including Half Moon Cay), and northern Honduras (including the Bay Islands).

Casual or accidental in southern British Columbia, Oregon, California (primarily the Farallon Islands), Arizona (Chiricahua Mountains), New Mexico (Clayton), northeastern Keewatin, Clipperton Island (sight reports), Martinique, Guadeloupe, eastern Peru, Greenland, the British Isles, and continental Europe (some records may pertain to *C. bicknelli*); sight reports for the Aleutian Islands (Shemya) and Washington.

Notes.—See comments under *C. fuscescens* and *C. bicknelli*.

Catharus bicknelli (Ridgway). Bicknell's Thrush.

Hylocichla aliciae bicknelli Ridgway, 1882, Proc. U. S. Natl. Mus. 4, p. 377. (near the summit of Slide Mountain, Ulster County, New York.)

Habitat.—Stunted deciduous and coniferous forest, often near mountain-tops; in migration and winter, a variety of wooded habitats, primarily broadleaf forest and woodland.

Distribution.—*Breeds* (at least formerly) in southern Quebec (including the Magdalen Islands), the Maritime Provinces, eastern New York (Catskill and Adirondack mountains), western Massachusetts, central and northern Vermont, New Hampshire, and central Maine.

Winters in Cuba, Hispaniola, and Puerto Rico, probably elsewhere in the mountains of the Greater Antilles.

Migrates through the eastern United States east of the Appalachians; recorded from southern New England south to South Carolina, the Bahama Islands, and Bermuda.

Notes.—Ouellet (1993) showed that *C. bicknelli* is best treated as a species distinct from *C. minimus,* differing in vocalizations, morphology, breeding habitat, migration routes, and winter range. See comments under *C. fuscescens.*

Catharus ustulatus (Nuttall). Swainson's Thrush.

Turdus ustulatus Nuttall, 1840, Man. Ornithol. U. S. Can. (ed. 2) 1: vi, 400, 830. (forests of the Oregon = Fort Vancouver, Washington.)

Habitat.—Dense scrub, coniferous woodland (especially spruce) and aspen-poplar forest with dense undergrowth, second growth, and willow or alder thickets; in migration and winter, a variety of wooded habitats, primarily broadleaf forest and woodland.

Distribution.—*Breeds* [*swainsoni* group] from western and central Alaska, central Yukon and western Mackenzie south to southwestern and south-coastal Alaska (west to the base of the Alaska Peninsula), east-central California, central Nevada, central Arizona, northern New Mexico, and east to central Montana, southwestern South Dakota, eastern Wyoming, extreme northwestern Nebraska, and from southern Mackenzie, northern Saskatchewan, north-central Manitoba, northern Ontario, central Quebec, southern Labrador, and Newfoundland south to southwestern and central Saskatchewan, southern Manitoba, northern Minnesota, northern Wisconsin, northern Michigan, southern Ontario, southern Quebec, southern New York, northern Pennsylvania, and Massachusetts, also in eastern West Virginia, western Virginia (Mount Rogers), and (formerly) western Maryland; and [*ustulatus* group] humid coastal region from southeastern Alaska south to southern California, and inland to central Washington, central Oregon, and eastern California.

Winters [*ustulatus* group] mostly from Nayarit and southern Tamaulipas (casually from California, southern Texas, and the Gulf coast) south through Middle America to Panama; and [*swainsoni* group] primarily in South America east to Guyana and western Brazil, and south to northwestern Argentina.

Migrates [*swainsoni* group] through southern Canada, the United States (less commonly in southwestern portion) and Middle America (rare in Baja California and northwestern Mexico), less frequently through the Bahamas, western Cuba, the Isle of Pines, Hispaniola, Jamaica, the Cayman and Swan islands, and Isla Providencia (in the western Caribbean Sea).

Casual or accidental [*swainsoni* group] on Meighen Island (Franklin District), in the Revillagigedo Islands (Socorro Island; sight report), and in Bermuda, Iceland, the British Isles, continental Europe, and the Ukraine.

Notes.—Groups: *C. swainsoni* (Tschudi, 1845) [Olive-backed Thrush] and *C. ustulatus* [Russet-backed Thrush]. See comments under *C. fuscescens.*

Catharus guttatus (Pallas). Hermit Thrush.

Muscicapa guttata Pallas, 1811, Zoogr. Rosso-Asiat. 1: 465. (in insulis Americae vicinis praesertim Kadiak = Kodiak Island, Alaska.)

Habitat.—Open coniferous and mixed coniferous-deciduous forest and forest edge, and dry sandy and sparse jack-pine, less frequently in deciduous forest and thickets; in migration and winter, also chaparral, riparian woodland, arid pine-oak association, tall desert-scrub, and suburbs with extensive shrub layer.

Distribution.—*Breeds* from western and central Alaska, southern Yukon, southern Mackenzie, northern Saskatchewan, northern Manitoba, northern Ontario, central Quebec, southern Labrador, and Newfoundland south to southern Alaska (west to the Alaska Peninsula, and Shumagin and Kodiak islands), in the mountains to south-central and eastern California (to Santa Rosa and Clark mountains), southern Nevada, central and southeastern Arizona, southern New Mexico, and extreme western Texas, and east of the Rockies to southwestern and central Alberta, central Saskatchewan, southern Manitoba, north-central and northeastern Minnesota, central Wisconsin, central Michigan, southern Ontario, southeastern Ohio, central Pennsylvania, eastern West Virginia, western Virginia (Mount Rogers), western Maryland, eastern Tennessee, western North Carolina, southern New Jersey, and southern New York (including Long Island); also isolated breeding in the Black Hills of southwestern South Dakota.

Winters from southwestern British Columbia, the northern United States, southern Ontario, and New England (casually or irregularly in the northern portions of the breeding range) south to southern Baja California (including islands), through Mexico (mostly in the interior, not recorded Yucatan Peninsula) to Guatemala and El Salvador, and to southern Texas, the Gulf coast, southern Florida, and the northern Bahamas (south to New Providence and Cat Island).

Casual or accidental on Southampton Island (The Post) and Bermuda, and in Iceland, the British Isles, Sweden, Germany, and Luxembourg.

Notes.—See comments under *C. fuscescens*.

Genus *HYLOCICHLA* Baird

Hylocichla Baird, 1864, Rev. Amer. Birds 1: 12. Type, by original designation, *Turdus mustelinus* Gmelin.

Notes.—*Hylocichla* was formerly considered closer to *Turdus* than to *Catharus* (Dilger 1956, Bourns 1967), but recent studies (Hendrickson and Yow 1973, Avise et al. 1980, Winker and Rappole 1988) show that it is closer to *Catharus*. Whether the distinctive morphology of *Hylocichla* (Gibson et al. 1976) warrants recognition as a genus is controversial; see Winker and Rappole (1988) for reasons for merging *Hylocichla* into *Catharus*.

Hylocichla mustelina (Gmelin). Wood Thrush.

Turdus mustelinus Gmelin, 1789, Syst. Nat. 1(2): 817. Based on the "Tawny Thrush" Latham, Gen. Synop. Birds 2(1): 29. (in Noveboraco = New York.)

Habitat.—Deciduous forest and woodland, locally in dense second-growth, mixed woodland, and parks and suburbs with dense shrub layer; in migration and winter, a variety of wooded habitats, primarily broadleaf forest and woodland.

Distribution.—*Breeds* from southeastern North Dakota, central and eastern Minnesota, northern Wisconsin, northern Michigan, southern Ontario, southwestern Quebec, northern Vermont, central New Hampshire, southwestern Maine, southern New Brunswick, and western Nova Scotia south to east-central Texas, the Gulf coast, and northern Florida, and west to eastern South Dakota, central Nebraska, central Kansas, and eastern Oklahoma; casual breeding to southern Manitoba, southwestern North Dakota, and central South Dakota.

Winters from southern Louisiana (casual) and southern (rarely eastern) Texas south through eastern Mexico (including the Yucatan Peninsula and islands) and Middle America (primarily Caribbean slope, but recorded in El Salvador and rarely on the Pacific slope from southeastern Oaxaca southward) to Panama (most common in Bocas del Toro and Chiriquí) and northwestern Colombia (Chocó).

Migrates casually through Cuba, the Bahama Islands (New Providence, Grand Bahama, Cay Lobos), and the Cayman Islands.

Casual in western North America from Oregon, Utah, Montana, Saskatchewan, and Manitoba south to California, Arizona, and New Mexico, also in Prince Edward Island; a sight report for Idaho. Accidental in Bermuda and Puerto Rico, and in Curaçao, Guyana, Iceland, the British Isles, and the Azores.

Genus *TURDUS* Linnaeus

Turdus Linnaeus, 1758, Syst. Nat. (ed. 10) 1: 168. Type, by subsequent designation (G. R. Gray, 1840), *Turdus viscivorus* Linnaeus.

Mimocichla [subgenus] Sclater, 1859, Proc. Zool. Soc. London, p. 336. Type, by subsequent designation (Baird, 1864), *Turdus rubripes* Temminck = *Turdus plumbeus* Linnaeus.

Notes.—See comments under *Hylocichla*.

Turdus merula Linnaeus. Eurasian Blackbird.

Turdus Merula Linnaeus, 1758, Syst. Nat. (ed. 10) 1: 170. (in Europæ sylvis = Sweden.)

Habitat—Woodland, forest, scrub, and gardens.

Distribution.—*Resident* (or partly migratory) [*merula* group] virtually throughout the Palearctic; and [*simillimus* group] in India and Southeast Asia.

Accidental [*merula* group] in Quebec (specimen, Outremont, island of Montreal, 23 November 1970; McNeil and Cyr 1971). The origin of this individual has been questioned (DeBenedictis 1991).

Introduced and established [*merula* group] in Australia and New Zealand, and on associated islands.

Notes.—Also known as European Blackbird and, in Old World literature, the Blackbird. Groups: *T. merula* [Eurasian Blackbird] and *T. simillimus* Jerdon, 1839 [Nilgiri Blackbird].

Turdus obscurus Gmelin. Eyebrowed Thrush.

Turdus obscurus Gmelin, 1789, Syst. Nat. 1(2): 816. Based on the "Dark Thrush" Latham, Gen. Synop. Birds 2(1): 31. (in Sibiriae silvis, ultra lacum Baical = Lake Baikal.)

Habitat.—Dense coniferous and mixed woodland, usually near water; in migration and winter, also deciduous woodland, farmland, and scrub.

Distribution.—*Breeds* from northern Siberia and Kamchatka south to northern Mongolia, Sakhalin, the Kuril Islands, and Japan (Honshu).

Winters from India, Southeast Asia, southeastern China, and Taiwan south to the Andaman Islands, Java, Borneo, the Philippines, and Palau Islands.

Migrates through Mongolia, Manchuria, eastern China, Korea, Japan, and the Ryukyu Islands, to the western Aleutians (Near Islands), and casually east and north to the Pribilofs and Alaska mainland (Wales, Barrow).

Casual in western Europe.

Notes.—Also known as Eye-browed Thrush.

Turdus naumanni Temminck. Dusky Thrush.

Turdus naumanni Temminck, 1820, Man. Ornithol. (ed. 2) 1: 170. (en Silésie et en Autriche. . .en Hongrie, etc., error = Siberia.)

Habitat.—Open coniferous and mixed forest, forest edge, taiga, and deciduous scrub; in migration and winter, fields, farmland, and open woodland.

Distribution.—*Breeds* [*eunomus* group] from northern Siberia east to Kamchatka; and [*naumanni* group] from southern Siberia east to Lake Baikal, northern Manchuria, Amurland, and the Sea of Okhotsk.

Winters [*eunomus* group] from Japan and the Ryukyu Islands south to southern China and Taiwan, rarely west to Southeast Asia and India; and [*naumanni* group] from southern Manchuria, northern China, and Korea south to eastern China, rarely to Taiwan and the Ryukyu Islands.

Casual [*eunomus* group] in Alaska (western Aleutians, St. Lawrence Island, Barrow), British Columbia (Langley), the British Isles, western Europe and the Commander Islands. Accidental [*eunomus* group] in southeastern Alaska (Petersburg); and [*naumanni* group] in Great Britain; a sight report from the central Aleutians (Adak).

Notes.—Groups: *T. eunomus* Temminck, 1831 [Dusky Thrush], and *T. naumanni* [Naumann's Thrush].

Turdus pilaris Linnaeus. Fieldfare.

Turdus pilaris Linnaeus, 1758, Syst. Nat. (ed. 10) 1: 168. (in Europa = Sweden.)

Habitat.—Coniferous and mixed woodland edge (birch, pine, spruce), brushy and rocky slopes, and birch, alder, or willow thickets; in migration and winter, primarily open country and agricultural areas bordering wooded areas.

Distribution.—*Breeds* from southern Greenland, Scandinavia, northern Russia, and northern Siberia south to central Europe, central Russia, southern Siberia, and Lake Baikal, occasionally in the Faeroe Islands.

Winters from Iceland, the Faeroe Islands, British Isles, southern Scandinavia, and central Europe south to the Mediterranean region, Asia Minor, Iran, Turkestan, and northwestern India, casually to the eastern Atlantic islands and northern Africa.

Casual or accidental in Alaska (Point Barrow, St. Lawrence Island), Keewatin (Foxe Basin), Franklin District (Jens Munk Island), Ontario (Long Point, Toronto), Quebec (Rigaud), Newfoundland, New Brunswick (Caraquet), Massachusetts (Concord), Connecticut (Stamford), and Minnesota (Cook County); sight reports for Nova Scotia, New York, and Delaware.

Turdus iliacus Linnaeus. Redwing.

Turdus iliacus Linnaeus, 1766, Syst. Nat. (ed. 12) 1: 292. (in Europa = Sweden.)

Habitat.—Coniferous and mixed forest and woodland (birch, spruce, pine), taiga, and damp thickets; in winter, moist agricultural fields, pastures, and lawns mixed with wooded areas and open woodland.

Distribution.—*Breeds* from Iceland across northern Eurasia to central Siberia, and *winters* south to the British Isles, continental Europe, and the Mediterranean region, in migration casually to Greenland.

Casual in Newfoundland at St. Anthony (25 June-11 July 1950, photograph; Montevecchi et al. 1981) and Sable Island (25 November-23 December 1989, photograph; 1990, Amer. Birds 44: 223, 231); a report with photographs (since lost) from New York (Jamaica Bay, Long Island, 1959); a sight report from Newfoundland (St. John's).

Notes.—*Turdus iliacus* is sometimes known as *T. musicus* Linnaeus, 1758, but the latter name has been suppressed by the International Commission on Zoological Nomenclature.

Turdus nigrescens Cabanis. Sooty Robin.

Turdus nigrescens Cabanis, 1861, J. Ornithol. 8 (1860): 324. (Volcán de Irazú, Costa Rica.)

Habitat.—Montane Evergreen Forest Edge, Semihumid/Humid Montane Scrub, Second-growth Scrub (2150–3500 m; Subtropical and Temperate zones).

Distribution.—*Resident* in the mountains of Costa Rica (cordilleras Central and de Talamanca) and extreme western Panama (western Chiriquí).

Notes.—Also known as Sooty Thrush. Ridgely and Tudor (1989) and Sibley and Monroe (1990) used "Thrush" instead of "Robin" for this species and several other New World species of *Turdus*. Because "Robin" is applied to many species outside the genus *Turdus*, including species outside the Turdidae, we favor retaining long-established English names.

Turdus infuscatus (Lafresnaye). Black Robin.

Merula infuscata Lafresnaye, 1844, Rev. Zool. [Paris] 7: 41. (du Mexique = Mexico.)

Habitat.—Montane Evergreen Forest, Pine-Oak Forest (900–3100 m; Subtropical and Temperate zones).

Distribution.—*Resident* in the mountains from Guerrero, México, Hidalgo, eastern San

Luis Potosí and southwestern Tamaulipas south through Veracruz, Oaxaca, Chiapas, Guatemala, and El Salvador to central Honduras.

Notes.—Also known as Black Thrush. *Turdus infuscatus* and the South American *T. serranus* Tschudi, 1844 [Glossy-black Thrush], constitute a superspecies. See comments under *T. nigrescens.*

Turdus plebejus Cabanis. Mountain Robin.

Turdus plebejus Cabanis, 1861, J. Ornithol. 8 (1860): 323. (Costa Rica.)

Habitat.—Montane Evergreen Forest, Pine-Oak Forest, Secondary Forest (900–3500 m; Subtropical and lower Temperate zones).

Distribution.—*Resident* in the mountains from southeastern Oaxaca and Chiapas south through Guatemala, El Salvador, Honduras, north-central Nicaragua, and Costa Rica to western Panama (Chiriquí and Bocas del Toro). Some down-slope movement during peak of wet season in Costa Rica and probably elsewhere.

Notes.—Also known as Mountain Thrush and American Mountain Thrush. See comments under *T. nigrescens.*

Turdus fumigatus Lichtenstein. Cocoa Thrush.

Turdus fumigatus Lichtenstein, 1823, Verz. Doubl. Zool. Mus. Berlin, p. 38. (Brazil = Rio Espirito Santo.)

Habitat.—Gallery Forest, Tropical Lowland Evergreen Forest (0–1400 m; Tropical and lower Subtropical zones).

Distribution.—*Resident* [*personus* group] in the Lesser Antilles (St. Vincent and Grenada); [*hauxwelli* group] Amazonia from southeastern Colombia and southern Venezuela south to central Bolivia and western Brazil; and [*fumigatus* group] in South America from northern Venezuela, Trinidad, and the Guianas south to Amazonian and eastern Brazil.

Notes.—Groups: *T. personus* (Barbour, 1911) [Lesser Antillean Thrush], *T. hauxwelli* Lawrence, 1869 [Hauxwell's Thrush], and *T. fumigatus* [Cocoa Thrush]. Species limits in this group are uncertain; see summaries in Snow (1985) and Ridgely and Tudor (1989). *Turdus fumigatus* is sometimes (e.g., Ripley *in* Mayr and Paynter 1964, Meyer de Schauensee 1966, 1970) considered conspecific with *T. obsoletus,* but the two differ in voice and habitat; the two species appear to constitute a superspecies (Sibley and Monroe 1990).

Turdus obsoletus Lawrence. Pale-vented Thrush.

Turdus obsoletus Lawrence, 1862, Ann. Lyc. Nat. Hist. N. Y. 7: 470. (Atlantic side of the Isthmus of Panama, along the line of the Panama Railroad = Canal Zone.)

Habitat.—Montane Evergreen Forest, Tropical Lowland Evergreen Forest, Secondary Forest (500–2900 m; Tropical and lower Subtropical zones).

Distribution.—*Resident* from central Costa Rica (Caribbean slope of Cordillera Central and Cordillera de Talamanca) south through Panama (locally in foothills east to the Canal area, and in eastern Darién) and western Colombia to western Ecuador.

Notes.—See comments under *T. fumigatus.*

Turdus grayi Bonaparte. Clay-colored Robin.

Turdus Grayi Bonaparte, 1838, Proc. Zool. Soc. London (1837), p. 118. (Guatamala = San Jose, Dept. Escuintla, Guatemala; Dickerman, 1981, Bull. Brit. Ornithol. Club 101: 285–289.)

Habitat.—Tropical Lowland Evergreen Forest Edge, Tropical Deciduous Forest, Secondary Forest (0–2500 m; Tropical and lower Subtropical zones).

Distribution.—*Resident* on Pacific slope from southeastern Oaxaca south, and on Gulf-Caribbean slope from central Nuevo León, Hidalgo, and San Luis Potosí south, along both slopes of Middle America to northern Colombia. Breeds casually in the Rio Grande Valley of Texas.

Winters rarely north to southern Texas (lower Rio Grande Valley)
Casual in south-central and coastal Texas.
Introduced elsewhere in Mexico (e.g., Acapulco, Guerrero).
Notes.—Also known as Clay-colored Thrush, Gray's Thrush, and Garden Thrush. See comments under *T. nigrescens.*

Turdus nudigenis Lafresnaye. Bare-eyed Robin.

Turdus nudigenis Lafresnaye, 1848, Rev. Zool. [Paris] 11: 4. (Caracas [Venezuela].)

Habitat.—Open forest and woodland, second growth, plantations, and gardens (Tropical and lower Subtropical zones).
Distribution.—*Resident* [*nudigenis* group] in the Lesser Antilles (Martinique, St. Lucia, St. Vincent, the Grenadines, and Grenada), and in South America from eastern Colombia, Venezuela (including Margarita and Patos islands), Tobago, Trinidad, and the Guianas south, east of the Andes, to northern Brazil; and [*maculirostris* group] western Ecuador and extreme northwestern Peru.
An attempted introduction on Barbados was unsuccessful.
Notes.—Also known as Bare-eyed Thrush, American Bare-eyed Thrush, Naked-eyed Thrush, and Yellow-eyed Thrush. The English name of *T. nudigenis* was changed from Bare-eyed Thrush of the A.O.U. (1983) to Bare-eyed Robin (A.O.U. 1985) to avoid confusion with the African species, *T. tephronotus,* also called Bare-eyed Thrush. Groups: *T. nudigenis* [Bare-eyed Robin] and *T. maculirostris* Berlepsch and Taczanowski, 1883 [Ecuadorian Robin]; the latter was treated as a species by Ridgely and Tudor (1989) and Sibley and Monroe (1990). See comments under *T. grayi.*

Turdus jamaicensis Gmelin. White-eyed Thrush.

Turdus jamaicensis Gmelin, 1789, Syst. Nat. 1(2): 809. Based on the "Jamaica Thrush" Latham, Gen. Synop. Birds 2(1): 20. (in Jamaica.)

Habitat.—Montane Evergreen Forest, Tropical Lowland Evergreen Forest, Secondary Forest (0–1800 m).
Distribution.—*Resident* on Jamaica.

Turdus assimilis Cabanis. White-throated Robin.

Turdus assimilis Cabanis, 1850, Mus. Heineanum 1: 4. (Xalapa = Jalapa, Veracruz.)

Habitat.—Montane Evergreen Forest, Tropical Lowland Evergreen Forest, Tropical Deciduous Forest (0–3100 m; Tropical and Subtropical zones).
Distribution.—*Resident* [*assimilis* group] from southeastern Sonora, southwestern Chihuahua, Sinaloa, western Durango, Nayarit, Jalisco, Michoacán, México, Hidalgo, southeastern San Luis Potosí and southern Tamaulipas south along both slopes of Middle America (absent from the Yucatan Peninsula) to central Panama (east to western Panamá province, including Isla Coiba); and [*daguae* group] in eastern Panama (eastern Darién), western Colombia, and western Ecuador.
Winters [presumably *personatus* group] to Canal area of Panama.
Accidental [*assimilis* group] in southern Texas (18–25 Feb. 1990, Cameron County; photos, Lasley and Krzywonski 1991, DeBenedictis 1992).
Notes.—Also known as White-throated Thrush. Groups: *T. assimilis* [White-throated Thrush] and *T. daguae* Berlepsch, 1897 [Dagua Thrush]. *Turdus assimilis* and the South American *T. albicollis* Vieillot, 1818 [White-necked Thrush], constitute a superspecies (Sibley and Monroe 1990). Many authors (e.g., Wetmore 1957, Wetmore et al. 1984, Ripley *in* Mayr and Paynter 1964) consider them conspecific, but see Monroe (1968) and Ridgely and Tudor (1989). See comments under *T. nigrescens.*

Turdus rufopalliatus Lafresnaye. Rufous-backed Robin.

Turdus rufo-palliatus Lafresnaye, 1840, Rev. Zool. [Paris] 3: 259. (al Monterey en Californie, error = Acapulco, Guerrero.)

Habitat.—[*rufopalliatus* group] Tropical Deciduous Forest, Gallery Forest (0–2500 m; Tropical and Subtropical zones); [*graysoni* group] Tropical Deciduous Forest.

Distribution.—*Resident* [*rufopalliatus* group] from southern Sonora south through Sinaloa, western Durango, Nayarit, Jalisco, Colima, Michoacán, México, Distrito Federal, Morelos, and Guerrero to western Puebla and Oaxaca (east to the Isthmus of Tehuantepec); and [*graysoni* group] in the Tres Marias Islands and, probably, coastal Nayarit (San Blas region).

Casual [*rufopalliatus* group] north to southern California (north to Orange and Inyo counties), southern Arizona (north to Phoenix area), southwestern New Mexico, and western Texas (Langtry, Falcon Dam).

Notes.—Also known as Rufous-backed Thrush. Phillips (1981) suggested that the two groups represent distinct species, *T. rufopalliatus* [Rufous-backed Robin] and *T. graysoni* (Ridgway, 1882) [Grayson's Robin], with the latter resident (rather than a casual vagrant) in coastal Nayarit and thus sympatric with the former. See comments under *T. nigrescens*.

Turdus rufitorques Hartlaub. Rufous-collared Robin.

Turdus (Merula) rufitorques Hartlaub, 1844, Rev. Zool. [Paris] 7: 214. (Guatemala.)

Habitat.—Montane Evergreen Forest, Pine-Oak Forest, Secondary Forest (1500–3300 m; Subtropical and lower Temperate zones).

Distribution.—*Resident* in the mountains of Chiapas, Guatemala, El Salvador, and (possibly as a vagrant only) western and central Honduras (east to Cerro Uyuca).

Notes.—*Turdus rufitorques* and *T. migratorius* appear to constitute a superspecies.

Turdus migratorius Linnaeus. American Robin.

Turdus migratorius Linnaeus, 1766, Syst. Nat. (ed. 12) 1: 292. Based mainly on "The Fieldfare of Carolina" Catesby, Nat. Hist. Carolina 1: 29, pl. 29. (in America septentrionali = South Carolina.)

Habitat.—Coniferous and deciduous woodland and edge, parks and suburbs with lawns; in winter, in a variety of habitats with at least some trees, primarily where fruiting trees and shrubs are present (Subtropical and Temperate zones).

Distribution.—*Breeds* [*migratorius* group] from western and northern Alaska, northern Yukon, northern Mackenzie, southern Keewatin, northern Manitoba, northern Ontario, northern Quebec, Labrador, and Newfoundland south to southern Alaska (west to the Alaska Peninsula and Kodiak Island), southern California (rarely southeastern desert regions), northern Baja California, southern Nevada, central and southeastern Arizona, northern Sonora, in the mountains of Mexico to central Oaxaca (west of the Isthmus of Tehuantepec) and west-central Veracruz, and to central and southern Texas, the Gulf coast, and (casually) central Florida.

Winters [*migratorius* group] from southern Alaska (casually) and southernmost Canada and northern United States south to southern Baja California (casually to Guadalupe Island), throughout Mexico (rarely to the Yucatan Peninsula, and Cozumel and Holbox islands) to Guatemala, and to southern Texas, the Gulf coast, southern Florida, Bermuda, and (at least irregularly) western Cuba, casually to the northern Bahama Islands (south to San Salvador).

Resident [*confinis* group] in the mountains of southern Baja California (Cape San Lucas district).

Casual or accidental [*migratorius* group] in the Pribilofs (St. Paul), Aleutians (Amchitka), Greenland, Iceland, the British Isles, and continental Europe; sight reports from Jamaica, Dominican Republic, Mona Island, and Puerto Rico.

Notes.—Formerly known in American literature as the Robin. Groups: *T. migratorius* [American Robin] and *T. confinis* Baird, 1864 [San Lucas Robin]. See comments under *T. rufitorques*.

Turdus swalesi (Wetmore). La Selle Thrush.

Haplocichla swalesi Wetmore, 1927, Proc. Biol. Soc. Wash. 40: 55. (Massif de la Selle, 6,000 ft., Haiti.)

Habitat.—Montane Evergreen Forest (1400–2100 m).
Distribution.—*Resident* in the mountains of Hispaniola.

Turdus aurantius Gmelin. White-chinned Thrush.

Turdus aurantius Gmelin, 1789, Syst. Nat. 1(2): 832. Based largely on "Le Merle de la Jamaique" Brisson, Ornithologie 2: 277. (in Jamaicae montibus silvosis = Jamaica.)

Habitat.—Montane Evergreen Forest, Tropical Lowland Evergreen Forest, Secondary Forest (0–1800 m).
Distribution.—*Resident* on Jamaica.

†*Turdus ravidus* (Cory). Grand Cayman Thrush.

Mimocichla ravida Cory, 1886, Auk 3: 499. (Island of Grand Cayman, West Indies.)

Habitat.—Woodland.
Distribution.—EXTINCT. Formerly *resident* on Grand Cayman, in the Cayman Islands. Last recorded in 1938 in the eastern part of the island; several recent thorough searches have had negative results.
Notes.—*Turdus ravidus* and *T. plumbeus* are sometimes placed in the genus *Mimocichla;* the two species appear to constitute a superspecies (Sibley and Monroe 1990).

Turdus plumbeus Linnaeus. Red-legged Thrush.

Turdus plumbeus Linnaeus, 1758, Syst. Nat. (ed. 10) 1: 169. Based on "The Red-leg'd Thrush" Catesby, Nat. Hist. Carolina 1: 30, pl. 30. (in America = Andros and Eleuthera islands, Bahamas.)

Habitat.—Tropical Deciduous Forest, Tropical Lowland Evergreen Forest, Montane Evergreen Forest, Secondary Forest (0–1200 m).
Distribution.—*Resident* [*plumbeus* group] in the northern Bahama Islands (south to Andros and Cat Island), Cuba (and nearby cays), the Isle of Pines, Cayman Islands (Cayman Brac, with reports from Grand Cayman based on an escaped individual), and (formerly) the Swan Islands (in the western Caribbean Sea); and [*ardosiaceus* group] in Hispaniola (including Gonâve, Tortue, and Saona islands), Puerto Rico, and Dominica (in the Lesser Antilles).
Notes.—Groups: *T. ardosiaceus* Vieillot, 1823 [Eastern Red-legged Thrush], and *T. plumbeus* [Western Red-legged Thrush]. See comments under *T. ravidus.*

Genus *CICHLHERMINIA* Bonaparte

Cichlherminia Bonaparte, 1854, C. R. Acad. Sci. Paris 38: 2. Type, by subsequent designation (G. R. Gray, 1855), *Turdus lherminieri* Lafresnaye.

Cichlherminia lherminieri (Lafresnaye). Forest Thrush.

Turdus L'Herminieri Lafresnaye, 1844, Rev. Zool. [Paris] 7: 167. (Guadeloupe.)

Habitat.—Tropical Lowland Evergreen Forest, Secondary Forest (0–1000 m).
Distribution.—*Resident* in the Lesser Antilles (Montserrat, Guadeloupe, Dominica, and St. Lucia).

Genus *IXOREUS* Bonaparte

Ixoreus Bonaparte, 1854, C. R. Acad. Sci. Paris 38: 3 (note). Type, by original designation, *Turdus naevius* Gmelin.

Hesperocichla Baird, 1864, Rev. Amer. Birds 1: 12. Type, by monotypy, *Turdus naevius* Gmelin.

Notes.—This genus and *Ridgwayia* are sometimes merged in the Old World genus *Zoothera* Vigors, 1832 (e.g., Ripley *in* Mayr and Paynter 1964).

Ixoreus naevius (Gmelin). Varied Thrush.

Turdus naevius Gmelin, 1789, Syst. Nat. 1(2): 817. Based on the "Spotted Thrush" Latham, Gen. Synop. Birds 2(1): 27. (in sinu Americae Natca = Nootka Sound, Vancouver Island, British Columbia.)

Habitat.—Humid coastal and interior montane coniferous forest, deciduous forest with dense understory (especially alder); in migration and winter, also open woodland and chaparral, but favors shady, cool areas.

Distribution.—*Breeds* from western and northern Alaska, northern Yukon, and northwestern and western Mackenzie south through central and southern Alaska (west to the base of the Alaska Peninsula and Kodiak Island), British Columbia (including the Queen Charlotte and Vancouver islands), west-central Alberta, northwestern Montana, northern Idaho, Washington, and Oregon (except southeastern portion) to extreme northwestern California (Del Norte and Humboldt counties), casually to west-central California (San Mateo and Santa Cruz counties).

Winters from southern Alaska (coastally west to Kodiak Island), coastal and southern British Columbia, northern Idaho, and western Montana (rarely) south through Washington, Oregon, Utah, and California to northern Baja California and Arizona.

Casual widely in eastern North America from southern Alberta, southern Saskatchewan, Manitoba, central Ontario, southwestern Quebec, Maine, New Brunswick, Prince Edward Island, and Nova Scotia south to New Mexico, Texas, Louisiana, Oklahoma, Kansas, Nebraska, Missouri, Illinois, Indiana, Ohio, Pennsylvania, West Virginia, Tennessee, Alabama, and in Atlantic coastal states from New Jersey south to southern Florida; also on Guadalupe Island, off southern Baja California. Accidental in Great Britain.

Genus *RIDGWAYIA* Stejneger

Ridgwayia Stejneger, 1883, Proc. U. S. Natl. Mus. 5 (1882): 460. Type, by original designation, *Turdus pinicola* Sclater.

Notes.—See comments under *Ixoreus*.

Ridgwayia pinicola (Sclater). Aztec Thrush.

Turdus pinicola Sclater, 1859, Proc. Zool. Soc. London, p. 334. (Pine-forests of the tableland above Jalapa, [Veracruz,] Southern Mexico.)

Habitat.—Pine-Oak Forest, Pine Forest (1850–3100 m; Subtropical and Temperate zones).

Distribution.—*Resident* in the mountains from southern Chihuahua and west-central Coahuila south through Sinaloa, Durango, Nayarit, Jalisco, Michoacán, Guerrero, the Distrito Federal, Hidalgo, and Puebla to west-central Veracruz and central Oaxaca (west of the Isthmus of Tehuantepec).

Casual in southeastern Arizona and western Texas (Chisos Mountains); sight reports for southeastern Texas (Port Aransas) and eastern San Luis Potosí (near El Naranjo).

Family **TIMALIIDAE**: Babblers

Notes.—DNA-DNA hybridization data (Sibley and Ahlquist 1990) suggest that the Timaliidae are more closely related to the Sylviidae than is indicated by their traditional placement next to the Turdidae. See comments under Sylviidae.

Genus *GARRULAX* Lesson

Garrulax Lesson, 1831, Traité Ornithol., livr. 8, p. 647. Type, by subsequent designation (Ripley, 1961), *Garrulax rufifrons* Lesson.

Garrulax pectoralis (Gould). Greater Necklaced Laughingthrush.

> *Ianthocincla pectoralis* Gould, 1836, Proc. Zool. Soc. London (1835), p. 186. (in Nepaliâ = Nepal.)

Habitat.—Lowland humid forest of monkeypod, hau, and kukui; in native range, forest and dense second-growth.

Distribution.—*Resident* from the Himalayan region of southwestern China and Nepal southeast to northern Burma, northern Thailand, northern Laos, and southeastern China (including Hainan).

Introduced and established in the Hawaiian Islands (possibly as early as 1920, on Kauai).

Notes.—Also known as Black-gorgeted Laughingthrush.

Garrulax canorus (Linnaeus). Hwamei.

> *Turdus Canorus* Linnaeus, 1758, Syst. Nat. (ed. 10) 1: 169. Based on "The Brown Indian Thrush" Edwards, Nat. Hist. Birds 4: 184, pl. 184, and Albin, Nat. Hist. Birds 3: 18, pl. 19. (in Benghala, China = Amoy, Fukien, China.)

Habitat.—Forest and scrub; in Hawaii, also wooded suburbs.

Distribution.—*Resident* from central to southeastern China (including Taiwan and Hainan).

Introduced and established in the Hawaiian Islands (in 1900), where common on Kauai, Maui, and Hawaii, and uncommon or local on Oahu and Molokai.

Notes.—Also known as Melodious Laughingthrush, Spectacled Laughingthrush, Hwamei Laughingthrush, Chinese Thrush, or Hwa-mei.

Genus *LEIOTHRIX* Swainson

> *Leiothrix* Swainson, 1832, in Swainson and Richardson, Fauna Bor.-Amer. 2 (1831): 233, 490. Type, by original designation, *Parus furcatus* Temm[inck]. Pl. Col. = *Sylvia lutea* Scopoli.

Leiothrix lutea (Scopoli). Red-billed Leiothrix.

> *Sylvia (lutea)* Scopoli, 1786, Del. Flor. Faun. Insubr., fasc. 2, p. 96. (China = mountains of Anhwei, China.)

Habitat.—Forest and dense second growth.

Distribution.—*Resident* in the Himalayas from Nepal and northern India east to northern Burma and central China.

Introduced and established in the Hawaiian Islands (in 1918, now common on Molokai, Maui, and Hawaii, formerly common but now rare on Kauai and Oahu).

Notes.—Also known as Pekin Nightingale, Pekin Robin, or Japanese Hillrobin.

Genus *CHAMAEA* Gambel

> *Chamæa* Gambel, 1847, Proc. Acad. Nat. Sci. Philadelphia 3: 154. Type, by original designation, *Parus fasciatus* Gambel.

Notes.—This genus was formerly placed in the monotypic family Chamaeidae; see Sibley and Ahlquist (1982b) for placement in the Timaliidae.

Chamaea fasciata (Gambel). Wrentit.

> *Parus fasciatus* Gambel, 1845, Proc. Acad. Nat. Sci. Philadelphia 2: 265. (California = Monterey.)

Habitat.—Chaparral, coastal sage scrub, and brushy areas, primarily in lowlands; locally in suburbs with dense shrub layer.

Distribution.—*Resident* in coastal regions from northwestern Oregon south to northwestern Baja California (south to lat. 30°N.), and in interior regions of northern and central California.

Family **ZOSTEROPIDAE**: White-eyes

Notes.—DNA-DNA hybridization data (Sibley and Ahlquist 1990) suggest that the Zosteropidae are more closely related to Sylviinae, Timaliidae, and Pycnonotidae than is indicated by their traditional placement near the Nectariniidae and Meliphagidae (the latter placed next to the Laniidae in our arrangement).

Genus *ZOSTEROPS* Vigors and Horsfield

Zosterops Vigors and Horsfield, 1826, Trans. Linn. Soc. London 15: 234. Type, by subsequent designation (Lesson, 1828), *Motacilla maderaspatana* Linnaeus.

Zosterops japonicus Temminck and Schlegel. Japanese White-eye.

Zosterops japonicus Temminck and Schlegel, 1847, in Siebold, Fauna Jpn., Aves, p. 57, pl. 22. (Japon = Decima, Nagasaki, Japan.)

Habitat.—Forest, second growth, and scrub, from sea level to the upper limit of forest, also cultivated lands and gardens.

Distribution.—*Resident* from eastern China, Taiwan, and Japan south to northern Indochina, southern China, Hainan, the northern Philippines, and the Ryukyu and Volcano islands.

Introduced and established in the Hawaiian Islands (in 1929, now widespread and common on the main islands from Kauai eastward).

Notes.—Also known as Chinese White-eye. *Zosterops japonicus* is sometimes regarded as conspecific with *Z. palpebrosus* (Temminck, 1824), of India and Southeast Asia, but the two species overlap in southern China.

Family **MIMIDAE**: Mockingbirds and Thrashers

Notes.—Morphological (Beecher 1953b) and biochemical (Stallcup 1961, Sibley and Ahlquist 1980, 1984, 1985, 1990) data support a close relationship between the Mimidae and Sturnidae, contrary to the traditional placement of the Mimidae near Turdidae or Troglodytidae.

Genus *DUMETELLA* Wood

Dumetella S. D. W.=C. T. Wood, 1837, Analyst 5: 206. Type, by monotypy, *Turdus felivox* Vieillot = *Muscicapa carolinensis* Linnaeus.
Lucar Coues, 1875, Proc. Acad. Nat. Sci. Philadelphia 27: 349. Type, by monotypy, *Muscicapa carolinensis* Linnaeus.

Notes.—See comments under *Melanoptila*.

Dumetella carolinensis (Linnaeus). Gray Catbird.

Muscicapa carolinensis Linnaeus, 1766, Syst. Nat. (ed. 12) 1: 328. Based mainly on "The Cat-Bird" Catesby, Nat. Hist. Carolina 1: 66, pl. 66. (in Carolina = Virginia.)

Habitat.—Thickets, dense brushy areas, undergrowth of forest edge, hedgerows, and suburbs with dense shrub layer.

Distribution.—*Breeds* from southern British Columbia (except Vancouver Island), central Alberta, central Saskatchewan, southern Manitoba, south-central Ontario, southern Quebec, New Brunswick, Prince Edward Island, Nova Scotia, and Newfoundland south to central New Mexico (locally), north-central and eastern Texas, the Gulf states, and northern Florida (casually farther south), and west to eastern Washington, northeastern Oregon, southern Idaho, north-central Utah, and central and northeastern Arizona; also in Bermuda.

Winters from north-central and eastern Texas, southern Arkansas (rare), the central portions of the Gulf states, central Georgia, and in the Atlantic coastal lowlands from southern New England (casually north to Montana, South Dakota, the northern United States from Minnesota eastward, southern Ontario, and Quebec; many records to December only) south along the Gulf-Caribbean slope of Middle America (also on the Pacific slope of southern Oaxaca, and casually in the interior of Guatemala, Honduras, and Costa Rica) to central Panama (east to the Canal area), and in Bermuda, the Bahamas, Greater Antilles (Cuba, the Isle of Pines, rarely Jamaica, Hispaniola, and Tortue Island), the Cayman Islands, Puerto Rico, and islands in the western Caribbean Sea (San Andrés, Providencia).

Casual in east-central and southeastern Alaska, northeastern British Columbia, northern Manitoba, northeastern Ontario, California, Nevada, Arizona, the Lesser Antilles (Anguilla), and northern Colombia; a sight report from southern Baja California. Accidental in James Bay (North Twin Island), the British Isles, and Germany.

Notes.—Also known as Common Catbird, Northern Catbird, and the Catbird.

Genus *MELANOPTILA* Sclater

Melanoptila Sclater, 1858, Proc. Zool. Soc. London (1857), p. 275. Type, by monotypy, *Melanoptila glabrirostris* Sclater.

Notes.—This genus is sometimes merged in *Dumetella* (e.g., Paynter 1955).

Melanoptila glabrirostris Sclater. Black Catbird.

Melanoptila glabrirostris Sclater, 1858, Proc. Zool. Soc. London (1857), p. 275. (In rep. Honduras, prope urbem Omoa = Omoa, Honduras.)

Habitat.—Tropical Deciduous Forest, Tropical Lowland Evergreen Forest Edge, Secondary Forest, Second-growth Scrub (Tropical Zone).

Distribution.—*Resident* in the Yucatan Peninsula (including Cozumel and Mujeres islands, and Cayo Culebra), northern Guatemala (Petén), Belize, and (questionably) extreme northern Honduras (Omoa).

Accidental in southern Texas (Brownsville).

Genus *MIMUS* Boie

Mimus Boie, 1826, Isis von Oken, col. 972. Type, by monotypy, *Turdus polyglottos* Linnaeus.

Mimus polyglottos (Linnaeus). Northern Mockingbird.

Turdus polyglottos Linnaeus, 1758, Syst. Nat. (ed. 10) 1: 169. Based mainly on "The Mock-Bird" Catesby, Nat. Hist. Carolina 1: 27, pl. 27. (in Virginia.)

Habitat.—A variety of open and partly open situations from areas of scattered brush or trees to forest edge and semi-desert (absent from forest interior), especially in scrub, thickets, gardens, towns, and around cultivated areas; in many areas, virtually restricted to the vicinity of human habitations during breeding season (Tropical to Temperate zones).

Distribution.—*Breeds* regularly from northern California, northwestern Nevada, northern Utah, southeastern Wyoming, southwestern South Dakota, eastern Nebraska, southern Iowa, central Illinois, southern Michigan, northern Ohio, extreme southern Ontario, central Pennsylvania, New York, and New England, sporadically or locally north to southwestern British Columbia, Washington, southern Idaho, southern Alberta, southern Saskatchewan, southern Manitoba, central and northeastern Minnesota, southern Wisconsin, northern Michigan, central Ontario, southern Quebec, New Brunswick, Nova Scotia, and (casually) Newfoundland, south to southern Baja California (including many offshore islands), through Mexico (including the Tres Marias Islands, and on Socorro Island in the Revillagigedos, where possibly introduced) to Oaxaca (west of the Isthmus of Tehuantepec) and Veracruz, and to southeastern Texas, the Gulf coast, southern Florida (including the Florida Keys), the Bahama Islands, and Greater Antilles (east to Anegada in the Virgin Islands, and recently on Little Cayman in the Cayman Islands).

Winters primarily from northern California, southern Nevada, southwestern Utah, Arizona, southern New Mexico, southeastern Colorado, Kansas, southeastern Iowa, Illinois, Indiana, Ohio, Pennsylvania, southern New York, and southern Maine through remainder of breeding range. Small numbers winter sporadically farther north through remainder of breeding range; northern limits of winter distribution have expanded in recent decades. The suggestion by

Phillips (1986) that northernmost records pertain to escapes from captivity is highly questionable.

Introduced and established in the Hawaiian Islands (main islands from Kauai eastward, wandering casually west to French Frigate Shoals), and in Bermuda; an introduced population in Barbados, in the Lesser Antilles, has become extirpated.

Casual north to southern and east-central Alaska, northern British Columbia, southwestern Keewatin, northern Manitoba, northern Ontario, and Prince Edward Island. Accidental on Isla Isabel off Nayarit, Guadalupe Island, Clarion Island, and in the British Isles.

Notes.—Also known as the Mockingbird and Common Mockingbird. *Mimus polyglottos* and *M. gilvus* hybridize, occasionally but not freely, in Oaxaca and Veracruz (Wetmore 1943, Davis and Miller *in* Mayr and Greenway 1960). Therefore, we follow most recent authors (e.g., Binford 1989, Sibley and Monroe 1990) in treating the two as separate species that form a superspecies (cf. Phillips 1962, 1986).

Mimus gilvus (Vieillot). Tropical Mockingbird.

> *Turdus gilvus* Vieillot, 1808, Hist. Nat. Ois. Amer. Sept. 2 (livr. 12) 15: pl. 68 bis. (la Guiane et les contrées les plus chaudes de l'Amérique septentrionale = French Guiana.)

Habitat.—Arid Lowland Scrub, Arid Montane Scrub, Second-growth Scrub, Tropical Lowland Evergreen Forest Edge (0–2600 m; Tropical and Subtropical zones).

Distribution.—*Resident* [*gilvus* group] locally from eastern Oaxaca (Isthmus of Tehuantepec) and extreme southern Veracruz south along both slopes of Middle America (including the Yucatan Peninsula and adjacent islands of Mujeres, Holbox, and Cozumel) to Honduras, and in the southern Lesser Antilles (from Guadeloupe, Désirade, and Antigua southward), and in South America from northern Colombia, Venezuela (including islands from the Netherlands Antilles east to Tobago and Trinidad) and the Guianas south to northern Amazonian Brazil and along the coast to southeastern Brazil; and [*magnirostris* group] on Isla San Andrés, in the western Caribbean Sea.

Introduced and established [*gilvus* group] in central Panama (Canal area and adjacent regions of Colón and Panamá provinces); introductions on Barbados and Nevis, in the Lesser Antilles, have failed.

Notes.—Groups: *M. gilvus* [Tropical Mockingbird] and *M. magnirostris* Cory, 1887 [St. Andrew Mockingbird]. See comments under *M. polyglottos*.

Mimus gundlachii Cabanis. Bahama Mockingbird.

> *Mimus Gundlachii* Cabanis, 1855, J. Ornithol. 3: 470. (Cuba.)

Habitat.—Arid Lowland Scrub, Second-growth Scrub, Tropical Deciduous Forest Edge, Tropical Lowland Evergreen Forest Edge.

Distribution.—*Resident* in the Bahama Islands, on cays off the northern coast of Cuba (Cayo Tío Pepe east to Cayo Coco), and along the arid coast of southern Jamaica (Hellshire Hills and Portland Point).

Occurs regularly and apparently with increasing frequency in southern Florida (including the Florida Keys).

Genus *OREOSCOPTES* Baird

> *Oreoscoptes* Baird, 1858, in Baird, Cassin, and Lawrence, Rep. Explor. Surv. R. R. Pac. 9: xix, xxxv, 346. Type, by monotypy, *Orpheus montanus* Townsend.

Oreoscoptes montanus (Townsend). Sage Thrasher.

> *Orpheus montanus* C. K. Townsend, 1837, J. Acad. Nat. Sci. Philadelphia 7: 192. (Plains of the Rocky Mountains = Sandy Creek, lat. 42° N., long. 109° 30' W., Wyoming.)

Habitat.—Sagebrush plains or slopes; in migration and winter, also arid scrub, grassland with scattered bushes, open pinyon-juniper woodland, primarily in arid or semi-arid situations.

Distribution.—*Breeds* from extreme south-central British Columbia, central Idaho, south-western, and south-central Montana (also locally in southeastern Alberta and southwestern Saskatchewan), northern and southeastern Wyoming, Colorado, and southwestern South Dakota (rare) south through eastern Washington and eastern Oregon to east-central California (Inyo County, formerly to Ventura and San Bernardino counties), southern Nevada, northeastern Arizona, west-central and northern New Mexico, northern Texas (possibly), western Oklahoma (possibly), and (casually) southwestern Kansas.

Winters from east of the Sierras in southern California (rarely), southern Nevada, northern Arizona, central New Mexico, central Texas, and southwestern Oklahoma south to southern Baja California, northern Sonora, Chihuahua, Durango, Guanajuato, northern Nuevo León, northern Tamaulipas, and southern Texas. Casual in southwestern California and Colorado.

Migrates through much of Great Basin and western Great Plains, including areas away from breeding localities, and northern Mexico, casually north to Alberta and northern Montana, and east to southern Manitoba, the Dakotas, western Nebraska, western Kansas, and in the Gulf region from eastern Texas and northeastern Arkansas east to northwestern Florida (recorded east to Gilchrist County).

Casual to southwestern British Columbia, western Washington, western Oregon, and coastal California (including Channel Islands), east across southern Manitoba and the Great Lakes region (western and southern Ontario, Minnesota, Wisconsin, northern Illinois, Michigan) to the Atlantic coastal region (recorded from Massachusetts south to North Carolina). Accidental on Guadalupe Island.

Genus *MIMODES* Ridgway

Mimodes Ridgway, 1882, Proc. U. S. Natl. Mus. 5: 45. Type, by monotypy, *Harporhynchus graysoni* Lawrence.

Mimodes graysoni (Lawrence). Socorro Mockingbird.

Harporhynchus graysoni (Baird MS) Lawrence, 1871, Ann. Lyc. Nat. Hist. N. Y. 10: 1. (Socorro Island, Mexico.)

Habitat.—Arid Lowland Scrub (0–700 m)
Distribution.—*Resident* on Socorro Island, in the Revillagigedo Islands, off western Mexico.
Notes.—Also known as Socorro Thrasher.

Genus *TOXOSTOMA* Wagler

Toxostoma Wagler, 1831, Isis von Oken, col. 528. Type, by monotypy, *Toxostoma vetula* Wagler = *Orpheus curvirostre* Swainson.

Toxostoma rufum (Linnaeus). Brown Thrasher.

Turdus rufus Linnaeus, 1758, Syst. Nat. (ed. 10) 1: 169. Based on the "Fox-coloured Thrush" Catesby, Nat. Hist. Carolina 1: 28, pl. 28. (in America septentrionali & meridionali = South Carolina.)

Habitat.—Thickets and bushy areas in deciduous or mixed forest clearings and forest edge, shrubby areas, and suburbs with extensive shrubs.
Distribution.—*Breeds* from east-central Alberta, central Saskatchewan, southern Manitoba, central Ontario, southwestern Quebec, Vermont, New Hampshire, southern Maine, and southern New Brunswick south to east-central Texas (south to Nueces County), the Gulf coast, and southern Florida (including the Florida Keys), and west to western Montana, eastern Wyoming, and eastern Colorado.

Winters in southeastern Arizona, central and southern New Mexico, and from western and northern Texas, eastern Oklahoma, southern Missouri, western Tennessee, central Kentucky, North Carolina, and southern Maryland (casually north to southern Ontario, and the northern United States from Montana eastward) south to southern Texas, the Gulf coast, and southern Florida.

Casual from northern and east-central Alaska, southern British Columbia, northern Manitoba, Washington, Idaho, and Utah south to southern California, northern Sonora, Sinaloa, Nayarit, and Tamaulipas, and to Prince Edward Island, Nova Scotia, Newfoundland, the Bahama Islands (Grand Bahama, Harbour Island), and western Cuba. Accidental in southern Hudson Bay, Bermuda, Curaçao, the British Isles, and Germany.

Notes.—*Toxostoma rufum, T. longirostre,* and *T. guttatum* constitute a superspecies (Mayr and Short 1970).

Toxostoma longirostre (Lafresnaye). Long-billed Thrasher.

Orpheus longirostris Lafresnaye, 1838, Rev. Zool.[Paris] 1: 55. (du Mexique et de la Californie = Mexico.)

Habitat.—Riparian Thickets, Arid Lowland Scrub, Tropical Deciduous Forest Edge (0–1550 m; Subtropical Zone).

Distribution.—*Resident* from primarily in Gulf lowlands in northeastern Coahuila, northern Nuevo León, and southern Texas (north to the Midland and San Antonio areas) south to eastern San Luis Potosí, northern Querétaro, northeastern Hidalgo, northeastern Puebla, and central Veracruz.

Casual in southeastern Coahuila. Accidental in Colorado (Jefferson County and Barr) and southeastern Veracruz.

Notes.—See comments under *T. rufum.*

Toxostoma guttatum (Ridgway). Cozumel Thrasher.

Harporhynchus guttatus Ridgway, 1885, Proc. Biol. Soc. Wash. 3: 21. (Cozumel Island, Yucatan.)

Habitat.—Arid Lowland Scrub, Tropical Deciduous Forest Edge (Tropical Zone).
Distribution.—*Resident* on Cozumel Island, off Quintana Roo.
Notes.—See comments under *T. rufum.*

Toxostoma cinereum (Xántus de Vesey). Gray Thrasher.

Harporhynchus cinereus Xántus de Vesey, 1860, Proc. Acad. Nat. Sci. Philadelphia 11 (1859): 298. (Cape St. Lucas, Lower California.)

Habitat.—Arid Lowland Scrub (Tropical Zone).
Distribution.—*Resident* in Baja California from lat. 31°7′ N. (on the Pacific coast) and Animas Bay (on the east coast) south to Cape San Lucas.
Notes.—Also known as San Lucas Thrasher. *Toxostoma cinereum* and *T. bendirei* appear to constitute a superspecies (Mayr and Short 1970).

Toxostoma bendirei (Coues). Bendire's Thrasher.

Harporhynchus Bendirei Coues, 1873, Amer. Nat. 7: 330 (footnote). (Tucson, Ariz[ona].)

Habitat.—Desert, primarily in areas with tall open vegetation, cholla cactus, Joshua trees, and yucca, and adjacent juniper woodland, locally in agricultural areas with adjacent scrub and arid grassland with scattered bushes and yuccas.

Distribution.—*Breeds* from southeastern California (primarily northeastern and south-central San Bernardino County), southern Nevada, southern Utah, south-central Colorado (Saguache and Costilla counties), and western and central New Mexico (east to Sandoval and Socorro counties) south to central Sonora.

Winters from southern Arizona, and extreme southwestern New Mexico south through Sonora to northern Sinaloa.

Casual to coastal southern California (including Channel Islands), primarily in fall (when rare but regular), north to central California (to the Farallon Islands, and Marin and Sacramento counties) and north-central Utah, east-central and southwestern Colorado, and southern Sinaloa. Accidental in Alberta (Jasper); sight reports for Saskatchewan and northeastern Baja California.

Notes.—See comments under *T. cinereum.*

Toxostoma ocellatum (Sclater). Ocellated Thrasher.

Harporhynchus ocellatus Sclater, 1862, Proc. Zool. Soc. London, p. 18, pl. iii. (In Mex. merid., prov. Oaxaca . . . at Oaxaca = Oaxaca City, Oaxaca; Binford, 1989, Ornithol. Monogr. 43, p. 344.)

Habitat.—Arid Montane Scrub, Pine-Oak Forest (1500–3000 m; Subtropical and Temperate zones).

Distribution.—*Resident* in the interior of central Mexico from northeastern Guanajuato and west-central Hidalgo south through México, Puebla, and west-central Veracruz to central Oaxaca (east to Santiago Matatlán area).

Notes.—*Toxostoma ocellatum* and *T. curvirostre* appear to constitute a superspecies (Sibley and Monroe 1990).

Toxostoma curvirostre (Swainson). Curve-billed Thrasher.

Orpheus curvirostris Swainson, 1827, Philos. Mag. (n.s.) 1: 369. (Table land, Mexico.)

Habitat.— Arid Lowland Scrub, Arid Montane Scrub; primarily in areas with relatively dense vegetation, but locally in desert grassland with scattered cactus; also in suburbs of desert towns (0–3300 m; upper Tropical and Subtropical zones).

Distribution.—*Resident* from northwestern Arizona, central and northeastern New Mexico, southeastern Colorado, western Oklahoma, extreme southwestern Kansas, and western and central Texas (east to Travis and Refugio counties) south to northwestern Nayarit (including San Esteban and Tiburón islands off Sonora), through the Mexican Plateau to central Oaxaca (east to San Pedro Totolapan area) and Veracruz, and to central Tamaulipas.

Wanders casually west to southeastern California, and east to South Dakota, southwestern Minnesota, Iowa, Nebraska, central Kansas, central Oklahoma, eastern Texas, and southwestern Louisiana; also southwestern Wisconsin (Buffalo County, present four years). Casual in Idaho and western Florida (Santa Rosa County and St. George Island); a sight report for southwestern Saskatchewan.

Notes.—See comments under *T. ocellatum.*

Toxostoma redivivum (Gambel). California Thrasher.

Harpes rediviva Gambel, 1845, Proc. Acad. Nat. Sci. Philadelphia 2: 264. (near Monterey, in Upper California.)

Habitat.—Lowland and coastal chaparral, riparian woodland thickets, and locally in suburbs with extensive shrubs.

Distribution.—*Resident* in California north to Humboldt and Shasta counties (west of the Cascades-Sierra Nevada and the deserts), and in northwestern Baja California (south to lat. 30° N.).

Casual in southwestern Oregon (Medford, O'Brien).

Notes.—*Toxostoma redivivum* and *T. crissale* appear to constitute a superspecies (Sibley and Monroe 1990).

Toxostoma crissale Henry. Crissal Thrasher.

Toxostoma crissale Henry, 1858, Proc. Acad. Nat. Sci. Philadelphia 10: 117. (Fort Thorn [Doña Ana County, New Mexico].

Habitat.—Riparian Thickets, Arid Montane Scrub, Arid Lowland Scrub (0–2400 m).

Distribution.—*Resident* from southeastern California (north to southern Inyo County), southern Nevada, southwestern Utah, northwestern and central Arizona, central New Mexico, and western Texas south to northeastern Baja California, central Sonora, and central Chihuahua, and locally south in the Mexican Plateau to central Mexico (recorded Coahuila,

Zacatecas, San Luis Potosí, and Hidalgo). Some nonbreeding dispersal slightly north of breeding range in Arizona and Utah.

Notes.—The long-used specific name *dorsale* has been suppressed by the International Commission on Zoological Nomenclature (I.C.Z.N. 1983) in favor of *crissale,* which was originally intended by Henry (see Hubbard 1976). See comments under *T. redivivum.*

Toxostoma lecontei Lawrence. Le Conte's Thrasher.

Toxostoma Le Contei Lawrence, 1851, Ann. Lyc. Nat. Hist. N. Y. 5: 121. (California near the junction of the Gila and Colorado Rivers = Fort Yuma, California.) Phillips (1986) considered the type locality to be the Gila River, Arizona, but we continue to follow Grinnell (1932).

Habitat.—Relatively barren, open desert scrub, particularly saltbush and creosote bush associations with dry, sandy washes.

Distribution.—*Resident* [*lecontei* group] in southern California (the Carrizo Plain of eastern San Luis Obispo County, and the San Joaquin Valley desert from Fresno County south to Kern County); and from eastern California (east of the Sierra Nevada north to southern Mono and Inyo counties), southern Nevada, southwestern Utah, and western and south-central Arizona south to northeastern Baja California and western Sonora; and [*arenicola* group] in west-central Baja California (Pacific coast from lat. 29° N. south to lat. 26° N.).

Casual [*lecontei* group] in northwestern Arizona.

Notes.—Groups: *T. lecontei* [Le Conte's Thrasher] and *T. arenicola* (Anthony, 1897) [Rosalia Thrasher]; see Zink et al. (1997).

Genus *RAMPHOCINCLUS* Lafresnaye

Ramphocinclus Lafresnaye, 1843, Rev. Zool. [Paris] 6: 66. Type, by original designation, *Turdus brachyurus* Vieillot.

Ramphocinclus brachyurus (Vieillot). White-breasted Thrasher.

Turdus brachyurus Vieillot, 1818, Nouv. Dict. Hist. Nat. (nouv. éd.) 20: 255. (Martinique.)

Habitat.—Tropical Deciduous Forest (0–300 m).
Distribution.—*Resident* on Martinique and St. Lucia, in the Lesser Antilles.

Genus *MELANOTIS* Bonaparte

Melanotis Bonaparte, 1850, Consp. Gen. Avium 1(2): 276. Type, by monotypy, *Turdus melanotis* Temminck = *Orpheus caerulescens* Swainson.

Melanotis caerulescens (Swainson). Blue Mockingbird.

Orpheus cærulescens Swainson, 1827, Philos. Mag. (n.s.) 1: 369. (Table land, Mexico.)

Habitat.—Montane Evergreen Forest Edge, Pine-Oak Forest, Tropical Deciduous Forest, Secondary Forest (0–3200 m; upper Tropical to lower Temperate zones).

Distribution.—*Resident* from central Sonora, southwestern Chihuahua, western Durango, Sinaloa, Nayarit (including the Tres Marias Islands), Jalisco, Guanajuato, eastern San Luis Potosí, and southern Tamaulipas south to central Oaxaca (west of the Isthmus of Tehuantepec) and central Veracruz. Some nonbreeding dispersal into adjacent lowlands.

Casual in southern Arizona (Patagonia, Cave Creek Canyon; photographs published in Amer. Birds 46: 332, 1992, and in DeBenedictis 1996), southern Nuevo León, and (questionably) western Chiapas (Ocozocoautla).

Notes.—*Melanotis caerulescens* and *M. hypoleucus* constitute a superspecies (Sibley and

Monroe 1990); Hellmayr (1934) treated them as conspecific, but see Davis and Miller *in* Mayr and Greenway (1960).

Melanotis hypoleucus Hartlaub. Blue-and-white Mockingbird.

> *Melanotis hypoleucus* Hartlaub, 1852, Rev. Mag. Zool. (2)4: 460. (Guatemala.)

Habitat.—Montane Evergreen Forest Edge, Pine-Oak Forest, Secondary Forest (900–3000 m; Subtropical and lower Temperate zones).
Distribution.—*Resident* in the mountains of Chiapas, Guatemala, El Salvador, and western Honduras (east to the Tegucigalpa region).
Notes.—See comments under *M. caerulescens.*

Genus *MARGAROPS* Sclater

> *Cichalopia* (not Bonaparte, 1854) Bonaparte, 1857, Rev. Mag. Zool. (2)9: 205. Type, by original designation, *Turdus densirostris* Vieillot = *Turdus fuscatus* Vieillot.
> *Margarops* Sclater, 1859, Proc. Zool. Soc. London, p. 335. New name for *Cichalopia* Bonaparte, 1857, preoccupied.
> *Allenia* Cory, 1891, Auk 8: 42. Type, by original designation, *Turdus montanus* Lafresnaye = *Muscicapa fusca* Müller.

Margarops fuscus (Müller). Scaly-breasted Thrasher.

> *Muscicapa fusca* P. L. S. Müller, 1776, Natursyst., Suppl., p. 170. (Martinique.)

Habitat.—Arid Lowland Scrub, Tropical Lowland Evergreen Forest, Tropical Deciduous Forest, Secondary Forest (0–900 m).
Distribution.—*Resident* in the Lesser Antilles (St. Martin, Saba, St. Eustatius, and Barbuda south to Grenada and Barbados, possibly extirpated on Barbuda and Grenada).
Casual in the Grenadines.
Notes.—Often treated in the monotypic genus *Allenia* (e.g., Davis and Miller *in* Mayr and Greenway 1960).

Margarops fuscatus (Vieillot). Pearly-eyed Thrasher.

> *Turdus fuscatus* Vieillot, 1808, Hist. Nat. Ois. Amer. Sept. 2 (1807): 1, pl. 57 bis. (les grande îles Antilles et particulièrement à Porto-Ricco et à Saint-Domingue = Puerto Rico.)

Habitat.—Arid Lowland Scrub, Tropical Lowland Evergreen Forest, Tropical Deciduous Forest, Secondary Forest (0–900 m).
Distribution.—*Resident* in the southern Bahama Islands (north to Eleuthera), Hispaniola (questionably on the mainland, but found on Beata Island), Puerto Rico (including Mona, Desecheo, Vieques, Culebra, and Culebrita islands), the Virgin Islands, and Lesser Antilles (south to St. Lucia); and on islands north of Venezuela from Bonaire east to Los Hermanos. Accidental (possibly formerly resident) on Barbados.

Genus *CINCLOCERTHIA* Gray

> *Stenorhynchus* (not Lamarck, 1819) Gould, 1836, Proc. Zool. Soc. London (1835), p. 186. Type, by monotypy, *Stenorhynchus ruficauda* Gould.
> *Cinclocerthia* G. R. Gray, 1840, List Genera Birds, p. 17. New name for *Stenorhynchus* Gould, preoccupied.

Cinclocerthia ruficauda (Gould). Brown Trembler.

> *Stenorhynchus ruficauda* Gould, 1836, Proc. Zool. Soc. London (1835), p. 186. (No locality given = Dominica.)

Habitat.—Tropical Lowland Evergreen Forest, Tropical Deciduous Forest, Secondary Forest (0–900 m).

Distribution.—*Resident* in the Lesser Antilles from Saba, St. Eustatius (where possibly extirpated), and St. Kitts south to Dominica, and on St. Vincent.

Notes.—Although *C. ruficauda* and *C. gutturalis* usually have been considered conspecific [*Cinclocerthia ruficauda,* Trembler], we treat these distinctive forms as allospecies (Storer 1989).

Cinclocerthia gutturalis (Lafresnaye). Gray Trembler.

Ramphocinclus gutturalis Lafresnaye, 1843, Rev. Zool. [Paris] 6: 67. (des Antilles = Martinique.)

Habitat.—Tropical Lowland Evergreen Forest, Tropical Deciduous Forest, Secondary Forest (0–900 m).

Distribution.—*Resident* in the Lesser Antilles on Martinique and St. Lucia.

Notes.—See comments under *C. ruficauda.*

Family **STURNIDAE:** Starlings

Notes.—See comments under Mimidae.

Genus *STURNUS* Linnaeus

Sturnus Linnaeus, 1758, Syst. Nat. (ed. 10) : 167. Type, by tautonymy, *Sturnus vulgaris* Linnaeus (*Sturnus,* prebinomial specific name, in synonymy).

Sturnus vulgaris Linnaeus. European Starling.

Sturnus vulgaris Linnaeus, 1758, Syst. Nat. (ed. 10) 1: 167. (in Europa, Africa = Sweden.)

Habitat.—Generally in human-disturbed habitats, including cultivated lands, pastures, suburbs, and cities; usually avoids natural, undisturbed areas such as forest, grasslands, and desert.

Distribution.—*Breeds* from Iceland, the Faeroe and Shetland islands, northern Scandinavia, northern Russia, and central Siberia south to the Azores, southern Europe, Asia Minor, Iran, the Himalayas, northern Mongolia, and Lake Baikal.

Winters from the breeding range south to northern Africa, India, and northeastern China (casually to Thailand).

Casual in Labrador (about 1878) and Greenland (regularly).

Introduced in the United States (New York City, 1890); now breeds from east-central and southeastern Alaska, southern Yukon, northern British Columbia (including the Queen Charlotte Islands), southern Mackenzie, southern Keewatin, northern Manitoba, northern Ontario, northern Quebec, southern Labrador, and Newfoundland south to central Baja California, northern Sinaloa, southern New Mexico, southern Texas, the Gulf coast, southern Florida (to Key West), and Bermuda, with an isolated population in Mexico City and a breeding record from Veracruz. Winters throughout the breeding range and south to Veracruz, the Bahama Islands (south to Grand Turk), and eastern Cuba. Also introduced and established on Jamaica and Puerto Rico, and in South Africa, Australia, New Zealand, and Polynesia. Reported casually in the Hawaiian Islands (Oahu), on Bermuda, in the Virgin Islands (St. Croix), the Cayman Islands (Cayman Brac), and in the summer north to western and northern Alaska, northern Mackenzie, and Southampton Island; an individual recorded in Panama (Canal area) was questionably a natural vagrant.

Notes.—Also known as the Starling or Common Starling. *Sturnus vulgaris* and *S. unicolor* Temminck, 1820 [Spotless Starling], of the western Mediterranean region, constitute a superspecies (Sibley and Monroe 1990).

Genus *ACRIDOTHERES* Vieillot

Acridotheres Vieillot, 1816, Analyse, p. 42. Type, by subsequent designation (G. R. Gray, 1840), *Paradisaea tristis* Linnaeus.

Acridotheres tristis (Linnaeus). Common Myna.

Paradisæa tristis Linnaeus, 1766, Syst. Nat. (ed. 12) 1: 167. Based on "Le Merle des Philippines" Brisson, Ornithologie 2: 278, pl. 26, fig. 1. (in Philippinis, error = Pondichéry.)

Habitat.—Open country, forest edge, agricultural areas, and suburbs; in Asia, open country, primarily in the vicinity of human habitation.

Distribution.—*Resident* from eastern Iran, Turkestan, and the Himalayas south to India, Sri Lanka, southeastern Asia, and the Andaman Islands.

Introduced and established in the Hawaiian Islands (in 1865, now abundant on all main islands from Kauai eastward, and recently on Midway), South Africa, Malaya, Australia, New Zealand, and on many islands in the South Atlantic, Indian, and Pacific oceans; a population in southern Florida known since 1983 is increasing and expanding (Stevenson and Anderson 1994).

Notes.—Also known as Indian Myna or House Myna.

Acridotheres cristatellus (Linnaeus). Crested Myna.

Gracula cristatella Linnaeus, 1758, Syst. Nat. (ed. 10) 1: 109. Based on "The Chinese Starling or Blackbird" Edwards, Nat. Hist. Birds 1: 19, pl. 19. (in China.)

Habitat.—Open country, cultivated lands, and around human habitation.

Distribution.—*Resident* in central and eastern China, Taiwan, and northern Indochina.

Introduced and established in southwestern British Columbia (Vancouver region), Japan, and the Philippines (Luzon). Reports in northwestern Oregon (Portland) and Florida (Dade County) are based on escaped cage birds. Also reported in Puerto Rico, status uncertain.

Genus *GRACULA* Linnaeus

Gracula Linnaeus, 1758, Syst. Nat. (ed. 10) 1: 108. Type, by subsequent designation (G. R. Gray, 1840), *Gracula religiosa* Linnaeus.

Gracula religiosa Linnaeus. Hill Myna.

Gracula religiosa Linnaeus, 1758, Syst. Nat. (ed. 10) 1: 108. (in Asia = Java.)

Habitat.—Primarily open woodland; in Old World, forest, second growth, and scrub.

Distribution.—*Resident* [*religiosa* group] from India (except southern peninsular), southeastern Asia, extreme southern China, and Hainan south to the Andaman and Nicobar islands, and the East Indies (east to Palawan and Alor); and [*indica* group] in southern peninsular India and Sri Lanka.

Introduced and established [*religiosa* group] in Puerto Rico (casual vagrant to Mona and Vieques islands), and in the Indian Ocean on Christmas Island; escapes in the Hawaiian Islands (Oahu, 1960 and 1961) and southern Florida have persisted for years without evidence of establishment.

Notes.—Also known as Talking Myna or Indian Hill Myna and, in Old World literature, as the Grackle. Groups: *G. religiosa* [Eastern Hill-Myna] and *G. indica* (Cuvier, 1829) [Southern Hill-Myna].

Family **PRUNELLIDAE**: Accentors

Notes.—Sibley and Ahlquist (1981a, 1990) provided evidence from DNA-DNA hybridization indicating that this family is most closely related to the Ploceidae and, along with the Motacillidae, belongs to a group of families that includes the nine-primaried oscines.

Genus *PRUNELLA* Vieillot

Prunella Vieillot, 1816, Analyse, p. 43. Type, by monotypy, "Fauvette de haie" Buffon = *Motacilla modularis* Linnaeus.

Prunella montanella (Pallas). Siberian Accentor.

> *Motacilla montanella* Pallas, 1776, Reise Versch. Prov. Russ. Reichs 3: 695. (in Dauuriam = Dauria.)

Habitat.—Breeds in open coniferous or mixed woodland (spruce, birch) and riverine scrub; in winter, open woodland with scrub and second growth.

Distribution.—*Breeds* in the mountains of Siberia.

Winters from southern Manchuria and Japan south to central China, in migration occurring through Mongolia.

Casual in Alaska (Point Barrow, St. Lawrence and Nunivak islands, and Shemya in the Aleutians); sight reports from Fairbanks, Kenai Peninsula, and Juneau. Accidental in British Columbia, Washington, and Idaho.

Notes.—Also known as Mountain Accentor.

Family **MOTACILLIDAE**: Wagtails and Pipits

Notes.—For relationships of the family, see Sibley and Ahlquist (1981b, 1990) and comments under Prunellidae.

Genus *MOTACILLA* Linnaeus

> *Motacilla* Linnaeus, 1758, Syst. Nat. (ed. 10) 1: 184. Type, by tautonymy, *Motacilla alba* Linnaeus (*Motacilla,* prebinomial specific name, listed in synonymy).

Motacilla flava Linnaeus. Yellow Wagtail.

> *Motacilla flava* Linnaeus, 1758, Syst. Nat. (ed. 10) 1: 185. (in Europa = Sweden.)

Habitat.—Breeds in tundra with thickets of dwarf willow or birch; in Eurasia, also wet meadows, moorlands, edges of wetlands, and coastal scrub; in winter, cultivated fields, moist grassy fields, and mudflats, often roosting in reedbeds and cane-fields. Often associated with livestock.

Distribution.—*Breeds* in North America in northern and western Alaska (south to St. Lawrence and Nunivak islands, and on the mainland to the Nushagak River), northern Yukon, and extreme northwestern Mackenzie; and in the Palearctic from the British Isles, southern Scandinavia, northern Russia, and northern Siberia south to northwestern Africa, the Mediterranean region, Asia Minor, Iran, Turkestan, northern Mongolia, central Manchuria, Kamchatka, and the Kuril and Commander islands.

Winters in the Old World from northern Africa, India, Southeast Asia, eastern China, and the Philippines south to southern Africa, the East Indies, and (rarely) northern Australia.

Migrates regularly through coastal western Alaska and the western Aleutians, and in the Old World throughout Europe, the Mediterranean region, and Asia (except unsuitable regions in central Asia and the Himalayas), including Japan and Korea.

Casual in the western Aleutians, Pribilof Islands, central and south-coastal Alaska, central Yukon, British Columbia, western Washington, California, Iceland, the Faeroe Islands, northern Scandinavia, the eastern Atlantic islands, and New Guinea; a sight report from Alabama.

Notes.—Variation in this species is complex, and relationships between morphologically distinguishable groups are uncertain (Sammalisto 1961, Vaurie 1957b, 1959). If more than one species is recognized, North American populations and records would pertain to the eastern Eurasian *M. tschutschensis* Gmelin, 1789 [Alaska Yellow-Wagtail].

Motacilla citreola Pallas. Citrine Wagtail.

> *Motacilla citreola* Pallas, 1776, Reise versch. Prob. Russ. Reischs., 3: 696. (in Siberia orientaliore = East Siberia.)

Habitat.—Wet meadows, marshes, scrubby tundra, and along banks of slow streams and lakes, almost always near water; in winter, marshes, edges of wetlands, irrigated ricefields, and reedbeds.

Distribution.—*Breeds* in central Eurasia from Russia to Siberia, Mongolia, and China, south to northern Afghanistan and through the Himalayas to the Tibetan plateau.

Winters to Iran, southern Afghanistan, India, northern Thailand, and Burma.

Accidental in Mississippi (Starkville, Oktibbeha County, 31 January-1 February 1992; 1992, Amer. Birds 46: 278; photograph in DeBenedictis 1995).

Motacilla cinerea Tunstall. Gray Wagtail.

> *Motacilla Cinerea* Tunstall, 1771, Ornithol. Br., p. 2. Based on the "Gray Water Wagtail" Pennant, Br. Zool., and "La Bergeronette jaune" Brisson, Ornithologie 3: 471, pl. 23, fig. 3. (No locality given = Wycliffe, Yorkshire, England.)

Habitat.—Along watercourses, most frequently swift flowing streams in mountainous country, less frequently along seashores or sluggish streams, in open country such as pastures and meadows with nearby rocky areas and brush nearby, and around human habitation; in winter, primarily open areas in lowlands next to shorelines with little or no vegetation.

Distribution.—*Breeds* from the British Isles, southern Scandinavia, central Russia, and central Siberia south to the eastern Atlantic islands, northwestern Africa, the Mediterranean region, Asia Minor, Iran, the Himalayas, northern Mongolia, Manchuria, northern Korea, and Japan.

Winters from northern Africa, Arabia, Iraq, southern Iran, Afghanistan, India, Southeast Asia, southern China, and Taiwan south to central Africa, Sri Lanka, the Malay Peninsula, East Indies, and western New Guinea.

Migrates casually (primarily in spring) through the Commander and western Aleutians (Attu, Agattu, Shemya, Buldir, Amchitka), occasionally reaching the Pribilofs (St. Paul) and St. Lawrence Island.

A sight report for California (Salinas River).

Motacilla alba Linnaeus. White Wagtail.

> *Motacilla alba* Linnaeus, 1758, Syst. Nat. (ed. 10) 1: 185. (in Europa = Sweden.)

Habitat.—Arctic coastal cliffs, villages, and debris, locally gravel flats of rivers; in Eurasia, almost any kind of open country from tundra and desert edge to margins of watercourses, towns, and cultivated areas. Often associated with livestock.

Distribution.—*Breeds* [*alba* group] in North America in western Alaska from Cape Lisburne south to St. Lawrence Island and Norton Sound, probably farther south; and in the Old World from Greenland, Iceland, and northern Eurasia south (except most of British Isles) to the northern Mediterranean region, Asia Minor, southern Russia, southern Siberia, and northern China; [*yarrelli* group] in the British Isles, rarely the adjacent coasts of continental Europe; and [*personata* group] in Iran, extreme southern Russia, western China, and Pakistan.

Winters [*alba* group] from the southern parts of the breeding range in Eurasia south to southern Africa, the coasts of the Indian Ocean, East Indies, and Philippines.

Migrates [*alba* group] through the eastern Atlantic islands, and islands from Japan south to the Philippines.

Resident [*subpersonata* group] in Morocco.

Casual or accidental [*alba* group] in the Pribilofs, central Alaska (Fairbanks), Washington (Whidbey Island), California (Point Piedra Blanca, Oxnard), Louisiana (Cameron Parish), and Baja California (La Paz); sight reports for British Columbia, Sonora, and Trinidad. An old report from northern Quebec is questionable. See further comments under *M. lugens.*

Notes.—Known in the Old World as Pied Wagtail. Groups: *M. alba* [White Wagtail], *M. yarrelli* Gould, 1837 [British Pied Wagtail], *M. personata* Gould, 1861 [Masked Wagtail], *M. subpersonata* Meade-Waldo, 1901 [Moroccan Wagtail]. *Motacilla alba* and *M. lugens* are sympatric with limited hybridization in Kamchatka and southern Ussuriland (Kistchinski and Lobkov 1979); they formerly were considered conspecific (Dement'ev and Gladkov 1954). *Motacilla alba, M. lugens, M. grandis* Sharpe, 1885 [Japanese Wagtail], *M. aguimp* Dumont, 1821 [African Pied Wagtail], and *M. madaraspatensis* Gmelin, 1789 [White-browed Wagtail] appear to constitute a superspecies (Sibley and Monroe 1990). For further notes on taxonomy and species limits, see Stepanyan (1978) and Cramp (1988).

Motacilla lugens Gloger. Black-backed Wagtail.

Motacilla lugens Gloger, 1829, Isis von Oken, col. 771. (Kamchatka.)

Habitat.—Primarily near seacoasts, also in forest edge, second-growth woodland, and around towns and human habitation.

Distribution.—*Breeds* occasionally in western and southwestern Alaska (Nome, and Attu in Aleutian Islands), and in eastern Asia from southern Ussuriland, Sakhalin, Kamchatka, and (possibly) the Commander Islands south to the Kuril Islands and northern Japan.

Winters from eastern China, Korea, and Japan south to southeastern China, Taiwan, the Seven Islands of Izu and Bonin Islands.

Migrates through Manchuria, northeastern China, and (mostly in spring) the western Aleutian Islands (Near Islands, casually east to Amchitka and Adak).

Casual or accidental on St. Lawrence Island, and in southeastern Alaska (Glacier Bay), Oregon (Eugene, Lower Elk River), California (McKinleyville, Tiburon, Watsonville, Port Hueneme), and North Carolina (Cedar Island). Sight reports or photographs of individuals in the Aleutians, southeastern Alaska, British Columbia, western Washington, Arizona (Grand Canyon), and elsewhere in Oregon and California are indeterminate as to species (Morlan 1981), as are sight reports from Michigan and Barbados.

Notes.—See comments under *M. alba.*

Genus *ANTHUS* Bechstein

Anthus Bechstein, 1805, Gemein. Naturgesch. Dtsch. (ed. 2) 2: 302. Type, by subsequent designation (Sharpe, 1885), *Alauda trivialis* Linnaeus.

Anthus trivialis (Linnaeus). Tree Pipit.

Alauda trivialis Linnaeus, 1758, Syst. Nat. (ed. 10) 1: 166. (in Svecia = Sweden.)

Habitat.—Open and partly open situations with scattered trees and bushes.
Distribution.—*Breeds* through most of Eurasia.
Winters south to tropical Africa and India.
Accidental in Alaska (Cape Prince of Wales, 23 June 1972; Kessel 1989).
Notes.—Also known as Brown Tree-Pipit.

Anthus hodgsoni Richmond. Olive-backed Pipit.

Anthus maculatus (not Vieillot, 1818) "Hodgson" Jerdon, 1864, Birds India "3" [= 2 (2)]: 873. (India = Bengal.)
Anthus hodgsoni Richmond, 1907, in Blackwelder, Publ. Carnegie Inst., no. 54, 1(2): 493. New name for *Anthus maculatus* Jerdon, preoccupied.

Habitat.—Taiga, edges of coniferous and mixed forest, bogs, alpine scrub, and montane forest, including clearings and adjacent meadows; in winter, open woodland, tree plantations, second growth, and farm groves.

Distribution.—*Breeds* from northeastern Russia and central Siberia south to the Himalayas, western China, Mongolia, Japan, and the Kuril Islands.

Winters from India, Southeast Asia, eastern China, Korea, and Japan south to southeastern China, the Philippines, Taiwan. and the Ryukyu Islands.

Migrates casually through the western Aleutians (Attu, Agattu, Shemya, Buldir), occasionally reaching the Pribilofs (St. Paul) and St. Lawrence Island.

Accidental in Nevada (Reno); a sight report for Baja California and the Hawaiian Islands (Kure).

Notes.—Also known as Olive Tree-Pipit, Indian Tree-Pipit, Oriental Tree-Pipit, Hodgson's Tree-Pipit, or Spotted Pipit.

Anthus gustavi Swinhoe. Pechora Pipit.

Anthus gustavi Swinhoe, 1863, Proc. Zool. Soc. London, p. 90. (Amoy, [China].)

Habitat.—Woody and shrubby tundra, swampy scrub, and wet meadows with sedges and reeds; in migration and winter, open woodland and marshes.

Distribution.—*Breeds* [*gustavi* group] from northeastern Siberia (east to the Bering Strait) south to Kamchatka and the Commander Islands; and [*menzbieri* group] in southern Ussuriland.

Winters [*gustavi* group] from eastern China, Korea, and the Ryukyu Islands south to the East Indies and Moluccas; and [*menzbieri* group] presumably in southern China.

Casual [*gustavi* group] in Alaska on St. Lawrence Island and in the western Aleutians (Attu), also in Great Britain, Norway, Finland, Poland, and Iceland.

Notes.—Groups: *A. gustavi* [Pechora Pipit] and *A. menzbieri* Shulpin, 1928 [Menzbier's Pipit].

Anthus cervinus (Pallas). Red-throated Pipit.

> *Motacilla cervina* Pallas, 1811, Zoogr. Rosso-Asiat. 1: 511. (Siberia near the Kolyma, and Kamchatka = Kolyma.)

Habitat.—Rocky areas with mat tundra in coastal mountains and lowlands; in the Old World, wet grassy areas in tundra; in migration and winter, open grasslands and cultivated fields, most frequently near water.

Distribution.—*Breeds* in North America in western Alaska (St. Lawrence Island, and on the mainland from Cape Lisburne south to Wales, probably also on Little Diomede and Sledge islands) and possibly northern Yukon; and in Eurasia from northern Scandinavia east across northern Russia and northern Siberia to the Chukotski Peninsula, possibly also Kamchatka and the Kuril Islands.

Winters in the Old World from northern Africa east across Asia Minor, Iran, and India to southeastern China, and south to central Africa, Southeast Asia, the East Indies, and Philippines.

Migrates through the western Aleutian islands (east to Shemya and Buldir), and in the Old World through central Eurasia from Italy east to Sakhalin, Korea, the Ryukyu Islands, and Taiwan, rarely through northwestern, central and southern California (in fall primarily along coasts and in the Channel Islands), the Faeroe Islands, and British Isles.

Casual or accidental in the Hawaiian Islands (Kure), Gulf of Alaska (Middleton Island), northeastern Arizona, Baja California, Colima, and Michoacán; sight reports for British Columbia and Washington.

Anthus rubescens (Tunstall). American Pipit.

> *Alauda Rubescens* Tunstall, 1771, Ornithol. Br., p. 2. Based on "The Lark from Pensilvania" Edwards, Glean. Nat. Hist. 2: 185, pl. 297. (Pennsylvania = Philadelphia, Pennsylvania.)

Habitat.—Tundra, rocky Arctic and alpine slopes, and alpine meadows (breeding); seacoasts, beaches, mudflats, wet meadows, sandy areas, pastures, and cultivated fields (nonbreeding).

Distribution.—*Breeds* in North America throughout Alaska (including the eastern Aleutian Islands), from northern Yukon south through British Columbia, southwestern Alberta, Washington, and western Montana, locally on mountain tops from Oregon, Utah, and Colorado south to California (the Sierra Nevada, and on Mt. San Gorgonio), northern Baja California (possibly), northern Arizona (San Francisco and White mountains), and northern New Mexico, and from the Canadian Arctic islands (northern Banks east to northern Baffin islands) south to south-central and southeastern Mackenzie, southern Keewatin, northern Manitoba, extreme northern Ontario, southern Labrador, Newfoundland, and, locally, southeastern Quebec (Gaspé Peninsula), New Hampshire (Mt. Washington), and northern Maine (Mt. Katahdin); and in eastern Siberia west to the Taimyr Peninsula and south to northern Transbaicalia, northern Ussuriland, Sakhalin, Kamchatka, and the Kuril Islands.

Winters in coastal areas north to southern British Columbia and southern New York (casually in Alaska in the Aleutians and on Kodiak Island, and from the southern United States casually in the interior and northeast as far as southern Canada) south to Guatemala, southern Mexico (including the Yucatan Peninsula), the Gulf coast, southern Florida, and (rarely) the West Indies (Bahama Islands south to San Salvador, Jamaica, and Swan, Providencia, and San Andrés islands); and in eastern Asia south to eastern China, Southeast Asia, Japan, and the Ryukyu Islands.

Migrates regularly throughout North America between the breeding and wintering ranges.

Casual or accidental in the Hawaiian Islands (Kure), Clipperton Island (sight report), El Salvador, and Bermuda, and in Iceland, the British Isles, Germany, and Italy.

Notes.—Formerly regarded as conspecific with *A. spinoletta* (Linnaeus, 1758) [Water Pipit] but sympatric with the latter in the Transbaicalia region of southern Siberia (Nazarenko 1978). Also strongly genetically differentiated from *A. spinoletta* (Zink et al. 1995). For further notes on taxonomy and species limits, see Stepanyan (1978) and Knox (1988a).

Anthus spragueii (Audubon). Sprague's Pipit.

Alauda Spragueii Audubon, 1844, Birds Amer. (octavo ed.) 7: 334, pl. 486. (Near Ft. Union [western North Dakota].)

Habitat.—Well-drained short-grass prairie (breeding); also in pastures and fields with medium-height grass (nonbreeding).

Distribution.—*Breeds* from north-central British Columbia (locally), north-central Alberta, central Saskatchewan, and west-central and southern Manitoba south to Montana, western South Dakota, North Dakota, and northwestern Minnesota.

Winters from south-central and southeastern Arizona, southern New Mexico, central and eastern Texas, southern Kansas, southern Oklahoma, Arkansas, southern Missouri, Tennessee, northwestern Mississippi, and Louisiana south through Mexico (except the northwestern portion) to northern Michoacán, Puebla, and central Veracruz, casually north to southern California.

Migrates primarily through the eastern Great Plains, casually west (primarily in fall) to southwestern Alberta, California, and northwestern Mexico.

Casual in Illinois, Michigan, western Ontario, Ohio, Massachusetts, and the Gulf and southern Atlantic states (Mississippi east and north to South Carolina); sight reports from Guerrero, Maine, Delaware, Virginia, and North Carolina.

Notes.—A close relationship between *A. spragueii* and the South American *A. furcatus* Lafresnaye and d'Orbigny, 1837, has been suggested (Hall 1961); they may constitute a superspecies (Mayr and Short 1970).

Anthus lutescens Pucheran. Yellowish Pipit.

Anthus lutescens Pucheran, 1855, Arch. Mus. Nat. Hist. Paris 7: 343. (Brésil = vicinity of Rio de Janeiro.)

Habitat.—Pastures/Agricultural Lands, Low Seasonally Wet Grassland (0–1300 m; Tropical Zone).

Distribution.—*Resident* on the Pacific slope of Panama (western Chiriquí east to eastern Panamá province, also both slopes in the Canal area); and in South America west of the Andes in coastal Peru and northern Chile, and locally east of the Andes from eastern Colombia, Venezuela, and the Guianas south to central Argentina, Uruguay, and southeastern Brazil.

Family **BOMBYCILLIDAE**: Waxwings

Notes.—Sibley and Ahlquist (1990) presented evidence from DNA-DNA hybridization that the Bombycillidae, which in their classification included also the Ptilogonatidae and Dulidae, are most closely related to a group of families, the Muscicapoidea, that includes the Cinclidae, Muscicapidae, Turdidae, Sturnidae, and Mimidae.

Genus *BOMBYCILLA* Vieillot

Bombycilla Vieillot, 1808, Hist. Nat. Ois. Amer. Sept., 1: 88. Type, by monotypy, *Bombycilla cedrorum* Vieillot.

Bombycilla garrulus (Linnaeus). Bohemian Waxwing.

> *Lanius Garrulus* Linnaeus, 1758, Syst. Nat. (ed. 10) 1: 95. (in Europa & America boreali = Sweden.)

Habitat.—Open coniferous or deciduous forest and edge, muskeg, and, less frequently, mixed coniferous-deciduous woodland; in migration and winter, also parks and suburbs with fruiting trees and shrubs.

Distribution.—*Breeds* in North America from western and northern Alaska, northern Yukon, northwestern and southern Mackenzie, northern Saskatchewan, northern Manitoba, northern Ontario, and extreme west-central Quebec south to south-coastal Alaska, and through interior British Columbia and northern and southwestern Alberta to northern Washington, northern Idaho, and northwestern Montana; and in Eurasia from northern Scandinavia east across northern Russia to northern Siberia, and south to Amurland and Kamchatka.

Winters in North America from central, south-coastal and southeastern Alaska, northern British Columbia, southwestern Mackenzie, central Alberta, central Saskatchewan, southern Manitoba, central Ontario, southern Quebec, Prince Edward Island, New Brunswick, Nova Scotia, and Newfoundland south irregularly or sporadically to southern California, northern (casually southern) Arizona, northern (casually southern) New Mexico, northern Texas, Oklahoma, northwestern Arkansas, southern Illinois, central Indiana, northern Ohio, West Virginia, Pennsylvania, and New Jersey (casually to Maryland and District of Columbia); sight reports south to southern Texas and Virginia; and in Eurasia from the breeding range south to the British Isles, central and southeastern Europe, Asia Minor, Iran, Turkestan, Mongolia, Manchuria, Ussuriland, Korea, Japan, and the Kuril Islands.

Casual in the Pribilofs (St. Paul), Aleutians (Attu, Amchitka), Greenland, Iceland, the Faeroe Islands, Mediterranean region and islands off Japan (south to the Volcano Islands).

Notes.—Also known as Greater Waxwing and, in Old World literature, as the Waxwing.

Bombycilla cedrorum Vieillot. Cedar Waxwing.

> *Bombycilla cedrorum* Vieillot, 1808, Hist. Nat. Ois. Amer. Sept., 1, livr. 10,: 88, pl. 57. (Amérique depuis le Canada jusqu'au Mexique; restricted to Pennsylvania by Burleigh, 1963, Proc. Biol. Soc. Washington 76: 177–180.)

Habitat.—A variety of open woodland types, either deciduous or coniferous, forest edge, second growth, parks, and orchards; in migration and winter, occurring wherever there are fruiting trees and shrubs.

Distribution.—*Breeds* from southeastern Alaska, central British Columbia, northern Alberta, northern Saskatchewan, northern Manitoba, northern Ontario, south-central Quebec, New Brunswick, Prince Edward Island, Nova Scotia, and Newfoundland south to northern California (primarily Del Norte and Humboldt counties, casually to Orange County in southern California), northern Utah (rarely), Colorado (locally), western Oklahoma (rarely), Kansas, northwestern Arkansas, central Missouri, southern Illinois, east-central Mississippi, northern Alabama, northern Georgia, and South Carolina. Recorded in summer (and breeding suggested) in northern New Mexico.

Winters from southern British Columbia, central Alberta, central Saskatchewan, southern Manitoba, southern Ontario, southern Quebec, New York, New England, New Brunswick, and Nova Scotia south through the continental United States, Middle America to central Panama (the Canal area and Pearl Islands), and Bermuda, irregularly to the Bahama Islands, the Greater Antilles, and the Cayman Islands.

Casual in central and south-coastal Alaska (Fairbanks, Cordova, Middleton Island), in the Revillagigedo Islands (Socorro Island; sight reports), the Lesser Antilles (Guadeloupe and Dominica), Netherlands Antilles (Aruba), Colombia, and northern Venezuela.

Family **PTILOGONATIDAE**: Silky-flycatchers

Notes.—Sometimes included in the Bombycillidae (e.g., Sibley and Monroe 1990). See comments under Bombycillidae.

Genus *PHAINOPTILA* Salvin

Phainoptila Salvin, 1877, Proc. Zool. Soc. London, p. 367. Type, by original designation, *Phainoptila melanoxantha* Salvin.

Phainoptila melanoxantha Salvin. Black-and-yellow Silky-flycatcher.

Phainoptila melanoxantha Salvin, 1877, Proc. Zool. Soc. London, p. 367. (Costa Rica = San Francisco, Costa Rica.)

Habitat.—Montane Evergreen Forest (1200–3000 m; Subtropical and Temperate zones).
Distribution.—*Resident* in the mountains of Costa Rica (Cordillera de Guanacaste to Cordillera de Talamanca) and western Panama (east to Veraguas).

Genus *PTILOGONYS* Swainson

Ptiliogonys [sic] Swainson, 1827, Philos. Mag. (n.s.) 1: 268. Type, by monotypy, *Ptiliogonys cinereus* Swainson.

Notes.—The usual citation, with the spelling *Ptilogonys,* is to Swainson, 1824, a work that was not published (see Browning 1989b). *Ptiliogonys* may be considered an incorrect spelling and *Ptilogonys,* as later used by Swainson, a justifiable emendation (Sibley and Monroe 1990: 506).

Ptilogonys cinereus Swainson. Gray Silky-flycatcher.

Ptiliogonys [sic] *cinereus* Swainson, 1827, Philos. Mag. (n.s.) 1: 368. (Tableland of Mexico, Real del Monte [Hidalgo]; Browning, 1989, Auk 106: 743–746.)

Habitat.—Pine-Oak Forest, Pine Forest (1100–3200 m; Subtropical and Temperate zones).
Distribution.—*Resident* in the highlands from southern Sonora, Sinaloa, southern Chihuahua, western Durango, Zacatecas, central Nuevo León, and southwestern Tamaulipas south to central Guatemala.
Accidental in southern (Laguna Atascosa N.W.R.; Lasley and Pincelli 1986, DeBenedictis 1991) and western (El Paso; 12 Jan.—5 March 1995; 1995, Nat. Aud. Soc. Field Notes 49: 168–169) Texas. Reports from California and Arizona are usually regarded as escaped cagebirds.

Ptilogonys caudatus Cabanis. Long-tailed Silky-flycatcher.

Ptilogonys caudatus Cabanis, 1861, J. Ornithol. 8 (1860): 402. (Irazú, Costa Rica.)

Habitat.—Montane Evergreen Forest, Secondary Forest (1800–3000 m; Subtropical and Temperate zones).
Distribution.—*Resident* in the mountains of Costa Rica (north to the Cordillera Central) and western Panama (western Chiriquí).

Genus *PHAINOPEPLA* Baird

Phainopepla Baird, 1858, in Baird, Cassin, and Lawrence, Rep. Explor. Surv. R. R. Pac. 9: xix, xxxiv, 923. Type, by original designation, *Ptilogonys nitens* Swainson.

Phainopepla nitens (Swainson). Phainopepla.

Ptilogonys nitens Swainson, 1838, Animals in Menageries, *in* Lardner, Cabinet Cyclopedia 98: 285. (Mexico.)

Habitat.—Desert washes, mesquite, juniper and oak woodland, tall brush, and riparian woodland, mainly where fruiting mistletoe present (Tropical to Temperate zones).
Distribution.—*Breeds* from interior northern California (also once on Santa Catalina Island), southern Nevada, southern Utah, southern (casually western) New Mexico, and western Texas south to southern Baja California, Jalisco, Guanajuato, San Luis Potosí, and west-central Veracruz.

Winters from central California, southern Nevada, central Arizona, southern New Mexico, and western Texas south to northwestern Oaxaca and Veracruz.

Regular in fall on Channel Islands (off California). Casual or accidental in southern Oregon, Colorado, southern Texas, Nebraska (Alliance), southern Ontario (Wallacetown, London), Wisconsin, and Rhode Island (Block Island); sight reports for Guadalupe Island and Massachusetts.

Family **DULIDAE**: Palmchats

Notes.—Sometimes included in the Bombycillidae (e.g., Sibley and Monroe 1990). See comments under Bombycillidae.

Genus *DULUS* Vieillot

Dulus Vieillot, 1816, Analyse, p. 42. Type, by monotypy, "Tanagra esclave" Buffon = *Tanagra dominica* Linnaeus.

Dulus dominicus (Linnaeus). Palmchat.

Tanagra dominica Linnaeus, 1766, Syst. Nat. (ed. 12) 1: 316. Based on "Le Tangara de S. Domingue" Brisson, Ornithologie 3: 37, pl. 2, fig. 4. (in Dominica = Santo Domingo, Hispaniola.)

Habitat.—Secondary Forest, Tropical Deciduous Forest, Tropical Lowland Evergreen Forest Edge, nesting primarily in royal palm (0–1800 m).

Distribution.—*Resident* on Hispaniola (including Gonâve Island).

Family **PEUCEDRAMIDAE**: Olive Warbler

Genus *PEUCEDRAMUS* Henshaw

Peucedramus Henshaw, 1875, Ann. Rep. Geogr. Explor. West 100th Merid., p. 201. Type, by original designation, *Sylvia olivacea* Giraud = *Sylvia taeniata* Du Bus de Gisignies.

Notes.—The elevation to family rank of *Peucedramus* is based on morphology and breeding biology (George 1962, 1968) and on biochemical systematics (DNA-DNA hybridization data; Sibley and Ahlquist 1990, Harshman 1994), supporting the distinctiveness of this species with reference to the other members of the nine-primaried assemblage.

Peucedramus taeniatus (Du Bus de Gisignies). Olive Warbler.

Sylvia tæniata Du Bus de Gisignies, 1847, Bull. Acad. R. Sci. Lett. Beaux-Arts Belg. 14: 104. (le Mexique = San Cristóbal, Chiapas.)

Habitat.—Pine Forest, Pine-Oak Forest; locally firs (1700–3100 m).

Distribution.—*Breeds* from central and southeastern Arizona, southwestern New Mexico, northern Chihuahua, northern Coahuila, southern Nuevo León, and western Tamaulipas south through the highlands of Mexico, Guatemala, El Salvador, and Honduras to north-central Nicaragua.

Winters primarily through the breeding range, although most individuals winter south of Arizona and New Mexico; recorded in winter also in Nayarit. Some movement to lower elevations in winter in northern portion of range.

Casual in western Texas and south-central New Mexico.

Family **PARULIDAE**: Wood-Warblers

Genus *VERMIVORA* Swainson

Vermivora Swainson, 1827, Philos. Mag. (n.s.) 1, p. 434. Type, by monotypy, *Sylvia solitaria* Wilson = *Certhia pinus* Linnaeus.

Helminthophaga (not Bechstein, 1803) Cabanis, 1850, Mus. Heineanum 1: 20. Type, by original designation, *Motacilla chrysoptera* Linnaeus.

Helminthophila Ridgway, 1882, Bull. Nuttall Ornithol. Club 7: 53. New name for *Helminthophaga* Cabanis, preoccupied.

Notes.—The genera *Vermivora, Parula,* and *Dendroica* are closely related (Lowery and Monroe *in* Paynter 1968); some authors (e.g., Griscom, *in* Griscom and Sprunt 1957: 349) suggest that all be merged in *Vermivora.* In a study of genetic variation using allozymes, however, three species of *Vermivora* clustered separately from four species of *Dendroica* (Barrowclough and Corbin 1978); unfortunately, the more *Dendroica*-like species of *Vermivora,* such as *V. pinus* and *V. chrysoptera,* were not included. We also suspect that *Vermivora* is not a monophyletic group. Relationships in this assemblage require further study.

†*Vermivora bachmanii* (Audubon). Bachman's Warbler.

Sylvia Bachmanii Audubon, 1833, Birds Amer. (folio) 2: pl. 185 (1834, Ornithol. Biogr. 2: 483). (a few miles from Charleston [= Edisto River], in South Carolina.)

Habitat.—Moist deciduous woodland and swamp; in migration and winter also open woodland, pine, and scrub (see comments below).

Distribution.—Probably extinct. *Bred* formerly in northeastern Arkansas, southeastern Missouri, southwestern Kentucky, central Alabama, and southeastern South Carolina. Recorded during breeding season (and possibly breeding) from south-central Missouri and Virginia south to Louisiana, Mississippi, and southern Alabama.

Wintered in Cuba and the Isle of Pines. Accidental in Florida.

In *migration* recorded from the Gulf coast region (from Florida to Louisiana), Florida Keys, and Bahama Islands (Cay Sal).

Although the species is still reported on the basis of song or sightings, the last confirmed record was in 1962 near Charleston, South Carolina; the photo of a female in Florida in 1977 (Barber 1985) is not definitive, nor is a sight report of a female in Cuba in 1980 (Ripley and Moreno 1980). *Vermivora bachmanii* might have been a bamboo specialist, and the historical decline of "cane" (= bamboo) in the southeastern United States may be linked to the disappearance of this species (Remsen 1986).

Vermivora pinus (Linnaeus). Blue-winged Warbler.

Certhia Pinus Linnaeus, 1766, Syst. Nat. (ed. 12) 1: 187. Based largely on "The Pine-Creeper" Edwards, Glean. Nat. Hist. 2: 140, pl. 277. (in America septentrionali = Philadelphia, Pennsylvania.)

Habitat.—Second-growth dominated by shrubs, from over-grown fields to forest edge; in migration may be found in any wooded habitat; in winter, favors second-growth.

Distribution.—*Breeds* from eastern Nebraska (formerly), Missouri, central Iowa, southeastern Minnesota, southern Wisconsin, central Michigan, northern Ohio, southern Ontario, central New York, southern Vermont, southern New Hampshire, and extreme southern Maine south to northeastern Oklahoma (casually), northern Arkansas, central Tennessee, northern Alabama, northern Georgia, southwestern North Carolina, western and northern Virginia, Maryland, and northern Delaware. Summer records for western South Carolina and Colorado, but breeding not confirmed. Breeding distribution has expanded dramatically to the north and northeast over the last century.

Winters from Puebla, Veracruz, and Oaxaca south through Middle America (both slopes, including the Yucatan Peninsula, but less commonly on the Pacific drainage) to central Panama (east to the Canal area and eastern Panamá province). Many winter sight reports from southeastern United States, especially Florida, but few confirmed records. Casual in Bermuda, the Bahamas, and the Greater Antilles, and accidental in coastal California, Texas, North Carolina, and Mississippi; December-early January reports from Kentucky and New York.

Migrates through the eastern United States (casually west to the eastern foothills of the Rockies and central and southern Texas; also rare in the extreme southeast), eastern Mexico

(Gulf slope), and Bermuda, rarely through Cuba, Jamaica, Hispaniola, and the Bahama and Cayman islands. Recorded annually in Newfoundland.

Casual north to southern Saskatchewan, southern Quebec, New Brunswick, and Nova Scotia, west to California, Arizona, New Mexico, and western Texas, and south to northern Colombia; sight reports for Washington, Oregon, southern Manitoba, Alberta, northern Baja California, and the Caicos and Virgin islands.

Notes.—This species hybridizes regularly and extensively with *V. chrysoptera* in a dynamic situation, producing variable hybrids that have resulted in the naming of two extreme types, *V. "leucobronchialis"* Brewster, 1874 and *V. "lawrencii"* Herrick, 1875. The hybrids are more variable than these hybrid types would suggest. In many regions *V. chrysoptera* has been replaced by *V. pinus,* the extent of interbreeding diminishing with this shift, but the situation is complex and locally variable. See Parkes (1951), Short (1963), Ficken and Ficken (1968, 1970), Gill and Murray (1972), Murray and Gill (1976), Gill (1980, 1987, 1997), and references therein. The two species constitute a superspecies (Mayr and Short 1970).

Vermivora chrysoptera (Linnaeus). Golden-winged Warbler.

> *Motacilla chrysoptera* Linnaeus, 1766, Syst. Nat. (ed. 12) 1: 333. Based on "The Golden-winged Fly-catcher" Edwards, Glean. Nat. Hist. 2: 189, pl. 299. (in Pensylvania = near Philadelphia, Pennsylvania.)

Habitat.—Second-growth dominated by shrubs and dense herbaceous growth, from overgrown fields to forest edge, bogs; in migration and winter, primarily forest edge and tall second-growth, especially in foothills and mountains.

Distribution.—*Breeds* in southern Manitoba, northern Minnesota, Wisconsin, Michigan, northern Illinois (locally), extreme northern Indiana, southern Ontario, extreme southwestern Quebec, New York, western Vermont, New Hampshire (locally), western Massachusetts, and northwestern Connecticut, and south through Pennsylvania, northern New Jersey, western Maryland, West Virginia, extreme eastern Kentucky, eastern Tennessee, western North Carolina, and northern Georgia. Formerly bred in southeastern Iowa, Missouri, northern Ohio, central Illinois, southern Connecticut, Rhode Island, and northwestern South Carolina. Breeding range has been contracting in the southern and eastern portions of its range, but expanding in the northern portion. Bred once in northeastern North Dakota and once in Colorado. Recorded in summer (and possibly breeding) in southeastern Maine.

Winters from Chiapas and Guatemala (casually southern Veracruz and the Yucatan Peninsula) south through Middle America (mostly on the Caribbean drainage north of Panama) to central Colombia and northern Venezuela, and rarely in the Greater Antilles (east to Puerto Rico). Accidental in southern Texas, southern Arizona, and coastal California.

Migrates through eastern North America east of the Rockies (rare along the Great Plains and in the extreme southeast) south to south-central Texas and the Gulf coast, recorded rarely in eastern Mexico (Gulf-Caribbean slope), Bermuda, and the northwestern Bahama Islands.

Casual or accidental in southern Saskatchewan, Oregon, California, Arizona, Colorado, New Mexico, western Texas, New Brunswick, Nova Scotia, Newfoundland, Greenland, and Great Britain; sight reports for northern Baja California, Nevada, Idaho, Wyoming, Clipperton Island, the Virgin Islands (St. John), Trinidad, and Ecuador.

Notes.—See comments under *V. pinus.*

Vermivora peregrina (Wilson). Tennessee Warbler.

> *Sylvia peregrina* Wilson, 1811, Amer. Ornithol. 3: 83, pl. 25, fig. 2. (banks of the Cumberland River in Tennessee.)

Habitat.—Coniferous and deciduous woodland (usually open, with brushy undergrowth, and with herbaceous ground-cover), alder and willow thickets (especially in western portions of range), edges of bogs, and open deciduous second growth; in migration and winter in a variety of wooded habitats (especially where flowering trees present) and dense scrub, also (especially in fall) weed fields (especially giant ragweed).

Distribution.—*Breeds* from southeastern Alaska (rare), southeastern Yukon, northwestern and southern Mackenzie, northern Saskatchewan, northern Manitoba, northern Ontario, north-central Quebec, southern Labrador, and Newfoundland south to south-central British Columbia, southwestern and south-central Alberta, northwestern Montana (rare and local), southern Saskatchewan, southern Manitoba, northern Minnesota, extreme northern Wisconsin, northern Michigan, southern Ontario, northeastern New York, northeastern Vermont, northern New Hampshire, central Maine, and Nova Scotia.

Winters from Guerrero and southern Veracruz south through Middle America (including islands off the Caribbean coast) to Colombia, northern Ecuador, and northern Venezuela. Regular on Bermuda and the western West Indies, and regular to casual in coastal California, southern Arizona, the Gulf Coast, and southern Florida, but few records are later than December. Sight reports from Tennessee, Georgia, Illinois, and New York.

Migrates regularly through central and eastern North America (west to western Montana and the Rockies), eastern Mexico, Bermuda, the Bahama Islands, Greater Antilles (east to Hispaniola, rarely to the Virgin Islands), the Cayman Islands, and islands in the western Caribbean Sea (Providencia, San Andrés), also rarely but regularly through California (more commonly in fall).

Casual elsewhere in western North America from southwestern British Columbia and Colorado south to northern Baja California, northern Sonora, southeastern Arizona, southern New Mexico, and western Texas, also in central Alaska and the British Isles. Accidental on Clipperton Island and the Revillagigedo Islands (Socorro Island, sight reports), and in Greenland, Iceland, and the Faeroe Islands.

Vermivora celata (Say). Orange-crowned Warbler.

Sylvia celatus Say, 1823, in Long, Exped. Rocky Mount. 1: 169 (note). (Engineer Cantonment near Council Bluff = Omaha, Nebraska.)

Habitat.—Open, brushy deciduous and mixed deciduous-coniferous woodland, dense chaparral, riparian thickets, and aspen groves (especially in Rocky Mountain region); in migration and winter, a variety of wooded habitat edges, especially with dense undergrowth.

Distribution.—*Breeds* from western and northern Alaska, Yukon, northwestern and southern Mackenzie, northern Alberta, northern Saskatchewan, northern Manitoba, northern Ontario, central Quebec, and central Labrador south to southern Alaska (west to the Alaska Peninsula and Kodiak Island), southwestern and central California (including the Channel Islands), northwestern Baja California (including Los Coronados and Todos Santos islands), locally in Nevada, southern Utah, southeastern Arizona, southern New Mexico, and extreme western Texas (Guadalupe and, probably, Davis mountains), and, east of the Rockies, to southern Saskatchewan, southern Manitoba, northeastern North Dakota (probably), central Ontario, south-central Quebec, and southern Labrador.

Winters from coastal British Columbia (rare) south coastally to coastal California, and from northern California, southern Nevada, central Arizona, southern New Mexico (rarely), Texas (not Panhandle), central Oklahoma, central Arkansas, the central portions of the Gulf states, South Carolina, eastern North Carolina, and southeastern Virginia (casually north to the northern contiguous United States and southeastern Alaska) south to southern Baja California, Guatemala, El Salvador, Belize (questionably), the Yucatan Peninsula (rarely), and southern Florida, rarely to Bermuda and the Bahama Islands.

Migrates regularly through the United States primarily west of the Appalachians.

Casual north to northern Alaska and northern Mackenzie, and in the Pribilof Islands, the Maritime Provinces, Newfoundland, and Cuba. Accidental in Greenland. A report from Costa Rica requires verification.

Vermivora ruficapilla (Wilson). Nashville Warbler.

Sylvia ruficapilla Wilson, 1811, Amer. Ornithol. 3: 120, pl. 27, fig. 3. (near Nashville, Tennessee.)

Habitat.—Open, brushy deciduous or coniferous woodland, second growth, regenerating burns and clear-cuts, forest-bordered bogs and brush, and brushy riparian growth; in migration and winter, a variety of woodland and scrub habitats.

Distribution.—*Breeds* from extreme southwestern and southern interior British Columbia, southern Alberta (rarely), and western Montana south through Washington (except western portion), Oregon, and central Idaho to northwestern and south-central California (to San Bernardino Mountains), and extreme west-central Nevada (Carson Range); and from central Saskatchewan, central Manitoba, central Ontario, southern Quebec (including Anticosti and Magdalen islands), extreme southwestern Newfoundland (casually), New Brunswick, Prince Edward Island, and Nova Scotia south to southern Manitoba, northeastern North Dakota, northern and east-central Minnesota, southern Wisconsin, central Michigan, southeastern Ontario, northeastern West Virginia, western Maryland, western Virginia (rare), southeastern Pennsylvania (rare), northern New Jersey, southeastern New York, northern Connecticut, and Rhode Island. Formerly bred south to Illinois, northeastern Ohio, and southern Connecticut. Casual in Labrador.

Winters from southern Sonora, Durango, Nuevo León, and extreme southern Texas south through Mexico (sight reports only from the Yucatan Peninsula) to Guatemala, Belize, El Salvador, and central Honduras; also rarely or irregularly in coastal California, and casually north to western Washington and southern Arizona, and along the Gulf coast, southern Florida, the Bahama and Cayman Islands, Cuba, and Jamaica. Several December records farther north in the United States and Nova Scotia.

Migrates regularly through California, Utah, Arizona, New Mexico, and the central United States from the Plains states east to the Appalachians, rarely through southern Baja California, the Rockies, and southeastern United States.

Casual in Bermuda and Greenland; sight reports from southern Alaska (Middleton Island), Costa Rica, and Panama (Chiriquí).

Notes.—*Vermivora ruficapilla* and *V. virginiae* are closely related and constitute a superspecies (Johnson 1976, Brush and Johnson 1976); Mayr and Short (1970) also included *V. crissalis* in this superspecies. See comments under *V. crissalis*.

Vermivora virginiae (Baird). Virginia's Warbler.

Helminthophaga virginiae Baird, 1860, in Baird, Cassin, and Lawrence, Birds N. Amer., p. xi, Atlas, pl. 79, fig. 1. (Cantonment [= Fort] Burgwyn, N.M.)

Habitat.—Brushy arid montane woodland, oak thickets, mountain mahogany groves, coniferous scrub, and chaparral; in migration and winter, also in arid scrub, open woodland, and second growth.

Distribution.—*Breeds* from in montane areas in the Great Basin region in eastern California (White Mountains, eastern slope of Sierras in Mono and Inyo counties; Clark Mountain, New York Mountains), Nevada (except northwest), southeastern Idaho, Utah, southwestern Wyoming, western Colorado, northern New Mexico; and also in southern California (San Bernardino and San Gabriel mountains), central Wyoming, eastern ranges of Rocky Mountains in Colorado and New Mexico, central and southeastern Arizona, central and southern New Mexico, and western Texas (Guadalupe and, probably, Davis mountains).

Winters from southern Nayarit and Guanajuato south to Morelos and central Oaxaca (west of the Isthmus of Tehuantepec), casually north to southern California. Accidental in Rio Grande Valley of Texas.

Migrates from southern California, Arizona, New Mexico, and western and northern Texas south through northern Mexico (except Baja California), rarely but regularly through southern and central coastal California and east to western Kansas, western Oklahoma, and northern Texas.

Casual or accidental in southern Oregon, northern coastal California, southeastern Texas, southwestern Louisiana, Ontario, Nova Scotia, Labrador (Goose Bay), Michigan (Dearborn), and New Jersey; sight reports for New Brunswick, Missouri, northern Baja California, Belize, northern Guatemala (Petén), and the Bahamas (Grand Bahama).

Notes.—See comments under *V. ruficapilla*.

Vermivora crissalis (Salvin and Godman). Colima Warbler.

Helminthophila crissalis Salvin and Godman, 1889, Ibis, p. 380. (Sierra Nevada de Colima, Mexico.)

Habitat.—Pine-Oak Forest; in migration and winter, also open woodland and scrub; primarily in brushy, humid Pine-Oak Forest (1800–3000 m).

Distribution.—*Breeds* in southwestern Texas (Chisos Mountains), western and central Coahuila, western and southern Nuevo León, northeastern Zacatecas, northern San Luis Potosí and southwestern Tamaulipas (Miquihuana).

Winters from southern Sinaloa south through Jalisco, Colima, and Michoacán to Guerrero, casually to northern Oaxaca.

Casual in southern Texas (Santa Ana, sight report).

Notes.—For a detailed discussion of range and habitat, see Lanning et al. (1990). The view of Phillips et al. (1964) that *V. crissalis* is conspecific with *V. virginiae* and *V. ruficapilla,* despite radical differences in plumage, song, and body size, has not been entertained seriously by subsequent authors. See comments under *V. ruficapilla.*

Vermivora luciae (Cooper). Lucy's Warbler.

Helminthophaga luciæ J. G. Cooper, 1861, Proc. Calif. Acad. Sci. (1)2: 120. (Fort Mojave, near lat. 35° in the Colorado Valley [Arizona].)

Habitat.—Gallery Forest, Arid Lowland Scrub, primarily mesquite or mesquite-cottonwood woodland along streams and washes, locally also in montane canyons with broadleaf woodland; in migration and winter, arid brush and thickets (0–1500 m).

Distribution.—*Breeds* from southeastern California (north to Inyo County), southern Nevada, and southern Utah south to northeastern Baja California, southern Arizona, northern Sonora, southwestern New Mexico, and western Texas (Brewster, Hudspeth, and Presidio counties), and once in extreme southwestern Colorado.

Winters in western Mexico from southern Sonora south to Oaxaca, casually north to central coastal and southern California and upper Rio Grande valley of Texas.

Migrates through northwestern Mexico, rarely southern California (casually north to Point Reyes and the Farallon Islands).

Casual or accidental in Oregon (Florence), Baja California (away from Río Colorado), southern Louisiana (Cameron Parish, Mississippi River delta), and Massachusetts (Ipswich).

Genus PARULA Bonaparte

Parula Bonaparte, 1838, Geogr. Comp. List, p. 20. Type, by monotypy, *Sylvia americana* Latham = *Parus americanus* Linnaeus.
Oreothlypis Ridgway, 1884, Auk 1: 169. Type, by original designation, *Compsothlypis gutturalis* Cabanis.

Notes.—See comments under *Vermivora.*

Parula gutturalis (Cabanis). Flame-throated Warbler.

Compsothlypis gutturalis Cabanis, 1861, J. Ornithol. 8 (1860): 329. (Irazú, Costa Rica.)

Habitat.—Montane Evergreen Forest (1800–3000 m; Subtropical and lower Temperate zones).

Distribution.—*Resident* in the highlands of Costa Rica (Cordillera Central, Dota Mountains, and Cordillera de Talamanca) and western Panama (western Chiriquí).

Notes.—Often placed in the genus *Vermivora* (Eisenmann 1955) or, occasionally, in the monotypic genus *Oreothlypis* (Ridgway 1902).

Parula superciliosa (Hartlaub). Crescent-chested Warbler.

Conirostrum superciliosum Hartlaub, 1844, Rev. Zool. [Paris] 7: 215. (Guatemala.)

Habitat.—Pine-Oak Forest, Montane Evergreen Forest (900–3400 m; Subtropical and lower Temperate zones).

Distribution.—*Resident* in the highlands from southeastern Sonora, southern Chihuahua, western Durango, Nayarit, Jalisco, northern Nuevo León, southern San Luis Potosí, and western Tamaulipas south through Mexico, Guatemala, El Salvador, and Honduras to north-central Nicaragua. Northernmost populations are partly migratory.

Casual north to southern Arizona (Huachuca Mountains, Ramsey Canyon, Patagonia) and Sonora. Sight report from Texas (Big Bend National Park).

Notes.—Also known as Hartlaub's Warbler or Spot-breasted Warbler. Often included in the genus *Vermivora* (Eisenmann 1955).

Parula americana (Linnaeus). Northern Parula.

Parus americanus Linnaeus, 1758, Syst. Nat. (ed. 10) 1: 190. Based on "The Finch-Creeper" Catesby, Nat. Hist. Carolina 1: 64, pl. 64. (in America septentrionali = South Carolina.)

Habitat.—Open humid deciduous forest, riparian woodland, swamps, locally humid co-niferous forest, all with at least some tree lichens or Spanish moss for nest sites; in migration and winter, also humid lowland forest, second growth, and scrub.

Distribution.—*Breeds* from southeastern Manitoba, central Ontario, southern Quebec, New Brunswick, Prince Edward Island, and Nova Scotia south (but rare or absent in much of upper Midwest-Great Lakes region and southern New England) to south-central and southern Texas (west to Tarrant, Kerr, and Hidalgo counties), the Gulf coast, and southern Florida (to Collier and Palm Beach counties), and west to the eastern edge of the Plains states (extreme eastern Nebraska, eastern Kansas, eastern Oklahoma, eastern Texas); and casually in central and southern California, central Arizona (Verde Valley), New Mexico (near Bernalillo), Rio Grande Valley of Texas, and northern Sonora.

Winters from southern Tamaulipas (sparingly), Veracruz, and Oaxaca (casually from north-ern California, southern Arizona, northern Sonora, and coastal Louisiana; perhaps annually in southern Texas) south through Mexico (primarily on the Gulf-Caribbean drainage and offshore islands) to Guatemala and Belize, rarely to Nicaragua and Costa Rica, also sight reports from the Caribbean coast of Panama; and from central Florida, Bermuda, and the Bahama Islands south throughout the West Indies to Tobago, casually to Curaçao and Isla Los Roques, off Venezuela. Accidental in Illinois. Several December records from central United States north to southern Canada

Migrates primarily through eastern North America, Bermuda, and northeastern Mexico, rarely but regularly to California, casually elsewhere in western North America from British Columbia, Alberta, Saskatchewan, Montana (sight report), and Wyoming southward.

Casual or accidental in Newfoundland, Greenland, Iceland, the British Isles, and France. Sight report for Alaska (Middleton Island).

Notes.—Also known as Parula Warbler. Moldenhauer (1992) and Regelski and Molden-hauer (1996) described a major song difference between eastern and western populations of this species. *Parula americana* and *P. pitiayumi* constitute a superspecies (Mayr and Short 1970).

Parula pitiayumi (Vieillot). Tropical Parula.

Sylvia pitiayumi Vieillot, 1817, Nouv. Dict. Hist. Nat. (nouv. éd.) 11: 276. Based on "Pico de Punzon del celeste pecho de oro" Azara, Apunt. Hist. Nat. Páx. Parag. 1: 421 (no. 109). (Paraguay.)

Habitat.—Montane Evergreen Forest, Tropical Lowland Evergreen Forest, Tropical De-ciduous Forest, Secondary Forest, Gallery Forest; in Texas, primarily in live oaks with Spanish moss (0–2600 m; Tropical and Subtropical zones).

Distribution.—*Resident* [*pitiayumi* group] from southern Sonora, southwestern Chihua-hua, Sinaloa, western Durango, Nayarit (including the Tres Marias and Isabela islands), Jalisco, San Luis Potosí, Nuevo León, and southern Texas (lower Rio Grande Valley north to King Ranch; casually to Edwards Plateau and Big Bend areas) south locally through Middle America to Panama (including Isla Coiba), and in South America from Colombia, Venezuela (including Margarita Island), Tobago, Trinidad, and the Guianas south, west of the Andes to northwestern Peru and east of the Andes to northern Argentina and southern Brazil (except absent from most of Amazonia); and [*graysoni* group] on Socorro Island, in the Revillagigedo Islands. Northernmost populations [*pitiayumi* group] are partly migratory.

Casual [*pitiayumi* group] in southern Baja California, southern Arizona, southwestern Texas (Big Bend, Edwards Plateau), coastal Texas, and southwestern Louisiana, and [*graysoni* group] in southern Baja California (confirmation of these records is needed).

Notes.—Also known as Olive-backed Warbler. Groups: *P. pitiayumi* [Tropical Parula] and *P. graysoni* (Ridgway, 1887) [Socorro Warbler]. See comments under *P. americana*.

Genus *DENDROICA* Gray

Dendroica G. R. Gray, 1842, List Genera Birds, app., p. 8. Type, by original designation, *Motacilla coronata* Linnaeus.

Notes.—See comments under *Vermivora* and *Catharopeza*.

Dendroica petechia (Linnaeus). Yellow Warbler.

Motacilla petechia Linnaeus, 1766, Syst. Nat. (ed. 12) 1: 334. Based on "The Yellow Red-pole" Edwards, Glean. Nat. Hist. 1: 99, pl. 256, fig. 2. (in America septentrionali = Barbados.)

Habitat.—[*aestiva* group] Primarily riparian woodlands and thickets, particularly those dominated by willow or cottonwood, also locally in early successional stages dominated by saplings, wooded suburbs, shelterbelts, regenerating burns and clearcuts, and aspen woodland; in migration and winter, also open woodland, brushy areas, tall weeds, mangroves, and marsh and forest edge (Tropical to Temperate zones); [*petechia* group] Mangrove Forest, Arid Lowland Scrub, Tropical Deciduous Forest, Secondary Forest; and [*erithachorides* group] Mangrove Forest, Secondary Forest, Arid Lowland Scrub (Tropical Zone).

Distribution.—*Breeds* [*aestiva* group] from northwestern and north-central Alaska, northern Yukon, northwestern and central Mackenzie, northern Saskatchewan, northern Manitoba, northern Ontario, central Quebec, central Labrador, and Newfoundland south to central Alaska (west to the Alaska Peninsula and Unimak Island), northern Baja California, through the central plateau region of Mexico to northern Guerrero, Puebla, and southeastern San Luis Potosí, and to central and northeastern Texas (formerly), central Oklahoma, central Arkansas, central Alabama, central Georgia, extreme northwestern South Carolina, and central North Carolina.

Winters [*aestiva* group] from southern (casually northern) California, southwestern Arizona, northern Mexico, the southern Gulf Coast (primarily December records), and the Bahama Islands south through Middle America, the southern Lesser Antilles (north to St. Vincent), and South America (mostly east of the Andes) to Peru and Amazonian Brazil. Rare to casual in Florida, and annual in December in Newfoundland.

Resident [*petechia* group] from southern Florida (Florida Bay area and the Florida Keys) and the Bahama Islands south throughout the West Indies (south to St. Lucia, Barbados, and the Grenadines, and including the Cayman, Providencia, and San Andrés islands), to the northern coast of Venezuela (west to Falcón) and islands offshore, and on Cozumel Island (off Quintana Roo); and [*erithachorides* group] from southern Baja California (south of lat. 27° N.), Sonora, and southern Tamaulipas south along both coasts of Middle America (including the Bay Islands off Honduras and Cocos Island off Costa Rica) to eastern Panama (on the Pacific coast east only to western Darién, but including Escudo, Coiba, and the Pearl islands), along the west coast of South America from northwestern Colombia south to central Peru (also the Galapagos Islands), and east along the northern coast of Colombia to northwestern Venezuela (east to the Paraguana Peninsula).

Migrates [*aestiva* group] through Texas and the Gulf Coast region south of the breeding range, Florida, Bermuda, and Cuba.

Casual or accidental [*aestiva* group] in northern Alaska, islands in the Bering Sea (St. Lawrence Island, Nunivak, and the Pribilofs), the Queen Charlotte Islands, Southampton Island (Northwest Territories), Baffin Island, northern Bolivia, Greenland, Iceland, and the British Isles; and [*erithachorides* group] in the Revillagigedo Islands (Socorro; sight reports) and southern Texas (Cameron County, Rockport).

Notes.—Groups: *D. aestiva* (Gmelin, 1789) [Yellow Warbler], *D. petechia* [Golden Warbler], and *D. erithachorides* Baird, 1858 [Mangrove Warbler]. Klein and Brown (1994) have clarified relationships among populations in this complex.

Dendroica pensylvanica (Linnaeus). Chestnut-sided Warbler.

> *Motacilla pensylvanica* Linnaeus, 1766, Syst. Nat. (ed. 12) 1: 333. Based on "The Red-throated Fly-catcher" Edwards, Glean. Nat. Hist. 2: 193, pl. 301. (in Pensylvania = Philadelphia.)

Habitat.—Early successional stages of regenerating deciduous forest, locally in thickets of mountain laurel and, in extreme western portion of range, tall deciduous woodland; in migration in any wooded habitat; in winter, tropical forest edge and second-growth.

Distribution.—*Breeds* from northeastern British Columbia (local), east-central Alberta, central Saskatchewan, central Manitoba, central Ontario, central Quebec, New Brunswick, Prince Edward Island, and Nova Scotia south to north-central North Dakota, central Minnesota, eastern Nebraska (formerly), central Iowa, southern Missouri, northern Arkansas, northern Illinois, south-central Indiana, and central Ohio, in the Appalachians south through West Virginia, eastern Kentucky, western Virginia, eastern Tennessee, and eastern North Carolina to northeastern Alabama, north-central Georgia, and northwestern South Carolina, and to central Maryland and Delaware. Casual in north-central and east-central Colorado.

Winters from Oaxaca, southern Veracruz, Chiapas, and Guatemala (casually farther north to southern California, southern Arizona, and in southern Florida) south through Middle America (primarily on the Caribbean slope north of Costa Rica) to eastern Panama, casually to northern Colombia, Venezuela, and Trinidad. Casual (mainly December) in southern Texas and southern Louisiana and accidental in Bermuda (sight report).

Migrates primarily through the eastern United States (east of the Rockies), Bermuda (only casually in spring), Bahama Islands, Greater Antilles (Cuba and Jamaica, also sight reports from Hispaniola, Puerto Rico, and the Virgin Islands), and eastern Mexico (also Nayarit, otherwise not recorded Pacific slope north of Guerrero), rarely through western North America from southern British Columbia, Idaho, and Montana south to southern California, Arizona, and New Mexico.

Casual or accidental in southern interior British Columbia, Bermuda, Barbados, and Greenland; accidental in Great Britain; sight reports from southern Alaska (Middleton Island), central Baja California, and western Ecuador.

Dendroica magnolia (Wilson). Magnolia Warbler.

> *Sylvia magnolia* Wilson, 1811, Amer. Ornithol. 3: 63, pl. 23, fig. 2. (the Little Miami, near its junction with the Ohio . . . [and] not far from fort Adams on the Mississippi = Fort Adams, Mississippi.)

Habitat.—Open moist coniferous (especially spruce and fir) or mixed coniferous-deciduous woodland, forest edge, and second growth; in migration and winter, a variety of wooded habitats and tall weeds (especially giant ragweed).

Distribution.—*Breeds* from southeastern Alaska (probably), northeastern British Columbia, southeastern Yukon, west-central and southern Mackenzie, northern Saskatchewan, north-central Manitoba, northern Ontario, and Labrador (locally), Newfoundland, and south-central and eastern Quebec (including Anticosti and Magdalen islands) south to south-central British Columbia, south-central Alberta, central Saskatchewan, southern Manitoba, north-central and northeastern Minnesota, northern Wisconsin, central Michigan, southern Ontario, north-central and south-central Ohio (local), southeastern West Virginia, western Virginia, western Maryland, northeastern Pennsylvania, northwestern New Jersey, and Connecticut. Also locally in southern Wisconsin (Baraboo Hills), west-central Indiana (Montgomery County), and in the high mountains of eastern Tennessee and western North Carolina. Summer records for California and Colorado.

Winters from Oaxaca, Puebla, San Luis Potosí, central Veracruz, Bermuda, the Greater Antilles, and the Cayman and Bahama islands (casually north to central California, southwestern Arizona, northern Sonora, southern Texas, the Gulf coast, and Virginia) south through Middle America to western Panama (rarely east to Canal area and eastern Panamá province), and east in the West Indies (at least rarely) to the Virgin Islands; also, rare in southern Florida, and casual in California, Arizona, and coastal Texas. Many December records from eastern North America, north to southern Canada.

Migrates primarily through eastern North America east of the Rockies, rarely but regularly in western North America.

Casual or accidental in western and northern Alaska, Newfoundland, Barbados, northwestern Colombia, Greenland, and the British Isles; sight reports for northern Baja California, Clipperton Island, the Lesser Antilles, Trinidad, Tobago, and northern Venezuela.

Notes.—*Dendroica lutea,* based on *Muscicapa lutea* Linnaeus, 1776, has been officially suppressed (I.C.Z.N. 1956c).

Dendroica tigrina (Gmelin). Cape May Warbler.

> *Motacilla tigrina* Gmelin, 1789, Syst. Nat. 1(2): 985. Based on "Le Figuier brun de Canada" Brisson, Ornithologie 3: 515, pl. 27, fig. 4. (in Canada.)

Habitat.—Primarily spruce forest, usually in open stands and often mixed with other trees, spruce bogs; in migration and winter, a variety of wooded habitats, especially in flowering trees and palms.

Distribution.—*Breeds* from southeastern Yukon, northeastern British Columbia, southwestern and south-central Mackenzie, northern Alberta, northern Saskatchewan, central Manitoba, central Ontario, south-central Quebec, New Brunswick, Prince Edward Island, Nova Scotia, and southwestern Newfoundland south to central Alberta, central Saskatchewan, southeastern Manitoba, northeastern Minnesota, northern Wisconsin, northern (casually central) Michigan, southern Ontario, northeastern New York, northeastern Vermont, northern New Hampshire, and east-central Maine. Recorded in summer (and possibly breeding) on Anticosti Island (Quebec).

Winters in coastal southern Florida, Bermuda, the West Indies (primarily the Bahamas and Greater Antilles, less commonly in the Lesser Antilles), the Caribbean slope of Middle America from Veracruz (rarely San Luis Potosí) and the Yucatan Peninsula to Honduras. Rare also on Pacific slope from Oaxaca to El Salvador (casually from Sonora to Jalisco). Rare also in Nicaragua, Costa Rica, and Panama; recorded casually in winter also in California, southern Arizona, southern Canada, the central and eastern United States, Trinidad, Tobago, the Netherlands Antilles, and Caribbean islands off Colombia and Venezuela..

Migrates primarily through the midwestern, eastern, and southeastern states, rarely (occurring mostly in spring) south of Arkansas and Tennessee and west of Alabama.

Casual north and west to northern, central and south-coastal Alaska (Point Barrow, Fairbanks, Middleton Island), Labrador, elsewhere in western North America south to California, southern Nevada, southern Arizona, New Mexico, and Chihuahua, and to Isla Providencia (in the western Caribbean Sea); sight reports for Washington, Sonora, Revillagigedo Islands (Socorro), northern Colombia, and Great Britain.

Dendroica caerulescens (Gmelin). Black-throated Blue Warbler.

> *Motacilla caerulescens* Gmelin, 1789, Syst. Nat. 1(2): 960. Based on "La Fauvette bleuâtre de St. Domingue" Buffon, Hist. Nat. Ois. 5: 164. (in insula S. Dominici = Hispaniola.)

Habitat.—Deciduous or mixed deciduous-coniferous woodland and second growth, usually with dense undergrowth, and on mountain or hill country slopes; in migration and winter, also other forest types, open woodland, and scrub.

Distribution.—*Breeds* locally in eastern Saskatchewan, southeastern Manitoba (probably), and from southwestern and central Ontario, southern Quebec, New Brunswick, Prince Edward Island, and Nova Scotia south to extreme northeastern Minnesota, northern Wisconsin, central Michigan, southern Ontario, northeastern Ohio (formerly), in the Appalachians through West Virginia, western Maryland, eastern Kentucky, western Virginia, eastern Tennessee, and western North Carolina to extreme northeastern Georgia and northwestern South Carolina, and to northeastern Pennsylvania, northern New Jersey, southern New York, and southern New England. Recorded in summer (and possibly breeding) on Anticosti and Magdalen islands. Summer records for Oregon, Arizona, and Colorado.

Winters from southern Florida (rare) and the Bahama Islands south through the Greater Antilles (east to Tortola in the Virgin Islands), and the Cayman Islands, and in the Yucatan

Peninsula and Belize, casually in British Columbia, Washington, Oregon, California, Arizona, the Gulf Coast, Bermuda, St. Martin, Antigua, Guadeloupe, Dominica, and the Swan Islands. Rare to casual along Caribbean coast from southern Veracruz through Middle America to northern Colombia and Venezuela. One January specimen from Idaho, and scattered records in eastern North America north to Minnesota, Ontario, and New York.

Migrates through eastern North America east of the Rockies (rarely west to eastern Texas), rarely to California (mostly in fall), and casually elsewhere in western North America (recorded from interior British Columbia, Oregon, Alberta, Saskatchewan, and Montana south to southern Baja California, southern Arizona, southern New Mexico, southern Texas, and Veracruz). Rare but regular in Newfoundland.

Casual or accidental on St. Kitts (sight report), Nuevo León, Greenland, and Iceland.

Dendroica coronata (Linnaeus). Yellow-rumped Warbler.

> *Motacilla coronata* Linnaeus, 1766, Syst. Nat. (ed. 12) 1: 333. Based on "The Golden-crowned Fly-catcher" Edwards, Glean. Nat. Hist. 2: 187, pl. 298. (in Pensylvania = Philadelphia.)

Habitat.—Primarily open coniferous or mixed coniferous-deciduous forest and woodland; in migration and winter, virtually any wooded habitat, including suburbs, low scrub (especially *Myrica* thickets in eastern portion of winter range), and weedy fields.

Distribution.—*Breeds* [*coronata* group] from western and central Alaska, northern Yukon, northwestern and central Mackenzie, southwestern Keewatin, northern Manitoba, northern Ontario, northern Quebec, northern Labrador, and Newfoundland south to southern and southeastern Alaska, northern British Columbia, central and southwestern Alberta, southern Saskatchewan, north-central North Dakota (probably), northern Minnesota, northern Wisconsin, central Michigan, southern Ontario, in the Appalachians to eastern West Virginia and northwestern Virginia, and to eastern Pennsylvania, extreme northeastern Maryland (casually), and Massachusetts; and [*auduboni* group] from extreme southeastern Alaska, south-coastal and central British Columbia (including Vancouver Island), southern Alberta, southwestern Saskatchewan (Cypress Hills), central and southeastern Montana, southwestern North Dakota, western South Dakota, and northwestern Nebraska south to south-central and eastern California (to Cuyumaca and New York mountains), northern Baja California (Sierra San Pedro Mártir), central and southeastern Arizona, southern New Mexico, western Chihuahua, New Mexico, and extreme western Texas (Guadalupe and, probably, Davis mountains), also in the mountains of western Durango, eastern Chiapas (Volcán Tacaná), and western Guatemala.

Winters [*coronata* group] from the Pacific states, Arizona, Colorado, and Kansas east across the central United States to southern Ontario and New England (occasionally farther north) south through the southern United States, Middle America, and the West Indies to eastern Panama (including the Pearl Islands), islands off Middle America (including Socorro in the Revillagigedo Islands), islands in the western Caribbean Sea, and Barbados; and [*auduboni* group] from southwestern British Columbia, southeastern Washington, Idaho, western Montana (rarely), Colorado, and central and southern Texas south (mostly in highlands) to southern Baja California, the Revillagigedo Islands (Socorro), and through Mexico to Guatemala and western Honduras.

Casual or accidental [*coronata* group] north to King William and Southampton islands, and in Tobago, Colombia, Venezuela, Greenland, Iceland, the British Isles, and Siberia (Chukotski Peninsula); and [*auduboni* group] on Attu in the Aleutian Islands, and in eastern North America from southern Ontario, southern Quebec, Newfoundland, and Massachusetts south to Arkansas, Louisiana, Ohio, Alabama, Pennsylvania, New Jersey, and North Carolina. Sight reports for southern Florida, Bermuda, and western Panama (Chiriquí). Reports [*auduboni* group] from Costa Rica are regarded as erroneous.

Notes.—The two groups have often been regarded as distinct species, *D. coronata* [Myrtle Warbler] and *D. auduboni* (J. K. Townsend, 1837) [Audubon's Warbler]; free interbreeding occurs in a narrow hybrid zone in mountain passes in the Jasper Park area, Alberta, and the Pine Pass area, British Columbia (Hubbard 1969, Barrowclough 1980).

Dendroica nigrescens (Townsend). Black-throated Gray Warbler.

Sylvia nigrescens J. K. Townsend, 1837, J. Acad. Nat. Sci. Philadelphia 7: 191. (No locality given = near Fort William, Portland, Oregon.)

Habitat.—Open, dry coniferous or mixed coniferous-deciduous woodland with brushy undergrowth, pinyon-juniper, pine-oak association, and oak woodland; in migration and winter, also in a variety of forest, woodland, and scrub habitats.

Distribution.—*Breeds* from southwestern British Columbia (including Vancouver Island), western Washington, central Oregon, southern Idaho, central and southern Wyoming, and northwestern and central Colorado south, primarily in mountains, to northern Baja California, south-central and eastern California (to Laguna and New York mountains), central and southeastern Arizona, northeastern Sonora, southern New Mexico, and (possibly) extreme western Texas (Guadalupe Mountains).

Winters from central California (casually north to Washington and once in British Columbia), southern Arizona, and southern Texas south to central Oaxaca (west of Isthmus of Tehuantepec) and Veracruz. Casually along the Gulf coast to southern Florida.

Migrates regularly between breeding and wintering grounds, and east to western Kansas.

Casual north to Alberta and Saskatchewan, across the northeastern region from eastern Montana, South Dakota, Minnesota, Wisconsin, Michigan, southern Ontario, Quebec, New York, Massachusetts, New Brunswick, Nova Scotia, and Newfoundland south to Ohio, Kentucky, Pennsylvania, New Jersey, and Virginia, and through the Gulf states from eastern Texas east to southeastern Georgia and southern Florida; sight reports from other midwestern and eastern states, Alaska (Mitkof Island), and Guatemala (Dueñas).

Notes.—*Dendroica nigrescens, D. virens, D. occidentalis,* and *D. townsendi* have been subjected to phylogenetic analysis based on mtDNA restriction sites by Bermingham et al. (1992), who found that *D. townsendi* and *D. occidentalis* were sister species and that *D. nigrescens* was the basal species in the group. See comments under *D. townsendi.*

Dendroica chrysoparia Sclater and Salvin. Golden-cheeked Warbler.

Dendrœca chrysoparia Sclater and Salvin, 1860, Proc. Zool. Soc. London, p. 298. (In reip. Guatemalensis provincia Veræ Pacis, inter montes = Tactic, Alta Verapaz, Guatemala.)

Habitat.—Mixed oak-juniper woodland, often mixed with ash, maple, sycamores, and other deciduous trees; in migration in a variety of open woodland, scrub, and thicket habitats; in winter, montane pine and pine-oak association.

Distribution.—*Breeds* in central Texas from Dallas County south to the Edwards Plateau region (south to Medina and Bexar counties, and west to Real and Kerr counties).

Winters in the highlands of Chiapas, Guatemala, Honduras, and north-central Nicaragua.

Migrates rarely through Mexico (reported Coahuila, Nuevo León, and Tamaulipas; a record from Puebla is questionable, one from Sinaloa is erroneous).

Accidental in California (Farallon Islands) and Florida (Pinellas County); sight reports from eastern Texas, Morelos, and the Virgin Islands.

Notes.—See comments under *D. townsendi.*

Dendroica virens (Gmelin). Black-throated Green Warbler.

Motacilla virens Gmelin, 1789, Syst. Nat. 1(2): 985. Based on "The Black-throated Green Fly-catcher" Edwards, Glean. Nat. Hist. 2: 190, pl. 300. (in Pensilvania = Philadelphia.)

Habitat.—Open coniferous (primarily balsam fir or spruce) or mixed deciduous-coniferous woodland and edge, also in cypress swamps in southeastern coastal portion of range; in migration and winter, a variety of wooded habitats, but in Middle America in winter confined mostly to montane regions (but typically at lower elevations than *D. townsendi* and *D. occidentalis*).

Distribution.—*Breeds* from northeastern British Columbia, northern Alberta, north-central Saskatchewan, central Manitoba, central Ontario, central Quebec, southern Labrador,

and Newfoundland south to central Alberta, central Saskatchewan, southern Manitoba, northern and east-central Minnesota, northern Wisconsin, southern Michigan (locally to southern
Wisconsin, northern Illinois, south-central Indiana, southern Ohio), Pennsylvania, New Jersey, and southern New England, and south through Appalachian region through eastern
Kentucky, West Virginia, western Maryland, western Virginia, eastern Tennessee, western
North Carolina, central Alabama, extreme northern Georgia, and northwestern South Carolina; also in northwestern Arkansas (Ozark Mountains), and the coastal plains from southeastern Virginia to eastern South Carolina (Charleston County). Summer records for Washington, California, Arizona, and Colorado.

   Winters from Colima (casually north to coastal California), Nuevo León, southern and
southeastern Texas, extreme southeastern Louisiana, southern Florida, Bermuda (rare), and
the Bahama Islands south through eastern and southern Mexico (west to San Luis Potosí,
Hidalgo, Morelos, Puebla, and Oaxaca), Central America, Cuba, the Isle of Pines, the Cayman
Islands, and Jamaica (casually east to the Virgin Islands) to central Panama (east to the
Canal area and eastern Panamá province, rarely to Darién). Accidental in southeastern Arizona. Early winter records for many states along the Atlantic Coast and also Nova Scotia.

   Migrates primarily through North America east of the Rockies and through Middle America (including both lowlands from Oaxaca southward), rarely to California, Arizona, Sonora,
and New Mexico, casually elsewhere in western North America north to southern British
Columbia, southern Alberta, and southern Saskatchewan.

   Casual or accidental in southeastern Alaska (Chichagof Island), southwestern British Columbia, Northwest Territories, the Revillagigedo Islands (Socorro Island), Clipperton Island
(sight report), and the Lesser Antilles (St. Martin, Barbuda, Guadeloupe, Dominica, Barbados), Netherlands Antilles, and Trinidad, and in Colombia, Venezuela, Greenland, off
Iceland, and Germany.

   Notes.—See comments under *D. townsendi.*

Dendroica townsendi (Townsend). Townsend's Warbler.

   Sylvia Townsendi (Nuttall MS) J. K. Townsend, 1837, J. Acad. Nat. Sci. Philadelphia
   7: 191. (forests of the Columbia River = Fort Vancouver, Washington.)

   Habitat.—Tall and moist coniferous and mixed coniferous-deciduous forest; in migration
and winter, also humid forest, pine-oak association, oak woodland, and tall second growth,
primarily in montane situations.

   Distribution.—*Breeds* from east-central Alaska, southern Yukon, northwestern and central
British Columbia, and extreme west-central Alberta (once in Cypress Hills of southwestern
Saskatchewan) south to south-coastal and southeastern Alaska, northwestern Washington,
central and northeastern Oregon, central Idaho, western Montana, and (casually) northwestern
Wyoming. One summer record from coastal California.

   Winters from extreme southwestern British Columbia (rare) and coastal Washington south
to coastal southern California (rarely to northern Baja California), and also rarely in Sierra
Nevada foothills in California, southern Arizona, southwestern Texas (Chisos and Davis
mountains). Also from northern Mexico (Sonora east to Nuevo León) south through the
highlands of Mexico and Central America (except Belize) to Costa Rica (casually to western
Panama). Casual or accidental in winter in the Queen Charlotte Islands, eastern Oregon,
southern Nevada, Utah, southern New Mexico, and the southeastern United States.

   Migrates primarily through the western United States west of the Great Plains and western
Texas, rarely through the Mexican lowlands.

   Casual or accidental in the western Aleutians (Shemya), northern Alaska (Point Barrow),
the Revillagigedo Islands (Socorro), Great Plains region (from central Alberta, southeastern
Saskatchewan, North Dakota, and Minnesota south to Nebraska, Kansas, western Oklahoma,
Iowa, and Illinois), the eastern region (from southern Ontario, Newfoundland, New York,
New Hampshire, and Nova Scotia south to Pennsylvania, New Jersey, Massachusetts, Rhode
Island, the Gulf states from eastern Texas east to Florida), Bermuda, Bahamas (Grand Turk
Island and Grand Bahama), Cuba (Cayo Coco), and northern Colombia; sight reports from
Michigan, Indiana, Ohio, Maine, and North Carolina.

   Notes.—*Dendroica townsendi, D. occidentalis, D. virens,* and *D. chrysoparia* constitute
a superspecies (Mengel 1964). *Dendroica townsendi* and *D. occidentalis* hybridize to a

limited extent where parapatric (Morrison and Hardy 1983). See comments under *D. nigrescens*.

Dendroica occidentalis (Townsend). Hermit Warbler.

> *Sylvia occidentalis* J. K. Townsend, 1837, J. Acad. Nat. Sci. Philadelphia 7: 190. (forests of the Columbia River = Fort Vancouver, Washington.)

Habitat.—Coniferous forest, usually cool and moist, especially where Douglas-fir present; in migration, a variety of wooded habitats; in winter, primarily montane forest and pine-oak association.

Distribution.—*Breeds* from western Washington south through the coast ranges and Cascades (mostly western slopes) to northern California (Marin County), and south in interior through the Sierra Nevada Mountains (to Kern County), including extreme west-central Nevada; also small populations in Santa Cruz Mountains of central California and in the San Gabriel and San Bernardino mountains of southern California .

Winters locally in coastal California (mainly from Point Reyes south to Santa Barbara County; casually north to western Oregon and south to San Diego County), and from Sinaloa and Durango south through the highlands of Mexico and Central America (except Belize) to north-central Nicaragua. Casual in interior California, southern Arizona, and southern Texas; accidental in Missouri and Nova Scotia.

Migrates through the southwestern states (from California and Arizona east to southern New Mexico and western Texas), Baja California, and most of Mexico (except the Yucatan Peninsula).

Casual in Utah, Colorado, and along the Gulf coast from southeastern Texas to southeastern Louisiana. Accidental in Kansas, Minnesota, Wisconsin, southern Ontario, and Newfoundland; sight reports for Wyoming, Minnesota, southern Quebec, New Brunswick, Massachusetts, Connecticut, Costa Rica, and western Panama (Chiriquí).

Notes.—See comments under *D. townsendi*.

Dendroica fusca (Müller). Blackburnian Warbler.

> *Motacilla fusca* P. L. S. Müller, 1776, Natursyst., Suppl., p. 175. (Guyana = French Guiana.)

Habitat.—Mature coniferous (primarily hemlock, balsam fir, and spruce) and mixed coniferous-deciduous forest, locally in deciduous forest in Appalachians; in migration, a variety of wooded habitats; in winter, primarily Montane Evergreen Forest, Secondary Forest.

Distribution.—*Breeds* from central Alberta (local), central Saskatchewan, central Manitoba, central Ontario, southern Quebec, New Brunswick, Prince Edward Island, Nova Scotia, and southwestern Newfoundland south to southern Manitoba, central Minnesota, central Wisconsin, southwestern Michigan, southern Ontario, northern Indiana (probably), eastern Ohio (local), Pennsylvania, in the Appalachians through West Virginia, western Maryland, eastern Kentucky, western Virginia, eastern Tennessee, and western North Carolina to north-central Georgia and northwestern South Carolina (breeding not confirmed), and to northern New Jersey, southeastern New York, and Massachusetts. Recorded in summer (and possibly breeding) in South Dakota, Colorado, central Ontario, and central Quebec.

Winters from Costa Rica (rare) Panama (primarily Darién), Colombia, and northern Venezuela south in Andes of Ecuador to central Peru, casually to northern Bolivia. Casual in winter in coastal California, accidental in coastal Oregon, and one January record from Ontario; many winter sight reports for Gulf Coast and Florida, but no documented winter records from anywhere in eastern United States.

Migrates regularly through the eastern United States (west to the Plains states and central Texas), Bermuda, Bahama Islands, Greater Antilles (except Jamaica), the Cayman Islands, eastern Mexico, both slopes of Middle America from Oaxaca and Veracruz southward (more frequently on the Caribbean slope), islands in the western Caribbean Sea (Swan, Providencia, and San Andrés), and the Netherlands Antilles.

Casual in western North America (most frequently recorded in coastal areas in fall) from British Columbia, Washington, Montana, and Colorado south to northern Baja California (annual in small numbers in coastal central and southern California), southern Arizona, and southern New Mexico, also in the Lesser Antilles (Barbados, Grenada), Tobago, Trinidad (sight reports), and Greenland. Accidental in Surinam, Brazil, at sea off Iceland, and the British Isles (sight reports).

Dendroica dominica (Linnaeus). Yellow-throated Warbler.

> *Motacilla dominica* Linnaeus, 1766, Syst. Nat. (ed. 12) 1: 334. Based mainly on "Le Figuier cendré de S. Domingue" Brisson, Ornithologie 3: 520, pl. 27, fig. 3. (in Jamaica, Dominica = Hispaniola.)

Habitat.—Pine forest, sycamore-bald cypress swamp, riparian woodland (especially sycamores), and live oak woodland; in migration and winter, a variety of wooded habitats, especially pines and palms.

Distribution.—*Breeds* from central Iowa (rare), extreme southern Wisconsin, extreme southwestern Michigan, northern Ohio, central Pennsylvania, central New Jersey, and Connecticut (casually southern New York) south to eastern Kansas (local), central Oklahoma, south-central and eastern Texas (west to Uvalde and Real counties), the Gulf coast, and central Florida, and also in the northern Bahama Islands (Grand Bahama, Abaco).

Winters from southeastern Texas, the Gulf coast (rare), and South Carolina, rarely to southeastern North Carolina (casually farther north, and to central California, Arizona, and Sinaloa; accidental as far northwest as Idaho) south through Middle America (primarily the Gulf-Caribbean slope and, in Chiapas and northern Central America, the interior highlands), Bermuda (rare), the Bahama Islands, Greater Antilles (east to the Virgin Islands), Cayman Islands, and to Costa Rica (casually to Panama).

Migrates rarely west to Wyoming, eastern Colorado, and New Mexico, casually to Utah and southern Arizona. Recorded annually in small numbers in California and Newfoundland.

Casual or accidental north to southern Oregon, Idaho, southern Manitoba, Minnesota, central Ontario, southern Quebec, New Brunswick, Nova Scotia, and Newfoundland, Clipperton Island, and to the Lesser Antilles (Montserrat, Guadeloupe); sight reports for south-central Montana, Saskatchewan, Nevada, northern Baja California, and Colombia.

Notes.—Mengel (1964) considered *D. dominica, D. graciae,* and *D. adelaidae* to constitute a superspecies; *D. pityophila* also appears to be closely related to *D. graciae* and to belong to this group, but it is sympatric with *D. dominica* in the Bahamas.

Dendroica graciae Baird. Grace's Warbler.

> *Dendroica graciæ* (Coues MS) Baird, 1865, Rev. Amer. Birds 1: 210. (Fort Whipple, near Prescott, Arizona.)

Habitat.—Pine Forest, Pine-Oak Forest, lowland pine savanna (Middle America), locally spruce-fir forest in northern portions of range (600–2800 m; Tropical to Temperate zones).

Distribution.—*Breeds* from southern Nevada, southern Utah, southwestern Colorado, northern New Mexico, and western Texas (Guadalupe and Davis mountains) south through the mountains of western Mexico (east to western Chihuahua, Durango, and western Zacatecas), Guatemala, El Salvador, and Honduras to north-central Nicaragua; also in the lowland pine savanna of Belize, eastern Honduras, and northeastern Nicaragua. Summer records from mountains of eastern and southern California.

Winters from Sonora and Chihuahua south through the breeding range (occurring east at least to northern Oaxaca), being generally resident from central Mexico southward. Casual in winter in coastal southern California and accidental in lower Colorado River Valley of Nevada.

Casual in California (see above), southwestern Texas (El Paso, Big Bend), and Front Range of central Colorado.

Notes.—See comments under *D. dominica.*

Dendroica adelaidae Baird. Adelaide's Warbler.

> *Dendroica adelaidæ* Baird, 1865, Rev. Amer. Birds 1: 212. (Puerto Rico.)

Habitat.—Tropical Lowland Evergreen Forest, Tropical Deciduous Forest, Arid Lowland Scrub (0–700 m).

Distribution.—*Resident* on Puerto Rico (including Vieques Island), and in the Lesser Antilles on Barbuda and St. Lucia.

Notes.—Lowery and Monroe *in* Paynter (1968) proposed that *D. adelaidae* and *D. graciae* were each other's closest relative. See comments under *D. dominica*.

Dendroica pityophila (Gundlach). Olive-capped Warbler.

Sylvicola pityophila Gundlach, 1858, Ann. Lyc. Nat. Hist. N. Y. 6: 160. (Cuba.)

Habitat.—Pine Forest (0–2000 m).

Distribution.—*Resident* in the northern Bahama Islands (Grand Bahama and Abaco) and Cuba (Pinar del Río and Oriente provinces).

Notes.—See comments under *D. dominica*.

Dendroica pinus (Wilson). Pine Warbler.

Sylvia pinus Wilson, 1811, Amer. Ornithol. 3: 25, pl. 19, fig. 4. (Southern States = Georgia.)

Habitat.—Pine forest and pine woodland; in migration and winter, also deciduous forest and woodland and pine groves in parks and suburbs.

Distribution.—*Breeds* in southeastern Manitoba (possibly also locally in eastern Saskatchewan), northern Minnesota, northern Wisconsin, northern Michigan, southern Ontario, southern Quebec, central Maine, and southwestern New Brunswick south to eastern Oklahoma and eastern Texas (west to Bastrop and Matagorda counties), the Gulf coast, southern Florida (to Long Pine Key, Everglades National Park) and the northern Bahama Islands (Grand Bahama, Abaco, Andros, and New Providence), but scarce, local, or absent from much of the Midwest south of the Great Lakes region and north of central Missouri, southern Illinois, and southern Indiana; also on Hispaniola.

Winters from eastern Texas, southeastern Oklahoma, Arkansas, southern Tennessee, North Carolina, eastern Virginia, eastern Maryland, and Delaware south to south-central Texas, the Gulf coast, Florida, Bermuda (rare), and through the breeding range in the Bahamas and on Hispaniola. Casual north (often early winter only) to the southern Great Lakes region, New York, and New England, and south to southern Texas, extreme northern Tamaulipas, and southern Florida; also casual in California.

Casual north to Newfoundland, Prince Edward Island, west to southeastern Alberta, southern Saskatchewan, Montana, Wyoming, eastern Colorado, western Kansas, and eastern New Mexico, also to California (primarily coastal region), Arizona, the Florida Keys, Cuba, and Cay Sal (in the Bahamas). Accidental in Greenland; sight reports for Oregon and Nuevo León. Sight reports from August and early September from Costa Rica require documentation.

Dendroica kirtlandii (Baird). Kirtland's Warbler.

Sylvicola kirtlandii Baird, 1852, Ann. Lyc. Nat. Hist. N. Y. 5: 217, pl. 6. (near Cleveland, Ohio.)

Habitat.—Scrubby jack-pine with openings; in winter, in low scrub, thickets, and (rarely) deciduous woodland.

Distribution.—*Breeds* in northern Michigan (from Otsego, extreme southwestern Presque Isle, and Alpena counties south to Kalkaska, northwestern Clare, Roscommon, Ogemaw, and Iosco counties) and (formerly) southern Ontario; has recently (1995, 1996) bred in Upper Peninsula of Michigan. Recorded in summer (and possibly breeding) in west-central Wisconsin (Jackson, Douglas, and Washburn counties).

Winters evidently in the Bahamas, but winter distribution largely unknown.

Casual (generally in migration) in Minnesota, northern Illinois, Indiana, Ohio, western Pennsylvania, southwestern Quebec, South Carolina, and southern Florida; sight reports from Kentucky, West Virginia, North Carolina, Alabama, and Georgia; recorded (prior to 1901) from eastern Missouri and Virginia.

Dendroica discolor (Vieillot). Prairie Warbler.

Sylvia discolor Vieillot, 1809, Hist. Nat. Ois. Amer. Sept. 2 (1808, livr. 17): 37, pl. 98. (États-Unis et les grandes Îles Antilles = the Antilles.)

Habitat.—Brushy second growth, dry scrub, brushy ridgetops, regenerating pine clear-cuts, low pine-juniper, pine barrens, and mangroves; in migration and winter also in a variety of woodland, second growth, and brushy situations.

Distribution.—*Breeds* from eastern Oklahoma, central Missouri, southern Illinois, central Indiana, central Ohio, Pennsylvania, southern New York, southern Vermont, southern New Hampshire, and extreme southern Maine south to eastern Texas, central Louisiana, southern Mississippi, southern Alabama, and southern Florida and the Florida Keys from Volusia County and Cedar Keys south to Marquesas Keys. Also locally north to eastern Nebraska (formerly), extreme eastern Kansas, extreme southeastern Iowa (probably, at least formerly), central Illinois, northern Michigan, southern Ontario, and northern New York. Summer records from Manitoba, North Dakota, and Wisconsin.

Winters from central Florida (casually from southern Texas, the Gulf coast, and Virginia, most records from December to early January only), Bermuda (rare), and the Bahama Islands south throughout most of the West Indies (casual in southern Lesser Antilles) to islands off the coast of northern Middle America (off Quintana Roo, Belize, and Honduras), and casually in coastal California, coastal Georgia, coastal South Carolina, southeastern North Carolina, the Gulf Coast to eastern Texas, southern Veracruz, and the Pacific coast from Nayarit to El Salvador. Early winter records along Atlantic coast to Massachusetts and Nova Scotia, and in Kentucky.

Migrates casually west through the Plains states and central Texas. Recorded in small numbers annually in California (primarily fall in coastal areas), Nova Scotia, New Brunswick, and Newfoundland.

Casual or accidental north to south-coastal and southeastern Alaska (Middleton Island, Ketchikan), southern Quebec, and Prince Edward Island, and to Oregon, Nevada, New Mexico, Arizona, eastern Montana, Wyoming, eastern Colorado, northern Baja California, Cocos Island, and Colombia; sight reports for Washington, New Mexico, South Dakota, Minnesota, Newfoundland, Guatemala (off the Pacific coast), Caribbean Nicaragua (pine savanna), Costa Rica, Panama, Clipperton Island, and Trinidad.

Notes.—*Dendroica discolor* and *D. vitellina* are considered to be each other's closest relatives (Lowery and Monroe *in* Paynter 1968) and to constitute a superspecies (Mayr and Short 1970).

Dendroica vitellina Cory. Vitelline Warbler.

Dendroica vitellina Cory, 1886, Auk 3: 497. (Island of Grand Cayman, West Indies.)

Habitat.—Tropical Deciduous Forest, Arid Lowland Scrub.
Distribution.—*Resident* in the Cayman (including Grand Cayman, Little Cayman, and Cayman Brac) and Swan (especially Little Swan) islands, in the Caribbean Sea.
Notes.—See comments under *D. discolor.*

Dendroica palmarum (Gmelin). Palm Warbler.

Motacilla palmarum Gmelin, 1789, Syst. Nat. 1(2): 951. Based on the "Bimbelé ou fausse Linotte" Buffon, Hist. Nat. Ois. 5: 330. (in insula S. Dominici = Hispaniola.)

Habitat.—Open bogs at the edge of boreal coniferous forest, and occasionally partly open situations with scattered trees and heavy undergrowth, usually near water; in migration and winter, primarily second growth habitats, weedy fields, hedgerows, and edges of marsh and mangrove woodland.

Distribution.—*Breeds* from extreme southeastern Yukon, west-central and southern Mackenzie, northern Alberta, northern Saskatchewan, northern Manitoba, northern Ontario, central Quebec, southern Labrador, and Newfoundland south to northeastern British Columbia, central Alberta, central Saskatchewan, southern Manitoba, north-central and northeastern Minnesota, northern Wisconsin, northern Michigan, southern Ontario, central Maine, New

Brunswick, and Nova Scotia; also rare and local in northern New York, Vermont, and northern New Hampshire.

Winters from southeastern Texas, central Louisiana, southern Mississippi, central Alabama, northern Georgia, South Carolina, eastern North Carolina, coastal Maryland, and coastal Delaware (casually north to Missouri, the Ohio Valley, and New England; often in early winter only) south to the Gulf Coast of southern Florida, Bermuda, the Bahama Islands, Greater Antilles (east to the Virgin Islands), Cayman Islands, islands in the western Caribbean Sea, and the Yucatan Peninsula (including islands offshore and off Belize); also regularly in coastal areas of Washington, Oregon, and California (casually southwestern British Columbia), from Baja California and Sonora south through the Pacific lowlands to Oaxaca, and in the lowland pine savanna of eastern Honduras and northeastern Nicaragua.

Migrates primarily through the central United States (from Montana and the Plains states eastward to the Atlantic seaboard), regularly through coastal California in fall, and casually elsewhere in western North America (from British Columbia, Idaho, and Wyoming south to northern Baja California, southern Arizona, and New Mexico).

Casual in Alaska (north to Barrow, west to Nunivak Island, and from Kodiak and Middleton islands to Ketchikan), Guerrero, Veracruz, Costa Rica, Panama, and in the Netherlands Antilles; accidental in Colombia and Venezuela (photograph; June 1995) and Great Britain; sight reports for Clipperton Island.

Dendroica castanea (Wilson). Bay-breasted Warbler.

Sylvia castanea Wilson, 1810, Amer. Ornithol. 2: 97, pl. 14, fig. 4. (Pennsylvania.)

Habitat.—Boreal coniferous forest (especially spruce, balsam fir) with openings, occasionally adjoining second growth or deciduous scrub; in migration and winter, a variety of wooded habitats, but primarily second-growth forest and forest edge.

Distribution.—*Breeds* from extreme southeastern Yukon, northeastern British Columbia, southwestern Mackenzie, northern Alberta, northern Saskatchewan, central Manitoba, central Ontario, central Quebec, New Brunswick, Prince Edward Island, Nova Scotia, and western Newfoundland south to east-central British Columbia, central Alberta, central Saskatchewan, southern Manitoba, north-central and northeastern Minnesota, northern Michigan, southern Ontario, southern Quebec, northern New York, northern Vermont (rare), northern New Hampshire, and southern Maine; also bred once in Colorado (Douglas County) and West Virginia (mated to a *D. fusca*). Recorded in summer in northern Wisconsin.

Winters from Costa Rica (Caribbean lowlands), Panama (Caribbean slope throughout, Pacific slope from eastern Veraguas eastward) east through Colombia to northwestern Venezuela (including Curaçao and Tortuga Island), casually in eastern Venezuela and Trinidad. Casual in coastal southern California and Georgia. Many undocumented records for Florida. Recorded casually in early winter north to the southern United States.

Migrates primarily through the eastern United States (west to central North Dakota and the eastern Plains states, and central and southern Texas), Bermuda (rare), the Bahamas (fall, rare), Cuba, the Cayman Islands, Jamaica, islands in the western Caribbean Sea (Providencia, San Andrés), and Middle America (from southern Veracruz and the Yucatan Peninsula south to Panama, casual further north), rarely (mostly along the coast) in western North America from Oregon, Idaho, and Montana south to southern California, southern Arizona, and New Mexico.

Casual in Labrador, Sonora, Clipperton and the Revillagigedo islands, the eastern Greater Antilles (recorded from Hispaniola, Mona Island, Puerto Rico, and St. Croix in the Virgin Islands), Lesser Antilles (St. Vincent, Barbados), Greenland, and Great Britain; sight reports for central Alaska and Ecuador.

Dendroica striata (Forster). Blackpoll Warbler.

Muscicapa striata J. R. Forster, 1772, Philos. Trans. R. Soc. London 62: 406, 428. (Severn River = Fort Severn, west coast of Hudson Bay.)

Habitat.—Cool, wet boreal coniferous forest (primarily spruce), usually dominated by low trees; locally, also mixed coniferous-deciduous second growth, regenerating burns, bogs, and alder thickets; in migration and winter, a variety of wooded habitats.

Distribution.—*Breeds* from western and north-central Alaska, central Yukon, northern Mackenzie, southern Keewatin, northern Manitoba, northern Ontario, northern Quebec, northern Labrador, and Newfoundland south to southern Alaska (west to the Alaska Peninsula), south-central British Columbia, southwestern and central Alberta, central Saskatchewan, central Manitoba, north-central Ontario, southern Quebec, eastern New York, northwestern Massachusetts (Mt. Graylock), central New Hampshire, east-central Maine, and Nova Scotia. One breeding record for northeastern Pennsylvania.

Winters from Colombia, Venezuela, and the Guianas south, mostly east of the Andes, to northeastern Peru and Amazonian Brazil. Casual in Panama, Costa Rica, and Trinidad.

Migrates primarily in spring through the West Indies, Bahama Islands, and eastern North America (west to Montana, the Plains states, and central and southern Texas); and in fall mostly across northeastern North America from New England and the Maritime Provinces south to West Virginia and Virginia, thence mostly at sea (but see Notes below) over Bermuda and the Lesser Antilles (north, at least irregularly, to Puerto Rico and the Virgin Islands) to northern South America (including islands north of Venezuela), also regularly in California.

Casual elsewhere in western North America from southwestern British Columbia, Utah, and New Mexico south to northern Baja California, southern Arizona, and Chihuahua, and in Argentina, southeastern Brazil, Greenland, Iceland, the British Isles, and France. Accidental on Cornwallis Island, and in Oaxaca (Tehuantepec City), Chile, and the Galapagos Islands; sight reports for Idaho, Yucatán, Belize, and Clipperton Island.

Notes.—Transoceanic migration in this species has been questioned by Murray (1989) and is currently the subject of vigorous debate. See Nesbit et al. (1995) and references therein. *Dendroica breviunguis,* based on *Alauda (Anthus) breviunguis* Spix, 1824, sometimes used for this species, is not valid because *Muscicapa striata* Forster, 1772, is unaffected by *Motacilla striata* Pallas, 1764, the latter species now currently placed in the Old World genus *Muscicapa*; see Banks and Browning (1995).

Dendroica cerulea (Wilson). Cerulean Warbler.

> *Sylvia cerulea* Wilson, 1810, Amer. Ornithol. 2: 141, pl. 17, fig. 5. (Pennsylvania = Philadelphia.)

Habitat.—Mature deciduous forest; in migration, a variety of wooded (broadleaf) habitats; in winter, primarily Montane Evergreen Forest.

Distribution.—*Breeds* from central and southeastern Minnesota, central Wisconsin, central Michigan, southeastern Ontario, New York, Connecticut, and Rhode Island south through central and northeastern Iowa and Missouri to southern Arkansas, east-central Mississippi, central Alabama, eastern North Carolina, central Virginia, northeastern Maryland, northern Delaware, and northern New Jersey. Also rarely or formerly in southeastern South Dakota, northern Michigan, southwestern Quebec, northwestern Vermont, central Massachusetts, southeastern Nebraska, eastern Oklahoma, north-central Texas (to Dallas area), northern Louisiana, northern Georgia, and northwestern South Carolina.

Winters from Colombia and Venezuela south, mostly along the eastern slope of the Andes, to southern Peru, perhaps northern Bolivia.

Migrates through the southeastern United States (west to central and southern Texas in spring), Cuba, the Isle of Pines, the Cayman Islands, Jamaica, and, uncommonly, along the Caribbean slope and offshore islands from southern Veracruz, Chiapas, and the Yucatan Peninsula south to Panama (also the Pearl Islands, off Pacific Panama, but not recorded from Nicaragua), casually through the Bahama Islands (recorded from Cay Lobos, New Providence). Common spring migrant in Maya Mountains of Belize.

Casual north to southwestern Manitoba, North Dakota, northern Minnesota, northern Wisconsin, central Ontario, New Hampshire, Maine, New Brunswick, and Nova Scotia, in western North America to California, northern Baja California, southern Nevada, southeastern Arizona, Colorado, and New Mexico; sight reports for Newfoundland, Bermuda, and southeastern Brazil.

Dendroica plumbea Lawrence. Plumbeous Warbler.

> *Dendrœca plumbea* Lawrence, 1877, Ann. N. Y. Acad. Sci. 1 (1877): 47. (Dominica.)

Habitat.—Tropical Lowland Evergreen Forest, Tropical Deciduous Forest, Montane Evergreen Forest (0–900 m).

Distribution.—*Resident* in the Lesser Antilles (Dominica, Marie Galante, Guadeloupe, and Terre-de-Haut, possibly only a casual vagrant to the latter).

Notes.—Kepler and Parkes (1972) regarded *D. plumbea, D. pharetra, D. angelae*, and *Catharopeza bishopi* as more closely related to one another than to any other member of *Dendroica* and as possibly constituting a superspecies; see comments under *C. bishopi*.

Dendroica pharetra (Gosse). Arrowhead Warbler.

> *Sylvicola pharetra* Gosse, 1847, Birds Jamaica, p. 163. (Bognie woods, on the top of Bluefields Peak, Jamaica.)

Habitat.—Montane Evergreen Forest (300–1600 m).
Distribution.—*Resident* on Jamaica.
Notes.—See comments under *D. plumbea*.

Dendroica angelae Kepler and Parkes. Elfin-woods Warbler.

> *Dendroica angelae* Kepler and Parkes, 1972, Auk 89: 3. (ridge between the Río Sabana and Río Espíritu Santo valleys, approximately 2.5 km west of Highway 191 on the El Toro trail, Sierra de Luquillo, Puerto Rico [elevation 780 m].)

Habitat.—Elfin Forest, Montane Evergreen Forest (650–1050 m).
Distribution.—*Resident* on Puerto Rico (Sierra de Luquillo, Maricao).
Notes.—See comments under *D. plumbea*.

Genus *CATHAROPEZA* Sclater

> *Catharopeza* Sclater, 1880, Ibis, pp. 40, 73, 74. Type, by original designation, *Leucopeza bishopi* Lawrence.

Notes.—Sometimes merged in *Dendroica* (Bond 1967, Kepler and Parkes 1972) and often considered to be most closely related to that genus (e.g., Lowery and Monroe *in* Paynter 1968). Robbins and Parker (1997b), however, presented data on voice, behavior, and morphology that suggest that *Catharopeza* is more closely related to *Phaeothlypis*.

Catharopeza bishopi (Lawrence). Whistling Warbler.

> *Leucopeza bishopi* Lawrence, 1878, Ann. N. Y. Acad. Sci. 1 (1877): 151. (St. Vincent.)

Habitat.—Tropical Lowland Evergreen Forest (300–1000 m)
Distribution.—*Resident* on St. Vincent, in the Lesser Antilles.

Genus *MNIOTILTA* Vieillot

> *Mniotilta* Vieillot, 1816, Analyse, p. 45. Type, by monotypy, "Figuier varié" Buffon = *Motacilla varia* Linnaeus.

Mniotilta varia (Linnaeus). Black-and-white Warbler.

> *Motacilla varia* Linnaeus, 1766, Syst. Nat. (ed. 12) 1: 333. Based on the "Small Black and White Creeper" Sloane, Voy. Jamaica 2: 309, pl. 265, fig. 1, and "Le Figuier varié de S. Domingue" Brisson, Ornithologie 3: 529, pl. 27, fig. 5. (in Jamaica, Dominica = Hispaniola.)

Habitat.—Extensive tracts of deciduous and mixed deciduous-coniferous forest and woodland, primarily where tall trees present; in migration and winter, a variety of wooded habitats.
Distribution.—*Breeds* from extreme southeastern Yukon, west-central and southwestern

Mackenzie, northern Alberta, central Saskatchewan, central Manitoba, northern Ontario, south-central Quebec, southern Labrador (probably), and Newfoundland south (at least locally) to northeastern British Columbia, central Alberta, southern Saskatchewan, eastern Montana, southwestern South Dakota, western Nebraska, central Kansas, south-central and eastern Texas, central Louisiana, southern Mississippi, southern Alabama, central Georgia, central South Carolina, and southeastern North Carolina. Recorded in summer in California, Arizona, and Colorado.

Winters from southern and coastal northern California (rarely), southern Arizona (rarely), Coahuila, Nuevo León, southern Texas, the Gulf Coast (rare), Florida (casually farther north to eastern North Carolina), Bermuda, and the Bahama Islands south through Middle America and the West Indies (less commonly in the Lesser Antilles) to western Ecuador, Colombia, northern Venezuela, the Netherlands Antilles, and Trinidad; sight reports for northern Peru. Accidental in Minnesota. Many early winter records in eastern United States north to southern Canada.

Migrates most commonly east of the Rockies, regularly (but rarely) through Bermuda and in western North America from southwestern British Columbia, Idaho, and Montana southward.

Casual or accidental in northern and southeastern Alaska (Colville River delta, Hyder), and northeastern Manitoba, and in Iceland, the Faeroe Islands, and the British Isles.

Genus *SETOPHAGA* Swainson

Setophaga Swainson, 1827, Philos. Mag. (n.s.) 1: 368. Type, by subsequent designation (Swainson, 1827), *Motacilla ruticilla* Linnaeus.

Setophaga ruticilla (Linnaeus). American Redstart.

Motacilla Ruticilla Linnaeus, 1758, Syst. Nat. (ed. 10) 1: 186. Based mostly on "The Red-start" Catesby, Nat. Hist. Carolina 1: 67, pl. 67, and "The Small American Redstart" Edwards, Nat. Hist. Birds 1: 80, pl. 80. (in America = Virginia.)

Habitat.—Open deciduous and mixed deciduous-coniferous woodland, riparian woodland (especially cottonwoods and willows), and second growth, locally birch or aspen woodland; in migration and winter, a variety of wooded habitats, especially edges of humid and semi-humid tropical forest and mangroves.

Distribution.—*Breeds* from southeastern Alaska, southern Yukon, west-central and southern Mackenzie, north-central Saskatchewan, north-central Manitoba, north-central Ontario, south-central Quebec, southern Labrador, and Newfoundland south, at least locally (or formerly) through interior British Columbia, central Washington, and eastern Oregon to northwestern California (irregularly in Del Norte and Humboldt counties), Idaho, northern Utah (formerly), south-central Colorado (rarely), central Arizona (rarely), eastern Oklahoma, eastern Texas, central Louisiana, central Mississippi, southern Alabama, northwestern Florida, southern Georgia, central South Carolina, central North Carolina, and southern Virginia; also casually in Cuba.

Winters from southern Baja California, Sinaloa, Veracruz, central Florida, and the Bahama Islands (rarely from California, southern Arizona, southern Texas, and the Gulf coast, casually farther north, mostly in early winter) south through Middle America, Bermuda, and the West Indies, and in South America from Colombia, Venezuela (including islands from the Netherlands Antilles east to Tobago and Trinidad), and the Guianas south to coastal lowlands of Peru (sight reports) and northwestern Brazil.

Migrates throughout North America (more commonly in the eastern portion).

Casual north to central and south-coastal Alaska (Denali National Park, Homer, Middleton Island), northern Mackenzie, Banks Island, northern Manitoba, and northeastern Quebec, in the Revillagigedo Islands (San Benedicto and Socorro islands; sight reports), Clipperton Island, at sea near the Azores, Greenland, Iceland, the British Isles, and France.

Genus *PROTONOTARIA* Baird

Protonotaria Baird, 1858, in Baird, Cassin, and Lawrence, Rep. Explor. Surv. R. R. Pac. 9: xix, xxxi, 235, 239. Type, by monotypy, *Motacilla protonotarius* Gmelin = *Motacilla citrea* Boddaert.

Protonotaria citrea (Boddaert). Prothonotary Warbler.

> *Motacilla citrea* Boddaert, 1783, Table Planches Enlum., p. 44. Based on "Figuier à ventre et tête jaunes de la Louisiane" Daubenton, Planches Enlum., pl. 704, fig. 2. (Louisiana.)

Habitat.—Swamps, wet bottomland forest, and riparian forest; in migration and winter, also dry woodland, scrub, and mangroves.

Distribution.—*Breeds* from east-central and southeastern Minnesota, central Wisconsin, southern Michigan, extreme southern Ontario (locally), central New York (locally), and northern New Jersey (casually in Connecticut and Rhode Island) south to south-central and eastern Texas (west to Medina County), the Gulf coast, and central (locally also southern) Florida, and west to extreme eastern Nebraska, eastern Kansas, and central Oklahoma.

Winters from southern Veracruz (rare) and the Yucatan Peninsula south on the Caribbean slope of Middle America (including nearby islands) to Nicaragua, on both slopes of Costa Rica and Panama, and in South America from Colombia, northwestern Ecuador, and northern Venezuela (including islands from the Netherlands Antilles east to Tobago and Trinidad), in Puerto Rico and (rarely) the Virgin Islands, and casually east to Surinam and north in the Antilles. Casual in winter in coastal California, coastal Texas, southern Florida, and Bermuda. Accidental in Illinois and Georgia. Casual in December in southern Louisiana.

Migrates through the southeastern United States (west to central and southern Texas), Bermuda, the Bahamas, Cuba, the Isle of Pines, the Cayman Islands, and islands in the western Caribbean Sea, rarely east to the Virgin Islands and Lesser Antilles.

Casual north to northern Ontario, Labrador (sight report), Newfoundland (sight reports), southern Quebec, Nova Scotia, and Maine, and in western North America from southern Washington, Oregon, Nevada, and southern Saskatchewan (sight report) south to southern California, Los Coronado Islands, southern Arizona, and southern New Mexico, and in Sonora, Jalisco, Nuevo León, Clipperton Island (sight reports), Hispaniola, the Galapagos Islands, and Brazil.

Genus *HELMITHEROS* Rafinesque

> *Helmitheros* Rafinesque, 1819, J. Phys. Chim. Hist. Nat. 88: 418. Type, by original designation, *Helmitheros migratorius* Rafinesque = *Motacilla vermivora* Gmelin.

Notes.—See comments under *Limnothlypis*.

Helmitheros vermivorus (Gmelin). Worm-eating Warbler.

> *Motacilla vermivora* Gmelin, 1789, Syst. Nat. 1(2): 951. Based mainly on "The Worm-eater" Edwards, Glean. Nat. Hist. 2: 200, pl. 305. (in Pensilvania = Philadelphia.)

Habitat.—Deciduous forest and damp, bushy ravines with dense undergrowth; also locally in regenerating clear-cuts; in migration, a variety wooded habitats; in winter, primarily broadleaf forest with dense undergrowth.

Distribution.—*Breeds* from northeastern Kansas, northern Missouri, southern and eastern Iowa (rarely), southern Wisconsin (locally), southwestern Michigan (locally), southern and east-central Ohio, northern Pennsylvania, central and southern New York, and Massachusetts south to extreme eastern Oklahoma, northeastern (locally to southeastern) Texas, south-central Louisiana, southern Mississippi, southwestern Alabama, northwestern Florida (locally), northern (locally to central) Georgia, northwestern and (locally) coastal South Carolina, and North Carolina. Recorded in summer (and possibly breeding) in southern Ontario.

Winters from southern Tamaulipas, Oaxaca, Chiapas, and the Yucatan Peninsula south through Middle America (more commonly on the Gulf-Caribbean slope north of central Costa Rica) to central Panama (east to the Canal area and eastern Panamá province), and on Bermuda, the Bahama Islands, Greater Antilles (east to the Virgin Islands), the Cayman Islands, and rarely in peninsular Florida and casually in California and coastal Texas. Recorded in early winter in Louisiana.

Migrates through the southeastern United States (west to eastern Colorado and central and southern Texas), eastern Mexico (mostly Gulf slope), and islands in the western Caribbean Sea (Swan, Providencia).

Casual north to southern Saskatchewan, Manitoba, Minnesota, southern Quebec, New-foundland, New Brunswick, and Nova Scotia, west to Wyoming, North Dakota, eastern South Dakota, Nebraska, western Texas, California, Nevada, Arizona, New Mexico, and Colorado; sight reports for Oregon, Utah, northern Baja California, Nayarit, and St. Pierre et Miquelon. Accidental in northern St. Martin, Antigua, and Venezuela.

Notes.—*Vermivora americ* Linnaeus, 1776 (including the genus), has been officially suppressed (I.C.Z.N. 1956c).

Genus *LIMNOTHLYPIS* Stone

Limnothlypis Stone, 1914, Science (n.s.) 40: 26. Type, by original designation, *Sylvia swainsonii* Audubon.

Notes.—Sometimes merged in *Helmitheros* (Griscom and Sprunt 1957, Mayr and Short 1970).

Limnothlypis swainsonii (Audubon). Swainson's Warbler.

Sylvia Swainsonii Audubon, 1834, Birds Amer. (folio) 2: pl. 198 (1834, Ornithol. Biogr. 2: 563). (Edisto River, near Charleston in South Carolina.)

Habitat.—Bottomland forest, woodland, and swamps with dense undergrowth and sparse ground cover, dense second-growth, and canebrakes, also in moist montane deciduous forest with rhododendron thickets, and locally in regenerating pine forest; in winter, primarily humid forest with dense undergrowth; more widespread in migration.

Distribution.—*Breeds* locally from southeastern Oklahoma, southern Missouri, southern Illinois, southwestern and eastern Kentucky, southern West Virginia, extreme western and extreme southeastern Virginia, southeastern Maryland, and southern Delaware (at least formerly) south to east-central Texas (west to Gonzales, Bastrop, Lee, and Brazos counties), the Gulf coast, and northern Florida. Summer records north to southwestern Pennsylvania.

Winters in Cuba (including Cayo Real), the Cayman Islands, Jamaica, Puerto Rico, the Virgin Islands, Veracruz (rare), the Yucatan Peninsula, eastern Guatemala (Petén), and Belize; casual in Bermuda and the northern Bahama Islands (Grand Bahama); one early December specimen from Florida Keys.

Migrates through the southeastern United States (west to southern Texas), the Bahama Islands, Tamaulipas, and Chiapas. Rare but regular on Bermuda; one record for Swan Islands.

Casual north to eastern Colorado, southern Nebraska, eastern Kansas, northern Illinois, southern Ontario, central Ohio, Pennsylvania, central New York, and Massachusetts; sight reports for New Mexico. Accidental in Arizona, Wisconsin, Maine, and Nova Scotia (Seal Island).

Genus *SEIURUS* Swainson

Seiurus Swainson, 1827, Philos. Mag. (n.s.) 1: 369. Type, by subsequent designation (Swainson, 1827), *Motacilla aurocapilla* Linnaeus.

Seiurus aurocapillus (Linnaeus). Ovenbird.

Motacilla aurocapilla Linnaeus, 1766, Syst. Nat (ed. 12) 1: 334. Based on "The Golden-crowned Thrush" Edwards, Glean. Nat. Hist. 5: 91, pl. 252. (in Pensylvania, error = at sea, apparently off Haiti.)

Habitat.—Mature upland deciduous and mixed deciduous-coniferous forest, rarely in bottomland woodland, usually with sparse undergrowth and abundant leaf-litter; in migration and winter, a variety of wooded habitats.

Distribution.—*Breeds* from northeastern British Columbia, extreme southeastern Yukon, southern Mackenzie, northern Alberta, central Saskatchewan, central Manitoba, northern Ontario, central Quebec (including Anticosti and Magdalen islands), and Newfoundland south to southern Alberta, central and eastern Montana, northeastern Wyoming, central Colorado (local), Nebraska, extreme eastern Kansas, southeastern Oklahoma, western Arkansas, southwestern Tennessee, northern Alabama, northern Georgia, western South Carolina, and central and northeastern North Carolina.

Winters from Sinaloa, southern Texas (rare), southern Louisiana (rare), and North Carolina (casually north to northern California, the Great Lakes region and New England; most records from December only) south through Middle America (both slopes, more commonly on the Gulf-Caribbean) and Bermuda and the West Indies to Panama (casual east of the Canal area and eastern Panamá province) and northern Venezuela (including islands from the Netherlands Antilles east to Tobago and Trinidad), casually in Colombia and western Ecuador.

Migrates primarily through eastern North America from the Rockies eastward, and casually to rarely elsewhere in western North America from southwestern British Columbia, Washington, Idaho, and Montana south to California, Baja California, northwestern Mexico, New Mexico, and western Texas.

Casual or accidental in Alaska (Prudhoe Bay, Fairbanks), southwestern British Columbia, Guadalupe Island (off Baja California), Clipperton Island (sight reports), Greenland, Iceland, and the British Isles.

Seiurus noveboracensis (Gmelin). Northern Waterthrush.

> *Motacilla noveboracensis* Gmelin, 1789, Syst. Nat. 1(2): 958. Based on "The New York Warbler" Latham, Gen. Synop. Birds 2(2): 436. (in Louisiana, et Noveboraci sepibus = New York.)

Habitat.—Thickets near slow-moving streams, ponds, swamps, and bogs; in migration and winter, a variety of wooded habitats, generally near water, often in mangroves.

Distribution.—*Breeds* from western and north-central Alaska, northern Yukon, northwestern and southern Mackenzie, northern Saskatchewan, northern Manitoba, northern Ontario, northern Quebec, northern Labrador, and Newfoundland south to southern Alaska (west to the base of the Alaska Peninsula), central British Columbia, northeastern Washington, northern Idaho, western and central Montana, southwestern and central Alberta, southeastern Saskatchewan, southern Manitoba, northern North Dakota, northeastern Minnesota, central Wisconsin, southern Michigan, southern Ontario, extreme northeastern Ohio, southeastern West Virginia, western Maryland, Pennsylvania, New York, Connecticut, and Rhode Island; one breeding record from north-central North Carolina (Caswell County). One breeding record from Colorado. Recorded in summer (and probably breeding) in the central Cascade Mountains of Oregon.

Winters from southern Baja California, Sinaloa, San Luis Potosí, Tamaulipas, southern Florida, the Bahama Islands, and Bermuda (casually north to British Columbia, the Gulf coast, and Virginia) south through Middle America and the West Indies, and in northern South America from Colombia, Venezuela (including islands from Netherlands Antilles east to Tobago and Trinidad), and the Guianas south to Ecuador. Recorded annually in winter in southern coastal California, southern Texas, and southern Louisiana.

Migrates regularly throughout most of North America, most commonly east of the Rockies.

Casual on St. Lawrence Island, northern Alaska, coastal British Columbia, Banks Island, northern Baja California, Peru, Greenland, the British Isles, France, the Canary Islands, and Siberia (Chukotski Peninsula); sight reports for the Revillagigedo Islands (Socorro) and Clipperton Island.

Seiurus motacilla (Vieillot). Louisiana Waterthrush.

> *Turdus motacilla* Vieillot, 1809, Hist. Nat. Ois. Amer. Sept. 2 (1808, livr. 14): 9, pl. 65. (Kentucky.)

Habitat.—Along shaded, fast-flowing, usually rocky streams in forest and woodland, and locally in swamps; in migration and winter, a variety of wooded habitats, usually near fast-flowing water.

Distribution.—*Breeds* from eastern Nebraska (formerly), eastern Kansas, north-central Iowa, east-central and southeastern Minnesota, west-central Wisconsin, central Michigan, southern Ontario, central and northeastern New York, central Vermont, central New Hampshire, and southern Maine south to west-central Oklahoma, central Texas (west to Bandera

County), central Louisiana, southern Mississippi, southern Alabama, northern Florida (south to the Gainesville area), central and southwestern Georgia, central South Carolina, and North Carolina; recorded in summer in southern Quebec.

Winters from southern Sonora, southern Nuevo León, southwestern Tamaulipas, and the Bahama Islands (casually north to southern California, southeastern Arizona, southern Florida, and accidental in Maryland) south through Middle America (both slopes, although more commonly on the Gulf-Caribbean) and the West Indies (south to St. Vincent in the Lesser Antilles) to eastern Panama, northern Colombia (rare), northwestern Venezuela, and Trinidad.

Migrates primarily through the southeastern United States (west to central and southern Texas) and northern Mexico; also Bermuda (rare).

Casual north to northeastern Minnesota, northern Michigan, Nova Scotia, and in California, Baja California, eastern Colorado, and New Mexico. Accidental in Greenland. Sight reports for the Dakotas and New Brunswick.

Genus *OPORORNIS* Baird

Oporornis Baird, 1858, in Baird, Cassin, and Lawrence, Rep. Explor. Surv. R. R. Pac. 9: xix, xxxii, 240, 246. Type, by original designation, *Sylvia agilis* Wilson.

Notes.—Sometimes merged in *Geothlypis* (Lowery and Monroe *in* Paynter 1968).

Oporornis formosus (Wilson). Kentucky Warbler.

Sylvia formosa Wilson, 1811, Amer. Ornithol. 3: 85, pl. 25, fig. 3. (Kentucky.)

Habitat.—Humid deciduous forest with dense undergrowth, dense second growth, shady ravines, and swamp edges; in migration, a variety of wooded habitats; in winter, primarily broadleaf forest with dense undergrowth.

Distribution.—*Breeds* from eastern Nebraska, central and northeastern Iowa, southern Wisconsin, northern Illinois, northern Indiana, extreme southern Michigan, northern Ohio, Pennsylvania, northern New Jersey, south-central (formerly) and southeastern New York, and (presumably) extreme southwestern Connecticut south to south-central and eastern Texas (west to Kerrville), the Gulf coast (east to Suwanee County in Florida), central Georgia, and South Carolina, and west to eastern Kansas and central Oklahoma. One breeding record for southern Minnesota. In 1992, many summered and may have attempted to breed in California. Summer records for Ontario and Massachusetts.

Winters from Nayarit, Oaxaca, southern Veracruz, and the Yucatan Peninsula south through Middle America (primarily the Caribbean slope, rare and local on the Pacific slope north of central Costa Rica) to Panama, and rarely to northern Colombia and northern Venezuela. Casual in coastal California, Puerto Rico, the Virgin Islands, and the Netherlands Antilles. Accidental in northern Louisiana, Bermuda, and Cuba (sight report).

Migrates primarily through the southeastern United States (west to eastern Colorado, eastern New Mexico, and western Texas), northeastern Mexico, Cuba, Hispaniola, Jamaica, and the Cayman Islands, rarely east to Puerto Rico, the Virgin and Bahama islands, and Bermuda.

Casual north to eastern Montana, North Dakota, Minnesota, southern Ontario, central New York, northern New England, Nova Scotia, and Newfoundland, in western North America from California east through Utah, Arizona, and northern Sonora to eastern Colorado and New Mexico, and in the Lesser Antilles (Guadeloupe); sight reports for northern Alaska, Washington, Oregon, Alberta, Saskatchewan, Manitoba, Wyoming, the Dakotas, Nevada, and southern Quebec.

Oporornis agilis (Wilson). Connecticut Warbler.

Sylvia agilis Wilson, 1812, Amer. Ornithol. 5: 64, pl. 39, fig. 4. (Connecticut.)

Habitat.—Spruce and tamarack bogs, jack pine barrens (locally), also open poplar or aspen woodland in western portion of range; in migration and winter, a variety of wooded and semi-open habitats.

Distribution.—*Breeds* from northeastern British Columbia (rare, local) east across central

Alberta, central Saskatchewan, central Manitoba, and northern Ontario to south-central Quebec, and south to southern Manitoba, northern Minnesota, northern Wisconsin, northern Michigan, and south-central Ontario.

Winter range poorly understood, and only a few documented records are known from December to February. Recorded from northeastern Colombia and Venezuela south to Amazonian and central Brazil.

Migrates through the Atlantic states (primarily in fall, rarely north to southern New England, New Brunswick, and Nova Scotia), the east-central United States west of the Appalachians and east of the Rockies (mostly in spring, casually west to eastern Colorado and central Texas), and in both seasons through the southeastern states, Bermuda (rare), Bahama Islands, Netherlands Antilles, and Venezuela.

Casual or accidental in southern British Columbia, Newfoundland, California (mostly Farallon Islands), Utah, southern Arizona, Montana, Nebraska, Kansas, Oklahoma, Newfoundland (sight report), western Panama (Bocas del Toro), the Greater Antilles (Hispaniola, and Mona Island off Puerto Rico), the Lesser Antilles (St. Martin), and southern Peru; sight reports for Oregon, Wyoming, Clipperton Island (sight report), and islands off Belize and Caribbean Honduras.

Oporornis philadelphia (Wilson). Mourning Warbler.

Sylvia Philadelphia Wilson, 1810, Amer. Ornithol. 2: 101, pl. 14, fig. 6. (within a few miles of Philadelphia, Pennsylvania.)

Habitat.—Open brushy deciduous woodland and second growth (especially burns, regenerating clear-cuts); in migration and winter, thickets, weedy fields, scrub, and woodland undergrowth, primarily in humid regions.

Distribution.—*Breeds* from northeastern British Columbia, southeastern Yukon, northeastern and central Alberta, central Saskatchewan, central Manitoba, central Ontario, south-central and southeastern Quebec, and Newfoundland south to southern Manitoba, north-central and northeastern North Dakota, central Minnesota, central Wisconsin, northeastern Illinois, southern Michigan, and northern Ohio, in the higher Appalachians to eastern West Virginia, western Maryland, and northwestern Virginia, and to northeastern Pennsylvania, southeastern New York, and western Massachusetts. Casual in western North Carolina.

Winters from southern Nicaragua south through Costa Rica and Panama to western Colombia, eastern Ecuador (rare), and southern Venezuela. Accidental in southern California and Oaxaca.

Migrates primarily through the Mississippi and Ohio valleys (west to eastern Montana, the Plains states, and central Texas, casually to central Colorado, eastern New Mexico, and western Texas), rarely in the southeastern states (only casually in South Carolina, Georgia, and Florida east of panhandle), and regularly through eastern and southern Mexico, northern Central America, and Bermuda.

Casual or accidental in south-coastal Alaska (Middleton Island), south-central British Columbia, California (mostly Farallon Islands), Nevada, Wyoming, northern Arizona, Hispaniola, Puerto Rico, Curaçao, and Greenland; sight reports from Washington, Oregon, southern Baja California, Cuba, the Bahama Islands, and Vieques Island (off Puerto Rico).

Notes.—*Oporornis philadelphia* and *O. tolmiei* are each other's closest relatives (Lowery and Monroe *in* Paynter 1968), hybridize (Cox 1973), and constitute a superspecies (Pitocchelli 1990).

Oporornis tolmiei (Townsend). MacGillivray's Warbler.

Sylvia Tolmiei J. K. Townsend, 1839, Narr. Journey Rocky Mount., etc., p. 343. (the Columbia = Fort Vancouver, Washington.)

Habitat.—Coniferous forest edge, brushy hillsides, regenerating clearcuts and burns, and willow-alder riparian thickets; in migration and winter, a variety of open wooded habitats, weedy fields.

Distribution.—*Breeds* from southeastern Alaska, southern Yukon, northern British Columbia, western and southern Alberta, extreme southwestern Saskatchewan, central Montana, and southwestern South Dakota south, primarily in the mountains, to southern California (San Jacinto Mountains), southeastern Arizona, and southern New Mexico; also in southeastern Coahuila and Nuevo León (Cerro Potosí).

Winters from southern Baja California, southern Sonora, Chihuahua, Coahuila, and Nuevo León south, mostly in the highlands, through Middle America (except Belize) to western Panama (Chiriquí, casually east to the Canal area). Casual in coastal California, southern Arizona, southern Texas, and southern Louisiana.

Migrates primarily through western North America from the western Great Plains and central Texas westward, casually east to Minnesota, central South Dakota, eastern Kansas, northwestern Missouri, Illinois, eastern Texas, and southern Louisiana.

Casual or accidental in northern Alaska, Northwest Territories, northeastern British Columbia, Illinois, Massachusetts, and Georgia.

Notes.—See comments under *O. philadelphia.*

Genus *GEOTHLYPIS* Cabanis

Trichas (not Gloger, March 1827) Swainson, June 1827, Philos. Mag. (n.s.) 1: 433. Type, by monotypy, *Trichas personatus* Swainson = *Turdus trichas* Linnaeus.
Geothlypis Cabanis, 1847, Arch. Naturgesch. 13: 316, 349. New name for *Trichas* Swainson, preoccupied.
Chamæthlypis Ridgway, 1887, Man. N. Amer. Birds, p. 225. Type, by original designation, *Geothlypis poliocephala* Baird.

Notes.—See comments under *Oporornis.*

Geothlypis trichas (Linnaeus). Common Yellowthroat.

Turdus Trichas Linnaeus, 1766, Syst. Nat. (ed. 12) 1: 293. Based on "The Maryland Yellow-Throat" Edwards, Glean. Nat. Hist. 1: 56, pl. 257, fig. 2. (in America septentrionali = Maryland.)

Habitat.—Marshes (especially cattail), thickets near water, bogs, brushy pastures, old fields, and, locally, undergrowth at edge of humid forest; in migration and winter more widespread, but mostly in marshy, brushy, or weedy areas (Tropical to Temperate zones).

Distribution.—*Breeds* [*trichas* group] from southeastern Alaska (west and north to Glacier Bay), central Yukon, southwestern Northwest Territories, northern Alberta, northern Saskatchewan, northern Manitoba, northern Ontario, central Quebec, and Newfoundland south to northern Baja California, in Mexico to Veracruz (and possibly Oaxaca), and to southern Texas, the Gulf coast, and southern Florida.

Winters [*trichas* group] from northern California (rarely or casually to southwestern British Columbia and Washington), southern Arizona, southern New Mexico (rarely), southern Texas, the Gulf states, and Maryland (casually north to Colorado and Missouri; recorded annually in the southern Great Lakes) south through Middle America, the Greater Antilles (east to the Virgin Islands), Bermuda, and the Cayman and Bahama islands to central Panama (east to the Canal area and eastern Panamá province, casually to Darién), and casually to northern Colombia and the Lesser Antilles (Dominica); questionably reported from northern Venezuela and Tobago.

Resident [*chapalensis* group] in Jalisco.

Migrates [*trichas* group] broadly through North America and also through Bermuda and islands in the western Caribbean Sea.

Casual [*trichas* group] in central and south-coastal Alaska, Hudson Bay, northern Labrador, on Clipperton Island (sight report), Greenland, and the British Isles.

Notes.—Groups: *G. chapalensis* Nelson, 1903 [Chapala Yellowthroat] and *G. trichas* [Common Yellowthroat]. Species limits and relationships within the genus are generally poorly understood and require further study.

Geothlypis beldingi Ridgway. Belding's Yellowthroat.

Geothlypis beldingi Ridgway, 1882, Proc. U. S. Natl. Mus. 5: 344. (San José del Cabo, Baja California.)

Habitat.—Freshwater Marshes, possibly Saltwater/Brackish Marshes.
Distribution.—*Resident* in central (north to lat 28° N.) and southern Baja California.
Notes.—Also known as Peninsular Yellowthroat. See comments under *G. trichas*.

Geothlypis flavovelata Ridgway. Altamira Yellowthroat.

Geothlypis flavovelata Ridgway, 1896, Proc. U. S. Natl. Mus. 18 (1895): 119. (Alta Mira, near Tampico, Tamaulipas, Mexico.)

Habitat.—Freshwater Marshes (Tropical Zone).
Distribution.—*Resident* in central and southern Tamaulipas, extreme eastern San Luis Potosí and northern Veracruz.
Notes.—Also known as Yellow-crowned Yellowthroat. See comments under *G. trichas*.

Geothlypis rostrata Bryant. Bahama Yellowthroat.

Geothlypis rostratus Bryant, 1867, Proc. Boston Soc. Nat. Hist. 11 (1866): 67. (Nassau, New Providence, Bahamas.)

Habitat.—Arid Lowland Scrub; thickets in open pine woodland.
Distribution.—*Resident* in the northern Bahama Islands (Grand Bahama, Andros, New Providence, Eleuthera, Little Abaco, Great Abaco and Cat Island.
Reports from Florida are unsatisfactory.
Notes.—See comments under *G. trichas*.

Geothlypis semiflava Sclater. Olive-crowned Yellowthroat.

Geothlypis semiflava Sclater, 1860, Proc. Zool. Soc. London, p. 273. (In rep. Equator = Babahoyo, Ecuador.)

Habitat.—Riparian Thickets, Second-growth Scrub (0–1800 m; Tropical and lower Subtropical zones).
Distribution.—*Resident* in Middle America from northeastern Honduras (Río Segovia [= Coco]) south in the Caribbean lowlands of Nicaragua and Costa Rica (locally also on the Pacific slope in the Arenal region) to western Panama (Bocas del Toro); and in South America in western Colombia and western Ecuador.

Geothlypis speciosa Sclater. Black-polled Yellowthroat.

Geothlypis speciosa Sclater, 1859, Proc. Zool. Soc. London (1858), p. 447. (In Mexico = headwaters of the Río Lerma, México.)

Habitat.—Freshwater Marshes (1700–2900 m; Subtropical and Temperate zones).
Distribution.—*Resident* in the highlands of eastern Michoacán (Lago Patzcuaro, Lago Cuitzeo), southern Guanajuato (Lago Yuriria, Presa Solis), México (upper Río Lerma, Lago Zumpango), and (formerly) Distrito Federal (Lago Texcoco).

Geothlypis nelsoni Richmond. Hooded Yellowthroat.

Geothlypis cucullata Salvin and Godman, 1889, Ibis, p. 237. (Cofre de Perote, Jalapa, [Veracruz,] Mexico.) Not *Sylvia cucullata* Latham, 1790 = *Geothlypis aequinoctialis* (Gmelin).
Geothlypis nelsoni Richmond, 1900, Auk 17: 179. New name for *G. cucullata* Salvin and Godman, preoccupied.

Habitat.—Pine-Oak Forest Edge (2000–3100 m; Subtropical and Temperate zones).
Distribution.—*Resident* from southeastern Coahuila and central Nuevo León south through eastern San Luis Potosí, Hidalgo, Puebla, central Veracruz, and Distrito Federal to western and central Oaxaca.

Geothlypis aequinoctialis (Gmelin). Masked Yellowthroat.

Motacilla aequinoctialis Gmelin, 1789, Syst. Nat. 1(2): 972. Based on "Figuier olive de Cayenne" Daubenton, Planches Enlum., pl. 685, fig. 1. (in Cayenna = Cayenne.)

Habitat.—Riparian Thickets, Freshwater Marshes, Arid Montane Scrub, Second-growth Scrub (0–2100 m; Tropical Zone, in Panama known only from upper Tropical Zone).

Distribution.—*Resident* [*chiriquensis* group] in southwestern Costa Rica (Cañas Gordas district) and western Panama (Volcán de Chiriquí, in western Chiriquí); [*auricularis* group] on the Pacific slope from western Ecuador to central Peru; and [*aequinoctialis* group] in eastern Colombia, Venezuela, Trinidad, the Guianas, and northeastern Brazil, and from southeastern Peru, eastern Bolivia, and central Argentina east to Uruguay and southern Brazil.

Notes.—Groups: *G. chiriquensis* Salvin, 1872 [Chiriqui Yellowthroat], *G. auricularis* Salvin, 1884 [Black-lored Yellowthroat] (see Ridgely and Tudor 1989), and *G. aequinoctialis* [Masked Yellowthroat]. Based on allozymic divergence and disjunct distributions, Escalante-Pliego (1991) suggested that more than one species may be included within *G. aequinoctialis*; resolution of this issue awaits more extensive sampling and detailed analysis. Lowery and Monroe *in* Paynter (1968) considered *G. chiriquensis* to be a species.

Geothlypis poliocephala Baird. Gray-crowned Yellowthroat.

Geothlypis poliocephala Baird, 1865, Rev. Amer. Birds. 1: 225. (Mazatlán, Sinaloa.)

Habitat.—Second-growth Scrub, Riparian Thickets, lowland pine savanna; dense grass with adjacent brush, weedy fields (0–1500 m; Tropical and Subtropical zones).

Distribution.—*Resident* from northern Sinaloa, southern Tamaulipas, and (formerly) southern Texas (primarily Brownsville area) south along both slopes of Middle America to western Panama (western Chiriquí). Two recent records and two sight reports from southern Texas.

Notes.—Also known as Ground Chat. Often placed in the monotypic genus *Chamaethlypis*, but see Eisenmann (1962b).

Genus *MICROLIGEA* Cory

Ligea (not Illiger, 1801 [Crustacea], nor Drybowski, 1876 [Mollusca]) Cory, 1884, Auk 1: 1. Type, by original designation, *Ligea palustris* Cory.

Ligia (not Weber, 1795 [Crustacea], Fabricius 1798 [Crustacea], nor Dupre, 1829 [Lepidoptera]) Cory, 1884, Birds Haiti San Domingo, p. 34. Emendation of *Ligea* Cory, preoccupied.

Microligea Cory, 1884, Auk 1: 290. New name for *Ligea* Cory and *Ligia* Cory, preoccupied.

Notes.—Although probably parulid, relationships of this genus otherwise are uncertain, Formerly included *Microligea montana,* now placed in the genus *Xenoligea* (Lowery and Monroe *in* Paynter 1968).

Microligea palustris (Cory). Green-tailed Warbler.

Ligea palustris Cory, 1884, Auk 1: 1, pl. 1. (Santo Domingo = Río Villa, Dominican Republic.)

Habitat.—Tropical Lowland Evergreen Forest, Tropical Deciduous Forest, Secondary Forest; frequents dense undergrowth of montane forest, less frequently in scrub of semi-arid lowlands (0–2000 m).

Distribution.—*Resident* on Hispaniola (in Haiti mostly in low elevations of northwestern Haiti and high elevations in Massif de la Selle, more widespread in the Dominican Republic), including Beata Island.

Notes.—Also known as Gray-breasted Ground Warbler or Green-tailed Ground Warbler.

Genus *TERETISTRIS* Cabanis

Teretistris Cabanis, 1855, J. Ornithol. 3: 475, 476. Type, by original designation, *Anabates fernandinae* Lembeye.

Teretistris fernandinae (Lembeye). Yellow-headed Warbler.

> *Anabates fernandinae* Lembeye, 1850, Aves Isla Cuba, p. 66, pl. 5, fig. 2. (Cuba = western Cuba.)

Habitat.—Tropical Lowland Evergreen Forest, Tropical Deciduous Forest (0–500 m).
Distribution.—*Resident* in western Cuba (east to southwestern Las Villas and western Matanzas provinces, also Cayo Cantiles) and the Isle of Pines.

Teretistris fornsi Gundlach. Oriente Warbler.

> *Teretistris fornsi* Gundlach, 1858, Ann. Lyc. Nat. Hist. N. Y. 6: 274. (eastern part of Cuba.)

Habitat.—Tropical Deciduous Forest, Tropical Lowland Evergreen Forest, Pine Forest, Arid Lowland Scrub (0–1500 m).
Distribution.—*Resident* in eastern Cuba (ranging west along the north coast to eastern Matanzas province, also on Cayo Coco, Cayo Romano, Cayo Saetía, Cayo Guajaba, and Cayo Sabinal).

Genus *LEUCOPEZA* Sclater

> *Leucopeza* Sclater, 1876, Proc. Zool. Soc. London, p. 14. Type, by monotypy, *Leucopeza semperi* Sclater.

Leucopeza semperi Sclater. Semper's Warbler.

> *Leucopeza semperi* Sclater, 1876, Proc. Zool. Soc. London, p. 14, pl. 2. (St. Lucia.)

Habitat.—Tropical Lowland Evergreen Forest (400–900 m).
Distribution.—*Resident* (at least formerly) in the highlands of St. Lucia (in the Lesser Antilles); possibly extinct. Last confirmed report in 1972.

Genus *WILSONIA* Bonaparte

> *Wilsonia* Bonaparte, 1838, Geogr. Comp. List, p. 23. Type, by subsequent designation (Ridgway, 1881), *Motacilla mitrata* Gmelin = *Muscicapa citrina* Boddaert.

Wilsonia citrina (Boddaert). Hooded Warbler.

> *Muscicapa Citrina* Boddaert, 1783, Table Planches Enlum., p. 41. Based on "Gobe-mouche de la Louisiane" Daubenton, Planches Enlum., pl. 666, fig. 2. (Louisiana.)

Habitat.—Deciduous or mixed deciduous-pine forest with dense understory, especially along streams, rivers, and ravines, second growth; in migration and winter, a variety of wooded habitats.
Distribution.—*Breeds* from central and northeastern Iowa (rare and local), southeastern Minnesota (casually), central Wisconsin (local), southern Michigan (locally farther north), extreme southern Ontario, central and southeastern New York, Massachusetts (casually), Connecticut, and Rhode Island south to central and eastern Texas (south to Matagorda County and west to Bastrop County), the Gulf coast, and northern Florida, and west to southeastern Nebraska (formerly), eastern Kansas (casually) and eastern Oklahoma, with casual breeding in southern California (Kern and Los Angeles counties, 1992). Summer records for Colorado and Arizona.
Winters primarily on Gulf-Caribbean slope of Middle America from southern Tamaulipas (rare) to Panama (east rarely to the Canal area, including Isla Coiba), rarely or casually on Pacific Slope of Middle America, and (rare) in Bermuda, the Bahamas, and the Greater Antilles; casual in Washington, coastal California, southern Texas, southern Louisiana, South Carolina, and southern Florida, and in northern Colombia, northern Venezuela, the Lesser Antilles, and the Netherlands Antilles.
Migrates regularly through the eastern Plains states (west to eastern Colorado, eastern New Mexico, and western Texas), southeastern states, the Antilles (east to the Virgin Islands,

and casually to Saba, St. Kitts [sight report], and Martinique), the Cayman and Bahama islands, Bermuda, and islands in the western Caribbean Sea, rarely to California.

Casual elsewhere in western North America from Northwest Territories, Washington, Oregon, Idaho, and Montana south to Arizona and New Mexico; also north to southeastern Alberta, southern Saskatchewan, northern Ontario, northern Minnesota, southern Quebec, Newfoundland, New Brunswick, and Nova Scotia; also in Trinidad; sight reports for British Columbia, Utah, northern Baja California, and the British Isles.

Wilsonia pusilla (Wilson). Wilson's Warbler.

> *Muscicapa pusilla* Wilson, 1811, Amer. Ornithol. 3: 103, pl. 26, fig. 4. (southern States, . . . lower parts . . . of New Jersey and Delaware = southern New Jersey.)

Habitat.—Breeds in riparian thickets (especially alder-willow), moist undergrowth, dense second-growth, and bogs; in migration and winter, occupies a variety of open woodland, thickets, brush, scrub, and forest undergrowth.

Distribution.—*Breeds* from western and northern Alaska, northern Yukon, northwestern and east-central Mackenzie, northern Saskatchewan, northern Manitoba, northern Ontario, northern Quebec, northern Labrador, and Newfoundland south to southern Alaska (west to the Alaska Peninsula and Unimak Island), central coastal California (and in mountains of the interior to San Bernardino Mountains; formerly south to San Diego County), west-central and northeastern Nevada, south-central Utah, southwestern Colorado, and northern New Mexico, and to southwestern and east-central Alberta, central Saskatchewan, southern Manitoba, extreme north-central and northeastern Minnesota, extreme northwestern Wisconsin, northern Michigan (Upper Peninsula, rare), south-central Ontario, southern Quebec, extreme northeastern New York (Adirondacks), northern Vermont (rare), central Maine, and central Nova Scotia.

Winters from coastal California (rare), southern Baja California, southern Sonora, southern Texas, southern Louisiana, and Florida (rarely southern Mississippi and southern Alabama) south through Middle America (rarely in the Yucatan Peninsula) to western Panama (Chiriquí), rarely to central Panama. Casual north to British Columbia, Arizona, New Mexico, Kentucky, Ontario, Connecticut, and Nova Scotia. One record for Alaska (Kodiak).

Migrates regularly through North America west of the Appalachians, less commonly through the Atlantic and southeastern states, rarely through the Bahama Islands and the Greater Antilles (Cuba, Jamaica, and Puerto Rico).

Accidental in northern Baffin Island, Colombia, Greenland, and Great Britain. A sight report for the Revillagigedo Islands (Socorro Island).

Notes.—Also known as Pileolated Warbler or Black-capped Warbler.

Wilsonia canadensis (Linnaeus). Canada Warbler.

> *Muscicapa canadensis* Linnaeus, 1766, Syst. Nat. (ed. 12) 1: 327. Based on "Le Gobe-mouche cendré de Canada" Brisson, Ornithologie 2: 406, pl. 39, fig. 4. (in Canada.)

Habitat.—Moist woodland with dense undergrowth (especially aspen-poplar), bogs, and tall scrub along streams; in migration and winter, a variety of wooded habitats.

Distribution.—*Breeds* from extreme southeastern Yukon, northeastern British Columbia, northern Alberta, central Saskatchewan, central Manitoba, northern Ontario, south-central Quebec (including Anticosti Island), New Brunswick, Prince Edward Island, and Nova Scotia south to central Alberta, southern Manitoba, northern Minnesota, southern Wisconsin, northern Illinois (local), southern Michigan, northern Indiana (local), and southeastern Ohio (local), through the Appalachians to eastern Kentucky, eastern Tennessee, northwestern Georgia, western North Carolina, western Virginia, western Maryland, and east-central Pennsylvania, and to northern New Jersey, southeastern New York, and southern New England.

Winters in South America (rarely or casually in Middle America north to Costa Rica) from northern Colombia and Venezuela south, mostly on the east slope of the Andes, to southern Peru and border of southern Venezuela and northern Brazil (Tepui region). A December record for Honduras. No documented winter records for the United States (or anywhere north of Costa Rica).

Migrates mostly through North America east of the Rockies (rarely through the southeastern states in spring), Middle America (absent on Pacific slope of Mexico north of Oaxaca) and, rarely, Newfoundland, Bermuda, and the Bahama Islands (Grand Bahama, New Providence, Exuma).

Casual in western North America in eastern Oregon, Montana, California, Nevada, Utah, Arizona, New Mexico, and Colorado, and in the Greater Antilles (Cuba, Jamaica, Puerto Rico, and the Virgin Islands); sight reports for southwestern British Columbia and Wyoming. Accidental in Alaska (Barrow), southern Mackenzie District, the Lesser Antilles (Guadeloupe), Bonaire, Greenland, and Iceland; sight reports for Baja California and Clipperton Island.

Genus *CARDELLINA* Bonaparte

Cardellina (Du Bus de Gisignies MS) Bonaparte, 1850, Consp. Gen. Avium 1(2): 312. Type, by subsequent designation (Baird, 1865), *Cardellina amicta* Du Bus de Gisignies = *Muscicapa rubrifrons* Giraud.

Cardellina rubrifrons (Giraud). Red-faced Warbler.

Muscicapa rubrifrons Giraud, 1841, Descr. Sixteen New Spec. N. Amer. Birds, pl. [7], fig. 1 and text. (Texas, error = Mexico.)

Habitat.—Pine Forest, Pine-Oak Forest, Riparian Thickets; locally also mixed aspen-coniferous woodland (1500–3100 m; upper Subtropical and Temperate zones).

Distribution.—*Breeds* from central Arizona and southwestern New Mexico (casually in the Sandia Mountains) south through Sonora, western Chihuahua, and Sinaloa to western Durango.

Winters from Sinaloa and Durango south through the highlands of Mexico (ranging east to west-central Veracruz) and Guatemala to El Salvador and western Honduras. One February record from Arizona.

Casual or accidental in California (Farallon Islands, and southern California mainland, where it possibly breeds), Wyoming, Colorado, western and southern Texas, and southwestern Louisiana; a sight report for southern Nevada.

Genus *ERGATICUS* Baird

Ergaticus Baird, 1865, Rev. Amer. Birds. 1: 237, 264. Type, by original designation, *Setophaga rubra* Swainson.

Ergaticus ruber (Swainson). Red Warbler.

Setophaga rubra Swainson, 1827, Philos. Mag. (n.s.) 1: 368. (woods of Valladolid, Mexico = Morelia, Michoacán.)

Habitat.—Pine Forest, Pine-Oak Forest (2100–3200 m; upper Subtropical and Temperate zones, to lower Subtropical Zone in winter).

Distribution.—*Resident* [*melanauris* group] in the mountains of southwestern Chihuahua, eastern Sinaloa, and western Durango; and [*ruber* group] from Jalisco, Michoacán, and Guerrero east to Hidalgo, eastern Puebla, central Veracruz, and central Oaxaca (west of the Isthmus of Tehuantepec).

Ranges in winter [both groups] to lower elevations.

Notes.—Groups: *E. melanauris* Moore, 1937 [Black-eared Warbler] and *E. ruber* [Red Warbler]. *Ergaticus ruber* and *E. versicolor* may constitute a superspecies (Sibley and Monroe 1990).

Ergaticus versicolor (Salvin). Pink-headed Warbler.

Cardellina versicolor Salvin, 1863, Proc. Zool. Soc. London, p. 188, pl. 24, fig. 1. (Volcán de Fuego, Totonicapam, and Chilasco, Guatemala.)

Habitat.—Pine-Oak Forest, Montane Evergreen Forest (2100–3000 m; Subtropical and Temperate zones).

Distribution.—*Resident* in the mountains of central and southeastern Chiapas, and Guatemala (east to the Sierra de las Minas).

Notes.—See comments under *E. ruber.*

Genus *MYIOBORUS* Baird

Erythrosoma [subgenus] Swainson, 1832, in Swainson and Richardson, Fauna Bor.-Amer. 2 (1831): 201. Type, by subsequent designation (Richmond, 1917), *Setophaga picta* Swainson. *Nomen oblitum.*

Myioborus Baird, 1865, Rev. Amer. Birds. 1: 237, 257. Type, by original designation, *Setophaga verticalis* Lafresnaye and d'Orbigny = *Setophaga miniata* Swainson.

Myioborus pictus (Swainson). Painted Redstart.

Setophaga picta Swainson, 1829, Zool. Illus. (2)1: pl. 3 and text. (Real del Monte, Hidalgo, Mexico.)

Habitat.—Pine-Oak Forest, Pine Forest; prefers moist, shaded canyons (1100–3100 m; upper Tropical to lower Temperate zones).

Distribution.—*Breeds* from northwestern and central Arizona, southwestern New Mexico, western Texas (Chisos and Davis mountains), and central Nuevo León south through the mountains of Middle America to north-central Nicaragua; summers casually, and breeds or attempts to breed occasionally, in southern California (Laguna Mountains, San Bernardino Mountains, and Clark Mountain).

Winters from southeastern Arizona (rare), eastern Sonora, central Chihuahua, central Nuevo León, and central Tamaulipas south through the remainder of the breeding range. Casual in California.

Casual migrant in (mostly southern) California, southwestern Arizona, southern Nevada, southern Utah, western Montana, Colorado, and northern and eastern New Mexico. Accidental in Ohio, Michigan, southern Ontario, New York, Massachusetts, and Louisiana; sight reports for British Columbia, Baja California, Wisconsin, central and southeastern Texas, Alabama, and Georgia.

Notes.—Formerly placed in the genus *Setophaga,* but see Parkes (1961).

Myioborus miniatus (Swainson). Slate-throated Redstart.

Setophaga miniata Swainson, 1827, Philos. Mag. (n.s.) 1: 368. (woods of Valladolid, Mexico = Morelia, Michoacán.)

Habitat.—Montane Evergreen Forest, Secondary Forest, Pine-Oak Forest (600–2500 m; upper Tropical and Subtropical zones).

Distribution.—*Resident* from southern Sonora, southern Chihuahua, Durango, Zacatecas, southeastern Coahuila, southern Nuevo León, and San Luis Potosí south through the mountains of Mexico, Guatemala, and El Salvador to Honduras; and from Costa Rica and Panama (Chiriquí, Veraguas, eastern Panamá, Darién) and in the coastal mountains of Venezuela, the Tepui region of Venezuela, extreme northern Brazil, and Guyana, and in the Andes from Venezuela and Colombia south, on the western slope to northwestern Peru and on the eastern slope to central Bolivia.

Accidental in spring in southeastern New Mexico (Lea County) and southern Arizona (Miller Canyon, also sight reports from Cave Creek Canyon); and a sight report for western Texas (Big Bend).

Myioborus torquatus (Baird). Collared Redstart.

Setophaga torquata Baird, 1865, Rev. Amer. Birds. 1: 261. (San José, Costa Rica.)

Habitat.—Semihumid/Humid Montane Scrub, Secondary Forest, Elfin Forest (1400–3500 m; upper Subtropical and Temperate zones).

Distribution.—*Resident* in the mountains of Costa Rica (northwest to the Cordillera de Tilarán) and western Panama (Chiriquí and adjacent Bocas del Toro).

Genus *EUTHLYPIS* Cabanis

Euthlypis Cabanis, 1850, Mus. Heineanum 1: 18. Type, by original designation, *Euthlypis lachrymosa* Cabanis = *Basileuterus lachrymosa* Bonaparte.

Euthlypis lachrymosa (Bonaparte). Fan-tailed Warbler.

Basileuterus lachrymosa (Lichtenstein MS) Bonaparte, 1850, Consp. Gen. Avium 1(2): 314. (Mexico = Laguna Huetulacán, Veracruz.)

Habitat.—Tropical Deciduous Forest, Tropical Lowland Evergreen Forest, Montane Evergreen Forest, Gallery Forest; usually in steep, shaded, rocky canyons (100–1900 m; Tropical and Subtropical zones).

Distribution.—*Resident* on the Pacific slope of Mexico from southern Sonora south to Guatemala, El Salvador, and Honduras (locally also in interior valleys) to central Nicaragua and on the Gulf slope of Mexico from eastern San Luis Potosí and southern Tamaulipas to Veracruz and north-central Oaxaca.

Casual or accidental in northern Baja California (Santo Domingo), northeastern Sonora, and southeastern Arizona (about six records).

Genus *BASILEUTERUS* Cabanis

Basileuterus Cabanis, 1849, in Schomburgk, Reisen Brit.-Guiana 3 (1848): 666. Type, by monotypy, *Basileuterus vermivorus* Cabanis = *Setophaga auricapilla* Swainson = *Sylvia culicivora* Deppe.

Notes.—See comments under *Phaeothlypis*.

Basileuterus culicivorus (Deppe). Golden-crowned Warbler.

Sylvia culicivora "Lichtenst[ein]." W. Deppe, 1830, Preis. Verz. Säugeth. Vögel, etc., Mex., p. 2. (Mexico = Jalapa, Veracruz.)

Habitat.—Tropical Lowland Evergreen Forest, Montane Evergreen Forest, Secondary Forest (0–2100 m; Tropical and Subtropical zones).

Distribution.—*Resident* [*culicivorus* group] in Nayarit and Jalisco, and from Nuevo León and Tamaulipas south on the Gulf-Caribbean slope of San Luis Potosí, Veracruz, Hidalgo, Puebla, Veracruz, Tabasco, southern Campeche, and Quintana Roo, and on both slopes from Guerrero and Oaxaca south through Chiapas and Central America to western Panama (Chiriquí, Veraguas, and Herrera); [*cabanisi* group] in the Santa Marta Mountains and Andes of Colombia and northern Venezuela; and [*auricapillus* group] northeastern Colombia (Boyacá), the coastal mountains of Venezuela, and Trinidad; the Tepui region of Venezuela and western Guyana; and eastern and central Brazil from Maranhão south to Uruguay, Paraguay, and northeastern Argentina and southwest to central Bolivia and northwestern Argentina.

Casual [*culicivorus* group] in southern Texas (about eight records, mainly in winter in lower Rio Grande Valley).

Notes.—Groups: *B. culicivorus* [Stripe-crowned Warbler], *B. cabanisi* Berlepsch, 1879 [Cabanis's Warbler], and *B. auricapillus* (Swainson, 1838) [Golden-crowned Warbler].

Basileuterus rufifrons (Swainson). Rufous-capped Warbler.

Setophaga rufifrons Swainson, 1838, Animals in Menageries, *in* Lardner, Cabinet Cyclopedia 98: 294. (Mexico = Real del Arriba, México.)

Habitat.—Tropical Deciduous Forest, Tropical Lowland Evergreen Forest Edge, Secondary Forest, Pine-Oak Forest, Arid Montane Scrub (0–2800 m; Tropical and Subtropical zones).

Distribution.—*Resident* [*rufifrons* group] from northern Sonora, western Chihuahua, Sinaloa, western Durango, Nayarit, Jalisco, Guanajuato, San Luis Potosí, central Nuevo León, and western Tamaulipas south through Mexico (except southeastern and the Yucatan Peninsula) to central Guatemala; [*salvini* group] in southern Veracruz, Tabasco, northern Oaxaca, northern Chiapas, Belize, and northern Guatemala; and [*delattrii* group] from southeastern Chiapas, southern Guatemala, El Salvador, and Honduras south through Nicaragua, Costa Rica, Panama (including Isla Coiba), and northern Colombia to northwestern Venezuela.

Casual [*rufifrons* group] in southeastern Arizona (mainly Huachuca, Whetstone, Pajaritos, and Chiricahua mountains, with attempted nesting in Cave Creek Canyon in 1977), and western and southern Texas (Brewster, Webb, Kendall, and Uvalde counties, and Corpus Christi; also a sight report from Starr County).

Notes.—The groups have frequently been treated as species (Hellmayr 1935): *B. rufifrons* [Rufous-capped Warbler], *B. salvini* Cherrie, 1892 [Salvin's Warbler], and *B. delattrii* Bonaparte, 1854 [Chestnut-capped Warbler], but intergradation between *salvini* and *delattrii* occurs in Guatemala, El Salvador, and Honduras (Monroe 1968, *contra* Howell and Webb 1995).

Basileuterus belli (Giraud). Golden-browed Warbler.

Muscicapa belli Giraud, 1841, Descr. Sixteen New Spec. N. Amer. Birds, pl. [4], fig. 2 and text. (Texas, error = Mount Orizaba, Veracruz.)

Habitat.—Montane Evergreen Forest, Pine-Oak Forest (1300–3100 m; Subtropical and Temperate zones).

Distribution.—*Resident* from southeastern Sinaloa, western Durango, Nayarit, Jalisco, Michoacán, México, Hidalgo, eastern San Luis Potosí, and southwestern Tamaulipas south through the mountains of southern Mexico, Guatemala, and El Salvador to central Honduras.

Notes.—Also known as Bell's Warbler.

Basileuterus melanogenys Baird. Black-cheeked Warbler.

Basileuterus melanogenys Baird, 1865, Rev. Amer. Birds 1: 248. ("San José ?," Costa Rica.)

Habitat.—Elfin Forest, Montane Evergreen Forest, Secondary Forest; prefers bamboo-choked ravines and understory of oak forest (1200–3500 m; Subtropical and Temperate zones).

Distribution.—*Resident* in the mountains of Costa Rica (Cordillera Central southward) and western Panama (Chiriquí and Veraguas).

Notes.—*Basileuterus melanogenys* and *B. ignotus* constitute a superspecies and are sometimes treated as conspecific (Lowery and Monroe *in* Paynter 1968).

Basileuterus ignotus Nelson. Pirre Warbler.

Basileuterus melanogenys ignotus Nelson, 1912, Smithson. Misc. Collect. 60(3): 21. (Mount Pirri, at 5,200 feet altitude, near head of Rio Limon, [Darién,] eastern Panama.)

Habitat.—Montane Evergreen Forest, Elfin Forest (1200–1500 m; Subtropical and lower Temperate zones).

Distribution.—*Resident* in the mountains of eastern Panama (Cerro Pirre and Cerro Tacarcuna, eastern Darién).

Notes.—See comments under *B. melanogenys*.

Basileuterus tristriatus (Tschudi). Three-striped Warbler.

Myiodioctes tristriatus Tschudi, 1844, Arch. Naturgesch. 10: 283. (Republica Peruana = San Pedro plantation, near Lurín, error [= valley of Vitoc, depto. de Junín, Peru].)

Habitat.—Montane Evergreen Forest, Secondary Forest (800–2500 m; upper Tropical and Subtropical zones).

Distribution.—*Resident* in the mountains of Costa Rica (north to Cordillera de Tilarán) and western Panama (east to Veraguas); in eastern Panama (eastern Panamá province and Darién); in coastal mountains of Venezuela; in Santa Marta Mountains and Andes from Colombia south, on the western slope to central Ecuador and on the eastern slope to central Bolivia.

Genus *PHAEOTHLYPIS* Todd

Phaeothlypis Todd, 1929, Proc. U. S. Natl. Mus. 74(7): 8. Type, by original designation, *Muscicapa fulvicauda* Spix.

Notes.—Sometimes merged in *Basileuterus* (Ridgely and Tudor 1989, Sibley and Monroe 1990). See comments under *Catharopeza.*

Phaeothlypis fulvicauda (Spix). Buff-rumped Warbler

Muscicapa fulvicauda Spix, 1825, Avium Spec. Nov. Bras. 2: 20, pl. 28, fig. 2. (No locality given = São Paulo de Olivença, Rio Solimões, Brazil.)

Habitat., --Tropical Lowland Evergreen Forest, usually along rocky and rapidly flowing streams and rivers (0–1100 m; Tropical Zone).
Distribution.—*Resident* on the Caribbean slope of Honduras (west to the Sula Valley) and Nicaragua, on both slopes of Costa Rica (except the dry northwest) and Panama, and in South America from Colombia south, west of the Andes to northwestern Peru and east of the Andes in central Colombia, eastern Ecuador, eastern Peru, western Amazonian Brazil, and northern Bolivia.
Notes.—*Phaeothlypis fulvicauda* and *P. rivularis* (Wied, 1821), of eastern South America, constitute a superspecies and are often considered conspecific (Meyer de Schauensee 1970).

Genus *ZELEDONIA* Ridgway

Zeledonia Ridgway, 1889, Proc. U. S. Natl. Mus. 11 (1888): 537. Type, by monotypy, *Zeledonia coronata* Ridgway.

Notes.—Formerly considered related to the muscicapid assemblage (with turdid affinities) and placed in the monotypic family Zeledoniidae, but now regarded as parulid (see Sibley 1968).

Zeledonia coronata Ridgway. Wrenthrush.

Zeledonia coronata Ridgway, 1889, Proc. U. S. Natl. Mus. 11 (1888): 538. (Laguna del Volcán de Poás, Costa Rica.)

Habitat.—Montane Evergreen Forest, Elfin Forest (1500–3500 m; Subtropical and Temperate zones).
Distribution.—*Resident* in the highlands of Costa Rica (north to Cordillera de Tilarán) and western Panama (western Chiriquí and Veraguas).

Genus *ICTERIA* Vieillot

Icteria Vieillot, 1807, Hist. Nat. Ois. Amer. Sept. 1 (livr. 1): iv, 85. Type, by monotypy, *Icteria dumicola* Vieillot = *Turdus virens* Linnaeus.

Notes.—Although placement of this genus in the Parulidae has been questioned frequently (e.g., Eisenmann 1962b, Ficken and Ficken 1962, Mayr and Short 1970), molecular data support its traditional placement (Sibley and Ahlquist 1982c).

Icteria virens (Linnaeus). Yellow-breasted Chat.

Turdus virens Linnaeus, 1758, Syst. Nat. (ed. 10) 1: 171. Based on "The yellow brested Chat" Catesby, Nat. Hist. Carolina 1: 50, pl. 50. (in America = South Carolina, 200 or 300 miles from the sea.)

Habitat.—Dense second-growth, riparian thickets, and brush (Tropical to Temperate zones).

Distribution.—*Breeds* from southern British Columbia, southern Alberta, southern Saskatchewan, western and central North Dakota, southern Minnesota (casually?), southern Wisconsin, southern Michigan, extreme southern Ontario (local), and central New York (formerly north to Connecticut and Rhode Island, casually to southern Vermont and southern New Hampshire) south to south-central Baja California, on Pacific slope to northern Sinaloa, in interior over plateau to Zacatecas, (formerly) on Atlantic slope to southern Tamaulipas, and to the Gulf coast and northern Florida.

Winters from southern Baja California, southern Sinaloa, southern Texas, southern Louisiana, and southern Florida (casually northward, primarily in early winter only, to western Oregon, California, the Great Lakes region, New York, and New England) south through Middle America to western Panama (rarely to western Bocas del Toro). Casual in Bermuda and the Bahama Islands.

Migrates rarely through Bermuda and the northern Bahama Islands (Grand Bahama, Abaco, Bimini, Andros).

Casual north to western Washington, eastern North Dakota, southern Manitoba, northern Minnesota, northern Michigan, northern Ontario, southern Quebec, New Brunswick, Nova Scotia, and Newfoundland. Accidental or casual in Cuba, Grand Cayman, and Greenland.

Genus *GRANATELLUS* Bonaparte

Granatellus (Du Bus de Gisignies MS) Bonaparte, 1850, Consp. Gen. Avium 1(2): 312. Type, by monotypy, *Granatellus venustus* Bonaparte.

Notes.—Systematic position uncertain; it may not be a parulid (Lowery and Monroe *in* Paynter 1968).

Granatellus venustus Bonaparte. Red-breasted Chat.

Granatellus venustus (Du Bus de Gisignies MS) Bonaparte, 1850, Consp. Gen. Avium 1(2): 312. (Mexico = near Comitán, Chiapas.)

Habitat.—Tropical Deciduous Forest (0–1200 m; Tropical and lower Subtropical zones).
Distribution.—*Resident* [*venustus* group] in the Pacific lowlands of Mexico from northern Sinaloa and western Durango south to Chiapas; and [*francescae* group] in the Tres Marias Islands (Isla María Madre).
Notes.—Groups: *G. venustus* [Red-breasted Chat] and *G. francescae* Baird, 1865 [Tres Marias Chat]. *Granatellus venustus, G. sallaei,* and the South American *G. pelzelni* Sclater, 1865 [Rose-breasted Chat], may constitute a superspecies (Sibley and Monroe 1990).

Granatellus sallaei (Bonaparte). Gray-throated Chat.

Setophaga sallæi (Bonaparte and Sclater MS) Bonaparte, 1856, C. R. Acad. Sci. Paris 42: 957. (southern Mexico = Córdoba, Veracruz.)

Habitat.—Tropical Deciduous Forest (Tropical Zone).
Distribution.—*Resident* from southern Veracruz and the Yucatan Peninsula south in the Gulf-Caribbean lowlands of Tabasco, northern Oaxaca, and northern Chiapas to northern Guatemala and Belize.
Notes.—See comments under *G. venustus.*

Genus *XENOLIGEA* Bond

Xenoligea [subgenus] Bond, 1967, Birds W. Indies, 12th Suppl., p. 20. Type, by original designation, *Microligea montana* Chapman.

Notes.—Formerly treated as a subgenus of *Microligea.* Relationships of *Xenoligea* are uncertain. Although here placed within Parulidae, the genus possibly has thraupid affinities (Lowery and Monroe *in* Paynter 1968).

Xenoligea montana (Chapman). White-winged Warbler.

Microligea montana Chapman, 1917, Bull. Amer. Mus. Nat. Hist. 37: 330. (Loma Tina, 1566 m, 18°47′ N, 70°49′ W., Azua Peninsula, Dominican Republic.)

Habitat.—Montane Evergreen Forest (950–2000 m).
Distribution.—*Resident* in the higher mountains of Hispaniola.
Notes.—Also known as White-winged Ground Warbler.

Family **COEREBIDAE**: Bananaquits

Genus *COEREBA* Vieillot

Cœreba Vieillot, 1809, Hist. Nat. Ois. Amer. Sept. 2 (livr. 21): 70. Type, by monotypy, *Certhia flaveola* Linnaeus.

Coereba flaveola (Linnaeus). Bananaquit.

Certhia flaveola Linnaeus, 1758, Syst. Nat. (ed. 10) 1: 119. Based mainly on "Luscinia s. Philomela e fusco & luteo varia" Sloane, Voy. Jamaica 2: 307, pl. 259, fig. 3, and "The Black and Yellow Creeper" Edwards, Nat. Hist. Birds 3: 122, pl. 122, upper fig. (in America = Jamaica.)

Habitat.—Tropical Lowland Evergreen Forest Edge, Secondary Forest, Tropical Lowland Evergreen Forest, Tropical Deciduous Forest, Arid Lowland Scrub, Second-growth Scrub (0–1500 m; Tropical to lower Temperate zones).

Distribution.—*Resident* [*bahamensis* group] in the Bahama Islands (from Grand Bahama and Little Abaco south to Great Inagua and Turks Islands); and [*flaveola* group] throughout the Antilles (including many small cays and islands in the western Caribbean Sea, but absent from Cuba and the Swan Islands), and on mainland and nearby islands from central Veracruz, northern Oaxaca, and Chiapas (also the islands of Cancun, Cozumel, and Cayo Culebra) south through the Gulf-Caribbean lowlands of northern Central America to Nicaragua (including islas Providencia and San Andrés), on both slopes of Costa Rica (except the dry northwest) and Panama (including Coiba and the Pearl islands), and in South America from Colombia (including Isla Gorgona), Venezuela (including islands from the Netherlands Antilles east to Tobago and Trinidad), and the Guianas south, west of the Andes to northwestern Peru and east of the Andes to southern Bolivia, Paraguay, extreme northeastern Argentina, and southern Brazil.

Ranges irregularly [*bahamensis* group] to southern Florida (north to Brevard County; most frequently recorded in Palm Beach and Broward counties). Casual off Cuba (Cayo Tío Pepe, Gibara).

Notes.—Groups: *C. bahamensis* (Reichenbach, 1853) [Bahama Bananaquit] and *C. flaveola* [Common Bananaquit]. See Seutin et al. (1994) for relationships among populations in the Caribbean region.

Family **THRAUPIDAE**: Tanagers

Genus *CONIROSTRUM* Lafresnaye and d'Orbigny

Conirostrum Lafresnaye and d'Orbigny, 1838, Mag. Zool. [Paris] 8(2): pl. 77–79, p. 25. Type, by monotypy, *Conirostrum cinereum* Lafresnaye and d'Orbigny.

Conirostrum leucogenys (Lafresnaye). White-eared Conebill.

Dacnis Leucogenys Lafresnaye, 1852, Rev. Mag. Zool. (2) 4: 470. (Colombiâ = Bogotá.)

Habitat.—Tropical Lowland Evergreen Forest Edge, Gallery Forest, Secondary Forest (0–1300 m; Tropical Zone).

Distribution.—*Resident* from eastern Panama (eastern Panamá province in the Bayano River valley, and Darién) east to northern Colombia and northern Venezuela.

Genus *NESOSPINGUS* Sclater

Nesospingus Sclater, 1885, Ibis, p. 273. Type, by monotypy, *Chlorospingus speculiferus* Lawrence.

Nesospingus speculiferus (Lawrence). Puerto Rican Tanager.

Chlorospingus ? *speculiferus* Lawrence, 1875, Ibis, p. 383, pl. 9, fig. 1. (Porto Rico.)

Habitat.—Montane Evergreen Forest, Secondary Forest (200–1200 m).
Distribution.—*Resident* in the highlands of Puerto Rico.

Genus *CHLOROSPINGUS* Cabanis

Chlorospingus Cabanis, 1851, Mus. Heineanum 1: 139. Type, by virtual monotypy, *Chlorospingus leucophrys* Cabanis = *Arremon ophthalmicus* Du Bus de Gisignies.

Chlorospingus ophthalmicus (Du Bus de Gisignies). Common Bush-Tanager.

Arremon ophthalmicus Du Bus de Gisignies, 1847, Bull. Acad. R. Sci. Lett. Beaux-Arts Belg., 14, p. 106. (Mexico = Jalapa, Veracruz.)

Habitat.—Montane Evergreen Forest, Secondary Forest (1000–2500 m; upper Tropical and Subtropical zones, in nonbreeding season to lower Tropical Zone, in South America also to lower Temperate Zone).
Distribution.—*Resident* [*ophthalmicus* group] in the highlands from Guerrero, Puebla, Hidalgo, southeastern San Luis Potosí south through Middle America to western Panama (western Chiriquí and Bocas del Toro), and in South America in the coastal Mountains of Venezuela, locally in the Western Andes of Colombia and Ecuador, in the Central Andes of Colombia, and in the Eastern Andes of Venezuela and Colombia south to northwestern Argentina; and [*punctulatus* group] in the highlands of western Panama (Veraguas and Coclé).
Notes.—Species limits within the genus are poorly understood. The two groups have sometimes (e.g., Storer *in* Paynter 1970) been regarded as separate species, *C. ophthalmicus* [Brown-headed Bush-Tanager] and *C. punctulatus* Sclater and Salvin, 1869 [Dotted Bush-Tanager], but intergradation was reported by Olson (1993b); *C. inornatus* is sometimes regarded as a race of *C. ophthalmicus,* whereas *C. tacarcunae* is considered a race of *C. ophthalmicus* (Zimmer 1947) or a race of *C. flavigularis* (Hellmayr 1936).

Chlorospingus tacarcunae Griscom. Tacarcuna Bush-Tanager.

Chlorospingus tacarcunae Griscom, 1924, Amer. Mus. Novit., no. 141, p. 11. (Mt. Tacarcuna, east slope, alt. 4600 ft., eastern Panama.)

Habitat.—Montane Evergreen Forest, Elfin Forest, Montane Evergreen Forest Edge (850–1500 m; upper Tropical and lower Subtropical zones).
Distribution.—*Resident* in eastern Panama in western San Blas (Cerro Brewster), eastern Panamá province (Cerro Azul, Cerro Jefe) and eastern Darién (Cerro Tacarcuna, Cerro Mali).
Notes.—See comments under *C. ophthalmicus.*

Chlorospingus inornatus (Nelson). Pirre Bush-Tanager.

Hylospingus inornatus Nelson, 1912, Smithson. Misc. Collect. 60(3): 18. (Mount Pirri, at 5,200 feet altitude, eastern Panama.)

Habitat.—Montane Evergreen Forest, Elfin Forest, Montane Evergreen Forest Edge (800–1650 m; upper Tropical and Subtropical zones).
Distribution.—*Resident* in eastern Panama in eastern Darién (Cerro Pirre, Cerro Sapo, and Cana).
Notes.—See comments under *C. ophthalmicus.*

Chlorospingus pileatus Salvin. Sooty-capped Bush-Tanager.

Chlorospingus pileatus Salvin, 1865, Proc. Zool. Soc. London (1864), p. 581. (Volcan de Cartago [= Irazú], Costa Rica.)

Habitat.—Montane Evergreen Forest, Elfin Forest, Secondary Forest (1500–3000 m; Subtropical and lower Temperate zones).

Distribution.—*Resident* in the mountains of Costa Rica (north to the Cordillera de Tilarán) and western Panama (Chiriquí and Veraguas).

Notes.—Includes *C. zeledoni* Ridgway, 1905 [Volcano Bush-Tanager], of the Irazú and Turrialba volcanoes in central Costa Rica, now shown to be a color morph of *C. pileatus* (Johnson and Brush 1972).

Chlorospingus flavigularis (Sclater). Yellow-throated Bush-Tanager.

Pipilopsis flavigularis Sclater, 1852, Rev. Mag. Zool. (2)4: 8. (Nouvelle-Grenade = Bogotá, Colombia.)

Habitat.—Montane Evergreen Forest, Secondary Forest, Tropical Lowland Evergreen Forest Edge (250–1600 m; Tropical and lower Subtropical zones).

Distribution.—*Resident* [*hypophaeus* group] in western Panama (Bocas del Toro and Veraguas); and [*flavigularis* group] in South America in the Andes from Colombia south, on the western slope to southwestern Ecuador and on the eastern slope to northern Bolivia.

Notes.—Differences in iris color and behavior suggest that the two groups may represent separate species (Isler and Isler 1987), *C. hypophaeus* Sclater and Salvin, 1868 [Drab-breasted Bush-Tanager] and *C. flavigularis* [Yellow-throated Bush-Tanager]. See comments under *C. ophthalmicus*.

Chlorospingus canigularis (Lafresnaye). Ashy-throated Bush-Tanager.

Tachyphonus canigularis Lafresnaye, 1848, Rev. Zool. [Paris] 11: 11. (ad Bogotam, in Colombia = Bogotá, Colombia.)

Habitat.—Montane Evergreen Forest, Tropical Lowland Evergreen Forest, Tropical Deciduous Forest, Tropical Lowland Evergreen Forest Edge (300–2600 m; Subtropical Zone).

Distribution.—*Resident* [*olivaceiceps* group] in the mountains of central Costa Rica (primarily Caribbean slope from Río Reventazón to the Cordillera Central) and extreme western Panama (western Bocas del Toro, sight report only); and [*canigularis* group] in South America from Colombia and northwestern Venezuela south to northwestern Peru and eastern Ecuador.

Notes.—Groups: *C. olivaceiceps* Underwood, 1898 [Olive-crowned Bush-Tanager] and *C. canigularis* [Ashy-throated Bush-Tanager].

Genus *HEMITHRAUPIS* Cabanis

Hemithraupis Cabanis, 1850, Mus. Heineanum 1 (1851): 21. Type, by original designation, *Hylophilus ruficeps* Wied = *Nemosia ruficapilla* Vieillot.

Hemithraupis flavicollis (Vieillot). Yellow-backed Tanager.

Nemosia flavicollis Vieillot, 1818, Nouv. Dict. Hist. Nat. (nouv. éd.) 22: 491. (l'Amérique méridionale = Cayenne.)

Habitat.—Tropical Lowland Evergreen Forest, Secondary Forest (0–1000 m; Tropical and lower Subtropical zones).

Distribution.—*Resident* from extreme eastern Panama (Río Tuira and Cana, in eastern Darién), northern Colombia, southern Venezuela, and the Guianas south, east of the Andes, to northern Bolivia and Amazonian and southeastern Brazil.

Genus *CHRYSOTHLYPIS* Berlepsch

Chrysothlypis Berlepsch, 1912, Verh. V Int. Ornithol. Kongr., Berlin (1911), p. 1080. Type, by original designation, *Tachyphonus chrysomelas* Sclater and Salvin.

Chrysothlypis chrysomelaena (Sclater and Salvin). Black-and-yellow Tanager.

Tachyphonus chrysomelas Sclater and Salvin, 1869, Proc. Zool. Soc. London, p. 440, pl. 32. (Cordillera del Chucú, Veraguas, Panama.)

Habitat.—Montane Evergreen Forest, Tropical Lowland Evergreen Forest (350–1600 m; upper Tropical and lower Subtropical zones).

Distribution.—*Resident* in Costa Rica (primarily Caribbean slope north to Arenal) and Panama (Chiriquí, Veraguas, Coclé, western and eastern Panamá province, and Darién).

Notes.—For use of *chrysomelaena* instead of *chrysomelas,* see Deignan (1961).

Genus *PHAENICOPHILUS* Strickland

Phænicophilus Strickland, 1851, in Jardine, Contrib. Ornithol. 1: 104. Type, by original designation, *Phaenicophilus palmarum* (Linn.) = *Turdus palmarum* Linnaeus.

Phaenicophilus palmarum (Linnaeus). Black-crowned Palm-Tanager.

Turdus palmarum Linnaeus, 1766, Syst. Nat. (ed. 12) 1: 295. Based in part on "Le Palmiste a teste [= tête] noire" Brisson, Ornithologie 2: 303, pl. 29, fig. 2. (in Cayennæ Palmis, error = Santo Domingo, Hispaniola.)

Habitat.—Secondary Forest, Tropical Lowland Evergreen Forest, Tropical Deciduous Forest, Montane Evergreen Forest, Mangrove Forest, Arid Lowland Scrub (0–2000 m).

Distribution.—*Resident* on Hispaniola (except the southern peninsula of Haiti west of the Trouin Valley) and adjacent Saona Island.

Notes.—This species and the next are very closely related and have been considered conspecific (e.g., Hellmayr 1936). A narrow hybrid zone, with little or no introgression, occurs north of Marigot, Haiti (McDonald and Smith 1990, 1994).

Phaenicophilus poliocephalus (Bonaparte). Gray-crowned Palm-Tanager.

Dulus poliocephalus Bonaparte, 1851, Rev. Mag. Zool. (2)3: 178. (Hispaniola = Haiti.)

Habitat.—Secondary Forest, Tropical Lowland Evergreen Forest, Tropical Deciduous Forest, Montane Evergreen Forest, Mangrove Forest, Arid Lowland Scrub (0–2400 m).

Distribution.—*Resident* in southwestern Hispaniola (Massif de la Hotte area, in southwestern Haiti, and on adjacent islands (Gonâve, Île-à-Vache, and Grand Cayemite).

Notes.—See comments under *P. palmarum.*

Genus *CALYPTOPHILUS* Cory

Calyptophilus Cory, 1884, Auk 1: 3. Type, by monotypy, *Phoenicophilus frugivorus* Cory.

Calyptophilus tertius Wetmore. Western Chat-Tanager.

Calyptophilus tertius Wetmore, 1929, Smithsonian Misc. Coll. 81 (13): 2. (higher slopes of Morne La Hotte, Haiti.)

Habitat.—Montane Evergreen Forest (1500-2200 m).

Distribution.—*Resident* on the higher mountains of the massifs de la Hotte and la Selle, southern Haiti, and extreme southwestern Dominican Republic, Hispaniola.

Notes.—See Wetmore and Swales (1931) for treatment of this and *C. frugivorus* as separate species (also followed by Pregill and Olson 1981). For a contrary opinion, see Bond and Dod (1977) and Bond (1982). Also known as Highland Chat-Tanager.

Calyptophilus frugivorus (Cory). Eastern Chat-Tanager.

Phænicophilus frugivorus Cory, 1883, Q. J. Boston Zool. Soc. 2: 45. (Santo Domingo = Almercen [= Villa Rivas], Dominican Republic.)

Habitat.—Tropical Deciduous Forest (0-2000 m).

Distribution.—*Resident* in the western Dominican Republic (east to Semaná province), and on Gonâve Island.

Notes.—Also known as Lowland Chat-Tanager. See comments under *C. tertius.*

Genus *RHODINOCICHLA* Hartlaub

Rhodinocichla Hartlaub, 1853, J. Ornithol. 1: 33. Type, by original designation, *Furnarius roseus* Lesson.

Notes.—Systematic position of this genus is uncertain. Similarities in plumage colors, pattern, and sexual dimorphism suggest that it may be related to the "paruline" genus *Granatellus* (Storer *in* Paynter 1970).

Rhodinocichla rosea (Lesson). Rosy Thrush-Tanager.

Furnarius roseus Lesson, 1832, Illus. Zool., livr. 2, pl. 5. (du Brésil et du district peu connu de San-Jose, error = Caracas, Venezuela.)

Habitat.—Tropical Deciduous Forest, Secondary Forest, Gallery Forest (0–1700 m; Tropical and lower Subtropical zones).

Distribution.—*Resident* in the Pacific lowlands of Mexico from Sinaloa to western Michoacán (Coahuayana); on the Pacific slope of southern Middle America from southwestern Costa Rica east to central Panama (to eastern Panamá province, also on the Caribbean slope in Coclé, Colón, and the Canal area); and in South America in northern and central Colombia, and northern Venezuela.

Notes.—Also known as Rose-breasted Thrush-Tanager.

Genus *MITROSPINGUS* Ridgway

Mitrospingus Ridgway, 1898, Auk 15: 225. Type, by original designation, *Tachyphonus cassini* [sic] Lawrence.

Mitrospingus cassinii (Lawrence). Dusky-faced Tanager.

Tachyphonus Cassinii Lawrence, 1861, Ann. Lyc. Nat. Hist. N. Y. 7: 297. (on the Atlantic side of the Isthmus of Panama, along the line of the Panama Railroad = Canal Zone.)

Habitat.—Tropical Lowland Evergreen Forest Edge, Secondary Forest (0–1200 m; Tropical and lower Subtropical zones).

Distribution.—*Resident* from Costa Rica (Caribbean lowlands) south through Panama (entire Caribbean slope, and locally in the Pacific lowlands in Veraguas, eastern Panamá province, and Darién), and locally in northwestern Colombia (east to Antioquia) and the Pacific lowlands of western Colombia and western Ecuador.

Genus *CHLOROTHRAUPIS* Salvin and Godman

Chlorothraupis (Ridgway MS) Salvin and Godman, 1883, Biol. Cent.-Amer. (Aves) 1: 297. Type, by subsequent designation (Ridgway, 1884), *Phoenicothraupis carmioli* Lawrence.

Chlorothraupis carmioli (Lawrence). Olive Tanager.

Phœnicothraupis carmioli Lawrence, 1868, Ann. Lyc. Nat. Hist. N. Y. 9: 100. (Angostura, Costa Rica.)

Habitat.—Tropical Lowland Evergreen Forest, Secondary Forest (0–1200 m; Tropical and lower Subtropical zones).

Distribution.—*Resident* [*carmioli* group] in eastern Nicaragua (Caribbean slope), Costa Rica (Caribbean slope, locally on Pacific slope in low passes), and Panama (entire Caribbean slope, and Pacific slope from eastern Panamá province to Darién, generally north and east of the valleys of Río Chepo and Río Chucunaque); and [*frenata* group] in South America on the eastern slope of the Andes from southeastern Colombia south to central Bolivia.

Notes.—Groups: *C. carmioli* [Olive Tanager] and *C. frenata* Berlepsch, 1907 [Yellow-lored Tanager]. *Chlorothraupis carmioli* and *C. olivacea* constitute a superspecies (Sibley and Monroe 1990).

Chlorothraupis olivacea (Cassin). Lemon-spectacled Tanager.

> *Orthogonys olivaceus* Cassin, 1860, Proc. Acad. Nat. Sci. Philadelphia 12: 140. (Cordilleras Mountains, on the River Truando, New Granada = Río Truandó, northwestern Colombia.)

Habitat.—Tropical Lowland Evergreen Forest, Montane Evergreen Forest, Secondary Forest (0–1500 m; Tropical Zone).

Distribution.—*Resident* in extreme eastern Panama (eastern Darién, generally south and west of the valleys of Río Chepo and Río Chucunaque), western Colombia, and northwestern Ecuador.

Notes.—Also known as Lemon-browed Tanager or Yellow-browed Tanager, the latter applied also to *Tangara guttata*. See comments under *C. carmioli*.

Genus *EUCOMETIS* Sclater

> *Comarophagus* (not Boie, 1826) Bonaparte, 1851, C. R. Acad. Sci. Paris 32: 81. Type, by subsequent designation (G. R. Gray, 1855), *Tanagra penicillata* Spix.
> *Eucometis* Sclater, 1856, Proc. Zool. Soc. London, p. 117. New name for *Comarophagus* Bonaparte, preoccupied.

Eucometis penicillata (Spix). Gray-headed Tanager.

> *Tanagra penicillata* Spix, 1825, Avium Spec. Nov. Bras. 2: 36, pl. 49, fig. 1. (No locality given = Fonte Bõa, Rio Solimões, Brazil.)

Habitat.—Tropical Lowland Evergreen Forest, Gallery Forest, River-edge Forest, Secondary Forest (0–600 m; Tropical and lower Subtropical zones).

Distribution.—*Resident* [*cristata* group] on the Gulf-Caribbean slope from Oaxaca (Isthmus of Tehuantepec), southern Veracruz, and the Yucatan Peninsula south to Honduras, on both slopes of Nicaragua (rare on the Pacific slope), Costa Rica (primarily Pacific slope, locally on Caribbean drainage), and Panama (locally on Pacific slope throughout, on Caribbean slope from Canal area eastward), and in northern and eastern Colombia and northwestern Venezuela; and [*penicillata* group] from southeastern Colombia, Venezuela, and the Guianas south to central Bolivia, northern Paraguay, and central and eastern Brazil.

Notes.—Groups: *E. cristata* (Du Bus de Gisignies, 1855) [Gray-crested Tanager] and *E. penicillata* [Gray-headed Tanager].

Genus *LANIO* Vieillot

> *Lanio* Vieillot, 1816, Analyse, p. 40. Type, by original designation, "Tangara mordoré" Buffon = *Tangara fulva* Boddaert.

Lanio aurantius Lafresnaye. Black-throated Shrike-Tanager.

> *Lanio Aurantius* Lafresnaye, 1846, Rev. Zool. [Paris] 9: 204. (in Colombiâ, error = Guatemala.)

Habitat.—Tropical Lowland Evergreen Forest (0–1200 m; Tropical Zone).

Distribution.—*Resident* from central Veracruz and northern Oaxaca south on the Gulf-Caribbean slope of Tabasco, Chiapas, southern Campeche, southern Quintana Roo, Guatemala, and Belize to northern Honduras (east to the La Ceiba region).

Notes.—*Lanio aurantius* and *L. leucothorax* constitute a superspecies (Sibley and Monroe 1990).

Lanio leucothorax Salvin. White-throated Shrike-Tanager.

> *Lanio leucothorax* Salvin, 1865, Proc. Zool. Soc. London (1864), p. 581. (Tucurriqui, Costa Rica.)

Habitat.—Tropical Lowland Evergreen Forest (0–750 m; Tropical and lower Subtropical zones).

Distribution.—*Resident* from eastern Honduras (Olancho) south through Nicaragua (Caribbean slope) and Costa Rica (both slopes, absent from the dry northwest) to western Panama (western Bocas del Toro, Chiriquí, Veraguas, Coclé).

Notes.—See comments under *L. aurantius*.

Genus *HETEROSPINGUS* Ridgway

Heterospingus Ridgway, 1898, Auk 15: 225. Type, by original designation, *Tachyphonus rubrifrons* Lawrence.

Heterospingus rubrifrons (Lawrence). Sulphur-rumped Tanager.

Tachyphonus rubrifrons Lawrence, 1865, Proc. Acad. Nat. Sci. Philadelphia 17: 106. (Line of the Pan[ama]. R[ail]. Road, near Lion Hill Station = Lion Hill, Canal Zone.)

Habitat.—Tropical Lowland Evergreen Forest (0–900 m; Tropical Zone).

Distribution.—*Resident* in eastern Costa Rica (Caribbean lowlands west to the Río Reventazón) and Panama (entire Caribbean slope, and Pacific lowlands in eastern Panamá province and Darién, with a sight report from Veraguas).

Notes.—*Heterospingus rubrifrons* and *H. xanthopygius* have been considered conspecific (e.g., Storer *in* Paynter 1970, Wetmore et al. 1984); they constitute a superspecies (Sibley and Monroe 1990).

Heterospingus xanthopygius (Sclater). Scarlet-browed Tanager.

Tachyphonus xanthopygius Sclater, 1855, Proc. Zool. Soc. London (1854), p. 158, pl. 69. (in Nov. Grenada = Bogotá, Colombia.)

Habitat.—Tropical Lowland Evergreen Forest (0–1100 m; Tropical Zone).

Distribution.—*Resident* in eastern Panama (eastern Darién), western Colombia, and western Ecuador.

Notes.—See comments under *H. rubrifrons*.

Genus *TACHYPHONUS* Vieillot

Tachyphonus Vieillot, 1816, Analyse, p. 33. Type, by monotypy, "Tangara noir" Buffon = *Tangara rufa* Boddaert.

Tachyphonus luctuosus d'Orbigny and Lafresnaye. White-shouldered Tanager.

Tachyphonus luctuosus d'Orbigny and Lafresnaye, 1837, Mag. Zool. [Paris] 7(2): 29, pl. 77–79. (Guarayos [Bolivia].)

Habitat.—Tropical Lowland Evergreen Forest, River-edge Forest, Secondary Forest (0–1000 m; Tropical and Subtropical zones).

Distribution.—*Resident* from eastern Honduras (Caribbean slope west to La Ceiba region) south through Nicaragua (Caribbean slope), Costa Rica (both slopes, absent from the dry northwest), and Panama (entire Caribbean slope, and Pacific lowlands in western Chiriquí, eastern Panamá and Darién), and in South America from Colombia, Venezuela, Trinidad and the Guianas south, west of the Andes to northwestern Peru and east of the Andes to central Bolivia and central and eastern Brazil.

Tachyphonus delatrii Lafresnaye. Tawny-crested Tanager.

Tachyphonus Delatrii Lafresnaye, 1847, Rev. Zool. [Paris] 10: 72. (St-Bonaventure = Buenaventura, Colombia.)

Habitat.—Tropical Lowland Evergreen Forest, Montane Evergreen Forest, Secondary Forest (0–900 m; Tropical and lower Subtropical zones).

Distribution.—*Resident* from eastern Honduras (sight report) and eastern Nicaragua (Caribbean slope) south through Costa Rica (primarily Caribbean slope), Panama (entire Caribbean slope, and Pacific slope in Veraguas and Darién), and western Colombia (including Gorgona Island) to western Ecuador.

Tachyphonus rufus (Boddaert). White-lined Tanager.

> *Tangara rufa* Boddaert, 1783, Table Planches Enlum., p. 44. Based on "Le Tangaroux de Cayenne" Daubenton, Planches Enlum., pl. 711. (Cayenne.)

Habitat.—Secondary Forest, Gallery Forest, Tropical Lowland Evergreen Forest, Second-growth Scrub (0–1500 m; Tropical and lower Subtropical zones).

Distribution.—*Resident* in Costa Rica (primarily Caribbean lowlands, recently spreading to the southwestern Pacific lowlands) and Panama (entire Caribbean slope, on Pacific slope from western Panamá province eastward), and in South America in northwestern Ecuador, in the Andean region from Colombia (including the Santa Marta Mountains) south to south-central Peru, along the coast and Andes of Venezuela (including Isla Margarita, Trinidad and Tobago), and in the Guianas, eastern Brazil (Amapá south to Mato Grosso and Bahia, mainly east of the Rio Tapajos), eastern Bolivia (Santa Cruz), central Paraguay, and north-eastern Argentina (Misiones south to northern Buenos Aires).

Genus *HABIA* Blyth

> *Habia* Blyth, 1840, in Cuvier, Anim. Kingdom, p. 184. Type, by subsequent designation (Oberholser, 1922), *Tanagra flammiceps* Temminck = *Saltator rubicus* Vieillot.

Habia rubica (Vieillot). Red-crowned Ant-Tanager.

> *Staltator* [sic] *rubicus* Vieillot, 1817, Nouv. Dict. Hist. Nat. (nouv. éd.) 14: 107. Based on "Habia Roxiza" Azara, Apunt. Hist. Nat. Páx. Parag. 1: 351 (no. 85). (Paraguay.)

Habitat.—Tropical Lowland Evergreen Forest, Tropical Deciduous Forest, Secondary Forest, Montane Evergreen Forest (0–1000 m; Tropical Zone).

Distribution.—*Resident* from Nayarit south to south-central Oaxaca, and from southern Tamaulipas and southeastern Chiapas south along both slopes of Middle America (including the Yucatan Peninsula) to Nicaragua, in Costa Rica (Pacific lowlands), and Panama (primarily Pacific lowlands, locally on Caribbean slope)); also in northern South America (isolated populations in northern Colombia, northern Venezuela, and Trinidad), in Amazonia from Colombia (Meta and Vaupes) south to central Bolivia and central Brazil, and in eastern Brazil (Pernambuco south to central Rio Grande do Sul), southeastern Paraguay, and extreme northeastern Argentina (Misiones).

Habia fuscicauda (Cabanis). Red-throated Ant-Tanager.

> *Phoenicothraupis fuscicauda* Cabanis, 1861, J. Ornithol. 9: 86. (Costa Rica.)

Habitat.—Tropical Lowland Evergreen Forest Edge, River-edge Forest, Secondary Forest, Mangrove Forest (0–1200 m; Tropical and lower Subtropical zones).

Distribution.—*Resident* [*salvini* group] from southeastern San Luis Potosí, southern Tamaulipas, Puebla, Veracruz, northern Oaxaca, and northern and southeastern Chiapas south along both slopes of Middle America (including the Yucatan Peninsula, and Meco and Mujeres islands) to Honduras and northeastern Nicaragua; [*fuscicauda* group] in southern Nicaragua, Costa Rica (mostly Caribbean slope, and Pacific coast south to the Río Grande de Tárcoles), Panama (the Caribbean slope to Bocas de Toro and the Pacific slope locally in Veraguas and the Canal area) and northern Colombia (at least formerly, west through Sucre and Córdoba to the Río Sinú).

Notes.—Also known as Dusky-tailed Ant-Tanager. Groups: *H. salvini* (Berlepsch, 1883) [Salvin's Ant-Tanager] and *H. fuscicauda* [Red-throated Ant-Tanager]. *Habia fuscicauda* and the South American *H. gutturalis* (Sclater, 1854) [Sooty Ant-Tanager] constitute a superspecies (Sibley and Monroe 1990). See comments under *H. atrimaxillaris*.

Habia atrimaxillaris (Dwight and Griscom). Black-cheeked Ant-Tanager.

> *Phœnicothraupis atrimaxillaris* Dwight and Griscom, 1924, Amer. Mus. Novit., no. 142, p. 4. (Puerto Jimenez, Golfo Dulce, Prov. de Puntarenas, Costa Rica.)

Habitat.—Tropical Lowland Evergreen Forest, Secondary Forest (Tropical Zone).

Distribution.—*Resident* in the Pacific lowlands of southwestern Costa Rica (Golfo Dulce region).

Notes.—Storer *in* Paynter (1970) proposed that *atrimaxillaris* might be a subspecies of *H. fuscicauda.*

Genus *PIRANGA* Vieillot

> *Piranga* Vieillot, 1807, Hist. Nat. Ois. Amer. Sept. 1 (livr. 1): iv. Type, by monotypy, *Muscicapa rubra* Linnaeus = *Fringilla rubra* Linnaeus.
>
> *Spermagra* Swainson, 1827, Philos. Mag. (n.s.) 1: 437. Type, by monotypy, *Spermagra erythrocephala* Swainson.

Piranga roseogularis Cabot. Rose-throated Tanager.

> *Pyranga roseo-gularis* Cabot, 1846, Boston J. Nat. Hist. 5: 416. (road from Chemax to Yalahao, Yucatan = Yalahau, Quintana Roo.)

Habitat.—Tropical Deciduous Forest, Secondary Forest (Tropical Zone).

Distribution.—*Resident* in the Yucatan Peninsula (including Cozumel, Meco, and Mujeres islands), northern Guatemala (Petén), and northern Belize.

Piranga flava (Vieillot). Hepatic Tanager.

> *Saltator Flavus* Vieillot, 1822, in Bonnaterre and Vieillot, Tabl. Encycl. Méth. (Ornithol.) 2(91): 791. Based on "Habia Amarilla" Azara, Apunt. Hist. Nat. Páx. Parag. 1: 358 (no. 87). (Paraguay.)

Habitat.—Pine-Oak Forest, Gallery Forest, Tropical Deciduous Forest, Secondary Forest, Montane Evergreen Forest Edge, Tropical Lowland Evergreen Forest Edge, lowland pine savanna; mainly in highlands north of Costa Rica except in lowland pine savanna; the migratory northern populations range in nonbreeding season to lowland woodland and forest (600–3000 m; Tropical to Temperate zones).

Distribution.—*Breeds* [*hepatica* group] from southeastern California (San Bernardino and Kingston mountains, and Clark Mountain, probably also the New York Mountains), northwestern and central Arizona, southeastern Colorado, northern New Mexico, western Texas, Nuevo León, and Tamaulipas south through the highlands of Middle America (also the Isthmus of Tehuantepec lowlands) to north-central Nicaragua, and in the lowland pine savanna of Belize, extreme eastern Honduras, and northeastern Nicaragua.

Winters [*hepatica* group] from northern Mexico (casually from central and southern California and southern Arizona) south through the breeding range, occurring also in lowland areas in northern Mexico.

Casual [*hepatica* group] north elsewhere in California (to Inyo County and the Farallon Islands), and to Baja California, southern Nevada (probably breeds), and southeastern Wyoming, and east to southeastern Texas and southwestern Louisiana. Accidental in Illinois (Beverly).

Resident [*lutea* group] in Costa Rica (Cordillera Central southward) and Panama (both slopes), in the Andes of northern South America (locally in northern Colombia and northern Venezuela, also Trinidad), western Colombia (Cauca Valley), and on east slope from northern Peru south to Bolivia (Cochabamba); also west of the Andes from Colombia (Valle) south through western Ecuador to Peru (Lima), and south of the Orinoco in southern Venezuela (Amazonas and Bolivar), northern Brazil, central Guyana, and central Surinam; and [*flava* group] in South America from eastern Brazil (Roraima) and southern Guyana south through much of central and eastern Brazil to eastern Bolivia, northern Argentina (Mendoza, Córdoba, and northern Buenos Aires), western Uruguay, and southeastern Brazil.

Notes.—Groups: *P. hepatica* Swainson, 1827 [Hepatic Tanager], *P. lutea* (Lesson, 1834)

[Tooth-billed Tanager], and *P. flava* [Red Tanager]. The three groups may represent two or three species (Ridgely and Tudor 1989).

Piranga rubra (Linnaeus). Summer Tanager.

> *Fringilla rubra* Linnaeus, 1758, Syst. Nat. (ed. 10) 1: 181. Based on "The Summer Red-Bird" Catesby, Nat. Hist. Carolina 1: 56, pl. 56. (in America = South Carolina.)

Habitat.—Open deciduous woodland, swamps, pine and pine-oak woodland, and cottonwood riparian woodland; in migration and winter in a wide variety of wooded habitats with tall trees.

Distribution.—*Breeds* from southeastern California (west to Los Angeles and Kern counties, and north to southern Inyo County), southern Nevada, southwestern Utah, central Arizona, central New Mexico, central Texas, west-central Oklahoma, eastern Kansas, southeastern Nebraska, southern Iowa, central (rarely northern) Illinois, southern Wisconsin (formerly), central Indiana, southern (rarely northern) Ohio, southwestern Pennsylvania, West Virginia, Virginia, eastern Maryland and New Jersey south to northeastern Baja California, southeastern Sonora, northern Durango, southeastern Coahuila, central Nuevo León, southern Texas, the Gulf coast, and southern Florida.

Winters from southern Baja California, southern Sinaloa, and Veracruz south through Middle America and South America (including Trinidad) west of the Andes to western Ecuador and east of the Andes to northern Bolivia and Amazonian Brazil, rarely north to central coastal and southern California and southern Arizona, and casually in Louisiana, southern Florida, the Bahama Islands, and Cuba.

Migrates regularly through eastern Colorado, northern Mexico, the Bahama Islands, Cuba, Jamaica, the Cayman Islands, and islands in the western Caribbean Sea (Swan, Providencia, and San Andrés).

Casual or accidental north to Oregon, Montana, southwestern Saskatchewan, central Manitoba, Minnesota, Wisconsin, northern Michigan, southern Ontario, southwestern Quebec, New Brunswick, Nova Scotia, and Newfoundland, to Bermuda (most often in the fall), the Lesser Antilles (Mustique in the Grenadines, and Barbados), Clipperton Island, and to the Galapagos Islands, Curaçao, Chile, and Great Britain; sight reports from Idaho and the Revillagigedo Islands (Socorro Island).

Piranga olivacea (Gmelin). Scarlet Tanager.

> *Tanagra olivacea* Gmelin, 1789, Syst. Nat. 1(2): 889. Based primarily on the "Olive Tanager" Latham, Gen. Synop. Birds 2(1): 218. (in Cayenna et Noveboraco = New York.)

Habitat.—Deciduous forest and mature deciduous woodland, especially where oaks common, less frequently in mixed deciduous-coniferous forest; in migration and winter, a variety of wooded habitats with tall trees.

Distribution.—*Breeds* from central North Dakota, eastern Saskatchewan (probably), southern Manitoba, central Ontario, southwestern Quebec, central Maine, southern New Brunswick, and Nova Scotia south to central Nebraska, eastern Kansas, north-central and southeastern Oklahoma, northwestern and north-central Arkansas, west-central Tennessee, northern Alabama, northern Georgia, northwestern South Carolina, western North Carolina, Virginia, and Maryland.

Winters from Panama (rarely, in the lowlands) and Colombia south, east of the Andes, through eastern Ecuador and Peru to northern Bolivia.

Migrates primarily through the eastern United States (west to central Texas, rarely to eastern Colorado and eastern New Mexico), Middle America (primarily the Gulf-Caribbean slope north of Costa Rica, and in Veracruz, Chiapas, and the Yucatan Peninsula), and the West Indies, casually west to the eastern slopes of the Rockies, in Bermuda (most numerous in the fall), and to the Netherlands Antilles and Isla Los Roques (off Venezuela).

Casual in western North America from southern British Columbia, southern Alberta, and Montana south to California, Baja California, Arizona, and New Mexico, and in northeastern North America north to Prince Edward Island and Newfoundland. Accidental in Alaska (Point Barrow) and Clipperton Island, and in Iceland and the British Isles.

Notes.— Mayr and Short (1970) considered *P. olivacea* and *P. ludoviciana* to constitute a superspecies.

Piranga ludoviciana (Wilson). Western Tanager.

Tanagra ludoviciana Wilson, 1811, Amer. Ornithol. 3: 27, pl. 20, fig. 1. (prairies of the Missouri, between the Osage and Mandan nations = about two miles north of Kamiah, Idaho County, Idaho.)

Habitat.—Open coniferous, mixed coniferous-deciduous woodland, and aspen forest, primarily in mountains; in migration and winter, a variety of wooded habitats, in Middle America mostly in highland pine, pine-oak association, and humid forest edge.

Distribution.—*Breeds* from southeastern Alaska (probably), northern British Columbia, southern Mackenzie, northern Alberta, and central Saskatchewan south to northern Baja California, central and southeastern Arizona, southern New Mexico, and western Texas; also in western South Dakota and northwestern Nebraska; one isolated breeding record from southern Wisconsin (Jefferson County, 1877) is questionable.

Winters from coastal southern California, Baja California, Jalisco, and southern Tamaulipas (casually north to south-coastal British Columbia, southern Oregon, southern Arizona, and southern Texas) south through Middle America (mostly highlands) to Costa Rica, casually in the Gulf Coast region from southeastern Texas and Arkansas east to southern Florida.

Migrates regularly east to western Nebraska, western Kansas, western Oklahoma, and central Texas.

Casual north to central Alaska, southern Yukon, and the Queen Charlotte Islands, and across northeastern North America from Iowa and southern Manitoba and Minnesota east through Wisconsin, Illinois, Michigan, southern Ontario, and southern Quebec to New Brunswick, Nova Scotia, and Newfoundland, and south to New York, Pennsylvania, Maryland, Virginia, and South Carolina; sight reports elsewhere in eastern North America. Accidental in northern Alaska (Point Barrow), the Bahama Islands (New Providence), Cuba (Cárdenas), and Panama (western Chiriquí).

Notes.—See comments under *P. olivacea.*

Piranga bidentata Swainson. Flame-colored Tanager.

Pyranga bidentata Swainson, 1827, Philos. Mag. (n.s.) 1: 438. (Temiscaltipec, Mexico = Temascaltepec, México.)

Habitat.—Montane Evergreen Forest, Pine-Oak Forest, Secondary Forest (800–2500 m; Subtropical and Temperate zones).

Distribution.—*Resident* from southern Chihuahua, central Nuevo León, and southern Tamaulipas south through the interior of Mexico (also the Tres Marias Islands off Nayarit), Guatemala, El Salvador, and Honduras to north-central Nicaragua; in the mountains of Costa Rica (primarily the Cordillera Central) and western Panama (western and central Chiriquí).

Breeds rarely in southeastern Arizona (Chiricahua, Santa Rita, and Huachuca mountains). Casual elsewhere in southern Arizona (Patagonia).

Notes.—Also known as Streak-backed Tanager.

Piranga leucoptera Trudeau. White-winged Tanager.

Pyranga leucoptera Trudeau, 1839, J. Acad. Nat. Sci. Philadelphia 8: 160. (Mexico.)

Habitat.—Montane Evergreen Forest, Pine-Oak Forest, Montane Evergreen Forest Edge, Secondary Forest (800–2200 m; upper Tropical and Subtropical zones).

Distribution.—*Resident* from southeastern San Luis Potosí and southern Tamaulipas south (west to Hidalgo, México, Guerrero, and northern Oaxaca) through Middle America (mostly in the highlands, not recorded Yucatan Peninsula) to western Panama (Chiriquí, Veraguas, Herrera); and in South America in the Andes from Colombia and Venezuela south on the western slope to southwestern Ecuador and on the eastern slope to central Bolivia; also in the Tepui region of Venezuela and extreme northwestern Brazil.

Piranga erythrocephala (Swainson). Red-headed Tanager.

> *Spermagra erythrocephala* Swainson, 1827, Philos. Mag. (n.s.) 1: 437. (Temiscaltipec, Mexico = Temascaltepec, México.)

Habitat.—Pine-Oak Forest, Montane Evergreen Forest, Tropical Deciduous Forest (900–2600 m; Subtropical and lower Temperate zones).

Distribution.—*Resident* from southeastern Sonora and Chihuahua south through Sinaloa, Durango, Nayarit, Jalisco, Michoacán, México (Temascaltepec), Morelos, and Guerrero to Oaxaca (west of the Isthmus of Tehuantepec).

Genus *RAMPHOCELUS* Desmarest

> *Ramphocelus* Desmarest, 1805, Hist. Nat. Tangaras, Manakins, Todiers, livr. 1, pl. 28 (and text), p. [1]. Type, by subsequent designation (G. R. Gray, 1855), *Tanagra brasilia* [sic] Linnaeus.
>
> *Phlogothraupis* Sclater and Salvin, 1873, Nomencl. Avium Neotrop., pp. 21, 155. Type, by original designation, *Tanagra (Tachyphonus) sanguinolentus* Lesson.

Ramphocelus sanguinolentus (Lesson). Crimson-collared Tanager.

> *Tanagra (Tachyphonus) sanguinolentus* Lesson, 1831, Cent. Zool., p. 107, pl. 39. (Mexico.)

Habitat.—Tropical Lowland Evergreen Forest Edge, Secondary Forest (0–1200 m; Tropical and lower Subtropical zones).

Distribution.—*Resident* from southern Veracruz, Tabasco, northern Oaxaca, Chiapas, and southern Quintana Roo south on the Gulf-Caribbean slope of Central America to western Panama (Bocas del Toro, Veraguas, and western Panamá province, locally also on Pacific slope of Panama in Veraguas).

Notes.—Often placed in the monotypic genus *Phlogothraupis*; see Stiles and Skutch (1989) for reasons for not including this species in *Ramphocelus*.

Ramphocelus dimidiatus Lafresnaye. Crimson-backed Tanager.

> *Ramphocelus dimidiatus* Lafresnaye, 1837, Mag. Zool. [Paris] 7(2): 2, pl. 81. (du sud du Mexique et de Carthagène, Nouvelle-Grenade = Cartagena, Colombia.)

Habitat.—Secondary Forest, Tropical Lowland Evergreen Forest Edge, Second-growth Scrub (0–1700 m; Tropical and lower Subtropical zones).

Distribution.—*Resident* in Panama (both slopes west to Chiriquí and Veraguas, including Coiba and the Pearl islands), northern and western Colombia, and western Venezuela.

Notes.—*Ramphocelus dimidiatus* and the South American *R. melanogaster* (Swainson, 1838) [Huallaga Tanager], *R. carbo* (Pallas, 1764) [Silver-beaked Tanager], and *R. bresilius* (Linnaeus, 1766) [Brazilian Tanager] appear to constitute a superspecies (Storer *in* Paynter 1970).

Ramphocelus passerinii Bonaparte. Passerini's Tanager.

> *Ramphocelus Passerinii* Bonaparte, 1831, Antologia [Florence] 44 (130): 164. (in Insula Cuba, error = Guatemala.)

Habitat.—Tropical Lowland Evergreen Forest Edge, Secondary Forest, Second-growth Scrub (0–1700 m; Tropical and lower Subtropical zones).

Distribution.—*Resident* from northeastern Oaxaca, extreme southeastern Veracruz, Tabasco, and Chiapas south on the Gulf-Caribbean slope of Central America from Belize to western Panama (Bocas del Toro), and on Pacific slope in Costa Rica (central Guanacaste, northern Puntarenas).

Notes.—Recognition of *R. passerinii* and *R. costaricensis* as separate species follows Hackett (1996). *Ramphocelus passerinii* (including *R. costaricensis*) and *R. flammigerus* constitute a superspecies (Storer *in* Paynter 1970).

Ramphocelus costaricensis Cherrie. Cherrie's Tanager.

Ramphocelus costaricensis Cherrie, 1891, Auk 8: 62. (Pozo Azul [de Pirrís], Costa Rica.)

Habitat.—Tropical Lowland Evergreen Forest Edge, Secondary Forest, Second-growth Scrub (0–1350 m; Tropical and lower Subtropical zones).

Distribution.—*Resident* on Pacific slope of Costa Rica (central Puntarenas, south) and western Panama (Chiriquí and [formerly?] western Veraguas).

Notes.—See comments under *R. passerinii.*

Ramphocelus flammigerus (Jardine and Selby). Flame-rumped Tanager.

Ramphopis flammigerus Jardine and Selby, 1833, Illus. Ornithol. 3: pl. 131. (Columbia River, error = Antioquia, Colombia.)

Habitat.—Tropical Lowland Evergreen Forest Edge, Secondary Forest, Second-growth Scrub (0–800 m; Tropical Zone).

Distribution.—*Resident* [*icteronotus* group] in Panama (west to Bocas del Toro and Veraguas, more commonly on the Caribbean slope), western Colombia and western Ecuador; and [*flammigerus* group] in western Colombia (east of the preceding, from the middle Cauca Valley south to Nariño).

Notes.—The two morphologically distinct groups are sometimes regarded as separate species, *R. icteronotus* Bonaparte, 1838 [Yellow-rumped Tanager], and *R. flammigerus* [Flame-rumped Tanager], but they intergrade in the Río San Juan region of western Colombia (Sibley 1958). See comments under *R. passerinii.*

Genus *SPINDALIS* Jardine and Selby

Spindalis Jardine and Selby, 1837, Illus. Ornithol. (n.s.), pt. 2, pl. 9. Type, by monotypy, *Spindalis bilineatus* Jardine and Selby = *Tanagra nigricephala* Jameson = *Fringilla zena* Linnaeus.

Spindalis zena (Linnaeus). Stripe-headed Tanager.

Fringilla Zena Linnaeus, 1758, Syst. Nat. (ed. 10) 1: 181. Based on "The Bahama Finch" Catesby, Nat. Hist. Carolina 1: 42, pl. 42. (Bahama Islands = New Providence.)

Habitat.—Montane Evergreen Forest, Tropical Lowland Evergreen Forest, Secondary Forest, Second-growth Scrub (0–2000 m).

Distribution.—*Resident* [*zena* group] in Bahama Islands, Cuba, the Isle of Pines, Grand Cayman, and Cozumel Island off the Yucatan Peninsula; [*dominicensis* group] Hispaniola (including Gonâve Island) and Puerto Rico; and [*nigricephala* group] in Jamaica.

Ranges [*zena* group] rarely to southern Florida (north to the Palm Beach area).

Notes.—Groups: *S. zena* [Stripe-headed Tanager], *S. dominicensis* (Bryant, 1866) [Hispaniolan Tanager] and *S. nigricephala* (Jameson, 1835) [Jamaican Tanager].

Genus *THRAUPIS* Boie

Thraupis Boie, 1826, Isis von Oken, col. 974. Type, by virtual monotypy, *Tanagra archiepiscopus* Desmarest = *Tanagra ornata* Sparrman.

Thraupis episcopus (Linnaeus). Blue-gray Tanager.

Tanagra Episcopus Linnaeus, 1766, Syst. Nat. (ed. 12) 1: 316. Based on "L'Evesque" Brisson, Ornithologie 3: 40, pl. 1, fig. 2. (in Brasilia, error = probably Cayenne.)

Habitat.—Tropical Lowland Evergreen Forest Edge, Secondary Forest, River-edge Forest, Second-growth Scrub (0–2600 m; Tropical and Subtropical zones).

Distribution.—*Resident* from southeastern San Luis Potosí, Veracruz, Puebla, northern Oaxaca, Tabasco, northern and southeastern Chiapas, southern Campeche, and southern

Quintana Roo south along both slopes of Central America to Panama (including Escudo de Veraguas, Coiba, and the Pearl Islands), and in South America from Colombia, Venezuela, Tobago, Trinidad and the Guianas south, west of the Andes to northwestern Peru and east of the Andes to northern Bolivia and Amazonian Brazil.

Introduced or escaped about 1960 in southern Florida (southern Broward and Dade counties) but disappeared in mid 1970s (Robertson and Woolfenden 1992).

Notes.—Formerly called *T. virens* (Linnaeus, 1766); *T. episcopus* has been ruled to have priority by the I.C.Z.N. (1968). *Thraupis episcopus* and the South American *T. sayaca* (Linnaeus, 1766) [Sayaca Tanager] and *T. glaucocolpa* (Cabanis, 1850) [Glaucous Tanager] constitute a superspecies (Sibley and Monroe 1990).

Thraupis abbas (Deppe). Yellow-winged Tanager.

> *Tanagra Abbas* "Lichtens[tein]." W. Deppe, 1830, Preis.-Verz. Säugeth. Vögel, etc., Mex., p. 2. (Mexico = Jalapa, Veracruz; Binford, 1989, Ornithol. Monogr. 43, p. 345.)

Habitat.—Tropical Lowland Evergreen Forest Edge, Secondary Forest, Gallery Forest (0–1600 m; Tropical and Subtropical zones).

Distribution.—*Resident* from southeastern San Luis Potosí, southwestern Tamaulipas, Veracruz, México, Puebla, northern Oaxaca, and northern and southeastern Chiapas south along both slopes of Middle America (including the Yucatan Peninsula) to Honduras and eastern Nicaragua (Zelaya).

Notes.—Also known as Abbot's Tanager.

Thraupis palmarum (Wied). Palm Tanager.

> *Tanagra palmarum* Wied, 1821, Reise Bras. 2: 76. (Canavieras, Bahia, Brazil.)

Habitat.—Tropical Lowland Evergreen Forest Edge, Secondary Forest, Gallery Forest, Montane Evergreen Forest, River-edge Forest (0–1200 m; Tropical and occasionally lower Subtropical zones).

Distribution.—*Resident* in eastern Nicaragua, on both slopes of Costa Rica (rare in the dry northwest) and Panama (except for dry Pacific slope from Veraguas to western Panamá province, but including Isla Coiba), and in South America from Colombia, Venezuela, Trinidad and the Guianas south, west of the Andes to western Ecuador and east of the Andes to southern Bolivia, eastern Paraguay, and southern Brazil.

Genus *BANGSIA* Penard

> *Bangsia* Penard, 1919, Auk 36: 539. Type, by original designation, *Buthraupis arcaei caeruleigularis* Cherrie [= Ridgway] = *Buthraupis arcaei* Sclater and Salvin.

Notes—*Bangsia* is sometimes (e.g., Storer *in* Paynter 1970, Isler and Isler 1987) merged in the genus *Buthraupis* Cabanis.

Bangsia arcaei (Sclater and Salvin). Blue-and-gold Tanager.

> *Buthraupis arcæi* Sclater and Salvin, 1869, Proc. Zool. Soc. London, p. 439, pl. 31. (Cordillera del Chucú, Veraguas, Panama.)

Habitat.—Tropical Lowland Evergreen Forest, Montane Evergreen Forest, Tropical Lowland Evergreen Forest Edge (300–1200 m; Tropical and lower Subtropical zones).

Distribution.—*Resident* in Costa Rica (the Caribbean slope north to the Cordillera de Tilarán) and western Panama (in Chiriquí, on both slopes in Veraguas, and in the Cerro Jefe area of eastern Panamá province).

Genus *EUPHONIA* Desmarest

> *Euphonia* Desmarest, 1806, Hist. Nat. Tangaras, Manakins, Todiers, livr. 10, table [pl. 27]. Type, by monotypy, *Euphonia olivacea* Desmarest = *Euphonia minuta* Cabanis.

Pyrrhuphonia Bonaparte, 1850, C. R. Acad. Sci. Paris 31: 423. Type, by subsequent designation (G. R. Gray, 1855), *Fringilla jamaica* Linnaeus.

Notes.—The generic name *Tanagra* Linnaeus, 1764, has been suppressed for the purposes of the Law of Priority (but not the Law of Homonymy) by the I.C.Z.N. (1968).

Euphonia jamaica (Linnaeus). Jamaican Euphonia.

Fringilla jamaica Linnaeus, 1766, Syst. Nat. (ed. 12) 1: 323. Based mainly on *Passer Coeruleo fuscus* Sloane, Voy. Jamaica 2: 311, pl. 257, fig. 3. (in Jamaica.)

Habitat.—Tropical Lowland Evergreen Forest, Secondary Forest, Tropical Lowland Evergreen Forest Edge (0–1000 m).
Distribution.—*Resident* on Jamaica.
Notes.—Often placed in the monotypic genus *Pyrrhuphonia,* but see Storer *in* Paynter (1970).

Euphonia affinis (Lesson). Scrub Euphonia.

Tanagra (Euphonia) affinis Lesson, 1842, Rev. Zool. [Paris] 5: 175. (Realejo [Nicaragua].)

Habitat.—Tropical Deciduous Forest, Gallery Forest, Secondary Forest, Tropical Lowland Evergreen Forest Edge (0–1000 m; Tropical Zone).
Distribution.—*Resident* [*godmani* group] in the Pacific lowlands from southeastern Sonora south to central Guerrero; and [*affinis* group] from eastern San Luis Potosí, southern Tamaulipas, Veracruz, Puebla, and northern and southwestern Oaxaca (north to near Santiago Pinotepa Nacional) and the Yucatan Peninsula south along both slopes of Middle America to Honduras, and in the Pacific lowlands of Nicaragua to northwestern Costa Rica (Guanacaste).
Notes.—Also known as Lesson's Euphonia or Black-throated Euphonia. Groups: *Euphonia godmani* Brewster, 1889 [Pale-vented Euphonia] and *E. affinis* [Scrub Euphonia].

Euphonia luteicapilla (Cabanis). Yellow-crowned Euphonia.

Phonasca luteicapilla Cabanis, 1860, J. Ornithol. 8 (1860): 332. (Costa Rica.)

Habitat.—Tropical Lowland Evergreen Forest Edge, Tropical Deciduous Forest, Secondary Forest (0–900 m; Tropical and lower Subtropical zones).
Distribution.—*Resident* in eastern Nicaragua, Costa Rica (both slopes, except the dry northwest), and Panama (east to the Canal area and eastern Darién).

Euphonia laniirostris d'Orbigny and Lafresnaye. Thick-billed Euphonia.

Euphonia laniirostris d'Orbigny and Lafresnaye, 1837, Mag. Zool. [Paris] 7(2): 30, pl. 77–79. (Yuracares, Bolivia.)

Habitat.—River-edge Forest, Gallery Forest, Secondary Forest, Tropical Deciduous Forest, Tropical Lowland Evergreen Forest Edge (0–1800 m; Tropical and Subtropical zones).
Distribution.—*Resident* [*melanura* group] in Costa Rica (primarily the humid southwest), Panama (both slopes), and South America from northern and eastern Colombia and northern Venezuela south, east of the Andes, to eastern Peru and western Amazonian Brazil; and [*laniirostris* group] west of the Andes from western Colombia to northwestern Peru, and east of the Andes in central Peru (west of *melanura*), northern Bolivia, and adjacent Amazonian Brazil.
Notes.—Groups: *E. melanura* Sclater, 1851 [Black-tailed Euphonia] and *E. laniirostris* [Thick-billed Euphonia].

Euphonia hirundinacea Bonaparte. Yellow-throated Euphonia.

Euphonia hirundinacea Bonaparte, 1838, Proc. Zool. Soc. London (1837), p. 117. (Guatamala = Pacific slope, San Jose to Ixtepec, Guatemala.)

Habitat.—Tropical Lowland Evergreen Forest Edge, Gallery Forest, Secondary Forest, Tropical Deciduous Forest (0–1200 m; Tropical and lower Subtropical zones).

Distribution.—*Resident* from southeastern San Luis Potosí, southern Tamaulipas, Veracruz, Puebla, and northern and (possibly) southeastern Oaxaca south along both slopes of Middle America (including the Yucatan Peninsula) to Costa Rica (most commonly in the dry northwest); reports from western Panama are questionable (Wetmore et al. 1984).

Notes.—Also known as Bonaparte's Euphonia. With the use of *Euphonia* instead of the suppressed *Tanagra*, *E. hirundinacea* Bonaparte, 1838, is no longer preoccupied by *Tanagra hirundinacea* Lesson, 1831; thus the frequently used *T. lauta* Bangs and Penard, 1919 becomes a synonym of *E. hirundinacea.*

Euphonia musica (Gmelin). Antillean Euphonia.

Pipra musica Gmelin, 1789, Syst. Nat. 1(2): 1004. Based on "L'Organiste" Daubenton, Planches Enlum., pl. 809, fig. 1. (in insula S. Dominici = Hispaniola.)

Habitat.—Tropical Lowland Evergreen Forest, Tropical Deciduous Forest, Secondary Forest, Tropical Lowland Evergreen Forest Edge (0–2000 m).

Distribution.—*Resident* on Hispaniola (including Gonâve Island) and Puerto Rico, and in the Lesser Antilles (Saba, Barbuda, Antigua, Montserrat, Guadeloupe, Dominica, Martinique, St. Lucia, St. Vincent, and Grenada); there are no recent records for Barbuda, Montserrat, St. Vincent or Grenada.

Casual elsewhere in the Lesser Antilles (St. Barthélemy, St. Kitts, Terre-de-haut, Bequia).

Notes.—*Euphonia musica, E. elegantissima,* and the South American *E. cyanocephala* (Vieillot, 1818) [Golden-rumped Euphonia] constitute a superspecies (Sibley and Monroe 1990) and are sometimes considered to be conspecific, with the English name Blue-hooded Euphonia.

Euphonia elegantissima (Bonaparte). Elegant Euphonia.

Pipra elegantissima Bonaparte, 1838, Proc. Zool. Soc. London (1837), p. 112. (Mexico.)

Habitat.—Pine-Oak Forest, Montane Evergreen Forest, Secondary Forest, Montane Evergreen Forest Edge (1000–2500 m; upper Tropical and Subtropical zones).

Distribution.—*Resident* from southeastern Sonora, southwestern Chihuahua, Sinaloa, western Durango, Nayarit, Jalisco, Guanajuato, San Luis Potosí, central Nuevo León, and southern Tamaulipas south through the highlands of Middle America to western Panama (Chiriquí, Veraguas, Coclé).

Notes.—See comments under *E. musica*. Called Blue-hooded Euphonia by A. O. U. (1983).

Euphonia fulvicrissa Sclater. Fulvous-vented Euphonia.

Euphonia fulvicrissa Sclater, 1857, Proc. Zool. Soc. London (1856), p. 276. ("S[anta]. Martha in New Grenada" = locality uncertain.)

Habitat.—Tropical Lowland Evergreen Forest, Secondary Forest, Tropical Lowland Evergreen Forest Edge (0–1000 m; Tropical Zone).

Distribution.—*Resident* in central and eastern Panama (west to northern Coclé and western Panamá province), and in South America in western Colombia (east to the northern Eastern Andes and the middle Magdalena Valley) and along the Pacific slope south to northwestern Ecuador.

Euphonia imitans (Hellmayr). Spot-crowned Euphonia.

Tanagra imitans Hellmayr, 1936, Field Mus. Nat. Hist. Publ. (Zool. Ser.) 13(9): 63. (El Pózo, Río Térraba, Costa Rica.)

Habitat.—Tropical Lowland Evergreen Forest, Secondary Forest, Tropical Lowland Evergreen Forest Edge (0–1350 m; Tropical and lower Subtropical zones).

Distribution.—*Resident* in southwestern Costa Rica (Pacific slope west to the Gulf of Nicoya) and extreme western Panama (western Chiriquí).

Accidental in central Costa Rica (San José, possibly an escaped cage bird; a record from Miravalles is erroneous).

Notes.—Also known as Tawny-bellied Euphonia.

Euphonia gouldi Sclater. Olive-backed Euphonia.

Euphonia Gouldi Sclater, 1857, Proc. Zool. Soc. London, p. 66, pl. 24. (In Guatimala et Mexico Meridionali = Guatemala.)

Habitat.—Tropical Lowland Evergreen Forest, Tropical Lowland Evergreen Forest Edge (0–900 m; Tropical Zone).

Distribution.—*Resident* from Veracruz, northern Oaxaca, Tabasco, Chiapas, and southern Quintana Roo south in the Gulf-Caribbean lowlands of Central America to Costa Rica (also known from the Pacific slope of the Cordillera de Guanacaste) and central Panama (Bocas del Toro, western Veraguas, and Canal area).

Notes.—Also known as Gould's Euphonia.

Euphonia minuta Cabanis. White-vented Euphonia.

Euphonia minuta Cabanis, 1849, in Schomburgk, Reisen Br.-Guiana 3 (1848): 671. (British Guiana.)

Habitat.—Tropical Lowland Evergreen Forest, River-edge Forest, Secondary Forest, Tropical Lowland Evergreen Forest Edge (0–1000 m; Tropical and lower Subtropical zones).

Distribution.—*Resident* locally on the Caribbean slope of Guatemala, southern Belize, and Nicaragua, and widely on both slopes of Costa Rica (except the dry northwest) and Panama (more widespread on the Caribbean slope), and in South America south along the Pacific slope to northwestern Ecuador, and east of the Andes from southern Colombia, Venezuela south of the Orinoco, and the Guianas south to central Bolivia and Amazonian Brazil (south to southern Amazonas and Pará, rarely to northern Mato Grosso). A report from Chiapas (Palenque) is questionable.

Notes.—The name *E. olivacea* Desmarest, 1806, has been suppressed for the purposes of the Law of Priority (but not the Law of Homonymy) by the I.C.Z.N. (1968).

Euphonia anneae Cassin. Tawny-capped Euphonia.

Euphonia Anneæ Cassin, 1865, Proc. Acad. Nat. Sci. Philadelphia 17: 172. (Santa Rosa, Costa Rica.)

Habitat.—Tropical Lowland Evergreen Forest, Montane Evergreen Forest, Secondary Forest (600–1500 m, locally to 350 m; upper Tropical and Subtropical zones).

Distribution.—*Resident* in Costa Rica (Caribbean slope north to the Cordillera de Guanacaste), Panama (locally on both slopes), and extreme northwestern Colombia (Gulf of Urubá region).

Euphonia xanthogaster (Sundevall). Orange-bellied Euphonia.

Euphone xanthogaster Sundevall, 1834, Vetensk.-Akad. Handl. (1833), p. 310, pl. 10, fig. 1. (Brazil = Rio de Janeiro.)

Habitat.—Montane Evergreen Forest, Tropical Lowland Evergreen Forest, Secondary Forest (0–2300 m; Tropical and Subtropical zones).

Distribution.—*Resident* in eastern Panama (Darién), and South America from Colombia, Venezuela, and Guyana south, west of the Andes to western Ecuador, and east of the Andes to northern Bolivia (in Andean foothills) and western Amazonian Brazil; also in eastern Brazil from Bahia south to Rio de Janeiro.

Genus *CHLOROPHONIA* Bonaparte

Chlorophonia Bonaparte, 1851, Rev. Mag. Zool. (2)3: 137. Type, by subsequent designation (G. R. Gray, 1855), *Tanagra viridis* Vieillot = *Pipra cyanea* Vieillot.

Chlorophonia flavirostris Sclater. Yellow-collared Chlorophonia.

Chlorophonia flavirostris P. L. Sclater, 1861, Proc. Zool. Soc. London, p. 129. (Ecuador.)

Habitat.—Montane Evergreen Forest, Montane Evergreen Forest Edge (600–1700 m; upper Tropical and Subtropical zones).

Distribution.—*Resident* on the western slope of the Andes of southwestern Colombia and northwestern Ecuador.

Accidental on Cerro Pirre, eastern Darién, Panama (photograph [Capparella 1986]).

Chlorophonia occipitalis (Du Bus de Gisignies). Blue-crowned Chlorophonia.

Euphonia occipitalis Du Bus de Gisignies, 1847, Esquisses Ornithol., livr. 3, pl. 14. (Le Mexique = Mexico.)

Habitat.—Montane Evergreen Forest, to Tropical Lowland Evergreen Forest and Secondary Forest in nonbreeding season (1000–2500 m; Subtropical Zone, to Tropical Zone in nonbreeding season).

Distribution.—*Resident* from central Veracruz and northern and southeastern Oaxaca south through Chiapas, Guatemala, El Salvador, and Honduras to north-central Nicaragua.

Notes.—*Chlorophonia occipitalis* and *C. callophrys* constitute a superspecies (Sibley and Monroe 1990) and have been treated as conspecific (e.g., Storer *in* Paynter 1970).

Chlorophonia callophrys (Cabanis). Golden-browed Chlorophonia.

Triglyphidia callophrys Cabanis, 1861, J. Ornithol. 8 (1860): 331. (Costa Rica.)

Habitat.—Montane Evergreen Forest, Montane Evergreen Forest Edge (750–2500 m; upper Tropical and Subtropical zones).

Distribution.—*Resident* in the highlands of Costa Rica (north to the Cordillera de Guanacaste) and western Panama (Chiriquí and Veraguas), descending to lower elevations in nonbreeding season.

Notes.—See comments under *C. occipitalis.*

Genus *TANGARA* Brisson

Tangara Brisson, 1760, Ornithologie 3: 3. Type, by tautonymy, *Tangara* Brisson = *Aglaia paradisea* Swainson = *Aglaia chilensis* Vigors.

Tangara inornata (Gould). Plain-colored Tanager.

Calliste inornata Gould, 1855, Proc. Zool. Soc. London, p. 158. (Santa Fé de Bogota [Colombia].)

Habitat.—Tropical Lowland Evergreen Forest, Secondary Forest, Tropical Lowland Evergreen Forest Edge (0–1000 m; Tropical Zone).

Distribution.—*Resident* in Costa Rica (Caribbean slope only, north to Sarapiquí region), Panama (entire Caribbean slope, and Pacific slope west to Cerro Campana in western Panamá province) and northern Colombia.

Tangara cabanisi (Sclater). Azure-rumped Tanager.

Calliste s. *Callispiza Sclateri* (not *Calliste sclateri* Lafresnaye, 1854) Cabanis, 1866, J. Ornithol. 14: 163. (Costa Cuca, western Guatemala.)
Calliste cabanisi Sclater, 1868, Ibis, p. 71, pl. 3. New name for *Calliste sclateri* Cabanis, preoccupied.

Habitat.—Montane Evergreen Forest (1100–1700 m; Subtropical Zone).

Distribution.—*Resident* in the highlands (Sierra Madre de Chiapas, primarily Pacific slope) of Chiapas and western Guatemala (Volcán Santa María).

Notes.—Also known as Cabanis's Tanager.

Tangara palmeri (Hellmayr). Gray-and-gold Tanager.

Calospiza palmeri Hellmayr, 1909, Rev. Fr. Ornithol. 1: 49. (Sipi, Rio Sipi, Choco, Colombia.)

Habitat.—Tropical Lowland Evergreen Forest, Montane Evergreen Forest, Tropical Lowland Evergreen Forest Edge (0–1100 m; Tropical and lower Subtropical zones).

Distribution.—*Resident* in eastern Panama (cerros Sapo, Quía, and Tacarcuna, in eastern Darién), and on the Pacific slope of western Colombia and northwestern Ecuador.

Tangara florida (Sclater and Salvin). Emerald Tanager.

Calliste florida Sclater and Salvin, 1869, Proc. Zool. Soc. London, p. 416, pl. 28. (Costa Rica.)

Habitat.—Tropical Lowland Evergreen Forest, Montane Evergreen Forest, Secondary Forest (0–1200 m; upper Tropical and lower Subtropical zones).

Distribution.—*Resident* in the highlands of Costa Rica (primarily in the Cordillera Central), Panama (entire Caribbean slope, and Pacific slope from eastern Panamá province eastward), western Colombia, and northwestern Ecuador.

Tangara icterocephala (Bonaparte). Silver-throated Tanager.

Calliste icterocephala Bonaparte, 1851, C. R. Acad. Sci. Paris 32: 76. (Ecuador = valley of Punta Playa, south of Quito.)

Habitat.—Montane Evergreen Forest, Tropical Lowland Evergreen Forest, Secondary Forest, Tropical Lowland Evergreen Forest Edge (600–1600 m; upper Tropical and Subtropical zones).

Distribution.—*Resident* in the highlands of Costa Rica (north to Cordillera de Guanacaste, more frequently found on Caribbean slope), Panama (both slopes); in South America in the Western Andes of Colombia and Ecuador and the northern Central Andes of Colombia.

Tangara guttata (Cabanis). Speckled Tanager.

Callispiza guttata Cabanis, 1850, Mus. Heineanum 1 (1851): 26. (Roraima, Guiana = Cerro Roraima, Bolívar, Venezuela.)

Habitat.—Montane Evergreen Forest, Tropical Lowland Evergreen Forest, Secondary Forest, Tropical Lowland Evergreen Forest Edge (300–2000 m; upper Tropical and Subtropical zones).

Distribution.—*Resident* in Costa Rica (north to Cordillera de Tilarán), Panama (entire Caribbean slope, and Pacific slope in western Chiriquí, Veraguas, eastern Panamá province, and eastern Darién), Colombia, Venezuela, Trinidad, Surinam, and extreme northern Brazil.

Notes.—*Tangara guttata* clearly has priority over *T. chrysophrys* (Sclater, 1851); see Storer *in* Paynter 1970: 370, footnote). See comments under *Chlorothraupis olivacea*.

Tangara gyrola (Linnaeus). Bay-headed Tanager.

Fringilla Gyrola Linnaeus, 1758, Syst. Nat. (ed. 10) 1: 181. Based on "The Red-headed Green-Finch" Edwards, Nat. Hist. Birds 1: 23, pl. 23. (in America = Surinam.)

Habitat.—Montane Evergreen Forest, Tropical Lowland Evergreen Forest, Secondary Forest, Tropical Lowland Evergreen Forest Edge (0–1800 m; Tropical and Subtropical zones).

Distribution.—*Resident* [*gyroloides* group] in Costa Rica (north to the Cordillera Central) and Panama (both slopes), and in South America from Colombia south, west of the Andes to southwestern Ecuador and east of the Andes to central Bolivia, and western Amazonian Brazil; [*viridissima* group] in northeastern Colombia, northern Venezuela, and Trinidad; and [*gyrola* group] in southeastern Venezuela, the Guianas, and extreme northern Brazil.

Notes.—Distinct morphological characters suggest that the three groups might be recognized as species, *T. gyroloides* (Lafresnaye, 1847) [= *T. albertinae* (Pelzeln, 1877)] [Bay-

and-blue Tanager], *T. viridissima* (Lafresnaye, 1847) [Bay-and-green Tanager], and *T. gyrola* [Bay-headed Tanager] (Sibley and Monroe 1990).

Tangara lavinia (Cassin). Rufous-winged Tanager.

> *Calliste Lavinia* Cassin, 1858, Proc. Acad. Nat. Sci. Philadelphia 10: 178. (Isthmus of Darien, New Grenada [= Panama].)

Habitat.—Tropical Lowland Evergreen Forest, Secondary Forest (0–1000 m; Tropical and lower Subtropical zones).

Distribution.—*Resident* from Honduras (east of the Sula Valley) south on the Caribbean slope (mostly) of Central America to Costa Rica, on both slopes of Panama, and in western Colombia (including Gorgona Island) and northwestern Ecuador; erroneously reported from Guatemala.

Tangara cucullata (Swainson). Lesser Antillean Tanager.

> *Aglaia Cucullata* Swainson, 1834, Ornithol. Drawings, pt. 1, pl. 7. (No locality given = Grenada, Lesser Antilles.)

Habitat.—Tropical Lowland Evergreen Forest, Secondary Forest, Tropical Lowland Evergreen Forest Edge (0–850 m).

Distribution.—*Resident* on St. Vincent and Grenada, in the Lesser Antilles.

Notes.—Also known as Hooded Tanager, a name now generally applied to the South American *Nemosia pileata* (Boddaert, 1783).

Tangara larvata (Du Bus de Gisignies). Golden-hooded Tanager.

> *Calliste larvata* Du Bus de Gisignies, 1846, Esquisses Ornithol., livr. 2, pl. 9. (Tabasco, Mexico.)

Habitat.—Tropical Lowland Evergreen Forest Edge, Secondary Forest (0–1200 m; Tropical and lower Subtropical zones).

Distribution.—*Resident* from southern Veracruz, northern Oaxaca, Tabasco, and Chiapas south on the Gulf-Caribbean slope of Central America to Nicaragua, on both slopes of Costa Rica (absent from the dry northwest) and Panama (entire Caribbean slope, and Pacific slope in western Chiriquí, western Veraguas, eastern Panamá province, and Darién), and in western Colombia and northwestern Ecuador.

Notes.—Also known as Golden-masked Tanager. *Tangara larvata* and the South American *T. nigrocincta* (Bonaparte, 1838) [Masked Tanager] have been treated as a single species by some authors (e.g., Meyer de Schauensee 1966, 1970). Eisenmann (1957) provided rationale for treating them as separate species; they constitute a superspecies (Storer 1969).

Tangara dowii (Salvin). Spangle-cheeked Tanager.

> *Calliste dowii* Salvin, 1863, Proc. Zool. Soc. London, p. 168. (San José [= Rancho Redondo de San José], Costa Rica.)

Habitat.—Montane Evergreen Forest, Montane Evergreen Forest Edge (1100–3200 m; Subtropical and lower Temperate zones).

Distribution.—*Resident* in the mountains of Costa Rica (north to the Cordillera de Tilarán) and western Panama (east to Veraguas).

Notes.—Some authors (e.g., Storer *in* Paynter 1970, Isler and Isler 1987) consider *T. dowii* and *T. fucosa* as conspecific; we follow Sibley and Monroe (1990) in treating them as separate species that form a superspecies.

Tangara fucosa Nelson. Green-naped Tanager.

> *Tangara fucosus* Nelson, 1912, Smithson. Misc. Collect. 60(3): 17. (Mount Pirri, at 5,000 feet altitude, near head of Rio Limon, eastern Panama.)

Habitat.—Montane Evergreen Forest, Elfin Forest, Montane Evergreen Forest Edge (1400–2000 m; Subtropical Zone).

Distribution.—*Resident* in extreme eastern Panama (eastern Darién on Cerro Mali and Cerro Pirre).

Notes.—Also known as Pirre Tanager. See comments under *T. dowii.*

Genus *DACNIS* Cuvier

Dacnis Cuvier, 1816, Règne Anim. 1 ("1817"): 395. Type, by monotypy, *Motacilla cayana* Linnaeus.

Notes.—The genera *Dacnis, Chlorophanes* and *Cyanerpes,* formerly placed in the family Coerebidae, are now considered to be thraupids related to the genus *Tangara* (Storer *in* Paynter 1970).

Dacnis venusta Lawrence. Scarlet-thighed Dacnis.

Dacnis venusta Lawrence, 1862, Ann. Lyc. Nat. Hist. N. Y. 7: 464. (Atlantic side of the Isthmus of Panama, along the line of the Panama Railroad = Canal Zone.)

Habitat.—Montane Evergreen Forest, Tropical Lowland Evergreen Forest, Secondary Forest, Tropical Lowland Evergreen Forest Edge (0–1450 m; Subtropical Zone, to Tropical Zone in nonbreeding season).

Distribution.—*Resident* on both slopes of Costa Rica (north to the Cordillera de Guanacaste) and Panama, and in western Colombia and northwestern Ecuador.

Dacnis cayana (Linnaeus). Blue Dacnis.

Motacilla cayana Linnaeus, 1766, Syst. Nat. (ed. 12) 1: 336. Based in part on "Le Pipit bleu de Cayenne" Brisson, Ornithologie 3: 534, pl. 28, fig. 1. (in Cayana = Cayenne.)

Habitat.—Tropical Lowland Evergreen Forest, River-edge Forest, Secondary Forest, Tropical Lowland Evergreen Forest Edge (0–1200 m; Tropical Zone).

Distribution.—*Resident* on the Caribbean slope of northeastern Honduras (Olancho, Gracias a Dios) and Nicaragua, on both slopes of Costa Rica (except the dry northwest) and Panama, and in South America from Colombia, Venezuela, Trinidad and the Guianas south, west of the Andes to southwestern Ecuador and east of the Andes to central Bolivia, eastern Paraguay, northeastern Argentina, and southern Brazil.

Dacnis viguieri Salvin and Godman. Viridian Dacnis.

Dacnis viguieri (Oustalet MS) Salvin and Godman, 1883, Biol. Cent.-Amer. (Aves) 1: 246, pl. 15A, fig. 3. (Isthmus of Panama, on the shores of the Gulf of Darien.)

Habitat.—Tropical Lowland Evergreen Forest, Tropical Lowland Evergreen Forest Edge (0–600 m; Tropical Zone).

Distribution.—*Resident* in extreme eastern Panama (eastern Darién) and northwestern Colombia (northern Chocó and Córdoba).

Genus *CHLOROPHANES* Reichenbach

Chlorophanes Reichenbach, 1853, Hand. Spec. Ornithol., cont. xi, Scansoriae B. Tenuirostres, p. 233. Type, by monotypy, *Coereba atricapilla* Vieillot = *Motacilla spiza* Linnaeus.

Notes.—See comments under *Dacnis.*

Chlorophanes spiza (Linnaeus). Green Honeycreeper.

Motacilla Spiza Linnaeus, 1758, Syst. Nat. (ed. 10) 1: 188. Based on "The Green Blackcap Fly-catcher" Edwards, Nat. Hist. Birds 1: 25, pl. 25, upper fig. (in Surinami = Surinam.)

Habitat.—Tropical Lowland Evergreen Forest, River-edge Forest, Gallery Forest, Secondary Forest, Tropical Lowland Evergreen Forest Edge (0–1600 m; Tropical and lower Subtropical zones).

Distribution.—*Resident* from northern Oaxaca, Chiapas, and southern Campeche (Pacaytún) south on the Caribbean slope of Central America to Nicaragua, on both slopes of Costa Rica (except the dry northwest) and Panama, and in South America from Colombia, Venezuela, Trinidad and the Guianas south, west of the Andes to northwestern Peru and east of the Andes to central Bolivia and Amazonian and southeastern Brazil.

Genus *CYANERPES* Oberholser

Cyanerpes Oberholser, 1899, Auk 16: 32. Type, by original designation, *Certhia cyanea* Linnaeus.

Notes.—See comments under *Dacnis*.

Cyanerpes lucidus (Sclater and Salvin). Shining Honeycreeper.

Cœreba lucida Sclater and Salvin, 1859, Ibis, p. 14. (Guatemala.)

Habitat.—Tropical Lowland Evergreen Forest, Secondary Forest, Tropical Lowland Evergreen Forest Edge (0–1500 m; Tropical and lower Subtropical zones).

Distribution.—*Resident* locally on the Caribbean slope of Chiapas, Guatemala, southern Belize, Honduras, and northern Nicaragua, and on both slopes of Costa Rica (except the dry northwest) and Panama, and in extreme northwestern Colombia (Chocó).

Notes.—Sometimes regarded as conspecific with *C. caeruleus* (e.g., Hellmayr 1938), but they are sympatric in eastern Panama and northwestern Colombia; *C. lucidus* and *C. caeruleus* constitute a superspecies (Sibley and Monroe 1990).

Cyanerpes caeruleus (Linnaeus). Purple Honeycreeper.

Certhia cærulea Linnaeus, 1758, Syst. Nat. (ed. 10) 1: 118. Based on "The Blue Creeper" Edwards, Nat. Hist. Birds 1: 21, pl. 21, upper fig. (Surinami = Surinam.)

Habitat.—Tropical Lowland Evergreen Forest, River-edge Forest, Secondary Forest, Tropical Lowland Evergreen Forest Edge, Montane Evergreen Forest (0–1100 m; Tropical and lower Subtropical zones).

Distribution.—*Resident* in extreme eastern Panama (Jaqué and Cerro Quía, in eastern Darién), and in South America from Colombia, Venezuela, Trinidad and the Guianas south, west of the Andes to west-central Ecuador and east of the Andes to central Bolivia and Amazonian and eastern Brazil.

Notes.—See comments under *C. lucidus*.

Cyanerpes cyaneus (Linnaeus). Red-legged Honeycreeper.

Certhia cyanea Linnaeus, 1766, Syst. Nat. (ed. 12) 1: 188. Based in part on "The Black and Blue Creeper" Edwards, Glean. Nat. Hist. 2: 114, pl. 264, upper fig. (in Brasilia, Cayania = Surinam.)

Habitat.—Tropical Lowland Evergreen Forest, Secondary Forest, Gallery Forest, Tropical Lowland Evergreen Forest Edge (0–1200 m; Tropical and Subtropical zones).

Distribution.—*Resident* (mostly) from Guerrero, Puebla, eastern San Luis Potosí and Veracruz south along both slopes of Middle America (including the Yucatan Peninsula) to Panama (including Coiba and the Pearl islands), and in South America from Colombia, Venezuela, Trinidad, Tobago, and the Guianas south, west of the Andes to northwestern Ecuador and east of the Andes locally to southern Bolivia, and central and southeastern Brazil. Generally withdraws from the Gulf-Caribbean slope of Mexico in winter.

Casual on Cozumel Island. Records from Cuba (where possibly established), Jamaica, and Bonaire are probably based on escaped caged birds.

Genus *TERSINA* Vieillot

Tersina Vieillot, 1819, Nouv. Dict. Hist. Nat. (nouv. éd.) 33: 401. Type, by monotypy, *Tersina caerulea* Vieillot = *Hirundo viridis* Illiger.

Notes.—This genus was formerly placed in the monotypic family Tersinidae but see Sibley (1973).

Tersina viridis (Illiger). Swallow Tanager.

Hirundo viridis Illiger, 1811, Prodromus, p. 229. Based on "L'Hirondelle verte" Temminck, Cat. Syst. Cab. Ornithol., Quadr., p. 245. (Sandwich Islands, error = eastern Brazil.)

Habitat.—Tropical Lowland Evergreen Forest Edge, Secondary Forest, River-edge Forest, Gallery Forest; in breeding season restricted to areas with banks for nest sites (0–1600 m; Tropical and Subtropical zones).

Distribution.—*Resident* in eastern Panama (eastern Panamá province and eastern Darién), and in South America south, west of the Andes to northwestern Ecuador and east of the Andes to central Bolivia, Paraguay, northeastern Argentina, and southern Brazil. Southernmost populations apparently are migratory, at least in part.

One photographed on Grand Cayman in 1982 may have been an escaped individual.

Family **EMBERIZIDAE**: Emberizids

Notes.—The first 16 genera (*Volatinia* through *Emberizoides*) in this family are considered to be tanagers rather than emberizids on the basis of genetic data by Bledsoe (1988b) and Sibley and Ahlquist (1990). Two of these genera (*Euneornis* and *Diglossa*) were listed as thraupids by Storer *in* Paynter (1970) but were moved to the Emberizinae by the A.O.U. (1983).

Genus *VOLATINIA* Reichenbach

Volatinia Reichenbach, 1850, Avium Syst. Nat., pl. 79. Type, by subsequent designation (G. R. Gray, 1855), *Tanagra jacarinia* [sic] Linnaeus.

Volatinia jacarina (Linnaeus). Blue-black Grassquit.

Tanagra jacarina Linnaeus, 1766, Syst. Nat. (ed. 12) 1: 314. Based mainly on "Jacarini" Marcgrave, Hist. Nat. Bras., p. 210. (in Brasilia = northeastern Brazil.)

Habitat.—Second-growth Scrub, Low Seasonally Wet Grassland, Arid Lowland Scrub, Pastures/Agricultural Lands, Riparian Thickets (0–1100 m; Tropical, rarely lower Subtropical zones).

Distribution.—*Resident* from southern Sonora, Sinaloa, western Durango, Nayarit, Jalisco, Michoacán, México, Morelos, Puebla, southeastern San Luis Potosí, and southern Tamaulipas south along both slopes of Middle America (including the Yucatan Peninsula) to Panama (including Coiba and the Pearl islands), and in South America from Colombia, Venezuela (including Margarita Island), Tobago, Trinidad, and the Guianas south, west of the Andes to extreme northern Chile and east of the Andes to central Argentina; also on Grenada, in the Lesser Antilles.

Casual on Isla Cancun (off Quintana Roo); an individual captured in Cuba was likely an escaped cage bird.

Genus *SPOROPHILA* Cabanis

Spermophila (not Richardson, 1825) Swainson, 1827, Zool. J. 3: 348. Type, by subsequent designation (G. R. Gray, 1840), *Pyrrhula falcirostris* Temminck.
Sporophila Cabanis, 1844, Arch. Naturgesch. 10: 291. New name for *Spermophila* Swainson, preoccupied.

Notes.—See comments under *Oryzoborus*.

Sporophila schistacea (Lawrence). Slate-colored Seedeater.

> *Spermophila schistacea* Lawrence, 1863, Ann. Lyc. Nat. Hist. N. Y. 7: 474. (along the line of the Panama Railroad, on the Atlantic side of Isthmus of Panama = Lion Hill, Canal Zone.)

Habitat.—Tropical Lowland Evergreen Forest Edge, Second-growth Scrub, Secondary Forest, mainly where bamboo is seeding (Neudorf and Blanchfield 1994) (0–1500 m; Tropical Zone).

Distribution.—*Resident* locally in southern Belize, northern Honduras (Lancetilla, Tela), Costa Rica (upper Térraba valley northwest to the Río Tarcoles), and Panama (both slopes), and in South America, west of the Andes in Colombia and northwestern Ecuador, and east of the Andes in northern Colombia and Venezuela east to northeastern Brazil, and also locally in extreme western Amazonia from Colombia to central Bolivia.

Two specimens reportedly taken in Oaxaca (confluence of the Río Coatzacoalcos and Río Sarabia) are of questionable origin (Binford 1989).

Sporophila americana (Gmelin). Variable Seedeater.

> *Loxia americana* Gmelin, 1789, Syst. Nat. 1(2): 863. Based on the "Blackbreasted Grosbeak" Latham, Gen. Synop. Birds 2: 148. (America = Cayenne.)

Habitat.—Second-growth Scrub, Tropical Lowland Evergreen Forest Edge, Tropical Deciduous Forest, Secondary Forest (0–1500 m; Tropical and lower Subtropical zones).

Distribution.—*Resident* [*corvina* group] from northern Oaxaca, southern Veracruz, and Tabasco south on the Gulf-Caribbean slope of Central America to western Panama (Bocas del Toro); [*aurita* group] from the Pacific slope of southwestern Costa Rica (north to the Gulf of Nicoya) south through Panama (both slopes, except for Bocas del Toro), western Colombia, and western Ecuador to northwestern Peru; and [*americana* group] in southeastern Colombia, northeastern Venezuela, Tobago, northeastern Peru, and Amazonian Brazil.

Notes.—Groups: *S. corvina* (Sclater, 1860) [Black Seedeater], *S. aurita* (Bonaparte, 1850) [Variable Seedeater], and *S. americana* [Wing-barred Seedeater]. Although there are differences in morphology and vocalizations between the *corvina* and *aurita* groups, intergradation occurs in central Panama (Olson 1981a). Stiles (1996b) presented evidence that *Sporophila "aurita"* represents intergrades between *S.* [*americana*] *corvina* and *S. a hicksi*, and that *corvina* (including subspecies *ophthalmica* and *hicksi*) is a separate species from *S. americana*.

Sporophila torqueola (Bonaparte). White-collared Seedeater.

> *Spermophila torqueola* Bonaparte, 1850, Consp. Gen. Avium 1(2): 495. (Mexico = Ciudad México.)

Habitat.—Second-growth Scrub, Arid Lowland Scrub, Arid Montane Scrub, Riparian Thickets (0–2000 m; Tropical and lower Subtropical zones).

Distribution.—*Resident* [*torqueola* group] on the Pacific slope and in the interior of Mexico from central Sinaloa and western Durango south through Nayarit, Jalisco, Colima, Guanajuato, Michoacán, Guerrero, México, Morelos, and western Puebla to central Oaxaca (vicinity of Oaxaca City); and [*morelleti* group] from southern Texas (western Rio Grande Valley from Falcon Dam area to San Ygnacio; formerly more widespread), Nuevo León, and Tamaulipas south on the Gulf-Caribbean slope through eastern San Luis Potosí, Veracruz, northern Oaxaca, Tabasco, and the Yucatan Peninsula (including Mujeres, Cozumel, and Cancun islands), and on both slopes of Middle America from Chiapas, Guatemala, and Belize south to extreme western Panama (Bocas del Toro and Chiriquí).

Reports from California and Arizona are considered to be of escapes.

Notes.—Groups: *S. torqueola* [Cinnamon-rumped Seedeater] and *S. morelleti* (Bonaparte, 1851) [White-collared Seedeater or Morellet's Seedeater]. This species is highly variable and relationships between various populations are not well understood (Binford 1989).

Sporophila nigricollis (Vieillot). Yellow-bellied Seedeater.

> *Pyrrhula nigricollis* Vieillot, 1823, in Bonnaterre and Vieillot, Tabl. Encycl. Méth. (Ornithol.) 3(93): 1027. (Brésil = Brazil.)

Habitat.—Second-growth Scrub, Semihumid/Humid Montane Scrub, Pastures/Agricultural Lands (0–2300 m; Tropical and Subtropical zones).

Distribution.—*Resident* in southwestern Costa Rica (Puntarenas) and Panama (Pacific slope, including Taboga and the Pearl islands, and Caribbean slope in Colón and the Canal area), and in South America from Colombia, Venezuela (including Chacachacare Island), Tobago, Trinidad, Guyana, and Surinam south, west of the Andes to northwestern Peru, and east of the Andes (absent from central Amazonia) to southern Bolivia, extreme northeastern Argentina, and southern Brazil; also in the southern Lesser Antilles (Grenada, and Carriacou in the Grenadines).

Accidental in St. Vincent (in the Lesser Antilles).

Sporophila minuta (Linnaeus). Ruddy-breasted Seedeater.

Loxia minuta Linnaeus, 1758, Syst. Nat. (ed. 10) 1: 176. (Surinami = Surinam.)

Habitat.—Low Seasonally Wet Grassland, Second-growth Scrub (0–1100 m; Tropical and Subtropical zones).

Distribution.—*Resident* on the Pacific slope of Middle America from Jalisco (rarely north to Nayarit) south to Nicaragua, in southwestern Costa Rica (upper Térraba Valley) and Panama (Pacific slope throughout, and Caribbean from the Canal area east to western San Blas); and in South America from Colombia, Venezuela, Tobago, Trinidad, and the Guianas south, west of the Andes to northwestern Ecuador and east of the Andes to northern Amazonian Brazil.

Notes.—For reasons for treating *S. hypoxantha* Cabanis, 1851 [Tawny-bellied Seedeater] of southern South America as a separate species from *S. minuta,* see Short (1969); this treatment has been followed by most authors (e.g., Ridgely and Tudor 1989, Ouellet 1992).

Genus *ORYZOBORUS* Cabanis

Oryzoborus Cabanis, 1851, Mus. Heineanum 1: 151. Type, by subsequent designation (G. R. Gray, 1855), *Loxia torrida* "Gmelin" [= Scopoli] = *Loxia angolensis* Linnaeus.

Notes.—Sometimes merged in *Sporophila* (Olson 1981b).

Oryzoborus nuttingi Ridgway. Nicaraguan Seed-Finch.

Oryzoborus nuttingi Ridgway, 1884, Proc. U. S. Natl. Mus. 6: 401. (Los Sábalos, [Río San Juan,] Nicaragua.)

Habitat.—Riparian Thickets, Tropical Lowland Evergreen Forest, Second-growth Scrub (0–500 m; Tropical Zone).

Distribution.—*Resident* in the Caribbean lowlands of Nicaragua, northern Costa Rica (Laguna de Arenal, near Finca La Selva), and western Panama (Bocas del Toro).

Notes.—Also known as Pink-billed Seed-Finch. Sometimes regarded as a subspecies of *O. maximiliani* Cabanis, 1851 [Great-billed Seed-Finch] but here considered a separate species, following Stiles (1984).

Oryzoborus funereus Sclater. Thick-billed Seed-Finch.

Oryzoborus funereus Sclater, 1859, Proc. Zool. Soc. London, p. 378. (Suchapam, Oaxaca.)

Habitat.— Second-growth Scrub, Secondary Forest, Tropical Lowland Evergreen Forest Edge (0–1100 m; Tropical Zone).

Distribution.—*Resident* from central Veracruz, northern Oaxaca, Tabasco, and Chiapas south on the Gulf-Caribbean slope of Central America to Costa Rica (also on Pacific slope in Térraba region), and in Panama (both slopes, including Coiba and the Pearl islands), western Colombia, and western Ecuador.

Notes.—Although *O. funereus* and South American *O. angolensis* (Linnaeus, 1766) [Chestnut-bellied Seed-Finch] hybridize to a limited extent in the Magdalena Valley of northern Colombia (Olson 1981c), no hybrid swarm exists. They are treated as a single species by many authors (e.g., Ridgely and Tudor 1989, Sibley and Monroe 1990), in which case the appropriate English name is Lesser Seed-Finch.

Genus *AMAUROSPIZA* Cabanis

Amaurospiza Cabanis, 1861, J. Ornithol. 9: 3. Type, by original designation, *Amaurospiza concolor* Cabanis.

Amaurospizopsis Griscom, 1934, Bull. Mus. Comp. Zool. Harv. 75: 412. Type, by original designation, *Amaurospizopsis relictus* Griscom.

Notes.—Paynter (1970) suggested that *Amaurospiza* might belong in the Cardinalidae.

Amaurospiza concolor Cabanis. Blue Seedeater.

Amaurospiza concolor Cabanis, 1861, J. Ornithol. 9: 3. (Costa Rica = Miravalles, Costa Rica.)

Habitat.—Montane Evergreen Forest Edge (especially seeding bamboo) (1000–2200 m; upper Tropical and Subtropical zones).

Distribution.—*Resident* [*relicta* group] in the mountains of Jalisco, Colima (sight report), Guerrero, Morelos, and south-central Oaxaca; and [*concolor* group] locally in Chiapas (Cintalapa, Tuxtla Gutiérrez), Belize, El Salvador (Cerro Verde), Honduras (Lago de Yojoa, Arenal), Nicaragua, Costa Rica, Panama (Chiriquí, Veraguas, western Panamá province, Canal area), southwestern Colombia, and northwestern Ecuador.

Notes.—Groups: *A. relicta* (Griscom, 1934) [Slate-blue Seedeater] and *A. concolor* [Blue Seedeater].

Genus *MELOPYRRHA* Bonaparte

Melopyrrha Bonaparte, 1853, C. R. Acad. Sci. Paris 37: 924. Type, by subsequent designation (G. R. Gray, 1855), *Loxia nigra* Linnaeus.

Melopyrrha nigra (Linnaeus). Cuban Bullfinch.

Loxia nigra Linnaeus, 1758, Syst. Nat. (ed. 10) 1: 175. Based on "The Little Black Bullfinch" Catesby, Nat. Hist. Carolina 1: 68, pl. 68, and "The Black Bullfinch" Albin, Nat. Hist. Birds 3: 65, pl. 69. (in America australi = Cuba.)

Habitat.—Tropical Lowland Evergreen Forest, Pine Forest, Secondary Forest (90–900 m).

Distribution.—*Resident* on Cuba (including some coastal cays), the Isle of Pines, and Grand Cayman Island.

Birds reported from southern Florida were probably escapes from captivity (Robertson and Woolfenden 1992).

Genus *TIARIS* Swainson

Tiaris Swainson, 1827, Philos. Mag. (n.s.) 1: 438. Type, by monotypy, *Tiaris pusillus* Swainson = *Emberiza olivacea* Linnaeus.

Tiaris canora (Gmelin). Cuban Grassquit.

Loxia canora Gmelin, 1789, Syst. Nat. 1(2): 858. Based on the "Brown-cheeked Grosbeak" Latham, Gen. Synop. Birds 2(1): 155. (in nova Hispania, error = Cuba.)

Habitat.—Tropical Lowland Evergreen Forest Edge, Secondary Forest, Pine Forest, Arid Lowland Scrub, Second-growth Scrub.

Distribution.—*Resident* on Cuba. Old reports from the Isle of Pines are not confirmed. Introduced and established in the Bahama Islands (New Providence).

Several reports from southern Florida are probably based on escaped cage birds; reportedly bred in Dade County in 1960 but no population has become established (Stevenson and Anderson 1994). An old report from Sombrero Key is based on *T. bicolor*.

Notes.—Also known as Melodious Grassquit.

Tiaris olivacea (Linnaeus). Yellow-faced Grassquit.

> *Emberiza olivacea* Linnaeus, 1766, Syst. Nat. (ed. 12) 1:309. Based on "Le Bruant de S. Domingue" Brisson, Ornithologie 3: 300, pl. 13, fig. 5. (in Dominica = Hispaniola.)

Habitat.—Second-growth Scrub, Arid Lowland Scrub (0–2300 m; Tropical and Subtropical zones).

Distribution.—*Resident* from central Nuevo León, eastern San Luis Potosí, and southern Tamaulipas south along the Gulf-Caribbean slope of Mexico (including the Yucatan Peninsula, and Cozumel and Holbox islands), Guatemala, and Belize, in El Salvador, on both slopes of Honduras, in Nicaragua (Caribbean slope only), on both slopes of Costa Rica and Panama (including Isla Coiba), and in western and central Colombia, northwestern Ecuador, and northwestern Venezuela; also in the Greater Antilles (east to Puerto Rico, and including the Cayman Islands).

Introduced (discovered in 1974) and established in the Hawaiian Islands (in the highlands of Oahu).

Accidental in southern Texas (22–24 Jan. 1990, Santa Ana; Amer. Birds 44: 222, 289; DeBenedictis 1992) and southern Florida (near Homestead, 7–12 July 1990, Smith et al. 1991; Dry Tortugas, 20–24 April 1994, photo, 1994, Nat. Audubon Soc. Field Notes 48: 191); a sight report from Nuevo León.

Tiaris bicolor (Linnaeus). Black-faced Grassquit.

> *Fringilla bicolor* Linnaeus, 1766, Syst. Nat. (ed. 12) 1: 324. Based on "The Bahama Sparrow" Catesby, Nat. Hist. Carolina 1: 37, pl. 37. (in America = Bahama Islands.)

Habitat.—Arid Lowland Scrub, Second-growth Scrub, Tropical Deciduous Forest Edge, Tropical Lowland Evergreen Forest Edge (0–1300 m; Tropical Zone).

Distribution.—*Resident* throughout the West Indies (except Cuba, where confined to various cays off the northern coast and off the southern coast on Cayo Cantiles), on islands in the western Caribbean Sea (Providencia, Santa Catalina, and San Andrés), and in northern Colombia and northern Venezuela (including islands from the Netherlands Antilles east to Tobago and Trinidad).

Casual in southern Florida (Palm Beach County south to Sombrero Key). Accidental in eastern Cuba (near Holguín).

Genus *LOXIPASSER* Bryant

> *Loxipasser* Bryant, 1866, Proc. Boston Soc. Nat. Hist. 10: 254. Type, by original designation, *Spermophila anoxantha* Gosse.

Loxipasser anoxanthus (Gosse). Yellow-shouldered Grassquit.

> *Spermophila anoxantha* Gosse, 1847, Birds Jamaica, p. 247 (footnote). (Mount Edgecumbe, Jamaica.)

Habitat.—Tropical Lowland Evergreen Forest Edge, Secondary Forest Edge, Montane Evergreen Forest Edge (0–1800 m).

Distribution.—*Resident* on Jamaica.

Notes.—Also known as Yellow-backed Finch.

Genus *LOXIGILLA* Lesson

> *Loxigilla* Lesson, 1831, Traité Ornithol., livr. 6, p. 443. Type, by subsequent designation (G. R. Gray, 1855), *Fringilla noctis* Linnaeus.

Loxigilla portoricensis (Daudin). Puerto Rican Bullfinch.

Loxia portoricensis Daudin, 1800, Traité Ornithol. 2: 411. (Puerto Rico.)

Habitat.—Montane Evergreen Forest, Tropical Lowland Evergreen Forest, Tropical Deciduous Forest, Secondary Forest, Mangrove Forest (0–1000 m).
Distribution.—*Resident* on Puerto Rico and on St. Kitts in the Lesser Antilles (at least formerly, last reported there in 1929).
A report from the Virgin Islands (St. Johns) is regarded as based on an escaped individual.

Loxigilla violacea (Linnaeus). Greater Antillean Bullfinch.

Loxia violacea Linnaeus, 1758, Syst. Nat. (ed. 10) 1: 176. Based on "The Purple Grossbeak" Catesby, Nat. Hist. Carolina 1: 40, pl. 40. (in America = Bahama Islands.)

Habitat.—Tropical Lowland Evergreen Forest, Montane Evergreen Forest, Secondary Forest, Arid Lowland Scrub (0–2000 m).
Distribution.—*Resident* throughout the Bahama Islands, and in the Greater Antilles on Hispaniola (including Tortue, Gonâve, Saona, Beata, and Catalina islands, and Île-à-Vache) and Jamaica; a sight report for southern Florida (Hypoluxo Island) may have been of an escaped cage-bird (Stevenson and Anderson 1994).

Loxigilla noctis (Linnaeus). Lesser Antillean Bullfinch.

Fringilla noctis Linnaeus, 1766, Syst. Nat. (ed. 12) 1: 320. Based mainly on "Le Père noir" Brisson, Ornithologie 3: 118, pl. 7, fig. 1. (in Jamaica, Mexico, Martinica = Martinique.)

Habitat.—Tropical Lowland Evergreen Forest, Secondary Forest, Tropical Deciduous Forest (0–900 m).
Distribution.—*Resident* in the Virgin Islands (on St. John, since 1971, possibly introduced) and Lesser Antilles (from Anguilla and Saba south to St. Vincent and Barbados, also on Grenada).

Genus *EUNEORNIS* Fitzinger

Euneornis Fitzinger, 1856, Sitzungsber. K. Akad. Wiss. Wien, Math.-Naturwiss. Kl. 21(2): 316. Type, by original designation, *Motacilla campestris* Linnaeus.

Notes.—Systematic position uncertain; formerly placed in the Coerebidae or the Thraupidae (Storer *in* Paynter 1970).

Euneornis campestris (Linnaeus). Orangequit.

Motacilla campestris Linnaeus, 1758, Syst. Nat. (ed. 10) 1: 184. Based on "The American Hedge-Sparrow" Edwards, Nat. Hist. Birds 3: 122, pl. 122, lower fig. (in Jamaica.)

Habitat.—Tropical Lowland Evergreen Forest, Secondary Forest (0–1500 m).
Distribution.—*Resident* on Jamaica.

Genus *MELANOSPIZA* Ridgway

Melanospiza Ridgway, 1897, Proc. U. S. Natl. Mus. 19 (1886): 466. Type, by original designation, *Loxigilla richardsoni* Cory.

Melanospiza richardsoni (Cory). St. Lucia Black Finch.

Loxigilla richardsoni Cory, 1886, Auk 3: 382. (Mountains of Santa Lucia, West Indies.)

Habitat.—Tropical Lowland Evergreen Forest Edge, Secondary Forest (0–1000 m).
Distribution.—*Resident* on St. Lucia, in the Lesser Antilles.

Genus *PINAROLOXIAS* Sharpe

Pinaroloxias Sharpe, 1885, Cat. Birds Brit. Mus. 10: ix, 3, 52. Type, by monotypy, *Cactornis inornata* Gould.

Pinaroloxias inornata (Gould). Cocos Finch.

Cactornis inornata Gould, 1843, Proc. Zool. Soc. London, p. 104. (Bow Island, Low Archipelago, Polynesia, error = Cocos Island.)

Habitat.—Tropical Lowland Evergreen Forest (0–800 m)
Distribution.—*Resident* on Cocos Island, off Costa Rica.

Genus *HAPLOSPIZA* Cabanis

Haplospiza Cabanis, 1851, Mus. Heineanum 1: 147. Type, by original designation, *Haplospiza unicolor* Cabanis.
Spodiornis Sclater, 1866, Proc. Zool. Soc. London, p. 322. Type, by original designation, *Spodiornis jardinii* Sclater = *Phrygilus rusticus* Tschudi.

Notes.—See comments under *Acanthidops*.

Haplospiza rustica (Tschudi). Slaty Finch.

Phrygilus rusticus (Lichtenstein MS) Tschudi, 1844, Arch. Naturgesch. 10: 290. (Republica Peruana = Peru.)

Habitat.—Montane Evergreen Forest Edge (especially where bamboo is seeding), Tropical Lowland Evergreen Forest Edge (1500–2500 m; upper Subtropical and Temperate zones).
Distribution.—*Resident* locally in the highlands of Middle America in Veracruz (Jalapa), Chiapas (Volcán Tacaná), El Salvador, Honduras (El Chorro), northwestern Nicaragua (near Matagalpa), Costa Rica (cordilleras Central and Talamanca), and western Panama (western Chiriquí and western Panamá province); and in South America in the Andes from Colombia and Venezuela south to northern Bolivia.
Notes.—Often treated in the monotypic genus *Spodiornis*.

Genus *ACANTHIDOPS* Ridgway

Acanthidops Ridgway, 1882, Proc. U. S. Natl. Mus. 4 (1881): 335. Type, by original designation, *Acanthidops bairdii* Ridgway.

Notes.—Closely related to the genus *Haplospiza* and possibly not separable generically from it (Paynter 1970).

Acanthidops bairdii Ridgway. Peg-billed Finch.

Acanthidops bairdii Ridgway, 1882, Proc. U. S. Natl. Mus. 4 (1881): 336. (Volcan de Irazú, Costa Rica.)

Habitat.—Montane Evergreen Forest Edge, especially where bamboo is seeding (1500–3000 m; Temperate Zone).
Distribution.—*Resident* in Costa Rica (Tilarán, Central, and Talamanca cordilleras). Casual in western Panama (Cerro Punta, Chiriquí, January–March 1979).

Genus *DIGLOSSA* Wagler

Diglossa Wagler, 1832, Isis von Oken, col. 280. Type, by monotypy, *Diglossa baritula* Wagler.

Notes.—Formerly placed in the family Coerebidae or in the Thraupidae (Storer *in* Paynter 1970).

Diglossa baritula Wagler. Cinnamon-bellied Flowerpiercer.

> *Diglossa baritula* Wagler, 1832, Isis von Oken, col. 281. (Mexico.)

Habitat.—Montane Evergreen Forest Edge, Pine-oak Forest Edge, Secondary Forest, Second-growth Scrub (1500–3350 m; Subtropical and Temperate zones).
Distribution.—*Resident* in the highlands from Jalisco, Guanajuato, Hidalgo, and Veracruz south through southern Mexico, Guatemala, El Salvador, and Honduras to north-central Nicaragua.
Notes.—Also known as Cinnamon Flowerpiercer. *Diglossa baritula* and *D. plumbea* constitute a superspecies, which is a sister group to the South American *D. sittoides* (d'Orbigny and Lafresnaye, 1838) [Rusty Flowerpiercer] (Hackett 1995). *Diglossa plumbea* and *D. sittoides* were merged into *baritula* by Paynter (1970) and Wetmore et al. (1984).

Diglossa plumbea Cabanis. Slaty Flowerpiercer.

> *Diglossa plumbea* Cabanis, 1861, J. Ornithol. 8(1860): 411. (Costa Rica.)

Habitat.—Montane Evergreen Forest Edge, Semihumid/Humid Montane Scrub, Second-growth Scrub (1200–3300 m; upper Subtropical and Temperate zones).
Distribution.—*Resident* in the mountains of Costa Rica (north to Cordillera de Guanacaste) and western Panama (western Chiriquí and Veraguas).
Notes.—See comments under *D. baritula*.

Genus SICALIS Boie

> *Sicalis* Boie, 1828, Isis von Oken, col. 324. Type, by subsequent designation (Cabanis, 1846), *Emberiza brasiliensis* Gmelin = *Fringilla flaveola* Linnaeus.

Notes.—Bledsoe (1988b) suggested that *Sicalis* belongs in the Thraupidae.

Sicalis flaveola (Linnaeus). Saffron Finch.

> *Fringilla flaveola* Linnaeus, 1766, Syst. Nat. (ed. 12) 1: 321. (No locality given = Surinam.)

Habitat.—Pastures/Agricultural Lands, Second-growth Scrub; extensive lawns (Tropical and lower Subtropical zones).
Distribution.—*Resident* [*flaveola* group] in South America west of the Andes in western Ecuador and northwestern Peru, and east of the Andes in northern and eastern Colombia, northern Venezuela, the Guianas, and northeastern Brazil; and [*pelzelni* group] in eastern Bolivia, Paraguay, eastern and southern Brazil, and Uruguay south to central Argentina.
Introduced and established [*flaveola* group] in the Hawaiian Islands (since 1966, presently in small numbers on Oahu, and along the North Kona coast of Hawaii), central Panama (Canal area), Jamaica, and Puerto Rico (Río Piedras to Dorado).
Notes.—Groups: *S. flaveola* [Saffron Finch] and *S. pelzelni* Sclater, 1872 [Pelzeln's Finch].

Sicalis luteola (Sparrman). Grassland Yellow-Finch.

> *Emberiza luteola* Sparrman, 1789, Mus. Carlson., fasc. 4, pl. 93. (No locality given = Surinam.)

Habitat.—Low Seasonally Wet Grassland, Pastures/Agricultural Lands (0–3500 m; Tropical, locally to Temperate zones).
Distribution.—*Resident* [*chrysops* group] locally in Middle America in Puebla, Morelos (Pacific drainage), central and southern Veracruz, northern Chiapas, Tabasco, western Campeche, central Guatemala (Dueñas, at least formerly), Belize (possibly), the Mosquitia of eastern Honduras, and northeastern Nicaragua, Costa Rica (Guanacaste, one record), and Panama (Coclé and eastern Panamá province); [*luteola* group] lowlands of South America in Colombia, Venezuela, Trinidad, the Guianas, and northern Brazil; and [*bogotensis* group] in the Andes from Colombia south to Peru.
Introduced and established [*luteola* group] in the Lesser Antilles on Barbados, whence it

has since spread to the Grenadines (Mustique), St. Vincent, St. Lucia, Martinique, Guade-loupe, and Antigua.

Notes.—Also known as Yellow Grass-Finch. Groups: *S. chrysops* Sclater, 1862 [Northern Yellow-Finch], *S. luteola* [Grassland Yellow-Finch], and *S. bogotensis* Chapman, 1924 [Montane Yellow-Finch]. *Sicalis luteiventris* (Meyen, 1834) [Misto Yellow-Finch], of southern South America, may also be conspecific with *S. luteola* (Ridgely and Tudor 1989).

Genus *EMBERIZOIDES* Temminck

Emberizoïdes Temminck, 1822, Planches Color., livr. 19, text to pl. 114. Type, by subsequent designation (G. R. Gray, 1840), *Emberizoides marginalis* Temminck = *Sylvia herbicola* Vieillot.

Emberizoides herbicola (Vieillot). Wedge-tailed Grass-Finch.

Sylvia herbicola Vieillot, 1817, Nouv. Dict. Hist. Nat. (nouv. éd.) 11: 192. Based on "Cola aguda encuentro amarillo" Azara, Apunt. Hist. Nat. Páx. Parag. 2: 257 (no. 230). (Paraguay.)

Habitat.—Low Seasonally Wet Grassland, Second-growth Scrub (0–1900 m; Tropical and Subtropical zones).

Distribution.—*Resident* locally in southwestern Costa Rica (Térraba region) and western and central Panama (Chiriquí, Cerro Campana, and the Tocumen-Chepo area in eastern Panamá province); and in South America in Colombia (except far western and southern portions), Venezuela, the Guianas, and northeastern Brazil, and from eastern Peru (local), eastern Bolivia, and eastern Argentina east to Atlantic Brazil and Paraguay.

Notes.—Also known as Wedge-tailed Ground-Finch.

Genus *PAROARIA* Bonaparte

Paroaria Bonaparte, 1832 (1831), G. Arcad. Sci. Lett. Arti [Rome] 52: 206. Type, by original designation, *Fringilla cucullata* Vieillot = *Loxia coronata* Miller.

Notes.—Sometimes treated as a cardinalid, but appears to be emberizine, or possibly thraupine of uncertain relationships (see Paynter 1970).

Paroaria coronata (Miller). Red-crested Cardinal.

Loxia coronata J. F. Miller, 1776, Var. Subj. Nat. Hist., pt. 1, pl. 2. (No locality given = Rio Grande do Sul, Brazil.)

Habitat.—Scrub, brushy areas, parks, and residential areas, mostly in humid regions.

Distribution.—*Resident* from northern Bolivia, Paraguay, Uruguay, and extreme southern Brazil south to northern Argentina.

Introduced and established in the Hawaiian Islands in 1928 on Oahu (where now common), presently also on Molokai and, locally, on Kauai, Lanai, and Maui; and Puerto Rico (Dorado); occurs in southern Florida but as yet there is no persistent wild population (Robertson and Woolfendon 1992).

Notes.—Also known as Brazilian Cardinal.

Paroaria capitata (d'Orbigny and Lafresnaye). Yellow-billed Cardinal.

Tachyphonus capitatus d'Orbigny and Lafresnaye, 1837, Mag. Zool. [Paris] 7(2): 29, pl. 77–79. (Corrientes, rep. Argentina.)

Habitat.—Primarily dry kiawe thickets; in South America, forest and woodland, and adjacent partly open situations with scattered trees, primarily in semi-arid habitats.

Distribution.—*Resident* from southeastern Bolivia, central Brazil (western Mato Grosso), and Paraguay south to northern Argentina.

Introduced and established in the Hawaiian Islands (since 1933, presently in small numbers along the Kona coast of Hawaii and spreading).

Genus *LYSURUS* Ridgway

Lysurus Ridgway, 1898, Auk 15: 225. Type, by original designation, *Buarremon crassirostris* Cassin.

Lysurus crassirostris (Cassin). Sooty-faced Finch.

Buarremon crassirostris Cassin, 1865, Proc. Acad. Nat. Sci. Philadelphia 17: 170. (Barranca, Costa Rica.)

Habitat.—Montane Evergreen Forest (600–2000 m; Subtropical and lower Temperate zones).

Distribution.—*Resident* in the mountains from central Costa Rica (Aguacate Mountains southward) south through Panama (recorded Chiriquí, Bocas del Toro, Veraguas, Coclé, and eastern Darién) to northern Colombia (Cerro Tacarcuna).

Notes.—*Lysurus crassirostris* and the South American *L. castaneiceps* (Sclater, 1860) [Olive Finch] constitute a superspecies; Paynter (1970) and Wetmore et al. (1984) treated them as conspecific.

Genus *PSELLIOPHORUS* Ridgway

Pselliophorus Ridgway, 1898, Auk 15: 225. Type, by original designation, *Tachyphonus tibialis* Lawrence.

Notes.—Sometimes merged in *Atlapetes*.

Pselliophorus tibialis (Lawrence). Yellow-thighed Finch.

Tachyphonus tibialis Lawrence, 1864, Ann. Lyc. Nat. Hist. N. Y. 8: 41. (San Jose, Costa Rica.)

Habitat.—Montane Evergreen Forest, Secondary Forest (1500–3400 m; Subtropical and Temperate zones).

Distribution.—*Resident* in the mountains from central Costa Rica (north to Cordillera de Tilarán) to extreme western Panama (western Chiriquí).

Notes.—*Pselliophorus tibialis* and *P. luteoviridis* are closely related and constitute a superspecies. Paynter (1970) suggested that *P. luteoviridis* might be a subspecies of *P. tibialis,* but see Wetmore et al. (1984).

Pselliophorus luteoviridis Griscom. Yellow-green Finch.

Pselliophorus luteoviridis Griscom, 1924, Amer. Mus. Novit., no. 141, p. 10. (Cerro Flores, alt. 6000 ft., eastern Chiriqui, Panama.)

Habitat.—Montane Evergreen Forest (1200–1800 m; upper Subtropical and Temperate zones).

Distribution.—*Resident* in the mountains of western Panama (eastern Chiriquí and adjacent Veraguas).

Notes.—See comments under *P. tibialis*.

Genus *PEZOPETES* Cabanis

Pezopetes Cabanis, 1861, J. Ornithol. 8 (1860): 415. Type, by monotypy, *Pezopetes capitalis* Cabanis.

Notes.—Paynter (1970) suggested that *Pezopetes* might belong in the genus *Atlapetes*.

Pezopetes capitalis Cabanis. Large-footed Finch.

Pezopetes capitalis Cabanis, 1861, J. Ornithol. 8 (1860): 415. (Costa Rica.)

Habitat.—Montane Evergreen Forest Edge, Montane Evergreen Forest, Second-growth Scrub (2150–3350 m; upper Subtropical and Temperate zones).

Distribution.—*Resident* in the mountains from central Costa Rica (Cordillera Central southward) to extreme western Panama (western Bocas del Toro and western Chiriquí).

Genus *ATLAPETES* Wagler

Atlapetes Wagler, 1831, Isis von Oken, col. 526. Type, by monotypy, *Atlapetes pileatus* Wagler.

Notes.—Members of this genus are sometimes known under the English group name Atlapetes. See comments under *Pezopetes* and *Pselliophorus,* and under *Buarremon.*

Atlapetes albinucha (d'Orbigny and Lafresnaye). White-naped Brush-Finch.

Embernagra albinucha d'Orbigny and Lafresnaye, 1838, Rev. Zool. [Paris] 1: 165. (Cartagène, error = Caribbean slope of Mexico; see Paynter [1964a].)

Habitat.—Montane Evergreen Forest Edge, Pine-Oak Forest, Secondary Forest, Semi-humid/Humid Montane Scrub, Second-growth Scrub (1000–3350 m; Subtropical and lower Temperate zones).

Distribution.—*Resident* [*albinucha* group] in the highlands on the Gulf slope in Veracruz, Hidalgo, eastern San Luis Potosí, Puebla, northern Oaxaca, and northern Chiapas; a report from the valley of México is considered doubtful, and those from Colombia are regarded as erroneous; and [*gutturalis* group] in the highlands of southern Chiapas, Guatemala, El Salvador, Honduras, north-central Nicaragua, Costa Rica, western Panama (Chiriquí, Veraguas, Coclé, Herrera), and Colombia.

Notes.—Groups: *A. albinucha* (d'Orbigny and Lafresnaye, 1838) [White-naped Brush-Finch] and *A. gutturalis* (Lafresnaye, 1843) [Yellow-throated Brush-Finch]. Although *A. gutturalis* has been treated as a species for most of this century (e.g., Ridgway 1901, Hellmayr 1938, A.O.U. 1983, Sibley and Monroe 1990), Paynter (1964a, 1978) showed that *albinucha* and *gutturalis* cannot intergrade because of separation by a dry valley and that they differ only in the amount of yellow on the underparts.

Atlapetes pileatus Wagler. Rufous-capped Brush-Finch.

Atlapetes pileatus Wagler, 1831, Isis von Oken, col. 526. (Mexico.)

Habitat.—Pine-Oak Forest, Montane Evergreen Forest Edge, Semihumid/Humid Montane Scrub (1225–3400 m; Subtropical and Temperate zones).

Distribution.—*Resident* in the Mexican highlands from western Chihuahua, Sinaloa, western Durango, Nayarit, Jalisco, Guanajuato, San Luis Potosí, central Nuevo León, and southwestern Tamaulipas south to central Oaxaca (west of the Isthmus of Tehuantepec), Puebla, and western Veracruz.

Genus *BUARREMON* Bonaparte

Buarremon Bonaparte, 1850, Consp. Gen. Av., i, p. 483. Type, by subsequent designation (Gray, 1855), *Embernagra torquata* Lafresnaye and d'Orbigny.

Notes.—Members of the is genus were formerly placed in *Atlapetes,* but see Remsen and Graves (1995).

Buarremon brunneinuchus (Lafresnaye). Chestnut-capped Brush-Finch.

Embernagra brunnei-nucha Lafresnaye, 1839, Rev. Zool. [Paris] 2: 97. (Mexico = Jalapa, Veracruz.)

Habitat.—Montane Evergreen Forest, Pine-Oak Forest, Secondary Forest (upper Tropical to lower Temperate zones).

Distribution.—*Resident* [*apertus* group] in the Sierra de los Tuxtlas in southern Veracruz; and [*brunneinuchus* group] locally in the highlands from Guerrero, Hidalgo, eastern San Luis Potosí, and northern Veracruz south through Oaxaca, Chiapas, central Guatemala, northern El Salvador, Honduras, Nicaragua, and Costa Rica (Cordillera de Tilarán southward) to

Panama (Bocas del Toro, Chiriquí, Veraguas, Coclé, western Panamá province, eastern Darién), and in South America in the Andes from Colombia and northern Venezuela south to southern Peru.

Notes.—Groups: *B. brunneinuchus* [Chestnut-capped Brush-Finch] and *B. apertus* Wetmore, 1942 [Plain-breasted Brush-Finch].

Buarremon virenticeps Bonaparte. Green-striped Brush-Finch.

Buarremon virenticeps Bonaparte, 1855, C. R. Acad. Sci. Paris 41: 657. (Mexico = Desierto de los Leones, near Ciudad México, Distrito Federal.)

Habitat.—Montane Evergreen Forest, Pine-Oak Forest (1500–3000 m; Subtropical and Temperate zones).

Distribution.—*Resident* in the mountains, primarily on the Pacific slope, from southern Sinaloa and western Durango south through Nayarit, Jalisco, Colima, and Michoacán to México, Distrito Federal, Morelos, and western Puebla.

Notes.—*Buarremon virenticeps* is merged with *B. torquatus* by Paynter (1970) and Wetmore et al. (1984), but see Paynter (1978) and Ridgely and Tudor (1989).

Buarremon torquatus (Lafresnaye and d'Orbigny). Stripe-headed Brush-Finch.

Embernagra torquata Lafresnaye and d'Orbigny, 1837, Mag. Zool. [Paris] 7(2): 34. (Yungas, Bolivia.)

Habitat.—Montane Evergreen Forest, Tropical Lowland Evergreen Forest, Secondary Forest, Elfin Forest (300–1500 m; upper Tropical and Subtropical zones).

Distribution.—*Resident* [*atricapillus* group] from the highlands of southwestern Costa Rica (north to the Gulf of Nicoya), east through Panama to northern Colombia; and [*torquatus* group] in South America in the Andes in Venezuela, and from Colombia south to northwestern Argentina.

Notes.—Groups: *B. atricapillus* Lawrence, 1874 [Black-headed Brush-Finch], and *B. torquatus* (Lafresnaye and d'Orbigny, 1837) [Stripe-headed Brush-Finch]. Following Paynter (1970), Wetmore et al. (1984), and Remsen and Graves (1995), *B. atricapillus* is treated in *torquatus*; it was treated as a separate species by A.O.U. (1983) and Ridgely and Tudor (1989).

Genus *ARREMON* Vieillot

Arremon Vieillot, 1816, Analyse, p. 32. Type, by monotypy, "L'Oiseau Silencieux" Buffon = *Tanagra taciturna* Hermann.

Notes.—See comments under *Arremonops*.

Arremon aurantiirostris Lafresnaye. Orange-billed Sparrow.

Arremon aurantiirostris Lafresnaye, 1847, Rev. Zool. [Paris] 10: 72. (Panama.)

Habitat.—Tropical Lowland Evergreen Forest (0–1200 m; Tropical Zone).

Distribution.—*Resident* from northern Oaxaca, southern Veracruz, Tabasco, and Chiapas south through the Gulf-Caribbean lowlands of Central America to Nicaragua, on both slopes of Costa Rica (except the dry northwest), and Panama, and in South America from Colombia south, west and east of the Andes to northern Peru.

Genus *ARREMONOPS* Ridgway

Arremonops Ridgway, 1896, Man. North Amer. Birds, ed. 2, pp. 434, 605. Type, by original designation, *Embernagra rufivirgata* Lawrence.

Notes.—Sometimes merged in *Arremon*.

Arremonops rufivirgatus (Lawrence). Olive Sparrow.

Embernagra rufivirgata Lawrence, 1851, Ann. Lyc. Nat. Hist. N. Y. 5: 112, pl. 5, fig. 2. (Rio Grande in Texas = Brownsville, Texas.)

Habitat.—Tropical Deciduous Forest, Arid Lowland Scrub, Riparian Thickets (0–1625 m; Tropical and lower Subtropical zones).

Distribution.—*Resident* [*superciliosus* group] on the Pacific slope from central Sinaloa south to central Oaxaca (east to Huamelula) and the Central Valley of Chiapas, and in northwestern Costa Rica (Guanacaste); and [*rufivirgatus* group] in the Gulf-Caribbean lowlands from central Texas (north to Uvalde, McMullen, Bee, and Refugio counties), Coahuila, and Nuevo León south through eastern Mexico (including the Yucatan Peninsula) to northern Guatemala (Petén) and Belize.

Notes.—Groups: *A. rufivirgatus* [Olive Sparrow] and *A. superciliosus* (Salvin, 1865) [Pacific Sparrow]. *Arremonops rufivirgatus* and the South American *A. tocuyensis* Todd, 1912 [Tocuyo Sparrow], appear to constitute a superspecies (Mayr and Short 1970).

Arremonops chloronotus (Salvin). Green-backed Sparrow.

Embernagra chloronota Salvin, 1861, Proc. Zool. Soc. London, p. 202. (In Prov. Veræ Pacis regione calida = Choctum, Alta Verapaz, Guatemala.)

Habitat.—Tropical Lowland Evergreen Forest Edge, Tropical Deciduous Forest Edge, Secondary Forest, Second-growth Scrub (0–900 m; Tropical Zone).

Distribution.—*Resident* from Tabasco, northern Chiapas, and the southern and eastern Yucatan Peninsula south through northern Guatemala and Belize to northern Honduras (west of the Sula Valley, and disjunctly in Olancho).

Notes.—Although once considered conspecific with *A. conirostris,* differences in morphology, juvenal plumage, and vocalizations in northern Honduras confirm the specific distinctness of *A. chloronotus* (Monroe 1963b).

Arremonops conirostris (Bonaparte). Black-striped Sparrow.

Arremon conirostris Bonaparte, 1851, Consp. Gen. Avium 1(2): 488. (Brasil, error = Colombia.)

Habitat.—Tropical Lowland Evergreen Forest Edge, Tropical Deciduous Forest Edge, Secondary Forest, Riparian Thickets, Second-growth Scrub (0–1600 m; Tropical and lower Subtropical zones).

Distribution.—*Resident* on the Caribbean slope of Honduras (west to the Sula Valley) and Nicaragua, on both slopes of Costa Rica (rare in the dry northwest) and Panama (including Coiba and the Pearl islands), and in South America in northern Colombia, Venezuela, and extreme northern Brazil, and west of the Andes in southwestern Colombia and western Ecuador.

Notes.—See comments under *A. chloronotus.*

Genus *MELOZONE* Reichenbach

Melozone Reichenbach, 1850, Avium Syst. Nat., pl. 79. Type, by subsequent designation (Sharpe, 1888), *Pyrgita biarcuata* Prévost and Des Murs.

Melozone kieneri (Bonaparte). Rusty-crowned Ground-Sparrow.

Pyrgisoma kieneri Bonaparte, 1851, Consp. Gen. Avium 1(2): 486. (ex Am[erica]. occ[identale]. = San Blas, Nayarit.)

Habitat.—Tropical Deciduous Forest, Secondary Forest, Arid Montane Scrub, Tropical Deciduous Forest Edge (0–1500 m; upper Tropical and Subtropical zones).

Distribution.—*Resident* from southeastern Sonora south through Sinaloa, western Durango, Nayarit, Jalisco, Guanajuato, Colima, Michoacán, México, Morelos, and Guerrero, to southwestern Puebla and central Oaxaca (west of the Isthmus of Tehuantepec).

Notes.—*Melozone kieneri* and *M. biarcuatum* were considered conspecific by Hellmayr (1938), but see Miller et al. (1957).

Melozone biarcuatum (Prévost and Des Murs). Prevost's Ground-Sparrow.

Pyrgita biarcuata Prévost and Des Murs, 1846, Voy. Venus, Atlas, Zool., Ois., pl. 6. (No locality given = Guatemala.)

Habitat.—Tropical Deciduous Forest, Montane Evergreen Forest Edge, Secondary Forest (600–1800 m; Subtropical and lower Temperate zones).

Distribution.—*Resident* [*biarcuatum* group] in the highlands of Chiapas, Guatemala, El Salvador, and western Honduras (east to the Sula and Comayagua valleys); and [*cabanisi* group] in central Costa Rica (Aguacate Mountains east to Turrialba).

Notes.—Groups: *M. biarcuatum* [Prevost's Ground-Sparrow] and *M. cabanisi* (Sclater and Salvin, 1868) [White-faced Ground-Sparrow]. See comments under *M. kieneri.*

Melozone leucotis Cabanis. White-eared Ground-Sparrow.

Melozone leucotis Cabanis, 1861, J. Ornithol. 8(1860): 413. (Costa Rica.)

Habitat.—Montane Evergreen Forest Edge (500–2000 m; upper Tropical to Temperate zones).

Distribution.—*Resident* in the highlands (primarily on the Pacific slope) of southeastern Chiapas, Guatemala, El Salvador, north-central Nicaragua, and central Costa Rica (Cordillera de Tilarán and central highlands).

Genus *PIPILO* Vieillot

Pipilo Vieillot, 1816, Analyse, p. 32. Type, by monotypy, "Pinson aux yeux rouges" Buffon = *Fringilla erythrophthalma* Linnaeus.
Chlorura Sclater, 1862, Cat. Collect. Amer. Birds, p. 117. Type, by monotypy, *Fringilla chlorura* Audubon.
Oreospiza (not Keitel, 1857) Ridgway, 1896, Man. N. Amer. Birds, ed. 2, p. 439. Type, by monotypy, *Fringilla chlorura* Audubon.
Oberholseria Richmond, 1915, Proc. Biol. Soc. Wash. 28: 180. New name for *Oreospiza* Ridgway, preoccupied.

Notes.—The generic name *Hortulanus* Vieillot, 1807, sometimes used for *Pipilo,* has no standing (Banks and Browning 1995).

Pipilo chlorurus (Audubon). Green-tailed Towhee.

Fringilla chlorura Audubon, 1839, Ornithol. Biogr. 5: 336. (No locality given = Ross' Creek, ca. 20 miles southwest Blackfoot, Bingham County, Idaho.)

Habitat.—Chaparral, brushy hillsides, riparian scrub, primarily in mountains in breeding season; to lowland habitats in nonbreeding season.

Distribution.—*Breeds* from southwestern and central Oregon, southeastern Washington, southern Idaho, southwestern and south-central Montana, northwestern and southeastern Wyoming, and north-central Colorado south to southern California (primarily interior mountains), northern Baja California, southern Nevada, central Arizona, southern New Mexico, and western Texas (Davis Mountains, presumably breeding; casually in Chisos Mountains).

Winters from southern (casually central) California, southern Arizona, southern New Mexico, and western and central Texas south to southern Baja California, Jalisco, Guanajuato, Querétaro, Morelos, Hidalgo, San Luis Potosí, and Tamaulipas.

Migrates east through western Nebraska, western Kansas, western Oklahoma, and west-central Texas.

Casual north to southwestern British Columbia, southern Saskatchewan, and northern Manitoba, and over most of eastern North America from Minnesota, Wisconsin, northern Michigan, southern Ontario, southwestern Quebec, New Hampshire, Maine, and Nova Scotia south to Louisiana, Mississippi, Alabama, Georgia, Florida, Cuba, and Cayo Coco; a sight report for central Oaxaca.

Notes.—Often treated in the monotypic genus *Chlorura* (or *Oberholseria*), but see Sibley (1955).

Pipilo ocai (Lawrence). Collared Towhee.

> *Buarremon Ocai* Lawrence, 1865, Ann. Lyc. Nat. Hist. N. Y. 8: 126. (Jalapa, Mexico = Las Vigas, west of Jalapa, Veracruz.)

Habitat.—Pine-Oak Forest Edge, Montane Evergreen Forest Edge, Second-growth Scrub (1500–3750 m; Subtropical and Temperate zones).

Distribution.—*Resident* in the mountains from western Jalisco and extreme northeastern Colima southeast through north-central Michoacán, Guerrero (Sierra Madre del Sur), and eastern Puebla to west-central Veracruz and central Oaxaca (west of the Isthmus of Tehuantepec).

Notes.—Hybridizes extensively with *P. maculatus* in western portions of the range but on a limited basis or not at all in the eastern portions (Sibley 1954, Sibley and West 1959).

Pipilo maculatus Swainson. Spotted Towhee.

> *Pipilo maculata* Swainson, 1827, Philos. Mag., new ser., 1, p. 434. (Real del Monte, [Hidalgo], Mexico.)

Habitat.—Open woodland, chaparral, scrub-oak, and riparian thickets (Subtropical and Temperate Zones).

Distribution.—*Breeds* [*maculatus* group] from southern British Columbia (including Vancouver Island), southern Alberta, and southern Saskatchewan south to southern California (including Santa Cruz, Santa Rosa, Santa Catalina, and San Clemente islands), northwestern Baja California (also mountains of southern Baja California and, formerly, Guadalupe Island), southern Nevada, west-central and southern Arizona, and through the Mexican highlands to Chiapas and central Guatemala, and east to the central Dakotas, central Nebraska, eastern Colorado, eastern New Mexico, and extreme western Texas.

Winters [*maculatus* group] from southern British Columbia, Nevada, Utah, Colorado, Nebraska, and Iowa (casually farther north) south to northern Baja California (also in mountains of southern Baja California), northern Sonora, through the Mexican breeding range to central Guatemala, and east to central Oklahoma and south-central Texas.

Resident [*socorroensis* group] on Socorro Island, in the Revillagigedo Islands, off western Mexico.

Casual [*maculatus* group] in southeastern Alaska and northern Manitoba, and east to Ontario, Minnesota, Iowa, Illinois, Michigan, Ohio, Pennsylvania, Massachusetts, New York, New Jersey, Arkansas, Louisiana, and Alabama. A record from the British Isles may pertain to an escaped cage-bird.

Notes.—Formerly considered conspecific with *P. erythrophthalmus* (Sibley and West 1959) but see A.O.U. (1995). The Socorro Island form has been treated as a distinct species *P. socorroensis* Grayson, 1867 [Socorro Towhee], but see Mayr and Short (1970: 82). See also comments under *P. ocai*.

Pipilo erythrophthalmus (Linnaeus). Eastern Towhee.

> *Fringilla erythrophthalma* Linnaeus, 1758, Syst. Nat., ed. 10, 1: p. 180. Based on the "Towhee-bird" Catesby, Nat. Hist. Carolina 1, p. 34, pl. 34. (in America = South Carolina.)

Habitat.—Dense second growth, undergrowth of open woodland, forest edge (Temperate zone).

Distribution.—*Breeds* from southeastern Saskatchewan, southern Manitoba, northeastern North Dakota, northern Minnesota, northern Wisconsin, northern Michigan, southern Ontario, southwestern Quebec, northern New York, Vermont, central New Hampshire, and southwestern Maine south to extreme northeastern Texas (at least formerly), northern and eastern Arkansas, northeastern and south-central Louisiana, the Gulf coast (from Mississippi eastward), and southern Florida (excluding the Florida Keys), and west to northeastern Colorado, western Iowa, southeastern Nebraska, eastern Kansas, and eastern Oklahoma.

Winters from eastern Colorado (rare), southeastern Nebraska, Iowa, the southern Great Lakes region, southern New York, and Massachusetts (rarely farther north) south to southern Texas, the Gulf coast, and southern Florida (rarely the Florida Keys).

Casual north to northern Ontario, southern Quebec, New Brunswick, Prince Edward Island, Nova Scotia, and Newfoundland, and west to Montana and Colorado. Accidental in the British Isles.

Notes.—*Pipilo erythrophthalmus* and *P. maculatus* were formerly considered conspecific [Rufous-sided Towhee], but see A.O.U. (1995).

Pipilo albicollis Sclater. White-throated Towhee.

> *Pipilo albicollis* Sclater, 1858, Proc. Zool. Soc. London, p. 304. (San Miguel de las Peras, Oaxaca, Southern Mexico.)

Habitat.—Arid Montane Scrub, Pine-Oak Forest (1150–2800 m; Subtropical and Temperate zones).

Distribution.—*Resident* in the interior valleys of eastern Guerrero, southern Puebla, and central Oaxaca (west of the Isthmus of Tehuantepec).

Notes.—*Pipilo rutilus* W. Deppe, 1830, sometimes used for this species, is now regarded as a synonym of *P. fuscus.*

Pipilo fuscus Swainson. Canyon Towhee.

> *Pipilo fuscus* Swainson, 1827, Philos. Mag. (n.s.) 1: 434. (Temiscaltepec, Mexico = Temascaltepec, México.)

Habitat.–Brushlands, arid scrub, mesquite, riparian thickets, and around human habitation.

Distribution.—*Resident* from northern Arizona, central and northeastern New Mexico, southeastern Colorado, extreme northwestern Oklahoma, and western and central Texas south to northern Sinaloa (including Isla Tiburón, off Sonora), and in the Mexican highlands to northwestern Oaxaca, west-central Veracruz, Puebla, and southwestern Tamaulipas.

Casual in northwestern Wyoming, southwestern Kansas, and southern Texas.

Notes.–See comments under *P. crissalis. Pipilo fuscus* is more closely related to *P. albicollis* than to *P. crissalis* (Zink 1988, Zink and Dittmann 1991).

Pipilo crissalis (Vigors). California Towhee.

> *Fringilla crissalis* Vigors, 1839, in Beechey, Zool. Voy. "Blossom", p. 19. (No locality given = Monterey, Monterey County, California.)

Habitat.—Chaparral, brush, riparian thickets, and suburbs.

Distribution.—*Resident* from southwestern Oregon south through California (from the western slopes of the Sierra Nevada and Argus Range westward, and west of the southeastern desert region) to southern Baja California.

Accidental on Todos Santos Island, off Baja California.

Notes.–Molecular and morphometric studies indicate that *P. crissalis* is distinct from *P. fuscus,* with which it was previously merged, and more closely related to *P. aberti* than to *P. fuscus* (Zink 1988, Zink and Dittmann 1991); *P. crissalis* and *P. fuscus* also differ also in vocalizations (Davis 1951, Marshall 1964).

Pipilo aberti Baird. Abert's Towhee.

> *Pipilo aberti* Baird, 1852, in Stansbury, Explor. Valley Great Salt Lake Utah, p. 325. ("New Mexico" = Gila Bend, Maricopa County, Arizona.)

Habitat.—Riparian Thickets, Arid Lowland Scrub (0–1250 m).

Distribution.—*Resident* from southeastern California (west to Salton Sea), extreme southern Nevada, southwestern Utah, central and southern Arizona, and southwestern New Mexico south to northeastern Baja California and northwestern Sonora.

Genus *AIMOPHILA* Swainson

> *Aimophila* Swainson, 1837, Class. Birds 2: 287. Type, by subsequent designation (G. R. Gray, 1840), *Aimophila rufescens* (Swainson) = *Pipilo rufescens* Swainson.

Notes.—Relationships within this genus are poorly understood, and it is probably polyphyletic as now constituted (Wolf 1977 and references therein). See comments under *Amphispiza*. The classification presented here follows the proposed phylogeny of Wolf (1977), with four clades of species: (1) *ruficauda-humeralis-mystacalis-sumichrasti-carpalis*; (2) *cassinii-botterii-aestivalis*; (3) *ruficeps-notosticta-rufescens*; and (4) *quinquestriata*.

Aimophila ruficauda (Bonaparte). Stripe-headed Sparrow.

Chondestes ruficauda Bonaparte, 1853, C. R. Acad. Sci. Paris 37: 918. (Nicaragua.)

Habitat.—Arid Lowland Scrub, Arid Montane Scrub, Tropical Deciduous Forest (0–2000 m; Tropical and lower Subtropical zones).

Distribution.—*Resident* along the Pacific slope from southern Durango and Nayarit south through Jalisco, Michoacán, Guerrero, Morelos, southern Puebla, Oaxaca, Chiapas, Guatemala (also in arid interior in Motagua Valley), El Salvador, Honduras, and Nicaragua to northwestern Costa Rica (Guanacaste).

Notes.—Also known as Russet-tailed Sparrow.

Aimophila humeralis (Cabanis). Black-chested Sparrow.

Haemophila humeralis (Lichtenstein MS) Cabanis, 1851, Mus. Heineanum 1: 132. (Mexico = Tehotepec, Puebla.)

Habitat.—Arid Lowland Scrub, Arid Montane Scrub (0–1500 m; Tropical and lower Subtropical zones).

Distribution.—*Resident* from southern Jalisco south through Colima, Michoacán, Guerrero, Morelos, and southern Puebla to extreme southwestern Oaxaca (near San José Estancia Grande).

Aimophila mystacalis (Hartlaub). Bridled Sparrow.

Zonotrichia mystacalis Hartlaub, 1852, Rev. Mag. Zool. (2)4: 3. (Rio Frio entre Puebla et la ville de Mexico = Río Frío, between Puebla and Mexico City.)

Habitat.—Arid Montane Scrub (900–1900 m; upper Tropical to lower Temperate zones).

Distribution.—*Resident* in the eastern portion of México, southwestern Morelos, southern Puebla, west-central Veracruz, and central Oaxaca (west of the Isthmus of Tehuantepec).

Aimophila sumichrasti (Lawrence). Cinnamon-tailed Sparrow.

Hæmophila sumichrasti Lawrence, 1871, Ann. Lyc. Nat. Hist. N. Y. 10: 6. (Tuchitan, Tehuantepec, Mexico = Juchitán, Oaxaca; Binford, 1989, Ornithol. Monogr. 43, p. 347.)

Habitat.—Arid Lowland Scrub, Tropical Deciduous Forest Edge (0–950 m; Tropical Zone).

Distribution.—*Resident* on the Pacific slope of Oaxaca (west to Rancho Las Animas) and extreme southwestern Chiapas.

Notes.—Also known as Sumichrast's Sparrow.

Aimophila carpalis (Coues). Rufous-winged Sparrow.

Peucæa carpalis Coues, 1873, Amer. Nat. 7: 322 (footnote). (Tucson, Ariz[ona].)

Habitat.—Arid Lowland Scrub, usually where grassy (0–1500 m; Subtropical Zone).

Distribution.—*Resident* from south-central Arizona (north to Tucson area) south through central and southeastern Sonora to central Sinaloa.

Aimophila cassinii (Woodhouse). Cassin's Sparrow.

Zonotrichia Cassinii Woodhouse, 1852, Proc. Acad. Nat. Sci. Philadelphia 6: 60. (near San Antonio, Texas.)

Habitat.—Northern Temperate Grassland, Arid Lowland Scrub (0–1800 m).

Distribution.—*Breeds* from southeastern Arizona, New Mexico (except the northwestern part of state), central and northeastern Colorado, central eastern Wyoming, southwestern Nebraska, west-central Kansas, and west-central Oklahoma south to northern Chihuahua, western San Luis Potosí, northern Tamaulipas, and central and southern Texas. In recent years singing males have appeared sporadically, sometimes in large numbers, from southern California east across southern Arizona, in northwestern New Mexico, and north to south-western South Dakota, although breeding has not been confirmed in these regions.

Winters from southeastern Arizona, southern New Mexico (rarely), Sonora, Chihuahua, and western and south-central Texas south to southern Sinaloa, Zacatecas, Guanajuato, San Luis Potosí, and Tamaulipas.

Casual or accidental in California (north to Humboldt County), southern Nevada, northern Illinois, Michigan, northern Indiana, southern Ontario, Nova Scotia, Maine, and New Jersey; a sight report for Missouri.

Aimophila aestivalis (Lichtenstein). Bachman's Sparrow.

Fringilla aestivalis Lichtenstein, 1823, Verz. Doubl. Zool. Mus. Berlin, p. 25. (Georgia.)

Habitat.—Open, grassy pine woods with scattered bushes or understory, brushy or over-grown hillsides, and overgrown fields with thickets and brambles.

Distribution.—*Breeds* from south-central Missouri, central and northeastern Illinois, central Indiana, central Ohio, southwestern Pennsylvania (now rarely), and central Maryland south to eastern Oklahoma, eastern Texas, the Gulf coast, and south-central Florida; now generally absent (or very local) as a breeding bird in the northeastern portion of the breeding range north of Tennessee and North Carolina.

Winters from eastern Texas, the Gulf states, and Atlantic coast (from southeastern North Carolina) south through the remainder of the breeding range (casually elsewhere in the northern parts of the breeding range), and to southern Florida.

Casual north to northeastern Kansas, southeastern Michigan, southern Ontario (Pt. Pelee; possibly breeding), New York, and New Jersey.

Notes.—Also known as Pine-woods Sparrow.

Aimophila botterii (Sclater). Botteri's Sparrow.

Zonotrichia botterii Sclater, 1858, Proc. Zool. Soc. London (1857), p. 214. (vicinity of Orizaba, [Veracruz,] in Southern Mexico.)

Habitat.—[*botterii* group] Northern Temperate Grassland (0–2000 m); [*petenica* group] Northern Temperate Grassland, Pine Forest, lowland pine savanna (0–1600 m); (Tropical and Subtropical zones).

Distribution.—*Breeds* [*botterii* group] from southeastern Arizona, extreme southwestern New Mexico (probably), eastern Sonora, Sinaloa, Durango, Zacatecas, San Luis Potosí, Tamaulipas, and southern coastal Texas (north to Kleberg and Nueces counties) south through Mexico to Chiapas.

Winters [*botterii* group] from northern Mexico south throughout the remainder of the breeding range.

Resident [*petenica* group] locally in Tabasco, Yucatán, Guatemala (lowlands of Petén, and central highlands), Belize, eastern Honduras, northwestern and northeastern Nicaragua, and northwestern Costa Rica (base of Cordillera de Guanacaste).

Casual [*botterii* group] in southern Texas just north of the breeding range.

Notes.—The two groups have sometimes been regarded as distinct species, *A. botterii* [Botteri's Sparrow] and *A. petenica* (Salvin, 1863) [Peten Sparrow]; extensive variability and apparent intergradation in Tabasco and Veracruz, and similarity in vocalizations, suggest strongly that a single species should be recognized (Wolf 1977).

Aimophila ruficeps (Cassin). Rufous-crowned Sparrow.

Ammodromus ruficeps Cassin, 1852, Proc. Acad. Nat. Sci. Philadelphia 6: 184. (Calaveras River [east of Stockton], California.)

Habitat.—Arid rocky and hilly regions with brush, scattered scrub or short trees, and grassy or weedy patches, also in Mexico in arid scrub and pine-oak association (Subtropical and lower Temperate zones).

Distribution.—*Resident* from central California (north to Mendocino and Tehama counties, and including Santa Cruz, Anacapa, and Santa Catalina islands, with an isolated colony in eastern San Bernardino County), southwestern Utah, northwestern and central Arizona, central and northeastern New Mexico, southeastern Colorado, western (locally west-central and southeastern) Oklahoma, north-central Texas, and west-central Arkansas south to southern Baja California (including Todos Santos Island), throughout Mexico to Oaxaca (west of the Isthmus of Tehuantepec), southern Puebla, west-central Veracruz, and southern Tamaulipas, and to western and central Texas.

Casual in southwestern Kansas and southeastern Texas.

Aimophila rufescens (Swainson). Rusty Sparrow.

Pipilo rufescens Swainson, 1827, Philos. Mag. (n.s.) 1: 434. (Temiscaltipec, Mexico = Temascaltepec, México.)

Habitat.—Arid Montane Scrub, Pine-Oak Forest, Tropical Deciduous Forest, lowland pine savanna (0–2700 m; Tropical to lower Temperate zones).

Distribution.—*Resident* from north-central and eastern Sonora, western Chihuahua, Sinaloa, northwestern Durango, Nayarit, Jalisco, Guanajuato, eastern San Luis Potosí, and southern Tamaulipas south through Middle America (except the Yucatan Peninsula) to north-central and northeastern Nicaragua and northwestern Costa Rica (base of Cordillera de Guanacaste).

Aimophila notosticta (Sclater and Salvin). Oaxaca Sparrow.

Peucæa notosticta Sclater and Salvin, 1868, Proc. Zool. Soc. London, p. 322. (Mexico = probably Puebla.)

Habitat.—Arid Montane Scrub (1500–1900 m; Subtropical Zone).

Distribution.—*Resident* in northwestern and central Oaxaca (east to Santiago Matatlán area) and probably adjacent southwestern Puebla.

Aimophila quinquestriata (Sclater and Salvin). Five-striped Sparrow.

Zonotrichia quinquestriata Sclater and Salvin, 1868, Proc. Zool. Soc. London, p. 323. (Mexico = Bolaños, Jalisco.)

Habitat.—Arid Montane Scrub; in winter, also to more open grassy areas (50–1850 m; Subtropical Zone; to Tropical Zone in winter).

Distribution.—*Breeds* from southeastern Arizona (very locally) south through southeastern Sonora and southwestern Chihuahua.

Winters in central Sonora, northern Sinaloa, and southwestern Chihuahua, probably farther south.

Resident in northern Jalisco.

Accidental off Mazatlán (Isla Pájaros), southern Sinaloa.

Notes.—Treated as a member of the genus *Amphispiza* by the A.O.U. (1983) based on unpublished data, but see Phillips and Phillips Farfan (1993). This species differs, however, from other *Aimophila* in juvenal plumage, molt pattern, plumage pattern, vocalizations, and habitat (Wolf 1977).

Genus *ORITURUS* Bonaparte

Oriturus Bonaparte, 1851, Consp. Gen. Avium 1(2): 469. Type, by subsequent designation (Bonaparte, 1856), *Oriturus mexicanus* Bonaparte = *Aimophila superciliosa* Swainson.

Oriturus superciliosus (Swainson). Striped Sparrow.

Aimophila superciliosa Swainson, 1838, Animals in Menageries, *in* Lardner, Cabinet Cyclopedia 98: 314, fig. 63e-g. (Mexico.)

Habitat.—Northern Temperate Grassland, Pine Forest, Pine-Oak Forest (2100–3300 m; upper Subtropical and Temperate zones).

Distribution.—*Resident* from eastern Sonora, Chihuahua, Durango, western Zacatecas, Aguascalientes, and San Luis Potosí south to western Oaxaca, Puebla, and west-central Veracruz.

Genus *TORREORNIS* Barbour and Peters

Torreornis Barbour and Peters, 1927, Proc. N. Engl. Zool. Club 9: 96. Type, by monotypy, *Torreornis inexpectata* Barbour and Peters.

Torreornis inexpectata Barbour and Peters. Zapata Sparrow.

Torreornis inexpectata Barbour and Peters, 1927, Proc. N. Engl. Zool. Club. 9: 96. (Santo Tomás, Peninsula de Zapata, Cuba.)

Habitat.—Arid Lowland Scrub.

Distribution.—*Resident* locally in southwestern Cuba (Ciénaga de Zapata area), southeastern Cuba (from Baitiquiri to near Imías and Cajobabo, Oriente province), and Cayo Coco (off northern Camagüey province).

Genus *SPIZELLA* Bonaparte

Spizella Bonaparte, 1831 (1832), G. Arcad. Sci. Lettr. Arti [Rome] 52: 205. Type, by original designation, *Fringilla pusilla* Wilson.

Spizella arborea (Wilson). American Tree Sparrow.

Fringilla arborea Wilson, 1810, Amer. Ornithol. 2: 123, pl. 16, fig. 3. (eastern Pennsylvania.)

Habitat.—Open willow, scrub, scrub conifers, and bogs; in migration and winter also in weedy fields, fence-rows, and brush.

Distribution.—*Breeds* from northern Alaska, northern Yukon, northern Mackenzie, Banks Island (probably), central interior Keewatin, northern Quebec, and Labrador south to southern Alaska (Bristol Bay, Alaska Peninsula, and Wrangell Mountains), south-central British Columbia, southeastern Yukon, southern Mackenzie, northern Alberta, northern Saskatchewan, northern Manitoba, northern Ontario, James Bay, central Quebec, and northern Newfoundland.

Winters from south-coastal and southeastern Alaska (rarely) and southern Canada (British Columbia east to New Brunswick, Prince Edward Island, and Nova Scotia) south to eastern Oregon, northeastern California, central Nevada, northern and east-central Arizona, central New Mexico, north-central Texas, Arkansas, Tennessee, and North Carolina, casually to coastal and southern California, southern New Mexico, southern Texas, Louisiana, Mississippi, Alabama, and South Carolina; sight reports for southwestern Arizona and northern Florida.

Migrates regularly throughout central and southern Canada (including Newfoundland), and rarely in eastern California. Accidental in California in summer.

Notes.—Formerly known in American literature as the Tree Sparrow.

Spizella passerina (Bechstein). Chipping Sparrow.

Fringilla passerina (Borkhausen MS) Bechstein, 1798, in Latham, Allg. Uebers. Vögel 3(2): 544, pl. 120, fig. 1. (Canada = City of Quebec, Quebec.)

Habitat.—Open coniferous forest (especially early second growth) and forest edge (especially pine), oak woodland, pine-oak association, and open woodland and parks; in migration and winter also in a variety of open woodland, and brushy and shrubby habitats (Tropical to Temperate zones).

Distribution.—*Breeds* from east-central and southeastern Alaska, central Yukon, central Mackenzie, northern Saskatchewan, northern Manitoba, northern Ontario, southern Quebec, and southwestern Newfoundland south to northern Baja California (Sierra San Pedro Mártir), southwestern and east-central California, southern Nevada, and central and southeastern Arizona, through the highlands of Mexico and northern Central America to north-central Nicaragua, in the Caribbean lowland pine savanna of Guatemala, Belize, eastern Honduras, and northeastern Nicaragua, and to central and eastern Texas, the Gulf coast, and northwestern Florida.

Winters from central California, southern Nevada, central Arizona, central New Mexico, northern Texas, southern Oklahoma, Arkansas, Tennessee, Virginia, and southern New England (casually farther north) south throughout Mexico to the Isthmus of Tehuantepec, throughout the breeding range from Oaxaca and Chiapas southward, and to the Gulf coast and southern Florida, casually to the northern Bahama Islands.

Migrates rarely but regularly, at least in fall, through Bermuda.

Casual or accidental in northern Alaska, the Queen Charlotte Islands, northern Newfoundland, Costa Rica, and Cuba.

Spizella pallida (Swainson). Clay-colored Sparrow.

> *Emberiza pallida* Swainson, 1832, in Swainson and Richardson, Fauna Bor.-Amer. 2 (1831): 251. (Carlton-house, Saskatchewan.)

Habitat.—Shrubby areas and thickets, especially near water, tall brush in meadows, bushy openings or burns in open coniferous or deciduous forest, and dry pastures with a few shrubs; in migration and winter also in brushy and weedy fields, fence-rows, and arid scrub.

Distribution.—*Breeds* from west-central and southern Mackenzie, eastern British Columbia, northwestern and central Saskatchewan, northern Manitoba, and central and northeastern Ontario south to eastern Washington, southern Alberta, western Montana, northern and southeastern Wyoming, western Nebraska (casually), western Kansas (casually), northwestern Iowa, southern Wisconsin, northern Illinois, central and southeastern Michigan, southern Ontario, southwestern Quebec, and (sporadically) western New York.

Winters from southern Baja California, northern Sonora, southern Coahuila, central Nuevo León, and central Texas (casually farther north) south through Mexico (mostly in the highlands) to Oaxaca and Veracruz, casually to Chiapas and western Guatemala (Sacapulas).

Migrates through the Great Plains east to the Mississippi Valley, rarely west to southeastern Arizona and southern California, and rarely or casually (most frequently in fall) from New York, Maine, New Brunswick, Prince Edward Island, Nova Scotia, and Newfoundland south through Pennsylvania, West Virginia, and the Atlantic states to the Gulf coast, Florida, and South Carolina, and casually to the northern Pacific coast (southern British Columbia southward) and Cuba.

Casual in southeastern Alaska, southwestern British Columbia, Idaho, Bermuda, the Bahama Islands, and off Quintana Roo (Cozumel Island). Accidental in northern Alaska (Marsh Creek).

Spizella breweri Cassin. Brewer's Sparrow.

> *Spizella Breweri* Cassin, 1856, Proc. Acad. Nat. Sci. Philadelphia 8: 40. (western North America, California, and New Mexico = Black Hills, South Dakota.)

Habitat.—Brushland, especially sagebrush; in migration and winter also in desert scrub and creosote bush.

Distribution.—*Breeds* [*taverneri* group] from southwestern Yukon, northwestern British Columbia, and west-central Alberta south to mountains of coastal southern and southeastern British Columbia and southwestern Alberta; and [*breweri* group] from central southern British Columbia, southern Alberta, southwestern Saskatchewan and southwestern North Dakota south (generally east of the Cascades and the coast ranges) to eastern and southern California (to western Riverside County, Mt. Pinos, and the San Gabriel and San Bernardino mountains, formerly elsewhere), southern Nevada, central Arizona, northwestern New Mexico, Colorado (except southeast), southwestern Kansas, northwestern Nebraska, and southwestern South Dakota.

Winters [*breweri* group] from southern interior (casually central and coastal) California, southern Nevada, western and central Arizona, southern New Mexico, and western and central Texas south to southern Baja California and Sonora (including Isla Tiburón), in the Mexican highlands to Jalisco and Guanajuato; winter range [*taverneri* group] poorly known, recorded in migration from Arizona, New Mexico, and western Texas.

Migrates [*breweri* group] regularly through western Kansas and western Oklahoma.

Accidental [*breweri* group] in southeastern Alaska, southern Manitoba, Illinois, Nova Scotia, and Massachusetts, also a sight (and sound) report for Minnesota; and [*taverneri* group] in east-central Alaska.

Notes.—Differences in vocalizations, ecology, and morphology suggest that the two groups may be distinct species, *S. taverneri* Swarth and Brooks, 1925 [Timberline Sparrow] and *S. breweri* [Brewer's Sparrow] (J. Barlow, unpublished data; see also Doyle 1997).

Spizella pusilla (Wilson). Field Sparrow.

Fringilla pusilla Wilson, 1810, Amer. Ornithol. 2: 131, pl. 16, fig. 2. (Pennsylvania = Philadelphia.)

Habitat.—Old fields, brushy hillsides, overgrown pastures, thorn scrub, deciduous forest edge, sparse second growth, and fence-rows.

Distribution.—*Breeds* from eastern Montana, North Dakota (except northeastern), central Minnesota, north-central Wisconsin, northern Michigan, southeastern Saskatchewan, southern Ontario, southwestern Quebec, southern Maine, and southern New Brunswick (at least formerly) south to northeastern Colorado (ca, western Kansas, western Oklahoma, central and southern Texas (west to Irion County), the Gulf coast (east to north-central Florida), and southern Georgia; also in southern Manitoba (Winnipeg).

Winters from Kansas, Missouri, Illinois, southern Michigan, northern Ohio, Pennsylvania, central New York, and Massachusetts (casually farther north) south to southeastern New Mexico, northern Coahuila, central Nuevo León, northern Tamaulipas, the Gulf coast, and southern Florida.

Casual north to southeastern Quebec (including the Magdalen Islands), New Brunswick, Prince Edward Island, Nova Scotia, and Newfoundland, and west to Wyoming, eastern Colorado, California, Arizona, and central New Mexico, and on Bermuda; a sight report for Newfoundland.

Notes.—*Spizella pusilla* and *S. wortheni* constitute a superspecies (Sibley and Monroe 1990).

Spizella wortheni Ridgway. Worthen's Sparrow.

Spizella wortheni Ridgway, 1884, Proc. U. S. Natl. Mus. 7: 259. (Silver City, New Mexico.)

Habitat.—Arid Montane Scrub, mesquite-juniper and yucca-juniper grasslands (1200–2500 m; upper Tropical and Subtropical zones).

Distribution.—*Resident* in southeastern Coahuila and western Nuevo León, and, at least formerly, in central Chihuahua, northwestern and southeastern Zacatecas, and southwestern Tamaulipas; also formerly recorded (only during non-breeding season) in southern San Luis Potosí, northern Puebla, and west-central Veracruz.

Accidental in New Mexico (Silver City, 16 June 1884), the type specimen.

Notes.—See comments under *S. pusilla*.

Spizella atrogularis (Cabanis). Black-chinned Sparrow.

Spinites atrogularis Cabanis, 1851, Mus. Heineanum 1: 133. (Mexico.)

Habitat.—Chaparral, sagebrush, arid scrub, and brushy hillsides (Subtropical, and lower Temperate zones).

Distribution.—*Breeds* from north-central California, southern Nevada, southwestern Utah, central Arizona, central (rarely northeastern) New Mexico, western Texas (Guadalupe, and Chisos mountains), central Nuevo León, and southwestern Tamaulipas south to northern

Baja California, and in the Mexican highlands to Guerrero, Puebla, and northwestern Oaxaca (east to Asunción Nochixtlán).

Winters from coastal California (casually), southern Arizona, southern New Mexico, western Texas (sporadic), and Nuevo León south to southern Baja California, and through the remainder of the breeding range in Mexico.

Casual in southern Oregon; sight reports in winter from central Texas.

Genus *POOECETES* Baird

Pooecetes Baird, 1858, in Baird, Cassin, and Lawrence, Rep. Explor. Surv. R. R. Pac. 9: xx, xxxix [on pp. 439 and 447, as *"Poocætes"*]. Type, by monotypy, *Fringilla graminea* Gmelin.

Pooecetes gramineus (Gmelin). Vesper Sparrow.

Fringilla graminea Gmelin, 1789, Syst. Nat. 1(2): 922. Based on the "Grass Finch" Latham, Gen. Synop. Birds 2(1): 273. (in Noveboraco = New York.)

Habitat.—Plains, prairie, dry shrublands, savanna, weedy pastures, fields, sagebrush, arid scrub, and woodland clearings.

Distribution.—*Breeds* from central British Columbia, southern Mackenzie, northern Alberta, northwestern and central Saskatchewan, north-central Manitoba, central and (formerly) northeastern Ontario, south-central Quebec, New Brunswick, Prince Edward Island, and Nova Scotia south to western Oregon, northern and eastern California (to Del Norte, Inyo, and San Bernardino counties), central Nevada, southwestern Utah, northern and east-central Arizona, south-central New Mexico, Colorado, Missouri, eastern Tennessee, and North Carolina, generally local south of northern Illinois, central Ohio, and (east of the Appalachians) Maryland.

Winters from central California, southern Nevada, southwestern Utah, southern Arizona, southern New Mexico, western and north-central Texas, southern Oklahoma, Arkansas, southern Illinois (rarely), Kentucky (rarely), West Virginia, southern Pennsylvania, and Connecticut (casually farther north) south to southern Baja California, in the Mexican interior to Oaxaca, Veracruz, and Chiapas, and to southern Texas, the Gulf coast, and central Florida.

Casual in Yucatán, central Guatemala, southern Florida, the Bahama Islands (Grand Bahama), and Bermuda.

Genus *CHONDESTES* Swainson

Chondestes Swainson, 1827, Philos. Mag. (n.s.) 1: 435. Type, by monotypy, *Chondestes strigatus* Swainson = *Fringilla grammaca* Say.

Chondestes grammacus (Say). Lark Sparrow.

Fringilla grammaca Say, 1823, in Long, Exped. Rocky Mount. 1: 139. (Prairies on the Missouri between the Kansas and Platte = Bellefontaine, four miles from mouth of Missouri River, Missouri.)

Habitat.—Open situations with scattered bushes and trees, prairie, forest edge, cultivated areas, orchards, fields with bushy borders, and savanna.

Distribution.—*Breeds* from western Oregon, eastern Washington, southern interior British Columbia, southeastern Alberta, southern Saskatchewan, southern Manitoba, northwestern and central Minnesota, western Wisconsin, southern Michigan (formerly), central Ontario, Ohio, and central Pennsylvania (formerly) south to southern California (chiefly west of the Sierra Nevada), northern Baja California (probably), central Nevada, southern Arizona, northeastern Sonora, southern Chihuahua, Durango, Zacatecas, Nuevo León, northern Tamaulipas, southern and eastern Texas, Louisiana, central Alabama, south-central North Carolina, and western Virginia, with breeding very local and irregular east of the Mississippi Valley.

Winters from northern California, southern Arizona, southern New Mexico (rarely), north-central and eastern Texas and the Gulf coast (rarely to southern Florida) south through

Mexico to southern Baja California, Oaxaca, and Chiapas; casual farther north in western and interior North America and on the Atlantic coast from New York south.

Casual in southwestern British Columbia, and in the northeast from southern Quebec, New Brunswick, Nova Scotia, and Newfoundland southward, and south to Yucatán, Quintana Roo, Guatemala, El Salvador, Honduras, Cuba, Bermuda, and the northern Bahama Islands. Accidental in the British Isles. Sight reports from the Revillagigedo Islands (Socorro Island) and central Panama (Tocumen).

Genus *AMPHISPIZA* Coues

Amphispiza Coues, 1874, Birds Northwest (Misc. Publ. U. S. Geol. Surv. Terr.), p. 234. Type, by original designation, *Emberiza bilineata* Cassin.

Notes.—Sometimes merged in *Aimophila* (but see Paynter 1970).

Amphispiza bilineata (Cassin). Black-throated Sparrow.

Emberiza bilineata Cassin, 1850, Proc. Acad. Nat. Sci. Philadelphia 5: 103, pl. 3. (Texas, on the Rio Grande.)

Habitat.—Desert scrub, thorn brush, mesquite, and juniper; in migration and winter also occasionally in grassy areas and weedy fields away from desert regions (Tropical and Subtropical zones).

Distribution.—*Breeds* from eastern Washington, south-central and southeastern Oregon, southwestern Idaho, western and southern Colorado, extreme western Oklahoma, and north-central Texas south through eastern California (primarily Colorado, Mojave, and Great Basin deserts) to southern Baja California (including many islands), northern Jalisco, Guanajuato, Querétaro, Hidalgo, Tamaulipas, and central and southern Texas.

Winters from southeastern (casually central) California, southern Nevada, central and southeastern Arizona, southern New Mexico, and central and southern Texas south through the remainder of the breeding range.

Casual in western North America west and north of the breeding range from Washington, southern interior British Columbia, southern Alberta, and western Montana southward, and on the Los Coronados Islands. Recorded annually in coastal central and southern California. Casual or accidental in eastern North America (recorded in southern Saskatchewan, North Dakota, South Dakota, Nebraska, Iowa, Kansas, Missouri, Minnesota, Wisconsin, northern Illinois, Michigan, southern Ontario, Ohio, southern Quebec, New Jersey, Virginia, and north-central Florida).

Amphispiza belli (Cassin). Sage Sparrow.

Emberiza Belli Cassin, 1850, Proc. Acad. Nat. Sci. Philadelphia 5: 104, pl. 4. (California near Sonoma.)

Habitat.—[*nevadensis* group] Sagebrush and salt-bush (*Atriplex*) desert scrub; in migration and winter also in arid plains with sparse bushes, grasslands, and open situations with scattered brush; [*belli* group] chaparral (dominated by *Adenostoma fasciculatum* or *Artemesia californica*) and salt-bush desert scrub.

Distribution.—*Breeds* [*nevadensis* group] primarily in Great Basin from central interior Washington, eastern Oregon, southern Idaho, southwestern Wyoming, and northwestern Colorado south to eastern California (south to the Owens Valley), southern Nevada, southwestern Utah, northeastern Arizona, and northwestern New Mexico. One breeding record for eastern Montana.

Winters [*nevadensis* group] from southern California, central Nevada, southwestern Utah, northern Arizona, and central New Mexico south to central Baja California, northern Sonora, northern Chihuahua, and western Texas.

Resident [*belli* group] in western California (from Trinity County south, including San Clemente Island) to central Baja California; and also in San Joaquin Valley and Mojave Desert areas of east-central California. The latter populations (*A. b. canescens*) undergo post-breeding, up-slope migrations into coastal and Sierran foothills (Johnson and Marten 1992).

Casual [*nevadensis* group] in the Pacific coastal region from southwestern British Columbia southward, and to western Montana, eastern Wyoming, eastern Colorado, western Kansas, and western Oklahoma, and in Nova Scotia; a sight report for Nebraska.

Notes.—The two groups, *A. nevadensis* (Ridgway, 1873) [Sage Sparrow] and *A. belli* [Bell's Sparrow], differ in morphology, ecology, and genetics, and generally behave as reproductively isolated species in areas where both are found (Johnson and Marten 1992). In spite of the closer appearance of the subspecies *canescens* to *nevadensis, canescens* is more closely related to *bellii* (Johnson and Marten 1992). The two groups were treated as separate species by Rising (1996), but *canescens* was mistakenly placed in *nevadensis.*

Genus *CALAMOSPIZA* Bonaparte

Calamospiza Bonaparte, 1838, Geogr. Comp. List, p. 30. Type, by monotypy, *Fringilla bicolor* Townsend = *Calamospiza melanocorys* Stejneger.

Notes.—Paynter (1970) suggested that *Calamospiza* is closely related to the genus *Plectrophenax.*

Calamospiza melanocorys Stejneger. Lark Bunting.

Fringilla bicolor (not Linnaeus, 1766) J. K Townsend, 1837, J. Acad. Nat. Sci. Philadelphia 7: 189. (plains of Platte River = western Nebraska.)
Calamospiza melanocorys Stejneger, 1885, Auk 2: 49. New name for *Fringilla bicolor* Townsend, preoccupied.

Habitat.—Plains, prairies, meadows, and sagebrush; in migration and winter also in cultivated lands, brushy areas, and desert.

Distribution.—*Breeds* from southern Alberta, southern Saskatchewan, southwestern Manitoba (irregularly), and southeastern North Dakota south to eastern New Mexico, northern Texas (Panhandle), western Oklahoma (Panhandle), eastern Kansas, and northwestern Missouri; also casually in southern California (San Bernardino County), Utah, southwestern Colorado (Navajo Springs), northwestern New Mexico (Star Lake), and west-central Texas (northern Trans-Pecos and Edwards Plateau).

Winters from central California (casually), southern Nevada, central Arizona, southern New Mexico, north-central Texas, southwestern Kansas, and western Oklahoma south to southern Baja California, Jalisco, Guanajuato, Hidalgo, Tamaulipas, and southern and eastern Texas.

Casual elsewhere in western North America from central British Columbia, central Alberta, and northern Manitoba southward, and in eastern North America from Minnesota, Wisconsin, central Ontario, southern Quebec, New Brunswick, and Nova Scotia south to the Gulf coast and Florida.

Genus *PASSERCULUS* Bonaparte

Passerculus Bonaparte, 1838, Geogr. Comp. List, p. 33. Type, by subsequent designation (G. R. Gray, 1840), *Fringilla savanna* Wilson = *Emberiza sandwichensis* Gmelin.

Notes.—*Passerculus* is sometimes merged in *Ammodramus* (Paynter 1970), which is almost certainly the sister genus (Zink and Avise 1990).

Passerculus sandwichensis (Gmelin). Savannah Sparrow.

Emberiza sandwichensis Gmelin, 1789, Syst. Nat. 1(2): 875. Based on the "Sandwich Bunting" Latham, Gen. Synop. Birds 2(1): 202. (in Unalaschca et sinu Sandwich = Unalaska, Alaska.)

Habitat.—Open areas, especially grasslands, tundra, meadows, bogs, farmlands, grassy areas with scattered bushes, and marshes; [*beldingi* and *rostratus* groups] Saltwater/Brackish Marshes; (Subtropical and Temperate zones).

Distribution.—*Breeds* [*princeps* group] on Sable Island and the adjacent mainland of Nova Scotia; [*sandwichensis* group] from western and northern Alaska, northern Yukon, northern Mackenzie, northern Keewatin, northern Ontario, islands in James Bay, northern Quebec, northern Labrador, and Newfoundland south to southwestern Alaska (including Nunivak Island and the Aleutians west to Amukta), coastal regions of west-central California (Monterey region), the interior of east-central California (locally to San Bernardino County), southern Nevada, southern Utah, east-central Arizona, northern New Mexico, central Colorado, Nebraska, Iowa, Kentucky, eastern Tennessee, western Virginia, central Maryland, western North Carolina (possibly), southeastern Pennsylvania, and northern New Jersey, on the Pacific coast of Baja California from El Rosario south to Magdalena Bay, and locally in the interior highlands of Mexico from Chihuahua and Coahuila south to Guerrero and Puebla, and in southwestern Guatemala; and [*rostratus* group] from northeastern Baja California (San Felipe, mouth of the Colorado River) south along the coast of Sonora to northern Sinaloa (lat. 25° N.), probably also the San Benito Islands off the Pacific coast.

Winters [*princeps* group] along the Atlantic coast from central Nova Scotia south to northeastern Florida; [*sandwichensis* group] from southwestern British Columbia, southern Nevada, southwestern Utah, northern Arizona, central New Mexico, Kansas, Missouri, Tennessee, southern Kentucky, and, east of the Appalachians, from Massachusetts (casually north to Alaska, the northern United States, southern Ontario, and Nova Scotia) south to southern Baja California (including most adjacent islands), throughout most of Mexico (including the Yucatan Peninsula) to Guatemala, Belize, El Salvador, and northern Honduras, and to southern Texas, the Gulf coast, southern Florida, Bermuda, the Bahama Islands (south to Rum Cay), Cuba, the Isle of Pines, and Cayman and Swan islands; and [*rostratus* group] in salt marshes from central coastal and southern California (casually north to the San Mateo County and the Channel Islands) south to southern Baja California (along both coasts), and the coasts of Sonora and northern Sinaloa.

Resident [*beldingi* group] in salt marshes of coastal southern California (north to Santa Barbara region) and Baja California (including the Todos Santos Islands).

Casual or accidental [*sandwichensis* group] on St. Lawrence Island and in the Pribilofs and western Aleutians (Shemya), north to Seymour, Cornwallis, and Southampton islands, in the British Isles, and in northeastern Asia (Chukotski Peninsula, Koryak highlands) and Japan; sight reports for the Hawaiian Islands (Kure) and central Panama.

Notes.—Groups: *P. princeps* Maynard, 1872 [Ipswich Sparrow], *P. sandwichensis* [Savannah Sparrow], *P. beldingi* Ridgway, 1885 [Belding's Sparrow], and *P. rostratus* (Cassin, 1852) [Large-billed Sparrow]. The *rostratus* group appears to be genetically distinct (Zink et al. 1991), but more study needs to be done on the populations in Baja California.

Genus *AMMODRAMUS* Swainson

Ammodramus Swainson, 1827, Philos. Mag. (n.s.) 1: 435. Type, by monotypy, *Ammodramus bimaculatus* Swainson = *Fringilla savannarum* Gmelin.

Centronyx Baird, 1858, in Baird, Cassin, and Lawrence, Rep. Explor. Surv. R. R. Pac. 9: 440. Type, by monotypy, *Emberiza bairdii* Audubon.

Ammospiza Oberholser, 1905, Smithson. Misc. Collect. 48: 68. Type, by original designation, *Oriolus caudacutus* Gmelin.

Passerherbulus "Maynard" Stone, 1907, Auk 24: 193. Type, by original designation, *Ammodramus lecontei* Audubon = *Emberiza leconteii* Audubon.

Thryospiza Oberholser, 1917, Ohio J. Sci. 17: 332. Type, by original designation, *Fringilla maritima* Wilson.

Nemospiza Oberholser, 1917, Ohio J. Sci. 17: 335. Type, by original designation, *Emberiza henslowii* Audubon.

Notes.—Generic limits within this group have been treated in a variety of ways, and the genus may not be monophyletic. The linear sequence below is based on the phylogeny proposed by Zink and Avise (1990). See comments under each species and also under *Passerculus*.

Ammodramus savannarum (Gmelin). Grasshopper Sparrow.

Fringilla Savannarum Gmelin, 1789, Syst. Nat. 1(2): 921. Based on the "Savanna Finch" Latham, Gen. Synop. Birds 2(1): 270. (in Jamaicae = Jamaica.)

Habitat.—Prairie, old fields, open grasslands, cultivated fields, and savanna (Tropical to Temperate zones).

Distribution.—*Breeds* from eastern Washington, southern interior British Columbia, southern Alberta, southern Saskatchewan, southern Manitoba, western and southern Ontario, southwestern Quebec, northern Vermont, central New Hampshire, and southern Maine south to southern California (west of the Sierra Nevada), central Nevada (rare and local), northern Utah, eastern Colorado, eastern New Mexico, northern Texas, Arkansas, northern and east-central Mississippi, central Alabama, central Georgia, central North Carolina, and south-eastern Virginia, and from southeastern Arizona, southwestern New Mexico, and south-central Texas south to northern Sonora and northern Chihuahua; also in central peninsular Florida (primarily Kissimmee Prairie region). Populations are declining and distribution is shrinking in eastern parts of the range.

Winters from central (casually northern) California, southern Arizona, southern New Mexico (rarely), Texas, central Missouri (rarely), Tennessee, and North Carolina (casually farther north) south through Mexico and northern Central America to north-central Costa Rica, and in the Bahamas (south to San Salvador), Cuba, and the Isle of Pines.

Resident locally in Middle America in Veracruz, Chiapas, Guatemala (Petén, Izabál), Belize, Honduras (interior highlands and eastern pine savanna), northwestern Costa Rica, and Panama (Pacific lowlands in western Chiriquí, eastern Coclé and eastern Panamá province); in the Greater Antilles (Jamaica, Hispaniola, and Puerto Rico, including Vieques Island); and in western Colombia (Cauca Valley), western Ecuador (formerly), and the Netherlands Antilles (Curaçao and Bonaire).

Casual elsewhere west to the Pacific coast from southwestern British Columbia southward, and east to New Brunswick, Prince Edward Island, Nova Scotia, and Newfoundland; also on Bermuda (regular in fall), in the Swan Islands, and northwestern Panama (Bocas del Toro).

Ammodramus bairdii (Audubon). Baird's Sparrow.

> *Emberiza Bairdii* Audubon, 1844, Birds Amer. (octavo ed.) 7: 359, pl. 500. (Prairie of the upper Missouri = near Old Fort Union, North Dakota.)

Habitat.—Short-grass prairie with scattered low bushes and matted vegetation; in migration and winter also in open grasslands and overgrown fields.

Distribution.—*Breeds* from southern Alberta, southern Saskatchewan, and southern Manitoba south to central and eastern Montana, northern South Dakota, and southeastern North Dakota.

Winters from southeastern Arizona, southern New Mexico (casually), and the high-plains grasslands of Trans-Pecos Texas south to northern Sonora, Durango, Chihuahua, and Coahuila.

Migrates through the Plains states from western Kansas east to western Minnesota, and south through eastern and southern New Mexico, and casually west to western Montana. Many sight records refer to misidentified Savannah Sparrows.

Accidental or casual in California (Farallon Islands, San Diego), southern Texas, Oklahoma, Wisconsin, New York (Montauk), and Maryland (Ocean City); a sight report for Ohio.

Ammodramus henslowii (Audubon). Henslow's Sparrow.

> *Emberiza Henslowii* Audubon, 1829, Birds Amer. (folio) 1: pl. 70 (1831, Ornithol. Biogr. 1: 360). (opposite Cincinnati, in state of Kentucky.)

Habitat.—Open fields and meadows with grass interspersed with weeds or shrubby vegetation, especially in damp or low-lying areas; in migration and winter also in grassy areas adjacent to pine woods or second-growth woodland.

Distribution.—*Breeds* from southeastern South Dakota (at least formerly), southeastern Minnesota, north-central Wisconsin, northern Michigan, southern Ontario, northern New York, and southern Quebec (casually New England) south to central Kansas, northeastern Oklahoma, southwestern and central Missouri, southern Illinois, northern Kentucky, central West Virginia, eastern Virginia, northern Tennessee (rarely), and central and eastern North

Carolina; also (at least formerly) in eastern Texas (Harris County). The breeding range in the northwestern and eastern portions has decreased in recent years.

Winters in coastal states from South Carolina south to southern Florida, and west to Arkansas and southeastern Texas, casually north to Illinois, Indiana, and New England, and casually south to southern Texas.

Sight reports for Colorado, North Dakota, New Brunswick, Nova Scotia, and the Bahama Islands.

Notes.—Formerly placed in the genus *Passerherbulus*.

Ammodramus leconteii (Audubon). Le Conte's Sparrow.

> *Fringilla caudacuta* (not *Oriolus caudacutus* Gmelin) Latham, 1790, Index Ornithol. 1: 459. (in Georgiæ americanæ interioribus = interior of Georgia.)
>
> *Emberiza le conteii* Audubon, 1844, Birds Amer. (octavo ed.) 7: 338, pl. 488. (wet portions of prairies of upper Missouri = Fort Union, North Dakota.)

Habitat.—Moist grass or sedge meadows, damp matted grass and shrubby tangles on edges of marshes and bogs, and areas of moist or dry, tall, rank grass; in migration and winter also in weedy fields, broomsedge, and cattails.

Distribution.—*Breeds* from northeastern British Columbia, southern Mackenzie, northern Alberta, northern Saskatchewan, central Manitoba, north-central Ontario, and west-central Quebec south to southern Alberta, northwestern and northeastern Montana, southern Saskatchewan, North Dakota (except southwestern), central Minnesota, northern Wisconsin, and northern Michigan, casually south to southeastern South Dakota, northeastern Illinois (formerly), and southern Ontario.

Winters from west-central Kansas (rarely), southern Missouri, central Illinois (rarely), southern Indiana (rarely), western Tennessee, central Alabama, south-central Georgia, and South Carolina south to eastern New Mexico (rarely), eastern and southern Texas, the Gulf coast, and Florida.

Migrates regularly through the Great Plains (east to the Mississippi Valley), irregularly through the Great Lakes region and Ohio Valley, and casually to the east coast from Maine southward.

Casual north to Nova Scotia and southern Yukon, west to south-coastal British Columbia, Washington, Oregon, and California, and south to Arizona and Coahuila (Sabinas).

Notes.—In the past usually treated in the literature as *Passerherbulus caudacutus* (Latham, 1790) or *Ammospiza leconteii* (Murray 1968). Its closest relatives are *A. caudacutus, A. nelsoni,* and *A. maritimus* (Zink and Avise 1990).

Ammodramus nelsoni Allen. Nelson's Sharp-tailed Sparrow.

> *Ammodramus caudacutus* var. *nelsoni* Allen, 1875, Proc. Bost. Soc. Nat. Hist., 17, p. 293. (Calumet marshes, Cook Co., n.e. Illinois.)

Habitat.—Freshwater marshes and wet meadows in interior and brackish marshes along coast; in winter in salt and brackish marshes.

Distribution.—*Breeds* from northeastern British Columbia, southern Mackenzie, northern Alberta, central Saskatchewan, and northern Manitoba south to south-central Alberta, southern Saskatchewan, northeastern Montana, southern Manitoba, North Dakota (except southwestern), southeastern South Dakota (probably), northwestern and central Minnesota, and central Wisconsin (probably); in northern Ontario and northwestern Quebec near Hudson Bay and around James Bay; and in southern Quebec (along the St. Lawrence River from Lac St. Pierre eastward), and along the Atlantic coast from eastern Quebec (including the Magdalen Islands), New Brunswick, Prince Edward Island, and Nova Scotia south to southern Maine (Scarborough Marsh, Popham Beach).

Winters in coastal marshes along the mid- to south Atlantic coast south to southern Florida, along the Gulf coast west to southern Texas and northern Tamaulipas, and rarely in coastal California.

Migrates presumably through the interior United States, rarely but regularly through the Great Lakes region but casually elsewhere from Colorado and the Great Plains east to

Michigan, western Pennsylvania, and central New York, and casually in the west away from coastal areas.

Casual in northern Baja California; a sight report for northeastern Washington. A report from the Yucatan Peninsula is erroneous.

Notes.—Often treated in the genus *Ammospiza* (Murray 1968). See notes under *A. caudacutus*.

Ammodramus caudacutus (Gmelin). Saltmarsh Sharp-tailed Sparrow.

> *Oriolus caudacutus* Gmelin, 1788, Syst. Nat. 1 (1), p. 394. Based mainly on the "Sharp-tailed Oriole" Latham, Gen. Synop. Birds 1 (2), p. 448. (in Noveboraco = New York.)

Habitat.—Salt marshes.

Distribution.—*Breeds* along the Atlantic coast from southern Maine (Scarborough, Popham Beach) south to North Carolina (Pea Island).

Winters in coastal marshes from New York (casually from Massachusetts) south to the central east coast of Florida, rarely on the eastern Gulf coast.

Casual in coastal Texas.

Notes.— Often treated in the genus *Ammospiza* (Murray 1968). This and the previous species have been considered conspecific but differ in morphology, song, and habitat, with overlap in a secondary contact zone in southern Maine (Greenlaw 1993, Rising and Avise 1993).

Ammodramus maritimus (Wilson). Seaside Sparrow.

> *Fringilla maritima* Wilson, 1811, Amer. Ornithol. 4: 68, pl. 34, fig. 2. (sea islands along our Atlantic coast = Great Egg Harbor, New Jersey.)

Habitat.—Salt marshes, especially *Spartina* grass, rushes, and tidal reeds, also [*mirabilis* group] marsh prairie *(Muhlenbergia)*.

Distribution.—*Breeds* [*maritimus* group] from southern New Hampshire and Massachusetts south along the Atlantic coast to northeastern Florida (south to the St. John's River, formerly to New Smyrna Beach); and along the Gulf coast from western Florida (south to Tampa Bay) west to southeastern Texas (south to Corpus Christi area).

Winters [*maritimus* group] along the Atlantic coast from Massachusetts south through the remainder of the breeding range, casually to southern Florida (Flamingo region); and along the Gulf coast throughout the breeding range and south to the mouth of the Rio Grande.

Resident [*nigrescens* group] formerly along the coast of east-central Florida (eastern Orange and northern Brevard counties), now extinct; and [*mirabilis* group] in southern Florida (southwestern Collier, Monroe, and southern Dade counties).

Casual [*maritimus* group] north to Maine (possibly breeding in southern Maine), southern New Brunswick, and Nova Scotia, and inland in North Carolina (Raleigh).

Notes.—Groups: *A. maritimus* [Common Seaside-Sparrow], *A. nigrescens* Ridgway, 1873 [†Dusky Seaside-Sparrow], and *A. mirabilis* (Howell, 1919) [Cape Sable Sparrow or Cape Sable Seaside-Sparrow]. Often treated in the genus *Ammospiza*.

Genus *XENOSPIZA* Bangs

> *Xenospiza* Bangs, 1931, Proc. N. Engl. Zool. Club 12: 86. Type, by original designation, *Xenospiza baileyi* Bangs.

Notes.—Sometimes merged in *Ammodramus* (e.g., Paynter 1970).

Xenospiza baileyi Bangs. Sierra Madre Sparrow.

> *Xenospiza baileyi* Bangs, 1931, Proc. N. Engl. Zool. Club 12: 87. (Bolaños, Jalisco, Mexico.)

Habitat.—Pine Forest, Northern Temperate Grassland (2400–3050 m; upper Subtropical and Temperate zones).

Distribution.—*Resident* in the highlands of Durango, Jalisco, Morelos, and the Distrito Federal.

Genus *PASSERELLA* Swainson

Passerella Swainson, 1837, Class. Birds 2: 288. Type, by monotypy, *P. iliaca* Wilson, iii. 22. f. 4 = *Fringilla iliaca* Merrem.

Notes.—Some authors (e.g., Paynter 1964b, 1970) merge *Passerella* and *Melospiza* in *Zonotrichia*. A broader generic concept would merge these also in *Junco* (see Mayr and Short 1970: 85). See Zink (1982) for rationale for retaining them as separate genera, and for support for the monophyly of *Zonotrichia* and *Melospiza*.

Passerella iliaca (Merrem). Fox Sparrow.

Fringilla iliaca Merrem, 1786, Avium Rar. Icones Descr. 2: 37, pl. 10. (North America = Quebec.)

Habitat.—Undergrowth of deciduous or coniferous forest, forest edge, woodland thickets, scrub, cut-over lands, chaparral, riparian woodland, streamside undergrowth, low willow and alder thickets, and montane brushland; in migration and winter a variety of wooded habitats with dense thickets.

Distribution.—Breeds [*iliaca* group] from northwestern and interior Alaska, northern Yukon, northwestern and central eastern Mackenzie, northern Manitoba, northern Ontario, northern Quebec, and northern Labrador south to southwestern and southern interior Alaska, northern, central interior, and southeastern British Columbia (Mount Revelstoke), southwestern and central Alberta, central Saskatchewan, southern Manitoba, north-central Ontario, southeastern Quebec, and southern Newfoundland; [*unalaschensis* group] on the eastern Aleutian Islands (west to Unalaska), the Shumagin and Semidi islands, the Alaska Peninsula, the Kodiak Island group, the Kenai Peninsula, southeastern Alaska, and the coastal districts of British Columbia (including the Queen Charlotte Islands) south to northwestern Washington (Destruction Island, Lopez Island); [*schistacea* group] southeastern British Columbia (Crowsnest Pass), southwestern Alberta (Waterton Lakes Park), northern Idaho, and western Montana south through the mountains of north-central and eastern Oregon to extreme central eastern California (White Mountains), central Nevada (Shoshone, Toyabe, and Monitor mountains), northeastern Nevada, northern Utah (Raft River, Deep Creek, and Wasatch mountains) southwestern Wyoming, and central Colorado; and [*megarhyncha* group] in the mountains from southwestern and south-central British Columbia south through central and eastern Washington, central and southern Oregon through northern California in the northern and inner Coast Ranges and in the Sierra Nevada to the Mono Lake district and the mountains of southern California (Mount Pinos, San Gabriel, San Bernardino, and San Jacinto mountains).

Winters [*iliaca* group] in Pacific Coastal region (rare) from Washington south to northwestern Baja California, and from southern Minnesota, southern Wisconsin, southern Michigan, southern Ontario, northern Vermont, Maine, and southern New Brunswick south to southern Texas, Louisiana, Mississippi, Alabama, and southern Florida, and casually to rarely in interior California and southern Arizona; [*unalaschensis* group] in Pacific coastal region from central British Columbia south through Washington and Oregon to southern California, rarely to northwestern Baja California; [*schistacea* group] from northern interior California, central Arizona, and northern New Mexico south to southern California, northern Baja California, southern Arizona and western Texas; and [*megarhyncha* group] central California south to southern California, northern Baja California, and southern Arizona.

Migrates regularly throughout eastern North America between the breeding and wintering ranges.

Casual or accidental [*iliaca* group] in Bermuda, Greenland, and Europe, and [*unalaschensis* group] Japan.

Notes.—Groups: *P. iliaca* [Red Fox-Sparrow], *P. unalaschensis* (Gmelin, 1789) [Sooty Fox-Sparrow], *P. schistacea* Baird, 1858 [Slate-colored Fox-Sparrow], and *P. megarhyncha* Baird, 1858 [Thick-billed Fox-Sparrow]. Correspondence of genetic evidence and plumage types suggest that the groups may represent biological species, but there is at least limited hybridization among them, especially between the *schistacea* and *megarhyncha* groups (Zink 1986, 1991, 1994). Additional study is needed in areas of contact of members of the groups. Three of the four groups were treated as separate species by Rising (1996), who considered the *schistacea* and *megarhyncha* groups to be conspecific.

Genus *MELOSPIZA* Baird

Melospiza Baird, 1858, in Baird, Cassin, and Lawrence, Rep. Explor. Surv. R. R. Pac. 9: xx, xl, 440, 476. Type, by original designation, *Fringilla melodia* Wilson.

Heliospiza Baird, 1858, in Baird, Cassin, and Lawrence, Rep. Explor. Surv. R. R. Pac. 9: xx, xl, 476. Type, by original designation, *Fringilla palustris* Wilson = *Fringilla georgiana* Latham.

Notes.—See comments under *Passerella.*

Melospiza melodia (Wilson). Song Sparrow.

Fringilla melodia Wilson, 1810, Amer. Ornithol. 2: 125, pl. 16, fig. 4. (Canada to Georgia = Philadelphia, Pennsylvania.)

Habitat.—Brushy, shrubby, and deep grassy areas along watercourses and seacoasts, in marshes (cattail, bulrush, and salt), and, mostly in northern and eastern portions of the range, in forest, edge, bogs, brushy clearings, thickets, hedgerows, suburbs, and brushy pastures (upper Subtropical and Temperate zones).

Distribution.—*Breeds* from southern Alaska (including the Aleutians west to Attu), south-central Yukon, northern British Columbia, south-central Mackenzie, northern Saskatchewan, northern Manitoba, northern Ontario, south-central Quebec, and southwestern Newfoundland south to south-central Baja California and northern Sonora, locally in the Mexican highlands to Michoacán, México, Tlaxcala, and Puebla, and to northern New Mexico, northeastern Kansas, north-central Arkansas, southern Tennessee, northern Alabama, northern Georgia, and northwestern and coastal South Carolina.

Winters from southern Alaska (resident in the Aleutians), coastal and southern British Columbia, the northern United States, southern Ontario, southwestern Quebec, Prince Edward Island, and Nova Scotia south throughout the remainder of the breeding range, and to southern Texas, the Gulf coast, and southern Florida, rarely to Bermuda, northern Sonora, and northern Nuevo León.

Casual or accidental in the northern Bahama Islands, and in Norway and the British Isles.

Melospiza lincolnii (Audubon). Lincoln's Sparrow.

Fringilla Lincolnii Audubon, 1834, Birds Amer. (folio) 2: pl. 193. (Labrador = near mouth of Natashquan River, Quebec.)

Habitat.—Bogs, wet meadows, and riparian thickets, dry brushy clearings, mostly in northern and montane areas; in migration and winter also in brushy areas, thickets, hedgerows, understory of open woodland, forest edge, clearings, and scrubby areas.

Distribution.—*Breeds* from western and central Alaska, central Yukon, northwestern and southern Mackenzie, northern Saskatchewan, northern Manitoba, northern Ontario, northern Quebec, central Labrador, and Newfoundland south to south-coastal and southeastern Alaska, in the mountains to southern California (south to San Jacinto Mtns.), extreme west-central Nevada (absent as a breeding bird from most mountains in the Great Basin), east-central Arizona, and southern New Mexico, and to southwestern and south-central Alberta, central Saskatchewan, southern Manitoba, north-central and northeastern Minnesota, northern Wisconsin, central Michigan, southern Ontario, northern New York, northwestern Massachusetts, southern Vermont, northern New Hampshire, central Maine, New Brunswick, Prince Edward Island, and Nova Scotia.

Winters from southwestern British Columbia, California, southern Nevada, southwestern Utah, Arizona, central New Mexico, Oklahoma, eastern Kansas, Missouri, southern Kentucky, and northern Georgia (casually north to southern Alaska and the northern United States) south (casual Yucatan Peninsula) to southern Baja California, through northern Middle

America to El Salvador and Honduras, and to southern Texas, the Gulf coast, and central Florida, Bermuda (rare), casually to Costa Rica and Panama (east to the Canal area), southern Florida, the Bahama Islands (south to Little Inagua), and Cuba.

Migrates regularly throughout continental North America between the breeding and wintering ranges, and (rarely) through the Greater Antilles (east to Puerto Rico).

Accidental in Greenland.

Melospiza georgiana (Latham). Swamp Sparrow.

> *Fringilla georgiana* Latham, 1790, Index Ornithol. 1: 460. (in Georgiæ americanæ interioribus = interior of Georgia.)

Habitat.—Emergent vegetation around watercourses, marshes, bogs, and wet meadows; in migration and winter also in weedy fields, brush, thickets, scrub, and forest edge.

Distribution.—*Breeds* from west-central and southern Mackenzie, northern Saskatchewan, northern Manitoba, northern Ontario, central Quebec, southern Labrador, and Newfoundland south to east-central British Columbia, south-central Alberta, central Saskatchewan, southern Manitoba, the eastern Dakotas, central Nebraska, northern Missouri (formerly), northern Illinois, northern Indiana, central Ohio, southeastern West Virginia, Maryland, and Delaware.

Winters from Nebraska, Iowa, the Great Lakes region, central New York, and Massachusetts (casually farther north) south to western and southern Texas, the Gulf coast, and southern Florida, and, in smaller numbers, west across central and southern New Mexico and Utah (rarely) to southeastern Arizona and California, also south to northern Guerrero and central Veracruz, rarely west to Sonora, and on Bermuda.

Casual elsewhere in western North America from south-coastal and southeastern Alaska, southern British Columbia, and Montana southward, and in the Bahama Islands (New Providence, Exumas); a sight report for southern Yukon.

Genus *ZONOTRICHIA* Swainson

> *Zonotrichia* [subgenus] Swainson, 1832, in Swainson and Richardson, Fauna Bor.-Amer. 2 (1831): 254–257, 493. Type, by subsequent designation (Bonaparte, 1832), *Fringilla pensylvanica* Latham = *Fringilla albicollis* Gmelin.

Notes.—See comments under *Passerella*. The sequence of species follows Zink (1982); cf. Zink et al. (1991).

Zonotrichia capensis (Müller). Rufous-collared Sparrow.

> *Fringilla capensis* P. L. S. Müller, 1776, Natursyst., Suppl., p. 165. Based on "Bruent, du Cap de Bonne-Espérance" Daubenton, Planches Enlum., pl. 386, fig. 2. (Cape of Good Hope, error = Cayenne.)

Habitat.—Arid Lowland Scrub, Arid Montane Scrub, Second-growth Scrub, Secondary Forest, Semihumid/Humid Montane Scrub, Pastures/Agricultural Lands (0–4000 m; Subtropical and Temperate, locally also Tropical zones).

Distribution.—*Resident* in the Greater Antilles in the mountains of Hispaniola; in the highlands of Middle America from Chiapas south through Guatemala and El Salvador to Honduras, and in Costa Rica and western Panama (east to western Panamá province); and in South America virtually throughout except Amazonia.

Notes.—Also known as Andean Sparrow.

Zonotrichia albicollis (Gmelin). White-throated Sparrow.

> *Fringilla albicollis* Gmelin, 1789, Syst. Nat. 1(2): 921. Based on the "White-throated Sparrow" Edwards, Glean. Nat. Hist. 2: 198, pl. 304. (in Pensilvania = Philadelphia.)

Habitat.—Coniferous and mixed coniferous-deciduous forest, forest edge, clearings, bogs, brush, and open woodland; in migration and winter also in deciduous forest and woodland, scrub, and gardens.

Distribution.—*Breeds* from southeastern Yukon, west-central and southern Mackenzie, northern Saskatchewan, northern Manitoba, northern Ontario, north-central Quebec, central Labrador, and Newfoundland south to central interior and northeastern British Columbia, central Alberta, central and southeastern Saskatchewan, north-central North Dakota, northern and east-central Minnesota, northern Wisconsin, central Michigan, northern Ohio (formerly), northern and east-central West Virginia (irregularly), northern Pennsylvania, northern New Jersey, northern New York, New Brunswick, and Nova Scotia; recorded in summer in northwestern Montana, but not known to breed.

Winters from Kansas, southern Minnesota, southern Wisconsin, southern Michigan, northern Ohio, Pennsylvania, central New York, and Massachusetts (casually north to southern Canada from Manitoba eastward) south to Nuevo León, northern Tamaulipas, southern Texas, the Gulf coast, and southern Florida, and (less commonly) west across western Texas, New Mexico, Utah, and Arizona to California (virtually statewide) and northern Baja California (casually to Guadalupe Island, and north to southwestern British Columbia and western Montana), and also on Bermuda.

Migrates regularly through North America east of the Rockies, casually through western North America from southern British Columbia and the breeding range southward.

Casual north to northern Alaska, Northwest Territories (Baffin and Coats islands), Iceland, the British Isles, and continental Europe; a sight report from Puerto Rico.

Zonotrichia querula (Nuttall). Harris's Sparrow.

Fringilla querula Nuttall, 1840, Man. Ornithol. U. S. Can. (ed. 2) 1: 555. (few miles west of Independence, Missouri.)

Habitat.—Brush and stunted trees in coniferous forest-tundra ecotone; in migration and winter in thickets, open woodland, forest edge, windbreaks, hedgerows, and scrub.

Distribution.—*Breeds* from northwestern and east-central Mackenzie and southern Keewatin south to northeastern Saskatchewan, northern Manitoba, and northwestern Ontario (Fort Severn).

Winters primarily from northern Nebraska and central Iowa south to south-central and central coastal Texas, and rarely but regularly north to southeastern Alaska (Juneau area southward), southern British Columbia, Idaho, Montana, northeastern Saskatchewan, and North Dakota, west to southern California (mostly east of the Sierra Nevada), southern Nevada, southern Utah, southern Arizona, and southern New Mexico, and east to western Tennessee, Arkansas, and northwestern Louisiana.

Migrates regularly through the northern Great Plains region from Alberta, Saskatchewan, Manitoba, and Minnesota south to Nebraska and Iowa, and east to Lake Michigan.

Casual in northern, western and south-coastal Alaska and northeastern British Columbia; and in eastern North America from western and southern Ontario, southern Quebec, Maine, and Nova Scotia south to the Gulf coast and southern Florida. Accidental on Banks Island.

Zonotrichia leucophrys (Forster). White-crowned Sparrow.

Emberiza leucophrys J. R. Forster, 1772, Philos. Trans. R. Soc. London 62: 340. (Severn River, west shore of Hudson Bay.)

Habitat.—Stunted trees and shrubs, wet meadows with willows, brushy edges of woodland and forest, thickets, chaparral, coastal brushland in the fog belt, gardens, and parks; in migration and winter also farmlands and brushy desert areas.

Distribution.—*Breeds* from western and northern Alaska, northern Yukon, northern Mackenzie, and central Keewatin south to southern Alaska (west to the Alaska Peninsula), in coastal areas and mountains (somewhat disjunctly in southern portion) to southern California (to Santa Barbara and San Bernardino counties), southern Nevada, northern and east-central Arizona, and northern New Mexico, and from northern Saskatchewan (also in Cypress Hills of southeastern Alberta and southwestern Saskatchewan) and northern Manitoba east across northern Ontario and northern Quebec to southern Labrador, northern Newfoundland, and south-central Quebec.

Winters from southern British Columbia (casually north to central Alaska and Yukon),

Washington, Idaho, Montana, and the central United States (from Nebraska and Kansas east to central Ohio and southern West Virginia, casually farther north) south to southern Baja California, Michoacán, Querétaro, San Luis Potosí, Tamaulipas, southern Texas, the Gulf coast (east to northwestern Florida), and south-central Georgia, and regularly in small numbers north to southern Ontario and central New York, and east to coastal areas from Massachusetts south to southern Florida, the Bahama Islands, Cuba, and Jamaica, casually to the Yucatan Peninsula and Belize (sight report). Casual in Bermuda.

Migrates regularly through North America between the breeding and wintering ranges and, in the northeast, from southern Ontario eastward (less commonly in the Maritime Provinces and New England), and south to Pennsylvania, Maryland, and Delaware; regular in fall on Bermuda.

Casual or accidental on islands in the Bering Sea (Pribilofs, Nunivak) and in the western Aleutians (Shemya); north to Banks and southern Baffin islands, and to the Melville Peninsula; on Fletcher's Ice Island (in the Arctic Ocean west of northern Ellesmere Island); and Cuba; and in Greenland, Iceland, the British Isles, the Netherlands, France, and Japan. An individual photographed in Panama (Canal area) may have been a man-assisted vagrant.

Zonotrichia atricapilla (Gmelin). Golden-crowned Sparrow.

Emberiza atricapilla Gmelin, 1789, Syst. Nat. 1(2): 875. Based mainly on the "Black-crowned Bunting" Latham, Gen. Synop. Birds 2(1): 202, pl. 45. (in Sinu Natka, et insulis Sandwich = Prince William Sound, Alaska.)

Habitat.—Montane thickets and scrub, dwarf conifers, and brushy canyons; in migration and winter in dense brush, thickets, chaparral, and gardens.

Distribution.—*Breeds* from western and north-central Alaska and south-central Yukon south to southern Alaska (west to Unimak in the eastern Aleutian Islands), southern British Columbia, extreme northern Washington (Okanogan County), and southwestern Alberta (Banff).

Winters from southern Alaska (west to Kodiak) and coastal and interior southern British Columbia south, mostly west of the Cascades and Sierra Nevada, to northern Baja California, southern California, and southern Arizona (rarely), casually east to Utah, Colorado, and central New Mexico, and south to Baja California (including offshore islands) and northern Sonora.

Migrates casually through the Pribilofs and western Aleutians (Attu, Amchitka) and St. Lawrence Island, and east to southern Alberta, southern Saskatchewan, and Idaho.

Casual in northern Alaska, northwestern Mackenzie, and from Montana, Nebraska, Minnesota, southern Manitoba (sight report), western and southern Ontario, New York, Massachusetts, Maine, and Nova Scotia south to Kansas, Missouri, Illinois, Pennsylvania, and New Jersey, also along the Gulf coast east to eastern Texas and southern Louisiana. Accidental in southern Florida (Florida Keys), northeastern Siberia, and Japan; a questionable sight report for Nayarit.

Notes.—Mayr and Short (1970) considered *Z. atricapilla* and *Z. albicollis* to represent a superspecies, but Zink (1982), Zink et al. (1991), and Zink and Blackwell (1996) showed that *atricapilla* and *Z. leucophrys* are sister species.

Genus *JUNCO* Wagler

Junco Wagler, 1831, Isis von Oken, col. 526. Type, by monotypy, *Junco phaeonotus* Wagler.

Notes.—See comments under *Passerella*. Species limits here follow Mayr and Short (1970).

Junco vulcani (Boucard). Volcano Junco.

Zonotrichia vulcani Boucard, 1878, Proc. Zool. Soc. London, p. 57, pl. 4. (Volcan of Irazu, altitude of 10,000 feet, Costa Rica.)

Habitat.—Semihumid/Humid Montane Scrub, Paramo Grassland (2700–3600 m; upper Temperate Zone).

Distribution.—*Resident* on the high mountains of Costa Rica (Irazú and Turrialba volcanoes, and northern portion of Cordillera de Talamanca) and extreme western Panama (Volcán Barú, in western Chiriquí).

Notes.—Mayr and Short (1970) considered *J. vulcani, J. hyemalis,* and *J. phaeonotus* to constitute a superspecies.

Junco hyemalis (Linnaeus). Dark-eyed Junco.

> *Fringilla hyemalis* Linnaeus, 1758, Syst. Nat. (ed. 10) 1: 183. Based on "The Snowbird" Catesby, Nat. Hist. Carolina 1: 36, pl. 36. (in America = South Carolina.)

Habitat.—Coniferous and deciduous forest, forest edge, clearings, bogs, open woodland, brushy areas adjacent to forest, and burned-over lands; in migration and winter in a variety of open woodland, brushy, and grassy habitats, and suburbs; [*insularis* group] Pine Forest, Pine-Oak Forest (0–1300 m).

Distribution.—*Breeds* [*hyemalis* group] from western and northern Alaska, central Yukon, northwestern and central Mackenzie, southern Keewatin, northern Manitoba, northern Ontario, islands in southern James Bay, northern Quebec, northern Labrador, and Newfoundland south to southwestern and south-coastal Alaska, southern Yukon, northern British Columbia, south-central Alberta, south-central Saskatchewan, southern Manitoba, northern and east-central Minnesota, northern Wisconsin, central Michigan, southern Ontario, and northeastern Ohio, in the Appalachians through eastern Kentucky, western Virginia, eastern Tennessee, and western North Carolina to northern Georgia and northwestern South Carolina, and to southeastern New York, northern New Jersey, and southern New England; [*oreganus* group] from south-coastal and southeastern Alaska, coastal and central British Columbia (including the Queen Charlotte and Vancouver islands), west-central and southern Alberta, and extreme southwestern Saskatchewan south to southern California (to Orange County, including Santa Catalina Island), and in the mountains to northern Baja California, western Nevada, eastern Oregon, northern Utah, southern Idaho, and northwestern Wyoming; [*aikeni* group] from southeastern Montana and western South Dakota south to northeastern Wyoming and northwestern Nebraska; and [*caniceps* group] in the mountains from southern Idaho, northern Utah, and southern Wyoming south to eastern California (Clark Mountain and Grapevine Mountains), central Arizona, southern New Mexico, and western Texas (Guadalupe Mountains).

Winters [*hyemalis* group] from central (casually) and south-coastal Alaska (west to Kodiak), coastal and southern British Columbia and southern Canada (east to Newfoundland) south to northern Baja California, northern Sonora, central Chihuahua, southern Texas, the Gulf coast, and northern (casually southern) Florida (in smaller numbers in the western and southeastern portion of the winter range); irregularly on Bermuda; [*oreganus* group] from south-coastal and southeastern Alaska, southern British Columbia, and the northwestern United States (east to the Dakotas, Minnesota, Oklahoma, and Kansas) south to northern Baja California, northern Sonora, Durango, southern Chihuahua, and central Texas; rare but regular in midwestern United States; [*aikeni* group] from the breeding range south to eastern Colorado, western Oklahoma, and western Kansas, rarely to northern Arizona, northern and eastern New Mexico, and northeastern Colorado; and [*caniceps* group] from Nevada, southern Idaho, southern Wyoming, and western Nebraska south to southern California (rarely), northern Sonora, northern Sinaloa, northern Durango, Chihuahua, and western Texas, casually to north-central Texas.

Resident [*insularis* group] on Guadalupe Island, off Baja California.

Casual or accidental [*hyemalis* group] north to the Arctic coast of Alaska and to islands in the Bering Sea, and to Banks, Southampton, and southern Baffin islands, Veracruz, the Bahama Islands (Grand Bahama, New Providence), and Jamaica, and in Iceland, the British Isles, continental Europe and eastern Siberia; sight reports for Puerto Rico and the Virgin Islands (St. Thomas); [*oreganus* group] in the eastern Aleutians (Unalaska), north to Banks Island, and through much of eastern North America from Michigan, southern Ontario, southwestern Quebec, Maine, and Nova Scotia south to the Gulf coast (east to southern Louisiana and central Alabama), Tennessee, and South Carolina; [*aikeni* group] to California, southern Idaho, eastern Nebraska, central Oklahoma, and northern Texas, and in North Dakota (sight report) and Michigan (Presque Isle County); and [*caniceps* group] west to the Pacific coast from southern British Columbia south to coastal northern California, and east to eastern Montana, the Dakotas, southern Manitoba, Minnesota, Illinois, Arkansas, and Louisiana; sight reports for Idaho and eastern Texas.

Notes.—Groups: *J. hyemalis* [Slate-colored Junco], *J. oreganus* (J. K. Townsend, 1837) [Oregon Junco], *J. aikeni* Ridgway, 1873 [White-winged Junco], *J. caniceps* (Woodhouse, 1853) [Gray-headed Junco], and *J. insularis* Ridgway, 1876 [Guadalupe Junco]. The form *insularis* is an isolated population closest to the *oreganus* group; Mirsky (1976) suggested that it should be recognized as a species because of vocal differences. The remaining groups intergrade in varying degrees. Several other forms may warrant recognition as groups: *Junco mearnsi* Ridgway, 1897 [Pink-sided Junco], of the *oreganus* group, breeding from southeastern Alberta and southwestern Saskatchewan to eastern Idaho and northwestern Wyoming, and *J. dorsalis* Henry, 1858 [Red-backed Junco], of the *caniceps* group, breeding from northern and central Arizona and central New Mexico to western Texas. For detailed information on groups, see Miller (1941). See comments under *J. vulcani*.

Junco phaeonotus Wagler. Yellow-eyed Junco.

Junco phaeonotus Wagler, 1831, Isis von Oken, col. 526. (Mexico.)

Habitat.—Pine Forest, Pine-Oak Forest (1200–4300 m; upper Subtropical and Temperate zones).

Distribution.—*Resident* [*phaeonotus* group] from northeastern Sonora, southern Arizona, extreme southwestern New Mexico (Animas, casually Big Hatchet mountains), Chihuahua, north-central Coahuila, Nuevo León, and southwestern Tamaulipas south through the mountains to western Veracruz and central Oaxaca (west of the Isthmus of Tehuantepec); [*bairdi* group] in the Cape district of southern Baja California; [*fulvescens* group] in the interior of Chiapas (from vicinity of San Cristóbal south to Teopisca); and [*alticola* group] in the mountains of extreme southeastern Chiapas (Volcán Tacaná area) and western Guatemala.

Casual [*phaeonotus* group] in western Texas.

Notes.—Groups: *J. phaeonotus* [Mexican Junco], *J. bairdi* Ridgway, 1883 [Baird's Junco], *J. fulvescens* Nelson, 1897 [Chiapas Junco], and *J. alticola* Salvin, 1863 [Guatemala Junco]. See comments under *J. vulcani*.

Genus *CALCARIUS* Bechstein

Calcarius Bechstein, 1802, Ornithol. Taschenb. Dtsch. 1: 130. Type, by monotypy, *Fringilla lapponica* Linnaeus.

Rhynchophanes Baird, 1858, in Baird, Cassin, and Lawrence, Rep. Explor. Surv. R. R. Pac. 9: xx, xxxviii, 432. Type, by monotypy, *Plectrophanes maccownii* [sic] Lawrence.

Notes.—Paynter (1970) suggested that *Calcarius* was closely related to and perhaps should be merged into the genus *Emberiza*.

Calcarius mccownii (Lawrence). McCown's Longspur.

Plectrophanes McCownii Lawrence, 1851, Ann. Lyc. Nat. Hist. N. Y. 5: 122. (high prairies of Western Texas.)

Habitat.—Sparse short-grass plains, plowed and stubble fields, and bare or nearly bare ground.

Distribution.—*Breeds* from southeastern Alberta, southern Saskatchewan, southwestern North Dakota (formerly much of North Dakota), and southwestern Minnesota (formerly) south through central Montana to southeastern Wyoming, northeastern Colorado, and northwestern Nebraska.

Winters from southeastern California (rarely), central Arizona, central New Mexico, west-central Kansas, and central Oklahoma (casually north to southwestern Oregon and southeastern Colorado) south to northeastern Sonora, Chihuahua, northern Durango, Zacatecas, and western and south-central Texas (rare in recent years in eastern portions of range).

Migrates rarely through eastern and coastal southern California.

Casual north and west to southern British Columbia, Idaho, Nevada, northern Arizona, and Utah, and east to southern Manitoba (sight report), Minnesota, Missouri, and eastern Texas. Accidental in Michigan (Whitefish Point), New York (Long Island), Massachusetts (Bridgewater), and Louisiana (Jefferson Davis Parish, New Orleans).

Notes.—Formerly placed in the monotypic genus *Rhynchophanes*.

Calcarius lapponicus (Linnaeus). Lapland Longspur.

Fringilla lapponica Linnaeus, 1758, Syst. Nat. (ed. 10) 1: 180. (in Lapponia = Lapland.)

Habitat.—Arctic tundra in wet meadows, grassy tussocks, and scrub; in migration and winter in plowed fields, stubble, and open grasslands.

Distribution.—*Breeds* in North America from western and northern Alaska, northern Yukon, and Banks, Prince Patrick, Melville, and northern Ellesmere islands south to islands in the Bering Sea, the Aleutians, south-coastal Alaska (east to the Susitna River highlands and Middleton Island), northern Mackenzie, southern Keewatin, northeastern Manitoba, extreme northern Ontario, northern Quebec, and northern Labrador; and in the Palearctic from Greenland, northern Scandinavia, northern Russia, and northern Siberia south to southern Scandinavia, central and eastern Siberia, Kamchatka, and the Commander Islands.

Winters in North America from coastal southern Alaska (casually), southern British Columbia, the northern United States, southern Ontario, and Nova Scotia south to northern California, northern Utah, Colorado, Oklahoma, northwestern Texas (locally in southeastern Texas), Arkansas, southwestern Louisiana (locally), Tennessee, and Maryland, rarely to southern California, southern and central Arizona, southern New Mexico, northeastern and eastern Texas, the Gulf coast, and northern (casually southern) Florida; and in the Palearctic from northern Europe and northern Siberia south to central Europe, southern Russia, Mongolia, China, Korea, and Japan.

Migrates in North America throughout Alaska and Canada, and in Eurasia throughout the regions between the breeding and wintering ranges, including Iceland.

Casual on Bermuda. Accidental in southern Baja California (Isla Cerralvo) and Yucatán (Celestún); a sight report for Veracruz.

Notes.—In Old World literature known as Lapland Bunting.

Calcarius pictus (Swainson). Smith's Longspur.

Emberiza (Plectrophanes) picta Swainson, 1832, in Swainson and Richardson, Fauna Bor.-Amer. 2 (1831): 250, pl. 49. (Carlton House, on the banks of the Saskatchewan [River].)

Habitat.—Dry, grassy, and hummocky tundra; in migration and winter in fields with short grass, prairies, and grassy margins of airports.

Distribution.—*Breeds* in east-central Alaska (Susitna River highlands, Wrangell Mountains region) and adjacent northwestern British Columbia, and from northern Alaska (Brooks Range) east across northern Yukon and northern and east-central Mackenzie to southern Keewatin, northeastern Manitoba, and extreme northern Ontario.

Winters from Kansas south to west-central Oklahoma and east-central Texas, and east to Arkansas and northwestern Louisiana (rare).

Migrates primarily through the northern Great Plains east to central Illinois, casually from central and southern British Columbia east to Montana, and to Michigan, southern Ontario, Ohio, and central Alabama.

Casual or accidental in coastal and southwestern British Columbia, California, Nevada, Arizona, Quebec, Connecticut, New York, New Jersey, West Virginia, Maryland, North Carolina, and South Carolina; sight reports for Massachusetts and Nova Scotia.

Calcarius ornatus (Townsend). Chestnut-collared Longspur.

Plectrophanes ornata J. K. Townsend, 1837, J. Acad. Nat. Sci. Philadelphia 7: 189. (prairies of Platte River = near forks of Platte River, western Nebraska.)

Habitat.—Short-grass plains, and prairies; in migration and winter also in open cultivated fields.

Distribution.—*Breeds* from southern Alberta, southern Saskatchewan, and southern Manitoba south, east of the Rockies, to northeastern Colorado, western Kansas (formerly), north-central Nebraska, and western Minnesota.

Winters from coastal, southern, and eastern California (rarely), northern Arizona, central and eastern New Mexico, eastern Colorado, and central Kansas south to northern Sonora, Chihuahua, Zacatecas, San Luis Potosí, and southern Texas, casually east to northern Louisiana and south to Puebla, Veracruz, and México.

Migrates regularly west through California and Nevada.

Casual elsewhere in western North America from southwestern British Columbia south to Baja California; north to northern Alberta and northern Manitoba; and in eastern North America from Wisconsin, northern Michigan, southern Ontario, New Brunswick, Nova Scotia, and Newfoundland south to Missouri, Arkansas, Louisiana, along the Atlantic coast south to North Carolina, and in northern Florida; sight reports for southeastern Alaska, southern Florida, and Guerrero.

Genus *EMBERIZA* Linnaeus

Emberiza Linnaeus, 1758, Syst. Nat. (ed. 10) 1: 176. Type, by subsequent designation (G. R. Gray, 1840), *Emberiza citrinella* Linnaeus.

Emberiza leucocephalos Gmelin. Pine Bunting.

Emberiza leucocephalos S. G. Gmelin, 1771, Nov. Comm. Acad. Imp. Sci. Petrop., 15, p. 480, pl. 23, fig. 3. (Astrakhan.)

Habitat.—Sparse coniferous forests.

Distribution.—*Breeds* in eastern Russia across the Ural Mountains and Siberia to the upper Kolyma and the coastal ranges of the Pacific and northeastern Tsinghai.

Winters in much of the breeding range and south to Israel, Iraq, and southern Iran to northwestern India, and central China.

Resident as a disjunct population in Kansu and Tsinghai provinces, China.

Accidental in Alaska (Attu Island, 18–19 November 1985, photograph deposited in VIREO, Wagner 1990; 23 September–10 October 1993, D. D. Gibson, specimen, Univ. Alaska Mus. 6385; 1994, National Audubon Soc. Field Notes 48:142, 160).

Notes.—The specific name is sometimes erroneously emended to *leucocephala*. This species hybridizes extensively in western Siberia with *E. citrinella* Linnaeus, 1758 [Yellowhammer], with which it is sometimes merged (Dement'ev and Gladkov 1954, Byers et al. 1995).

Emberiza pusilla Pallas. Little Bunting.

Emberiza pusilla Pallas, 1776, Reise Versch. Proc. Russ. Reichs 3: 647. (Daurian Range, southern Chita, southeastern Siberia.)

Habitat.—Breeds in birch and willow scrub in tundra; winters in scrub and cultivated lands.

Distribution.—*Breeds* from northern Finland, northern Russia, and northern Siberia south to Lake Baikal, Anadyrland, and the Sea of Okhotsk.

Winters in the northern parts of India and Southeast Asia, rarely in the British Isles, continental Europe, North Africa, the Near East, and Philippines.

Accidental in Alaska in the Chukchi Sea (280 km northwest of Icy Cape, 6 September 1970; Watson et al. 1974), on St. Lawrence Island (Gambell, 1996), and in the Aleutian Islands (Shemya, 8 September 1977) and California (Point Loma, San Diego County, 21–24 October 1991, photograph; 1992, Amer. Birds 46: 153).

Emberiza rustica Pallas. Rustic Bunting.

Emberiza rustica Pallas, 1776, Reise Versch. Prov. Russ. Reichs 3: 698. (Dauria = Transbaicalia.)

Habitat.—Low bushes and wet grassy areas of taiga, undergrowth of open coniferous-deciduous woodland, and thickets along streams; in migration and winter in scrub, brushy areas, grasslands, open woodland and cultivated lands.

Distribution.—*Breeds* from northern Scandinavia, northern Russia, and northern Siberia southeast to southeastern Siberia, northern Sakhalin, the Sea of Okhotsk, and Kamchatka.

Winters in eastern China, Japan, and, rarely, the Commander Islands.

Migrates regularly through the western Aleutian Islands (Near Islands, casually east to Adak), occasionally reaching the Pribilofs (St. Paul) and St. Lawrence Island, and rarely through the British Isles, continental Europe, and the Middle East.

Casual in south-coastal and southeastern Alaska (Homer, Mitkof Island), southwestern British Columbia (Tofino, Jordan River), Washington (Kent), and northern and central California (Humboldt County, Half Moon Bay, and Kern County); a sight report for Oregon.

Emberiza aureola Pallas. Yellow-breasted Bunting.

Emberiza Aureola Pallas, 1773, Reise Versch. Prov. Russ. Reichs. 2: 711. (Irtysh River, south-central Siberia.)

Habitat.—Scrub and fields.

Distribution.—*Breeds* in Eurasia from Finland east to Kamchatka, and south to northern China, Korea, and Japan.

Winters in southern Asia and the Philippines.

Accidental in Alaska (Attu, in the Aleutian Islands, 26 May 1988; Gibson and Kessel 1992); sight reports from Attu, Buldir, and St. Lawrence Island.

Emberiza variabilis Temminck. Gray Bunting.

Emberiza variabilis Temminck, 1835, Planches Color., livr. 98, pl. 583, fig. 2. (northern Japan.)

Habitat.—Breeds in thickets, bamboo, and undergrowth of coniferous-deciduous woodland; winters in scrub, thickets, and woodland undergrowth.

Distribution.—*Breeds* in southern Kamchatka, the Kuril Islands, Sakhalin, and possibly northern Japan.

Winters in Japan and the Ryukyu Islands.

Accidental in Alaska (Shemya, in the Aleutian Islands, 18 May 1977; Gibson and Hall 1978); a sight report for Attu.

Emberiza pallasi (Cabanis). Pallas's Bunting.

Cynchramus Pallasi Cabanis, 1851, Mus. Heineanum 1: 130 (footnote). Based on *Emberiza schoeniclus* var. ß Pallas, Zoogr. Rosso-Asiat. 2: 48. (No locality given = near Selenga River, Transbaicalia.)

Habitat.—Birch and river thickets in tundra and taiga, and in reed beds.

Distribution.—*Breeds* from central and eastern Siberia south to Mongolia and Manchuria.

Winters from the southern part of the breeding range and Ussuriland south to northern China, Korea, and Japan, casually west to the British Isles.

Accidental in northern Alaska (Barrow, 11 June 1968; Pitelka 1974); a sight report for St. Lawrence Island.

Emberiza schoeniclus (Linnaeus). Reed Bunting.

Fringilla Schœniclus Linnaeus, 1758, Syst. Nat. (ed. 10) 1: 182. (in Europa = Sweden.)

Habitat.—Reed beds, rushes, and riparian thickets; in migration and winter also wet meadows, pastures, and open country.

Distribution.—*Breeds* [*schoeniclus* group] from the British Isles, Scandinavia, northern Russia, and northern Siberia south to the Mediterranean region, Asia Minor, Iran, Turkestan, southern Siberia, Kamchatka, and northern Japan.

Winters [*schoeniclus* group] from the southern portions of the breeding range south to the Mediterranean region, Iraq, northwestern India, northeastern China, and southern Japan.

Migrates [*schoeniclus* group] casually (in spring) through the western Aleutian Islands (Attu, Shemya, Buldir).

Resident [*intermedia* group] from northwestern Africa east to the Near East and southwestern Russia; and [*pyrrhuloides* group] in south-central Asia from the Caspian Sea and Afghanistan east to Mongolia

Notes.—Groups: *E. schoeniclus* [Northern Reed-Bunting], *E. intermedia* Degland, 1849 [Dark Reed-Bunting], and *E. pyrrhuloides* Pallas, 1811 [Pale Reed-Bunting].

Genus *PLECTROPHENAX* Stejneger

Plectrophenax Stejneger, 1882, Proc. U. S. Natl. Mus. 5: 33. Type, by original designation, *Emberiza nivalis* Linnaeus.

Plectrophenax nivalis (Linnaeus). Snow Bunting.

Emberiza nivalis Linnaeus, 1758, Syst. Nat., ed. 10, 1, p. 176. (in alpibus Lapponiæ, Spitsbergæ ad sinum Hudsonis = Lapland.)

Habitat.—Arctic rocky shores, cliffs, stony escarpments, and dry tundra, also nesting in bird houses, empty oil barrels, cabins, and other artificial structures; in migration and winter in grassy or weedy fields, stubble, beaches, and roadsides.

Distribution.—*Breeds* in North America from northern Alaska, northern Yukon, northwestern Mackenzie, and Banks, Prince Patrick, Ellef Ringnes, Axel Heiberg, and northern Ellesmere islands south to southern Alaska (including the Aleutian Islands), extreme northwestern British Columbia, southwestern and central Yukon, east-central Mackenzie, central and southeastern Keewatin, Southampton and Belcher islands, northern Quebec, and northern Labrador; and in the Palearctic from Greenland, Spitsbergen, Franz Josef Land, Novaya Zemlya, and northern Siberia south to the British Isles, northern Scandinavia, central Siberia, Kamchatka, and the Commander Islands.

Winters in North America from west-central and southern Alaska, southern Canada (British Columbia east to southern Labrador and Newfoundland) south to central Oregon, northern Utah, Colorado, central Kansas, central Missouri, northern Kentucky (rare), and North Carolina, casually to California (to Kern County), northeastern New Mexico, Oklahoma, eastern Texas, Arkansas, central Mississippi, Tennessee, Georgia, and northern Florida, and irregularly to Bermuda; and in the Palearctic from the breeding range south to central continental Europe, the Mediterranean region (casually), Asia Minor (casually), southern Russia, Manchuria, Sakhalin, the Kuril Islands, and (casually) Japan.

Casual or accidental in the northwestern Hawaiian Islands, northwestern Arizona, the Bahamas (Cat Island), eastern Atlantic islands, and northern Africa; sight reports for western and northern Texas.

Notes.—*Plectrophenax nivalis* and *P. hyperboreus* are closely related, with limited hybridization occurring (Sealy 1969); they constitute a superspecies and may be conspecific (Mayr and Short 1970, Paynter 1970).

Plectrophenax hyperboreus Ridgway. McKay's Bunting.

Plectrophenax hyperboreus Ridgway, 1884, Proc. U. S. Natl. Mus. 7: 68. (St. Michael's, Alaska.)

Habitat.—Open rocky ground, beaches, and shores of tundra pools; in migration and winter in open rocky or sandy areas.

Distribution.—*Breeds* in Alaska on islands in the Bering Sea (Hall and St. Matthew, also rarely on St. Paul in the Pribilofs and on St. Lawrence).

Winters on the coast of western and southeastern Alaska (Nome to Cold Bay, including Nunivak Island), casually to the Aleutians (Adak, Unalaska) and south-coastal Alaska (Kodiak Island, Homer).

Accidental in British Columbia (Vancouver Island), Washington (Ocean Shores), and Oregon (mouth of Columbia River).

Notes.—See comments under *P. nivalis*.

Family **CARDINALIDAE**: Cardinals, Saltators, and Allies

Genus *SALTATOR* Vieillot

Saltator Vieillot, 1816, Analyse, p. 32. Type, by monotypy, "Grand Tanagra" Buffon = *Tanagra maxima* Müller.
Pitylus Cuvier, 1829, Règne Anim. (nouv. éd.) 1: 413. Type, by subsequent designation (G. R. Gray, 1840), *Loxia grossa* Linnaeus.

Notes.—Biochemical and morphological evidence (Hellack and Schnell 1977, Tamplin et al. 1993, Demastes and Remsen 1994) supports the merger of *Pitylus* into *Saltator*.

Saltator albicollis Vieillot. Lesser Antillean Saltator.

Saltator albicollis Vieillot, 1817, Nouv. Dict. Hist. Nat. (nouv. éd.) 14, p. 107. (Cayenne, error = Martinique.)

Habitat.—Shrubby Second Growth, Arid Lowland Scrub (Tropical and lower Subtropical zones).
Distribution.—*Resident* in the Lesser Antilles (Guadeloupe, Dominica, Martinique, and St. Lucia).
Accidental on Nevis, in the Lesser Antilles.
Notes.—See note under *S. striatipectus*.

Saltator striatipectus Lafresnaye. Streaked Saltator.

Saltator striatipictus [sic] Lafresnaye, 1847, Rev. Zool. (Paris), 10, p. 73. (Cali, Valle de Cauca, Colombia.)

Habitat.—Tropical Deciduous Forest, Secondary Forest (0–1850 m; Tropical and lower Subtropical zones).
Distribution.—*Resident* on the Pacific slope of southwestern Costa Rica (El General region) and Panama (including Coiba, Coibita, Taboga, and the Pearl islands, and on the Caribbean slope from the Canal area to western San Blas), and in South America from northern Colombia, northern Venezuela (also Patos, Monos, Chacachacare islands), and Trinidad south, west of the Andes, to western Peru.
Notes.—The original spelling *"striatipictus"* is regarded as a *lapsus calami* (Paynter 1970). *Saltator albicollis* and *S. striatipectus* are treated as separate species, based on the analysis of Seutin et al. (1993).

Saltator coerulescens Vieillot. Grayish Saltator.

Saltator cœrulescens Vieillot, 1817, Nouv. Dict. Hist. Nat. (nouv. éd.) 14: 105. Based on "Habia Ceja blanca" Azara, Apunt. Hist. Nat. Páx. Parag. 1: 344 (no. 81). (Paraguay.)

Habitat.—Second-growth Scrub, Secondary Forest, Tropical Lowland Evergreen Forest Edge, Tropical Deciduous Forest, Gallery Forest (0–1300 m; Tropical and lower Subtropical zones).
Distribution.—*Resident* [*grandis* group] from Sinaloa, western Durango, eastern San Luis Potosí and southern Tamaulipas south along both slopes of Middle America (including the Yucatan Peninsula, but unrecorded Pacific slope of Nicaragua) to central Costa Rica; and [*coerulescens* group] in South America from northern and eastern Colombia, Venezuela (including Monos and Chacachacare islands) Trinidad, and the Guianas south, east of the Andes, to northern Argentina, Uruguay, and south-central Brazil.
Notes.—Groups: *S. grandis* (W. Deppe, 1830) [Middle American Saltator] and *S. coerulescens* [Grayish Saltator].

Saltator maximus (Müller). Buff-throated Saltator.

Tanagra maxima P. L. S. Müller, 1776, Natursyst., Suppl., p. 159. Based on "Tanagra, des grands bois de Cayenne" Daubenton, Planches Enlum., pl. 205. (Cayenne.)

Habitat.—Tropical Lowland Evergreen Forest Edge, Secondary Forest, Montane Evergreen Forest Edge (0–1500 m; Tropical and Subtropical zones).
Distribution.—*Resident* from northern Oaxaca, southern Veracruz, Tabasco, Chiapas, southern Campeche, and southern Quintana Roo south on the Gulf-Caribbean slope of Central America to Nicaragua, on both slopes of Costa Rica (absent from the dry northwest) and Panama, and in South America from Colombia, Venezuela, and the Guianas south, west of the Andes to northwestern Peru and east of the Andes to central Bolivia and central and southeastern Brazil.
Accidental in El Salvador (Montecristo).

Saltator atriceps (Lesson). Black-headed Saltator.

Tanagra (Saltator) atriceps Lesson, 1832, Cent. Zool., p. 208, pl. 69. (Mexico = Veracruz.)

Habitat.—Tropical Lowland Evergreen Forest Edge, Secondary Forest, Second-growth Scrub (0–1300 m; Tropical and lower Subtropical zones).
Distribution.—*Resident* from Guerrero, southeastern San Luis Potosí and southern Tamaulipas south along both slopes of Middle America (including the Yucatan Peninsula) to Honduras, and in Nicaragua (Pacific slope only), Costa Rica (mostly Caribbean slope), and Panama (both slopes, east to Darién).

Saltator grossus (Linnaeus). Slate-colored Grosbeak.

Loxia grossa Linnaeus, 1766, Syst. Nat. (ed. 12) 1: 307. Based on "Le Gros-bec bleu d'Amérique" Brisson, Ornithologie 6, (suppl.): 89, pl. 5, fig. 1. (in America = Cayenne.)

Habitat.—Tropical Lowland Evergreen Forest (0–1200 m; Tropical and lower Subtropical zones).
Distribution.—*Resident* on the Caribbean slope of Nicaragua and Costa Rica, on both slopes of Panama (more widespread on the Caribbean), and in South America from Colombia, southern Venezuela, and the Guianas south, west of the Andes to western Ecuador and east of the Andes to northern Bolivia and Amazonian and eastern Brazil; a sight report for northeastern Honduras.
Notes.—*Saltator grossus* and the South American *S. fuliginosus* (Daudin, 1800) [Black-throated Grosbeak] constitute a superspecies (Sibley and Monroe 1990); Paynter (1970) treated them as conspecific. Both were formerly placed in the genus *Pitylus* (see Note under *Saltator*).

Genus *CARYOTHRAUSTES* Reichenbach

Caryothraustes Reichenbach, 1850, Avium Syst. Nat., pl. 78. Type, by subsequent designation (Sclater and Salvin, 1869), *"Pitylus" [= Coccothraustes] viridis = Loxia canadensis* Linnaeus.

Notes.—See comments under *Rhodothraupis*.

Caryothraustes poliogaster (Du Bus de Gisignies). Black-faced Grosbeak.

Pitylus poliogaster Du Bus de Gisignies, 1847, Bull. Acad. R. Sci. Lett. Beaux-Arts Belg. 14: 105. (Guatemala.)

Habitat.—Tropical Lowland Evergreen Forest (0–900 m; Tropical and lower Subtropical zones).
Distribution.—*Resident* from northern Oaxaca, southern Veracruz, Tabasco, Chiapas, southern Campeche, and southern Quintana Roo south along the Gulf-Caribbean slope of Central America to western Panama (Bocas del Toro and both slopes of Veraguas, casually or formerly to Coclé, western Panamá province and the Canal area).
Notes.—*Caryothraustes poliogaster* and *C. canadensis* constitute a superspecies (Sibley and Monroe 1990); Paynter (1970) considered them to be conspecific.

Caryothraustes canadensis (Linnaeus). Yellow-green Grosbeak.

Loxia canadensis Linnaeus, 1766, Syst. Nat. (ed. 12) 1: 304. Based on "Le Gros-bec de Cayenne" Brisson, Ornithologie 3: 229, pl. 11, fig. 3. (in Canada, error = Cayenne.)

Habitat.—Tropical Lowland Evergreen Forest (0–900 m; Tropical and lower Subtropical zones).

Distribution.—*Resident* in extreme eastern Panama (Cana, in eastern Darién); and in South America from southeastern Colombia, southern Venezuela, and the Guianas south through Amazonian and central Brazil to southeastern Brazil.

Notes.—Also known as Green Grosbeak. See comments under *C. poliogaster.*

Genus *RHODOTHRAUPIS* Ridgway

Rhodothraupis Ridgway, 1898, Auk 15: 226. Type, by original designation, *Fringilla celaeno* Lichtenstein = *Tanagra celaeno* Deppe.

Notes.—Paynter (1970) suggested that *Rhodothraupis* might be merged with the genus *Caryothraustes.*

Rhodothraupis celaeno (Deppe). Crimson-collared Grosbeak.

Tanagra Celaeno Lichtenst[ein]." W. Deppe, 1830, Preis.-Verz. Säugeth. Vögel, etc., Mex., p. 2. (Mexico = Papantla, Veracruz.)

Habitat.—Tropical Deciduous Forest, Gallery Forest, Secondary Forest (0–1200 m; Tropical and lower Subtropical zones).

Distribution.—*Resident* from east-central Nuevo León and southern Tamaulipas south through eastern San Luis Potosí and northern Veracruz to northeastern Puebla.

Casual in southern Texas (Laredo, McAllen, Santa Ana National Wildlife Refuge, Aransas National Wildlife Refuge, Sabal Palms Audubon Sanctuary).

Genus *CARDINALIS* Bonaparte

Cardinalis Bonaparte, 1838, Proc. Zool. Soc. London (1837), p. 111. Type, by subsequent designation (G. R. Gray, 1840), *Cardinalis virginianus* Bonaparte = *Loxia cardinalis* Linnaeus.

Pyrrhuloxia Bonaparte, 1850, Consp. Gen. Avium 1(2): 500. Type, by monotypy, *Cardinalis sinuatus* Bonaparte.

Richmondena Mathews and Iredale, 1918, Austral Avian Rec. 3: 145. Type, by original designation, *Loxia cardinalis* Linnaeus.

Cardinalis cardinalis (Linnaeus). Northern Cardinal.

Loxia cardinalis Linnaeus, 1758, Syst. Nat. (ed. 10) 1: 172. Based mainly on "The Red-Bird" Catesby, Nat. Hist. Carolina 1: 38, pl. 38. (in America septentrionali = South Carolina.)

Habitat.—Thickets, brushy fields, deciduous and mixed forest with dense undergrowth, forest edge, suburbs, and, in arid regions, in scrub and riparian woodland (Tropical to Temperate zones).

Distribution.—*Resident* [*cardinalis* group] from central Baja California, southeastern California (along the Colorado River), central and southeastern Arizona, southern New Mexico, western and northern Texas, northeastern Colorado, western Kansas, west-central Nebraska, central and eastern North Dakota (at least formerly), southeastern South Dakota, southeastern Manitoba (Winnipeg), central Minnesota, northern Wisconsin, southern Ontario, southwestern Quebec, northern New York, New Brunswick, and southern Nova Scotia south to southern Baja California (including Cerralvo, Santa Margarita, Carmen, and San Jóse islands), Sonora (including Isla Tiburón), in the Tres Marias islands (off Nayarit), in the interior to Guanajuato and Hidalgo, along the Gulf-Caribbean slope to the Yucatan Peninsula (including Holbox and Mujeres islands), northern Guatemala (Petén), and central Belize, and to the Gulf coast and southern Florida (including the Florida Keys); and [*carneus* group] along the Pacific coast of Mexico from Colima to Oaxaca (Isthmus of Tehuantepec). The range in eastern North America has been gradually expanding northward.

Introduced and established [*cardinalis* group] in the Hawaiian Islands (common on all main islands from Kauai eastward), coastal southern California, and Bermuda.

Casual or accidental [*cardinalis* group] west and north to northern Utah, southern Alberta, central Saskatchewan, Prince Edward Island, and Newfoundland.

Notes.—Groups: *C. cardinalis* [Common Cardinal] and *C. carneus* (Lesson, 1842) [Long-crested Cardinal]. Also known as the Cardinal or Common Cardinal. *Cardinalis cardinalis* and the South American *C. phoeniceus* Bonaparte, 1838 [Vermilion Cardinal], may constitute a superspecies (Mayr and Short 1970, Paynter 1970).

Cardinalis sinuatus Bonaparte. Pyrrhuloxia.

Cardinalis sinuatus Bonaparte, 1838, Proc. Zool. Soc. London (1837), p. 111. (Western parts of Mexico = Zacatecas.)

Habitat.—Arid Lowland Scrub, Arid Montane Scrub, Riparian Thickets (0–2200 m; Tropical and Subtropical zones).

Distribution.—*Resident* from central Baja California (north to lat. 27°N.), Sonora, southern Arizona, southern New Mexico, and western and south-central Texas south to southern Baja California, northern Nayarit, northeastern Jalisco, northern Michoacán, Querétaro, southeastern San Luis Potosí and southern Tamaulipas. Some nonbreeding dispersal in northern portions of range into nearby habitats.

Casual north to southern California (San Miguel Island, and north to Los Angeles and San Bernardino counties, attempted nesting in latter in 1977), central Arizona, central New Mexico, Colorado, southwestern Kansas, east-central Texas, and extreme western Oklahoma. Reports from Nevada and Puebla are open to question.

Notes.—Frequently placed in the monotypic genus *Pyrrhuloxia*.

Genus *PHEUCTICUS* Reichenbach

Pheucticus Reichenbach, 1850, Avium Syst. Nat., pl. 78. Type, by subsequent designation (G. R. Gray, 1855), *Pitylus aureoventris* d'Orbigny and Lafresnaye.

Hedymeles Cabanis, 1851, Mus. Heineanum 1: 152. Type, by subsequent designation (G. R. Gray, 1855), *Loxia ludoviciana* Linnaeus.

Pheucticus chrysopeplus (Vigors). Yellow Grosbeak.

Coccothraustes chrysopeplus Vigors, 1832, Proc. Zool. Soc. London, Comm. Sci. Corresp., pt. 2, p. 4. (Mexico = San Blas, Nayarit.)

Habitat.—Montane Evergreen Forest Edge, Tropical Lowland Evergreen Forest Edge, Tropical Deciduous Forest, Gallery Forest (0–2800 m; upper Tropical to lower Temperate zones).

Distribution.—*Resident* from southern Sonora (north to central Sonora in summer), southwestern Chihuahua, Sinaloa, and western Durango south in the highlands to northern Guerrero, Morelos, western Puebla, and central Oaxaca (west of the Isthmus of Tehuantepec); and in southern Chiapas and central Guatemala.

Casual in central and southeastern Arizona. A record from California is regarded as an escaped cage-bird.

Notes.—*Pheucticus chrysopeplus, P. tibialis,* and the South American *P. chrysogaster* (Lesson, 1832) [Golden-bellied Grosbeak] constitute a superspecies. Hellmayr (1938), Paynter (1970), and others treat them as subspecies of a single species; we follow Eisenmann (1955), Sibley and Monroe (1990), and others in treating them as allospecies in a superspecies complex.

Pheucticus tibialis Lawrence. Black-thighed Grosbeak.

Pheucticus tibialis (Baird MS) Lawrence, 1867, Ann. Lyc. Nat. Hist. N. Y. 8: 478. ("Eervantes" [= Cervántes], Costa Rica.)

Habitat.—Montane Evergreen Forest Edge (1000–2600 m; upper Subtropical and Temperate zones).

Distribution.—*Resident* in the mountains of Costa Rica (north to the Cordillera de Tilarán) and western Panama (east to Coclé).

Notes.—See comments under *P. chrysopeplus.*

Pheucticus ludovicianus (Linnaeus). Rose-breasted Grosbeak.

Loxia ludoviciana Linnaeus, 1766, Syst. Nat. (ed. 12) 1: 306. Based on "Le Gros-bec de la Louisiane" Brisson, Ornithologie 3: 247, pl. 12, fig. 2. (in Ludovicia = Louisiana.)

Habitat.—Open deciduous forest and forest edge (especially poplar and aspen), woodland, and tall second growth; in migration and winter, a variety of wooded habitats.

Distribution.—*Breeds* from northeastern British Columbia, southwestern and south-central Mackenzie, northern Alberta, central Saskatchewan, southern Manitoba, central Ontario, southern Quebec, New Brunswick, Prince Edward Island, Nova Scotia, and Newfoundland south to central and southeastern Alberta, southern Saskatchewan, north-central North Dakota, eastern South Dakota, central Nebraska, central (formerly northwestern) Kansas, eastern (formerly central) Oklahoma, southern Missouri, southern Illinois, central Indiana, southern Ohio, eastern Kentucky, eastern Tennessee, northern Georgia, western North Carolina, western Virginia, West Virginia, Maryland, and Delaware, casually west to eastern Wyoming, northeastern Colorado, New Mexico, Arizona, and central California (1992, male paired with female *P. melanocephalus*).

Winters from Nayarit and southeastern San Luis Potosí south through Middle America to northern and eastern Colombia, Venezuela, Ecuador, and east-central Peru, rarely in southern Texas, southern Louisiana, southern Mississippi, southern Alabama, western Cuba, and Bermuda (uncommonly); recorded occasionally in winter within the breeding range, and in Oregon, Utah, and California.

Migrates regularly through the southeastern states (west to the Rockies) and northeastern Mexico, irregularly through Bermuda, the Bahama Islands, Greater Antilles (east to the Virgin Islands), the Cayman Islands, and islands in the western Caribbean Sea (Swan, Providencia, and San Andrés), and casually elsewhere in western North America from southern British Columbia, Idaho, and Montana south to Arizona and northwestern Mexico.

Casual or accidental in the Lesser Antilles (Barbuda, Marie Galante, Dominica, Barbados), Greenland, the British Isles, Sweden, France, Spain, Yugoslavia, and Malta; sight reports for southeastern Alaska and the Revillagigedo Islands.

Notes.—*Pheucticus ludovicianus* and *P. melanocephalus* hybridize to varying degrees where their ranges overlap in the Great Plains (West 1962, R. L. Kroodsma 1974a, b). Considered conspecific by some (e.g., Phillips et al. 1964, Phillips 1994), they are considered here as forming a superspecies (Mayr and Short 1970, Paynter 1970).

Pheucticus melanocephalus (Swainson). Black-headed Grosbeak.

Guiraca melanocephala Swainson, 1827, Philos. Mag. (n.s.) 1: 438. (Temiscaltipec, Mexico = Temascaltepec, México.)

Habitat.—Deciduous forest and woodland, cottonwood riparian woodland, pine-oak association, oak scrub, and pinyon-juniper woodland; in migration and winter, a variety of wooded habitats (Subtropical and Temperate zones).

Distribution.—*Breeds* from coastal southern British Columbia, southern Alberta, southwestern Saskatchewan, northeastern Montana, and central North Dakota south to northern Baja California, southern California, southern Nevada, central and southeastern Arizona, and, in the Mexican highlands, to Guerrero and Oaxaca (west of the Isthmus of Tehuantepec), and east to western South Dakota, central Nebraska, central Kansas, eastern New Mexico, and western Texas.

Winters from coastal California (rarely), southern Baja California, northern Mexico, southeastern Texas, and (rarely) southern Louisiana south to central Oaxaca and Veracruz.

Casual in eastern North America from southern Manitoba, Minnesota, Wisconsin, Michigan, western and southern Ontario, southwestern Quebec, New York, Maine, New Brunswick, and Nova Scotia south to the Gulf coast and Florida (recorded most frequently in New England and along the Atlantic coast south to South Carolina); sight reports for south-coastal Alaska (Middleton Island) and the Queen Charlotte Islands; a sight report for Costa Rica and an old record from Yucatán are highly questionable.

Notes.—See comments under *P. ludovicianus.*

Genus *CYANOCOMPSA* Cabanis

Cyanocompsa Cabanis, 1861, J. Ornithol. 9: 4. Type, by original designation, *Fringilla [Cyanoloxia] parellina* Bonaparte.

Notes.—*Cyanocompsa* and *Guiraca* are sometimes merged in *Passerina* (Phillips et al. 1964, Paynter 1970).

Cyanocompsa cyanoides (Lafresnaye). Blue-black Grosbeak.

Coccoborus cyanoides Lafresnaye, 1847, Rev. Zool. [Paris] 10: 74. (Panama.)

Habitat.—Tropical Lowland Evergreen Forest, Secondary Forest (0–1250 m; Tropical and lower Subtropical zones).

Distribution.—*Resident* from southern Veracruz, northern Oaxaca, Tabasco, Chiapas, southern Campeche, and southern Quintana Roo south on the Gulf-Caribbean slope of Central America to Nicaragua, on both slopes of Costa Rica (except the dry northwest) and Panama, and in South America from Colombia, Venezuela, and the Guianas south, west of the Andes to western Ecuador and east of the Andes to central Bolivia and Amazonian Brazil.

Cyanocompsa parellina (Bonaparte). Blue Bunting.

Cyanoloxia parellina (Lichtenstein MS) Bonaparte, 1850, Consp. Gen. Avium 1(2): 502. (Alvarado, Veracruz, Mexico.)

Habitat.—Tropical Deciduous Forest, Tropical Lowland Evergreen Forest Edge, Pine-Oak Forest (0–1850 m; Tropical and lower Subtropical zones).

Distribution.—*Resident* from central Sinaloa, eastern San Luis Potosí, northern Nuevo León, and central Tamaulipas south locally along both slopes of Middle America (including the Yucatan Peninsula and Isla Mujeres) to north-central Nicaragua.

Casual in southern and coastal Texas and southwestern Louisiana (Cameron Parish).

Genus *GUIRACA* Swainson

Guiraca Swainson, 1827, Philos. Mag. (n.s.) 1: 438. Type, by subsequent designation (Swainson, 1827), *Loxia caerulea* "Wilson" [= Linnaeus].

Notes.—See comments under *Cyanocompsa.*

Guiraca caerulea (Linnaeus). Blue Grosbeak.

Loxia cærulea Linnaeus, 1758, Syst. Nat. (ed. 10) 1: 175. Based on "The blew Gross-bec" Catesby, Nat. Hist. Carolina 1: 39, pl. 39. (in America = South Carolina.)

Habitat.—Brushy and weedy fields, scrub, young second-growth woods, riparian thickets (upper Tropical to lower Temperate zones, in nonbreeding season also to lower Tropical Zone).

Distribution.—*Breeds* from northern California, western and southern Nevada, southern Idaho, south-central Montana (once), south-central North Dakota, southwestern Minnesota, central and northeastern Illinois, northwestern Indiana, northern Ohio, southern Pennsylvania, and southeastern New York (once) south to northern Baja California and southern Arizona, in the highlands and Pacific lowlands of Middle America through Mexico, Guatemala, El Salvador, Honduras, and Nicaragua to central Costa Rica, and to southern Tamaulipas, the Gulf coast, and central (casually southern) Florida, with the range expanding along northern edge.

Winters from southern Baja California and northern Mexico (rarely from the Gulf coast and southern Florida, casually elsewhere in the North American breeding range and north to New England) south through Middle America to central Panama (Canal area).

Migrates from California and the North American breeding range south over most of Middle America, and through Bermuda (where one winter record), the Bahama Islands, Greater Antilles (east to the Virgin Islands), Cayman Islands, and Swan Islands.

Casual north to Oregon, southeastern British Columbia, southern Saskatchewan, Wisconsin, central Ontario, southern Quebec, New Brunswick, Nova Scotia, and Newfoundland. Accidental in southeastern Alaska (Petersburg) and Ecuador; sight reports from Michigan and Colombia.

Genus *PASSERINA* Vieillot

Passerina Vieillot, 1816, Analyse, p. 30. Type, by subsequent designation (G. R. Gray, 1840), "Le Ministre" Buffon = *Tanagra cyanea* Linnaeus.

Notes.—See comments under *Cyanocompsa*.

Passerina rositae (Lawrence). Rose-bellied Bunting.

Cyanospiza rositæ (Sumichrast MS) Lawrence, 1874, Ann. Lyc. Nat. Hist. N. Y. 10: 397. (Tehuantepec, Mexico = Rancho de Cacoprieto, Oaxaca; Binford, 1989, Ornithol. Monogr. 43, p. 345.)

Habitat.—Hilly areas in Tropical Deciduous Forest (0–1250 m; Tropical Zone).

Distribution.—*Resident* in southeastern Oaxaca (Isthmus of Tehuantepec region west to the Chivela, Matías Romero, and Juchitán areas) and extreme western Chiapas (La Trinidad).

Notes.—Also known as Rosita's Bunting.

Passerina amoena (Say). Lazuli Bunting.

Emberiza amœna Say, 1823, in Long, Exped. Rocky Mount. 2: 47 (note). (Rocky Mountains, source of the Arkansas = near Canyon City, Colorado.)

Habitat.—Arid brushy areas in canyons, riparian thickets, chaparral, scrub oak, and open woodland; in migration and winter, also open grassy and weedy areas.

Distribution.—*Breeds* from south-central British Columbia, southern Alberta, southern Saskatchewan, central North Dakota, and northeastern South Dakota south to northwestern Baja California, southern California, southern Nevada, central Arizona, central New Mexico, and central Texas (Kerr County, with summer records also for Trans-Pecos and the Panhandle), and east to western Nebraska, western Kansas, and western Oklahoma.

Winters from southern Arizona and Chihuahua (casually north to central California and extreme western Texas) south to Guerrero and central Veracruz.

Migrates regularly through the southwestern United States and northwestern Mexico (including Baja California), rarely west to southwestern British Columbia, north to central Alberta, and east to eastern and southern Texas.

Casual in eastern North America (recorded Manitoba, Minnesota, Wisconsin, Missouri, Illinois, Louisiana, Ontario, Pennsylvania, Maine, Maryland, South Carolina, and Florida). Accidental in southern Mackenzie; sight reports for southeastern Alaska, Arkansas, Virginia, and central Oaxaca.

Notes.—*Passerina amoena* and *P. cyanea* hybridize to a limited extent where their ranges overlap in the Great Plains region (Sibley and Short 1959, Emlen et al. 1975, R. L. Kroodsma 1975, Thompson 1976) but are locally sympatric with little or no interbreeding in the southwestern United States. Evidence of behavioral isolating mechanisms (Baker et al. 1990) indicates that although formerly treated by some (e.g., Phillips et al. 1964) as conspecific, they are better considered to constitute a superspecies (Mayr and Short 1970).

Passerina cyanea (Linnaeus). Indigo Bunting.

Tanagra cyanea Linnaeus, 1766, Syst. Nat. (ed. 12) 1: 315. Based on "The blew Linnet" Catesby, Nat. Hist. Carolina 1: 45, pl. 45. (in Carolina = South Carolina.)

Habitat.—Deciduous forest edge and regenerating clearings, open woodland, second growth, shrubby areas, scrub, and riparian woodland; in migration and winter, a variety of open forest, woodland, scrub, and weedy habitats.

Distribution.—*Breeds* from southeastern British Columbia (Creston), southeastern Saskatchewan, southern Manitoba, northern Minnesota, south-central Ontario, southwestern Quebec, southern Maine, southern New Brunswick, and Nova Scotia south to southern New Mexico, Texas (west to Big Bend and south to San Patricio County), the Gulf coast, and central Florida, and west to Montana, eastern Colorado, western Kansas, and central New Mexico; recorded breeding sporadically also in Colorado, southwestern Utah, central and southeastern Arizona, and southern California.

Winters from Nayarit, San Luis Potosí (rarely from southern Texas, the Gulf coast, and Florida, casually in winter elsewhere in the North American breeding range and in coastal California) and Bermuda south through Middle America (including most adjacent islands), the Greater Antilles (east to the Virgin Islands), and the Cayman and Bahama islands to Panama (rare east of the Canal area) and northwestern Colombia.

Migrates through the United States east of the Rockies, Mexico (except the northwestern portion), northern Middle America, Bermuda, the western Greater Antilles, and Bahama Islands; rarely (but regularly) through California, Baja California, northwestern Mexico, southern Arizona, and New Mexico; and casually elsewhere in western North America from southern British Columbia, Idaho, southern Alberta, and southern Saskatchewan southward.

Casual or accidental north to northwestern and south-coastal Alaska (Wainwright, Anchorage), northern Manitoba, central Quebec, Prince Edward Island, Newfoundland, and Iceland; also to Revillagigedo Islands (Socorro Island; sight report) and Europe (where likely escapes).

Notes.—See comments under *P. amoena.*

Passerina versicolor (Bonaparte). Varied Bunting.

> *Spiza versicolor* Bonaparte, 1838, Proc. Zool. Soc. London (1837), p. 120. (near Temascallepec [= Temascaltepec, state of México].)

Habitat.—Arid Montane Scrub, Arid Lowland Scrub, Riparian Thickets (0–1900 m; Tropical and Subtropical zones).

Distribution.—*Resident* from southern Baja California, northern Sonora, south-central and southeastern Arizona, southern New Mexico, and western and southern Texas (Culberson and Crockett counties, and the Rio Grande Valley) south through Mexico (except the Yucatan Peninsula) to central Oaxaca (east to Rancho Las Animas), and in Chiapas and Guatemala. Withdraws from the southwestern United States and northern plateau of Mexico in winter. Casual in southeastern California. Accidental in Ontario (Long Point).

Passerina leclancherii Lafresnaye. Orange-breasted Bunting.

> *Passerina (Spiza) Leclancherii* Lafresnaye, 1840, Rev. Zool. [Paris] 3: 260. (Acapulo [sic], au Mexique = Acapulco, Guerrero.)

Habitat.—Tropical Deciduous Forest, Arid Lowland Scrub (0–1200 m; Tropical and lower Subtropical zones).

Distribution.—*Resident* on the Pacific slope from Colima, Jalisco, and Michoacán south through Guerrero, southern Puebla, and southern Oaxaca to southwestern Chiapas (Arriaga).

An individual netted in southern Texas (Hidalgo County) in 1972 was almost certainly an individual escaped from captivity.

Notes.—Also known as Leclancher's Bunting.

Passerina ciris (Linnaeus). Painted Bunting.

> *Emberiza Ciris* Linnaeus, 1758, Syst. Nat. (ed. 10) 1: 179. Based mainly on "The Painted Finch" Catesby, Nat. Hist. Carolina 1: 44, pl. 44. (in America = South Carolina.)

Habitat.—Partly open situations with dense brush and scattered trees, riparian thickets, and weedy and shrubby areas; in migration and winter, a variety of open weedy, grassy, and scrub habitats, and in open woodland.

Distribution.—*Breeds* from southeastern New Mexico, northern Texas, western and central Oklahoma, west-central Kansas, southern Missouri, and southwestern Tennessee south to southern Chihuahua, northern Coahuila, southern Texas, and southern Louisiana, and east along the Gulf coast to southern Alabama (locally in the Apalachicola region of western Florida); and from central South Carolina and southeastern North Carolina south, primarily on barrier islands and the adjacent mainland coast, to central Florida.

Winters from Sinaloa, southern Tamaulipas, southern Florida, and the northwestern Bahama Islands south through Cuba, Jamaica, and Middle America (both slopes) to western Panama (east to western Panamá province), casually north to southern Arizona and western and southern Texas.

Migrates west rarely to southern California and southeastern Arizona.

Casual north to southeastern Wyoming, Minnesota, Wisconsin, Michigan, Ontario, New Brunswick, and Nova Scotia, west to Oregon, California, and Nevada, and on Bermuda. Some of these reports may be based on escaped individuals, but many are not.

Notes.—Thompson (1991) suggested that the eastern and western populations might represent two species.

Genus *SPIZA* Bonaparte

Spiza Bonaparte, 1824, J. Acad. Nat. Sci. Philadelphia 4: 45. Type, by subsequent designation (Bonaparte, 1827), *Emberiza americana* Gmelin.

Notes.—Affinities of this genus are uncertain (Sibley and Monroe 1990); it may be an icterid or an aberrant cardinalid (Paynter 1970). It is an outgroup to the other cardinalids (Tamplin et al. 1993).

Spiza americana (Gmelin). Dickcissel.

Emberiza americana Gmelin, 1789, Syst. Nat. 1(2): 872. Based on the "Black-throated Bunting" Pennant, Arct. Zool. 2: 363, pl. 17. (in Noveboraco = New York.)

Habitat.—Grassland, meadows, savanna, cropland (especially alfalfa), and brushy fields; in migration and winter, also a variety of open country, second growth, and scrub.

Distribution.—*Breeds* from eastern Montana, southern Saskatchewan, southern Manitoba, western and southern Minnesota, northern Wisconsin, northern Michigan, southern Ontario, and central New York south to northeastern Wyoming, eastern Colorado, northeastern New Mexico (rarely), western and southern Texas, southern Louisiana, central Mississippi, central (rarely southern) Alabama, central and southeastern Georgia, and South Carolina, at least formerly also in the Atlantic lowlands from Massachusetts to North Carolina; breeding sporadic and irregular in eastern portion of range.

Winters from Nayarit south, primarily along the Pacific slope, through Middle America to northern and eastern Colombia, Venezuela (most abundant wintering area), Trinidad, and the Guianas, locally in small numbers also in coastal lowlands from southern New England south to Florida and west to coastal and southern Texas, casually north to the southern Great Lakes region and northwest to eastern Colorado.

Migrates through the eastern United States and Bahama Islands through Middle America (both slopes), and casually through California, Baja California, southern Arizona, eastern and southern New Mexico, Cuba, Jamaica, Puerto Rico, the Cayman Islands, islands in the western Caribbean Sea (Swan, Providencia, San Andrés, and Albuquerque Cay), and the Netherlands Antilles (Aruba).

Casual north to southern British Columbia, southern Alberta, southern Quebec, southern New Brunswick, Prince Edward Island, Nova Scotia, and Newfoundland, and to Bermuda and Clipperton Island. Accidental in Norway.

Family **ICTERIDAE**: Blackbirds

Genus *DOLICHONYX* Swainson

Dolichonyx Swainson, 1827, Philos. Mag. (n.s.) 1: 435. Type, by monotypy, *Fringilla oryzivora* Linnaeus.

Dolichonyx oryzivorus (Linnaeus). Bobolink.

> *Fringilla oryzivora* Linnaeus, 1758, Syst. Nat. (ed. 10) 1: 179. Based mainly on "The Rice-Bird" Catesby, Nat. Hist. Carolina 1: 14, pl. 14. (in Cuba, . . . in Carolinam = South Carolina.)

Habitat.—Tall grass areas, flooded meadows, prairie, deep cultivated grains, and alfalfa and clover fields; in migration and winter, also in rice fields and marshes.

Distribution.—*Breeds* from central and southern interior British Columbia, southern Alberta, southern Saskatchewan, southern Manitoba, central Ontario, southern Quebec (including Magdalen Islands), New Brunswick, Prince Edward Island, Nova Scotia, and Newfoundland south to eastern and south-central Washington, eastern Oregon, northeastern Nevada (local), northern Utah, eastern Colorado, Kansas, northern Missouri, central Illinois, central Indiana, southern Ohio, southern Pennsylvania, and central New Jersey, and locally to north-central Kentucky, extreme northeastern Tennessee, western North Carolina, western Virginia, and western and central Maryland, also isolated breeding in east-central Arizona; recorded in summer (but without positive evidence of breeding) north to southwestern and northeastern British Columbia, central Alberta, central Saskatchewan, northern Ontario, and eastern Quebec, and south to northern California, central Nevada, and north-central New Mexico.

Winters in southern South America (mostly east of the Andes) in eastern Bolivia, central Brazil, Paraguay, and (primarily) northern Argentina. Limits of winter range (versus areas where only occurring as migrant) not well known.

Migrates regularly through the southeastern United States (west to the Great Plains and central Texas), the West Indies, Yucatan Peninsula, Belize, islands in the Caribbean Sea (Swan, Providencia, and San Andrés), the northern coast of South America, Costa Rica (fall only; Caribbean lowlands, rarely on Pacific slope), Panama, and northern South America from Colombia, Venezuela (also islands off the northern coast), and the Guianas southward; also rarely through western North America south to California, southern Nevada, Arizona, and southern New Mexico.

Casual or accidental in Alaska (Point Barrow, Hyder), Labrador, southern Baja California, Honduras (Isla Utila in the Bay Islands), Nicaragua (Río Escondido), Cocos Island (off Costa Rica), Bermuda, the Galapagos Islands, northern Chile, Greenland, the British Isles, Norway, France, Gibraltar, and Italy; sight reports for southern Mackenzie, Veracruz, and Clipperton Island.

Genus *AGELAIUS* Vieillot

> *Agelaius* Vieillot, 1816, Analyse, p. 33. Type, by original designation, "Troupiale Commandeur" Buffon = *Oriolus phoeniceus* Linnaeus.

Notes.—Although Lanyon (1994) showed that *Agelaius* is not a monophyletic genus, those species found in the Check-list area form a monophyletic group.

Agelaius phoeniceus (Linnaeus). Red-winged Blackbird.

> *Oriolus phœniceus* Linnaeus, 1766, Syst. Nat. (ed. 12) 1: 161. Based mainly on "The red wing'd Starling" Catesby, Nat. Hist. Carolina 1: 13, pl. 13. (in America septentrionali = Charleston, South Carolina.)

Habitat.—Fresh-water and brackish marshes, bushes and small trees along watercourses, and upland cultivated fields; in migration and winter, also in open cultivated lands, plowed fields, pastures, and prairie (Tropical to Temperate zones, in Central America restricted to Tropical and lower Subtropical zones).

Distribution.—*Breeds* [*phoeniceus* group] from east-central, south-coastal and southeastern Alaska (west to Anchorage and north to Fairbanks), southern Yukon, west-central and southern Mackenzie, northern Saskatchewan, central Manitoba, northern Ontario, southern Quebec (including Anticosti and Magdalen islands), New Brunswick, Prince Edward Island, Nova Scotia, and southwestern Newfoundland south to northern Baja California, locally through Mexico (including the Yucatan Peninsula and Holbox Island) and along both coasts of Central America to Nicaragua and northern Costa Rica (Guanacaste, Río Frío), and to southern Texas, the Gulf coast, and southern Florida (including the Florida Keys); also in the northern Bahama Islands (south to Andros and Eleuthera).

Winters [*phoeniceus* group] from southern British Columbia, Idaho, Montana, North Dakota, southern Minnesota, the southern Great Lakes region, southern Ontario, and New England (casually farther north) south throughout the remainder of the breeding range, with the southwestern and most of Middle American populations being sedentary.

Resident [*gubernator* group] in Mexican Plateau region from Durango and Zacatecas south to México, Distrito Federal, and Puebla.

Casual [*phoeniceus* group] north to western and northern Alaska, northern Mackenzie, and Victoria Island, and in Trinidad.

Notes.—Groups: *A. phoeniceus* Linnaeus, 1766 [Red-winged Blackbird] and *A. gubernator* [Bicolored Blackbird]. Hardy and Dickerman (1965) found that where the two groups come in contact they differ in vocalizations, breeding habitat, juvenal plumage, female plumage, epaulet color of males, and bill shape; they also found that interbreeding was limited at one locality (Lerma marshes) but extensive at another (Laguna Rosario). Lanyon (1994) confirmed the traditional interpretation that *A. phoeniceus* and *A. tricolor* are sister taxa (but *A. assimilis* was not available for analysis).

Agelaius assimilis Lembeye. Red-shouldered Blackbird.

Agelaius assimilis Lembeye, 1850, Aves Isla Cuba, p. 64, pl. 9, fig. 3. (Cuba.)

Habitat.—Trees and tall grasses at the margins of fresh-water marshes.

Distribution.—*Resident* in western Cuba and the Isle of Pines.

Notes.—Formerly considered conspecific with *A. phoeniceus*, but separated on the basis of studies by Whittingham et al. (1992) and Garrido and Kirkconnell (1996); the two species constitute a superspecies.

Agelaius tricolor (Audubon). Tricolored Blackbird.

Icterus tricolor Audubon, 1837, Birds Amer. (folio) 4: pl. 388, fig. 1 (1839, Ornithol. Biogr. 5: 1). (No locality given = Santa Barbara, California.)

Habitat.—Fresh-water marshes of cattails, tule, bulrushes, and sedges; in migration and winter, also in open cultivated lands and pastures.

Distribution.—*Breeds* from northwestern and eastern Oregon (east of the coast ranges) south through interior California, and along the coast from central California (Sonoma County) south to northwestern Baja California (south to lat. 30° N.).

Winters from northern California (Glenn County southward) south throughout the breeding range and adjacent agricultural areas.

Casual in northwestern and southeastern California.

Notes.—See comments under *A. phoeniceus*.

Agelaius humeralis (Vigors). Tawny-shouldered Blackbird.

Leistes humeralis Vigors, 1827, Zool. J. 3: 442. (neighborhood of Havana, Cuba.)

Habitat.—Arid Lowland Scrub, Pastures/Agricultural Lands, Second-growth Scrub (0–900 m).

Distribution.—*Resident* in Cuba (including Cayo Cantiles and Archipelago de las Jardines) and western Hispaniola (west-central Haiti in vicinity of Port-de-Paix, lower Artibonite River, and St. Marc).

Casual in Florida (Florida Keys, including Dry Tortugas, also a sight report from Marathon).

Notes.—*Agelaius humeralis* and *A. xanthomus* constitute a superspecies (Sibley and Monroe 1990); they are sister taxa (Lanyon 1994).

Agelaius xanthomus (Sclater). Yellow-shouldered Blackbird.

Icterus xanthomus Sclater, 1862, Cat. Collect. Amer. Birds., p. 131. (Mexico, error = Puerto Rico.)

Habitat.—Arid Lowland Scrub, Pastures/Agricultural Lands, Riparian Thickets.
Distribution.—*Resident* on Puerto Rico (presently restricted to the southwestern and northeastern sections, including Mona Island).
Notes.—See comments under *A. humeralis.*

Genus *NESOPSAR* Sclater

Nesopsar Sclater, 1859, Ibis, p. 457 (footnote). Type, by original designation, *N. nigerrimus* = *Icterus nigerrimus* Osburn.

Nesopsar nigerrimus (Osburn). Jamaican Blackbird.

Icterus nigerrimus Osburn, 1859, Zoologist 17: 6662. (lower mountains of Jamaica.)

Habitat.—Montane Evergreen Forest (500–1500 m).
Distribution.—*Resident* on Jamaica.

Genus *STURNELLA* Vieillot

Sturnella Vieillot, 1816, Analyse, p. 34. Type, by monotypy, "Stourne, ou Merle à fer-à-cheval" Buffon = *Alauda magna* Linnaeus.
Leistes Vigors, 1825, Zool. J. 2: 191. Type, by original designation, *Oriolus americanus* Gmelin = *Emberiza militaris* Linnaeus.

Sturnella militaris (Linnaeus). Red-breasted Blackbird.

Emberiza militaris Linnaeus, 1758, Syst. Nat. (ed. 10) 1: 178. Based mainly on *Turdus hæmatodos* Linnaeus, Mus. Adolphi Friderici 1: 18. (in America, Asia = Surinam.)

Habitat.—Pastures/Agricultural Lands, Low Seasonally Wet Grassland, Freshwater Marshes (0–1600 m; Tropical Zone).
Distribution.—*Resident* in southwestern Costa Rica (Puntarenas province; first detected in 1974), Panama (entire Pacific slope, and Caribbean lowlands in Colón and the Canal area), and South America from northern Colombia, Venezuela, Tobago, Trinidad, and the Guianas south, east of the Andes, to northeastern Peru, and Amazonian and central Brazil. Expanding its range north in Costa Rica.
Notes.—Often (e.g., Blake *in* Paynter 1968) considered conspecific with South American *S. superciliaris* (Bonaparte, 1850) [White-browed Blackbird], but see Short (1968). Often placed in the genus *Leistes* (e.g., Blake *in* Paynter 1968, Parker and Remsen 1987, Sibley and Monroe 1990), but we follow Short (1968).

Sturnella magna (Linnaeus). Eastern Meadowlark.

Alauda magna Linnaeus, 1758, Syst. Nat. (ed. 10) 1: 167. Based on "The Large Lark" Catesby, Nat. Hist. Carolina 1: 33, pl. 33. (in America, Africa = South Carolina.)

Habitat.—Grassland, savanna, open fields, pastures, and cultivated lands (Tropical to Temperate zones).
Distribution.—*Breeds* [*magna* group] from southwestern South Dakota, northern Minnesota, northern Wisconsin, northern Michigan, central Ontario, southwestern Quebec, Maine, southern New Brunswick, and central Nova Scotia south through the eastern United States (west to western Nebraska, northeastern Colorado [probably], central Kansas, and eastern Texas) and Middle America (except Baja California and northwestern Mexico) to central Panama (Pacific slope east to eastern Panamá province), and to the Gulf coast, southern Florida (rarely the Florida Keys), Cuba (including cayos Coco, Romano, and Saetía), and the Isle of Pines; and in South America from northern and eastern Colombia, Venezuela, Guyana, and Surinam south, east of the Andes, to Amazonian Brazil.
Winters [*magna* group] from northern Texas, Kansas, Nebraska, southern Minnesota, central Wisconsin, southern Michigan, southern Ontario, New York, and New England (casually farther north) south throughout the remainder of the breeding range, with the West Indian, Middle American and South American populations being essentially sedentary.

Resident [*lilianae* group] from northwestern, central and southern Arizona, central New Mexico, and western and central Texas south to northeastern Sonora and northwestern and central Chihuahua, with some dispersal in winter.

Casual [*magna* group] north to southern Manitoba, west-central and eastern Quebec, Prince Edward Island, and Newfoundland; a sight report [*lilianae* group] of a singing bird in Baja California.

Notes.—Groups: *S. magna* [Eastern Meadowlark] and *S. lilianae* Oberholser, 1930 [Lilian's Meadowlark]. The two groups differ in plumage, morphology, and habitat preferences (Lanyon 1962, Rohwer 1972, 1976), but are quite similar in vocalizations (Lanyon 1962). *Sturnella magna* and *S. neglecta* rarely interbreed (Lanyon 1957, 1966, Rohwer 1972, 1973) and their hybrids are sterile (Lanyon 1979); they constitute a superspecies (Mayr and Short 1970).

Sturnella neglecta Audubon. Western Meadowlark.

> *Sturnella neglecta* Audubon, 1844, Birds Amer. (octavo ed.) 7: 339, pl. 489. (Missouri River above Fort Croghan = Old Fort Union, North Dakota.)

Habitat.—Grassland, savanna, cultivated fields, and pastures (Subtropical and Temperate zones).

Distribution.—*Breeds* from central British Columbia (including Vancouver Island), north-central Alberta, central Saskatchewan, southern Manitoba, western Ontario, northwestern Minnesota, northern Wisconsin, northern Michigan, southern Ontario, and northwestern Ohio south to northwestern Baja California, (irregularly also on Guadalupe Island) southern California, northwestern Sonora, western and central Arizona, in the Mexican highlands to eastern Jalisco, Guanajuato, San Luis Potosí, southern Nuevo León, and western Tamaulipas, and to west-central Texas, northwestern Louisiana, southwestern Tennessee, southern Illinois, northern Indiana, central Ohio, western Pennsylvania (possibly), and western New York.

Winters from southern British Columbia, southern Alberta, southern Saskatchewan, southern Manitoba, southern Wisconsin, and southwestern Michigan south to southern Baja California, Michoacán, México, northern Veracruz, southern Texas, and the Gulf coast east to northwestern (possibly central) Florida, occurring east regularly to western Kentucky, central Tennessee, and Alabama.

Introduced and established in the Hawaiian Islands (Kauai).

Casual or accidental north to northern Alaska (Anaktuvuk Pass), southern Mackenzie, northern Alberta, northern Manitoba, northern Ontario, southwestern Quebec, and New Brunswick, and east to southeastern New York and Georgia; singing birds, presumably this species, have been recorded in New England and New Jersey.

Notes.—See comments under *S. magna*.

Genus *XANTHOCEPHALUS* Bonaparte

> *Xanthocephalus* Bonaparte, 1850, Consp. Gen. Avium 1(2): 431. Type, by monotypy, *Psarocolius perspicillatus* Wagler = *Icterus xanthocephalus* Bonaparte.

Xanthocephalus xanthocephalus (Bonaparte). Yellow-headed Blackbird.

> *Icterus icterocephalus* (not *Oriolus icterocephalus* Linnaeus, 1766 = *Agelaius icterocephalus*) Bonaparte, 1825, Amer. Ornithol. 1: 27, figs. 1–2. (Pawnee villages on the river Platte = along the Loup River, just west of Fullerton, Nance County, Nebraska.) *Nomen oblitum.*
>
> *Icterus xanthocephalus* Bonaparte, 1826, J. Acad. Nat. Sci. Philadelphia 5: 223. New name for *Icterus icterocephalus* Bonaparte.

Habitat.—Fresh-water marshes of cattail, tule or bulrushes; in migration and winter also in open cultivated lands, pastures, and fields.

Distribution.—*Breeds* from western Oregon, central Washington, central interior and northeastern British Columbia, northern Alberta, north-central Saskatchewan, central Manitoba, extreme western Ontario, northern Minnesota, northern Michigan, and extreme southern Ontario south to southern California, northeastern Baja California, southwestern and east-central Arizona, southwestern and northeastern New Mexico, northern Texas (Panhandle), western Oklahoma (Panhandle), central Kansas, and western and northern Missouri, central Illinois, northwestern Indiana, and northwestern Ohio. Formerly bred in northern Tamaulipas.

Winters from Washington, Oregon, California, central Arizona, Colorado, southeastern Texas, and (rarely) the Gulf Coast (east to Florida) south to southern Baja California, northern Guerrero (perhaps irregularly to southeastern Oaxaca), Chiapas, Puebla, and central Veracruz.

Casual north to western and northern Alaska (including in the Arctic Ocean 100 miles west of Point Hope), southern Mackenzie, and northern Manitoba, and over eastern North America from southern Quebec, New Brunswick, Nova Scotia, and Newfoundland south; also recorded Yucatan (sight report), Costa Rica (Palo Verde), Panama (eastern Panamá province), Cuba, the northern Bahama Islands (Grand Bahama, San Salvador), Barbados, at sea in the Atlantic Ocean (300 miles northeast of New York City), and in Greenland, Iceland, Great Britain, Norway, Sweden, Denmark, and France; sight reports for the Revillagigedo Islands (Socorro Island) and off Yucatán.

Genus *DIVES* Deppe

> *Dives* "Lichtenst[ein]." W. Deppe, 1830, Preis.-Verz. Säugeth. Vögel, etc., Mex., p. 1. Type, by tautonymy, *Icterus dives* Deppe.
> *Ptiloxena* Chapman, 1892, Bull. Amer. Mus. Nat. Hist. 4: 307. Type, by original designation, *Quiscalus atroviolaceus* d'Orbigny.

Notes.—Freeman and Zink (1995) found that *Dives* and *Euphagus* are each others' closest relatives. An analysis of blood proteins (Smith and Zimmerman 1976) suggested a close relationship between *Euphagus* and *Quiscalus* (including *Cassidix*), but did not analyze *Dives*.

Dives dives (Deppe). Melodious Blackbird.

> *Icterus dives* "Lichtenst[ein]." W. Deppe, 1830, Preis.-Verz. Säugeth. Vögel, etc., Mex., p. 1. (Valle Real, Veracruz = Valle Nacional, Oaxaca; Binford, 1990, Wilson Bull. 102: 153.)

Habitat.—Tropical Lowland Evergreen Forest Edge, Secondary Forest, Gallery Forest (0–2000 m; Tropical and lower Subtropical zones).

Distribution.—*Resident* from southeastern San Luis Potosí, southern Tamaulipas, Puebla, México, and northern Oaxaca south on the Gulf-Caribbean slope of Middle America (including the Yucatan Peninsula) to north-central Nicaragua, and on the Pacific slope in El Salvador, casually to northwestern Costa Rica (to Tarcoles area).

Notes.—Also known as Singing Blackbird. *Dives dives* and the South American *D. warszewiczi* (Cabanis, 1861) [Scrub Blackbird] constitute a superspecies (Sibley and Monroe 1990); some authors (e.g., Hellmayr 1937) consider them conspecific.

Dives atroviolacea (d'Orbigny). Cuban Blackbird.

> *Quiscalus atroviolaceus* d'Orbigny, 1839, in La Sagra, Hist. Fis. Pol. Nat. Cuba, Ois., p. 121, pl. 19. (Cuba.)

Habitat.—Tropical Lowland Evergreen Forest Edge, Gallery Forest, Secondary Forest (0–500 m).

Distribution.—*Resident* on Cuba; reports from the Isle of Pines are doubtful.

Notes.—Sometimes placed in the monotypic genus *Ptiloxena*.

Genus *EUPHAGUS* Cassin

> *Euphagus* Cassin, 1867, Proc. Acad. Nat. Sci. Philadelphia 18 (1866): 413. Type, by monotypy, *Psarocolius cyanocephalus* Wagler.

Notes.—See comments under *Dives*.

Euphagus carolinus (Müller). Rusty Blackbird.

Turdus Carolinus P. L. S. Müller, 1776, Natursyst., Suppl., pl. 140. (Carolina.)

Habitat.—Moist woodland (primarily coniferous), bushy bogs, and wooded edges of watercourses; in migration and winter also open woodland, scrub, pastures, and cultivated lands.

Distribution.—*Breeds* from western and north-central Alaska, northern Yukon, northwestern and central Mackenzie, southern Keewatin, northern Manitoba, northern Ontario, northern Quebec, north-central Labrador, and Newfoundland south to southwestern and south-coastal Alaska, northwestern and interior British Columbia, southwestern and south-central Alberta, central Saskatchewan, central Manitoba, northeastern Minnesota, northern Michigan (rarely), southern Ontario, southern Quebec, northeastern New York, western Massachusetts, central New Hampshire, central Maine, and Nova Scotia.

Winters from central (casually) and south-coastal Alaska, southern British Columbia, central Alberta, southern Saskatchewan, southern Manitoba, southern Ontario, and the northern United States (east of the Rockies) south to central and southeastern Texas, the Gulf coast, and northern Florida, and west to Montana, central Colorado, and eastern New Mexico, rarely in southern Arizona and coastal California.

Migrates regularly through southeastern Alaska, northern British Columbia, and (rarely) eastern California.

Casual elsewhere in western North America from Idaho and western Montana south to northern Baja California, Sonora (sight report), to islands in the Bering Sea (St. Lawrence, and St. Paul in the Pribilofs), and to southern Florida. Accidental in Siberia and Greenland.

Euphagus cyanocephalus (Wagler). Brewer's Blackbird.

Psarocolius cyanocephalus Wagler, 1829, Isis von Oken, col. 758. (Temascaltepec, Mexico = Oaxaca City, Oaxaca; Binford, 1989, Ornithol. Monogr. 43, p. 348.)

Habitat.—Shrubby and bushy areas (especially near water), riparian woodland, aspen parklands, cultivated lands, marshes, and around human habitation; in migration and winter also in pastures and fields.

Distribution.—*Breeds* from southwestern and central interior British Columbia (including Vancouver Island), southwestern Mackenzie, north-central Alberta, central Saskatchewan, southern Manitoba, central Ontario, and northern New York south to northwestern Baja California, southern California, southern Nevada, central Arizona, southern New Mexico, western and northern Texas, Oklahoma, Colorado, northwestern Nebraska, southern Minnesota, southern Wisconsin, northeastern Illinois, northwestern Indiana, and southern Michigan. The breeding range has recently expanded along its eastern border.

Winters from southern British Columbia, central Alberta, Montana, the eastern edge of the Rockies, Kansas, Oklahoma, Missouri, the northern portions of the Gulf states, northern Georgia, and western South Carolina (casually farther north) south to southern Baja California, Jalisco, western Oaxaca, and central Veracruz, irregularly farther south to southeastern Oaxaca (Isthmus of Tehuantepec), southwestern Chiapas, Campeche, southern Texas, the Gulf coast, and southern Florida.

Migrates regularly as far east as the Appalachians from Ohio southward.

Casual north to southeastern Alaska and southern Keewatin, and in the northeast from southern Quebec (sight reports), New York, New England, and Nova Scotia southward. Accidental in northern Alaska (Barrow) and western Guatemala (Hacienda Chancol).

Genus *QUISCALUS* Vieillot

Quiscalus Vieillot, 1816, Analyse, p. 36. Type, by subsequent designation (G. R. Gray, 1840), *Gracula quiscala* [sic] Linnaeus.

Cassidix Lesson, 1831, Traité Ornithol., livr. 6, p. 433. Type, by subsequent designation (G. R. Gray, 1840), *Cassidix mexicanus* Lesson = *Corvus mexicanus* Gmelin.

Holoquiscalus Cassin, 1867, Proc. Acad. Nat. Sci. Philadelphia 18 (1866): 404. Type, by subsequent designation (Sclater, 1884), *Quiscalus crassirostris* Swainson = *Oriolus niger* Boddaert.

Notes.—See comments under *Dives*.

Quiscalus quiscula (Linnaeus). Common Grackle.

Gracula Quiscula Linnaeus, 1758, Syst. Nat. (ed. 10) 1: 109. Based mainly on "The Purple Jack-Daw" Catesby, Nat. Hist. Carolina 1: 12, pl. 12. (in America septentrionali = coast of South Carolina.)

Habitat.—Partly open situations with scattered trees, open woodland (coniferous or deciduous), forest edge, and suburbs; in migration and winter also in open situations, cultivated lands, pastures, fields, and marshes.

Distribution.—*Breeds* from northeastern British Columbia, southern Mackenzie, northern Alberta, northwestern and central Saskatchewan, central and northeastern Manitoba, central Ontario, southern Quebec (including Anticosti Island), New Brunswick, Prince Edward Island, Nova Scotia, and southwestern Newfoundland south to Nevada, northern and eastern Utah, central Colorado, central and southeastern New Mexico, central and southeastern Texas (south to Corpus Christi region), the Gulf coast, and southern Florida (including the Florida Keys).

Winters from North Dakota, the southern Great Lakes region, southern Ontario, New England, and Nova Scotia (casually farther north) south to southern New Mexico, central and southern Texas (rarely also western Texas in the Big Bend region), the Gulf coast, and southern Florida.

Casual in western North America from northern and western Alaska south through western and southern British Columbia, Washington, and Oregon to southern California and Arizona; accidental in Denmark (possibly an escape); sight reports from northern Tamaulipas are unverified.

Notes.—Groups: *Q. quiscula* [Purple Grackle] and *Q. versicolor* Vieillot, 1819 [Bronzed Grackle]. The two groups were formerly considered separate species, but see Chapman (1935), Huntington (1952), Yang and Selander (1968), and Zink et al. (1991).

Quiscalus major Vieillot. Boat-tailed Grackle.

Quiscalus major Vieillot, 1819, Nouv. Dict. Hist. Nat. (nouv. éd.) 28: 487. (Mexico and Louisiana = New Orleans, Orleans Parish, Louisiana.)

Habitat.—Brackish marshes in coastal areas, and adjacent open situations, pastures, and cultivated lands.

Distribution.—*Resident* along the Atlantic coast from New York (Long Island) and New Jersey southward, throughout peninsular Florida, and west along the Gulf coast to southeastern Texas (south to Aransas and Calhoun counties, casually farther south).

Casual inland to central New York and New England.

Notes.—See comments under *Q. mexicanus*.

Quiscalus mexicanus (Gmelin). Great-tailed Grackle.

Corvus mexicanus Gmelin, 1788, Syst. Nat. 1(1): 375. Based in part on the "Mexican Crow" Latham, Gen. Synop. Birds 1(1): 396. (in nova Hispania = Veracruz, Veracruz.)

Habitat.—Second-growth Scrub, Pastures/Agricultural Lands, Mangrove Forest, Secondary Forest (0–2300 m; Tropical and Subtropical zones).

Distribution.—*Resident* in southwestern and east-central California and northeastern Baja California, and from central Nevada, north-central Utah, central Colorado, southern Nebraska, northern Iowa, northern Missouri, western Arkansas, and southwestern Louisiana south along both slopes of Middle America (including the Yucatan Peninsula, islands and cays off the Yucatan Peninsula and Belize, and the Bay Islands off Honduras) to Costa Rica (formerly Pacific coast only; now widespread), and Panama (Pacific slope throughout, Caribbean slope in Bocas del Toro, the Canal area, and San Blas, and widely on islands off the Pacific coast and off San Blas), and along both coasts of South America from Colombia east to northwestern Venezuela and south to Ecuador and northwestern Peru. The breeding range has expanded greatly in the last century, and is apparently continuing to do so. Some populations at the northern edge of the breeding range leave in winter.

Casual to the Hawaiian Islands (Oahu), and north to the Queen Charlotte Islands, northeastern Montana, south-central Idaho, southern Wyoming, Minnesota, central Illinois, Indiana, western and southern Ontario, and Ohio; sight reports for southeastern South Dakota, Michigan, and Mississippi, and elsewhere in northern Baja California.

Notes.—Although *Q. mexicanus* and *Q. major* were long considered conspecific, sympatry without interbreeding is known from southwestern Louisiana to southeastern Texas (Selander and Giller 1961, Pratt 1991); they should probably be regarded as constituting a superspecies (Mayr and Short 1970); they are sister taxa (e.g., Freeman and Zink 1995). *Quiscalus mexicanus, Q. major,* and *Q. palustris* are often placed in the genus *Cassidix.*

†*Quiscalus palustris* (Swainson). Slender-billed Grackle.

Scaphidurus palustris Swainson, 1827, Philos. Mag. (n.s.) 1: 437. (marshes and borders of the lakes round Mexico [City] = marshes at headwaters of Río Lerma, México.)

Habitat.—Fresh-water marshes and lake margins (lower Temperate Zone).
Distribution.—EXTINCT. Formerly *resident* in marshes in the upper reaches of the Río Lerma, México.
Notes.—See comments under *Q. mexicanus.*

Quiscalus nicaraguensis Salvin and Godman. Nicaraguan Grackle.

Quiscalus nicaraguensis Salvin and Godman, 1891, Ibis, p. 612. (Momotombo, Lake Managua [Nicaragua].)

Habitat.—Fresh-water Marshes, Pastures/Agricultural Lands (Tropical Zone).
Distribution.—*Resident* in southwestern Nicaragua (vicinity of Lake Managua and Lake Nicaragua) and extreme northern Costa Rica (Río Frío district).
Notes.—This species is sometimes treated in the genus *Cassidix.*

Quiscalus niger (Boddaert). Greater Antillean Grackle.

Oriolus niger Boddaert, 1783, Table Planches Enlum., p. 31. Based on "Troupiale Noir, de St. Domingue" Daubenton, Planches Enlum., pl. 534. (Santo Domingo = Port au Prince, Haiti.)

Habitat.—Pastures/Agricultural Lands, Second-growth Scrub (0–1800 m).
Distribution.—*Resident* on Cuba (including nearby cays), the Isle of Pines, Cayman Islands (including Cayman Brac), Jamaica, Hispaniola (including Gonâve, Tortue, and Beata islands, and Île-à-Vache), and Puerto Rico (including Vieques Island).
Notes.—*Quiscalus niger* and *Q. lugubris* appear to constitute a superspecies (Sibley and Monroe 1990). These two species are sometimes treated in the genus *Holoquiscalus.*

Quiscalus lugubris Swainson. Carib Grackle.

Quiscalus lugubris Swainson, 1838, Animals in Menageries, *in* Lardner, Cabinet Cyclopedia 98: 299, fig. "50c" [= 54c]. (Brazil, error = Guyana.)

Habitat.—Second-growth Scrub, Pastures/Agricultural Lands (0–600 m; Tropical Zone).
Distribution.—*Resident* in the Lesser Antilles (Montserrat, Guadeloupe, Marie Galante, Dominica, Martinique, St. Lucia, St. Vincent, Grenada, the Grenadines, and Barbados), Trinidad, northern Venezuela (including islands nearby), the Guianas, and extreme northeastern Brazil.

Introduced and established on St. Martin, Barbuda, Antigua, and (formerly) St. Kitts.
Notes.—Also known as Lesser Antillean Grackle. See comments under *Q. niger.*

Genus *MOLOTHRUS* Swainson

Molothrus Swainson, 1832, in Swainson and Richardson, Fauna Bor.-Amer. 2 (1831): 275, 277. Type, by original designation, *Fringilla pecoris* Gmelin = *Oriolus ater* Boddaert.

Tangavius Lesson, 1839, Rev. Zool. [Paris] 2: 41. Type, by monotypy, *Tangavius involucratus* Lesson = *Psarocolius aeneus* Wagler.

Notes.—Lanyon (1992) found that this genus is not monophyletic unless it is expanded to include *Scaphidura*; see also Freeman and Zink (1995).

Molothrus bonariensis (Gmelin). Shiny Cowbird.

Tanagra bonariensis Gmelin, 1789, Syst. Nat. 1(2): 898. Based on "Tangavio" Buffon, Hist. Nat. Ois. 4: 241, and Daubenton, Planches Enlum., pl. 710. (in Bonaria = Buenos Aires, Argentina.)

Habitat.—Tropical Deciduous Forest, Riparian Thickets, Tropical Lowland Evergreen Forest Edge, Arid Lowland Scrub, Second-growth Scrub, Pastures/Agricultural Lands (0–2000 m; Tropical and Subtropical zones).

Distribution.—*Resident* on Puerto Rico (since 1955), Vieques Island (where recorded initially about 1860, possibly as an introduction), Virgin Islands, Barbados (probably an introduction), and Grenada, in recent years spreading to the Cayman Islands and throughout the Antilles (except Jamaica); and in eastern Panama (eastern Panamá province, San Blas, and Darién), and from Colombia, Venezuela, Tobago, Trinidad, and the Guianas south over most of South America to central Chile and central Argentina.

Recently established in southern Florida (Smith and Sprunt 1987), now occurring regularly north to central Florida and rarely to western Florida and southern Georgia.

Ranges casually west to Oklahoma and central Texas, and north to North Carolina. Accidental in Maine.

Notes.—Also known as Glossy Cowbird.

Molothrus aeneus (Wagler). Bronzed Cowbird.

Psarocolius aeneus Wagler, 1829, Isis von Oken, col. 758. (Mexico = Mexico City.)

Habitat.—Pine-Oak Forest, Tropical Deciduous Forest, Second-growth Scrub, Pastures/Agricultural Lands (0–3000 m; Tropical and Subtropical zones).

Distribution.—*Resident* [*aeneus* group] from southeastern California, west-central and southern Arizona, southern New Mexico, western, west-central and southern Texas (with an isolated breeding population in the New Orleans area, Louisiana) south through Middle America (including the Yucatan Peninsula, but absent from Baja California) to central Panama (on the Caribbean slope in Bocas del Toro, and east to eastern Panamá province on the Pacific slope); and [*armenti* group] in coastal central northern Colombia. Northern populations [*aeneus* group] are mostly migratory.

Casual or accidental [*aeneus* group] in central eastern and southwestern California, central New Mexico, Colorado, Missouri, southern Mississippi, southern Alabama, and Florida; a sight report for northern Baja California.

Notes.—Often placed in the genus *Tangavius*. Groups: *M. aeneus* [Bronzed Cowbird] and *M. armenti* Cabanis, 1851 [Bronze-brown Cowbird]. The two groups were formerly considered separate species (e.g., Meyer de Schauensee 1970), but see Dugand and Eisenmann (1983). Also known as Red-eyed Cowbird.

Molothrus ater (Boddaert). Brown-headed Cowbird.

Oriolus ater Boddaert, 1783, Table Planches Enlum., p. 37. Based on "Troupiale, de la Caroline" Daubenton, Planches Enlum., pl. 606, fig. 1. (Carolina.)

Habitat.—Woodland, forest (primarily deciduous) and forest edge; in migration and winter also in open situations, cultivated lands, fields, pastures, and scrub (Tropical to Temperate zones).

Distribution.—*Breeds* from south-coastal (rarely) and southeastern (probably) Alaska, northern British Columbia, southern Mackenzie, northern Alberta, north-central Saskatchewan, southern Manitoba, central Ontario, southern Quebec, New Brunswick, Prince Edward Island, Nova Scotia, and southern Newfoundland south (including Vancouver Island) to southern Baja California, southeastern Oaxaca, Guerrero, Michoacán, Guanajuato, San Luis Potosí, northern Tamaulipas, southern Texas, the Gulf coast, and southern Florida.

Winters from southwestern British Columbia, western Washington, western Oregon, California, southern Utah, northern New Mexico, Kansas, central Missouri, the southern Great Lakes region, southern Ontario, New England, southern New Brunswick, and Nova Scotia (casually farther north) south to southern Baja California, Oaxaca (Isthmus of Tehuantepec), central Veracruz, southern Texas, the Gulf coast, and southern Florida.

Casual north to western and northern Alaska, northern Manitoba, and southern Labrador, and the Revillagigedo Islands (Socorro Island), Bermuda, the northern Bahama Islands, and Cuba.

Genus *SCAPHIDURA* Swainson

Scaphidura Swainson, 1837, Class. Birds 2: 272. Type, by virtual monotypy, *Scaphidura barita* Swainson = *Oriolus oryzivorus* Gmelin.
Psomocolax Peters, 1929, Proc. Biol. Soc. Wash. 42: 123. Type, by original designation, *Oriolus oryzivorus* Gmelin.

Notes.—See comments under *Molothrus*.

Scaphidura oryzivora (Gmelin). Giant Cowbird.

Oriolus oryzivorus Gmelin, 1788, Syst. Nat. 1(1): 386. Based on the "Rice Oriole" Latham, Gen. Synop. Birds 1(2): 423. (in Cayenna = Cayenne.)

Habitat.—Tropical Lowland Evergreen Forest Edge, Second-growth Scrub, usually in vicinity of colonies of oropendolas or caciques (0–2000 m; Tropical and lower Subtropical zones).

Distribution.—*Resident* from northern Oaxaca, southern Veracruz, Tabasco, Chiapas, and southern Quintana Roo south on the Gulf-Caribbean slope of Central America to Honduras, in Nicaragua (both slopes), Costa Rica (Caribbean slope and central plateau), and Panama (both slopes, more widespread on Caribbean), and in South America from Colombia, Venezuela, Trinidad, and the Guianas south, west of the Andes to western Ecuador and east of the Andes to southern Bolivia, eastern Paraguay, extreme northeastern Argentina, and southern Brazil.

Notes.—Also known as Rice Grackle.

Genus *ICTERUS* Brisson

Icterus Brisson, 1760, Ornithologie 1: 30; 2: 85. Type, by tautonymy, *Icterus* Brisson = *Oriolus icterus* Linnaeus.
Pendulinus Vieillot, 1816, Analyse, p. 33. Type, by subsequent designation (Sclater, 1883), *Oriolus spurius* Linnaeus.
Bananivorus Bonaparte, 1853, C. R. Acad. Sci. Paris 37: 834. Type, by original designation, *Oriolus bonana* Linnaeus.
Andriopsar Cassin, 1867, Proc. Acad. Nat. Sci. Philadelphia 19: 49. Type, by subsequent designation (Sclater, 1883), *Psarocolius gularis* Wagler.

Icterus dominicensis (Linnaeus). Black-cowled Oriole.

Oriolus dominicensis Linnaeus, 1766, Syst. Nat. (ed. 12) 1: 163. Based on "Le Carouge de S. Domingue" Brisson, Ornithologie 2: 121, pl. 12, fig. 3. (in Dominica = Hispaniola.)

Habitat.—[*prosthemelas* group] Tropical Lowland Evergreen Forest Edge, Secondary Forest (0–1200 m); [*dominicensis* group] Tropical Lowland Evergreen Forest Edge, Secondary Forest (0–1000 m); (Tropical Zone).

Distribution.—*Resident* [*prosthemelas* group] from southern Veracruz, northern Oaxaca, Tabasco, Chiapas, and the Yucatan Peninsula south on the Caribbean slope of Central America to extreme western Panama (western Bocas del Toro); and [*dominicensis* group] in the northern Bahama Islands (Andros, Great Abaco, and Little Abaco), Cuba, the Isle of Pines, Hispaniola (including Tortue and Gonâve islands, and Île-à-Vache), and Puerto Rico.

Notes.—Groups: *I. prosthemelas* (Strickland, 1850) [Black-cowled Oriole] and *I. dominicensis* [Greater Antillean Oriole]. *Icterus dominicensis, I. laudabilis, I. oberi,* and *I. bonana* appear to constitute a superspecies (Blake *in* Paynter 1968, Sibley and Monroe 1990).

Icterus laudabilis Sclater. St. Lucia Oriole.

Icterus laudabilis Sclater, 1871, Proc. Zool. Soc. London, p. 270, pl. 21. (St. Lucia.)

Habitat.—Tropical Lowland Evergreen Forest, Tropical Deciduous Forest, Secondary Forest (0–900 m).
Distribution.—*Resident* on St. Lucia, in the Lesser Antilles.
Notes.—See comments under *I. dominicensis.*

Icterus oberi Lawrence. Montserrat Oriole.

Icterus oberi Lawrence, 1880, Proc. U. S. Natl. Mus. 3: 351. (Montserrat.)

Habitat.—Tropical Lowland Evergreen Forest, Montane Evergreen Forest (200–900 m).
Distribution.—*Resident* on Montserrat, in the Lesser Antilles.
Notes.—See comments under *I. dominicensis.*

Icterus bonana (Linnaeus). Martinique Oriole.

Oriolus Bonana Linnaeus, 1766, Syst. Nat. (ed. 12) 1: 162. Based primarily on "Le Carouge" Brisson, Ornithologie 2: 115, pl. 12, fig. 2. (in America meridionali = Martinique.)

Habitat.—Tropical Deciduous Forest, Tropical Lowland Evergreen Forest, Mangrove Forest, Secondary Forest (0–700 m).
Distribution.—*Resident* on Martinique, in the Lesser Antilles.
Notes.—See comments under *I. dominicensis.*

Icterus wagleri Sclater. Black-vented Oriole.

Icterus wagleri Sclater, 1857, Proc. Zool. Soc. London, p. 7. (No locality given = Mexico.)

Habitat.—Pine-Oak Forest, Tropical Deciduous Forest, Gallery Forest (100–2500 m; upper Tropical to lower Temperate zones).
Distribution.—*Resident* from southern Sonora, central Chihuahua, Coahuila, and Nuevo León south through the highlands of Mexico, Guatemala, El Salvador, and Honduras to central Nicaragua. Seasonal movements little understood.
Accidental in southern Arizona (Patagonia) and Texas (Big Bend, Kingsville, Austin).
Notes.—Also known as Wagler's Oriole.

Icterus maculialatus Cassin. Bar-winged Oriole.

Icterus maculialatus Cassin, 1848, Proc. Acad. Nat. Sci. Philadelphia 3 (1847): 332. (near Vera Cruz, Mexico, error = Vera Paz, Guatemala.)

Habitat.—Pine-Oak Forest, Secondary Forest (500–2100 m; upper Tropical and Subtropical zones).
Distribution.—*Resident* on the Pacific slope from eastern Oaxaca and Chiapas south through Guatemala to El Salvador. Seasonal movements little understood.
Casual in southeastern Oaxaca (Sierra Madre de Chiapas), possibly resident.

Icterus spurius (Linnaeus). Orchard Oriole.

Oriolus spurius Linnaeus, 1766, Syst. Nat. (ed. 12) 1: 162. Based mainly on "The Bastard Baltimore" Catesby, Nat. Hist. Carolina 1: 48, pl. 48. (in America septentrionali = South Carolina.)

Habitat.—Scrub, second growth, brushy hillsides, partly open situations with scattered trees, open woodland, mesquite, and orchards; [*fuertesi* group] Gallery Forest, Secondary Forest; shrubby dunes (Subtropical and lower Temperate zones, in winter to Tropical Zone).

Distribution.—*Breeds* [*spurius* group] from southeastern Saskatchewan, southern Manitoba, central Minnesota, central Wisconsin, central Michigan, southern Ontario, central New York, southern Vermont, and northern Massachusetts south to eastern Chihuahua, Coahuila, southern Texas, the Gulf coast, and central Florida, west to eastern Montana, eastern Wyoming, eastern Colorado, and southeastern New Mexico, and on the Mexican Plateau from central Durango and Zacatecas to Jalisco, northern Michoacán, México, and Hidalgo (probably also in central Sonora); and [*fuertesi* group] in southern Tamaulipas and northern Veracruz.

Winters [*spurius* group] from Sinaloa, Guerrero, Puebla, and central Veracruz (casually north to coastal California and southern Texas, with occasional reports farther north) south through Middle America (including islands along the coast) to Colombia and northwestern Venezuela; and [*fuertesi* group] presumably in central Mexico (recorded Guerrero, Morelos, and southern Chiapas).

Migrates [*spurius* group] regularly through Mexico (west to southern Sinaloa), southern Florida (including the Keys), and Cuba, casually through California, Baja California, and southern Arizona, and rarely to southwestern New Mexico, Sonora, the Bahama Islands (Eleuthera, New Providence), Jamaica, and the Swan Islands.

Casual [*spurius* group] west to Washington, Oregon, Wyoming, central Colorado, and northern New Mexico, and north to south-central Manitoba, southern Quebec, New Brunswick, and Nova Scotia; and [*fuertesi* group] in southern Texas (Brownsville).

Notes.—Groups: *I. spurius* [Orchard Oriole] and *I. fuertesi* Chapman [Ochre Oriole or Fuertes's Oriole]. Although *fuertesi* is usually regarded as a subspecies of *I. spurius,* it differs from *spurius* in some song features and juvenal plumage (Chapman 1911, Graber and Graber 1954). Molecular data (Freeman and Zink 1995) confirm the traditional view that *I. spurius* and *I. cucullatus* are closely related and are probably sister taxa.

Icterus cucullatus Swainson. Hooded Oriole.

> *Icterus cucullatus* Swainson, 1827, Philos. Mag. (n.s.) 1: 436. (Temiscaltipec, Mexico = Temascaltepec, México.)

Habitat.—Riparian woodland, palm groves, mesquite, arid scrub, deciduous woodland, and around human habitation (Tropical and Subtropical zones).

Distribution.—*Breeds* from northern coastal and central California, southern Nevada, southwestern Utah, central Arizona, southern New Mexico, and western and southern Texas (one breeding record also from Bell County, in central Texas) south to southern Baja California and Sonora, and on Caribbean slope through Mexico, including the Yucatan Peninsula (also Mujeres, Holbox, Contoy, and Cozumel islands) to coastal Belize.

Winters from southern Baja California and southern Sonora (rarely from southern California, southern Arizona, and southern Texas) south on Pacific slope to western Oaxaca, and on Caribbean slope from southern Tamaulipas to Belize.

Casual north to southwestern Washington, west-central Oregon, eastern Texas, and Louisiana (Cameron Parish, Baton Rouge). Accidental in Ontario (Long Point) and Cuba; a sight report for the Revillagigedo Islands (Socorro).

Notes.—See comments under *I. spurius.*

Icterus chrysater (Lesson). Yellow-backed Oriole.

> *Xanthornus chrysater* Lesson, 1844, Echo Monde Savant (2)11: 204. (Mexico.)

Habitat.—Tropical Deciduous Forest, Pine-Oak Forest, Tropical Lowland Evergreen Forest Edge, Secondary Forest, lowland pine savanna (0–2500 m; Tropical and Subtropical zones).

Distribution.—*Resident* from southern Veracruz (Sierra de los Tuxtlas), southeastern Oaxaca (Sierra Madre de Chiapas), northern Chiapas, and the Yucatan Peninsula south through the interior of Central America to northern Nicaragua and, locally, the Gulf-Caribbean lowlands to northeastern Nicaragua; and from Panama (west to Veraguas) east through Colombia to northern Venezuela. Apparently at least partly migratory in El Salvador and probably elsewhere in northern Central America.

Notes.—Includes the lowland form in Colombia, once regarded as a distinct species, *I. hondae* Chapman, 1914 [Honda Oriole], but see Olson (1981d). Howell and Webb (1995) suggested that *I. chrysater* was closely related to *I. graduacauda.*

Icterus auricapillus Cassin. Orange-crowned Oriole.

> *Icterus auricapillus* Cassin, 1848, Proc. Acad. Nat. Sci. Philadelphia 3 (1847): 332. (Mexico and South America = Santa Marta, Colombia.)

Habitat.—Tropical Deciduous Forest, Tropical Lowland Evergreen Forest, Secondary Forest, Gallery Forest (0–800 m; Tropical and Subtropical zones).

Distribution.—*Resident* from eastern Panama (eastern Panamá province, western San Blas, Darién) east across northern Colombia to Venezuela.

Icterus mesomelas (Wagler). Yellow-tailed Oriole.

> *Psarocolius mesomelas* Wagler, 1829, Isis von Oken, col. 755. (Mexico = Chalcaltianges, Veracruz.)

Habitat.—Tropical Deciduous Forest, Secondary Forest, Tropical Lowland Evergreen Forest Edge, Gallery Forest (0–1600 m; Tropical Zone).

Distribution.—*Resident* from central Veracruz, northern Oaxaca, Tabasco, Chiapas, and the Yucatan Peninsula south along the Gulf-Caribbean slope of Middle America to Panama (also on the Pacific slope from western Panamá province eastward), and in South America from Colombia and northwestern Venezuela south, west of the Andes, to western Peru.

Icterus icterus (Linnaeus). Troupial.

> *Oriolus Icterus* Linnaeus, 1766, Syst. Nat. (ed. 12) 1: 161. Based primarily on "Le Troupiale" Brisson, Ornithologie 2: 86, pl. 8, fig. 1. (in America calidiore = Cumaná, Sucre, Venezuela.)

Habitat.—Semi-arid woodland and mangroves; in South America, Gallery Forest, Secondary Forest, River-edge Forest, Tropical Deciduous Forest (0–700 m; Tropical Zone).

Distribution.—*Resident* [*icterus* group] from northern and eastern Colombia, and western and northern Venezuela (also islands to north); [*croconotus* group] in southeastern Colombia, southwestern Guyana, eastern Ecuador, and eastern Peru; and [*jamacaii* group] in Amazonian Brazil, Bolivia, Paraguay, and northern Argentina.

Introduced and established [*icterus* group] on Puerto Rico, Mona Island, and St. Thomas (including Water Island) in the Virgin Islands; also reported from southern Florida, Jamaica, St. John, Antigua, Dominica, Grenada, and Trinidad, presumably based on escaped cage birds.

Notes.—Groups: *I. icterus* [Troupial], *I. croconotus* (Wagler, 1829) [Orange-backed Oriole], and *I. jamacaii* (Gmelin, 1788) [Campo Oriole]. *Icterus icterus* and *I. jamacaii* (including *I. croconotus*) are sometimes considered distinct species (e.g., Hilty and Brown 1986; cf. Ridgely and Tudor 1989). The molecular data of Freeman and Zink (1995) strongly suggest that *I. icterus* is only distantly related to other orioles and that the genus *Icterus* is paraphyletic.

Icterus pustulatus (Wagler). Streak-backed Oriole.

> *Psarocolius pustulatus* Wagler, 1829, Isis von Oken, col. 757. (Mexico = Cuernavaca, Morelos; Binford, 1989, Ornithol. Monogr. 43, p. 348.)

Habitat.—Tropical Deciduous Forest, Gallery Forest, Secondary Forest, Arid Lowland Scrub (0–1900 m; Tropical and lower Subtropical zones).

Distribution.—*Resident* [*pustulatus* group] in the Pacific lowlands from Sonora and Chihuahua south to Nayarit; [*graysonii* group] in the Tres Marias Islands, off Nayarit; and [*sclateri* group] on the Pacific slope from Jalisco south to northwestern Oaxaca and western Chiapas, in the arid interior of western Chiapas, Guatemala, and Honduras, and in the Pacific lowlands from El Salvador south to northwestern Costa Rica (Guanacaste). Northwestern populations are partially migratory.

Breeds [*pustulatus* group] casually in Pinal and Santa Cruz counties, Arizona.

Casual [*pustulatus* group] in southern California and eastern Arizona; sight reports for southern Oregon and Baja California.

Notes.—The three groups have sometimes been regarded as distinct species, *I. pustulatus* [Scarlet-headed Oriole], *I. graysonii* Cassin, 1867 [Tres Marias Oriole], and *I. sclateri* Cassin, 1867 [Streak-backed Oriole], although *pustulatus* and *sclateri* intergrade in southwestern Mexico (Binford 1989). See notes under *I. galbula*.

Icterus auratus Bonaparte. Orange Oriole.

Icterus auratus (Du Bus de Gisignies MS) Bonaparte, 1850, Consp. Gen. Avium 1(2): 435. (Yucatan.)

Habitat.—Tropical Deciduous Forest, Secondary Forest (0–200 m; Tropical Zone).

Distribution.—*Resident* in southeastern Mexico on the Yucatan Peninsula (Campeche, Yucatán, and Quintana Roo) and northeastern Belize.

Icterus leucopteryx (Wagler). Jamaican Oriole.

Oriolus mexicanus (not Linnaeus, 1766) Leach, 1814, Zool. Misc. 1: 8, pl. 2. (St. Andrews, Jamaica.)

Psarocolius Leucopteryx Wagler, 1827, Syst. Avium, sig. 22, genus *Psarocolius*, sp. 16. New name for *Oriolus mexicanus* Leach, preoccupied.

Habitat.—Secondary Forest, Tropical Lowland Evergreen Forest, Montane Evergreen Forest (0–1000 m).

Distribution.—*Resident* on Jamaica, Grand Cayman (where extirpated, not recorded since 1967; Bradley [1995]), and Isla San Andrés, in the western Caribbean Sea.

Icterus pectoralis (Wagler). Spot-breasted Oriole.

Psarocolius pectoralis Wagler, 1829, Isis von Oken, col. 755. (Mexico = San Pedro Totulapan, Oaxaca; Binford, 1989, Ornithol. Monogr. 43, p. 348–349.)

Habitat.—Tropical Deciduous Forest, Gallery Forest, Secondary Forest (0–1500 m; Tropical Zone).

Distribution.—*Resident* in the Pacific lowlands from Colima and Guerrero south to central Costa Rica (vicinity of Puntarenas), and locally in arid interior valleys and on the Caribbean slope of Guatemala and Honduras.

Introduced and established in southeastern Florida (Palm Beach, Broward, and Dade counties, rarely north to Brevard County) and apparently also on Cocos Island.

Icterus gularis (Wagler). Altamira Oriole.

Psarocolius gularis Wagler, 1829, Isis von Oken, col. 754. (Mexico = Tehuantepec City, Oaxaca; Binford, 1989, Ornithol. Monogr. 43, p. 349.)

Habitat.—Tropical Deciduous Forest, Gallery Forest, Secondary Forest (0–1500 m; Tropical and lower Subtropical zones).

Distribution.—*Resident* from extreme southern Texas (lower Rio Grande valley), eastern Nuevo León, and eastern San Luis Potosí south on the Gulf-Caribbean slope (including the Yucatan Peninsula) to Belize and (locally) Honduras, and from México and Guerrero south along the Pacific slope to west-central Nicaragua (also locally in the arid interior valleys of Guatemala and Honduras).

Notes.—Also known as Lichtenstein's Oriole or Black-throated Oriole.

Icterus graduacauda Lesson. Audubon's Oriole.

Icterus graduacauda Lesson, 1839, Rev. Zool. [Paris] 2: 105. (Mexico.)

Habitat.—Gallery Forest, Pine-Oak Forest, Tropical Lowland Evergreen Forest, Tropical Deciduous Forest (0–2500 m; upper Tropical and Subtropical zones).

Distribution.—*Resident* on Pacific slope from Nayarit to central Oaxaca, and on Caribbean slope from southern Texas (north to Val Verde, Bee, and Nueces counties) and Nuevo León south to central Veracruz. Old records from Chiapas and Guatemala (Santo Tomás) are questionable.

Notes.—Also known as Black-headed Oriole, a name now restricted to an Old World group of species in the genus *Oriolus*. See comments under *I. chrysater*.

Icterus galbula (Linnaeus). Baltimore Oriole.

Coracias Galbula Linnaeus, 1758, Syst. Nat. ed. 10, 1, p. 108. Based on "The Baltimore-Bird" Catesby, Nat. Hist. Carolina 1, p. 48, pl. 48. (in America = Virginia.)

Habitat.—Breeds in open woodland, deciduous forest edge, riparian woodland, orchards, and planted shade trees (Temperate Zone); in migration and winter in humid forest edge, second growth, and scrub.

Distribution.—*Breeds* from northeastern British Columbia, central Alberta, central Saskatchewan, southern Manitoba, western Ontario, northern Michigan, southern Ontario, southwestern Quebec, central Maine, southern New Brunswick, Prince Edward Island, and central Nova Scotia south to eastern Texas, central Louisiana, central Mississippi, central Alabama, north-central Georgia, western South Carolina, central North Carolina, central Virginia, Maryland, and Delaware, and west to central Montana, the western edge of the Great Plains (also single breeding records from northeastern Colorado and Key West, Florida).

Winters from Nayarit and Veracruz (rarely from coastal California and Sonora) south through Middle America to northern Colombia, northern Venezuela, and Trinidad, regularly in small numbers in the Atlantic states north to Virginia, in the Greater Antilles east to the Virgin Islands, and casually elsewhere in eastern North America north to the Great Lakes region, southern Ontario, and New England;

Migrates regularly through the central and southeastern United States (west to Montana, eastern New Mexico, and western Texas) and northeastern Mexico, rarely through coastal California, the northern Bahama Islands, the Cayman Islands, and Yucatan Peninsula, and casually elsewhere in western North America west to Washington, Oregon, Arizona, and northwestern Mexico.

Casual north to northern Manitoba, western and southern Ontario, eastern Quebec, Nova Scotia, and Newfoundland, and in the Lesser Antilles (Sombrero, St. Kitts, Barbados), also in Greenland, Iceland, the British Isles, Norway, and the Netherlands.

Notes.—This species has been considered conspecific with *I. bullockii* (with the English name Northern Oriole) because of limited interbreeding in a few areas in the Great Plains. In some areas, a hybrid zone with virtually no pure phenotypes has been found, suggesting complete breakdown of reproductive isolating mechanisms (Sibley and Short 1964, Anderson 1971, Misra and Short 1974, Rising 1970, 1983), whereas in other areas the distribution of phenotypes suggests selection against interbreeding (Rising 1970, 1973). Corbin and Sibley (1977) found a dramatic shift in phenotypes away from hybrids and toward pure parentals in areas sampled 15 years previously, but Rising (1983) found little evidence for temporal change in another contact zone. Thus, the nature of contact between these two taxa varies geographically and temporally, thereby defying traditional, typological, static classification schemes. We treat these taxa as two separate biological species because the number of important differences between them suggests in concert that gene flow between them is restricted. They differ in: male, female, and immature plumages; vocalizations (Rising 1970); thermoregulatory abilities (Rising 1969); allele frequencies (Corbin et al. 1979); number of molts (Rohwer and Manning 1990); molt-migration schedule (Rohwer and Manning 1990); nest-site placement and dispersion (Rising 1970); and body size (Sibley and Short 1964, Rising 1973, 1983). Although many of these characters vary geographically within taxa that we treat as one species, we know of no case in which there are so many discrete, abrupt, concordant differences between populations treated as one species. Furthermore, Freeman and Zink's (1995) molecular data indicate that *I. bullockii* and *I. pustulatus* are more closely related than either is to *I. galbula*. See notes under *I. abeillei*.

Icterus bullockii (Swainson). Bullock's Oriole.

Xanthornus Bullockii Swainson, 1827, Philos. Mag., new ser., 1, p. 436. ("Table land" [of Mexico]; restricted to Temascáltepec by van Rossem, 1945, Occas. Pap. Mus. Zool. Louisiana State Univ. 21: 238.)

Habitat.—Open and fragmented woodland of cottonwoods, willows, sycamores, and oaks, especially near fields, grasslands, and savannahs.

Distribution.—*Breeds* from southern British Columbia (including Vancouver Island), southern Alberta, southwestern Saskatchewan, Montana, southwestern North Dakota, and central South Dakota south to northern Baja California, northwestern Sonora, northern Durango, Coahuila, and central and southern Texas, and east to western Nebraska, western Kansas, and western Oklahoma.

Winters sparsely in the southernmost part of the breeding range, and from southern Sonora, México, and Puebla south to Guatemala (casually to northwestern Costa Rica), and in small numbers in the Gulf coast region from eastern and southern Texas east to southern Georgia and Florida.

Migrates regularly through western North America west of the Rockies.

Casual in northeastern North America from Minnesota, western and southern Ontario, New York, New Brunswick, Maine, and Nova Scotia south through New England to New Jersey; a sight report from southeastern Alaska.

Notes.—This and the next species have been combined with *I. galbula* with the English name Northern Oriole. See notes under *I. galbula* and *I. abeillei*.

Icterus abeillei (Lesson). Black-backed Oriole.

Xanthornus Abeillei Lesson, 1839, Rev. Zool. [Paris] 2: 101. (Mexico.)

Habitat.—Pine-Oak Forest, Gallery Forest (1500–3000 m); (Subtropical and Temperate zones, in winter to Tropical Zone).

Distribution.—*Breeds* the central volcanic belt of Mexico from central Durango, Zacatecas, San Luis Potosí, and southern Nuevo León south in the Central Plateau of Mexico to Michoacán, México, Morelos, Puebla, and central Veracruz.

Winters in central and south-central Mexico south to Oaxaca.

Notes.—Long ago merged with *I. bullockii* on the basis of hybridization in Durango reported by Miller (1906), and carried with *bullockii* into the merger with *I. galbula* (see A.O.U. 1995). However, the small sample of hybrid specimens is close to *bullockii,* and the oriole population at the area of contact is evidently intermittent (Rising 1973); thus, the evidence for free interbreeding between *abeillei* and *bullockii* is weak. Also known as Abeillé's Oriole.

Icterus parisorum Bonaparte. Scott's Oriole.

Icterus Parisorum Bonaparte, 1838, Proc. Zool. Soc. London (1837), p. 110. (Mexico.)

Habitat.—Arid Montane Scrub, Arid Lowland Scrub, Pine-Oak Forest (0–3000 m; upper Tropical to lower Temperate zones).

Distribution.—*Breeds* from southern California (north in the interior to Santa Barbara and Inyo counties), southern Nevada, southern Idaho (once), southern Utah, western Colorado, southwestern Wyoming, northern New Mexico, and western Texas (locally east to the Edwards Plateau in Kerr, Kendall, and Comal counties) south to southern Baja California, southeastern Sonora, Durango, southeastern Coahuila, and, locally, to Michoacán and northwestern Oaxaca.

Winters from southern California (rarely), central Baja California, southern Sonora, Coahuila, and western Nuevo León south to Guerrero and central Oaxaca (west of the Isthmus of Tehuantepec), Puebla, and Hidalgo.

Casual north to southern Oregon, central Idaho, central Colorado, and southwestern Kansas, and east to Louisiana. Accidental in Washington (Chehalis), Minnesota (Duluth), Wisconsin (Adams), and western Ontario (Silver Islet Landing).

Genus *AMBLYCERCUS* Cabanis

Amblycercus Cabanis, 1851, Mus. Heineanum 1: 186. Type, by monotypy, *Amblyramphus prevostii* Lesson = *Sturnus holosericeus* Deppe.

Amblycercus holosericeus (Deppe). Yellow-billed Cacique.

Sturnus holosericeus "Lichtenst[ein]." W. Deppe, 1830, Preis.-Verz. Säugeth. Vögel, etc., Mexico, p. 1. (Mexico = Alvarado, Veracruz.)

Habitat.—Montane Evergreen Forest, Tropical Lowland Evergreen Forest, Secondary Forest (0–3000 m; Tropical to Temperate zones).

Distribution.—*Resident* [*holosericeus* group] from southeastern San Luis Potosí, southern Tamaulipas, Veracruz, Puebla, and northern and (possibly) southeastern Oaxaca south along both slopes of Middle America (including the Yucatan Peninsula) to Panama and northern Colombia, south, west of the Andes to northwestern Peru; and [*australis* group] in South America in the Santa Marta Mountains and Andes of Colombia and northern Venezuela to northern Bolivia.

Notes.—Groups: *A. holosericeus* [Prévost's Cacique] and *A. australis* Chapman, 1919 [Chapman's Cacique]; see Kratter (1993) and Freeman and Zink (1995). Sometimes (e.g., Blake *in* Paynter 1968) merged in the genus *Cacicus,* but see, for example, Freeman and Zink (1995), who found that *A. holosericeus* was only distantly related to most members of *Cacicus.*

Genus *CACICUS* Lacépède

Cacicus Lacépède, 1799, Tabl. Mamm. Ois., p. 6. Type, by subsequent designation (Zimmer, 1930), *Oriolus haemorrhous* Linnaeus.
Cassiculus Swainson, 1827, Philos. Mag. (n.s.) 1: 436. Type, by original designation, *Cassiculus coronatus* Swainson = *Icterus melanicterus* Bonaparte.

Notes.—This genus may be paraphyletic (Freeman and Zink 1995).

Cacicus uropygialis (Lafresnaye). Scarlet-rumped Cacique.

Cassiculus uropygialis Lafresnaye, 1843, Rev. Zool. [Paris] 6: 290. (Colombia = Bogotá.)

Habitat.—Tropical Lowland Evergreen Forest, Secondary Forest (0–1100 m; Tropical and lower Subtropical zones).

Distribution.—*Resident* [*microrhynchus* group] on the Caribbean slope of northeastern Honduras (Olancho, Gracias a Dios) and Nicaragua, and on both slopes of Costa Rica (absent from the dry northwest) and Panama (except eastern Darién); [*pacificus* group] in extreme southeastern Panama (eastern Darién), western Colombia, and western Ecuador; and [*uropygialis* group] in South America from northeastern Colombia and northwestern Venezuela south, east of the Andes, to eastern Ecuador and northeastern Peru.

Notes.—Groups: *C. microrhynchus* (Sclater and Salvin, 1865) [Scarlet-rumped Cacique], *C. pacificus* Chapman, 1915 [Pacific Cacique], and *C. uropygialis* [Subtropical Cacique]; see Ridgely and Tudor (1989). The *microrhynchus* group is sometimes called Small-billed Cacique or Flame-rumped Cacique, the *uropygialis* group, Curve-billed Cacique.

Cacicus cela (Linnaeus). Yellow-rumped Cacique.

Parus Cela Linnaeus, 1758, Syst. Nat. (ed. 10) 1: 191. Based on *Parus niger, rostro albo* Linnaeus, Mus. Adolphi Friderici 2: . . (in Indiis, error = Surinam.)

Habitat.—River-edge Forest, Tropical Lowland Evergreen Forest Edge, Secondary Forest (0–100 m; Tropical Zone).

Distribution.—*Resident* [*vitellinus* group] in Panama (west on Pacific slope to Veraguas and on Caribbean slope to the Canal area) and northern Colombia; and [*cela* group] in western Ecuador and northwestern Peru, and from eastern Colombia, Venezuela, Trinidad, and the Guianas south, east of the Andes, to southern Bolivia and central and eastern Brazil.

Notes.—Groups: *C. vitellinus* (Lawrence, 1864) [Saffron-rumped Cacique] and *C. cela* [Yellow-rumped Cacique].

Cacicus melanicterus (Bonaparte). Yellow-winged Cacique.

Icterus melanicterus Bonaparte, 1825, J. Acad. Nat. Sci. Philadelphia 4: 389. (Mexico = restricted to Temáscaltepec, México, by van Rossem, 1945, Occ. Pap. Mus. Zool. Louisiana State Univ. 21: 234, but this locality is certainly erroneous.)

Habitat.—Tropical Deciduous Forest, Secondary Forest (0–1500 m; Tropical Zone).

Distribution.—*Resident* in the Pacific lowlands from extreme southern Sonora (at least formerly) south to western Chiapas (Tonalá, Monserrate) and, disjunctly, southeastern Guatemala.

Notes.—Also known as Mexican Cacique. Often placed in the monotypic genus *Cassiculus*.

Genus *PSAROCOLIUS* Wagler

Psarocolius Wagler, 1827, Syst. Avium 1: sig. "22" [= 23]. Type, by subsequent designation (G. R. Gray, 1855), *Oriolus cristatus* Gmelin = *Xanthornus decumanus* Pallas.
Eucorystes (not Bell, 1862) Sclater, 1883, Ibis, p. 147. Type, by monotypy, *Cassicus* [sic] *wagleri* Gray.
Zarhynchus Oberholser, 1899, Proc. Acad. Nat. Sci. Philadelphia 51: 215. New name for *Eucorystes* Sclater, preoccupied.

Notes.—This genus may be paraphyletic (Freeman and Zink 1995).

Subgenus *PSAROCOLIUS* Wagler

Psarocolius decumanus (Pallas). Crested Oropendola.

Xanthornus decumanus Pallas, 1769, Spic. Zool. 1(6): 1, pl. 1. (America = Surinam.)

Habitat.—Tropical Lowland Evergreen Forest, Secondary Forest, River-edge Forest (0–1200 m; Tropical and lower Subtropical zones).

Distribution.—*Resident* in Panama (Pacific slope of western Chiriquí, Veraguas, and from the Canal area east to Darién, and on the Caribbean slope recorded from western Colón and northern Coclé east to the Canal area), and in South America from northern and eastern Colombia, Venezuela, Tobago, Trinidad, and the Guianas south, east of the Andes, to northern Argentina and southern Brazil.

Psarocolius wagleri (Gray). Chestnut-headed Oropendola.

Cacicus Wagleri G. R. Gray, 1845, Genera Birds 2: 342, pl. 85. (No locality given = Cobán, Alta Verapaz, Guatemala.)

Habitat.—Tropical Lowland Evergreen Forest, Secondary Forest (0–1200 m; Tropical and lower Subtropical zones).

Distribution.—*Resident* from north-central Oaxaca, southern Veracruz, Tabasco, and Chiapas south on the Gulf-Caribbean slope of Central America to Honduras, on both slopes of Nicaragua, Costa Rica (absent from the dry northwest), and Panama, and in western Colombia and western Ecuador.

Notes.—Also known as Wagler's Oropendola. Often placed in the monotypic genus *Zarhynchus*.

Subgenus *GYMNOSTINOPS* Sclater

Gymnostinops Sclater, 1886, Cat. Birds Brit. Mus. 11: xvi, 309, 312. Type, by subsequent designation (Ridgway, 1902), *Cacicus montezuma* Lesson.

Psarocolius montezuma (Lesson). Montezuma Oropendola.

Cacicus Montezuma Lesson, 1830, Cent. Zool., livr. 2, p. 33, pl. 7. (Mexico.)

Habitat.—Tropical Lowland Evergreen Forest, Secondary Forest (0–1000 m; Tropical and lower Subtropical zones).

Distribution.—*Resident* from southeastern San Luis Potosí, Veracruz, eastern Puebla, northern Oaxaca, Tabasco, Chiapas, Campeche, and Quintana Roo south on the Gulf-Caribbean slope of Central America (also on Pacific slope of Nicaragua) to central Panama (east to the Canal area).

Notes.—*Psarocolius montezuma, P. guatimozinus,* and two South American species, *P. cassini* (Richmond, 1898) [Chestnut-mantled Oropendola] and *P. bifasciatus* (Spix, 1824) [Olive Oropendola], appear to constitute a superspecies (Blake *in* Paynter 1968, Sibley and Monroe 1990); see also Ridgely and Tudor (1989).

Psarocolius guatimozinus (Bonaparte). Black Oropendola.

Ostinops guatimozinus Bonaparte, 1853, C. R. Acad. Sci. Paris 37: 833. (Guaripata [= Garrapata], middle Rio Magdalena, near Malena, Antioquia, Colombia.)

Habitat.—Tropical Lowland Evergreen Forest, River-edge Forest (0–800 m; Tropical Zone).

Distribution.—*Resident* in eastern Panama (Darién) and northwestern Colombia.

Notes.—See comments under *P. montezuma.*

Family **FRINGILLIDAE**: Fringilline and Cardueline Finches and Allies

Subfamily FRINGILLINAE: Fringilline Finches

Genus *FRINGILLA* Linnaeus

Fringilla Linnaeus, 1758, Syst. Nat. (ed. 10) 1: 179. Type, by tautonymy, *Fringilla coelebs* Linnaeus (*Fringilla,* prebinomial specific name, in synonymy).

Fringilla coelebs Linnaeus. Common Chaffinch.

Fringilla cælebs Linnaeus, 1758, Syst. Nat. (ed. 10) 1: 179. (in Europa = Sweden.)

Habitat.—Open and partly open country, forest, and woodland.

Distribution.—*Breeds* throughout Eurasia south to the eastern Atlantic islands, Mediterranean region, Asia Minor, Iran, southern Russia, and western Siberia.

Winters in the southern part of the breeding range and south to northern Africa and southwestern Asia.

Casual in northeastern North America from Newfoundland, Nova Scotia, and Maine south to Massachusetts, where presumably natural vagrants (Vickery 1980, DeBenedictis 1996). Reports from Wyoming, Indiana, Ohio, Louisiana, and California are more likely to represent escaped cage-birds.

Notes.—Known in Old World literature as the Chaffinch.

Fringilla montifringilla Linnaeus. Brambling.

Fringilla montifringilla Linnaeus, 1758, Syst. Nat. (ed. 10) 1: 179. (in Europa = Sweden.)

Habitat.—Mixed deciduous-coniferous forest, forest edge, and birch and willow scrub; in migration and winter also in woodland and weedy fields.

Distribution.—*Breeds* from northern Scandinavia, northern Russia, and northern Siberia south to southern Scandinavia, central Russia, Transbaicalia, northern Amurland, Anadyrland, Kamchatka, and the Sea of Okhotsk. One nesting record from Attu, Aleutian Islands, in May 1996.

Winters from the British Isles and southern portions of the breeding range south to the Mediterranean region, northern Africa, the Near East, Iran, northwestern India, Tibet, China, Taiwan, and Japan, casually to the Faeroe Islands, Iceland, Madeira, and the Philippines.

Migrates regularly through the western Aleutian Islands (Near Islands, casually east to Adak), and casually islands in the Bering Sea (St. Lawrence, and St. Paul in the Pribilofs) and through western and south-coastal Alaska (Hooper Bay east to Cordova).

Casual in western North America from northern and southeastern Alaska, British Columbia, central Alberta, Saskatchewan, Manitoba, and North Dakota south to central California, Nevada, northern Utah, Colorado, and Minnesota, and east to Michigan, Indiana, Ohio, Ontario, Quebec (sight report), Pennsylvania, New York, Massachusetts, New Jersey, and Nova Scotia. Although some records from the northeastern states may be of escaped cage birds, the majority of North American records appear to be based on natural vagrants.

Subfamily CARDUELINAE: Cardueline Finches

Genus *LEUCOSTICTE* Swainson

Leucosticte [subgenus] Swainson, 1832, in Swainson and Richardson, Fauna Bor.-Amer. 2 (1831): 265. Type, by monotypy, *Linaria (Leucosticte) tephrocotis* Swainson.

Leucosticte tephrocotis (Swainson). Gray-crowned Rosy-Finch.

Linaria (Leucosticte) tephrocotis Swainson, 1832, in Swainson and Richardson, Fauna Bor.-Amer., 2 (1831), p. 265, pl. 50. (on the Saskatchewan = Carleton House, Saskatchewan.)

Habitat.—Barren, rocky, or grassy areas and cliffs among glaciers or beyond timberline; in migration and winter also in open situations, fields, cultivated lands, brushy areas, and around human habitation.

Distribution.—*Breeds* from western and north-central Alaska (north to the Seward Peninsula and Brooks Range), central Yukon, British Columbia, and southwestern Alberta south to southern Alaska (including St. Matthew, Nunivak, and the Pribilof and Aleutian islands), and through the Cascades, Sierra Nevada, and Rocky Mountains to northeastern Oregon, east-central California (to Tulare and Inyo counties), central Idaho, and northwestern Montana, also in the Commander Islands.

Winters from the Aleutians, southern mainland Alaska (rarely), British Columbia, southern Alberta, and central Saskatchewan south to western Oregon, central and eastern California, central Nevada, central Utah, northern New Mexico, northwestern Nebraska, and southwestern North Dakota.

Casual on St. Lawrence Island, east to Manitoba, Minnesota, Iowa, Wisconsin, Illinois, Michigan, and Ohio, and south to southern California (Ventura County). Accidental in Ontario (Thunder Bay, Dryden), Quebec (St. Norbert, sight report), and Maine (Gorham).

Notes.—The three American *Leucosticte* species are sometimes (e.g., Mayr and Short 1970) treated as subspecies of the Asian *L. arctoa* (Pallas, 1811) [Rosy Finch]; limited hybridization between *L. tephrocotis* and *L. atrata* occurs from west-central Idaho to central Montana. If the three American species are merged into a single species distinct from *L. arctoa, L. tephrocotis* [American Rosy-Finch] would be the appropriate name.

Leucosticte atrata Ridgway. Black Rosy-Finch.

Leucosticte atrata Ridgway, 1874, Amer. Sportsman, 4, p. 241. (Cañon City, Colorado.)

Habitat.—Barren, rocky, or grassy areas and cliffs among glaciers or beyond timberline; in migration and winter also in open situations, fields, cultivated lands, brushy areas, and around human habitation.

Distribution.—*Breeds* in the mountains from central Idaho, southwestern and south-central Montana, and northwestern and north-central Wyoming south to northeastern and east-central Nevada (south to the Snake Mountains) and central Utah (to the Tushar and La Sal mountains).

Winters from central Idaho and western and southeastern Wyoming south to eastern California (at least casually), southern Nevada, northern Arizona, and northern New Mexico.

Casual in eastern Oregon and eastern Montana. Accidental in Ohio (Conneaut).

Notes.—See *L. tephrocotis.*

Leucosticte australis Ridgway. Brown-capped Rosy-Finch.

> *Leucosticte tephrocotis,* var. *australis* Ridgway, 1874, Bull. Essex Inst., 5, p. 189 (1873). (Mt. Lincoln, Colorado.) See Banks and Browning (1979).

Habitat.—Barren, rocky, or grassy areas and cliffs among glaciers or beyond timberline; in migration and winter also in open situations, fields, cultivated lands, brushy areas, and around human habitation.

Distribution.—*Breeds* in the mountains from southeastern Wyoming (Medicine Bow Range) south through Colorado to northern New Mexico (Santa Fe region).

Winters generally at lower elevations in the breeding range.

Notes.—See *L. tephrocotis.*

Genus *PINICOLA* Vieillot

> *Pinicola* Vieillot, 1807, Hist. Nat. Ois. Amer. Sept. 1: iv, pl. 1, fig. 13. Type, by monotypy, *Pinicola rubra* Vieillot = *Loxia enucleator* Linnaeus.

Pinicola enucleator (Linnaeus). Pine Grosbeak.

> *Loxia Enucleator* Linnaeus, 1758, Syst. Nat. (ed. 10) 1: 171. (in Sveciæ summæ, Canadæ Pinetis = Sweden.)

Habitat.—Open coniferous (less commonly mixed coniferous-deciduous) forest and forest edge; in migration and winter also in deciduous forest, woodland, and second growth.

Distribution.—*Breeds* in North America from western and central Alaska, northern Yukon, northwestern and central Mackenzie, northern Manitoba, northern Ontario, northern Quebec, northern Labrador, and Newfoundland south to southern Alaska (west to the base of the Alaska Peninsula and Kodiak Island), British Columbia (including the Queen Charlotte Islands), western Alberta, central California (southern Sierra Nevada), extreme west-central Nevada, northern and east-central Arizona, northern New Mexico, and, east of the Rockies, to northern Alberta, northern Saskatchewan, central and southeastern (rarely) Manitoba, south-central Ontario, northern Michigan (rarely), southwestern Quebec, northern New Hampshire, northern Vermont (probably), central Maine, and Nova Scotia; and in the Palearctic from northern Scandinavia east across northern Russia to northern Siberia, and south to northern Mongolia, Sakhalin, the Kuril Islands, Kamchatka, and Japan.

Winters in North America from western and central Alaska, southern Yukon, southern Mackenzie, and southern Canada (east to southern Labrador and Newfoundland) south through the breeding range, casually or sporadically as far as central New Mexico, northern and north-central Texas, northwestern Oklahoma, north-central Arkansas, Missouri, Kentucky, Virginia, and the Carolinas; and in the Old World south to northern Europe, the Amur River, and Ussuriland, casually to the British Isles and central Europe.

Casual or accidental in the Pribilof, western Aleutian (Attu), and Commander islands, and in Bermuda and Greenland.

Genus *CARPODACUS* Kaup

> *Carpodacus* Kaup, 1829 (April), Skizz. Entw.-Ges. Eur. Thierw. 1: 161. Type, by subsequent designation (G. R. Gray, 1842), *Fringilla rosea* Pallas.
>
> *Erythrina* Brehm, 1829 (July), Isis von Oken 22, cols. 724-736. Type, by monotypy, *E. albifrons* Brehm = *Loxia erythrina* Pallas. See Banks and Browning (1995).

Burrica Ridgway, 1887, Man. N. Amer. Birds, p. 390. Type, by original designation, *Fringilla mexicana* Müller.

Carpodacus erythrinus (Pallas). Common Rosefinch.

Loxia erythrina Pallas, 1770, Novi Comm. Acad. Sci. Petropol. 14: 587, pl. 23, fig. 1. (Volga and Samara Rivers.)

Habitat.—Swampy woods, brushy meadows, thickets, forest edge, clearings, cultivated areas, and around human habitation.

Distribution.—*Breeds* from southern Finland, northern Russia, and northern Siberia south to central Europe, Asia Minor, the Himalayas, Mongolia, and northern China.

Winters primarily from India east through Southeast Asia to southern China.

Migrates irregularly through the western Aleutians (Attu, Shemya, Buldir) and St. Lawrence Island, occasionally reaching the Pribilofs (St. Paul) and the mainland of western Alaska (Old Chevak), also in the British Isles, western Europe, and Japan.

Notes.—Also known as Scarlet Grosbeak. Mayr and Short (1970) considered *C. erythrinus* and *C. purpureus* to constitute a superspecies.

Carpodacus purpureus (Gmelin). Purple Finch.

Fringilla purpurea Gmelin, 1789, Syst. Nat. 1(2): 923. Based mainly on "The Purple Finch" Catesby, Nat. Hist. Carolina 1: 41, pl. 41. (in Carolina = South Carolina.)

Habitat.—Open coniferous (especially fir and spruce) and mixed coniferous-deciduous forest, forest edge, open woodland, and second growth; in migration and winter also in deciduous forest, tall brush, weedy areas, and around human habitation.

Distribution.—*Breeds* from central and northeastern British Columbia, southern Yukon, southwestern Mackenzie, northern and central Alberta, central Saskatchewan, south-central Manitoba, northern Ontario, southern Quebec (including Anticosti Island), and Newfoundland south (west of the Cascades and Sierra Nevada, except in Washington) to southern California, and (east of the Great Plains) to central Alberta, southeastern Saskatchewan, north-central North Dakota, northwestern and central Minnesota, central Wisconsin, central Michigan, northern Ohio, West Virginia, central Pennsylvania, and southeastern New York.

Winters from southwestern British Columbia south through western Washington, central and western Oregon, and California to northern Baja California, and (rarely) east across central and southern Arizona to southern New Mexico; and from southern Manitoba, southern Ontario, southern Quebec, New Brunswick, Prince Edward Island, Nova Scotia, and Newfoundland south to central and southeastern Texas, the Gulf coast, and central (casually southern) Florida.

Casual elsewhere in western North America from east-central, south-coastal and southeastern Alaska, eastern Washington, Idaho, and western Montana south to northern Arizona, New Mexico, and extreme western Texas, and north to Franklin District (off Resolution Island) and Labrador (Cartwright). Accidental on St. Lawrence Island, in the Bering Sea.

Notes.—See comments under *C. erythrinus*.

Carpodacus cassinii Baird. Cassin's Finch.

Carpodacus cassinii Baird, 1854, Proc. Acad. Nat. Sci. Philadelphia 7: 119. (Camp 104, Pueblo Creek, New Mexico = 10 miles east of Gemini Peak, Yavapai County, Arizona.)

Habitat.—Open coniferous forest; in migration and winter also in deciduous woodland, second growth, scrub, brushy areas, and partly open situations with scattered trees.

Distribution.—*Breeds* from southern interior British Columbia, extreme southwestern Alberta, north-central and southeastern Montana, northern Wyoming, southwestern South Dakota (probably), and northwestern Nebraska (rarely) south (generally east of the Cascades and coast ranges) to southern California, northern Baja California (Sierra San Pedro Mártir), southern Nevada, northern Arizona, and northern New Mexico.

Winters from southern British Columbia, northwestern Montana, and east-central Wyoming south to northern Baja California, southern Arizona, and western Texas, and in the Mexican highlands to Durango, Zacatecas, western San Luis Potosí, and Coahuila, casually to coastal and southeastern California, the Tres Marias Islands (off Nayarit), Michoacán, México, and west-central Veracruz.

Casual or irregular north to south-coastal Alaska (Homer, Middleton Island), southwestern British Columbia, southeastern Alberta, and east to northern Minnesota, western Nebraska, western Kansas, western Oklahoma, and central Texas; a sight report for North Dakota.

Notes.—Also known as Cassin's Purple Finch.

Carpodacus mexicanus (Müller). House Finch.

> *Fringilla mexicana* P. L. S. Müller, 1776, Natursyst., Suppl., p. 165. (Mexico = valley of México.)

Habitat.—Arid scrub and brush, thornbush, oak-juniper, pine-oak association, chaparral, open woodland, urban areas, cultivated lands, and savanna (Subtropical and Temperate zones).

Distribution.—*Breeds* [*mexicanus* group] from southwestern and southern interior British Columbia (including Vancouver Island), northern Idaho, Montana, north-central and south-eastern Wyoming, southwestern South Dakota, western Nebraska, west-central Kansas, and western Oklahoma south to southern Baja California (including the Channel Islands off California, and most islands off Baja California, except Guadalupe and the San Benito Islands), central Sonora (including Tiburón and San Pedro Mártir islands), in the Mexican highlands south to central Oaxaca, central Chiapas, and west-central Veracruz, and to eastern San Luis Potosí, Nuevo León, southwestern Tamaulipas, and western and south-central Texas.

Winters [*mexicanus* group] throughout the breeding range and east to southern Texas.

Resident [*mcgregori* group] formerly on the San Benito Islands, off Baja California, where now extinct (last recorded in 1938), and possibly also on Cedros Island (two records, latest in 1925), where a representative of the *mexicanus* group is now common; and [*amplus* group] on Guadalupe Island, off southern Baja California.

Introduced and established [*mexicanus* group] in the Hawaiian Islands (about 1859, now common on all main islands from Kauai eastward, straggling casually west to Nihoa); and in eastern North America on Long Island, New York (early 1950's), now breeding from Kansas, eastern North Dakota, southern Manitoba, Minnesota, southern Wisconsin, north-central Michigan, southern Ontario, southern Quebec, New Brunswick, Prince Edward Island, Nova Scotia, and (possibly) Newfoundland south to north-central and eastern Texas, the Gulf coast (east to the Florida Panhandle), Georgia, and South Carolina.

Casual [*mexicanus* group] north to southern Alberta and southern Saskatchewan; a sight report from southeastern Alaska (Haines). Reports from Europe probably pertain to escapes from captivity.

Notes.—Groups: *C. mexicanus* [Common House-Finch], *C. mcgregori* Anthony, 1897 [McGregor's House-Finch], and *C. amplus* Ridgway, 1876 [Guadalupe House-Finch].

Genus *LOXIA* Linnaeus

> *Loxia* Linnaeus, 1758, Syst. Nat. (ed. 10) 1: 171. Type, by tautonymy, *Loxia curvirostra* Linnaeus (*Loxia,* prebinomial specific name, in synonymy).

Loxia curvirostra Linnaeus. Red Crossbill.

> *Loxia curvirostra* Linnaeus, 1758, Syst. Nat. (ed. 10) 1: 171. (in Europæ = Sweden.)

Habitat.—Coniferous and mixed coniferous-deciduous forest, humid pine-oak association, lowland pine savanna, and suburban areas; in migration and winter also in deciduous forest, woodland, second growth, scrub, weedy fields, and gardens (Subtropical and Temperate zones, locally to Tropical Zone in lowland pine savanna).

Distribution.—*Breeds* in North America from south-coastal and southeastern Alaska (west to the base of the Alaska Peninsula and Kodiak Island), British Columbia (including the Queen Charlotte and Vancouver islands), southern Yukon, southern Mackenzie, northern Alberta, northwestern and central Saskatchewan, central Manitoba, central Ontario, southern

Quebec, New Brunswick, Prince Edward Island, Nova Scotia, and Newfoundland south to northern Baja California, southern California, southern Nevada, central and southeastern Arizona, in the Middle American highlands through Mexico, Belize, Guatemala, and Honduras to north-central Nicaragua (also in lowland pine savanna in Belize, eastern Honduras, and northeastern Nicaragua), in the Rockies and Plains region east to southeastern Montana, northeastern Wyoming, western South Dakota, northwestern Nebraska, central Colorado, northeastern and central New Mexico (probably), and extreme western Texas (Guadalupe and, probably, Davis mountains), and to southern Manitoba, North Dakota, northern Minnesota, central Wisconsin, northern and central Illinois, southern Michigan, southern Ontario, Pennsylvania, West Virginia, western Virginia (also in the Great Smoky Mountains of eastern Tennessee, western North Carolina, and northwestern Georgia), southeastern New York, and Massachusetts (with isolated breeding in south-central Iowa, northeastern Kansas, Ohio, central and southeastern Arkansas, and east-central Mississippi); and in the Old World from the British Isles, northern Scandinavia, northern Russia, and northern Siberia south to northwestern Africa, the Mediterranean region, Caucasus, Himalayas, southern China, Vietnam, northern Philippines, and Japan.

Winters throughout the breeding range, wandering irregularly and sporadically in the nonbreeding season, occurring in North America south to central Baja California (including Santa Cruz Island off California, and Guadalupe and Cedros islands off Baja California), Sinaloa, southern and eastern Texas, the northern portions of the Gulf states, and casually to southern Georgia and central Florida; and in the Old World casually to the Faeroe Islands, Iceland, Greenland, Bear Island, and Jan Mayen.

Casual or accidental in the Pribilof and Aleutian islands, St. Lawrence Island, Bermuda, and El Salvador.

Notes.—Known in Old World literature as the Crossbill. Apparently at least nine species, differing in morphology and vocalizations, exist in North America, with some breeding sympatrically and mating assortatively (Groth 1988, 1993a, 1993b); however, morphological overlap among some species currently prevents assignment with certainty of some existing type specimens to the groups defined by call types (Groth 1993a). Additional species-level taxa almost certainly exist among the populations outside North America currently assigned to *Loxia curvirostra* (Groth 1993a).

Loxia leucoptera Gmelin. White-winged Crossbill.

> *Loxia leucoptera* Gmelin, 1789, Syst. Nat. 1(2): 844. Based on "The White-winged Crossbill" Latham, Gen. Synop. Birds 2(1): 108. (in sinu Hudsonis et Noveboraco = Hudson Bay and New York.)

Habitat.—Coniferous forest (especially spruce, fir, or larch), mixed coniferous-deciduous woodland, and forest edge; in migration and winter also in deciduous forest and woodland.

Distribution.—*Breeds* in North America from western and central Alaska, northern Yukon, northern and east-central Mackenzie, northern Saskatchewan, central Manitoba, northern Ontario, northern Quebec, north-central Labrador, and Newfoundland south to southern Alaska (west to the base of the Alaska Peninsula and Kodiak Island), interior British Columbia, Washington, northeastern Oregon (with isolated populations breeding irregularly in northern Utah, southwestern Colorado, and probably north-central New Mexico), western Montana, northwestern Wyoming, central and southwestern Alberta, central Saskatchewan, southeastern Manitoba, North Dakota, northern Minnesota, northern Wisconsin, northern Michigan, southern Ontario, southwestern Quebec, central New York, northern Vermont, New Hampshire, Maine, New Brunswick, and Nova Scotia; in the Greater Antilles in the mountains of Hispaniola (Dominican Republic, and the Massif de La Selle of southeastern Haiti); and in the Palearctic from northern Scandinavia east across northern Russia to northern Siberia, and south to Lake Baikal and Transbaicalia.

Winters in North America throughout the breeding range, wandering irregularly and sporadically south to western Washington, southern Oregon, southern Idaho, northern Utah, Colorado, central and northeastern New Mexico, northern Texas (Lubbock, Amarillo), central Oklahoma, Arkansas, Kentucky, Virginia, and North Carolina; in Hispaniola in the breeding range; and in the Old World irregularly south to central Europe, Sakhalin, Japan, and the Seven Islands of Izu.

Casual in the Bering Sea (Pribilofs, St. Lawrence Island, and at sea), coastal British Columbia, southern Utah, northern Manitoba, southern Baffin Island, Bermuda, Greenland, the Faeroe Islands, and British Isles; sight reports for northwestern California, northern Florida, and Jamaica.

Notes.—Vocal differences between New World and Old World populations suggest that more than one species is involved (Elmberg 1993).

Genus *CARDUELIS* Brisson

Carduelis Brisson, 1760, Ornithologie 1: 36; 3: 53. Type, by tautonymy, *Carduelis* Brisson = *Fringilla carduelis* Linnaeus.

Subgenus *ACANTHIS* Borkhausen

Acanthis Borkhausen, 1797, Dtsch. Fauna 1: 248. Type, by subsequent designation (Stejneger, 1884), *Fringillaria linaria* Linnaeus = *Fringilla flammea* Linnaeus.

Carduelis flammea (Linnaeus). Common Redpoll.

Fringilla flammea Linnaeus, 1758, Syst. Nat. (ed. 10) 1: 182. (in Europa = Norrland, Sweden.)

Habitat.—Forest, scrub and shrubby areas, and open tundra with bushes or dwarf trees; in migration and winter in open woodland, weedy fields, fence rows, and cultivated lands.

Distribution.—*Breeds* in North America from western and northern Alaska, northern Yukon, northern Mackenzie, southern Victoria Island, northern Keewatin, northern Quebec, Baffin Island, and northern Labrador south to the eastern Aleutians (Unalaska), south-coastal and southeastern Alaska, northwestern British Columbia, central Alberta, northern (casually southern) Saskatchewan, northern Manitoba, northern Ontario, central and southeastern Quebec, and Newfoundland; and in the Palearctic from Greenland, Iceland, northern Scandinavia, northern Russia, and northern Siberia south to the British Isles, central Europe (Alps), central Russia, southern Siberia, Amurland, Sakhalin, and Kamchatka.

Winters in North America from central Alaska, southern Mackenzie, northern Saskatchewan, northern Manitoba, central Ontario, southern Quebec, central Labrador, and Newfoundland south to the northern United States, irregularly or casually to western Oregon, northern California, northern Nevada, northern Utah, central Colorado, Kansas, northern Oklahoma, Arkansas, northern Alabama, and South Carolina; and in the Old World from the southern part of the breeding range south to southern Europe, the northern Mediterranean region, Balkans, Turkestan, Mongolia, eastern China, and Japan.

Migrates regularly through the Aleutian Islands.

Introduced and established in New Zealand and on Lord Howe Island.

Casual on Bermuda. Accidental in north-central Texas; sight reports for the Hawaiian Islands (Midway, Kure).

Notes.—Known in Old World literature as the Redpoll. *Carduelis flammea* and *C. hornemanni* are often placed in the genus *Acanthis* (e.g., Howell et al. *in* Paynter 1968); they appear to constitute a superspecies (Mayr and Short 1970). See comments under *C. hornemanni*.

Carduelis hornemanni (Holböll). Hoary Redpoll.

Linota hornemanni Holböll, 1843, in Krøyer, Naturhist. Tidskr. 4: 398. (Greenland = Ameralikfjord, Greenland.)

Habitat.—Shrubby areas, including sparse low vegetation in open tundra; in migration and winter in open situations, fields, and open woodland.

Distribution.—*Breeds* [*exilipes* group] in North America in western and northern Alaska (south to Hooper Bay), northern Yukon, northwestern British Columbia, northern and east-central Mackenzie, southern Victoria Island, Keewatin, northeastern Manitoba, Southampton Island, northern Quebec, and northern Labrador, and in Eurasia from northern Scandinavia east across northern Russia to northern and eastern Siberia; and [*hornemanni* group] in North America on Ellesmere, Bylot, and northern Baffin islands, and in northern Greenland.

Winters [*exilipes* group] in North America in the breeding range (except extreme northern areas) and south, irregularly, to southern Canada (British Columbia eastward), Montana, Wyoming, South Dakota, Iowa, Wisconsin, northern Illinois, central Indiana, northern Ohio, New York, West Virginia, Maryland, and New England (sight reports from Washington, Oregon, Idaho, Nebraska, and Virginia need verification), and in the Palearctic irregularly to the British Isles, central Europe, central Asia, Japan, Kamchatka, and the Commander Islands; and [*hornemanni* group] in southern Greenland, casually south to northern Manitoba, Keewatin, northern Michigan, southern Ontario, southern Quebec, Labrador, and the British Isles.

Accidental [*hornemanni* group] in central Alaska (Fairbanks).

Notes.—Also known as Arctic Redpoll. The two groups may represent separate species, *C. exilipes* (Coues, 1862) [Hoary Redpoll] and *C. hornemanni* [Hornemann's Redpoll]. Species limits in redpolls are complex and controversial. Some authors consider all forms, including both *C. flammea* and *C. exilipes,* to be members of a single species (e.g., Salomonsen 1951, Harris et al. 1965, Troy 1985), whereas others recognize four species (*C. flammea, C. exilipes, C. hornemanni,* and *C. rostrata* (Coues, 1862) [Greater Redpoll] (e.g., Todd 1963, Herremans 1990). Molau (1985) found no evidence for hybridization between *C. f. flammea* and *C. h. exilipes* in Sweden; Knox (1988b) refuted evidence for hybridization between *C. f. flammea* and *C. h. exilipes,* or between *C. f. rostrata* and *C. h. hornemanni.* Thus, at least two species are probably involved, and that treatment is followed here. Differences in vocalizations between *C. flammea* and *C. hornemanni* in Eurasia also suggest species rank (Knox 1988b, Herremans 1989, references therein). Nevertheless, the possibility that the two species may represent morphotypes of the same species cannot yet be completely eliminated (Seutin et al. 1992). See comments under *C. flammea.*

Subgenus SPINUS Koch

Spinus C. L. Koch, 1816, Syst. Baier. Zool. 1: 232. Type, by tautonymy, *Fringilla spinus* Linnaeus.

Loximitris Bryant, 1868, Proc. Boston Soc. Nat. Hist. 11 (1866): 93. Type, by monotypy, *Chrysomitris dominicensis* Bryant.

Carduelis spinus (Linnaeus). Eurasian Siskin.

Fringilla Spinus Linnaeus, 1758, Syst. Nat., ed. 10, 1, p. 181. (in Europæ juniperetis = Sweden.)

Habitat.—Coniferous woodland, and birch and alder thickets.

Distribution.—*Breeds* from the British Isles and Scandinavia discontinuously across Eurasia to Siberia, and south to southern Europe, northern Iran, northeastern China, and Japan.

Winters in much of the breeding range south to the Mediterranean region, the Middle East, eastern China, and the Philippines.

Accidental in Alaska (Attu, in the Aleutians, 21-22 May 1993, specimen, Univ. Alaska Museum; 1995, Amer. Birds 47: 445; also a sight report 4 June 1978, Roberson 1980: 482). The species has been recorded in southern Ontario (Etobicoke), St. Pierre et Miquelon, Maine (Kittery), Massachusetts (New Bedford and Rockport), and New Jersey (Bloomfield), with additional unconfirmed reports from Wisconsin, New Jersey, Massachusetts (two additional reports), Newfoundland, and Nova Scotia (McLaren et al. 1989). However, there is still question as to the natural origin of these latter birds and they may represent escaped individuals (DeBenedictis 1995).

Notes.—Mayr and Short (1970) considered *C. spinus* and *C. pinus* to constitute a superspecies.

Carduelis pinus (Wilson). Pine Siskin.

Fringilla pinus Wilson, 1810, Amer. Ornithol. 2: 133, pl. 17, fig. 1. (Bush-hill in the neighborhood of Philadelphia, Pennsylvania.)

Habitat.—Coniferous and mixed coniferous-deciduous forest, woodland, parks, and suburban areas; in migration and winter in a variety of woodland and forest habitats, partly open situations with scattered trees, open fields, pastures, and savanna (Temperate Zone).

Distribution.—*Breeds* from central and south-coastal Alaska, central Yukon, southwestern Mackenzie, northwestern and east-central Saskatchewan, central Manitoba, northern Ontario, central Quebec, southern Labrador, and Newfoundland south to south-central California, northern Baja California (to Sierra San Pedro Mártir), southern Nevada, northern and southeastern Arizona, southern New Mexico, western Texas, Chihuahua, Coahuila, the central volcanic belt of Mexico, southwestern Oklahoma, Kansas, Missouri, central Illinois, central Indiana, southwestern and northern Ohio, Pennsylvania, and southern New Jersey, and in the Appalachians south to western Virginia and western North Carolina, with nesting irregular and sporadic in southern areas of the range east of the Rockies. Recorded in summer (and probably breeding) in the mountains of eastern Tennessee.

Winters throughout the breeding range but mainly in the southern part, and also south, irregularly, into northern Mexico to about 30°N in Baja California and east to about 25°N in Tamaulipas, and to the Gulf coast of the United States and northern Florida (casually to the Florida Keys).

Resident in the mountains of central Chiapas and western Guatemala.

Casual or accidental in the Pribilofs (St. Paul) and eastern Aleutians (Unimak), on St. Lawrence, Bathurst, Cornwallis, and Coats islands, and in northern Manitoba, southern Baja California, and Bermuda.

Notes.—This and the following eight species are often treated in the genus *Spinus*.

Carduelis atriceps (Salvin). Black-capped Siskin.

Chrysomitris atriceps Salvin, 1863, Proc. Zool. Soc. London, p. 190. (near Quetzaltenango, 8,000 ft., Guatemala.)

Habitat.—Pine Forest, Pine-Oak Forest, Second-growth Scrub (2300-3100 m; Temperate Zone).

Distribution.—*Resident* in the mountains of Chiapas (interior highlands, and Sierra Madre de Chiapas) and Guatemala (Western Highlands).

Notes.—See comments under *C. pinus*.

Carduelis notata Du Bus de Gisignies. Black-headed Siskin.

Carduelis notata Du Bus de Gisignies, 1847, Bull. Acad. Roy. Sci. Lett. Beaux-Arts Belg. 14: 106. (Mexico = Jalapa, Veracruz.)

Habitat.—Pine-Oak Forest, Montane Evergreen Forest, Pine Forest, Secondary Forest (600-3100 m; Tropical to Temperate zones).

Distribution.—*Resident* from southeastern Sonora, western Chihuahua, Sinaloa, Durango, Zacatecas, eastern San Luis Potosí, southwestern Tamaulipas, and Veracruz south through the highlands of southern Mexico and northern Central America to north-central Nicaragua (also in the lowland pine savanna of northeastern Nicaragua and probably adjacent Honduras).

Notes.—See comments under *C. pinus*.

Carduelis xanthogastra (Du Bus de Gisignies). Yellow-bellied Siskin.

Chrysomitris xanthogastra Du Bus de Gisignies, 1855, Bull. Acad. Roy. Sci. Lett. Beaux-Arts Belg. 22: 152. (Ocaña, Colombia.)

Habitat.—Montane Evergreen Forest, Secondary Forest, Second-growth Scrub (1000-3000 m; upper Tropical and Subtropical zones).

Distribution.—*Resident* in the highlands of Costa Rica (Cordillera Central, Dota Mountains, and Cordillera de Talamanca) and western Panama (western Chiriquí); and in South America from Colombia and northern Venezuela south to southwestern Ecuador, and in central Bolivia.

Notes.—See comments under *C. pinus*.

Carduelis cucullata Swainson. Red Siskin.

Carduelis cucullata Swainson, 1820, Zool. Illus. (1)1(2): pl. 7 and text. ("Spanish Main" = Cumaná, Venezuela.)

Habitat.—Open grassy areas with shrubs and bushes, and scrubby hillsides (upper Tropical Zone).

Distribution.—*Resident,* at least formerly, in northeastern Colombia, northern Venezuela (including Monos and Gasparee islands), and Trinidad; recorded in the original range during the last 30 years only in Colombia, perhaps approaching extinction there.

Introduced and established in southeastern Puerto Rico.

Notes.—See comments under *C. pinus.*

Carduelis dominicensis (Bryant). Antillean Siskin.

Chrysomitris dominicensis Bryant, 1867, Proc. Boston Soc. Nat. Hist. 11 (1866): 93. (Port au Prince, Haiti.)

Habitat.—Pine Forest, Secondary Forest, Second-growth Scrub (700-3000 m).

Distribution.—*Resident* on Hispaniola (in the Dominican Republic from the province of La Vega westward, and in southeastern Haiti in the Massif de la Selle and probably also Massif de la Hotte).

Notes.—This species is sometimes placed in *Spinus* or in the monotypic genus *Loximitris.*

Carduelis psaltria (Say). Lesser Goldfinch.

Fringilla psaltria Say, 1823, in Long, Exped. Rocky Mount. 2: 40 (note). (Arkansas River near the mountains = near Colorado Springs, Colorado.)

Habitat.—Partly open situations with scattered trees, woodland edge, second growth, open fields, pastures, and around human habitation (upper Tropical to lower Temperate zones).

Distribution.—*Resident* from southwestern Washington, western Oregon, northern California, southern Idaho (once), northern Utah, southern Wyoming (possibly), southwestern and central Colorado, and western Oklahoma south to southern Baja California, through Middle America (including the Tres Marías Islands off Nayarit, and Isla Mujeres off Quintana Roo, but in Nicaragua primarily on the Pacific slope), and in South America in Colombia, northern Venezuela, western Ecuador, and northwestern Peru.

Introduced and established on Cuba (at least formerly).

Casual or accidental in British Columbia, Montana, southwestern South Dakota, Nebraska, Kansas, Missouri (Kansas City), Arkansas, southern Louisiana (Cameron, Gretna), Kentucky (Elizabethtown), and Maine (Georgetown); sight reports for North Dakota, southern Ontario, and North Carolina.

Notes.—Also known as Dark-backed Goldfinch or Arkansas Goldfinch. See comments under *C. pinus.*

Carduelis lawrencei Cassin. Lawrence's Goldfinch.

Carduelis lawrencei Cassin, 1850, Proc. Acad. Nat. Sci. Philadelphia 5: 105. (Sonoma and San Diego, California = Sonoma, California.)

Habitat.—Oak woodland, chaparral, riparian woodland, pinyon-juniper association, and weedy areas, in arid regions but usually near water.

Distribution.—*Breeds* from north-central (casually northwestern) California south (west of the Sierra Nevada) to southern California, and in northwestern Baja California and (formerly) western and southern Arizona.

Winters irregularly from north-central California, central Arizona, southwestern New Mexico (rarely), and western Texas (casually) south to northern Baja California (to lat. 30° S.), northern Sonora, and southern Arizona.

Casual in southern Oregon and southern Nevada.

Notes.—See comments under *C. pinus.*

Carduelis tristis (Linnaeus). American Goldfinch.

> *Fringilla tristis* Linnaeus, 1758, Syst. Nat. (ed. 10) 1: 181. Based on "The American Goldfinch" Catesby, Nat. Hist. Carolina 1: 43, pl. 43. (in America septentrionali = South Carolina.)

Habitat.—Weedy fields, cultivated lands, open deciduous and riparian woodland, forest edge, second growth, orchards, and farmlands.

Distribution.—*Breeds* from southern British Columbia (including Vancouver Island), north-central Alberta, central Saskatchewan, west-central and southern Manitoba, central Ontario, southern Quebec (including Anticosti Island), New Brunswick, Prince Edward Island, Nova Scotia, and southwestern Newfoundland south to southern California (west of the Sierra Nevada and southeastern deserts), eastern Oregon, central Nevada, southern Utah, southern Colorado, northern New Mexico (probably), central Oklahoma, extreme northeastern Texas, northern Louisiana, northern Mississippi, central Alabama, central Georgia, and South Carolina.

Winters from southern British Columbia, the northern United States, southern Manitoba, southern Ontario, southwestern Quebec, New Brunswick, and Nova Scotia south to northern Baja California, northern Sonora, southern New Mexico, western and southern Texas, the Gulf coast, and southern Florida (including Florida Keys), and eastern Mexico south to Veracruz.

Casual north to southeastern Alaska, northern Ontario, central Quebec, and southern Labrador, and in Bermuda, the northern Bahama Islands (Grand Bahama, Abaco, Bimini), and Cuba (Cárdenas).

Notes.—See comments under *C. pinus*.

Subgenus *CARDUELIS* Brisson

Carduelis carduelis (Linnaeus). European Goldfinch.

> *Fringilla carduelis* Linnaeus, 1758, Syst. Nat. (ed. 10) 1: 180. (in Europæ juniperetis = Sweden.)

Habitat.—Partly open situations with scattered trees, open woodland, weedy areas, pastures, cultivated lands, forest edge, clearings, and around human habitation.

Distribution.—*Breeds* in Eurasia from the British Isles, central Scandinavia, central Russia, and southern Siberia south to the eastern Atlantic islands, Mediterranean region, northern Africa, the Near East, Himalayas, and Mongolia, the northern populations partially migratory.

Winters in the southern parts of the breeding range.

Introduced in Bermuda, Uruguay, and the Australian region; also introduced widely elsewhere in North America (Oregon, Missouri, Ohio, Pennsylvania, New York, New Jersey, Massachusetts) but not presently established in any of these localities. Occasional reports from North America in these areas and elsewhere (California, Wisconsin, Illinois, and widely in the northeastern United States) almost certainly are based on birds escaped from captivity.

Notes.—Known in Old World literature as the Goldfinch.

Carduelis sinica (Linnaeus). Oriental Greenfinch.

> *Fringilla sinica* Linnaeus, 1766, Syst. Nat. (ed. 12) 1: 321. Based on "Le Pinçon de la Chine" Brisson, Ornithologie 3: 175, pl. 7, fig. 2. (in China = Macao.)

Habitat.—Open woodland (including pine) and cultivated areas with trees or bushes.

Distribution.—*Breeds* from Amurland, Ussuriland, Sakhalin, the Kuril Islands, and Kamchatka south to central and eastern China, Japan, and the Bonin and Volcano islands.

Winters mostly in the southern portions of the breeding range, casually south to Taiwan.

Migrates casually through the western Aleutian Islands (Attu, Shemya, Buldir). A bird reported from California is regarded as of questionable origin.

Notes.—Also known as Chinese Greenfinch.

Genus *SERINUS* Koch

Serinus C. L. Koch, 1816, Syst. Baier. Zool. 1: 228, pl. 6A, fig. 50. Type, by monotypy, *Serinus hortulanus* Koch = *Fringilla serinus* Linnaeus.

Serinus mozambicus (Müller). Yellow-fronted Canary.

Fringilla mozambica P. L. S. Müller, 1776, Natursyst., Suppl., p. 163. (Mozambique.)

Habitat.—Primarily parks and open woodland (Hawaii) or coastal sea grape forest (Puerto Rico); in Africa, open woodland, grasslands, cultivated areas, and parks.

Distribution.—*Resident* throughout most of Africa south of the Sahara and east to Ethiopia and Somalia.

Introduced and established in the Hawaiian Islands (since 1964, common locally in western Hawaii and in small numbers on Oahu), northeastern Puerto Rico, and the Mascarene Islands (in the Indian Ocean).

Notes.—Also known as Green Singing-Finch.

Serinus canaria (Linnaeus). Common Canary.

Fringilla Canaria Linnaeus, 1758, Syst. Nat. (ed. 10) 1: 181. (in Canariis insulis = Canary Islands.)

Habitat.—Primarily groves of ironwood trees; in native range, open woodland and cultivated districts with trees and shrubs.

Distribution.—*Resident* in the Azores, Madeira, and western Canary Islands.

Introduced and established in the Hawaiian Islands (on Midway since at least 1912, presently surviving in small numbers) and on Bermuda. Escaped cage birds occur widely in continental areas of North America and Puerto Rico but have not established breeding populations.

Notes.—Also known as the Canary.

Genus *PYRRHULA* Brisson

Pyrrhula Brisson, 1760, Ornithologie 1: 36. Type, by tautonymy, *Pyrrhula* Brisson = *Loxia pyrrhula* Linnaeus.

Pyrrhula pyrrhula (Linnaeus). Eurasian Bullfinch.

Loxia Pyrrhula Linnaeus, 1758, Syst. Nat. (ed. 10) 1: 171. (in Europæ sylvis = Sweden.)

Habitat.—Coniferous and mixed coniferous-deciduous forest, less commonly open deciduous woodland and parks; in migration and winter also in scrub and partly open situations with scattered trees.

Distribution.—*Breeds* [*pyrrhula* group] from the British Isles, northern Scandinavia, northern Russia, and northern Siberia south to southern Europe, the Balkans, northern Iran, Ussuriland, Sakhalin, Japan, the Kuril Islands, and Kamchatka; [*cineracea* group] in southern Siberia and northern Mongolia.

Winters throughout the breeding range and [*pyrrhula* group] south to southern Europe and central China; and [*cineracea* group] south to Korea, northern China, and southern Japan.

Migrates [*pyrrhula* group] casually in Alaska on St. Lawrence and Nunivak islands, through the western Aleutians (Attu, Shemya), and to the mainland of western and south-coastal Alaska (Aniak, Nulato, Anchorage); sight reports from central and southeastern Alaska.

Resident [*murina* group] in the Azores.

Notes.—Known in Old World literature as the Bullfinch. Groups: *P. pyrrhula* [Eurasian Bullfinch], *P. cineracea* Cabanis, 1872 [Baikal Bullfinch], and *P. murina* Godman, 1866 [Azores Bullfinch].

Genus *COCCOTHRAUSTES* Brisson

Coccothraustes Brisson, 1760, Ornithologie 1: 36, 3: 218. Type, by tautonymy, *Coccothraustes* Brisson = *Loxia coccothraustes* Linnaeus.
Hesperiphona Bonaparte, 1850, C. R. Acad. Sci. Paris 31: 424. Type, by original designation, *Fringilla vespertina* Cooper.

Coccothraustes abeillei (Lesson). Hooded Grosbeak.

Guiraca Abeillei Lesson, 1839, Rev. Zool. [Paris] 2: 41. (Mexico.)

Habitat.—Montane Evergreen Forest, Pine-Oak Forest, Pine Forest (900-3200 m; Subtropical and Temperate zones).
Distribution.—*Resident* in the mountains of Sinaloa, southern Chihuahua, and Durango; and from Michoacán, México, Hidalgo, southeastern San Luis Potosí, southwestern Tamaulipas, and west-central Veracruz south through Guerrero, Oaxaca, and Chiapas to central Guatemala and northern El Salvador.
Notes.—Also known as Abeillé's Grosbeak. See comments under *C. vespertinus.*

Coccothraustes vespertinus (Cooper). Evening Grosbeak.

Fringilla vespertina W. Cooper, 1825, Ann. Lyc. Nat. Hist. N. Y. 1: 220. (Sault Ste. Marie, near Lake Superior [Michigan].)

Habitat.—Coniferous (primarily spruce and fir) and mixed coniferous-deciduous woodland, second growth, and occasionally parks; in migration and winter in a variety of forest and woodland habitats, and around human habitation (Subtropical and Temperate zones).
Distribution.—*Breeds* from southwestern and north-central British Columbia, northern Alberta, central Saskatchewan, southern Manitoba, central Ontario, southern Quebec (including Anticosti Island), New Brunswick, Prince Edward Island, Nova Scotia, and Newfoundland south, in the mountains, to central California (southern Sierra Nevada), west-central and eastern Nevada, central and southeastern Arizona, southern New Mexico, in the Mexican highlands to Michoacán, México, Puebla, and west-central Veracruz, and, east of the Rockies, to southwestern South Dakota (Black Hills), north-central and northeastern Minnesota, northern Wisconsin, central Michigan, southern Ontario, northern New York, and central Massachusetts, casually in northern New Jersey.
Winters throughout the breeding range and south, sporadically, to southern California, southern Arizona, Oaxaca (Cerro San Felipe, where possibly resident), western and central Texas, the northern portions of the Gulf states, Georgia, and South Carolina, casually to the Gulf coast and central Florida.
Casual in east-central, south-coastal and southeastern Alaska, southern Mackenzie, and on Bermuda. Accidental in the British Isles (St. Kilda).
Notes.—*Coccothraustes vespertinus* and *C. abeillei* are often placed in the genus *Hesperiphona.*

Coccothraustes coccothraustes (Linnaeus). Hawfinch.

Loxia Coccothraustes Linnaeus, 1758, Syst. Nat. (ed. 10) 1:. 171. (in Europa australiori = Italy.)

Habitat.—Mixed deciduous-coniferous or deciduous forest, woodland, parks, bushy areas, scrub, and cultivated lands.
Distribution.—*Breeds* from the British Isles, southern Scandinavia, central Russia, and central Siberia south to northwestern Africa, the Mediterranean region, Asia Minor, northern Iran, Transbaicalia, Amurland, Manchuria, Ussuriland, Sakhalin, and Japan.
Winters throughout the breeding range and south to northern Africa, southern Iran, northwestern India, northern China, and the Ryukyu, Bonin, and Volcano islands.
Casual in the western and central Aleutians (from Attu to Adak), Pribilofs (St. Paul), and as far north as St. Lawrence Island and the mainland of western Alaska (Noatak River).

Subfamily DREPANIDINAE: Hawaiian Honeycreepers

Notes.—Generic and specific limits of the Hawaiian Honeycreepers have been subjects of numerous recent studies, but remain in dispute (e.g., Raikow 1977, Sibley and Ahlquist 1982d, Pratt 1979, 1992a, 1992b, Johnson et al. 1989, Tarr and Fleischer 1993, Olson and James 1995). The taxonomy presented here differs from that in the A.O.U. Checklist 6th Ed. (1983) principally by incorporating additional species-level splits among superspecies that occur on more than one of the Hawaiian islands.

Genus *TELESPIZA* Wilson

Telespyza [= error for *Telespiza*] S. B. Wilson, 1890, Ibis, p. 341. Type, by monotypy, *Telespyza* [sic] *cantans* Wilson.

Notes.—Relationships among the seven genera from *Telespiza* through *Chloridops* were debated for decades. All species in these genera were treated by Amadon (1950) under the single genus *Psittirostra,* whereas Greenway (*in* Paynter 1968) treated *Psittirostra* as distinct, with the rest combined into the genus *Loxioides.* Banks and Laybourne (1977) and Pratt (1979) advocated recognizing the separate genera, and this treatment has been followed by subsequent authors (e.g. A.O.U. 1983, Pratt et al. 1987, Sibley and Monroe 1990, Olson and James 1982).

Telespiza cantans Wilson. Laysan Finch.

Telespyza [sic] *cantans* S. B. Wilson, 1890, Ibis, p. 341, pl. 9. (Midway Island, North Pacific, error = Laysan Island.)

Habitat.—*Scaevola* thickets, bunch-grass, and low bushy areas.
Distribution.—*Resident* on Laysan Island, in the Hawaiian Islands.
Introduced and established on islets in Pearl and Hermes Reef, formerly also on Midway (but now extirpated).
Notes.—*Telespiza cantans* and *T. ultima* have been considered conspecific (e.g., Amadon 1950, Greenway *in* Paynter 1968), but Banks and Laybourne (1977) showed that they are distinct species. Sibley and Monroe (1990) considered them to constitute a superspecies, but fossils indicate that these taxa were broadly sympatric before human arrival (James and Olson 1991).

Telespiza ultima Bryan. Nihoa Finch.

Telespiza ultima Bryan, 1917, Auk 34: 70, 71. (Nihoa Island, Hawaiian Group.)

Habitat.—Rock outcroppings and shrub-covered slopes.
Distribution.—*Resident* on Nihoa Island, in the Hawaiian Islands.
Introductions to French Frigate Shoals in 1967 failed.
Notes.—See comments under *T. cantans.*

Genus *PSITTIROSTRA* Temminck

Psittirostra Temminck, 1820, Man. Ornithol. (ed. 2) 1: 70. Type, by monotypy, *Loxia psittacea* Gmelin.

Notes.—See comments under *Telespiza.*

Psittirostra psittacea (Gmelin). Ou.

Loxia psittacea Gmelin, 1789, Syst. Nat. 1(2): 844. Based on the "Parrot-billed Grosbeak" Latham, Gen. Synop. Birds 2(1): 108, pl. 42. (Sandwich Islands = Hawaii.)

Habitat.—Humid montane forest.
Distribution.—Probably extinct. *Resident* until recently in very small numbers in the mountains of Kauai (Alakai plateau; last documented sighting in 1989) and Hawaii (Mauna Loa; extirpated 1984), formerly also on Oahu (last reported in late 1890's), Molokai (last

reported 1907, extirpated before 1948), Lanai (last reported in 1923, extirpated by 1932), and Maui (last reported before 1930), in the Hawaiian Islands.

Genus *DYSMORODREPANIS* Perkins

Dysmorodrepanis Perkins, 1919, Ann. Mag. Nat. Hist., ser. 9, 3, p. 250. Type, by monotypy, *Dysmorodrepanis munroi* Perkins.

Notes.—See comments under *Telespiza*.

†*Dysmorodrepanis munroi* Perkins. Lanai Hookbill.

Dysmorodrepanis munroi Perkins, 1919, Ann. Mag. Nat. Hist., ser. 9, 3, p. 251. (Kaiholena Valley, Island of Lanai.)

Habitat.—Forest.
Distribution.—EXTINCT. Known only from a single specimen taken in 1913 on Lanai, in the Hawaiian Islands.
Notes.—Formerly (Greenway 1939, Amadon 1950) thought to be based on an aberrant specimen of *Psittirostra psittacea* but shown to be a valid species by James et al. (1989).

Genus *LOXIOIDES* Oustalet

Loxioides Oustalet, 1877, Bull. Sci. Soc. Philom. Paris (7)1: 99. Type, by monotypy, *Loxioides bailleui* Oustalet.

Notes.—See comments under *Telespiza*.

Loxioides bailleui Oustalet. Palila.

Loxioides bailleui Oustalet, 1877, Bull. Sci. Soc. Philom. Paris (7)1: 100. (Hawaii.)

Habitat.—Dry mamane-naio forest at higher elevations.
Distribution.—*Resident* in the mountains of Hawaii (Mauna Kea; formerly on the western slope of Mauna Loa and on Hualalai), in the Hawaiian Islands.

Genus *RHODACANTHIS* Rothschild

Rhodacanthis Rothschild, 1892, Ann. Mag. Nat. Hist. (6)10: 110. Type, by subsequent designation (Bryan and Greenway, 1944), *Rhodacanthis palmeri* Rothschild.

Notes.—See comments under *Telespiza*.

†*Rhodacanthis flaviceps* Rothschild. Lesser Koa-Finch.

Rhodacanthis flaviceps Rothschild, 1892, Ann. Mag. Nat. Hist. (6)10: 111. (Kona, Hawaii, Sandwich group.)

Habitat.—Humid montane forest, primarily koa.
Distribution.—EXTINCT. Formerly *resident* at higher elevations in the mountains of the Kona district of Hawaii, in the Hawaiian Islands (last collected in 1891).
Notes.—Also known as Yellow-headed Koa-Finch.

†*Rhodacanthis palmeri* Rothschild. Greater Koa-Finch.

Rhodacanthis Palmeri Rothschild, 1892, Ann. Mag. Nat. Hist. (6)10: 111. (Kona, Hawaii, Sandwich Islands.)

Habitat.—Humid montane forest, primarily koa.
Distribution.—EXTINCT. Formerly *resident* at higher elevations in the mountains of the Kona district of Hawaii, in the Hawaiian Islands (last collected in 1896).
Notes.—Also known as Orange Koa-Finch.

Genus *CHLORIDOPS* Wilson

Chloridops S. B. Wilson, 1888, Proc. Zool. Soc. London, p. 218. Type, by monotypy, *Chloridops kona* Wilson.

Notes.—See comments under *Telespiza.*

†*Chloridops kona* Wilson. Kona Grosbeak.

Chloridops kona S. B. Wilson, 1888, Proc. Zool. Soc. London, p. 218. (Kona, Hawaii.)

Habitat.—Medium-sized trees (especially naio) on lava flows with little ground cover.
Distribution.—EXTINCT. Formerly *resident* on Hawaii (Kona district; last reported in about 1894), in the Hawaiian Islands.
Notes.—Also known as Grosbeak Finch.

Genus *PSEUDONESTOR* Rothschild

Pseudonestor Rothschild, 1893, Bull. Brit. Ornithol. Club 1: 35. Type, by monotypy, *Pseudonestor xanthophrys* Rothschild.

Pseudonestor xanthophrys Rothschild. Maui Parrotbill.

Pseudonestor xanthophrys Rothschild, 1893, Bull. Brit. Ornithol. Club 1: 36. (Island of Maui, Sandwich Islands.)

Habitat.—Humid montane forest, especially koa.
Distribution.—*Resident* in small numbers in the mountains of eastern Maui (windward slopes of Haleakala), in the Hawaiian Islands.
Notes.—Also known as the Pseudonestor.

Genus *HEMIGNATHUS* Lichtenstein

Hemignathus Lichtenstein, 1839, Abh. Phys. Kl. Akad. Wiss. Berlin (1838), p. 449. Type, by subsequent designation (G. R. Gray, 1841), *Hemignathus lucidus* Lichtenstein.
Heterorhynchus Lafresnaye, 1839, Mag. Zool. [Paris] 9: pl. 10. Type, by monotypy, *Heterorhynchus olivaceus* Lafresnaye = *Hemignathus lucidus* Lichtenstein.
Viridonia Rothschild, 1892, Ann. Mag. Nat. Hist. (6)10: 112. Type, by monotypy, *Viridonia sagittirostris* Rothschild.
Akialoa Olson and James, 1995, Proc. Biol. Soc. Wash. 108: 384. Type, by original designation, *Certhia obscura* Gmelin.

Notes.—Generic limits of *Hemignathus* and allies are controversial and subjects of current study. Despite protestations to the contrary (e.g., Amadon 1986, Olson and James 1988, 1995), we continue to follow Pratt (1979) in treating the enlarged genus as a natural assemblage, but this will no doubt change as current genetic analyses become available for evaluation. The enlarged genus contains three groups, referred to by Olson and James (1995) as the Amakihis, the Akialoas, and the Nukupuus (the last including the Akiapolaau). Olson and James (1988, 1995) treated these three groups as separate genera and proposed a new generic name for the Akialoas because the traditional genus for this group (*Heterorhynchus*) has the same type species as the genus *Hemignathus,* and therefore is not a valid name.

Hemignathus virens (Gmelin). Hawaii Amakihi.

Certhia virens Gmelin, 1788, Syst. Nat. 1(1): 479. Based on the "Olive-green Creeper" Latham, Gen. Synop. Birds 1(2), p. 740. (in insulis Sandwich = Hawaii, restricted to Kona district, Island of Hawaii by Medway, 1981, Pacific Sci. 35: 105-175.)

Habitat.—Humid ohia forest, drier mamane-naio forest, and subalpine scrub, mostly at higher elevations but seasonally to lowland forest, including some exotic plantings; also a small population in remnant lowland dry forest in South Kohala District of Hawaii.

Distribution.—*Resident* in the Hawaiian Islands on [*wilsoni* group] Molokai, Lanai (formerly), and Maui, and [*virens* group] Hawaii.

Notes.—This and the following four species are sometimes placed in *Viridonia* (e.g., Greenway *in* Paynter 1968) or *Loxops* (Amadon 1947, 1950, James and Olson 1991). The following two species, *H. flavus* and *H. kauaiensis,* have been considered conspecific with *virens* (e.g., Greenway *in* Paynter 1968) but are here considered members of a superspecies based on studies by Johnson et al. (1989) and Tarr and Fleischer (1993). Johnson et al. (1989) showed that the group on Molokai, Maui, and Lanai (*H. wilsoni* Rothschild, 1893 [Maui Amakihi]) is genetically closest to *virens.* If the four taxa (*virens, wilsoni, flavus,* and *kauaiensis*) are treated as races of a single species, they are known collectively as Common Amakihi.

Hemignathus flavus (Bloxam). Oahu Amakihi.

> *Nectarinia flava* Bloxam, 1827, *in* Byron, Voyage H. M. S. Blonde, App. 3, p. 249. (Oahu.)
>
> *Himatione chloris* Cabanis, 1850, Mus. Heineanun, 1, p. 99. (Oahu.)

Habitat.—Humid montane forest, often with *Eucalyptus*; formerly to sea level.

Distribution.—*Resident* in the Hawaiian Islands on Oahu.

Notes.—Olson (1996) showed that the name *H. flavus* Bloxam, 1827, has priority over *H. chloris* Cabanis. See notes under *H. virens.*

Hemignathus kauaiensis Pratt. Kauai Amakihi.

> *Himatione stejnegeri* Wilson, 1890, Proc. Zool. Soc. London, 1889, p. 446.
>
> *Hemignathus kauaiensis* Pratt, 1989, 'Elepaio, 49: 14. New name for *Himatione stejnegeri* Wilson, preoccupied.

Habitat.—Humid koa/ohia forest above 1100 m, formerly lower.

Distribution.—*Resident* in the Hawaiian Islands on Kauai.

Notes.—If this species is not placed in the genus *Hemignathus,* its specific name reverts to *stejnegeri.* See notes under *H. virens.*

Hemignathus parvus (Stejneger). Anianiau.

> *Himatione parva* Stejneger, 1887, Proc. U. S. Natl. Mus. 10: 94. (Kauai.)

Habitat.—Humid montane forest, primarily ohia.

Distribution.—*Resident* in the mountains of Kauai (Kokee, and the Alakai plateau) in the Hawaiian Islands.

Notes.—Also known as Lesser Amakihi. See comments under *H. virens.*

†*Hemignathus sagittirostris* (Rothschild). Greater Amakihi.

> *Viridonia sagittirostris* Rothschild, 1892, Ann. Mag. Nat. Hist. (6)10: 112. (Mauna Kea, Hawai[i], Sandwich group.)

Habitat.—Humid montane forest at middle elevations.

Distribution.—EXTINCT. Formerly *resident* in the mountains of Hawaii (windward slopes of Mauna Kea; last collected in 1901, and not confirmed since), in the Hawaiian Islands.

Notes.—See comments under *H. virens.*

†*Hemignathus obscurus* (Gmelin). Lesser Akialoa.

> *Certhia obscura* Gmelin, 1788, Syst. Nat. 1(2): 470. Based on the "Hook-billed green Creeper" Latham, Gen. Synop. Birds 1(2): 703, pl. 33, fig. 1. (in insulis Sandwich = Hawaii.)

Habitat.—Humid montane forest, especially ohia, locally in lowland forest.

Distribution.—EXTINCT. Formerly *resident* in the mountains of Hawaii (last collected in 1903, and not confirmed since), in the Hawaiian Islands.

Notes.—*Hemignathus obscurus* and *H. ellisianus* are sometime treated as conspecific (e.g., Greenway *in* Paynter 1968, Olson and James 1982), in which case *H. obscurus* [Akialoa] is the appropriate name. Treated as *Akialoa obscura* [Hawaii Akialoa] by Olson and James (1995). See comments under *H. ellisianus*.

Hemignathus ellisianus (Gray). Greater Akialoa.

Drepanis (Hemignathus) ellisianus G. R. Gray, 1860, Cat. Birds Trop. Islands Pacific, p. 9. (Oahu.)
Hemignathus procerus Cabanis, 1890, J. Ornithol. 39: 331. (Kauai.)

Habitat.—Humid montane forest.

Distribution.—Probably extinct. Formerly *resident* [*stejnegeri* group] in the mountains of Kauai (Alakai plateau; last collected in 1960, sight report in 1969), [*ellisiana* group] in the mountains of Oahu (last recorded 1837, sight report in 1892), and [*lanaiensis* group] Lanai (last collected 1892, sight report 1894), in the Hawaiian Islands.

Notes.—The *ellisianus* and *lanaiensis* groups were formerly (A.O.U. 1983) merged with *H. obscurus* [Hawaiian Akialoa] and the *stejnegeri* group was kept separate under the name *H. procerus* Cabanis, 1890 [Kauai Akialoa]. See Olson and James (1988) for replacement of *procerus* by *stejnegeri* Wilson, 1889. Because *obscurus* is morphologically the most distinctive member of the complex (Pratt 1979, Olson and James 1982), we recognize it as a separate species and merge the others under the oldest name, *ellisianus*. Olson and James (1995) recommended that each island's population be recognized as a separate species in the genus *Akialoa*: *A. ellisiana* [~~Kauai~~ Akialoa], *A. lanaiensis* (Rothschild, 1893) [Lanai Akialoa], and *A. stejnegeri* (Wilson, 1989) [Kauai Akialoa].

(margin note:)Oahu

Hemignathus lucidus Lichtenstein. Nukupuu.

Hemignathus lucidus Lichtenstein, 1839, Abh. Phys. Kl. Akad. Wiss. Berlin (1838), p. 451, pl. 5. (Oahu.)

Habitat.—Humid montane forest, especially ohia and koa.

Distribution.—Possibly extinct, or *resident* locally in precariously small numbers in the Hawaiian Islands, with unverified sightings in recent years on Kauai (Alakai plateau region) and eastern Maui (windward slopes of Haleakala); formerly also on Oahu (last recorded in 1839).

Hemignathus munroi Pratt. Akiapolaau.

Heterorhynchus wilsoni (not *Himatione wilsoni* Rothschild, April 1893) Rothschild, November 1893, Avifauna Laysan, p. 75. (Hawaii.)
Hemignathus munroi Pratt, 1979, Dissert. Abstracts 40: 1581. New name for *Heterorhynchus wilsoni,* preoccupied.

Habitat.—Montane forest, especially koa or mamane-naio but also in mamane-naio parklands.

Distribution.—*Resident* in small numbers in widely separated areas on Hawaii (windward slopes of Mauna Kea and forested regions of Mauna Loa), in the Hawaiian Islands.

Notes.—Formerly known as *H. wilsoni,* but enlarging the genus *Hemignathus* to include the Amakihi and Nukupuu complexes (Pratt 1979) required the new name *munroi.* If this species is not placed in the genus *Hemignathus,* then its specific name reverts to *wilsoni.*

Genus *OREOMYSTIS* Stejneger

Oreomyza (not Pokorny, February 1887, Insecta) Stejneger, April 1887, Proc. U. S. Natl. Mus. 10: 99. Type, by original designation, *Oreomyza bairdi* Stejneger.
Oreomystis Stejneger, 1903, Proc. Biol. Soc. Wash. 16: 11. New name for *Oreomyza* Stejneger, preoccupied.

Notes.—Relationships in the "Hawaiian Creeper" complex were reviewed by Pratt (1992a), who showed that two genera are involved, *Oreomystis* and *Paroreomyza*. Pratt (1979) questioned the familial affinities of *Paroreomyza,* but Johnson et al. (1989) presented allozyme evidence for the sister-group relationship between *Oreomystis* and *Paroreomyza*.

Oreomystis bairdi (Stejneger). Akikiki.

Oreomyza bairdi Stejneger, 1887, Proc. U. S. Natl. Mus. 10: 99. (Kauai.)

Habitat.—Humid montane forest, especially ohia.
Distribution.—*Resident* in small numbers in the mountains of Kauai (Alakai plateau and, until recently, Kokee), in the Hawaiian Islands.
Notes.—Known also as the Kauai Creeper.

Oreomystis mana (Wilson). Hawaii Creeper.

Himatione mana S. B. Wilson, 1891, Ann. Mag. Nat. Hist. (6)7: 460. (Hawaii.)

Habitat.—Humid montane forest, especially koa-ohia.
Distribution.—*Resident* on Hawaii, in the Hawaiian Islands.
Notes.—Placed in the genus *Loxops* by Olson and James (1995) and previous authors. Placement within *Loxops* also is supported by recent biochemical evidence (Fleischer et al. in press).

Genus *PAROREOMYZA* Perkins

Paroreomyza [subgenus] Perkins, 1901, Ibis, p. 583. Type, by original designation, *Oreomyza* [= *Himatione*] *maculata* Cabanis.

Notes.—See comments under *Oreomystis*.

Paroreomyza maculata (Cabanis). Oahu Alauahio.

Himatione maculata Cabanis, 1850, Mus. Heineanum 1: 100 (footnote). (Oahu.)

Habitat.—Humid montane forest.
Distribution.—Probably extinct. Formerly *resident* in the mountains of Oahu (Waianae and Koolau ranges; last reported in 1986), in the Hawaiian Islands.
Notes.—Also known as Oahu Creeper.

Paroreomyza flammea (Wilson). Kakawahie.

Loxops flammea S. B. Wilson, 1890, Proc. Zool. Soc. London (1889), p. 445. (Kalae, Molokai.)

Habitat.—Humid montane forest.
Distribution.—Probably extinct. Formerly *resident* in the mountains of Molokai (last reported in 1962), in the Hawaiian Islands.
Notes.—Also known as Molokai Creeper.

Paroreomyza montana (Wilson). Maui Alauahio.

Himatione montana S. B. Wilson, 1890, Proc. Zool. Soc. London (1889), p. 446. (Lanai.)

Habitat.—Humid montane forest and subalpine scrub.
Distribution.—*Resident* in the mountains of eastern Maui (slopes of Haleakala, formerly also on western Maui); and formerly on Lanai (last recorded in 1937), in the Hawaiian Islands.
Notes.—Also known as Maui Creeper.

Genus *LOXOPS* Cabanis

Loxops Cabanis, 1847, Arch. Naturgesch. 13: 330. Type, by original designation, *Fringilla coccinea* Gmelin.

Loxops caeruleirostris (Wilson). Akekee.

> *Chrysomitridops caeruleirostris* Wilson, 1890, Proc. Zool. Soc. London, p. 373. (Kauai.)

Habitat.—Humid montane forest, preferring ohia.
Distribution.—*Resident* in the mountains of Kauai (Kokee, and the Alakai plateau), in the Hawaiian Islands.
Notes.—Sometimes called the Kauai Akepa. *Loxops caeruleirostris,* formerly considered a subspecies of *L. coccineus* (e.g., Greenway *in* Paynter 1968), was recognized as a distinct species by Pratt (1989b).

Loxops coccineus (Gmelin). Akepa.

> *Fringilla coccinea* Gmelin, 1789, Syst. Nat., 1(2), p. 921. Based on the "Scarlet Finch" Latham, Gen Synop. Birds, 2(1), p. 270. (in insulis Sandwich = Hawaii.)

Habitat.—Humid montane forest, primarily ohia-koa.
Distribution.—*Resident* in the mountains [*wolstenholmei* group] on Oahu (formerly, not recorded since the early 1900's); [*ochraceus* group] on eastern Maui (probably extinct); and [*coccineus* group] on Hawaii (rare and local).
Notes.—Sometimes called the Common Akepa. Groups: *L. wolstenholmei* Rothschild, 1893 [Oahu Akepa], *L. ochraceus* Rothschild, 1893 [Maui], and *L. coccineus* [Hawaii Akepa]. *Loxops rufus,* based on *Fringilla rufa* Bloxam, 1827, and generally used for the Oahu Akepa, is preoccupied by *Fringilla rufa* Wilson, 1811 [= *Passerella iliaca*] (Olson 1986). See comments under *L. caeruleirostris.*

Genus *CIRIDOPS* Newton

> *Ciridops* Newton, 1892, Nature 45: 469. Type, by monotypy, *Fringilla anna* Dole.

†*Ciridops anna* (Dole). Ula-ai-hawane.

> *Fringilla anna* Dole, 1878, in Thrum, Hawaiian Almanac Annual (1879), p. 49. (Hawaii.)

Habitat.—Montane forest, especially loulu palm.
Distribution.—EXTINCT. Formerly *resident* in the mountains of Hawaii (Kona and Hilo districts, and Kohala Mountains, last collected in early 1890's), in the Hawaiian Islands.

Genus *VESTIARIA* Jarocki

> *Vestiaria* Jarocki, 1821, Zoologia 2: 75. Type, by monotypy, *Certhia vestiaria* Latham = *Certhia coccinea* Forster.

Notes.—Pratt (1979) proposed merging this genus with *Drepanis.*

Vestiaria coccinea (Forster). Iiwi.

> *Certhia coccinea* J. R. Forster, 1780, Göttinger Mag. Wiss. 1: 347. (O-Waihi = Kona district, Hawaii; Olson, 1989, Bull. Brit. Ornithol. Club 109: 203-204.)

Habitat.—Native montane forest.
Distribution.—*Resident* on Kauai, Oahu (very small numbers), Maui, and Hawaii, formerly Molokai and Lanai, in the Hawaiian Islands.

Genus *DREPANIS* Temminck

> *Drepanis* Temminck, 1820, Man. Ornithol. (ed. 2) 1: 86. Type, by subsequent designation (G. R. Gray, 1840), *Certhia pacifica* Gmelin.

Notes.—See comments under *Vestiaria.*

†*Drepanis pacifica* (Gmelin). Hawaii Mamo.

Certhia pacifica Gmelin, 1788, Syst. Nat. 1(1): 470. Based on the "Great Hook-billed Creeper" Latham, Gen. Synop. Birds 1(2): 703. (in insula amicis maris australis, error = Hawaii.)

Habitat.—Humid montane forest, specializing on lobeliad flowers.
Distribution.—EXTINCT. Formerly *resident* in the mountains of Hawaii (last recorded in 1898), in the Hawaiian Islands.
Notes.—Also known as the Mamo.

†*Drepanis funerea* Newton. Black Mamo.

Drepanis funerea Newton, 1894, Proc. Zool. Soc. London (1893), p. 690. (Molokai.)

Habitat.—Humid montane forest, specializing on lobeliad flowers.
Distribution.—EXTINCT. Formerly *resident* in the mountains of Molokai (last recorded in 1907), in the Hawaiian Islands.
Notes.—Also known as Perkins's Mamo.

Genus *PALMERIA* Rothschild

Palmeria Rothschild, 1893, Ibis, p. 113. Type, by monotypy, *Palmeria mirabilis* Rothschild = *Himatione dolei* Wilson.

Palmeria dolei (Wilson). Akohekohe.

Himatione dolei S. B. Wilson, 1891, Proc. Zool. Soc. London, p. 166. (Maui.)

Habitat.—Humid montane forest, especially ohia.
Distribution.—*Resident* in the mountains of eastern Maui (windward slopes of Haleakala), formerly also on Molokai (last reported in 1907), in the Hawaiian Islands.
Notes.—Also known as Crested Honeycreeper.

Genus *HIMATIONE* Cabanis

Himatione Cabanis, 1850, Mus. Heineanum 1: 99. Type, by monotypy, *Certhia sanguinea* Gmelin.

Himatione sanguinea (Gmelin). Apapane.

Certhia sanguinea Gmelin, 1788, Syst. Nat. 1(1): 479. Based on the "Crimson Creeper" Latham, Gen. Synop. Birds 1(2): 739. (in insulis Sandwich = Hawaii.)

Habitat.—Humid montane forests, primarily ohia-koa, but occasionally in mixed native-exotic forest, and [*freethii* group] in brushy areas and bunch-grass.
Distribution.—*Resident* [*sanguinea* group] in the mountains in the Hawaiian Islands (all main islands from Kauai eastward); and [*freethii* group] formerly on Laysan Island (extirpated in 1923).
Accidental [*sanguinea* group] on Niihau.
Notes.—Groups: *H. sanguinea* [Apapane] and *H. freethii* Rothschild, 1892 [Laysan Honeycreeper].

Genus *MELAMPROSOPS* Casey and Jacobi

Melamprosops Casey and Jacobi, 1974, Occas. Pap. Bernice P., Bishop Mus., no. 12, p. 217. Type, by original designation, *Melamprosops phaeosoma* Casey and Jacobi.

Notes.—The affinity of this recently discovered genus within the Drepanidinae is unknown, and Pratt (1992b) presented evidence that it may not belong in this group at all.

Melamprosops phaeosoma Casey and Jacobi. Poo-uli.

Melamprosops phaeosoma Casey and Jacobi, 1974, Occas. Pap. Bernice P., Bishop. Mus., no. 12, p. 219. (Haleakala Volcano, Maui, Hawaii.)

Habitat.—Humid montane forest, primarily ohia.

Distribution.—*Resident* in precariously small numbers in the mountains of Maui (Hanawi region of the windward slopes of Haleakala), in the Hawaiian Islands.

Notes.—Known also as Black-faced Honeycreeper.

Family **PASSERIDAE**: Old World Sparrows

Genus *PASSER* Brisson

Passer Brisson, 1760, Ornithologie 1: 36; 3: 71. Type, by subsequent designation (G. R. Gray, 1840), *Passer domesticus* Brisson = *Fringilla domestica* Linnaeus.

Passer domesticus (Linnaeus). House Sparrow.

Fringilla domestica Linnaeus, 1758, Syst. Nat. (ed. 10) 1: 183. (in Europa = Sweden.)

Habitat.—Vicinity of human habitation (Tropical to Temperate zones).

Distribution.—*Resident* from the British Isles, northern Scandinavia, northern Russia, and northern Siberia south to northwestern Africa, the Mediterranean region, northeastern Africa, Arabia, India (including Sri Lanka), and Southeast Asia.

Introduced (initially in 1850 at Brooklyn, New York, with several subsequent introductions elsewhere in the northeast through 1867) and established in North America, presently resident from central and southeastern British Columbia, southwestern Mackenzie, northwestern and central Saskatchewan, northern Manitoba, central Ontario, southern Quebec (including Anticosti and Magdalen islands), and Newfoundland south throughout southern Canada, the continental United States, and most of Mexico to Veracruz, Oaxaca, and Chiapas, locally in Central America (where range expanding rapidly in recent years) south to Panama (east to eastern Panamá province); also in the Hawaiian Islands (Honolulu in 1871, since spreading throughout all main islands), Bahama Islands (Grand Bahama, New Providence), Cuba (late 1890's), Jamaica (1903-1966, 1992-1993), Hispaniola (1978), Puerto Rico (1978), the Virgin Islands (St. Thomas, early 1950's), Aruba, Curaçao, South America (western Colombia to Chile, and eastern Brazil to Paraguay, Argentina, and the Falkland Islands), southern and eastern Africa, islands in the Indian Ocean, Australia, and New Zealand. Sight report from the Revillagigedo Islands (Socorro Island).

Passer montanus (Linnaeus). Eurasian Tree Sparrow.

Fringilla montana Linnaeus, 1758, Syst. Nat. (ed. 10) 1: 183. (in Europa = Bagnacavallo, Ravenna, Italy.)

Habitat.—Open woodland, fields, cultivated lands, and around human habitation.

Distribution.—*Resident* from the British Isles, northern Scandinavia, northern Russia, and northern Siberia south to the Mediterranean region, Iran, Afghanistan, northern India, Southeast Asia, Sumatra, Java, Bali, the Himalayas, Sea of Okhotsk, and on Pacific islands from Sakhalin and the Kuril Islands south through Japan to Hainan, Taiwan, and the Ryukyu Islands.

Introduced and established at St. Louis, Missouri (1870), whence it has spread into east-central Missouri and western Illinois, with stragglers reported in southern Manitoba, southern Ontario, Minnesota, Wisconsin, southeastern Iowa (West Branch), Indiana (Marshall), and western Kentucky (Lone Oak); sight reports to northern Illinois; introduced in Bermuda (now extirpated), and established in Borneo, Sulawesi, the Philippines, Micronesia, and Australia.

Notes.—Also known as European Tree Sparrow and, in Old World literature, as the Tree Sparrow.

Family **PLOCEIDAE**: Weavers

Subfamily PLOCEINAE: Typical Weavers

Genus *PLOCEUS* Cuvier

Ploceus Cuvier, 1816, Règne Anim. 1: 383. Type, by subsequent designation (G. R. Gray, 1840), *Loxia philippina* Linnaeus.

Ploceus cucullatus (Müller). Village Weaver.

  Oriolus cucullatus P. L. S. Müller, 1776, Natursyst., Suppl., p. 87. (Senegal.)

Habitat.—Forest, woodland, scrub, brush, vegetation near water, and around human habitation.

Distribution.—*Resident* [*cucullatus* group] in West Africa from Senegal eastward, and across the Congo region to Sudan, Eritrea, Ethiopia, Uganda, and western Kenya; [*collaris* group] from Gabon to northern Angola; and [*nigriceps* group] from southern Somalia south through eastern Kenya and Tanzania to southern Africa.

  Introduced [*cucullatus* group] and established on Hispaniola (including Saona and Catalina islands).

Notes.—Also known as Black-headed Weaver. Groups: *P. cucullatus* [Black-headed Weaver], *P. collaris* Vieillot, 1819 [Mottled Weaver], and *P. nigriceps* (Layard, 1867) [Layard's Weaver].

Genus *EUPLECTES* Swainson

  Euplectes Swainson, 1829, Zool. Illus. (2) 1: text to pl. 37. Type, by original designation, *"Loxia"* [= *Emberiza*] *orix* Linnaeus.

Notes.—Members of this genus are sometimes known under the group name Bishopbird.

Euplectes franciscanus (Isert). Orange Bishop.

  Loxia franciscanus Isert, 1789, Schrift. Ges. Nat. Freund. Berlin 19: 332. (Accra.)

Habitat.—Open grassland and edges of swamps, rice, and cane fields; weedy areas.

Distribution.—*Resident* in Africa from Senegal and Sudan south to Cameroon, eastern Congo region, northern Uganda, and northeastern Kenya.

  Introduced and established in southern California and Puerto Rico; introductions in the Hawaiian Islands (Oahu) and Bermuda are not known to have become established.

Notes.—Formerly (A.O.U. 1983) considered conspecific with *E. orix* (Linnaeus, 1758) [Red Bishop] but seperated following Hall and Moreau (1970). Johnston and Garrett (1994) noted that this species rather than *orix* is present in southern California. Also known as Northern Red Bishop.

Euplectes afer (Gmelin). Yellow-crowned Bishop.

  Loxia afra Gmelin, 1789, Syst. Nat. 1(2): 857. Based mainly on the "Black-bellied Grosbeak" Latham, Gen. Synop. Birds 2(1): 155. (in Africa = Senegal.)

Habitat.—Swamps, marshes, and tall grass areas in wet situations.

Distribution.—*Resident* [*afer* group] in western and central Africa from Senegal east to Sudan, Ethiopia, and northern Kenya, and south to northern Angola and Zaire; and [*taha* group] in eastern and southern Africa from central Angola, southeastern Zaire, southern Sudan, and central Ethiopia south to southern Africa.

  Introduced and established [*afer* group] on Puerto Rico; introductions in the Hawaiian Islands (Oahu) have not become established.

Notes.—Also known as Golden Bishop, Napoleon Bishop, or Napoleon Weaver. Groups: *E. afer* [Yellow-crowned Bishop] and *E. taha* Smith, 1836 [Taha Bishop].

Family **ESTRILDIDAE**: Estrildid Finches

Subfamily ESTRILDINAE: Estrildine Finches

Genus *URAEGINTHUS* Cabanis

  Uraeginthus Cabanis, 1851, Mus. Heineanum 1: 171. Type, by subsequent designation (G. R. Gray, 1855), *Fringilla bengalus* Linnaeus.

Uraeginthus bengalus (Linnaeus). Red-cheeked Cordonbleu.

> *Fringilla bengalus* Linnaeus, 1766, Syst. Nat. (ed. 12) 1: 323. Based on "Le Bengali" Brisson, Ornithologie 3: 203, pl. 10, fig. 1. (in Bengala, error = Senegal.)

Habitat.—Weedy and grassy fields; in Africa, thornbush, savanna, forest edge, cultivated lands, and around human habitation.

Distribution.—*Resident* in Africa from Senegal east to Sudan, Eritrea, and Somalia, and south to Angola, Zambia, and Tanzania.

Introduced and established in very small numbers in the Hawaiian Islands (since 1965 on Oahu, where now extirpated, and locally in Puuanahulu area on Hawaii).

Genus *ESTRILDA* Swainson

> *Estrilda* Swainson, 1827, Zool. J. 3: 349. Type, by original designation, *Loxia astrild* Linnaeus.

Estrilda caerulescens (Vieillot). Lavender Waxbill.

> *Fringilla cærulescens* Vieillot, 1817, Nouv. Dict. Hist. Nat. (nouv. éd.) 12: 176. (Zone Torride = Senegal.)

Habitat.—Weedy and grassy fields; in Africa, bush country, scrub, gardens, and around human habitation.

Distribution.—*Resident* in West Africa from Senegal to Nigeria, and inland to western Central African Republic, southwestern Chad, and northern Cameroon.

Introduced and established in the Hawaiian Islands (first reported in 1965, nearly extirpated from Hawaii but becoming increasingly common on the Kona coast of Hawaii).

Notes.—Also known as Red-tailed Lavender Waxbill or Lavender Fire-Finch.

Estrilda melpoda (Vieillot). Orange-cheeked Waxbill.

> *Fringilla melpoda* Vieillot, 1817, Nouv. Dict. Hist. Nat. (nouv. éd.) 12: 177. (India and west coast of Africa = Senegal.)

Habitat.—Fields with tall grass; in Africa, savanna, grasslands, cultivated lands, and around human habitation.

Distribution.—*Resident* in West Africa from Senegal and Gambia east to Chad, and south to Angola and Zambia.

Introduced and established in the Hawaiian Islands (first reported in 1965, now in small numbers on Oahu, with recent sight reports from Maui), Bermuda (reported 1975, well established and breeding since 1982), and on Puerto Rico.

Estrilda troglodytes (Lichtenstein). Black-rumped Waxbill.

> *Fringilla Troglodytes* Lichtenstein, 1823, Verz. Doubl. Zool. Mus. Berlin, p. 26. (Senegambia.)

Habitat.—Fields with tall grass; in Africa, bush country, swampy areas, and brushy habitats.

Distribution.—*Resident* in Africa from Senegal and Gambia east to Sudan, Eritrea, and Ethiopia, and south to northeastern Zaire and northwestern Uganda.

Introduced and established in the Hawaiian Islands (first reported in 1965, now in small numbers on Oahu and Hawaii) and on Puerto Rico.

Notes.—Also known as Red-eared Waxbill.

Estrilda astrild (Linnaeus). Common Waxbill.

> *Loxia Astrild* Linnaeus, 1758, Syst. Nat. (ed. 10) 1: 173. Based on "The Wax Bill" Edwards, Nat. Hist. Birds 4: 179, pl. 179, lower fig. (in Canariis, America, Africa = Cape Town, South Africa.)

Habitat.—Weedy and grassy fields, usually near water; in Africa, open country, grasslands, cultivated lands, open woodland, and around human habitation.

Distribution.—*Resident* throughout Africa south of the Sahara.

Introduced and established in the Hawaiian Islands (Oahu), Bermuda (first reported 1973, now poorly established), and Puerto Rico.

Notes.—Also known as the Waxbill.

Genus *AMANDAVA* Blyth

Amandava Blyth, 1836, in White, Nat. Hist. Selbourne, p. 44, footnote. Type, by monotypy, *Amandava punctata* Blyth = *Fringilla amandava* Linnaeus.

Amandava amandava (Linnaeus). Red Avadavat.

Fringilla Amandava Linnaeus, 1758, Syst. Nat. (ed. 10) 1: 180. Based on "Amandava" Albin, Nat. Hist. Birds 3: 72, pl. 77. (in india orientali = Calcutta, West Bengal.)

Habitat.—Weedy and grassy fields, especially at edges of marshes; in Asia, second growth, grasslands, scrub, reed beds, and cultivated lands.

Distribution.—*Resident* from Pakistan, India, and southern Nepal south through Southeast Asia and Java to the Lesser Sunda Islands (east to Timor).

Introduced and established in the Hawaiian Islands (on Oahu, between 1900 and 1910, now also on Kauai and Hawaii), Fiji, Puerto Rico, Spain, Sumatra, and Singapore.

Notes.—Also known as Strawberry Finch or Red Munia.

Genus *LONCHURA* Sykes

Lonchura Sykes, 1832, Proc. Zool. Soc. London, p. 94. Type, by subsequent designation (G. R. Gray, 1840), *Fringilla nisoria* Temminck = *Loxia punctulata* Linnaeus.

Spermestes Swainson, 1837, Birds W. Afr. 1: 201. Type, by monotypy, *Spermestes cucullata* Swainson.

Euodice Reichenbach, 1863, Singvögel, p. 46. Type, by subsequent designation (Sharpe, 1890), *Loxia cantans* Gmelin = *Loxia malabarica* Linnaeus.

Lonchura malabarica (Linnaeus). Warbling Silverbill.

Loxia malabarica Linnaeus, 1758, Syst. Nat. (ed. 10) 1: 175. (in Indiis = Malabar.)

Habitat.—Dry, grassy brush and scrub; in Africa, scrub and brush, and around human habitation.

Distribution.—*Resident* [*cantans* group] in Africa from Senegal east to Sudan, Ethiopia, and Somalia, and south to Kenya and northern Tanzania, also in southern Arabia; and [*malabarica* group] in southern Asia from eastern Arabia east to India.

Introduced and established [*malabarica* group] in the Hawaiian Islands (first reported in 1973 on Hawaii, recently spreading to Maui, Lanai, and Molokai, with sight reports from Kauai, Oahu, and Kahoolawe), and on Puerto Rico. A pair successfully bred on Merritt Island, Florida, in June 1965 (1965, Amer. Birds 19: 537; reported as *Euodice cantans*), but the species has not become established there.

Notes.—Also known as the Silverbill. Groups: *L. cantans* (Gmelin) 1789 [African Silverbill] and *L. malabarica* [White-throated Silverbill]. Sometimes placed in the genus *Euodice*.

Lonchura cucullata (Swainson). Bronze Mannikin.

Spermestes cucullata Swainson, 1837, Birds W. Afr. 1: 201. (West Africa = Senegal.)

Habitat.—Open areas with grass, including lawns, in lowlands (primarily below 300 m); in Africa, open country, bush, cultivated lands, and around human habitation.

Distribution.—*Resident* in Africa from Senegal east to Sudan, Ethiopia, and Kenya, and south to Angola, Zambia, and Rhodesia (including Zanzibar and other coastal islands in the Gulf of Guinea and along the Indian Ocean).

Introduced and established in Puerto Rico (common in coastal lowlands, but rare in hill country).

Notes.—Also known as Bronze Munia or Hooded Weaver. Often placed in the genus *Spermestes*.

Lonchura punctulata (Linnaeus). Nutmeg Mannikin.

Loxia punctulata Linnaeus, 1758, Syst. Nat. (ed. 10) 1: 173. Based on "The Gowry Bird" Edwards, Nat. Hist. Birds 1: 40, pl. 40. (in Asia = Calcutta, India.)

Habitat.—Open areas and second growth with tall grass; in Asia, second growth, scrub, grasslands, cultivated lands, and around human habitation.

Distribution.—*Resident* from India, Nepal, southern China, Hainan, and Taiwan south to Sri Lanka, and through Southeast Asia to the East Indies (east to Sulawesi and Tanimbar) and Philippines.

Introduced and established in the Hawaiian Islands (about 1865, presently widespread on all main islands), in lowland central Jamaica, in Australia, and on islands in the Indian Ocean. Pairs bred successfully in Florida at Cocoa Beach in 1964 (1964, Amer. Birds 18: 504-505) and on Merritt Island in 1965 (1965, Amer. Birds 19: 537), but no population has become established; also reported (status uncertain) on Hispaniola and Puerto Rico.

Notes.—Also known as Spotted Munia, Spice Finch, Ricebird, or Scaly-breasted Mannikin.

Lonchura malacca (Linnaeus). Chestnut Mannikin.

Loxia malacca Linnaeus, 1766, Syst. Nat. (ed. 12) 1: 302. Based mainly on "Le Grosbec de Java" Brisson, Ornithologie 3: 237, pl. 13, fig. 1. (in China, Java, Malacca, error = Belgaum, India.)

Habitat.—Open areas with tall grass; in Asia, second growth, scrub, grasslands, cultivated lands, marshes, and around human habitation.

Distribution.—*Resident* [*malacca* group] in southern India and Sri Lanka; and [*atricapilla* group] from northern and eastern India, Nepal, Southeast Asia, southern China, Hainan, and Taiwan south to Sri Lanka, the Greater Sunda Islands, and Philippines.

Introduced and established [*atricapilla* group] in the Hawaiian Islands (first observed in 1959 on Oahu, presently also occurs on Kauai and possibly Hawaii), on Puerto Rico, and in the Moluccas and Micronesia. A pair bred successfully in 1965 on Merritt Island, Florida (1965, Amer. Birds 19: 537), but no population became established.

Notes.—Also known as Black-headed Munia, Black-headed Mannikin, Chestnut Munia, or Black-headed Nun. Groups: *L. malacca* [Indian Black-headed Munia] and *L. atricapilla* (Vieillot, 1807) [Southern Black-headed Munia].

Genus *PADDA* Reichenbach

Padda Reichenbach, 1850, Avium Syst. Nat., pl. 76, fig. 4. Type, by monotypy, *Loxia oryzivora* Linnaeus.

Padda oryzivora (Linnaeus). Java Sparrow.

Loxia oryzivora Linnaeus, 1758, Syst. Nat. (ed. 10) 1: 173. Based in part on "The Cock Padda or Rice-bird" Edwards, Nat. Hist. Birds 1: 41, pl. 41. (in Asia & Æthiopia = Java.)

Habitat.—Primarily open grassy areas of parks and lawns; in Indonesia, scrub, mangroves, cultivated lands, and around human habitation.

Distribution.—*Resident* on Java and Bali, in the East Indies.

Introduced and established in the mid-1960's in the Hawaiian Islands (now widespread on Oahu, common on the Kona coast of Hawaii, and in small numbers on Kauai and Maui; earlier introductions on Oahu in 1865 did not become established), in southern Florida (Miami region, now extirpated), on Puerto Rico (San Juan area), and widely elsewhere, especially in Sri Lanka, Southeast Asia, Sulawesi, the Lesser Sunda Islands, Philippines, and Moluccas.

Notes.—Also known as Java Finch.

Subfamily VIDUINAE: Whydahs

Genus *VIDUA* Cuvier

Vidua Cuvier, 1816, Règne Anim. 1: 388. Type, by tautonymy, *Emberiza vidua* Linnaeus = *Fringilla macroura* Pallas.

Vidua macroura (Pallas). Pin-tailed Whydah.

Fringilla macroura Pallas, 1764, in Vroeg, Cat. Raissoné Ois., Adumbr., p. 3. (East Indies, error = Angola.)

Habitat.—Areas of short grass and lawns; in Africa, arid bush country, grassland, scrub, cultivated areas, and around human habitation.

Distribution.—*Resident* in Africa from Senegal east to Eritrea, and south to southern Africa, including Zanzibar and other coastal islands.

Introduced and established on Puerto Rico; escapes in the Hawaiian Islands (Oahu) probably bred in the mid-1970s, but are now extirpated.

APPENDIX

Part 1. Species reported from the A.O.U. Check-list area with insufficient evidence for placement on the main list. Species on this list have been reported (published) as occurring in the geographic area covered by this Check-list. However, their occurrence is considered hypothetical for one of more of the following reasons:

1. Physical evidence for their presence (e.g., specimen, photograph, video-tape, audio-recording) is lacking, of disputed origin, or unknown. See the Preface for further discussion.
2. The natural occurrence (unrestrained by humans) of the species is disputed.
3. An introduced population has failed to become established.
4. Inclusion in previous editions of the Check-list was based exclusively on records from Greenland, which is now outside the A.O.U. Check-list area.

Phoebastria irrorata (Salvin). Waved Albatross.

> *Diomedea irrorata* Salvin, 1883, Proc. Zool. Soc. London, p. 430. (Callao Bay, Peru.)

This species breeds on Hood Island in the Galapagos and on Isla de la Plata off Ecuador, and ranges at sea along the coasts of Ecuador and Peru. A specimen was taken just outside the North American area at Octavia Rocks, Colombia, near the Panama-Colombia boundary (8 March 1941, R. C. Murphy). There are sight reports from Panama, west of Piñas Bay, Darién, 26 February 1941 (Ridgely 1976), and southwest of the Pearl Islands, 27 September 1964. Also known as Galapagos Albatross.

Thalassarche chrysostoma (Forster). Gray-headed Albatross.

> *Diomedea chrysostoma* J. R. Forster, 1785, Mém. Math. Phys. Acad. Sci. Paris 10: 571, pl. 14. (voisinage du cercle polaire antarctique & dans l'Ocean Pacifique = Isla de los Estados [= Staten Island], off Tierra del Fuego.)

This species breeds on islands off Cape Horn, in the South Atlantic, in the southern Indian Ocean, and off New Zealand. Reports from Oregon (mouth of the Columbia River), California (coast near Golden Gate), and Panama (Bay of Chiriquí) are unsatisfactory (see A.O.U. 1957: 643, and Wetmore 1965).

Macronectes giganteus (Gmelin). Antarctic Giant-Petrel.

> *Procellaria gigantea* Gmelin, 1789, Syst. Nat. 1 (2): 563. Based in part on the "Giant Petrel" Latham, Gen. Synop. Birds 3(2): 396, pl. 100. (in oceano, potissimum australi, circa Staatenland, Terra del fuego = Isla los Estados [= Staten Island], off Tierra del Fuego.)

This species breeds in Antarctica and on subantarctic islands and ranges at sea throughout southern oceans. A report from the "coast of Oregon" (immature specimen taken by Town-send) is generally regarded to be in error as to locality (see Stone 1930, but for conflicting opinion, see also Fisher 1965). There are sight reports near Midway, Hawaiian Islands: 9 December 1962, dark-phased individual, plus two other probables in December 1959 and December 1961 (Fisher, *loc. cit.*). Also known as Giant Fulmar or Southern Giant-Petrel. Two forms, *M. giganteus,* a more southern breeding form, and *M. halli* Mathews, 1912, were formerly considered conspecific, but are widely sympatric in the northern portion of the range of *M. giganteus* (Bourne and Warham 1966, Hunter 1987). The above reports may pertain to either form.

Fulmarus glacialoides (Smith). Southern Fulmar.

> *Procellaria glacialoides* Smith, 1840, Illus. Zool. S. Afr., pt. 11, pl. 51. (neighbourhood of the South African coast.)

This species breeds around Antarctica and on Antarctic islands in the South Atlantic and southern Indian oceans, and ranges at sea in southern oceans north to southern Australia,

New Zealand, central South America, and South Africa. A report from off western Mexico (near Mazatlán, Sinaloa; Friedmann et al. 1950) and the locality of Townsend's specimen reported from the "mouth of the Columbia River, Oregon" (Stone 1930) are regarded as erroneous (Bourne 1967, Banks 1988b).

Daption capense (Linnaeus). Cape Petrel.

Procellaria capensis Linnaeus, 1758, Syst. Nat. (ed. 10) 1: 132. Based primarily on "The white and black Spotted Peteril" Edwards, Nat. Hist. Birds 2: 90, pl. 90, right fig. (ad Cap. b. Spei = Cape of Good Hope.)

This species breeds on Antarctic and subantarctic islands in the South Atlantic and southern Indian oceans and in New Zealand waters. Reports from Maine (Harpswell, Cumberland County, June 1873; Norton 1922), Ireland, continental Europe, Sicily, and Sri Lanka, as well as sight reports in the Pacific Ocean off California and Atlantic Ocean off North Carolina, have been questioned; a report from off the coast of Acapulco, Guerrero, is "indefinite" (Friedmann et al. 1957), and an early California specimen ("coast of California, opposite Monterey," before 1853; Lawrence 1853) is regarded as erroneously labeled (Lee 1993). Thus all Northern Hemisphere reports are highly questionable. Also known as Pintado Petrel or Cape Pigeon.

Pterodroma solandri (Gould). Solander's Petrel.

Procellaria Solandri Gould, 1844, Proc. Zool. Soc. London, p. 57. (Australia = Bass Strait.)

This species breeds in the South Pacific on Lord Howe and (formerly) Norfolk islands; pelagic distribution little-known, but recorded primarily in southwestern Pacific off Australia and New Zealand north to approximately Tropic of Cancer. An individual found dead in the Hawaiian Islands (Kauai, 25 November 1986; 1987, 'Elepaio 47: 29) and previously reported as *P. solandri* is an example of *P. ultima* (R. Clapp, pers. comm.). Additional sightings of this species in Hawaiian waters are unsubstantiated (Pyle 1988). All California sightings are referable to *P. ultima* or are unidentifiable; none has been substantiated. A sight report and photograph from off Westport, Washington, 11 September 1983, by T. R. Wahl, are not definitive. Also known as Providence Petrel.

Pterodroma rostrata (Peale). Tahiti Petrel.

Procellaria rostrata Peale, 1848, U. S. Explor. Exped. 8: 296. (Mountains about 600 feet on Tahiti, Society Islands.)

This species breeds on New Caledonia and in the Society and Marquesas islands, and ranges widely in the South Pacific. Because of failure to distinguish this species from *P. alba,* sight reports in Hawaiian waters are inconclusive (Pyle 1988); there are also sight reports near Clipperton and the Revillagigedo islands.

Pterodroma alba (Gmelin). Phoenix Petrel.

Procellaria alba Gmelin, 1789, Syst. Nat. 1 (2): 565. Based on the "White-breasted Petrel" Latham, Gen. Synop. Birds 3(2): 400. (in insulis Turturum et nativitatis Christi = Turtle and Christmas islands.)

This species breeds on islands in the South Pacific and is rather sedentary. Reports from Hawaiian waters are uncertain because of the failure to distinguish this species from *P. rostrata* (Pyle 1988).

Pterodroma feae (Salvadori). Fea's Petrel.

Oestralata feae Salvadori, 1899, Ann. Mus. Civ. Genova 40: 305. (San Nicholas Island, Cape Verde Islands.)

This North Atlantic species, along with *Pterodroma madeira* Mathews, 1934 [Madeira

Petrel], has been separated from *P. mollis* (Gould, 1844) [Soft-plumaged Petrel] by Bourne (1983). Reports of birds of the complex off North Carolina in 1981 (Lee 1984) were attributed to *mollis* (A.O.U. 1985). More recent reports off North Carolina, including a bird photographed in 1991 (1992, Amer. Birds, 46: 130; 1992, Chat 56: 52) and a bird seen off Georgia in 1984 (Haney et al. 1993) are considered likely to be *feae*. Because *feae* and *madeira* may not be distinguishable in the field or in photographs, available information is insufficient for inclusion of the species in the main list (see also DeBenedictis 1996). Bretagnolle (1995) suggested on the basis of vocal similarities that *P. madeira* may be conspecific with *P. feae*.

Pterodroma defilippiana (Giglioli and Salvadori). Defilippe's Petrel.

> *Æstrelata defilippiana* Giglioli and Salvadori, 1869, Ibis, p. 63. (off coast between Calao, Peru, and Valparaíso, Chile.)

The report of this southern species from Hawaiian waters (A.O.U. 1989: 537) pertains to *P. externa.* There are no valid reports of *P. defilippiana* from the A.O.U. check-list area.

Procellaria cinerea Gmelin. Gray Petrel.

> *Procellaria cinerea* Gmelin, 1789, Syst. Nat. 1 (2): 563. Based on the "Cinereous Fulmar" Latham, Gen. Synop. Birds 3(2): 405. (intra circulum Antarcticum = Antarctic seas, lat. 48° S.)

This species, frequently placed in the genus *Adamastor,* breeds on islands in the South Pacific, South Atlantic, and southern Indian oceans, ranging at sea throughout all southern oceans between lat. 25° and 55° S. A specimen from California (off Monterey prior to 1853) is considered to be labeled erroneously (Lee 1993). Also known as Black-tailed Shearwater.

Procellaria aequinoctialis Linnaeus. White-chinned Petrel.

> *Procellaria aequinoctialis* Linnaeus, 1758, Syst. Nat. (ed. 10) 1: 132. Based on "The Great Peteril" Edwards, Nat. Hist. Birds, p. 89, pl. 89. ("Cape of Good Hope" = South Georgia.)

This species breeds on subantarctic islands and ranges at sea, mostly in the South Atlantic and southern Indian oceans. An individual found in Texas (Rollover Pass, Galveston County, 27 April 1986, photograph; 1990, Amer. Birds 44: 1158) is of controversial origin. A recent report from North Carolina (October 1996, Nat. Audubon Soc. Field Notes 51: 39) is under review.

Oceanites gracilis (Elliot). White-vented Storm-Petrel.

> *Thalassidroma gracilis* Elliot, 1859, Ibis, p. 391. (West Coast of America = coast of Chile.)

The breeding grounds of this species are largely unknown, but nests have been found on islands off north-central Chile. It ranges regularly to the Galapagos Islands and along the Pacific coast of South America from Colombia to Chile. There are sight reports by R. C. Murphy in September 1937 in the Gulf of Panama and at Humboldt Bay, just south of the Darién border in Colombia (Ridgely and Gwynne 1989).

Fregetta grallaria (Vieillot). White-bellied Storm-Petrel.

> *Procellaria grallaria* Vieillot, 1818, Nouv. Dict. Hist. Nat. (nouv. éd.) 25 (1817): 418. (Nouvelle-Hollande = New South Wales, Australia.)

Lawrence (1851) reported the capture of seven individuals in the harbor of St. Marks, Florida; one specimen was preserved and given to the Academy of Natural Sciences at Philadelphia, but its present location is unknown. The report has been listed under *F. tropica* (Gould, 1844) [Black-bellied Storm-Petrel] (see A.O.U. 1957) as well as *F. grallaria* (see

Palmer 1962). It is uncertain to which of these two species the specimen pertains, and even more doubtful that the locality is correct.

Oceanodroma hornbyi (Gray). Ringed Storm-Petrel.

> *Thalassidroma Hornbyi* G. R. Gray, 1854, Proc. Zool. Soc. London (1853), p. 62. (north-west coast of America, error = west coast of South America.)

The type locality originally given for this species, normally found off the Pacific coast of South America from Ecuador to Chile, is deemed in error (Murphy 1936). No other specimens have been reported from North America.

Spheniscus mendiculus Sundevall. Galapagos Penguin.

> *Spheniscus mendiculus* Sundevall, 1871, Proc. Zool. Soc. London, pp. 126, 129. (Galapagos Islands.)

An immature of this Galapagos endemic was captured at Puerto Armuelles, Chiriquí, Panama, in February 1955 (Eisenmann 1956); because it is unlikely, although not impossible, that this individual reached Panamanian waters on its own, the occurrence is a probable result of transport by humans.

Phalacrocorax perspicillatus Pallas. Pallas's Cormorant.

> *Phalacrocorax perspicillatus* Pallas, 1811, Zoogr. Rosso-Asiat. 2: 305. (in Beringii = Bering Island.)

North American reports of this species, known only from Bering Island in the Commander Islands and extinct since 1852, are unsatisfactory.

Phalacrocorax bougainvillii (Lesson). Guanay Cormorant.

> *Carbo Bougainvillii* Lesson, 1837, in Bougainville, J. Navig. Thétis Espérance 2: 331. (Valparaíso, Chile.)

This species breeds on islands off the coast of Peru, central Chile, and southern Argentina, and ranges north to Colombia and Ecuador. There are sight reports by R. C. Murphy in Panama, off Ensenada de Guayabo Chiquito, southern Darién, 21 May 1941. A flock of 100 individuals (from which specimens were obtained) was just south of the A.O.U. Check-list area in Colombia in March and April 1941 (Ridgely 1976). The reported introduction of this species in 1953 on Isla San Gerónimo, Baja California (see A.O.U. 1957: 34), is erroneous.

Phalacrocorax kenyoni (Siegel-Causey). Amchitka Cormorant.

> *Stictocarbo kenyoni* Siegel-Causey, 1991, Occas. Pap. Mus. Nat. Hist. Kansas 140: 5. (Constantine Harbor, Amchitka Island, Alaska.)

The status of this recently described species from Amchitka Island, Alaska, is uncertain, pending acquisition of additional specimen material; at present it is known only from skeletal material.

Phalacrocorax gaimardi (Lesson and Garnot). Red-legged Cormorant.

> *Carbo Gaimardi* Lesson and Garnot, 1828, in Duperrey, Voy. Coquille, Zool., Atlas 1(7): pl. 48; 1830, 1(14): 601. (Lima, au Pérou = San Lorenzo Island, roadstead of Lima, Peru.)

There is a sight report of this species for Texas (Galveston, 28 December 1946; Oberholser 1974). Its normal range is the Pacific coast of South America, and an individual in eastern Texas (even if its identity were fully verified) would probably represent an escape from captivity, perhaps a ship-transported bird.

Mesophoyx intermedia (Wagler). Intermediate Egret.

> *Ardea intermedia* Wagler, 1829, Isis von Oken, col. 659. (Java.)

The specimen of this Old World species, also known as Yellow-billed Egret or Lesser Egret, reportedly taken at Vancouver, British Columbia, may actually have been obtained elsewhere (Brooks 1923, Godfrey 1986).

Platalea leucorodia Linnaeus. Eurasian Spoonbill.

> *Platalea Leucorodia* Linnaeus, 1758, Syst. Nat. (ed. 10) 1: 139. (in Europa = Sweden.)

This widespread Old World species has been included in previous check-lists on the basis of one specimen from Greenland, where accidental. There are no known reports from the A.O.U. area now treated. Also known as European Spoonbill, White Spoonbill, Common Spoonbill, or the Spoonbill.

Ciconia ciconia (Linnaeus). White Stork.

> *Ardea Ciconia* Linnaeus, 1758, Syst. Nat. (ed. 10) 1: 142. (in Europe, Asia, Africa = Sweden.)

There is one sight report of this Palearctic stork from Antigua, Lesser Antilles (Gricks 1994).

Phoenicopterus chilensis Molina. Chilean Flamingo.

> *Phoenicopterus chilensis* Molina, 1782, Saggio Storia Nat. Chili, pp. 242, 344. (Chile.)

Individuals of this South American species have been reported in California, Delaware, and other states; they are regarded as escaped individuals. Many other reports of this species have not reached the scientific literature because the birds are assumed to be escapes from captivity.

Anser anser (Linnaeus). Graylag Goose.

> *Anas Anser* Linnaeus, 1758, Syst. Nat. (ed. 10) 1: 123. Based on "The Laughing-Goose" Edwards, Nat. Hist. Birds 3: 153, pl. 153. (in Europa & America maxime boreali = Sweden.)

An individual of this widespread Eurasian species captured on the Housatonic River near Lenox, Massachusetts, 2 December 1932, was considered later to be a domestic bird (Snyder 1957). More recent sight reports, mostly in the eastern United States, are thought also to pertain to escapes from captivity; a report from Attu (1987, Amer. Birds 41: 476) pertains to *Anser fabalis* (1988, Amer. Birds 42: 121).

Anser indicus Latham. Bar-headed Goose.

> *Anser indica* Latham, 1790, Index Ornithol. 2: 839. (in India; hyeme gregaria; e Thibeto = India in winter, and Tibet.)

Individuals of this central Asian species reported from California, Saskatchewan, Illinois, Pennsylvania, Ohio, Quebec, Texas, and elsewhere in North America are probable escapes from captivity (Palmer 1976; for discussion see Lahrman 1994).

Branta ruficollis (Pallas). Red-breasted Goose.

> *Anser ruficollis* Pallas, 1769, Spic. Zool. 1 (6): 21, pl. 4. (lower Ob, southern Russia.)

This western Siberian species has been reported in North America between September and April from California (six reports, 1890s to 1969), Maine (1962), and Texas (1969–1970). It is widely kept by aviculturists, and these reports probably pertain to escapes from captivity (Palmer 1976).

Tadorna ferruginea (Pallas). Ruddy Shelduck.

> *Anas ferruginea* Pallas, 1764, in Vroeg, Cat. Raisonn Ois., Adumbr., p. 5. (No locality given = Tartary.)

This Eurasian species has been reported as accidental in western Greenland. Reports from California, and in eastern North America from Iowa, Indiana, Ohio, Quebec, Vermont, Rhode Island, Pennsylvania, and New Jersey south to Florida, probably pertain to escapes from captivity.

Tadorna tadorna (Linnaeus). Common Shelduck.

> *Anas Tadorna* Linnaeus, 1758, Syst. Nat. (ed. 10) 1: 122. (in Europæ maritimis = Sweden.)

This Eurasian species, known in Old World literature as the Shelduck and kept widely in captivity, has been reported from Quebec (Cap Saint-Ignace, 1982), Massachusetts (Ipswich Bay, 1921), and Delaware (Bombay Hook, 1970–1976); these reports likely pertain to es- caped individuals. Several other reports of birds definitely known to have escaped have appeared in the literature.

Aix galericulata (Linnaeus). Mandarin Duck.

> *Anas galericulata* Linnaeus. 1758, Syst. Nat. (ed. 10) 1: 128. Based on "The Chinese Teal" of Edwards, Nat. Hist. Birds, p. 102, pl. 102. (China).

An introduced population of this Eurasian species may be established as a breeding species in Sonoma County, California. The first nest was recorded in 1972, and by the mid-1980s, the population had grown to several hundred (Shurtleff and Savage 1996). Reports from elsewhere are regarded as escapees from captivity.

Netta rufina (Pallas). Red-crested Pochard.

> *Anas rufina* Pallas, 1773, Reise Versch. Prov. Russ. Reichs 2: 713. (in Mari Caspio lacubusque vastissimis deserti Tatarici = Caspian Sea.)

The report of a specimen of this Eurasian species from Long Island Sound (1881) is unsatisfactory; the specimen cannot be located. Sight reports of individuals in Washington and in eastern North America almost certainly pertain to individuals escaped from captivity.

Aythya baeri (Radde). Baer's Pochard.

> *Anas (Fuligula) Baeri* Radde, 1863, Reisen Süd. Ost-Sib. 2: 376, pl. 15. (in der oberen Salbatsche-Ebene auf dem rechten Amurufer = upper Salbatch Plains, middle Amur River, eastern Siberia.)

This species has been included in the North American avifauna on the basis of two specimens (one still extant) reportedly taken about 1841 by Peale in "Oregon" (= southern British Columbia to Oregon; Friedmann 1949). The extant specimen does not agree with examples of *A. baeri* in plumage or bill shape and may be a hybrid (P. Rasmussen, pers. comm., *contra* Palmer 1976).

Aythya nyroca (Güldenstädt). Ferruginous Duck.

> *Anas nyroca* Güldenstädt, 1770, Novi Commentarii Acad. Sci. Imp. Petropolitanae 14 (1769): 403 (southern Russia.)

This Eurasian species was reported on Bermuda, 5 January-1 March 1987 (Amos 1991), but the report was evidently undocumented.

Accipiter nisus (Linnaeus). Eurasian Sparrowhawk.

> *Falco Nisus* Linnaeus, 1758, Syst. Nat. (ed. 10) 1: 92. (in Europa = Sweden.)

An immature female believed to be this Old World species was reported from New Jersey

(Cape May, 24 October 1978; 1979, New Jersey Audubon Suppl. 5: 11); the individual photographed is not identifiable.

Buteo polyosoma (Quoy and Gaimard). Red-backed Hawk.

> *Falco polyosoma* Quoy and Gaimard, 1824, in Freycinet, Voy. Uranie Phys., Zool., 3: 92, pl. 14. (Falkland Islands.)

An individual thought to be of this Andean and southern South American species was reported from Colorado (Gunnison, first from mid-August-31 October 1987, photographs; 1988, Amer. Birds 42: 112); the bird returned the next year and was paired with a *B. swainsoni*. Identification as another South American species, *B. poecilochrous* Gurney, 1879, cannot be ruled out; furthermore, the origin of the bird remains highly questionable (Allen 1988).

Buteo buteo (Linnaeus). Common Buzzard.

> *Falco Buteo* Linnaeus, 1758, Syst. Nat. (ed. 10) 1: 1. (in Europa = Sweden.)

An individual thought to be of this Eurasian species was reported from Alaska (Nizki, in the Aleutian Islands, 26 May 1983; 1983, Amer. Birds 37: 902); this sight report of a highly variable species often difficult to identify in the field is unsatisfactory.

Hieraaetus pennatus (Gmelin). Booted Eagle.

> *Falco pennatus* Gmelin, 1788, Syst. Nat. 1: 272. Based on "Booted Falcon" Latham, Gen. Synop. Birds 1, p. 75. (No locality given, France suggested by Swann, 1922, Synop. Accipitres, ed. 2, p. 113.)

This species of southern Eurasia was reported on Bermuda, 8–13 September 1989; an African origin and transportation by Hurricane Gabrielle were postulated (Amos 1991). The report was evidently undocumented.

Rallus aquaticus Linnaeus. Water Rail.

> *Rallus aquaticus* Linnaeus, 1758, Syst. Nat. (ed. 10) 1: 153. (in Europa = Great Britain.)

This Eurasian species was included in former check-lists on the basis of several stragglers taken in Greenland. There are no known reports from the A.O.U. area now treated.

Porphyrio porphyrio (Linnaeus). Purple Swamphen.

> *Fulica Porphyrio* Linnaeus, 1758, Syst. Nat. (ed. 10) 1: 152. (in Asia, America = lands bordering the western Mediterranean Sea.)

An individual thought to be a molting sub-adult and possibly from one of the Middle Eastern subspecies appeared in suburban Wilmington, Delaware, 5 December 1990, and it remained two weeks (1991, Amer. Birds 45: 255). Its origin is questionable, but given the unusual dispersal abilities of many Rallidae, a natural origin cannot be dismissed.

Hoploxypterus cayanus (Latham). Pied Lapwing.

> *Charadrius cayanus* Latham, 1790, Index Ornithol. 2: 749. Based mainly on "Le Pluvier armé de Cayenne" Buffon, Hist. Nat. Ois. 8: 102. (in Cayana = Cayenne.)

The report of this South American species from Honduras, based on a reputed specimen from the "Aloor River" [= Río Ulúa] region (1855–1856), is unsatisfactory (Monroe 1968).

Charadrius pecuarius Temminck. Kittlitz's Plover.

> *Charadrius pecuarius* Temminck, 1823, Planches Color., livr. 31, pl. 183. (Cape of Good Hope.)

A banded individual of this African species was photographed at the mouth of the San

Diego river, San Diego County, California, 26 December 1970, but the origin of this individual is highly questionable (Langham 1991).

Charadrius veredus Gould. Oriental Plover.

> *Charadrius veredus* Gould, 1848, Proc. Zool. Soc. London, p. 38. (Northern Australia.)

This Asiatic species was included in former check-lists on the basis of a record from Greenland (A.O.U. 1957: 165–166, footnote, as *C. asiaticus veredus*). There are no known reports from the A.O.U. area now treated.

Gallinago media (Latham). Great Snipe.

> *Scolopax Media* Latham, 1787, Gen. Synop. Birds, suppl., 1: 292. (Lancashire, England.)

This Eurasian species, which winters in Africa, was supposedly photographed in New Jersey (Cape May, 7 September 1963; 1964, Audubon Field Notes 18: 21), but the report has not been verified.

Catharacta chilensis (Bonaparte). Chilean Skua.

> *Stercorarius antarcticus* b. *chilensis* Bonaparte, 1856, Consp. Gen. Avium 2 (1857): 207. (ex Am[erica]. m[eridionale]. = Chile.)

Birds reported to be of this Southern Hemisphere species in Pacific waters off the coast of North America have been re-identified as *C. maccormicki* (Devillers 1977a). A pre-1853 specimen reportedly taken off Monterey, California, was re-identified as *C. lonnbergi,* and the locality is probably erroneous (Lee 1993).

Larus cirrocephalus Vieillot. Gray-hooded Gull.

> *Larus cirrocephalus* Vieillot, 1818, Nouv. Dict. Hist. Nat. (nouv. éd) 21: 502. (Brazil = Rio de Janeiro.)

This species breeds on bays, estuaries, and lagoons along the Pacific coast of Ecuador and Peru, the Atlantic coast of South America from southern Brazil to central Argentina, and in tropical and southern Africa and Madagascar; it winters in coastal areas and on inland lakes near the breeding areas, occasionally north along the coasts of South America and Africa. There is a sight report of an adult in Panama, Panama Bay at Panama City, 25 September 1955 (Ridgely 1976).

Larus dominicanus Lichtenstein. Kelp Gull.

> *Larus dominicanus* Lichtenstein, 1823, Verz. Doubl. Zool. Mus. Berlin, p. 502. (Coasts of Brazil.)

This species breeds from Tierra del Fuego north to southwestern Ecuador and southern Brazil, and elsewhere at subantarctic latitudes in the Southern Hemisphere. A pair of "mated" gulls and possibly a third individual appeared in 1989 in coastal Louisiana and were tentatively identified as *L. dominicanus.* The following summer, one bred with *L. argentatus,* the only report of breeding of the latter species in Louisiana (1990, Amer. Birds 44: 1147); additional individuals identified as *L. dominicanus* have been reported there in subsequent years. Three records from the Yucatan in 1991, 1993, and 1994 have been accompanied by photos (Howell et al. 1993), as have reports from Texas and Indiana. Because of the difficulty of positive identification to species without a specimen, and also because it seems unlikely that a sub-Antarctic species would colonize the subtropical Gulf of Mexico, the species is retained in the Appendix until confirmation is obtained. Also known also as Dominican Gull and Southern Black-backed Gull.

Creagrus furcatus (Néboux). Swallow-tailed Gull.

> *Larus furcatus* Néboux, 1846, Voy. Venus, Atlas, Zool., Ois., pl. 10. (rade de Monterey, Haute-Californie, error = Galapagos Islands.)

This species breeds on the Galapagos Islands and ranges to the Pacific coast of South America. A sight report from Panama (northwest of Piñas Bay, Darién, 18 July 1957; Robins 1958) is unsatisfactory. The identification of a bird from California (Monterey Bay, 6–8 June 1985, photograph; 1985, Amer. Birds 39: 879–880, 958–959) is not questioned, but the origin of the bird is uncertain (DeBenedictis 1996). There is also a published report referring to a photograph from the Bay of Panama, 14 June 1983 (Reed 1988), but the photograph has not been examined.

Sterna sumatrana Raffles. Black-naped Tern.

Sterna Sumatrana Raffles, 1822, Trans. Linn. Soc. London 13 (2): 329. (Sumatra.)

This species ranges throughout much of the Indian Ocean, and in the Pacific from southeastern China, and the Ryukyu, Caroline, Gilbert, and Phoenix islands south to Australia, New Caledonia, and the Loyalty Islands. Old reports from the Hawaiian Islands (Kauai, Hawaii) are erroneous and based on specimens of *S. hirundo* (Clapp et al. 1983).

Sterna trudeaui Audubon. Trudeau's Tern.

Sterna Trudeaui Audubon, 1838, Birds Amer. (folio) 4: pl. 409, fig. 2 (1839, Ornithol. Biogr. 5: 125). (Great Egg Harbor, New Jersey.)

This species breeds in Chile, southern Brazil (Rio Grande do Sul province), Uruguay, and Argentina (Santa Fé, Entre Ríos, and Buenos Aires provinces), and winters along the coast of Chile, occasionally to Peru. The type was supposedly taken at Great Egg Harbor, New Jersey; the natural occurrence of this species in North America is highly questionable. Also known also as Snowy-crowned Tern.

Cepphus carbo Pallas. Spectacled Guillemot.

Cepphus Carbo Pallas, 1811, Zoogr. Rosso-Asiat. 2: 350. (circa insulas Aleuticas, error = Kuril Islands.)

The original type locality of this Asiatic species, known also as Sooty Guillemot, is regarded as erroneous; there is no evidence for its occurrence in North American waters.

Columba goodsoni Hartert. Dusky Pigeon.

Columba goodsoni Hartert, 1902, Bull. Brit. Ornithol. Club 12: 42. (S[an]. Javier, Pambilar, and Carondelet, n.w. Ecuador = Pambilar, Ecuador.)

This species is a resident of western Colombia and western Ecuador. There is a sight report of two individuals in Panama (upper Tuira valley, Darién, 7 March 1981; Ridgely and Gwynne 1989).

Nandayus nenday (Vieillot). Black-hooded Parakeet.

Psittacus nenday Vieillot, 1823, in Bonnaterre and Vieillot, Tabl. Encycl. Méth. (Ornithol.) 3 (93): 1400. (Paraguay.)

This southern South American species, known also as Nanday Parakeet or Conure, is widely reported in the United States and Puerto Rico as an escape. Breeding has been reported in peninsular Florida, where it may be established (Robertson and Woolfenden 1992), and in southern California, where it seems to have existed for more than 15 years (Johnston and Garrett 1994). A small population that existed at Coney Island, Brooklyn, New York, has now disappeared.

Forpus xanthopterygius (Spix). Blue-winged Parrotlet.

Psittacula xanthopterygius Spix, 1824, Avium Spec. Nov. Bras. 1: 42, pl. 31. (Amazon Basin.)

This South American species was doubtfully reported from Panama, as *F. passerinus spengeli* (Hartlaub, 1885) by Wetmore (1968). The blue-rumped forms, including *spengeli,* were separated from the green-rumped *passerinus* by Gyldenstolpe (1945).

Brotogeris chiriri (Vieillot). Yellow-chevroned Parakeet.

> *Psittacus chiriri* Vieillot, 1817 (1818), Nouv. Dict. Hist. Nat. (nouv. éd.) 25: 359. (Paraguay, ex. Azara.)

Although details of introduction are unknown and establishment is uncertain, this South American species has been replacing *B. versicolurus* [White-winged Parakeet] in southern California (Johnston and Garrett 1994) and Florida (Smith and Smith 1993) in recent years. The two forms have been treated as conspecific but are considered separate species on the basis of morphological differences and near sympatry in southern Pará, Brazil (Pinto and Camargo 1957).

Amazona amazonica (Linnaeus). Orange-winged Parrot.

> *Psittacus amazonicus* Linnaeus, 1766, Syst. Nat. (ed. 12) 1: 147. Based mainly on "Le Perroquet Amazone" Brisson, Ornithologie 4: 256. (in Surinamo = Surinam.)

Small numbers of this recently introduced South American species are now resident and apparently breeding in Puerto Rico (San Juan area, Mayaguez, Salinas, Río Piedras). Populations in southern Florida are considered to be escaped individuals or their descendants (Robertson and Woolfenden 1992).

Coccyzus pumilus Strickland. Dwarf Cuckoo.

> *Coccyzus pumilus* Strickland, 1853, in Jardine, Contrib. Ornithol. (1852): 28, pl. 82. (Trinidad, error = Venezuela.)

This species is found in northern Colombia and northern Venezuela (including Margarita Island). There is a sight report in Panama (Tocumen, eastern Panamá province, 9 February 1979; Braun and Wolf 1987).

Coccyzus lansbergi Bonaparte. Gray-capped Cuckoo.

> *Coccyzus lansbergi* Bonaparte, 1850, Consp. Gen. Avium 1 (1): 112. (Sta. Fé de Bogotá [Colombia].)

This South American species is resident in northern Colombia, northern Venezuela, and western Ecuador, migrating, at least in part, south to western Peru. This species was listed from Panama initially by Shelley (in Sclater and Shelley 1891: 303), but it seems clear from the comments of Wetmore et al. (1984) that there are no reports from Panama prior to 1980. There are more recent sight reports in Panama (Tocumen, eastern Panamá province, 10 February 1980, 7 January 1982, 23 December 1985; Braun and Wolf 1987).

Anthracothorax viridigula (Boddaert). Green-throated Mango.

> *Trochilus viridigula* Boddaert, 1783, Table Planches Enlum., p. 41. Based on Daubenton, Planches Enlum., pl. 671, fig. 1. (Cayenne.)

This species is found from eastern Venezuela, Trinidad, and the Guianas south to northeastern Brazil. There is a sight report of an immature individual on Union Island in the Grenadines, Lesser Antilles (Bond 1956: 91, footnote).

Chlorostilbon mellisugus (Linnaeus). Blue-tailed Emerald.

> *Trochilus mellisugus* Linnaeus, 1758, Syst. Nat. (ed. 10) 1: 121. (In Indiis = Cayenne.)

Simon (1921: 290) erroneously listed "*Prasitis melanorrhynchus pumila* (Gould)" = *Chlorostilbon pumilus* Gould, 1872, from the Republic of Panama (Wetmore 1968). That subspecies, known from western Colombia and western Ecuador, is placed in the species *mellisugus* by Meyer de Schauensee (1966) but was referred to *C. gibsoni* (Fraser, 1840) by Peters (1945). Stiles (1996a), who reviewed the taxonomy of this group, agreed with the latter author.

Amazilia chionopectus (Gould). White-chested Emerald.

> *Thaumatias chionopectus* Gould, 1859, Monogr. Trochil., pt. 18, pl. [8] and text. (Trinidad).

This species is found in the Guianas, northeastern Venezuela, and on Trinidad. Four specimens in the Museum of Comparative Zoology are labeled "Grenada W. I. Peter Gellineau"; because these are of a typical Trinidad "trade skin" make, they are regarded as mislabeled (Ridgway 1911: 431, footnote).

Amazilia tobaci (Gmelin). Copper-rumped Hummingbird.

> *Trochilus Tobaci* Gmelin, 1788, Syst. Nat. 1 (1): 498. Based on the "Tobago Hummingbird" Latham, Gen. Synop. Birds 1(2): 781. (in insula Tobago.)

This species is known primarily from Tobago, Trinidad, and Venezuela. Specimens in the Boucard collection, labeled "Grenada," may have been taken on Tobago (Bond 1956: 91, footnote), and the occurrence of the species in the Lesser Antilles is doubtful.

Acestrura heliodor (Bourcier). Gorgeted Woodstar.

> *Ornismya heliodor* Bourcier, 1840, Rev. Zool. [Paris] 3: 275. (Santa-Fé de Bogota [Colombia].)

A resident of humid mountain forest in northwestern South America, this species was erroneously reported from eastern Panama (see account of *Calliphlox mitchellii* in Robbins et al. 1985).

Ramphastos brevis Meyer de Schauensee. Choco Toucan.

> *Ramphastos ambiguus brevis* Meyer de Schauensee, 1945, Proc. Acad. Nat. Sci. Philadelphia 97: 14. (Rio Mechengue, 2500 ft., Cauca, western Colombia.)

This species, found in the Pacific lowlands of western Colombia and western Ecuador, was attributed to eastern Panama (as *Ramphastos ambiguus*) by Ridgway (1914) on the basis of a specimen in the Museum of Comparative Zoology reported from Loma del León (eastern Darién). Wetmore (1968) and subsequent authors regard the locality as uncertain, and recent field workers in eastern Darién have failed to discover it.

Thamnophilus multistriatus Lafresnaye. Bar-crested Antshrike.

> *Thamnophilus multistriatus* Lafresnaye, 1844, Rev. Zool. [Paris] 7: 82. (Colombie = Bogotá, Colombia.)

This species, known from the northern Andes in extreme western Venezuela and Colombia, was reported by Sclater (1890) from Panama; there is apparently no basis for this listing, and the report is considered erroneous (Wetmore 1972).

Urocissa erythrorhyncha (Boddaert). Red-billed Blue-Magpie.

> *Corvus erythrorynchus* [sic] Boddaert, 1783, Table Planches Enlum., p. 38. Based on the "Geay de la Chine à bec rouge" Daubenton, Planches Enlum., pl. 622. (China = Canton, China.)

A few individuals of this Southeast Asian species were released on Oahu in the Hawaiian

Islands in the mid-1960s They persisted at least into 1970 and bred (Berger 1972), but no population became established. The species was also introduced in Puerto Rico but did not become established (Raffaele 1983).

Corvus frugilegus Linnaeus. Rook.

Corvus frugilegus Linnaeus, 1758, Syst. Nat. (ed. 10) 1: 105. (in Europa = Sweden.)

This Eurasian species was included in former check-lists on the basis of a report from southeastern Greenland. There are no known reports from the A.O.U. area now treated. Also known as Eurasian Rook.

Corvus corone Linnaeus. Carrion Crow.

Corvus Corone Linnaeus, 1758, Syst. Nat. (ed. 10) 1: 105. (in Europa = England.)

The distinct form of this Eurasian species occurring in Ireland, Scotland, and from eastern Europe eastward, formerly treated as a separate species, *C. cornix* Linnaeus, 1758 [Hooded Crow], has been included previously on the basis of specimens from Greenland, which is no longer included in the A.O.U. area. A report from southeastern California (Salton Sea) is considered an escape from captivity.

Melanocorypha calandra (Linnaeus). Calandra Lark.

Alauda calandra Linnaeus, 1766, Syst. Nat.(ed. 12) 1: 288. (Pyrenees.)

A specimen of this Old World species was obtained at Glenolden, Pennsylvania, on 6 May 1928, after being observed since 15 April (1928, Cassinia [Proc. Delaware Valley Ornithol. Club] 27: 35); it was most likely an escaped cage-bird.

Parus major Linnaeus. Great Tit.

Parus major Linnaeus, 1758, Syst. Nat.(ed. 10) 1: 189. (in Europa = Sweden.)

There is a sight report of this Eurasian species in Alaska (Little Diomede Island, 2 September 1988; 1989, Amer. Birds 43: 153; see DeBenedictis 1994a).

Parus varius Temminck and Schlegel. Varied Tit.

Parus varius Temminck and Schlegel, 1848, in Siebold, Fauna Jpn., Aves, p. 71, pl. 35. (Japon = Honshu, Japan.)

This species, a native of eastern Asia south to Japan, was introduced into the Hawaiian Islands about 1890 (on Kauai, Oahu, Maui, and Hawaii) and established on Kauai and Oahu. Numbers diminished during the 1940s, and it was last reported in the 1960s (Pyle 1979).

Phylloscopus trochilus (Linnaeus). Willow Warbler.

Motacilla Trochilus Linnaeus, 1758, Syst. Nat. (ed. 10) 1: 188. (in Europa = Sweden.)

A specimen, reported as this widespread Eurasian species (which has also straggled to Greenland), was taken at Barrow, Alaska, on 10 June 1952 (Pitelka 1974); however, re-examination of the specimen indicated that it is an example of *P. borealis* (Roberson and Pitelka 1983).

Copsychus saularis (Linnaeus). Magpie Robin.

Gracula Saularis Linnaeus, 1758, Syst. Nat. (ed. 10) 1: 109. Based mainly on the "Dialbird" Albin, Nat. Hist. Birds 3: 17, pl. 17–18. (in Asia = Bengal.)

Various introductions of this southern Asian species were made in the Hawaiian Islands (Kauai and Oahu) between 1922 and 1950, but there is no evidence of establishment; there have been no reliable reports since 1967.

Saxicola rubetra (Linnaeus). Whinchat.

> *Motacilla Rubetra* Linnaeus, 1758, Syst. Nat. (ed. 10) 1: 186. (in Europa = Sweden.)

A sight report of this European species from Massachusetts (Lincoln, 22 October 1964; 1965, Audubon Field Notes 19:8) is considered unsatisfactory.

Garrulax caerulatus (Hodgson). Gray-sided Laughing-thrush.

> *Cinclosoma Caerulatus* Hodgson, 1836, Asiat. Res. 19: 147. (Nepal.)

Introduced in the Hawaiian Islands (Oahu), this laughing-thrush from southern Asia was frequently reported in the northern Koolau Mountains along the Poamoho Trail during the 1940s and 1950s; well-substantiated reports in the same locality in 1978 (Taylor and Collins 1979) and 1986 (Bremer 1987) suggest that the species may persist in small numbers.

Acridotheres javanicus Cabanis. White-vented Myna.

> *Acridotheres javanicus* Cabanis, 1850, Mus. Heineanum 1 (1851): 205. (Java.)

A native of southeast Asia, this species has been introduced in Puerto Rico (Bayamón area), but its present status is uncertain (Raffaele 1983).

Anthus pratensis (Linnaeus). Meadow Pipit.

> *Anthus pratensis* Linnaeus, 1758, Syst. Nat. (ed. 10) 1: 166. (in Europæ pratis = Sweden.)

This Palearctic species breeds in Greenland and has been included in previous Check-lists on that basis.

Euphonia mesochrysa Salvadori. Bronze-green Euphonia.

> *Euphonia mesochrysa* Salvadori, 1873, Atti R. Accad. Sci. Torino, Cl. Sci. Fis. Math. Nat. 8: 193. (No locality given = Bogotá, Colombia.)

The locality "Honduras" on the label of a specimen in the Academy of Natural Sciences at Philadelphia is regarded as erroneous (Monroe 1968); the species is found in the Andes from Colombia to Bolivia.

Piranga rubriceps Gray. Red-hooded Tanager.

> *Pyranga rubriceps* G. R. Gray, 1844, Genera Birds 2: 364, pl. 89, lower fig. (No locality given = Bogotá, Colombia.)

A specimen of this South American species was taken at Dos Pueblos [= Naples], Santa Barbara County, California, about 1871 (Bryant 1887). It is assumed to have been an escape from captivity (Ridgway 1902: 776; Grinnell and Miller 1944). Also known as Gray's Tanager.

Sporophila bouvronides (Lesson). Lesson's Seedeater.

> *Pyrrhula bouvronides* Lesson, 1831, Traité Ornith., livre 6: 450. (No locality given; Trinidad designated by Hellmayr [1938].)

This species breeds in South America in northern and eastern Colombia, Venezuela, Tobago, Trinidad, Guyana, and Surinam; it winters south to northern Peru and Amazonian Brazil. There are sight reports in Panama (Yaviza, Darién, 30 April 1979, two pairs, J. Pujals; Ridgely 1981). Although *S. bouvronides* and *S. lineola* (Linnaeus, 1758) [Lined Seedeater], a southern South American breeder that migrates to northern South America in nonbreeding season (Silva 1995 and references therein), have been considered conspecific (e.g., A.O.U. 1983), species limits were clarified by Schwartz (1975).

Icterus nigrogularis (Hahn). Yellow Oriole.

>*Xanthornus nigrogularis* Hahn, 1819, Vögel Asien, Afr., etc., lief 5, pl. 1. (Jamaica, Mexico, and Cayenne = Brazil.)

One or two specimens said to have come from the Isthmus of Panama formed the basis for the description of *Icterus xanthornus dubusii* Dubois, 1875; *nigrogularis* is a replacement name for *xanthornus,* which was preoccupied. The origin of these specimens of this South American species is indefinite, but they were probably not from Panama, where there are no other records (Hellmayr 1937). Wetmore et al. (1972) did not mention the species.

Carduelis magellanica (Vieillot). Hooded Siskin.

>*Fringilla magellanica* Vieillot, 1805, Ois. Chant., pl. 30. (southern America and vicinity of Straits of Magellan, error = Buenos Aires, Argentina.)

A specimen of this widespread South American species taken at Henderson, Kentucky, was described and figured by Audubon (1838: pl. 394, fig. 2; 1839: 46); the origin of the specimen is uncertain.

Carduelis chloris (Linnaeus). European Greenfinch.

>*Loxia chloris* Linnaeus, 1758, Syst. Nat. (ed. 10) 1: 174. (in Europa = Sweden.)

An individual of this European finch was present and photographed at St. John, New Brunswick, 31 March-3 April 1977 (1977, Amer. Birds 31: 977); although this report as well as a more recent sight report from Quebec may represent natural vagrants, a pattern of such vagrancy in a cage-bird species should be demonstrated before the species is removed from hypothetical status. Also known as the Greenfinch.

Lagonosticta rubricata (Lichtenstein). African Fire-Finch.

>*Fringilla rubricata* Lichtenstein, 1823, Verz. Doubl. Zool. Mus. Berlin, p. 27. (terra Caffrorum = Uitenhage, Cape Province, Africa.)

Successful breeding of escaped pairs of this widespread African species was reported at Pacific Grove, Monterey County, California, in 1965 and 1966 (1966, Amer. Birds 20: 90, 598), but no population became established. It was also introduced in the 1960s in the Hawaiian Islands, but it has since disappeared; there is no evidence that the species was ever established (R. L. Pyle, in litt.).

Part 2. Forms of doubtful status or of hybrid origin that have been given a formal scientific name. Because these taxa are of uncertain specific status or of presumed hybrid origin, their generic placement is also uncertain. Therefore, we retain the original generic and specific names even when certain that the generic designation is incorrect; the probable generic relationships are indicated in the comments under each species. An exception is made for Brewster's and Lawrence's warblers, which are known to be intrageneric hybrids.

Anas breweri Audubon.

>*Anas breweri* Audubon, 1838, Ornithol. Biogr. 3: 302. (Lake Barataria, Louisiana).

This bird is a hybrid between *A. platyrhynchos* and *A. strepera.* (Cockrum 1952).

Lophortyx leucoprosopon Reichenow.

>*Lophortyx leucoprosopon* Reichenow, 1895, Ornithol. Monatsber. 3: 11. (Origin unknown).

Known only from a pair in a private aviary, believed to have been bought from a sailor arriving at Hamburg, Germany, this quail is regarded as a hybrid between *Callipepla douglasii* and *C. gambelii* (Hellmayr and Conover 1942).

Tringa cooperi Baird. Cooper's Sandpiper.

> *Tringa cooperi* Baird, 1858, *in* Baird, Cassin, and Lawrence, Rep. Explor. Surv. R. R. Pac. 9: 716. (Raynour South, Long Island [New York].)

Known only from the unique type specimen, taken in May 1833. Although probably a representative of the present genus *Calidris,* the status of this form remains undetermined (Ridgway 1919, Cox 1989).

Calidris paramelanotos Parker. Cox's Sandpiper.

> *Calidris paramelanotos* Parker, 1982, S. Austral. Nat. 56: 63. (Price Saltfields, upper Gulf St. Vincent, South Australia.)

Christidis et al. (1996) have shown on the basis of molecular data that this form is a hybrid between Curlew Sandpiper (*Calidris ferruginea*) and Pectoral Sandpiper (*C. melanotos*). It has been found during nonbreeding seasons in Australia (Cox 1989 and references therein). Reports from Massachusetts (Kasprzyk et al. 1987, Vickery et al. 1987) have been disputed by Monroe (1991), who noted that this observation "cannot be definitely ascribed to anything."

Larus nelsoni Henshaw. Nelson's Gull.

> *Larus nelsoni* Henshaw, 1884, Auk 1: 250. (St. Michael, Alaska.)

This gull is regarded as a hybrid between *L. hyperboreus* and *L. argentatus* (Jehl 1987).

Zenaida plumbea Gosse. Plumbeous Dove.

> *Zenaida plumbea* Gosse, 1849, Illustr. Birds Jamaica, pl. 85. (Jamaica.)

This bird is known only from Gosse's colored plate. No specimens are known, although it may have occurred on Jamaica until the mid-1850s (Ridgway 1916).

Conurus labati Rothschild. Guadeloupe Parakeet.

> *Conurus labati* Rothschild, 1905, Bull. Brit. Ornith. Club 16: 13. (Guadeloupe, Lesser Antilles.)

Described from accounts by early travelers, this bird is believed to have been endemic to Guadeloupe, Lesser Antilles. No specimens are known.

Anodorhynchus martinicus Rothschild. Martinique Macaw.

> *Anadorhynchus* [sic] *martinicus* Rothschild, 1905, Bull. Brit. Ornith. Club 16: 14. (Martinique, Lesser Antilles.)

Described from the account of an early traveler, this bird was believed to be endemic to Martinique, Lesser Antilles. No specimens are known.

Anodorhynchus purpurascens Rothschild. Guadeloupe Violet Macaw.

> *Anadorhynchus* [sic] *purpurascens* Rothschild, 1905, Bull. Brit. Ornith. Club 16: 13. (Guadeloupe, Lesser Antilles.)

Based on a description by an early traveler, this bird was apparently restricted to the island of Guadeloupe, Lesser Antilles. No specimens are known.

Ara atwoodi Clark. Dominican Macaw.

> *Ara atwoodi* Clark, 1908, Auk 25: 310. (Dominica.)

This bird, apparently occurring on Dominica, Lesser Antilles, was named on the basis of a description in an early book. No specimens are known.

Ara erythrocephala Rothschild. Red-headed Green Macaw.

> *Ara erythrocephala* Rothschild, 1905, Bull. Brit. Ornith. Club 16: 14. (Mountains of Trelawny and St. Anne's, Jamaica.)

This bird was reported only from Jamaica. One bird, perhaps a captive, was mentioned by Gosse (1847), but there are no specimens.

Ara erythrura Rothschild. Red-tailed Macaw.

> *Ara erythrura* Rothschild, 1907, Extinct Birds, p. 54, pl. 15. ("One of the West Indian Islands.")

Described from the accounts of early travelers, this bird was believed to occur on an unspecified Antillean island. No specimens are known.

Ara gossei Rothschild. Yellow-headed Macaw.

> *Ara gossei* Rothschild, 1905, Bull. Brit. Ornith. Club 16: 14. (Mountains of Hanover Parish, about 10 miles east of Lucea, Jamaica.)

This bird was reported only from Jamaica. A specimen collected about 1765 was described by Gosse (1847), although he apparently did not see the bird.

Ara guadeloupensis Clark. Guadeloupe Macaw.

> *Ara guadeloupensis* Clark, 1905, Auk 22: 272. (Guadeloupe, Lesser Antilles.)

Described from accounts of early travelers, this bird evidently occurred on Guadeloupe and Martinique, Lesser Antilles. No specimens are known.

Amazilia bangsi Ridgway. Bangs's Hummingbird.

> *Amizilis* [sic] *bangsi* Ridgway, 1910, Proc. Biol. Soc. Wash. 23: 54. (Volcán de Miravalles, Costa Rica.)

This hummingbird is regarded as a hybrid between *Amazilia rutila* and *A. tzacatl* (Bangs 1930).

Amazilia ocai Gould. d'Oca's Hummingbird.

> *Amazilia Ocai* Gould, 1859, Ann. Mag. Nat. Hist., ser. 3, 4: 96. (Xalapa, southern Mexico = Jalapa, Veracruz.)

This unique hummingbird is regarded as a hybrid between *Amazilia cyanocephala* and *A. beryllina* (Berlioz 1932).

Thaumatias lerdi d'Oca.

> *Thaumatias lerdi* d'Oca, 1875, La Naturaleza 3: 24. (Paso del Macho, Vera Cruz, Mexico.)

This is often considered to be the same as *Amazilia ocai* (Peters 1945).

Saucerottia florenceae van Rossem and Hachisuka. Florence's Hummingbird.

> *Saucerottia florenceae* van Rossem and Hachisuka, 1938, Trans. San Diego Soc. Nat. Hist. 8: 408. (Rancho Santa Barbara, 5000 feet, 20 miles northeast of Guirocoba, Sonora.)

The unique type is probably an intrageneric hybrid in *Amazilia* (Peters 1945).

Cyanomyia salvini Brewster. Salvin's Hummingbird.

> *Cyanomyia salvini* Brewster, 1893, Auk 10: 214. (Nacosari, Sonora, Mexico.)

This form is regarded as a hybrid between *Amazilia violiceps* and *Cynanthus latirostris* (Griscom 1934).

Trochilus violajugulum Jeffries. Violet-throated Hummingbird.

> *Trochilus violajugulum* Jeffries, 1888, Auk 5: 168. (Santa Barbara, California.)

This form is regarded as a hybrid between *Archilochus alexandri* and *Calypte anna* (Ridgway 1911, Banks and Johnson 1961).

Phasmornis mystica Oberholser. Chisos Hummingbird.

> *Phasmornis mystica* Oberholser, 1974, Bird Life Texas 1: 485. (Boot Spring, Chisos Mts., Texas.)

Described from the unique type (subsequently lost) as a new species (and genus), this form probably represents a hybrid (of unknown parentage) or an aberrant individual of *Archilochus alexandri* (Browning 1978).

Selasphorus floresii Gould. Floresi's Hummingbird.

> *Selasphorus floresii* Gould, 1861, Monogr. Trochil., pt. 23, pl. [10] and text; vol. 3, pl. 139. (Bolaños, Jalisco, Mexico.)

This hummingbird is regarded as a hybrid between *S. sasin* and *Calypte anna* (Banks and Johnson 1961).

Celeus immaculatus Berlepsch. Immaculate Woodpecker.

> *Celeus immaculatus* Berlepsch, 1880, Ibis, p. 113. (Agua Dulce, Panama.)

Both the identity and source of the unique type specimen of *C. immaculatus* have been questioned (see Wetmore 1968). The type locality was based on the "make" of the type specimen, a trade skin of uncertain origin. Short (1982) considered the specimen to be an aberrant example of the extralimital *Celeus elegans* [Chestnut Woodpecker]; he did not comment on the locality.

Vireosylva propinqua Baird. Vera Paz Vireo.

> *Vireosylvia* [sic] *propinqua* Baird, 1866, Rev. Amer. Birds 1: 345, 348. (Cobán, Vera Paz, Guatemala.)

This form is probably a hybrid between *Vireo flavifrons* and *V. solitarius* (Ridgway 1904).

Regulus cuvieri Audubon. Cuvier's Kinglet.

> *Regulus cuvieri* Audubon, 1829, Birds Amer. (folio), 1, pl. 55 (1831, Ornithol. Biogr. 1: 288). (Fatland Ford, about ten miles west of Norristown, Pennsylvania.)

This form is known only from Audubon's description and plate of a specimen taken in 1812 but not saved. It probably represents an aberrant plumage of *R. satrapa* (*fide* Watson, *in* Parkes 1985).

Vermivora lawrencii (Herrick). Lawrence's Warbler.

> *Helminthophaga Lawrencii* Herrick, 1875, Proc. Acad. Nat. Sci. Philadelphia 26 (1874): 220). (bank of the Passaic, near Chatham, New Jersey.)

This warbler is a hybrid between *Vermivora pinus* and *V. chrysoptera,* displaying the face pattern of *V. chrysoptera*. It has been recorded from the contact zone between the two species and from much of their nonbreeding distributions (Parkes 1951). See comments under *V. pinus.*

Vermivora leucobronchialis (Brewster). Brewster's Warbler.

> *Helminthophaga leucobronchialis* Brewster, 1874, Amer. Sportsman 5 (3): 33. (Newtonville, Massachusetts.)

This warbler is a hybrid between *Vermivora pinus* and *V. chrysoptera,* displaying the face pattern of *V. pinus.* It has been recorded from the contact zone between the two species and from much of their nonbreeding distributions (Parkes 1951). See comments under *V. pinus.*

Helminthophaga cincinnatiensis Langdon. Cincinnati Warbler.

> *Helminthophaga cincinnatiensis* Langdon, 1880, J. Cincinnati Soc. Nat. Hist. 3: 119. (Madisonville, Hamilton Co., Ohio.)

This warbler is regarded as a hybrid between *Vermivora pinus* and *Oporornis formosus* (Ridgway 1880, McCamey 1950, Graves 1988).

Dendroica potomac Haller. Sutton's Warbler.

> *Dendroica potomac* Haller, 1940, Cardinal 5: 50. (Berkeley County, elev. 450 ft., twelve miles south of Martinsburg, West Virginia.)

This warbler is generally regarded as a hybrid between *Dendroica dominica* and *Parula americana* (Brooks 1945, Morse 1989). Sightings have been reported from West Virginia, Virginia, District of Columbia, South Carolina, Florida, Indiana, and Texas (Carlson 1981).

Sylvia carbonata Audubon. Carbonated Warbler.

> *Sylvia carbonata* Audubon, 1829, Birds Amer. (folio), 1. pl. 60 (1831, Ornithol. Biogr. 1, p. 308. (near Henderson, Kentucky.)

The two birds represented in Audubon's description and plate are probably young *Dendroica tigrina* (Parkes 1985).

Sylvia montana Wilson. Blue Mountain Warbler.

> *Sylvia montana* Wilson, 1812, Amer. Ornithol. 5: 113, pl. 44, fig 2. (near the Blue Mountains [Pennsylvania].)

This form is known only from descriptions and paintings by Wilson of a bird from Pennsylvania (not Virginia, as often stated) and by Audubon of a bird from California (Parkes 1985). They have not been identified with certainty but are not in the Old World genus *Sylvia.*

Sylvania microcephala Ridgway. Small-headed Flycatcher.

> *Muscicapa minuta* (not Gmelin, 1789) Wilson, 1812, Amer. Ornithol. 6: 62, pl. 50, fig. 5. (New Jersey.)
> *Sylvania microcephala* Ridgway, 1885, Proc. U. S. Natl. Mus. 8: 354, New name for *Muscicapa minuta* Wilson, preoccupied.

This bird is known only from the works of Wilson and Audubon, whose specimens were from New Jersey and Kentucky, respectively (Parkes 1985). When Ridgway proposed a new name for *minuta,* preoccupied in *Muscicapa,* he transferred it to the genus *Sylvania,* a synonym of modern *Wilsonia,* but generic placement is uncertain; thus, we retain the former generic designation. Sometimes called Small-headed Warbler (A.O.U. 1957).

Emberiza townsendii (Audubon). Townsend's Bunting.

> *Emberiza townsendii* Audubon, 1834, Ornithol. Biogr. 2: 183. (near New Garden, Chester County, Pennsylvania.)

Known only from the unique type, taken 11 May 1833 by John K. Townsend, this bird is often treated in the genus *Spiza*. Parkes (1985) suggested that it is a female *Spiza americana* that lacks the normal carotenoid pigment in its plumage.

Aegiothus brewsterii Ridgway. Brewster's Linnet.

> *Aegiothus (flavirostris* var.) *brewsterii* Ridgway, 1872, Amer. Nat. 6: 433. (Waltham, Massachusetts.)

Known only from the type, taken 1 November 1870, this form is possibly a hybrid between *Carduelis flammeus* and *C. pinus* (Ridgway 1901).

FRENCH NAMES OF NORTH AMERICAN BIRDS

A French name is provided for each species appearing in the main list and the appendix of the 7th Edition of the Check-list of North American Birds. Except for a few cases, the French names are those of the Standing Committee on French Names of the Birds of the World (Commission internationale des noms français des oiseaux) (International Ornithological Committee—I.O.C.), and derived from the publication: NOMS FRANÇAIS DES OISEAUX DU MONDE. 1993. Éditions MultiMondes, Sainte-Foy, Québec, Canada. 452 pages. Some French names have been added or modified because of new taxonomic decisions and reflect these taxonomic changes. They have been reviewed by the North American members of the Standing Committee on French Names and will be included in the next edition of the world list of French names. This list follows the taxonomic sequence and arrangement of the Check-list.

TINAMIDAE
Tinamus major	Grand Tinamou
Nothocercus bonapartei	Tinamou de Bonaparte
Crypturellus soui	Tinamou soui
Crypturellus cinnamomeus	Tinamou cannelle
Crypturellus boucardi	Tinamou de Boucard
Crypturellus kerriae	Tinamou de Kerr

GAVIIDAE
Gavia stellata	Plongeon catmarin
Gavia arctica	Plongeon arctique
Gavia pacifica	Plongeon du Pacifique
Gavia immer	Plongeon huard
Gavia adamsii	Plongeon à bec blanc

PODICIPEDIDAE
Tachybaptus dominicus	Grèbe minime
Podilymbus podiceps	Grèbe à bec bigarré
Podilymbus gigas	Grèbe de l'Atitlan
Podiceps auritus	Grèbe esclavon
Podiceps grisegena	Grèbe jougris
Podiceps nigricollis	Grèbe à cou noir
Aechmophorus occidentalis	Grèbe élégant
Aechmophorus clarkii	Grèbe à face blanche

DIOMEDEIDAE
Thalassarche chlororhynchos	Albatros à nez jaune
Thalassarche cauta	Albatros à cape blanche
Thalassarche melanophris	Albatros à sourcils noirs
Phoebetria palpebrata	Albatros fuligineux
Diomedea exulans	Albatros hurleur
Phoebastria immutabilis	Albatros de Laysan
Phoebastria nigripes	Albatros à pieds noirs
Phoebastria albatrus	Albatros à queue courte

PROCELLARIIDAE
Fulmarus glacialis	Fulmar boréal
Pterodroma neglecta	Pétrel des Kermadec
Pterodroma arminjoniana	Pétrel de la Trinité du Sud
Pterodroma ultima	Pétrel de Murphy
Pterodroma inexpectata	Pétrel maculé
Pterodroma cahow	Pétrel des Bermudes
Pterodroma hasitata	Pétrel diablotin
Pterodroma externa	Pétrel de Juan Fernandez
Pterodroma phaeopygia	Pétrel des Galapagos
Pterodroma cervicalis	Pétrel à col blanc
Pterodroma hypoleuca	Pétrel des Bonin
Pterodroma nigripennis	Pétrel à ailes noires
Pterodroma cookii	Pétrel de Cook
Pterodroma longirostris	Pétrel de Stejneger
Bulweria bulwerii	Pétrel de Bulwer
Bulweria fallax	Pétrel de Jouanin
Procellaria parkinsoni	Puffin de Parkinson
Calonectris leucomelas	Puffin leucomèle
Calonectris diomedea	Puffin cendré
Puffinus creatopus	Puffin à pieds roses
Puffinus carneipes	Puffin à pieds pâles
Puffinus gravis	Puffin majeur
Puffinus pacificus	Puffin fouquet
Puffinus bulleri	Puffin de Buller
Puffinus griseus	Puffin fuligineux
Puffinus tenuirostris	Puffin à bec grêle
Puffinus nativitatis	Puffin de la Nativité
Puffinus puffinus	Puffin des Anglais
Puffinus auricularis	Puffin de Townsend
Puffinus opisthomelas	Puffin cul-noir
Puffinus lherminieri	Puffin d'Audubon
Puffinus assimilis	Petit Puffin

HYDROBATIDAE
Oceanites oceanicus	Océanite de Wilson
Pelagodroma marina	Océanite frégate
Hydrobates pelagicus	Océanite tempête

Oceanodroma furcata	Océanite à queue fourchue
Oceanodroma leucorhoa	Océanite cul-blanc
Oceanodroma homochroa	Océanite cendré
Oceanodroma castro	Océanite de Castro
Oceanodroma tethys	Océanite téthys
Oceanodroma melania	Océanite noir
Oceanodroma macrodactyla	Océanite de Guadalupe
Oceanodroma markhami	Océanite de Markham
Oceanodroma tristrami	Océanite de Tristram
Oceanodroma microsoma	Océanite minute

PHAETHONTIDAE

Phaethon lepturus	Phaéton à bec jaune
Phaethon aethereus	Phaéton à bec rouge
Phaethon rubricauda	Phaéton à brins rouges

SULIDAE

Sula dactylatra	Fou masqué
Sula nebouxii	Fou à pieds bleus
Sula variegata	Fou varié
Sula leucogaster	Fou brun
Sula sula	Fou à pieds rouges
Morus bassanus	Fou de Bassan

PELECANIDAE

Pelecanus erythrorhynchos	Pélican d'Amérique
Pelecanus occidentalis	Pélican brun

PHALACROCORACIDAE

Phalacrocorax penicillatus	Cormoran de Brandt
Phalacrocorax brasilianus	Cormoran vigua
Phalacrocorax auritus	Cormoran à aigrettes
Phalacrocorax carbo	Grand Cormoran
Phalacrocorax urile	Cormoran à face rouge
Phalacrocorax pelagicus	Cormoran pélagique

ANHINGIDAE

Anhinga anhinga	Anhinga d'Amérique

FREGATIDAE

Fregata magnificens	Frégate superbe
Fregata minor	Frégate du Pacifique
Fregata ariel	Frégate ariel

ARDEIDAE

Botaurus pinnatus	Butor mirasol
Botaurus lentiginosus	Butor d'Amérique
Ixobrychus sinensis	Blongios de Chine
Ixobrychus exilis	Petit Blongios
Tigrisoma lineatum	Onoré rayé
Tigrisoma fasciatum	Onoré fascié
Tigrisoma mexicanum	Onoré du Mexique
Ardea herodias	Grand Héron
Ardea cinerea	Héron cendré
Ardea cocoi	Héron cocoi
Ardea alba	Grande Aigrette
Egretta eulophotes	Aigrette de Chine
Egretta garzetta	Aigrette garzette
Egretta gularis	Aigrette à gorge blanche
Egretta thula	Aigrette neigeuse
Egretta caerulea	Aigrette bleue
Egretta tricolor	Aigrette tricolore
Egretta rufescens	Aigrette roussâtre
Bubulcus ibis	Héron garde-boeufs
Butorides virescens	Héron vert
Butorides striatus	Héron strié
Agamia agami	Héron agami
Pilherodius pileatus	Héron coiffé
Nycticorax nycticorax	Bihoreau gris
Nyctanassa violacea	Bihoreau violacé
Cochlearius cochlearius	Savacou huppé

THRESKIORNITHIDAE

Eudocimus albus	Ibis blanc
Eudocimus ruber	Ibis rouge
Plegadis falcinellus	Ibis falcinelle
Plegadis chihi	Ibis à face blanche
Mesembrinibis cayennensis	Ibis vert
Theristicus caudatus	Ibis mandore
Ajaia ajaja	Spatule rosée

CICONIIDAE

Jabiru mycteria	Jabiru d'Amérique
Mycteria americana	Tantale d'Amérique

CATHARTIDAE

Coragyps atratus	Urubu noir
Cathartes aura	Urubu à tête rouge
Cathartes burrovianus	Urubu à tête jaune
Gymnogyps californianus	Condor de Californie
Sarcoramphus papa	Sarcoramphe roi

PHOENICOPTERIDAE

Phoenicopterus ruber	Flamant rose

ANATIDAE

Dendrocygna viduata	Dendrocygne veuf
Dendrocygna autumnalis	Dendrocygne à ventre noir
Dendrocygna arborea	Dendrocygne des Antilles
Dendrocygna bicolor	Dendrocygne fauve
Anser fabalis	Oie des moissons
Anser brachyrhynchus	Oie à bec court
Anser albifrons	Oie rieuse

Anser erythropus	Oie naine
Chen canagica	Oie empereur
Chen caerulescens	Oie des neiges
Chen rossii	Oie de Ross
Branta canadensis	Bernache du Canada
Branta sandvicensis	Berrnache néné
Branta bernicla	Bernache cravant
Branta leucopsis	Bernache nonnette
Cygnus olor	Cygne tuberculé
Cygnus buccinator	Cygne trompette
Cygnus columbianus	Cygne siffleur
Cygnus cygnus	Cygne chanteur
Sarkidiornis	
melanotos	Canard à bosse
Neochen jubata	Ouette de l'Orénoque
Cairina moschata	Canard musqué
Aix sponsa	Canard branchu
Anas strepera	Canard chipeau
Anas falcata	Canard à faucilles
Anas penelope	Canard siffleur
Anas americana	Canard d'Amérique
Anas rubripes	Canard noir
Anas platyrhynchos	Canard colvert
Anas fulvigula	Canard brun
Anas wyvilliana	Canard des Hawaï
Anas laysanensis	Canard de Laysan
Anas poecilorhyncha	Canard à bec tacheté
Anas discors	Sarcelle à ailes
	bleues
Anas cyanoptera	Sarcelle cannelle
Anas clypeata	Canard souchet
Anas bahamensis	Canard des Bahamas
Anas acuta	Canard pilet
Anas querquedula	Sarcelle d'été
Anas formosa	Sarcelle élégante
Anas crecca	Sarcelle d'hiver
Aythya valisineria	Fuligule à dos blanc
Aythya americana	Fuligule à tête rouge
Aythya ferina	Fuligule milouin
Aythya collaris	Fuligule à collier
Aythya fuligula	Fuligule morillon
Aythya marila	Fuligule milouinan
Aythya affinis	Petit Fuligule
Polysticta stelleri	Eider de Steller
Somateria fischeri	Eider à lunettes
Somateria spectabilis	Eider à tête grise
Somateria mollissima	Eider à duvet
Histrionicus	
histrionicus	Arlequin plongeur
Camptorhynchus	
labradorius	Eider du Labrador
Melanitta	Macreuse à front
perspicillata	blanc
Melanitta fusca	Macreuse brune
Melanitta nigra	Macreuse noire
Clangula hyemalis	Harelde kakawi
Bucephala albeola	Petit Garrot
Bucephala clangula	Garrot à oeil d'or
Bucephala islandica	Garrot d'Islande
Mergellus albellus	Harle piette
Lophodytes	
cucullatus	Harle couronné
Mergus merganser	Grand Harle
Mergus serrator	Harle huppé

Nomonyx dominicus	Érismature routoutou
Oxyura jamaicensis	Érismature rousse
ACCIPITRIDAE	
Pandion haliaetus	Balbuzard pêcheur
Leptodon cayanensis	Milan de Cayenne
Chondrohierax	
uncinatus	Milan bec-en-croc
Elanoides forficatus	Milan à queue
	fourchue
Gampsonyx	
swainsonii	Élanion perle
Elanus leucurus	Élanion à queue
	blanche
Rostrhamus sociabilis	Milan des marais
Rostrhamus hamatus	Milan à long bec
Harpagus bidentatus	Milan bidenté
Ictinia	
mississippiensis	Milan du Mississippi
Ictinia plumbea	Milan bleuâtre
Haliaeetus	Pygargue à tête
leucocephalus	blanche
Haliaeetus albicilla	Pygargue à queue
	blanche
Haliaeetus pelagicus	Pygargue empereur
Busarellus nigricollis	Busarelle à tête
	blanche
Circus cyaneus	Busard Saint-Martin
Accipiter soloensis	Épervier de Horsfield
Accipiter	
superciliosus	Épervier nain
Accipiter striatus	Épervier brun
Accipiter cooperii	Épervier de Cooper
Accipiter gundlachi	Épervier de Cuba
Accipiter bicolor	Épervier bicolore
Accipiter gentilis	Autour des palombes
Geranospiza	
caerulescens	Buse échasse
Leucopternis	
plumbea	Buse plombée
Leucopternis	
princeps	Buse barrée
Leucopternis	
semiplumbea	Buse semiplombée
Leucopternis	
albicollis	Buse blanche
Asturina nitida	Buse cendrée
Buteogallus	
anthracinus	Buse noire
Buteogallus subtilis	Buse des mangroves
Buteogallus	
urubitinga	Buse urubu
Buteogallus	
meridionalis	Buse roussâtre
Parabuteo unicinctus	Buse de Harris
Harpyhaliaetus	
solitarius	Buse solitaire
Buteo magnirostris	Buse à gros bec
Buteo lineatus	Buse à épaulettes
Buteo ridgwayi	Buse de Ridgway
Buteo platypterus	Petite Buse
Buteo brachyurus	Buse à queue courte
Buteo swainsoni	Buse de Swainson
Buteo albicaudatus	Buse à queue blanche

Buteo albonotatus	Buse à queue barrée
Buteo solitarius	Buse d'Hawaï
Buteo jamaicensis	Buse à queue rousse
Buteo regalis	Buse rouilleuse
Buteo lagopus	Buse pattue
Morphnus guianensis	Harpie huppée
Harpia harpyja	Harpie féroce
Aquila chrysaetos	Aigle royal
Spizastur melanoleucus	Aigle noir et blanc
Spizaetus tyrannus	Aigle tyran
Spizaetus ornatus	Aigle orné

FALCONIDAE

Micrastur ruficollis	Carnifex barré
Micrastur mirandollei	Carnifex ardoisé
Micrastur semitorquatus	Carnifex à collier
Daptrius americanus	Caracara à gorge rouge
Caracara plancus	Caracara huppé
Milvago chimachima	Caracara à tête jaune
Herpetotheres cachinnans	Macagua rieur
Falco tinnunculus	Faucon crécerelle
Falco sparverius	Crécerelle d'Amérique
Falco columbarius	Faucon émerillon
Falco subbuteo	Faucon hobereau
Falco femoralis	Faucon aplomado
Falco rufigularis	Faucon des chauves-souris
Falco deiroleucus	Faucon orangé
Falco rusticolus	Faucon gerfaut
Falco peregrinus	Faucon pèlerin
Falco mexicanus	Faucon des prairies

CRACIDAE

Ortalis vetula	Ortalide chacamel
Ortalis cinereiceps	Ortalide à tête grise
Ortalis ruficauda	Ortalide à ventre roux
Ortalis wagleri	Ortalide à ventre marron
Ortalis poliocephala	Ortalide de Wagler
Ortalis leucogastra	Ortalide à ventre blanc
Penelope purpurascens	Pénélope panachée
Chamaepetes unicolor	Pénélope unicolore
Penelopina nigra	Pénélope pajuil
Oreophasis derbianus	Oréophase cornu
Crax rubra	Grand Hocco

PHASIANIDAE

Alectoris chukar	Perdrix choukar
Francolinus pondicerianus	Francolin gris
Francolinus francolinus	Francolin noir
Francolinus erckelii	Francolin d'Erckel
Tetraogallus himalayensis	Tétraogalle de l'Himalaya

Perdix perdix	Perdrix grise
Coturnix japonica	Caille du Japon
Gallus gallus	Coq bankiva
Lophura leucomelanos	Faisan leucomèle
Phasianus colchicus	Faisan de Colchide
Pavo cristatus	Paon bleu
Bonasa umbellus	Gélinotte huppée
Centrocercus urophasianus	Tétras des armoises
Falcipennis canadensis	Tétras du Canada
Lagopus lagopus	Lagopède des saules
Lagopus mutus	Lagopède alpin
Lagopus leucurus	Lagopède à queue blanche
Dendragapus obscurus	Tétras sombre
Tympanuchus phasianellus	Tétras à queue fine
Tympanuchus cupido	Tétras des prairies
Tympanuchus pallidicinctus	Tétras pâle
Meleagris gallopavo	Dindon sauvage
Meleagris ocellata	Dindon ocellé
Numida meleagris	Pintade de Numidie

ODONTOPHORIDAE

Dendrortyx barbatus	Colin barbu
Dendrortyx macroura	Colin à longue queue
Dendrortyx leucophrys	Colin à sourcils blancs
Oreortyx pictus	Colin des montagnes
Callipepla squamata	Colin écaillé
Callipepla douglasii	Colin élégant
Callipepla californica	Colin de Californie
Callipepla gambelii	Colin de Gambel
Philortyx fasciatus	Colin barré
Colinus virginianus	Colin de Virginie
Colinus nigrogularis	Colin à gorge noire
Colinus cristatus	Colin huppé
Odontophorus gujanensis	Tocro de Guyane
Odontophorus melanotis	Tocro à face noire
Odontophorus dialeucos	Tocro du Panama
Odontophorus leucolaemus	Tocro à poitrine noire
Odontophorus guttatus	Tocro tacheté
Dactylortyx thoracicus	Colin chanteur
Cyrtonyx montezumae	Colin arlequin
Cyrtonyx ocellatus	Colin ocellé
Rhynchortyx cinctus	Colin ceinturé

RALLIDAE

Coturnicops noveboracensis	Râle jaune
Micropygia schomburgkii	Râle ocellé

Laterallus ruber	Râle roux	*Charadrius wilsonia*	Pluvier de Wilson
Laterallus albigularis	Râle à menton blanc	*Charadrius hiaticula*	Pluvier grand-gravelot
Laterallus exilis	Râle grêle		
Laterallus jamaicensis	Râle noir	*Charadrius semipalmatus*	Pluvier semipalmé
Crex crex	Râle des genêts	*Charadrius melodus*	Pluvier siffleur
Rallus longirostris	Râle gris	*Charadrius dubius*	Pluvier petit-gravelot
Rallus elegans	Râle élégant	*Charadrius vociferus*	Pluvier kildir
Rallus limicola	Râle de Virginie	*Charadrius montanus*	Pluvier montagnard
Aramides axillaris	Râle à cou roux	*Charadrius morinellus*	Pluvier guignard
Aramides cajanea	Râle de Cayenne		
Amaurolimnas concolor	Râle concolore	**HAEMATOPODIDAE**	
Porzana palmeri	Marouette de Laysan	*Haematopus ostralegus*	Huîtrier pie
Porzana porzana	Marouette ponctuée	*Haematopus palliatus*	Huîtrier d'Amérique
Porzana carolina	Marouette de Caroline	*Haematopus bachmani*	Huîtrier de Bachman
Porzana sandwichensis	Marouette des Hawaï	**RECURVIROSTRIDAE**	
Porzana flaviventer	Marouette à sourcils blancs	*Himantopus himantopus*	Échasse blanche
		Himantopus mexicanus	Échasse d'Amérique
Neocrex colombianus	Râle de Colombie	*Recurvirostra americana*	Avocette d'Amérique
Neocrex erythrops	Râle à bec peint		
Cyanolimnas cerverai	Râle de Zapata	**JACANIDAE**	
Pardirallus maculatus	Râle tacheté	*Jacana spinosa*	Jacana du Mexique
Porphyrula martinica	Talève violacée	*Jacana jacana*	Jacana noir
Porphyrula flavirostris	Talève favorite		
Gallinula chloropus	Gallinule poule-d'eau	**SCOLOPACIDAE**	
Fulica atra	Foulque macroule	*Tringa nebularia*	Chevalier aboyeur
Fulica alai	Foulque des Hawaï	*Tringa melanoleuca*	Grand Chevalier
Fulica americana	Foulque d'Amérique	*Tringa flavipes*	Petit Chevalier
Fulica caribaea	Foulque à cachet blanc	*Tringa stagnatilis*	Chevalier stagnatile
		Tringa totanus	Chevalier gambette
HELIORNITHIDAE		*Tringa erythropus*	Chevalier arlequin
Heliornis fulica	Grébifoulque d'Amérique	*Tringa glareola*	Chevalier sylvain
		Tringa ochropus	Chevalier cul-blanc
EURYPYGIDAE		*Tringa solitaria*	Chevalier solitaire
Eurypyga helias	Caurale soleil	*Catoptrophorus semipalmatus*	Chevalier semipalmé
ARAMIDAE		*Heteroscelus incanus*	Chevalier errant
Aramus guarauna	Courlan brun	*Heteroscelus brevipes*	Chevalier de Sibérie
		Actitis hypoleucos	Chevalier guignette
GRUIDAE		*Actitis macularia*	Chevalier grivelé
Grus canadensis	Grue du Canada	*Xenus cinereus*	Chevalier bargette
Grus grus	Grue cendrée	*Bartramia longicauda*	Maubèche des champs
Grus americana	Grue blanche	*Numenius minutus*	Courlis nain
		Numenius borealis	Courlis esquimau
BURHINIDAE		*Numenius phaeopus*	Courlis corlieu
Burhinus bistriatus	Oedicnème bistrié	*Numenius tahitiensis*	Courlis d'Alaska
		Numenius madagascariensis	Courlis de Sibérie
CHARADRIIDAE		*Numenius tenuirostris*	Courlis à bec grêle
Vanellus vanellus	Vanneau huppé	*Numenius arquata*	Courlis cendré
Vanellus chilensis	Vanneau téro	*Numenius americanus*	Courlis à long bec
Pluvialis squatarola	Pluvier argenté	*Limosa limosa*	Barge à queue noire
Pluvialis apricaria	Pluvier doré	*Limosa haemastica*	Barge hudsonienne
Pluvialis dominica	Pluvier bronzé	*Limosa lapponica*	Barge rousse
Pluvialis fulva	Pluvier fauve		
Charadrius mongolus	Pluvier de Mongolie		
Charadrius collaris	Pluvier d'Azara		
Charadrius alexandrinus	Pluvier à collier interrompu		

Limosa fedoa   Barge marbrée
Arenaria interpres   Tournepierre à collier
Arenaria
  melanocephala   Tournepierre noir
Aphriza virgata   Bécasseau du ressac
Calidris tenuirostris   Bécasseau de
       l'Anadyr
Calidris canutus   Bécasseau maubèche
Calidris alba   Bécasseau sanderling
Calidris pusilla   Bécasseau semipalmé
Calidris mauri   Bécasseau d'Alaska
Calidris ruficollis   Bécasseau à col roux
Calidris minuta   Bécasseau minute
Calidris temminckii   Bécasseau de
       Temminck
Calidris subminuta   Bécasseau à longs
       doigts
Calidris minutilla   Bécasseau minuscule
Calidris fuscicollis   Bécasseau à croupion
       blanc
Calidris bairdii   Bécasseau de Baird
Calidris melanotos   Bécasseau à poitrine
       cendrée
Calidris acuminata   Bécasseau à queue
       pointue
Calidris maritima   Bécasseau violet
Calidris ptilocnemis   Bécasseau des
       Aléoutiennes
Calidris alpina   Bécasseau variable
Calidris ferruginea   Bécasseau cocorli
Calidris himantopus   Bécasseau à échasses
Eurynorhynchus
  pygmeus   Bécasseau spatule
Limicola falcinellus   Bécasseau falcinelle
Tryngites
  subruficollis   Bécasseau roussâtre
Philomachus pugnax   Combattant varié
Limnodromus griseus   Bécassin roux
Limnodromus
  scolopaceus   Bécassin à long bec
Lymnocryptes
  minimus   Bécassine sourde
Gallinago gallinago   Bécassine des marais
Gallinago stenura   Bécassine à queue
       pointue
Scolopax rusticola   Bécasse des bois
Scolopax minor   Bécasse d'Amérique
Phalaropus tricolor   Phalarope de Wilson
Phalaropus lobatus   Phalarope à bec étroit
Phalaropus fulicaria   Phalarope à bec large

GLAREOLIDAE
Glareola maldivarum   Glaréole orientale

LARIDAE
Catharacta skua   Grand Labbe
Catharacta
  maccormicki   Labbe de McCormick
Stercorarius
  pomarinus   Labbe pomarin
Stercorarius
  parasiticus   Labbe parasite
Stercorarius
  *longicaudu*s   Labbe à longue
       queue

Larus atricilla   Mouette atricille
Larus pipixcan   Mouette de Franklin
Larus minutus   Mouette pygmée
Larus ridibundus   Mouette rieuse
Larus philadelphia   Mouette de
       Bonaparte
Larus heermanni   Goéland de
       Heermann
Larus modestus   Goéland gris
Larus belcheri   Goéland siméon
Larus crassirostris   Goéland à queue
       noire
Larus canus   Goéland cendré
Larus delawarensis   Goéland à bec cerclé
Larus californicus   Goéland de
       Californie
Larus argentatus   Goéland argenté
Larus cachinnans   Goéland leucophée
Larus thayeri   Goéland de Thayer
Larus glaucoides   Goéland arctique
Larus fuscus   Goéland brun
Larus schistisagus   Goéland à manteau
       ardoisé
Larus livens   Goéland de Cortez
Larus occidentalis   Goéland d'Audubon
Larus glaucescens   Goéland à ailes
       grises
Larus hyperboreus   Goéland bourgmestre
Larus marinus   Goéland marin
Xema sabini   Mouette de Sabine
Rissa tridactyla   Mouette tridactyle
Rissa brevirostris   Mouette des brumes
Rhodostethia rosea   Mouette rosée
Pagophila eburnea   Mouette blanche
Sterna nilotica   Sterne hansel
Sterna caspia   Sterne caspienne
Sterna maxima   Sterne royale
Sterna elegans   Sterne élégante
Sterna bergii   Sterne huppée
Sterna sandvicensis   Sterne caugek
Sterna dougallii   Sterne de Dougall
Sterna hirundo   Sterne pierregarin
Sterna paradisaea   Sterne arctique
Sterna forsteri   Sterne de Forster
Sterna albifrons   Sterne naine
Sterna antillarum   Petite Sterne
Sterna superciliaris   Sterne argentée
Sterna aleutica   Sterne des
       Aléoutiennes
Sterna lunata   Sterne à dos gris
Sterna anaethetus   Sterne bridée
Sterna fuscata   Sterne fuligineuse
Phaetusa simplex   Sterne à gros bec
Chlidonias
  leucopterus   Guifette leucoptère
Chlidonias hybridus   Guifette moustac
Chlidonias niger   Guifette noire
Larosterna inca   Sterne inca
Anous stolidus   Noddi brun
Anous minutus   Noddi noir
Procelsterna cerulea   Noddi bleu
Gygis alba   Gygis blanche
Rynchops niger   Bec-en-ciseaux noir

ALCIDAE

Alle alle	Mergule nain
Uria aalge	Guillemot marmette
Uria lomvia	Guillemot de Brünnich
Alca torda	Petit Pingouin
Pinguinus impennis	Grand Pingouin
Cepphus grylle	Guillemot à miroir
Cepphus columba	Guillemot colombin
Brachyramphus perdix	Guillemot à long bec
Brachyramphus marmoratus	Guillemot marbré
Brachyramphus brevirostris	Guillemot de Kittlitz
Synthliboramphus hypoleucus	Guillemot de Xantus
Synthliboramphus craveri	Guillemot de Craveri
Synthliboramphus antiquus	Guillemot à cou blanc
Ptychoramphus aleuticus	Starique de Cassin
Aethia psittacula	Starique perroquet
Aethia pusilla	Starique minuscule
Aethia pygmaea	Starique pygmée
Aethia cristatella	Starique cristatelle
Cerorhinca monocerata	Macareux rhinocéros
Fratercula arctica	Macareux moine
Fratercula corniculata	Macareux cornu
Fratercula cirrhata	Macareux huppé

PTEROCLIDIDAE [Incertae sedis]

Pterocles exustus	Ganga à ventre brun

COLUMBIDAE

Columba livia	Pigeon biset
Columba cayennensis	Pigeon rousset
Columba speciosa	Pigeon ramiret
Columba squamosa	Pigeon à cou rouge
Columba leucocephala	Pigeon à couronne blanche
Columba flavirostris	Pigeon à bec rouge
Columba inornata	Pigeon simple
Columba fasciata	Pigeon à queue barrée
Columba caribaea	Pigeon de la Jamaïque
Columba subvinacea	Pigeon vineux
Columba nigrirostris	Pigeon à bec noir
Streptopelia orientalis	Tourterelle orientale
Streptopelia risoria	Tourterelle rieuse
Streptopelia turtur	Tourterelle des bois
Streptopelia decaocto	Tourterelle turque
Streptopelia chinensis	Tourterelle tigrine
Geopelia striata	Géopélie zébrée
Zenaida asiatica	Tourterelle à ailes blanches
Zenaida aurita	Tourterelle à queue carrée
Zenaida auriculata	Tourterelle oreillarde
Zenaida macroura	Tourterelle triste
Zenaida graysoni	Tourterelle de Socorro
Ectopistes migratorius	Tourte voyageuse
Columbina inca	Colombe inca
Columbina passerina	Colombe à queue noire
Columbina minuta	Colombe pygmée
Columbina talpacoti	Colombe rousse
Claravis pretiosa	Colombe bleutée
Claravis mondetoura	Colombe mondétour
Leptotila verreauxi	Colombe de Verreaux
Leptotila rufaxilla	Colombe à front gris
Leptotila wellsi	Colombe de Grenade
Leptotila jamaicensis	Colombe de la Jamaïque
Leptotila cassini	Colombe de Cassin
Geotrygon veraguensis	Colombe de Veragua
Geotrygon chrysia	Colombe à joues blanches
Geotrygon mystacea	Colombe à croissants
Geotrygon albifacies	Colombe des nuages
Geotrygon chiriquensis	Colombe du Chiriqui
Geotrygon carrikeri	Colombe de Tuxtla
Geotrygon lawrencii	Colombe de Lawrence
Geotrygon costaricensis	Colombe du Costa Rica
Geotrygon goldmani	Colombe de Goldman
Geotrygon caniceps	Colombe de Gundlach
Geotrygon versicolor	Colombe versicolore
Geotrygon violacea	Colombe à nuque violette
Geotrygon montana	Colombe rouviolette
Starnoenas cyanocephala	Colombe à tête bleue

PSITTACIDAE

Melopsittacus undulatus	Perruche ondulée
Psittacula krameri	Perruche à collier
Pyrrhura picta	Conure versicolore
Pyrrhura hoffmanni	Conure de Hoffmann
Myiopsitta monachus	Conure veuve
Conuropsis carolinensis	Conure de Caroline
Aratinga holochlora	Conure verte
Aratinga strenua	Conure de Ridgway
Aratinga finschi	Conure de Finsch
Aratinga chloroptera	Conure maîtresse
Aratinga euops	Conure de Cuba
Aratinga nana	Conure naine
Aratinga canicularis	Conure à front rouge
Aratinga pertinax	Conure cuivrée
Ara severa	Ara vert
Ara militaris	Ara militaire
Ara ambigua	Ara de Buffon
Ara chloropterus	Ara chloroptère

Ara macao	Ara rouge
Ara tricolor	Ara tricolore
Ara ararauna	Ara bleu
Rhynchopsitta	
pachyrhyncha	Conure à gros bec
Rhynchopsitta terrisi	Conure à front brun
Bolborhynchus	
lineola	Toui catherine
Forpus passerinus	Toui été
Forpus cyanopygius	Toui du Mexique
Forpus conspicillatus	Toui à lunettes
Brotogeris jugularis	Toui à menton d'or
Brotogeris	
versicolurus	Toui à ailes variées
Touit costaricensis	Toui du Costa Rica
Touit dilectissima	Toui à front bleu
Pionopsitta pyrilia	Caïque de Bonaparte
Pionopsitta	
haematotis	Caïque à capuchon
Pionus menstruus	Pione à tête bleue
Pionus senilis	Pione à couronne blanche
Amazona albifrons	Amazone à front blanc
Amazona xantholora	Amazone du Yucatan
Amazona	
leucocephala	Amazone de Cuba
Amazona collaria	Amazone sasabé
Amazona ventralis	Amazone d'Hispaniola
Amazona vittata	Amazone de Porto Rico
Amazona agilis	Amazone verte
Amazona	Amazone à joues
viridigenalis	vertes
Amazona finschi	Amazone à couronne lilas
Amazona autumnalis	Amazone diadème
Amazona farinosa	Amazone poudrée
Amazona oratrix	Amazone à tête jaune
Amazona	Amazone à nuque
auropalliata	d'or
Amazona	Amazone à front
ochrocephala	jaune
Amazona arausiaca	Amazone de Bouquet
Amazona versicolor	Amazone de Sainte-Lucie
Amazona guildingii	Amazone de Saint-Vincent
Amazona imperialis	Amazone impériale

CUCULIDAE

Cuculus canorus	Coucou gris
Cuculus saturatus	Coucou oriental
Coccyzus	
erythropthalmus	Coulicou à bec noir
Coccyzus americanus	Coulicou à bec jaune
Coccyzus euleri	Coulicou d'Euler
Coccyzus minor	Coulicou manioc
Coccyzus ferrugineus	Coulicou de Cocos
Coccyzus	
melacoryphus	Coulicou de Vieillot
Saurothera merlini	Tacco de Cuba
Saurothera vetula	Tacco de la Jamaïque

Saurothera	
longirostris	Tacco d'Hispaniola
Saurothera vieilloti	Tacco de Porto Rico
Hyetornis rufigularis	Piaye cabrite
Hyetornis pluvialis	Piaye de pluie
Piaya cayana	Piaye écureuil
Piaya minuta	Petit Piaye
Tapera naevia	Géocoucou tacheté
Dromococcyx	
phasianellus	Géocoucou faisan
Morococcyx	Géocoucou de
erythropygus	Lesson
Geococcyx velox	Géocoucou véloce
Geococcyx	
californianus	Grand Géocoucou
Neomorphus	Géocoucou de
geoffroyi	Geoffroy
Crotophaga major	Ani des palétuviers
Crotophaga ani	Ani à bec lisse
Crotophaga	
sulcirostris	Ani à bec cannelé

TYTONIDAE

Tyto alba	Effraie des clochers
Tyto glaucops	Effraie d'Hispaniola

STRIGIDAE

Otus flammeolus	Petit-duc nain
Otus sunia	Petit-duc d'Orient
Otus kennicottii	Petit-duc des montagnes
Otus asio	Petit-duc maculé
Otus seductus	Petit-duc du Balsas
Otus cooperi	Petit-duc de Cooper
Otus trichopsis	Petit-duc à moustaches
Otus choliba	Petit-duc choliba
Otus barbarus	Petit-duc bridé
Otus guatemalae	Petit-duc guatémaltèque
Otus clarkii	Petit-duc de Clark
Otus nudipes	Petit-duc de Porto Rico
Otus lawrencii	Petit-duc de Cuba
Lophostrix cristata	Duc à aigrettes
Pulsatrix	
perspicillata	Chouette à lunettes
Bubo virginianus	Grand-duc d'Amérique
Nyctea scandiaca	Harfang des neiges
Surnia ulula	Chouette épervière
Glaucidium gnoma	Chevêchette naine
Glaucidium jardinii	Chevêchette des Andes
Glaucidium	Chevêchette à tête
griseiceps	grise
Glaucidium sanchezi	Chevêchette du Tamaulipas
Glaucidium	Chevêchette du
palmarum	Colima
Glaucidium	
brasilianum	Chevêchette brune
Glaucidium siju	Chevêchette de Cuba

Micrathene whitneyi	Chevêchette des saguaros	*Caprimulgus indicus*	Engoulevent jotaka
Athene cunicularia	Chevêche des terriers	**NYCTIBIIDAE**	
Ciccaba virgata	Chouette mouchetée	*Nyctibius grandis*	Grand Ibijau
Ciccaba nigrolineata	Chouette à lignes noires	*Nyctibius griseus*	Ibijau gris
		Nyctibius jamaicensis	Ibijau jamaïcain
Strix occidentalis	Chouette tachetée		
Strix varia	Chouette rayée	**STEATORNITHIDAE**	
Strix fulvescens	Chouette fauve	*Steatornis caripensis*	Guacharo des cavernes
Strix nebulosa	Chouette lapone		
Asio otus	Hibou moyen-duc		
Asio stygius	Hibou maître-bois	**APODIDAE**	
Asio flammeus	Hibou des marais	*Cypseloides niger*	Martinet sombre
Pseudoscops clamator	Hibou strié	*Cypseloides storeri*	Martinet de Storer
		Cypseloides cryptus	Martinet à menton blanc
Pseudoscops grammicus	Hibou de la Jamaïque	*Cypseloides cherriei*	Martinet à points blancs
Aegolius funereus	Nyctale de Tengmalm	*Streptoprocne rutila*	Martinet à collier roux
Aegolius acadicus	Petite Nyctale		
Aegolius ridgwayi	Nyctale immaculée	*Streptoprocne zonaris*	Martinet à collier blanc
		Streptoprocne semicollaris	Martinet à nuque blanche
CAPRIMULGIDAE		*Chaetura pelagica*	Martinet ramoneur
Lurocalis semitorquatus	Engoulevent à queue courte	*Chaetura vauxi*	Martinet de Vaux
Chordeiles acutipennis	Engoulevent minime	*Chaetura chapmani*	Martinet de Chapman
Chordeiles minor	Engoulevent d'Amérique	*Chaetura brachyura*	Martinet polioure
		Chaetura andrei	Martinet d'André
Chordeiles gundlachii	Engoulevent piramidig	*Chaetura spinicauda*	Martinet spinicaude
Nyctidromus albicollis	Engoulevent pauraqué	*Chaetura cinereiventris*	Martinet à croupion gris
Phalaenoptilus nuttallii	Engoulevent de Nuttall	*Chaetura martinica*	Martinet chiquesol
Siphonorhis americanus	Engoulevent de la Jamaïque	*Hirundapus caudacutus*	Martinet épineux
Siphonorhis brewsteri	Engoulevent grouillécor	*Aerodramus bartschi*	Salangane de Guam
		Apus apus	Martinet noir
Nyctiphrynus mcleodii	Engoulevent aztèque	*Apus pacificus*	Martinet de Sibérie
Nyctiphrynus yucatanicus	Engoulevent du Yucatan	*Apus melba*	Martinet à ventre blanc
Nyctiphrynus ocellatus	Engoulevent ocellé	*Aeronautes saxatalis*	Martinet à gorge blanche
Caprimulgus carolinensis	Engoulevent de Caroline	*Panyptila cayennensis*	Martinet de Cayenne
Caprimulgus rufus	Engoulevent roux	*Panyptila sanctihieronymi*	Martinet de San Geronimo
Caprimulgus cubanensis	Engoulevent peut-on-voir	*Tachornis phoenicobia*	Martinet petit-rollé
Caprimulgus salvini	Engoulevent de Salvin		
Caprimulgus badius	Engoulevent maya	**TROCHILIDAE**	
Caprimulgus ridgwayi	Engoulevent de Ridgway	*Glaucis aenea*	Ermite bronzé
		Glaucis hirsuta	Ermite hirsute
Caprimulgus vociferus	Engoulevent bois-pourri	*Threnetes ruckeri*	Ermite de Rucker
Caprimulgus noctitherus	Engoulevent de Porto Rico	*Phaethornis guy*	Ermite vert
		Phaethornis superciliosus	Ermite à brins blancs
Caprimulgus saturatus	Engoulevent montagnard	*Phaethornis anthophilus*	Ermite anthophile
Caprimulgus cayennensis	Engoulevent coré	*Phaethornis longuemareus*	Ermite nain
Caprimulgus maculicaudus	Engoulevent à queue étoilée	*Eutoxeres aquila*	Bec-en-faucille aigle
		Androdon aequatorialis	Colibri d'équateur
		Doryfera ludovicae	Porte-lance de Louise

Phaeochroa cuvieri	Colibri de Cuvier	*Lepidopyga*	
Campylopterus	Campyloptère à	*coeruleogularis*	Colibri faux-saphir
curvipennis	queue large	*Hylocharis grayi*	Saphir ulysse
Campylopterus	Campyloptère de	*Hylocharis eliciae*	Saphir d'Elicia
excellens	Wetmore	*Hylocharis leucotis*	Saphir à oreilles
Campylopterus rufus	Campyloptère roux		blanches
Campylopterus		*Hylocharis xantusii*	Saphir de Xantus
hemileucurus	Campyloptère violet	*Goldmania violiceps*	Colibri à calotte
Florisuga mellivora	Colibri jacobin		violette
Colibri delphinae	Colibri de Delphine	*Goethalsia bella*	Colibri du Pirré
Colibri thalassinus	Colibri thalassin	*Trochilus polytmus*	Colibri à tête noire
Anthracothorax		*Amazilia candida*	Ariane candide
prevostii	Mango de Prévost	*Amazilia luciae*	Ariane de Lucy
Anthracothorax	Mango à cravate	*Amazilia amabilis*	Ariane aimable
nigricollis	noire	*Amazilia decora*	Ariane charmante
Anthracothorax		*Amazilia boucardi*	Ariane de Boucard
veraguensis	Mango de Veragua	*Amazilia*	Ariane à couronne
Anthracothorax		*cyanocephala*	azur
dominicus	Mango doré	*Amazilia cyanifrons*	Ariane à front bleu
Anthracothorax		*Amazilia beryllina*	Ariane béryl
viridis	Mango vert	*Amazilia cyanura*	Ariane à queue bleue
Anthracothorax	Mango de la	*Amazilia saucerrottei*	Ariane de Sophie
mango	Jamaïque	*Amazilia edward*	Ariane d'Edward
Eulampis jugularis	Colibri madère	*Amazilia tzacatl*	Ariane à ventre gris
Eulampis		*Amazilia*	
holosericeus	Colibri falle-vert	*yucatanensis*	Ariane du Yucatan
Chrysolampis		*Amazilia rutila*	Ariane cannelle
mosquitus	Colibri rubis-topaze	*Amazilia violiceps*	Ariane à couronne
Orthorhyncus			violette
cristatus	Colibri huppé	*Amazilia viridifrons*	Ariane à front vert
Klais guimeti	Colibri à tête violette	*Eupherusa eximia*	Colibri à épaulettes
Abeillia abeillei	Colibri d'Abeillé	*Eupherusa*	
Lophornis		*cyanophrys*	Colibri d'Oaxaca
brachylopha	Coquette du Guerrero	*Eupherusa poliocerca*	Colibri du Guerrero
Lophornis delattrei	Coquette de Delattre	*Eupherusa*	
Lophornis helenae	Coquette d'Hélène	*nigriventris*	Colibri à ventre noir
Lophornis adorabilis	Coquette adorable	*Elvira chionura*	Colibri elvire
Discosura conversii	Coquette à queue fine	*Elvira cupreiceps*	Colibri à tête cuivrée
Chlorostilbon		*Microchera*	Colibri à coiffe
auriceps	Émeraude couronnée	*albocoronata*	blanche
Chlorostilbon	Émeraude de	*Chalybura buffonii*	Colibri de Buffon
forficatus	Cozumel	*Chalybura urochrysia*	Colibri à queue
Chlorostilbon			bronzée
canivetii	Émeraude de Canivet	*Lampornis*	
Chlorostilbon		*viridipallens*	Colibri vert-d'eau
assimilis	Émeraude du Panama	*Lampornis sybillae*	Colibri de Sybil
Chlorostilbon		*Lampornis*	Colibri à gorge
ricordii	Émeraude de Ricord	*amethystinus*	améthyste
Chlorostilbon bracei	Émeraude de New	*Lampornis*	
	Providence	*clemenciae*	Colibri à gorge bleue
Chlorostilbon	Émeraude	*Lampornis*	
swainsonii	d'Hispaniola	*hemileucus*	Colibri à gorge lilas
Chlorostilbon	Émeraude de Porto	*Lampornis calolaema*	Colibri à gorge
maugaeus	Rico		pourprée
Cynanthus sordidus	Colibri sombre	*Lampornis*	Colibri à ventre
Cynanthus latirostris	Colibri circé	*castaneoventris*	châtain
Cyanophaia bicolor	Colibri à tête bleue	*Lamprolaima rhami*	Colibri à gorge
Thalurania ridgwayi	Dryade du Mexique		grenat
Thalurania		*Heliodoxa jacula*	Brillant fer-de-lance
colombica	Dryade couronnée	*Eugenes fulgens*	Colibri de Rivoli
Thalurania fannyi	Dryade de Fanny	*Haplophaedia*	
Panterpe insignis	Colibri insigne	*aureliae*	Érione d'Aurélie
Damophila julie	Colibri julie	*Heliothryx barroti*	Colibri féérique

Heliomaster		*Todus mexicanus*	Todier de Porto Rico
longirostris	Colibri corinne		
Heliomaster		MOMOTIDAE	
constantii	Colibri de Constant	*Hylomanes momotula*	Motmot nain
Calliphlox evelynae	Colibri des Bahamas	*Aspatha gularis*	Motmot à gorge
Calliphlox bryantae	Colibri magenta		bleue
Calliphlox mitchellii	Colibri de Mitchell	*Momotus mexicanus*	Motmot à tête rousse
Doricha enicura	Colibri à queue	*Momotus momota*	Motmot houtouc
	singulière	*Baryphthengus martii*	Motmot roux
Doricha eliza	Colibri élise	*Electron carinatum*	Motmot à bec caréné
Tilmatura dupontii	Colibri zémès	*Electron*	
Calothorax lucifer	Colibri lucifer	*platyrhynchum*	Motmot à bec large
Calothorax pulcher	Colibri charmant	*Eumomota*	Motmot à sourcils
Archilochus colubris	Colibri à gorge rubis	*superciliosa*	bleus
Archilochus			
alexandri	Colibri à gorge noire	ALCEDINIDAE	
Mellisuga minima	Colibri nain	*Ceryle torquata*	Martin-pêcheur à
Mellisuga helenae	Colibri d'Helen		ventre roux
Calypte anna	Colibri d'Anna	*Ceryle alcyon*	Martin-pêcheur
Calypte costae	Colibri de Costa		d'Amérique
Stellula calliope	Colibri calliope	*Chloroceryle*	Martin-pêcheur
Atthis heloisa	Colibri héloïse	*amazona*	d'Amazonie
Atthis ellioti	Colibri d'Elliot	*Chloroceryle*	
Selasphorus		*americana*	Martin-pêcheur vert
platycercus	Colibri à queue large	*Chloroceryle inda*	Martin-pêcheur
Selasphorus rufus	Colibri roux		bicolore
Selasphorus sasin	Colibri d'Allen	*Chloroceryle aenea*	Martin-pêcheur nain
Selasphorus flammula	Colibri flammule		
Selasphorus ardens	Colibri ardent	BUCCONIDAE	
Selasphorus scintilla	Colibri scintillant	*Nystalus radiatus*	Tamatia barré
		Notharchus	
TROGONIDAE		*macrorhynchos*	Tamatia à gros bec
Priotelus temnurus	Trogon de Cuba	*Notharchus*	
Priotelus roseigaster	Trogon damoiseau	*pectoralis*	Tamatia à plastron
Trogon		*Notharchus tectus*	Tamatia pie
melanocephalus	Trogon à tête noire	*Malacoptila*	Tamatia de
Trogon citreolus	Trogon citrin	*panamensis*	Lafresnaye
Trogon viridis	Trogon à queue	*Micromonacha*	
	blanche	*lanceolata*	Barbacou lancéolé
Trogon bairdii	Trogon de Baird	*Nonnula ruficapilla*	Barbacou à couronne
Trogon violaceus	Trogon violacé		rousse
Trogon mexicanus	Trogon montagnard	*Monasa morphoeus*	Barbacou à front
Trogon elegans	Trogon élégant		blanc
Trogon collaris	Trogon rosalba		
Trogon	Trogon à ventre	GALBULIDAE	
aurantiiventris	orange	*Brachygalba salmoni*	Jacamar sombre
Trogon rufus	Trogon aurore	*Galbula ruficauda*	Jacamar à queue
Trogon melanurus	Trogon à queue noire		rousse
Trogon massena	Trogon de Masséna	*Jacamerops aurea*	Grand Jacamar
Trogon clathratus	Trogon échelette		
Euptilotis neoxenus	Trogon oreillard	RAMPHASTIDAE	
Pharomachrus		*Capito*	Cabézon à calotte
auriceps	Quetzal doré	*maculicoronatus*	tachetée
Pharomachrus	Quetzal	*Eubucco bourcierii*	Cabézon à tête rouge
mocinno	resplendissant	*Semnornis frantzii*	Cabézon de Frantzius
		Aulacorhynchus	
UPUPIDAE		*prasinus*	Toucanet émeraude
Upupa epops	Huppe fasciée	*Pteroglossus*	
		torquatus	Araçari à collier
TODIDAE		*Pteroglossus frantzii*	Araçari de Frantzius
Todus multicolor	Todier de Cuba	*Selenidera spectabilis*	Toucanet à oreilles
Todus subulatus	Todier à bec large		d'or
Todus angustirostris	Todier à bec étroit	*Ramphastos*	
Todus todus	Todier de la	*sulfuratus*	Toucan à carène
	Jamaïque		

Ramphastos
   swainsonii — Toucan de Swainson

PICIDAE
Jynx torquilla — Torcol fourmilier
Picumnus olivaceus — Picumne olivâtre
Nesoctites
   micromegas — Picumne des Antilles
Melanerpes lewis — Pic de Lewis
Melanerpes
   herminieri — Pic de la Guadeloupe
Melanerpes
   portoricensis — Pic de Porto Rico
Melanerpes
   erythrocephalus — Pic à tête rouge
Melanerpes
   formicivorus — Pic glandivore
Melanerpes
   chrysauchen — Pic masqué
Melanerpes
   pucherani — Pic de Pucheran
Melanerpes striatus — Pic d'Hispaniola
Melanerpes
   radiolatus — Pic de la Jamaïque
Melanerpes
   chrysogenys — Pic élégant
Melanerpes
   hypopolius — Pic alezan
Melanerpes
   pygmaeus — Pic du Yucatan
Melanerpes
   rubricapillus — Pic à couronne rouge
Melanerpes
   uropygialis — Pic des saguaros
Melanerpes
   hoffmannii — Pic de Hoffman
Melanerpes aurifrons — Pic à front doré
Melanerpes carolinus — Pic à ventre roux
Melanerpes
   superciliaris — Pic à sourcils noirs
Sphyrapicus
   thyroideus — Pic de Williamson
Sphyrapicus varius — Pic maculé
Sphyrapicus nuchalis — Pic à nuque rouge
Sphyrapicus ruber — Pic à poitrine rouge
Xiphidiopicus
   percussus — Pic poignardé
Dendrocopos major — Pic épeiche
Picoides scalaris — Pic arlequin
Picoides nuttallii — Pic de Nuttall
Picoides pubescens — Pic mineur
Picoides villosus — Pic chevelu
Picoides stricklandi — Pic de Strickland
Picoides borealis — Pic à face blanche
Picoides albolarvatus — Pic à tête blanche
Picoides tridactylus — Pic tridactyle
Picoides arcticus — Pic à dos noir
Veniliornis fumigatus — Pic enfumé
Veniliornis kirkii — Pic à croupion rouge
Piculus simplex — Pic à ailes rousses
Piculus callopterus — Pic bridé
Piculus
   chrysochloros — Pic vert-doré
Piculus rubiginosus — Pic or-olive

Piculus auricularis — Pic à tête grise
Colaptes punctigula — Pic de Cayenne
Colaptes auratus — Pic flamboyant
Colaptes chrysoides — Pic chrysoïde
Colaptes fernandinae — Pic de Fernandina
Celeus loricatus — Pic cannelle
Celeus castaneus — Pic roux
Dryocopus lineatus — Pic ouentou
Dryocopus pileatus — Grand Pic
Campephilus
   haematogaster — Pic superbe
Campephilus
   melanoleucos — Pic de Malherbe
Campephilus
   guatemalensis — Pic à bec clair
Campephilus
   principalis — Pic à bec ivoire
Campephilus
   imperialis — Pic impérial

FURNARIIDAE
Synallaxis albescens — Synallaxe albane
Synallaxis brachyura — Synallaxe ardoisé
Synallaxis
   erythrothorax — Synallaxe à poitrine rousse
Cranioleuca
   erythrops — Synallaxe à face rouge
Cranioleuca vulpina — Synallaxe renard
Xenerpestes minlosi — Queue-grise des feuilles

Premnoplex
   brunnescens — Anabasitte tachetée
Margarornis bellulus — Anabasitte superbe
Margarornis
   rubiginosus — Anabasitte rousse
Pseudocolaptes
   lawrencii — Anabate chamois
Hyloctistes subulatus — Anabate forestier
Syndactyla subalaris — Anabate vergeté
Anabacerthia
   variegaticeps — Anabate à lunettes
Philydor fuscipennis — Anabate à croupion roux
Philydor rufus — Anabate roux
Automolus
   ochrolaemus — Anabate à gorge fauve
Automolus
   rubiginosus — Anabate rubigineux
Thripadectes
   rufobrunneus — Anabate des ravins
Xenops minutus — Sittine brune
Xenops rutilans — Sittine striée
Sclerurus mexicanus — Sclérure à gorge rousse
Sclerurus albigularis — Sclérure à gorge grise
Sclerurus
   guatemalensis — Sclérure écaillé
Lochmias nematura — Picerthie de Saint-Hilaire

DENDROCOLAPTIDAE
Dendrocincla
   fuliginosa — Grimpar enfumé
Dendrocincla
   anabatina — Grimpar à ailes rousses

Dendrocincla		*Herpsilochmus*	
homochroa	Grimpar roux	*rufimarginatus*	Grisin à ailes rousses
Sittasomus		*Microrhopias*	
griseicapillus	Grimpar fauvette	*quixensis*	Grisin étoilé
Deconychura	Grimpar à longue	*Formicivora grisea*	Grisin de Cayenne
longicauda	queue	*Terenura callinota*	Grisin à croupion
Glyphorynchus			roux
spirurus	Grimpar bec-en-coin	*Cercomacra*	
Xiphocolaptes		*tyrannina*	Grisin sombre
promero-		*Cercomacra*	
pirhynchus	Grimpar géant	*nigricans*	Grisin de jais
Dendrocolaptes		*Gymnocichla*	
sanctihomae	Grimpar vermiculé	*nudiceps*	Alapi à tête nue
Dendrocolaptes		*Myrmeciza longipes*	Alapi à ventre blanc
picumnus	Grimpar varié	*Myrmeciza exsul*	Alapi à dos roux
Xiphorhynchus picus	Grimpar talapiot	*Myrmeciza*	
Xiphorhynchus		*laemosticta*	Alapi tabac
susurrans	Grimpar cacao	*Myrmeciza*	
Xiphorhynchus		*immaculata*	Alapi immaculé
flavigaster	Grimpar à bec ivoire	*Hylophylax*	
Xiphorhynchus		*naevioides*	Fourmilier grivelé
lachrymosus	Grimpar maillé	*Myrmornis torquata*	Palicour de Cayenne
Xiphorhynchus		*Gymnopithys*	Fourmilier à joues
erythropygius	Grimpar tacheté	*leucaspis*	blanches
Lepidocolaptes		*Phaenostictus*	
leucogaster	Grimpar givré	*mcleannani*	Fourmilier ocellé
Lepidocolaptes			
souleyetii	Grimpar de Souleyet	**FORMICARIIDAE**	
Lepidocolaptes affinis	Grimpar moucheté	*Formicarius analis*	Tétéma coq-de-bois
Campylorhamphus		*Formicarius*	
trochilirostris	Grimpar à bec rouge	*nigricapillus*	Tétéma à tête noire
Campylorhamphus		*Formicarius*	Tétéma à poitrine
pusillus	Grimpar à bec brun	*rufipectus*	rousse
		Pittasoma michleri	Grallaire à tête noire
		Grallaria	
THAMNOPHILIDAE		*guatimalensis*	Grallaire écaillée
Cymbilaimus lineatus	Batara fascié	*Hylopezus*	
Taraba major	Grand Batara	*perspicillatus*	Grallaire à lunettes
Thamnophilus		*Hylopezus dives*	Grallaire buissonnière
doliatus	Batara rayé	*Grallaricula*	
Thamnophilus		*flavirostris*	Grallaire ocrée
nigriceps	Batara noir		
Thamnophilus		**RHINOCRYPTIDAE**	
bridgesi	Batara capucin	*Scytalopus*	
Thamnophilus		*panamensis*	Mérulaxe du Panama
atrinucha	Batara à nuque noire	*Scytalopus*	
Xenornis setifrons	Batara masqué	*chocoensis*	Mérulaxe du Choco
Thamnistes		*Scytalopus*	
anabatinus	Batara rousset	*argentifrons*	Mérulaxe argenté
Dysithamnus mentalis	Batara gorgeret		
Dysithamnus		**TYRANNIDAE**	
striaticeps	Batara strié	*Ornithion semiflavum*	Tyranneau à ventre
Dysithamnus			jaune
puncticeps	Batara ponctué	*Ornithion*	Tyranneau à tête
Myrmotherula		*brunneicapillum*	brune
brachyura	Myrmidon pygmée	*Camptostoma*	
Myrmotherula	Myrmidon du	*imberbe*	Tyranneau imberbe
surinamensis	Surinam	*Camptostoma*	
Myrmotherula		*obsoletum*	Tyranneau passegris
fulviventris	Myrmidon fauve	*Phaeomyias murina*	Tyranneau souris
Myrmotherula	Myrmidon à flancs	*Nesotriccus ridgwayi*	Tyranneau de Cocos
axillaris	blancs	*Capsiempis flaveola*	Tyranneau flavéole
Myrmotherula		*Tyrannulus elatus*	Tyranneau roitelet
schisticolor	Myrmidon ardoisé	*Myiopagis gaimardii*	Élénie de Gaimard

Myiopagis caniceps	Élénie grise
Myiopagis cotta	Élénie de la Jamaïque
Myiopagis viridicata	Élénie verdâtre
Elaenia martinica	Élénie siffleuse
Elaenia flavogaster	Élénie à ventre jaune
Elaenia chiriquensis	Élénie menue
Elaenia frantzii	Élénie montagnarde
Elaenia fallax	Élénie sara
Serpophaga cinerea	Tyranneau des torrents
Mionectes olivaceus	Pipromorphe olive
Mionectes oleagineus	Pipromorphe roussâtre
Leptopogon amaurocephalus	Pipromorphe à tête brune
Leptopogon superciliaris	Pipromorphe à tête grise
Phylloscartes flavovirens	Tyranneau jaune-vert
Phylloscartes superciliaris	Tyranneau à sourcils roux
Phyllomyias burmeisteri	Tyranneau pattu
Phyllomyias griseiceps	Tyranneau nain
Zimmerius vilissimus	Tyranneau gobemoucheron
Sublegatus arenarum	Tyranneau des palétuviers
Pseudotriccus pelzelni	Tyranneau bronzé
Myiornis atricapillus	Microtyran à calotte noire
Lophotriccus pileatus	Microtyran chevelu
Lophotriccus pilaris	Microtyran coiffé
Oncostoma cinereigulare	Tyranneau à bec courbe
Oncostoma olivaceum	Tyranneau de Lawrence
Poecilotriccus sylvia	Todirostre de Desmarest
Todirostrum cinereum	Todirostre familier
Todirostrum nigriceps	Todirostre à tête noire
Cnipodectes subbrunneus	Platyrhynque brun
Rhynchocyclus brevirostris	Platyrhynque à bec court
Rhynchocyclus olivaceus	Platyrhynque olivâtre
Tolmomyias sulphurescens	Platyrhynque jaune-olive
Tolmomyias assimilis	Platyrhynque à miroir
Platyrinchus cancrominus	Platyrhynque à queue courte
Platyrinchus mystaceus	Platyrhynque à moustaches
Platyrinchus coronatus	Platyrhynque à tête d'or
Onychorhynchus coronatus	Moucherolle royal
Terenotriccus erythrurus	Moucherolle rougequeue
Myiobius villosus	Moucherolle hérissé
Myiobius sulphureipygius	Moucherolle à croupion jaune
Myiobius atricaudus	Moucherolle à queue noire
Myiophobus fasciatus	Moucherolle fascié
Lathrotriccus euleri	Moucherolle d'Euler
Aphanotriccus capitalis	Moucherolle à poitrine fauve
Aphanotriccus audax	Moucherolle à bec noir
Xenotriccus callizonus	Moucherolle ceinturé
Xenotriccus mexicanus	Moucherolle aztèque
Mitrephanes phaeocercus	Moucherolle huppé
Contopus cooperi	Moucherolle à côtés olive
Contopus pertinax	Moucherolle de Coues
Contopus lugubris	Moucherolle ombré
Contopus ochraceus	Moucherolle ocré
Contopus sordidulus	Pioui de l'Ouest
Contopus virens	Pioui de l'Est
Contopus cinereus	Moucherolle cendré
Contopus caribaeus	Moucherolle tête-fou
Contopus pallidus	Moucherolle de la Jamaïque
Contopus hispaniolensis	Moucherolle d'Hispaniola
Contopus latirostris	Moucherolle gobemouche
Empidonax flaviventris	Moucherolle à ventre jaune
Empidonax virescens	Moucherolle vert
Empidonax alnorum	Moucherolle des aulnes
Empidonax traillii	Moucherolle des saules
Empidonax albigularis	Moucherolle à gorge blanche
Empidonax minimus	Moucherolle tchébec
Empidonax hammondii	Moucherolle de Hammond
Empidonax wrightii	Moucherolle gris
Empidonax oberholseri	Moucherolle sombre
Empidonax affinis	Moucherolle des pins
Empidonax difficilis	Moucherolle côtier
Empidonax occidentalis	Moucherolle des ravins
Empidonax flavescens	Moucherolle jaunâtre
Empidonax fulvifrons	Moucherolle beige
Empidonax atriceps	Moucherolle à tête noire
Sayornis nigricans	Moucherolle noir
Sayornis phoebe	Moucherolle phébi
Sayornis saya	Moucherolle à ventre roux
Pyrocephalus rubinus	Moucherolle vermillon

Fluvicola pica	Moucherolle pie	*Tyrannus forficatus*	Tyran à longue queue
Colonia colonus	Moucherolle à longs brins	*Tyrannus savana*	Tyran des savanes
Machetornis rixosus	Moucherolle querelleur	**INCERTAE SEDIS**	
		Sapayoa aenigma	Sapayoa à bec large
Attila spadiceus	Attila à croupion jaune	*Schiffornis turdinus*	Antriade turdoïde
		Piprites griseiceps	Piprite à tête grise
Sirystes sibilator	Tyran siffleur	*Lipaugus unirufus*	Piauhau roux
Rhytipterna holerythra	Aulia roux	*Laniocera rufescens*	Aulia tacheté
Myiarchus yucatanensis	Tyran du Yucatan	*Pachyramphus versicolor*	Bécarde barrée
Myiarchus barbirostris	Tyran triste	*Pachyramphus rufus*	Bécarde cendrée
Myiarchus tuberculifer	Tyran olivâtre	*Pachyramphus cinnamomeus*	Bécarde cannelle
Myiarchus panamensis	Tyran du Panama	*Pachyramphus polychopterus*	Bécarde à ailes blanches
Myiarchus cinerascens	Tyran à gorge cendrée	*Pachyramphus albogriseus*	Bécarde pie
Myiarchus nuttingi	Tyran de Nutting	*Pachyramphus major*	Bécarde du Mexique
Myiarchus crinitus	Tyran huppé	*Pachyramphus aglaiae*	Bécarde à gorge rose
Myiarchus tyrannulus	Tyran de Wied	*Pachyramphus homochrous*	Bécarde unicolore
Myiarchus nugator	Tyran bavard	*Pachyramphus niger*	Bécarde de la Jamaïque
Myiarchus validus	Tyran à queue rousse		
Myiarchus sagrae	Tyran de La Sagra	*Tityra semifasciata*	Tityre masqué
Myiarchus stolidus	Tyran grosse-tête	*Tityra inquisitor*	Tityre à tête noire
Myiarchus antillarum	Tyran de Porto Rico		
Myiarchus oberi	Tyran janeau	**COTINGIDAE**	
Deltarhynchus flammulatus	Tyran flammé	*Cotinga amabilis*	Cotinga céleste
Pitangus lictor	Tyran licteur	*Cotinga ridgwayi*	Cotinga turquoise
Pitangus sulphuratus	Tyran quiquivi	*Cotinga nattererii*	Cotinga bleu
Megarynchus pitangua	Tyran pitangua	*Carpodectes hopkei*	Cotinga blanc
		Carpodectes antoniae	Cotinga à bec jaune
Myiozetetes cayanensis	Tyran de Cayenne	*Carpodectes nitidus*	Cotinga neigeux
Myiozetetes similis	Tyran sociable	*Querula purpurata*	Coracine noire
Myiozetetes granadensis	Tyran à tête grise	*Cephalopterus glabricollis*	Coracine ombrelle
Conopias albovittata	Tyran diadème	*Procnias tricarunculata*	Araponga tricaronculé
Myiodynastes hemichrysus	Tyran à ventre d'or		
Myiodynastes chrysocephalus	Tyran à casque d'or	**PIPRIDAE**	
		Chloropipo holochlora	Manakin vert
Myiodynastes maculatus	Tyran audacieux	*Manacus candei*	Manakin à col blanc
Myiodynastes luteiventris	Tyran tigré	*Manacus aurantiacus*	Manakin à col orange
Legatus leucophaius	Tyran pirate	*Manacus vitellinus*	Manakin à col d'or
Empidonomus varius	Tyran tacheté	*Corapipo altera*	Manakin à fraise
Tyrannus melancholicus	Tyran mélancolique	*Chiroxiphia lanceolata*	Manakin lancéolé
Tyrannus couchii	Tyran de Couch	*Chiroxiphia linearis*	Manakin fastueux
Tyrannus vociferans	Tyran de Cassin	*Pipra pipra*	Manakin à tête blanche
Tyrannus crassirostris	Tyran à bec épais	*Pipra coronata*	Manakin à tête bleue
Tyrannus verticalis	Tyran de l'Ouest	*Pipra erythrocephala*	Manakin à tête d'or
Tyrannus tyrannus	Tyran tritri	*Pipra mentalis*	Manakin à cuisses jaunes
Tyrannus dominicensis	Tyran gris		
Tyrannus caudifasciatus	Tyran tête-police	**OXYRUNCIDAE**	
		Oxyruncus cristatus	Oxyrhynque huppé
Tyrannus cubensis	Tyran géant	**MELIPHAGIDAE**	
		Moho braccatus	Moho de Kauai
		Moho apicalis	Moho d'Oahu

Moho bishopi	Moho de Bishop
Moho nobilis	Moho d'Hawaï
Chaetoptila	
angustipluma	Méliphage kioéa

LANIIDAE

Lanius cristatus	Pie-grièche brune
Lanius ludovicianus	Pie-grièche migratrice
Lanius excubitor	Pie-grièche grise

VIREONIDAE

Vireo brevipennis	Viréo ardoisé
Vireo griseus	Viréo aux yeux blancs
Vireo crassirostris	Viréo à bec fort
Vireo pallens	Viréo des mangroves
Vireo bairdi	Viréo de Cozumel
Vireo caribaeus	Viréo de San Andrés
Vireo modestus	Viréo de la Jamaïque
Vireo gundlachii	Viréo de Cuba
Vireo latimeri	Viréo de Porto Rico
Vireo nanus	Viréo d'Hispaniola
Vireo bellii	Viréo de Bell
Vireo atricapillus	Viréo à tête noire
Vireo nelsoni	Viréo nain
Vireo vicinior	Viréo gris
Vireo osburni	Viréo d'Osburn
Vireo flavifrons	Viréo à gorge jaune
Vireo plumbeus	Viréo plombé
Vireo cassinii	Viréo de Cassin
Vireo solitarius	Viréo à tête bleue
Vireo carmioli	Viréo à ailes jaunes
Vireo huttoni	Viréo de Hutton
Vireo hypochryseus	Viréo doré
Vireo gilvus	Viréo mélodieux
Vireo leucophrys	Viréo à calotte brune
Vireo philadelphicus	Viréo de Philadelphie
Vireo olivaceus	Viréo aux yeux rouges
Vireo flavoviridis	Viréo jaune-verdâtre
Vireo altiloquus	Viréo à moustaches
Vireo magister	Viréo du Yucatan
Hylophilus flavipes	Viréon à pattes claires
Hylophilus ochraceiceps	Viréon à calotte rousse
Hylophilus aurantiifrons	Viréon à front d'or
Hylophilus decurtatus	Viréon menu
Vireolanius melitophrys	Smaragdan ceinturé
Vireolanius pulchellus	Smaragdan émeraude
Vireolanius eximius	Smaragdan à sourcils jaunes
Cyclarhis gujanensis	Sourciroux mélodieux

CORVIDAE

Perisoreus canadensis	Mésangeai du Canada
Cyanocitta stelleri	Geai de Steller
Cyanocitta cristata	Geai bleu
Calocitta colliei	Geai à face noire
Calocitta formosa	Geai à face blanche
Cyanocorax dickeyi	Geai panaché
Cyanocorax affinis	Geai à poitrine noire
Cyanocorax yncas	Geai vert
Cyanocorax morio	Geai enfumé
Cyanocorax melanocyaneus	Geai houppé
Cyanocorax sanblasianus	Geai de San Blas
Cyanocorax yucatanicus	Geai du Yucatan
Cyanocorax beecheii	Geai à dos violet
Cyanolyca cucullata	Geai couronné
Cyanolyca pumilo	Geai à gorge noire
Cyanolyca nana	Geai nain
Cyanolyca argentigula	Geai à gorge argentée
Cyanolyca mirabilis	Geai masqué
Aphelocoma coerulescens	Geai à gorge blanche
Aphelocoma insularis	Geai de Santa Cruz
Aphelocoma californica	Geai buissonnier
Aphelocoma ultramarina	Geai du Mexique
Aphelocoma unicolor	Geai unicolore
Gymnorhinus cyanocephalus	Geai des pinèdes
Nucifraga columbiana	Cassenoix d'Amérique
Pica pica	Pie bavarde
Pica nuttalli	Pie à bec jaune
Corvus monedula	Choucas des tours
Corvus brachyrhynchos	Corneille d'Amérique
Corvus caurinus	Corneille d'Alaska
Corvus palmarum	Corneille palmiste
Corvus nasicus	Corneille de Cuba
Corvus leucognaphalus	Corneille d'Hispaniola
Corvus jamaicensis	Corneille de la Jamaïque
Corvus imparatus	Corneille du Mexique
Corvus sinaloae	Corneille du Sinaloa
Corvus ossifragus	Corneille de rivage
Corvus hawaiiensis	Corneille d'Hawaï
Corvus cryptoleucus	Corbeau à cou blanc
Corvus corax	Grand Corbeau

MONARCHIDAE

Chasiempis sandwichensis	Monarque élépaïo

ALAUDIDAE

Alauda arvensis	Alouette des champs
Eremophila alpestris	Alouette hausse-col

HIRUNDINIDAE

Progne subis	Hirondelle noire
Progne cryptoleuca	Hirondelle de Cuba
Progne dominicensis	Hirondelle à ventre blanc
Progne sinaloae	Hirondelle du Sinaloa

Progne chalybea	Hirondelle chalybée	**TROGLODYTIDAE**	
Progne elegans	Hirondelle gracieuse	*Donacobius*	
Progne tapera	Hirondelle tapère	*atricapillus*	Troglodyte à miroir
Tachycineta bicolor	Hirondelle bicolore	*Campylorhynchus*	Troglodyte à tête
Tachycineta albilinea	Hirondelle des	*albobrunneus*	blanche
	mangroves	*Campylorhynchus*	
Tachycineta		*zonatus*	Troglodyte zoné
euchrysea	Hirondelle dorée	*Campylorhynchus*	
Tachycineta	Hirondelle à face	*megalopterus*	Troglodyte zébré
thalassina	blanche	*Campylorhynchus*	
Tachycineta	Hirondelle des	*chiapensis*	Troglodyte géant
cyaneoviridis	Bahamas	*Campylorhynchus*	Troglodyte à nuque
Pygochelidon	Hirondelle bleu et	*rufinucha*	rousse
cyanoleuca	blanc	*Campylorhynchus*	
Notiochelidon pileata	Hirondelle à tête	*gularis*	Troglodyte tacheté
	noire	*Campylorhynchus*	Troglodyte de
Neochelidon tibialis	Hirondelle à cuisses	*jocosus*	Boucard
	blanches	*Campylorhynchus*	Troglodyte du
Stelgidopteryx	Hirondelle à ailes	*yucatanicus*	Yucatan
serripennis	hérissées	*Campylorhynchus*	
Stelgidopteryx	Hirondelle à gorge	*brunneicapillus*	Troglodyte des cactus
ruficollis	rousse	*Salpinctes obsoletus*	Troglodyte des
Riparia riparia	Hirondelle de rivage		rochers
Petrochelidon	Hirondelle à front	*Catherpes mexicanus*	Troglodyte des
pyrrhonota	blanc		canyons
Petrochelidon fulva	Hirondelle à front		
	brun	*Hylorchilus*	
Hirundo rustica	Hirondelle rustique	*sumichrasti*	Troglodyte à bec fin
Delichon urbica	Hirondelle de fenêtre	*Hylorchilus navai*	Troglodyte de Nava
		Thryothorus spadix	Troglodyte moine
		Thryothorus	Troglodyte à gorge
PARIDAE		*atrogularis*	noire
Poecile carolinensis	Mésange de Caroline	*Thryothorus*	Troglodyte à ventre
Poecile atricapillus	Mésange à tête noire	*fasciatoventris*	noir
Poecile gambeli	Mésange de Gambel	*Thryothorus*	Troglodyte à calotte
Poecile sclateri	Mésange grise	*nigricapillus*	noire
Poecile rufescens	Mésange à dos	*Thryothorus*	Troglodyte des
	marron	*semibadius*	ruisseaux
Poecile hudsonicus	Mésange à tête brune	*Thryothorus*	
Poecile cinctus	Mésange lapone	*leucopogon*	Troglodyte balafré
Baeolophus		*Thryothorus*	
wollweberi	Mésange arlequin	*thoracicus*	Troglodyte flammé
Baeolophus inornatus	Mésange unicolore	*Thryothorus rutilus*	Troglodyte des
Baeolophus griseus	Mésange des pinèdes		halliers
Baeolophus bicolor	Mésange bicolore	*Thryothorus*	Troglodyte à poitrine
		maculipectus	tachetée
		Thryothorus rufalbus	Troglodyte rufalbin
REMIZIDAE		*Thryothorus sinaloa*	Troglodyte du
Auriparus flaviceps	Auripare verdin		Sinaloa
		Thryothorus	
		pleurostictus	Troglodyte barré
AEGITHALIDAE		*Thryothorus*	Troglodyte de
Psaltriparus minimus	Mésange	*ludovicianus*	Caroline
	buissonnière	*Thryothorus felix*	Troglodyte joyeux
		Thryothorus leucotis	Troglodyte à face
			pâle
SITTIDAE		*Thryothorus*	
Sitta canadensis	Sittelle à poitrine	*modestus*	Troglodyte modeste
	rousse	*Thryomanes bewickii*	Troglodyte de
Sitta carolinensis	Sittelle à poitrine		Bewick
	blanche	*Thryomanes sissonii*	Troglodyte de
Sitta pygmaea	Sittelle pygmée		Socorro
Sitta pusilla	Sittelle à tête brune	*Ferminia cerverai*	Troglodyte de Zapata
		Troglodytes aedon	Troglodyte familier
CERTHIIDAE			
Certhia americana	Grimpereau brun		

Troglodytes tanneri	Troglodyte de Clarion	*Polioptila albiloris*	Gobemoucheron à face blanche
Troglodytes rufociliatus	Troglodyte à sourcils roux	*Polioptila plumbea*	Gobemoucheron tropical
Troglodytes ochraceus	Troglodyte ocré	*Polioptila schistaceigula*	Gobemoucheron ardoisé
Troglodytes troglodytes	Troglodyte mignon	**MUSCICAPIDAE**	
Cistothorus platensis	Troglodyte à bec court	*Ficedula narcissina*	Gobemouche narcisse
Cistothorus palustris	Troglodyte des marais	*Ficedula mugimaki*	Gobemouche mugimaki
Uropsila leucogastra	Troglodyte à ventre blanc	*Ficedula parva*	Gobemouche nain
Thryorchilus browni	Troglodyte des volcans	*Muscicapa sibirica*	Gobemouche de Sibérie
Henicorhina leucosticta	Troglodyte à poitrine blanche	*Muscicapa griseisticta*	Gobemouche à taches grises
Henicorhina leucophrys	Troglodyte à poitrine grise	*Muscicapa dauurica*	Gobemouche brun
Microcerculus philomela	Troglodyte philomèle	**TURDIDAE**	
Microcerculus marginatus	Troglodyte siffleur	*Luscinia calliope*	Rossignol calliope
Cyphorhinus phaeocephalus	Troglodyte chanteur	*Luscinia svecica*	Gorgebleue à miroir
		Luscinia cyane	Rossignol bleu
CINCLIDAE		*Tarsiger cyanurus*	Rossignol à flancs roux
Cinclus mexicanus	Cincle d'Amérique	*Copsychus malabaricus*	Shama à croupion blanc
PYCNONOTIDAE		*Oenanthe oenanthe*	Traquet motteux
Pycnonotus cafer	Bulbul à ventre rouge	*Saxicola torquata*	Tarier pâtre
Pycnonotus jocosus	Bulbul orphée	*Sialia sialis*	Merlebleu de l'Est
		Sialia mexicana	Merlebleu de l'Ouest
REGULIDAE		*Sialia currucoides*	Merlebleu azuré
Regulus satrapa	Roitelet à couronne dorée	*Myadestes townsendi*	Solitaire de Townsend
Regulus calendula	Roitelet à couronne rubis	*Myadestes occidentalis*	Solitaire à dos brun
		Myadestes elisabeth	Solitaire de Cuba
SYLVIIDAE		*Myadestes genibarbis*	Solitaire siffleur
Cettia diphone	Bouscarle chanteuse	*Myadestes melanops*	Solitaire masqué
Locustella ochotensis	Locustelle de Middendorff	*Myadestes coloratus*	Solitaire varié
		Myadestes unicolor	Solitaire ardoisé
Locustella lanceolata	Locustelle lancéolée	*Myadestes myadestinus*	Solitaire kamao
Acrocephalus familiaris	Rousserolle obscure	*Myadestes woahensis*	Solitaire d'Oahu
Phylloscopus sibilatrix	Pouillot siffleur	*Myadestes lanaiensis*	Solitaire de Lanai
Phylloscopus fuscatus	Pouillot brun	*Myadestes obscurus*	Solitaire d'Hawaï
Phylloscopus borealis	Pouillot boréal	*Myadestes palmeri*	Solitaire puaïohi
Microbates cinereiventris	Microbate cendré	*Catharus gracilirostris*	Grive à bec noir
Ramphocaenus melanurus	Microbate à long bec	*Catharus aurantiirostris*	Grive à bec orange
Polioptila caerulea	Gobemoucheron gris-bleu	*Catharus fuscater*	Grive ardoisée
		Catharus occidentalis	Grive roussâtre
Polioptila lembeyei	Gobemoucheron de Cuba	*Catharus frantzii*	Grive à calotte rousse
Polioptila californica	Gobemoucheron de Californie	*Catharus mexicanus*	Grive à tête noire
		Catharus dryas	Grive tavelée
Polioptila melanura	Gobemoucheron à queue noire	*Catharus fuscescens*	Grive fauve
		Catharus minimus	Grive à joues grises
Polioptila nigriceps	Gobemoucheron à coiffe noire	*Catharus bicknelli*	Grive de Bicknell
		Catharus ustulatus	Grive à dos olive
		Catharus guttatus	Grive solitaire
		Hylocichla mustelina	Grive des bois
		Turdus merula	Merle noir
		Turdus obscurus	Merle obscur
		Turdus naumanni	Grive de Naumann

Turdus pilaris	Grive litorne	*Melanotis hypoleucus*	Moqueur bleu et blanc
Turdus iliacus	Grive mauvis		
Turdus nigrescens	Merle fuligineux	*Margarops fuscus*	Moqueur grivotte
Turdus infuscatus	Merle enfumé	*Margarops fuscatus*	Moqueur corossol
Turdus plebejus	Merle de montagne	*Cinclocerthia*	
Turdus fumigatus	Merle cacao	*ruficauda*	Trembleur brun
Turdus obsoletus	Merle cul-blanc	*Cinclocerthia*	
Turdus grayi	Merle fauve	*gutturalis*	Trembleur gris
Turdus nudigenis	Merle à lunettes		
Turdus jamaicensis	Merle aux yeux blancs	**STURNIDAE**	
		Sturnus vulgaris	Étourneau sansonnet
Turdus assimilis	Merle à gorge blanche	*Acridotheres tristis*	Martin triste
		Acridotheres	
Turdus rufopalliatus	Merle à dos roux	*cristatellus*	Martin huppé
Turdus rufitorques	Merle à col roux	*Gracula religiosa*	Mainate religieux
Turdus migratorius	Merle d'Amérique		
Turdus swalesi	Merle de La Selle	**PRUNELLIDAE**	
Turdus aurantius	Merle à miroir	*Prunella montanella*	Accenteur montanelle
Turdus ravidus	Merle de Grande Caïman	**MOTACILLIDAE**	
Turdus plumbeus	Merle vantard	*Motacilla flava*	Bergeronnette printanière
Cichlherminia		*Motacilla citreola*	Bergeronnette citrine
lherminieri	Grive à pieds jaunes	*Motacilla cinerea*	Bergeronnette des ruisseaux
Ixoreus naevius	Grive à collier		
Ridgwayia pinicola	Grive aztèque	*Motacilla alba*	Bergeronnette grise
		Motacilla lugens	Bergeronnette lugubre
TIMALIIDAE		*Anthus trivialis*	Pipit des arbres
Garrulax pectoralis	Garrulaxe à plastron	*Anthus hodgsoni*	Pipit à dos olive
Garrulax canorus	Garrulaxe hoamy	*Anthus gustavi*	Pipit de la Petchora
Leiothrix lutea	Léiothrix jaune	*Anthus cervinus*	Pipit à gorge rousse
Chamaea fasciata	Cama brune	*Anthus rubescens*	Pipit d'Amérique
		Anthus spragueii	Pipit de Sprague
ZOSTEROPIDAE		*Anthus lutescens*	Pipit jaunâtre
Zosterops japonicus	Zostérops du Japon		
		BOMBYCILLIDAE	
MIMIDAE		*Bombycilla garrulus*	Jaseur boréal
Dumetella		*Bombycilla cedrorum*	Jaseur d'Amérique
carolinensis	Moqueur chat		
Melanoptila		**PTILOGONATIDAE**	
glabrirostris	Moqueur noir	*Phainoptila*	Phénoptile noir et jaune
Mimus polyglottos	Moqueur polyglotte	*melanoxantha*	
Mimus gilvus	Moqueur des savanes	*Ptilogonys cinereus*	Ptilogon cendré
Mimus gundlachii	Moqueur des Bahamas	*Ptilogonys caudatus*	Ptilogon à longue queue
Oreoscoptes	Moqueur des	*Phainopepla nitens*	Phénopèple luisant
montanus	armoises		
Mimodes graysoni	Moqueur de Socorro	**DULIDAE**	
Toxostoma rufum	Moqueur roux	*Dulus dominicus*	Esclave palmiste
Toxostoma			
longirostre	Moqueur à long bec	**PEUCEDRAMIDAE**	
Toxostoma guttatum	Moqueur de Cozumel	*Peucedramus*	
Toxostoma cinereum	Moqueur gris	*taeniatus*	Fauvine des pins
Toxostoma bendirei	Moqueur de Bendire		
Toxostoma ocellatum	Moqueur ocellé	**PARULIDAE**	
Toxostoma	Moqueur à bec	*Vermivora bachmanii*	Paruline de Bachman
curvirostre	courbe	*Vermivora pinus*	Paruline à ailes bleues
Toxostoma redivivum	Moqueur de California		
Toxostoma crissale	Moqueur cul-roux	*Vermivora*	Paruline à ailes dorées
Toxostoma lecontei	Moqueur de Le Conte	*chrysoptera*	
		Vermivora peregrina	Paruline obscure
Ramphocinclus	Moqueur gorge-	*Vermivora celata*	Paruline verdâtre
brachyurus	blanche	*Vermivora ruficapilla*	Paruline à joues grises
Melanotis			
caerulescens	Moqueur bleu		

Vermivora virginiae	Paruline de Virginia	Oporornis agilis	Paruline à gorge grise
Vermivora crissalis	Paruline de Colima		
Vermivora luciae	Paruline de Lucy	Oporornis philadelphia	Paruline triste
Parula gutturalis	Paruline embrasée	Oporornis tolmiei	Paruline des buissons
Parula superciliosa	Paruline à croissant	Geothlypis trichas	Paruline masquée
Parula americana	Paruline à collier	Geothlypis beldingi	Paruline de Belding
Parula pitiayumi	Paruline à joues noires	Geothlypis flavovelata	Paruline à couronne jaune
Dendroica petechia	Paruline jaune	Geothlypis rostrata	Paruline des Bahamas
Dendroica pensylvanica	Paruline à flancs marron	Geothlypis semiflava	Paruline des bambous
Dendroica magnolia	Paruline à tête cendrée	Geothlypis speciosa	Paruline à face noire
Dendroica tigrina	Paruline tigrée	Geothlypis nelsoni	Paruline de Nelson
Dendroica caerulescens	Paruline bleue	Geothlypis aequinoctialis	Paruline équatoriale
Dendroica coronata	Paruline à croupion jaune	Geothlypis poliocephala	Paruline à calotte grise
Dendroica nigrescens	Paruline grise	Microligea palustris	Paruline aux yeux rouges
Dendroica chrysoparia	Paruline à dos noir	Teretistris fernandinae	Paruline de Fernandina
Dendroica virens	Paruline à gorge noire	Teretistris fornsi	Paruline d'Oriente
Dendroica townsendi	Paruline de Townsend	Leucopeza semperi	Paruline pied-blanc
		Wilsonia citrina	Paruline à capuchon
Dendroica occidentalis	Paruline à tête jaune	Wilsonia pusilla	Paruline à calotte noire
Dendroica fusca	Paruline à gorge orangée	Wilsonia canadensis	Paruline du Canada
Dendroica dominica	Paruline à gorge jaune	Cardellina rubrifrons	Paruline à face rouge
		Ergaticus ruber	Paruline rouge
Dendroica graciae	Paruline de Grace	Ergaticus versicolor	Paruline à tête rose
Dendroica adelaidae	Paruline d'Adélaïde	Myioborus pictus	Paruline à ailes blanches
Dendroica pityophila	Paruline à calotte verte	Myioborus miniatus	Paruline ardoisée
Dendroica pinus	Paruline des pins	Myioborus torquatus	Paruline ceinturée
Dendroica kirtlandii	Paruline de Kirtland	Euthlypis lachrymosa	Paruline des rochers
Dendroica discolor	Paruline des prés	Basileuterus culicivorus	Paruline à couronne dorée
Dendroica vitellina	Paruline des Caïmans	Basileuterus rufifrons	Paruline à calotte rousse
Dendroica palmarum	Paruline à couronne rousse	Basileuterus belli	Paruline à sourcils dorés
Dendroica castanea	Paruline à poitrine baie	Basileuterus melanogenys	Paruline sombre
Dendroica striata	Paruline rayée	Basileuterus ignotus	Paruline du Pirré
Dendroica cerulea	Paruline azurée	Basileuterus tristriatus	Paruline triligne
Dendroica plumbea	Paruline caféiette	Phaeothlypis fulvicauda	Paruline à croupion fauve
Dendroica pharetra	Paruline de la Jamaïque	Zeledonia coronata	Paruline de Zeledon
Dendroica angelae	Paruline d'Angela	Icteria virens	Paruline polyglotte
Catharopeza bishopi	Paruline de Saint-Vincent	Granatellus venustus	Paruline multicolore
		Granatellus sallaei	Paruline à plastron
Mniotilta varia	Paruline noir et blanc	Xenoligea montana	Paruline quatre-yeux
Setophaga ruticilla	Paruline flamboyante		
Protonotaria citrea	Paruline orangée	**COEREBIDAE**	
Helmitheros vermivorus	Paruline vermivore	Coereba flaveola	Sucrier à ventre jaune
Limnothlypis swainsonii	Paruline de Swainson		
Seiurus aurocapillus	Paruline couronnée	**THRAUPIDAE**	
Seiurus noveboracensis	Paruline des ruisseaux	Conirostrum leucogenys	Conirostre oreillard
Seiurus motacilla	Paruline hochequeue	Nesospingus speculiferus	Tangara de Porto Rico
Oporornis formosus	Paruline du Kentucky		

Chlorospingus ophthalmicus	Tangara des buissons	*Ramphocelus costaricensis*	Tangara du Costa Rica
Chlorospingus tacarcunae	Tangara du Tacarcuna	*Ramphocelus flammigerus*	Tangara flamboyant
Chlorospingus inornatus	Tangara du Pirré	*Spindalis zena*	Tangara à tête rayée
Chlorospingus pileatus	Tangara à sourcils brisés	*Thraupis episcopus*	Tangara évêque
Chlorospingus flavigularis	Tangara à gorge jaune	*Thraupis abbas*	Tangara à miroir jaune
Chlorospingus canigularis	Tangara à gorge grise	*Thraupis palmarum*	Tangara des palmiers
Hemithraupis flavicollis	Tangara à dos jaune	*Bangsia arcaei*	Tangara jaune et bleu
		Euphonia jamaica	Organiste de la Jamaïque
Chrysothlypis chrysomelaena	Tangara loriot	*Euphonia affinis*	Organiste de brousse
Phaenicophilus palmarum	Tangara à couronne noire	*Euphonia luteicapilla*	Organiste à calotte jaune
Phaenicophilus poliocephalus	Tangara quatre-yeux	*Euphonia laniirostris*	Organiste à bec épais
Calyptophilus tertius	Tangara de Wetmore	*Euphonia hirundinacea*	Organiste à gorge jaune
Calyptophilus frugivorus	Tangara cornichon	*Euphonia musica*	Organiste louis-d'or
Rhodinocichla rosea	Tangara quéo	*Euphonia elegantissima*	Organiste à capuchon
Mitrospingus cassinii	Tangara obscur	*Euphonia fulvicrissa*	Organiste cul-roux
Chlorothraupis carmioli	Tangara olive	*Euphonia imitans*	Organiste moucheté
		Euphonia gouldi	Organiste olive
Chlorothraupis olivacea	Tangara à lunettes	*Euphonia minuta*	Organiste cul-blanc
Eucometis penicillata	Tangara à tête grise	*Euphonia anneae*	Organiste à couronne rousse
Lanio aurantius	Tangara à gorge noire	*Euphonia xanthogaster*	Organiste à ventre orange
Lanio leucothorax	Tangara à gorge blanche	*Chlorophonia flavirostris*	Organiste à col jaune
Heterospingus rubrifrons	Tangara à croupion jaune	*Chlorophonia occipitalis*	Organiste à calotte bleue
Heterospingus xanthopygius	Tangara à sourcils roux	*Chlorophonia callophrys*	Organiste à sourcils jaunes
Tachyphonus luctuosus	Tangara à épaulettes blanches	*Tangara inornata*	Calliste gris
Tachyphonus delatrii	Tangara de Delattre	*Tangara cabanisi*	Calliste azuré
Tachyphonus rufus	Tangara à galons blancs	*Tangara palmeri*	Calliste or-gris
		Tangara florida	Calliste émeraude
Habia rubica	Tangara à couronne rouge	*Tangara icterocephala*	Calliste safran
Habia fuscicauda	Tangara à gorge rouge	*Tangara guttata*	Calliste tiqueté
		Tangara gyrola	Calliste rouverdin
Habia atrimaxillaris	Tangara à joues noires	*Tangara lavinia*	Calliste à ailes rousses
Piranga roseogularis	Tangara à gorge rose	*Tangara cucullata*	Calliste dos-bleu
Piranga flava	Tangara orangé	*Tangara larvata*	Calliste à coiffe d'or
Piranga rubra	Tangara vermillon	*Tangara dowii*	Calliste pailleté
Piranga olivacea	Tangara écarlate	*Tangara fucosa*	Calliste à nuque verte
Piranga ludoviciana	Tangara à tête rouge	*Dacnis venusta*	Dacnis à cuisses rouges
Piranga bidentata	Tangara à dos rayé	*Dacnis cayana*	Dacnis bleu
Piranga leucoptera	Tangara bifascié	*Dacnis viguieri*	Dacnis vert
Piranga erythrocephala	Tangara érythrocéphale	*Chlorophanes spiza*	Guit-guit émeraude
		Cyanerpes lucidus	Guit-guit brillant
Ramphocelus sanguinolentus	Tangara ceinturé	*Cyanerpes caeruleus*	Guit-guit céruléen
		Cyanerpes cyaneus	Guit-guit saï
Ramphocelus dimidiatus	Tangara à dos rouge	*Tersina viridis*	Tersine hirondelle
Ramphocelus passerinii	Tangara à croupion rouge	**EMBERIZIDAE**	
		Volatinia jacarina	Jacarini noir
		Sporophila schistacea	Sporophile ardoisé
		Sporophila americana	Sporophile variable

Sporophila torqueola	Sporophile à col blanc	*Pipilo maculatus*	Tohi tacheté
Sporophila nigricollis	Sporophile à ventre jaune	*Pipilo erythrophthalmus*	Tohi à flancs roux
Sporophila minuta	Sporophile petit-louis	*Pipilo albicollis*	Tohi à gorge blanche
Oryzoborus nuttingi	Sporophile de Nutting	*Pipilo fuscus*	Tohi des canyons
		Pipilo crissalis	Tohi de Californie
Oryzoborus funereus	Sporophile à bec fort	*Pipilo aberti*	Tohi d'Abert
Amaurospiza concolor	Sporophile bleu	*Aimophila ruficauda*	Bruant ligné
Melopyrrha nigra	Sporophile négrito	*Aimophila humeralis*	Bruant à plastron
Tiaris canora	Sporophile petit-chanteur	*Aimophila mystacalis*	Bruant à moustaches
		Aimophila sumichrasti	Bruant à queue rousse
Tiaris olivacea	Sporophile grand-chanteur	*Aimophila carpalis*	Bruant à épaulettes
		Aimophila cassinii	Bruant de Cassin
Tiaris bicolor	Sporophile cici	*Aimophila aestivalis*	Bruant des pinèdes
Loxipasser anoxanthus	Sporophile mantelé	*Aimophila botterii*	Bruant de Botteri
		Aimophila ruficeps	Bruant à calotte fauve
Loxigilla portoricensis	Sporophile de Porto Rico	*Aimophila rufescens*	Bruant roussâtre
Loxigilla violacea	Sporophile petit-coq	*Aimophila notosticta*	Bruant d'Oaxaca
Loxigilla noctis	Sporophile rougegorge	*Aimophila quinquestriata*	Bruant pentaligne
Euneornis campestris	Pique-orange de la Jamaïque	*Oriturus superciliosus*	Bruant rayé
Melanospiza richardsoni	Moisson pied-blanc	*Torreornis inexpectata*	Bruant de Zapata
Pinaroloxias inornata	Spizin de Cocos	*Spizella arborea*	Bruant hudsonien
Haplospiza rustica	Haplospize ardoisé	*Spizella passerina*	Bruant familier
Acanthidops bairdii	Bec-en-cheville gris	*Spizella pallida*	Bruant des plaines
Diglossa baritula	Percefleur cannelle	*Spizella breweri*	Bruant de Brewer
Diglossa plumbea	Percefleur ardoisé	*Spizella pusilla*	Bruant des champs
Sicalis flaveola	Sicale bouton-d'or	*Spizella wortheni*	Bruant de Worthen
Sicalis luteola	Sicale des savanes	*Spizella atrogularis*	Bruant à menton noir
Emberizoides herbicola	Grand Tardivole	*Pooecetes gramineus*	Bruant vespéral
Paroaria coronata	Paroare huppé	*Chondestes grammacus*	Bruant à joues marron
Paroaria capitata	Paroare à bec jaune	*Amphispiza bilineata*	Bruant à gorge noire
Lysurus crassirostris	Tohi masqué	*Amphispiza belli*	Bruant de Bell
Pselliophorus tibialis	Tohi à cuisses jaunes	*Calamospiza melanocorys*	Bruant noir et blanc
Pselliophorus luteoviridis	Tohi jaune-vert	*Passerculus sandwichensis*	Bruant des prés
Pezopetes capitalis	Tohi à grands pieds	*Ammodramus savannarum*	Bruant sauterelle
Atlapetes albinucha	Tohi à calotte blanche	*Ammodramus bairdii*	Bruant de Baird
Atlapetes pileatus	Tohi à calotte rousse	*Ammodramus henslowii*	Bruant de Henslow
Buarremon brunneinuchus	Tohi à nuque brune	*Ammodramus leconteii*	Bruant de Le Conte
Buarremon virenticeps	Tohi à raies vertes	*Ammodramus nelsoni*	Bruant de Nelson
Buarremon torquatus	Tohi à tête rayée	*Ammodramus caudacutus*	Bruant à queue aiguë
Arremon aurantiirostris	Tohi à bec orange	*Ammodramus maritimus*	Bruant maritime
Arremonops rufivirgatus	Tohi olive	*Xenospiza baileyi*	Bruant des sierras
Arremonops chloronotus	Tohi à dos vert	*Passerella iliaca*	Bruant fauve
Arremonops conirostris	Tohi ligné	*Melospiza melodia*	Bruant chanteur
Melozone kieneri	Tohi de Kiener	*Melospiza lincolnii*	Bruant de Lincoln
Melozone biarcuatum	Tohi à face blanche	*Melospiza georgiana*	Bruant des marais
Melozone leucotis	Tohi oreillard	*Zonotrichia capensis*	Bruant chingolo
Pipilo chlorurus	Tohi à queue verte	*Zonotrichia albicollis*	Bruant à gorge blanche
Pipilo ocai	Tohi à collier	*Zonotrichia querula*	Bruant à face noire

Zonotrichia
  leucophrys   Bruant à couronne
                      blanche
Zonotrichia
  atricapilla   Bruant à couronne
                      dorée
Junco vulcani   Junco des volcans
Junco hyemalis   Junco ardoisé
Junco phaeonotus Junco aux yeux
                      jaunes

Calcarius mccownii   Bruant de McCown
Calcarius lapponicus Bruant lapon
Calcarius pictus   Bruant de Smith
Calcarius ornatus   Bruant à ventre noir
Emberiza   Bruant à calotte
  leucocephalos   blanche
Emberiza pusilla   Bruant nain
Emberiza rustica   Bruant rustique
Emberiza aureola   Bruant auréole
Emberiza variabilis Bruant gris
Emberiza pallasi   Bruant de Pallas
Emberiza schoeniclus Bruant des roseaux
Plectrophenax nivalis Bruant des neiges
Plectrophenax
  hyperboreus   Bruant blanc

CARDINALIDAE
Saltator albicollis   Saltator gros-bec
Saltator striatipectus Saltator strié
Saltator coerulescens Saltator gris
Saltator maximus   Saltator des grands-
                           bois
Saltator atriceps   Saltator à tête noire
Saltator grossus   Cardinal ardoisé
Caryothraustes   Cardinal à ventre
  poliogaster   blanc
Caryothraustes
  canadensis   Cardinal flavert
Rhodothraupis
  celaeno   Cardinal à collier
Cardinalis cardinalis Cardinal rouge
Cardinalis sinuatus   Cardinal pyrrhuloxia
Pheucticus
  chrysopeplus   Cardinal jaune
Pheucticus tibialis   Cardinal à cuisses
                           noires
Pheucticus   Cardinal à poitrine
  ludovicianus   rose
Pheucticus
  melanocephalus   Cardinal à tête noire
Cyanocompsa
  cyanoides   Évêque bleu-noir
Cyanocompsa
  parellina   Évêque paré
Guiraca caerulea   Guiraca bleu
Passerina rositae   Passerin à ventre rose
Passerina amoena   Passerin azuré
Passerina cyanea   Passerin indigo
Passerina versicolor   Passerin varié
Passerina
  leclancherii   Passerin arc-en-ciel
Passerina ciris   Passerin nonpareil
Spiza americana   Dickcissel
                           d'Amérique

ICTERIDAE
Dolichonyx
  oryzivorus   Goglu des prés
Agelaius phoeniceus   Carouge à épaulettes
Agelaius assimilis   Carouge de Cuba
Agelaius tricolor   Carouge de
                           Californie
Agelaius humeralis   Petit Carouge
Agelaius xanthomus   Carouge de Porto
                           Rico
Nesopsar nigerrimus   Carouge de la
                           Jamaïque
Sturnella militaris   Sturnelle militaire
Sturnella magna   Sturnelle des prés
Sturnella neglecta   Sturnelle de l'Ouest
Xanthocephalus
  xanthocephalus   Carouge à tête jaune
Dives dives   Quiscale chanteur
Dives atroviolacea   Quiscale violet
Euphagus carolinus   Quiscale rouilleux
Euphagus
  cyanocephalus   Quiscale de Brewer
Quiscalus quiscula   Quiscale bronzé
Quiscalus major   Quiscale des marais
Quiscalus mexicanus   Quiscale à longue
                           queue
Quiscalus palustris   Quiscale de Mexico
Quiscalus   Quiscale du
  nicaraguensis   Nicaragua
Quiscalus niger   Quiscale noir
Quiscalus lugubris   Quiscale merle
Molothrus
  bonariensis   Vacher luisant
Molothrus aeneus   Vacher bronzé
Molothrus ater   Vacher à tête brune
Scaphidura oryzivora   Vacher géant
Icterus dominicensis   Oriole à capuchon
Icterus laudabilis   Oriole de Sainte-
                           Lucie
Icterus oberi   Oriole de Montserrat
Icterus bonana   Oriole de la
                           Martinique
Icterus wagleri   Oriole cul-noir
Icterus maculialatus   Oriole unifascié
Icterus spurius   Oriole des vergers
Icterus cucullatus   Oriole masqué
Icterus chrysater   Oriole noir et or
Icterus auricapillus   Oriole à tête d'or
Icterus mesomelas   Oriole à queue jaune
Icterus icterus   Oriole troupiale
Icterus pustulatus   Oriole à dos rayé
Icterus auratus   Oriole orange
Icterus leucopteryx   Oriole de la
                           Jamaïque
Icterus pectoralis   Oriole maculé
Icterus gularis   Oriole à gros bec
Icterus graduacauda   Oriole d'Audubon
Icterus galbula   Oriole de Baltimore
Icterus bullockii   Oriole à ailes
                           blanches
Icterus abeillei   Oriole d'Abeillé
Icterus parisorum   Oriole jaune-verdâtre
Amblycercus
  holosericeus   Cassique à bec jaune

Cacicus uropygialis	Cassique à dos rouge
Cacicus cela	Cassique cul-jaune
Cacicus melanicterus	Cassique à ailes jaunes
Psarocolius decumanus	Cassique huppé
Psarocolius wagleri	Cassique à tête brune
Psarocolius montezuma	Cassique de Montezuma
Psarocolius guatimozinus	Cassique noir

FRINGILLIDAE

Fringilla coelebs	Pinson des arbres
Fringilla montifringilla	Pinson du Nord
Leucosticte tephrocotis	Roselin à tête grise
Leucosticte atrata	Roselin noir
Leucosticte australis	Roselin à tête brune
Pinicola enucleator	Durbec des sapins
Carpodacus erythrinus	Roselin cramoisi
Carpodacus purpureus	Roselin pourpré
Carpodacus cassinii	Roselin de Cassin
Carpodacus mexicanus	Roselin familier
Loxia curvirostra	Bec-croisé des sapins
Loxia leucoptera	Bec-croisé bifascié
Carduelis flammea	Sizerin flammé
Carduelis hornemanni	Sizerin blanchâtre
Carduelis spinus	Tarin des aulnes
Carduelis pinus	Tarin des pins
Carduelis atriceps	Tarin sombre
Carduelis notata	Chardonneret à tête noire
Carduelis xanthogastra	Chardonneret à ventre jaune
Carduelis cucullata	Chardonneret rouge
Carduelis dominicensis	Chardonneret des Antilles
Carduelis psaltria	Chardonneret mineur
Carduelis lawrencei	Chardonneret gris
Carduelis tristis	Chardonneret jaune
Carduelis carduelis	Chardonneret élégant
Carduelis sinica	Verdier de Chine
Serinus mozambicus	Serin du Mozambique
Serinus canaria	Serin des Canaries
Pyrrhula pyrrhula	Bouvreuil pivoine
Coccothraustes abeillei	Gros-bec à capuchon
Coccothraustes vespertinus	Gros-bec errant
Coccothraustes coccothraustes	Gros-bec casse-noyaux
Telespiza cantans	Psittirostre de Laysan
Telespiza ultima	Psittirostre de Nihoa
Psittirostra psittacea	Psittirostre psittacin
Dysmorodrepanis munroi	Psittirostre de Munro
Loxioides bailleui	Psittirostre palila

Rhodacanthis flaviceps	Petit Psittirostre
Rhodacanthis palmeri	Psittirostre de Palmer
Chloridops kona	Psittirostre à gros bec
Pseudonestor xanthophrys	Psittirostre de Maui
Hemignathus virens	Amakihi familier
Hemignathus flavus	Amakihi d'Oahu
Hemignathus kauaiensis	Amakihi de Kauai
Hemignathus parvus	Petit Amakihi
Hemignathus sagittirostris	Grand Amakihi
Hemignathus obscurus	Hémignathe akialoa
Hemignathus ellisianus	Hémignathe à long bec
Hemignathus lucidus	Hémignathe nukupuu
Hemignathus munroi	Hémignathe akiapolaau
Oreomystis bairdi	Grimpeur de Kauai
Oreomystis mana	Grimpeur d'Hawaï
Paroreomyza maculata	Grimpeur d'Oahu
Paroreomyza flammea	Grimpeur de Molokai
Paroreomyza montana	Grimpeur de Maui
Loxops caeruleirostris	Loxopse de Kauai
Loxops coccineus	Loxopse des Hawaï
Ciridops anna	Ciridopse d'Anna
Vestiaria coccinea	Iiwi rouge
Drepanis pacifica	Drépanide mamo
Drepanis funerea	Drépanide noir
Palmeria dolei	Palmérie huppée
Himatione sanguinea	Picchion cramoisi
Melamprosops phaeosoma	Po-o-uli masqué

PASSERIDAE

Passer domesticus	Moineau domestique
Passer montanus	Moineau friquet

PLOCEIDAE

Ploceus cucullatus	Tisserin gendarme
Euplectes franciscanus	Euplecte franciscain
Euplectes afer	Euplecte vorabé

ESTRILDIDAE

Uraeginthus bengalus	Cordonbleu à joues rouges
Estrilda caerulescens	Astrild queue-de-vinaigre
Estrilda melpoda	Astrild à joues orange
Estrilda troglodytes	Astrild cendré
Estrilda astrild	Astrild ondulé
Amandava amandava	Bengali rouge
Lonchura malabarica	Capucin bec-de-plomb
Lonchura cucullata	Capucin nonnette
Lonchura punctulata	Capucin damier

Lonchura malacca	Capucin à dos marron	*Charadrius veredus*	Pluvier oriental
		Gallinago media	Bécassine double
Padda oryzivora	Padda de Java	*Catharacta chilensis*	Labbe du Chili
Vidua macroura	Veuve dominicaine	*Larus cirrocephalus*	Mouette à tête grise
		Larus dominicanus	Goéland dominicain
APPENDIX (Part 1)		*Creagrus furcatus*	Mouette à queue fourchue
Phoebastria irrorata	Albatros des Galapagos	*Sterna sumatrana*	Sterne diamant
		Sterna trudeaui	Sterne de Trudeau
Thalassarche chrysostoma	Albatros à tête grise	*Cepphus carbo*	Guillemot à lunettes
Macronectes giganteus	Pétrel géant	*Columba goodsoni*	Pigeon de Goodson
		Nandayus nenday	Conure nanday
Fulmarus glacialoides	Fulmar argenté	*Forpus xanthopterygius*	Toui de Spix
Daption capense	Damier du Cap	*Brotogeris chiriri*	Toui à ailes jaunes
Pterodroma solandri	Pétrel de Solander	*Amazona amazonica*	Amazone aourou
Pterodroma rostrata	Pétrel de Tahiti	*Coccyzus pumilus*	Coulicou nain
Pterodroma alba	Pétrel à poitrine blanche	*Coccyzus lansbergi*	Coulicou à tête grise
		Anthracothorax viridigula	Mango à cravate verte
Pterodroma feae	Pétrel gongon	*Chlorostilbon mellisugus*	Émeraude orvert
Pterodroma defilippiana	Pétrel de Defillipe	*Amazilia chionopectus*	Ariane à poitrine blanche
Procellaria cinerea	Puffin gris	*Amazilia tobaci*	Ariane de Félicie
Procellaria aequinoctialis	Puffin à menton blanc	*Acestrura heliodor*	Colibri héliodore
Oceanites gracilis	Océanite d'Elliot	*Ramphastos brevis*	Toucan du Choco
Fregetta grallaria	Océanite à ventre blanc	*Thamnophilus multistriatus*	Batara de Lafresnaye
Oceanodroma hornbyi	Océanite de Hornby	*Urocissa erythrorhyncha*	Pirolle à bec rouge
Spheniscus mendiculus	Manchot des Galapagos	*Corvus frugilegus*	Corbeau freux
Phalacrocorax perspicillatus	Cormoran de Pallas	*Corvus corone*	Corneille noire
Phalacrocorax bougainvillii	Cormoran de Bougainville	*Melanocorypha calandra*	Alouette calandre
		Parus major	Mésange charbonnière
Phalacrocorax kenyoni	Cormoran de Kenyon	*Parus varius*	Mésange variée
Phalacrocorax gaimardi	Cormoran de Gaimard	*Phylloscopus trochilus*	Pouillot fitis
Mesophoyx intermedia	Héron intermédiaire	*Copsychus saularis*	Shama dayal
Platalea leucorodia	Spatule blanche	*Saxicola rubetra*	Tarier des prés
Ciconia ciconia	Cigogne blanche	*Garrulax caerulatus*	Garrulaxe à flancs gris
Phoenicopterus chilensis	Flamant du Chili		
Anser anser	Oie cendrée	*Acridotheres javanicus*	Martin à ventre blanc
Anser indicus	Oie à tête barrée	*Anthus pratensis*	Pipit farlouse
Branta ruficollis	Bernache à cou roux	*Euphonia mesochrysa*	Organiste mordoré
Tadorna ferruginea	Tadorne casarca	*Piranga rubriceps*	Tangara à capuchon
Tadorna tadorna	Tadorne de Belon	*Sporophila bouvronides*	Sporophile faux-bouvron
Aix galericulata	Canard mandarin	*Icterus nigrogularis*	Oriole jaune
Netta rufina	Nette rousse	*Carduelis magellanica*	Chardonneret de Magellan
Aythya baeri	Fuligule de Baer		
Aythya nyroca	Fuligule nyroca	*Carduelis chloris*	Verdier d'Europe
Accipiter nisus	Épervier d'Europe	*Lagonosticta rubricata*	Amarante foncé
Buteo polyosoma	Buse tricolore		
Buteo buteo	Buse variable		
Hieratus pennatus	Aigle botté	APPENDIX (Part 2)	
Rallus aquaticus	Râle d'eau		
Porphyrio porphyrio	Talève sultane	*Anas breweri*	Canard de Brewer
Hoploxypterus cayanus	Vanneau de Cayenne	*Lophortyx leucoprosopon*	Colin de Reichenow
Charadrius pecuarius	Pluvier pâtre	*Tringa cooperi*	Bécasseau de Cooper

Calidris		*Trochilus*	
paramelanotos	Bécasseau de Cox	*violajugulum*	Colibri de Jeffries
Larus nelsoni	Goéland de Nelson	*Phasmornis mystica*	Colibri des Chisos
Zenaida plumbea	Tourterelle plombée	*Selasphorus floresii*	Colibri de Flores
Conurus labati	Conure de Labat	*Celeus immaculatus*	Pic immaculé
Anodorhynchus		*Vireosylvia*	
martinicus	Ara de Martinique	*propinqua*	Viréo de Vera Paz
Anodorhynchus		*Regulus cuvieri*	Roitelet de Cuvier
purpurascens	Ara violet	*Vermivora lawrencii*	Paruline de Lawrence
Ara atwoodi	Ara de la Dominique	*Vermivora*	
Ara erythrocephala	Ara de Jamaïque	*leucobronchialis*	Paruline de Brewster
Ara erythrura	Ara à queue rouge	*Helminthophaga*	Paruline de
Ara gossei	Ara de Gosse	*cincinnatiensis*	Cincinnati
Ara guadeloupensis	Ara de Guadeloupe	*Dendroica potomac*	Paruline de Sutton
Amazilia bangsi	Ariane de Bangs	*Sylvia carbonata*	Paruline charbonnière
Amazilia ocai	Ariane de Gould	*Sylvia montana*	Paruline des
Thaumatias lerdi	Colibri d'Oca		montagnes
Saucerottia		*Sylvania*	
florenceae	Colibri de Florence	*microcephala*	Paruline à petite tête
Cyanomyia salvini	Colibri de Salvin	*Emberiza townsendii*	Bruant de Townsend
		Aegiothus brewsterii	Sizerin de Brewster

List of Supplements to the A.O.U. Check-list

Supplements to the Check-list have been published at irregular intervals to call attention to taxonomic or other decisions of the Committee between editions. These Supplements are valuable in tracking references for such actions and in tracing the nomenclatural history of species or groups of birds. The first Supplement was published separately. Later Supplements were published in *The Auk* (year, volume, and pages are given below). Annual reports of the Committee were published in *The Auk* from 1905 to 1908, and annual lists of proposed changes were published from 1916 to 1924. Other taxonomic decisions were noted by the Committee in reports in *The Auk* in 1973, 1984, 1990, and 1998 as noted below. This list was compiled by Roger B. Clapp (1–18), Robert W. Dickerman (19–32), and Richard C. Banks (33–41).

Supple-ment	Year	Where Published	Supple-ment	Year	Where Published
*	1886	First Check-list	22	1947	*Auk* 64: 445–452
1	1889	Separate Publication	23	1948	*Auk* 65: 438–443
2	1890	*Auk* 7: 60–66	24	1949	*Auk* 66: 281–285
3	1891	*Auk* 8: 83–90	25	1950	*Auk* 67: 368–370
4	1892	*Auk* 9: 105–108	26	1951	*Auk* 68: 367–369
5	1893	*Auk* 10: 59–63	27	1952	*Auk* 69: 308–312
6	1894	*Auk* 11: 46–51	28	1953	*Auk* 70: 359–361
7	1895	*Auk* 12: 163–169	29	1954	*Auk* 71: 310–312
*	1895	Second Edition	30	1955	*Auk* 72: 292–295
8	1897	*Auk* 14: 117–135	31	1956	*Auk* 73: 447–449
9	1899	*Auk* 16: 97–133	*	1957	Fifth Edition
10	1901	*Auk* 18: 295–320	32	1973	*Auk* 90: 411–419
11	1902	*Auk* 19: 315–342	–	1973	*Auk* 90: 887
12	1903	*Auk* 20: 331–368	33	1976	*Auk* 93: 875–879
13	1904	*Auk* 21: 411–424	34	1982	*Auk* 99: 1CC–16CC
14	1908	*Auk* 25: 343–399	*	1983	Sixth Edition
15	1909	*Auk* 26: 294–303	–	1984	*Auk* 101: 348
*	1910	Third Edition	35	1985	*Auk* 102: 680–686
16	1912	*Auk* 29: 380–387	36	1987	*Auk* 104: 591–596
17	1920	*Auk* 37: 439–449	37	1989	*Auk* 106: 532–538
18	1923	*Auk* 40: 513–525	–	1990	*Auk* 107: 274
*	1937	Fourth Edition	38	1991	*Auk* 108: 750–754
19	1944	*Auk* 61: 441–464	39	1993	*Auk* 110: 675–682
20	1945	*Auk* 62: 436–449	40	1995	*Auk* 112: 819–830
21	1946	*Auk* 63: 428–432	41	1997	*Auk* 114: 542–552
			–	1998	*Auk* 115: 280

LITERATURE CITED

ABBOTT, D. J., III, AND D. W. FINCH. 1978. First Variegated Flycatcher *(Empidonomus varius)* record for the United States. Amer. Birds 32: 161–163.

ABLE, K. P. 1996. In memoriam: Burt L. Monroe, Jr., 1930–1994. Auk 113: 924–927.

AHLQUIST, J. E., A. H. BLEDSOE, J. E. RATTI, AND C. G. SIBLEY. 1987. Divergence of the single-copy DNA sequences of the Western Grebe *(Aechmophorus occidentalis)* and Clark's Grebe *(A. clarkii),* as indicated by DNA-DNA hybridization. Postilla 200.

AID, C. S., G. G. MONTGOMERY, AND D. W. MOCK. 1985. Range extension of the Peruvian Booby to Panama during the 1983 El Niño. Colonial Waterbirds 8: 67–68.

AINLEY, D. G. 1980. Geographic variation in Leach's Storm-Petrel. Auk 97: 837–853.

AINLEY, D. G. 1983. Further notes on variation in Leach's Storm-Petrel. Auk 100: 230–233.

ALDRICH, J. W. 1946. Speciation in the white-cheeked geese. Wilson Bull. 58: 94–103.

ALDRICH, J. W., AND K. P. BAER. 1970. Status and speciation in the Mexican Duck *(Anas diazi).* Wilson Bull. 82: 63–73.

ALLEN, A. A. 1934. A new bird for North America. Univ. State New York Bull. Schools 20: 134–135.

ALLEN, S. 1988. Some thoughts on the identification of Gunnison's Red-backed Hawk *(Buteo polyosoma)* and why it's not a natural vagrant. C[olorado]. F[ield]. O[rnithol]. J. 22: 9–13.

AMADON, D. 1947. Ecology and the evolution of some Hawaiian birds. Evolution 1: 63–68.

AMADON, D. 1950. The Hawaiian honeycreepers (Aves: Drepaniidae). Bull. Amer. Mus. Nat. Hist. 95: 158–192.

AMADON, D. 1966. The superspecies concept. Syst. Zool. 15: 246–249.

AMADON, D. 1982. A revision of the sub-buteonine hawks (Accipitridae, Aves). Amer. Mus. Novitates 2741.

AMADON, D. 1986. The Hawaiian honeycreepers revisited. 'Elepaio 46: 83–84.

AMADON, D., AND J. BULL. 1988. Hawks and owls of the world: a distributional and taxonomic list. Proc. Western Foundation Vertebrate Zool. 3: 295–357.

AMERICAN ORNITHOLOGISTS' UNION [A.O.U.]. 1957. Check-list of North American birds, 5th ed. Lord Baltimore Press, Baltimore, Maryland.

AMERICAN ORNITHOLOGISTS' UNION [A.O.U.]. 1983. Check-list of North American birds, 6th ed. American Ornithologists' Union, Washington, D.C.

AMERICAN ORNITHOLOGISTS' UNION [A.O.U.]. 1985. Thirty-fifth supplement to American Ornithologists' Union check-list of North American birds. Auk 102: 680–686.

AMERICAN ORNITHOLOGISTS' UNION [A.O.U.]. 1989. Thirty-seventh supplement to the American Ornithologists' Union check-list of North American birds. Auk 106: 532–538.

AMERICAN ORNITHOLOGISTS' UNION [A.O.U.]. 1990. Errata. Auk 107: 274.

AMERICAN ORNITHOLOGISTS' UNION [A.O.U.]. 1991. Thirty-eighth supplement to the American Ornithologists' Union check-list of North American birds. Auk 108: 750–754.

AMERICAN ORNITHOLOGISTS' UNION [A.O.U.]. 1993. Thirty-ninth supplement to the American Ornithologists' Union check-list of North American birds. Auk 110: 675–682.

AMERICAN ORNITHOLOGISTS' UNION [A.O.U.]. 1995. Fortieth supplement to the American Ornithologists' Union check-list of North American birds. Auk 112: 819–830.

AMERICAN ORNITHOLOGISTS' UNION [A.O.U.]. 1997. Forty-first supplement to the American Ornithologists' Union check-list of North American birds. Auk 114: 542–552.

AMERSON, A. B., JR. 1971. The natural history of French Frigate Shoals, northwestern Hawaiian Islands. Atoll Res. Bull. 150.

AMOS, E. J. R. 1991. A guide to the birds of Bermuda. E. J. R. Amos, Warwick, Bermuda.

ANDERSON, B. W. 1971. Man's influence on hybridization in two avian species in South Dakota. Condor 73: 342–347.

ANDERSON, W., AND A. W. MILLER. 1953. Hybridization of Cinnamon and Blue-winged Teal in northeastern California. Condor 55: 152–153.

ANKNEY, C. D., AND D. G. DENNIS. 1988. Response to Hepp et al. Auk 105: 807–808.

ANKNEY, C. D., D. G. DENNIS, L. N. WISHARD, AND J. E. SEEB. 1986. Low genic variation between Black Ducks and Mallards. Auk 103: 701–709.

ARNOLD, K. A. 1978. First United States record of Paint-billed Crake (*Neocrex erythrops*). Auk 95: 945–946.

ATKINSON, P. W., M. J. WHITTINGHAM, H.G. D. S. GARZA, A. M. KENT, AND R. T. MAIER. 1993. Notes on the ecology, conservation and taxonomic status of *Hylorchilus* wrens. Bird Conserv. International 3: 75–85.

ATWOOD, J. L. 1988. Speciation and geographic variation in Black-tailed Gnatcatchers. Ornithol. Monogr. 42.

AUDUBON, J. J. 1838. Birds of America (folio), vol. 4. J. J. Audubon, London.

AUDUBON, J. J. 1839. Ornithological biography, vol. 5. Adam Black, Edinburgh.

AVISE, J. C., C. D. ANKNEY, AND W. S. NELSON. 1990. Mitochondrial gene trees and the evolutionary relationship of Mallard and Black Ducks. Evolution 44: 1109–1119.

AVISE, J. C., AND C. F. AQUADRO. 1987. Malate dehydrogenase isozymes provide a phylogenetic marker for the Piciformes (woodpeckers and allies). Auk 104: 324–328.

AVISE, J. C., J. C. PATTON, AND C. F. AQUADRO. 1980. Evolutionary genetics of birds. I. Relationships among North American thrushes and allies. Auk 97: 135–147.

AVISE, J. C., AND R. M. ZINK. 1988. Molecular genetic distances between avian sibling species: Long-billed and Short-billed dowitchers, Boat-tailed and Great-tailed grackles, and Tufted and Black-crested titmice. Auk 105: 516–528.

BAILEY, A. M. 1947. Wryneck from Cape Prince of Wales, Alaska. Auk 64: 456.

BAKER, M. C., AND A. E. M. BAKER. 1990. Reproductive behavior of female buntings: isolating mechanisms in a hybridizing pair of species. Evolution 44: 332–338.

BALDRIDGE, F. A., L. F. KIFF, S. K. BALDRIDGE, AND R. B. HANSEN. 1983. Hybridization of a Blue-throated Hummingbird in California. Western Birds 14: 17–30.

BANGS, O. 1930. Types of birds now in the Museum of Comparative Zoology. Bull. Mus. Comp. Zool. 70: 147–426.

BANKS, R. C. 1983. The correct name for the Hawaiian Crow. 'Elepaio 44: 1–2.

BANKS, R. C. 1988a. An old record of the Pearly-breasted Cuckoo in North America and a nomenclatural critique. Bull. Brit. Ornithol. Club 108: 87–91.

BANKS, R. C. 1988b. Supposed northern records of the Southern Fulmar. Western Birds 19: 121–124.

BANKS, R. C. 1990a. Taxonomic status of the Rufous-bellied Chachalaca (*Ortalis wagleri*). Condor 92: 749–753.

BANKS, R. C. 1990b. Taxonomic status of the coquette hummingbird of Guerrero, Mexico. Auk 107: 191–192.

BANKS, R. C., AND M. R. BROWNING. 1979. Correct citations for some North American bird taxa. Proc. Biol. Soc. Wash. 92: 195–203.

BANKS, R. C., AND M. R. BROWNING. 1995. Comments on the status of revived old names for some North American birds. Auk 112: 633–648.

BANKS, R. C., AND C. J. DOVE. 1992. The generic name for Crested Caracaras (Aves: Falconidae). Proc. Biol. Soc. Wash. 105: 420–425.

BANKS, R. C., AND N. K. JOHNSON. 1961. A review of North American hybrid hummingbirds. Condor 63: 3–28.

BANKS, R. C., AND R. C. LAYBOURNE. 1977. Plumage sequence and taxonomy of Laysan and Nihoa finches. Condor 79: 343–348.

BAPTISTA, L. F. 1978. A revision of the Mexican *Piculus* (Picidae) complex. Wilson Bull. 90: 159–181.

BAPTISTA, L. F., W. I. BOARMAN, AND P. KANDIANIDIS. 1983. Behavior and taxonomic status of Grayson's Dove. Auk 100: 907–919.

BAPTISTA, L. F., AND R. B. JOHNSON. 1982. Song variation in insular and mainland California Brown Creepers (*Certhia familiaris*). J. für Ornithologie 123: 131–144.

BARBER, R. D. 1985. A recent record of the Bachman's Warbler in Florida. Florida Field Nat. 13: 64–66.

BARLOW, J. C., J. A. DICK, D. H. BALDWIN, AND R. A. DAVIS. 1969. New records of birds from British Honduras. Ibis 111: 399–402.

BARLOW, J. C., AND R. D. JAMES. 1975. Aspects of the biology of the Chestnut-sided Shrike-Vireo. Wilson Bull. 87: 320–334.

BARLOW, J. C., AND S. V. NASH. 1985. Behavior and nesting biology of the St. Andrew Vireo. Wilson Bull. 97: 265–272.

BARRE, N., P. FELDMANN, G. TAYALAY, P. ROC, M. ANSELME, AND P. W. SMITH. 1996. Status of the Eurasian Collared-Dove (*Streptopelia decaocto*) in the French Antilles. El Pitirre 9: 2–3.

BARROWCLOUGH, G. F. 1980. Genetic and phenotypic differentiation in a wood warbler (genus *Dendroica*) hybrid zone. Auk 97: 655–668.

BARROWCLOUGH, G. F., AND K. W. CORBIN. 1978. Genetic variation and differentiation in the Parulidae. Auk 95: 691–702.

BARROWCLOUGH, G. F., AND R. J. GUTIÉRREZ. 1990. Genetic variation and differentiation in the Spotted Owl *(Strix occidentalis)*. Auk 107: 737–744.

BAUER, R. D. 1979. Historical and status report of the Tule White-fronted Goose. Pages 44–55 *in* Management and Biology of Pacific Flyway Geese (R. L. Jarvis and J. C. Bartonek, Eds.). OSU Book Stores, Corvallis, Oregon.

BEARDSLEE, C. S., AND H. D. MITCHELL. 1965. Birds of the Niagara Frontier Region. Bull. Buffalo Soc. Nat. Hist. 22: 1–478.

BEECHER, W. J. 1953a. Feeding adaptations and systematics in the avian order Piciformes. J. Wash. Acad. Sci. 43: 293–299.

BEECHER, W. J. 1953b. A phylogeny of the oscines. Auk 70: 270–333.

BEHRSTOCK, R. A. 1983. Colombian Crake (*Neocrex columbianus*) and Paint-billed Crake (*N. erythrops*): first breeding records for Central America. Amer. Birds 37: 956–957.

BEHRSTOCK, R. A. 1996. Voices of Stripe-backed Bittern, Least Bittern and Zigzag Heron, with notes on distribution. Cotinga 5: 55–61.

BELL, D. A. 1996. Genetic differentiation, geographic variation and hybridization in gulls of the *Larus glaucescens-occidentalis* complex. Condor 98: 527–546.

BERGER, A. J. 1972. Hawaiian Birdlife. Univ. Hawaii Press, Honolulu.

BERGER, A. J. 1981. Hawaiian Birdlife, 2nd ed. Univ. Hawaii Press, Honolulu.

BERMINGHAM, E., S. ROWHER, S. FREEMAN, AND C. WOOD. 1992. Vicariance biogeography in the Pleistocene and speciation in North American wood warblers: a test of Mengel's model. Proc. Natl. Acad. Sci. USA 89: 6624–6628.

BERLIOZ, J. 1932. Notes critiques sur quelques Trochilidés du British Museum. Oiseau (n.s.) 2: 530–534.

BINFORD, L. C. 1989. A distributional survey of the birds of the Mexican state of Oaxaca. Ornithol. Monogr. 43.

BJÖRKLUND, M. 1994. Phylogenetic relationships among Charadriiformes: reanalysis of previous data. Auk 111: 825–832.

BLAKE, E. R. 1953. Birds of Mexico. Univ. Chicago Press, Chicago, Illinois.

BLAKE, E. R. 1977. Manual of Neotropical Birds, vol. 1. Univ. Chicago Press, Chicago, Illinois.

BLEDSOE, A. H. 1988a. Status and hybridization of Clapper and King rails in Connecticut. Connecticut Warbler 8: 61–65.

BLEDSOE, A. H. 1988b. Nuclear DNA evolution and phylogeny of the New World nine-primaried oscines. Auk 105: 504–515.

BLEIWEISS, R., J. A. W. KIRSCH, AND J. C. MATHEUS. 1994. DNA-DNA hybridization evidence for subfamily structure among hummingbirds. Auk 111: 8–19.

BLEM, C. R. 1980. A Paint-billed Crake in Virginia. Wilson Bull. 92: 393–394.

BLOCKSTEIN, D. E., AND J. W. HARDY. 1989. The Grenada Dove (*Leptotila wellsi*) is a distinct species. Auk 106: 339–340.

BOCHENSKI, Z. 1994. The comparative osteology of grebes (Aves: Podicipediformes) and its systematic implications. Acta Zool. Cracov. 37: 191–346.

BOCK, C. E. 1971. Pairing in hybrid flicker populations in eastern Colorado. Auk 88: 921–924.

BOCK, W. J. 1959. The status of the Semipalmated Plover. Auk 76: 98–100.

BOND, J. 1956. Check-list of birds of the West Indies, ed. 4. Academy of Natural Sciences, Philadelphia, Pennsylvania.

BOND, J. 1959. Fourth supplement to the check-list of birds of the West Indies. Academy of Natural Sciences, Philadelphia, Pennsylvania.

BOND, J. 1967. Twelfth supplement to the Check-list of birds of the West Indies (1956). Academy of Natural Sciences, Philadelphia, Pennsylvania.

BOND, J. 1982. Twenty-fourth supplement to the Check-list of birds of the West Indies (1956). Academy of Natural Sciences, Philadelphia, Pennsylvania.

BOND, J., AND A. DOD. 1977. A new race of Chat Tanager (*Calyptophilus frugivorus*) from the Dominican Republic. Notulae Naturae No. 451.

BORROR, D. J. 1972. Yellow-green Vireo in Arizona, with notes on vireo songs. Condor 74: 80–86.

BOURNE, W. R. P. 1967. Long-distance vagrancy in the petrels. Ibis 109: 141–167.

BOURNE, W. R. P. 1983. The Soft-plumaged Petrel, the Gon-gon and the Freira, *Pterodroma mollis, P. feae* and *P. madeira*. Bull. Brit. Ornithol. Club 103: 52–58.

BOURNE, W. R. P., AND J. R. JEHL, JR. 1982. Variation and nomenclature of Leach's Storm-Petrel. Auk 99: 793–797.

BOURNE, W. R. P., E. J. MACKRILL, A. M. PETERSON, AND P. YÉSOU. 1988. The Yelkouan Shearwater, *Puffinus (puffinus?) yelkouan*. Brit. Birds 81: 306–319.

BOURNE, W. R. P., AND J. WARHAM. 1966. Geographical variation in the Giant Petrels of the genus *Macronectes*. Ardea 54: 45–67.

BOURNS, T. K. R. 1967. Serological relationships among some North American thrushes. Can. J. Zool. 45: 97–99.

BRADBURY, R. C. 1992. First Florida record of Variegated Flycatcher (*Empidonomus varius*) at Garden Key, Dry Tortugas. Florida Field Nat. 20: 42–44.

BRADLEY, P. E. 1995. Birds of the Cayman Islands. Revised ed. Caerulea Press, Italy.

BRAUN, D., G. B. KITTO, AND M. J. BRAUN. 1984. Molecular population genetics of tufted and black-crested forms of *Parus bicolor*. Auk 101: 170–173.

BRAUN, M. J., AND M. B. ROBBINS. 1986. Extensive protein similarity of the hybridizing chickadees *Parus atricapillus* and *P. carolinensis*. Auk 103: 667–675.

BRAUN, M. J., AND D. E. WOLF. 1987. Recent records of vagrant South American land birds in Panama. Bull. Brit. Ornithol. Club 107: 115–117.

BREMER, D. 1987. The Waipio, Oahu, Christmas bird count: 1986 results and a review of the first decade, 1977–1986. 'Elepaio 47: 53–58.

BRETAGNOLLE, V. 1995. Systematics of the Soft-plumaged Petrel *Pterodroma mollis* (Procellariidae): new insights from the study of vocalizations. Ibis 137: 207–218.

BRITISH ORNITHOLOGISTS' UNION (B.O.U.). 1974. Records committee: eighth report. Ibis 116: 578–579.

BRITISH ORNITHOLOGISTS' UNION (B.O.U.). 1992. Checklist of birds of Britain and Ireland, 6th ed. British Ornithologists' Union, Tring, Herts., U.K.

BRODKORB, P. 1960. The skeleton and systematic position of *Gampsonyx*. Auk 77: 88–89.

BRODSKY, L. M., AND P. J. WEATHERHEAD. 1984. Behavioral and ecological factors contributing to American Black Duck—Mallard hybridization. J. Wildl. Manage. 48: 846–852.

BROM, T. G. 1990. Villi and the phylogeny of Wetmore's order Piciformes (Aves). Zool. J. Linnaean Soc. 98: 63–72.

BROOKS, A. 1923. A comment on the occurrence of *Mesophoyx intermedia* in North America. Condor 25: 180–181.

BROOKS, M. 1945. George Sutton and his warbler. Audubon Mag. 47: 145–150.

BROWN, J. L., AND E. G. HORVATH. 1989. Geographic variation in group size, ontogeny, rattle calls, and body size in *Aphelocoma ultramarina*. Auk 106: 124–128.

BROWN, J. L., AND S. H. LI. 1995. Phylogeny of social behavior in *Aphelocoma* jays: a role for hybridization? Auk 112: 464–472.

BROWN, L., AND D. AMADON. 1968. Eagles, hawks, and falcons of the world. 2 Vols. Country Life Books, Hamlyn, Middlesex, U.K.

BROWN, R. G. B. 1967. Species isolation between the Herring Gull *Larus argentatus* and Lesser Black-backed Gull *L. fuscus*. Ibis 109: 310–317.

BROWNING, M. R. 1977. The types and type-localities of *Oreortyx pictus* (Douglas) and *Oreortyx plumiferus* Gould. Proc. Biol. Soc. Wash. 90: 808–812.

BROWNING, M. R. 1978. An evaluation of the new species and subspecies proposed in Oberholser's *Bird Life of Texas*. Proc. Biol. Soc. Wash. 91: 85–122.

BROWNING, M. R. 1989a. The correct name for the Olivaceous Cormorant, "Maiague" of Piso (1658). Wilson Bull. 101: 101–106.

BROWNING, M. R. 1989b. The correct citation and spelling of *Ptiliogonys* and type locality of *Ptiliogonys cinereus*. Auk 106: 743–746.

BROWNING, M. R. 1993. Species limits of the cave swiftlets (*Collocalia*) in Micronesia. Avocetta 17: 101–106.

BROWNING, M. R., AND B. L. MONROE, JR. 1991. Clarifications and corrections of the dates of issue of some publications containing descriptions of North American birds. Archives Natur. Hist. 18: 381–405.

BRUMFIELD, R. T., AND A. P. CAPPARELLA. 1996. Genetic differentiation and taxonomy in the House Wren species group. Condor 98: 547–556.

BRUSH, A. H., AND N. K. JOHNSON. 1976. The evolution of color differences between Nashville and Virginia's warblers. Condor 78: 412–414.

BRYANT, W. E. 1887. *Piranga rubriceps* and *Tringa fuscicollis* in California. Auk 4: 78–79.

BUCKLEY, P. A., AND F. G. BUCKLEY. 1984. Cayenne Tern new to North America, with comments on its relationship to Sandwich Tern. Auk 101: 396–398.

BURTON, P. J. K. 1971. Comparative anatomy of head and neck in the Spoon-billed Sandpiper, *Eurynorhynchus pygmeus,* and its allies. J. Zool. London 163: 145–163.

BURTON, P. J. K. 1984. Anatomy and evolution of the feeding apparatus in the avian orders Coraciiformes and Piciformes. Bull Brit. Mus. (Nat. Hist.) Zool. 47: 331–443.

BYERS, C., J. CURSON, AND U. OLSSON. 1995. Sparrows and buntings. A guide to the sparrows and buntings of North America and the world. Houghton Mifflin, Boston, Massachusetts.

BYRD, G. V., J. L. TRAPP, AND D. D. GIBSON. 1978. New information on Asiatic birds in the Aleutian Islands, Alaska. Condor 80: 309–315.

CAMPBELL, R. W., N. K. DAWE, I. MCTAGGART-COWAN, J. M. COOPER, G. W. KAISER, AND M. C. E. MCNALL. 1990. The birds of British Columbia, vol. 2. Royal British Columbia Museum and Canadian Wildlife Service.

CAPPARELLA, A. P. 1986. First record of Yellow-collared Chlorophonia for Middle America. Amer. Birds 40: 194–195.

CARDIFF, S. W., AND J. V. REMSEN, JR. 1994. Type specimens of birds in the Louisiana State University Museum of Natural Science. Occ. Papers Mus. Nat. Sci. Louisiana St. Univ. 68: 1–32.

CARDILLO, R., A. FORBES-WATSON, AND R. RIDGELY. 1983. The Western Reef-Heron *(Egretta gularis)* at Nantucket Island, Massachusetts. Amer. Birds 37: 827–829.

CARLSON, C. W. 1981. The Sutton's Warbler - a critical review and summation of current data. Atlantic Natur. 34: 1–11.

CHAPMAN, F. M. 1911. Description of a new oriole (*Icterus fuertesi*) from Mexico. Auk 28: 1–4.

CHAPMAN, F. M. 1922. The distribution of the swallows of the genus *Pygochelidon.* Amer. Mus. Novitates 30.

CHAPMAN, F. M. 1935. Further remarks on the relationships of the grackles of the subgenus *Quiscalus.* Auk 52: 21–29.

CHRISTIAN, P. D., L. CHRISTIDIS, AND R. SCHODDE. 1992. Biochemical systematics of the Charadriiformes (shorebirds: relationships between Charadrii, Scolopaci and Lari). Australian J. Zool. 40: 291–302.

CHRISTIDIS, L., AND W. E. BOLES. 1994. The taxonomy and species of birds of Australia and its territories. Royal Australasian Ornithologists Union, Monogr. 2.

CHRISTIDIS, L., K. DAVIES, M. WESTERMAN, P. D. CHRISTIAN, AND R. SCHODDE. 1996. Molecular assessment of the taxonomic status of Cox's Sandpiper. Condor 98: 459–463.

CHU, P. C. 1994. Historical examination of delayed plumage maturation in the shorebirds (Aves: Charadriiformes). Evolution 48: 327–350.

CHU, P. C. 1995. Phylogenetic reanalysis of Strauch's osteological data set for the Charadriiformes. Condor 97: 174–196.

CICERO, C. 1996. Sibling species of titmice in the *Parus inornatus* complex (Aves: Paridae). Univ. Calif. Publ. Zool. 128: 1–217.

CICERO, C., AND N. K. JOHNSON. 1992. Genetic differentiation between populations of Hutton's Vireo (Aves: Vireonidae) in disjunct allopatry. Southwest. Nat. 37: 344–348.

CICERO, C., AND N. K. JOHNSON. 1995. Speciation in sapsuckers (*Sphyrapicus*): III. Mitochondrial-DNA sequence divergence at the cytochrome-*b* locus. Auk 112: 547–563.

CLAPP, R. B. 1984. First records of Juan Fernandez (*Pterodroma e. externa*) and Stejneger's (*Pterodroma longirostris*) petrels from Hawaii. 'Elepaio 44: 97–98.

CLAPP, R. B. 1989. First record of the Little Tern, *Sterna albifrons,* from Hawaii. 'Elepaio 49: 41–46.

CLAPP, R. B., R. C. LAYBOURNE, AND R. L. PYLE. 1983. Status of the Common Tern (*Sterna hirundo*) in the tropical Pacific, with a note on records of the Black-naped Tern (*Sterna sumatrana*) in Hawaii. 'Elepaio 43: 97–100.

CLAPP, R. B., AND P. W. WOODWARD. 1968. New records of birds from the Hawaiian Leeward Islands. Proc. U. S. Natl. Mus. 124.

CLARK, W. S., AND R. C. BANKS. 1992. The taxonomic status of the White-tailed Kite. Wilson Bull. 104: 571–579.

CLENCH, M. H. 1995. Body pterylosis of woodcreepers and ovenbirds (Dendrocolaptidae and Furnariidae). Auk 112: 800–804.

COCKRUM, E. L. 1952. A check-list and bibliography of hybrid birds in North America north of Mexico. Wilson Bull. 64: 140–159.

COHEN, B. L., A. J. BAKER, K. BLECHSCHMIDT, D. L. DITTMANN, R. W. FURNESS, J. A. GERWIN, A. J. HELBIG, J. DE KORTE, H. D. MARSHALL, R. L. PALMA, H.-U. PETER, R. RAMLI, I. SIEBOLD, M. S. WILLCOX, R. H. WILSON, and R. M. ZINK. 1997. Enigmatic phylogeny of skuas (Aves: Stercorariidae). Proc. Royal Soc. London 264: 181–190.

CONANT, S., R. CLAPP, L. HURUKI, AND B. CHOY. 1991. A new tern (*Sterna*) breeding record for Hawaii. Pacific Sci. 45: 348–354.

CONNORS, P. G. 1983. Taxonomy, distribution, and evolution of golden plovers (*Pluvialis dominica* and *Pluvialis fulva*). Auk 100: 607–620.

CONNORS, P. G., B. J. MCCAFFERY, AND J. L. MARON. 1993. Speciation in golden-plovers, *Pluvialis dominica* and *P. fulva*: evidence from the breeding grounds. Auk 110: 9–20.

CONTRERAS B., A. J. 1988. New records from Nuevo León, Mexico. Southwest. Nat. 33: 251–252.

COOKE, F., AND F. G. COOCH. 1968. The genetics of polymorphism in the goose *Anser caerulescens*. Evolution 22: 289–300.

COOKE, F., D. T. PARKIN, AND R. F. ROCKWELL. 1988. Evidence of former allopatry of the two color phases of Lesser Snow Geese (*Chen caerulescens caerulescens*). Auk 105: 467–479.

COOKE, F., R. F. ROCKWELL, AND D. B. LANK. 1995. The Snow Geese of La Perouse Bay: Natural selection in the wild. Oxford Univ. Press, New York.

CORBIN, K. W. 1968. Taxonomic relationships of some *Columba* species. Condor 70: 1–13.

CORBIN, K. W., AND C. G. SIBLEY. 1977. Rapid evolution in orioles of the genus *Icterus*. Condor 79: 335–342.

CORBIN, K. W., C. G. SIBLEY, AND A. FERGUSON. 1979. Genic changes associated with the establishment of sympatry in orioles of the genus *Icterus*. Evolution 33: 624–633.

CORY, C. B. 1918. Catalogue of birds of the Americas. Field Mus. Nat. Hist. Publ., Zool. Ser., vol. 13, pt. 2, no. 1.

CORY, C. B. 1919. Catalogue of birds of the Americas. Field Mus. Nat. Hist. Publ., Zool. Ser., vol. 13, pt. 2, no. 2.

CORY, C. B., AND C. E. HELLMAYR. 1925. Catalogue of birds of the Americas. Field Mus. Nat. Hist. Publ., Zool. Ser., vol. 13, pt. 4.

COX, G. W. 1973. Hybridization between Mourning and MacGillivray's warblers. Auk 90: 190–191.

COX, J. B. 1989. Notes on the affinities of Cooper's and Cox's sandpipers. South Australian Ornith. 30: 169–181.

CRACRAFT, J. 1983. Species concepts and speciation analysis. Pages 159–187 *in* Current Ornithology, Vol. 1 (R. F. Johnston, ed.). Plenum Press, New York.

CRACRAFT, J. 1985. Monophyly and phylogenetic relationships of the Pelecaniformes: a numerical cladistic analysis. Auk 102: 834–853.

CRAMP, S. (Ed.). 1985. Handbook of the birds of Europe, the Middle East and North Africa, vol. 4. Oxford Univ. Press, Oxford, U.K.

CRAMP, S. (Ed.). 1988. Handbook of the birds of Europe, the Middle East and North Africa, vol. 5. Oxford Univ. Press, Oxford, U.K.

CRAMP, S., AND K. E. L. SIMMONS. (Eds.). 1977. Handbook of the birds of Europe, the Middle East and North Africa: the birds of the western Palearctic, vol. 1. Oxford Univ. Press, Oxford, U.K.

CRAMP, S., AND K. E. L. SIMMONS. (Eds.). 1983. Handbook of the birds of Europe, the Middle East and North Africa: the birds of the western Palearctic, vol. 3. Oxford Univ. Press, Oxford, U.K.

CROWE, T. M. 1978. The evolution of guinea-fowl (Galliformes, Phasianidae, Numidinae): taxonomy, phylogeny, speciation and biogeography. Ann. S. Afr. Mus. 16: 43–136.

DAU, C. P., AND J. PANIYAK. 1977. Hoopoe, a first record for North America. Auk 94: 601.

DAVIS, J. 1951. Distribution and variation of the brown towhees. Univ. Calif. Publ. Zool. 52: 1–120.

DAVIS, J. 1965. Natural history, variation, and distribution of the Strickland's Woodpecker. Auk 82: 537–590.

DAVIS, L. I. 1958. Acoustic evidence of relationships in North American crows. Wilson Bull. 70: 151–167.

DAVIS, L. I. 1972. A field guide to the birds of Mexico and Central America. Univ. of Texas Press, Austin, Texas.

DAVIS, L. I. 1978. Acoustic evidence of relationship in potoos. Pan Amer. Studies 1: 4–21.

DAY, R. H., E. P. KNUDTSON, D. W. WOOLINGTON, AND R. P. SCHULMEISTER. 1979. *Caprimulgus indicus, Eurynorhynchus pygmeus, Otus scops,* and *Limicola falcinellus* in the Aleutian Islands, Alaska. Auk 96: 189–190.

DeBENEDICTIS, P. A. 1991. ABA Checklist report, 1990. Birding 23: 190–196.

DeBENEDICTIS, P. A. 1992. ABA Checklist report, 1991. Birding 24: 280–286.

DeBENEDICTIS, P. A. 1994a. ABA Checklist report, 1992. Birding 26: 93–102.

DeBENEDICTIS, P. A. 1994b. ABA Checklist Committee report, 1993. Birding 26: 320–326.

DeBENEDICTIS, P. A. 1995. ABA Checklist Committee report, 1994. Birding 27: 367–368.

DeBENEDICTIS, P. A. 1996. ABA Checklist Committee Report, 1995. Birding 28: 399–405.

DEIGNAN, H. G. 1961. Type specimens of birds in the United States National Museum. Bull. U. S. Natl. Mus. 221.

DEL HOYO, J., A. ELLIOTT, AND J. SARGATAL (Eds.). 1992. Handbook of the birds of the world. Vol. 1. Lynx Edicions, Barcelona, Spain.

DELGADO B., F. S. 1985. A new subspecies of the Painted Parakeet (*Pyrrhura picta*) from Panama. Pages 17–20 *in* Neotropical Ornithology (P. A. Buckley, M. S. Foster, E. S. Morton, R. S. Ridgely, and F. G. Buckley, Eds.). Ornithol. Monogr. No. 36.

DELACOUR, J., AND D. AMADON. 1973. Curassows and related birds. American Museum of Natural History, New York.

DELACOUR, J., AND J. T. ZIMMER. 1952. The identity of *Anser nigricans* Lawrence 1846. Auk 69: 82–84.

DEMASTES, J. W., AND J. V. REMSEN, JR. 1994. The genus *Caryothraustes* (Cardinalinae) is not monophyletic. Wilson Bull. 106: 733–738.

DEMENT'EV, G. P., AND N. A. GLADKOV. (Eds.). 1954. Birds of the Soviet Union, vol. 5. Trans. 1970, Israel Prog. Sci. Translations, Jerusalem.

DESFAYES, M. 1964. An observation on the song of the Black-capped Chickadee. Condor 66: 438–439.

DEVILLERS, P. 1977a. The skuas of the North American Pacific Coast. Auk 94: 417–429.

DEVILLERS, P. 1977b. Observations at a breeding colony of *Larus (belcheri) atlanticus.* Gerfaut 67: 22–43.

DEVILLERS, P. 1978. Distribution and relationships of South American Skuas. Gerfaut 68: 374–417.

DICKERMAN, R. W. 1968. Notes on the Ocellated Rail *(Micropygia schomburgkii)* with first record for Central America. Bull. Brit. Ornithol. Club 88: 25–30.

DICKERMAN, R. W., AND J. GUSTAFSON. 1996. The Prince of Wales Spruce Grouse: a new subspecies from southeastern Alaska. Western Birds 27: 41–47.

DILGER, W. C. 1956. Relationships of the thrush genera *Catharus* and *Hylocichla.* Syst. Zool. 5: 174–182.

DITTMANN, D. L., AND R. M. ZINK. 1991. Mitochondrial DNA variation among phalaropes and allies. Auk 108: 771–779.

DIXON, K. L. 1989. Contact zones of avian congeners on the southern Great Plains. Condor 91: 15–22.

DIXON, K. L. 1990. Constancy of margins of the hybrid zone in titmice of the *Parus bicolor* complex in coastal Texas. Auk 107: 184–188.

DORST, J. 1947. Révision systématique du genre *Corvus.* Oiseau et R. F. O. 17: 44–87.

DOYLE, T. J. 1997. The Timberline Sparrow, *Spizella (breweri) taverneri,* in Alaska, with notes on breeding habitat and vocalizations. West. Birds 28: 1–12.

DROST, C. A., AND D. B. LEWIS. 1995. Xantus' Murrelet (*Synthliboramphus hypoleucus*). *In* The Birds of North America, No. 164 (A. Poole and F. Gill, Eds.). Academy of Natural Sciences, Philadelphia, and American Ornithologists' Union, Washington, D.C.

DUGAND, A., AND E. EISENMANN. 1983. Rediscovery of, and new data on, *Molothrus armenti* Cabanis. Auk 100: 991–992.

EISENMANN, E. 1955. The species of Middle American birds. Trans. Linn. Soc. New York 7: 1–128.

EISENMANN, E. 1956. Galapagos Penguin in Panamá. Condor 58: 74–75.

EISENMANN, E. 1957. Notes on the birds of the Province of Bocas del Toro, Panama. Condor 59: 247–262.

EISENMANN, E. 1959a. The correct specific name of the Quetzal, *Pharomachrus mocinno.* Auk 76: 108.

EISENMANN, E. 1959b. South American migrant swallows of the genus *Progne* in Panama and northern South America: with comments on their identification and molt. Auk 76: 529–532.

EISENMANN, E. 1962a. Notes on nighthawks of the genus *Chordeiles* in southern Middle America, with a description of a new race of *Chordeiles minor* breeding in Panamá. Amer. Mus. Novitates 2094.

EISENMANN, E. 1962b. On the genus "*Chamaethlypis*" and its supposed relationship to *Icteria.* Auk 79: 265–267.

EISENMANN, E. 1965. The tiger-herons *(Tigrisoma)* of Argentina. Hornero 10: 225–234.

EISENMANN, E. 1966. *Falco rufigularis*—the correct name of the Bat Falcon. Condor 68: 208–209.

EISENMANN, E. 1970. [Review of:] A distributional survey of the birds of Honduras. Wilson Bull. 82: 106–109.

EISENMANN, E., AND T. R. HOWELL. 1962. The taxonomic status of the hummingbirds *Chalybura melanorrhoa* and *Chalybura urochrysia.* Condor 64: 300–310.

ELLIS, D. H, AND C. P. GRANT. 1983. The Pallid Falcon *Falco kreyenborgi* is a color phase of the austral Peregrine Falcon *(Falco peregrinus cassini).* Auk 100: 269–271.

EMLEN, S. T., J. D. RISING, AND W. L. THOMPSON. 1975. A behavioral and morphological study of sympatry in the Indigo and Lazuli buntings of the Great Plains. Wilson Bull. 87: 145–179.

EMSLIE, S. D. 1996. A fossil scrub-jay supports a recent systematic decision. Condor 98: 675–680.

ELLSWORTH, D. L., R. L. HONEYCUTT, N. J. SILVY, K. D. RITTENHOUSE, AND M. H. SMITH. 1994. Mitochondrial-DNA and nuclear-gene differentiation in North American prairie grouse (genus *Tympanuchus*). Auk 111: 661–671.

ELLSWORTH, D. L., R. L. HONEYCUTT, AND N. J. SILVY. 1995. Phylogenetic relationships among North American grouse inferred from restriction endonuclease analysis of mitochondrial DNA. Condor 97: 492–502.

ELLSWORTH, D. L., R. L. HONEYCUTT, AND N. J. SILVY. 1996. Systematics of grouse and ptarmigan determined by nucleotide sequences of the mitochondrial cytochrome-ß gene. Auk 113: 811–822.

ELMBERG, J. 1993. Song differences between North American and European White-winged Crossbills. Auk 110: 385.

ESCALANTE-PLIEGO, B. P. 1991. Genetic differentiation in yellowthroats (Parulidae: *Geothlypis*). Acta XX Congressus Internationalis Ornithologici, pp. 333–341.

ESCALANTE-PLIEGO, P., AND A. T. PETERSON. 1992. Geographic variation and species limits in Middle American woodnymphs *(Thalurania).* Wilson Bull. 104: 205–219.

ESPINOSA DE LOS MONTEROS, A., AND J. CRACRAFT. 1997. Intergeneric relationships of the New World jays inferred from cytochrome *b* gene sequences. Condor 99: 490–502.

FEDUCCIA, A. 1973. Evolutionary trends in the Neotropical ovenbirds and woodhewers. Ornithol. Monogr. 13.

FICKEN, M. S., AND R. W. FICKEN. 1962. Some aberrant characters of the Yellow-breasted Chat. Auk 79: 718–719.

FICKEN, M. S., AND R. W. FICKEN. 1968. Reproductive isolating mechanisms in the Blue-winged Warbler - Golden-winged Warbler complex. Evolution 22: 166–179.

FICKEN, M. S., AND R. W. FICKEN. 1970. Comments on introgression and reproductive isolating mechanisms in the Blue-winged Warbler - Golden-winged Warbler complex. Evolution 24: 254–256.

FIRSOVA, L. W., AND A. V. LEVADA. 1982. Ornithological finds at the south of Koriak Plateau. Ornithologia 17: 112–118 (in Russian).

FISHER, H. I. 1965. Bird records from Midway Atoll, Pacific Ocean. Condor 67: 355–357.

FJELDSÅ, J. 1976. The systematic affinities of the sandgrouse, Pteroclididae. Videns. Medd. Dansk Naturh. Foren. 139: 179–243.

FJELDSÅ, J. 1982a. Some behavior patterns of four closely related grebes *Podiceps nigricollis, P. gallardoi, P. occipitalis* and *P. taczanowskii,* with reflections on phylogeny and adaptive aspects of the evolution of displays. San. Ornithol. Foren. Tidsskr. 76: 37–68.

FJELDSÅ, J. 1982b. Biology and systematic relations of the Andean Coot *"Fulica americana ardesiaca"* (Aves, Rallidae). Steenstrupia 8: 1–21.

FJELDSÅ, J. 1983. Biology and systematic relations of the Andean Coot *"Fulica americana ardesiaca"* (Aves, Rallidae). Bull. Brit. Ornithol. Club 103: 18–21.

FJELDSÅ, J. 1985. Origin, evolution, and status of the avifauna of Andean wetlands. Pages 85–112 *in* Neotropical ornithology (P. A. Buckley, M. S. Foster, E. S. Morton, R. S. Ridgely, and F. G. Buckley, Eds.). Ornithol. Monogr. 36.

FJELDSÅ, J., AND N. KRABBE. 1990. Birds of the High Andes. Zoological Museum, Univ. Copenhagen, Copenhagen, Denmark.

FJELDSÅ, J., N. KRABBE, AND R. S. RIDGELY. 1987. Great Green Macaw *Ara ambigua* collected in northwest Ecuador, with taxonomic comments on *Ara militaris*. Bull. Brit. Ornith. Club 107: 28–31.

FLEISCHER, R. C., C. E. MCINTOSH, AND C. L. TARR. In press. Evolution on a volcanic conveyor belt: using phylogeographic reconstructions and K-Ar based ages of the Hawaiian Islands to estimate molecular evolution rates. Molecular Evolution.

FORSHAW, J. M. 1973. Parrots of the World, 1st ed. Lansdowne Press, Melbourne, Australia.

FREEMAN, S., AND R. M. ZINK. 1995. A phylogenetic study of the blackbirds based on variation in mitochondrial DNA restriction sites. Syst. Biol. 44: 409–420.

FRIEDMANN, H. 1949. The Baer Pochard, a bird new to the North American fauna. Condor 51: 43–44.

FRIEDMANN, H., L. GRISCOM, AND R. T. MOORE. 1950. Distributional check-list of the birds of Mexico, part. 1. Pac. Coast Avifauna 29.

FRIESEN, V. L., A. J. BAKER, AND J. F. PIATT. 1996. Phylogenetic relationships within the Alcidae inferred from total molecular evidence. Molecular Biol. Evol. 13: 359–367.

FFRENCH, R. 1991. A guide to the birds of Trinidad and Tobago, 2nd ed. Comstock Publ. Assocs., Ithaca, New York.

GARRIDO, O., AND A. KIRKCONNELL. 1996. Taxonomic status of the Cuban form of the Red-winged Blackbird. Wilson Bull. 108: 372–374.

GASTON, A. J., AND R. DECKER. 1985. Interbreeding of Thayer's Gulls, *Larus thayeri,* and Kumlien's Gulls, *Larus kumlieni,* on Southampton Island, Northwest Territories. Can. Field-Nat. 99: 257–259.

GEORGE, W. G. 1962. The classification of the Olive Warbler, *Peucedramus taeniatus*. Amer. Mus. Novitates 2103.

GEORGE, W. G. 1968. A second report on the basihyale in American songbirds, with remarks on the status of *Peucedramus*. Condor 70: 392–393.

GERBER, D. T. 1986. Female Golden-fronted Woodpecker or mutant female Red-bellied Woodpecker? Amer. Birds 40: 203–204.

GIBSON, A. R., M. A. GATES, AND R. ZACH. 1976. Phenetic affinities of the Wood Thrush, *Hylocichla mustelina* (Aves: Turdinae). Can. J. Zool. 54: 1679–1687.

GIBSON, D. D. 1981. Migrant birds at Shemya Island, Aleutian Islands, Alaska. Condor 83: 65–77.

GIBSON, D. D., AND G. E. HALL. 1978 *Emberiza variabilis* and *Ficedula parva* new to North America and the Aleutian Islands, Alaska. Auk 95: 428–429.

GIBSON, D. D., AND B. KESSEL. 1992. Seventy-four new avian taxa documented in Alaska 1976–1991. Condor 94: 454–467.

GILL, F. B. 1980. Historical aspects of hybridization between Blue-winged and Golden-winged warblers. Auk 97: 1–18.

GILL, F. B. 1987. Allozymes and genetic similarity of Blue-winged and Golden-winged warblers. Auk 104: 444–449.

GILL, F. B. 1988. Report of the American Birding Association Checklist Committee 1987–1988. Birding 20: 70–76.

GILL, F. B. 1997. Local cytonuclear extinction of the Golden-winged Warbler. Evolution 51: 519–525.

GILL, F. B., D. H. FUNK, AND B. SILVERIN. 1989. Protein relationships among titmice (*Parus*). Wilson Bull. 101: 182–187.

GILL, F. B., AND J. A. GERWIN. 1989. Protein relationships among hermit hummingbirds. Proc. Acad. Nat. Sci. Philadelphia 141: 409–421.

GILL, F. B., AND B. G. MURRAY. 1972. Discrimination behavior and hybridization of the Blue-winged and Golden-winged warblers. Evolution 26: 282–293.

GILL, F. B., AND B. SLIKAS. 1992. Patterns of mitochondrial DNA divergence in North American crested titmice. Condor 94: 20–28.

GILL, F. B., F. J. STOKES, AND C. STOKES. 1973. Contact zones and hybridization in the Jamaican hummingbird, *Trochilus polytmus* (L.). Condor 75: 170–176.

GODFREY, W. E. 1986. The birds of Canada, 2nd ed. National Museum of Natural Sciences, Ottawa.

GOODGE, W. R. 1972. Anatomical evidence for phylogenetic relationships among woodpeckers. Auk 89: 65–85.

GOODWIN, D. 1976. Crows of the world. Cornell Univ. Press, Ithaca, New York.

GOODWIN, D. 1983. Pigeons and doves of the world, 3rd ed. Cornell Univ. Press, Ithaca, New York.

GOSSE, P. H. 1847. The birds of Jamaica. John Van Voorst, London.

GOSSELIN, M., N. DAVID, AND P. LaPORTE. 1986. Hybrid Yellow-legged Gull from the Madeleine Islands. Amer. Birds 40: 58–60.

GOULD, P. J., AND W. B. KING. 1967. Records of four species of *Pterodroma* from the central Pacific Ocean. Auk 84: 591–594.

GRABER, R. R., AND J. W. GRABER. 1954. Comparative notes on Fuertes and Orchard orioles. Condor 56: 274–282.

GRANT, P. R., AND B. R. GRANT. 1992. Hybridization of bird species. Science 256: 193–197.

GRAVES, G. R. 1988. Evaluation of *Vermivora* x *Oporornis* hybrid wood-warblers. Wilson Bull. 100: 285–289.

GRAVES, G. R., AND S. L. OLSON. 1987. *Chlorostilbon bracei* Lawrence, an extinct species of hummingbird from New Providence Island, Bahamas. Auk 104: 296–302.

GRAY, A. P. 1958. Bird hybrids. Commonwealth Agriculture Bureaux, Farnham Royal, Bucks, U.K.

GREENLAW, J. S. 1993. Behavioral and morphological diversification in Sharp-tailed Sparrows (*Ammodramus caudacutus*) of the Atlantic coast. Auk 110: 286–303.

GREENWAY, J. C., JR. 1939. *Dysmorodrepanis munroi* probably not a valid form. Auk 56: 479–480.

GRICKS, N. P. 1994. Vagrant White Stork *Ciconia ciconia* (Aves: Ciconiidae) found in Antigua: a first record for the West Indies. El Pitirre 7: 2.

GRIFFITHS, C. 1994. Monophyly of the Falconiformes based on syringeal morphology. Auk 111: 787–805.

GRINNELL, J. 1932. Type localities of birds described from California. Univ. Calif. Publ. Zool. 38: 243–324.

GRISCOM, L. 1932. The distribution of bird-life in Guatemala. Bull. Amer. Mus. Nat. Hist. 64: 1–439.

GRISCOM, L. 1934. The ornithology of Guerrero, Mexico. Bull. Mus. Comp. Zool. 75: 367–422.

GRISCOM, L, AND A. SPRUNT, JR. 1957. The warblers of America. Devin-Adair, New York.

GROTH, J. G. 1988. Resolution of cryptic species in Appalachian Red Crossbills. Condor 90: 745–760.

GROTH, J. G. 1993a. Evolutionary differentiation in morphology, vocalizations, and allozymes among nomadic sibling species in the North American Red Crossbill complex. Univ. Calif. Publ. Zool. 127: 1–143.

GROTH, J. G. 1993b. Call matching and positive assortative mating in Red Crossbills. Auk 110: 398–401.

GRUDZIEN, T. A., W. S. MOORE, J. R. COOK, AND D. TAGLE. 1987. Genic population structure and gene flow in the Northern Flicker (*Colaptes auratus*) hybrid zone. Auk 104: 654–664.

GUTIÉRREZ, R. J., R. M. ZINK, AND S. Y. YANG. 1983. Genic variation, systematic, and biogeographical relationships of some galliform birds. Auk 100: 33–47.

GYLDENSTOLPE, N. 1945. The bird fauna of the Rio Juruá in western Brazil. Kungl Svenska Vet. Handlingar 22: 1–338.

HACKETT, S. J. 1993. Phylogenetic and biogeographic relationships in the Neotropical genus *Gymnopithys* (Formicariidae). Wilson Bull. 105: 301–315.

HACKETT, S. J. 1995. Molecular systematics and zoogeography of flowerpiercers in the *Diglossa baritula* complex. Auk 112: 156–170.

HACKETT, S. J. 1996. Molecular phylogenetics and biogeography of tanagers in the genus *Ramphocelus* (Aves). Molecular Phylogenetics Evolution 5: 368–382.

HACKETT, S. J., AND K. V. ROSENBERG. 1990. Comparison of phenotypic and genetic differentiation in South American antwrens. Auk 107: 473–489.

HAEMIG, P. D. 1989. A comparative experimental study of exploratory behavior in Santa Cruz Island and mainland California Scrub Jays *Aphelocoma coerulescens*. Bird Behav. 8: 38–42.

HAFFER, J. 1967. Speciation in Colombian forest birds west of the Andes. Amer. Mus. Novitates 2294.

HAFFER, J. 1974. Avian speciation in tropical South America. Publ. Nuttall Ornithol. Club No. 14.

HAGEY, L. R., C. D. SCHTEINGART, H.-T. YON-NU, S. S. ROSSI, D. ODELL, AND A. F. HOFFMAN. 1990. B-phocacholic acid in bile; biochemical evidence that the flamingo is related to an ancient goose. Condor 92: 593–597.

HAINEBACH, K. 1992. First records of Xantus' Hummingbird in California. Western Birds 23: 133–136.

HALL, B. P. 1961. The taxonomy and identification of pipits (genus *Anthus*). Bull. Brit. Mus. (Nat. Hist.), Zool. 7: 243–289.

HALL, B. P., AND R. E. MOREAU. 1970. An atlas of speciation in African passerine birds. British Museum (Natural History), London.

HALL, G. E., AND E. A. CARDIFF. 1978. First North American records of Siberian House Martin *Delichon urbica lagopoda*. Auk 95: 429.

HAMER, T. E., E. D. FORSMAN, A. D. FUCHS, AND M. L. WALTERS. 1994. Hybridization between Barred and Spotted owls. Auk 111: 487–492.

HAND, J. L. 1981. A comparison of vocalizations of Western Gulls (*Larus occidentalis occidentalis* and *L. o. livens*). Condor 83: 289–301.

HANDLEY, C. O., JR. 1950. The Brant of Prince Patrick Island, Northwest Territories. Wilson Bull. 62: 128–132.

HANEY, J. C., C. A. FAANES, AND W. R. P. BOURNE. 1993. An observation of Fea's Petrel, *Pterodroma feae* (Procellariiformes, Procellariidae), off the southeastern United States, with comments on the taxonomy and conservation of soft-plumaged and related petrels in the Atlantic Ocean. Brimleyana 18: 115–123.

HARDY, J. W. 1967. *Rhynchopsitta terrisi* is probably a valid species: a reassessment. Condor 69: 527–528.

HARDY, J. W. 1969. A taxonomic revision of the New World jays. Condor 71: 360–375.

HARDY, J. W. 1990a. Voices of the New World jays, crows, and their allies, family Corvidae. ARA Records, Gainesville, Florida.

HARDY, J. W. 1990b. The Fish Crow *(Corvus ossifragus)* and its Mexican relatives: vocal clues to evolutionary relationships. Florida Field Nat. 18: 74–80.

HARDY, J. W., B. B. COFFEY, JR., AND G. B. REYNARD. 1988. Voices of New World nightbirds, owls, nightjars, & their allies, 3rd ed. ARA Records, Gainesville, Florida.

HARDY, J. W., B. B. COFFEY, JR., AND G. B. REYNARD. 1989. Voices of the New World owls. ARA Records, Gainesville, Florida.

HARDY, J. W., AND D. J. DELANEY. 1987. The vocalizations of the Slender-billed Wren *(Hylorchilus sumichrasti)*: who are its close relatives? Auk 104: 528–530.

HARDY, J. W., AND R. W. DICKERMAN. 1965. Relationships between two forms of the Red-winged Blackbird in Mexico. Living Bird 4: 107–130.

HARDY, J. W., T. A. PARKER, III, AND B. B. COFFEY, JR. 1991. Voices of the woodcreepers. ARA Records, Gainesville, Florida.

HARDY, J. W., AND R. STRANECK. 1989. The Silky-tailed Nightjar and other Neotropical caprimulgids: unraveling some mysteries. Condor 91: 193–197.

HARPER, F. 1936. The *Vultur sacra* of William Bartram. Auk 53: 381–392.

HARRIS, M. P., F. I. NORMAN, AND R. H. S. McCOLL. 1965. A mixed population of redpoll in northern Norway. Brit. Birds 58: 288–294.

HARSHMAN, J. 1994. Reweaving the tapestry: what can we learn from Sibley and Ahlquist (1990)? Auk 111: 377–388.

HARTERT, E. 1917. Notes on game birds. Novitates Zool. 24: 275–292.

HAYMAN, P., J. MARCHANT, AND T. PRATER. 1986. Shorebirds: an identification guide. Houghton Mifflin, Boston.

HEIDRICH, P., C. KÖNIG, AND M. WINK. 1995a. Molecular phylogeny of South American screech owls of the *Otus atricapillus* complex (Aves: Strigidae) inferred from nucleotide sequences of the mitochondrial cytochrome *b* gene. Z. Naturforsch. 50c: 294–302.

HEIDRICH, P., C. KÖNIG, AND M. WINK. 1995b. Bioakustik, Taxonomie und molekulare Systematik amerikanischer Sperlingskäuze (Strigidae: *Glaucidium* spp.). Stuttgarter Beitr. Naturk., Ser. A, 534: 1–47.

HEINDEL, M. T., AND M. A. PATTEN. 1996. Eighteenth report of the California Bird Records Committee. Western Birds. 27: 1–29.

HEINTZELMAN, D. S. 1961. Kermadec Petrel in Pennsylvania. Wilson Bull. 73: 262–267.

HELLACK, J. J., AND G. D SCHNELL. 1977. Phenetic analysis of the subfamily Cardinalinae using external and skeletal characteristics. Wilson Bull. 89: 130–148.

HELLMAYR, C. E. 1929. Catalogue of birds of the Americas. Field Mus. Nat. Hist. Publ., Zool. Ser., vol. 13., pt. 6.

HELLMAYR, C. E. 1934. Catalogue of birds of the Americas. Field Mus. Nat. Hist. Publ., Zool. Ser., vol. 13., pt. 7.

HELLMAYR, C. E. 1935. Catalogue of birds of the Americas. Field Mus. Nat. Hist. Publ., Zool. Ser., vol. 13., pt. 8.

HELLMAYR, C. E. 1936. Catalogue of birds of the Americas. Field Mus. Nat. Hist. Publ., Zool. Ser., vol. 13., pt. 9.

HELLMAYR, C. E. 1937. Catalogue of birds of the Americas. Field Mus. Nat. Hist. Publ., Zool. Ser., vol. 13., pt. 10.

HELLMAYR, C. E. 1938. Catalogue of birds of the Americas. Field Mus. Nat. Hist. Publ., Zool. Ser., vol. 13., pt. 11.

HELLMAYR, C. E., AND B. CONOVER. 1942. Catalogue of birds of the Americas. Field Mus. Nat. Hist. Publ., Zool. Ser., vol. 13., pt. 1, no. 1.

HELLMAYR, C. E., AND B. CONOVER. 1948. Catalogue of birds of the Americas. Field Mus. Nat. Hist. Publ., Zool. Ser., vol. 13., pt. 1, no. 3 .

HELLMAYR, C. E., AND B. CONOVER. 1949. Catalogue of birds of the Americas. Field Mus. Nat. Hist. Publ., Zool. Ser., vol. 13., pt. 1, no. 4 .

HENDRICKSON, H. T., AND M. YOW. 1973. The relationships of the Wood Thrush *(Hylocichla mustelina)*: some indications from the electrophoresis of blood proteins. Condor 75: 301–305.

HEPP, G. R., J. M. NOVAK, K. T. SCRIBNER, AND P. W. STANGEL. 1988. Genetic distance and hybridization of Black Ducks and Mallards: a morph of a different color? Auk 105: 804–807.

HERREMANS, M. 1989. Vocalizations of Common, Lesser and Arctic redpolls. Dutch Birding 11: 9–15.

HERREMANS, M. 1990. Taxonomy and evolution in redpolls *Carduelis flammea-hornemanni*; a multivariate study of their biometry. Ardea 78: 441–458.

HICKEY, C. M., P. CAPITOLO, AND B. WALKER. 1996. First record of Lanceolated Warbler in California. Western Birds 27: 197–201.

HILTY, S. L., AND W. L. BROWN. 1986. A guide to the birds of Colombia. Princeton Univ. Press, Princeton, New Jersey.

HINKELMANN, C. 1996. Systematics and geographic variation in long-tailed hermit hummingbirds, the *Phaethornis superciliosus-malaris-longirostris* species group (Trochilidae), with notes on their biogeography. Ornitologia Neotropical 7: 119–148.

HOFFMAN, W., P. W. SMITH, AND P. WELLS. 1990. A record of the European Turtle-Dove in the Florida Keys. Florida Field Nat. 18: 88–90.

HOFFMAN, W., J. A. WIENS, AND J. M. SCOTT. 1978. Hybridization between gulls (*Larus glaucescens* and *L. occidentalis*) in the Pacific Northwest. Auk 95: 441–458.

HÖHN, E. O. 1958. The supposed occurrence and nesting of the Slaty-backed Gull in the western Arctic region of Canada. Can. Field-Nat. 72: 5–6.

HOLMAN, J. A. 1961. Osteology of living and fossil New World quails (Aves, Galliformes). Bull. Florida Mus. Biol. Sci. 6: 131–233.

HOLYOAK, D. T., AND J.-C. THIBAULT. 1976. La variation géographique de *Gygis alba*. Alauda 44: 457–473.

HOWELL, A. H. 1932. Florida bird life. Florida Dept. Game and Fresh Water Fish, Coward-McCann, New York.

HOWELL, S. N. G. 1993. Taxonomy and distribution of the hummingbird genus *Chlorostilbon* in Mexico and northern Central America. Euphonia 2: 25–37.

HOWELL, S. N. G. 1994. The specific status of black-faced antthrushes of Middle America. Cotinga 1: 21–25.

HOWELL, S. N. G., J. CORREA S., AND J. GARCIA B. 1993. First records of the Kelp Gull in Mexico. Euphonia 2: 71–80.

HOWELL, S. N. G., AND M. B. ROBBINS. 1995. Species limits of the Least Pygmy-Owl (*Glaucidium minutissimum*) complex. Wilson Bull. 107: 7–25.

HOWELL, S. N. G., AND S. WEBB. 1995. A guide to the birds of Mexico and northern Central America. Oxford Univ. Press, New York.

HOWELL, T. R. 1952. Natural history and differentiation in the Yellow-bellied Sapsucker. Condor 54: 237–282.

HUBBARD, J. P. 1969. The relationships and evolution of the *Dendroica coronata* complex. Auk 86: 393–432.

HUBBARD, J. P. 1976. The nomenclatural history of the Crissal Thrasher (Aves: Mimidae). Nemouria 20.

HUBBARD, J. P. 1977. The biological and taxonomic status of the Mexican Duck. Bull. New Mexico Dept. Game Fish 16.

HUGHES, J. M. 1996. Phylogenetic analysis of the Cuculidae (Aves: Cuculiformes) using behavioral and ecological characters. Auk 86: 393–432.

HUNTER, S. 1987. Species and sexual isolating mechanisms in sibling species of giant petrels *Macronectes*. Polar Biol. 7: 295–301.

HUNTER, L. A. 1988. Status of the endemic Atitlan Grebe in Guatemala: is it extinct? Condor 90: 906–912.

HUNTINGTON, C. E. 1952. Hybridization in the Purple Grackle, *Quiscalus quiscula*. Syst. Zool. 1: 149–170.

HUPP, J. W., AND C. E. BRAUN. 1991. Geographic variation among Sage Grouse in Colorado. Wilson Bull. 103: 255–261.

IMBER, M. J. 1985. Origins, phylogeny and taxonomy of the gadfly petrels *Pterodroma* spp. Ibis 127: 197–229.

INGOLD, J. L., L. A. WEIGT, AND S. L. GUTTMAN. 1988. Genetic differentiation between North American kinglets and comparisons with three allied passerines. Auk 105: 386–390.

INGOLFSSON, A. 1987. Hybridization of Glaucous and Herring gulls in Iceland. Studies Avian Biol. 10: 131–140.

INGOLFSSON, A. 1993. The variably plumaged gulls of Iceland. Auk 110: 409–410.

INT. COMM. ZOOL. NOMENCL. [I.C.Z.N.]. 1952. Opin. Decl. Rend. 1(C): 101, Direction 17.

INT. COMM. ZOOL. NOMENCL. [I.C.Z.N.]. 1956a. Opin. Decl. Rend 13: 3, Opin. 401.

INT. COMM. ZOOL. NOMENCL. [I.C.Z.N.]. 1956b. Opin. Decl. Rend. 13: 121, Opin. 406.

INT. COMM. ZOOL. NOMENCL. [I.C.Z.N.]. 1956c. Opin. Decl. Rend. 13: 205–232, Opin. 412.

INT. COMM. ZOOL. NOMENCL. [I.C.Z.N.]. 1964. International Code of Zoological Nomenclature. I.C.Z.N. London.

INT. COMM. ZOOL. NOMENCL. [I.C.Z.N.]. 1968. Opinion 852. Bull. Zool. Nomen. 25: 74–79.

INT. COMM. ZOOL. NOMENCL. [I.C.Z.N.]. 1983. Opinion 1249. Bull. Zool. Nomen. 40: 83–84.

INT. COMM. ZOOL. NOMENCL. [I.C.Z.N.]. 1985. International Code of Zoological Nomenclature. 3rd ed. International Trust for Zoological Nomenclature, London.

INT. COMM. ZOOL. NOMENCL. [I.C.Z.N.]. 1992. Bull. Zool. Nomen. 49: 178–179.

ISLER, M., AND P. ISLER. 1987. The tanagers, natural history, distribution, and identification. Smithsonian Institution, Washington, D.C.

ISLER, M., P. ISLER, AND B. M. WHITNEY. 1997. Biogeography and systematics of the *Thamnophilus punctatus* (Thamnophilidae) complex. Pages 355–382 *in* Studies in Neotropical ornithology honoring Ted Parker (Remsen, J. V., Jr., Ed.). Ornithol. Monogr. 48.

JACOB, J. 1983. Zur systematischen Stellung von *Vultur gryphus* (Cathartiformes). J. für Ornithologie 124: 83–86.

JAMES, H. F., AND S. L. OLSON. 1991. Descriptions of thirty-two new species of birds from the Hawaiian Islands. Part II. Passeriformes. Ornithol. Monogr. 46: 1–88.

JAMES, H. F., R. L. ZUSI, AND S. L. OLSON. 1989. *Dysmorodrepanis munroi* (Fringillidae: Drepanidinae), a valid genus and species of Hawaiian finch. Wilson Bull. 101: 159–170.

JAMES, R. D. 1981. Factors affecting variation in the primary song of North American Solitary Vireos. Can. J. Zool. 59: 2001–2009.

JEHL, J. R., JR. 1968a. The systematic position of the Surfbird, *Aphriza virgata*. Condor 70: 206–210.

JEHL, J. R., JR. 1968b. Relationships in the Charadrii (shorebirds): a taxonomic study based on color patterns of the downy young. San Diego Soc. Nat. Hist. Memoir No. 3.

JEHL, J. R., JR. 1974. The near-shore avifauna of the Middle American West Coast. Auk 91: 681–699.

JEHL, J. R., JR. 1985. Hybridization and evolution of oystercatchers on the Pacific coast of Baja California. Pages 484–504 *in* Neotropical ornithology (P. A. Buckley, M. S. Foster, E. S. Morton, R. S. Ridgely, and F. G. Buckley, Eds.). Ornithol. Monogr. 36.

JEHL, J. R., JR. 1987. A review of "Nelson's Gull *Larus nelsoni*." Bull. Brit. Ornithol. Club 107: 86–91.

JEHL, J. R., JR., AND S. I. BOND. 1975. Morphological variation and species limits in murrelets of the genus *Endomychura*. Trans. San Diego Soc. Nat. Hist. 18: 9–24.

JOHNSGARD, P. A. 1961. Evolutionary relationships among the North American Mallards. Auk 78: 3–43.

JOHNSGARD, P. A. 1967. Sympatry changes and hybridization incidence in Mallards and Black Ducks. Amer. Midl. Nat. 77: 51–63.

JOHNSGARD, P. A. 1974. Taxonomy and relationships of the northern swans. Wildfowl 25: 155–161.

JOHNSGARD, P. A. 1978. Ducks, geese, and swans of the world. Univ. Nebraska Press, Lincoln, Nebraska.

JOHNSGARD, P. A. 1983. The grouse of the world. Univ. Nebraska Press, Lincoln, Nebraska.

JOHNSGARD, P. A., AND R. E. WOOD. 1968. Distributional changes and interaction between Prairie Chickens and Sharp-tailed Grouse in the midwest. Wilson Bull. 80: 173–188.

JOHNSON, N. K. 1963. Biosystematics of sibling species of flycatchers in the *Empidonax hammondii-oberholseri-wrightii* complex. Univ. Calif. Publ. Zool. 66: 79–238.

JOHNSON, N. K. 1969. Review: Three papers on variation in flickers (*Colaptes*) by Lester L. Short, Jr. Wilson Bull. 81: 225–230.

JOHNSON, N. K. 1976. Breeding distribution of Nashville and Virginia's warblers. Auk 93: 219–230.

JOHNSON, N. K. 1980. Character variation and evolution of sibling species in the *Empidonax difficilis-flavescens* complex (Aves: Tyrannidae). Univ. Calif. Publ. Zool. 112: 1–151.

JOHNSON, N. K. 1994a. Old-school taxonomy versus modern biosystematics: Species-level decisions in *Stelgidopteryx* and *Empidonax*. Auk 111: 773–780.

JOHNSON, N. K. 1994b. Pioneering and natural expansion of breeding distributions in western North American birds. Studies Avian Biol. 15: 27–44.

JOHNSON, N. K. 1995. Speciation in vireos. I. Macrogeographic patterns of allozymic variation in the *Vireo solitarius* complex in the contiguous United States. Condor 97: 903–919.

JOHNSON, N. K., AND A. H. BRUSH. 1972. Analysis of polymorphism in the Sooty-capped Bush Tanager. Syst. Zool. 21: 245–262.

Johnson, N. K., and C. B. Johnson. 1985. Speciation in sapsuckers (*Sphyrapicus*): II. Sympatry, hybridization and mate preference in *S. ruber daggetti* and *S. nuchalis*. Auk 102: 1–15.

JOHNSON, N. K., AND J. A. MARTEN. 1988. Evolutionary genetics of flycatchers. II. Differentiation in the *Empidonax difficilis* group. Auk 105: 177–191.

JOHNSON, N. K., AND J. A. MARTEN. 1992. Macrogeographic patterns of morphometric and genetic variation in the Sage Sparrow complex. Condor 94: 1–19.

JOHNSON, N. K., J. A. MARTEN, AND C. J. RALPH. 1989. Genetic evidence for the origin and relationships of Hawaiian Honeycreepers (Aves: Fringillidae). Condor 91: 379–396.

JOHNSON, N. K., AND H. J. PEETERS. 1963. The systematic position of certain hawks in the genus *Buteo*. Auk 80: 417–446.

JOHNSON, N. K., AND R. M. ZINK. 1983. Speciation in sapsuckers (*Sphyrapicus*): I. Genetic differentiation. Auk 100: 871–884.

JOHNSON, N. K., AND R. M. ZINK. 1985. Genetic evidence for relationships in the avian family Vireonidae. Condor 90: 428–445.

JOHNSON, N. K., R. M. ZINK, AND J. A. MARTEN. 1988. Genetic evidence for relationships among the Red-eyed, Yellow-green, and Chivi vireos. Wilson Bull. 97: 421–435.

JOHNSTON, D. W. 1961. The biosystematics of American crows. Univ. Washington Press, Seattle.

JOHNSTON, D. W. 1971. Ecological aspects of hybridizing chickadees (*Parus*) in Virginia. Amer. Mid. Natur. 85: 124–134.

JOHNSTON, R. F. 1961. The genera of American ground doves. Auk 78: 372–378.

JOHNSTON, R. F. 1962. The taxonomy of pigeons. Condor 64: 69–74.

JOHNSTON, R. F., AND K. L. GARRETT. 1994. Population trends of introduced birds in western North America. Pages 221–231 *in* A century of avifaunal change in western North America (J. R. Jehl, Jr., and N. K. Johnson, Eds.). Studies of Avian Biology 15.

JONES, I. L. 1993. Least Auklet (*Aethia pusilla*). *In* The birds of North America, No. 69 (A. Poole and F. Gill, Eds.). Academy of Natural Sciences, Philadelphia, and American Ornithologists' Union, Washington, D.C.

JUNGE, G. C. A., AND K. H. VOOUS. 1955. The distribution and the relationship of *Sterna eurygnatha* Saunders. Ardea 43: 226–247.

KASPRZYK, M. J., R. A. FORSTER, AND B. A. HARRINGTON. 1987. First Northern Hemisphere record and first juvenile description of Cox's Sandpiper *(Calidris paramelanotos)*. Amer. Birds 41: 1359–1365.

KEITH, A. 1940. The Arizona Jay, *Aphelocoma siberii arizonae,* found in Kansas. Trans. Kansas Acad. Science 43: 427.

KENYON, K. W., AND R. E. PHILLIPS. 1965. Birds from the Pribilof Islands and vicinity. Auk 82: 633.

KEPLER, C. B., AND K. C. PARKES. 1972. A new species of warbler (Parulidae) from Puerto Rico. Auk 89: 1–18.

KESSEL, B. 1989. Birds on the Seward Peninsula, Alaska. Univ. Alaska Press, Fairbanks.

KESSEL, B., AND D. D. GIBSON. 1978. Status and distribution of Alaskan birds. Studies Avian Biol. 1: 1–100.

KILTIE, R. A., AND J. W. FITZPATRICK. 1984. Reproduction and social organization of the Black-capped Donacobius *(Donacobius atricapillus)* in southeastern Peru. Auk 101: 804–811.

KISTCHINSKI, A. A. 1980. [Birds of the Koryak Highlands]. Nauka, Moscow.

KISTCHINSKI, A. A., AND E. G. LOBKOV. 1979. [Spatial relationships between some bird subspecies in the Beringian forest-tundra]. Moskov. Obs. I Spyt. Prirody, Otd. Biol., Bull. (n.s.) 5: 11–23.

KLEIN, N. K., AND W. M. BROWN. 1994. Intraspecific molecular phylogeny in the Yellow Warbler (*Dendroica petechia*) and implications for avian biogeography in the West Indies. Evolution 48: 1914–1932.

KNOWLES, K. 1995. A Newfoundland invasion by European vagrants. Birders Journal 4: 144–147.

KNOX, A. 1988a. Taxonomy of the Rock/Water Pipit superspecies *Anthus petrosus, spinoletta* and *rubescens*. Brit. Birds 81: 206–211.

KNOX, A. 1988b. The taxonomy of redpolls. Ardea 76: 1–26.

KOENIG, W. D. 1984. Clutch size of the Gilded Flicker. Condor 86: 89–90.

KÖNIG, C. 1982. Zur systematischen Stellung der Neuweltgeier (Cathartidae). J. für Ornithologie 123: 259–267.

KÖNIG, C. 1991. Zur Taxonomie und ökologie der Sperlingskäuze (*Glaucidium* spp.) des Andenraumes. Ökol. Vøgel (Ecol. Birds) 13: 15–76.

KÖNIG, C. 1994. Lautäuberungen als interspezifische Isolationmechanismen bei Eulen der Gattung *Otus* aus dem südlichen Südamerika. Stuttgarter Beitr. Naturk., Ser. A, 511: 1–35.

KRATTER, A. W. 1993. Geographic variation in the Yellow-billed Cacique (*Amblycercus holosericeus*), a partial bamboo specialist. Condor 95: 641–651.

KROGMAN, B. 1978. The Tule Goose mystery—a problem in taxonomy. Amer. Birds 32: 164–166.

KROGMAN, B. 1979. A systematic study of *Anser albifrons* in California. Pages 29–43 *in* Symposium on Management and Biology of Pacific Flyway Geese, Northwest Section (R. L. Jarvis and J. C. Bartonek, Eds.). The Wildlife Society, Corvallis, Oregon.

KROODSMA, D. E. 1988. Two species of Marsh Wren (*Cistothorus palustris*) in Nebraska? Nebraska Bird Review 56: 40–42.

KROODSMA, D. E. 1989. Two North American song populations of the Marsh Wren reach distributional limits in the central Great Plains. Condor 91: 332–340.

KROODSMA, D. E., AND R. A. CANADY. 1985. Differences in repertoire size, singing behavior, and associated neuroanatomy among marsh wren populations have a genetic basis. Auk 102: 439–446.

KROODSMA, R. L. 1974a. Species recognition behavior of territorial male Rose-breasted and Black-headed grosbeaks (*Pheucticus*). Auk 91: 54–64.

KROODSMA, R. L. 1974b. Hybridization in grosbeaks (*Pheucticus*) in North Dakota. Wilson Bull. 86: 230–236.

KROODSMA, R. L. 1975. Hybridization in buntings (*Passerina*) in North Dakota and eastern Montana. Auk 92: 66–80.

KURODA, N. 1954. On the classification and phylogeny of the order Tubinares, particularly the shearwaters (*Puffinus*). Herald Co., Ltd., Tokyo, Japan.

LAHRMAN, F. W. 1994. A Bar-headed Goose seen in Regina - a possible first record for North America. Blue Jay 52: 137–140.

LAMMERTINK, M., AND A. R. ESTRADA. 1995. Status of the Ivory-billed Woodpecker *Campephilus principalis* in Cuba: almost certainly extinct. Bird Conserv. Int. 5: 53–59.

LANGHAM, J. M. 1991. Twelfth report of the California Bird Records Committee. Western Birds 22: 97–130.

LANNING, D. V., J. T. MARSHALL, AND J. T. SHIFTLETT. 1990. Range and habitat of the Colima Warbler. Wilson Bull. 102: 1–13.

LANYON, S. M. 1985. Molecular perspective on higher-level relationships in the Tyrannidae (Aves). Syst. Zool. 34: 404–418.

LANYON, S. M. 1992. Interspecific brood parasitism in blackbirds (Icterinae): a phylogenetic perspective. Science 255: 77–79.

LANYON, S. M. 1994. Polyphyly of the blackbird genus *Agelaius* and the importance of assumptions of monophyly in comparative studies. Evolution 48: 679–693.

LANYON, S. M., AND J. G. HALL. 1994. Re-examination of barbet monophyly using mitochondrial-DNA sequence data. Auk 111: 389–397.

LANYON, S. M., AND R. M. ZINK. 1987. Genetic variation in piciform birds: monophyly and generic and familial relationships. Auk 104: 724–732.

LANYON, W. E. 1957. The comparative biology of the meadowlarks (*Sturnella*) in Wisconsin. Publ. Nuttall Ornith. Club No. 1.

LANYON, W. E. 1960. Relationship of the House Wren (*Troglodytes aedon*) of North America and the Brown-throated Wren (*Troglodytes brunneicollis*) of Mexico. Proc. 12th Intern. Ornith. Congress: 450–458.

LANYON, W. E. 1962. Specific limits and distribution of meadowlarks of the desert grassland. Auk 79: 183–207.

LANYON, W. E. 1966. Hybridization in meadowlarks. Bull. Amer. Mus. Nat. Hist. 134: 1–25.

LANYON, W. E. 1967. Revision and probable evolution of the *Myiarchus* flycatchers of the West Indies. Bull. Amer. Mus. Nat. Hist. 136: 329–370.

LANYON, W. E. 1978. Revision of the *Myiarchus* flycatchers of South America. Bull. Amer. Mus. Nat. Hist. 161: 429–627.

LANYON, W. E. 1979. Hybrid sterility in meadowlarks. Nature 279: 557–558.

LANYON, W. E. 1984. The systematic position of the Cocos Flycatcher. Condor 86: 42–47.

LANYON, W. E. 1985. A phylogeny of the myiarchine flycatchers. Ornithol. Monogr. 36: 361–380.

LANYON, W. E. 1986. A phylogeny of the thirty-three genera in the *Empidonax* assemblage of tyrant flycatchers. Amer. Mus. Novitates 2846.

LANYON, W. E. 1988a. Phylogenetic affinities of the flycatcher genera *Myiobius* Darwin and *Terenotriccus* Ridgway. Amer. Mus. Novitates 2915.

LANYON, W. E. 1988b. A phylogeny of the flatbill and tody-tyrant assemblages of tyrant flycatchers. Amer. Mus. Novitates 2923.

LANYON, W. E., AND S. M. LANYON. 1986. Generic status of Euler's Flycatcher: a morphometric and biochemical study. Auk 103: 341–350.

LASLEY, G. W., AND M. KRZYWONSKI. 1991. First United States record of the White-throated Robin. Amer. Birds 45: 230–231.

LASLEY, G. W., AND T. PINCELLI. 1986. Gray Silky-flycatcher in Texas. Birding 18: 34–36.

LASLEY, G. W., C. SEXTON, AND D. HILLSMAN. 1988. First record of the Mottled Owl (*Ciccaba virgata*) in the United States. Amer. Birds 42: 23–24.

LAWRENCE, G. N. 1851. Additions to North American ornithology. Ann. Lyc. Nat. Hist. N. Y. 5: 117–119.

LAWRENCE, G. N. 1853. Additions to North American ornithology —no. 3. Ann. Lyc. Nat. Hist. N. Y. 6: 4–7.

LEE, D. S. 1979. Second record of the South Trinidad Petrel (*Pterodroma arminjoniana*) for North America. Amer. Birds 38: 151–163.

LEE, D. S. 1984. Petrels and storm-petrels in North Carolina's offshore waters: including species previously unrecorded for North America. Amer. Birds 38: 151–163.

LEE, D. S. 1993. Comments on four pre-1853 seabirds reportedly obtained off Monterey, California. Auk 110: 402–404.

LEE, P. L., D. H. CLAYTON, R. GRIFFITHS, AND R. D. M. PAGE. 1996. Does behavior reflect phylogeny in swiftlets (Aves: Apodidae)? A test using cytochrome b mitochondrial DNA sequences. Proc. Natl. Acad. Sci. USA 93: 7091–7096.

LEHMAN, P., AND J. L. DUNN. 1985. A little-known species reaches North America. Amer. Birds 39: 247–250.

LEVY, C. 1994. The Spotted Rail *Pardirallus maculatus* in Jamaica. El Pitirre 7: 2–3.

LIGON, J. D. 1967. Relationships of the cathartid vultures. Univ. Mich. Mus. Zool., Occas. Pap. 651.

LIGON, J. D. 1968. Observations on Strickland's Woodpecker, *Dendrocopos stricklandi*. Condor 70: 83–84.

LIGON, J. D. 1974. Comments on the systematic relationships of the Piñon Jay (*Gymnorhinus cyanocephalus*). Condor 76: 468–470.

LIVEZY, B. C. 1991. A phylogenetic analysis and classification of Recent dabbling ducks (Tribe Anatini) based on comparative morphology. Auk 108: 471–507.

LIVEZY, B. C. 1995a. A phylogenetic analysis of the whistling and White-backed ducks (Anatidae: Dendrocygninae) using morphological characters. Annals Carnegie Mus. 64: 65–97.

LIVEZY, B. C. 1995b. Phylogeny and comparative ecology of stiff-tailed dicks (Anatidae: Oxyurini). Wilson Bull. 107: 214–234.

LIVEZY, B. C. 1995c. Phylogeny and evolutionary ecology of modern seaducks (Anatidae: Mergini). Condor 97: 233–255.

LIVEZY, B. C. 1996a. A phylogenetic analysis of geese and swans (Anseriformes: Anserinae), including selected fossil species. Syst. Biol. 45: 415–450.

LIVEZY, B. C. 1996b. A phylogenetic analysis of modern pochards (Anatidae: Aythyini). Auk 113: 74–93.

LOSADA, S. A., AND S. N. G. HOWELL. 1996. Distribution, variation, and conservation of Yellow-headed Parrots in northern Central America. Cotinga 5: 46–53.

LOWERY, G. H., JR., AND D. G. BERRETT. 1963. A new Carolina Wren (Aves: Troglodytidae) from southern Mexico. Occ. Papers Mus. Zool. Louis. St. Univ. 24: 1–3.

LOWERY, G. H., JR., AND W. W. DALQUEST. 1951. Birds from the State of Veracruz, Mexico. Univ. Kansas Publ. Mus. Nat. Hist. 3: 533–649.

LOWERY, G. H., JR., AND J. P. O'NEILL. 1969. A new species of antpitta from Peru and a revision of the Subfamily Grallariinae. Auk 86: 1–12.

MACINNES, C. D., AND E. B. CHAMBERLAIN. 1963. The first record of the Double-striped Thick-knee in the United States. Auk 80: 79–80.

MACLEAN, G. L. 1967. Die Systematische Stellung der Flughühner (Pteroclididae). J. für Ornithologie 108: 203–217.

MACTAVISH, B. 1994. Eurasian Oystercatcher, first for North America. Birders Journal 3: 168–171.

MACTAVISH, B. 1996. Common Redshank in Newfoundland. Birding 28: 302–307.

MANNING, T. H., E. O. HÖHN, AND A. H. MACPHERSON. 1956. The birds of Banks Island. Bull. Nat. Mus. Canada No. 143.

MARANTZ, C. A. 1997. Geographic variation of plumage patterns in the woodcreeper genus *Dendrocolaptes* (Dendrocolaptidae). Pages 399–430 *in* Studies in Neotropical ornithology honoring Ted Parker (Remsen, J. V., Jr., Ed.). Ornithol. Monogr. 48.

MARÍN, M. 1993. First record of the White-flanked Antwren (*Myrmotherula axillaris*) in Mexico. Ornitologia Neotropical 4: 97–98.

MARÍN, M. 1997. Species limits and distribution of some New World spine-tailed swifts (*Chaetura* spp.). Pages 399–499 *in* Studies in Neotropical ornithology honoring Ted Parker (Remsen, J. V., Jr., Ed.). Ornithol. Monogr. 48.

MARÍN A., M., L. F. KIFF, AND L. PEÑA G. 1989. Notes on Chilean birds, with descriptions of two new subspecies. Bull. Brit. Ornithol. Club 109: 66–82.

MARÍN A., M., AND F. G. STILES. 1992. On the biology of five species of swifts (Apodidae, Cypseloidinae) in Costa Rica. Proc. Western Foundation Vertebr. Zool. 4: 287–351.

MARION, L., P. YÉSOU, P. J. DUBOIS, AND P. NICOLAU-GUILLAUMET. 1985. Coexistence progressive de la reproduction de *Larus argentatus* et de *Larus cachinnans* sur les côtes atlantiques françaises. Alauda 53: 81–87.

MARSHALL, J. T., JR. 1956. Summer birds of the Rincon Mountains, Saguaro National Monument, Arizona. Condor 58: 81–97.

MARSHALL, J. T., JR. 1964. Voice in communication and relationships among Brown Towhees. Condor 66: 345–356.

MARSHALL, J. T., JR. 1967. Parallel variation in North and Middle American Screech-Owls. Monogr. West. Foundation Vertebrate Zool. 1: 1–72.

MARSHALL, J. T., JR. 1978. Systematics of smaller Asian night birds based on voice. Ornithol. Monogr. 25.

MARSHALL, J. T., R. A. BEHRSTOCK, AND C. KÖNIG. 1991. (Review of) Voices of the New World nightjars and their allies (Caprimulgiformes: Steatornithidae, Nyctibiidae, and Caprimulgidae) by J. W. Hardy, B. B. Coffey, Jr., and G. B. Reynard, and (Review of) Voices of the New World owls (Strigiformes: Tytonidae, Strigidae) by J. W. Hardy. Wilson Bull. 103: 311–315.

MASSEY, B. W. 1976. Vocal differences between American Least Terns and the European Little Tern. Auk 93: 760–773.

MAURER, D. R., AND R. J. RAIKOW. 1981. Appendicular morphology, phylogeny, and classification of the avian order Coraciiformes (including Trogoniformes). Annals Carnegie Mus. 50: 417–434.

MAYR, E. 1956. Is the Great White Heron a good species? Auk 73: 71–77.

MAYR, E. 1963. *Gallinago* versus *Capella.* Ibis 105: 402–403.

MAYR, E., AND D. AMADON. 1951. A classification of recent birds. Amer. Mus. Novitates 1496.

Mayr, E., and G. W. Cottrell. (Eds.). 1979. Check-list of birds of the World, vol. 1, 2nd ed. Museum of Comparative Zoology, Cambridge, Massachusetts.

MAYR, E., AND G. W. COTTRELL. (Eds.). 1986. Check-list of birds of the world, vol. 11. Museum of Comparative Zoology, Cambridge, Massachusetts.

MAYR, E., AND J. C. GREENWAY, JR. (Eds.). 1960. Check-list of birds of the world, vol. 9. Museum of Comparative Zoology, Cambridge, Massachusetts.

MAYR, E., AND J. C. GREENWAY, JR. (Eds.). 1962. Check-list of birds of the world, vol. 15. Museum of Comparative Zoology, Cambridge, Massachusetts.

MAYR, E., AND R. A. PAYNTER, JR. (Eds.). 1964. Check-list of birds of the world, vol. 10. Museum of Comparative Zoology, Cambridge, Massachusetts.

MAYR, E., AND L. L. SHORT. 1970. Species taxa of North American birds. Publ. Nuttall Orn. Club 9.

MCATEE, W. L. 1947. Cuban Nighthawk a species, rather than a race, additional to the Check-list. Auk 64: 455–456.

MCCAMEY, F. 1950. A puzzling hybrid warbler from Michigan. Jack-Pine Warbler 28: 67–72.

MCCASKIE, G., AND R. E. WEBSTER. 1990. A second Wedge-tailed Shearwater in California. Western Birds 21: 139–140.

MCCRACKEN, K. G., AND F. H. SHELDON. 1997. Avian vocalizations and phylogenetic signal. Proc. Nat. Acad. Sciences USA 94: 3833–3836.

MCDONALD, M. A., AND M. H. SMITH. 1990. Speciation, heterochrony, and genetic variation in Hispaniolan Palm-tanagers. Auk 107: 707–717.

MCDONALD, M. A., AND M. H. SMITH. 1994. Behavioral and morphological correlates of heterochrony in Hispaniolan Palm-tanagers. Condor 96: 433–446.

MCHENRY, E. N., AND J. C. DYES. 1983. First record of juvenal "white-phase" Great Blue Heron in Texas. Amer. Birds 37: 119.

MCKINNEY, F. 1965. The displays of the American Green-winged Teal. Wilson Bull. 77: 112–121.

MCKITRICK, M. C. 1985. Monophyly of the Tyrannidae (Aves): comparison of morphology and DNA. Syst. Zool. 34: 35–45.

MCKITRICK, M. C., AND R. M. ZINK. 1988. Species concepts in ornithology. Condor 90: 1–14.

MCLAREN, I. A., J. MORLAN, P. W. SMITH, M. GOSSELIN, AND S. F. BAILEY. 1989. Eurasian Siskins in North America—distinguishing females from green-morph Pine Siskins. Amer. Birds 43: 1268–1274, 1381.

MCNEIL, R., AND J. BURTON. 1971. First authentic North American record of the British Storm Petrel *(Hydrobates pelagicus).* Auk 88: 671–672.

MCNEIL, R., AND A. CYR. 1971. European Blackbird *(Turdus merula)* in Quebec. Auk 88: 919–920.

MEANLEY, B. 1969. Natural history of the King Rail. North Amer. Fauna 67.

MEDWAY, D. G. 1981. The contribution of Cook's third voyage to the ornithology of the Hawaiian Islands. Pacific Sci. 35: 105–175.

MEISE, W. 1928. Die Verbreitung der Aaskrähe (Formenkreis *Corvus corone* L.). J. für Ornithologie 76: 1–203.

MENGEL. R. M. 1964. The probable history of species formation in some northern wood warblers (Parulidae). Living Bird 3: 9–43.

MEYER DE SCHAUENSEE, R. 1966. The species of birds of South America and their distribution. Livingston Publ. Co., Narberth, Pennsylvania.

MEYER DE SCHAUENSEE, R. 1970. A guide to the birds of South America. Livingston Publ. Co., Wynnewood, Pennsylvania.

MEYERRIECKS, A. J. 1957. Field observations pertaining to the systematic status of the Great White Heron in the Florida Keys. Auk 74: 469–478.

MICKEVICH, M. F., AND L. R. PARENTI. 1980. [Review of] The phylogeny of the Charadriiformes (Aves): a new estimate using the method of character compatibility analysis by J. G. Strauch. Syst. Zool. 29: 108–113.

MILLER, A. H. 1941. Speciation in the avian genus *Junco.* Univ. Calif. Publ. Zool. 44: 173–434.

MILLER, A. H. 1964. Mockingbird. Pp. 479–481 *in* A new dictionary of birds (A. L. Thomson, Ed.). Nelson, London.

MILLER, A. H., H. FRIEDMANN, L. GRISCOM, AND R. T. MOORE. 1957. Distributional checklist of the birds of Mexico. Part 2. Pac. Coast Avifauna 33: 1–436.

MILLER, A. H., AND L. MILLER. 1951. Geographic variation of the Screech Owls of the deserts of western North America. Condor 53: 161–177.

MILLER, W. DEW. 1906. List of birds collected in northwestern Durango, Mexico, by J. H. Batty, during 1903. Bull. Amer. Mus. Nat. Hist. 22: 161–183.

MINDELL, D. P. 1983. Harlan's Hawk *(Buteo jamaicensis harlani)*: a valid subspecies. Auk 100: 161–169.

MIRSKY, E. N. 1976. Song divergence in hummingbird and junco populations on Guadeloupe Island. Condor 78: 230–235.

MISRA, R. K., AND L. L. SHORT. 1974. A biometric analysis of oriole hybridization. Condor 76: 137–146.

MOBLEY, J. A., AND R. O. Prum. 1995. Phylogenetic relationships of the Cinnamon Tyrant, *Neopipo cinnamomea,* to the tyrant flycatchers (Tyrannidae). Condor 97: 650–662.

MOFFITT, J. 1938. Two southern petrels in the North Pacific. Auk 55: 255–259.

MOLAU, U. 1985. Gråsiskkomplexet i Sverige. Vår Fågelvärld 44: 5–20.

MOLDENHAUER, R. R. 1992. Two song populations of the Northern Parula. Auk 109: 215–222.

MONROE, B. L., JR. 1955. A gull new to North America. Auk 72; 208.

MONROE, B. L., JR. 1963a. A revision of the *Lampornis viridipallens* complex (Aves: Trochilidae). Occ. Papers Mus. Zool. Louis. State Univ. 27: 1–10.

MONROE, B. L., JR. 1963b. Notes on the avian genus *Arremonops* with description of a new subspecies form Honduras. Occas. Pap. Mus. Zool. Louis. State Univ. 28: 1–12.

MONROE, B. L., JR. 1968. A distributional survey of the birds of Honduras. Ornithol. Monogr. 7.

MONROE, B. L., JR. 1989. The correct name of the Terek Sandpiper. Bull. Brit. Ornithol. Club 109: 106–107.

MONROE, B. L., JR. 1991. A reconsideration of the Massachusetts "Cox's Sandpiper." Amer. Birds 45: 232–233.

MONROE, B. L., JR., AND T. R. HOWELL. 1966. Geographic variation in Middle American parrots of the *Amazona ochrocephala* complex. Occ. Pap. Mus. Zool. Louis. State Univ. 34: 1–18.

MONROE, B. L., JR., AND M. R. BROWNING. 1992. A re-analysis of *Butorides.* Bull. Brit. Ornithol. Club 112: 81–85.

MONROE, B. L., JR., AND C. G. SIBLEY. 1993. A world checklist of birds. Yale Univ. Press, New Haven Connecticut.

MONTEVECCHI, W. A., B. MACTAVISH, AND I. R. KIRKHAM. 1981. First North American photographic record of the Redwing *(Turdus iliacus).* Amer. Birds 35: 147.

MOORE, W. S. 1987. Random mating in the Northern Flicker hybrid zone: implications for the evolution of bright and contrasting plumage patterns in birds. Evolution 41: 539–546.

MOORE, W. S., AND D. B. BUCHANAN. 1985. Stability of the Northern Flicker hybrid zone. Evolution 39: 135–151.

MOORE, W. S., J. H. GRAHAM, AND J. PRICE. 1991. Geographic variation of mitochondrial DNA in the Northern Flicker *(Colaptes auratus).* Molecular Biol. Evolution 8: 327–344.

MOORE, W. S., AND W. D. KOENIG. 1986. Comparative reproductive success of Yellow-shafted, Red-shafted, and hybrid flickers across a hybrid zone. Auk 103: 42–51.

MOORE, W. S., AND J. T. PRICE. 1993. Nature of selection in the Northern Flicker hybrid zone and its implications for speciation theory. Pages 196–225 *in* Hybrid zones and the evolutionary process (R. G. Harrison, Ed.). Oxford Univ. Press, Oxford.

MORGAN, J. G., T. L. EUBANKS, JR., V. EUBANKS, AND L. N. WHITE. 1985. Yucatan Vireo appears in Texas. Amer. Birds 39: 245–246.

MORGAN, J. G., AND L. M. FELTNER. 1985. A Neotropical bird flies north: the Greenish Elaenia. Amer. Birds 39: 242–244.

MORLAN, J. 1981. Status and identification of forms of White Wagtail in western North America. Cont. Birdlife 2: 37–50.

MORLAN, J., AND R. A. ERICKSON. 1983. A Eurasian Skylark at Point Reyes, California, with notes on skylark identification and systematics. W. Birds 14: 113–126.

MORONY, J. J., JR., W. J. BOCK, AND J. FARRAND, JR. 1975. Reference list of the birds of the world. American Museum of Natural History, New York.

MORRISON, M. L., AND J. W. HARDY. 1983. Hybridization between Hermit and Townsend's warblers. Murrelet 64: 65–72.

MORSE, D. H. 1989. American warblers. Harvard Univ. Press, Cambridge, Massachusetts.

MOUM, T., S. JOHANSEN, K. E. ERIKSTAD, AND J. F. PIATT. 1994. Phylogeny and evolution of the auks based on mitochondrial DNA sequences. Proc. Natl. Acad. Sci. USA 91: 7912–7916.

MURPHY, R. C. 1936. Oceanic birds of South America. 2 vols. McMillan Co., New York.

MURPHY, R. C. 1938. The Wandering Albatross in the Bay of Panama. Condor 40: 126.

MURPHY, R. C. 1952. The Manx Shearwater, *Puffinus puffinus,* as a species of world-wide distribution. Amer. Mus. Novitates 1586.

MURRAY, B. G., JR. 1968. The relationships of sparrows in the genera *Ammodramus, Passerherbulus,* and *Ammospiza* with a description of a hybrid Le Conte's X Sharp-tailed Sparrow. Auk. 85: 586–593.

MURRAY, B. G., JR. 1989. A critical review of the transoceanic migration of the Blackpoll Warbler. Auk 106: 8–17.

MURRAY, B. G., JR., AND F. B. GILL. 1976. Behavioral interactions of Blue-winged and Golden-winged warblers. Wilson Bull. 88: 231–254.

MURRAY, B. W., W. B. MCGILLIVRAY, J. C. BARLOW, R. N. BEECH, AND C. STROBECK. 1994. The use of cytochrome *B* sequence variation in estimation of phylogeny in the Vireonidae. Condor 96: 1037–1054.

NAZARENKO, A. A. 1978. [On species validity of *Anthus rubescens* Tunstall (Aves: Motacillidae)]. Zool. Zh. 57: 1743–1744.

NESBIT, I. C. T., D. C. MCNAIR, W. POST, AND T. C. WILLIAMS. 1995. Transoceanic migration of the Blackpoll Warbler: summary of scientific evidence and response to criticisms by Murray. J. Field. Ornithol. 66: 612–622.

NEUDORF, D. L., AND P. J. BLANCHFIELD. 1994. The Slate-colored Seedeater (*Sporophila schistacea*): a bamboo specialist? Ornitologia Neotropical 5: 129–132.

NICHOLSON, C. P., AND S. J. STEADMAN. 1988. The official list of Tennessee birds, Addendum I. Migrant 59: 1–4.

NIELSEN, B. P. 1975. Affinities of *Eudromias morinellus* (L.) to the genus *Charadrius* (L.). Ornis Scandinavica 6: 65–82.

NORBERG, R. Å. 1977. Occurrence and independent evolution of bilateral ear asymmetry in owls and implications in owl taxonomy. Philos. Trans. R. Soc. London 280: 375–408.

NORRIS, R. A. 1958. Comparative biosystematics and life history of the nuthatches *Sitta pygmaea* and *Sitta pusilla.* Univ. Calif. Publ. Zool. 56: 119–300.

NORTON, A. H. 1922. The Pintado Petrel *(Daption capense)* in Maine. Auk 39: 101–103.

NORTON, R. L. 1984. Cayenne X Sandwich terns nesting in Virgin Islands, Greater Antilles. J. Field Ornith. 55: 243–246.

NUECHTERLEIN, G. L. 1981. Courtship behavior and reproductive isolation between Western Grebe color morphs. Auk 98: 335–349.

NUECHTERLEIN, G. L., AND R. W. STORER. 1982. The pair-formation displays of the Western Grebe. Condor 94: 351–369.

NUNN, G. B., J. COOPER, P. JOUVENTIN, C. J. R. ROBERTSON, AND G. G. ROBERTSON. 1996. Evolutionary relationships among extant albatrosses (Procellariiformes: Diomedeidae) established from complete cytochrome-*b* gene sequences. Auk 113: 784–801.

OBERHOLSER, H. C. 1921. Notes on North American birds. X. Auk 38: 79–82.

OBERHOLSER, H. C. 1974. The bird life of Texas. Univ. Texas Press, Austin.

OLSON, S. L. 1970. A study of seedsnipe in southern South America by G. L. Maclean (a review). Bird-Banding 41: 258–259.

OLSON, S. L. 1972. The generic distinction of the Hispaniolan Woodpecker, *Chryserpes striatus* (Aves: Picidae). Proc. Biol. Soc. Wash. 85: 499–508.

OLSON, S. L. 1973. A classification of the Rallidae. Wilson Bull. 85: 381–416.

OLSON, S. L. 1978. Greater Ani (*Crotophaga major*) in Mexico. Auk 95: 766–767.

OLSON, S. L. 1981a. The nature of the variability in the Variable Seedeater in Panama (*Sporophila americana*: Emberizinae). Proc. Biol. Soc. Wash. 94: 380–390.

OLSON, S. L. 1981b. Interaction between the two subspecies groups of the seed-finch *Sporophila angolensis* in the Magdalena Valley, Colombia. Auk 98: 379–381.

OLSON, S. L. 1981c. A revision of the subspecies of *Sporophila* ("*Oryzoborus*") *angolensis* (Aves: Emberizidae). Proc. Biol. Soc. Wash. 94: 43–51.

OLSON, S. L. 1981d. Systematic notes on certain oscines from Panama and adjacent areas (Aves: Passeriformes). Proc. Biol. Soc. Wash. 94: 363–373.

OLSON, S. L. 1982. The distribution of fused phalanges of the inner toe in the Accipitridae. Bull. Brit. Ornith. Club 102: 8–12.

OLSON, S. L. 1983. Evidence for a polyphyletic origin of the Piciformes. Auk 100: 126–133.

OLSON, S. L. 1986. The correct specific name for the Akepa of Oahu (Drepanidini, *Loxops*). Bull. Brit. Ornithol. Club 106: 148–149.

OLSON, S. L. 1989. Notes on some Hawaiian birds from Cook's third voyage. Bull. Brit. Ornithol. Club 109: 201–205.

OLSON, S. L. 1993a. Contributions to avian biogeography from the archipelago and lowlands of Bocas del Toro, Panama. Auk 110: 100–108.

OLSON, S. L. 1993b. Intergradation between the bush-tanagers *Chlorospingus punctulatus* and *C. ophthalmicus* in western Panama (Aves: Thraupidae). Auk 110: 148–150.

OLSON, S. L. 1994. The endemic vireo of Fernando de Noronha (*Vireo gracilirostris*). Wilson Bull. 106: 1–17.

OLSON, S..L. 1995. The genera of owls in the Asioninae. Bull. Brit. Ornithol. Club 115: 35–39.

OLSON, S. L. 1996. The contribution of the voyage of H.M.S. Blonde (1825) to Hawaiian ornithology. Archives Nat. Hist. 23: 1–42.

OLSON, S. L., AND A. FEDUCCIA. 1980. Relationships and evolution of flamingos (Aves: Phoenicopteridae). Smithsonian Contrib. Zool. 316: 1–73.

OLSON, S. L., AND H. F. JAMES. 1982. Prodromus of the fossil avifauna of the Hawaiian Islands. Smithsonian Contrib. Zool. 365: 1–59.

OLSON, S. L., AND H. F. JAMES. 1988. Nomenclature of the Kauai Amakihi and Kauai Akialoa (Drepanidini). 'Elepaio 48: 13–14.

OLSON, S. L., AND H. F. JAMES. 1995. Nomenclature of the Hawaiian Akialoas and Nukupuus (Aves: Drepanidini). Proc. Biol. Soc. Wash. 108: 373–387.

OLSON, S. L., AND K. I. WARHEIT. 1988. A new genus for *Sula abbotti*. Bull. Brit. Ornithol. Club 108: 9–12.

ORENSTEIN, R. I., AND J. C. BARLOW. 1981. Variation in the jaw musculature of the avian family Vireonidae. Life Sci. Contrib. Royal Ontario Mus. 128.

ORENSTEIN, R. I., AND H. D. PRATT. 1983. The relationships and evolution of the Southwest Pacific warbler genera *Vitia* and *Psamathia* (Sylviinae). Wilson Bull. 95: 184–198.

OUELLET, H. 1977. Relationships of woodpecker genera *Dendrocopos* Koch and *Picoides* Lacépède (Aves: Picidae). Ardea 65: 165–183.

OUELLET, H. 1992. Speciation, zoogeography, and taxonomic problems in the Neotropical genus *Sporophila* (Aves: Emberizinae). Bull. Brit. Ornithol. Club 112A: 225–235.

OUELLET, H. 1993. Bicknell's Thrush: taxonomic status and distribution. Wilson Bull. 105: 545–572.

PALMER, R. S. 1962. Handbook of North American birds, vol. 1 [Gaviiformes-Phoenicopteriformes]. Yale Univ. Press, New Haven, Connecticut.

PALMER, R. S. 1976. Handbook of North American birds. Vol. 2, Waterfowl (Part 1). Yale Univ. Press, New Haven, Connecticut.

PARKER, J. W. 1981. Comment on Mississippi Kite specimens collected by S. W. Woodhouse in Indian Territory. Bull. Oklahoma Ornithol. Soc. 14: 29–31.

PARKER, T. A., III, A. CASTILLO U., M. GELL-MANN AND O. ROCHA O. 1991. Records of new and unusual birds from northern Bolivia. Bull. Brit. Ornithol. Club 111: 120–138.

PARKER, T. A., III, T. S. SCHULENBERG, M. KESSLER, AND W. H. WUST. 1995. Natural history and conservation of the endemic avifauna in north-west Peru. Bird Conserv. Intern. 5: 201–232.

PARKER, T. A., III, AND J. V. REMSEN, JR. 1987. Fifty-two Amazonian bird species new to Bolivia. Bull. Brit. Ornith. Club 107: 94–107.

PARKES, K. C. 1951. The genetics of the Golden-winged and Blue-winged warbler complex. Wilson Bull. 63: 5–15.

PARKES, K. C. 1961. Taxonomic relationships among the American redstarts. Wilson Bull. 74: 374–379.

PARKES, K. C. 1985. Audubon's mystery birds. Natural History 94 (4): 88–93.

PARMALEE, D. F. 1988. The hybrid skua: the southern ocean enigma. Wilson Bull. 100: 345–346.

PATTEN, S., JR., AND A. R. WIESBROD. 1974. Sympatry and interbreeding of Herring and Glaucous-winged gulls in southeastern Alaska. Condor 76: 343–344.

PAXTON, R. O. 1968. Wandering Albatross in California. Auk 85: 502–504.

PAYNE, R. B. 1974. Species limits and variation of the New World Green Herons *Butorides virescens* and Striated Herons *Butorides striatus*. Bull. Brit. Ornithol. Club 94: 81–88.

PAYNE, R. B. AND C. J. RISLEY. 1976. Systematics and evolutionary relationships among the herons (Ardeidae). Misc. Publ. Univ. Michigan Mus. Zool. 150.

PAYNTER, R. A., JR. 1955. The ornithogeography of the Yucatan Peninsula. Bull. Peabody Mus. Yale Univ. 9: 1–347.

PAYNTER, R. A., JR. 1964a. The type locality of *Atlapetes albinucha*. Auk 81: 223–224.

PAYNTER, R. A., JR. 1964b. Generic limits of *Zonotrichia*. Condor 66: 277–281.

PAYNTER, R. A., JR. (Ed.) 1967. Check-list of birds of the world, vol. 12. Museum of Comparative Zoology, Cambridge, Massachusetts.

PAYNTER, R. A., JR. (Ed.) 1968. Check-list of birds of the world, vol. 14. Museum of Comparative Zoology, Cambridge, Massachusetts.

PAYNTER, R. A., JR. (Ed.) 1970. Check-list of birds of the world, vol. 13. Museum of Comparative Zoology, Cambridge, Massachusetts.

PAYNTER, R. A., JR. 1978. Biology and evolution of the avian genus *Atlapetes* (Emberizinae). Bull. Mus. Comp. Zool. 148: 323–369.

PEREZ-RIVERA, R. A. 1996. El Guacamayo azul y amarillo (*Ara ararauna*) exótico residente de Puerto Rico. El Pitirre 9: 3–4.

PETERS, J. L. 1931. Check-list of birds of the world, vol. 1. Museum of Comparative Zoology, Cambridge, Massachusetts.

PETERS, J. L. 1934. Check-list of birds of the world, vol. 2. Museum of Comparative Zoology, Cambridge, Massachusetts.

PETERS, J. L. 1940. Check-list of birds of the world, vol. 4. Museum of Comparative Zoology, Cambridge, Massachusetts.

PETERS, J. L. 1945. Check-list of birds of the world, vol. 5. Museum of Comparative Zoology, Cambridge, Massachusetts.

PETERS, J. L. 1948. Check-list of birds of the world, vol. 6. Museum of Comparative Zoology, Cambridge, Massachusetts.

PETERS, J. L. 1951. Check-list of birds of the world, vol. 7. Museum of Comparative Zoology, Cambridge, Massachusetts.

PETERSEN, W. R., B. J. NIKULA, AND D. W. HOLT. 1986. First record of Brown-chested Martin for North America. Amer. Birds 40: 192–193.

PETERSON, A. T. 1993. Species status of *Geotrygon carrikeri*. Bull. Brit. Ornithol. Club 113: 166–168.

PETERSON, A. T. 1991. Gene flow in scrub jays: frequency and direction of movement. Condor 93: 926–934.

PETERSON, A. T. 1992. Phylogeny and rates of molecular evolution in the *Aphelocoma* jays (Corvidae). Auk 109: 133–147.

PETERSON, A. T., AND D. B. BURT. 1992. A phylogenetic analysis of social evolution and habitat use in the *Aphelocoma* jays. Anim. Behav. 44: 859–866.

PHILLIPS, A., J. MARSHALL, AND G. MONSON. 1964. The birds of Arizona. Univ. Arizona Press, Tucson.

PHILLIPS, A. R. 1962. Notas sistematicas sobre aves mexicanas. I. An. Inst. Biol. Univ. Nac. Autón. Méx. 32: 333–381.

PHILLIPS, A. R. 1965. Notas sistematicas sobre aves mexicanas. III. Rev. Soc. Mex. Hist. Nat. 25 (1964): 217–242.

PHILLIPS, A. R. 1981. Subspecies vs. forgotten species: The case of Grayson's Robin *(Turdus graysoni)*. Wilson Bull. 93: 301–309.

PHILLIPS, A. R. 1986. The known birds of North and Middle America, pt. 1. A. R. Phillips, Denver.

PHILLIPS, A. R. 1991. The known birds of North and Middle America. pt. II. A. R. Phillips, Denver.

PHILLIPS, A. R. 1994. A review of the northern *Pheucticus* grosbeaks. Bull. Brit. Ornithol. Club 114: 162–176.

PHILLIPS, A. R., AND K. C. PARKES. 1955. Taxonomic comments on the Western Wood Pewee. Condor 57: 244.

PHILLIPS, A. R., AND R. PHILLIPS F. 1993. Distribution, migration, ecology, and relationships of the Five-striped Sparrow, *Aimophila quinquestriata.* Western Birds 24: 65–72.

PITELKA, F. A. 1945. Differentiation of the Scrub Jay, *Aphelocoma coerulescens,* in the Great Basin and Arizona. Condor 47: 23–26.

PITELKA, F. A. 1950. Geographic variation and the species problem in the shore-bird genus *Limnodromus.* Univ. Calif. Publ. Zool. 50: 1–107.

PITELKA, F. A. 1951. Speciation and ecologic distribution in American jays of the genus *Aphelocoma.* Univ. Calif. Publ. Zool. 50: 195–464.

PITELKA, F. A. 1974. An avifaunal review from the Barrow region and north slope of Arctic Alaska. Arctic Alpine Res. 6: 161–184.

PINTO, O. M. DE O., AND E. A. DE CAMARGO. 1957. Sobre uma coleçâo de aves da regiâo de Cachimbo (sul do Estado do Pará). Papeis Avulsos do Depto. de Zool., Secretaria da Agricultura, São Paulo, Brasil.

PITOCCHELLI, J. 1990. Plumage, morphometric, and song variation in Mourning *(Oporornis philadelphia)* and MacGillivray's *(O. tolmiei)* warblers. Auk 107: 161–171.

PITTAWAY, R., AND P. BURKE. 1996. Cory's Least Bittern. Ontario Birds 14: 26–40.

PORTENKO, L. A. 1972. Birds of the Chukchi Peninsula and Wrangel Island. Vol. 1. Nauka, Leningrad.

PRAGER, E. R., AND A. C. WILSON. 1975. Slow evolutionary loss of the potential for interspecific hybridization in birds: a manifestation of slow regulatory evolution. Proc. Nat. Acad. Sci. U.S.A. 72: 200–204.

PRATT, H. D. 1979. A systematic analysis of the endemic avifauna of the Hawaiian Islands. Dissert. Abstracts 40: 1581.

PRATT, H. D. 1982. Relationships and speciation of the Hawaiian thrushes. Living Bird 19 (1980–81): 73–90.

PRATT, H. D. 1987. Occurrence of the North American Coot *(Fulica americana americana)* in the Hawaiian Islands, with comments on the taxonomy of the Hawaiian Coot. 'Elepaio 47: 25–28.

PRATT, H. D. 1988. A new name for the eastern subspecies of the Brown-backed Solitaire *Myadestes occidentalis.* Bull. Brit. Ornith. Club 108: 135–136.

PRATT, H. D. 1989a. A new name for the Kauai Amakihi (Drepanidinae: *Hemignathus).* 'Elepaio 49: 13–14.

PRATT, H. D. 1989b. Species limits in the akepas (Drepanidinae: *Loxops).* Condor 91: 933–940.

PRATT, H. D. 1991. Hybridization of Great-tailed and Boat-tailed grackles *(Quiscalus)* in Louisiana. J. Louis. Ornith. 2: 2–14.

PRATT, H. D. 1992a. Systematics of the Hawaiian "creepers" *Oreomystis* and *Paroreomyza.* Condor 94: 836–846.

PRATT, H. D. 1992b. Is the Poo-uli a Hawaiian honeycreeper (Drepanidinae)? Condor 94: 172–180.

PRATT, H. D., P. L. BRUNER, AND D. G. BERRETT. 1987. A field guide to the birds of Hawaii and the tropical Pacific. Princeton Univ. Press, Princeton, New Jersey.

PREGILL, G. K., AND S. L. OLSON. 1981. Zoogeography of West Indian vertebrates in relation to Pleistocene climatic cycles. Ann. Rev. Ecol. Syst. 12: 75–98.

PRUM, R. O. 1988. Phylogenetic interrelationships of the barbets (Aves: Capitonidae) and toucans (Aves: Ramphastidae) based on morphology with comparisons to DNA-DNA hybridization. Zool. J. Linnean Soc. 92: 313–343.

PRUM, R. O. 1990. Phylogenetic analysis of the evolution of display behavior in the Neotropical manakins (Aves: Pipridae). Ethology 84: 202–231.

PRUM, R. O. 1992. Syringeal morphology, phylogeny, and evolution of the Neotropical manakins (Aves: Pipridae). Amer. Mus. Novitates 3043.

PRUM, R. O. 1994. Phylogenetic analysis of the evolution of alternative social behavior in the manakins (Aves: Pipridae). Evolution 48: 1657–1675.

PRUM, R. O., AND W. E. LANYON. 1989. Monophyly and phylogeny of the *Schiffornis* group (Tyrannoidea). Condor 91: 444–461.

PULICH, W. M. 1968. The occurrence of the Crested Hummingbird, *Orthorhynchus cristatus exilis,* in the United States. Auk 85: 322.

PYLE, P., AND B. EILERTS. 1986. Pelagic seabird observations from northwestern Hawaiian Island waters. 'Elepaio 46: 181–183.

PYLE, R. 1979. Preliminary list of the birds of Hawaii. 'Elepaio 40: 55–58.

PYLE, R. 1988. Checklist of the birds of Hawaii—1988. 'Elepaio 48: 95–106.

PYLE, R. 1990. First record of Great Crested Tern in Hawai'i. 'Elepaio 50: 21–22.

QUINN, T. W., G. F. SHIELDS, AND A. C. WILSON. 1991. Affinities of the Hawaiian Goose based on two types of mitochondrial DNA data. Auk 108: 585–593.

RAFFAELE, H. A. 1983. A guide to the birds of Puerto Rico and the Virgin Islands. Fondo Educativo Interamericano, San Juan, Puerto Rico.

RAIKOW, R. J. 1977. The origin and evolution of the Hawaiian honeycreepers (Drepanididae). Living Bird 15: 95–117.

RAIKOW, R. J. 1978. Appendicular myology and relationships of the New World nine-primaried oscines (Aves: Passeriformes). Bull. Carnegie Mus. Nat. Hist. 7: 1–43.

RAIKOW, R. J. 1994. A phylogeny of the woodcreepers (Dendrocolaptinae). Auk 111: 104–114.

RAIKOW, R. J., AND J. CRACRAFT. 1983. Monophyly of the Piciformes: a reply to Olson. Auk 100: 134–138.

RAITT, R. J. 1967. Relationships between black-eared and plain-eared forms of bushtits (*Psaltriparus*). Auk 84: 503–528.

RAMO, C., AND B. BUSTO. 1985. Comportamiento reproductivo del Corocoro *(Eudocimus ruber)* en los llanos de Venezuela. Mem. Soc. Cienc. Nat. La Salle 123: 77–113.

RAMO, C., AND B. BUSTO. 1987. Hybridization between the Scarlet Ibis *(Eudocimus ruber)* and the White Ibis *(Eudocimus albus)* in Venezuela. Colonial Waterbirds 10: 111–114.

RAND, A. L. 1960. Races of the Short-tailed Hawk, *Buteo brachyurus.* Auk 77: 448–459.

RAND, A. L., AND M. A. TRAYLOR, JR. 1953. The systematic position of the genera *Ramphocaenus* and *Microbates.* Auk 70: 334–337.

RATTI, J. T. 1979. Reproductive separation and isolating mechanisms between sympatric dark- and light-phase Western Grebes. Auk 96: 573–586.

REA, A. 1983. Cathartid affinities; a brief overview. Pages 26–56 *in* Vulture biology and management (S. R. Wilbur and J. A. Jackson, Eds.). Univ. California Press, Berkeley, California.

REED, J. R. 1988. Inca Terns in the Bay of Panama during the 1982–1983 El Niño event. Amer. Birds 42: 172–173.

REGELSKI, D. J., AND R. R. MOLDENHAUER. 1996. Discrimination behavior between regional song forms in the Northern Parula. Wilson Bull. 108: 335–341.

REMSEN, J. V., JR. 1986. Was Bachman's Warbler a bamboo specialist? Auk 103: 216–219.

REMSEN, J. V., JR. 1995. The importance of continued collecting of specimens to ornithology and bird conservation. Bird Conservation International 5: 145–180.

REMSEN, J. V., JR. 1997. [Review of:] "The Birds of South America. Volume II." by R. S. Ridgely and G. Tudor. Auk 114: 147–152.

REMSEN, J. V., JR., AND W. S. GRAVES, IV. 1995. Distribution patterns of *Buarremon* brush-finches (Emberizidae) and interspecific competition in Andean birds. Auk 112: 225–236.

REMSEN, J. V., JR., M. A. HYDE, AND A. CHAPMAN. 1993. The diets of Neotropical trogons, motmots, barbets, and toucans. Condor 95: 178–192.

REMSEN, J. V., JR., AND T. A. PARKER III. 1990. Seasonal distribution of the Azure Gallinule (*Porphyrula flavirostris*), with comments on vagrancy in rails and gallinules. Wilson Bull. 102: 380–299.

REYNARD, G. B. 1962. The rediscovery of the Puerto Rican Whip-poor-will. Living Bird 1: 51–60.

REYNARD, G. B., O. H. GARRIDO, AND R. L. SUTTON. 1993. Taxonomic revision of the Greater Antillean Pewee. Wilson Bull. 105: 217–227.

RIDGELY, R. S. 1976. A guide to the birds of Panama. Princeton Univ. Press, Princeton, New Jersey.

RIDGELY, R. S. 1981. A guide to the birds of Panama (with new material). Princeton Univ. Press, Princeton, New Jersey.

RIDGELY, R. S., AND J. A. GWYNNE. 1989. A guide to the birds of Panama, with Costa Rica, Nicaragua, and Honduras (2nd ed.). Princeton Univ. Press, Princeton, New Jersey.

RIDGELY, R. S., AND G. TUDOR. 1989. The birds of South America, vol. 1. Univ. Texas Press, Austin.

RIDGELY, R. S., AND G. TUDOR. 1994. The birds of South America, vol. 2. Univ. Texas Press, Austin.

RIDGWAY, R. 1880. Note on *Helminthophaga cincinnatiensis,* Langdon. Bull. Nuttall Ornithol. Club 5: 237–238.

RIDGWAY, R. 1901. The birds of North and Middle America. Bull. U.S. Natl. Mus., no. 50, pt. 1.

RIDGWAY, R. 1902. The birds of North and Middle America. Bull. U.S. Natl. Mus., no. 50, pt. 2.

RIDGWAY, R. 1904. The birds of North and Middle America. Bull. U.S. Natl. Mus., no. 50, pt. 3.

RIDGWAY, R. 1907. The birds of North and Middle America. Bull. U.S. Natl. Mus., no. 50, pt. 4.

RIDGWAY, R. 1911. The birds of North and Middle America. Bull. U.S. Natl. Mus., no. 50, pt. 5.

RIDGWAY, R. 1914. The birds of North and Middle America. Bull. U.S. Natl. Mus., no. 50, pt. 6.

RIDGWAY, R. 1916. The birds of North and Middle America. Bull. U.S. Natl. Mus., no. 50, pt. 7.

RIDGWAY, R. 1919. The birds of North and Middle America. Bull. U.S. Natl. Mus., no. 50, pt. 8.

RIPLEY, S. D. 1977. Rails of the world. David R. Godine, Boston.

RIPLEY, S. D., AND A. MORENO. 1980. A recent sighting of Bachman's Warbler in Cuba. Birding 12: 211–212.

RISING, J. D. 1968. A multivariate assessment of interbreeding between the chickadees, *Parus atricapillus* and *P. carolinensis.* Syst. Zool. 17: 160–169.

RISING, J. D. 1969. A comparison of metabolism and comparative water loss of Baltimore and Bullock orioles. Comp. Biochem. Physiol. 31: 915–925.

RISING, J. D. 1970. Morphological variation and evolution in some North American orioles. Syst. Zool. 19: 315–351.

RISING, J. D. 1973. Morphological variation and status of the orioles, *Icterus galbula, I. bullockii,* and *I. abeillei,* in the northern Great Plains and in Durango, Mexico. Can. J. Zool. 51: 1267–1273.

RISING, J. D. 1983a. The Great Plains hybrid zones. Pp. 131–157 *in* Current Ornithology (R. F. Johnston, ed.). Plenum Press, New York.

RISING, J. D. 1983b. The progress of oriole hybridization in Kansas. Auk 100: 885–897.

RISING, J. D. 1996. A guide to the identification and natural history of the sparrows of the United States and Canada. Academic Press, San Diego.

RISING, J. D., AND J. C. AVISE. 1993. Application of genealogical-concordance principles to the taxonomy and evolutionary history of the Sharp-tailed Sparrow (*Ammodramus caudacutus*). Auk 110: 844–856.

ROBBINS, M. B., M. J. BRAUN, AND E. A. TOBEY. 1986. Morphological and vocal variation across a contact zone between the chickadees *Parus atricapillus* and *P. carolinensis.* Auk 103: 655–666.

ROBBINS, M. B., AND S. N. G. HOWELL. 1995. A new species of pygmy-owl from the eastern Andes. Wilson Bull. 107: 1–6.

ROBBINS, M. B., AND T. A. PARKER III. 1997a. Voice and taxonomy of *Caprimulgus* (*rufus*) *otiosus* (Caprimulgidae), with a reevaluation of *Caprimulgus rufus* subspecies. Pages 601–607 *in* Studies in Neotropical ornithology honoring Ted Parker (Remsen, J. V., Jr., Ed.). Ornithol. Monogr. 48.

ROBBINS, M. B., AND T. A. PARKER III. 1997b. What is the closest living relative of *Catharopeza* (Parulinae)? Pages 595–599 *in* Studies in Neotropical ornithology honoring Ted Parker (Remsen, J. V., Jr., Ed.). Ornithol. Monogr. 48.

ROBBINS, M. B., T. A. PARKER III, AND S. E. ALLEN. 1985. The avifauna of Cerro Pirre, Darién, eastern Panama. Pages 198–232 *in* Neotropical ornithology (P. A. Buckley, M. S. Foster, E. S. Morton, R. S. Ridgely, and F. G. Buckley, Eds.). Ornithol. Monogr. 36.

ROBBINS, M. B., AND R. S. RIDGELY. 1990. The avifauna of an upper tropical cloud forest in southwestern Ecuador. Proc. Acad. Nat. Sci. Philadelphia 143: 145–159.

ROBBINS, M. B., AND R. S. RIDGELY. 1991. *Sipia rosenbergi* (Formicariidae) is a synonym of *Myrmeciza* [*laemosticta*] *nigricauda,* with comments on the validity of the genus *Sipia.* Bull. Brit. Ornithol. Club 111: 11–18.

ROBBINS, M. B., G. H. ROSENBERG, F. SORNOZA M., AND M. A. JÁCOME. 1997. Taxonomy and nest description of the Tumbes Swallow (*Tachycineta* [*albilinea*] *stolzmanni*). Pages 609–612 *in* Studies in Neotropical ornithology honoring Ted Parker (Remsen, J. V., Jr., Ed.). Ornithol. Monogr. 48.

ROBERSON, D. 1980. Rare Birds of the West Coast of North America. Woodcock Publications, Pacific Grove, California.

ROBERSON, D., AND L. F. BAPTISTA. 1988. White-shielded coots in North America: a critical evaluation. Amer. Birds 42: 1241–1246.

ROBERSON, D., AND F. A. PITELKA. 1983. Occurrence of Willow Warbler *(Phylloscopus trochilus)* in North America refuted. Condor 85: 258.

ROBERTSON, W. B., JR., AND G. E. WOOLFENDEN. 1992. Florida bird species: an annotated list. Florida Ornithol. Soc., Spec. Publ. 6.

ROBINS, C. R. 1958. Observations on oceanic birds in the Gulf of Panama. Condor 60: 300–302.

ROGERS, C. H. 1939. The swifts of Panamá. Auk 56: 82.

ROHWER, S. A. 1972. A multivariate assessment of interbreeding between the meadowlarks, *Sturnella.* Syst. Zool. 21: 313–338.

ROHWER, S. A. 1973. Significance of sympatry to behavior and evolution of Great Plains meadowlarks. Evolution 27: 44–57.

ROHWER, S. 1976. Specific distinctness and adaptive differences in southwestern meadowlarks. Occ. Papers Mus. Nat. Hist. Univ. Kansas 44: 1–14.

ROHWER, S., AND J. MANNING. 1990. Differences in timing and number of molts for Baltimore and Bullock's orioles: implications to hybrid fitness and theories of delayed plumage maturation. Condor 92: 125–140.

ROWLEY, J. S., AND R. T. ORR. 1964. The status of Frantzius' Nightingale Thrush. Auk 81: 308–314.

SABO, S. R. 1982. The rediscovery of the Bishop's O'o' on Maui. 'Elepaio 42: 69–70.

SALOMONSEN, F. 1951. The birds of Greenland. Part III. Munksgaard, Copenhagen.

SAMMALISTO, L. 1961. An interpretation of variation in the dark-headed forms of the Yellow Wagtail. Brit. Birds 54: 54–69.

SCHMUTZ, S. M., J. MAKER, AND J. K. SCHMUTZ. 1989. Karyotypes of two threatened prairie raptors, *Buteo regalis* and *Athene cunicularia.* Page 54 *in* Abstracts of Annual Meeting of Genetic Society of Canada. Canadian Society for Plant Molecular Biology, Univ. of Calgary, June 1989.

SCHUCHMANN, K.-L. 1978. Allopatriche artbildung bei der Kolibriggatung Trochilus. Ardea 66: 156–172.

SCHWARTZ, A., AND R. F. KLINIKOWSKI. 1965. Additional observations on West Indian birds. Not. Nat., Acad. Nat. Sci. Philadelphia 376.

SCHWARTZ, P. 1972. *Micrastur gilvicollis,* a valid species sympatric with *M. ruficollis* in Amazonia. Condor 74: 399–415.

SCHWARTZ, P. 1975. Solved and unsolved problems in the *Sporophila lineola/bouvronides* complex (Aves: Emberizidae). Ann. Carnegie Mus. 45: 277–285.

SCLATER, P. L. 1890. Catalogue of birds in the British Museum, vol. 15. London.

SCLATER, P. L., AND G. E. SHELLEY. 1891. Catalogue of birds in the British Museum, vol. 19. London.

SCOTT, D. M., C. D. ANKNEY, AND C. H. JAROSCH. 1976. Sapsucker hybridization in British Columbia: changes in 25 years. Condor 78: 253–257.

SEALY, S. G. 1969. Apparent hybridization between Snow Bunting and McKay's Bunting on St. Lawrence Is., Alaska. Auk 86: 350–351.

SEALY, S. G., H. R. CARTER, W. D. SHUFORD, K. D. POWERS, AND C. A. CHASE III. 1982. Long-distance vagrancy of the Asiatic Marbled Murrelet in North America, 1979–1989. Auk 99: 778–781.

SELANDER, R. K. 1964. Speciation in wrens of the genus *Campylorhynchus*. Univ. Calif. Publ. Zool. 74: 1–259.

SELANDER, R. K. 1965. Hybridization of Rufous-naped Wrens in Chiapas, México. Auk 82: 206–214.

SELANDER, R. K., AND D. R. GILLER. 1959. Interspecific relations of woodpeckers in Texas. Wilson Bull. 71: 106–124.

SELANDER, R. K., AND D. R. GILLER. 1961. Analysis of sympatry of Great-tailed and Boat-tailed grackles. Condor 63: 29–86.

SELANDER, R. K., AND D. R. GILLER. 1963. Species limits in the woodpecker genus *Centurus* (Aves). Bull. Amer. Mus. Nat. Hist. 124: 217–273.

SEUTIN, G., P. T. BOAG, AND L. M. RATCLIFFE. 1992. Plumage variability in redpolls from Churchill, Manitoba. Auk 109: 771–785.

SEUTIN, G., J. BRAWN, R. E. RICKLEFS, AND E. BERMINGHAM. 1993. Genetic divergence among populations of a tropical passerine, the Streaked Saltator (*Saltator albicollis*). Auk 104: 97–108.

SEUTIN, G., N. K. KLEIN, R. E. RICKLEFS, AND E. BERMINGHAM. 1994. Historical biogeography of the Bananaquit (*Coereba flaveola*) in the Caribbean region: a mitochondrial DNA assessment. Evolution 48: 1041–1061.

SHELDON, F. H. 1987. Phylogeny of herons estimated from DNA-DNA hybridization data. Auk 104: 97–108.

SHELDON, F. H., AND F. B. GILL. 1996. A reconsideration of songbird phylogeny, with emphasis on the evolution of titmice and their sylvioid relatives. Syst. Biol. 45: 473–495.

SHELDON, F. H., K. G. MCCRACKEN, AND K. D. STUEBING. 1995. Phylogenetic relationships of the Zigzag Heron (*Zebrilus undulatus*) and White-crested Bittern (*Tigriornis leucolophus*) estimated by DNA-DNA hybridization. Auk 112: 672–679.

SHELDON, F. H., B. SLIKAS, M. KINNARNEY, F. B. GILL, E. ZHAO, AND B. SILVERIN. 1992. DNA-DNA hybridization evidence of phylogenetic relationship among major lineages of *Parus*. Auk 109: 173–185.

SHELDON, F. H., AND D. W. WINKLER. 1993. Intergeneric phylogenetic relationships of swallows estimated by DNA-DNA hybridization. Auk 110: 798–824.

SHIELDS, G. F. 1982. Comparative avian cytogenetics: a review. Condor 84: 45–58.

SHIELDS, G. F. 1990. Analysis of mitochondrial DNA of Pacific Black Brant (*Branta bernicla nigricans*). Auk 107: 620–623.

SHORT, L. L., JR. 1963. Hybridization in the wood warblers *Vermivora pinus* and *V. chrysoptera*. Proc. 13th Intern. Ornithol. Congr.: 147–160.

SHORT, L. L., JR. 1965a. Hybridization in the flickers (*Colaptes*) of North America. Bull. Amer. Mus. Nat. Hist. 129: 307–428.

SHORT, L. L., JR. 1965b. Variation in West Indian flickers (Aves, *Colaptes*). Bull. Florida State Mus. 10: 1–42.

SHORT, L. L., JR. 1967a. A review of the genera of grouse (Aves, Tetraoninae). Amer. Mus. Novitates 2289.

SHORT, L. L., JR. 1967b. Variation in central American flickers. Wilson Bull. 79: 5–21.

SHORT, L. L., JR. 1968. Variation of Ladder-backed Woodpeckers in southwestern North America. Proc. Biol. Soc. Wash. 81: 1–10.

SHORT, L. L., JR. 1969. Relationships among some South American seedeaters (*Sporophila*), with a record of *S. hypochroma* for Argentina. Wilson Bull. 81: 216–219.

SHORT, L. L., JR. 1972. Relationships among the four species of superspecies *Celeus elegans* (Aves, Picidae). Amer. Mus. Novitates 2487.

SHORT, L. L., JR. 1974. Habits of three endemic West Indian woodpeckers (Aves, Picidae). Amer. Mus. Novitates 2549.

SHORT, L. L., JR. 1975. A zoogeographic analysis of the South American Chaco avifauna. Bull. Amer. Mus. Nat. Hist. 154: 163–352.

SHORT, L. L., JR. 1982. Woodpeckers of the world. Delaware Museum of Natural History, Greenville, Delaware.

SHURTLEFF, L. L., AND C. SAVAGE. 1996. The Wood Duck and the Mandarin. Univ. California Press, Berkeley, California.

SIBLEY, C. G. 1954. Hybridization in the red-eyed towhees of Mexico. Evolution 8: 252–290.

SIBLEY, C. G. 1955. The generic allocation of the Green-tailed Towhee. Auk 72: 420–423.

SIBLEY, C. G. 1958. Hybridization in some Colombian tanagers, avian genus *Ramphocelus*. Proc. Amer. Phil. Soc. 102: 448–453.

SIBLEY, C. G. 1968. The relationships of the "Wren-Thrush," *Zeledonia coronata* Ridgway. Postilla 125.

SIBLEY, C. G. 1970. A comparative study of the egg-white proteins of passerine birds. Bull. Peabody Mus. Nat. Hist. 32: 1–131.

SIBLEY, C. G. 1973. The relationships of the Swallow-Tanager *Tersina viridis*. Bull. Brit. Ornith. Club 93: 75–79.

SIBLEY, C. G., AND J. E. AHLQUIST. 1972. A comparative study of the egg white proteins of non-passerine birds. Peabody Mus. Nat. Hist. Bull. 39: 1–276.

SIBLEY, C. G., AND J. E. AHLQUIST. 1980. The relationships of the "primitive insect eaters" (Aves: Passeriformes) as indicated by DNA x DNA hybridization. Proc. 17th Intl. Ornith. Congr.: 1215–1220.

SIBLEY, C. G., AND J. E. AHLQUIST. 1981a. The relationships of the accentors (*Prunella*) as indicated by DNA-DNA hybridization. J. für Ornithologie 122: 369–378.

SIBLEY, C. G., AND J. E. AHLQUIST. 1981b. The relationships of wagtails and pipits (Motacillidae) as indicated by DNA-DNA hybridization. Oiseau et R.F.O. 51: 189–199.

SIBLEY, C. G., AND J. E. AHLQUIST. 1982a. The relationships of the vireos (Vireonidae) as indicated by DNA-DNA hybridization. Wilson Bull. 94: 114–128.

SIBLEY, C. G., AND J. E. AHLQUIST. 1982b. The relationships of the Wrentit as indicated by DNA-DNA hybridization. Condor 84: 40–44.

SIBLEY, C. G., AND J. E. AHLQUIST. 1982c. The relationships of the Yellow-breasted Chat (*Icteria virens*) and the alleged slowdown in the rate of macromolecular evolution in birds. Postilla 187: 1–18.

SIBLEY, C. G., AND J. E. AHLQUIST. 1982d. The relationships of the Hawaiian honeycreepers (Drepanidini) as indicated by DNA-DNA hybridization. Auk 99: 130–140.

SIBLEY, C. G., AND J. E. AHLQUIST. 1984. The relationships of the starlings (Sturnidae: Sturnini) and the mockingbirds (Sturnidae: Mimini). Auk 101: 230–243.

SIBLEY, C. G., AND J. E. AHLQUIST. 1985. The phylogeny and classification of the passerine birds, based on comparisons of the genetic material, DNA. Proc. 18th Intl. Ornith. Congr.: 83–121.

SIBLEY, C. G., AND J. E. AHLQUIST. 1990. Phylogeny and classification of birds. Yale Univ. Press, New Haven, Connecticut.

SIBLEY, C. G., S. M. LANYON, AND J. E. AHLQUIST. 1985. The relationships of the Sharpbill (*Oxyruncus cristatus*). Condor 86: 48–52.

SIBLEY, C. G., AND B. L. MONROE, JR. 1990. Distribution and taxonomy of birds of the world. Yale Univ. Press, New Haven, Connecticut.

SIBLEY, C. G., AND B. L. MONROE, JR. 1993. A supplement to distribution and taxonomy of birds of the world. Yale Univ. Press, New Haven, Connecticut.

SIBLEY, C. G., AND L. L. SHORT, JR. 1959. Hybridization in the buntings (*Passerina*) of the Great Plains. Auk 76: 443–463.

SIBLEY, C. G., AND L. L. SHORT, JR. 1964. Hybridization in the orioles of the Great Plains. Condor 66: 130–150.

SIBLEY, C. G., AND F. G. SIBLEY. 1964. Hybridization in the red-eyed towhees of Mexico: the populations of the southwestern plateau region. Auk 76: 326–338.

SIBLEY, C. G., AND D. A. WEST. 1958. Hybridization in the red-eyed towhees of Mexico: the eastern plateau populations. Condor 60: 85–104.

SIBLEY, C. G., AND D. A. WEST. 1959. Hybridization in the Rufous-sided Towhees of the Great Plains. Auk 76: 326–338.

SICK, H. 1984. Ornitologia Brasileira. Vol. 1. Editora Universidade Brasília, Brasília, Brazil.

SICK, H. 1993. Birds in Brazil. Princeton Univ. Press, Princeton, New Jersey.

SIEGEL-CAUSEY, D. 1988. Phylogeny of the Phalacrocoracidae. Condor 90: 885–905.

SIEGFRIED, W. R, 1976. Social organization in Ruddy and Macoa ducks. Auk 93: 560–570.

SILVA, J. M. C. DA. 1995. Seasonal distribution of the Lined Seedeater *Sporophila lineola.* Bull. Brit. Ornith. Club 115: 14–21.

SIMON, E. 1921. Histoire naturelle des Trochilidés. éncyclopedie Roret, Paris.

SIMPSON, S. F., AND J. CRACRAFT. 1981. The phylogenetic relationships of the Piciformes (class Aves). Auk 98: 481–494.

SLIKAS, B., F. H. SHELDON, AND F. B. GILL. 1996. Phylogeny of titmice (Paridae): I. Estimate of relationships among subgenera based on DNA-DNA hybridization. J. Avian Biol. 27: 70–82.

SLIPP, J. W. 1952. A record of the Tasmanian White-capped Albatross, *Diomedea cauta,* in American North Pacific waters. Auk 69: 458–459.

SLUD, P. 1964. The birds of Costa Rica: distribution and ecology. Bull. Amer. Mus. Nat. Hist. 128: 1–430.

SLUD, P. 1967. The birds of Cocos Island [Costa Rica]. Bull. Amer. Mus. Nat. Hist. 134: 263–295.

SMITH, G. A. 1982. *Pyrrhura* conures. Parrot Soc. Mag. 16: 365–372.

SMITH, J. I. 1987. Evidence of hybridization between Red-bellied and Golden-fronted woodpeckers. Condor 89: 377–386.

SMITH, J. K., AND E. G. ZIMMERMAN. 1976. Biochemical genetics and evolution of North American blackbirds, family Icteridae. Comp. Biochem. Physiol. 53B: 319–324.

SMITH, P. W. 1985. Jackdaws reach the New World. Amer. Birds 39: 255–258.

SMITH, P. W. 1987. The Eurasian Collared-Dove arrives in the Americas. Amer. Birds 41: 1371–1379.

SMITH, P. W., AND M. B. HUTT. 1984. First sight record of Western Reef-Herons for Barbados. Amer. Birds 38: 254–256.

SMITH, P. W., W. B. ROBERTSON, AND H. M. STEVENSON. 1988. West Indian Cave Swallows nesting in Florida, with comments on the taxonomy of *Hirundo fulva.* Florida Field Nat. 16: 86–90.

SMITH, P. W., AND S. A. SMITH. 1993. An exotic dilemma for birders: the Canary-winged Parakeet. Birding 25: 426–430.

SMITH, P. W., S. A. SMITH, AND W. HOFFMAN. 1991. A Yellow-faced Grassquit in Florida, with comments on importation of this and related species. Florida Field Nat. 19: 21–24.

SMITH, P. W., AND A. SPRUNT, IV. 1987. The Shiny Cowbird reaches the United States. Amer. Birds 41: 370–371.

SNELL, R. R. 1989. Status of *Larus* gulls at Home Bay, Baffin Island. Colonial Waterbirds 12: 12–23.

SNELL, R. R. 1993. Variably plumaged Icelandic Herring Gulls: high intraspecific variation in a founded population. Auk 110: 410–413.

SNOW, D. W. 1973. The classification of the Cotingidae (Aves). Breviora 409: 1–27.

SNOW, D. W. 1975. The classification of the manakins. Bull. Brit. Ornithol. Club 95: 20–27.

SNOW, D. W. 1982. The cotingas. Cornell Univ. Press, Ithaca, New York.

SNOW, D. W. 1985. Systematics of the *Turdus fumigatus/hauxwelli* group of thrushes. Bull. Brit. Ornith. Club 105: 30–37.

SNYDER, D. E. 1957. The Gray Lag-Goose in Massachusetts: correction. Auk 74: 394.

SNYDER, D. E. 1961. First record of the Least Frigate-bird *(Fregata ariel)* in North America. Auk 78: 265.

SPENCER, R., AND W. KOLODNICKI. 1988. First Azure Gallinule for North America. Amer. Birds 42: 25–27.

STAGER, K. E. 1964. The birds of Clipperton Island, eastern Pacific. Condor 66: 357–371.

STAHL, J.-C., J.-L. MOUGIN, P. JOUVENTIN, AND H. WEIMERKIRCH. 1984. Le Canard d'Eaton, *Anas eatoni dryglaskii,* des Iles Crozet: systematique, comportement alimentaire et biologie de reproduction. Gerfaut 74: 305–326.

STALLCUP, R., AND S. TERRILL. 1996. Albatrosses and Cordell Bank. Birding 28: 106–110.

STALLCUP, R., J. MORLAN, AND D. ROBERSON. 1988. First record of the Wedge-tailed Shearwater in California. Western Birds 19: 61–68.

STALLCUP, W. B. 1961. Relationships of some families of the suborder Passeres (songbird) as indicated by comparisons of tissue proteins. J. Grad. Res. Center Southern Methodist Univ. 29: 43–65.

STEADMAN, D. W. 1980. A review of the osteology and paleontology of turkeys (Aves: Meleagridinae). Contrib. Sci. Nat. Hist. Mus. Los Angeles County 330: 131–207.

STEIN, R. C. 1958. The behavioral, ecological and morphological characteristics of two populations of the Alder Flycatcher, *Empidonax traillii* (Audubon). New York State Mus. and Sci. Serv. Bull. 371: 1–63.

STEIN, R. C. 1963. Isolating mechanisms between populations of Traill's Flycatcher. Proc. Amer. Phil. Soc. 107: 21–50.

STEPANYAN, L. S. 1975. [Check-list and distribution of the avifauna of the U.S.S.R.]. Nauka, Moscow.

STEPANYAN, L. S. 1978. Sostav i raspredelenie ptits fauny SSSR, Passeriformes. Hayka, Moscow.

STEPANYAN, L. S. 1990. Conspectus of the ornithological fauna of the U.S.S.R. Nauka, Moscow.

STEVENSON, H. M., AND B. H. ANDERSON. 1994. The birdlife of Florida. University Press of Florida, Gainesville, Florida.

STEVENSON, H. M., E. EISENMANN, C. WINEGARNER, AND W. KARLIN. 1983. Notes on Common and Antillean nighthawks of the Florida Keys. Auk 100: 983–988.

STILES, F. G. 1981. The taxonomy of Rough-winged Swallows (*Stelgidopteryx;* Hirundinidae) in southern Central America. Auk 98: 282–293.

STILES, F. G. 1983a. Systematics of the southern forms of *Selasphorus* (Trochilidae). Auk 100: 311–325.

STILES, F. G. 1983b. The taxonomy of *Microcerculus* wrens (Troglodytidae) in Central America. Wilson Bull. 95: 169–183.

STILES, F. G. 1984. The Nicaraguan Seed-Finch *(Oryzoborus nuttingi)* in Costa Rica. Condor 86: 118–122.

STILES, F. G. 1996a. A new species of emerald hummingbird (Trochilidae, *Chlorostilbon*) from the Sierra de Chiribiquete, southeastern Colombia, with a review of the *C. mellisugus* complex. Wilson Bull. 108: 1–27.

STILES, F. G. 1996b. When black plus white equals gray: the nature of variation in the Variable Seedeater complex (Emberizinae: *Sporophila*). Ornitologia Neotropical 7: 75–107.

STILES, F. G., AND A. J. NEGRET. 1994. The nonbreeding distribution of the Black Swift: a clue from Colombia and unsolved problems. Condor 96: 1091–1094.

STILES, F. G., AND A. SKUTCH. 1989. A guide to the birds of Costa Rica. Cornell Univ. Press, Ithaca, New York.

STIVER, SAN J. 1984. Himalayan Snowcocks—Nevada's newest upland game. Calif.-Nevada Widl. Trans., pp. 55–58.

STONE, W. 1930. Townsend's Oregon Tubinares. Auk 47: 414–415.

STORER, R. W. 1945. Structural modifications in the hind limb in the Alcidae. Ibis 87: 433–456.

STORER, R. W. 1969. What is a tanager? Living Bird 8: 127–136.

STORER, R. W. 1976. The behavior and relationships of the Least Grebe. Trans. San Diego Soc. Nat. Hist. 18: 113–125.

STORER, R. W. 1978. Systematic notes on the loons (Gaviidae: Aves). Breviora 448.

STORER, R. W. 1989. Geographic variation and sexual dimorphism in the tremblers *(Cinclocerthia)* and White-breasted Thrasher *(Ramphocinclus)*. Auk 106: 249–258.

STORER, R. W. 1996. [Review of]: The comparative osteology of grebes (Aves: Podicipediformes) and its systematic implications. Auk 113: 974–975.

STORER, R. W., AND G. L. NUECHTERLEIN. 1985. An analysis of plumage and morphological characters of the two color forms of the Western Grebe *(Aechmophorus)*. Auk 102: 102–119.

STOTZ, D. F., J. W. FITZPATRICK, T. A. PARKER, III, AND D. K. MOSKOVITS. 1996. Neotropical birds. Univ. of Chicago Press, Chicago.

STRANG, C. A. 1977. Variation and distribution of Glaucous Gulls in western Alaska. Condor 79: 170–175.

STRAUCH, J. G., JR. 1978. The phylogeny of the Charadriiformes (Aves): a new estimate using the character compatibility analysis. Trans. Zool. Soc. London 34: 263–345.

STRAUCH, J. G., JR. 1979. [Review of]: the systematic affinities of the sandgrouse, Pteroclidae, by J. Fjeldså. Bird-Banding 50: 283–284.

STRAUCH, J. G., JR. 1985. The phylogeny of the Alcidae. Auk 102: 520–539.

SWIERCZEWSKI, E. V., AND R. J. RAIKOW. 1981. Hind limb morphology, phylogeny, and classification of the Piciformes. Auk 98: 466–480.

SZANTYR, M. S. 1985. A Barnacle Goose in Connecticut. Connecticut Warbler 5: 16–18.

TAMPLIN, J. W., J. W. DEMASTES, AND J. V. REMSEN, JR. 1993. Biochemical and morphometric relationships among some members of the Cardinalinae. Wilson Bull. 105: 93–113.

TANNER, J. T. 1952. Black-capped and Carolina chickadees in the southern Appalachian Mountains. Auk 69: 407–424.

TARR, C. L., AND R. C. FLEISCHER. 1993. Mitochondrial-DNA variation and evolutionary relationships in the Amakihi complex. Auk 110: 825–831,

TAYLOR, A. L., JR., AND M. S. COLLINS. 1979. Rediscovery and identification of the "mystery" *Garrulax* on Oahu. 'Elepaio 39: 79–81.

TEXAS ORNITHOLOGICAL SOCIETY [T.O.S.]. 1995. Checklist of the birds of Texas, 3rd ed. Austin, Texas.

THIELCKE, G. 1962. Versuche mit Klangattrappan zur Klärung der Verwandtschaft der Baumläufer *Certhia familiaris* L., *C. brachydactyla* Brehm und *C. americana* Bonaparte. J. für Ornithologie 103: 266–271.

THOMPSON, C. 1991. Is the Painted Bunting actually two species? Problems determining species limits between allopatric populations. Condor 93: 987–1000.

THOMPSON, W. L. 1976. Vocalizations of the Lazuli Bunting. Condor 78: 195–207.

THÖNEN, W. 1969. Auffalender Unterschied zwischen den instrumentalen Balzlautender europäischen und nordamericknischen Bekassine *Gallinago gallinago*. Orn. Beobachter 66: 6–13.

TOBISH, T. G. 1985. The first record of *Locustella lanceolata* for North America. Auk 102: 645.

TODD, W. E. C. 1963. Birds of the Labrador Peninsula and adjacent areas. Univ. Toronto Press, Toronto.

TOMER, J. S., R. B. CLAPP, AND J. C. HOFFMAN. 1996. *Fregata minor,* Great Frigatebird, in Oklahoma. Bull. Oklahoma Ornithol. Soc. 29: 34–35.

TOMKOVICH, P. S. 1991. External morphology of the Spoon-billed Sandpiper *(Eurynorhynchus pygmaeus)* at Chukotski Peninsula. Ornithology 25: 135–144.

TRAYLOR, M. A., JR. 1977. A classification of the tyrant flycatchers (Tyrannidae). Bull. Mus. Comp. Zool. 148: 128–184.

TRAYLOR., M. A., JR. 1979a. Two sibling species of *Tyrannus* (Tyrannidae). Auk 96: 221–233.

TRAYLOR., M. A., JR. (Ed.) 1979b. Check-list of birds of the world, vol. 8 . Museum of Comparative Zoology, Cambridge, Massachusetts.

TRAYLOR, M. A., JR. 1982. Notes on tyrant flycatchers (Aves: Tyrannidae). Fieldiana (Zool.), New Series, no. 13.

TRAYLOR., M. A., JR. 1988. Geographic variation and evolution in South American *Cistothorus platensis* (Aves: Troglodytidae). Fieldiana (Zool). No. 48.

TRAYLOR, M. A., Jr., AND J. W. FITZPATRICK. 1982. A survey of the tyrant flycatchers. Living Bird 19: 7–50.

TROY, D. M. 1985. A phenetic analysis of the redpolls *Carduelis flammea flammea* and *C. hornemanni exilipes.* Auk 102: 82–96.

TUCK, L. M. 1972. The snipes: a study of the genus *Capella.* Canadian Wildlife Service Monogr. Ser. 5: 1–428.

URBAN, E. K., C. H. FRY, AND S. KEITH. 1986. The birds of Africa, vol. II. Academic Press, London.

VAN ROSSEM, A. J. 1934. Critical notes on Middle American birds. Bull. Mus. Comp. Zool. 77: 387–490.

VAN ROSSEM, A. J. 1938. Notes on some Mexican and Central American wrens of the genera *Heleodytes, Troglodytes,* and *Nannorchilus,* and four new races. Bull. Brit. Ornith. Club 59: 10–15.

VAN TETS, G. F., C. W. MEREDITH, P. J. FULLAGAR, AND P. M. DAVIDSON. 1988. Osteological differences between *Sula* and *Morus,* and a description of an extinct new species of *Sula* from Lord Howe and Norfolk islands, Tasman Sea. Notornis 35: 35–57.

VAN TYNE, J. 1943. A peculiar Goshawk from Labrador. Auk 60: 267–268.

VAURIE, C. 1953. A generic revision of flycatchers of the tribe Muscicapini. Bull. Amer Mus. Nat. Hist. 100: 455–538.

VAURIE, C. 1957a. Systematic notes on Palearctic birds, no. 30. The Certhiidae. Amer Mus. Novitates 1855.

VAURIE, C. 1957b. Systematic notes on Palearctic birds, no. 25. Motacillidae: the genus *Motacilla.* Amer. Mus. Novitates 1832.

VAURIE, C. 1959. The birds of the Palearctic fauna. Passeriformes. Witherby, London.

VAURIE, C. 1965. The birds of the Palearctic fauna. Non-Passeriformes. Witherby, London.

VAURIE, C. 1980. Taxonomy and geographical distribution of the Furnariidae (Aves, Passeriformes). Bull. Amer. Mus. Nat. Hist. 166: 1–357.

VAURIE, C., AND D. SNOW 1957. Systematic notes on Palearctic birds. No. 27. Paridae: the genera *Parus* and *Sylviparus.* With supplementary notes. Amer. Mus. Novitates 1852: 1–43.

VERBEEK, N. A. M. 1972. Comparison of displays of the Yellow-billed Magpie. J. für Ornithologie 113: 297–314.

VICKERY, P. D. 1980. The Spring migration. Northeastern Maritime region. Amer. Birds 34: 754–757.

VICKERY, P. D., D. W. FINCH, AND P. K. DONAHUE. 1987. Juvenile Cox's Sandpiper *(Calidris paramelanotos)* in Massachusetts, a first New World occurrence and a hitherto undescribed plumage. Amer. Birds 41: 1366–1369.

VIELLIARD, J. 1989. Uma nova espécie de *Glaucidium* (Aves, Strigidae) da Amazônia. Rev Bras. Zool. 6: 685–693.

VLUG, J. J., AND J. FJELDSÅ. 1990. Working bibliography of grebes of the world with summaries of current taxonomy and of distributional status. Zoological Museum, Copenhagen.

VOOUS, K. H. 1957. A specimen of the Spotted Crake, *Porzana porzana,* for the Lesser Antilles. Ardea 45: 89–90.

VOOUS, K. H. 1964. Wood owls of the genera *Strix* and *Ciccaba.* Zool. Meded. 39: 471–478.

VOOUS, K. H. 1973. List of recent Holarctic bird species. Ibis 115: 612–638.

VOOUS, K. H. 1977. List of recent Holarctic bird species. Academic Press, London.

VOOUS, K. H. 1988. Owls of the Northern Hemisphere. MIT Press, Cambridge, Massachusetts.

VUILLEUMIER, F. 1970. Generic relations and speciation patterns in the caracaras (Aves: Falconidae). Breviora 355.

WAGNER, G. F. 1989. Great Spotted Woodpecker at Attu Island, Alaska: first record for the near islands and for North America. Amer. Birds 43: 254–257.

WAGNER, G. F. 1990. Pine Bunting on Attu Island, Alaska. Amer. Birds 44: 1089–1091.

WALTERS, M. 1995. On the status of *Ara tricolor* Bechstein. Bull. Brit. Ornith. Club 115: 168–170.

WARD, D. 1992. The behavioral and morphological affinities of some vanelline plovers (Vanellinae: Charadriiformes: Aves). J. Zoology 228: 625–640.

WATSON, G. E. 1962a. Sympatry in Palearctic *Alectoris* partridges. Evolution 16: 11–19.

WATSON, G. E. 1962b. Three sibling species of *Alectoris* partridge. Ibis 1962: 353–367.

WATSON, G. E., J. P. ANGLE, AND M. R. BROWNING. 1974. First North American record of Little Bunting in eastern Chukchi Sea. Auk 91: 417.

WATSON, G. E., S. L. OLSON, AND J. R. MILLER. 1991. A new subspecies of the Double-crested Cormorant, *Phalacrocorax auritus,* from San Salvador, Bahama Islands. Proc. Biol. Soc. Wash. 104: 356–369.

WEBBER, T., AND J. W. HARDY. 1985. Breeding and behaviour of Tamaulipas Crows, *Corvus imparatus,* in captivity. Avicultural Mag. 91: 191–198.

WEBER, J. W. 1981a. The *Larus* gulls of the Pacific Northwest's interior, with taxonomic comments on several forms (Part I). Continental Birdlife 2: 1–10.

WEBER, J. W. 1981b. The *Larus* gulls of the Pacific Northwest's interior, with taxonomic comments on several forms (Part II—Conclusion). Continental Birdlife 2: 74–91.

WEST, D. A. 1962. Hybridization in grosbeaks (*Pheucticus*) of the Great Plains. Auk 79: 399–424.

WETHERBEE, D. K. 1985. The extinct Cuban and Hispaniolan macaws (*Ara,* Psittacidae), and description of a new species, *Ara cubensis.* Carib. J. Sci. 21: 169–175.

WETMORE, A. 1926. Observations on the birds of Argentina, Paraguay, Uruguay, and Chile. U.S. Nat. Mus. Bull. 133: 1–448.

WETMORE, A. 1930. A systematic classification of the birds of the world. Proc. U.S. Nat. Mus. 76: 1–8.

WETMORE, A. 1943. The birds of southern Veracruz, Mexico. Proc. U.S. Nat. Mus. 95: 215–340.

WETMORE, A. 1957. The birds of Isla Coiba, Panamá. Smithson. Misc. Coll. 134: 1–105.

WETMORE, A. 1960. A classification of the birds of the world. Smithsonian Misc. Coll. 139: 1–37.

WETMORE, A. 1965. The birds of the Republic of Panamá, part 1. Smithsonian Misc. Collect., vol. 150.

WETMORE, A. 1968. The birds of the Republic of Panamá, part 2. Smithsonian Misc. Collect., vol. 150.

WETMORE, A. 1972. The birds of the Republic of Panamá, part 3. Smithsonian Misc. Collect., vol. 150.

WETMORE, A., R. F. PASQUIER, AND S. L. OLSON. 1984. The birds of the Republic of Panamá, part 4. Smithsonian Misc. Collect., vol. 150.

WETMORE, A., AND B. H. SWALES. 1931. The birds of Haiti and the Dominican Republic. U.S. Nat. Mus. Bull. 155: 1–483.

WHITNEY, B. M., AND G. H. ROSENBERG. 1993. Behavior, vocalizations and possible relationships of *Xenornis setifrons* (Formicariidae), a little-known Chocó endemic. Condor 95: 227–231.

WHITTINGHAM, L. A., A. KIRKCONNELL, AND L. M. RATCLIFFE. 1992. Differences in song and sexual dimorphism between Cuban and North American Red-winged Blackbirds (*Agelaius phoeniceus*). Auk 109: 928–933.

WILDS, C., AND D. CZAPLAK. 1994. Yellow-legged Gulls (*Larus cachinnans)* in North America. Wilson Bull. 106: 344–356.

WILEY, J. W. 1993. Natural range expansion and local extirpation of an exotic psittacine – an unsuccessful colonization attempt. Ornitologia Neotropical 4: 43–54.

WILLIAMSON, F. S. L., AND L. J. PEYTON. 1963. Interbreeding of Glaucous-winged and Herring gulls in the Cook Inlet region, Alaska. Condor 65: 24–28.

WILLIS, E. O. 1967. The behavior of Bicolored Antbirds. Univ. Calif. Publ. Zool. 79: 1–132.

WILLIS, E. O. 1982. The behavior of Black-banded Woodcreepers (*Dendrocolaptes picumnus*). Condor 84: 272–285.

WILLIS, E. O. 1983a. Three *Dendrocincla* woodcreepers (Aves; Dendrocolaptidae) as army ant followers. Ciencia e Cultura 25: 201–204.

WILLIS, E. O. 1983b. Trans-Andean *Xiphorhynchus* (Aves, Dendrocolaptidae) as army ant followers. Rev. Brasil. Biol. 43: 125–131.

WILLIS, E. O. 1992. Compartemento e ecologia do Arapaçu-Barrado (*Dendrocolaptes certhia*) Aves, Dendrocolaptidae. Bol. Mus. Paraense Emílio Goeldi 8: 151–216.

WINGATE, D. B. 1958. House Martin *(Delichon urbica)* and Canary *(Serinus canaria)* in Bermuda. Auk 75: 359–360.

WINGATE, D. B. 1983. A record of the Siberian Flycatcher *(Muscicapa sibirica)* from Bermuda: an extreme extra-limital vagrant. Auk 100: 212–213.

WINK, M., P. HEIDRICK, AND D. RISTOW. 1993. Genetic evidence for speciation of the Manx

Shearwater *Puffinus puffinus* and Mediterranean Shearwater *Puffinus yelkouan*. Vogelwelt 114: 226–232.

WINK, M. 1995. Phylogeny of Old and New World vultures (Aves: Accipitridae and Cathartidae) inferred from nucleotide sequences of the mitochondrial cytochrome ß gene. Z. Naturforsch. 50c: 868–882.

WINKER, K. 1995. *Xiphorhynchus striatigularis* (Dendrocolaptidae): *Nomen monstrositatum*. Auk 112: 1066–1070.

WINKER, K. 1996. The crumbling infrastructure of biodiversity: the avian example. Conservation Biology 10: 703–707.

WINKER, K., J. T. KLICKA, AND G. VOELKER. 1996. Sexual size dimorphism in birds from southern Veracruz, Mexico. II. *Thryothorus maculipectus* and *Henicorhina* [*leucosticta*] *prostheleuca*. J. Field Ornith. 67: 236–251.

WINKER, K., AND J. H. RAPPOLE. 1988. The relationship between *Hylocichla* and *Catharus* (Turdinae). Auk 105: 392–394.

WOLF, L. L. 1977. Species relationships in the avian genus *Aimophila*. Ornithol. Monogr. No. 23.

WOOLFENDEN, G. E., AND J. W. FITZPATRICK. 1984. The Florida Scrub Jay: demography of a cooperative-breeding bird. Monogr. Pop. Biol. No. 20, Princeton Univ. Press, Princeton.

YAMASHINA, [Y.]. 1939. Note sur le Tétras falcipene de Sibérie. Oiseau et la Rev. Fr. Ornithol., n.s., 9: 3–9.

YANG, S. Y., AND R. K. SELANDER. 1968. Hybridization in the Grackle *Quiscalus quiscula* in Louisiana. Syst. Zool. 17: 107–143.

YÉSOU, P. 1991. The sympatric breeding of *Larus fuscus, L. cachinnans* and *L. argentatus* in western France. Ibis 133: 256–263.

YOUNG, J. R., J. W. HUPP, J. W. BRADBURY, AND C. E. BRAUN. 1994. Phenotypic divergence of secondary sexual traits among Sage Grouse, *Centrocercus urophasianus*, populations. Anim. Behav. 47: 1353–1362.

YOVANOVICH, G. D. L. 1995. Collared Plover in Uvalde, Texas. Birding 27: 102–104.

ZEILLEMAKER, C. F., M. S. ELTZROTH, AND J. E. HAMERNICK. 1985. First North American record of the Black-winged Stilt. Amer. Birds 39: 241.

ZIMMER, B., AND K. BRYAN. 1993. First United States record of Tufted Flycatcher. Amer. Birds 47: 48–50.

ZIMMER, J. T. 1935. Studies of Peruvian birds. No. 17. Notes on the genera *Syndactyla, Anabacerthia, Philydor,* and *Automolus*. Amer. Mus. Novitates 785.

ZIMMER, J. T. 1937. Studies of Peruvian birds. No. 25. Notes on the genera *Thamnophilus, Thamnocharis, Gymnopithys,* and *Ramphocaenus*. Amer. Mus. Novitates 917.

ZIMMER, J. T. 1942. Studies of Peruvian birds. No. 41. The genera *Hylophilus, Smaragdolanius,* and *Cyclarhis*. Amer. Mus. Novitates 785.

ZIMMER, J. T. 1947. Studies of Peruvian birds. No. 52. Notes on the genera *Sericossypha, Chlorospingus, Cnemoscopus, Hemispingus, Conothraupis, Chlorornis, Lamprospiza, Cissopis,* and *Schistochlamys*. Amer. Mus. Novitates 1367.

ZINK, R. M. 1982. Patterns of genic and morphologic variation among sparrows in the genera *Zonotrichia, Melospiza, Junco,* and *Passerella*. Auk 99: 632–649.

ZINK, R. M. 1986. Patterns and evolutionary significance of geographic variation in the *schistacea* group of the Fox Sparrow (*Passerella iliaca*). Ornithol. Monogr. 40.

ZINK, R. M. 1988. Evolution of Brown Towhees: allozymes, morphometrics and species limits. Condor 90: 72–82.

ZINK, R. M. 1991. The geography of mitochondrial DNA variation in two sympatric sparrows. Evolution 45: 329–339.

ZINK, R. M. 1994. The geography of mitochondrial DNA variation, population structure, hybridization, and species limits in the Fox Sparrow (*Passerella iliaca*). Evolution 48: 96–111.

ZINK, R. M. 1996. Species concepts, speciation, and sexual selection. J. Avian Biol. 27: 1–6.

ZINK, R. M., AND J. C. AVISE. 1990. Patterns of mitochondrial DNA and allozyme evolution in the avian genus *Ammodramus*. Syst. Zool. 39: 148–161.

ZINK, R. M., AND R. C. BLACKWELL. Patterns of allozyme, mitochondrial DNA, and morphometric variation in four sparrow genera. Auk 113: 59–67.

ZINK, R. M., R. C. BLACKWELL, AND O. ROJAS-SOTO. 1997. Species limits in the Le Conte's Thrasher. Condor 99: 132–138.

ZINK, R. M., AND D. L. DITTMANN. 1991. Evolution of Brown Towhees: mitochondrial DNA evidence. Condor 93: 98–105.

ZINK, R. M., D. L. DITTMANN, AND W. L. ROOTES. 1991. Mitochondrial DNA variation and the phylogeny of *Zonotrichia*. Auk 108: 578–584.

ZINK, R. M., D. L. DITTMANN, S. W. CARDIFF, AND J. D. RISING. 1991. Mitochondrial DNA variation and the taxonomic status of the Large-billed Savannah Sparrow. Condor 93: 1016–1019.

ZINK, R. M., AND N. K. JOHNSON. 1984. Evolutionary genetics of flycatchers. I. Sibling species in the genera *Empidonax* and *Contopus*. Syst. Zool. 33: 205–216.

ZINK, R. M., S. ROWHER, A. V. ANDREEV, AND D. L. DITTMANN. 1995. Trans-Beringia comparisons of mitochondrial DNA differentiation in birds. Condor 97: 639–649.

ZONFRILLO, B. 1988 Notes and comments on the taxonomy of Jouanin's Petrel *Bulweria fallax* and Bulwer's Petrel *Bulweria bulwerii*. Bull. Brit. Ornith. Club 108: 71–75.

INDEX

Compiled by Beth Sakumura

C

X

Y

Z

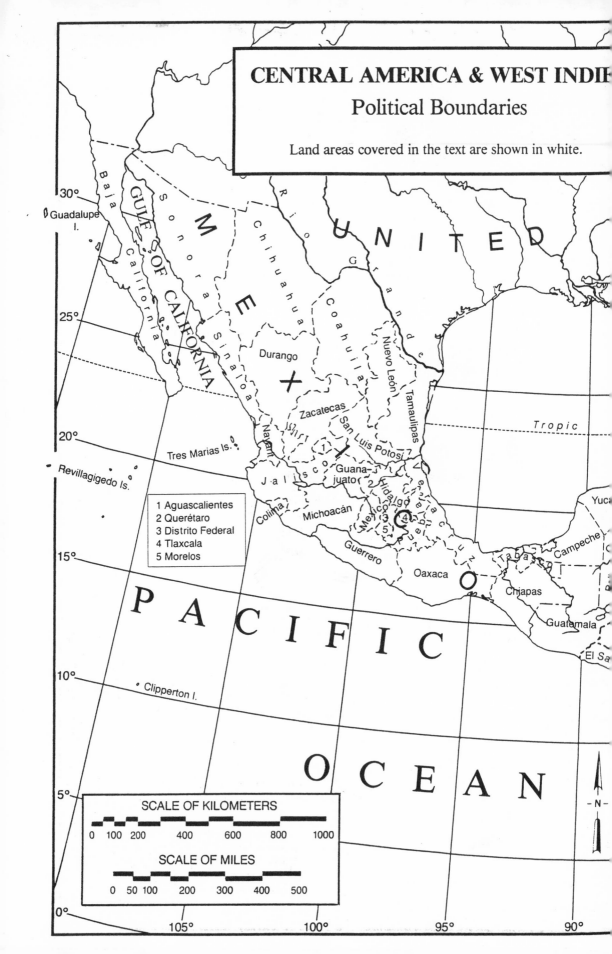

CENTRAL AMERICA & WEST INDIE

Political Boundaries

Land areas covered in the text are shown in white.

1 Aguascalientes
2 Querétaro
3 Distrito Federal
4 Tlaxcala
5 Morelos

SCALE OF KILOMETERS

0 100 200   400   600   800   1000

SCALE OF MILES

0 50 100   200   300   400   500